Middle English
Metrical Romances

Middle English
Metrical Romances

edited by

Walter Hoyt French

and

Charles Brockway Hale

TWO VOLUMES BOUND AS ONE
VOLUME I

NEW YORK / RUSSELL & RUSSELL

FIRST PUBLISHED IN 1930
REISSUED, 1964, BY RUSSELL & RUSSELL
A DIVISION OF ATHENEUM PUBLISHERS, INC.
BY ARRANGEMENT WITH WALTER H. FRENCH
L. C. CATALOG CARD NO: 64-18606
PRINTED IN THE UNITED STATES OF AMERICA

PREFACE

Although the metrical romances are the first large body of English fiction, and have long been of interest to distinguished scholars, no recent collection has been available for study in the classroom. This book is designed to make such study possible. It aims at comprehensiveness: nineteen of the romances included are complete; the rest are represented in selections, usually of about a thousand lines. Each of the conventionally recognized types is represented by at least one poem, as are all dialects and periods. No piece has been included for purely linguistic or historical reasons; each has some further merit or interest.

Immediate surprise may be occasioned by our failure to include "Sir Gawain and the Green Knight" and the two poems on the death of Arthur. We feel, however, that for the two alliterative poems our method of glossing would not be serviceable, and that for profitable study they require the apparatus possible only in a separate text. As for the stanzaic poem, since complete editions are readily available, we have omitted it in favor of other texts now less accessible.

Since every student must refer frequently to the manuals of Professor Wells and Miss Hibbard, it seems needless to repeat information given there; hence the introductions to the individual romances are intended to supplement rather than summarize their discussions.

Much the same might be said of the lists of books in our footnotes.

Because of the linguistic difficulties involved, it has seemed wise to gloss the texts in a special way. The commoner words and expressions, which a student might be expected to know after a first course in Middle English, or will soon learn because of their frequent occurrence, have been put in a vocabulary at the end of the book. Since no vocabularies have previously been made for several of the poems included here, we have cited frequently from them ("The Earl of Toulouse," "Sir Degaré," "Sir Perceval of Galles," etc.). Rare words, strained constructions, and uncommon idioms have been glossed at the foot of the page; accuracy of definition has been aimed at rather than poetical phrasing. Special notes on difficult lines have also been given at the foot of the page, below the glosses.

As a basis for the text for each poem, we have used what seemed to us the best single manuscript of it, and have reproduced this with as little alteration as possible. Brackets indicate that the parts are supplied, without distinction as to whether they are wholly conjectural or mostly illegible in the manuscript. Standard abbreviations, such as those for *-er* and *and*, have been expanded without note. Capitals, punctuation, and word-division have been normalized, except the pronoun "I," which is capitalized only in "Eger and Grime," where it is so written in the manuscript. Bad rhymes have seldom been tampered with; the restoration of the correct form is usually easy, and may be a useful exercise for the student.

Most of the northern and north-midland poems included here were written down in court-hand, and hence present peculiar problems in transcription. The scribes terminated many words with flourishes, the exact significance of which is disputed. English editors usually have transcribed every cross-stroke as -*e;* German editors have disregarded all flourishes except one or two of known significance (-*ur, pat, with*). The latter has seemed to us the more reasonable course. Any one reading many manuscripts in court-hand soon learns that at least some of the flourishes meant nothing to the scribes who wrote them; and there seems to be no good reason why they should have greater significance for the editor who transcribes them. To prevent misunderstanding, however, we have stated in our preface to each poem in court-hand our conventions in tr, nscribing it.

In numbering the lines, we were unwilling to mak innovations, and wherever possible, have followed the numbering in some text frequently referred to in significant articles. Complications that result from this practice have been indicated in the notes.

This book owes much to the scholarly work of English, German, and American editors who have explained many obscure allusions and unintelligible lines in the poems. Their contributions to the understanding of the text have usually been acknowledged in the notes; we wish to say here, however, that we have found their work most helpful and suggestive, and have greatly admired their philological learning and insight. Though the responsibility for anything appearing in the book is ours, the credit is often theirs.

The texts of most of the poems have been prepared from rotographs. This would of course have been impossible but for the ready coöperation of librarians and other authorities in English and American libraries. Acknowledgments for special kindnesses are made in introductions to the separate pieces; the editors wish here to express their thanks to the librarians and members of the staff of the Cornell University Library, Harvard University Library, and the Library of the University of Maryland, for various kinds of assistance; to the Heckscher Research Foundation of Cornell University for a grant that made possible the purchase of many rotographs; to the Oxford University Press for permission to reproduce texts of "King Horn" and "Sir Orfeo"; to Messrs. Ginn and Company for permission to use notes from their editions of "The Squire of Low Degree" and "The Seven Sages of Rome"; to Mr. George Fogg and Mr. W. B. Thomas of the University of Maryland for their kind assistance in the task of preparing the manuscript and reading the proof; to Professor G. L. Hamilton of Cornell University, for many helpful suggestions, especially regarding the selections from "King Alexander"; and to Professors Joseph Q. Adams and Harry Caplan of Cornell University, for encouragement and advice.

CONTENTS

(The poems are complete unless marked "selections.")

INTRODUCTION

ERRATA

p. 188, note on line 283: *read* PMLA 44. 377

p. 259, line 2219: *read* Alas! that thou

p. 288, first line: *read* were sometyme

p. 326, note on line 79: Latin should read *fletuque fluit, laniatque* . . .

p. 333, line 328: *read* him no lenger

p. 350, line 143: *read* "Tellyd

p. 374, note to line 873: *read* PMLA 22. 238;

p. 378, line 997: *last word read* nyme:

p. 412, line 980: *read* no fayrer

p. 998, note to line to 219 should be to 229.

INTRODUCTION

These sections are designed partly to set forth a few facts that may well be borne in mind while studying the romances, but mainly as a working bibliography for rather general subjects not confined to any one piece.

For information of all sorts, see Wells; Hibbard; "The Cambridge History of English Literature," vols. 1, 2, 3; and for the most recent studies, the March number of the Publications of the Modern Language Association; and the Bibliography of the Modern Humanities Research Association.

I. History in the Romances.

Political, economic, and constitutional history meant little to the romance-writers, who were satisfied with any sort of politics that would complicate a plot. Occasionally a story clearly reflects a particular event (cf. "Athelston"); but usually history was transformed beyond recognition. The books here mentioned are useful mainly in giving an idea of the social conditions at the time when the poems were composed.

Cross, A. L., "A History of England and Greater Britain"; also a revision of it called "A Shorter History of England and Greater Britain" (see its bibliographies); Trevelyan, G. M., "England in the Age of Wycliffe" (deals with the social unrest of the period); Froissart (full of the sort of material the romancers liked). See also Section III.

II. The History of the Metrical Romances.

A. The early history of the legends of chivalry is obscure; but they seem to have originated as a type in France before 1100. Many of them are heroic in tone, and exalt military virtues. Their material came from tradition and what passed for history; but this was glorified, so that the unedifying squabbles of quarrelsome barons were given dignity and importance. Though they deal almost wholly with the passion' and interests proper to a fighter intent upon his business,

3

they seem somehow to have expressed the beliefs, interests, and aspirations of a large national group.

B. Before 1150, however, the knightly tale was being circulated by professional entertainers who plied their trade, not in military camps, but in French and Norman and English cities, castles, and manors. They addressed a peace-time audience, which included many women. Here the monotonous heroism and combativeness of the martial epics were out of place; the audience wanted more subtle and varied entertainment. Hence, the minstrels grafted genteel and courtly manners and sentiments on the old stock, pillaged extensively from the fanciful stories of the Celts and the cynical stories of the Arabs, and evolved a form which held sway in literature for over three hundred years. Its peculiarities are the presence of women as principal actors, the prominence of love as a motive for activity, the exaltation of honor and courage, an insistence on the superiority of courtesy to rudeness, a sentimental belief in the paradoxes of feudal loyalty, and a frank enthusiasm for the unreal and fanciful as it came to them from other literatures.

C. On settling in France, the Normans had given up their own sagas and had readily adopted French literature and literary fashions. After they came to England, they continued to read and compose typically French pieces; but they preserved a few of the native legends, some of them in English. When, about 1300, it was evident that the English language had prevailed over the French, professional entertainers and scribes soon worked out a technique for adapting and translating. Most of the English Charlemagne-romances date from this time; and about four-fifths of the surviving English romances were written during the next hundred years.

D. In the early fifteenth century, the type became increasingly unfashionable, though many pieces were copied in manuscripts. About 1480 Caxton printed translations of some of the interminable French composites, and also the great English compilation, Malory's "Morte D'Arthur." Even in the sixteenth and seventeenth centuries, antiquarians printed single romances or had them copied; to this chance is due the preservation of "Eger and Grime" and "The Squire of Low Degree." But though they were rarely set down in permanent form, they were still recited to crowds in Shakespeare's youth.

The great time of production, however, was the fourteenth century; and it is principally to that time that the following sections refer.

No single book is devoted to this subject; information may be found in Schofield; "The Cambridge History of English Literature"; W. P. Ker, "English Literature—Medieval"; G. Saintsbury, "The Flourishing of Romance and the Rise of Allegory"; C. M. Dixon, "English Epic and Heroic Poetry." See also works cited under the national divisions in Section IV.

III. Life in the Middle Ages.

Only items and customs mentioned frequently in the romances and largely unfamiliar to-day are dealt with here.

A. Castles. 1. Most castles were large, so that the community could find shelter in time of danger and so that many extra fighters could be accommodated on short notice. As foundation, a mound was thrown up, the excavation around it forming a ditch, over which was thrown a narrow drawbridge. This led to a large gate, with a smaller gate (wicket) cut in it, to save opening the other for unmounted visitors. At the edge of the ditch, the outer wall was built; the buildings inside were erected against this, so that in the center was a court-yard. The principal building was a large hall, with ante-rooms (chambers) and a kitchen opening off from it. A good deal of the cooking was done in the open. The upper rooms (solars) were reserved for women, members of the household, and distinguished guests; often a bed was the only piece of furniture. Every castle had a chapel, sometimes outside the walls.

2. The hall was the center of life in the castle, all meals, public meetings, and entertainments being held there. Its appointments were few: at one end, chairs on a canopied dais for the great folk; along the side-walls, benches for the retainers and lesser guests. A fire was kindled in the center of the floor, and part of the smoke went out a hole in the roof. At the lower end of the hall the beggars sat on the ground. Minstrels performed either on the floor or in a gallery; and from other galleries the women might look on after the meal was over and they had left the floor.

See Davis, Chs. 2, 3, and the bibliography; Wright, Chs. 2, 5, 6, 7, 8, and 19; Salzman, Ch. 4; Dale, Ch. 4; and S. O. Addy, "The Evolution of the English House" (1898). Many more titles may be found in D. D. Griffith's "Bibliography of Chaucer, 1908–1929," *Univ. of Washington Pub. in Lang. and Lit.* IV. 1. 50 ff.

B. Meals. Two meals were served each day: dinner about 9 A.M. (prime), and supper about 5 P.M.; but the latter was sometimes prolonged to a late hour. To summon the guests, special minstrels (waits) blew on pipes or trumpets. After assembling and before starting to eat, all washed their hands, basins and towels being passed around by the servants. One or more of the tables might be fixed to the floor and permanent; but most of them were temporary—boards laid on trestles. The diners sat only on the side nearer the wall, the other being left to the servers. The table was set with knives and serving-spoons, but not with forks, and food was conveyed to the mouth with the fingers. Large slices of bread (trenchers) served as plates, and either disappeared with the other food during the course of the meal or were afterwards given to the poor or to the numerous dogs. The courses were substantial, and consisted mostly of meat and game in rich sauces; especially noteworthy are the many birds served at each meal. Vegetables are rarely mentioned. The last course consisted of sweets and wines, both highly spiced.

Especially complete and full is the information in Chs. 5, 16, and 21 in Wright; many recipes, menus, and rules of etiquette are in Furnivall.

C. Dress. Small details in costume changed considerably between 1200 and 1400, but the general forms remained the same.

1. Men wore over- and under-tunics (sleeved garments that slipped over the head and extended to the knee), with a girdle at the waist. Over these might be worn a sleeveless mantle or cape, sometimes thrown about the shoulders and clasped, sometimes with a hole for the head. It might be trimmed and lined with costly furs and jewels; further extravagances were wide sleeves and a fur muffler (tippet). The hose were long and often bright-colored; and when, in the fourteenth century, the tunic and mantle were greatly shortened, so that they became practically a blouse and cape, the hose were made even more decorative. Shoes were high, and pointed at the toe. Head-coverings were of two common types: servants, wayfarers, and the clergy wore hoods, either round at the top or pointed, and joined to the mantle; other persons wore hats with crowns and brims of various shapes and proportions. Sometimes a hat was worn over a hood.

2. Women wore long tight tunics, and over them full mantles, clasped about the shoulders. About 1400 their head-dresses were very elaborate.

Davis, Ch. 4, is very useful; cf. his bibliography. See also A. Abrams, "English Life and Manners in the Late Middle Ages" (1913); Quennell, several plates; and Wright.

D. Arms and Armor. An armed knight wore a cloth garment (actoun) under his armor; then came a suit of ring mail (brinie, hauberk), forming a hood at the head, mittens at the ends of the sleeves, and covering the legs. At first the rings were sewn on a leather tunic; later (1300), ch n mail, with welded links, was used instead. During the fou teenth century, armor became increasingly bulky; addition breast-plates, pieces for the arms and legs, and large helme came into use; these last were at first cylindrical, then conica and had movable visors in front, so that the whole face could be covered. The weapons usually carried were a spear, a sword, and a shield; knights in romances seldom resort to daggers or axes, and gunpowder is unheard of. In battle, the knight was careful to wear some coat-of-arms that would permit his companions to distinguish him from the enemy.

Knights were attended by young men (squires), often apprentices in the business of fighting, who were given an exacting course of training both at home and in the field.

War in the romances is unlike the reality. Its grimmer side is overshadowed by the successes of a popular character; strategy and mass-manoeuvers give way to single combats. By 1325, the center of interest is not the warring group, but the single knight-errant; the tournament is substituted for the battlefield as the proving-ground for the hero.

See Davis, Ch. 5; Salzman, Ch. 9; Quennell, *passim*. For information on medieval warfare, see notes to "The Destruction of Troy."

E. Feudal Relations. In the Middle Ages, the relations between men were determined, not by wealth or wages, but by the conditions under which they held land. The king of a country owned or claimed it all; from him, favored lords (knights) held large sections, in return for which they undertook to render him military service; their tenants (thanes) held smaller sections from them, and undertook to render specified services as rental. Usually these were agricultural, but might be military; "war in the Middle Ages was not an exceptional and disturbing occurrence, but part of the normal conditions of life" (Salzman).

The romances show three attitudes of mind toward feudal service, and any of them may be uppermost for the moment in the writer's mind. (1) Legally, violation of a feudal law was a serious offense, and the vassal liable to severe penalties.[1] (2) In the French pieces was a romantic view of the relationship: it was held both sacred and honorable. (3) English romancers did not go so far: though in their works feudal duties are taken for granted, these are performed only so long as the overlord has power; and retainers are shameless in supporting the winner in a struggle.

F. Miscellaneous. **1.** For information about the church, pilgrims, hermits, and related matters, see *The Catholic Encyclopedia;* Jusserand; and especially Cutts, who has much material.

2. For wayfarers, see the last two works mentioned.

IV. Sources of Material.

The statement that the source of a story is, say, Celtic. does not mean that all the material in it originated in Celtic countries. Though a few motives in folklore come demonstrably from history, and others are known to have grown up in particular places, the vast majority were so widely current

---

[1] See Pollock and Maitland.

in the Middle Ages that it is now impossible to be certain where they originated (for example, magic finger-rings, magic swords).

In this discussion, the statement that a piece has a Celtic source means that, somewhere in the formation of the story, a narrator has so decisively impressed on it the technique, concepts, and habits of thought familiar in surviving Celtic literature that writers of other ages and races cannot modify or eliminate these without harm to the story. Thus, despite its descent from the famous Greek story, "Sir Orfeo" is from a Celtic source, because it has been so thoroughly assimilated to Celtic methods and traditions.

A. The romances first current in England came from France and dealt with Charlemagne's wars with the Saracens. They were further distinguished by their militant Christianity and their hatred of Saracens and idolatry. Probably their strong national and religious feeling interfered with their popularity in England; at any rate, they never were so popular there as in Latin countries. Some of their material is now familiar in English literature because later writers assigned it to their own heroes.

B. English legends are few, and except for a few relics of local tradition, have no distinctive material. Three poems customarily grouped here survive only in unique manuscripts, but seem to have had considerable currency in particular localities. Though all but "Gamelyn" seem to have some basis in history, they deal with the facts very freely. Their principal characters desire power or revenge, not love or honor. War with them is an unpleasant necessity, not a diversion; they fight without finesse or artistry, often with cudgels or fists; and the heroes are likely to be of common origin, or to have served an apprenticeship among common people. Though the plots lack other distinctive traits, they are interesting and exciting.

C. The most charming romances are Celtic. Much of the material in them has been shown to have been current among the people of Ireland, Wales, Scotland, and Armorica; and, about 1150, this found its way, probably in translation, into

the hands of French poets, notably Chrétien de Troyes and
Marie de France (c. 1190). (For the view that Chrétien
gave final form to this material, see Bruce.) Most of the
English pieces profess to be translations of French versions
now lost. They fall into two classes, Arthurian and noncyclical. In both the actors are supernatural beings, although
their divinity is often concealed by English adapters; and the
plots often involve a visit to the Celtic Otherworld. The
Arthurian cycle is a study in itself, and really belongs to
comparative literature, for the continental and Celtic poems
on the legend are nearly all of greater antiquity than the
English and must come into any discussion of them.

D. (1) Classical stories from Greek and Roman literature
were primarily for the learned, and hence were mostly translations or faithful abridgments. The Middle Ages knew the
past through sources different from our own: the Troy-legend
came to them through Latin versions of the early Christian
era; the Alexander-legend came through a redaction of about
900 A.D. Other stories were worked over in France or Celtic
countries before coming to England. But usually classical
stories are easily recognizable.

(2) The noncyclical oriental pieces are recognizable by one
or another of three characteristics: their central incident is a
sharp trick, by which some one is outwitted; they require
pretentious magical apparatus, like the horse in the Squire's
Tale; and the women are likely to be vicious or perfidious.
Their more repulsive traits made them suitable material for
exempla; but that they are often set in the midst of Christian
moralizing should blind no one to their real origin.

E. Writers either followed their sources very closely or
treated them with the greatest freedom; in fact, a serviceable
division of romances is into scholarly and popular. Before
1350, many of them were mere translations, usually abridged,
and made by people with literary training, some of whom may
have been members of the clergy. Naturally, they were
deferential to their authorities. But when, toward the end
of the century, itinerant reciters had seen the value of the
stories, they adapted them to the demands of their public;

the minstrel retained nothing that failed to thrill or amuse, and rationalised everything puzzling. Sometimes this is unfortunate (for example, in "Sir Perceval"); but as a rule the abridgments are well contrived to attain the reciter's purpose.

There is no single book on the subject; but much material may be found in Wells, Hibbard, Child, Wimberly, and Schofield. See also W. E. Lawrence's "Medieval Story."

On the Charlemagne romances, see the prefaces to the editions in the Early English Text Society's publications; J. L. Weston, "The Romance Cycle of Charlemagne and his Peers" (London, 1901); G. Saintsbury's "Flourishing of Romance and the Rise of Allegory"; and G. B. Fundenburg's "Feudal France in the French Epic."

On the Arthurian legend, see Bruce, Chambers, and Loomis; A. C. L. Brown has published many important papers. Bruce summarizes numerous articles, and has an extensive bibliography.

For other Celtic pieces, see Hibbard, and the prefaces to separate editions of the texts.

No good general study of the oriental pieces has been made. Special studies are in most of the standard editions of single poems.

On minstrels, see E. K. Chambers, "The Medieval Stage"; Jusserand; and Cutts. There is no good study of their methods.

V. Grammar.

A. General. All short unstressed vowels tended to become short **-e**. Inflectional endings were being dropped throughout the Middle English period, the southern dialect being the most tenacious of them, the midland least so.

B. The Noun. Inflectional endings are, for the singular, nominative and accusative, nothing or **-e**; genitive, **-es, -is**; dative, **-e**; for the plural, all cases, **-es** or **-is**.

1. The **-e** of the nominative is sometimes a reduction of an old case-ending; sometimes represents an original **-e**; and sometimes, especially in feminines of the OE. first declension, is an inorganic **-e** by analogy to the oblique cases.

2. The genitive singular sometimes lacks the **-s** in (a) nouns of relationship, especially those ending in **-r** (*his fader soule*); (b) nouns of the OE. weak declension (*herte blode*); (c) proper nouns (*Mary grace*). The adverbial genitive is common (*lives*, alive).

3. **-E** as the sign of the dative is common only before 1300.

4. As in modern English, the plurals of some nouns are formed by a change of the stem-vowel (*man, men*). A few are formed in (e)n(e) (*eyen; foon*). A few monosyllables show no change in form (*hors; net*). Most of these, however, are also found with plurals in **-s.**

C. The Adjective. There is no change in form except that in the strong declension the plural generally ends in **-e.**

1. Predicate adjectives and those of more than two syllables are usually uninflected.

2. An OE. genitive form survives in *aller, alther, alder* (cf. *alle* in the vocabulary).

3. Most adjectives form their comparatives in **-er;** a few without (*bet,* better; *leng,* longer; *nere,* nearer). Most of these, however, are also found with comparatives in **-er.** Superlatives are usually formed in **-est, -ost.**

D. The Verb. The infinitive form usually ends in **e(n);** sometimes in **i(n).** Weak verbs form their preterits in **-ed(e), -d(e),** or **-t(e),** and their past participles in **-(e)d** or **-t.** Strong verbs form their past tenses by a change of the stem vowel (*binden, band, bunden*); such forms are noted in the vocabulary.

1. Up to 1350, the present tense and the present participle were differently formed and inflected in the different dialects:

	Singular			Plural	Pres. Part.
	1	2	3		
Northern	(e),	(e)s, (is)	(e)s (is)	(e)s (is)	ande
Midland	(e),	(e)st	(e)th	(e)n	ende
Southern	(e),	(e)st	(e)th	(e)th	inde

2. After 1350, the endings appear with less consistency, and ᶜter 1425 are seldom written.

(*a*) The **-en** of the present infinitive and present plural is soon reduced to **-e.**

(*b*) In all forms the **-e** is frequently syncopated in a light syllable (*slideth, slit; findeth, fint; sworen, sworn*).

(*c*) The pronoun is sometimes attached to the verb (*shaltu,* shalt thou; *yeuenet,* given it; *dones,* put it; *willi,* I will), especially in questions.

(*d*) The prefix **i-, y-** is common with past participles in the midlands and the south, but rare in the north. In the older southern poems (the "Brut," "Horn"), it is fairly frequent with present infinitives and with preterits.

E. The Adverb. In form, adverbs are very like adjectives, the usual ending being -e, which became silent and was frequently not written. Historically, the ending -ly, -liche belongs to adjectives, and was still used with them as well as with adverbs in Middle English.

F. The Pronoun. Personal pronouns are as in modern English, and have also certain forms not now current: *ic,* *ich* (I); *sho, ho, he, heo* (she); *he, hi, hie* (they); *here, hem* (their, them). See the vocabulary under *he, she,* and *I.*

G. Dialectal Differences. Morphological differences in the three main dialects have been indicated (cf. D.1.). Phonological differences include the following:

OLD ENGLISH	IN NORTH	IN MIDLANDS	IN SOUTH
long -a (*stan*)	a ai (*stane*)	o (*ston*)	o (*ston*)
initial s- (*sang*)	s (*sang*)	s (*song*)	z (*zong*)
initial g- (*giefan*)	g (*give*)*	y,ʒ (*yeve*)	y,ʒ (*yeve*)
c- before -e or -i (*cirice*)	k (*kirk*)*	ch (*chirche*)	ch (*churche*)
-y- (*fyllan*)	i (*fille*)	i (*fille*)	u (*vulle*)
initial f- (as above)†			

H. Spellings. Although early scribes had individual preferences, Middle English spellings are usually either phonetic (*hwat*) or much as in modern English. Exceptions are the use of qu- or qw- for wh- (*quat,* what); -th for -ht (*rith, riht*); the prefixing of an unnecessary h- (*habide*); the omission of h- where needed (*wat,* what); the interchange of u- and v- (*loue, vs*); the occasional use of ʒ- for s- (*seruantʒ,* servants). See A. C. Wyld's "Short History of English."

---

* These peculiarities are due to the influence in the north of cognate Scandinavian words, which had hard sounds before -e and -i.

† Between vowels, this change was common in all dialects.

For fuller discussions of Middle English Grammar, cf. S. Moore, "Historical Outlines of English Phonology and Middle English Grammar"; J. W. and E. N. Wright, "An Elementary Historical New English Grammar"; L. Morsbach, "Mittelenglische Grammatik"; Richard Jordan, "Handbuch der Mittelenglischen Grammatik"; K. Sisam, "Fourteenth Century Verse and Prose."

VI. Meters in the Romances.

Few of the romances are metrically perfect, because most of them are preserved in copies made long after their composition and by persons not familiar with their dialect. Hence many a bad rhyme can be made good by substituting the proper dialectal form ("Eger and Grime" 7–8, for *younge— thing*, read *ʒyng—thing*; "Squire" 39–40, for *one—plane*, *ane—plane*).

The accent of words in Middle English was by no means so fixed as it is in modern English. Especially in French words, it was possible to vary the accentuation (cf. the treatment of the name Havelok, note to line 632; also *meyne*, "Squire" 442, and *meyne*, "Squire" 503; *burgeys*, "Havelok" 1328, and *burgeys*, "Havelok" 2012).

A. The Line.

1. Cadence.—Most romances, except the alliterative ones, are written in iambic tetrameter, a meter imported from France and domesticated with great success. But through the influence of Old English poetry, Middle English poets tended to count accents more carefully than syllables.

(a) The line may end either on a stressed or a light syllable:

I tok hit out and haue hit er   "Degaré" 125

Þe cloþ was spred, þe bord was sette   "Launfal" 341

(b) A common variant is the same line, minus the first light syllable:

Traytours, yelde you to me   "Sultan" 2212

Sket cam tiding intil Ubbe   "Havelok" 1926

(c) Permissible irregularities are not numerous, the most common being the substitution of a trochee in the first foot or after a cesural pause, or the substitution of an anapest:

Harping and piping ful god won   "Havelok" 2325

He fallythe that puttis hymselfe so farre   "Ipomadon" 1121

(*d*) In the middle of the line, a weak syllable is sometimes omitted, especially when the cesura occurs there, and in northern poems:

Al so briht, al so shir "Havelok" 1253

Of late, there has grown a theory that the basic metrical unit is a double foot, consisting of four syllables. For discussion, see *PMLA* 42.113 and Young.

(*e*) A few pieces are in other meters; these will be discussed in the introductions to those pieces.

2. Elision and Syncopation.—(*a*) Until 1300, final -e and -e- in light syllables were pronounced at line ends and within the line when the succeeding word began with a consonant other than **h-** or **y-**. During the next hundred years, it continued to be pronounced in most localities, but not consistently. In the north, it was sometimes written to indicate the length of a preceding vowel, and had no phonetic value. Sometimes it was a mere scribal flourish. In general, poets used it as a metrical filler; whether it is pronounced depends on the requirements of the meter:

"Sir Kay, I wote wele," sayd þe Quene "Ywain" 82

Bi grete God, þat aw þis day *ibid.* 92

(*b*) Before an initial vowel, **h-** or **y-**, -e and -en are usually elided:

Al bitechen into to hire hond "Havelok" 203

(*c*) -E is sometimes syncopated in such words as *euerich, hauede, leuedi,* where it is pronounced lightly or not at all:

Þe leuedi wreiȝ him warm apliȝt "Degaré" 843

3. Expansion.—(*a*) The letter *r* seems to have been trilled so strongly as frequently to equal another syllable in such words as *lord, erl, arm, world.* Cf. Skeat's introduction to "Havelok" xiv.

(*b*) A light syllable is frequently missing after a word ending in a hard consonant (k, t, d, g); possibly these letters were so strongly pronounced as sometimes to be equivalent to a separate syllable (ke, te, de, ge):

Þe sharpe swerd let wade "Havelok" 2645

(c) Many apparent irregularities in meter are due to copyists, who omitted inflexional endings, especially those preserved in other dialects and discarded in their own.

B. Groups of Lines.

1. Rhyme.—As in modern English, words rhyme on all the sounds following the last stressed vowel. A few consonantal pairs are exceptions: -m and -n (*Grime—fine*, "Eger" 43), -t and -d (*reward—part*, "Cleges" 364), -d and -g (*hand—dange*, "Eger" 165), -t and -c or -k (*fet—ek*, "Havelok" 1303). Some poets admitted misrhymes, the *"rime riche"* (that is, the rhyming of syllables identical in sound but different in meaning: *selve* (self)—*selve* (salve), "Beryn" 3587–8), and assonance (*gate—skape*, "Gamelyn" 575). Such variations are infrequent before 1350. Set phrases, or rhyme-tags, for aiding a poet to find a rhyme (cf. VII.A.8) are common in all romances; see Hibbard, 143.

2. Stanzas and Strophes—Romances were usually written in one of three common meters:

(a) Tetrameter couplets. Generally one line or the other has a final cesura, but run-on lines are found.

(b) Tail-rhyme stanzas (rime couée). The unit is a three-line group—a tetrameter couplet followed by a trimeter. Stanzas usually consist of twelve lines, the trimeters (b) rhyming with each other: AAbCCbDDbEEb ("Sir Launfal"). Sometimes the poet carried the A-rhyme through two or more of the tetrameter couplets (AAbAAbCCb, etc.), but this was a rather intricate rhyme-scheme for a language so poor in rhymes as English.

(c) Layamon's meter represents a transition from Old English, and is dealt with in the preface to the "Brut." After 1350, some twenty-five poems, mostly northern, appeared in alliterative meters. They do not rhyme, and their cadence is a matter of dispute. Every line has two parts, each con-

taining two principal stresses; and at least one stressed syllable
in each half-line must alliterate, while all four may. The
number of light syllables is less a matter of rule. There may
be several or none between accented syllables. (For the opposite view—that the cadence is iambic and the line tends to
contain fourteen syllables—see *PMLA* 42.113 and W. E.
Leonard, *University of Wisconsin Studies in Language and
Literature* 11.)

For ofte hārmes were heñte · þat heĺpe we ne myʒte
"Chevelere" 3.

Alliteration is common as an ornament in rhymed poetry,
especially in the north.

For complete discussions of meter, see:

Saintsbury, G. A., "A History of English Prosody from the Twelfth
Century to the Present Day." Vol. 1 (Oxford, 1906).

Kaluza, Max, "Englische Metrik in Historische Entwicklung" (Berlin,
1909).

The same, translated by A. C. Dunstan, under the title of "A Short
History of English Versification from the Earliest Times to the Present
Day" (N. Y., 1911).

Schipper, J., "Grundriss der Englischen Metrik" (Leipsic, 1895). "History of English Versification" (Oxford, 1910).

Young, Sir George, "An English Prosody on Inductive Lines" (Cambridge, 1928).

VII. A Few Essentials.

A student of the romances would do well to learn at once
a few peculiarities of Middle English.

A. Constructions. 1. Impersonal verbs were much more
common than nowadays, because Middle English still retained
the dative case. The telltale *it* is often missing, but the case
of the pronoun or the inverted order mark the construction.
Common verbs of the sort are *þuʒte* (*hym to gode þuʒte:* it
seemed good to him); *like* (*hyr lykede welle:* it pleased her
greatly); *ought* (*us ought to go*); *seme* (*hym semede:* it seemed
to him).

2. Genitives frequently show no case-ending. See V.B.2.

3. As in colloquial modern English, verbs of action were
often omitted when their auxiliaries are expressed (*of the mete*

non he myȝth: of the food he could not [eat]), or when an adverb of place or direction is present (*he out wiþ his swerde*).

4. Verbs of wishing and willing which introduce a clause are similarly omitted (*what is thi name? anon that thou tell mee*).

5. One is often used with demonstratives in inverted order, or with comparatives in correlative clauses (*an hard doome now is this on; A better man than he was one*).

6. Writers pass easily from indirect to direct discourse.

7. In old and northern poems, when emphasis is desirable, a fact is often understated or the contrary denied. (*He was not the last;* that is, he was among the first.) See the prefaces to "King Horn" and to Layamon's "Brut."

8. Rhyme-tags and fillers are a common resort of metrists, and in translating should not be taken too seriously. The main classes are: (1) synonyms for *quickly: wel sone, in hie, anon, fast,* etc.; (2) emphatic phrases assuring the hearer of the truth of a statement: *wit ye for sothe, withouten les, iwisse,* etc.; (3) phrases vaguely complimentary: *worthy in wede, lufsome under line, stiffe in stour.* These last are commonly alliterative.

B. Contractions. 1. In questions and imperatives, the pronoun *thou* frequently becomes enclitic with the verb, which often shows slight changes as a result: *wostow* (knowest thou); *slepestu* (sleepest thou); *wiltu* (wilt thou), *wurstu* (be thou). See also V.D.2.c.

2. Before vowels, **-e** of the definite article is sometimes elided: *þerl* (the earl).

3. The word *ne*, not, is frequently combined with the following verb if it begins with a vowel or **h-** or **w-**, and the final **-e** disappears: *not* (*ne wot,* knew not); *nastu* (*ne hast thou); nadrinke* (*ne adrinke,* not drown); see also the vocabulary under N.

C. Meanings of Words. 1. In Middle English, the following words very rarely mean what they do in modern English. Their usual meanings are: *also*—as, so; *agayn*—back; *doute*—fear; *hope*—believe, expect (usually in an unpleasant sense); *sone*—at once, straightway; *þo*—then, those; *understand* —believe, receive.

2. The following words frequently have the same significance as in modern English, but often have another. Only the latter is given: *and*—if; *but*—unless, except; *do*—cause; *graunte*— agree; *kinde*—nature, natural, proper; *lef*—dear; *leve*—believe, permit; *mete*—food, meal; *or*—before; *oþer*—or; *rede*—advise, advice; *so*—as; *þanne*—when; *þer*—where; *wher*—whither, whether.

GENERAL BIBLIOGRAPHY

The books in this list are referred to in the notes under the first word given here.

Ballads—see CHILD.

"Beowulf and the Fight at Finnsburg," FRIEDRICH KLAEBER (1922).

B.S.—BRADLEY, HENRY, and STRATMANN, FRANCIS HENRY—"A Middle English Dictionary" (Oxford, 1891).

BRAND, JOHN—"Observations on Popular Antiquities."

BRUCE, J. D.—"The Evolution of Arthurian Romance" (*Hesperia* 8, 9), second edition, 1928.

CHAMBERS, E. K.—"Arthur of Britain" (London, 1927).

"Chanson (La) de Roland"—edited by T. A. JENKINS (1924).

CHILD, FRANCIS JAMES—"The English and Scottish Popular Ballads" (1882–98).

CUTTS, EDWARD L.—"Scenes and Characters of the Middle Ages."

DALE, EDMUND—"National Life and Character in the Mirror of Early English Literature" (1907).

DAVIS, H. W. C.—"Medieval England" (a re-edition of F. P. BARNARD'S "Companion to English History"; Oxford, 1924).

DICKMAN, A. J.—"Le Rôle du Surnaturel dans les Chansons de Geste" (Iowa thesis, 1925).

FRAZER, SIR JAMES GEORGE—"The Golden Bough: A Study in Magic and Religion." References to this are according to Frazer's own scheme.

French romances. The reference is to the latest edition unless otherwise specified.

FROISSART, JOHN—"The Chronicles of England, France, and Spain," etc. (Everyman's Library translation).

FURNIVALL, FREDERICK J.—"Early English Meals and Manners" (*EETS* 32).

GAUTIER, LEON—"La Chevalerie" (1890). A translation was made by Henry Frith.

HIBBARD, LAURA A.—"Medieval Romance in England" (Oxford, 1924).

JUSSERAND, JEAN JULES—"English Wayfaring Life in the Middle Ages" (translated by Lucy Toulmin Smith).
LOOMIS, R. S.—"Celtic Myth and Arthurian Romance" (New York, 1927).
MALORY, SIR THOMAS—"Morte D'Arthur."
Periodicals.—The abbreviations for these are the same as in Wells's Manual.
"Pelerinage de Charlemagne"—edited by EDUARD KOSCHWITZ under the title "Karls des Grossen Reise nach Jerusalem und Constantinopel" (second edition).
POLLOCK, SIR FREDERICK, and MAITLAND, FREDERICK WILLIAM— "The History of English Law before the Time of Edward I" (1898).
QUENNELL, MARJORIE and C. H. B.—"A History of Everyday Things in England,"—1066–1499 (Batsford). A book for school children, but full of pictures and information.
Romances not in this volume. References are always to the standard text. Where several versions are in print, the version alluded to is indicated. See Wells for full bibliography.
SALZMAN, LOUIS F.—"English Life in the Middle Ages" (1926).
STRUTT, JOSEPH—"The Sports and Pastimes of the People of England" (Cox's revision, 1903).
WELLS, JOHN EDWIN—"A Manual of the Writings in Middle English, 1050–1400." Three supplements have appeared.
WIMBERLY, LOWRY C.—"Folklore in the English and Scottish Ballads" (University of Chicago Press, 1928).
WRIGHT, THOMAS—"A History of Domestic Manners and Sentiments in England during the Middle Ages." References by page are to the edition of 1862.

THE MATTER OF ENGLAND

KING HORN

The text is from Hall's edition (Oxford, 1901), which should be consulted for its very full notes, by the kind permission of the Oxford Press. The text of the Cambridge Manuscript (Gg. 4.27.2) is printed here, with insertions of important lines from the other manuscripts. For convenience in reference, however, the line-numbering is that of Hall and Lumby, the lines inserted from other manuscripts being set in brackets, and not included in the numbering; their numbering in Hall's text is given in a note.

The writer's dialect was south midland of about 1225. He frequently writes -u for a sound that in modern English has become -i or -e: *wulleȝ*, will; *ȝut*, yet. -U and -v also represent the southern vocalizing of -f: *biualle*, befall. Genitives are often without a final -s: *his fader deþ*. Understatement is common: "more than a mile" means a considerable distance; "more than five" implies a good many.

> Alle beon he bliþe
> þat to my song lyþe:[1]
> A sang ihc schal ȝou singe
> Of Murry þe Kinge.
> King he was biweste[2]   5
> So longe so hit laste.[3]
> Godhild het his quen;
> Faire[4] ne miȝte non ben.
> He hadde a sone þat het Horn,
> Fairer ne miste non beo born,   10
> Ne no rein vpon birine,[5]
> Ne sunne vpon bischine.
> Fairer nis non þane he was,
> He was briȝt so þe glas,
> He was whit so þe flur;[6]   15
> Rose-red was his colur.

---

[1] listen.   [2] in the west country.   [3] i.e., all his life.   [4] fairer.   [5] rain upon [6] flower.

16. The two following lines are from MS. O. 17–8.

25

[He was fayr and eke bold,
And of fiftene winter hold.]
In none kingeriche
Nas non his iliche.[7]
Twelf feren he hadde
Þat [he] alle wiþ him ladde.   20
Alle riche mannes sones,
And alle hi were faire gomes,[8]
Wiþ him for to pleie,
And mest he luuede tweie;
Þat on him het Haþulf child,   25
And þat oþer Fikenild.
Aþulf was þe beste,
And Fikenylde þe werste.
Hit was vpon a someres day,
Also ihc ȝou telle may,   30
Murri þe gode King
Rod on his pleing[9]
Bi þe se side,
Ase he was woned ride.
[With him riden bote tvo;
Al to fewe ware þo]
He fond bi þe stronde,   35
Ariued on his londe,
Schipes fiftene
Wiþ Sarazins kene:
He axede what hi soȝte
Oþer to londe broȝte.   40
A payn[10] hit ofherde,
And hym wel sone answarede:
"Þi lond folk we schulle slon,
And alle þat Crist luueþ[11] vpon,
And þe selue riȝt anon,   45
Ne schaltu to-dai henne gon."
Þe Kyng aliȝte of his stede,
For þo he hauede nede,

---

[7] equal. [8] youths. [9] sport. [10] paynim, heathen. [11] believe.
34. The next two lines are from MS. O. 37-8.
39. MS. *isoȝte.*

And his gode kniӡtes two;
Al to fewe he hadde þo. 50
Swerd hi gunne gripe
And togadere smite.
Hy smyten vnder schelde
Þat sume hit yfelde:[12]
Þe King hadde al to fewe 55
Toӡenes so fele schrewe:[13]
So vele miӡten yþe[14]
Bringe hem þre to diþe.
 Þe pains come to londe
And neme hit in here honde: 60
Þat folc hi gunne quelle,[15]
And churchen for to felle:
Þer ne moste libbe
Þe fremde[16] ne þe sibbe,
Bute hi here laӡe asoke,[17] 65
And to here tȯke.
Of alle wymmanne,
Wurst was Godhild þanne;
For Murri heo weop sore
And for Horn ӡute more. 70
He wente vt of halle
Fram hire maidcncs alle
Vnder a roche of stone,
Þer hco liuede alone.
Þer heo seruede Gode 75
Aӡenes þc paynes forbode:[18]
Þer he seruede Criste
Þat no payn hit ne wiste:
Eure heo bad[19] for Horn child
Þat Jesu Crist him beo myld.[20] 80
Horn was in paynes honde
Wiþ his feren of the londe.
Muchel was his fairhede,[21]

---

[12] felt. [13] many villains. [14] easily. [15] kill. [16] strangers. [17] renounced their religion. [18] prohibition. [19] prayed. [20] gracious. [21] beauty.

73. Solitaries often dug caves in hillsides; see Cutts, p. 111.

For Ihesu Crist him makede.
Payns him wolde slen,   85
Oþer al quic flen,²²
ʒef his fairnesse nere:²³
þe children alle aslaʒe²⁴ were.
þanne spak on admirad—
Of wordes he was bald,—   90
"Horn, þu art wel kene,
And þat is wel isene;
þu art gret and strong,
Fair and euene long;²⁵
þu schalt waxe more   95
Bi fulle seue ʒere:
ʒef þu mote to liue go²⁶
And þine feren also,
ʒef hit so bifalle,
ʒe scholde slen vs alle: 100
þaruore²⁷ þu most to stere,²⁸
þu and þine ifere;
To schupe schulle ʒe funde,²⁹
And sinke to þe grunde;³⁰
þe se ʒou schal adrenche,³¹   105
Ne schal hit us noʒt ofþinche;³²
For if þu were aliue,
Wiþ swerd oþer wiþ kniue,
We scholden alle deie,
And þi fader deþ abeie."   110
þe children hi broʒte to stronde,
Wringinde here honde,
Into schupes borde³³
At þe furste worde.³⁴
Ofte hadde Horn beo wo,³⁵   115
Ac neure wurs þan him was þo.

---

²² flay alive.   ²³ if it were not for his beauty.   ²⁴ slain.   ²⁵ of average height;
i.e., tall.   ²⁶ remain alive.   ²⁷ therefore.   ²⁸ boat.   ²⁹ hasten.   ³⁰ bottom.
³¹ drown.   ³² make sorry.   ³³ aboard ship.   ³⁴ at once.   ³⁵ woe (n).

100. On the Saracen's premonition, cf. Dickman, 182–3.
106. A person exposed in a boat would die only if guilty; hence setting him adrift was not such a sin as shedding his innocent blood.

Þe se bigan to flowe,[36]
And Horn child to rowe;
Þe se þat schup so fasste drof
Þe children dradde þerof. 120
Hi wenden to-wisse[37]
Of here lif to misse,[38]
Al þe day and al þe niȝt
Til hit sprang dai-liȝt,
Til Horn saȝ on þe stronde 125
Men gon[39] in þe londe.
"Feren" quaþ he "ȝonge,
Ihc telle ȝou tiþinge:
Ihc here foȝeles singe,
And þat gras him springe.[40] 130
Bliþe beo we on lyue;
Vre schup is on ryue."[41]
Of schup hi gunne funde,
And setten fout to grunde;
Bi þe se side 135
Hi leten þat schup ride:[42]
Þanne spak him child Horn,
(In Suddene[43] he was iborn):
"Schup bi þe se flode,
Daies haue þu gode:[44] 140
Bi þe se brinke,
No water þe nadrinke:[45]
Ȝef þu cume to Suddenne,
Gret þu wel of myne kenne,
Gret þu wel my moder, 145
Godhild, Quen þe gode,
And seie þe paene kyng,
Jesu Cristes wiþering,[46]
Þat ihc am hol and fer[47]
On þis lond ariued her: 150
And seie þat hei schal fonde[48]
Þe dent of myne honde."

---

[36] i.e., it was flood tide. [37] expected surely. [38] lose. [39] going about. [40] sc. "see." [41] shore. [42] ride at anchor. [43] Isle of Man. [44] i.e., a pleasant lot be thine. [45] not sink. [46] enemy. [47] sound, well. [48] experience.

Þe children ȝede to tune,[49]
Bi dales and bi dune.[50]
Hy metten wiþ Almair King,   155
(Crist ȝeue him His blessing!)
King of Westernesse[1]
(Crist ȝiue him muchel blisse!).
He him spac to Horn child
Wordes þat were mild: 160
"Whannes beo ȝe, faire gumes,
Þat her to londe beoþ icume,
Alle þrottene,[2]
Of bodie swiþe kene?
Bi God þat me makede,   165
A swihc fair verade[3]
Ne sauȝ ihc in none stunde,
Bi westene londe:
Seie me wat ȝe seche."
Horn spak here speche,   170
He spak for hem alle,
Vor so hit moste biualle:[4]
He was þe faireste
And of wit þe beste.
    "We beoþ of Suddenne,   175
Icome of gode kenne,
Of Cristene blode,
And kynges suþe gode.
Payns þer gunne ariue
And duden hem of lyue.[5]   180
Hi sloȝen and todroȝe[6]
Cristene men inoȝe.
So Crist me mote rede,[7]
Vs he dude lede
Into a galeie,[8]   185
Wiþ þe se to pleie,[9]

---

[49] went their way. [50] by valleys and uplands. [1] the Wirral district in Cheshire(?). [2] thirteen. [3] company. [4] befall. [5] killed them. [6] tore asunder. [7] on my word as a Christian. [8] large row-boat. [9] enjoy ourselves.

155. The ceremonies are very like those in "Beowulf" 229 ff. The questions and speeches are so conventional as to be almost a formula.

Dai hit is igon and oþer,[10]
Wiþute sail and roþer:[11]
Vre schip bigan to swymme
To þis londes brymme.[12]   190
Nu þu miȝt vs slen and binde,
Ore[13] honde bihynde;
Bute ȝef hit beo þi wille,
Helpe þat we ne spille."
    þanne spak þe gode Kyng   195
(Iwis he nas no niþing):[14]
"Seie me, child, what is þi name;
Ne schaltu haue bute game."
þe child him answerde,
Sone so he hit herde: 200
"Horn ihc am ihote,
Icomen vt of þe bote,
Fram þe se side.
Kyng, wel mote þc tide."
þanne hym spak þe gode King,   205
"Wel bruc þu þi neuening.[15]
Horn, þu go wel schulle[16]
Bi dales and bi hulle;[17]
Horn, þu lude sune,[18]
Bi dales and bi dune;   210
So schal þi name springe
Fram kynge to kynge,
And þi fairnesse
Abute Westernesse,
þe strengþe of þine honde   215
Into eurech londe.
Horn, þu art so swete,
Ne may ihc þe forlete."[19]
Hom rod Aylmar þe Kyng
And Horn mid him, his fundling,[20]   220

---

[10] a second. [11] rudder. [12] edge. [13] our [14] villian. [15] naming; i.e., may your fame carry like the sound of a trumpet. [16] musically. [17] hill. [18] sound loudly. [19] part with. [20] foundling.

220. MS. *fundyng.*

And alle his ifere,
Þat were him so dere.
  Þe Kyng com into halle
Among his kniȝtes alle:
Forþ he clupede Aþelbrus,   225
Þat was stiward of his hus.
"Stiward, tak nu here
Mi fundlyng for to lere
Of þine mestere,[21]
Of wude and of riuere,[22]   230
And tech him to harpe
Wiþ his nayles scharpe,
Biuore me to kerue,[23]
And of þe cupe serue.
Þu tech him of alle þe liste[24]   235
Þat þu eure of wiste,
And his feiren þou wise[25]
Into oþere seruise:
Horn þu underuonge,[26]
And tech him of harpe and songe."   240
  Ailbrus gan lere
Horn and his yfere:
Horn in herte laȝte[27]
Al þat he him taȝte.
In þe curt and vte,   245
And elles al abute,
Luuede men Horn child,
And mest him louede Rymenhild,
Þe Kynges oȝene doȝter,
He was mest in þoȝte;[28]   250
Heo louede so Horn child
Þat neȝ heo gan wexe wild:
For heo ne miȝte at borde
Wiþ him speke no worde,
Ne noȝt in þe halle   255
Among þe kniȝtes alle,

---

[21] craft.   [22] i.e., hunting and hawking.   [23] carve.   [24] accomplishments.
[25] instruct.   [26] take in charge.   [27] seized.   [28] was most in her thoughts.
237. MS. *In his.*

Ne nowhar in non oþere stede:
Of folk heo hadde drede:
Bi daie ne bi niȝte
Wiþ him speke ne miȝte; 260
Hire soreȝe ne hire pine
Ne miȝte neure fine.²⁹
In heorte heo hadde wo,
And þus hire biþoȝte³⁰ þo:
Heo sende hire sonde 265
Aþelbrus to honde,
Þat he come hire to,
And also scholde Horn do
Al into bure,
For heo gan to lure;³¹ 270
And þe sonde seide
Þat sik lai þat maide,
And bad him come swiþe,
For heo nas noþing bliþe.
Þe stuard was in herte wo, 275
For he nuste what to do.
Wat Rymenhild hure þoȝte
Gret wunder him þuȝte,³²
Abute Horn þe ȝonge
To bure for to bringe. 280
He þoȝte vpon his mode³³
Hit nas for none gode:
He tok him anoþer,
Aþulf, Hornes broþer.
"Athulf," he sede, "riȝt anon 285
Þu schalt wiþ me to bure gon
To speke wiþ Rymenhild stille³⁴
And witen hure wille.
In Hornes ilike³⁵
Þu schalt hure biswike: 290
Sore ihc me ofdrede³⁶
He wolde Horn misrede."³⁷

²⁹ end. ³⁰ planned. ³¹ look gloomy, sick. ³² what she intended to do seemed
evil to him. ³³ in his mind. ³⁴ secretly. ³⁵ likeness; i.e., as Horn's substitute. ³⁶ fear greatly. ³⁷ she would advise Horn badly.

Aþelbrus gan Aþulf lede,
And into bure wiþ him ȝede:
Anon vpon Aþulf child 295
Rymenhild gan wexe wild:
He wende þat Horn hit were
þat heo hauede þere:
Heo sette him on bedde;
Wiþ Aþulf child he wedde;[38] 300
On hire armes tweie
Aþulf heo gan leie.
"Horn," quaþ heo, "wel longe
Ihc habbe þe luued stronge.
þu schalt þi trewþe pliȝte 305
On myn hond her riȝte,[39]
Me to spuse[40] holde,
And ihc þe lord to wolde."[41]
    Aþulf sede on hire ire[42]
So stille so hit were, [43] 310
"þi tale nu þu lynne,[44]
For Horn nis noȝt herinne.
Ne beo we noȝt iliche:
Horn is fairer and riche,
Fairer bi one ribbe[45] 315
þane eni man þat libbe:
þeȝ Horn were vnder molde
Oþer elles wher he wolde[46]
Oþer henne a þusend mile,
Ihc nolde him ne þe bigile." 320
    Rymenhild hire biwente,[47]
And Aþelbrus fule heo schente.
"Hennes þu go, þu fule þeof,[48]
Ne wurstu me neure more leof;
Went vt of my bur, 325
Wiþ muchel mesauentur.

---

[38] displayed passion.   [39] by giving the hand.   [40] wife.   [41] and I to own thee
as lord.   [42] ear.   [43] as quietly as could be.   [44] cease.   [45] rib; i.e., as woman's
beauty exceeds man's.   [46] or wherever else he cares to be.   [47] turned.   [48] thief.

299. Beds were the only furniture in most apartments, and hence
served for chairs or benches.

Schame mote þu fonge
And on hiȝe rode anhonge.[49]
Ne spek ihc noȝt wiþ Horn:
Nis he noȝt so vnorn;[50]   330
Hor[n] is fairer þane beo he:
Wiþ muchel schame mote þu deie."
   Aþelbrus in a stunde
Fel anon to grunde.
"Lefdi min oȝe,[51]   335
Liþe me a litel þroȝe.[1]
Lust whi ihc wonde[2]
Bringe þe Horn to honde.
For Horn is fair and riche,
Nis no whar his iliche.[3]   340
Aylmar, þe gode Kyng,
Dude him on mi lokyng;[4]
ȝef Horn were her abute,
Sore y me dute[5]
Wiþ him ȝe wolden pleie   345
Bitwex ȝou selue tweie;
þanne scholde wiþuten oþe[6]
þe Kyng maken vs wroþe.[7]
Rymenhild, forȝef me þi tene,
Lefdi, my Quene,   350
And Horn ihc schal þe fecche,
Wham so hit recche."[8]
   Rymenhild ȝef he cuþe
Gan lynne wiþ hire muþe:[9]
Heo makede hire wel bliþe;   355
Wel was hire þat siþe.
"Go nu," quaþ heo, "sone,
And send him after none,
On a squieres wise:[10]
Whane þe Kyng arise   360
To wude for to pleie,

---

[49] hang. [50] ugly. [51] own. [1] space. [2] hear why I hesitated. [3] equal. [4] placed him in my custody. [5] fear. [6] no doubt. [7] sorry. [8] may concern. [9] she stopped speaking as well as she could (i.e., entirely). [10] dressed as a squire.

359–60. In C. the order of these lines is reversed.

Nis non þat him biwreie.
He schal wiþ me bileue
Til hit beo nir eue,
To hauen of him mi wille;   365
After ne recche ihc what me[11] telle."
    Aylbrus wende hire fro;
Horn in halle fond he þo
Bifore þe Kyng on benche,
Wyn for to schenche.[12]   370
"Horn," quaþ he, "so hende,
To bure nu þu wende,
After mete stille,[13]
Wiþ Rymenhild to duelle;
Wordes suþe bolde,   375
In herte þu hem holde.
Horn, beo me wel trewe;
Ne schal hit þe neure rewe."
Horn in herte leide
Al þat he him seide;   380
He ȝeode in wel riȝte
To Rymenhild þe briȝte;
On knes he him sette,
And sweteliche hure grette.
Of his feire siȝte[14]   385
Al þe bur gan liȝte.
He spac faire speche—
Ne dorte[15] him no man teche.
"Wel þu sitte and softe,[16]
Rymenhild þe briȝte,   390
Wiþ þine maidenes sixe
Þat þe sitteþ nixte.[17]
Kinges stuard vre
Sende me into bure:
Wiþ þe speke ihc scholde: 395
Seie me what þu woldest:

---

[11] men.   [12] pour.   [13] quietly.   [14] because of his fair appearance.   [15] needed.
[16] comfortably.   [17] beside.

366. MS. *recchecche.*

Seie, and ich schal here
What þi wille were."
  Rymenhild vp gan stonde
And tok him bi þe honde: 400
Heo sette him on pelle[18]
Of wyn to drinke his fulle:
Heo makede him faire chere
And tok him abute þe swere.
Ofte heo him custe,[19]   405
So wel so hire luste.
"Horn," heo sede, "wiþute strif,[20]
þu schalt haue me to þi wif.
Horn, haue of me rewþe,
And plist[21] me þi trewþe."   410
  Horn þo him biþoȝte
What he speke miȝte.
"Crist," quaþ he, "þe wisse,
And ȝiue þe heuene blisse
Of þine husebonde,   415
Wher he beo in londe.[22]
Ihc am ibore to lowe
Such wimman to knowe.
Ihc am icome of þralle[23]
And fundling bifalle.   420
Ne feolle hit þe of cunde
To spuse beo me bunde:[24]
Hit nere no fair wedding
Bitwexe a þral and a king."
  þo gan Rymenhild mislyke,[25]   425
And sore gan to sike:
Armes heo gan buȝe:[26]
Adun he feol iswoȝe.[27]
  Horn in herte was ful wo,
And tok hire on his armes two.   430

---

[18] rich coverlet.   [19] kissed.   [20] i.e., no doubt.   [21] plight, pledge.   [22] i.e., whoever he may turn out to be.   [23] serf; i.e., serfdom.   [24] nor would it befit one of your (high) birth to be bound as wife to me.   [25] be displeased.   [26] bend; i.e., she threw up her arms.   [27] swooning.

420. For the foundling's duties in Celtic countries, cf. "The Destruction of Da Choca's Hostel," *Rev. Celt.* 21.157.

He gan hire for to kesse
Wel ofte mid ywisse.[28]
"Lemman," he sede, "dere,
Þin herte nu þu stere.[29]
Help me to kniȝte[30]   435
Bi al þine miȝte,
To my lord þe King,
Þat he me ȝiue dubbing:
Þanne is mi þralhod
Iwent into kniȝthod,   440
And i schal wexe more,
And do, lemman, þi lore."
 Rymenhild, þat swete þing,
Wakede of hire swoȝning.
"Horn," quaþ heo, "vel sone   445
Þat schal beon idone:
Þu schalt beo dubbed kniȝt
Are come seueniȝt.
Haue her þis cuppe
And þis ryng þervppe[31]   450
To Aylbrus þe stuard,
And se he holde foreward.
Seie ihc him biseche,
Wiþ loueliche speche,
Þat he adun falle   455
Bifore þe King in halle,
And bidde þe King ariȝte
Dubbe þe to kniȝte.
Wiþ seluer and wiþ golde
Hit wurþ him wel iȝolde.[32]   460
Crist him lene spede
Þin erende to bede."[33]
 Horn tok his leue,
For hit was neȝ eue.
Aþelbrus he soȝte   465

---

[28] certainly. [29] govern. [30] to knighthood. [31] in addition. [32] repaid (to Athelbrus). [33] to make known your business.

441. Since a thrall could not bear weapons, Horn could prove his worth only if he were made a knight.

And ȝaf him þat he broȝte,
And tolde him ful ȝare
Hu he hadde ifare,
And sede him his nede,
And bihet him his mede.   470
  Aþelbrus also swiþe
Wente to halle bliue.
"Kyng," he sede, "þu leste³⁴
A tale mid þe beste;³⁵
þu schalt bere crune   475
Tomoreȝe in þis tune;
Tomoreȝe is þi feste:
þer bihoueþ geste.³⁶
Hit nere noȝt forloren³⁷
For to kniȝti child Horn,   480
þine armes for to welde;
God kniȝt he schal ȝelde."³⁸
  þe King sede sone,
"þat is wel idone.
Horn me wel iquemeþ;³⁹   485
God kniȝt him bisemeþ.⁴⁰
He schal haue mi dubbing,
And after, wurþ mi derling.
And alle his feren twelf
He schal kniȝten himself: 490
Alle he schal hem kniȝtc
Bifore me þis niȝte."
Til þe liȝt of day sprang
Ailmar him þuȝte lang.
þe day bigan to springe;   495
Horn com biuore þe Kinge,
Mid his twelf yfere,—
Sume hi were luþere.⁴¹

---

³⁴ hearken to. ³⁵ a very good (wise) speech. ³⁶ acts of celebration. ³⁷ in vain.
³⁸ turn out. ³⁹ pleases. ⁴⁰ he gives promise of being a good knight. ⁴¹ wicked.

475. Kings often wore their crowns in ceremonies on certain feast-days, including Whitsunday and Easter.
488. MS. afterward.
490. Any knight could perform the ceremony of conferring knighthood.

Horn he dubbede to kniʒte
Wiþ swerd and spures briʒte; 500
He sette him on a stede whit:
þer nas no kniʒt hym ilik.
He smot him a litel wiʒt[42]
And bed him beon a god kniʒt.
Aþulf fel a knes þar 505
Biuore þe King Aylmar.
"King," he sede, "so kene,
Grante me a bene:[43]
Nu is kniʒ[t] Sire Horn
þat in Suddenne was iboren: 510
Lord he is of londe[44]
Ouer us þat bi him stonde;
þin armes he haþ and scheld
To fiʒte wiþ vpon þe feld:
Let him vs alle kniʒte 515
For þat is vre riʒte."
Aylmar sede sone ywis:
"Do nu þat þi wille is."
Horn adun liʒte
And makede hem alle kniʒtes. 520
Murie was þe feste
Al of faire gestes:[45]
Ac Rymenhild nas noʒt þer,
And þat hire þuʒte seue[46] ʒer:
After Horn heo sente, 525
And he to bure wente.
Nolde he noʒt go one:
Aþulf was his mone.[47]
Rymenhild on flore stod:
Hornes come[48] hire þuʒte god: 530
And sede "Welcome, Sire Horn,
And Aþulf kniʒt þe biforn.[49]
Kniʒt, nu is þi time

---

[42] gently. [43] boon. [44] i.e., undisputed; a mere intensifier. [45] deeds befitting festivity. [46] seven. [47] companion. [48] coming. [49] i.e., who entered before thee.

500. The essential part of the ceremony was girding on the sword.

For to sitte bi me;
Do nu þat þu er of spake: 535
To þi wif þu me take.
Ef þu art trewe of dedes,
Do nu ase þu sedes.
Nu þu hast wille þine,
Vnbind[50] me of my pine." 540
　"Rymenhild," quaþ he, "beo stille:
Ihc wulle don al þi wille,
Also hit mot bitide.
Mid spere i schal furst ride,
And mi kniȝthod proue, 545
Ar ihc þe ginne to woȝe.[1]
We beþ kniȝtes ȝonge,
Of o dai al isprunge;
And of vre mestere[2]
So is þe manere:[3] 550
Wiþ sume oþere kniȝte
Wel for his lemman fiȝte
Or he eni wif take:
Forþi me stondeþ þe more rape.[4]
Today, so Crist me blesse, 555
Ihc wulle do pruesse,[5]
For þi luue, in þe felde
Mid spere and mid schelde.
If ihc come to lyue,[6]
Ihc schal þe take to wyue." 560
　"Kniȝt," quaþ heo, "trewe,
Ihc wene ihc mai þe leue:
Tak nu her þis gold ring:
God him is þe dubbing;[7]
Þer is vpon þe ringe 565
Igraue[8] Rymenhild þe ȝonge:
Þer nis non betere anonder[9] sunne
Þat eni man of telle cunne.
For my luue þu hit were,[10]
And on þi finger þu him bere. 570

---

[50] release. [1] woo. [2] craft. [3] custom. [4] therefore my haste is the greater.
[5] deeds of valor. [6] return alive. [7] decoration. [8] engraved. [9] under. [10] wear.

Þe stones beoþ of suche grace[11]
Þat þu ne schalt in none place
Of none duntes beon ofdrad,[12]
Ne on bataille beon amad,[13]
Ef þu loke þeran   575
And þenke vpon þi lemman.
  And Sire Aþulf, þi broþer,
He schal haue anoþer.
Horn, ihc þe biseche
Wiþ loueliche speche,   580
Crist ʒeue god erndinge[14]
Þe aʒen to bringe."
  Þe kniʒt hire gan kesse,
And heo him to blesse.
Leue at hire he nam,   585
And into halle cam:
Þe kniʒtes ʒeden to table,
And Horne ʒede to stable:
Þar he tok his gode fole,[15]
Also blak so eny cole.[16]   590
Þe fole schok þe brunie[17]
Þat al þe curt gan denie.[18]
Þe fole bigan to springe,
And Horn murie to singe.
Horn rod in a while   595
More þan a myle.
He fond o schup stonde[19]
Wiþ heþene honde:[20]
He axede what hi soʒte
Oþer to londe broʒte.   600
  An hund him gan bihelde,
Þat spac wordes belde:[21]

---

[11] power. [12] afraid. [13] confused. [14] success. [15] steed. [16] charcoal. [17] chain mail. [18] resound. [19] riding at anchor. [20] hounds, a common term for Saracens. [21] bold.

571. Belief in the power of stones to avert injury was widespread. Cf. "Ywain and Gawain" 1530; "Sir Perceval" 1861.
  591. Steeds were protected with ring-mail.
  599. A customary salutation to persons landing in a country.

"Þis lond we wulleȝ wynne,
And sle þat þer is inne."
Horn gan his swerd gripe   605
And on his arme wype:
Þe Sarazins he smatte[22]
Þat his blod hatte:[23]
At eureche dunte
Þe heued of wente;   610
Þo gunne þe hundes gone
Abute Horn alone:
He lokede on þe ringe,
And þoȝte on Rimenilde;
He sloȝ þer on haste   615
On hundred bi þe laste,[24]
Ne miȝte no man telle[25]
Þat folc þat he gan quelle.[26]
Of alle þat were aliue,
Ne miȝte þer non þriue.   620
Horn tok þe maisteres heued,
Þat he hadde him bireued,
And sette hit on his swerde,
Anouen at þan orde.[27]
He verde[28] hom into halle,   625
Among þe kniȝtes alle,
"Kyng," he sede, "wel þu sitte,[29]
And alle þine kniȝtes mitte.[30]
To-day, after mi dubbing,
So i rod on mi pleing,   630
I fond o schup rowe
Mid watere al byflowc,[31]
Al wiþ Sarazines kyn,
And none londisse[32] men,
To-dai for to pine   635
Þe and alle þine.
Hi gonne me assaille:

---

[22] smote.   [23] grew hot.   [24] at least.   [25] count.   [26] kill.   [27] right at the point.
[28] went.   [29] i.e., may you continue to enjoy your present state.   [30] with
thee.   [31] surrounded.   [32] native.

632. Reading from O. 646. MS. C. has *þo hit gan to flowe.*

My swerd me nolde faille:
I smot hem alle to grunde,
Oþer ȝaf hem diþes wunde.[33]   640
Þat heued i þe bringe
Of þe maister-kinge.
Nu is þi wile iȝolde,[34]
King, þat þu me kniȝti woldest."
    A moreȝe þo þe day gan springe,   645
Þe King him rod an huntinge.
At hom lefte Fikenhild,
Þat was þe wurste moder child.[35]
Horn ferde into bure
To sen auenture.   650
He saȝ Rymenild sitte
Also he were of witte.[36]
Heo sat on þe sunne,[37]
Wiþ tieres al birunne.[38]
Horn sede, "Lef, þin ore;   655
Wi wepestu so sore?"
Heo sede, "Noȝt i ne wepe[39]
Bute ase i lay aslepe
To þe se my net i caste,
And hit nolde noȝt ilaste;[40]   660
A gret fiss at the furste
Mi net he gan to berste.
Ihc wene þat ihc schal leose
Þe fiss þat ihc wolde cheose."
    "Crist," quaþ Horn "and Seint Steuene   665
Turne þine sweuene.[41]
Ne schal i þe biswike,
Ne do þat þe mislike.

---

[33] death wound.   [34] willingness rewarded.   [35] child of woman; i.e., in the world.   [36] mad.   [37] i.e., in the window.   [38] in tears.   [39] i.e., this only do I weep.   [40] remain whole.   [41] turn your dream to joy.

638. Bad weapons, which broke at inopportune times, caused the death of many knights.
649. MS. *Heo.*
650. *Sen* may be a blunder for *seie,* recount.
651. MS. *Heo.*

I schal me make þin owe[42]
To holden and to knowe   670
For euerech oþere wiȝte,
And þarto mi treuþe i þe pliȝte."
Muchel was þe ruþe
þat was at þare truþe:
For Rymenhild weop ille,   675
And Horn let þe tires stille.[43]
"Lemman," quaþ he, "dere,
þu schalt more ihere.
þi sweuen schal wende,[44]
Oþer sum man schal vs schende.   680
þe fiss þat brak þe lyne,
Ywis he doþ us pine:
þat schal don vs tene,
And wurþ wel sone isene."
    Aylmar rod bi Sture,[45]   685
And Horn lai in bure.
Fykenhild hadde enuye
And sede þes folye:[46]
"Aylmar, ihc þe warne,
Horn þe wule berne:[47]   690
Ihc herde whar he sede,
And his swerd forþ leide,[48]
To bringe þe of lyue,
And take Rymenhild to wyue.
He liþ in bure   695
Vnder couerture,[1]
By Rymenhild þi doȝter,
And so he doþ wel ofte;
And þider þu go al riȝt,
þer þu him finde miȝt;   700
þu do him vt of londe,
Oþer he doþ þe schonde."[2]
    Aylmar aȝen gan turne
Wel modi and wel murne:[3]

---

[42] own.   [43] wept quietly.   [44] come to evil.   [45] the Mersey.   [46] mad speech.
[47] burn, destroy.   [48] i.e., bared his sword so as to swear on it; a superstitious
practice among heroes.   [1] bed linen.   [2] will do you injury.   [3] mournful.

He fond Horn in arme   705
On Rymenhilde barme.[4]
"Awei vt," he sede, "fule þeof,
Ne wurstu me neuremore leof!
Wend vt of my bure
Wiþ muchel messauenture.[5]   710
Wel sone, bute þu flitte,[6]
Wiþ swerde ihc þe anhitte.[7]
Wend vt of my londe,
Oþer þu schalt haue schonde."
    Horn sadelede his stede,   715
And his armes he gan sprede:[8]
His brunie he gan lace
So he scholde into place.[9]
His swerd he gan fonge:
Nabod he noȝt to longe.[10]   720
He ȝede forþ bliue
To Rymenhild his wyue.
He sede, "Lemman derling,
Nu hauestu þi sweuening.
Þe fiss þat þi net rente,   725
Fram þe he me sente.
Rymenhild, haue wel godne day:
No leng abiden i ne may.
In to vncuþe londe,
Wel more for to fonde,[11]   730
I schal wune þere
Fulle seue ȝere.
At seue ȝeres ende,
Ȝef i ne come ne sende,
Tak þe husebonde: 735
For me þu ne wonde.[12]
In armes þu me fonge,
And kes me wel longe."

---

[4] bosom.   [5] i.e., and bad luck go with you.   [6] unless you depart at once.   [7] lay
on.   [8] put armor on the steed.   [9] as if he were going to the battle-field.   [10] i.e.,
he hurried.   [11] to seek further adventures.   [12] hesitate.

732. Seven years was a conventional period for a lover's probation.

He custe him wel a stunde,[13]
And Rymenhild feol to grunde.   740
Horn tok his leue:
Ne miȝte he no leng bileue;
He tok Aþulf, his fere,
Al abute þe swere,
And sede, "Kniȝt so trewe,   745
Kep wel mi luue newe.
þu neure me ne forsoke:
Rymenhild þu kep and loke."[14]
His stede he gan bistride,
And forþ he gan ride: 750
To þe hauene he ferde,
And a god schup he hurede,[15]
þat him scholde londe
In westene londe.[16]
Aþulf weop wiþ iȝe,   755
And al þat him isiȝe.
[þe whyȝt[17] him gan stonde,
And drof tyl Hirelonde.]
To lond he him sette,
And fot on stirop sette.
He fond bi þe weie
Kynges sones tweie;   760
þat on him het Harild,
And þat oþer Berild.
Berild gan him preie
þat he scholde him seie
What his name were,   765
And what he wolde þere.
"Cutberd," he sede, "ihc hotc,
Icomen vt of þe bote,
Wel feor fram biweste
To seche mine beste."[18]   770
Berild gan him nier[19] ride

---

[13] a short while.   [14] guard.   [15] hired.   [16] i.e., Ireland.   [17] breeze.   [18] profit.
[19] nearer.

756. The two following lines are from O. 784–5.

And tok him bi þe bridel:
"Wel beo þu, kniȝt, ifounde;
Wiþ me þu lef²⁰ a stunde.
Also mote i sterue,²¹   775
þe King þu schalt serue.
Ne saȝ i neure my lyue²²
So fair kniȝt aryue."
Cutberd heo ladde into halle,
And he²³ a kne gan falle: 780
He sette him a knewelyng²⁴
And grette wel þe gode Kyng.
þanne sede Berild sone:
"Sire King, of him þu hast to done:²⁵
Bitak him þi lond to werie:²⁶   785
Ne schal hit no man derie,
For he is þe faireste man
þat eure ȝut on þi londe cam."
þanne sede þe King so dere:
"Welcome beo þu here.   790
Go nu, Berild, swiþe,
And make him ful bliþe,
And whan þu farst to woȝe,²⁷
Tak him þine gloue:
Iment þu hauest to wyue,²⁸   795
Awai he schal þe dryue.
For Cutberdes fairhede²⁹
Ne schal þe neure wel spede."
    Hit was at Cristesmasse,
Neiþer more ne lasse:³⁰   800
þer cam in at none
A geaunt suþe sone,

---

²⁰ remain. ²¹ die, i.e., surely. ²² in my life. ²³ they. ²⁴ kneeling. ²⁵ i.e., secure his services. ²⁶ guard. ²⁷ wooing. ²⁸ (where) you mean to marry.
²⁹ beauty. ³⁰ i.e., on Christmas Day itself.

786. MS. schat.
794. The king urges him to exchange gloves with Horn, probably as
a ceremony to show they had agreed not to be rivals in love.
799. Christmas Day was a conventional time for challenges from
heathen enemies.

Iarmed fram paynyme,[31]
And seide þes ryme:[32]
"Site stille, Sire Kyng,   805
And herkne þis tyþyng:
Her buþ paens ariued:
Wel mo þane fiue[33]
Her beoþ on þe sonde,
King, vpon þi londe;   810
On of hem wile fiȝte
Aȝen þre kniȝtes:
Ȝef oþer þre slen vre,
Al þis lond beo ȝoure:
Ȝef vre on ouercomeþ ȝour þreo,   815
Al þis lond schal vre beo.
Tomoreȝe be þe fiȝtinge,
Whane þe liȝt of daye springe."
   Þanne sede þe Kyng þurston,
"Cutberd schal beo þat on,   820
Berild schal beo þat oþer,
Þe þridde Alrid his broþer,
For hi beoþ þe strengeste
And of armes þe beste.
Bute what schal vs to rede?   825
Ihc wene we beþ alle dede."
   Cutberd sat at borde
And sede þes wordes,
"Sire King, hit nis no riȝte
On wiþ þre to fiȝte: 830
Aȝen one hunde,
Þre Cristen men to fonde.
Sire, i schal alone,
Wiþute more ymone,[34]
Wiþ mi swerd wel eþe[35]   835
Bringe hem þre to deþe."
   Þe Kyng aros amoreȝe,
Þat hadde muchel sorȝe,
And Cutberd ros of bedde,

---

[31] heathendom. [32] speech. [33] i.e., a good many. [34] companions. [35] easily.

Wiþ armes he him schredde:[36]   840
Horn his brunie gan on caste,
And lacede hit wel faste,
And cam to þe Kinge
At his vprisinge.
"King," he sede, "cum to fel[de],   845
For to bihelde
Hu we fiȝte schulle,
And togare[37] go wulle."
Riȝt at prime tide
Hi gunnen vt ride,   850
And funden on a grene
A geaunt suþe kene,
His feren him biside
Hore deþ to abide.
    Þe ilke bataille[38]   855
Cutberd gan assaille:
He ȝaf dentes inoȝe;
Þe kniȝtes felle iswoȝe.
His dent he gan wiþdraȝe,[39]
For hi were neȝ aslaȝe:[40]   860
And sede, "Kniȝtes, nu ȝe reste
One[41] while ef ȝou leste."
Hi sede hi neure nadde
Of kniȝte dentes so harde,
[Bote of þe King Murry,
Þat wes swiþe sturdy.]
He was of Hornes kunne,   865
Iborn in Suddenne.
    Horn him gan to agrise,[42]
And his blod arise.
Biuo[r] him saȝ he stonde
Þat[43] driuen him of londe,   870
And þat his fader sloȝ;

---

[36] arrayed. [37] together. [38] hostile forces. [39] withhold. [40] slain. [41] a. [42] shudder. [43] those who.

845. MS. *fel*.
864. The next two lines are from MS. L. 873-4.

To him his swerd he droʒ.
He lokede on his rynge,
And þoʒte on Rymenhilde.
Ho smot him þureʒ þe herte, 875
Þat sore him gan to smerte.[44]
Þe paens, þat er were so sturne,
Hi gunne awei vrne;
Horn and his compaynye
Gunne after hem wel swiþe hiʒe, 880
And sloʒen alle þe hundes
Er hi here schipes funde:
To deþe he hem alle broʒte;
His fader deþ wel dere hi boʒte.
Of alle þe Kynges kniʒtes, 885
Ne scaþede[45] wer no wiʒte,
Bute his sones tweie
Bifore him he saʒ deie.
Þe King bigan to grete
And teres for to lete. 890
Me leiden hem in bare[46]
And burden[47] hem ful ʒare.
   Þe King com into halle
Among his kniʒtes alle.
"Horn," he sede, "i seie þe, 895
Do as i schal rede þe.
Aslaʒen beþ mine heirs,
And þu art kniʒt of muchel pris,
And of grete strengþe,
And fair o bodie lengþe;[48] 900
Mi rengne[49] þu schalt welde,
And to spuse helde
Reynild, mi doʒter,
Þat sitteþ on þe lofte."[50]
   "O Sire King, wiþ wronge 905
Scholte ihc hit vnderfonge,[1]

---

[44] pain.　[45] injured.　[46] bier.　[47] buried.　[48] i.e., tall.　[49] realm.　[50] in an upper room.　[1] accept.

886. MS. *scapede þer.*

Þi doȝter, þat ȝe me bede,
Ower rengne for to lede.[2]
Wel more ihc schal þe serue,
Sire Kyng, or þu sterue.[3]   910
Þi sorwe schal wende
Or seue ȝeres ende:
Wanne hit is wente,
Sire King, ȝef me mi rente:[4]
Whanne i þi doȝter ȝerne,   915
Ne schaltu me hire werne."[5]
Cutberd wonede þere
Fulle seue ȝere
Þat to Rymenild he ne sente,
Ne him self ne wente.   920
Rymenild was in Westernesse
Wiþ wel muchel sorinesse.
   A king þer gan ariue
Þat wolde hire haue to wyue;
Aton[6] he was wiþ þe King   925
Of þat ilke wedding.
Þe daies were schorte,
Þat Rimenhild ne dorste[7]
Leten in none wise.
A writ he dude deuise;   930
Aþulf hit dude write,
Þat Horn ne luuede noȝt lite
Heo sende hire sonde
To euereche londe,
To seche Horn þe kniȝt   935
Þer me him finde miȝte.
Horn noȝt þer of ne herde
Til o dai þat he ferde
To wude for to schete.[8]
A knaue he gan imete.   940
Horn seden, "Leue fere,
Wat sechestu here?"

---

[2] to govern your kingdom.   [3] before you die.   [4] reward.   [5] refuse.   [6] at one,
agreed.   [7] dared.   [8] shoot arrows (at stags).

"Kniȝt, if beo þi wille,
I mai þe sone telle.
I seche fram biweste   945
Horn of Westernesse,
For a maiden Rymenhild,
þat for him gan wexe wild.
A king hire wile wedde
And bringe to his bedde: 950
King Modi of Reynes,[9]
On of Hornes enemis.
Ihc habbe walke wide,[10]
Bi þe se side;
Nis he nowar ifunde.   955
Walawai þe stunde!
Wailaway þe while!
Nu wurþ Rymenild bigiled."[11]
Horn iherde wiþ his ires,
And spak wiþ bidere[12] tires: 960
"Knaue, wel þe bitide;
Horn stondeþ þe biside.
Aȝen to hure þu turne,
And seie þat heo ne murne,[13]
For i schal beo þer bitime,[14]   965
A Soneday bi pryme."
þe knaue was wel bliþe
And hiȝede aȝen bliue.
þe knaue þere gan adrinkc:[15]
Rymenhild hit miȝte ofþinke.[16]   970
[þe see him con ded þrowe[17]
Vnder hire chambre wowe.][18]
Rymenhild undude þe dure-pin[19]
Of þe hus þer heo was in,
To loke wiþ hire iȝe,   975
If heo oȝt of Horn isiȝe:

[9] Furness, in northern Lancashire.   [10] traveled far.   [11] deceived, disappointed.
[12] bitter.   [13] mourn.   [14] betimes.   [15] drown.   [16] regret.   [17] threw him dead.
[18] wall.   [19] sliding bolt.
  969–70. MS. C. þe se bigan to þroȝe Vnder hire woȝe. These have been
omitted, and two lines from L. (981–2) substituted after 972.

Þo fond heo þe knaue adrent,[20]
Þat he hadde for Horn isent,
And þat scholde Horn bringe.
Hire fingres he gan wringe.   980
    Horn cam to Þurston þe Kyng,
And tolde him þis tiþing.
Þo he was iknowe
Þat Rimenhild was his oȝe;
Of[22] his gode kenne   985
Þe King of Suddenne,
And hu he sloȝ in felde
Þat[23] his fader quelde,[24]
And seide, "King þe wise,
ȝeld me mi seruise: 990
Rymenhild help me winne,
Þat þu noȝt ne linne:[25]
And i schal do to spuse[26]
Þi doȝter wel to huse:[27]
Heo schal to spuse haue   995
Aþulf, mi gode felaȝe,
God kniȝt mid þe beste
And þe treweste."
Þe King sede so stille,[28]
"Horn haue nu þi wille."   1000
He dude writes sende
Into Yrlonde
After kniȝtes liȝte,[29]
Irisse men to fiȝte.
To Horn come inoȝe   1005
Þat to schupe droȝe.
Horn dude him in þe weie[30]
On a god galeie.
Þe [wind] him gan to blowe
In a litel þroȝe.   1010
Þe se bigan to posse[31]
    Riȝt into Westernesse.

---

[20] drowned.   [22] sc. he acknowledged.   [23] him who.   [24] killed.   [25] cease.   [26] cause
to be married.   [27] i.e., preside over a good home.   [28] quietly.   [29] agile.   [30] set
out.   [31] push, drive.

Hi strike seil and maste
And ankere gunne caste,
Or eny day was sprunge 1015
Oþer belle irunge.
Þe word bigan to springe
Of Rymenhilde weddinge.
Horn was in þe watere,
Ne miȝte he come no latere. 1020
He let his schup stonde,[32]
And ȝede to londe.
His folk he dude abide[33]
Vnder wude side.[34]
Hor[n] him ȝede alone 1025
Also he sprunge of stone.[35]
A palmere he þar mette,
And faire hine grette:
"Palmere, þu schalt me telle
Al of þine spelle." 1030
He sede vpon[36] his tale:
"I come fram o brudale;[37]
Ihc was at o wedding
Of a maide Rymenhild:
Ne miȝte heo adriȝe[38] 1035
Þat heo ne weop wiþ iȝe;
Heo sede þat heo nolde
Ben ispused wiþ golde.[39]
Heo hadde on husebonde,
Þeȝ he were vt of londe: 1040
And in strong halle,
Biþinne[40] castel walle,
Þer i was atte ȝate,
Nolde hi me in late.

[32] ride at anchor. [33] caused to wait. [34] wood's edge. [35] i.e., alone. [36] in the course of. [37] bridal feast. [38] forbear. [39] i.e., a gold ring. [40] within.

1016. Bells were rung in religious establishments at early services.

1026. The first men were superstitiously believed to have sprung from stones, and therefore to have been solitary.

1044. Refusing to entertain all comers at a wedding was a mark of niggardliness.

Modi ihote hadde 1045
To bure þat me hire ladde:
Awai i gan glide:
Þat deol i nolde abide.
Þe bride wepeþ sore,
And þat is muche deole." 1050
Quaþ Horn, "So Crist me rede,
We schulle chaungi wede:[41]
Haue her cloþes myne,
And tak me þi sclauyne.[42]
Today i schal þer drinke 1055
Þat some hit schulle ofþinke."[43]
His sclauyn he dude dun legge,
And tok hit on his rigge,
He tok Horn his[44] cloþes:
Þat nere him noȝt loþe. 1060
Horn tok burdon and scrippe[45]
And wrong[46] his lippe.
He makede him a ful chere,
And al bicolmede[47] his swere.
He makede him vnbicomelich,[48] 1065
Hes he nas neuremore ilich,[49]
    He com to þe gateward,[50]
Þat him answerede hard:
Horn bad vndo softe[1]
Mani tyme and ofte, 1070
Ne miȝte he awynne[2]
Þat he come þerinne.
Horn gan to þe ȝate turne
And þat wiket vnspurne;[3]
Þe boye hit scholde abugge:[4] 1075
Horn þreu him ouer þe brigge[5]
Þat his ribbes him tobrake,
And suþþe com in atte gate.

---

[41] exchange garments. [42] sclavin, robe. [43] regret. [44] Horn's. [45] long staff and wallet. [46] twisted. [47] blackened, dirtied. [48] uncomely. [49] such as he never was at any time. [50] porter. [1] gently to unbar. [2] succeed. [3] kick open the wicket (cf. Int. III.A.1.). [4] rascal had to pay for it. [5] i.e., into the moat.

1052. A palmer's costume was a favorite disguise.

He sette him wel loӡe,[6]
In beggeres rowe; 1080
He lokede him abute
Wiþ his colmie snute;[7]
He seӡ Rymenhild sitte
Ase heo were of witte,[8]
Sore wepinge and ӡerne: 1085
Ne miӡte hure no man wurne.[9]
He lokede in eche halke:[10]
Ne seӡ he nowhar walke
Aþulf his felawe,
Þat he cuþe knowe.[11] 1090
Aþulf was in þe ture,[12]
Abute for to pure[13]
After his comynge,
Ӡef schup him wolde bringe.
He seӡ þe se flowe 1095
And Horn nowar rowe.
He sede vpon his songe,
"Horn, nu þu ert wel longe.
Rymenhild þu me toke[14]
Þat i scholde loke;[15] 1100
Ihc habbe ikept hure eure;
Com nu oþer neure:
I ne may no leng hure kepe.
For soreӡe nu y wepe."
Rymenhild ros of benche, 1105
Wyn for to schenche:[16]
After mete in sale,[17]
Boþe wyn and ale.
On horn he bar anhonde,
So laӡe[18] was in londe. 1110
Kniӡtes and squier

---

[6] low. [7] begrimed nose. [8] crazed. [9] stop. [10] corner. [11] so far as he could perceive. [12] tower. [13] look attentively. [14] entrusted. [15] protect. [16] pour. [17] hall. [18] custom.

1080, 1105. A few beggars were admitted to wedding feasts, and were served wine by the bride. The exploit of Horn has a close parallel in Gram's visit (Saxo Grammaticus, Ch. 1).

Alle dronken of þe ber,[19]
Bute Horn alone
Nadde þerof no mone.[20]
Horn sat vpon þe grunde;   1115
Him þuȝte he was ibunde.[21]
He sede, "Quen so hende,
To meward[22] þu wende;
Þu ȝef vs wiþ þe furste:[23]
Þe beggeres beoþ ofþurste."[24]   1120
    Hure horn heo leide adun,
And fulde him of a brun,[25]
His bolle of a galun,[26]
For heo wende he were a glotoun
He seide, "Haue þis cuppe,   1125
And þis þing þervppe:[27]
Ne saȝ ihc neure, so ihc wene,
Beggere þat were so kene."
Horn tok hit his ifere,
And sede, "Quen so dere,   1130
Wyn nelle ihc muche ne lite
Bute of cuppe white.[28]
Þu wenest i beo a beggere,
And ihc am a fissere,
Wel feor icome bi este[29]   1135
For fissen[30] at þi feste:
Mi net liþ her bi honde,[31]
Bi a wel fair stronde.
Hit haþ ileie þere
Fulle seue ȝere.   1140
Ihc am icome to loke
Ef eni fiss hit toke.[32]

---

[19] beer.   [20] share.   [21] i.e., he seemed overcome.   [22] toward me.   [23] serve us among the first.   [24] thirsty.   [25] brown bowl.   [26] gallon.   [27] have an amount equal to the capacity of the horn, and more as well.   [28] i.e., a horn.   [29] toward the east.   [30] to fish.   [31] i.e., Rimenhild.   [32] i.e., whether she has another lover.

1121. She distinguishes between the gentlefolk, who drink from the horn, and a beggar, who drinks from a bowl. Horn objects (1132).

1132. Drinking horns were usually made of horns of animals, and hence were white; bowls and other pottery were brown.

Ihc am icome to fisse:
Drynke null y of dyssh:
Drink to Horn of horne:[33]   1145
Feor ihc am iorne."[34]
Rymenhild him gan bihelde;
Hire heorte bigan to chelde.[35]
Ne kneu heo noȝt his fissing,
Ne Horn hymselue noþing:[36]   1150
Ac wunder hire gan þinke,
Whi he bad to Horn drinke.
Heo fulde[37] hire horn wiþ wyn,
And dronk to þe pilegrym.
Heo sede, "Drink þi fulle,   1155
And suþþe þu me telle
If þu eure isiȝe
Horn vnder wude liȝe."
Horn dronk of horn a stunde
And þreu þe ring to grunde.[38]   1160
[He seyde, "Qucn, nou seche
Qwat hys in þy drenche."]
Þe Quen ȝede to bure
Wiþ hire maidenes foure.
Þo fond heo what heo wolde,
A ring igrauen of golde
Þat Horn of hure hadde;   1165
Sore hure dradde
Þat Horn isterue were,
For þe ring was þere.
Þo sente heo a damesele
After þe palmere;   1170
"Palmere," quaþ heo, "trewe,
Þe ring þat þu þrewe,
Þu seie whar þu hit nome,

---

[33] to Horn from the horn. [34] travelled. [35] grow cold. [36] she did not recognize Horn at all. [37] filled. [38] the bottom of the horn.

1144. C. has *Drink to me of disse*. The substituted line is L. 1146.
1160. The next two lines are from O. 1198-9. On the incident, cf.
FF Communications 74.81.
1167. MS. *isteue*.

And whi þu hider come."
He sede, "Bi Seint Gile,[39]   1175
Ihc habbe go mani mile,
Wel feor bi ȝonde weste
To seche my beste.[40]
I fond Horn child stonde[41]
To schupeward in londe.[42]   1180
He sede he wolde agesse[43]
To ariue in Westernesse.
Þe schip nam to þe flode
Wiþ me and Horn þe gode;
Horn was sik and deide,   1185
And faire he me preide:
'Go wiþ þe ringe
To Rymenhild þe ȝonge.'
Ofte he hit custe,[44]
God ȝeue his saule[45] reste!"   1190
    Rymenhild sede at þe furste:[46]
"Herte, nu þu berste,
For Horn nastu namore,
Þat þe haþ pined so sore."
Heo feol on hire bedde,   1195
Þer heo knif hudde,[47]
To sle wiþ King loþe[48]
And hureselue boþe
In þat vlke niȝte,
If Horn come ne miȝte.   1200
To herte knif heo sette,
Ac Horn anon hire kepte.[49]
He wipede þat blake of his swere,
And sede: "Quen so swete and dere,
Ihc am Horn þin oȝe;   1205
Ne canstu me noȝt knowe?
Ihc am Horn of Westernesse;
In armes þu me cusse."
    Hi custe hem[50] mid ywisse,

---

[39] St. Gilles, great shrine near Nîmes. [40] profit. [41] i.e., about to embark.
[42] i.e., some place. [43] strive. [44] kissed. [45] soul. [46] at once. [47] hid. [48] with
which to slay her hated king. [49] caught up. [50] kissed each other.

And makeden muche blisse.   1210
  "Rymenhild," he sede, "y wende
Adun to þe wudes ende:
þer beþ myne kniʒtes
Redi to fiʒte,
Iarmed vnder cloþe;   1215
Hi schulle make wroþe
þe King and his geste
þat come to þe feste:
Today i schal hem teche
And sore hem areche."[1]   1220
  Horn sprong vt of halle
And let his sclauin[2] falle.
þe Quen ʒede to bure
And fond Aþulf in ture:
"Aþulf," heo sede, "be bliþe,   1225
And to Horn þu go wel swiþe:
He is vnder wude boʒe,[3]
And wiþ him kniʒtes inoʒe."
  Aþulf bigan to springe[4]
For þe tiþinge: 123v
After Horn he arnde[5] anon,
Also[6] þat hors miʒte gon.
He him ouertok ywis;
Hi makede suiþe muchel blis.
Horn tok his preie[7]   1235
And dude[8] him in þe weie.
He com in wel sone:
þe ʒates were vndone.
Iarmed ful þikke[9]
Fram fote to þe nekke,   1240
Alle þat were þerin
Biþute[10] his twelf ferin
And þe King Aylmare,
He dude hem alle to kare,[11]
þat at the feste were;   1245

---

[1] strike. [2] cloak. [3] bough. [4] caper (with joy). [5] ran; i.e., rode. [6] as fast as.
[7] band of warriors. [8] set. [9] completely. [10] except. [11] be sorry.

Here lif hi lete[12] þere.
Horn ne dude no wunder[13]
Of Fikenhildes false tunge.
Hi sworen oþes holde,[14]
Þat neure ne scholde[15]   1250
Horn neure bitraie,
Þeȝ he at diþe[16] laie.
Hi runge þe belle
Þe wedlak for to felle;[17]
Horn him ȝede with his[18]   1255
To þe Kinges palais,
Þer was bridale suete,
For riche men þer ete.[19]
Telle ne miȝte tunge
Þat gle þat þer was sunge.   1260
  Horn sat on chaere,
And bad hem alle ihere.
"King," he sede, "þu luste[20]
A tale mid þe beste.
I ne seie hit for no blame:[21]   1265
Horn is mi name;
Þu me to kniȝt houe,[22]
And kniȝthod haue proued:
To þe, King, men seide
Þat i þe bitraide;   1270
Þu makedest me fleme,[23]
And þi lond to reme;[24]
Þu wendest þat i wroȝte
Þat y neure ne þoȝte,
Bi Rymenhild for to ligge;   1275
And þat i wiþsegge.[25]
Ne schal ihc hit biginne,
Til i Suddene winne.

---

[12] they left, lost. [13] terrible deed. [14] of allegiance. [15] sc. they. [16] near death.
[17] celebrate. [18] his men. [19] i.e., a feast for nobles. [20] listen to. [21] reproach.
[22] elevated. [23] outlaw. [24] quit. [25] deny.

1257. MS. *brid and ale.*
1261. King's chair; most of the company sat on benches.
1268. Sc. "I"; often omitted if previously expressed.

Þu kep hure a stunde,
Þe while þat i funde²⁶   1280
Into min heritage,
And to mi baronage.
Þat lond i schal ofreche,²⁷
And do mi fader wreche.
I schal beo king of tune,   1285
And bere kinges crune;
Þanne schal Rymenhilde
Ligge bi þe kinge."
  Horn gan to schupe draȝe
Wiþ his Yrisse felaȝes,   1290
Aþulf wiþ him, his brother:
Nolde he non oþer.
Þat schup bigan to crude,²⁸
Þe wind him bleu lude;²⁹
Biþinne daies fiue   1295
Þat schup gan ariue,
Abute middelniȝte.
Horn him ȝede wel riȝte;
He tok Aþulf bi honde,
And vp he ȝede to londe.   1300
Hi founde vnder schelde
A kniȝt hende in felde.³⁰
[O þe shelde wes ydrawe
A croyȝ of Ihesu Cristes lawe.³¹]
Þe kniȝt him aslepe lay
Al biside þe way.
Horn him gan to take   1305
And sede, "Kniȝt, awake.
Seie what þu kepest?
And whi þu her slepest?
Me þinkþ bi þine crois liȝte,³²
Þat þu longest to vre Driȝte.³³   1310
Bute þu wule me schewe,
I schal þe tohewe."³⁴

_____

²⁶ work my way. ²⁷ obtain. ²⁸ make way. ²⁹ blew loudly. ³⁰ capable in combat. ³¹ religion. ³² shining cross. ³³ Lord. ³⁴ hew to pieces.

1302. The next two lines are from MS. L. 1313–4.

þe gode kniʒt vp aros;
Of þe wordes him gros:³⁵
He sede, "Ihc serve aʒenes my wille   1315
Payns³⁶ ful ylle.
Ihc was Cristene a while:
þo icom to þis ille³⁷
Sarazins blake,
þat dude me forsake:³⁸   1320
On Crist ihc wolde bileue.
On him³⁹ hi makede me reue,
To kepe þis passage⁴⁰
Fram Horn þat is of age,
þat wunieþ bieste,⁴¹   1325
Kniʒt wiþ þe beste;
Hi sloʒe wiþ here honde⁴²
þe king of þis londe,
And wiþ him fele hundred,
And þerof is wunder   1330
þat he ne comeþ to fiʒte:
God sende him þe riʒte,⁴³
And wind him hider driue,
To bringe hem of liue:⁴⁴
Hi sloʒen Kyng Murry,   1335
Hornes fader, king hendy.⁴⁵
Horn hi vt of londe sente;
Tuelf felaʒes wiþ him wente,
Among hem Aþulf þe gode,
Min oʒene child, my leue fode:⁴⁶   1340
Ef Horn child is hol and sund,
And Aþulf biþute⁴⁷ wund,
He luueþ him⁴⁸ so dere,
And is him so stere.⁴⁹
Miʒte i seon hem tueie,   1345

---

³⁵ he was terrified.   ³⁶ heathens.   ³⁷ isle.   ³⁸ give it up.   ³⁹ against Horn they made me guardian.   ⁴⁰ pass.   ⁴¹ dwells in the east; but a blunder for *biweste*.   ⁴² blunder for *He . . . his*.   ⁴³ God grant that right be on Horn's side.   ⁴⁴ kill them.   ⁴⁵ a courteous king.   ⁴⁶ child.   ⁴⁷ without.   ⁴⁸ i.e., Athulf loves Horn.   ⁴⁹ so faithful (?).

1315. MS. *He sede ihc haue.*

For ioie i scholde deie."
"Kniȝt, beo þanne bliþe,
Mest of alle siþe;[50]
Horn and Aþulf his fere
Boþe hi ben here."   1350
To Horn he gan gon
And grette him anon.
Muche ioie hi makede þere
þe while hi togadere were.
"Childre," he sede, "hu habbe ȝe fare?   1355
þat ihc ȝou seȝ hit is ful ȝare.
Wulle ȝe þis londe winne
And sle þat[1] þer is inne?"
He sede, "Leue Horn child,
ȝut lyueþ þi moder Godhild: 1360
Of ioie heo miste[2]
If heo þe aliue wiste."
   Horn sede on his rime,[3]
"Iblessed beo þe time
I com to Suddenne   1365
Wiþ mine Irisse menne:
We schulle þe hundes teche
To speken vre speche.[4]
Alle we hem schulle sle,
And al quic hem fle."[5]   1370
Horn gan his horn to blowe;
His folk hit gan iknowe;
Hi comen vt of stere,[6]
Fram Hornes banere;
Hi sloȝen and fuȝten,   1375
þe niȝt and þe vȝten;[7]
þe Sarazins cunde
Ne lefde þer non in þende.[8]
Horn let wurche
Chapeles and chirche;   1380
He let belles ringe

---

[50] more than ever before.   [1] whoever.   [2] she would fail to be joyful.   [3] speech.
[4] i.e., do something distasteful.   [5] flay alive.   [6] boat.   [7] time before dawn.
[8] at the last.

And masses let singe.
He com to his moder halle
In a roche walle.
Corn he let serie,[9] 1385
And makede feste merie;
Murie lif he wroȝte:[10]
Rymenhild hit dere boȝte.
　Fikenhild was prut[11] on herte,
And þat him dude smerte.[12] 1390
Ȝonge he ȝaf[13] and elde
Mid him for to helde.
Ston he dude lede,[14]
Þer he hopede spede,[15]
Strong castel he let sette,[16] 1395
Mid see him biflette,[17]
Þer ne miȝte liȝte
Bute foȝel wiþ fliȝte.
Bute whanne þe se wiþdroȝe,[18]
Miȝte come men ynoȝe. 1400
Fikenhild gan wende
Rymenhild to schende.
To woȝe[19] he gan hure ȝerne;
Þe Kyng ne dorste him werne.[20]
Rymenhild was ful of mode:[21] 1405
He wep teres of blode.
Þat niȝt Horn gan swete[22]
And heuie for to mete
Of Rymenhild his make[23]
Into schupe was itake: 1410
Þe schup bigan to blenche:[24]
His lemman scholde adrenche.[25]
Rymenhild wiþ hire honde
Wolde vp to londe:
Fikenhild aȝen hire pelte[26] 1415

---

[9] grain he ordered carried.　[10] i.e., led.　[11] arrogant.　[12] i.e., it got him into trouble.　[13] i.e., bribed.　[14] transported.　[15] where he expected it to do the most good.　[16] build.　[17] flowed about, surrounded.　[18] receded.　[19] woo.　[20] refuse.　[21] i.e., was reluctant.　[22] sweat.　[23] mate.　[24] lurch.　[25] drown.　[26] thrust her back.

Wiþ his swerdes hilte.
  Horn him wok of slape
So a man þat hadde rape.[27]
"Aþulf," he sede, "fela3e,
To schupe we mote dra3e.   1420
Fikenhild me haþ idon vnder,[28]
And Rymenhild to do wunder;
Crist, for his wundes fiue,
To-ni3t me þuder driue."
Horn gan to schupe ride,   1425
  His feren him biside.
Fikenhild, or þe dai gan springe,
Al ri3t[29] he ferde to þe Kinge,
After Rymenhild þe bri3te,
To wedden hire bi ni3te.   1430
He ladde hure bi þe derke[30]
Into his nywe[31] werke.
Þe feste hi bigunne
Er þat ros þe sunne.
Er þane Horn hit wiste,   1435
Tofore þe sunne vpriste,[32]
His schup stod vnder ture
At Rymenhilde bure.
Rymenhild, litel weneþ heo
Þat Horn þanne aliue beo.   1440
Þe castel þei ne knewe,
For he[33] was so nywe.
Horn fond sittinde Arnoldin,
Þat was Aþulfes cosin,
Þat þer was in þat tide,   1445
Horn for tabide.[34]
"Horn kni3t," he sede, "kinges sone,
Wel beo þu to londe icome.
Today haþ ywedde Fikenhild
Þi swete lemman Rymenhild.   1450
Ne schal i þe lie:
He haþ giled þe twie.[35]

---

[27] haste. [28] undermined. [29] at once. [30] in darkness. [31] new. [32] before the
rising of the sun. [33] it. [34] to await. [35] deceived thee twice.

Þis tur he let make
Al for þine sake.
Ne mai þer come inne   1455
No man wiþ none ginne.[36]
Horn, nu Crist þe wisse,
Of Rymenhild þat þu ne misse."[37]
    Horn cuþe al þe liste[38]
Þat eni man of wiste.   1460
Harpe he gan schewe,
And tok fela3es fewe,
Of kni3tes suiþe snelle
Þat schrudde[39] hem at wille.
Hi 3eden bi þe grauel[40]   1465
Toward þe castel;
Hi gunne murie[41] singe
And makede here gleowinge.[42]
    Rymenhild hit gan ihere,
And axede what hi were.   1470
Hi sede, hi weren harpurs,
And sume were gigours.[43]
He dude Horn in late[44]
Ri3t at halle gate.
He sette him on þe benche,   1475
His harpe for to clenche.[45]
He makede Rymenhilde lay,[46]
And heo makede walaway.
Rymenhild feol yswo3e,
Ne was þer non þat lou3e.   1480
Hit smot to Hornes herte
So bitere þat hit smerte.
He lokede on þe ringe
And þo3te on Rymenhilde:
He 3ede vp to borde[47]   1485
Wiþ gode suerdes orde:[48]
Fikenhildes crune[49]

---

[36] artifice. [37] lose. [38] cunning. [39] clad; i.e., disguised. [40] beach. [41] merrily.
[42] harping. [43] fiddlers. [44] she ordered Horn to be let in. [45] pluck. [46] song.
[47] the high table. [48] sword's edge. [49] top of head.

Þer he fulde adune,
And al his men arowe⁵⁰
Hi dude adun þrowe.   1490
Whanne hi weren asla3e,
Fikenhild hi dude todra3e.¹
Horn makede Arnoldin þare
King, after King Aylmare,
Of al Westernesse   1495
For his meoknesse.²
Þe King and his homage³
3euen Arnoldin trewage.⁴
    Horn tok Rymenhild bi þe honde
And ladde hure to þe stronde,   1500
And ladde wiþ him Aþelbrus,
Þe gode stuard of his hus.
Þe se bigan to flowe,⁵
And Horn gan to rowe.
Hi gunne for [to] ariue   1505
Þer King Modi was sire.⁶
Aþelbrus he makede þer king
For his gode teching:
He 3af alle þe kni3tes ore⁷
For Horn kni3tes lore.   1510
Horn gan for to ride;⁸
Þe wind him blcu wel wide.⁹
He ariuede in Yrlonde,
Þer he wo fonde,
Þer he dude Aþulf child   1515
Wedden maide Reynild.
Horn com to Suddenne
Among al his kenne;
Rymenhild he makede his quene;
So hit mi3te wel beon.   1520

---

⁵⁰ in a row, in order. ¹ rend in pieces. ² meekness. ³ vassals. ⁴ tribute. ⁵ i.e.,
at flood tide. ⁶ lord. ⁷ he was well-disposed toward all knights because of
Horn's counsel. ⁸ sail. ⁹ amply.

1488. MS. *ifulde.*
1514. MS. *fondede.* The line is corrupt; it may mean "which he had
found woeful" (because of Saracens).

Al folk hem miȝte rewe[10]
Þat loueden hem so trewe.
Nu ben hi boþe dede,—
Crist to heuene hem lede!
Her endeþ þe tale of Horn,   1525
Þat fair was and noȝt vnorn;[11]
Make we vs glade eure among,
For[12] þus him endeþ Hornes song.
Jesus, þat is of heuene king,
Ȝeue vs alle His suete blessing.   1530

AMEN.

EX—PLI—CIT.

HAVELOK THE DANE

HAVELOK THE DANE

"Havelok the Dane" is an early piece in which partly historical material is treated frankly as fiction. The dialect is north-midland of about 1285, and shows strong Norse influence; but the poet's style and ideas are those of French heroic poetry.

The unique manuscript is an unintelligent copy of another manuscript, and full of mistakes; yet it has been followed unless the error causes absurdity. Necessary words omitted by the scribe have been inserted, and palpable misspellings corrected; but his mannerisms in spelling have been retained. Noteworthy are the use of -*th* for -*ht* (*rith* = *riht*); of -*w* for -*u* (hw = hu); the needless addition of initial *h*- (*holde* = *old*); the omission of *h*- where necessary (*wat* = *hwat*); and the omission of final -*h* after *t*- (*herknet* = *hearkeneth*). He is liberal with negatives, especially in dependent clauses where they would now be omitted (cf. 249).

The problem of sources is difficult; the principal contributions are summarized by Miss Hibbard. But clearly there were two traditions, one showing the influence of French courtly literature, the other, a homely rhyme in English; and they had grown far apart by the time of the first surviving versions. The subject is further complicated by the indifference of the English poet to consistency and accuracy; obviously, he cared little for anything but dramatic scenes with a moral (see Creek's study). His talent in arranging and presenting these, however, is extraordinary.

With the kind permission of the authorities of the Bodleian Library, the text has been prepared from rotographs. The numbering of the lines is that of the edition of Skeat and Sisam, Oxford, 1915. Skeat, Holthausen, Sisam, and others have done much to make intelligible this very difficult text. Many of their emendations are credited to them in notes; those not otherwise credited are Skeat's. For references to Gaimar's "Estorie des Engles" and the "Lai d'Havelok," see A. Bell's edition of the latter (Manchester, 1925).

Herknet to me, godemen,
Wiues, maydnes, and alle men,
Of a tale þat ich you wile telle,
Wo-so it wile here and þer-to duelle.[1]
Þe tale is of Hauelok imaked;   5
Wil he was litel, he yede ful naked.
Hauelok was a ful god gome:[2]
He was ful god in eueri trome;[3]
He was þe wicteste man at nede
Þat þurte riden on ani stede.   10
Þat ye mowen nou yhere,
And þe tale ye mowen ylere,
At þe biginning of vre tale,
Fil me a cuppe of ful god ale;
And wile [y] drinken, her y spelle,[4]   15
Þat Crist vs shilde[5] alle fro helle!
Krist late vs heuere so for to do
Þat we moten comen him to;
And, witþat[6] it mote ben so,

---

[1] wait.   [2] man.   [3] company.   [4] relate (a story).   [5] shield.   [6] considering that.

Heading. The union of England and Denmark under Havelok is an essential part of all the versions of the story, and Robert Manning of Brunne rejected it only with great reluctance. It was so persistent that it was inserted in one of the MSS. of his translation of Langtoft's chronicle.

1–26. The minstrel-prologue is unusually full. The customary items, all present here, are (1) a request for attention; (2) an announcement of the subject; (3) an interesting fact or two about the story, to whet the listeners' curiosity; and (4) a prayer for the listeners, or a wish that the story may prove edifying, or an assurance that it is told with a view to moral improvement. The fashion was French (cf. the openings of "L'Entree d'Espaigne," "La Mort Aymeri de Narbonne"). The lines in "Havelok" give a good idea of the conditions under which the romance was read in public.

B[e]nedicamus Domino! 20
Here y schal biginnen a rym;
Krist us yeue wel god fyn![7]
The rym is maked of Hauelok,
A stalworþi man in a flok;[8]
He was þe wihtest man at nede 25
Þat may riden on ani stede.

It was a king bi are dawes,[9]
Þat in his[10] time were gode lawes:
He dede maken an ful wel holden;
Hym louede yung, him louede holde, 30
Erl and barun, dreng[11] and tayn,
Knict, bondeman, and swain,
Wydues, maydnes, prestes and clerkes,
And al for hise gode werkes.
He louede God with al his micth, 35
And holi kirke and soth ant ricth;
Ricth-wise[12] men he louede alle,
And oueral made hem forto calle;[13]
Wreieres and wrobberes[14] made he falle,
And hated hem so man doth galle;[15] 40
Vtlawes and theues made he bynde,
Alle that he micthe fynde,

---

[7] end; i.e., at its end, may Christ approve. [8] band. [9] former days. [10] *þat* *his* = whose. [11] military vassal. [12] righteous. [13] summoned them from everywhere. [14] traitors and informers. [15] filth.

25. MS. *þe stalworþeste*, the word being repeated from the preceding line.
27 ff. An unusual portrait of a king. In romances of French or Breton origin, a king is usually (1) a good-hearted dupe, (2) a thorough villain, (3) a convenient ornament introduced merely for literary gorgeousness, or (4) a *deus ex machina*, with astonishing power to effect difficult adjustments. Athelston, however, is more like the kings in "Beowulf:" brave, able to keep order, hard on his enemies, generous to his friends and to the weak and needy. There is a brief parallel in "William of Palerne" 5475-95. The poet's own king, Edward I, was noted for his zeal in revising and enforcing laws to maintain peace. On the decay of the character of the heroic king in the romances, see *PMLA* 21.279.
31. MS. *kayn*. In copying the form *tayn*, the scribe confused *c-* and *t-*, which looked much alike in manuscripts of the period.—Sisam.
37. MS. *rirth*.

And heye hengen on galwe-tre;[16]
For hem ne yede[17] gold ne fe.
In þat time a man þat bore   45
[Wel fifty pund, y wot, or more,]
Of red gold upon hiis bac,
In a male[18] hwit or blac,
Ne funde he non þat him misseyde,
N[e] with iuele on hond leyde.[19]   50
Þanne micthe chapmen[20] fare
Þuruth Englond wit here ware,
And baldelike[21] beye and sellen,
Oueral þer he wilen dwellen,
In gode burwes, and þer-fram   55
Ne funden he non þat dede hem sham,
Þat he ne weren sone to sorwe brouth,
An pouere maked, and browt to nouth.
Þanne was Engelond at hayse;
Michel was svich a king to preyse,   60
Þat held so Englond in grith![22]
Krist of heuene was him with.
He was Engelondes blome;[23]
Was non so bold louerd to Rome[24]
Þat durste upon his[25] bringhe   65
Hunger, ne othere wicke þinghe.

---

[16] gallows.   [17] availed (as a bribe).   [18] wallet.   [19] laid on a hand.   [20] merchants.   [21] boldly.   [22] peace.   [23] flower.   [24] lord as far as Rome.   [25] his (retainers).

46. Line supplied by Madden.

47. Gold was alloyed with copper, which gave it a reddish tinge. See *PMLA* 14.195; and cf. Zupitza's "Athelston" 312.

48. MS. *male with.*

50. The same anecdote has been told of several strong kings, including William the Conqueror. Of Alfred, Otterbourne says (52): *Legum enim rigorem sic exercuit ut armillas [bracelets] aureas in bivio stratas vel suspensas, nemo abripere est ausus.* For a parallel in romance, see "Guy of Warwick" (A.) 140. Cf. also Bede II. 16.

51. Itinerant packmen were numerous, and very important as almost the sole distributors of manufactured goods. See Jusserand II.ii.

60. Statements conveying the author's opinion are common in "Havelok" and rare elsewhere in romance.

64. MS. *lond to.* Craigie emends.

66. MS. *ne here.* Holthausen emends.

Hwan he felede[26] hise foos,
He made hem lurken, and crepen in wros:[27]
þe[i] hidden hem alle, and helden hem stille,
And diden al his herte wille.　　　　　　　　70
Ricth he louede of alle þinge,
To wronge micht him no man bringe,
Ne for siluer, ne for gold:—
So was he his soule hold.[28]
To þe faderles was he rath,[29]　　　　　　75
Wo-so dede hem wrong or lath,[30]
Were it clerc, or were it knicth,
He dede hem sone to hauen ricth;
And wo dide widuen[31] wrong,
Were he neure knicth so strong　　　　　　80
þat he ne made him sone kesten
In feteres, and ful faste festen;
And wo-so dide maydne shame
Of hire bodi, or brouth in blame,
Bute it were bi hire wille,　　　　　　　　85
He made him sone of limes spille.
He was þe beste knith at nede
þat heuere micthe riden on stede,
Or wepne wagge,[32] or folc vt lede;
Of knith ne hauede he neuere drede,　　　　90

---

[26] pursued.　　[27] corners.　　[28] loyal; i.e., careful of.　　[29] an aid.　　[30] injury.
[31] widows.　　[32] wield.

79. The basis for this passage may be Psalm 146:9: "The Lord preserveth the strangers; he relieveth the fatherless and widow; but the way of the wicked he turneth upside down." But it had become a commonplace in French romance; cf. "Entree d'Espaigne" 20.
79. MS. *diden.*
82. MS. *And in feteres ful.* The order in the MS. can be defended by assuming a loose construction: "cast and fasten in chains."
86. Even up to the time of the Commonwealth, mutilation was a legal punishment; it was occasionally forbidden, but continued to be practised.
87. MS. *ke waste.* The couplet was a favorite with the poet, and occurs elsewhere in romance, for instance in the "Brut." It is a translation of the common French phrase, *Ce fu li mieudres qui sor destrier sist.* The passage beginning here has nineteen rhymes on the same sound, and may be a deliberate imitation of the French assonant tirades. There are many shorter sequences in "Havelok" (e.g., 1740 ff.).

Þat he ne sprong forth so sparke of glede,[33]
And lete him [knawe] of hise hand-dede,
Hw he couÞe with wepne spede;
And oÞer he refte him hors or wede,
Or made him sone handes sprede,   95
And "Louerd, merci !" loude grede.[34]
He was large, and no wicth gnede;[35]
Hauede he non so god brede,
Ne on his bord non so god shrede,[36]
Þat he ne wolde Þorwit fede   100
Poure Þat on fote yede;
Forto hauen of Him Þe mede
Þat for vs wolde on rode blede,
Crist, that al kan wisse and rede
Þat euere woneth in ani Þede.[37]   105

Þe king was hoten AÞelwold,
Of word, of wepne he was bold;
In Engeland was neure knicth
Þat betere hel[d] Þe lond to ricth.
Of his bodi ne hauede he eyr   110
Bute a mayden, swiÞe fayr,
Þat was so yung Þat sho ne couÞe
Gon on fote, ne speke wit mouÞe.
Þan him tok an iuel strong,[38]
Þat he we[l] wiste and underfong,[39]   115
Þat his deth was comen him on,
And seyde, "Crist, wat shal y don?
Louerd, wat shal me to rede?
I woth ful wel ich haue mi mede:
[H]w shal nou mi douhter fare?   120

---

[33] coal.   [34] cry.   [35] generous and not at all stingy.   [36] bit (of food).   [37] country.
[38] violent illness.   [39] perceived.

94. One of the objects of war and fighting in the Middle Ages was
plunder. The victorious army carried off as much as it could; the victorious knight took the valuable armor and the steed of the vanquished.
The practice was deplored by moralists as unchristian, but is a matter
of course in the romances.

95. I.e., show them open, without a weapon.

Of hire haue ich michel kare;
Sho is mikel in mi þouth:
Of me self is me rith nowt.[40]
No selcouth[41] is þou me be wo:
Sho ne kan speke, ne sho kan go.   125
Yif scho couþe on horse ride,
And a thousande men bi hire syde,
And sho were comen intil helde,
And Engelond sho couþe welde,
And don of hem þat hire were queme,[42]   130
An hire bodi couþe yeme,
Ne wolde me neuere iuele like,[43]
Ne þou ich were in heuene-riche!"

Quanne[44] he hauede þis pleinte maked,
þerafter stronglike [he] quaked.   135
He sende writes sone onon
After his erles euereich on;
And after hise baruns, riche and poure,

---

[40] I (think) not at all of myself.   [41] wonder.   [42] pleasing.   [43] please me ill.
[44] when.

130. MS. *don hem of þar.* Garnett emends.

135. The poet or the scribe frequently omitted pronouns, especially when the subject of a second clause was the same as that of the first (cf. 456, 709, 1089). In this text, most of these have been supplied, because their omission seems to have been a mannerism of this writer alone. (For omission of the object, cf. 1947, 2372, 2502, 2511; of the verb itself, 1267, 1369, 2840.)

136. For information about messengers, see Jusserand II.ii. They were very expeditious, and traveled long distances. Cf. "Athelston" 13.

137 ff. When a king was dying, the great nobles hastened to the capital, either out of sympathy or a wish to maintain order and look after their interests in arranging for a successor. The romancers made a conventional scene of this, of which these lines are a good example. There seems to have been a formal ceremony of leave-taking: Matthew of Westminster writes of the death of John, "With great bitterness he cursed all his barons instead of bidding them farewell." For parallels from romance, cf. "Partonope" 7950; "La Mort Aymeri" 229 ff.; Malory I.iv; and (a very close one) "Arthour and Merlin" 64 ff. See also Froissart, Ch. 1, on the death of Robert of Scotland, and Ganelon's charge to his retainers ("Chanson" 364). See also Gautier XIX.

Fro Rokesburw al into Douere,
Þat he shulden comen swiþe   140
Til him, þat was ful vnbliþe,
To þat stede þe[r] he lay
In harde bondes, nicth and day.
He was so faste wit yuel fest[45]
Þat he ne mouthe hauen no rest;   145
He ne mouthe no mete hete,
Ne he ne mouchte no lyþe[46] gete,
Nè non of his iuel þat couþe red;[47]
Of him ne was nouth buten ded.

Alle þat þe writes herden   150
Sorful an sori til him ferden;
He wrungen hondes, and wepen sore,
And yerne preyden Cristes hore,[48]
Þat he [wolde] turnen him
Vt of þat yuel þat was so grim !   155
Þanne he weren comen alle
Bifor þe king into the halle,
At Winchestre þer he lay:
"Welcome," he seyde, "be ye ay !
Ful michel þank kan [y] yow   160
That ye aren comen to me now !"

Quanne he weren alle set,
And þe king aueden igret,
He greten, and gouleden, and gouen hem ille,[49]

---

[45] fastened.   [46] comfort.   [47] i.e., no competent physician.   [48] ore, grace.
[49] they mourned and howled and lamented.

139. Roxburgh was a fortress on the Scottish border, and changed
hands frequently. The poem was evidently written during an English
occupation of it; but the history of that subject is at present too obscure
to enable one to date the poem with its help.
142. MS. þe he.
158. The story seems to have grown up before London was the political
center of England. Athelwold is buried at Winchester; Goldeboru is confined at Dover; and important legislation is enacted at Lincoln.
160. Cf. "La Mort Aymeri" 31; the dying lord says to his barons:
Venu i estes, si vos en sai bon gre.

And he bad hem alle ben stille, 165
And seyde þat greting helpeth nouth,
"For al to dede am ich brouth.
Bute nov ye sen þat i shal deye,
Nou ich wille you alle preye
Of mi douther þat shal be 170
Yure leuedi after me,
Wo may yemen hire so longe,
Boþen hire and Engelonde,
Til þat she wman [be] of helde,
And þa[t] she mowe [hit] yemen and welde?" 175
He ansuereden, and seyden anon,
Bi Crist and bi seint Ion,
That þ'erl Godrigh of Cornwayle
Was trewe man, wituten faile;
Wis man of red, wis man of dede, 180
And men haueden of him mikel drede:
"He may hire alþer best yeme,
Til þat she mowe wel ben quene."

þe king was payed[50] of that rede;
A wel fair cloth bringen he dede, 185
And þeron leyde þe messebok,[1]
þe caliz,[2] and þe pateyn[3] ok,
þe corporaus,[4] þe messe-gere;[5]
þer-on he garte þe erl suere,

---

[50] pleased. [1] service-book. [2] chalice. [3] plate for the host. [4] fine linen cloth.
[5] implements of the mass.

166. Cf. "La Mort Aymeri" 272 ff.
167. Such alternations of direct and indirect discourse are very common in the romances. Cf. 182 below and Int. VII.A.6.
185. MS. *wol fair*.
186. A similar ceremony is in "Richard Coeur de Lion" 605. The Saracens in the "Chanson" swear on the Koran (610). Most of the articles mentioned here are used in "Ywain" 3907 ff. The penalty for swearing falsely was violent death sent from heaven; cf. "Joseph of Arimathea" 362; Chaucer's "Man of Law's Tale" 660 ff. In "Amis and Amiloun" the punishment is leprosy. See Addis and Arnold's *Catholic Dictionary*, under "Oath."
189. All these injunctions are conventional. Cf. 137.

Þat he sholde yemen hire wel,   190
Withuten lac,[6] wituten tel,[7]
Til þat she were tuelf winter hold,
And of speche were bold;
And þat she covþe of curteysye
Don, and speken of luue-drurye;[8]   195
And til þat she louen mouhte
Wom so hire to gode þoucte;[9]
And þat he shulde hire yeue
Þe hexte man þat micthe liue,
Þe beste, fayreste, the strangest ok;   200
Þat dede he him sweren on þe bok.
And þanne shulde he Engelond
Al bitechen into hire hond.

Quanne þat was sworn on þis wise,
Þe king dede þe mayden arise,   205
And þe erl hire bitaucte,
And al the lond he euere awcte—
Engelonde, eueri del—
And preide, he shulde yeme hire wel.

Þe king ne mowcte don no more,   210
But yerne preyede Godes ore,
And dede him hoslen[10] wel and shriue
I woth fif hundred siþes and fiue;
An ofte dede him sore swinge,[11]
And wit hondes smerte dinge,[12]   215

---

[6] fail.   [7] reproach.   [8] courtship.   [9] seemed (as) good to her.   [10] given the sacrament.   [11] beat.   [12] strike.

195. MS. *Gon and.*
196. MS. *mithe.*
199. MS. *þe beste*, anticipating the next line. The Lai says "plus fort."
204. MS. *his wise.*
206. For the metrical type, see VI.A.1.d. Cf. 577, 2714, 2843; Kaluza Sec. 122 ff.; Schipper I.440; Chaucer's "Works," ed. Skeat, VI. lxxxviii.
213. William of Malmesbury writes of the death of Henry I that he confessed, beat his breast, was absolved three times, and received unction.
214. Mortifying the flesh was thought a most efficacious penance. See *The Catholic Encyclopedia* under "Flagellation."

So þat þe blod ran of his fleys,
þat tendre was and swiþe neys,[13]
He made his quiste[14] swiþe wel
And sone gaf[15] it euereil[k] del.
Wan it was gouen, ne micte men finde   220
So mikel men micte him in winde,
Of his in arke,[16] ne in chiste,
In Engelond, þat noman wiste:
For al was youen, faire and wel,
þat him was leued no catel.   225

þanne he hauede ben ofte swngen,
Ofte shriuen, and ofte dungen,
"In manus tuas, lou[er]de," he seyde,
Her þat he þe speche leyde;
To Iesu Crist bigan to calle,   230
And deyede biforn his heymen[17] alle.
þan he was ded, þere micte men se
þe meste sorwe that micte be:
þer was sobbing, siking, and sor,
Handes wringing and drawing bi hor.[18]   235
Alle greten swiþe sore,
Riche and poure þat þere wore;
An mikel sorwe haueden alle,
Leuedyes in boure, knictes in halle.
    Quan þat sorwe was somdel laten[19]   240
And he haueden longe graten,

[13] tender.   [14] bequest, will.   [15] affirmed.   [16] coffer.   [17] nobles.   [18] hair.
[19] mitigated.

218 and 219 are transposed in the MS. Zupitza alters.

220 ff. The Church taught energetically that the rich should share with the poor, a doctrine the minstrels were not slow to disseminate. Generosity is always a leading trait of their heroes.

221. I.e., a sheet.

226. In this manuscript, -w sometimes stands for -wu, -wo, -ow.

228. Luke 23:46.

231. Cf. Froissart on the death of Robert (I.40): *Tout cil qui la estoient prisent a plorer de pite.* The entire account is very like the passage in "Havelok." Cf. also "La Mort Aymeri" 269: the queen, *toz ses chevex ronpi et descira,* etc.

Belles deden he sone ringen,
Monkes and prestes messe singen;
And sauteres[20] deden he manie reden,
Þat God self shulde his soule leden   245
Into heuene, biforn his Sone,
And þer wituten hende wone.
Þan he was to þe erþe brouth,
Þe riche erl ne foryat[21] nouth
Þat he ne dede al Engelond   250
Sone sayse[22] intil his hond;
And in þe castels let he do
Þe knictes he micte tristen to;[23]
And alle þe Englis dede he swere,
Þat he shulden him ghod fey beren;   255
He yaf alle men þat god [him] þoucte,[24]
Liuen and deyen til þat [he] moucte,[25]
Til þat þe kinges dowter wore
Tuenti winter hold, and more.

Þanne he hauede taken þis oth   260
Of erles, baruns, lef and loth,
Of knictes, cherles, fre and þewe,[26]
Iustises dede he maken newe,
Al Engelond to faren þorw,
Fro Douere into Rokesborw.   265

---

[20] groups of psalms.   [21] forgot.   [22] take as a possession.   [23] trust in.   [24] he granted all men whatever seemed good to him.   [25] i.e., to the ends of their lives.   [26] in service.

247. The subject is shifted from *God* to *his soule* in the midst of the sentence.

252. MS. *leth.* Holding the castles was a favorite way among the Normans of subjecting a region. Castles usually commanded the roads and waterways, and were invaluable as centers for military operations. See Pollock and Maitland I. 278.

257. MS. *þat him.*

263. Itinerant justices may have been known in Saxon times (Stubbs, "Constitutional History" 442). They seem not to have held permanent commissions, but to have been appointed in emergencies. Their function was to mitigate the injustice of local courts, which might be dominated by powerful nobles.

Schireues he sette, bedels, and greyues,
Grith-sergeans, wit longe gleyues,[27]
To yemen wilde wodes and paþes
Fro wicke men, that wolde don scaþes,[28]
And forto hauen alle at his cri,[29]   270
At his wille, at hise merci,
þat non durste ben him ageyn,
Erl ne barun, knict ne sweyn.[30]
Wislike,[31] for soth, was him wel[32]
Of folc, of wepne, of catel.   275
Soþlike, in a lite þrawe,
Al Engelond of him stod awe;[33]
Al Engelond was of him adrad
So his þe beste fro þe gad.[34]

þe kinges douther bigan þriue,   280
And wex þe fayrest wman on liue.
Of alle þewes[35] w[as] she wis
þat gode weren and of pris.
þe mayden Goldeboru was hoten;
For hire was mani a ter igroten.   285

Quanne þe Erl Godrich him herde
Of þat mayden, hw we[l] [s]he ferde,—
Hw wis sho was, [h]w chaste, hw fayr,
And þat sho was þe rithe eyr

---

[27] lances.   [28] mischief.   [29] cf. "beck and call."   [30] peasant.   [31] assuredly.
[32] plenty.   [33] stood in awe of him.   [34] goad.   [35] manners.

266. The sheriff was supposed to keep order in the county. The graves had a similar responsibility in the towns. Beadles did the police work of the churches. The peace-soldiers did the rough work necessary in maintaining order.
268. Marauding bands usually (but cf. 55) had their headquarters in the woods, and infested the forest roads. See Jusserand II.iii.
280. For *bigan* not followed by *to*, cf. 1357, 2795. The construction was not uncommon in early English, though the form with *to* was usual.
285. One of numerous prophetic lines. The poet seeks suspense by describing a pleasant state of things and then hinting darkly at calamity to ensue. The device is common in "Beowulf" and other Old English poems.

Of Engelond, of al þe rike— 290
Þo bigan Godrich to sike,
And seyde, "Weþer she sholde be
Quen and leuedi ouer me?
Hweþer sho sholde al Engelond,
And me, and mine, hauen in hire hond? 295
Daþeit hwo it hire thaue ![36]
Shal sho it neuere more haue.
Sholde ic yeue a fol, a þerne,[37]
Engelond, þou sho it yerne?
Daþeit[38] hwo it hire yeue 300
Euere-more hwil i liue !
Sho is waxen al to prud,
For gode metes, and noble shrud,[39]
Þat hic haue youen hire to offte;
Hic haue yemed hire to softe. 305
Shal it nouth ben als sho þenkes:
Hope maketh fol man ofte blenkes.[40]
Ich haue a sone, a ful fayr knaue:
He shal Engelond al haue !
He shal king, he shal ben sire, 310
So brouke i euere mi blake swire !"[41]

---

[36] cursed be he who endures it of her!   [37] servant maid.   [38] cursed be.
[39] clothing.   [40] "Hope often plays tricks on the foolish man."   [41] as I may
enjoy (the continued use) of my white neck! i.e., as sure as I'm alive.

292. In this poem soliloquies are frequent and give the motive for much
of the action. The device was known to French poets, and had been
much used by Chrétien. The English writer makes them brief and to
the point.
296. Daþeit is said to be derived from a contraction of odium Dei
habet. Cf. Jenkins' note to the "Chanson" 1047.
298. Tarne is glossed wenche in "Handlyng Sinne" 7353, and rhymes
with yerne.
310. For the omission of ben, cf. 607.
311 ff. Though sworn with so much earnestness and ceremony, oaths
were broken with surprising readiness and on trivial pretexts. They seem
to have been regarded as public acknowledgment of an agreement between parties. Some oaths were thought stronger than others, especially
those sworn on the Bible. In the Spanish ballad of the Cid and the king
(Wolf 52), the oaths exacted are so terrific that the king protests.

Hwan þis trayson was al þouth,
Of his oth ne was him nouth.
He let his oth al ouerga:
þerof ne yaf he nouth a stra;[42]   315
But sone dede hire fete,
Er he wolde heten ani mete,
Fro Winchestre, þer sho was,
Also a wicke traytur Iudas,
And dede leden hire to Doure,   320
þat standeth on þe seis-oure;[43]
And þerhinne dede hire fede
Pourelike in feble[44] wede.
þe castel dede he yemen so
þat non ne micte comen hire to   325
Of hire frend, with [hir] to speken,
þat heuere micte hire bale wreken.

Of Goldeb[oru] shul we nou laten,
þat nouth ne blinneth forto graten
þer sho liggeth in prisoun: 330

---

[42] straw.   [43] sea-shore.   [44] wretched.

317. This practice, though in the romances it had come to indicate
little more than haste and determination, was once bound up with magic.
By fasting, one could constrain his opponents, either human or supernatural, to cease their opposition to his will. For a discussion of the
subject, see the article by F. N. Robinson in the Putnam Anniversary
volume. As the true force of the vow became less apparent, it was made
more rhetorical and elaborate; William of Orange ("Aliscans") swears not
to drink, eat, change his clothing, or kiss any woman, and to sleep on
his saddle-cloth, until he meets his mistress. For other examples, see
Campion and Holthausen's "Sir Perceval" n. 929; Child I.257.

319. Writers of the Middle Ages hated Judas, and could scarcely mention him without disapproval. (Cf. "Amis and Amiloun" 1109; "Octavian" (S) 152.) Wretches sometimes swear by him (e.g., Mordred in
"Le Morte Arthure"). For much curious information about his reputation in the Middle Ages, see articles by Archer Taylor, *JEGP* 19.1; *American Journal of Philology* 167.234; *Washington University Studies*, Human-
istic Series VIII.i.3; IX.ii.135; P. F. Baum's article, *PMLA* 31.181; and
"Kittredge Anniversary Papers" 305.

Iesu Crist, that Lazarun
To liue broucte fro dede bondes,
He lese[45] hire wit hise hondes!
And leue sho mo[te] him yse
Heye hangen on galwe-tre,   335
Þat hire haued in sorwe brouth
So as[46] sho ne misdede nouth!

Sa[y] we nou forth in hure spelle!
In þat time, so it bifelle,
Was in þe lon[d] of Denemark   340
A riche king, and swyþe stark.
Þ[e] name of him was Birkabeyn,
He hauede mani knict and sueyn,
He was fayr man, and wicth,
Of bodi he was þe beste knicth   345
Þat euere micte leden uth here,[47]
Or stede onne ride, or handlen spere.
Þre children he hauede bi his wif;
He hem louede so his lif.
He hauede a sone [and] douhtres two,   350

---

[45] loose.   [46] when, although.   [47] army.

331. This popular formula has two parts. First, the speaker mentions
some divine miracles; and, since the restoring to life of Lazarus, Daniel,
and Jonah was especially impressive miracle-working, some or all of
these persons are mentioned. Second, the speaker argues *a fortiori* that
a lesser miracle—e.g., the rescue of some one still living—is easily possible.
Cf. Jenkins' note on the "Chanson" 2384, and the passage 3100 ff. In-
voking the aid of God for the hero of a story was common in French
romance. Cf. "La Mort Aymeri" 986, 1444; "William of Palerne"; and
in English, "Bevis of Hamtoun" 510, "Octavian" (N.) 436, and "Ferumbras" 3901.

334. This may not be meant literally; but a Spanish proverb lists the
sight of a thief on a gallows as one of the three most agreeable sights.
Pleasant or not, the Middle Ages were accustomed to it. Cf. 2480.

338 ff. The second introduction is a duplicate of the first; but the poet
handles it skillfully. The first story has two good scenes—the king's
death and Godrich's soliloquy. If repeated, these cannot be impressive;
hence, in the second story, the writer abridges the repeated parts and
invents a horrible scene to sustain the interest. In the French versions,
the two stories at the beginning are unlike.

Swiþe fayre, as fel it so.
He þat wile non forbere,[48]
Riche ne poure, king ne kaysere,[49]
Deth him tok þan he bes[t] wolde
Liuen,—but hyse dayes were fulde,[50]— 355
Þat he ne moucte no more liue,
For gol[d] ne siluer, ne for no gyue.

Hwan he þat wiste, raþe he sende
After prestes fer an hende,[1]
Chanounes[2] gode, and monkes boþe, 360
Him for to wisse, and to rede;
Him for to hoslen, an forto shriue,
Hwil his bodi were on liue.

Hwan he was hosled and shriuen,
His quiste maked, and for him gyuen,[3] 365
His knictes dede he alle site;
For þorw hem hc wolde wite
Hwo micte yeme hise children yunge,
Til þat he kouþen speken wit tunge;
Speken and gangen, on horse riden, 370
Knictes an sweynes bi here siden.
He spoken þer-offe and chosen sone
A riche man þat, under mone,
Was þe trewest, as he wende,
Godard, þe kinges oune frende; 375
And seyden, he moucthe hem best loke,
Yif þat hc hem vndertoke,
Til hise sone mouthe bere
Helm on heued, and leden vt here,[4]
In his hand a spere stark, 380

---

[48] spare.   [49] emperor.   [50] completed.   [1] both distant and near at hand.
[2] canons.   [3] executed.   [4] army.

360. The bad rhyme is a result of the copyist's substitution of the familiar *rede* for the cognate Norse form *rothe*. (Sisam.)
361. MS. *fort to.*
362. MS. *hoslon.*
373–4. MS. *man was; trewest þat.* The emendations are Zupitza's.

And king ben maked of Denemark.
He wel trowede þat he seyde,
And on Godard handes leyde;
And seyde, "Here biteche i þe
Mine children alle þre,   385
Al Denemark, and al mi fe,
Til þat mi sone of helde be;
But þat ich wille þat þo[u] suere
On auter and on messe-gere,
On þe belles þat men ringes,   390
On messe-bok þe prest on singes,
Þat þou mine children shalt we[l] yeme,
Þat hire kin be ful wel queme,[5]
Til mi sone mowe ben knicth;
Þanne biteche him þo his ricth:[6]   395
Denemark, and þat þertil longes,[7]
Casteles and tunes, wodes and wonges."[8]

Godard stirt up, an swor al þat
Þe king him bad, and siþen sat
Bi þe knictes, þat þer ware,   400
Þat wepen alle swiþe sare
For þe king, þat deide sone.—
Iesu Crist, that makede mone
On þe mirke[9] nith to shine,
Wite his soule fro helle pine;   405
And leue þat it mote wone
In heuene-riche with Godes sone!

Hwan Birkabeyn was leyd in graue,
Þe erl dede sone take þe knaue,
Hauelok, þat was þe broþer,   410
Swanborow, his sister, Helfled, þe toþer,

---

[5] so that their kinsmen shall approve.   [6] lit., "those his rights."   [7] appertains to it.   [8] fields.   [9] dark.

393. Napier suggested *hire kinde*, their rank. The "kin" are mentioned again only in l. 414.
410. MS. *þe eir*. Holthausen's emendation.

And in þe castel dede he hem do,
Þer non ne micte hem comen to
Of here kyn, þer þei sperd[10] were;
Þer he greten ofte sore, 415
Boþe for hunger and for kold,
Or he weren þre winter hold.
Feblelike[11] he gaf hem cloþes,
He ne yaf a note[12] of hise oþes;
He hem cloþede rith ne fedde, 420
Ne hem dede richelike bedde.
Þanne Godard was sikerlike
Vnder God þe moste swike,[13]
Þat eure in erþe shaped was,
Withuten on, þe wike Iudas. 425
Haue he þe malisun to-day
Of alle þat eure speken may!
Of patriark, and of pope,
And of prest with loken kope,[14]
Of monekes and hermites boþe, 430
And of þe leue holi rode
Þat[15] God himselue ran on blode![16]
Crist warie[17] him with his mouth!
Waried wrþe he of norþ and suth!

---

[10] bound. [11] wretchedly. [12] nut. [13] greatest traitor. [14] fastened cloaks.
[15] (on) which. [16] i.e., bled. [17] curse.

420. The poet sometimes omits the first of two correlative ne's. (Sisam)
421. MS. *hem ne dede richelike bebedde.* Cf. "La Mort Aymeri" 512 for the sense and construction. The beds of wealthy folk were elaborately and expensively furnished. Cf. Mead's note to "The Squire of Low Degree" 833; also Salzman 89, 105; and Wright Ch. XII.
426. Though the Church discouraged elaborate and rhetorical curses, some have been preserved. Burton's "History of Scotland" (III. 319) contains a fearfully inclusive formula for excommunication, three pages in length. The curse of Ernulphus (most accessible in "Tristram Shandy" III.x) is well known. Though the passage in "Havelok" is unusually long for the romances, it is brief and hasty in comparison with fully developed specimens.
432. For the syntax, with the preposition following the relative at a distance, cf. 463.
433. Cf. "Arthour and Merlin" (A) 3183.

Offe alle men þat speken kunne,   435
Of Crist, þat made mone and sunne!
Þanne he hauede of al þe lond
Al þe folk tilled[18] intil his hond,
And alle haueden sworen him oth,
Riche and poure, lef and loth,   440
Þat he sholden hise wille freme,[19]
And þat he shulde[n] him nouth greme,[20]
He þouthe a ful strong trechery,
A trayson and a felony,
Of þe children forto make: 445
Þe deuel of helle him sone take!

   Hwan þat was þouth, onon he ferde
To þe tour þer he woren sperde,[21]
Þer he greten for hunger and cold.
Þe knaue, þat was sumdel[22] bold,   450
Kam him ageyn, on knes him sette,
And Godard ful feyre he þer grette.
And Godard seyde, "Wat is yw?[23]
Hwi grete ye and goulen[24] nou?"
"For us hungreth swiþe sore,"   455
Seyden he, "[We] wolden more:
We ne haue to hete, ne we ne haue
Herinne neyther knith ne knaue
Þat yeueth us drinke, ne no mete,—
Haluendel[25] þat we moun ete!   460
Wo is us þat we weren born!
Weilawei! nis it no korn
Þat men micte maken of bred?[26]
Us hungreth: we aren ney ded!"

---

[18] drawn; i.e., subdued.   [19] perform.   [20] annoy.   [21] confined.   [22] rather.
[23] what's the matter?   [24] cry.   [25] half the amount.   [26] is there no grain from
which men can make bread?

435. MS. *man.* Holthausen's emendation.
436. MS. *maude.* The confusion of Christ and God indicated here is
very common in Middle English poetry; cf. "Roland and Vernagu" 96.
456. Sisam's emendation.
459. MS. *drinken.*
464. MS. *þs hungreth.*

Godard herde here wa,   465
Þeroffe yaf he nouth a stra,²⁷
But tok þe maydnes boþe samen,
Also it were up-on hiis gamen²⁸—
Also he wolde with hem leyke,²⁹
Þat weren for hunger grene and bleike.³⁰   470
Of boþen he karf on two here þrotes,
And siþen, hem al to grotes.³¹
Þer was sorwe, wo-so it sawe,
Hwan þe children bi þe wawe³²
Leyen and sprauleden in þe blod: 475
Hauelok it saw, and þe[r] bi stod.
Ful sori was þat seli³³ knaue;
Mikel dred he mouthe haue,
For at hise herte he saw a knif
For to reuen him hise lyf.   480
But þe k[n]aue, þat litel was,
He knelede bifor þat Iudas,
And seyde, "Louerd, merci nov!
Manrede,³⁴ louerd, biddi you!
Al Denemark i wile you yeue,   485
To þat forward þu late me liue;
Here hi wile on boke swere,
Þat neure more ne shal i bere
Ayen þe, louerd, shel[d] ne spere,
Ne oþer wepne that may you dere.   490
Louerd, haue merci of me!
To-day i wile fro Denemark fle,
Ne neuere more comen ageyn:
Sweren y wole, þat Bircabein
Neuere yete me ne gat!"³⁵   495
Hwan þe deuel he[r]de þat,
Sumdel bigan him forto rewe;
Withdrow þe knif, þat was lewe³⁶

---

²⁷ straw.   ²⁸ in sport.   ²⁹ play.   ³⁰ wan.   ³¹ bits.   ³²⌐wall (a tag).   ³³ innocent.
³⁴ homage.   ³⁵ begot.   ³⁶ warm.

490. MS. *wepne bere.*
498. The omission of the subject in the second part of a compound
sentence is common in this poem. Cf. 1409, 1420, 1428, etc.

Of þe seli[37] children blod.
Þer was miracle fair and god,   500
Þat he þe knaue nouth ne slou,
But fo[r] rewnesse him witdrow.
Of Auelok rewede him ful sore,
And þoucte he wolde þat he ded wore,
But-on þat he nouth wit his hend   505
Ne drepe[38] him nouth, þat fule fend!
Þoucte he, als he him bistod,
Starinde[39] als he were wod:
"Yif y late him liues go,
He micte me wirchen michel wo.   510
Grith[40] ne get y neuere mo,
He may [me] waiten[41] for to slo;
And yf he were brouct of liue,[42]
And mine children wolden þriue,
Louerdinges after me   515
Of al Denemark micten he be.
God it wite, he shal ben ded,—
Wile i taken non oþer red!
I shal do casten him in þe se,

---

[37] innocent.   [38] slew.   [39] staring.   [40] peace.   [41] lie in wait.   [42] killed.

502. For a similar relenting, see "King Horn" 87. Note especially how similar are the speeches of the murderers. In "Horn," the boy's fairness causes the Saracens to spare him; here, a miracle is invoked. As a rule, however, English writers avoided miracles, no matter how convenient. (Cf. note on "Sowdone of Babylon" 2810.) French poets used the device frequently (e.g., "Le Pelerinage de Charlemagne" 774); and see D. B. Easter, "Magic in the Romans d'Aventure." 37; Dickman 182; and cf. the prophecies in Celtic pieces; e.g., "Macdatho's Pig."

510. For similar premonitions, see the preceding, and Malory I. 28; Loomis 341. The motive is common in Germanic literature also.

519. MS. *she.* For this method of disposing of an enemy, see Hall's note on "King Horn" 87; by throwing the victim into the water, or exposing him in a boat, one could place the responsibility for receiving him or rejecting him on the element. Here the English poet seems to be dealing with a superstition that he barely understood, so that instead of committing the child to the waves on a raft or in a boat, and leaving his fate to heaven, he has Godrich remove all doubt of the outcome by specifying the anchor. The French poets replace this episode with an attack by pirates, after which Grim saves Havelok from the sea.

Þer i wile þat he drench[ed]⁴³ be;   520
Abouten his hals⁴⁴ an anker god,
Þat he ne flete⁴⁵ in the flod."
Þer anon he dede sende
After a fishere, þat he wende
Wolde al his wille do,   525
And sone anon he seyde him to:
"Grim, þou wost þu art mi þral;⁴⁶
Wilte⁴⁷ don mi wille al
Þat i wile bidden þe,
To-morwen shal [i] maken þe fre,   530
And aucte⁴⁸ þe yeuen and riche make,
Withþan⁴⁹ þu wilt þis child take,
And leden him with þe to-nicht,
Þan þou se[st] þe mone-lith,
Into þe se, and don him þerinne;   535
Al wile [i] taken on me þe sinne."
Grim tok þe child and bond him faste,
Hwil þe bondes micte laste,⁵⁰
Þat weren of ful strong line.
Þo was Hauelok in ful strong pine!   540
Wiste he neuere her wat was wo.
Iesu Crist, þat makede go
Þe halte and þe doumbe speke,
Hauelok, þe of Godard wreke!
    Hwan Grim him hauede faste bounden,   545
And siþen in an eld cloth wnden,
[He þriste in his muth wel faste]
A keuel of clutes, ful unwraste,¹
Þat he mouhte speke ne fnaste,²

---

⁴³ drowned. ⁴⁴ neck. ⁴⁵ float. ⁴⁶ serf. ⁴⁷ if you will. ⁴⁸ property. ⁴⁹ provided.
⁵⁰ i.e., the knots would hold until the bonds rotted away. ¹ a gag of very
filthy cloths. ² breathe.

525. MS. *þat wolde.*
542. MS. *to go.* Holthausen emends.
543-4. MS. *speken; wreken.*
546. The following line is supplied from the Cambridge fragment, and
not counted in the numbering. The rhymes are probably too badly disturbed for reconstruction; but l. 554 is feeble, and may be a filler; and
l. 548 might have ended *ne grede.* (For the rhyme, cf. 96.)

Hwere he wolde him bere or lede.
Hwan he hauede don þat dede,   550
Hwan þe swike³ him bad, he yede
þat he shulde him forth [lede]
And him drinchen in þe se—
þat forwarde makeden he.
In a poke,⁴ ful and blac,   555
Sone he caste him on his bac,
Ant bar him hom to hise cleue,⁵
And bitaucte him dame Leue,
And seyde, "Wite þou þis knaue,
Also thou with me lif haue:⁶   560
I shal dreinchen him in þe se;
For⁷ him shole we ben maked fre,
Gold hauen ynou, and oþer fe:
þat hauet mi louerd bihoten me."

Hwan dame [Leue] herde þat,   565
Vp she stirte, and nouth ne sat,
And caste þe knaue so harde adoune,
þat he crakede þer his croune
Ageyn a gret ston, þer it lay:
þo Hauelok micte sei, "Weilawei   570
þat euere was i kinges bern!
þat him⁸ ne hauede grip or ern,⁹
Leoun or wlf, wluine¹⁰ or bere,
Or oþer best, þat wolde him dere!"
So lay þat child to middel nicth,   575
þat Grim bad Leue bringen lict,
For to don on his cloþes:
"Ne thenkeste nowht of mine oþes
þat ich haue mi louerd sworen?
Ne wile i nouth be forloren.   580
I shal beren him to þe se—

---

³ villain (Godard). ⁴ bag. ⁵ hut. ⁶ i .e., on your life. ⁷ on account (of what we do with). ⁸ i.e., Godard. ⁹ vulture or eagle. ¹⁰ she-wolf.

551. MS. *him hauede.*—Holthausen.
567–8. MS. *adoun so harde/þat hise croune he þer crakede.*—Morris.

Þou wost þat [so] houes[11] me—
And i shal drenchen him þer-inne;
Ris up swiþe, an go þu binne,[12]
And blou þe fir, and lith a kandel."   585
Als she shulde hise cloþes handel
On forto don, and blawe þe fir,
She saw þerinne a lith ful shir,
Also brith so it were day,
Aboute þe knaue þer he lay.   590
Of hise mouth it stod a stem[13]
Als it were a sunnebem:
Also lith was it þer-inne
So þer brenden cerges[14] inne.
"Iesu Crist!" wat[15] dame Leue,   595
"Hwat is þat lith in vre cleue?
Ris up, Grim, and loke wat it menes:
Hwat is þe lith, as þou wenes?"
He stirten boþe up to the knaue
(For man shal god wille haue),[16]   600
Vnkeueleden[17] him, and swiþe unbounden,
And sone anon [upon] him funden,

---

[11] behooves.   [12] within.   [13] there issued a ray.   [14] candles.   [15] quoth.   [16] i.e.,
people are naturally kind.   [17] ungagged.

584. I.e., from the chamber into the hall.   See Introduction.
587. MS. þer fir.
591. In tradition and folklore, such lights usually play about the heads of heroes, not their mouths (cf. Achilles, "Iliad" xviii. 188; Cuchulainn in the "Tain bo Cuailnge"; "Horn" 384); and only beasts breathe fire. But both French poems agree with the English in having the ray issue from Havelok's mouth.   An analog is in Livy (I. xxxix): *Puero dormienti, cui Servio Tullio fuit nomen, caput arsisse ferunt multorum in conspectu. Plurimo igitur clamore ad tantae rei miraculum orto, excitos reges; et cum quidam familiarum aquam ad exstinguendum ferret, ab regina retentum; sedatoque eam tumultu moveri vetuisse puerum, donec sua sponte experrectus esset.   Mox cum somno et flammam abisse.*   Frazer (II.xiv) has a conjecture on the source of the story.   Cf. A. M. Hocart, "Kingship," p. 27; Hibbard 111; Charles Plummer, "Vitae Sanctorum Hiberniae" I.cxxxvii and St. Congal, Pt. 7; Loomis 46.   In the ballad "Lamkin" a severed head lights the house.
594. The perfect rhyme indicates corruption; on analogy with 2125, the second *inne* might be read *þrinne*.
597. MS. *sir up*.

Als he tirueden of his serk,[18]
On his rith shuldre a kyne-merk,[19]
A swiþe brith, a swiþe fair.   605
"Goddot!"[20] quath Grim, "þis[21] ure eir,
þat shal louerd of Denemark:
He shal ben king, strong and stark;
He shal hauen in his hand
A[l] Denemark and Engeland;   610
He shal do Godard ful wo,
He shal him hangen, or quik flo;[22]
Or he shal him al quic graue:[23]
Of him shal he no merci haue."
þus seide Grim, and sore gret,   615
And sone fel him[24] to þe fet,
And seide, "Louerd, haue merci
Of me, and Leue, þat is me bi!
Louerd, we aren boþe þine,
þine cherles, þine hine.[25]   620
Lowerd, we sholen þe wel fede
Til þat þu cone riden on stede,

---

[18] rolled back his shirt.   [19] king-mark.   [20] by heaven!   [21] this is.   [22] flay alive.
[23] bury alive.   [24] Havelok.   [25] bond-servants.

604. The king-mark seems to have been a shining golden cross (1263).
In "Richars li Biaus," the hero has two, as has the child in "Emare,"
who is of royal blood by both parents (505). Material on the subject
is scanty; cf. Hibbard 112; Miss Rickert's note on "Emare," *EETSES*
99; and "The Saga Book of the Viking Club" VI. 280. Other examples
are in "Macaire" I. 434; "Parise la Duchesse" 824-5; I. 169-173; and
"Boeve de Hantoun" V. 310. See also M. R. Cox's "Cinderella" 480, 487.
607. See note to 310.
610. Cf. "King Horn" 90 ff., where the Saracens foresee the hero's
vengeance. Such premonitions are as old as the Œdipus-story. See note
on 502.
621. They suffer a change of heart because they believed the body of
a king to be sacred. The belief is very old, and was enthusiastically
received by medieval writers. In "Richard Coeur de Lion," the German
emperor wishes Richard dead, but may not slay him or order him slain;
he compromises by having a lion placed in Richard's prison. In "Octavian," however, even a lion refuses to kill an anointed king (N. 481);
and in the alliterative "Morte Arthur" (2442), the king recklessly exposes
himself, saying that no knave can have the good fortune to kill an anointed
king.

Til þat þu cone ful wel bere
Helm on heued, sheld and spere.
He ne shal neuere, sikerlike,   625
[Wite,] Godard, þat fule swike.[26]
Þoru oþer man, louerd, þan þoru þe
Sal i neuere freman be.
Þou shalt me, louerd, fre maken,
For i shal yemen þe and waken;[27]   630
Þoru þe wile i fredom haue."
Þo was Haueloc a bliþe knaue;
He sat him up and crauede bred,
And seide, "Ich am ney ded,
Hwat for hunger, wat for bondes   635
Þat þu leidest on min hondes,
And for [þe] keuel at þe laste,
Þat in mi mouth was þrist faste:
Y was þe[r-]with so harde prangled[28]
Þat i was þe[r-]with ney strangled."   640
"Wel is me þat þu mayth hete!"[29]
Goddoth!" quath Leue, "y shal þe fete
Bred an chese, butere and milk,
Pastees and flaunes; al with suilk[30]
Shole we sone þe wel fede,   645
Louerd, in þis mikel nede;
Soth it is, þat men seyt and suereth:
Þer God wile helpen, nouth ne dereth."[31]

Þanne sho hauede brouth þe mete,
Haueloc anon bigan to ete   650
Grundlike,[32] and was ful bliþe;

---

[26] traitor.   [27] watch over.   [28] it was packed so tightly (in my mouth).   [29] eat.
[30] such (things).   [31] works injury.   [32] heartily.

625. MS. *neuere wite.*—Sisam.
632. The hero's name is pronounced in three different ways in the
poem: (1) Hăv e lŏk, (2) Hăv lŏk, (3) Hav lŏk. The scansion here requires the last.
644. Pasties were meat pies; flaunes were cakes containing either cus-
tard or cheese. For recipes, see Furnivall's "Early English Meals and
Manners" 287.

Couþe he nouth his hunger miþe.[33]
A lof he het, y woth and more,
For him hungrede swiþe sore.
Þre dayes þer-biforn, i wene,   655
Et he no mete, þat was wel sene.
Hwan he hauede eten and was fed,
Grim dede maken a ful fayr bed,
Vncloþede him, and dede him þer-inne,
And seyde, "Slep, sone, with michel winne!   660
Slep wel faste, and dred þe nouth:
Fro sorwe to ioie art þu brouth."
Sone so it was lith of day,
Grim it undertok, þe wey
To þe wicke traitour Godard,   665
Þat was [in] Denema[r]k a stiward,
And seyde, "Louerd, don ich haue
Þat þou me bede of þe knaue;
He is drenched in þe flod,
Abouten his hals[34] an anker god;   670
He is witerlike[35] ded:
Eteth he neure more bred.
He liþ drenched in þe se:—
Yif me gold [and] oþer fe,
Þat y mowe riche be;   675
And with þi chartre make fre,
For þu ful wel bihetet me
Þanne i last spak with þe."
Godard stod and lokede on him
Þoruthlike, with eyne grim,   680
And seyde, "Wiltu ben erl?
Go hom swiþe, fule drit-cherl;[36]
Go heþen,[37] and be eueremore
Þral and cherl, als þou er wore.

[33] hide.   [34] neck.   [35] surely.   [36] base slave.   [37] hence.

676. Villeins could be freed by their lords, and became in law the equals of men born free. E. L. Guilford ("Travelers and Traveling in the Middle Ages," p. 21) prints a charter in which a serf is freed by his master because of his performance of an unusual service. (See also Pollock and Maitland, "History of English Law" I. 427.)

Shal[tu] haue non oþer mede; 685
For litel³⁸ [shal] i do þe lede
To þe galues, so God me rede!
For þou haues don a wicke dede.
þou mait stonden her to longe,
Bute þou swiþe [h]eþen gonge!" 690

Grim þoucte to late þat he ran³⁹
Fro þat traytour, þa[t] wicke man;
And þoucte, "Wat shal me to rede?
Wite he him onliue, he wile [us] beþe
Heye hangen on galwe-tre: 695
Betere us is of londe to fle,
And berwen boþen ure liues,
And mine children, and mine wiues."
Grim solde sone al his corn,
Shep wit wolle, neth⁴⁰ wit horn, 700
Hors, and swin, [and geet⁴¹] with berd,
þe gees, þe hennes of þe yerd;
Al he solde, þat outh douthe,⁴²
þat he eure selle moucte,
And al he to þe peni drou.⁴³ 705
Hise ship he greyþede wel inow:
He dede it tere,⁴⁴ an ful wel pike,⁴⁵
þat it ne doutede sond ne krike;⁴⁶
þer-inne dide a ful god mast,

---

³⁸ i.e., on slight provocation. ³⁹ i.e., feared that he started away too late.
⁴⁰ cattle. ⁴¹ goats. ⁴² was worth anything. ⁴³ turned into money. ⁴⁴ tar.
⁴⁵ fill the seams with pitch. ⁴⁶ creek, shallow inlet.

698. *Children* is a genitive. Cf. Intro. V.B.2.
701. *And geet* supplied by Skeat.
702. The yard was a special enclosure for fowls; other animals were tied outside or allowed to range about. Cf. Chaucer's "Nun's Priest's Tale" 4400.
707. Cf. "Beowulf" 295.
709. Grim's boat was a fishing smack. For illustrations (somewhat wanting in perspective), see the British Museum's *Reproductions from Illuminated Manuscripts*, Series I.xxii and Series III.xiii; and the picture in Gollancz's edition of "Patience" (also in the facsimile text *EETS* 162, leaf 56). See Quennell, various references; J. F. Meigs, "The Story of the Seaman" (1924), especially Volume II.

Stronge kables, and ful fast,   710
Ores gode, an ful god seyl;
Þerinne wantede nouth a nayl,
Þat euere he sholde þerinne do.
Hwan he hauedet greyþed so,
Hauelok þe yunge he dede þerinne,   715
Him and his wif, hise sones þrinne,[47]
And hise two doutres, þat faire wore;
And sone dede he leyn in an ore,
And drou him to þe heye se,
Þere he mith alþerbest fle.   720
Fro londe woren he bote a mile—
Ne were [it] neuere but ane hwile—
Þat it ne bigan a wind to rise
Out of þe north—men calleth "bise"—
And drof hem intil Engelond,   725
Þat al was siþen in his hond—
His, þat Hauelok was þe name—
But or, he hauede michel shame,
Michel sorwe, and michel tene,
And yete he gat it al bidene;[48]   730
Als ye shulen nou forthwar[d][49] lere,
Yf that ye wilen þerto here.

    In Humber Grim bigan to lende,[50]
In Lindeseye, rith at þe north ende.
Þer sat is ship upon þe sond,   735
But Grim it drou up to þe lond;
And þere he made a litel cote[1]
To him and to hise flote.[2]

---

[47] three.   [48] completely.   [49] presently.   [50] land.   [1] hut.   [2] company.

718. Probably to steer. The steering-oar was on the right side facing
forward; hence, "starboard."
724. The word, meaning "north wind," is not in Gaimar or the Lai,
but is common in Old French literature: e.g. "Pelerinage de Charlemagne" 354.
730. MS. *and þrie he.*—Holthausen.
731. MS. *here.*
734. Lindsay was a district on the coast of Lincolnshire.

Bigan he þere for to erde,[3]
A litel hus to maken of erþe,   740
So þat he wel þore were
Of here herboru[4] herborwed þere;
And for þat Grim þat place aute,
Þe stede of Grim þe name laute;[5]
So þat Grimesbi calleth alle   745
Þat þeroffe speken alle;
And so shulen men callen it ay,
Bituene þis and domesday.

Grim was fishere swiþe god,
And mikel couþe on the flod;   750
Mani god fish þerinne he tok,
Boþe with neth, and with hok.
He tok þe sturgiun and þe qual[6]
And þe turbut and lax withal;[7]
He tok þe sele and þe hwel;[8]   755
He spedde ofte swiþe wel.
Keling[9] he tok, and tumberel,[10]
Hering and þe makerel,
Þe butte, þe schulle, þe þornebake.[11]
Gode paniers[12] dede he make,   760
On til him, and oþer þrinne[13]
Til hise sones, to beren fish inne
Vp o-londe, to selle and fonge;[14]

---

[3] dwell.   [4] shelter.   [5] took its name from Grim.   [6] whale.   [7] salmon as well.
[8] eel.   [9] cod.   [10] porpoise.   [11] flounder, plaice, and skate.   [12] baskets.   [13] three.
[14] receive (money).

739. MS. *erþe.*—Holthausen.

740. Probably *erþe* is a substitution for *erde*, a cognate form.   Cf.
middelerd (2244).   The walls of the huts were made by setting out two
rows of stones and filling in between with sod; the roof was a straw thatch.

745. Here and in 724 *calleth* may mean *call it.* (Cf. 714, 2005.) Skeat
emended . . . *Grimesbi it calle/ He þat . . . alle.*

755. The whale, seal, sturgeon, and porpoise are regularly included in
medieval menus (cf. Furnivall, who mentions all the sea creatures listed
here; and Barbazon's "Fabliaux et Contes" No. 86).   Fish were much
eaten in the Middle Ages both because they were permitted on fast-days
and because they could readily be salted and kept all winter.

763. Holthausen suggested that the correct rhymes were *chaunge* (exchange) and *graunge.*

Forbar[15] he neyþe[r] tun ne gronge[16]
Þat he ne to yede with his ware;   765
Kam he neuere hom hand-bare[17]
Þat he ne broucte bred and sowel[18]
In his shirte, or in his couel;[19]
In his poke[20] benes and korn;
Hise swink ne hauede he nowt forlorn.   770
And hwan he tok þe grete laumprei,
Ful we[l] he couþe þe rithe wei
To Lincolne, þe gode boru;
Ofte he yede it boru and þoru,
Til he hauede al wel sold,   775
And þerfore þe penies told.
Þanne he com þenne, he were bliþe,
For hom he brouthe fele siþe
Wastels, simenels with þe horn,[21]
Hise pokes fulle of mele an korn,   780
Netes flesh, shepes, and swines;
And hemp to maken of gode lines,
And stronge ropes to hise netes,
[Þat] in þe se he ofte setes.

Þusgate Grim him fayre ledde: 785
Him and his genge[22] wel he fedde
Wel twelf winter oþer more:
Hauelok was war þat Grim swank[23] sore
For his mete, and he lay at hom:
[He] thouthe, "Ich am nou no grom;[24]   790
Ich am wel waxen, and wel may eten
More þan euere Grim may geten.

---

[15] neglected.   [16] farm.   [17] empty-handed.   [18] relish.   [19] hood.   [20] bag.   [21] fine
bread, and cake twisted so as to look like a horn.   [22] household.   [23] worked.
[24] boy.

771. A "great" lamprey weighed as much as five pounds, and sold for
three shillings (see Thorold Rogers, "Agriculture and Prices"). It was
highly prized as a delicacy. Henry I is said to have brought on a fatal
illness by partaking too freely of lamprey.

773. The distance is some thirty miles.

775. MS. hauede wol wel.

784. MS. se weren.

Ich ete more, bi God on liue,
Þan Grim an hise children fiue!
It ne may nouth ben þus longe: 795
Goddot! y wile with hem gange,
For to leren sum god to gete;[25]
Swinken[26] ich wolde for mi mete.
It is no shame forto swinken;
Þe man þat may wel eten and drinken   800
Þat nouth ne haue, but-on swink long;
To liggen at hom it is ful strong.
God yelde him, þer i ne may,
Þat haueth me fed to þis day!
Gladlike i wile þe paniers bere;   805
Ich woth, ne shal it me nouth dere,
Þey þer be inne a birþene[27] gret
Al so heui als a neth.[28]
Shal ich neuere lengere dwelle;
To-morwen shal ich forth pelle."[29]   810

On þe morwen, hwan it was day,
He stirt up sone, and nouth ne lay;
And cast a panier on his bac,
With fish giueled[30] als a stac;
Also michel he bar him one   815
So he foure,[31] bi mine mone![32]
Wel he it bar, and solde it wel;
Þe siluer he brouthe hom il[k] del,
Al þat he þer-fore tok:
Withheld he nouth a ferþinges nok.   820

---

[25] win some useful thing. [26] work. [27] burden. [28] ox. [29] hasten. [30] heaped up. [31] he alone bore as much as the four of them. [32] on my word.

796. MS. *with þe.*—Holthausen.

800. A troublesome passage. Morsbach suggested that *nouth* was *ne + outh;* a rendering then would be: "The man who can eat and drink heartily ought not to have that [food and drink] without long toil." Skeat emended *þat* to *þar,* need.

818. Practically all coins were silver, other materials being too soft or too valueless. For small change, the pennies were cut into halves and quarters; the expression in 820 means "a corner of a penny, worth a farthing." See Davis, article on coinage.

So yede he forth ilke day,
þat he neuere at home lay.
So wolde he his mester[33] lere.—
Bifel it so, a strong dere[34]
Bigan to rise of korn[35] of bred,   825
þat Grim ne couþe no god red,
Hw he sholde his meiné fede;
Of Hauelok hauede he michel drede:
For he was strong, and wel mouthe ete
More þanne heuere mouthe he gete;   830
Ne he ne mouthe on þe se take
Neyþer lenge, ne þornbake,[36]
Ne non oþer fish þat douthe[37]
His meyné feden with he mouthe.
Of Hauelok he hauede kare,   835
Hwil[k]gat[38] þat he micthe fare.—
Of his children was him nouth:[39]
On Hauelok was al hise þouth,
And seyde, "Hauelok, dere sone,
I wene that we deye mone[40]   .840
For hunger, þis dere is so strong,
And hure mete is uten long.[41]
Betere is þat þu henne gonge
þan þu here dwelle longe;
Heþen þow mayt gangen to late;   845
þou canst ful wel þe ricthe gate[42]
To Lincolne, þe gode borw—
þou hauest it gon ful ofte þoru;
Of[43] me, ne is me nouth a slo.[44]
Betere is þat þu þider go,   850
For þer is mani god man inne:
þer þou mayt þi mete winne.

---

[33] trade.   [34] famine.   [35] grain.   [36] ling nor skate.   [37] availed.   [38] in what manner.   [39] i.e., he did not think of the welfare of his children.   [40] must.   [41] long out; i.e., exhausted.   [42] road, way.   [43] as for.   [44] sloe-berry; i.e., I am powerless.

824. In the French, Havelok is sent away by Grim because fishing and the company of fisherfolk are of no value to him in recovering his inheritance.

But wo is me! þou art so naked,
Of mi seyl y wolde þe were maked
A cloth, þou mithest inne gongen, 855
Sone, no cold þat þu ne fonge."

He tok þe sh[e]res of þe nayl,
And made him a couel⁴⁵ of þe sayl,
And Hauelok dide it sone on.
Hauede [he] neyþer hosen ne shon, 860
Ne none kines oþe[r] wede;
To Lincolne barfot he yede.
Hwan he kam þe[r], he was ful wil:⁴⁶
Ne hauede he no frend to gangen til;
Two dayes þer fastinde he yede, 865
Þat⁴⁷ non for his werk wolde him fede;
Þe þridde day herde he calle:
"Bermen,⁴⁸ bermen, hider forth alle!"
[Poure þat on fote yede]
Sprongen forth so sparke of glede.⁴⁹ 870
Hauelok shof dun[e] nyne or ten
Rith amidewarde þe fen,⁵⁰
And stirte forth to þe kok,
[Þer the erles mete he tok]
Þat he bouthe at þe brigge: 875
Þe bermen let he alle ligge,
And bar þe mete to þe castel,
And gat him þere a ferþing wastel.¹
Þet oþer day kepte he ok
Swiþe yerne þe erles kok, 880
Til þat he say him on þe b[r]igge,

---

⁴⁵ garment. ⁴⁶ perplexed. ⁴⁷ during which. ⁴⁸ porters. ⁴⁹ live coal. ⁵⁰ mud.
¹ cake worth a farthing.

869. Line supplied by Skeat.
870. MS. *on glede*.
874. Supplied by Madden.
875. The bridge spanned the Witham. The castle is about a half-mile away, up a steep hill.
878. Gaimar says that they gave him, from their own food, *gastels*, *Asquanz quartiers de simenels* (128).

And bi him mani fishes ligge.
Þe herles mete hauede he bouth
Of Cornwaile, and kalde oft:
"Bermen, bermen, hider swiþe !"   885
Hauelok it herde, and was ful bliþe
Þat he herde "bermen" calle:
Alle made he hem dun falle
Þat in his gate yeden and stode,
Wel sixtene laddes gode.   890
Als he lep þe kok til,
He shof hem alle upon an hyl;
Astirte² til him with his rippe,³
And bigan þe fish to kippe.⁴
He bar up wel a carte-lode   895
Of segges,⁵ laxes,⁶ of playces brode,
Of grete laumprees, and of eles;
Sparede he neyþer tos ne heles⁷
Til þat he to þe castel cam,
Þat men fro him his birþene nam.   900
Þan men haueden holpen him doun
With þe birþene of his croun,
Þe kok stod, and on him low,
And þoute him stalworþe man ynow,
And seyde, "Wiltu ben wit me?   905
Gladlike wile ich feden þe;
Wel is set⁸ þe mete þu etes,
And þe hire þat þu getes."
"Goddot !" quoth he, "leue sire,
Bidde ich you non oþer hire:⁹   910
But yeueþ me inow to ete,

² hastened.   ³ basket.   ⁴ seize.   ⁵ ? cuttlefish?   ⁶ salmon.   ⁷ i.e., he hurried.
⁸ invested.   ⁹ I ask you for no other wages.

883. *Bouth* might have been pronounced *boft* (Sisam).
884. MS. *cornwalie.* The phrase means, "the earl of Cornwall's food."
909. MS. *Soddot.*
911. Havelok's accomplishments are much more homely than is usual with heroes of romance. Cuchulainn ("Wooing of Emer") is a judge, warrior, counsellor, poet, and magician. Cf. "King Horn" 228, and "The Squire of Low Degree."

Fir[10] and water y wile you fete,
þe fir blowe, an ful wele maken;
Stickes kan ich breken and kraken,
And kindlen ful wel a fyr,   915
And maken it to brennen shir;
Ful wel kan ich cleuen shides,[11]
Eles to-turuen of here hides;[12]
Ful wel kan ich dishes swilen,[13]
And don al þat ye euere wilen."   920
Quoth þe kok, "Wile i no more;
Go þu yunder, and sit þore,
And y shal yeue þe ful fair bred,
And make þe broys in þe led.[14]
Sit now doun and et ful yerne: 925
Daþeit hwo þe mete werne !"[15]

Hauelok sette him dun anon
Also stille als a ston,
Til he hauede ful wel eten;
Þo hauede Hauelok fayre geten.[16]   930
Hwan he hauede eten inow,
He kam to þe welle, water updrow,
And filde þe[r] a michel so;[17]
Bad he non ageyn him go;
But bitwen his hondes he bar it in,   935
A[l] him one,[18] to þe kichin.
Bad he non him watcr to fetc,
Ne fro b[r]igge to bere þe mete.
He bar þe turues,[19] he bar þe star,[20]
Þe wode fro the brigge he bar;   940
Al þat euere shulden he nytte,[21]
Al he drow, and al he citte;[22]
Wolde he neuere hauen rest,
More þan he were a best.

---

[10] firewood. [11] split small sticks. [12] i.e., skin eels. [13] wash. [14] broth in the
kettle. [15] a curse on him who denies you food. [16] made out well. [17] tub.
[18] himself alone. [19] peat. [20] a fibrous plant used for fuel. [21] use. [22] cut.

937. Morsbach suggested omitting *to*.

Of alle men was he mest meke,   945
Lauhwinde ay, and bliþe of speke;
Euere he was glad and bliþe:
His sorwe he couþe ful wel miþe.²³
It²⁴ ne was non so litel knaue,
For to leyken, ne forto plawe,²⁵   950
Þat he ne wo[l]de with him pleye:
Þe children that y[e]den in þe weie
Of him, he deden al he[re] wille,
And with him leykeden here fille.
Him loueden alle, stille²⁶ and bolde,   955
Knictes, children, yunge and holde;
Alle him loueden þat him sowen,
Boþen heye men and lowe.
Of him ful wide þe word sprong,
Hw he was mike[l], hw he was strong,   960
Hw fayr man God him hauede maked,
But-on þat he was almest naked:
For he ne hauede nouth to shride²⁷
But a kouel ful unride,²⁸
Þat [was] ful, and swiþe wicke,   965
Was it nouth worth a fir-sticke.²⁹
Þe cok bigan of him to rewe,
And bouthe him cloþes, al spannewe;³⁰
He bouthe him boþe hosen and shon,
And sone dide him dones³¹ on.   970
Hwan he was cloþed, [h]osed, and shod,
Was non so fayr under God,

---

²³ hide. ²⁴ there. ²⁵ sport or play. ²⁶ shy. ²⁷ wear. ²⁸ very wretched cloak.
²⁹ piece of firewood. ³⁰ brand-new. ³¹ put them.

945. This extended picture of a popular hero is very like one in "Horn
et Rimenhild" (O.) 471 ff., and most of the items—his willingness to
serve others, his good-nature, his popularity, strength, and beauty—are
familiar in the romances.   Gareth is said by Malory never to have displeased man or child (cf. 955).
960. The form *mike* may be right, as noted by Grattan.
972. Great personal beauty is a stock quality of heroes of romance.
The elements are given in W. C. Curry's "Middle English Ideal of Personal Beauty."   It was taken as a sign of royal or aristocratic descent.
(Cf. 2300 and Hall's note to "King Horn" 10.)

Þat euere yete in erþe were,
Non þat euere moder bere;
It was neuere man þat yemede   975
In kinneriche, þat so wel semede
King or cayser forto be,
Þan he was shrid,[32] so semede he;
For þanne he weren alle samen
At Lincolne, at þe gamen,   980
And þe erles men woren al þore,
Þan was Hauelok bi þe shuldren more[33]
Þan þe meste þat þer kam:
In armes him noman nam
Þat he doune sone ne caste.   985
Hauelok stod ouer hem als a mast;
Als he was heie, al[s] he was long,
He was boþe stark and strong;
In Engelond [was] non hise per
Of strengþe þat euere kam him ner.   990
Als he was strong, so was he softe:
Þey a man him misdede ofte,
Neuere more he him misseyde,
Ne hond on him with yuele leyde.
Of bodi was he mayden-clene;   995
Neuere yete in game, ne in grene,
With hore[34] ne wolde [he] leyke ne lye,
No more þan it were a strie.[35]
In þat time al Hengelond
Þerl Godrich hauede in his hond,   1000

---

[32] clad.   [33] i.e., taller by a head and shoulders.   [34] harlot.   [35] hag.

984. At Grasmere and elsewhere, the kind of wrestling mentioned here is still popular. The contestants locked arms about each other or held the ends of a towel thrown about the other's shoulders, and attempted either to break the opponent's hold or to cause him to lose his balance. (See Strutt II.ii; Salzman 83; British Museum postcard of illumination in MS. Royal 10 E.iv.) Cf. "Gamelyn" and "Octavian" (S.) 895.

993. MS. *him misdede*, repeated from preceding line, and causing a bad rhyme.

996. Koelbing proposed *yete in gardine;* another proposal is to read *graine* (scarlet).

997. MS. *þit hire.*

And he gart komen into þe tun
Mani erl and mani barun;
And alle þat liues were
In Englond þanne wer þere
Þat þey haueden after sent   1005
To ben þer at þe parlement.
With hem com mani champioun,
Mani with ladde, blac and brown;
An fel it so þat yunge men,
Wel abouten nine or ten,   1010
Bigunnen þe[re] for to layke:[36]
Þider komen boþe stronge and wayke:
Þider komen lesse and more
Þat in þe borw þanne weren þore;
Chaunpiouns and starke laddes,   1015
Bondemen with here gaddes,[37]
Als he comen fro þe plow;
Þere was sembling[38] inow!
For it ne was non horse-knaue,[39]
Þo[uh] þei sholden in honde haue,[40]   1020

---

[36] sport.   [37] goads (for oxen).   [38] assembly.   [39] stable-boy.   [40] be on duty.

1006. Several parliaments were held at Lincoln, the earliest recorded being in 1213. But probably the reference here is not to history proper, since the Lai mentions the same event (284). On this subject and on the history of the word, see *Archiv* 146.187.

1007. MS. *chābioun.*

1008. Despite much evidence, the meaning of this phrase is uncertain. "Black" is generally agreed to refer to peasants only; "brown" is doubtful. (1) The phrase may mean "persons of all ranks." Sisam pointed out that the poet liked to indicate inclusiveness by coupling terms of opposite meaning. In 2181 ff., the sense seems to be general. Furthermore, gentle-folk as well as peasants engaged in putting the stone. Finally, brown was shown by Curry (87) to be a proper complexion of knights; and the Nut-brown Maid was a baron's daughter. (2) But in most ballads and romances, brown and black complexions are for the peasantry, red and white for nobles. See Curry 86; "Partonope" 8164; "King Estmere" 46; and dozens of instances may be found of the preference for the light complexion in Celtic pieces and their English imitations and adaptations. Hence the phrase may mean "all the lesser folk."

1016. Bondmen were practically slaves on farms. See Percy Folio MS. II. 33.

Þat he ne kam þider, þe leyk to se:
Biforn here fet þanne lay a tre,[41]
And putten[42] with a mikel ston
Þe starke laddes, ful god won.
Þe ston was mikel and ek greth,   1025
And al so heui so a neth;[43]
Grund-stalwrþe[44] man he sholde be
Þat mouthe liften it to his kne;
Was þer neyþer clerc ne prest,
Þat mithe liften it to his brest.   1030
Þerwit putten the chaunpiouns
Þat þider comen with þe barouns;
Hwo-so mithe putten þore
Biforn anoþer an inch or more,
Wore he yung, wore he hold,   1035
He was for a kempe told.[45]
Al-so þe[i] stoden an ofte stareden,
Þe chaunpiouns and ek the ladden;
And he maden mikel strout[46]
Abouten þe alþerbeste but,[47]   1040
Hauelok stod and lokede þer-til;
And of puttingge he was ful wil,[48]
For neuere yete ne saw he or
Putten the ston, or þanne þor.[49]

---

[41] beam (as a foul-mark). [42] put, cast. [43] ox. [44] very powerful. [45] counted a champion. [46] disputed fiercely. [47] effort. [48] ignorant. [49] before that time.

1023. MS. *pulten*. The sport was popular among Germanic peoples (cf. "Nibelungen Lied" 435, 532, etc.), though not confined to them (cf. the Perseus legend, the father being slain by a prodigious cast of a stone; and "The Voyage of Maelduin"). A picture of it is on a post-card of the British Museum, from Royal MS. 10. E.iv. Heroes of romance are often proficient in the sport; Florent ("Octavian") outscores his rivals by nine fathoms; Isumbras does well enough to make his competitors angry (607); and cf. Adam Bell at the king's court, and "Horn et Rimnild" 2567 ff. The sport is mentioned in a curious sermon in the *Bulletin of the Modern Humanities Research Association* II.v.106. Robert Manning says that in his day (1338) the stone which Havelok cast is said to be preserved in Lincoln Castle.

1036. *Champioun* means competent athlete, man of valor; *kempe* means an outstanding performer among many good ones.

1037. Sisam suggested *stadden*, looked on.

Hise mayster bad him gon þer-to,   1045
Als he couþe þer-with do.[50]
þo hise mayster it him bad,
He was of him sore adrad;
þerto he stirte sone anon,
And kipte[1] up þat heui ston   1050
þat he sholde puten wiþe;
He putte, at þe firste siþe,
Ouer alle þat þer wore
Twel[ue] fote and sumdel[2] more.
þe chaunpiouns þat put sowen;   1055
Shuldreden he ilc oþer and lowen:
Wolden he no more to putting gange,
But seyde, "We dwellen her to longe!"[3]
þis selkouth[4] mithe nouth ben hyd;
Ful sone it was ful loude kid[5]   1060
Of Hauelok, hw he warp[6] þe ston
Ouer þe laddes euerilkon;
Hw he was fayr, hw he was long,
Hw he was with, hw he was strong;
þoruth England yede þe speche,   1065
Hw he was strong and ek meke;
In the castel, up in þe halle,
þe knithes speken þerof alle,
So that Godrich it herde wel:
þe[i] speken of Hauelok, eueri del,[7]   1070
Hw he was strong man and hey,
Hw he was strong, and ek fri,
And þouthte Godrich, "þoru þis knaue
Shal ich Engelond al haue,
And mi sone after me;   1075
For so i wile þat it be.
The king Aþelwald me dide swere
Vpon al þe messe-gere

---

[50] to do the best he could.   [1] picked.   [2] somewhat.   [3] i.e., we are wasting our time.   [4] marvel.   [5] made known.   [6] threw.   [7] i.e., in every particular.

1048. Havelok is brave and cowardly by turns, whichever best suits the story; cf. 1682, 1153.

1067. Cf. "Horn et Rimnild" 474 (O.).

Þat y shu[l]de his douthe[r] yeue
Þe hexte [man] þat mithe liue.   1080
Þe beste, þe fairest, þe strangest ok;
Þat gart he me sweren on þe bok.
Hwere mithe i finden ani so hey
So Hauelok is, or so sley?[2]
Þou y southe heþen into Ynde,   1085
So fayr, so strong, ne mithe y finde.
Hauelok is þat ilke knaue
Þat shal Goldeborw haue !"
Þis þouthe [he] with trechery,
Wit traysoun, and wit felony;   1090
For he wende þat Hauelok wore
Sum cherles sone, and no more;
Ne shulde he hauen of Engellond
Onlepi forw[3] in his hond
With hire þat was þerof eyr,   1095
Þat boþe was god and swiþe fair.
He wende þat Hauelok wer a þral;
Þerþoru he wende hauen al
In Engelond, þat hire rith was—
He was werse þan Sathanas   1100
Þat Iesu Crist in erþe stoc ![4]
Hanged worþe he on an hok ![5]

After Goldebo[r]w sone he sende,
Þat was boþe fayr and hende,
And dide hire to Lincolne bringe;   1105
Belles dede he ageyn hire ringen,

[2] skillful.   [3] a single furrow.   [4] shut fast.   [5] oak.

1080. In the Lai there is the same play on the words "plus fort" (327).
1085. The Lai says "Rome" (367). But India was commonly used to
indicate great distance and remoteness; cf. "Partonope" 6209, 11907;
"Seven Sages" 2943; "La Mort Aymeri" 147.
1101. MS. *shop*, which does not rhyme or make sense. Hell was thought
to be in the interior of the earth.
1102. Criminals were often hanged on trees. Cf. "Bevis of Hamtoun"
(A) 1613, where one text reads, *I wolde i were hanged on an oke/ But y
were wroken*, etc. The form *ok*, without the final -*e*, in the oblique cases,
seems to have been common.

And ioie he made hire swiþe mikel;
But neþeles he was ful swikel.[6]
He seyde þat he sholde hire yeue
Þe fayreste man þat mithe liue.   1110
She answerede and seyde anon,
Bi Crist and bi seint Iohan,
Þat hire sholde noman wedde
Ne noman bringen hire to bedde,
But he were king or kinges eyr,   1115
Were he neuere man so fayr.

Godrich þe erl was swiþe wroth
Þat she swor swilk an oth,
And seyde, "Hwor þou wilt be
Quen and leuedi ouer me?   1120
Þou shalt hauen a gadeling[7]
Ne shalt þou hauen non oþer þing!
Þe shal spusen mi cokes knaue:
Shalt þou non oþer louerd haue!
Daþeit þat þe oþer yeue[8]   1125
Eueremore hwil i liue!
To-mo[r]we sholen ye ben weddeth,
And, maugre þin,[9] togidere beddeth.
Goldeborw gret and yaf hire ille;[10]
She wolde ben ded bi hire wille.   1130
On þe morwen hwan day was sprungen,
And day-belle at kirke rungen,

[6] treacherous.   [7] a low rascal.   [8] a curse on him who gives you anyone
else.   [9] in spite of you.   [10] grieved.

1114. MS. to hire.—Holthausen.
1119. The scribe has substituted hwor for the more common hweþer,
to the detriment of the meter.
1122. MS. king.
1124. MS. ne shalt.—Holthausen.
1127. MS. ye sholen.—Holthausen.
1132. I.e., for matins. Rural communities had commonly only two
ways of telling time: by the sun and by the church-bells. The poet
does not mention the great cathedral in Lincoln, though it was practically completed in his day; it was near the green (2829), the bridge
(881), and the castle.

After Hauelok sente þat Iudas
Þat werse was þanne Sathanas,
And seyde, "Mayster, wilte[11] wif?"   1135
"Nay," quoth Hauelok, "bi my lif!
Hwat sholde ich with wif do?
I ne may hire fede ne cloþe ne sho.
Wider sholde ich wimman bringe?
I ne haue none kines þinge.   1140
I ne haue hws, y ne haue cote,[12]
I ne haue stikke, y ne haue sprote,[13]
I ne haue neyþer bred ne sowel[14]
Ne cloth, but of an hold with couel.
Þis cloþes þat ich onne haue   1145
Aren þe kokes, and ich his knaue."
Godrich stirt up and on him dong[15]
[With dintes swiþe hard and strong,]
And seyde, "But þou hire take
Þat y wole yeuen þe to make,[16]   1150
I shal hangen þe ful heye,
Or y shal þristen uth þin heie."
Hauelok was one[17] and was adrad,
And grauntede him al þat he bad.
Þo sende he after hire sone,   1155
Þe fayrest wymman under mone;
And seyde til hire, [fals] and slike,[18]
Þat wicke þral, þat foule swike:[19]
"But þu þis man understonde,[20]
I shal flemen[21] þe of londe;   1160

---

[11] do you want.   [12] hut.   [13] twig (to burn).   [14] relish.   [15] struck.   [16] as a mate.   [17] alone.   [18] treacherous.   [19] traitor.   [20] accept.   [21] put to flight.

1136. Havelok's reluctance is also found in the French. (Cf. Gaimar 175 ff.)
1142. MS. ne i.
1148. Supplied by Skeat.
1153. MS. odrat.—Holthausen.
1157. Cf. Gower II. 365: He can so wel his wordes slike, where the word seems to mean "make suave." Yet Godrich's next speech involves little adroitness or finesse, and is not insinuating or insidious. See also B. S., who cite examples from the "Promptorium Parvulorum," Richard Rolle, and Palladius, all meaning "smooth" or "sleek."

Or þou shal[t] to þe galwes renne,
And þer þou shalt in a fir brenne."
Sho was adrad for he so þrette,[22]
And durste nouth þe spusing lette;
But þey hire likede swiþe ille,   1165
[Sho] þouthe it was Godes wille:
God, þat makes to growen þe korn,
Formede hire wimman to be born.
Hwan he hauede don[23] him, for drede,
Þat he sholde hire spusen[24] and fede,   1170
And þat she sholde til him holde,
Þer weren penies þicke tolde,
Mikel plenté upon þe bok:
He ys hire yaf, and she is tok.
He weren spused fayre and wel,   1175
Þe messe he dede—eueridel
Þat fel to spusing—a god cle[r]k,
Þe erchebishop uth of Yerk,
Þat kam to þe parlement,
Als God him hauede þider sent.   1180

Hwan he weren togydere in Godes lawe
Þat þe folc ful wel it sawe,

---

[22] because he so threatened her.   [23] i.e., when Godrich had caused Havelok.
[24] marry.

1161. *þou* is probably Havelok, and the same word in the next line
refers to Goldeborw. Men were sometimes hanged and then burned.
Female criminals were burned but not hanged.

1172. The Salisbury Missal says: *Ponat vir aurum vel argentum vel
aliquid et annulum super scutum vel librum.* Part of the money was the
clerk's fee, part was a symbol that the wife was endowed with the husband's worldly goods (see Gautier, Ch. XI), and part might be payment
for the wife's virginity. The Sarum Missal in English (ed. F. E. Warren)
gives as part of the service, *Wyth thys rynge I the wedde, and thys gold
and selvir I the geve.* For information about wedding customs, see Gautier
and *M Phil.* for 1905, 13, 18.

1174. MS. *as tok.*—Holthausen. *Ys = them.*

1177. MS. *and god.*

1182. The poem does not tell where the marriage was performed; but
Robert Mannyng of Brunne remarks, *Men said . . . ȝit þe chapelle standes
þer he weddid his wife.*

He ne wisten hwat he mouthen,[25]
Ne he ne wisten wat hem douthe,[26]
Þer to dwellen, or þenne to gonge.   1185
Þer ne wolden he dwellen longe,
For he wisten and ful wel sawe
Þat Godrich hem hatede, þe deuel him hawe!
And yf he dwelleden þer outh,
Þat[27] fel Hauelok ful wel on þouth   1190
Men sholde don his leman shame,
Or elles bringen in wicke blame,[28]
Þat were him leuere to ben ded.
Forþi he token anoþer red:
Þat þei sholden þenne fle   1195
Til Grim, and til hise sones þre;
Þer wenden he alþerbest to spede,
Hem forto cloþe and for to fede.
Þe lond he token under fote—
Ne wisten he non oþer bote—   1200
And helden ay the rithe [sti][29]
Til he komen to Grimesby.
Þanne he komen þere, þanne was Grim ded:
Of him ne haueden he no red;
But hise children, alle fyue,   1205
Alle weren yet on liue,
Þat ful fayre ayen hem neme
Hwan he wisten þat he keme,
And maden ioie swiþe mikel,
Ne weren he neuere ayen hem fikel.[30]   1210
On knes ful fayre he hem setten
And Hauelok swiþe fayre gretten,
And seyden, "Welkome, louerd dere!
And welkome be þi fayre fere!

---

[25] could (do).   [26] was of any avail.   [27] it occurred to Havelok.   [28] shameful disrepute.   [29] way.   [30] disloyal.

1191. In some regions, the lord had a right for a time to the bride of his retainer.   Malcolm III of Scotland raised considerable revenue by foregoing this privilege for a mark of silver.

1204. The Lai is equally brief in its obituary of Grim, but more feeling: *E li enfant grant doel feseient.* (570).

Blessed be þat ilke þrawe[31]   1215
þat þou hire toke in Godes lawe!
Wel is hus[32] we sen þe on lyue.
þou mithe us boþe selle and yeue;[33]
þou mayt us boþe yeue and selle,
Withþat[34] þou wilt here dwelle.   1220
We hauen, louerd, alle gode,
Hors and neth[35] and ship on flode,
Gold and siluer and michel auchte,[36]
þat Grim ure fader us bitawchte.
Gold and siluer and oþer fe   1225
Bad he us bitaken þe.
We hauen shep, we hauen swin;
Bileue[37] her, louerd, and al be þin!
þo[u] shalt ben louerd, þou shalt ben syre,
And we sholen seruen þe and hire;   1230
And hure sistres sholen do
Al that euere biddes sho:
He sholen hire cloþes washen and wringen,
And to hondes water bringen;
He sholen bedden hire and þe,   1235
For leuedi[38] wile we þat she be."
Hwan he þis ioie haueden maked,
Sithen stikes broken and kraked,
And þe fir brouth on brenne;
Ne was þer spared gos ne henne,   1240
Ne þe hende[39] ne þe drake:
Mete he deden plenté make;
Ne wantede þere no god mete,
Wyn and ale deden he fete,
And hem made glade and bliþe: 1245
Wesseyl ledden[40] he fele siþe.

---

[31] time. [32] us; i.e., we are glad. [33] i.e., into slavery. [34] if. [35] oxen. [36] wealth. [37] remain. [38] i.e., the mistress of the establishment. [39] duck. [40] they performed the ceremony of drinking healths.

1224. The time-sequence cannot be examined too closely. This line seems to contradict others (e.g., 858); a considerable interval must have elapsed.

1233. MS. cloþen.—Garnett.

1245. MS. made hem.

On þe nith, als Goldeborw lay,
Sory and sorwful was she ay,
For she wende she were biswike[41]
Þat sh[e w]ere yeuen un-kyndelike.[42]   1250
O nith[43] saw she þer-inne a lith,
A swiþe fayr, a swiþe bryth,
Al so brith, al so shir
So it were a blase of fir.
She lokede no[r]þ, and ek south,   1255
And saw it comen ut of his mouth
Þat lay bi hire in þe bed:
No ferlike þou she were adred!
Þouthe she, "Wat may this bimene?[44]
He beth heyman[45] yet, als y wene: 1260
He beth heyman er he be ded!"
On hise shuldre, of gold red
She saw a swiþe noble croiz;[46]
Of an angel she herde a uoyz:

"Goldeborw, lat þi sorwe be;   1265
For Hauelok, þat haueþ spuset þe,
He kinges sone and kinges eyr;
Þat bikenneth[47] þat croiz so fayr.
It bikenneth more: þat he shal
Denemark hauen, and Englond al;   1270
He shal ben king, strong and stark,
Of Engelond and Denemark:
Þat shal þu wit þin eyne sen,
And þo[u] shalt quen and leuedi ben!"

Þanne she hauede herd þe steuene[48]   1275
Of þe angel uth of heuene,
She was so fele siþes bliþe

---

[41] betrayed.   [42] because she was married out of her rank.   [43] in the night.
[44] betoken.   [45] nobleman.   [46] cross.   [47] indicates.   [48] voice.

1264. The angel is not in the French, his place being supplied by a
hermit; but angels as messengers from heaven are common in French
romance. See D. B. Easter, "Magic in the Romans d' Aventure," etc.
(Johns Hopkins Thesis, 1905, p. 33.)

Þat she ne mithe hire ioie mythe;[49]
But Hauelok sone anon she kiste,
And he slep and nouth ne wiste.   280
Hwan þat aungel hauede seyd,
Of his slep anon he brayd,
And seide, "Lemman, slepes þou?
A selkuth[50] drem dremede me nou:

Herkne nou hwat me haueth met![1]   1285
Me þouthe y was in Denemark set,
But on on þe moste hil
Þat euere yete kam i til.
It was so hey, þat y wel mouthe
Al þe werd se, als me þouthe.   1290
Als i sat upon þat lowe,[2]
I bigan Denemark for to awe,
Þe borwes and þe castles stronge;
And mine armes weren so longe
Þat i fadmede,[3] al at ones,   1295
Denemark, with mine longe bones;
And þanne y wolde mine armes drawe
Til me, and hem for to haue,[4]
Al that euere in Denemark liueden
On mine armes faste clyueden;   1300
And þe stronge castles alle
On knes bigunnen for to falle;
Þe keyes fellen at mine fet.—

---

[49] hide. [50] wondrous. [1] dreamed. [2] hill. [3] embraced. [4] = *awe*, possess.

1285. In Gaimar and the Lai, the details of the dream are entirely different. A parallel to this is in "William of Palerne" 2904 ff., where the queen dreams that her right hand stretches from Palermo over Rome, her left over all Spain; and "both kingdoms come to her will." It perplexes her, but is interpreted to mean rescue from her troubles and dominion over a large empire. Prophetic dreams of all sorts are common in the romances; cf. "Horn" 650; "Le Morte Arthur;" "Brut;" "Chanson;" "Pilgrimage of Charlemagne;" cf. Dickman 182.

1287. Literally, on one the highest hill. (Sisam) Cf. Int. VII. A.5.

1298. MS. *hom.* Probably a verb like *thought* was present in the writer's mind as he wrote the second clause.

1301. Possibly modelled on the dream of Joseph about the sheaves.

Anoþer drem dremede me ek:
þat ich fley[5] ouer þe salte se   1305
Til Engeland, and al with me
þat euere was in Denemark lyues
But bondemen and here wiues;
And þat ich kom til Engelond,
Al closede it intil min hond,   1310
And, Goldeborw, y gaf [it] þe:—
Deus![6] lemman, hwat may þis be?"
Sho answerede and seyde sone:
"Iesu Crist, þat made mone,
þine dremes turne to ioye, . . .   1315
þat wite þw that sittes in trone![7]
Ne non strong, king ne caysere,
So þou shalt be, fo[r] þou shalt bere
In Engelond corune yet.
Denemark shal knele to þi fet: 1320
Alle þe castles þat aren þer-inne
Shaltow, lemman, ful wel winne.
I woth so wel so ich it sowe,
To þe shole comen heye and lowe,
And alle þat in Denemark wone,   1325
Em and broþer, fader and sone,
Erl and baroun, dreng[8] an þayn,
Knithes and burgeys and sweyn,
And mad king heyelike[9] and wel.
Denemark shal be þin euere-ilc del: 1330
Haue þou nouth þeroffe douthe,

---

[5] flew.   [6] God; i.e., in heaven's name.   [7] throne.   [8] military vassal.   [9] solemnly.

1308 Whether husbandmen formed part of the expedition to England is hard to say, since the passage describing the voyage is omitted (2519).
1314. Cf. 436.
1316. The text seems imperfect here. 1316 probably belonged with a sequence of lines rhyming in—one; 1315 has been substituted for one of these, and its own sequence omitted.
1323. A dream was considered more trustworthy if it was repeated. Cf. "Pelerinage de Charlemagne," 71.
1327. MS. kayn. See note l. 31.
1329. Sudden shifts of subject are frequent in the romances.

Nouth þe worth of one nouthe,[10]
Þeroffe withinne þe firste yer
Shalt þou ben king, withouten were.[11]
But do nou als y wile rathe: 1335
Nimen we to Denema[r]k baþe,
And do þou nouth on frest þis fare;[12]
Lith and selthe[13] felawes are.
For shal ich neuere bliþe be
Til i with eyen Denemark se;   1340
For ich woth þat al þe lond
Shalt þou hauen in þin hon[d].
Prey Grimes sones, alle þre,
Þat he wenden forþ with þe;
I wot he wilen þe nouth werne:[14]   1345
With þe wende shulen he yerne,
For he louen þe hertelike.
Þou maght telle he aren quike,
Hwore-so he o worde[15] aren;
Þere ship þou do hem swithe yaren,   1350
And loke þat þou dwelle nouth:
Dwelling haueth ofte scaþe wrouth."

    Hwan Hauelok herde þat she radde,
Sone it was day, sone he him cladde,
And sone to þe kirke yede   1355
Or he dide ani oþer dede;
And bifor þe rode bigan falle,

---

[10] nut.   [11] doubt.   [12] do not postpone the journey.   [13] travel (?) and prosperity.   [14] refuse.   [15] in the world.
1333. In the French versions, the hermit specifies no time.
1334. MS. *king of euere il del*, repeated from 1330. Skeat's emendation.
1336. MS. *Nim in witl þe*. An alternative proposal is to read *Nim
me with þe to D. raþe*. The copyist seems to have been inattentive all
through the passage 1334 ff. Cf. Holthausen's note.
1338. Sisam suggested *Hith*, haste, for the troublesome *Lith*.
1348. MS. *til he.*—Skeat.
1351. MS. *dwellen*.
1355. Going to church before undertaking a critical enterprise was
usual in the French romances. Cf. "Chanson" 1133; "Partonope," 10828;
and see "Gawain" 592.
1357. For the construction, cf. 280.

Croiz and Crist bi[gan] to kalle,[16]
And seyde, "Louerd, þat al weldes,
Wind and water, wodes and feldes,   1360
For þe holi milce[17] of you,
Haue merci of me, louerd, nou,
And wreke me yet on mi fo,
Þat ich saw biforn min eyne slo
Mine sistres with a knif,   1365
And siþen wolde me mi lyf
Haue reft, for in þe se
Bad he Grim haue drenched me.
He [hath] mi lond with mikel vnrith,[18]
With michel wrong, with mikel plith,[19]   1370
For i ne misdede him neuere nouth,
And haueth me to sorwe brouth.
He haueth me do mi mete to þigge,[20]
And ofte in sorwe and pine ligge.
Louerd, haue merci of me,   1375
And late [me] wel passe þe se—
Þouh ich haue þeroffe douthe and kare—
With-uten stormes ouerfare,[21]
Þat y ne drenched [be] þerine,
Ne forfaren[22] for no sinne;   1380
And bringge me wel to þe lond
Þat Godard haldes in his hond,
Þat is mi rith, eueri del:
Iesu Crist, þou wost it wel!"

Þanne he hauede his bede[23] seyd,   1385

---

[16] invoke. [17] mercy. [18] injustice. [19] blame. [20] beg. [21] (let me) cross. [22] lost.
[23] prayer.

1364. The numerous summaries in the poem may have been designed
to give late-comers an idea of its course, or to refresh the memories of
those who might forget from one day to the next. Cf. the repetitions in
"Horn," "Octavian" (S.) 859, and the conclusion of "Le Bon Florent."
Elizabethan audiences seemed to like summaries in plays. Cf. also "Aliscans" 2637.
1372. MS. *haued.*
1377. MS. *þat ich.*

His offrende on þe auter²⁴ leyd,
His leue at Iesu Crist he tok,
And at his suete moder ok,
And at þe croiz þat he biforn lay;
Siþen yede sore grotinde awey.   1390

Hwan he com hom, he wore yare,
Grimes sones, forto fare
Into þe se, fishes to gete,
Þat Hauelok mithe wel of ete.
But Auelok þouthe al anoþer.²⁵   1395
First he ka[l]de þe heldeste broþer,
Roberd þe Rede, bi his name,
Wiliam Wenduth and H[uwe R]auen,
Grimes sones alle þre,
And sey[d]e, "Liþes nou alle to me;   1400
Louerdinges, ich wile you sheue
A þing of me þat ye wel knewe.
Mi fader was king of Denshe lond:
Denemark was al in his hond
Þe day þat he was quik and ded;   1405
But þanne hauede he wicke red,
Þat he me and Denemark al
And mine sistres bitawte a þral:
A deueles lime²⁶ [he] hus bitawte,
And al his lond and al hise authe,²⁷   1410
For y saw þat fule fend
Mine sistres slo with hise hend;
First he shar²⁸ a-two here þrotes,
And siþen hem al to grotes,²⁹

---

²⁴ altar.   ²⁵ intended something else.   ²⁶ limb; i.e., a scoundrel.   ²⁷ wealth.
²⁸ cut.   ²⁹ bits.

1386. For this practice, cf. "Sir Degare" 487; "Squire of Low Degree"
245, 706. Before entering the trial by ordeal, the knights in the "Chanson
de Roland" make large offerings (3861). Cf. also "Sir Gawain and the
Green Knight" 593; "Pelerinage de Charlemagne" 59.
1397. To restore the rhyme, Sisam suggested naven (ON. nafn), with
the same meaning.

And siþen bad [he] in þe se 1415
Grim, youre fader, drenchen me.
Deplike[30] dede he him swere
On bok, þat he sholde me bere
Vnto þe se, an drenchen ine,
And [he] wolde taken on him þe sinne. 1420
But Grim was wis and swiþe hende;
Wolde he nouth his soule shende;
Leuere was him to be forsworen
Þan drenchen me, and ben forlorn;
But sone bigan he forto fle 1425
Fro Denemark, forto berwen me.
For yif ich hauede þer ben funden,
Hauede [he] ben slayn or harde bunden,
And heye ben henged on a tre:
Hauede go[n] for[31] him gold ne fe. 1430
For-þi fro Denemark hider he fledde,
And me ful fayre and ful wel fedde,
So þat vn-to þis day
Haue ich ben fed and fostred ay.
But nou ich am up to þat helde 1435
Cumen, that ich may wepne welde,
And y may grete dintes yeue,
Shal i neuere hwil ich lyue
Ben glad, til that ich Denemark se;
I preie you þat ye wende with me, 1440
And ich may mak you riche men;
Ilk of you shal haue castles ten,
And þe lond þat þortil longes,
Borwes, tunes, wodes, and wonges[32] . . ."

[30] solemnly. [31] availed. [32] fields.

1444. A leaf has here been cut from the MS.; Madden believed it to contain 180 lines, and at this point added that number to the actual number of the lines following. The passage probably contained this information: The three sons agree, and exchange some of their property for a peddler's wares and a fine ring. They sail to Denmark and moor the boat; Hugh Raven remains in it. The others disembark and on the shore meet Ubbe, a Danish earl, who is out riding with his retinue near a town and castle. Havelok asks permission to sell his wares.

. . . "With swilk als ich byen shal: 1625
Þerof biseche [ich] you nou leue;
Wile ich speke with non oþer reue,[33]
But with þe, þat iustise are,
Þat y mithe seken mi ware
In gode borwes up and doun,   1630
And faren ich wile fro tun to tun."
A gold ring drow he forth anon
An hundred pund was worth þe ston
And yaf it Ubbe for to spede.[34]
He was ful wis þat first yaf mede;   1635
And so was Hauelok ful wis here:
He solde his gold ring ful dere:
Was neuere non so dere sold
Fro chapmen,[35] neyþer yung ne old:
Þat sholen ye forthward[36] ful wel heren,   1640
Yif þat ye wile þe storie heren.

Hwan Ubbe hauede þe gold ring,
Hauede he youenet[37] for no þing,
Nouth for þe borw euereil[k] del.
Hauelok bihel[d] he swiþe wel,   1645
Hw he was wel of bones maked,
Brod in þe sholdres, ful wel schaped,
Þicke in þe brest, of bodi long;
He semede wel to ben wel strong.

---

[33] magistrate; i.e., I will have nothing to do with lesser officers. [34] in the
hope of prospering.   [35] merchants.   [36] later.   [37] given it up.

1628. Read *with you*—Holthausen.
1629. Possibly a riddling speech like that in "King Horn" (1130); he
is to seek wares, i.e., recover his kingdom. But disguise as a merchant
was common, because it gave one a pretext for traveling anywhere and
entering castles. Cf. "Sir Ferumbras" 4373 and Jusserand II.ii.
1632. For other instances of giving rings as propitiatory gifts, cf. "Sir
Tristram" 623, "Piers Plowman" A.iii.202; "King Estmere" 46. The
practice is common in the romances.
1634. The name Ubbe was fairly common among the Danes. Cf. the
legend of St. Fremund told by Saxo Grammaticus.
1639. MS. *for*.
1640. MS. *shoren*.

"Deus !"[38] hwat Ubbe, "qui ne were he knith? 1650
I woth þat he is swiþe with !
Betere semede him to bere
Helm on heued, sheld and spere,
Þanne to beye and selle ware.
Allas, þat he shal þerwith fare ![39] 1655
Goddot ! wile he trowe me,[40]
Chaffare[41] shal he late be."
Neþeles he seyde sone:
"Hauelok, haue þi bone,
And y ful wel rede þ[e] 1660
Þat þou come and ete with me
To-day, þou and þi fayre wif,
Þat þou louest also þi lif.
And haue þou of hire no drede:
Shal hire no man shame bede. 1665
Bi þe fey that y owe to þe,
Þerof shal i meself borw[42] be."

Hauelok herde þat he bad,
And thow[43] was he ful sore [a]drad
With him to ete, for hise wif; 1670
For him wore leuere þat his lif
Him wore reft, þan she in blame
Felle, or lauthe[44] ani shame.
Hwanne he hauede his wille yat,[45]
Þe stede þat he onne sat 1675
Smot Ubbe with spures faste,
And forth awey, but at þe laste,
Or he fro him ferde,
Seyde he, þat his folk herde:
"Loke þat ye comen beþe, 1680

---

[38] God; i.e., in heaven's name. [39] i.e., pursue that trade. [40] by heaven, if he takes my advice. [41] trading. [42] surety. [43] then (?). [44] suffered. [45] assented.

1667. MS. *me serf.*

1675. It was traditional for kings or their representatives to meet travelers on the shore. Cf. note to "King Horn" 155; and cf. "Beowulf" 229 ff.

1680. For the rhyme, see 360.

For ich it wile, and ich it rede."

Hauelok ne durste, þe[y] he were adrad
Nouth withsitten[46] þat Ubbe bad:
His wif he dide with him lede;
Vn-to þe heye curt he y[e]de.   1685
Roberd hire ledde, þat was red,
Þat hauede þoled[47] for hire þe ded[48]
Or ani hauede hire misseyd,
Or hand with iuele onne leyd.
Willam Wendut was þat oþer   1690
Þat hire ledde, Roberdes broþer,
Þat was with at alle nedes:
Wel is him þat god man fedes![49]
Þan he weren comen to þe halle
Biforen Ubbe and hise men alle,   1695
Vbbe stirte hem ageyn,
And mani a knith and mani a sweyn,
Hem for to se and forto shewe.[50]
Þo stod Hauelok als a lowe[1]
Aboven [þo] þat þerinne wore,   1700
Rith al bi þe heued more
Þanne ani þat þerinne stod:
Þo was Ubbe bliþe of mod
Þat he saw him so fayr and hende;
Fro him ne mithe his herte wende—   1705
Ne fro him, ne fro his wif;
He louede hem sone so his lif.
Weren non in Denemark þat him þouthe
Þat he so mikel loue mouthe;
More he louede Hauelok one   1710
Þan al Denemark, bi mine wone![2]
Loke nou hw God helpen kan

---

[46] oppose.   [47] would have suffered.   [48] death itself.   [49] i.e., good retainers
are precious.   [50] inspect.   [1] hill.   [2] on my word.

1687. MS. þarned for; a confusion.
1712. "Octavian" (1145), which has many striking resemblances to
this poem, tells of the attraction between a king and his unrecognized
son, and of the dislike of the son for his base-born foster-father. (Cf.
especially 471.) Cf. also "Emare," where the king loves the little page.

O mani wise[3] wif and man!

Hwan it was comen time to ete,
Hise wif dede Ubbe sone in fete,   1715
And til hire seyde, al on gamen:
"Dame, þou and Hauelok shulen ete samen,
And Goldeboru shal ete wit me,
Þat is so fayr so flour on tre;
In al Denemark [n]is wimman   1720
So fayr so sche, bi seint Iohan!"
Þanne [he] were set, and bord leyd,
And þe beneysun[4] was seyd,
Biforn hem com þe beste mete
Þat king or cayser wolde ete: 1725
Kranes, swannes, ueneysun,
Lax,[5] lampreys, and god sturgun,[6]
Pyment[7] to drinke, and god claré,[8]
Win hwit and red, ful god plenté.
Was þerinne no page so lite   1730
Þat euere wolde ale bite.[9]
Of þe mete forto telle,
Ne of þe metes bidde i nout dwelle;
Þat is þe storie for to lenge,[10]
It wolde anuye þis fayre genge.[11]   1735
But hwan he haueden ilk þing deled,[12]
And fele siþes haueden wosseyled,[13]

---

[3] sort. [4] blessing. [5] salmon. [6] sturgeon. [7] spiced wine. [8] a mixture of
wine, honey, and spices. [9] drink. [10] prolong. [11] annoy this fair company.
[12] shared. [13] drunk healths.

1717. Possibly a reminiscence of the French story, where Goldeboru's
beauty incites a retainer to attack Havelok later.
1722. See Introduction, E.III.B.
1726. Birds formed a large part of a medieval bill-of-fare, and many
not now eaten were included. Feasts in the romances are numerous and
sumptuous; e.g., "Richard Coeur de Lion" 4221, "Morte Arthure" 177;
and see Henderson's note on "The Squire" of Low Degree" 317.
1731. I.e., every one had expensive drinks; wine was mostly imported,
ale being the common native drink.
1733. Skeat proposed win for metes.
1736. MS. þe kilþing.

And with gode drinkes seten longe,
And it was time for to gonge,
Il[k] man to þer he cam fro,   1740
Þouthe Ubbe, "Yf i late hem go,
Þus one foure,[14] withuten mo,
So mote ich brouke finger or to,[15]
For þis wimman bes mike[l] wo!
For hire shal men hire louerd slo."   1745
He tok sone knithes ten
And wel sixti oþer men
Wit gode bowes and with gleiues,[16]
And sende him unto þe greyues,[17]
Þe beste man of al þe toun,   1750
Þat was named Bernard Brun;
And bad him, als he louede his lif,
Hauelok wel y[e]men, and his wif,
And wel do wayten[18] al þe nith,
Til þe oþer day, þat it were lith.   1755
Bernard was trewe and swiþe with,
In al þe borw ne was no knith
Þat betere couþe on stede riden,
Helm on heued, ne swerd bi side.
Hauelok he gladlike understod[19]   1760
With mike[l] loue and herte god,
And dide greyþe a super riche,
Also he was no with chinche,[20]
To his bihoue[21] eueril[k] del,
Þat he mithe supe swiþe wel.   1765

Alſo he seten, and sholde soupe,
So comes a ladde in a ioupe,[22]

---

[14] four of them thus alone.   [15] as I (hope to) have the use of a finger or toe;
i.e., certainly.   [16] spears with a cutting hook near the end.   [17] house of the
grave (who was supposed to keep peace in the town).   [18] keep watch.   [19] received.   [20] stingy.   [21] advantage; i.e., taste.   [22] loose jacket.

1763. See 2941. The scribe has substituted the common *chinche* for
the less frequent cognate *chiche*, to the detriment of the rhyme (Sisam).

1767. All through the Middle Ages marauding bands were common in
England and France. They were easily assembled from laborers out of
work, men declared outlaws for crimes committed, and squires and land-

And with him sixti oþer stronge,
With swerdes drawen and kniues longe,
Ilkan in hande a ful god gleiue, 1770
And seyde, "Undo, Bernard þe greyue!
Vndo swiþe and lat us in,
Or þu art ded, bi seint Austin!"[23]
Bernard stirt up, þat was ful big,
And caste a brinie upon his rig, 1775
And grop an ax þat was ful god,
Lep to þe dore so he wore wod,
And seyde, "Hwat are ye, þat are þeroute,
Þat þus biginnen forto stroute?[24]
Goth henne swiþe, fule þeues, 1780
For bi þe Louerd þat man on leues,[25]
Shol ich casten þe dore open,
Summe of you shal ich drepen,
And þe oþre shal ich kesten
In feteres, and ful faste festen!" 1785
"Hwat haue ye seid?" quoth a ladde,
"Wenestu þat we ben adradde?
We shole[n] at þis dore gonge,
Maugre þin, carl, or outh longe."[26]
He gripen sone a bulder-ston,[27] 1790
And let it fleye, ful god won,[28]
Agen þe dore, þat it to-rof:[29]
Auelok it saw and þider drof,[30]
And þe barre sone vt-drow,

---

[23] Augustine. [24] make a disturbance. [25] believes in. [26] before any long time; i.e., at once. [27] large stone. [28] quantity; i.e., hard. [29] burst apart. [30] rushed.

owners eager for plunder. See notes on "Edward and the Shepherd;" Jusserand, II.iii; and cf. "Guy of Warwick" (C) 1636, "Octavian" 356. The motive in the raid on Bernard is said to be robbery (2017); in the French poems the outlaws want Goldeboru.

1775. The phrase is in Layamon (O. 6719).
1776. MS. *an ar.*
1785. On binding as a punishment, see 2442.
1792. The house is not a castle, but a flimsy structure. The Saxon population in England built their dwellings of wood, and were indignant with the Normans for erecting castles of stone.

þat was unride[31] and gret ynow,   1795
And caste þe dore open wide
And seide, "Her shal y now abide:
Comes swiþe vnto me;
Daþeyt hwo you henne fle !"[32]
"No," quodh on, "þat shaltou coupe,"[33]   1800
And bigan til him to loupe,[34]
In his hond his swerd ut-drawe;
Hauelok he wende þore haue slawe.
And with [him] comen oþer two,
þat him wolde of liue haue do.[35]   1805
Hauelok lifte up þe dore-tre,
And at a dint[36] he slow hem þre;
Was non of hem þat his hernes[37]
Ne lay þerute ageyn þe sternes.[38]
þe ferþe[39] þat he siþen mette,   1810
Wit þe barre so he him grette
Bifor þe heued þat þe rith eye
Vt of þe hole[40] made he fleye,
And siþe clapte him on þe crune
So þat he stan-ded[41] fel þor dune.   1815
þe fifte þat he ouertok
Gaf he a ful sor dint ok
Bitwen þe sholdres, þer he stod,
þat he spen[de][42] his herte blod.
þe sixte wende for to fle,   1820
And he clapte him with þe tre
Rith in þe fule necke so
þat he smot hise necke on to.
þanne þe sixe weren doun feld,
þe seuenþe brayd ut his swerd,   1825

---

[31] unwieldy.   [32] a curse on any of you who flee hence.   [33] pay for.   [34] run.
[35] do him to death.   [36] with one stroke.   [37] brains.   [38] stars.   [39] fourth.
[40] socket.   [41] stone-dead.   [42] shed.

1798. *Datheit* is repeated after *me* in the manuscript.
1813. This ghastly feat is common in French romance, from which it was often imitated by English writers. Cf. "Chanson" 2290; "Sowdone of Babylon"; "Fierabras" p. 64.
1819.—Holthausen. Sisam suggested *speu*, vomited.

And wolde Hauelok riht in þe eye;
And Haue[lok] le[t þe] barre fleye,
And smot him sone ageyn þe brest,
Þat hauede he neuere sch[r]ifte[43] of prest;
For he was ded on lesse hwile   1830
Þan men mouthe renne a mile.
Alle þe oþere weren ful kene:
A red þei taken hem bitwene
Þat he sholde[n] him bihalue,[44]
And brisen so þat wit no salue   1835
Ne sholde him helen leche non.
Þey drowen ut swerdes, ful god won,
And shoten[45] on him so don on bere
Dogges þat wolden him to-tere
Þanne men doth þe bere beyte.   1840
Þe laddes were kaske and teyte,[46]
And vmbiyeden him ilkon.
Sum smot with tre,[47] and sum wit ston;
Summe putten[48] with gleyue in bac and side
And yeuen wundes longe and wide   1845
In twenti stedes and wel mo,
Fro þe croune til þe to.
Hwan he saw þat, he was wod,
And was it ferlik hw he stod,
For þe blod ran of his sides   1850
So water þat fro þe welle glides;
But þanne bigan he for to mowe
With þe barre, and let hem shewe

---

[43] absolution; i.e., he died at once.   [44] surround.   [45] rushed.   [46] active and lively.   [47] i.e., clubs.   [48] thrust.

1826. On omitting the verb of motion, see Introduction VIII.A.3.

1831. For a catalogue of occurrences of this common comparison, see Campion and Holthausen's "Sir Perceval of Galles" n. 1033. For all sorts of minstrel tags, see Hibbard 143, n.

1840. In this sport, the bear was chained by his neck or hind leg, and dogs turned loose to worry him. They were likely to be killed or badly mauled, and the bear might suffer serious injury. Such contests were forbidden in 1835. Strutt has quotations and illustrations.

1842. MS. *vn bi yeden.*

Hw he cowþe sore smite;
For was þer non, long ne lite,   1855
Þat he mouthe ouertake,
Þat he ne garte his croune krake,
So þat on a litel stund
Felde he twenti to þe grund.

Þo bigan gret dine to rise,   1860
For þe laddes on ilke wise
Him asayleden wit grete dintes.
Ful fer he stoden, and with flintes
And gleyues schoten[49] him fro ferne,[50]
For drepen[1] him he wolden yerne;   1865
But dursten he newhen[2] him no more
Þanne he bor or leun wore.

Huwe Rauen þat dine herde,
And þowthe wel þat men misferde[3]
With his louerd, for his wif;   1870
And grop an ore and a long knif,
And þider drof also an hert,[4]
And cam þer on a litel stert,[5]
And saw how þe laddes wode
Hauelok his louerd umbistode,[6]   1875
And beten on him so doth þe smith
With þe hamer on þe stith.[7]

"Allas!" hwat Hwe, "þat y was boren—
Þat euere et ich bred of koren,
Þat ich here þis sorwe se!   1880
Roberd! Willam! hware ar ye?
Gripeth eþer unker[8] a god tre,
And late we nouth þise doges fle
Til ure louerd wreke [be];
Cometh swiþe and folwes me!   1885

---

[49] cast at. [50] afar. [1] murder. [2] draw near. [3] did amiss. [4] ran like a deer. [5] space. [6] surrounded. [7] anvil. [8] of you.

1863. MS. *Fro fer; him with;* both anticipations of the next line.
1873. MS. *cham.*

Ich haue in honde a ful god ore:
Daþeit wo ne smite sore!"
"Ya! leue,[9] ya!" quod Roberd sone,
"We hauen ful god lith of þe mone."
Roberd a staf grop, strong and gret,   1890
Þat mouth ful wel bere a net,[10]
And Willam Wendut grop a tre
Mikel grettere þan his þe,[11]
And Bernard held his ax ful faste—
I seye, was he nouth þe laste—   1895
And lopen[12] forth so he weren wode
To þe laddes, þer he stode,
And yaf hem wundes swiþe grete;
Þer mithe men wel se boyes[13] bete,
And ribbes in here sides breke,   1900
And Hauelok on hem wel wreke.
He broken armes, he broken knes,
He broken shankes, he broken thes.[14]
He dide þe blod þere renne dune
To þe fet rith fro the crune,   1905
For was þer spared heued non.
He leyden[15] on heuedes, ful god won,
And made croune[s] breke and crake
Of þe broune and of þe blake;
He maden here backes also bloute[16]   1910
Als he[re] wombes, and made hem rowte[17]
Als he weren kradelbarnes,[18]
So dos þe child þat moder þarnes.[19]

---

[9] i.e., yes, (my good) boy.   [10] sustain an ox.   [11] thigh.   [12] rushed.   [13] knaves.
[14] thighs.   [15] struck.   [16] soft.   [17] roar.   [18] children in cradles.   [19] loses.

1890. MS. *Roberd grop a staf.* The poet does not seem to be striving
for comic effect in arming his heroes with a door-bar, a staff, a cudgel,
and an oar.   But cf. "Sir Perceval" 2013, "Sir Degare" 325.
1893. MS. *þre.*
1895. An understatement, meaning that he was among the first.   See
Introduction VII. 7.
1909. See note to 1008 for significance of the phrase.

Daþeit hwo recke! for he it seruede,[20]
Hwat dide he þore! weren he werewed![21]   1915
So longe haueden he but and bet[22]
With neues under hernes[23] set,
Þat of þo sixti men and on
Ne wente awey þer liues non.

On þe morwen, hwan it was.day,   1920
Ilc on other wirwed[24] lay
Als it were dogges[25] þat weren henged;
And summe leye in dikes slenget,[26]
And summe in gripes[27] bi þe her
Drawen ware, and laten ther.   1925
Sket cam tiding intil Ubbe
Þat Hauelok hauede with a clubbe
Of hise slawen sixti and on
Sergaunz,[28] þe beste þat mithen gon.
"Deus!" quoth Ubbe, "hwat may þis be?   1930

---

[20] deserved.   [21] mauled.   [22] thrust and struck.   [23] fists under brains; see note.   [24] mauled.   [25] wretches.   [26] tossed in ditches.   [27] trenches.   [28] men-at-arms.

1914. MS. *we recke.*

1917. Holthausen proposed *under her neses set,* and there is a parallel in the Laxdaela Saga. "Sir Perceval" 2087 has *a dynt he ʒefe/ In the nekk with his nefe;* hence here *under her nekkes* seems a possible reading. Holthausen also suggested *heres* (ears).

1919. MS. *went þer away.* Sixty-one may seem an excessive number of victims for four men improperly armed; but it is moderate in comparison with the totals of other heroes. Perceval alone accounts for eleven score. Bishop Turpin, though exhausted, slays four hundred. Troilus in an ugly mood kills a thousand ("Geste Historiale" 9878).

1920. MS. *hhan.*

1922. "Dogs" probably means "wretches"; but animals were sometimes solemnly hanged for their misdeeds (see "The Criminal Prosecution and Capital Punishment of Animals," E. P. Evans, N. Y. 1906; frontispiece and p. 155 ff.).

1923. The point seems to be that they were given a hasty and ignominious burial. In "Richard Coeur de Lion" 3754 and 4557, the bodies of executed men are thrown into a "foul ditch." A similar indignity was inflicted on the dead Frenchmen in a song of about 1302 (Wright, "Political Songs of England"): they were *knulled y the putfalle.*

Betere is i nime miself and se
Wat þis baret oweth on wold,[29]
Þanne i sende yunge or old.
For yif i sende him unto,
I wene men sholde him shame do,   1935
And þat ne wolde ich for no þing:
I loue him wel, bi Heuene King!
Me wore leuere i wore lame
Þanne men dide him ani shame,
Or tok, or onne handes leyde   1940
Vnornelike,[30] or s[h]ame seyde."
He lep up on a stede lith,[31]
And with him mani a noble knith,
And ferde forth unto þe tun,
And dide calle Bernard Brun   1945
Vt of his hus, wan he þer cam;
And Bernard sone ageyn [him] nam,
Al to-tused[32] and al to-torn,
Ner also naked so he was born,
And al to-brised,[33] bac and þe.[34]   1950
Quoth Ubbe, "Bernard, hwat is þe?[35]
Hwo haues þe þus ille maked,[36]
Þus to-riuen,[37] and al mad naked?"
"Louerd, merci," quot he sone,
"To-nicht, also ros þe mone,   1955
Comen her mo þan sixti þeues,
With lokene copes[38] and wide sleues,
Me forto robben and to pine,
And for to drepe[39] me and mine.
Mi dore he broken up ful sket,   1960
And wolde me binden, hond and fet.

---

[29] what this tumult means. [30] roughly. [31] nimbly. [32] cut badly. [33] bruised
sorely. [34] i.e., all over. [35] what is wrong with you? [36] treated. [37] thrashed.
[38] clasped cloaks. [39] kill.

1931. MS. *his.* Cf. "Chanson" 1485: *Mielz est il molt que jo'l algë
ocidre.*
1932. MS. *þat þis baret on hwat is wold.* Emended by Holthausen
and Sisam.
1935. Probably another reminiscence of the French story, where Ubbe's
own retainers attack Havelok.

Wan þe godemen þat sawe,
Hauelok, and he þat bi þe wowe[40]
Leye, he stirten up sone onon,
And summe grop tre and sum grop ston,   1965
And driue hem ut, þei he weren crus,[41]
So dogges ut of milne-hous.[42]
Hauelok grop þe dore-tre,
And [at] a dint he slow hem þre.
He is þe beste man at nede   1970
Þat eueremar shal ride [on] stede!
Als helpe God, bi mine wone,
A þhousend of men his he worth one![43]
Yif he ne were,[44] ich were nou ded,
So haue ich don mi soule red![45]   1975
But it is of him mikel sinne:[46]
He maden him swilke woundes þrinne
Þat of þe alþerleste wounde
Were a stede brouht to grunde.
He haues a wunde in þe side,   1980
With a gleyue, ful unride;[47]
And he haues on þoru his arum—
Þerof is ful mikel harum!
And he haues on þoru his þhe,[48]
Þe vnrideste þat men may se;   1985
And oþe[re] wundes haues he stronge,
Mo than twenti, swiþe longe.
But siþen he hauede lauth þe sor[49]
Of þe wundes, was neuere bor
Þat so fauth so he fauth þanne;   1990
Was non þat hauede þe hern-panne[50]

---

[40] wall.   [41] fierce.   [42] mill.   [43] he alone is worth, etc.   [44] were it not for him.
[45] (as surely) as I have followed the best interests of my soul.   [46] pity.
[47] ugly.   [48] thigh.   [49] felt the smart.   [50] skull.

1964. I.e., the retainers, who slept on the benches along the walls.
Probably Havelok had a separate room. (See Wright, Ch. 8.) See 2087.
    1976. MS. *is hof*.
    1987. Bevis of Hamtoun survives thirty wounds "large and wyde."
Cf. Layamon 28578.

So hard þat he ne dede alto-crusshe
And alto-shiuere and alto-frusshe.[1]
He folwede hem so hund dos hare:
Daþeyt[2] on he wolde spare,   1995
Þat [he] ne made hem euerilk on
Ligge stille so doth þe ston:
And þer nis he nouth to frie,[3]
For oþer sholde he make hem lye
Ded, or þei him hauede slawen,   2000
Or alto-hewen, or alto-drawen.

Louerd, haui no more plith[4]
Of þat ich was þus grey[u]ed[5] to-nith.
Þus wolde þe þeues me haue reft:
But God þank, he hauenet sure keft.[6]   2005
But it is of him mikel scaþe:
I woth þat he bes ded ful raþe."

Quoth Ubbe, "Bernard, seyst þou soth?"
"Ya, sire, that i ne leye [o t]oth.[7]
Yif y, louerd, a word leye,   2010
To-morwen do me hengen heye."
Þe burgeys þat þerbi stode þore
Grundlike[8] and grete oþes swore,
Litle and mikle, yunge and holde,
Þat was soth þat Bernard tolde: 2015
Soth was þat he wolden him bynde,
And trusse[9] al þat he mithen fynde
Of hise, in arke or in kiste,[10]

---

[1] smash.   [2] i.e., never.   [3] blame.   [4] vexation.   [5] troubled.   [6] they have paid for it.   [7] (I say) that I do not lie in my teeth.   [8] heartily.   [9] pack.   [10] coffer or chest.

1992. MS. *cruhsse.*
2005. *Sure* = sourly, bitterly. (Skeat.)
2009. Sisam's emendation for the MS. *lepe oth.*
2013. The terms are not coördinate, and the *and* may be an insertion of the scribe.
2018. "Of his," with the noun understood, is probably an imitation of the French. Cf. "Chanson" 806: "Que l'emperedre nisun *des soens* n'i perdet."

Þat he mouthe in seckes þriste.[11]
"Louerd, awey he haueden[12] al born   2020
His þing, and himself al to-torn,
But als God self barw[13] him wel,
Þat he ne tinte no catel.[14]
Hwo mithe so mani stonde ageyn
Bi nither-tale,[15] knith or swein?   2025
He weren bi tale[16] sixti and ten,
Starke laddes, stalworþi men,
And on, þe mayster of hem alle,
Þat was þe name G[r]iffin Galle.
Hwo mouthe agey[n] so mani stonde,   2030
But als[17] þis man of ferne[18] londe
Haueth hem slawen with a tre?
Mikel ioie haue he !
God yeue him mikel god to welde,
Boþe in tun, and ek in felde !   2035
We[l] is set[19] þe mete he etes."
Quoth Ubbe, "Gos, him swiþe fetes,
Þat y mouthe his woundes se,
Yf that he mouthen holed[20] be.
For yf he mouthe couere[21] yet   2040
And gangen wel up-on hise fet,
Miself shal dubbe him to knith,
Forþi þat he is so with.
And yif he liuede, þo foule theues,
Þat weren of Kaym kin and Eues,   2045

[11] put in sacks.   [12] would have.   [13] rescued.   [14] lost no goods.   [15] nighttime.
[16] count.   [17] unless.   [18] distant.   [19] invested.   [20] be made whole.   [21] recover.

2020. MS. *he haueden al awey.*
2026. The number increases, as in Falstaff's account.
2036. MS. *We is set he etes mete /Quoth Ubbe, Doth, etc.*
2045. The Middle Ages were resentful toward Eve because she was
held responsible for the fall of man.   Here she is mentioned with Cain,
the reputed progenitor of the race of thieves, rascals, giants, and monsters.   See Klaeber's note to "Beowulf" 106.   Eve's character suffered
further because of the medieval belief that the devil was Cain's father.
For much information on the subject, see *PMLA* 21.878, and especially
916 ff.   In *MLR* 23.207 and 24.63, Crawford traces the connection of
Cain and the sea-demons.   Cf. also "Adam und Quain," E. Böklen,
Leipzig, 1907.

He sholden hange bi þe necke:
Of here ded daþeit wo recke,[22]
Hwan he yeden þus on nithes
To binde boþe burgmen and knithes!
For bynderes loue ich neuere mo: 2050
Of hem ne yeue ich nouht a slo."[23]

   Hauelok was bifore Ubbe browth,
Þat hauede for him ful mikel þouth,
And mikel sorwe in his herte
For hise wundes, þat we[re] so smerte.[24]   2055

   But hwan his wundes weren shewed
And a leche hauede knawed[25]
Þat he hem mouthe ful wel hele,
Wel make him gange, and ful wel mele,[26]
And wel a palefrey bistride,   2060
And wel upon a stede ride,
Þo let Ubbe al his care
And al his sorwe ouerfare,[27]
And seyde, "Cum now forth with me,
And Goldeboru þi wif with þe,   2065
And þine seriaunz[28] alle þre,
For nou wile y youre warant[29] be;
Wile y non of here frend
Þat þu slowe with þin hend
Moucte wayte þe [to] slo,   2070
Also þou gange to and fro.
I shal lene[30] þe a bowr
Þat is up in þe heye tour,
Til þou mowe ful wel go,
And wel ben hol of al þi wo.   2075
It[31] ne shal no þing ben bitwene
Þi bour and min, also y wene,

---

[22] a curse on any one who cares about their death.   [23] sloe-berry.
[24] painful.   [25] physician ascertained.   [26] speak.   [27] pass.   [28] men-at-arms.
[29] surety.   [30] lend.   [31] there.

But a fayr firrene wowe;[32]
Speke y loude or spek y lowe,
þou shalt ful wel heren me,   2080
And þan þu wilt, þou shalt me se.
A rof shal hile[33] us boþe o nith,
þat none of mine, clerk ne knith,
Ne sholen þi wif no shame bede,
No more þan min, so God me rede!"   2085

He dide unto þe borw bringe
Sone anon, al with ioynge,
His wif, and his serganz þre,
þe beste men þat mouthe be.
þe firste nith he lay þerinne,   2090
Hise wif, and his serganz þrinne,
Aboute þe middel of þe nith
Wok Ubbe, and saw a mikel lith
In þe bour þer Hauelok lay,
Also brith so it were day.   2095

"Deus!" quoth Ubbe, "hwat may þis be?
Betere is i go miself and se:
Hweþer he sitten nou and wesseylen,[34]
Or ani sotshipe to-deyle,[35]
þis tid nithes,[36] also foles;   2100
þan birþe[37] men casten hem in poles,[38]
Or in a grip,[39] or in þe fen:

---

[32] wall of fir-wood.   [33] cover.   [34] drink healths.   [35] take part in folly.   [36] time
of night.   [37] it behooves.   [38] ponds.   [39] ditch.

2078. The partition is of boards; Ubbe removes one of them later
(2106). Evidently it was flimsy and temporary. (See Wright, p. 111.)
Not only Ubbe, but Grim's sons, sleep in the apartment (2128; cf. Wright,
47), which is off the main hall (2121). Mead called attention to this
passage from the Prose Merlin (*EETS* 10, etc.), Ch. XII: *And the kyng
Lotte hadde do made a cowche in a chamber where he and his wif lay. And
Antor lay in mydell of the same chamber, and Kay and Arthur hadde made
her bedde atte the chamber dore of King Loot, in a corner, like as a squire
sholde ly.*
2094. MS. *bour þat.*
2099. MS. *or of ani shotshipe.*

Nou ne sitten none but wicke men,
Glotuns, reures,[40] or wicke þeues,
Bi Crist, þat alle folk onne leues !"[41]   2105

He stod and totede[42] in at a bord
Her he spak anilepi[43] word,
And saw hem slepen faste ilkon,
And lye stille so þe ston;
And saw al þat mikel lith   2110
Fro Hauelok cam, þat was so brith:
Of his mouth it com il[k] del—
þat was he war ful swiþe wel.
"Deus !" quoth he, "hwat may þis mene?"
He calde boþe arwe[44] men and kene,   2115
Knithes and serganz swiþe sleie,[45]
Mo þan an hundred, withuten leye,
And bad hem alle comen and se
Hwat þat selcuth[46] mithe be.
Als þe knithes were comen alle   2120
þer Hauelok lay, ut of þe halle,
So stod ut of his mouth a glem
Rith al swilk so þe sunne-bem,
þat al so lith wa[s] þare, bi heuene,
So þer brenden serges[47] seuene   2125
And an hundred serges ok:
þat durste hi sweren on a bok.
He slepen faste, alle fiue,
So he weren brouth of liue;[48]
And Hauelok lay on his lift[49] side,   2130
In his armes his brithe bride.
Bi þe pappes[50] he leyen naked:
So faire two weren neuere maked

---

[40] robbers.   [41] in whom all people believe.   [42] peeped.   [43] a single.   [44] timid.
[45] adroit.   [46] marvel.   [47] candles.   [48] i.e., dead.   [49] left.   [50] down to the breast.

2132. The custom of sleeping naked was very common, and persisted
through the sixteenth century. See Wright Ch. xv. In the time of
Elizabeth and James I, it was still often alluded to in imitations and
parodies of a well-known line in Kyd's "Spanish Tragedy" (II. iv),
What outcries pluck me from my naked bed?

In a bed to lyen samen
Þe knithes þouth of hem god gamen,   2135
Hem forto shewe and loken to.
Rith also he stoden alle so
And his bac was toward hem wend,
So weren he war of a croiz ful gent
On his rith shuldre, sw[iþ]e brith,   2140
Brithter þan gold ageyn þe lith,
So þat he wiste, heye and lowe,
Þat it was kunmerk[1] þat he sawe.
It sparkede[2] and ful brith shon
So doth þe gode charbucle-ston,[3]   2145
Þat men mouthe se by þe lith,
A peni chesen, so was it brith.
Þanne bihelden he him faste,[4]
So þat he knewen at þe laste
Þat he was Birkabeynes sone,   2150
Þat was here king, þat was hem wone
Wel to yeme and wel were[5]
Ageynes utenladdes here.[6]
"For it was neuere yet a broþer
In al Denemark so lich anoþer   2155
So þis man, þat is so fayr,
Als Birkabeyn: he is hise eyr."

He fellen sone at hise fet;
Was non of hem þat he ne gret:
Of ioie he weren alle so fawen   2160

---

[1] king-mark.   [2] sparkled.   [3] carbuncle.   [4] attentively.   [5] defend.   [6] the army
of invaders.

2143. MS. *kunrik.*—Holthausen.
2145. There was a widespread belief that precious stones gave off light
at night. Rabbinical tradition ascribed gems of the sort to Noah and
Abraham. Pliny may have been responsible for the spread of the belief.
(See G. F. Kunz, "The Curious Lore of Precious Stones," Ch. V; cf.
"Chanson" 2633, and "The Feast of Bricriu" II.)
2147. Pennies were smaller than modern dimes; hence a considerable
degree of brightness was necessary before they could be clearly distinguished.

So he him haueden of erþe drawen.[7]
Hise fet he kisten an hundred syþes,
Þe tos, þe nayles, and þe lithes,[8]
So þat he bigan to wakne
And wit hem ful sore to blakne;[9]   2165
For he wende he wolden him slo,
Or elles binde him and do wo.

Quoth Ubbe, "Louerd, ne dred þe nowth;
Me þinkes that i se þi þouth:
Dere sone, wel is me   2170
Þat y þe with eyn se!
Manred,[10] louerd, bede y þe:
Þi man auht i ful wel to be,
For þu art comen of Birkabeyn,
Þat hauede mani knith and sweyn,   2175
And so shalt þou, louerd, haue!
Þou þu be yet a ful yung knaue,
Þou shalt be king of al Denemark:—
Was þerinne neuere non so stark.
To-morwen shaltu manrede take   2180
Of þe brune and of þe blake—
Of alle þat aren in þis tun,
Boþe of erl and of barun
And of dreng and of thayn
And of knith and of sweyn.   2185
And so shaltu ben mad knith
Wit blisse, for þou art so with."

Þo was Hauelok swiþe bliþe,
And þankede God ful fele siþe.
On þe morwen, wan it was lith,   2190
And gon was þisternesse[11] of þe nith,
Vbbe dide upon a stede
A ladde lepe, and þider bede

---

[7] i.e., recovered him from the grave. [8] tips. [9] at their presence grew very
pale. [10] fealty. [11] darkness.

2181. On the phrase, see note to 1008.

Erles, barouns, drenges, theynes,
Klerkes, knithes, bu[r]geys, sweynes,   2195
Þat he sholden comen anon
Biforen him sone euerilkon,
"Also he louen here liues
And here children and here wiues."

Hise bode[12] ne durste he non at-sitte[13]   2200
Þat he ne neme, for to wite
Sone hwat wolde þe iustise;
And [he] bigan anon to rise,
And seyde sone, "Liþes me,
Alle samen, þeu[14] and fre.   2205
A þing ich wile you here shauwe
Þat ye alle ful wel knawe:
Ye witen wel þat al þis lond
Was in Birkabeynes hond
Þe day þat he was quic and ded,[15]   2210
And how þat he, bi youre red,
Bitauhte hise children þre
Godard to yeme, and al his fe.
Hauelok his sone he him tauhte,
And hise two douhtres, and al his auhte.[16]   2215
Alle herden ye him swere
On bok and on messe-gere
Þat he shulde yeme hem wel,
Withuten lac, withuten tel.[17]

He let his oth al ouergo[18]   2220
(Euere wurþe him yuel and wo !),
For þe maydnes here lif
Refte he boþen with a knif,
And him shulde ok haue slawen:
Þe knif was at his herte drawen !   2225

---

[12] command.   [13] resist.   [14] slave.   [15] i.e., the last day of his life.   [16] wealth.
[17] without fail or blame.   [18] i.e., disregarded it.

2201. MS. *meme.*
2207. MS. *he alle.*

But God him wolde wel haue saue;
He hauede reunesse[19] of þe knaue,
So þat he with his hend
Ne drop[20] him nouth, þat sor[i] fend!
But sone dide he a fishere   2230
Swiþe grete oþes swere
Þat he sholde drenchen him
In þe se, þat was ful brim.[21]
   Hwan Grim saw þat he was so fayr,
And wiste he was þe rith eir,   2235
Fro Denemark ful sone he fledde
Intil Englond, and þer him fedde
Mani winter; þat til þis day
Haues he ben fed and fostred[22] ay.
Lokes hware he stondes her!   2240
In al þis werd ne haues he per—
Non so fayr, ne non so long,
Ne non so mikel, ne non so strong.
In þis middelerd nis no knith
Half so strong, ne half so with.   2245
Bes of him ful glad and bliþe,
And cometh alle hider swiþe,
Manrede[23] youre louerd forto make,
Boþe brune and þe blake!
I shal miself do first þe gamen,[24]   2250
And ye siþen alle samen."

   O knes ful fayre he him sette
(Mouthe noþing him þerfro lette),

---

[19] pity.   [20] slew.   [21] fierce.   [22] nurtured.   [23] homage.   [24] i.e., go through the performance.

2244. *Middelerd* is a relic of old Scandinavian mythology. The universe was thought of as having three parts: above, the home of the gods; in the middle, this world; and beneath, the realms of the giants.
2252. The ceremony of taking service consisted of kneeling, placing one's hands between the lord's, and swearing that one would be a true servant of the lord, and remain ever loyal. In return, the vassal was given land and protection.

And bicam [h]is man rith þare,
Þat alle sawen þat þere ware.   2255

After him stirt up laddes ten
And bicomen hise men;
And siþen euerilk a baroun
Þat euere weren in al that toun;
And siþen drenges, and siþen thaynes,   2260
And siþen knithes, and siþen sweynes;
So þat or þat day was gon,
In al þe tun ne was nouth on
Þat he ne was his man bicomen:
Manrede of alle hauede he nomen.   2265

Hwan he hauede of hem alle
Manrede taken in the halle,
Grundlike²⁵ dide he hem swere
Þat he sholden him god feyth bere
Ageynes alle þat woren on liue;   2270
Þer-yen²⁶ ne wolde neuer on striue
Þat²⁷ he ne maden sone þat oth,
Riche and poure, lef and loth.
Hwan þat was maked, sone he sende
Vbbe, writes fer and hende,²⁸   2275
After alle þat castel yemede,
Burwes, tunes, sibbe an fremde,²⁹
Þat þider sholden [he] comen swiþe
Til him and heren tiþandes bliþe
Þat he hem alle shulde telle.   2280
Of hem ne wolde neuere on dwelle
Þat he ne come sone plattinde;³⁰
Hwo hors ne hauede, com gangande;
So þat withinne a fourtenith,

---

²⁵ solemnly.   ²⁶ thereagainst.   ²⁷ not one would resist making, etc.   ²⁸ far and near.   ²⁹ kinsman and stranger.   ³⁰ hurrying.

2260. Drengs were free tenants, subject to certain military duties. "Thane" was a title of honor given to a freeman holding lands of the king, or to a lord of a manor. See Pollock and Maitland I.279.
2264. MS. *it ne.*—Holthausen.

In al Denemark ne was no knith 2285
Ne conestable ne shireue
Þat com of Adam and of Eue
Þat he ne com biforn sire Ubbe:
He dredden him so þhef doth clubbe.
  Hwan he haueden alle þe king gret 2290
And he weren alle dun set,
Þo seyde Ubbe, "Lokes here
Vre louerd, swiþe dere,
Þat shal ben king of al þe lond,
And haue us alle under hond! 2295
For he is Birkabeynes sone,
Þe king þat was vmbe-stonde wone[31]
[Men] for to yeme, and wel were[32]
Wit sharp swerd and longe spere.
Lokes nou hw he is fayr! 2300
Sikerlike he is hise eyr.
Falles alle to hise fet:
Bicomes hise men ful sket."
He weren for Ubbe swiþe adrad,
And dide sone al þat he bad, 2305
And yet deden he sumdel more:
O bok ful grundlike he swore
Þat he sholde with him halde
Boþe ageynes stille and bolde,
Þat euere wo[l]de his bodi dere: 2310
Þat dide [he] hem o boke swere.

  Hwan he hauede manrede and oth
  Taken of lef and of loth,

---

[31] formerly wont. [32] defend.

2303. The phrase, in which "man" means "vassal," is common in French poetry. Cf. Jenkins' note, "Chanson" 39.
2307. The Bible was used because it was supposed to preclude the possibility of mental reservation. It was a survival of a pagan custom of swearing while touching something supposedly supernatural, with power to detect false intention and avenge violation of the oath. (See Frazer I. 70.)

Vbbe dubbede him to knith
With a swerd ful swiþe brith;   2315
And þe folk of al þe lond
Bitauhte him al in his hond,
Þe cunnriche eueril[k] del,
And made him king heylike[33] and wel.
Hwan he was king, þer mouthe men se   2320
Þe moste ioie þat mouhte be:
Buttinge[34] with sharpe speres,
Skirming with taleuaces[35] þat men beres,
Wrastling with laddes, putting of ston,
Harping and piping, ful god won,   2325
Leyk of mine, of hasard[36] ok,
Romanz-reding on þe bok;

---

[33] solemnly.   [34] tilting.   [35] fencing with (swords and) bucklers.   [36] play at backgammon and dice.

2314. The ceremony is described at some length in "Guy of Warwick" (C) 878; see also "Libeaus Desconus" 73 and "Horn" 495. The ritual is greatly simplified here; it might include special costumes, a vigil, and numerous symbolistic performances. Any knight might confer knighthood on any other free man. For other details, see Gautier, viii.

2316. The subject of the clause is "Ubbe;" his guardianship as a faithful steward is now at an end, and he returns his trust.

2320. Such scenes are as old as Geoffrey of Monmouth's chronicle (IX. xiv). See also "King Alisaunder" 193; "Octavian" 67; "Partonope" 12179; Layamon (C.) 8140. Tilting and sword-and-buckler play were recognized amusements for younger men; both were so dangerous that Edward I prohibited them; but his prohibition was ineffectual. Mine and hasard were gambling games played with dice and a board. On the subject of amusements, see Wright, Ch. 10, 24. For the reading of romances, see Scott's "Sir Tristrem" 290. Note that some of the gestes here were sung; the readers and singers were the aristocrats among minstrels, and trick drummers were not their equals. (See E. K. Chambers, "The Medieval Stage," for a full account.) Bulls were tied to stakes and worried by dogs, which tried to seize the animal's nose and underjaw, pinning them together; the dog must then hold on until the bull gave up. (See J. Timbs, "Abbeys and Castles of England," article on Stamford; Strutt, 193; "The Sportsman's Cyclopedia," (London 1831); a circumstantial and unfriendly account of a bull-baiting is given in William Taplin's "Sporting Dictionary" (London 1803). For a general bibliography of sports, see E. L. Guilford's "Sports and Pastimes of the Middle Ages.")

Þer mouthe men here þe gestes[37] singe,
Þe glevmen on þe tabour dinge;[38]
Þer mouhte men se þe boles beyte,[39]   2330
And þe bores, with hundes teyte;[40]
Þo mouthe men se eueril[k] gleu.
Þer mouthe men se hw grim[41] greu;
Was neuere yete ioie more
In al þis werd þan þo was þore.   2335
Þer was so mike[l] yeft[42] of cloþes,
Þat, þou i swore you grete othes,
I ne wore nouth þer-offe troud.[43]
Þat may i ful wel swere, bi God!
Þere was swiþe gode metes;   2340
And of wyn þat men fer fetes,
Rith al so mik[el] and gret plenté
So it were water of þe se.
Þe feste fourti dawes sat;
So riche[44] was neuere non so þat.   2345
Þe king made Roberd þere knith,
Þat was ful strong and ful.with,
And Willam Wendut hec, his broþer,
And Huwe Rauen, þat was þat oþer,
And made hem barouns alle þre,   2350
And yaf hem lond and oþer fe
So mikel þat ilker twent[i] knihtes
Hauede of genge,[45] dayes and nithes.

---

[37] narratives.   [38] minstrels beat the drum.   [39] bulls baited.   [40] lively.   [41] excitement (of bull-baiting).   [42] giving.   [43] believed.   [44] elaborate.   [45] in his company.

2331. *Bores* should be *beres*, bears.

2333. *Mouthe men see* is probably an adaptation of the convenient French phrase *la veissiez;* the sense of the passage is, "truly, there did excitement grow."

2338. MS. *croud*, a scribe's error for the form given, which in turn is a substitution for *trod*, believed. (Sisam's conjecture.)

2344. Froissart says the coronation celebration of Edward III lasted twelve days; but the romancers nearly always cause such events to last forty. Cf. Mead's note to "Squire" 1114.

Hwan þat feste was al don,
A thusand knihtes ful wel o bon[46]   2355
Withheld þe king, with him to lede,
Þat[47] ilkan hauede ful god stede,
Helm and sheld and brinie brith,
And al þe wepne þat fel to[48] kniht.
With hem fiue thusand gode   2360
Sergaunz, þat weren to fyht wode,[49]
With-held he, al of his genge.
Wile i namore þe storie lenge:[50]
Yet hwan he hauede of al þe lond
Þe casteles alle in his hond,   2365
And conestables[1] don þer-inne,
He swor he ne sholde neuer blinne
Til þat he were of Godard wreken,
Þat ich haue of ofte speken.
Hal[f] hundred knithes dede he calle,   2370
And hise fif thusand sergaunz alle,
And dide sweren on the bok
Sone, and on þe auter ok,
Þat he ne sholde neuere blinne,
Ne for loue ne for sinne,   2375
Til þat he haueden Godard funde
And brouth biforn him faste bunde.

Þanne he haueden swor[n] þis oth,
Ne leten he nouth, for lef ne loth,
Þat he ne foren swiþe rathe   2380
Þer he was, unto þe paþe
Þer he yet on hunting for

---

[46] well equipped.   [47] sc. "so furnished."   [48] befitted.   [49] men-at-arms crazy
to fight.   [50] prolong.   [1] military governors.

2355. Contrary to custom, in this poem the numbers are reasonable.
Gaimar gives Havelok 30,000 knights; and the forces in the romances of
Charlemagne are immense. But in fact, William I conquered England
with about 14,000 men; and a force of 50,000 was very large.

2382. Godard's indifference may have been part of the original story,
for the Lai also represents him as too proud to take arms against a mere
kitchen-knave.

With mikel genge, and swiþe stor.[2]
Robert, þat was of al þe ferd
Mayster, girt was wit a swerd,   2385
And sat upon a ful god stede,
Þat vnder him rith wolde wede;[3]
He was þe firste þat with Godard
Spak, and seyde, "Hede, cauenard![4]
Wat dos þu here at þis paþe?   2390
Cum to þe king, swiþe and raþe:
Þat sendes he þe word, and bedes
Þat þu þenke hwat þu him dedes
Hwan þu reftes with a knif
Hise sistres here lif,   2395
An siþen bede þu in þe se
Drenchen[5] him; þat herde he![6]
He is to þe swiþe grim:[7]
Cum nu swiþe unto him
Þat king is of þis kuneriche,[8]   2400
Þu fule man! þu wicke swike![9]
And he shal yelde þe þi mede,
Bi Crist, þat wolde on rode blede!"

Hwan Godard herde þat [he] þer þrette,[10]
With þe neue he Robert sette[11]   2405
Biforn þe teth a dint ful strong;
And Robert kipt[12] ut a knif long
And smot him þoru þe rith arum:
Þerof was ful litel harum![13]

Hwan his folk þat sau and herde,   2410
Hou Robert with here louerd ferde,
He haueden him wel ner browt of liue,[14]

---

[2] proud.   [3] was willing to gallop right furiously.   [4] heed knave!   [5] drown.
[6] i.e., he learned of it.   [7] hostile.   [8] kingdom.   [9] traitor.   [10] threatened.   [11] fist he
struck.   [12] plucked.   [13] i.e., and a good thing, too!   [14] i.e., killed.

2383. Froissart says that when Edward III went hunting, he had sixty
couples of greyhounds, as many hounds, and thirty falcons.
2385. MS. *was girt.*
2411. MS. *Hwou.*

Ne weren[15] his two breþren and oþre fiue,
Slowen of here laddes ten
Of Godardes alþerbeste men.   2415
Hwan þe oþre sawen þat, he fledden,
And Godard swiþe loude gredde:[16]
"Mine knithes, hwat do ye?
Sule ye þusgate fro me fle?
Ich haue you fed, and yet shal fede: 2420
Helpe me nu in þis nede,
And late ye nouth mi bodi spille,
Ne Hauelok don of me hise wille.
Yif ye it do, ye do you shame,
And bringeth youself in mikel blame."[17]   2425
Hwan he þat herden, he wenten ageyn
And slowen a kni[h]t and a sweyn
Of þe kinges oune men,
And woundeden abuten ten.
    Þe kinges men, hwan he þat sawe,   2430
Scuten on hem, heye and lowe,[18]
And euerilk fot[19] of hem slowe
But Godard one, þat he flowe[20]
So þe þef men dos henge,
Or hund men shole in dike slenge.[21]   2435
He bunden him ful swiþe faste
Hwil þe bondes wolden laste,[22]
Þat he rorede als a bole[23]
Þat wore parred[24] in an hole
With dogges forto bite and beite: 2440

---

[15] were it not for.   [16] shouted.   [17] dishonor.   [18] struck them everywhere.
[19] foot; i.e., person.   [20] flayed.   [21] throw in a ditch.   [22] i.e., the bonds would
come off only when the ropes rotted.   [23] bull.   [24] fastened.

2420. On this obligation of the master toward the servant, see the
Old English "Wanderer," and "Beowulf" 2864. But the line itself is
probably an imitation of similar lines in French poems; Baligant ("Chanson" 3374) exhorts his retainers: *Li mien baron, nodrit vos ai long tens.*
Thus he may command their services even in times of extreme peril; and
such an appeal is always heeded, no matter how fearful the odds.
    2424. MS. *ye id.*
    2427. MS. *and and a sweyn.*
    2439. MS. *þat he.*

Were þe bondes nouth to leite.[25]
He bounden him so fele sore
Þat he gan crien Godes ore
Þat he sholde his hend ofplette.[26]
Wolden he nouht þerfore lette   2445
Þat he ne bounden hond and fet
(Daþeit þat on þat þerfore let!),
But dunten[27] him so man doth bere,
And keste him on a scabbed mere:[28]
Hise nese went unto þe crice.[29]   2450
So ledden he þat fule swike
Til he biforn Hauelok was brouth,
Þat he haue[de] ful wo wrowht
Boþe with hungre and with cold
Or he were twel[ue] winter old,   2455
And with mani heui swink,[30]
With poure mete and feble[31] drink
And swiþe wikke cloþes,
For al hise manie grete othes.
Nu beyes he his holde blame: 2460
Old sinne makes newe shame.
Wan he was brouht so shamelike

---

[25] seek; i.e., were in evidence.   [26] strike off.   [27] beat.   [28] mare.   [29] i.e., facing backward.   [30] task.   [31] bad.

2444. Possibly *hend* is for *heu'd*, head. The sense would then be that he requested them to behead him at once, without further torture. Beheading was a mode of execution befitting a noble; hanging and beating were punishments for wretches and knaves.

2448. *But* refers to *ore* (l. 2443). Strutt (III.vi) mentions that a popular sport was whipping a blind bear; the contestants took the risk of being mauled if the animal reached them.

2452. MS. *was biforn hauelok.*

2453. MS. *haue.*

2454. MS. *hungred.*

2461. Förster discovered the same proverb in a manuscript collection, where it is given as an equivalent of a Latin proverb.

2462. In the MS., *brouht* follows *shamelike.*

Biforn þe king, þe fule swike,
þe king dede Ubbe swiþe calle
Hise erles and hise barouns alle,   2465
Dreng and thein, burgeis and knith,
And bad he sholden demen him rith,
For he kneu þe swike dam;[32]
Eueril[k] del, God was him gram.[33]
He setten hem dun bi þe wawe,[34]   2470
Riche and pouere, heye and lowe,
þe helde men, and ek þe grom,[35]
And made þer þe rithe dom,
And seyden unto þe king anon,
þat stille sat [al]-so þe ston: 2475
"We deme þat he be al quic flawen,[36]
And siþen to þe galwes drawe
At þis foule mere tayl—
þoru [h]is fet a ful strong nayl—
And þore ben henged wit two feteres;[37]   2480
And þare be writen þise leteres:
'þis is þe swike þat wende wel

---

[32] ? treacherous rogue.   [33] in every particular, God was angry with him.
[34] i.e., on the benches.   [35] youth.   [36] flayed alive.   [37] chains.

2463. The procedure in this trial is that of French romance, not of
English law. For full details, see Jenkins' note to the "Chanson" 3741.
The jury is of no fixed size. It is made up of the peers of the accused.
No one acts as prosecutor, although the complainant may state his case
(here abridged, 2467); and the defendant is not questioned. The king
can take no part in the actual trial, and must abide by the verdict. Cf.
also the trial in "Octavian."
    2468. Simon Fraser was adjudged a "lord swyke." (Wright, "Political
Songs of England" 212.)
    2476. MS. slawen.
    2479. Holthausen's emendation.
    2480. Most of these details are paralleled in a poem on the execution
of Simon Fraser. Criminals drawn to the gallows were placed on hurdles
or a cowhide so that they should not be battered to death on the way.
(See Salzman, 219.) The "foule mere" was an added humiliation, since
the knight was usually allowed to ride to his death on a charger. The
traces of the harness may have been attached to the nail (2479). Chains
were used (2480) in place of ropes so that the body might continue to
hang for a long time. (See Wright, Ch. XX.) For a parallel from the
romances, see "King Alisaunder" 4710 ff.

Þe king haue reft þe lond il[k] del,
And hise sistres with a knif
Boþe refte here lif.'   2485
Þis writ shal henge bi him þare;
Þe dom is demd: seye we na more."
    Hwan þe dom was demd and giue,
And he was wit þe prestes shriue,
And it ne mouhte ben non oþer,   2490
Ne for fader ne for broþer,
[But] þat he sholde þarne[38] lif,—
Sket cam a ladde with a knif,
And bigan rith at þe to
For to ritte, and for to flo,[39]   2495
And he bigan for to rore
So it were grim or gore,
Þat men mithe þeþen a mile
Here him rore, þat fule file.[40]
Þe ladde ne let no with[41] forþi,   2500
Þey he criede 'merci! merci!'—
Þat [he] ne flow [him] eueril[k] del
With knif mad of grunden stel.
Þei garte bringe þe mere sone,
Skabbed and ful iuele o bone,[42]   2505
And bunden him rith at hire tayl
With a rop of an old seyl,
And drowen him un-to þe galwes,
Nouth bi þe gate, but ouer þe falwes,[43]

---

[38] lose. [39] to cut and flay. [40] wretch. [41] any whit. [42] infirm. [43] plowed
fields.

2495. This barbarous punishment was not uncommon for serious offen-
ders. Mezeray writes that about 1280 two villains were flayed, dragged
at the tails of wild horses, and hanged. The Knight of La Tour-Landry
tells of a knight who was "quicke scorched" (p. 6). The murderer of
Richard I is said to have been flayed. In romances, cf. "Sowdone of
Babylon" 1853, 3078; "King Horn" 86; "Arthur and Gorlagon" § 17.
    2496–7. The least unsatisfactory emendation for this corrupt passage
is Littledale's: transpose the lines, read *goune* for *grim;* and render,
. . . *to cut and flay As if it were gown or gore* [*sewed strip*].
    2505. MS. *scabbeb.*

And henge [him] þore bi þe hals:[44]　　　2510
Daþeit hwo recke! he was fals.

Þanne he was ded, þat Sathanas,
Sket was seysed al þat his was
In þe kinges hand il[k] del—
Lond and lith[45] and oþer catel—　　　2515
And þe king ful sone it yaf
Vbbe in þe hond, wit a fayr staf,
And seyde, "Her ich sayse[46] þe
In al þe lond, in al þe fe. . . ."
Þo swor Hauelok he sholde make,　　　2520
Al for Grim, of monekes blake
A priorie to seruen inne ay
•Iesu Crist, til domesday,
For þe god he haueden him don
Hwil he was pouere and iuel o bon.[47]　　　2525
And þerof held he wel his oth,[48]

---

[44] neck.　[45] folk.　[46] seise, grant.　[47] infirm.　[48] = hot; promise (Sisam).

2513. A traitor's estate went, not to his heirs, but to the crown. Cf. the sentence passed on Godrich (2833).

2516. The staff was a symbol that Havelok was giving Ubbe land to hold. (This was not the staff of office commonly borne by stewards.) See P. Vinogradoff, "Villainage in England" 372. In a case cited in "Select Civil Pleas" (*Selden Society* III. xv), the symbol is a broken knife. See George Fundenburg's "Feudal France in the French Epic," under Festuca.

2519. Here the copyist omitted a passage, probably about twenty lines long, in which the journey to England is described. The French poems contribute little information; they mention, however, that the expedition disembarks at Grimsby and sends Godrich a demand that he restore England to its rightful owners.

2521. Cf. Charlemagne's endowment of a monastery where his sister is buried ("Chanson" 3730).

2522. Possibly Grimsby (or Wellow) Abbey, for an account of which see George Shaw's "Old Grimsby" 45. The monks were Augustinians. The abbey was given an advantageous charter by Henry II, though it was Henry I who founded it, in 1110. It prospered in spite of scandals until 1539, when it was surrendered to Henry VIII. About 1545 it was purchased from him by local land-owners and demolished, so that a farmhouse might be erected on the spot.

2525. MS. *we o.*

For ne it⁴⁹ made (God it woth!)
In þe tun þer Grim was grauen,⁵⁰
Þat of Grim yet haues þe name.
Of Grim bidde ich na more spelle.—   2530
But wan Godrich herde telle,
Of Cornwayle þat was erl,
Þat fule traytour, that mixed¹ cherl,
Þat Hauelok, was² king of Denemark,
And ferde with him, strong and stark,   2535
Comen Engelond withinne,
Engelond al for to winne,
And þat she þat was so fayr,
Þat was of Engelond rith eir,
Was comen up at Grimesbi,   2540
He was ful sorful and sori,
And seyde, "Hwat shal me to raþe?³
Goddoth! i shal do slon hem baþe!
I shal don hengen hem ful heye,
So mote ich brouke mi rith eie,   2545
But-yif he of mi lond fle!
Hwat wenden he to desherite me?"⁴
He dide sone ferd ut bidde,
Þat al þat euere mouhte o stede
Ride, or helm on heued bere,   2550
Brini on bac, and sheld and spere,
Or ani oþer wepne bere,
Hand-ax, syþe, gisarm,⁵ or spere,
Or aunlaz,⁶ and god long knif,
Þat als he louede leme or lif,   2555
Þat þey sholden comen him to,
With ful god wepne yboren so,
To Lincolne, þer he lay,
Of Marz þe seuentenþe day,

---

⁴⁹ i.e., the priory. ⁵⁰ buried. ¹ filthy. ² i.e., who was. ³ counsel. ⁴ do they
think to dispossess me? (*Hwat* is the sign of a question.) ⁵ battle-ax with
a blade at the end. ⁶ dagger.

2532. "who was earl of Cornwall."
2540. MS. *þat was.*—Zupitza.
2557. MS. *ye ber.*

So þat he couþe hem god þank;[7]   2560
And yif þat ani were so rank[8]
Þat he þanne ne come anon,
He swor bi Crist and Seint Iohan
Þat he sholde maken him þral,
And al his ofspring forth withal.   2565

Þe Englishe [men] þat herde þat,
Was non þat euere his bode [at]sat,[9]
For he him dredde swiþe sore,—
So runci[10] spore, and mikle more.
At þe day he come sone   2570
Þat he hem sette, ful wel o bone,[11]
To Lincolne, with gode stedes,
And al þe wepne þat knith ledes.[12]
Hwan he wore come, sket was þe erl yare
Ageynes Denshe men to fare,   2575
And seyde, "Lyþes nu, alle samen:
Haue ich gadred you for no gamen,
But ich wile seyen you forwi:
Lokes hware here at Grimesbi
Is uten-laddes here[13] comen,   2580
And haues nu þe priorie numen;
Al þat euere mithen he finde
He brenne kirkes, and prestes binde;
He strangleth monkes and nunnes boþe!
Wat wile ye, frend[es], heroffe rede?   2585
Yif he regne þusgate longe,
He moun us alle ouergange:[14]

---

[7] might be grateful.   [8] presumptuous.   [9] resisted his command.   [10] nag the spur.   [11] well equipped.   [12] bears.   [13] an army of foreigners.   [14] subdue.

2561. MS. *rang.*—Holthausen.
2580. MS. *Hise.*—Zupitza.
2583 ff. A common offense of raiders in the north of England. Langtoft says that the Scots warred against clerics; and Froissart writes that when they took Durham in 1346, they spared neither men, women, children, monks, canons, nor priests, and destroyed many churches. But such acts were commonly ascribed to the enemy in medieval warfare. Cf. "Arthour and Merlin" 4715, 5597, 6982, etc., "Horn" 50 ff.

He moun vs alle quic henge or slo,
Or þral maken and do ful wo,
Or elles reue us ure liues, 2590
And ure children and ure wiues.
But dos nu als ich wile you lere,
Als ye wile be with me dere:
Nimes nu swiþe forth and raþe,
And helpes me and yuself baþe, 2595
And slos upo[n] þe dogges swiþe!
For shal [i] neuere more be bliþe,
Ne hoseled ben, ne of prest shriuen,
Til þat he ben of londe driuen.
Nime we swiþe, and do hem fle, 2600
And folwes alle faste me;
For ich am he, of al þe ferd,[15]
Þat first shal slo with drawen swerd.
Daþeyt[16] hwo ne stonde faste
Bi me, hwil hise armes laste!" 2605
"Yc! lef,[17] ye!" quoth þe erl Gunter;
"Ya!" quoth þe erl of Cestre, Reyner.
And so dide alle·þat þer stode,
And stirte forth so he were wode.
Þo mouthe men se þe brinies[18] brihte 2610
On backes keste, and late rithe,[19]
Þe helmes heye on heued sette;
To armes al so swiþe plette,[20]
Þat þei wore on a litel stunde
Greyþet,[21] als men mithe telle a pund; 2615

[15] (native) army. [16] a curse on. [17] lord. [18] coats of mail. [19] thrown and straightened. [20] hastened. [21] ready.

2597. Cf. note to 317.
2602. The honor of striking the first blow was eagerly sought. See Gautier xviii.
2606. MS. *couth.* Expressions of approval of what has just been said are usual in French romance (e.g., "La Mort Aymeri" 873; "Pilgrimage").
2612. *Heye* modifies *helmes.*
2615. Since the English had no coins of greater value than a penny, counting out a pound was a fairly long task.

And lopen[22] on stedes sone anon,
And toward Grimesbi, ful god won,[23]
He foren softe bi þe sti,[24]
Til he come ney at Grimesbi.

Hauelok, þat hauede spired[25] wel   2620
Of here fare,[26] eueril[k] del,
With al his ferd cam hem ageyn.
Forbar[27] he noþer knith ne sweyn:
þe firste knith þat he þer mette
With þe swerd so he him grette!   2625
For his heued of he plette:[28]
Wolde he nouth for sinne lette.[29]
Roberd saw þat dint so hende,
Wolde he neuere þeþe[n] wende
Til þat he hauede anoþer slawen   2630
With þe swerd he held utdrawen.
Willam Wendut his swerd vtdrow,
And þe þredde so sore he slow,
þat he made upon þe feld
His lift arm fleye, with the swerd.   2635

Huwe Rauen ne forgat nouth
þe swerd he hauede þider brouth:
He kipte[30] it up and smot ful sore
An erl þat he saw priken[31] þore

---

[22] leaped. [23] a large force. [24] quietly along the road. [25] inquired. [26] actions.
[27] spared. [28] struck. [29] i.e., pity did not restrain him. [30] raised. [31] spurring.

2616. The battle is fought mostly on horseback, in Norman fashion.
The Saxons frequently rode to the field, but dismounted before going
into action. Cf. King Murry, "Horn" 47.

2622. The poet here thinks of Havelok as the rightful prince, and calls
his army the *ferd* (not *here*, as in 2580; and cf. 2602, 2942).

2628. The battle which follows is carefully worked up to a climax.
With it might be contrasted the courtly and chivalrous battle in "Partonope" 4000 ff.

2635. The rhyme-word should be *sheld;* references to cutting off the
left arm, which held the shield, are frequent in the romances. Cf. "Octavian" (N.) 1138; "Gest Historiale of the Destruction of Troy" 11,113;
"Libeaus Desconus" 2036 (a very close parallel); "Ipomedon" 3296.

Ful noblelike upon a stede, 2640
þat with him wolde al quic wede.[32]
He smot him on þe heued so
þat he þe heued clef[33] a-two,
And þat bi þe shu[l]dre-blade
þe sharpe swerd let wade[34] 2645
þorw the brest unto þe herte.
þe dint bigan ful sore to smerte,
þat þe erl fel dun anon
Al so ded so ani ston.
Quoth Ubbe, "Nu dwelle ich to longe !" 2650
And let his stede sone gonge
To Godrich, with a god spere
þat he saw anoþer bere,[35]
And smoth Godrich, and G[odrich] him,
Hetelike[36] with herte grim, 2655
So þat he boþe felle dune,
To þe erþe, first þe croune.
þanne he woren fallen dun boþen,
Grundlike[37] here swerdes utdrowen,
þat weren swiþe sharp and gode, 2660
And fouhten so þei woren wode,
þat þe swot ran fro þe crune
[To the fet riht þere adune.]
þer mouthe men se t[w]o knithes bete[38]
Ayþer on oþer dintes grete, 2665
So þat with alþerlest dint
Were al to-shiuered a flint.
So was bitwenen hem a fiht
Fro þe morwen ner to þe niht,

---

[32] gallop at a lively pace. [33] split. [34] pass. [35] whom he saw carrying another (spear). [36] furiously. [37] with a will. [38] strike.

2644. Prodigious blows are common in knightly tales; but those dealt by Irish heroes are easily the most startling. For instance, with one blow, Fiacha mac Firaba cuts off the sword-arms of twenty-nine warriors.

2651. MS. *leth.*

2662. *Swot* means either sweat or blood; here probably the latter, as heroes in the romances bleed profusely. Cf. 2685; also "Nibelungen Lied" 232.

2663. Supplied by Madden.

So þat þei nouth ne blunne,   2670
Til þat to sette bigan þe sunne.
Þo yaf Godrich þorw þe side
Vbbe a wunde ful unride,[39]
So þat þorw þat ilke wounde
Hauede [he] ben brouth to þe grunde   2675
And his heued al ofslawen,[40]
Yif God ne were, and Huwe Rauen,
Þat drow him fro Godrich awey
And barw[41] him so þat ilke day.
But er he were fro Godrich drawen,   2680
Þer were a þousind knihtes slawen
Bi boþe halue,[42] and mo ynowe[43]
Þer þe ferdes togidere slowe.
Þer was swilk dreping[44] of þe folk,
Þat on þe feld was neuere a polk[45]   2685
Þat it ne stod of blod so ful
Þat þe strem ran intil þe hul.[46]
Þo tarst[47] bigan Godrich to go
Vpon þe Danshe, and faste to slo,
And forth rith, also leuin[48] fares,   2690
Þat neuere kines[49] best ne spares,
Þanne his gon; for he garte alle
Þe Denshe men biforn him falle.
He felde browne, he felde blake,
Þat he mouthe ouertake.   2695

---

[39] ugly.   [40] struck off.   [41] rescued.   [42] on both sides.   [43] and plenty more.
[44] slaughter.   [45] puddle.   [46] hollow; i.e., flowed downhill.   [47] at first.   [48] lightning.   [49] no sort of beast.

2670. MS. *blinne.* All-day combats are frequent. Cf. "Sir Eglamoure";
"Roland and Vernagu."
2677. Cf. "Chanson de Roland" 3339: *Sempres chadist se Diu ne li
aidast;* the rescuer is Charlemagne. See Dickman 196.
2685. Cf. "King Alisaunder" 3855: *Theo blod of heom þat was slawen
Ran by flodes and by lauen* (pools). Also "Earl of Toulouse" 100; "Brut"
476.
2688. The text is not very sensible, since Godrich has been fighting all
day; possibly *tarst* is a miscopying for *faste.* For the repetition of the
word in the next line, cf. 711, 1002.
2690. For *leuin,* Skeat substituted *leun* (lion), which is more appropriate, although the text is perfectly possible.

Was neuere non þat mouhte þaue[50]
Hise dintes, noyþer knith ne knaue,
þat he felden so dos þe gres
Biforn þe syþe[1] þat ful sharp is.
Hwan Hauelok saw his folk so brittene,[2]   2700
And his ferd so swiþe littene,[3]
He cam driuende upon a stede,
And bigan til him to grede,
And seyde, "Godrich, wat is þe,[4]
þat þou fare þus with me   2705
And mine gode knihtes slos?
Sikerlike þou misgos.[5]
þou wost ful wel, yif þu wilt wite,
þat Aþelwold þe dide site
On knes, and sweren on messe-bok,   2710
On caliz, and on pateyn[6] hok,
þat þou hise douhter sholdest yelde,
þan she were wimman of elde,
Engelond eueril[k] del:
Godrich þe erl, þou wost it wel!   2715
Do nu wel, withuten fiht,
Yeld hire þe lond, for þat is rith.
Wile ich forgiue þe þe lathe,[7]
Al þi dede[8] and al mi wrathe,
For y se þu art so with,   2720
And of þi bodi so god knith."
"þat ne wile ich neuere mo,"
Quoth erl Godrich, "for ich shal slo
þe, and hire forhenge[9] heye.
I shal þrist[10] ut þi rith eye   2725
þat þou lokes with on me,
But þu swiþe heþen[11] fle."
He grop þe swerd ut sone anon
And hew on Hauelok ful god won,[12]

---

[50] endure.   [1] scythe.   [2] broken up.   [3] army diminished.   [4] what is wrong with
you.   [5] go wrong.   [6] chalice and paten.   [7] enmity.   [8] all of thy misdeeds.
[9] hang.   [10] thrust.   [11] hence.   [12] plenty; i.e., strokes enough.

2700. On the ensuing single combat, see *MLR* 17.113 and 18.22
2711. MS. *messe hok.*   Cf. 187.—Skeat.
2719. MS. *mi dede.*—Zupitza.

So þat he clef[13] his sheld on two. 2730
Hwan Hauelok saw þat shame do
His bodi þer bi-forn his ferd,
He drow ut sone his gode swerd
And smot him so upon þe crune
Þat Godrich fel to þe erþe adune. 2735
But Godrich stirt up swiþe sket[14]—
Lay he nowth longe at hise fet—
And smot him on þe sholdre so
Þat he dide þare undo
Of his brinie ringes mo 2740
Þan þat ich kan tellen fro;[15]
And woundede him rith in þe flesh,
Þat tendre was and swiþe nesh,[16]
So þat þe blod ran til his to:
Þo was Hauelok swiþe wo 2745
Þat he hauede of him drawen
Blod, and so sore him slawen.
Hertelike til him he wente,
And Godrich þer fulike shente:
For his swerd he hof[17] up heye, 2750
And þe hand he dide offleye
Þat he smot him with so sore:
Hw mithe he don him shame more?

Hwan he hauede him so shamed,
His hand ofplat[18] and yuele lamed, 2755
He tok him sone bi þe necke
Als a traytour (daþeyt wo recke!),
And dide him binde and fetere wel
With gode feteres al of stel;
And to þe quen he sende him, 2760

---

[13] split. [14] quickly. [15] about. [16] soft. [17] raised. [18] struck off.

2754. The disgrace of losing a hand in battle was as great as the inconvenience. Ipomedon tells one of his foes, thus mutilated, to remember the encounter whenever he drinks a glass of wine. The Saracen Queen thinks her husband's similar misfortune as great a one as the loss of Spain ("Chanson de Roland" 2719). Cf. also the dismemberment of giants in "Morte Arthure" and "Sir Perceval."

Þat birde[19] wel to him ben grim,
And bad she sholde don him gete[20]
And þat non ne sholde him bete
Ne shame do, for he was knith,
Til knithes haueden demd him rith.   2765
Þan þe Englishe men þat sawe,
Þat þei wisten, heye and lawe,
Þat Goldeboru, þat was so fayr,
Was of Engeland rith eyr,
And þat þe king hire hauede wedded   2770
And haueden ben samen bedded,
He comen alle to crie merci
Vnto þe king at one cri,[21]
And beden him sone manrede and oth
Þat he ne sholden, for lef ne loth,   2775
Neuere more ageyn him go
Ne ride, for wel ne for wo.[22]

Þe king ne wolde nouth forsake[23]
Þat he ne shulde of hem take
Manrede þat he beden, and ok   2780
Hold-oþes[24] sweren on þe bok;
But or bad he þat þider were[25] brouth
Þe quen, for hem—swilk was his þouth—
For to se and forto shawe[26]
Yif þat he hire wolde knawe.   2785
Þoru hem witen wolde he

---

[19] whom it behooved.   [20] guarded.   [21] with one voice.   [22] for good or ill; i.e., for any reason.   [23] neglect.   [24] oaths of allegiance.   [25] should be.   [26] make known.

2764. The prohibition was probably necessary; when Ganelon is tied to a stake awaiting trial, slaves beat him with staves—deservedly, thinks the poet ("Chanson de Roland" 3740).

2782. This curious manœuver is found only in the English version, and is one of numerous inconsistencies. Havelok knows that she is the rightful heir; and Goldeboru had been kept hidden from the people, so that they could identify her only with difficulty. But princes are readily recognised when they care to be (cf. "Orfeo"); and this is probably a convention of romance.

2786. MS. þoruth.

Yif þat she aucte quen to be.

Sixe erles weren sone yare
After hire for to fare;
He nomen onon and comen sone,   2790
And brouthen hire þat under mone
In al þe werd ne hauede per
Of hendeleik,[27] fer ne ner.
Hwan she was come þider, alle
Þe Englishe men bigunne to falle   2795
O knes, and greten swiþe sore,
And seyden, "Leuedi, K[r]istes ore
And youres! we hauen misdo mikel,
Þat we ayen you haue be fikel,[28]
For Englond auhte forto ben   2800
Youres, and we youre men.
Is non of us, yung ne old,
Þat he ne wot þat Aþelwold
Was king of þis kunerike,
And ye his eyr, and þat þe swike[29]   2805
Haues it halden with mikel wronge,
God leue him sone to honge!"

Quot Hauelok, "Hwan þat ye it wite,
Nu wile ich þat ye doun site,
And after Godrich haues wrouht,   2810
Þat haues him-self in sorwe brouth,
Lokes þat ye demen him rith,
For dom ne spareth clerk ne knith;
And siþen shal ich understonde
Of you, after lawe of londe,   2815
Manrede and holde-oþes boþe,
Yif ye it wilen and ek rothe."[30]

[27] courtesy.   [28] disloyal.   [29] traitor.   [30] counsel.

2801. MS. *forto ben youres/ And we youre men and youres.*—Holthausen.
2803. MS. *we ne.*
2811. MS. *in sorwe him self.*—Holthausen.
2813. MS. *spared.*—Holthausen.

Anon þer dune he hem sette,
For non þe dom ne durste lette,
And demden him to binden faste   2820
Vpon an asse swiþe unwraste,[31]
Andelong, nouht ouerþwert,[32]
His nose went unto þe stert,[33]
And so to Lincolne lede
Shamelike, in wicke wede;   2825
And hwan he cam unto þe borw,
Shamelike ben led þerþoru,
Bisouþe[34] þe borw, unto a grene
Þat þare is yet, als y wene,
And þere be bunden til a stake,   2830
Abouten him ful grete fir make,
And al to dust be brend rith þere;
And yet demden he þer more,
Oþer swikes for to warne:
Þat hise children sulde þarne[35]   2835
Euere-more þat eritage
Þat his was, for hise utrage.[36]

Hwan þe dom was demd and seyd,
Sket was þe swike on þe asse leyd,
And [led] him til þat ilke grene,   2840
And brend til asken[37] al bidene.
Þo was Goldeboru ful bliþe;
She þanked God fele syþe
Þat þe fule swike was brend
Þat wende wel hire bodi haue shend,   2845
And seyde, "Nu is time to take

[31] sorry, miserable. [32] endwise, not across. [33] turned toward the tail. [34] south
of. [35] lose. [36] presumption. [37] burned to ashes.

2821. Cf. the "malvais somier" of "Chanson de Roland" 481 and 1828;
and "Sir Ferumbras" 5671; also the Spanish ballad in Wolf's collection
(II.414). Simon Fraser was thus humiliated.

2825. Poor clothes amounted almost to a degradation in rank. The
sort of clothes one might wear was prescribed by law; the poorer classes
were forbidden to have expensive cloth.

2826. The scribe has substituted *cam* for the subjunctive *come* (Sisam).

Manrede of brune and of blake,
Þat ich se ride and go:
Nu ich am wreken of mi fo."

Hauelok anon manrede tok   2850
Of alle Englishe, on þe bok,
And dide hem grete oþes swere
Þat he sholden him god feyth bere
Ageyn alle þat woren liues
And þat sholde ben born of wiues.   2855

Þanne he hauede sikernesse
Taken of more and of lesse
Al at hise wille, so dide he calle
Þe erl of Cestre,[38] and hise men alle,
Þat was yung knith wituten wif,   2860
And seyde, "Sire erl, bi mi lif,
And þou wile mi conseyl tro,
Ful wel shal ich with þe do:
For ich shal yeue þe to wiue
Þe fairest þing þat is oliue: 2865
Þat is Gunnild of Grimesby,
Grimes douther, bi seint Dauy,
Þat[39] me forth broute and wel fedde
And ut of Denmark with me fledde,
Me for to berwen fro mi ded: 2870
Sikerlike þoru his red
Haue ich liued into þis day,
Blissed worþe his soule ay!
I rede þat þu hire take
And spuse and curteyse make,[40]   2875
For she is faýr and she is fre
And al so hende so she may be.

---

[38] Chester.   [39] i.e., Grim.   [40] ? make a fine lady.

2849. MS. wreke.
2856. MS. haueden.
2867. Probably St. David, the patron saint of Wales.
2870. MS. burwe.
2875. Sisam proposed curteysye (= treat courteously).

þertekene she is wel with me,⁴¹
þat shal ich ful wel shewe þe;
For ich giue þe a giue⁴²   2880
þat eueremore hwil ich liue
For hire shaltu be with me dere;
þat wile ich þat þis folc al here."
þe erl ne wolde nouth ageyn
þe king be, for knith ne sweyn,   2885
Ne of þe spusing seyen nay,
But spusede [hire] þat ilke day.
þat spusinge was [in] god time maked,⁴³
For it ne were neuere clad ne naked
In a þede samened two   2890
þat cam togidere, liuede so,
So þey diden al here liue.
He geten samen sones fiue,
þat were þe beste men at nede
þat mouthe riden on ani stede.—   2895
Hwan Gunnild was to Cestre brouth,
Hauelok þe gode ne forgat nouth
Bertram, þat was þe erles kok,
þat he ne dide [him] callen ok
And seyde, "Frend, so God me rede,   2900
Nu shaltu haue riche mede
For wissing⁴⁴ and þi gode dede
þat tu me dides in ful gret nede;
For þanne y yede in mi cuuel,⁴⁵
And ich ne hauede bred ne sowel,⁴⁶   2905
Ne y ne hauede no catel,
þou feddes and claddes me ful wel.
Haue nu forþi of Cornwayle
þe erldom il[k] del, withuten fayle,
And al þe lond þat Godrich held,   2910
Boþe in towne and ek in feld;
And þerto wile ich þat þu spuse

---

⁴¹ in addition, she is in favor with me. ⁴² i.e., make you a promise. ⁴³ i.e.,
was a happy inspiration. ⁴⁴ guidance. ⁴⁵ cloak. ⁴⁶ relish.

2905. MS. haue.

And fayre bring hire un-til huse
Grimes douther, Leuiue þe hende,
For þider shal she with þe wende.　　2915
Hire semes curteys[47] forto be,
For she is fayr so flour on tre;
þe heu[48] is swilk in hire ler
So þe rose in roser[49]
Hwan it is fayr sprad ut newe　　2920
Ageyn þe sunne brith and lewe."[50]
And girde him sone with þe swerd
Of þe erldom, biforn his ferd,
And with his hond he made him knith,
And yaf him armes, for þat was rith,　　2925
And dide him þere sone wedde
Hire þat was ful swete in bedde.

After þat he spused wore,
Wolde þe erl nouth dwelle þore,
But sone nam until his lond,　　2930
And seysed[1] it al in his hond,
And liuede þerinne, he and his wif,
An hundred winter in god lif,
And gaten mani children samen,
And liueden ay in blisse and gamen.—　　2935
Hwan þe maydens were spused boþe,
Hauelok anon bigan ful rathe
His Denshe men to feste[2] wel
Wit riche landes and catel,
So þat he weren alle riche:　　2940
For he was large and nouth chinche.[3]

þer-after sone, with his here,[4]

---

[47] it befits her to be a fine lady.　[48] color.　[49] rosebush.　[50] warm.　[1] took possession.　[2] endow.　[3] stingy.　[4] (hostile) army.

2922. For the ceremony, see Stubbs, "Constitutional History," II.392. The sword was the symbol of the governing power of the earl, just as the crown and scepter represented the power of the king.
2932. On long lives, see Dickman, 169.
2941. Cf. 1763.

For he to Lundone, forto bere
Corune, so þat it sawe
Henglishe ant Denshe, heye and lowe,   2945
Hou he it bar with mikel pride,
For his barnage þat was unride.[5]

þe feste of his coruning
Lastede with gret ioying
Fourti dawes and sumdel mo;   2950
þo bigunnen þe Denshe to go
Vnto þe king to aske leue,[6]
And he ne wolde hem nouth greue;
For he saw þat he woren yare
Into Denemark for to fare;   2955
But gaf hem leue sone anon
And bitauhte hem seint Iohan,
And bad Ubbe, his iustise,
þat he sholde on ilke wise
Denemark yeme and gete[7] so   2960
þat no pleynte[8] come him to.

Hwan he wore parted[9] alle samen,
Hauelok bilefte[10] wit ioie and gamen
In Engelond, and was þerinne
Sixti winter king with winne,   2965
And Goldeboru quen, þat i wene
So mikel loue was hem bitwene
þat al þe werd spak of hem two.
He louede hire and she him so,
þat neyþer owe[r][11] mithe be   2970
Fro oþer, ne no ioie se

---

[5] before his nobles, who were numerous.   [6] dismissal.   [7] guard.   [8] complaint.
[9] set out.   [10] remained.   [11] anywhere.

2943. For the ceremonies, see Freeman's "Norman Conquest" III.
appendix, note on *The Ancient Coronation Office.*
2946. MS. *Hwou.*
2949. MS. *laste.*
2970. MS. *oþe.*—Sisam.

But-yf he were togidere boþe;
Neuere yete ne weren he wroþe,
For here loue was ay newe;
Neuere yete wordes ne grewe   2975
Bitwene hem, hwarof ne lathe
Mithe rise, ne no wrathe.

He geten children hem bitwene
Sones and douthres rith fiuetene,
Hwarof þe sones were kinges alle—   2980
So wolde God it sholde bifalle,—
And þe douhtres alle quenes:
Him stondes wel þat god child strenes.[12]—
Nu haue ye herd þe gest[13] al þoru
Of Hauelok and of Goldeborw: 2985
Hw he weren born and hw fedde,
And hou he woren with wronge ledde
In here youþe, with trecherie,
With tresoun, and with felounye;
And hou þe swikes haueden tiht[14]   2990
Reuen hem þat was here rith,
And hou he weren wreken wel,
Haue ich sey[d] you eueril[k] del;
And forþi ich wolde biseken you
Þat hauen herd þe rim nu,   2995
Þat ilke of you, with gode wille,
Seye a pater-noster stille
For him þat haueth þe rym maked,
And þerfore fele nihtes waked,[15]
Þat Iesu Crist his soule bringe   3000
Biforn his fader at his endinge.
                              A—m—e—n.

---

[12] begets.   [13] story.   [14] intended.   [15] stayed awake.

2972. MS. to gidede.
2979. Cf. the ballad "Sir Cawline."
2984. The concluding lines tell much about the author, and seem to be
his own invention.
2987, 2990, 2992. MS. hwou. 2990. MS. haueden thit.

ATHELSTON

ATHELSTON

The dialect of the poem is north midland of 1350–1400. It has several northern peculiarities, such as the setting of two or three predicates in apposition, and the omission of relatives (cf. 253). On the various elements of the story, see Hibbard, 143 ff. A subsequent article is in *Archiv* 148.181, "Die Saga von König Athelston." The legend is dealt with in I. P. McKeehan's "St. Edmund of East Anglia," *U. of Colorado Studies*, XV.67.

Through the kind permission of the authorities of the library, the text has been prepared from the manuscript (175) in Caius College Library, Cambridge. No divisions are marked in it; those here are mostly like those in Zupitza's edition (*Englische Studien* xiii).

The copyist is prodigal with the letter F, frequently doubling it after a long vowel (*wyff*), and using it initially when no capital could have been intended. His spelling has been left undisturbed.

Lord þat is off myȝtys most,
Fadyr and Sone and Holy Gost,
    Bryng vs out off synne,
And lene vs grace so for to wyrke,
To loue boþe God and holy kyrke,   5
    Þat [we] may heuene wynne.
Lystnes, lordyngys þat ben hende,
Off ffalsnesse, hou it wil ende
    A man þat ledes hym þerin.
Off ffoure weddyd¹ breþeryn i wolc ȝow tcl,   10
Þat wolden yn Yngelond go dwel,
    Þat sybbe were nouȝt off kynde.

And alle foure messangeres þey were,
Þat wolden yn Yngelond lettrys bere,

¹ sworn.

11. Zupitza wished to alter to *wilen . . . gon;* but l. 20 indicates that the MS. reading is right.
13. For information about messengers, cf. Jusserand II.ii.

As it wes here kynde.[2]   15
By a fforest gan þey mete
Wiþ a cros, stood in a strete[3]
Be leff vndyr a lynde.[4]
And, as þe story telles me,
Ylke man was of dyuers cuntré: 20
In book iwreten we ffynde.
For loue of here metyng þare
Þey swoor hem weddyd breþeryn for euermare,
In trewþe trewely dede hem bynde.

Þe eldeste off hem ylkon,[5]   25
He was hyʒt Athelston,
Þe Kyngys cosyn dere;
He was off þe Kyngys blood,
Hys eemes sone, i vndyrstood:
Þerfore he neyʒyd hym nere.[6]   30
And at þe laste, weel and fayr,
Þe Kyng hym dyyd withouten ayr;
Þenne was þer non hys pere
But Athelston, hys eemes sone;
To make hym kyng wolde þey nouʒt schon,[7]   35
To corowne hym with gold so clere.

Now was he kyng semely to se,
He sendes afftyr hys breþeryn þree
And gaff hem here warysoun.[8]
Þe eldest broþir he made Eerl of Douere,   40
And þus þe pore man gan couere,[9]
Lord off tour and toun.
Þat oþer broþer he made Eerl of Stane—
Egelond was hys name,

---

[2] i.e., profession. [3] by a road. [4] exactly under a tree. [5] i.e., them all. [6] i.e.,
was closely related. [7] refuse. [8] reward. [9] restore (to affluence).

19. No original for the poem is known.
22. For bibliography on the sworn brotherhood, cf. Hibbard 145. By
various rites, the parties assumed a tie as binding as that of blood.
43. Stone is near Dartford. The localities mentioned are nearly all
on the road from London to Canterbury.

A man off gret renoun—   45
And gaff hym tyl hys weddyd wyff
Hys owne sustyr, Dame Edyff,
  Wiþ gret deuocyoun.[10]

Þe ferþe broþir was a clerk—
Mekyl he cowde off Goddys werk;   50
  His name, it was Alryke.
Cauntyrbury was vacant
And fel into þat Kyngys hand:
  He gaff it hym, þat wyke,[11]
And made hym bysschop of þat stede.   55
Þat noble clerk on book cowde rede,
  In þe world was non hym lyche.
Þus avaunsyd he hys broþer þorwȝ Goddys gras,
And Athelston hymseluen was
  A good kyng and a ryche.   60

And he þat was Eerl off Stane—
Sere Egeland was hys name—
  Was trewe, as ȝe schal here.
Þorwȝ þe myȝt off Goddys gras
He gat vpon þe Countas[12]   65
  Twoo knaue-chyldren dere.
Þat on was ffyfftene wyntyr old,
Þat oþer þryttene, as men me told.
  In þe world was non here pere:
Also whyt so lylye-fflour,   70
Red as rose off here colour,
  As bryȝt as blosme on brere.[13]

Boþe þe Eerl and hys wyff,
Þe Kyng hem louede as hys lyff,
  And here sones twoo,   75
And offten-syþe[14] he gan hem calle

---

[10] devotedness.   [11] place.   [12] countess.   [13] as blossom on briar.   [14] often-times.

56. Sc. ("so well.") The poet's diction often shows ellipsis.
66. *Knave* is the regular word for a male child.

Boþe to boure and to halle,
To counsayl whenne þey scholde goo.
Þerat Sere Wymound hadde gret envye,
Þat Eerl off Douere, wyttyrlye: 80
In herte he was ful woo.
He þouȝte al for here sake[15]
False lesyngys on hem to make,
To don hem brenne and sloo.

And þanne Sere Wymound hym beþouȝte,   85
"Here loue þus endure may nouȝte:
Þorwȝ wurd oure werk may sprynge."[16]
He bad hys men maken hem ȝare:
Vnto Londone wolde he fare
To speke wiþ þe Kynge.   90
Whenne þat he to Londone come,
He mette with þe Kyng ful sone.
He sayde, "Welcome, my derelyng."
Þe Kyng hym fraynyd soone anon,
Be what way he hadde igon,   95
Wiþouten ony dwellyng.[17]

"Come þou ouȝt[18] be Cauntyrbery,
Þere þe clerkys syngen mery
Boþe erly and late?
Hou faryth þat noble clerk,   100
Þat mekyl can on Goddys werk?
Knowest þou ouȝt hys state?
And come þou ouȝt be þe Eerl off Stane,
Þat wurþy lord in hys wane?[19]
Wente þou ouȝt þat gate?   105
Hou fares þat noble knyȝt
And hys sones fayr and bryȝt?
My sustyr, ȝiff þat þou wate?"

---

[15] i.e., for their ruin. [16] i.e., a rumor will forward our plan. [17] i.e., delay in
telling. [18] at all; i.e., by chance. [19] province.

77. I.e., both to public and to private counsel.
98. The monks of St. Augustine's in Canterbury were reputed to be
gay fellows and good singers.

"Sere," þanne he sayde, "wiþouten les,
Be Cauntyrbery my way i ches: 110
þere spak i wiþ þat dere.
Ryȝt weel gretes þee þat noble clerk,
þat mykyl can off Goddys werk:
In þe world is non hys pere.
And also be Stane my way i drowȝ:[20] 115
Wiþ Egeland i spak inowȝ
And with þe Countesse so clere.
þey fare weel, is nouȝt to layne,
And boþe here sones." þe Kyng was fayne,
And in his herte made glad chere. 120

"Sere Kyng," he sayde, "ȝiff it be þi wille
To chaumbyr þat þou woldest wenden tylle,
Counsayl for to here,
I schal þe telle a swete tydande:
þer comen neuere non swyche in þis lande 125
Off al þis hundryd ȝere."
þe Kyngys herte þan was ful woo
Wiþ þat traytour for to goo.
þey wente boþe forþ in ffere,
And, whenne þat þey were þe chaumbyr withinne, 130
False lesyngys he gan begynne
On hys weddyd broþer dere.

"Sere Kyng," he sayde, "woo were me
Ded þat i scholde see þe,
So moot i haue my lyff! 135
For by Hym þat al þis worl wan,[21]
þou hast makyd me a man,
And iholpe me ffor to þryff.[22]
For in þy land, sere, is a fals traytour:
He wole doo þe mykyl dyshonour 140
And brynge þe of lyue.

---

[20] took.　[21] i.e., Christ.　[22] prosper.

136. The form *worl*, for *world*, is correct.—Zupitza.
141. MS. *on lyue*.

He wole deposen þe slyly;
Sodaynly[23] þan schalt þou dy,
　　Be Crystys woundys ffyue!"

Þenne sayde þe Kyng, "So moot þou the,　　　　145
Knowe i þat man, and i hym see?
　　His name þou me telle."
"Nay," says þat traytour, "þat wole i nouȝt
For al þe gold þat euere was wrouȝt,
　　Be masse-book and belle,　　　　150
But-ȝiff þou me þy trowþe wil plyȝt
Þat þou sc[halt] neuere bewr[eye] þe knyȝt
　　Þat þe þe tale schal telle."
Þanne þe Kyng his hand vp rauȝte.
Þat false man his trowþe betauȝte:　　　　155
　　He was a deuyl off helle.

"Sere Kyng," he sayde, "þou madyst me kn[yȝt],
And now þou hast þy trowþe me plyȝt
　　Oure counsayl for to layne.
Sertaynly, it is non oþir　　　　160
But Egelane, þy weddyd broþir:
　　He wolde þat þou were slayne.
He dos þy sustyr to vndyrstande
He wole be kyng off þy lande,
　　And þus he begynnes here trayne.[24]　　　　165
He wole þe poysoun ryȝt slyly;
Sodaynly þanne schalt þou dy,
　　Be Hym þat suffryd payne."

Þanne swoor þe Kyng, "Be cros and roode,
Meete ne drynk schal do me goode[25]　　　　170
　　Tyl þat he be dede;
Boþe he and hys wyff, hys soones twoo,
Schole þey neuere be no moo

---

[23] i.e., by violence.　[24] lead astray.　[25] i.e., I shall touch neither.

150. For the peculiar force of such oaths, see "Havelok" 186.
166. *Poysoun* probably for *depoysen*, depose.　Cf. 142.—Z.

In Yngelond on þat stede."
'Nay," says þe traytour, "so moot i the,   175
Ded wole i nouзt my broþer se;—
  But do þy beste rede."[26]
No lengere þere þen wolde he lende:[27]
He takes hys leue—to Douere gan wende,
  God geue hym schame and dede!   180

Now is þat traytour hom iwent;
A messanger was afftyr sent
  To speke with þe Kyng.
I wene he bar his owne name:
He was hoten Athelstane: 185
  He was foundelyng.
Þe lettrys were imaad fullyche þare
Vnto Stane for to ffare
  Wiþouten ony dwellyng,
To ffette þe Eerl and his sones twoo   190
And þe Countasse alsoo,
  Dame Edyue, þat swete þyng.

And in þe lettre зit[28] was it tolde
Þat þe Kyng þe Eerlys sones wolde
  Make hem boþe knyзt,   195
And þerto his seel he sette.
Þe messanger wolde nouзt lette:
  Þe way he rydes ful ryзt.

Þe messanger, þe noble man,
Takes hys hors and forþ he wan,   200
  And hyes a ful good spede.
Þe Eerl in hys halle he fande;
He took hym þe lettre in his hande;
  Anon he bad hym rede:

---

[26] i.e., do as you think best. [27] tarry. [28] also.

186. The church encouraged the adoption of foundlings into families; and children so adopted were frequently given the name of their foster-parents. See Loomis 336 for other remarks and instances.

"Sere," he sayde also swyþe,   205
"Þis lettre ouȝte to make þe blyþe:
    Þertoo þou take good hede.
Þe Kyng wole for þe Cuntas sake
Boþe þy sones knyȝtes make:
    To London i rede þe spede.   210

Þe Kyng wole for þe Cuntas sake
Boþe þy sones knyȝtys make:
    Þe blyþere þou may be.
Þy ffayre wyff with þe þou bryng,
And þer be ryȝt no lettyng,   215
    Þat syȝte þat sche may see."
Þenne sayde þat Eerl with herte mylde,
"My wyff goþ ryȝt gret with chylde,
    And forþynkes²⁹ me,
Sche may nouȝt out off chaumbyr wyn   220
To speke with non ende³⁰ off here kyn
    Tyl sche delyueryd be."

But into chaumbyr þey gunne wende
To rede þe lettrys before þat hende,
    And tydyngys tolde here soone.   225
Þenne sayde þe Cuntasse, "So moot i the,
I wil nouȝt lette tyl i þere be
    To morwen, or it be noone.

To see hem knyȝtys, my sones ffre,
I wole nouȝt lette tyl i þere be: 230
    I schal no lengere dwelle.
Cryst forȝelde³¹ my lord þe Kyng,
Þat has grauntyd hem here dubbyng:
    Myn herte is gladyd welle."
Þe Eerl hys men bad make hem ȝare;   235
He and hys wyff, fforþ gunne þey fare:
    To London ffaste þey wente.
At Westemynstyr was þe Kyngys wone;

---

²⁹ regret.   ³⁰ any.   ³¹ requite.

Þere þey mette with Athelstone,
  Þat afftyr hem hadde sente.   240

Þe goode Eerl soone was hent
And feteryd faste, verrayment,
  And hys sones twoo.
Ful lowde þe Countasse gan to cry
And sayde, "Goode broþir, mercy.   245
  Why wole ȝe vs sloo?
What haue we aȝens ȝow done
Þat ȝe wole haue vs ded so soone?
  Me þynkiþ ȝe arn oure foo."
Þe Kyng as wood ferde in þat stede: 250
He garte hys [sustyr] to presoun lede;
  In herte he was ful woo.

Þenne a squyer, was þe Countasses ffrende,
To þe Qwene he gan wende,
  And tydyngys tolde here soone.   255
Gerlondes off chyryes off sche caste;
Into þe halle sche come at þe laste,
  Longe or it were noone.
"Sere Kyng, i am before þe come
Wiþ a chyld, douȝtyr or a sone: 260
  Graunte me my bone,
My broþir and sustyr þat i may borwe[32]
Tyl þe nexte day at morwe,
  Out off here paynys stronge,

Þat we mowe wete be comoun sent[33]   265
In þe playne[34] parlement . . ."
  "Dame" he sayde, "goo ffro me!
Þy bone schal nouȝt ygrauntyd be,

---

[32] act as surety for.   [33] know by general assent.   [34] full.

240. Half a stanza telling of the meeting has been lost.
256. Wearing garlands of flowers and cherry blossoms was a common
practice. Cf. Wright, ch. 13.
266. Four lines are lacking; their general sense is, "whether they are
guilty." MS. *playne playne*.

I doo þe to vndyrstande.
For be Hym þat weres þe corowne off þorn,   270
Þey schole be drawen and hangyd to-morn,
3yff i be kyng off lande !"

And whenne þe Qwene þese wurdes herde,
As sche hadde be beten wiþ 3erde[35]
Þe teeres sche leet doun falle.   275
Sertaynly as i 3ow telle,
On here bare knees doun sche felle,
And prayde 3it for hem alle.
"A, dame," he sayde, "verrayment,
Hast þou broke my comaundement;   280
Abyyd ful dere þou schalle."
Wiþ hys ffoot he wolde nou3t wonde;[36]
He slow3 þe chyld ry3t in here wombe;
Sche swownyd amonges hem alle.

Ladyys and maydenys þat þere were   285
Þe Qwene to here chaumbyr bere,
And þere was dool inow3.
Soone withinne a lytyl spase
A knaue-chyld iborn þer wase,
As bry3t as blosme on bow3:   290
He was boþe whyt and red;
Off þat dynt was he ded—
Hys owne fadyr hym slow3 !
Þus may a traytour baret[37] rayse
And make manye men ful euele at ayse—   295
Hymselff nou3t afftyr it low3.[38]

---

[35] rod.   [36] refrain.   [37] trouble.   [38] after (doing) it, he did not laugh; i.e., the consequences were serious.

271. This punishment was usually reserved for wretched criminals and traitors. They were dragged through the streets on a hurdle or a cowhide. Cf. "Havelok" 2480.
281. *Abyyd*=abye, pay for. The verbs were confused in Middle English.
283. On this episode, see *PMLA* 44.223.
291. The colors of the aristocracy. Cf. "Havelok" 1008.

But ȝit þe Qwene, as ȝe schole here,
Sche callyd vpon a messangere,
   Bad hym a lettre ffonge,
And bad hym wende to Cauntyrbery,   300
Þere þe clerkys syngen mery
   Boþe masse and euensonge.
"Þis lettre þou þe Bysschop take,
And praye hym, for Goddys sake,
   Come borewe hem out off here bande!³⁹   305
He⁴⁰ wole doo more for hym, i wene,
Þanne for me, þouȝ i be Qwene,
   I doo þe to vndyrstande.

An eerldom in Spayne i haue of land:
Al i sese⁴¹ into þyn hand,   310
   Trewely, as i þe hyȝt—
An hundryd besauntys⁴² off gold red.
Þou may saue hem from þe ded,
   ȝyff þat þyn hors be wyȝt."
"Madame, brouke weel þy moregeue⁴³   315
Also longe as þou may leue:
   Þerto haue i no ryȝt;
But off⁴⁴ þy gold and off þy ffee,
Cryst in heuene fforȝelde⁴⁵ it þe!
   I wole be þere to nyȝt.   320

Madame, þrytty myles off hard way
I haue reden siþ it was day:
   Ful sore i gan me swynke;⁴⁶
And for to ryde now ffyue and twenti þertoo,
An hard þyng it were to doo,   325

³⁹ rescue them from their bonds. ⁴⁰ (the king). ⁴¹ seise, give in possession.
⁴² besants, worth about a pound. ⁴³ enjoy (the use of) thy present; i.e.,
keep it. *More*=morrow. ⁴⁴ but (for the offer) of. ⁴⁵ reward. ⁴⁶ toil.

324. Zupitza proposed to read *fifti*, which mends the meter. The text
makes good sense as it stands: even a short ride would be tiring after
his trip to Stone. Jusserand tells, however, of messengers who made the
trip from Lyons in France to York, a distance of about 700 miles, in
ten days.

For soþe, ryʒt as me þynke.
Madame, it is nerhande passyd prime,
And me behoues al for to dyne,
Boþe wyn and ale to drynke.
Whenne i haue dynyd, þenne wole i fare: 330
God may couere⁴⁷ hem off here care
Or þat i slepe a wynke."

Whenne he hadde dynyd, he wente his way
Also faste as þat he may.
He rod be Charynge Cros   335
And entryd in to Fflete Strete
And seþþyn þorwʒ Londone, i ʒow hete,
Vpon a noble hors.
Þe messanger, þat noble man,
On Loundone Brygge sone he wan   340
(For his trauayle he hadde no los).⁴⁸
From Stone into Steppyngebourne,
For soþe, his way nolde he nouʒt tourne:
Sparyd he nouʒt for myre ne mos.⁴⁹

And þus hys way wendes he   345
Fro Osprynge to þe Blee.
Þenne myʒte he see þe toun
Off Cauntyrbery, þat noble wyke,⁵⁰
Þerin lay þat bysschop ryke,¹
Þat lord off gret renoun.   350
And whenne þey runggen vndernbelle,
He rod in Londone, as i ʒow telle:
He was non er² redy;
And ʒit to Cauntyrbery he wan:

⁴⁷ rescue. ⁴⁸ praise. ⁴⁹ mud nor bog. ⁵⁰ place. ¹ powerful. ² no earlier.

335 ff. The details of this journey are so full and accurate that it may
be traced on a map. Stone is seventeen miles from London toward Canterbury; Sittingbourne, forty-one; Osprynge, forty-seven; the Blean (a
wooded hill), fifty-one; and Canterbury, about fifty-five. The route was
the old pilgrims' road, and most of the localities are mentioned by Chaucer.
351. I.e., about six in the morning. Evensong was at about six in the
evening.

Longe or euensong began,   355
　　He rod mylys ffyffty.

Þe messanger noþyng abod:
Into þe palays forþ he rod
　　Þere þat þe Bysschop was inne.
Ryȝt welcome was þe messanger,   360
Þat was come ffrom þe Qwene so cleer,
　　Was off so noble kynne.
He took hym a lettre ful good speed
And sayde: "Sere Bysschop, haue þis and reed,"
　　And bad hym come wiþ hym.   365
Or he þe lettre hadde halff iredde,
For dool hym þouȝte hys herte bledde:
　　Þe teeres ffyl ouyr hys chyn.

Þe bysschop bad sadele hys palfray:
"Also ffaste as þay may,   370
　　Bydde my men make hem ȝare;
And wendes before," þe Bysschop dede say,
"To my maneres[3] in þe way—
　　For no þyng þat ȝe spare—
And loke at ylke ffyue mylys ende   375
A ffresch hors þat i ffynde
　　Schod and noþyng bare.[4]
Blyþe schal i neuere be
Tyl i my weddyd broþer see,
　　To keuere[5] hym out off care."   380

On nyne palfrays þe Bysschop sprong,
Ar it was day from euensong,[6]
　　In romaunce as we rede.
Certaynly, as i ȝow telle,
On Londone Brygge ded doun felle   385
　　Þe messangeres stede.
"Allas," he sayde, "þat i was born!
Now is my goode hors forlorn,

---

[3] manors.　[4] i.e., unsaddled.　[5] rescue.　[6] i.e., from even-song to day.

Was good at ylke a nede.
ȝistyrday vpon þe grounde   390
He was wurþ an hundryd pounde
    Ony kyng to lede."[7]

Þenne bespak þe Erchebysschop,
Oure gostly fadyr vndyr God,
    Vnto þe messangere.   395
"Lat be þy menyng[8] off þy stede,
And þynk vpon oure mykyl nede
    Þe whylys þat we ben here;
For ȝiff þat i may my broþer borwe
And bryngen hym out off mekyl sorwe,   400
    Þou may make glad chere,
And þy warysoun[9] i schal þe geue,
And God haue grauntyd þe to leue
    Vnto an hundryd ȝere."[10]

Þe Bysschop þenne nouȝt ne bod;   405
He took hys hors, and forþ he rod
    Into Westemynstyr so lyȝt[11]—
Þe messanger on his ffoot[12] alsoo—
Wiþ þe Bysschop come no moo,
    Neþer squyer ne knyȝt.   410
Vpon þe morwen þe Kyng aros
And takes þe way to þe kyrke; he gos
    As man off mekyl myȝt.
Wiþ hym wente boþe preest and clerk,
Þat mykyl cowde off Goddys werk,   415
    To praye God for þe ryȝt.

Whenne þat he to þe kyrke com,
Toffore þe rode he knelyd anon,
    And on hys knees he ffelle:

---

[7] bear.   [8] bemoaning.   [9] reward.   [10] i.e., it shall suffice if you live to be a hundred.   [11] quickly.   [12] afoot.

412. The line seems corrupt, and may have read originally *and to þe kyrke the way he goes.*

"God, þat syt in Trynyté,   420
A bone þat þou graunte me,
  Lord, as þou harewyd helle:
Gyltles men ʒiff þay be
þat are in my presoun ffree
  Forcursyd þere to ʒelle[13]—   425
Off þe gylt and þay be clene—
Leue[14] it moot on hem be sene
  þat garte hem þere to dwelle."

And whenne he hadde maad his prayer,
He lokyd vp into þe qweer;[15]   430
  þe Erchebysschop sawʒ he stande.
He was forwondryd off þat caas,[16]
And to hym he wente apas[17]
  And took hym be þe hande.
"Welcome," he sayde, "þou Erchebysschop,   435
Oure gostly fadyr vndyr God."
  He swoor be God leuande,[18]
"Wẹddyd broþer, weel moot þou spede,[19]
For i hadde neuere so mekyl nede,
  Siþ i took cros on hande.[20]   440

Goode weddyd broþer, now turne þy rede:[21]
Doo nouʒt þyn owne blood to dede
  But-ʒiff it wurþy were.
For Hym þat weres þe corowne off þorn,
Lat me borwe[22] hem tyl to morn,   445
  þat me mowe enquere
And weten alle be comoun asent
In þe playne[23] parlement
  Who is wurþy be schent.
And but-ʒiff ʒe wole graunte my bone,   450

---

[13] doomed there to shriek. [14] grant. [15] choir. [16] he marvelled at that event.
[17] quickly. [18] living. [19] i.e., may you be in a position to aid me. [20] i.e., became a bishop. [21] be better advised. [22] be surety for. [23] full.

424. "Free prison" was custody without confinement. Cf. "Avowis of Alexander" 5040: Cassamus *kepis hym allane, Bot [without] outher presoun or fastnine, But throw lele lufe and lauté fyne.*

It schal vs rewe boþe or none,
  Be God þat alle þyng lent."[24]

Þanne þe Kyng wax wroþ as wynde:
A wodere man myȝte no man fynde
  Þan he began to bee.   455
He swoor oþis be sunne and mone,
"Þey scholen be drawen and hongyd or none:
  Wiþ eyen þou schalt see!
Lay doun þy cros and þy staff,
Þy mytyr[25] and þy ryng þat i þe gaff;   460
  Out off my land þou fflee!
Hyȝe þe faste out off my syȝt!
Wher i þe mete, þy deþ is dyȝt;
  Non oþir þen schal it bee."

Þenne bespak þat Erchebysschop,   465
Oure gostly fadyr vndyr God,
  Smertly[26] to þe Kyng:
"Weel i wot þat þou me gaff
Boþe þe cros and þe staff,
  Þe mytyr and eke þe ryng.   470
My bysschopryche þou reues me,
And crystyndom forbede i þe!
  Preest schal þer non syngge;
Neyþer maydynchyld ne knaue
Crystyndom[27] schal þer non haue;   475
  To care i schal þe brynge.

I schal gare crye þorwȝ ylke a toun,
Þat kyrkys schole be broken doun—
  And stoken agayn[28] wiþ þorn;
And þou schalt lygge in an old dyke,   480
As it were an heretyke,

---

[24] loaned, gave.   [25] mitre, a bishop's headdress.   [26] sharply.   [27] i.e., baptism.
[28] stabbed; i.e., overgrown.

456. MS. *swoor be oþis.*—Z.
480. Heretics were refused burial in cemeteries.

Allas þat þou were born!

ȝiff þou be ded þat i may see,[29]
Asoylyd schalt þou neuere bee;
   Þanne is þy soule in sorwe;   485
And i schal wende in vncouþe [lond]
And gete me stronge men of hond;
   My broþir ȝit schal i borwe:
I schal brynge vpon þy lond
Hungyr and þyrst ful strong,   490
   Cold, drouȝþe, and sorwe;
I schal nouȝt leue on þy lond
Wurþ[30] þe gloues on þy hond,
   To begge ne to borwe."

Þe Bysschop has his leue tan;   495
By þat, his men were comen ylkan;
   Þey sayden, "Sere, haue good day."
He entryd into Flete Strete:
Wiþ lordys off Yngelond gan he mete
   Vpon a nobyl aray.   500
On here knees þey kneleden adoun
And prayden hym off his benysoun;[31]
   He nykkyd hem wiþ nay.[32]
Neyþer off cros neyþer off ryng
Hadde þey non kyns wetyng;[33]   505
   And þanne a knyȝt gan say.

A knyȝt þanne spak with mylde voys:
"Sere, where is þy ryng? where is þy croys?
   Is it ffro þe tan?"
Þanne he sayde, "ȝoure cursyd Kyng   510
Haþ me refft off al my þyng
   And off al my worldly wan,[34]
And i haue entyrdytyd[35] Yngelond:

---

[29] i.e., if I am present at your death. [30] i.e., anything worth. [31] blessing. [32] refused them by saying nay. [33] any sort of information. [34] store. [35] interdicted.

485. One dying under interdict was forbidden the sacrament of confession, and could not be absolved of his sins.

þer schal no preest synge masse with hond,
    Chyld schal be crystenyd non,   515
But-ȝiff he graunte me þat knyȝt,
His wyff and chyldryn fayr and bryȝt:
    He wolde with wrong hem slon.''

þe knyȝt sayde, "Bysschop, turne agayn·
Off þy body we are ful fayn;   520
    þy broþir ȝit schole we borwe.
And but he graunte vs oure bone,
Hys presoun schal be broken soone,
    Hymselff to mekyl sorwe.[36]
We scholen drawe doun boþe halle and boures,   525
Boþe hys castelles and hys toures:
    þey schole lygge lowe and holewe.[37]
þouȝ he be Kyng and were þe corown,
We scholen hym sette in a deep dunioun:[38]
    Oure crystyndom[39] we wole folewe.''   530

þanne, as þey spoken off þis þyng,
þer comen twoo knyȝtys ffrom þe Kyng
    And sayden, "Bysschop, abyde,
And haue þy cros and þy ryng,
And welcome, whyl þat þou wylt lyng:[40]   535
    It is nouȝt for to hyde.
Here he grauntys þe þe knyȝt,
Hys wyff and chyldryn fayr and bryȝt.
    Agayn i rede þou ryde.
He prayes þe par charyté   540
þat he myȝte asoylyd[41] be,
    And Yngelond long and wyde.''

Hereoff þe Bysschop was fful ffayn,
And turnys hys brydyl and wendes agayn;
    Barouns gunne wiþ hym ryde   545

---

[36] to his own great sorrow.   [37] empty.   [38] dungeon.   [39] Christianity.   [40] tarry.
[41] absolved.

514. The poet uses *synge* practically in the sense of *celebrate*.

Vnto þe brokene cros off ston.
Þedyr com þe Kyng ful soone anon,
   And þere he gan abyde.
Vpon hys knees he knelyd adoun
And prayde þe Bysschop off benysoun,   550
   And he gaff hym þat tyde:
Wiþ holy watyr and orysoun,[42]
He asoylyd þe Kyng þat weryd þe coroun,
   And Yngelond long and wyde.

Þenne sayde þe Kyng anon ryȝt,   555
"Here i graunte þe þat knyȝt
   And hys sones ffree,
And my sustyr, hende in halle:
Þou hast sauyd here lyuys alle:
   Iblessyd moot þou bee."   560
Þenne sayde þe Bysschop also soone,
"And i schal geuen swylke a dome
   Wiþ eyen þat þou schalt see!—
Ȝiff þay be gylty off þat dede,
Sorrere þe doome þay may drede,   565
   Þan schewe here schame to me."

Whanne þe Bysschop hadde sayd soo,
A gret ffyr was maad ryȝt þoo,
   In romaunce as we rede.
It was set, þat men myȝte knawe,   570
Nyne plowȝ-lengþe on rawe,[43]
   As red as ony glede.[44]
Þanne sayde þe Kyng, "What may þis mene?"
"Sere, off gylt and þay be clene,
   Þis doom hem thar[45] nouȝt drede."   575
Þanne sayde þe good Kyng Athelston,
"An hard doome now is þis on:
   God graunte vs alle weel to spede."

---

[42] prayer.   [43] the length of nine plow-shares in a row.   [44] hot coal.   [45] need.

546. The place was thought by Zupitza to be before the house of the
Bishop of Coventry, near the Strand.

565. "They shall fear the ordeal more than confession of their misdeeds."

þey fetten forþ Sere Egelan
(A trewere eerl was þer nan),   580
Before þe ffyr so bryȝt.
From hym þey token þe rede scarlet,
Boþe hosyn and schoon, þat weren hym met,[46]
þat fel al ffor a knyȝt.
Nyne syþe þe Bysschop halewid[47] þe way   585
þat his weddyd broþer scholde goo þat day,
To praye God for þe ryȝt.
He was vnblemeschyd, ffoot and hand:
þat sawȝ þe lordes off þe land,
And þankyd God off Hys myȝt.   590

þey offeryd hym with mylde chere
Vnto Seynt Powlys heyȝe awtere,
þat mekyl was off myȝt.
Doun vpon hys knees he felle
And þankyd God þat harewede helle,   595
And Hys Modyr so bryȝt.

And ȝit þe Bysschop þo gan say,
"Now schal þe chyldryn gon þe way

---

[46] suitable.   [47] consecrated.

585. The ordeal by hot iron as a means of testing innocence was familiar
enough to be provided for in service-books as a ceremony of the Church
(L. Rockinger, *Quellen und Erörterungen zur bayerischen und deutschen
Geschichte*, vii. 384; Franz Helbing, "Die Tortur," Ch. I; Ollard and
Crosse, "Dictionary of English Church History," under "Ordeal"). A
picture of St. Kunigund undergoing the ordeal of plow-shares is in Alwin
Schultz's "Das Höfische Leben zur Zeit der Minnesinger," I. 269; and
details about it, I. 175. The legendary basis of this story is apparent
because ordeals were permanently abolished in England in 1215, and no
record of one subsequent to that time is known (Pollock ix.4). But a
law of Edward the Confessor prescribed it for wives whose husbands had
been murdered; and see Reinhold Schmid's "Gesetze der Angelsachsen"
415; D. B. Easter, "Magic in the Romans d'Aventure" 36. Cf. also
Archiv 148.192; Hibbard 37; "Young Hunting," Child, No. 68; Sophocles'
"Antigone" 264; "Echtra Cormaic Tir Tairngiri" (Windisch's *Irische
Texte* III.1.209, 224–5.)
591. The expression is twice quoted in the *O.E.D.;* but the sense is
not defined.

þat þe fadyr ȝede."
Fro hem þey tooke þe rede scarlete,   600
þe hosen and schoon þat weren hem mete,
   And al here worldly wede.
þe ffyr was boþe hydous[48] and red:
þe chyldryn swownyd as þey were d[ed].
  þe Bysschop tyl hem ȝede,   605
Wiþ careful herte on hem gan look.
Be hys hand he hem vp took:
   "Chyldryn, haue ȝe no drede."

þanne þe chyldryn stood and lowȝ:
"Sere, þe fyr is cold i-nowȝ."   610
  þorwȝout þey wente apase:[49]
þey weren vnblemeschyd, foot and ha[nd]:
þat sawȝ þe lordys off þe land,
   And þankyd God off his grace.

þey offeryd hem with mylde chere   615
To Seynt Poulys þat hyȝe awtere:
  þis myracle schewyd was þere.
And ȝit þe Bysschop efft gan say,
"Now schal þe Countasse goo þe way
  þere þat þe chyldryn were."   620

þey fetten forþ þe lady mylde:
Sche was ful gret igon with chylde,
  In romaunce as we rede.
Before þe fyr when þat sche come,
To Iesu Cryst he prayde a bone,   625
  þat leet His woundys blede:[50]
"Now, God lat neuere þe Kyngys ffoo
Quyk out off þe ffyr goo."
  þeroff hadde sche no drede.

---

[48] hideous.   [49] rapidly.   [50] i.e., bled for mankind.

600. MS. *hym.*—Z.
611. MS. *he wente.*—Z.

Whenne sche hadde maad here prayer,   630
Sche was brou3t before þe ffeer,
  þat brennyd boþe fayr and ly3t.
Sche wente ffro þe lengþe into þe þrydde;[1]
Stylle sche stood þe ffyr amydde
  And callyd it merye and bry3t.   635
Harde schourys[2] þenne took here stronge
Boþe in bak and eke in wombe,
  And siþþen it ffel at sy3t.[3]

Whenne þat here paynys slakyd[4] was
And sche hadde passyd þat hydous pas,[5]   640
  Here nose barst[6] on bloode.
Sche was vnblemeschyd, ffoot and hand:
þat saw3 þe lordys off þe land,
  And þankyd God on rode.
þey comaundyd men here away to drawe,   645
As it was þe landys lawe;
  And ladyys þanne tyl here 3ode.
Sche knelyd doun vpon þe ground,
And þere was born Seynt Edemound:
  Iblessyd be þat ffoode.[7]   650

And whanne þis chyld iborn was,
It was brou3t into þe plas:[8]
  It was boþe hool and sound.
Boþe þe Kyng and Bysschop ffree,
þey crystnyd þe chyld, þat men my3t see,   655
  And callyd it Edemound.
"Halff my land," he sayde, "i þe geue,
Also longe as i may leue,
  Wiþ markys[9] and with pounde;
And al afftyr my dede,   660
Yngelond, to wysse and rede."
  Now iblessyd be þat stounde.

---

[1] along the line as far as the third. [2] severe pains. [3] befell that she sighed.
[4] lessened. [5] taken that horrible walk. [6] burst. [7] child. [8] open square (cf.
546). [9] marks (worth about thirteen shillings).

649. For a collection of documents about the saint, cf. "Corolla Sancti
Edmundi," F. Hervey, N. Y. 1907.

Þenne sayde þe Bysschop to þe Kyng,
"Sere, who made þis grete lesyng,
  And who wrouȝte al þis bale?" 665
Þanne sayde þe Kyng, "So moot i thee,
Þat schalt þou neuere wete for me,
  In burgh neyþer in sale;[10]
For i haue sworn be Seynt Anne
Þat i schal neuere bewreye þat manne 670
  Þat me gan telle þat tale.
Þey arn sauyd þorwȝ þy red:
Now lat al þis be ded,
  And kepe þis counseyl hale."[11]

Þenne swoor þe Bysschop, "So moot i the, 675
Now i haue power and dignyté
  For to asoyle þe as clene
As þou were houen[12] off þe ffount-ston:
Trustly[13] trowe þou þervpon
  And holde it for no wene.[14] 680
I swere boþe be book and belle,
But-ȝiff þou me his name telle,
  Þe ryȝt doom schal i deme:
Þy-selff schalt goo þe ryȝte[15] way
Þat þy broþer wente to day, 685
  Þouȝ it þe euele beseme!"[16]

Þenne sayde þe Kyng: "So moot i the,
Be schryffte[17] off mouþe telle i it þe;
  Þerto i am vnblyue.[18]
Sertaynly, it is non oþir 690
But Wymound, oure weddyd broþer;
  He wole neuere þryue."
"Allas," sayde þe Bysschop þan,

---

[10] hall. [11] secret intact. [12] raised. [13] confidently. [14] guess. [15] very same.
[16] though it ill befits you (a king). [17] confession. [18] reluctant.

669. St. Anne was the mother of the Virgin.
678. Medieval baptismal fonts were nearly always made of stone. At baptism, the child was purged of original sin, and hence became utterly guiltless for the moment.

"I wende he were þe treweste man,
    Þat euere ȝit leuyd on lyue.   695
And he wiþ þis ateynt[19] may bee,
He schal be hongyd on trees þree,[20]
    And drawen with hors ffyue."

And whenne þat þe Bysschop þe soþe hade,
Þat þat traytour þat lesyng made,   700
    He callyd a messaungere,
Bad hym to Doure þat he scholde founde
For to fette þat Eerl Wymounde:
    "Þat traytour has no pere.
Sey Egelane and hys sones be slawe,   705
Boþe ihangyd and todrawe;
    Doo as i þe lere.
Þe Countasse is in presoun done:
Schal sche neuere out off presoun come
    But-ȝiff it be on bere."[21]   710

Now wiþ þe messanger was no badde:[22]
He took his hors, as þe Bysschop radde,
    To Douere tyl þat he come.
Þe Eerl in hys halle he ffand:
He took hym þe lettre in his hand   715
    On hyȝ: wolde he nouȝt won[d]e.[23]
"Sere Egelane and his sones be slawe,
Boþe ihangyd and todrawe:
    Þou getyst þat eerldome.
Þe Countasse is in presoun done;   720
Schal sche neuere more out come,
    Ne see neyþer sunne ne mone."

Þanne þat Eerl made hym glade
And þankyd God þat[24] lesyng was made:
    "It haþ gete me þis eerldome."   725
He sayde, "Ffelawe, ryȝt weel þou bee.
Haue here besauntys[25] good plenté

---

[19] convicted of. [20] i.e., two upright beams and a cross-bar; gallows. [21] bier.
[22] delay. [23] hesitate. [24] that the. [25] besants (coins).

For þyn hedyr-come."²⁶
Þanne þe messanger made his mon:
"Sere, off ȝoure goode hors lende me on: 730
   Now graunte me my bone;
For ȝystyrday deyde my nobyl stede
On ȝoure arende²⁷ as i ȝede,
   Be þe way as i come."

"Myn hors be fatte and corn-fed,   735
And off þy lyff i am adred,"²⁸
   Þat Eerl sayde to hym þan,
"Þanne ȝiff myn hors scholde þe sloo,
My lord þe Kyng wolde be ful woo
   To lese swylk a man."   740

Þe messanger ȝit he brouȝte a stede,
On off þe beste at ylke a nede
   Þat euere on grounde dede gange,
Sadelyd and brydelyd at þe beste;
Þe messanger was ful preste;   745
   Wyȝtly on hym he sprange.
"Sere," he sayde, "haue good day:
Þou schalt come whan þou may.
   I schal make þe Kyng at hande."²⁹
With sporys faste he strook þe stede;   750
To Grauysende he come good spede:
   Is ffourly myle to ffande.

Þere þe messanger þe traytour abood,
And seþþyn boþe in same þey rod
   To Westemynstyr-wone.³⁰   755
In þe palays þere þay lyȝt,
Into þe halle þey come ful ryȝt,
   And mette wiþ Athelstone.
He wolde hauc kyssyd his lord swete;
He sayde: "Traytour, nouȝt ȝit lete,³¹   760

---

²⁶ for coming hither.   ²⁷ business.   ²⁸ i.e., a spirited horse might kill you.
²⁹ cause the king to be ready.   ³⁰ city.   ³¹ dare not to presume.
   751. Gravesend is east of London on the Thames.

Be God and be Seynt Ihon!
For þy falsnesse and þy lesyng
I slowȝ myn heyr, scholde haue ben kyng
When my lyf hadde ben gon."

Þere he denyyd faste þe Kyng   765
Þat he made neuere þat lesyng,
   Among hys peres alle.
Þe Bysschop has hym be þe hand tan;
Forþ in same þey are gan
   Into þe wyde halle.   770
Myȝte he neuere with crafft ne gynne[32]
Gare hym schryuen[33] off hys synne
   For nouȝt þat myȝte befalle.
Þenne sayde þe goode Kyng Athelston,
"Lat hym to þe ffyr gon   775
   To preue þe treweþe indede."

Whenne þe Kyng hadde sayd soo,
A gret ffyr was maad þoo,
   In romaunce as we rede.
It was set, þat men myȝten knawe,   780
Nyne plowȝ-lenge on rawe
   As red as ony glede.
Nyne syþis þe bysschop halewes[34] þe way
Þat þat traytour schole goo þat day,
   Þe wers hym gan to spede!   785
He wente ffro þe lengþe into þe þrydde,[35]
And doun he ffel þe ffyr amydde;
   Hys eyen wolde hym nouȝt lede.

Þan þe Eerlys chyldryn were war ful smerte[36]
And wyȝtly to þe traytour sterte   790
   And out off þe ffyr hym hade,
And sworen boþe be book and belle:
"Or þat þou deye, þou schalt telle

---

[32] trick. [33] confess. [34] consecrates. [35] as far along the line as the third. [36] very alert.

776. Zupitza proposed *treweþe wiþalle* for the rhyme.

Why þou þat lesyng made."
"Certayn, i can non oþer red,   795
Now i wot i am but ded:
   I telle ȝow noþyng gladde.[37]
Certayn, þer was non oþer wyte.[38]
He louyd hym to mekyl and me to lyte;
   þerffore enuye i hadde."   800

Whenne þat traytour so hadde sayde,
Fyue goode hors to hym were tayde[39]—
   Alle men myȝten see wiþ yȝe.
þey drowen hym þorwȝ ylke a strete,
And seþþyn to þe elmes, i ȝow hete,   805
   And hongyd hym ful hyȝe.
Was þer neuere man so hardy
þat durste ffelle hys ffalse body:
   þis hadde he ffor hys lye.
Now Iesu, þat is Heuene-kyng,   810
Leue neuere traytour haue betere endyng,
   But swych dome ffor to dye.

                 EXPLICIT.

---

[37] not willingly. [38] fault. [39] tied.

805. A grove of elms in Smithfield where criminals were executed.—Z.
812. *Dome* may be an error for *dede*, death.

GAMELYN

GAMELYN

The poem is important as a fore-runner of the Robin Hood Ballads, as a source of "As You Like It" (by way of Lodge's "Rosalynde"), and because Chaucer evidently contemplated using it in "The Canterbury Tales," in some of the manuscripts of which it is found.

The dialect is north midland of about the middle of the fourteenth century. Metrically, it inherits from Old English poetry the divided line, abundant alliteration, and a tendency to count accents, not syllables.

The text is that of Harleian Manuscript 7334, from Furnivall's edition in the *Chaucer Society Publications* (vol. 73). There are eight other manuscripts in existence. Skeat's edition (Oxford, 1893) should be consulted for copious notes, some of which have been used here.

Litheth, and lestneþ · and herkneþ aright,
And ȝe schul hecre a talkyng · of a doughty knight;
Sire Iohn of Boundys · was his right name;
He cowde of norture ynough · and mochil of game.
Thre sones þe knight [had] · þat with his body he wan;[1]   5
The eldest was a moche schrewe[2] · and sone he bygan.[3]
His breþeren loued wel here fader · and of him were agast;
The eldest deserued his fadres curs · and had it at þe last.
The goode kniȝt his fader · lyuede so ȝore,[4]
That deth was comen him to · and handled him ful sore.   10
The goode knight cared sore · sik þer he lay,
How his children scholde lyuen · after his day.
He hadde ben wyde-wher[5] · but non housbond he was;
Al þe lond þat he had · it was verrey purchas.[6]
Fayn he wold it were · dressed[7] amonges hem alle,   15

---

[1] begot.   [2] ruffian.   [3] i.e., to show it.   [4] long.   [5] far and wide.   [6] absolute ownership.   [7] divided.

1. "Hearken and listen," a frequent formula.
3. *Boundys* probably means "of the boundaries." It does not refer to any country.
13–4. He did not tend his land and gradually increase it; he bought it outright.

That ech of hem had his part · as it might falle.
Tho sent he into cuntré · after wise knightes
To helpe delen his londes · and dressen hem to rightes.
He sent hem word by lettres · þey schulden hye blyue,
Yf þey wolde speke with him · whil he was on lyue.   20
Tho þe knyghtes herden · sik þat he lay,
Hadde þey no reste · noþer night ne day,
Til þey comen to him · þer he lay stille
On his deþ-bedde · to abyde Goddes wille.
Þan seyde þe goode knight · syk þer he lay,   25
"Lordes, i ȝou warne · for soþ, wiþoute nay,
I may no lengere lyuen · heer in þis stounde;
For þurgh Goddes wille · deþ draweth me to grounde."
Ther nas non of hem alle · þat herd him aright,
Þat þey hadden reuþe · of þat ilke knight;   30
And seyde, "Sir, for Goddes loue · ne dismay ȝou nought;
God may do bote of bale · þat is now iwrought."
Then spak þe goode knight · sik ther he lay,
"Boote of bale God may sende · i wot it is no nay;
But i byseke ȝou, kniȝtes · for þe loue of me,   35
Goþ and dresseþ my lond · among my sones þre.
And sires, for þe loue of God · deleþ hem nat amys,
And forgetiþ nat Gamelyn · my ȝonge sone þat is.
Takeþ heed to þat on · as wel as to þat oþer;
Selde[8] ȝe see ony eyr · helpen his ʹbroþer."   40
Þo leete þey þe knight lyen · þat was nought in hele,[9]
And wenten into counseil · his londes for to dele;
For to delen hem alle · to oon, þat was her þought;
And for Gamelyn was ȝongest · he schuld haue nouȝt.
Al þe lond þat þer was · þey dalten it in two,   45
And leeten Gamelyn þe ȝonge · wiþoute lond go,
And ech of hem seyde · to oþer ful lowde
His breþeren might ȝeue him lond · whan he good cowde.[10]
Whan þey hadde deled · þe lond at here wille,
Þey come aȝein to þe knight · þer he lay ful stille,   50

8 seldom.   9 health.   10 reached years of discretion; usually about the age of
fourteen or fifteen.

21. Hl. þer; other MSS. þat.
30. The negative of l. 29 is to be carried over; a common construction.

And tolden him anon right · how þey hadden wrought;
And þe knight þere he lay · liked it right nought.
Than seyde þe knight · "By Seynt Martyn,
For al þat ȝe haue ydoon · ȝit is the lond myn.
For Goddes loue, neyhebours · stondeþ alle stille, 55
And i wil dele my lond · after my wille.
Iohan, myn eldeste sone · schal haue plowes[11] fyue,
That was my fadres heritage · whil he was on lyue;
And my myddeleste sone · fyf plowes of lond
That i halp for to gete · wiþ my right hond; 60
And al myn other purchas · of londes and leedes,[12]
þat i byqueþe Gamelyn · and alle my goode steedes;
And i byseke ȝow, goode men · þat lawe conne of londe,
For Gamelynes loue · þat my queste[13] stonde."
Thus dalte þe knight · his lond by his day, 65
Right on his deþ-bed · sik þer he lay;
And sone aftirward · he lay stoon stille,
And deyde whan tyme com · as it was Cristes wille.
And anon as he was deed · and vnder gras igraue,
Sone þe elder broþer · gyled þe ȝonge knaue; 70
He took into his hond · his lond and his leede,
And Gamelyn himselfe · to clothen and to feede.
He clothed him and fed him · yuel and eek wroþe,[14]
And leet his londes forfare · and his houses boþe;
His parkes and his woodes · and dede noþing wel; 75
And seþþen he it abought · on his faire fel.[15]
So longe was Gamelyn · in his broþeres halle,
For þe strengest, of good wil · þey doutiden him alle;[16]
þer was non þerinne · nowþer ȝong ne olde,
That wolde wraþþe Gamelyn · were he neuer so bolde. 80
Gamelyn stood on a day · in his broþeres ȝerde,[17]
And bygan wiþ his hond · to handlen his berde;[18]
He þought on his londes · þat layen vnsawe,[19]
And his faire okes · þat doun were idrawe.

---

[11] a measure of land. [12] serfs. [13] bequest. [14] ill. [15] paid for it with his skin.
[16] all avowedly (willingly) feared him as the strongest. [17] yard. [18] i.e., he
is of age.—Sk. [19] unsown.

53. St. Martin of Tours (fourth century).
71. Hl. *as his;* other MSS. *and his.*

His parkes were ibroken   ·   and his deer byreeued;   85
Of alle his goode steedes   ·   noon was him byleued;
His howses were vnhiled[20]   ·   and ful yuel dight;
Tho þoughte Gamelyn   ·   it wente nought aright.
Afterward cam his broþer   ·   walkynge þare,
And seyde to Gamelyn   ·   "Is our mete ȝare?"   90
Tho wraþþed him Gamelyn   ·   and swor by Goddes book,
"Thou schalt go bake þiself   ·   i will nouȝt be þy cook!"
"How? broþer Gamelyn   ·   how answerest þou now?
þou spake neuer such a word   ·   as þou dost now."
"By my faith," seyde Gamelyn   ·   "now me þinkeþ neede; 95
Of alle þe harmes þat i haue   ·   i tok neuer ar heede.
My parkes ben tobroken   ·   and my deer byreued,
Of myn armure and my steedes   ·   nought is me bileued;
Al þat my fader me byquaþ   ·   al goþ to schame,
And þerfor haue þou Goddes curs   ·   broþer, by þy name!"[21] 100
Than byspak his broþer   ·   þat rape was of rees,[22]
"Stond stille, gadelyng[23]   ·   and hold right þy pees.
Thou schalt be fayn for to haue   ·   þy mete and þy wede;
What spekest þou, Gamelyn   ·   of lond oþer of leede?"
Thanne seyde Gamelyn   ·   þe child þat was ying,   105
"Cristes curs mot he haue   ·   þat clepeþ me gadelyng!
I am no worse gadelyng   ·   ne no worse wight,
But born of a lady   ·   and geten of a knight."
Ne durst he nat to Gamelyn   ·   ner a foote go,
But clepide to him his men   ·   and seyde to hem þo,   110
"Goþ and beteþ þis boy   ·   and reueþ him his wyt,
And lat him leren[24] anoþer tyme   ·   to answere me bet."
Thanne seyde þe child   ·   ȝonge Gamelyn,
"Cristes curs mot þou haue!   ·   Broþer art þou myn,
And if i schal algate   ·   be beten anon,   115
Cristes curs mot þou haue   ·   but þou be þat oon!"[25]
And anon his broþer   ·   in þat grete hete
Made his men to fette staues   ·   Gamelyn to bete.

---

[20] unroofed.   [21] upon thy name.   [22] rage.   [23] vagabond.   [24] be taught.
[25] i.e., the one to beat me.

93. Omit *now?*
117. Hl. *þag.*

Whan þat euerich of hem · a staf had inome,
Gamelyn was war anon · þo he seigh hem come; 120
Þo Gamelyn seyh hem come · he loked oueral,
And was war of a pestel²⁶ · stood vnder a wal.
Gamelyn was light of foot · and þider gan he lepe,
And drof alle his broþeres men · right on an hepe.
He loked as a wilde lyoun · and leyde on good woon; 125
Tho his broþer say þat · he bigan to goon.
He fley vp intil a loft · and schette þe dore fast;
Thus Gamelyn wiþ þe pestel · made hem alle agast.
Some for Gamelynes loue · and some for his eyȝe,²⁷
Alle þey drowe by halues²⁸ · þo he gan to pleyȝe. 130
"What! how now!" seyde Gamelyn · "euel mot ȝe thee!
Wil ȝe bygynne contek²⁹ · and so sone flee?"
Gamelyn sought his broþer · whider he was flowe,
And saugh wher he loked · out at a wyndowe.
"Broþer," sayde Gamelyn · "com a litel ner, 135
And i wil teche þe a play · atte bokeler."³⁰
His broþer him answerde · and swor by Seynt Rycher,
"Whil þe pestel is in þin hond · i wil come no neer.
Broþer, i wil make þy pees · i swere by Cristes ore;
Cast away þe pestel · and wraþþe þe nomore." 140
"I mot neede," sayde Gamelyn · "wraþþe me at oones,
For thou wolde make þy men · to breke myne boones;
Ne had i hadde mayn · and might in myn armes,
To haue iput hem fro me · ·he wolde haue do me harmes."
"Gamelyn," sayde his broþer · "be þou nought wroþ; 145
For to seen þe haue harm · it were me right loþ.
I ne dide it nouȝt, broþer · but for a fondyng,³¹
For to loken or³² þou were strong · and art so ying."
"Com adoun þan to me · and graunte me my bone
Of þing i wil þe aske · and we schul saughte³³ sone." 150
Doun þan cam his broþer · þat fykil was and felle,
And was swiþe sore · agast of þe pestelle.

---

²⁶ a large instrument for grinding grain. ²⁷ awe of him. ²⁸ into two parties.
²⁹ quarrel. ³⁰ buckler. ³¹ test. ³² whether. ³³ be reconciled.

136. The swords and shields which were used at the game of sword and
buckler were frequently of wood.
144. All other MSS. *thei wolde.*

He seyde, "Broþer Gamelyn · aske me þy boone,
And loke þou me blame · but i graunte sone."
Thanne seyde Gamelyn · "Broþer, iwys,   155
And we schulle ben at oon[33] · þou most me graunte þis:
Al þat my fader me byquath · whil he was on lyue,
þou most do me it haue · ȝif we schul nat stryue."[34]
"That schalt þou haue, Gamelyn · i swere by Cristes ore!
Al þat þi fader the byquaþ · þough þou woldest haue more.[35]
Thy lond, þat lyþ laye[36] · ful wel it schal be sowe,   161
And þyn howses reysed vp · þat ben leyd so lowe."
Thus seyde þe knight · to Gamelyn wiþ mowthe,
And þought eek of falsnes · as he wel couþe.
The knight þought on tresoun · and Gamelyn on noon,   165
And went and kist his broþer · and whan þey were at oon,
Allas! ȝonge Gamelyn · noþing he ne wiste
Wiþ which a false tresoun · his broþer him kiste.
 Liþeth, and lestneþ · and holdeþ ȝour tonge,
And ȝe schul heere talkyng · of Gamelyn þe yonge.   170
Ther was þer bysiden · cryed[37] a wrastlyng,
And þerfor þer was sette vp · a ram and a ryng;
And Gamelyn was in good wil · to wende þerto,
For to preuen his might · what he cowþe do.
"Broþer," seyde Gamelyn · "by Seynt Richer,   175
Thou most lene me to-nyȝt · a litel courser
That is freisch to the spore[38] · on for to ryde;
I most on an erande · a litel her byside."
"By God," seyd his brother · "of steedes in my stalle
Go and chese þe þe best · and spare non of alle   180
Of steedes or of coursers · þat stonden hem bisyde;
And tel. me, goode broþer · whider þou wolt ryde."
"Her byside, broþer · is cryed a wrastlyng,
And þerfor schal be set vp · a ram and a ryng;
Moche worschip it were · broþer, to vs alle,   185

---

[33] be reconciled. [34] if we are not to quarrel. [35] i.e., and more if you should ask it. [36] fallow. [37] proclaimed. [38] spur.

165. Hl. *king.*

175. St. Richard, bishop of Chichester (13th century), was a pattern of brotherly love.—Sk.

181. Hl. *course;* others *coursers.*

Might i þe ram and þe ryng · bryng home to þis halle."
A steede þer was sadeled · smertely and skeet;[39]
Gamelyn did a paire spores · fast on his feet.
He set his foot in styrop · þe steede he bystrood,
And toward þe wrastelyng · þe ȝonge child rood. 190
Tho Gamelyn þe yonge · was ride out at þe gate,
The fals kniȝt his broþer · lokked it after þate,
And bysoughte Iesu Crist · þat is Heuen-kyng,
He mighte breke his nekke · in þat wrastlyng.
As sone as Gamelyn com · þer þe place was, 195
He lighte doun of his steede · and stood on þe gras;
And þer he herd a frankeleyn[40] · wayloway syng,
And bigan bitterly · his hondes for to wryng.
"Goode man," seyde Gamelyn · "why makestow þis fare?
Is þer no man þat may ȝou helpe · out of þis care?" 200
"Allas!" seyde þis frankeleyn · "þat euer was i bore!
For tweye stalworþe sones · i wene þat i haue lore;
A champioun is in þe place · þat haþ iwrought me sorwe,
For he haþ slayn my two sones · but if God hem borwe.[41]
I wold ȝeue ten pound · by Iesu Crist, and more, 205
Wiþ þe nones[42] i fand a man · to handil him sore!"
"Goode man," seyde Gamelyn · "wilt þou wel doon,
Hold myn hors whil my man · draweþ of my schoon;
And help my man to kepe · my cloþes and my steede,
And i wil into place go · to loke if i may speede." 210
"By God!" sayde þe frankeleyn · "anon it schal be doon;
I wil myself be þy man · and drawen of þy schoon,
And wende þou into þe place— · Iesu Crist þe speede—
And drede not of þy cloþes · nor of þy goode steede."
    Barfoot and vngert · Gamelyn in cam; 215
Alle þat weren in þe place · heede of him þey nam;
How he durst auntre him · of him to doon his might
That was so doughty champioun · in wrastlyng and in fight.
Vp sterte þe champioun · raply[43] and anoon;
Toward ȝonge Gamelyn · he bigan to goon, 220

---

[39] quickly. [40] freeholder. [41] restore. [42] if immediately. [43] quickly.

193. MS. reads ihū crist, throughout.
215. A wrestler's only costume was a breech clout.

And sayde, "Who is þy fader · and who is þy sire?
For soþe þou art a gret fool · þat þou come hire!"
Gamelyn answerde · þe champioun tho,
"Þou knewe wel my fader · whil he couþe go;⁴⁴
Whiles he was on lyue · by Seint Martyn!   225
Sir Iohn of Boundys was his name · and i, Gamelyn."
"Felaw," seyde þe champioun · "also mot i þryue.
I knew wel þy fader · whil he was on lyue;
And þiself, Gamelyn · i wil þat þou it heere,
Whil þou were a ʒong boy · a moche schrewe⁴⁵ þou were." 230
Þan seyde Gamelyn · and swor by Cristes ore,
"Now i am older woxe · þou schalt me fynd a more!"
"By God," sayde þe champioun · "welcome mote þou be!
Come þou ones in myn hond · schalt þou neuer þe."
It was wel wiþinne þe night · and þe moone schon,   235
Whan Gamelyn and þe champioun · togider gon to goon.
The champioun caste tornes⁴⁶ · to Gamelyn, þat was prest,
And Gamelyn stood stille · and bad him doon his best.
Thanne seyde Gamelyn · to þe champioun,
"Thou art fast aboute⁴⁷ · to brynge me adoun;   240
Now i haue iproued⁴⁸ · many tornes of þyne,
Thow most," he seyde, "prouen · on or tuo of myne."
Gamelyn to þe champioun · ʒede smartly anon;
Of alle þe tornes þat he cowþe · he schewed him but oon,
And kast him on þe left syde · þat þre ribbes tobrak,   245
And þerto his oon arm · þat ʒaf a gret crak.
Thanne seyde Gamelyn · smertly anoon,
"Schal it be holde for a cast⁴⁹ · or elles for noon?"
"By God," seyd þe champioun · "wheþer þat it bee,
He þat comes ones in þin hand · schal he neuer þee!"   250
Than seyde þe frankeleyn · þat had his sones þere,
"Blessed be þou, Gamelyn · þat euer þou bore were."
The frankleyn seyd to þe champioun · of him stood him
    noon eye,⁵⁰

⁴⁴ i.e., while he was alive. ⁴⁵ ruffian. ⁴⁶ tricks. ⁴⁷ trying hard. ⁴⁸ with-
stood. ⁴⁹ throw. ⁵⁰ the franklin stood in no awe of the champion.

237. The contestants locked arms around each other, and each tried to
force his opponent to release his hold or lose his balance and fall. Cf.
"Havelok" 984.

"This is yonge Gamelyn · þat taughte þe þis pleye."
Aӡein answerd the champioun · þat liked noþing well,   255
"He is alþer mayster · and his pley is riӡt fell;
Siþ i wrastled first · it is igo ful ӡore,
But i was neuere my lyf · handled so sore."
Gamelyn stood in þe place · allone wiþoute serk,[1]
And seyd, "If þer be eny mo · lat hem come to werk.   260
The champioun þat peyned him · to werke so sore,
It semeþ by his continaunce · þat he wil nomore."
Gamelyn in þe place · stood as stille as stoon
For to abyde wrastelyng · but þer com noon;
Ther was noon with Gamelyn · wolde wrastle more,   265
For he handled þe champioun · so wonderly sore.
Two gentilmen þer were · þat yemede þe place
Comen to Gamelyn— · God ӡeue him goode grace—
And sayde to him, "Do on · þyn hosen and þy schoon;
For soþe, at þis tyme · þis feire[2] is idoon."   270
And þan seyde Gamelyn · "So mot i wel fare,
I haue nought ӡet haluendel · sold vp my ware."
Tho seyde þe champioun · "So brouk i my sweere,
He is a fool þat þerof beyeþ · þou sellest it so deere."
Tho sayde þe frankeleyn · þat was in moche care,   275
"Felaw," he seyde, · "why lakkest[3] þou his ware?
By Seynt Jame in Galys · þat many man haþ sought,
Ӡet it is to good cheep[4] · þat þou hast ibought."
Tho þat wardeynes were · of þat wrastlyng
Come and broughte Gamelyn · þe ram and þe ryng,   280
And seyden, "Haue, Gamelyn · þe ryng and þe ram
For þe best wrasteler · þat euer here cam."
Thus wan Gamelyn · þe ram and þe ryng,
And wente wiþ moche ioye · home in þe mornyng.
His broþer seih wher he cam · with þe grete rowte,   285

[1] shirt. [2] fair. [3] decry. [4] too good a bargain.

256. Hl. a liþer; others, alþer, our alþer.
270. A proverb meaning that the things of the fair are all sold, and
there is no more business to be done.—Sk. This metaphor is continued
through the next eight lines.
277. The famous shrine of St. Iago de Compostella, in Galicia, northern
Spain.

And bad schitte þe gate · and holde him wiþoute.
The porter of his lord · was ful sore agast,
And stert anon to þe gate · and lokked it fast.
  Now litheþ, and lestneþ · boþe ȝong and olde,
And ȝe schul heere gamen · of Gamelyn þe bolde.   290
Gamelyn com þerto · for to haue comen in,
And þanne was it ischet · faste wiþ a pyn;[5]
Than seyde Gamelyn · "Porter, vndo þe yate,
For many good mannes sone · stondeþ þerate."
Than answerd þe porter · and swor by Goddes berd,   295
"Thow ne schalt, Gamelyn · come into þis ȝerde."
"Thow lixt,"[6] sayde Gamelyn · "so browke i my chyn."
He smot þe wyket[7] wiþ his foot · and brak awey þe pyn.
The porter seyh þo · it might no better be:
He sette foot on erþe · he bigan to flee.   300
"By my faiþ," seyde Gamelyn · "þat trauail is ilore,
For i am of foot as light as þou · þough þou haddest swore."[8]
Gamelyn ouertook þe porter · and his teene wrak,
And gert[9] him in þe nekke · þat þe bon tobrak,
And took him by þat oon arm · and þrew him in a welle, 305
Seuen fadmen[10] it was deep · as i haue herd telle.
Whan Gamelyn þe yonge · þus hadde pleyd his play,
Alle þat in þe ȝerde were · drewen hem away.
Þey dredden him ful sore · for werkes þat he wrouȝte,
And for þe faire company · þat he þider broughte   310
Gamelyn ȝede to þe gate · and leet it vp wyde;
He leet in alle maner men · þat gon in wold or ryde,
And seyde, "Ȝe be welcome · wiþouten eny greeue,
For we wiln be maistres heer · and aske no man leue.
Ȝestirday i lefte" · seyde ȝonge Gamelyn,   315
"In my broþer seller · fyue tonne[11] of wyn;
I wil not þat þis compaignye · parten atwynne,[12]
And ȝe will doon after me · while eny sope is þrynne;[13]
And if my broþer grucche[14] · or make foul cheere,

---

[5] bolt. [6] liest. [7] small gate in the portcullis. [8] sworn to the contrary.
[9] struck. [10] fathoms. [11] barrels. [12] asunder. [13] draught is therein. [14] grumble.

311. Opened the portcullis; he had kicked in the wicket.
316. In all MSS. numerals are regularly Roman.

Oþer for spense[15] of mete or drynk · þat we spenden heere, 320
I am oure catour[16] · and bere oure aller purs;
He schal haue for his grucchyng · Seint Maries curs.
My broþer is a nyggoun[17] · i swer by Cristes ore,
And we will spende largely[18] · þat he haþ spared ȝore;
And who þat makeþ grucchyng · þat we here dwelle, 325
He schal to þe porter · into þe draw-welle."
Seuen dayes and seuen nyght · Gamelyn held his feste,
With moche myrþ and solas · þat was þer and no cheste;[19]
In a litel toret · his brother lay isteke,[20]
And sey hem wasten his good · but durst he not speke. 330
Erly on a mornyng · on þe eighte day,
The gestes come to Gamelyn · and wolde gon here way.
"Lordes," seyde Gamelyn · "wil ȝe so hye?
Al þe wyn is not ȝet ydronke · so brouk i myn ye."
Gamelyn in his herte · was he ful wo, 335
Whan his gestes took her leue · from him for to go.
He wold þey had lenger abide · and þey seyde nay,
But bitaughte Gamelyn · God and good day.[21]
Thus made Gamelyn his fest · and brought it wel to ende,
And after his gestys · took leue to wende. 340
    Litheþ, and lestneþ · and holdeþ ȝoure tonge,
And ȝe schul heere gamen · of Gamelyn þe ȝonge;
Herkneþ, lordynges · and lesteneþ aright,
Whan alle gestes were goon · how Gamelyn was dight.
Al þe whil þat Gamelyn · heeld his mangerye,[22] 345
His broþer þought on him be wreke · wiþ his treccherie.
Tho Gamelyns gestes · were riden and igoon,
Gamelyn stood allone · frendes had he noon;
Tho after ful soone · wiþinne a litel stounde,
Gamelyn was itake · and ful hard ibounde. 350
Forþ com þe fals knight · out of þe selleer;[23]
To Gamelyn his broþer · he ȝede ful neer,
And sayde to Gamelyn · "Who made þe so bold

---

[15] cost. [16] caterer. [17] niggard. [18] freely. [19] quarreling. [20] fastened up.
[21] commended Gamelyn to God and bade him good day. [22] feast. [23] sollar,
upper chamber, but in 316, cellar.

326. I.e., a well from which water is drawn; *welle* commonly means
spring in Middle English.

For to stroye my stoor²³ · of myn houshold?"
"Broþer," seyde Gamelyn · "wraþþe þe right nouȝt,   355
For it is many day igon · siþþen it was bouȝt;
For, broþer, þou hast ihad · by Seynt Richer,
Of fiftene plowes of lond · þis sixtene ȝer,
And of alle þe beestes · þou hast forþ bred,
That my fader me biquath · on his deth-bed.   360
Of al þis sixtene ȝeer · i ȝeue þe þe prow,²⁴
For þe mete and þe drynk · þat we haue spended now."
Thanne seyde þe fals knyȝt— · euel mot he the—
"Herkne, broþer Gamelyn · what i wol ȝeue þe;
For of my body, broþer · geten heir haue i noon,   365
I wil make þe myn heir · i swere by Seint Iohn."
"Par ma foy," sayd Gamelyn · "and if it so be,
And þou þenke as þou seyst · God ȝelde it þe!"
Noþing wiste Gamelyn · of his broþeres gyle;
Therfore he him bigyled · in a litel while.   370
"Gamelyn," seyde he · "o thing i þe telle;
Tho þou þrewe my porter · in þe draw-welle,
I swor in þat wraþþe · and in þat grete moot²⁵
That þou schuldest be bounde · boþe hand and foot;
Therfore i þe biseche · brother Gamelyn,   375
Lat me nought be forsworn · brother art þou myn.
Lat me bynde þe now · boþe hand and feet
For to holde myn avow · as i þe biheet."
"Broþer," sayde Gamelyn · "also mot i þe,
Thou schalt not be forsworen · for þe loue of me."   380
Tho made þey Gamelyn to sitte · might he nat stonde,
Til þey had him bounde · boþe foot and honde.
The fals knight his broþer · of Gamelyn was agast,
And sent aftir feteres · to feteren him fast.
His broþer made lesynges · on him þer he stood,   385
And told hem þat comen in · þat Gamelyn was wood.
Gamelyn stood to a post · bounden in þe halle;
Tho þat comen in þer · loked on him alle.
Euer stood Gamelyn · euen vpright,
But mete ne drynk had he non · neiþer day ne night.   390

---

²³ waste the supplies.   ²⁴ profit.   ²⁵ anger.

Than seyde Gamelyn · "Broþer, by myn hals,[26]
Now i haue aspied · þou art a party fals;
Had i wist þat tresoun · þat þou haddest yfounde,
I wolde haue ȝeue þe strokes · or i had be bounde."
Gamelyn stood bounden · stille as eny stoon; 395
Two dayes and two nightes · mete had he noon.
Thanne seyde Gamelyn · þat stood ybounde stronge,
"Adam Spencer[27] · me þinkþ i faste to longe.
Adam Spencer · now i byseche þe,
For þe mochel loue · my fader loued þe, 400
Yf þou may come to þe keyes · lese[28] me out of bond,
And i wil parte[29] wiþ þe · of my free lond."
Thanne seyde Adam · þat was þe Spencer,
"I haue serued þy broþer · þis sixtene ȝeer;
If i leete þe goon · out of his bour, 405
He wolde say afterward · i were a traytour."
"Adam," sayde Gamelyn · "so brouk i myn hals,
þou schalt fynde my broþer · atte laste fals;
Therfor, broþer Adam · louse me out of bond,
And i wil parte wiþ þe · of my free lond." 410
"Vp[30] swich a forward," · seyde Adam, "iwys,
I wil do þerto · al þat in me is."
"Adam," seyde Gamelyn · "also mot i þe,
I wol hold þe couenaunt · and þou wil lose me."
Anon as Adames lord · to bedde was igoon, 415
Adam took þe keyes and leet · Gamelyn out anoon.
He vnlokked Gamelyn · boþe hand and feet,
In hope of auauncement · þat he him byheet.
Than seyde Gamelyn · "þanked be Goddes sonde!
Now i am loosed · boþe foot and honde; 420
Had i now eten · and dronken aright,
Ther is noon in þis hous · schulde bynde me þis night."
Adam took Gamelyn · as stille as ony stoon,
And ladde him into spence[31] · rapely and anon,
And sette him to soper · right in a priué stede; 425
He bad him do gladly · and Gamelyn so dede.

---

[26] neck. [27] steward. [28] release. [29] divide. [30] upon. [31] larder.

414. Hl. and most other MSS. omit *lose*.

Anon as Gamelyn hadde · eten wel and fyn,
And þerto ydronke wel · of þe rede wyn,
"Adam," seyde Gamelyn · "what is now þy reed?
Wher[32] i go to my broþer · and girde[33] of his heed?" 430
"Gamelyn," seyde Adam · "it schal not be so;
I can teche þe a reed · þat is worþ þe two.[34]
I wot wel, for soþe · þat þis is no nay:
We schul haue a mangery · right on Sonday.
Abbotes and priours · many heer schal be 435
And oþer men of holy chirche · as i telle þe.
Thow schalt stonde vp by þe post · as þou were hond-fast,
And i schal leue hem vnloke · awey þou may hem cast.
Whan þat þey haue eten · and waisschen here hondes,
Thou schalt biseke hem alle · to bryng þe out of bondes; 440
And if þey will borwe þe · þat were good game;
Then were þou out of prisoun · and i out of blame.
And if euerich of hem · say vnto vs nay,
I schal do anoþer[35] · i swere by þis day.
Thou schalt haue a good staf · and i wil haue anoþer, 445
And Cristes curs haue þat oon · þat faileþ þat oþer!"
"Ʒe, for Gode," sayde Gamelyn · "i say it for me,
If i fayle on my syde · yuel mot i þe.
If we schul algate · assoile hem of here synne,
Warne me, broþer Adam · whan i schal bygynne." 450
"Gamelyn," seyde Adam · "by Seynte Charité,
I wil warne þe byforn · whan þat it schal be.
Whan i twynk[36] on þe · loke for to goon,
And cast awey þe feteres · and com to me anoon."
"Adam," seide Gamelyn · "blessed be þy bones! 455
That is a good counseil · Ʒeuen for þe nones.
If þey werne[37] me þanne · to brynge me out of bendes,
I wol sette goode strokes · right on here lendes."[38]
Tho þe Sonday was icome · and folk to þe feste,
Faire þey were welcomed · boþe lest and meste; 460

---

[32] whether. [33] strike. [34] two of that. [35] something else. [36] wink. [37] deny.
[38] loins.

451. Saint Charity was the daughter of Saint Sophia, who named her
three daughters Faith, Hope, and Charity.—Sk.
456. Hl. Ʒeuyng.

And euer as þey atte halle · dore comen in,
They caste þeir eye · on ȝonge Gamelyn.
The fals knight his broþer · ful of trechery,
Alle þe gestes þat þer wer · atte mangery,
Of Gamelyn his broþer · he tolde hem with mouþe   465
Al þe harm and þe schame · þat he telle couþe.
Tho þey were serued · of messes[39] tuo oþer þre,
Than seyde Gamelyn · "How serue ȝe me?
It is nouȝt wel serued · by God þat al made,
That i sytte fastyng · and oþer men make glade !"   470
The fals knight his broþer · þer þat he stood,
Tolde alle his gestes · þat Gamelyn was wood;
And Gamelyn stood stille · and answerde nought,
But Adames wordes · he held in his þought.
Tho Gamelyn gan speke · dolfully wiþ-alle   475
To þe grete lordes · þat saten in þe halle:
"Lordes," he seyde · "for Cristes passioun,
Helpeþ brynge Gamelyn · out of prisoun."
Than seyde an abbot— · sorwe on his cheeke—
"He schal haue Cristes curs · and Seynte Maries eeke,   480
That þe out of prisoun · beggeþ oþer borwe;
But euer worthe hem wel · þat doþ þe moche sorwe."
After þat abbot · þan spak anoþer,
"I wold þin heed were of · þough þou were my broþer;
Alle þat þe borwe · foule mot hem falle !"   485
Thus þey seyde alle · þat were in þe halle.
Than seyde a priour— · yuel mot he þryue—
"It is moche skaþe,[40] boy · þat þou art on lyue."
"Ow !" seyde Gamelyn · "so brouk i my bon !
Now i haue aspyed · þat freendes haue i non.   490
Cursed mot he worþe · boþe fleisch and blood,
That euer do priour · or abbot ony good !"
Adam þe Spencer · took vp þe cloþ,
And loked on Gamelyn · and say þat he was wroth;
Adam on þe pantrye · litel he þought,[41]   495
But tuo goode staues · to hall-dore he brouȝt.
Adam loked on Gamelyn · and he was war anoon,

---

[39] courses.   [40] harm.   [41] i.e., thought of other things than serving food.

And cast awey þe feteres · and he bigan to goon.
Tho he com to Adam · he took þat oo staf
And bygan to worche · and goode strokes ȝaf. 500
Gamelyn cam into þe halle · and þe spencer boþe,
And loked hem aboute · as þey had be wroþe.
Gamelyn sprengeþ[42] holywater · wiþ an oken spire,[43]
That some þat stoode vpright · fel in þe fire.
Ther was no lewede man · þat in þe halle stood 505
That wolde do Gamelyn · enyþing but good,
But stood besyde · and leet hem boþe werche;
For þey hadde no rewþe · of men of holy cherche.
Abbot or priour · monk or chanoun[44]
That Gamelyn ouertok · anon þey ȝeeden doun. 510
Ther was non of hem alle · þat wiþ his staf mette
That he made him ouerþrowe · and quyt him his dette.
"Gamelyn," seyde Adam · "for Seynte Charité,
Pay large lyuerey[45] · for þe loue of me;
And i wil kepe þe dore · so euer here i masse! 515
Er þey been assoyled · þere schal noon passe."
"Dowt þe nought," seyde Gamelyn · "whil we ben in feere,
Kep þou wel þe dore · and i wol werche heere;
Stere[46] þe, good Adam · and lat þer noon flee,
And we schul telle largely[47] · how many þer be." 520
"Gamelyn," seyde Adam · "do hem but good;
þey ben men of holy chirche · draw of hem no blood.
Saue wel þe croune · and do hem non harmes,
But brek boþe her legges · and siþþen here armes."
Thus Gamelyn and Adam · wroughte right fast, 525
And pleyden wiþ þe monkes · and made hem agast.
Thider þey come rydyng · iolily wiþ swaynes,
And hom aȝen þey were ilad · in cartes and in waynes.[48]

---

[42] sprinkles. [43] spar, bar. [44] canon. [45] allowance (in food and clothing).
[46] bestir. [47] i.e., account for them all; knock all senseless. [48] wagons.

503. A reference to l. 449, as is also 516. *Spire* is probably a pun,
meaning (1) a club and (2) the aspergill, a bundle of twigs with which
holy water was sprinkled on the congregation.
504. The fireplace was in the middle of the hall floor; cf. Int. III.A.2.
512. Understand the negative from 511.
516. Hl. *schan* (probably for *schal ne*); other MSS. *schal(l)*.

Tho þey hadden al ydon · þan seyde a gray frere,
"Allas! sire abbot · what dide we now heere? 530
Tho þat we comen hider · it was a cold[49] reed;
Vs hadde ben better at home · wiþ water and breed."
Whil Gamelyn made ordres · of monkes and frere,
Euer stood his broþer · and made foul chere.
Gamelyn vp wiþ his staf · þat he wel knew, 535
And gert him in þe nekke · þat he ouerþrew;
A litel aboue þe girdel · þe riggebon tobarst;
And sette him in þe feteres · þer he sat arst.
"Sitte þer, broþer," · sayde Gamelyn,
"For to colyn[50] þy blood · as i dide myn." 540
As swiþe as þey hadde · iwroken hem on here foon,
They askeden watir · and wisschen anoon.
What some for here[1] loue · and some for awe,
Alle þe seruantȝ serued hem · of þe beste lawe.[2]
The scherreue was þennes · but a fyue-myle, 545
And al was ytold him · in a litel while,
How Gamelyn and Adam · had doon a sory rees,[3]
Bounden and iwounded men · aȝein þe kinges pees.
Tho bigan sone · strif for to wake,
And þe scherref aboute · Gamelyn for to take. 550
Now lytheþ and lestneþ · so God ȝif ȝou goode fyn,[4]
And ȝe schul heere good game · of ȝonge Gamelyn.
Four and twenty ȝonge men · þat heelden hem ful bolde
Come to þe schirref · and seyde þat þey wolde
Gamelyn and Adam · fetten away; 555
The scherref ȝaf hem leue · soþ as i ȝou say.
They hyeden faste · wold þey nought bylynne
Til þey come to þe ȝate · þer Gamelyn was inne.
They knokked on þe gate · þe porter was ny,
And loked out at an hol[5] · as man þat was sly. 560
The porter hadde byholde · hem a litel while;

[49] unprofitable. [50] cool. [1] of them. [2] according to best rules. [3] attack.
[4] ending. [5] peep-hole in the wicket.

531. Hl. omits *we*; others have it.
533. Satirical; the ceremony of ordaining priests and deacons was called "the laying on of hands."—Sk.
550. *About* takes the place of a verb of motion; cf. Int. VII.A.3.

He loued wel Gamelyn · and was adrad of gyle,
And leet þe wyket stonden · ysteke⁶ ful stylle,
And asked hem wiþoute · what was here wille.
For al þe grete company · þanne spak but oon,   565
"Vndo þe gate, porter · and lat vs in goon."
Than seyde þe porter · "So brouke i my chyn,
ȝe schul sey ȝour erand · er ȝe comen in."
"Sey to Gamelyn and Adam · if here wille be,
We wil speke wiþ hem · wordes two or þre."   570
"Felaw," seyde þe porter · "stond þere stille,
And i wil wende to Gamelyn · to witen his wille."
In went þe porter · to Gamelyn anoon,
And seyde, "Sir, i warne ȝou · her ben come ȝour foon;
The scherreues meyné · ben atte gate,   575
For to take ȝou boþe · schul ȝe na skape."
"Porter," seyde Gamelyn · "so moot i wel þe!
I wil allowe⁷ þe þy wordes · whan i my tyme se.
Go agayn to þe ȝate · and dwel wiþ hem a while,
And þou schalt se right sone · porter, a gyle."   580
"Adam," sayde Gamelyn · "looke⁸ þe to goon;
We haue foomen atte gate · and frendes neuer oon.
It ben þe schirrefes men · þat hider ben icome;
They ben swore togidere · þat we schul be nome."
"Gamelyn," seyde Adam · "hye þe right blyue,   585
And if i faile þe þis day · euel mot i þryue!
And we schul so welcome · þe scherreues men
That som of hem schul make · here beddes in þe fen."⁹
Atte posterne gate · Gamelyn out went,
And a good cart staf · in his hand he hente;   590
Adam hente sone · anoþer gret staf
For to helpe Gamelyn · and goode strokes ȝaf.
Adam felde tweyne · and Gamelyn felde þre;
The oþer setten feet on erþe · and bygonne fle.
"What," seyde Adam · "so euer here i masse!   595

---

⁶ fastened.   ⁷ reward for.   ⁸ be ready.   ⁹ mud.

588. Hl. *den;* others *fen.*
589 ff. They went out the postern, walked around, and made a flank
attack on the sheriff's men at the front gate.

I haue a draught of good wyn · drynk er ȝe passe!"
"Nay, by God!" sayde þay · "þy drynk is not good;
It wolde make mannes brayn · to lien in his hood."
Gamelyn stood stille · and loked him aboute,
And seih þe scherreue come · with a gret route. 600
"Adam," seyde Gamelyn · "what be now þy reedes?
Here comþ þe scherreue · and will haue oure heedes."
Adam sayde, "Gamelyn · my reed is now þis,
Abide we no lenger · lest we fare amys.
I rede þat we to wode goon · ar þat we be founde; 605
Better is vs þer loos · þan in town ybounde."
Adam took by þe hond · ȝonge Gamelyn,
And euerich of hem tuo · drank a draught of wyn,
And after took her coursers · and wenten her way;
Tho fond þe scherreue · nest but non ay.[10] 610
The scherreue lighte adoun · and went into þe halle,
And fond þe lord yfetered · faste wiþ-alle.
The scherreue vnfetered him · sone, and þat anoon,
And sent after a leche · to hele his rigge-boon.
  Lete we now þis fals knight · lyen in his care, 615
And talke we of Gamelyn · and loke how he fare.
Gamelyn into þe woode · stalkede[11] stille,
And Adam þe Spenser · liked ful ylle.
Adam swor to Gamelyn · by Seynt Richer,
"Now i see it is mery · to be a spencer. 620
That leuer me were · keyes for to bere,
Than walken in þis wilde woode · my clothes to tere."[12]
"Adam," seyde Gamelyn · "dismay þe right nought;
Many good mannes child · in care is ibrought."
And as þey stoode talkyng · boþen in feere, 625
Adam herd talkyng of men · and ŋeyh him þought þei were.
Tho Gamelyn vnder þe woode · loked aright,
Seuen score of ȝonge men · he saugh wel adight;
Alle satte atte mete · compas[13] aboute.
"Adam," seyde Gamelyn · "now haue we no doute; 630
After bale comeþ boote · þurgh grace of God Almight.

[10] egg. [11] went cautiously. [12] tear. [13] in a circle.

609. All other MSS. _cours._

Me þynkeþ of mete and drynk · þat i haue a sight."
Adam lokede þo · vnder woode-bowȝ,
And whan he seyh mete · he was glad ynough;
For he hopede to God · for to haue his deel,   635
And he was sore alonged[14] · after a good meel.
As he seyde þat word · þe mayster outlawe
Saugh Gamelyn and Adam · vnder woode-schawe.[15]
"ȝonge men," seyde þe maister · "by þe goode roode,
I am war of gestes · God send vs non but goode.   640
ȝonder ben tuo ȝonge men · wonder wel adight,
And parauenture þer ben mo · who-so loked aright.[16]
Ariseþ vp, ȝe ȝonge men · and fetteþ hem to me;
It is good þat we witen · what men þey bee."
Vp þer sterten seuene · fro þe dyner,   645
And metten with Gamelyn · and Adam Spenser.
Whan þey were neyh hem · þan seyde þat oon,
"ȝeldeth vp, ȝonge men · ȝour bowes and ȝour floon."[17]
Thanne seyde Gamelyn · þat yong was of elde,
"Moche sorwe mot he haue · þat to ȝou hem ȝelde!   650
I curse non oþer · but right myselue;
Þey[18] ȝe fette to ȝow fyue · þanne ȝe be twelue."[19]
Tho þey herde by his word · þat might was in his arm,
Ther was non of hem alle · þat wolde do him harm;
But sayd vnto Gamelyn · myldely and stille,   655
"Com afore our maister · and sey to him þy wille."
"Yonge men," sayde Gamelyn · "by ȝour lewté,[20]
What man is ȝour maister · þat ȝe wiþ be?"
Alle þey answerde · wiþoute lesyng,
"Oure maister is icrouned · of outlawes kyng."   660
"Adam," seyde Gamelyn · "go we in Cristes name;
He may neyþer mete ne drynk · werne vs for schame.
If that he be heende · and come of gentil blood,
He wol ȝeue vs mete an drink · and doon vs som good."
"By Seynt Iame," seyd Adam · "what harm þat i gete, 665

---

[14] stricken with desire.   [15] woods-thicket.   [16] if one looked carefully.   [17] arrows.   [18] though.   [19] i.e., twelve to two is fair odds.   [20] loyalty.

663. Noblemen were often outlaws; cf. Jusserand.

I wil auntre to þe dore · þat i hadde mete."
Gamelyn and Adam · wente forþ in feere,
And þey grette þe maister · þat þey founde þere.
Than seide þe maister · kyng of outlawes,
"What seeke ȝe ȝonge men · vnder woode-schawes?"   670
Gamelyn answerde · þe kyng wiþ his croune,
"He moste needes walke in woode · þat may not walke in
    towne.
Sire, we walke not heer · noon harm for to do,
But if we meete wiþ a deer · to scheete[21] þerto
As men þat ben hungry · and mow no mete fynde,   675
And ben harde bystad[22] · vnder woode-lynde."[23]
Of Gamelynes wordes · þe maister hadde rouþe,
And seyde, "Ȝe schal haue ynough · haue God my trouþe!"
He bad hem sitte þer adoun · for to take reste,
And bad hem ete and drynk · and þat of þe beste.   680
As þey sete and eeten · and dronke wel and fyn,
Than seyd þat oon to þat oþer · "Þis is Gamelyn."
Tho was þe maister outlawe · into counseil nome,
And told how it was Gamelyn · þat þider was icome.
Anon as he herde · how it was bifalle,   685
He made him maister vnder him · ouer hem alle.
Wiþin þe þridde wyke[24] · him com tydyng
To þe maister outlawe · þat þo was her kyng,
That he schulde come hom · his pees was imade;
And of þat goode tydyng · he was þo ful glad.   690
Tho seyde he to his ȝonge men · soþ for to telle,
"Me ben comen tydynges · i may no lenger dwelle."
Tho was Gamelyn anon · wiþoute taryyng,
Made maister outlawe · and crouned her kyng.

    Tho was Gamelyn crouned   kyng of outlawos,   695
And walked a while · vnder woode-schawes.
The fals knight his broþer · was scherreue and sire,
And leet his broþer endite[25] · for hate and for ire.
Tho were his bonde-men · sory and noþing glade,

---

[21] shoot at. [22] bestead. [23] forest-trees. [24] week. [25] indict.

666. There is no door; the phrase is probably proverbial. "Go up like
a wayfarer to an unfamiliar door."—Sk.

Whan Gamelyn her lord · wolues-heed[26] was cryed and
    made;   700
And sente out of[27] his men · wher þey might him fynde,
For to seke Gamelyn · vnder woode-lynde,
To telle him tydynges · how þe wynd was went,[28]
And al his good reued · and his men schent.
When þey had him founde · on knees þey hem sette, 705
And adoun wiþ here hood · and here lord grette:
"Sire, wraþþe ȝou nought · for þe goode roode,
For we haue brought ȝou tydynges · but þey be nat goode.
Now is þy broþer scherreue · and haþ þe baillye,[29]
And he haþ endited þe · and wolues-heed doþ þe crie." 710
"Allas!" seyde Gamelyn · "þat euer i was so slak
Þat i ne hadde broke his nekke · þo his rigge brak!
Goþ, greteþ hem wel · myn housbondes and wyf;[30]
I wol ben atte nexte schire[31] · haue God my lyf!"
Gamelyn came wel redy · to þe nexte schire,   715
And þer was his broþer · boþe lord and sire.
Gamelyn com boldelych · into þe moot-halle,[32]
And put adoun his hood · among þe lordes alle;
"God saue ȝou alle, lordynges · þat now here be,
But brokebak scherreue · euel mot þou þe!   720
Why hast þou do me · þat schame and vilonye,
For to late endite me · and wolues-heed me crye?"
Tho þought þe fals knight · for to ben awreke,
And leet take Gamelyn— · most he no more speke;
Might þer be no more grace · but Gamelyn atte last 725
Was cast into prisoun · and fetered ful fast.
Gamelyn haþ a broþer · þat highte Sir Ote,
As good a knight and heende · as mighte gon on foote.
Anon þer ȝede a messager · to þat goode knight,
And told him altogidere · how Gamelyn was dight. 730
Anon as Sire Ote herde · how Gamelyn was adight,
He was wonder sory · was he noþing light,
And leet sadle a steede · and þe way he nam,

---

[26] wolf's head, "an ancient Saxon formula of outlawry." [27] some of. [28] turned.
[29] bailiffship. [30] my farm-men and women. [31] shire-court. [32] judgment hall.

706. Drawing off the hood was a sign of respect to a superior.

And to his tweyne breþeren · anon right he cam.
"Sire," seyde Sire Ote · to þe scherreue þo,   735
"We ben but thre breþeren · schul we neuer be mo,
And þou hast yprisoned · þe best of vs alle;
Swich anoþer broþer[33] · yuel mot him bifalle !"
"Sire Ote," seide þe fals knight · "lat be þi curs;
By God, for þy wordes · he schal fare þe wurs !   740
To þe kynges prisoun · anon he is ynome,
And þer he schal abyde · til þe iustice come."
"Par de !" seyde Sir Ote · "better it schal be;
I bidde him to maynpris[34] · þat þou graunt him me
Til þe nexte sittyng · of delyueraunce,   745
And þanne lat Gamelyn · stande to his chaunce."
"Broþer, in swich a forthward · i take him to the;
And by þi fader soule · þat þe bygat and me,
But-if he be redy · whan þe iustice sitte,
Thou schalt bere þe iuggement · for al þi grete witte."   750
"I graunte wel," seide Sir Ote · "þat it so be.
Let delyuer him anon · and tak him to me."
Tho was Gamelyn delyuered · to Sire Ote his broþer,
And þat night dwellede · þat on wiþ þat oþer.
On þe morn seyde Gamelyn · to Sir Ote þe heende,   755
"Broþer," he seide, "i moot · forsothe fro þe wende,
To loke how my ȝonge men · leden here lyf,
Whether þey lyuen in ioie · or elles in stryf."
"By God," seyde Sire Ote · "þat is a cold reed !
Now i see þat al þe cark[35] · schall fallen on myn heed;   760
For whan þe iustice sitte · and þou be nought ifounde,
I schal anon be take · and in þy stede ibounde."
"Broþer," sayde Gamelyn · "dismaye þe nought,
For by Seint Iame in Gales · þat many man haþ sought,
If þat God almighty · hold my lyf and witt,   765
I wil be þer redy · whan þe iustice sitt."
Than seide Sir Ote to Gamelyn · "God schilde þe fro schame;

---

[33] i.e., as you. [34] ask in bail. [35] responsibility.

744. Hl. maympris.
754. Hl. dwelleden.
764. Cf. 277.

Com whan þou seest tyme · and bring vs out of blame."
Litheþ, and lestneþ · and holdeþ ȝou stille,
And ȝe schul here how Gamelyn · had al his wille.   770
Gamelyn wente aȝein · vnder woode-rys,[35]
And fond þere pleying · ȝonge men of prys.
Tho was ȝonge Gamelyn · glad and bliþe ynough,
Whan he fond his mery men · vnder woode-bough.
Gamelyn and his men · talked in feere,   775
And þey hadde good game · here maister to heere;
They tolden him of auentures · þat þey hadde founde,
And Gamelyn hem tolde aȝein · how he was fast ibounde.
Whil Gamelyn was outlawed · had he no cors;[36]
There was no man þat for him · ferde þe wors   780
But abbotes and priours · monk and chanoun;
Of hem left he noþing · whan he might hem nom.
Whil Gamelyn and his men · made merþes ryue,
The fals knight his broþer · yuel mot he þryue!
For he was fast about · boþe day and oþer,   785
For to hyre þe quest[37] · to hangen his broþer.
Gamelyn stood on a day · and as he biheeld
The woodes and þe schawes · in þe wilde feeld,
He þought on his broþer · how he him beheet
That he wolde be redy · whan þe iustice seet;   790
He þoughte wel þat he wolde · wiþoute delay,
Come afore þe iustice · to kepen his day.
And seide to his ȝonge men · "Dighteþ ȝou ȝare,
For whan þe iustice sitt · we moote be þare;
For i am vnder borwe[38] · til þat i come,   795
And my broþer for me · to prisoun schal be nome."
"By Seint Iame," seyde his ȝonge men · "and þou rede þerto,
Ordeyne how it schal be · and it schal be do."
Whil Gamelyn was comyng · þer þe iustice sat,
The fals knight his broþer · forȝat he nat þat,   800
To huyre[39] þe men on his quest · to hangen his broþer;
Though he hadde nought þat oon · he wolde haue þat oþer.
Tho cam Gamelyn · fro vnder woode-rys,

---

[35] wood-boughs.   [36] curse (from the common folk).   [37] bribe the jury.
[38] pledge; i.e., on bail.   [39] bribe.

And broughte wiþ him · his ȝonge men of prys.
"I se wel," seyde Gamelyn · "þe iustice is sette;   805
Go aforn, Adam · and loke how it spette."
Adam went into þe halle · and loked al aboute;
He seyh þere stonde · lordes gret and stoute,
And Sir Ote his broþer · fetered wel fast;
Þo went Adam out of halle · as he were agast.   810
Adam said to Gamelyn · and to his felaws alle,
"Sir Ote stant ifetered · in þe moot-halle."
"Ȝonge men," seide Gamelyn · "þis ȝe heeren alle;
Sir Ote stant ifetered · in þe moot-halle.
If God ȝif vs grace · wel for to doo,   815
He schal it abegge · þat broughte þertoo."[40]
Thanne sayde Adam · þat lokkes hadde hore,
"Cristes curs most he haue · þat him bond so sore!
And þou wilt, Gamelyn · do after my red,
Ther is noon in þe halle · schal bere awey his heed."   820
"Adam," seyde Gamelyn · "we wilne nought don so:
We wil slee þe giltyf · and lat þe oþer go.
I wil into þe halle · and wiþ þe iustice speke;
On hem þat ben gultyf · i wil ben awreke.
Lat non skape at þe dore · take, ȝonge men, ȝcme;[41]   825
For i wil be iustice þis day · domes to deme.
God spede me þis day · at my newe werk!
Adam, com on with me · for þou schalt be my clerk."
His men answereden him · and bad him doon his best,
"And if þou to vs haue neede · þou schalt fynd vs prest; 830
We wiln stande with þe · whil þat we may dure,
And but we werke manly · pay vs non hure."
"Yonge men," seyde Gamelyn · "so mot i wel þe!
As trusty a maister · ȝe schal fynde of me."
Right þere þe iustice · sat in þe halle,   835
In wente Gamelyn · amonges hem alle.
    Gamelyn leet vnfetere · his broþer out of beende.[42]
Thanne seyde Sir Ote · his broþer þat was heende,
"Thou haddest almost, Gamelyn · dwelled to longe,
For þe quest is oute on me[43] · þat i schulde honge."   840

---

[40] i.e., brought matters to such a pass.   [41] care.   [42] bonds.   [43] "verdict is delivered."

"Broþer," seyde Gamelyn · "so God ȝif me good rest,
This day þey schuln ben hanged · þat ben on þy quest;
And þe iustice boþe · þat is iugge-man,
And þe scherreue boþe · þurgh him it bigan."
Than seyde Gamelyn · to þe iustise, 845
"Now is þy power ydon · þou most nedes arise;
Thow hast ȝeuen domes · þat ben yuel dight,
I wil sitten in þy sete · and dressen hem aright."⁴⁴
The iustice sat stille · and roos nought anoon,
And Gamelyn · cleuede his cheeke boon. 850
Gamelyn took him in his arm · and no more spak,
But þrew him ouer þe barre · and his arm tobrak.
Durste non to Gamelyn · seye but good,
Forfered⁴⁵ of þe company · þat wiþoute stood.
Gamelyn sette him doun · in þe iustices sete, 855
And Sire Ote his broþer by him · and Adam at his feet.
Whan Gamelyn was iset · in þe iustices stede,
Herkneþ of a bourde⁴⁶ · þat Gamelyn dede:
He leet fetre þe iustice · and his fals broþer,
And dede hem come to þe barre · þat oon wiþ þat oþer. 860
Tho Gamelyn hadde þus ydoon · had he no rest,
Til he had enquered · who was on þe quest
For to deme his broþer · Sir Ote, for to honge;
Er he wiste which þey were · he þoughte ful longe.
But as sone as Gamelyn wiste · wher þey were, 865
He dede hem euerichone · fetere in feere,
And bringen hem to þe barre · and sette hem in rewe;⁴⁷
"By my faiþ," seyde þe iustice · "þe scherreue is a schrewe !"
Than seyde Gamelyn · to þe iustise,
"Thou hast yȝeue domes · of þe wors assise;⁴⁸ 870
And þe twelue sisours · þat weren of þe queste,
They schul ben hanged þis day · so haue i reste !"
Thanne seide þe scherreue · to ȝonge Gamelyn,
"Lord, i crie þe mercy · broþer art þou myn !"

---

⁴⁴ put in order. ⁴⁵ terrified. ⁴⁶ jest. ⁴⁷ row. ⁴⁸ of the worst quality.

843. Hl. *iugges man.*
856. Hl. *and two others sete.*

"Therefore," seyde Gamelyn · "haue þou Cristes curs, 875
For and þou were maister · ȝit i schulde haue wors."
For to make schort tale · and nouȝt to tarie longe,
He ordeyned him a queste · of his men so stronge;
The iustice and þe scherreue · boþe honged hye
To weyuen⁴⁹ wiþ ropes · and wiþ þe wynd drye; 880
And þe twelue sisours— · sorwe haue þat rekke!—
Alle þey were hanged · faste by þe nekke.
Thus ended þe fals knight · wiþ his treccherie,
That euer had ilad his lyf · in falsnes and folye.
He was hanged by þe nek · and nouȝt by þe purs;⁵⁰ 885
That was þe meede þat he had · for his fadres curs.
Sir Ote was eldest · and Gamelyn was ȝing,
Þay wenten wiþ here freendes · euen to þe kyng.
They made pees wiþ þe kyng · of þe best assise;¹
The kyng loued wel Sir Ote · and made him iustise. 890
And after, þe kyng made Gamelyn · boþe in est and west,
Chef iustice · of al his fre forest.
Alle his wighte ȝonge men · þe kyng forȝaf here gilt,
And sitthen in good office · þe kyng hem hath ipilt.²
Thus wan Gamelyn · his lond and his leede, 895
And wrak him of his enemys · and quyt hem here meede;
And Sire Ote his broþer · made him his heir,
And siþþen wedded Gamelyn · a wyf boþe good and feyr.
They lyueden togidere · whil þat Crist wolde,
And siþen was Gamelyn grauen vnder molde.³ 900
And so schal we alle · may þer no man fle;
God bryng vs to þe ioye · þat euer schal be.

---

⁴⁹ swing. ⁵⁰ i.e., did not buy off with a fine. ¹ on the best terms. ² put.
³ buried in the earth.

875. Hl. *Gamely.*
881. ". . . jurors—sorrow to him who pities them."

THE MATTER OF FRANCE

THE SULTAN OF BABYLON

This is a sample of the romance that gathered about Charlemagne and his court. The dialect is east midland of about 1400. The meter is unusual in its cadence and in having alternate rhyme; the odd-numbered lines are usually iambic with four stresses, but the even-numbered lines have either three or four stresses. Final -e is frequently pronounced.

The text and a few of the notes are from the edition of Dr. Hausknecht for the Early English Text Society. -R with a flourish has been expanded into -re, as that seems clearly the intention of the scribe.

In the first half of the story, here omitted, the Saracens sack Rome and then retreat to Spain, with Charlemagne in pursuit. In skirmishes before the city of Agremore, Roland and Oliver are captured by the Saracens, and the Sultan's son Ferumbras is captured and converted to Christianity by the French.

Nowe for to telle of Roulande
And of Olyuere, that worthy wos,
Howe thai were brought to þe Sowdan
By the Kinge of Boldas.
The Sowdan hem sore affrayned[1]   1495
What þat here names were.
Rouland saide and noght alayned:[2]
"Syr Roulande and Sire Olyuere,
Nevewes to Kinge Charles of Fraunce,
That worthy kinge and emperoure,   1500
That nowe are takyn by myschaunce
To be prisoneres here in thy toure."

---

[1] questioned closely.   [2] concealed.

1494. Lukafer, King of Baldas, "of Africa lord and governor," is one of the Sultan's chief vassals and advisers. Baldas probably means Bagdad; cf. Langlois. Babylon is Cairo, Egypt; cf. "Floris and Blancheflour."

"A, Olyuere, arte thou here
That haste my sone distroyede,[3]
And Rouland that arte his fere,   1505
That so ofte me hath anoyed?
To Mahounde i make a vowe here,
That to-morue, ere i do ete,
Ye shulle be flayn both qwik in fere,
And lives shalle ye bothe lete."   1510
Tho saide maide Florepas:
"My fader so dereworth[4] and dere,
Ye shulle be avysed of this cas,
How and in what manere
My brothir, þat is to prison take,   1515
May be delyuered by hem nowe,
By cause of these two knightes sake
That bene in warde here with you.
Wherefore i counsaile you, my fader dere
To have mynde of Sir Ferumbras.   1520
Pute hem in youre prison here,
Tille ye haue better space,[5]
So that ye haue my brother agayn
For hem þat ye haue here;
And certeyn elles wole he be slayn   1525
That is to you so lefe and dere."
"A, Floripp, iblessed thou bee;
Thy counsaile is goode at nede.
I wolde not leve my sone so free—
So Mahounde moost me spede—   1530
For al the realme of hethen Spayne,
That is so brode and large.
Sone clepe forth my gaylour[6] Bretomayne,
That he of hem hadde his charge.
Caste hem in your prison depe;   1535
Mete and drinke gyfe hem none;
Chayne hem faste, þat thay not slepe;
For here goode daies bene agone."

---

[3] i.e., Ferumbras.   [4] precious.   [5] i.e, more time to consult.   [6] jailer.

1527. This text follows the manuscript in abbreviating *Florıpas*.

Tho were thay cast in prison depe.
Every tyde the see came inne, 1540
Thay myght not see, so was it myrke;[7]
The watir wente to her chynne.
The salte watir hem greved sore;
Here woundis sore did smerte.
Hungir and thurste greved heme yet more; 1545
It wente yet more nere here herte.[8]
Who maye live withoute mete?
vi dayes hadde thay right none,
Ner[9] drinke that thay myght gete,
Bute loked vppon the harde stone. 1550
So on a daye, as God it wolde,
Floripas to hir garden wente
To geder'floures in morne colde.
Here maydyns from hir she sente,
For she herde grete lamentacion 1555
In the prison that was ther nye;
She supposed, by ymagynacion,
That it was the prisoners sory.
She wente here nerre to here more;
Thay wailed for defaute of mete. 1560
She rued on hem anoon ful sore;
She thought how she myght hem beste it gete.
She spake to her maistras[10] Maragounde,
Howe she wolde the prisoncres fcdc.
The develle of helle hir confounde! 1565
She wolde not assente to þat dede,
But saide, "Damesel, thou arte woode;
Thy fadir did vs alle defende,[11]
Both mete and drinke and othere goode
That no man shulde hem thider sende." 1570
Floripe bythought hir on a gyle;[12]
And cleped Maragounde anoon right
To the wyndowe to come a while

---

[7] dark. [8] hearts; i.e., affected their lives more. [9] nor. [10] governess. [11] for-bid. [12] trick.

1539. Hausknecht: read *dirke*.

And se ther a wonder syght:
"Loke oute," she saide, "and see aferre[13]   1575
The porpais[14] pley as thay were wode."
Maragounde lokede oute; Floripe come nere,
And shofed hire oute into the flode.
"Go there," she saide; "the devel the spede!
My counsail shaltowe never biwry.   1580
Whoso wole not helpe a man at nede,
On evel deth mote he dye!"
    She toke with hire maidyns two;
To Britomayne she wente hir waye,
And saide to him she moste go   1585
To viseten the prisoneris that daye;
And saide, "Sir, for alle loues,[15]
Lete me thy prisoneres seen.
I wole the gife both goolde and gloues,
And counsail[16] shalle it been."   1590
Brytomayne, that iaylor kene,
Answered to hir sone agayne
And saide, "Damesel, so mote i then,
Than were i worthy to be slayn.
Hath not youre fader charged me   1595
To kepe hem from every wyght?
And yet ye wole these traytours see!
I wole goo telle him anoon right."
He gan to turne him anone for to go,
To make a playnte on Floripas.   1600
She sued[17] him as faste as she myghte go,
For to gif him harde grace.[18]
With the keye cloge[19] þat she caught—
With goode wille she mente[20] than—
Such a stroke she hym there raught,   1605

---

[13] afar.   [14] porpoises.   [15] on the strength of your good will to me.   [16] a secret.   [17] followed.   [18] i.e., do him mischief.   [19] wooden block attached to keys.   [20] intended; i.e., (she struck) with a will.

1604. *Mente* is Hausknecht's emendation for MS. *maute*. The French reads: *Et Floripas le fiert, bien le sot aviser.* . . . But very possibly *smote* should be read; cf. 2011..

The brayne sterte oute of his hede-pan.²¹
To hire fader forth she goth
And saide, "Sire, i telle you here,
I saugh a sight that was me loth,
Howe the fals iailour fedde your prisonere,   1610
And how the covenaunte made was
Whan thai shulde delyuered be;
Wherefore i slough him with a mace.
Dere fadir, forgif it me!"
"My doghtir dere, that arte so free,   1615
The warde²² of hem now gif i the.
Loke here sorowe be evere newe
Tille that Ferumbras delyuered be."
  She thanked her fadere fele sithe,
And toke her maydyns, and forth she goth;   1620
To the prisone she hyed hire swyth.
The prison dore vp she dothe
And saide, "Sires, what be ye
That make here this ruly²³ moone?
What you lakkith, tellyth me?   1625
For we be here nowe alle alone."
Tho spake Roulande with hevy chere
To Floripe, that was bothe gente and fre,
And saide, "Lo, we two caytyfes²⁴ here
For defaute of mete dede moste be.   1630
vi dayes be comyn and goon
Sith we were loked in prison here,
That mete nor drinke hade we noon
To comforte with oure hevy chere.
But woolde God of myghtes moost   1635
The Sowdon wolde let vs oute goon:
We to fight with alle his ooste,
To be slayn in feelde anoon!
To murthir men for defaute of mete,
It is grete shame tille a kinge;   1640

---

²¹ skull.   ²² custody.   ²³ piteous.   ²⁴ captives.

1606. MS. *hede þan.*
1615. Read *trew*—H.

For every man most nedes ete,
Or ellis may he do no thinge."
Tho saide Floripe with wordes mylde,
"I wolde fayne ye were[25] now here;
From harme [and] skath[26] i wole you shelde,   1645
And gife you mete with right gode chere."
A rope to hem she lete down goon
That aboven was teyde faste;
She and hir maydyns drewe þer vppon,
Tille vp thay hadde hem at the last.   1650
She led hem into here chambir dere,
That arrayed for hem was right wele—
Both Roulande and Olyvere—
And gafe hem there a right gode mele.
And whan thay hadde eten alle her fille,   1655
A bath for hem was redy there;
Therto thay went ful fayre and stille,
And aftyr, to bedde, with right gode chere.
  Now Floripas chamber is here prisone,
Withouten wetinge[27] of the Sowdon;   1660
Thai were ful mery in that dongeon,
For of hem wiste man never oone.
Now lete we hem be and mery make
Tille God sende hem gode delyueraunce.
Aftir the tyme þat thay were take,   1665
What did Charles, the Kinge of Fraunce,
Therof wole we speke nowe;
Howe he cleped forth Sir Gy
And saide, "On my message shaltowe;[28]
Therfore make the faste redy   1670
To bidde the Sowden sende me my nevewes both
And the releqes also of Rome;
Or i shal make him so wroth,
He shall not wete what to done;
And by þat God þat hath me wroght,   1675

---

25 guard, protect. 26 harm. 27 knowledge. 28 sc. go.

1672. Ferumbras had removed the cross, crown, and nails of the cross
from St. Peter's to Agremore.

I shal him leve towre ner town.
This bargan shal so dere be bought
In dispite of his god Mahoun."
  Duke Neymes of Bauer²⁹ vp stert than
And saide, "Sir, hastowe no mynde³⁰   1680
How the cursed Sowdan Laban
Alle messengeris doth he shende?
Ye haue lost inowe; lese no mo;
Onworthily Olyuere and Roulande."
"By God, and thou shalt with him go,   1685
For al thy grete brode londe."
  Tho Ogere Danoys,³¹ þat worthy man,
"Sir," he saide, "be not wroth !
For he saith south." "Go thou than !
By Gode, thou shalte, be thou never so loth."   1690
  "A, Sire," quod Bery Lardeneys,³²
"Thou shalte hem se never more."
"Go thou forth in this same rees,³³
Or it shalle the repente ful sore."
  Folk Baliante saide to the Kinge,   1695
"Liste ye youre barons to lese?
Certis, this is a wondir thinge !"
"Go thou also; thou shalte not chese !"
  Aleroyse rose vp anone,
And to the Kinge þan gan he speke,   1700
And saide, "What thinke ye, sir, to done?"
"Dresse³⁴ the forth with hem eke !"

---

²⁹ Bavaria.   ³⁰ do you not remember.   ³¹ the Dane.   ³² Thierry d'Ardane.
³³ throng.   ³⁴ go.

1679. The knights whose names follow form, with Roland and Oliver,
the douzepers—twelve peers—ot Charlemagne. The list varies considerably in different accounts.

1680. The situation reverses the traditional one in the chansons, where,
instead of refusing, the knights are anxious to go. Cf. "Chanson de
Roland" 243 ff. The king has to forbid them.

1684. Understand "you have lost" from 1683.

1695. Mentioned only in this poem. Minstrels were not averse, for a
consideration, to substituting the names of their patron and members
of his family for those of minor characters; and hence the lesser folk in
any famous group do not remain the same in different episodes.

Miron of Brabane[35] spake an worde
And saide, "Sir, thou maiste do þy wille.
Knowist thou not that cruel lorde,　　　　　　　1705
How he wole thy barons spille?"
"Trusse the forth eke, sir dasaberde,[36]
Or i shalle the sone make!
For of all thinge thou arte aferde,
Yet arte thou neyther hurte ner take."　　　　　1710
　　Bisshope Turpyn[37] kneled adown
And saide, "Lege lorde, mercy!"
The Kinge him swore by Seynt Symon:[38]
"Thou goist eke; make the in hast redye!"
　　Bernarde of Spruwse,[39] þat worthy knyght,　1715
Saide, "Sir, avyse[40] you bette;
Set not of youre barons so light;[41]
Thou maiste haue nede to hem yette."
"Thou shalte goon eke for alle thy boost;
Haue done and make the fast yare!　　　　　　1720
Of my nede gyfe thou no coost;[42]
Therof haue thou right no care!"
　　Bryere of Mounteȝ,[43] þat marqwyȝ[44] bolde,
Was not aferde to him to speke.
To the Kinge sharply he tolde　　　　　　　　1725
His witte was not worth a leke.[45]
"Woltowe for angre thy barons sende
To þat tiraunte þat alle men sleith?
Or thou doist for þat ende:[46]
To bringe thy xii peres to the deth."　　　　　1730
The Kinge was wroth and swore in halle
By Him þat boght him with His blode:
"On my messange shall ye gon alle!
Be ye never so wroth or wode."
Thay toke here lefe, and forth thay yede;　　　1735
It availed not agayne him to sayne.
I pray God gif hem gode spede!
Ful harde it was to comen agayn.

---

[35] Brabant.　[36] get forth, sir simpleton.　[37] of Rheims.　[38] the apostle.　[39] Prussia?　[40] consider.　[41] i.e., set not such a low value on.　[42] cost, i.e., have no regard.　[43] Montdidier.　[44] marquis.　[45] leek.　[46] or else you intend merely this·

Nowe let hem passe, in Goddis name,
And speke we of the Sowdon: 1740
Howe he complayned him of his grame,[47]
And what that he myght beste done.
"Sortybraunnce and Bronlande," seyde he;
"Of counsail ye be fulle wyse.
How shal i do to avenge me 1745
Of Kinge Charles, and in what wyse?
He brennyth my toures and my citees,
And burges he levethe me never oon.
He stroieth my men, my londe, my fees;
Thus shalle it not longe goon. 1750
And yet me greveth most of alle
He hath made Ferumbras renay his laye.[48]
Therefore my counselors i calle,
To remedy this, howe thay best maye;
For me were lever that he were slayn 1755
Thane he a Cristen hounde shulde be,
Or with wolfes be rente and slayn
By Mahounde, myghty of dignyté!"
Tho answerde Sortybraunce and Broulande
And saide, "Gode counsaile we shal you gyfen; 1760
If thoue wilte do aftyr covenaunte,[49]
It shal you profit while you lyven.
Take xii knightis of worthy dede
And sende hem to Charles on message nowe.
Araye hem welle in roial wede, 1765
For thy honoure and for thy prowe.[50]
Bidde Charles sende thy sone to the
And voyde[1] thy londe in alle haste,
Or ellis thou shalt him honge on a tre
As hye as any shippes maste." 1770
"Nowe by Mahounde!" quod Laban,
"This counseil is both trewe and goode;
I shalle him leve[2] for no man

---

[47] wrath. [48] forswear his religion. [49] according to our advice. [50] advantage.
[1] vacate. [2] in double sense: leave alone, fail.

1757. This clause is the conclusion of l. 1755.
1759. H. reads to.

To parforme this, though he were woode."
He did his lettris write in haste;   1775
The knightes were called to goo þerwith,
That thay hyӡe hem to Charles faste
And charge hym vppon life and lithe.[3]
  Forth thai ride towarde Mantrible þan;
In a medowe was fayre and grene,   1780
Thai mette with Charles messageris ten.
Duke Neymes axed hem what thai wolde mene,
And saide, "Lordynges, whens come ye?
And whider ye are mente,[4] telle vs this tyde."
"From the worthy Sowdon," than saide he,   1785
"To Charles on message shalle we ride.
Euel tithyngges we shalle him telle
Fro Laban, that is lorde of Spayne.
Farewele, felowes; we may not dwelle."
"Abyde," quod Gy, "and turne agayne;   1790
We wole speke with you er ye goon,
For we be messengeris of his.
Ye shal aby, everichone;
So God brynge me to blis!"
Anoon here swerdes oute thay brayde   1795
And smoten down right al aboute
Tille the hethen were down layde;
Thai reseyued many a sore cloute.[5]
Thai smyten of here hedes alle;
Eche man toke one in his lappe: 1800
Fal what so euer byfalle,
To the Soudon wole they trappe.[6]
Tille thai come to Egremoure,
Thai stynte[7] for no worldes thinge.
  Anone thai fonde the Sawdan thore,   1805
At his mete proudely sittynge,
And þat maide faire Dame Floripas,

---

[3] command him upon (pain of losing) life and limb. [4] do you intend to go.
[5] blow. [6] go. [7] stopped.

1778. MS. *charke.*—H.
1779. Like many names in this poem, this is fictitious. It was reputed
to have a famous bridge.

And xiiii princes of grete price,
And Kinge Lukafere of Baldas,
That was both bolde, hardy, and wyse. 1810
Doughty Duke Neymes of Bauere
To the Sowdone his message tolde,
And saide "God, þat made heven so clere,
He saue[8] Kinge Charles so bolde
And confounde Laban and all his men 1815
That on Mahounde byleven,
And gife hem evel endinge, amen!—
To-morue, longe er it be even!
He commaundith the vppon thy life
His nevewes home to him sende, 1820
And the reliques of Rome, withoute strife;
And ellis getist thou an evel ende!
xii lurdeynes[9] mette vs on the waye;
Thai saide thay come streight fro the.
Thai made it[10] both stoute and gay; 1825
Here hedis here maistowe see.
Thai saide thai wolde to Charles goon,
Evel tidingges him to telle.
Loo! here here heddis euerychone;
Here soulis bene in helle." 1830
"O!" quod Lavane, "what may this be,
To suffre this amonge my knightes alle!
To be rebuked thus here of the
At mete in myn owen halle!
To Mahounde myghty i make a vowe, 1835
Ye shall be hanged alle ten,
Anoon as i have eten inowe,
In presence of alle my men."
Maide Floripas answered tho
And saide, "My derworth fadir dere! 1840
By my counsaile ye shal not so

---

[8] may He save. [9] knaves. [10] i.e., conducted themselves.

1810. Hausknecht reads *thas was.*
1816. MS. *byleved;* H. emends.
1821. MS. *Religes;* H. emends.

Tille ye haue your barons alle in fere,
That thai may se what is the best
For to delyuere my brother, Sir Ferumbras.
And aftirward, if þat ye liste,   1845
Ye may gife hem ful evel grace."
"Gramercy, doghter, thou saieste welle;
Take hem alle into thy warde.
Do feter hem faste in iren and stele
And set hem in stray3te garde.[11]   1850
Thus was i neuer rebukede er nowe;
Mahounde myghty gyfe hem sorowe!
Thay shalle be flayn[12] and honged on a bowe,
Longe ere prime to morowe."
Florip toke these messangeris   1855
And ladde hem vp into here toure,
There thai founde two of here feris;
Thay thanked thereof God of honoure.
Tho sayde Duke Neymys of Bauere:
"Gladde men we be nowe here   1860
To fynde Roulande and Olyuere
In helthe of bodye and of goode chere."
Thai kissed eche other with herte gladde
And thanked God of His grace;
And eche toolde othir howe thay sped hadde,   1865
And howe thay come into that place
By helpe of Mayde Florip hireself.
"God kepe hir in honoure!
For thus hath she brought vs hider alle twelfe,
To dwelle in hir owen boure."   1870
Tho thay wessh[13] and wente to mete,
And were served welle and fyne
Of suche goode as she myght gete,
Of venyson, brede, and gode wyne.
There thai were gladde and wel at ease;   1875
The Soudon ne wist it noght.
Aftyr thay slepe and toke her ese;

---

[11] strict   confinement.   [12] flayed.   [13] washed.

1854. MS. *tyme.*

Of no man than thay ne roght.
On the morowe Florip, that mayde fre,
To Duke Neymes spake in game: 1880
"Sir gentil knight," tho saide she,
"Telle me, what is your name."
"Whi axe[14] ye, my lady dere,
My name here to knowe alle?"
"For ye spake with so bolde chere   1885
To my fadir yestirdaye in his halle.
Be not ye the Duke of Burgoyne, Sir Gy,
Nevewe unto the Kinge Charles so fre?"
"Noe, certes, lady, it is not i;
It is yondir knight, þat ye may see."   1890
"A, him have i loved many a day;
And yet knowe i him noght.
For his loue i do alle that i maye
To chere you with dede and thought.
For his love wille i cristenede be   1895
And lefe Mahoundes laye.[15]
Spekith to him nowe for me,
As i you truste maye;
And but he wole graunte me his loue,
Of you askape shalle none here.   1900
By Him þat is almyghty aboue,
Ye shalle abye it ellis ful dere!"
Tho wente Duke Neymes to Sir Gye
And saide, "This ladye loveth the;
For thy loue she maketh us alle merye,   1905
And baptizede wole she be.
Ye shalle hir take to your wedded wife,
For alle vs she may saue."
"By God!" quod Gye, "þat gafe me life,
Hire wole i never haue;   1910
Wyle i neuer take hire ner no woman,
But Charles the Kinge hir me gife.
I hight him, as i was trewe man,

---

14 ask.   15 law, religion.

1885. MS. *he spake.*—H.

To holden it while i lyve."
Tho spake Roulande and Olyuere,   1915
Certyfyinge him of here myschefe,[16]
Tellinge him of the parelles[17] þat þay in were,
For to take this lady to his wedded wife.
"But thou helpe in this nede,
We be here in grete doute.   1920
Almyghty God shalle quyte thy mede;
Elles come we nevere hennys oute."
Thus thay treted[18] him to and fro;
At the laste he sayde he wolde.
Floripas thay cleped forth tho;   1925
And brought fourth a cuppe of golde,
Ful of noble myghty wyne,
And saide, "My loue and my lorde,
Myn herte, my body, my goode is thyn;"
And kissed him with that worde,   1930
And, "Sir," she saide, "drinke to me,
As the gyse[19] is of my londe;
And i shalle drinke agayn to the,
As to my worthy hosbonde."
Thay clipped and kissed both in fere   1935
And made grete ioye and game,
And so did alle that were there;
Thai made ful mery alle in same.
Tho spake Floripas to the barons boolde
And saide, "I haue armure inowe;   1940
Therfore i tel you what i wolde
þat ye dide for your prowe.[20]
To-morue, whan my fadir is at his soupere,
Ye shalle come in alle att onys;[21]
Loke ye spare for no fere;[22]   1945
Sle down and breke both bake and bones;
Kithe you knightis of hardynesse!
Ther is none helpe but in this wyse;

---

[16] assuring him of their misfortune.   [17] perils.   [18] argued with.   [19] custom.
[20] advantage.   [21] at once.   [22] i.e., don't spare on account of fear; strike
down, etc.

1942. MS. And þat.

Then moste ye shewen youre prowes,
And wynne this castel in this guyse."[23]   1950
Thai sayden alle it was welle saide,
And gladde thay were of this counsaile.
Here armure was forth layde
At souper the Sowdon to assaile.
Kinge Lucafere prayde the Sawdon   1955
That he wolde gif him lysence
To the prisoners for to goon,
To see the maner of her presence.
He gafe him lefe, and forth he wente
Vp vnto Floripas toure.   1960
To asspie the maner was his entent,
Hem to accuse agayne honoure.
Whan he come, he founde the dore fast istoke,[24]
He smote thereon with his fist,
That the barre began to broke.   1965
To make debate wel him list.
"Who artowe," quod Floripas,
"Þat maketh here such afraye?"[25]
"I am Kinge Lucafere of Baldas;
The Sowdon sente me hidir in faye;   1970
To seen his prisoneris is my desire,
And speke with hem everychon,
To talke with hem by the fire,
And speke of dedis of armes amonge."
Tho saide Duke Neymes, "Welcome be ye   1975
To us prisoners here!
What is your wille nowe telle ye;
For we be men of feble chere."
"I woolde wete of Charles the Kinge,
What man he is in his contré,   1980
And what meyné he hath, and of what thinge
He rekyneth moost his dignyté."
Duke Neymes saide, "An emperoure

---

[23] manner.   [24] shut.   [25] onslaught.

1963. Probably the right rhymes are *isteke; breke.*
1968. MS. *araye.*

And kinge he is of many a londe,
Of citeis, castels, and many a toure,   1985
Dukes, erles, barons bowynge to his honde."
"But saye me, felowe, what is your vse,
To do in contré[26] aftyr the none.
And what is the custome of your hous
Tille men to souper shalle gone?"   1990
"Sir, somme men iouste with spere and shelde,
And somme men carol[27] and singe gode songes;
Some shote[28] with dartis in the feelde,
And somme play at chesse amonge."
"Ye bene but foulis of gode dissporte;[29]   1995
I wole you tech a newe play.
Sitte down here by one assorte,[30]
And better myrthe never ye saye."
He teyde a tredde[31] on a pole
With an nedil theron ifest,   2000
And ther vppon a qwik cole;
He bade every man blowe his blast.
Duke Neymes hade a long berde;
Kinge Lucafere blewe even to hym;
That game hade he never before lered.   2005
He brent the here of Neymes berde to the skyne.
Duke Neymes than gan wex wroth
For he hade brente his berde so white;
To the chymneye forth he goth
And caught a bronde,[32] him with to smyte.   2010
With a goode wille he him smote
That both his eyen bresten oute.
He caste him in the fire al hote;
For sothe he hadde a right gode cloute.[33]
And with a fyre-forke[34] he helde him doune,   2015
Tille he were rosted to colis ilkadele;
His soule hade his god Mahoun.
Florip bade him warme him wele.
"Sires," tho saide Floripas,

---

[26] i.e., your country. [27] dance. [28] i.e., cast at a mark. [29] fools at amusing yourselves. [30] together. [31] thread. [32] a burning brand. [33] blow. [34] large fork used in making fires.

"Entendith[35] nowe al to me!   2020
This Lucafere of Baldas
Was a lorde of grete mayné:
My fadir hade him euer yn chere;
I telle you for sothe everydele,
He wolde anoon aftyr him enquere;   2025
And therefore loke ye arme you well!"
Florip wente in, as the maner was,
To here fadir at souper tyme.
No man spake worde of Kinge Baldas,
Ner no man knewe of his sharp pyne.   2030
The xii peris armed hem wel and fyne
With swerdes drawe and egre chere.
While thay mery[36] drinkyng the wyne
And sittinge alle at here soupere,
Thai reheted[37] the Sowdon and his barons alle   2035
And maden orders wondir fast;
Thai slowe down alle þat were in the halle,
And made hem wondirly sore agast.
Olyvere egerly sued[38] Laban
With swerd idrawe in his honde.   2040
Oute at the wyndowe lepte he þan
Vppon the salte see stronde,
And he skaped away from hime;
But woo was he[39] þerfore,
That he went awaye with lym   2045
To worche hem sorowe more.
Roulande than came rennynge
And axed where was Laban.
Olyvere answerede moornynge,
And saide howe he was agoon.   2050
Tho thai voided the courtes at the last
And slowen tho that wolde abyde,

---

[35] listen.   [36] make merry.   [37] assailed.   [38] followed.   [39] Oliver; the next *he* is Laban.

2036. *Maden orders* is a humorous way of saying "struck"; the reference is to the ceremony of the "laying on of hands" in installation into religious orders; cf. "Gamelyn" 533; "Bevis" 1869.
2042. MS. *strowde.*

And drewe the brigge and teyed it fast,
And shitte the gatis that were so wyde.
Laban, that by the ebbe escapede,   2055
Of harde,[40] er he come to londe;
He alle astonyed and awapide,[41]
For sorowe he wronge both his honde,
And made a vowe to Mahounde of myght
He wolde that cité wynne   2060
And never go thens by day nor nyght,
For foo, for frende, ner for kynne.
"And tho traytouris will i do honge
On a galowes hye withoute the gate;
And my doghter, þat hore stronge,[42]   2065
Ibrente shal be thereate."
To Mauntryble he gan sende anoon
Aftir men and tentis goode
And engynes to throwe with stoon
And goode armure many foolde.[43]   2070
The sege he did leyen abowte
On every side of that cité.
To wallis with engynes thai gan rowte,[44]
To breke the toures so fre.
Tho saide Florip, "Lordingges goode,   2075
Ye bene biseged in this toure;
As ye bene wight of mayne and moode,
Proveth here to saue youre honoure.
The toure is stronge, drede you nought,
And vitayle[45] we have plenté.   2080
Charles wole not leve you vnsought;
Truste ye welle alle to me.
Therefore go we soupe and make merye,
And takith ye alle your ease;
And xxx[ti] maydens, lo, here of Assye,[46]   2085
The fayrest of hem ye chese.

---

[40] heard it.   [41] amazed.   [42] vile wanton.   [43] in plenty.   [44] crowd.   [45] provisions.
[46] Asia.

2055. The flood tides cause the moat to fill with water; cf. 1504.
2057. MS. *a-mapide;* Hausknecht's emendation.
2085. MS. *Assyne.*

Take your sporte; and kith you knyghtes
Whan ye shalle haue to done;[47]
For to-morowe, when the day is light,
Ye mooste to the wallis goon   2090
And defende this place with caste of stoon
And with shotte of quarelles[48] and darte.
My maydyns and i shall bringe goode wone,[49]
So eueryche of us shalle bere hir parte."
On morowe the Sowdon made assaute   2095
To hem that were withinne,
And certes in hem was no defaute,
For of hem myght thay nought wynne.
Here shotte, here cast was so harde,
Thay durste not nyȝhe the walle.   2100
Thay drowen hem bakwarde;
Thay were beten overalle.
King Laban turnede to his tentes agayn;
He was nere wode for tene;
He cryede to Mahounde and Apolyne   2105
And to Termagaunte þat was so kene,
And saide "Ye goddes, ye slepe to longe;
Awake and helpe me nowe,
Or ellis i may singe of sorowe a songe,
And of mournynge right inowe.   2110
Wete ye not wele that my tresoure
Is alle withinne the walle?
Helpe me nowe, i saye therfore,
Or ellis i forsake you alle."
He made grete lamentacion;   2115
His goddis byganne to shake;
Yet that comfortede his medlacion,
Supposinge thay didde awake.

The Sultan decides to cut off Charlemagne's relieving expedition by ordering the giant Alagolofur to keep the bridge of Mantrible against the French. A messenger is sent to speak with Alagolofur.

Alagolofur rolled his yen   2175
    And smote with his axe on the stone,

---

[47] (to-morrow) prove yourselves knights when work is to be done. [48] bolts.
[49] plenty (of ammunition).

And swore by Termagaunte and Apolyne
That thereby shulde passen never one:
But-if he smote of his hede
And brought it to his lorde Laban,   2130
He wolde never ete no brede,
Nere never loke more on man.
xxiiii^ti cheynes he didde ouerdrawe[50]
That noo man passe myght
Neyther for loue nere for awe,[1]   2185
No tyme by daye nere by nyghte.
"Go, telle my lorde i shalle it kepe
On payne of my grete heede;[2]
Shalle ther no man goo ner crepe,
But he be take or dede."   2190
This geaunte hade a body longe
And hede like an libarde.[3]
Therto he was devely[4] stronge;
His skynne was blake and harde.
Of Ethiope he was bore,   2195
Of the kinde of Ascopartes.
He hade tuskes like a bore,
An hede like a liberde.
Laban nolde not forgete
The saute[5] to renewe;   2200
To wynne the toure he wolde not lete
Here trumpes lowde thay blewe;
Every man wente to the walle
With pikeys or with bowe;
Thai made assaute generalle,   2205
The walles downe to throwe.
But thay withinne bare hem soo,
Thay slowe of the Saresyns iii hundred.
Thay wroghten hem both care and woo;
Vppon her fightinge thay wondride.   2210

---

[50] he drew twenty-four chains across the bridge.   [1] fear.   [2] on pain (of losing)
my great head.   [3] leopard.   [4] duly.   [5] assault.

2183. The number is to be read "four and twenty."
2196. The Ascoparts were a race of giants. Cf. "Bevis of Hamtoun."

Tho cryed Laban to hem on hye,
"Traytours, yelde you to me;
Ye shall be hongede els by and bye
Vppon an hye galowe-tree."
Tho spake Florip to the Sowdon   2215
And sayde, "Thou fals tyraunte,
Were Charles come, thy pride were done
Nowe, cursede myscreaunte.
Alas! that hou ascapediste soo
By the wyndowe vppon the stronde;   2220
That thy nek hade broke a-twoo!
God sende the shame and shonde!"[6]
"A! stronge hore, God gife the sorowe!
Tho[u] venemouse serpente.
Withe wilde horses thou shalt be drawe to-morowe   2225
And on this hille be brente,
That al men may be ware by the,
That cursed bene of kynde.[7]
And thy love shalle honged be,
His hondes bounde him byhynde."   2230
He called forth Mavon, his engynoure,
And saide, "I charge the
To throwe a magnelle[8] to yon toure
And breke it downe on thre."
Mavon set vp his engyne   2235
With a stoon of vi c wight,[9]
That wente as even as eny lyne
And smote a cornell[10] down right.
Woo was Roulande and Olyuere
That þat myschief was befalle,   2240
And so were alle the xii peres;
But Florip than comforte hem alle:
"Sires," she saide, "beith of goode chere:
This toure is stronge inowe.
He may cast twies or thries or he hit ayen þer,   2245
For sothe i telle it you."

[6] harm.   [7] i.e., are unnatural.   [8] catapult.   [9] six hundredweight.   [10] battlement.

2225. This punishment was usually reserved for men.

Marsedage, the roialle kinge,
Rode in riche weede,
Fro Barbary commyng
Vppon a sturdy stede, 2250
Cryinge to hem vppon the walle:
"Traytouris, yelde you here!
Brenne you alle ellis i shalle,
By myghty god Iubytere."
Gy aspied that he came nere; 2255
A darte to hime he threwe ful even;
He smote him throwe herte and liver in fere.
Dame Floripe lough with loude steven,[11]
And saide, "Sir Gye, my loue so free,
Thou kanste welle hit the prikke.[12] 2260
He shall make no booste in his contré;
God giffe him sorowe thikke!"
Whan Laban herde of this myschief,
A sory man was he.
He trumped his mené to relefe;[13] 2265
For to cease that tyme mente he.
Mersadage, Kinge of Barbarye,
He did carye to his tente,
And beryed him by right of Sarsenye
With brennynge fire and riche oynemente, 2270
And songe the dirige of Alkaron,[14]
That bibill is of here laye,[15]
And wayled his deth everychon,
vii nyghtis and vii dayes.
Anoon the Sowdon, south to say, 2275
Sente iii hundrid of knightis
To kepe the brigge and the waye
Oute of that castil rightis,
That noon of hem shulde issue oute
To feche vitayle by no waye. 2280
He charged hem to wacche wel all abowte,
That thay forfamelid[16] myght dye.
Thus thay kepte the place vii dayes,

---

[11] voice. [12] bull's eye of a target. [13] i.e., sounded a trumpet for a retreat.
[14] dirge of the Koran. [15] religion. [16] starved.

Tille alle hire vitaile was nyȝe spente.[17]
The yates thai pas the streyte weyes.   2285
Tho helde thai hem within ishente.
Tho spake Roulande with hevy chere
Woordes lamentable,
Whan he saugh the ladies so whiȝte of lere
Faile[18] brede on here table,   2290
And saide, "Charles, thou curteys kinge,
Why forgetist thou vs so longe?
This is to me a wondir thinge;
Me thinkith thou doiste vs grete wronge
To let vs dye for faute of mete,   2295
Closed thus in a dongeon.
To morowe wol we asaye what we kon gete,
By God, that berithe the crown."
Tho saide Floripas, "Sires, drede noghte
For noon houngre that may befalle.   2300
I knowe a medycyne in my thoughte
To comforte you with alle.
I have a girdil in my forcere,[19]
Whoso girde hem therwith aboute,
Hunger ner thirste shal him neuer dere,   2305
Though he were vii yere withoute."
"O," quod Sir Gy, "my loue so trewe,
Iblessed mote ye be!
I pray you that ye wole us alle hit shewe,
That we may haue oure saulé."[20]   2310
She yede and set it forth anoon;
Thai proved alle the vertue,[21]
And diden it aboute hem euerychon.
It comforted alle, both moo and fewe,
As thai hade bene at a feste.   2315
So were thay alle wele at ease;
Thus were thai refresshed, both moost and lest

---

[17] exhausted.   [18] lack.   [19] coffer, chest.   [20] fill.   [21] power.

2285. Probably *pas* should read *par*, bar, close.

2303 ff. On the Saracen princess's understanding of magic, cf. Dickman 96. On the magic girdle, cf. G. L. Kittredge, "Sir Gawain and the Green Knight" 139.

And weren bifore in grete disese.
Laban wondred how thai myght endure
Withouten vitaile so longe.   2320
He remembred him on Floripas sencture,[22]
And of the vertue so stronge.
Tho wiste he welle that throgh famyne
Might he hem never wynne.
He cleped to him fals Mapyne,   2325
For he coude many a fals gynne.[23]
He coude scale castel and toure
And over the walles wende.
"Mapyne," he saide, "for myn honoure,
Thou mooste haue this in mynde: 2330
That hore, my doghter, a girdil hath she;
From hounger it savyth hem alle,
That wonnen may thay never be,
That[24] foule mote hir bifalle!
Kanstowe gete me that gyrdill by craft,   2335
A thousande pounde than shal i gefe the;
So that it be there not lefte,
But bringe it hithire to me.
Thou kanste see by nyghte as welle
As any man doth by daye.   2340
Whan thay bene in here beddes ful still,
Than go forth thider right in thy waye.
Thou shalt it in here chamber fynde,
Thou maist be thereofe sure."
"Sir, thereto i wole me bynde,   2345
If my life may endure."
Forth wente this fals Mapyne
By nyght into the toure—
God gife him evel endinge!—
Euen into Floripas boure.   2350
By a chemney he wente inne;
Fulle stilly there he soughte it.
He it founde and girde it aboute him,

---

[22] girdle.   [23] sleight, trick.   [24] i.e., and for that reason.

2326. *Fals* repeated from the preceding line?

And aftyr ful dere he boght it;
For by the light of a lampe there   2355
Floripas gan him aspye,
Alle afrayed[25] oute of hir slepe for fere,
But lowde than gan she crye,
And saide, "A thefe is in my boure;
Robbe me he wole or sloo."   2360
Therwith come Rouland fro his toure
To wete of hir woo.
He founde Mapyne bysyde hir bedde,
Stondinge amased for drede;
To the wyndowe he him ladde,[26]   2365
And there he smote of his hedde
And caste him oute into the see.
Of the gyrdille was he not ware;
But whan he wist the girdel hade he,
Tho hadde he sorowe and care.   2370
Floripe to the cheste wente
And aspyed hire gyrdel was goon.
"Alas!" she saide, "alle is it shente!
Sir, what haue ye done?
He hath my girdel aboute hym;   2375
Alas! þat harde while![27]
A rebelle hounde doth ofte grete tene;[28]
Howe be we alle begilede!"
Tho spake Roulande with chere boolde,
"Dameselle! beyth noughte aferde!   2380
If any vitaile be aboute this hoolde,[29]
We wole hem wynne withe dinte of swerde.
To morowe wole wee oute goon
And assaye howe it wole be.
I make a vowe to God alone,   2385
Assaile hem wole we!
And if thay haue any mete,
Parte[29a] withe hem wole we;
Or elles strokes thay shal gete

[25] startled.   [26] dragged.   [27] unlucky moment.   [28] mischief.   [29] castle.   [29a] divide.

2384. MS. *it wole it be.*

By God and Seynte Mary !"   2390
In the morne, er the larke songe,
Thai ordeynede hem to ride
To the Saresyns, þat hade so longe
Leyen hem besyde.
Duke Neymes and Ogere   2395
Were ordeynede to kepe the place;
The x othir of the xii peres
Wente oute to assaye here grace.[30]
Thay founden hem in logges[31] slepynge;
Of hem hade thay no thought.   2400
Thai slowen down þat came to honde;
Mahounde availed hem noghte.
In shorte tyme the ende was made;
Thay ten slough iii hundred there.
Tho founde thai vitaile, thay were glad,   2405
As moche as thay myghte home bere.
Duke Neymes and Ogere, that kept the toure,
Say hem with here praye.[32]
Thai thanked God hye of honoure
That thai spedde so þat day.   2410
Thay avaled[33] the brigge and lete him yn;
Florip and here maydyns were gladde,
And so were thay that were withyn,
For alle grete hounger thay hadde.
Thai eten and dronken right inowe   2415
And made myrth ever amonge.
But of the Sowdon Laban speke we nowe,
Howe of sorowe was his songe.
   Whan tidyngges came to him
That his men were slayn,   2420
And howe thai hade stuffed[34] hem also
With vitaile in agayne,
For sorowe he woxe nere wode.
He cleped Breulande and Sortybraunce
And tolde hem with angry mode   2425

---

[30] try their luck.   [31] lodges, tents.   [32] spoil.   [33] lowered.   [34] i.e., loaded.

2390. MS. *Mary myn avour;* Hausknecht's emendation.

Of his harde myschaunce.
"Remedye ordeyne me—
Ye be chief of my counsaile—
That i of hem may vengede be;
It shalle you bouth availe.[35]   2430
O ye goddes, ye faile at nede,
That i have honoured so longe;
I shalle you bren, so mote i spede,
In a fayre fyre ful stronge;
Shalle i neuer more on you bileve,   2435
But renaye[36] you playnly alle.
Ye shalle be brente this day er eve,
That foule mote you befalle !"
The fire was made, the goddes were broght
To have be caste thereinne.   2440
Tho alle his counsaile him bysought
He shulde of þat erroure blynne,
And saide, "Sir, what wole ye done?
Wole ye your goddis forsake?
Vengeaunce shalle than on you come,   2445
With sorowe, woo, and wrake ![37]
Ye moste make offrynge for youre offence,
For drede of grete vengeaunce,
With oyle, mylke, and ffrankencense,
By youre prestis ordynaunce."   2450
Tho he dide bere hem in ayen,
And to hem made dewe offerynge.
The prestis assoyled him of þat synne,
Ful lowly for him prayinge.
Tho he cleped his counselers,   2455
Brulande and Sortybraunce,
Axynge howe he myght destroye the xii peres,
That Mahounde gife hem myschaunce.
Thay cowde no more theron,
But late saile[38] ayen the toure.   2460
With xx[ti] thousande thai gan gon

---

[35] profit you both.   [36] deny.   [37] retaliation.   [38] assail.

2433. MS. *mete.*—H.

And bigonne a newe shoure[39]
To breke down the walles
With mattokes and with pike,
Tille iiii hundred of hem alle   2465
Lay slayne in the dike.[40]
So stronge was the cast of stoone,
The Saresyns drewe hem abakke
Tille it was at hye none;
Tho gonne thay ayen to shake.[41]   2470
Tho fayled hem cast[42] þat were withinne;
Tho cowde thai no rede,
For stoone was ther noone to wynne;
Tho were thay in grete drede.
Than saide Florip, "Beith not dismayde!   2475
Ye shalle be holpe anoon.
Here is syluer vessel; and now," she sayde,
"That shulle ye prove goode woon."
She set it forth; thay caste oute faste
Alle that came to honde.   2480
Off siluer and goolde vessel thay made waste
That was [cast] down vppon the sonde.
Whan thai saugh that roial sight,
Thai leften alle here dede;
And for the tresoure thay do fight,   2485
Who so myghte it awey lede.
Tho the Sowdon wexe nere wode,
Seinge this tresoure thus dispoyled;
That was to him so dere and goode
Laye in the dike thus defouled.   2490
He bade that thai shulde leue
And turne hem agayne in haste.
He wente home tille his tente than
With grete sorowe and mournyng mode.
Tofore his goddis whan he came,   2495
He cryed as he were wode:
"O fals goddis that ye beth,

[39] attack.   [40] ditch, moat.   [41] move.   [42] i.e., ammunition.

2482. MS. *wast* (repeated from 2481).

I have trustid to longe youre mode.
Me were levere to suffre dede
Than lif this life here lenger nowe. 2500
I haue almoste loste the breth;
xii fals traytours me overe-lede[43]
And stroyen alle þat i haue.
Ye fals goddis, the devel youe spede!
Ye make me nowe for to rave; 2505
Ye do fayle me at my nede."
In ire he smote Mahounde,
That was of goolde fulle rede,
That he fille down to the grounde
As he hade bene dede. 2510
Alle here bisshopes cryden oute
And saide, "Mahounde, thyn ore!"
And down to the erthe wele lowe thay loute,[44]
Howlynge and wepynge sore,
And saide, "Sire Sowdon, what haue ye done? 2515
Vengeaunce shalle on the falle,
But thou repente the here anone."
"Ye," quod he, "I shrewe[45] you alle!"
Thai made a fyre of frankencense
And blewen hornes of bras, 2520
And casten in milke and hony for the offence,
Tofore Mahoundes face.
Thay counsailed Laban to knele adown
And aske furgevenes in that place.
And so he didde and hade pardon 2525
Throgh prayere and specialle grace.
Then this was done, þan sayde Roulande
To his felowes xi:
"Here may we not longe holde londe,
By God that is in heven. 2530

---

[43] oppress. [44] bow. [45] curse.

2499. MS. *we were.*
2507. For a pagan king's revenge on his gods, cf. "Mort Aymeri de Narbonne," 935 ff. His peers rebuke him. Cf. also the "Chanson" 2582 ff. and note.
2521. MS. *milke hony.*

Therefore sende we to Charles the Kinge,
That he wolde reskowe vs sone;
And certyfye him of oure stray3te beinge,[46]
If ye thinke it be to done.
Richard of Normandye, ye most goon;   2535
I holde you both wyse and hende,
And we shalle tomorowe, as still as stoon,
The Saresyns awake er ye wynde.
And while we be mooste bysy in oure werke
And medel[47] with hem alle in fere,   2540
Stele ye awaye in the derke;
And spede you faste, ye were there !"[48]
On the morowe aftire the daye,
Thay were armede ful ryghte;
Thai rode forth stilly in here way—   2545
God gouerne hem, mooste of myght !
Floripe and here maydyns kept the toure
And woonde[49] vp the brigges on hye,
And prayde God to kepe here paramoure,
The Duke of Burgoyne, Sir Gye.   2550
She preyde to Rouland, er he wente,
To take goode hede of him,
That he were neyþer take nere shente,
As he wolde her loue wynne.
On thay set with herte stronge   2555
And alle hem sore afrayed.[50]
Richard the whiles away he wronge,[1]
While thai were alle dismayede.
Towarde the Mountrible he hyed him faste,
To passe if that he myghte.   2560
Thedir he came at the laste;
God kepe him for his moch myght !
His xii felowes besyed[2] hem soo
That many of hem thay sloughe.
Gye slowe[3] the Kinge of Babyloyne tho;   2565

---

[46] extremity.   [47] mix.   [48] if you hasten, you will (surely) arrive.   [49] drew (by windlasses).   [50] i.e., frightened all the Saracens.   [1] slipped.   [2] busied.   [3] struck [not killed].

2558. MS. *Thile.*

The Babyloynes of his hors him drowe,
And with force him drowe there
And bounde his hondes ful fast.
A new game thai gan him lere,
For in depe prison thay him caste.   2570
But Laban wolde him first se
To wete what he was.
"Telle me thy name nowe," quod he,
"Thy songe shalle be 'alas.' "
"Sire," he saide, "my name is Gye;   2575
I wole it never forsake.
It were to me grete vilanye
An othir name to take."
"O fals traytour," quod Laban,
"My doghtir, þat stronge hore,   2580
Hath me forsake and the hath tan;
Thou shalte be honged therfore."
Roulande made grete moone;
It wolde noon other be;
Homwarde thai gan goon.   2585
iii c Saresyns ther saye he,
That kepte the pace⁴ at the brigge-ende,
Armed wel in goode araye,
That thai sholde not in wende,
But be take or slayn þat daye.   2590
Roulande to his felowes saide:
"Beth alle of right gode chere!
And we shal make hem alle afrayde,
Ere we go to oure soupere."
There byganne a bykeringe⁵ bolde   2595
Of x bachelers⁶ that tyde,
Agayne iii c men itolde,⁷
That durste righte wel abyde.
Tho was Durnedale⁸ set a werke;
xl of hethen he sloughe;   2600
He spared neþere lewde⁹ ner clerke,
And Floripas thereof loughe.

---

⁴ pass. ⁵ engagement, struggle. ⁶ young knights. ⁷ by actual count. ⁸ Roland's sword. ⁹ layman.

The shotte, the caste was so stronge,
Syr Bryer was slayn there
With dartes, gauylokes,[10] and speres longe;   2605
xx[ti] on hym there were.
Roulande was woo and Olyuere;
Thay sloughen alle that thai mette.
Tho fledde the Turkes alle for fere;
Thay durste no longer lette,   2610
And saide thai were no men,
But develis abroken oute of helle,
"iii hundred of vs agayn hem ten!
Oure lorde Mahounde hem qwelle![11]
xl of vs here be ascaped,   2615
And hardde we be bistadde.[12]
Whoso wole of hem more be iaped,[13]
I holde him worsse than madde."
Tho Roulande and Olyuere
Maden grete woo and sorowe,   2620
And token the corps of Sir Bryere
And beryed it on the morowe.
Floripe asked Roulande anoone,
"Where is my loue Sir Gye?"
"Damesel," he saide, "he is goon,   2625
And therefore woo am i."
"Alas," she saide, "than am i dede,
Nowe Gye my lorde is slayn!
Shall i neuer more ete brede
Tille that i may se him agayn!"   2630
"Be stille," quod Roulande, "and haue no care·
We shal hym haue ful wele.
Tomorowe wele we thiderward fare
With spere and shelde of stele.
But we bringe him to this toure,   2635
Leeve me elles no more;—
With victorye and grete honoure,
Or thay shalle abye it ful sore."
On the morowe whan tha daye was clere,

---

[10] spears. [11] kill. [12] beset. [13] mocked.

Laban ordeynede Gye honged to be.   2640
He cleped forth Sir Tampere
And badde him do make a galowe tre,
"And set it even byfore the toure,
That þilke hore may him see;
For by Lord Mahounde of honoure,   2645
This traitour there shalle honged be.
Take withe the iii hundred knightes
Of Ethiopis, Indens, and Ascopartes,[14]
That bene boolde and hardy to fight
With wifles, fauchons, gauylokes[15] and dartes;   2650
Leste-þat lurdeynes[16] come skulkynge oute,
For ever thay haue bene shrewes.[17]
Loke eche of hem haue such a cloute
That thay neuer ete moo sewes."[18]
Forth thay wente with Sir Gye,   2655
That bounde was as a thefe faste,
Tille thay come the towre ful nye;
Thai rered the galowes in haste.
Roulande perceyued here doynge
And saide, "Felows, let armes!   2660
I am ful gladde of here comynge;
Hem shall not helpe her charmes."[19]
Oute thai riden a wele gode spede,
Thai ix towarde hem alle.
Florip with here maydyns toke gode hede,   2665
Biholdinge over the toure walle.
Thai met first with Sir Tampere,
God gife him evelle fyne![20]
Such a stroke lente hym Olyuere,
He clefe him down to the skyne.   2670
Rouland bare the Kinge of Ynde
Ther with his spere frome his stede.
iiii fote it passed his bak byhynde;

[14] Ethiopians, Indians, and the giant Ascopartes. [15] axes, swords, spears.
[16] knaves. [17] villains. [18] sauces. [19] their magic shall not help them. [20] end.

2650. MS. *gamylokes.*—H.
2660. Read *as armes!* (*aux armes*)—H.

His herte blode þere didde he blede.
He caught the stede—he was ful goode—   2675
And the swerde þat the Kinge hadde,
And rode to Gye, there he stode,
And onbounde hym and bade him be gladde.
And girde him with that goode swerde,
And lepen vppon here stedes.   2680
"Be thou," he saide, "righte nought aferde,
But helpe vs wightly at this nede."
An hundred of hem sone thay slowe
Of the beste of hem alle;
The remenaunte away fast thay flowe,   2685
That foule motte hem byfalle!
Rouland and his felowes were glad
That Gye was safe in dede.
Thay thanked God, that He hem hadde
Gyfen such grace to spede.   2690
As thay wente towarde the toure,
A litil bysyde the hye waye,
Thai saugh comynge with grete vigoure
An hundred vppon a laye.[21]
Costroye ther was, the admyrall,   2695
With vitaile grete plenté,
And the stondarte[22] of the Sowdon roial.
Towarde Mauntrible riden he,
iiii chariotes icharged[23] with flessh and brede
And two othere with wyne   2700
Of divers coulouris, yolowe, white, and rede,
And iiii somers[24] of spicery fyne.
Tho saide Roulande to Olyuere:
"With these meyné moste we shifte[25]
To haue parte of here vitailes here,   2705
For thereof us nedith, by my thrifte."[26]
"Howe, sires," he saide; "God you see!

---

[21] meadow.   [22] standard-bearer.   [23] loaded.   [24] pack horses.   [25] divide.   [26] welfare.

2689–90. H.'s reading for MS. . . . *that thay him hadde Gyfen thaye such*. . . .

We pray youe for youre curtesye
Parte of your vitaile graunte me,
For we may nother borowe ner bye." 2710
Tho spake Cosdroye, that admyral:
"Ye gete none here for noght.
Yf ye oght chalenge[27] in speciall,
It most be dere iboght."
"O gentil knightes," quod Olyuere, 2715
"He is no felowe þat wole haue alle."
"Go forth," quod the stondart; "thou getist noon here;
Thy parte shalle be fulle smalle."
"Forsoth," quod Roulande, "and shift we wole,
Gete the better, who gete maye! 2720
To parte with the nedy it is gode skille,[28]
And so shalle ye, by my faye."
He rode to the admyral with his swerde
And gafe him suche a cloute,
No wonder thogh he were aferde; 2725
Both his ey3en braste oute.
Olyuere met withe the proude stondarde;
He smote him through the herte:
That hade he for his rewarde;
That wounde gan sore smerte. 2730
Thai were slayn that wolde fight
Er durste bikure[29] abyde.
Thai forsoke her parte anoon right;
It lefte alle on that on side.
Forth thai drewen þat vitaile 2735
Streight in to the toure.
There was no man durst hem assayle,
For drede of here vigoure.
Floripe hem resceyved with honoure
And thanked Roulande fele sythe 2740
That she saugh Gye, hir paramoure;
That wolde she him[30] qwite and kithe.
Thai eten and dronken and made hem gladde;
Hem neded theraftyr fulle sore

---

[27] claim.   [28] practice.   [29] engagement.   [30] i.e., Roland.

Of suche as God hem sente hade,   2745
Inowe for iiii moonþes and more.
Florip saide to Roulande than,
"Ye moste chese you a love
Of alle my maydyns, white as swan."
Quod Rouland, "þat were myscheve;   2750
Oure lay[31] wole not þat we with youe dele
Tille that ye Cristyn be made;
Ner of your play we wole not fele,[32]
For than were we cursed in dede."
   Nowe shall ye here of Laban.   2755
Whan tidyngges to him were comen,
Tho was he a fulle sory man.
Whan he herde howe his vitaile were nomen
And howe his men were slayne,
And Gye was go safe hem froo,   2760
He defyed Mahounde and Apolyne,
Iubiter, Ascarot,[33] and Alcaron[34] also.
He commaundede a fire to be dight,
With picche and brymston to bren.
He made a vowe with alle his myght,   2765
"Thai shal be caste therinne !"
The prestes of here lawe, theron
Thai criden oute for drede
And saide, "Alas, what wole ye done?
The worse than moste ye spede !"   2770
The Sowdon made a grete othe
And swore by his hye trone
That though hem were never so loth,
Thai sholde be brente ichon.
Tho came the Bisshope Cramadas   2775
And kneled bifore the Sowdon,
And charged him by the hye name Sathanas
To saven his goddes ychon:
"For if ye brenne youre goddes here,
Ye wynnyn her malison;   2780

---

[31] law, religion.   [32] i.e., we will not wanton with you.   [33] gods imputed to the Saracens.   [34] the Koran, or, perhaps here, a god.

Than wole no man do you chere
In feelde, cité, nere in town."
The Sowdon was astonyed þan
And gan him sore repente
Of the foly that he bygan, 2785
And els hade he be shente.
A thousande of besauntes[34] he offred þaym to,
By counsail of Sir Cramadas,
To please with his goddys tho,
For fere of harde grace. 2790
The Sowdone commaunded euery daye
To assaile the toure with caste.[35]
But thay within gafe not an eye,[36]
For thai wroghte in wast.[37]
    Nowe speke we of Richarde of Normandy, 2795
That on message was sente,
Howe he spede and his meyné.
Whan he to Mauntrible wente,
He founde the brigge ichayned sore;
xxiiii[ti] were ouere drawen. 2800
Alagolofure stode there byfore,
That many a man hade slawene.
Whan Richard saugh ther was no gate[38]
But by Flagot, the flode,[39]
His message wolde he not lete; 2805
His hors was both bigge and goode.
He kneled, bisechinge God of his grace
To save him fro myschiefe.
A white hende[40] he saugh anoon in þat place,
That swam overe the cliffe. 2810
He blessed him in Godis name
And folowed the same waye
The gentil hende þat was so tame,

---

[34] gold coins. [35] bombardment. [36] egg. [37] i.e., in vain. [38] passage. [39] river (on which Mantrible was situated). [40] hind.

2810. The passage is abridged from the French, to the detriment of the sense. The river flows between cliffs, but rises through a miracle at this time so as to be nearly level with their tops. Thus Guy "swims across the cliffs."—H.

That on þat othir side gan playe.
He thanked God fele sythe,   2815
That him hade sente comforte.
He hied him in his message swiþe
To speke with Charles his lorde.
But i shalle you telle of a traytour,
That his name was called Genelyne;[41]   2820
He counseiled Charles for his honoure
To turne homewarde ageyn.
He saide, "The xii peres bene alle dede,
And ye spende your goode in vayne;
And therefore doth nowe by my rede,   2825
Ye shalle see hem no more certeyn."
The Kinge bileved þat he saide,
And homwarde gan he fare.
He of his xii dosiperes[42] was sore dismayed;
His herte woxe right fulle of care.   2830
Rycharde of Normandy came prikande
And hertly to ride begane.
Kinge Charles aspyed him comande;
He commaunded to abide euery man.
"What tidingges?" quod the Kinge to Richarde,   2835
"Howe fare my felowes alle?"
"My lorde," he saide, "God wote, ful harde,
For thai be byseged within ston walle,
Abydynge youre helpe and youre socoure,
As men þat haue grete nede.   2840
For Ihesues loue, Kinge of honoure,
Thiderward ye you spede !"
"O Genelyne," quod the Kinge,
"Nowe knowe i thy treson !
I shalle the qwite, be Seynte Fremounde,   2845
Whan this viage[43] is don."
The Kinge turned him ageyn,
And alle his ooste[44] him with,
Towarde Mountrible, certeyne—
And—graunte him gree and grith !—   2850

---

[41] Ganelon.   [42] Douzepers (twelve peers).   [43] journey.   [44] host, army.

Richarde him tolde of that place,
Howe stronge it was iholde
With a geaunte foule of face,
The brigge hath chayned many folde;
The river was both depe and brode;   2855
Ther myght no man over ryde.
"The last tyme that i over rode,
By myracle i passed þat tide.
Therfore, sir, i shal you telle
Howe ye mote governe you here: 2860
In yonde wode ye moste dwelle
Priuely in this manere,
And xii of vs shalle vs araye
In gyse of stronge marchauntes,
And fille oure somers withe fog and haye,[45]   2865
To passe the brigge-currauntes.[46]
We shalle be armed vnder the cote
With goode swerdes wele igyrde;
We moste paye tribute, wele i wote,
And elles over we may not sterte.   2870
But whan the chaynes be lete down
Ouer ther for to passe,
Than wole i þat ye come on,
In haste to that same place.
Whan i see tyme for to come,   2875
Than shalle i my horne blowe.
Loke ye be redy, alle and some,
For that shall ye welle knowe."
Forth thay wente in þat araye
To Mountrible, that cité.   2880
Alagolofure to hem gan seye,
"Felawes, wheder wole ye?"
Richarde spake to the geaunte
And saide, "Towarde the Sowdon
With dyu[e]rs chaffere, as trewe marchaunte,   2885
We purpose for to goon,
To shewen him of pellure and gryse,[47]

---

[45] load our horses with grass and hay.   [46] currents.   [47] kinds of fur.

Orfrays of Perse[48] imperyalle.
We wole the yefe tribute of assaye[49]
To passe by lycence in especyall."   2890
"Licence gete ye noon of me;
I am charged that noone shall passe,
For x lurdeyns[50] of Fraunce were here;
God yefe hem evell grace!
Thay passed this way to Egramoure;   2895
Thay haue done the Sowdon grete tene,
Thay have wonne his toure and his tresoure,
And yet holde thai it, i wene.
Wherfore, felawes, i arest you alle,
Tille i knowe what þat ye bene."   2900
Sire Focarde brayde oute his swerde withalle—
Wel sore he gan to tene—,
And saide, "Fye on the, Sarasyne!
For alle thy grete harde hede,
Shaltow never drinke water ner wyne;   2905
By God! thou shalte be dede."
He smote at him with egre chere,
But he gafe thereof right nought.
"Alas!" quod Richard, "thou combrest[1] vs here,
By God, that me dere hath boghte."   2910
The cheynes yet were alle faste;
The geaunte wexe nere wode;
Richard blewe his horne in haste,
That was both shrille and goode.
Kinge Charles hied him anoon   2915
Towarde the brigge so longe;
The geaunte faught with hem alone,
He was so harde and stronge.
With a clog[2] of an oke he faught,
That was wele bound with stele.   2920
He slough al þat evere he raught,[3]
So stronge was his dinte to dele.

---

[48] gold fringes of Persia.   [49] value.   [50] knaves.   [1] encumber; i.e., Focarde exposes the disguise.   [2] club, faggot.   [3] reached.

2889. For *assaye* perhaps read *assise*, value.

Richard raught him with a barre of bras
That he caught at the gate.
He brake his legges; he cryed "alas!"　2925
And felle alle chekmate.
Loude than gan he to yelle;
Thay herde him yelle through þat cité
Like the grete develle of helle,
And saide, "Mahounde, nowe helpe me!"　2930
iiii men him caught there,
So hevy he was and longe,
And cast him ouer into the rivere;
Chese he whither he wolde swymme or gong!
Anoon thay brast the chaynes alle　2935
That ouer the brigge were idrawe.
The Saresyns ronnen to the walle;
Many cristen men were there islawe.
Than came forth Dam Barrok, the bolde,
With a sithe[4] large and kene,　2940
And mewe[5] adown as þikke as shepe in folde,
That came byforne hir bydene.
This Barrok was a geaunesse,[6]
And wife she was to Astragote;
She did the Cristen grete distresse:　2945
She felled downe alle þat she smote.
There durst no man hire sithe abyde;
She grenned like a develle of helle.
King Charles with a quarel[7] þat tide
Smote hir, that she lowde gan yelle,　2950
Ouer the frounte[8] throughoute the brayn;
That cursede fende fille down dede.
Many a man hade she there slayn;
Might she never aftyr ete more brede!
Charles entred in the firste warde[9]　2955
With xv knightis and no moo;

---

[4] scythe. ¦ [5] mowed.　[6] giantess.　[7] dart.　[8] forehead.　[9] space between the outer and inner walls.

2923. A special primitive weapon is the only one effective against this giant.

2951. MS. *Euer the founte.*

Of hym his oste toke no garde;
He wende his oste hade entred also.
The Sarysyns ronne to the gate
And shet it wonder faste;   2960
Charles men come to late;
Tho was Charles sore agaste.
Betwene two wardes he was shit,
Defende he him if he can!
The Sarysyns with him thay mette;   2965
Grete parel was he in than.
Tho Genelyne saie the Kinge was inne
And the yates faste istoke[10]
(Ther myght no man to him wynne,
So was he faste withinne iloke),   2970
To his frendes he gan speke
And saide, "The Kinge is dede,
And alle xii peres eke.
On peyne," said he, "to lese myn hede,
Let vs hye to Fraunce warde!"[11]   2975
For i wele be crownede kinge;
I shalle you alle wele rewarde,
For i wole spare for no thinge."
Anoon thay assented to Genelyne;
Thay saugh ther was no better rede.   2980
The Frenssh men drewe hem al ayene;
Thay wende the Kinge hade bene dedde.
Tho Ferumbras with his meyné than
Came for to seke the Kinge,
And saugh hem turne, euery man;   2985
Him thought it was a wondir thing.
"Where is the Kinge?" quod Ferumbras.
Quod Genelyne, "Within the walle;
Shaltowe neuere more seen his face!"
"God gyf the an yvel falle!   2990
Turne agayne, thou traytoure,
And helpe to reskowe thy lorde.
And ye, sires, alle for youre honoure!"

---

[10] closed. [11] toward France.

Thay turned agayne with that worde;
Ferumbras with axe in honde   2995
Myghtyly brake up the gate;
Ther myght laste[12] him noon yron bonde.
He hade nerehonde icome to late.
The Kinge hadde fought so longe withynne
That onnethe myght he no more;   3000
Many ther were abouten him;
His men were wounded ful sore.
Ferumbras came with gode spede;
He made the Sarasyns to fle;
He reskowed the Kinge at his nede;   3005
xl Sarasyns sone killed he.
Thai ronnen aweye by every side;
Thai durste nowhere rowte;[13]
In shorte tyme was falled her pride;
Thay caught many a sore cloute!   3010
That cité was wonne that same daye,
And every toure therynne
Of Mountreble, þat was so gaye,
For alle here soubtile gynne,[14]
Fulle of tresoure and richesse,   3015
Of siluer and goolde and perré[15]
And clothes of goolde, wroght of Saresynes,
Of riche aray and roialté.
Richarde, Duke of Normandy,
Founde ii children of vii monþes oolde;   3020
xiiii fote longe were thay;
Thay were Barrakes sonnes so boolde;
Bygote thay were of Astragot.
Grete joye the Kinge of hem hade.
Hethen thay were both, wele i wote;   3025
Therfore hem to be cristenede he bade.
He called þat one of hem Roulande,
And that other he cleped Olyuere:
"For thai shalle be myghty men of honde."

---

[12] resist.   [13] gather.   [14] trickery.   [15] jewels.

3017. Fine Saracen cloths were much prized in Europe; cf. "Emaré."

To kepen hem he was fulle chere.   3030
Thay myght not leve; her dam[16] was dede;
Thai coude not kepe hem forth.
Thai wolde neyþer ete butter nere brede,
Ner no mete was to hem worthe.[17]
Here dammes mylke thay lakked there: 3035
Thay deyden for defaute of here dam.
Kinge Charles made hevy chere,
And a sory man was than.

After providing for the government of the city, Charlemagne pushes
on to Agremore, where he captures the Soudan. Ferumbras wishes his
father baptized, and preparations are made for this event.

Kinge Charles did calle Bisshope Turpyn
And bade him ordeyne a grete fat[18]
To baptyse the Sowdon yne;
"And loke what he shalle hat.[19]
Unarme him faste and bringe him nere: 3155
I shal his godfader be.
Fille it fulle of watere clere,
For baptysed shalle he be.
Make him naked as a childe;
He moste plunge therinne.   3160
For now most he be meke and mylde
And iwassh awaye his synne."
Turpyn toke him by the honde
And ladde him to the fonte.
He smote the bisshope with a bronde,   3165
And gaf him an evel bronte.[20]
He spitted in the water clere,
And cryed oute on hem alle,
And defied alle þat cristen were,
That foule mote him byfalle!   3170
"Ye and thou, hore serpentyne,

---

[16] mother. [17] valuable, suitable. [18] prepare a great vessel. [19] promise. [20] blow.

3034. MS. *mene.*—H.
3154. Probably the promise is to believe in the Christian religion. In
the French original, the Creed is given at length (p. 178), and the Saracen
required to subscribe to it.

And that fals cursed Ferumbras!
Mahounde gyfe hem both evel endyng,
And almyghty Sathanas!
By you came all my sorowe,   3175
And al my tresure forlorne.
Honged by ye both er tomorrowe!
In cursed tyme were ye born."
Ferumbras saide to the Kinge,
"Sir, ye see it wole not be;   3180
Lete him take his endynge,[21]
For he loueth not Cristyanté."
"Duke Neymes," quod Charles tho,
"Loke þat execucion be don;
Smyte of his hedde.—God gyfe him woo!—   3185
And goo we to mete anoone."
It was done as the Kinge commaunde:
His soule was fet to helle
To daunse in þat sory lande
With develes þat were ful felle.   3190
Dame Florip was baptysed than
And here maydyns alle,
And to Sir Gye imaryed;
The barons honoured hir alle.
Alle the londe of Spayne   3195
Kinge Charles gyfe hem two
To departe[22] bitwyxt hem twayne,
Ferumbras and Gy also.
And so thay livede in ioye and game,
And brethern both thay were;   3200
In pees and werre both isame,
There durste no man hem dere.
Kinge Charles turned home agayn
Towarde his contré;
He charged Sir Bryere of Bretayne   3205
His tresourere for to be:
To kepe the relikes of grete pris
And his other tresoure,

---

[21] i.e., die.   [22] divide between them . . . (and with) Ferumbras.

And bringe hem safe to Parys,
There to abide in store.[23]   3210
He saide "Farewell, Sir Ferumbras,
Ye and Gye, my dere frende,
And thy wyf Dame Floripas!
For to Fraunce nowe wole i wende.
Be ye togeder as breth[e]rn both,   3215
No man ye nedith to drede.
Be ye nevere togedere wroth,
But eyther helpe othir at his nede.
Vysityth me, whan ye haue space;
Into Fraunce makith your disporte—   3220
God wole you sende the better grace—
In age to do me comforte."
Thai toke leve of the Kinge
With ful hevy chere,
And turned agayn, both mornynge,   3225
With wepynge water clere.

In the remaining fifty lines, Charlemagne distributes the relics among
French churches, and orders the execution of the traitor Ganelon.

---

[23] i.e., to be stored.

THE MATTER OF BRITAIN

SIR DEGARÉ

The text is from the Auchinleck Manuscript. The division into strophes is according to capitals in the manuscript. A few lines from the Cambridge manuscript have been inserted where the text is defective, and a few substituted where it is corrupt; but, to avoid confusion, the numbering of the lines has been kept as in Laing's edition for the Abbotsford Club.

Through the kindness of the authorities of the National Library of Scotland, the University Library of Cambridge, the Bodleian Library, and the Department of Manuscripts of the British Museum, it has been possible to prepare the text from photographs of the manuscripts and prints in those libraries.

Most of the elements of the story are familiar and occur elsewhere frequently. Exceptions are the magic gloves and the pointless sword. The only careful study of this material is Miss Hibbard's (p. 301 ff.).* The piece seems to be a moralised Breton lay, and has some lines in common with "Lai le Freine." It has many striking resemblances to the first part of the Gregory-legend.

The manuscripts show that the story was current in two forms: in the earlier, as in MSS. A. and C., the hero's name is always rhymed with long -e; in the later, preserved in several prints and the Percy Folio Manuscript, the name is rhymed indifferently with -e or -ore. The later version, of which Wynkyn de Worde's print is the best text, is a revision of the earlier, and also shows borrowings from other pieces and the insertion of familiar details (see University of Chicago thesis by Muriel Carr, "Sir Degarre," 1923). It is inferior and often contradictory.

The scribe of the Auchinleck Manuscript wrote ȝ indiscriminately for ȝ, þ, and s (ȝhe : she or they; wiȝ: with). He reversed modern usage frequently in putting h before some vowels and omitting it before others (er, here; white, wit; wi, why; hese, ease). He often reversed the usual order of -h and -t (doht, doth; forht, forth). And is often written an, especially at the beginning of a line. Hi often is written for heo, she. The dialect is south midland, of the early fourteenth century. On the writing of -a- and -o-, see Miss Carr's "Medieval Scribe's Methods," *University of Wisconsin Studies in Language and Literature,* II. 153.

*See also the preface to Gustav Schleich's edition (1929).

Kniȝtus þat]werey sometme in lande]
Ferli fele[1] wolde fonde,
And sechen auentures bi niȝt and dai,
Hou ȝhe miȝte here strengthe asai;[2]
So dede a knyȝt, Sire Degarree: 5
Ich wille ȝou telle wat man was he.
    In Litel Bretaygne[3] was a kyng
Of gret poer[4] in alle þing,
Stif in armes vnder sscheld,
And mochel idouted[5] in þe feld.   10
Þer nas no man, verraiment,
Þat miȝte in werre[6] ne in tornament,
Ne in iustes for noþing,
Him out of his sadel bring,
Ne out of his stirop bringe his fot,   15
So stron[g] he was of bon and blod.
Þis Kyng [he hadde none hair][7]
But a maidenchild, [fre and] fair;
Here gentiresse[8] and hire beauté
Was moche renound in ich countré.   20
Þis maiden he loued als his lif:
Of hire was ded þe Quene his wif:
In trauailing here lif ȝhe les.
And þo þe maiden of age wes,
Kynges sones to him speke;   25
Emperours and dukes eke,
To hauen his doughter in mariage,
For loue of here heritage;
Ac þe Kyng answered euer
Þat no man sschal here halden euer   30
But-ȝif he mai in turneying
Him out of his sadel bring,

---

[1] wonderfully many.   [2] try.   [3] Brittany.   [4] power.   [5] feared.   [6] war.   [7] heir.
[8] gentle bearing.

1. Words in brackets supplied from Cambridge MS.
17. Words in brackets a guess, the MS. being illegible.
29 ff. Behind this situation is something of the same sort as in "Emaré."
See Frazer ii.270, v.43. Here it is thoroughly rationalized. See also Miss
Cox's "Cinderella" 190 ff.

And maken him lesen hise stiropes bayne;[9]
[Many assayed and myght not gayne.[10]
That ryche Kynge euery yere wolde   35
A solempne feste make and holde
On hys wyuys mynnyng-day,[11]
That was beryed in an abbay
In a foreste there besyde.
With grete meyné he wolde ryde,]   40
[H]ire dirige[12] do, and masse boþe;
[P]oure men fede, and naked cloþe;
[O]ffring brenge, gret plenté,
[A]nd fede þe couent[13] wiჳ gret daynté.
Towar[d] þe abbai als he con ride,   45
And mani knyჳtis bi his side,
His doughter also bi him rod.
Amidde þe forest hii abod;
Here chaumberleyn ჳhe clepede hire to,
And oþer dammaiseles two,   50
And seide þat hii moste aliჳte
To don here nedes and hire riჳte;
Þai aliჳt adoun alle þre,
Tweie damaiseles and ssche,
And longe while þer abiden,   55
Til al þe folk was forht iriden.
Þai wolden vp and after wolde,
And couþen nowt here way holde.
Þe wode was rough and þikke, iwis,
And þai token þe wai amys.   60
Þai moste souht,[14] and riden west

---

[9] both.   [10] succeed.   [11] minding-day.   [12] requiem.   [13] monastery.   [14] should
have gone south.

37. A minding-day is one set apart for prayers and penances for the
soul of a dead person. Giving to the poor was thought an act of merit;
and maintaining religious houses insured constant prayers toward any
desirable object.

57. *Wolden* for *stirten?*

60. The adventure has been rationalized. Cf. the story of Cuchulainn's
birth (*Irische Texte* 1; *Rev. Celt.* 9.2); the princess and fifty maids disappear for three years; they have gone, in the form of birds, to Emania,
where she becomes the bride of a fairy. See especially Version B.

Into þe þikke of þe forest.
Into a launde[15] hii ben icome,
And habbeȝ wel vndernome[16]
Þat þai were amis igon.   65
Þai liȝt adoun euerichon
And cleped and criede al ifere,
Ac no man ariȝt[17] hem ihere.
Þai nist what hem was best to don;
Þe weder was hot bifor þe non;   70
Hii leien hem doun vpon a grene,
Vnder a chastein[18] tre, ich wene,
And fillen aslepe euerichone
Bote þe damaisele alone:
Ȝhe wente aboute and gaderede floures,   75
And herknede song of wilde foules.
So fer in þe launde ȝhe goht, iwis,
Þat ȝhe ne wot neuere whare ȝe is.
To hire maidenes ȝhe wolde anon,
Ac hi ne wiste neuer wat wei to gon.   80
Whenne hi wende best to hem terne,
Aweiward þan hi goȝ wel ȝerne.
"Allas!" hi seide, "þat i was boren!
Nou ich wot ich am forloren!
Wilde bestes me willeȝ togrinde   85
Or ani man me sschulle finde!"
Þan segh hi swich a siȝt:
Toward hire comen a kniȝt,
Gentil, ȝong, and iolif[19] man;
A robe of scarlet he hadde vpon;   90
His visage was feir, his bodi ech weies;[20]

---

[15] heath.   [16] realized.   [17] at once.   [18] chestnut.   [19] handsome.   [20] in every way.

70–2. Cf. "Launfal" 220. The chestnut tree is especially a tree of the fairies.

73. Their sleep is of course an enchantment. Cf. "Orfeo" and the many stories of the theft of children while watchers sleep.

88. The fairy lover in the "Tain Bo Fraich" (*Rev. Celt.* 24) is similarly rationalized. Usually mortals do not realize that they are dealing with fairies until the fairies reveal themselves; here the revelation takes place, and the prophecies that usually accompany it are made.

Of countenaunce riȝt curteis;
Wel farende²¹ legges, fot, and honde:
Þer nas non in al þe Kynges londe
More apert²² man þan was he.   95
"Damaisele, welcome mote þou be;
Be þou afered of none wihȝte:
Iich am comen here a fairi knyȝte;
Mi kynde is armes for to were,
On horse to ride wiȝ scheld and spere;   100
Forþi afered be þou nowt:
I ne haue nowt but mi swerd ibrout.
Iich haue iloued þe mani a ȝer,
And now we beȝ vs selue²³ her,
Þou best mi lemman ar þou go,   105
Weþer þe likeȝ wel or wo."
Þo noþing ne coude do ȝhe
But wep and criede and wolde fle;
And he anon gan hire atholde,²⁴
And dide his wille, what he wolde.   110
He binam²⁵ hire here maidenhod,
And seththen vp toforen hire stod.
"Lemman," he seide, "gent and fre,
Mid schilde²⁶ i wot þat þou schalt be;
Siker ich wot hit worht a knaue;²⁷   115
Forþi mi swerd þou sschalt haue,
And whenne þat he is of elde
Þat he mai himself biwelde,²⁸
Tak him þe swerd, and bidde him fonde
To sechen his fader in eche londe.   120
Þe swerd his²⁹ god and auenaunt:³⁰
Lo, as i faugt wiȝ a geaunt,

---

²¹ conditioned, shaped. ²² attractive. ²³ ourselves, the two of us. ²⁴ seize.
²⁵ bereft. ²⁶ child. ²⁷ will be a son. ²⁸ protect. ²⁹ is. ³⁰ fitting; i.e., will
serve his purpose.

115. For similar predictions, see T. P. Cross's article on "Yonec" in the
University of North Carolina Studies in Philology; printed also in *Rev.
Celt.* 31.413 ff.

120. Otherworld creatures were reluctant to tell their names because
such knowledge gave mortals power over them, cf. Wimberly, 84. For
a popular exposition of this, see Edward Clodd's "Tom Tit Tot" 173.

I brak þe point in his hed;
And siththen, when þat he was ded,
I tok hit out and haue hit er,[31]   125
Redi in min aumener.[32]
3it parauenture time bi3
þat mi sone mete me wi3:
Be mi swerd i mai him kenne.
Haue god dai:[33] i mot gon henne."   130
þe kni3t passede as he cam.
Al wepende þe swerd 3he nam,
And com hom sore sikend,
And fond here maidenes al slepend.
þe swerd 3he hidde als 3he mi3te,   135
And awaked hem in hi3te,
And doht hem to horse[34] anon,
And gonne to ride euerichon.
þanne seghen hi ate last
Tweie squiers come prikend fast.   140
Fram þe Kyng þai weren isent,
To white[35] whider his doughter went.
þai browt hire into þe ri3te wai
And comen faire to þe abbay,
And do3 þe seruise in alle þingges,   145
Mani masse and riche offringes;
And whanne þe seruise was al idone,
And ipassed ouer þe none,[36]
þe Kyng to his castel gan ride;
His doughter rod bi his side.   150
And he 3eme3 his kyngdom oueral
Stoutliche, as a god king sschal.
Ac whan ech man was glad an blithe,
His doughter siked an sorewed swithe;
Here wombe greted[37] more and more;   155

---

[31] here.   [32] purse.   [33] farewell.   [34] orders them to mount.   [35] know.   [36] nones was past.   [37] increased.

123. In "The Voyage of Bran" (Nutt's ed. 51) a headless spear is used for identification.
133. Cambridge MS. has *went away*.

Þer-while ȝhe miȝte, ȝe hidde here sore.
On a dai, as hi wepende set,
On of hire maidenes hit vnderȝet.[38]
"Madame," ȝhe seide, "par charité,
Whi wepe ȝe now, telleȝ hit me." 160
"A! gentil maiden, kinde icoren,[39]
Help me, oþer ich am forloren!
Ich haue euer ȝete ben meke and milde:
Lo, now ich am wiȝ quike schilde![40]
ȝif ani man hit vnderȝete, 165
Men wolde sai be sti[41] and strete
Þat mi fader þe King hit wan[42]
(And i ne was neuere aqueint[43] wiȝ man!);
And ȝif he hit himselue wite,
Swich sorewe schal to him smite 170
Þat neuer bliȝe schal he be,
For al his ioie is in me,"
And tolde here al togeder þer
Hou hit was biȝete and wher.
"Madame," quad þe maide, "ne care þou nowt: 175
Stille[44] awai hit sschal be browt.
No man schal wite in Godes riche[45]
Whar hit bicomeȝ, but þou and iche."
Her time come, ȝhe was vnbounde,
And deliured al mid sounde;[46] 180
A knaue-schild þer was ibore;
Glad was þe moder þarfore.
Þe maiden seruede here at wille,
Wond[47] þat child in cloþes stille,
And laid hit in a cradel anon, 185
And was al prest þarwiȝ to gon.
ȝhit is moder was him hold:[48]
Four pound ȝhe tok of gold,
And ten of seluer also;
Vnder his fote ȝhe laid hit þo,— 190

---

[38] perceived. [39] lovely (one); a tag. [40] living child. [41] path. [42] begot. [43] familiar. [44] quietly. [45] domain. [46] health. [47] wrapped. [48] faithful.

167. Cf. note to l. 29.

For swich þing hit mi[ʒte] houe;[49]
And seththen ʒe tok a paire gloue
Þat here lemman here sente of fairi londe,
Þat nolde on no manne honde,
Ne on child ne on womman ʒhe nolde,   195
But on hire selue wel ʒhe wolde.
Þo glouen ʒe put vnder his hade,[50]
And siththen a letter ʒhe wrot and made,
And knit hit wiʒ a selkene þred
Aboute his nekke wel god sped[51]   200
Þat who hit founde sscholde iwite.
Þan was in þe lettre þous iwrite:
"Par charité, ʒif ani god man
Þis helples child finde can,
Lat cristen hit wiʒ prestes honde,   205
And bringgen hit to liue in londe,[1]
For hit is comen of gentil blod.
Helpeʒ hit wiʒ his owen god,[2]
Wiʒ tresor þat vnder his fet lis;
And ten ʒer eld whan þat he his,   210
Takeʒ him þis ilke glouen two,
And biddeʒ him, whareuere he go,
Þat he ne louie no womman in londe
But þis gloues willen on hire honde;
For siker on honde nelle þai nere[3]   215
But on his moder þat him bere."
    Þe maiden tok þe chil[d] here mide,
Stille awai in auen[4] tide,
Alle þe winteres longe niʒt.
Þe weder was cler, þe mone liʒt;   220
Þan warhtʒ[5] ʒe war anon

---

[49] be of aid.   [50] head.   [51] quickly; a tag.   [1] i.e., rear it.   [2] goods.   [3] never.
[4] evening.   [5] became she aware.

191. MS. *mi houe.*
192. The use of gloves as tokens is analyzed at length in Hall's "King Horn" 794; but no parallel to this is mentioned. Cf. "Cinderella" 234, etc.
214. This strange demand may be made so that her son must return to her. It has parallels in the Catskin story (Cox, "Cinderella" 178 ff., 190 ff.). The talisman is usually a ring.

Of an hermitage in a ston:
An holi man had þer his woniyng.
þider ȝhe wente on heying,[6]
An sette þe cradel at his dore,   225
And durste abide no lengore,
And passede forȝ anon riȝt.
Hom ȝhe com in þat oþer niȝt,
And fond þe leuedi al drupi,[7]
Sore wepinde, and was sori,   230
And tolde hire al togeder þer
Hou ȝhe had iben and wher.
    þe hermite aros erliche[8] þo,
And his knaue was vppe also,
An seide ifere here matines,[9]   235
And seruede God and hise seins.[10]
þe litel child þai herde crie,
And clepede after help on hie;
þe holi man his dore vndede,
And fond þe cradel in þe stede;   240
He tok vp þe cloþes anon
And biheld þe litel grom;[11]
He tok þe letter and radde wel sone
þat tolde him þat he scholde done.
    þe heremite held vp boþe his honde   245
An þonked God of al his sonde,
And bar þat child in to his chapel,
And for ioie he rong his bel.
He dede vp þe glouen and þe tresour
And cristned þe child wiȝ gret honour: 250
In þe name of þe Trinité,
He hit nemnede Degarré.
Degarré nowt elles ne is

---

[6] haste. [7] downcast. [8] early. [9] matins, morning prayers. [10] saints. [11] boy.

222. Probably it was excavated out of a soft rock cliff.
225. The entire passage is closely paralleled in "Lai le Freine."
229. MS. *drupin.*
247. The hermit's cell consisted of a chamber and a chapel, the latter usually with a belfry. He often had a servant. See Cutts.

But þing þat not neuer whar hit is,
Oþe[r] þing þat is neg3 forlorn also;   255
Forþi þe schild he nemnede þous þo.
Þe heremite þat was holi of lif
Hadde a soster þat was a wif;
A riche marchaunt of þat countré
Hadde hire ispoused into þat cité.   260
To hire þat schild he sente þo
Bi his knaue, and þe siluer also,
And bad here take gode hede
Hit to foster and to fede,
And 3if God Almi3ti wolde   265
Ten 3er his lif holde,[12]
A3en to him [h]i scholde hit wise:
He hit wolde teche of clergise.[13]
Þe litel child Degarré
Was ibrout into þat cité.   270
Þe wif and hire louerd ifere
Kept hit ase hit [þ]ere owen were.
Bi þat hit was ten 3er old,
Hit was a fair child and a bold,
Wel inorissched, god and hende;   275
Was non betere in al þat ende.[14]
He wende wel þat þe gode man
Had ben his fader þat him wan,[15]
And þe wif his moder also,
And þe hermite his vnkel bo;[16]   280
And whan þe ten 3er was ispent,
To þe hermitage he was sent,
And he was glad him to se,
He was so feir and so fre.
He tau3te him of clerkes lore   285

---

[12] continue.   [13] learning.   [14] region.   [15] begot.   [16] also.

254. Cf. French *égaré*, strayed. But all such etymologies are likely to
be equatings of unintelligible Celtic names with some familiar name or
term. Cf. Loomis 77; "Gawain" note p. 84.
   264. MS. *forster*.
   275. MS. *inorisscher*.

Oþer[17] ten wynter oþer more;
And [when] he was of twenti ʒer,
Staleworth he was, of swich pouer
þat þer ne wan[18] man in þat lond
þat o breid him miʒt astond.[19]   290
þo þe hermite seʒ, wiʒouten les,
Man for himself þat he wes,[20]
Staleworht to don ech werk,
And of his elde so god a clerk,
He tok him his florines and his gloues   295
þat he had kept to hise bihoues;[21]
Ac þe ten pound of starlings[22]
Were ispended in his fostrings.
He tok him þe letter to rede,
And biheld al þe dede.   300
"O leue hem,[23] par charité,
Was þis letter mad for me?"
"ʒe, bi oure Lord, vs helpe sschal!
þus hit was," and told him al.
He knelede adoun al so swiʒe,   305
And þonked þe ermite of his liue,
And swor he nolde stinte no stounde[24]
Til he his kinrede[25] hadde ifounde,
For in þe lettre was þous iwrite,
þat bi þe glouen he sscholde iwite   310
Wich were his moder and who,
ʒhif þat sche liuede þo,
For on hire honden hii wolde,
And on non oþer hii nolde.
Half þe florines he ʒaf þe hermite,   315
And haluendel[26] he tok him mide,
And nam his leue an wolde go.
"Nai," seide þe hermite, "schaltu no!
To seche þi ken miʒtou nowt dure[27]
Wiʒouten hors and god armure."   320

---

[17] another.   [18] contended.   [19] who could withstand one blow from him.   [20] i.e., capable of being his own master.   [21] needs.   [22] sterling.   [23] uncle.   [24] wait not a moment.   [25] kindred.   [26] half.   [27] persist.

288. MS. *Sstaleworth.*

"Nai," quad he, "bi Heuene-kyng,
Ich wil haue first anoþer þing."
He hew adoun, boþe gret and grim,
To beren in his hond wiȝ him,
A god sapling of an ok;   325
Whan he þarwiȝ ȝaf a strok,
Ne wer he neuer so strong a man
Ne so gode armes hadde vpon,
Þat he ne scholde falle to grounde;
Swich a bourdon[28] to him he founde.   330
Þo þenne God he him bitawt,
And aiþer fram oþer wepyng rawt.[29]
    Child Degarré wente his wai
Þourgh þe forest al þat dai.
No man he ne herd, ne non he seȝ,   335
Til hit was non ipassed heȝ;[30]
Þanne he herde a noise kete[31]
In o valai, an dintes grete.
Bliue þider he gan to te:[32]
What hit ware he wolde ise.   340
An Herl of þe countré, stout and fers,
Wiȝ a kniȝt and four squiers,
Hadde ihonted a der oþer two,
And al here houndes weren ago.[33]
Þan was þar a dragon grim,   345
Ful of filth and of venim,
Wiȝ wide þrote and teȝ grete,
And wynges bitere[34] wiȝ to bete.
As a lyoun he hadde fet,
And his tail was long and [gret].   350
Þe smoke com of his nose awai
Ase fer out of a chimenai.[35]
Þe knyȝt and squiers he had torent,
Man and hors to deþe chent.[36]

---

[28] pilgrim's staff. [29] tore himself. [30] past high noon (i.e., midday). [31] loud.
[32] hasten. [33] lost. [34] bitterly. [35] fire from a fireplace. [36] hurt.

345. On dragons and their ways, see "Dragons and Dragon-Lore,"
Ernest Ingersoll (1922), especially Ch. xi ff.
350. MS. illegible.

þe dragon þe Erl assaile gan, 355
And [he] defended him as a man,
And stoutliche leid on wiȝ his swerd,
And stronge strokes on him gerd;[37]
Ac alle his dentes ne greued him nowt:
His hide was hard so iren wrout.[38] 360
þerl flei[39] fram tre to tre—
Fein he wolde fram him be—,
And þe dragon him gan asail;
þe doughti Erl in þat batail
Ofsegh[40] þis child Degarré; 365
"Ha! help!" he seide, "par charité!"
þe dragoun seȝ þe child com;
He laft þe Erl and to him nom
Blowinde and ȝeniend[41] also
Als he him wolde swolewe þo. 370
Ac Degarré was ful strong;
He tok his bat,[42] gret and long,
And in þe forehefd[43] he him batereȝ
þat al þe forehefd he tospatereȝ.[44]
He fil adoun anon riȝt, 375
And frapte[45] his tail wiȝ gret miȝt
Vpon Degarrés side,
þat vp-so-doun[46] he gan to glide;
Ac he stert[47] vp ase a man
And wiȝ his bat leide vpan, 380
And altofrusst[48] him echa bon,
þat he lai ded, stille as [a] ston.
þerl[49] knelede adoun biliue
And ȝonked þe child of his liue,
And maked him wiȝ him gon 385

---

[37] struck. [38] as wrought iron. [39] the earl fled. [40] caught sight of. [41] yawning, gaping. [42] cudgel. [43] forehead. [44] scatter in pieces. [45] struck. [46] upside down. [47] started, leaped. [48] smashed. [49] the earl.

358. Monsters usually could not be injured with man-made weapons; they had to be fought with their own (cf. the sword in "Beowulf") or with primitive things like the club here, or even with bare hands. (Cf. Beowulf's first encounter with Grendel.)

367. MS. dagroun.

To his castel riȝt anon,
And wel at hese⁵⁰ he him made,
And proferd him al þat he hade,
Rentes, tresor, an eke lond,
For to holden in his hond.   390
Þanne answerede Degarré,
"Lat come ferst bifor me
Þi leuedi and oþer wimmen bold,¹
Maidenes and widues, ȝonge and olde,
And oþer damoiseles swete.   395
Ȝif mine glouen beȝ to hem mete²
For to done vpon here honde,
Þanne ich wil take þi londe;
And ȝif þai ben nowt so,
Iich wille take mi leue and go."   400
    Alle wimman were forht ibrowt
In that cuntré þat myght be soght:
Ech þe glouen assaie³ bigan,
Ac non ne miȝte don him on.
He tok his glouen and vp hem dede,⁴   405
And nam his leue in þat stede.
Þe Erl was gentil man of blod,
And ȝaf him a stede ful god
And noble armure, riche and fin,
When he wolde armen him þerin,   410
And a palefrai to riden an,
And a knaue to ben his man,
And ȝaf him a swerd briȝt,
And dubbed him þer to knyȝt,
And swor bi God Almiȝti   415
Þat he was better worthi
To vsen hors and armes also
Þan wiȝ his bat aboute to go.
    Sire Degarré was wel blithe,
And þanked þe Erl mani a siþe,   420

---

⁵⁰ ease.   ¹ fine.   ² suitable.   ³ try on.   ⁴ picked up.

402. MS. *Wide cuntreis and forht isowt.* The line is replaced with l. 398 of MS. C.

And lep vpon hiis palefrai,
And doht him for3[5] in his wai;
Vpon his stede ri3te[6] his man,
And ledde his armes als he wel can;
Mani a iorné þai ride and sette.[7]   425
So on a dai gret folk þei mette,
Erles and barouns of renoun,
Þat come fram a cité toun.[8]
He asked a seriaunt[9] what tiding,
And whennes hii come and what is þis þing?   430
"Sire," he seide, "verraiment,
We come framward a parlement.
Þe King a gret counseil made
For nedes þat he to don hade.
Whan þe parlement was plener,[10]   435
He lette crie fer and ner,
3if ani man were of armes so bold
Þat wi3 þe King iusti wold,
He sscholde hauc in mariage
His dowter and his heritage,   440
Þat is kingdom god and fair,
For he had non oþer hair.
Ac no man ne dar graunte þerto,
For mani hit assaie3[11] and mai nowt do:
Mani erl and mani baroun,   445
Kni3tes and squiers of renoun;
Ac ech man þat him iuste3 wi3 tit
Haþ of him a foul despit:[12]
Some he breke3 þe nekke anon,
And of some þe rig-bon;[13]   450
Some þourgh þe bodi he girt,[14]
Ech is maimed oþer ihirt;
Ac no man mai don him noþing,
Swich wonder chaunce haþ þe King.

[5] set out. [6] properly, as was right. [7] decide upon. [8] city. [9] man-at-arms.
[10] in full session. [11] try. [12] humiliation. [13] backbone. [14] thrusts.

421. MS. *palefrai hiis.*
424. Knights rode unarmed, and put on their armor only for combat.

Sire Degarré þous þenche[15] gan: 455
"Ich am a staleworht man,
And of min owen ich haue a stede,
Swerd and spere and riche wede;
And ȝif ich felle þe Kyng adoun,
Euere ich haue wonnen renoun; 460
And þei þat he me herte sore,[16]
No man wot wer ich was bore.
Wheþer deȝ oþer lif me bitide,
Aȝen þe King ich wille ride !"
In þe cité his in[17] he takkeȝ, 465
And resteȝ him and meri makeȝ.
On a dai wiȝ þe King he mette,
And knelede adoun and him grette:
"Sire King," he saide, "of muchel miȝt,
Mi louerd me sende hider [a]non riȝt 470
For to warne ȝou þat he
Bi þi leue wolde iuste wiȝ þe,
And winne þi dowter, ȝif he mai;
As þe cri was þis ender[18] dai,
Iustes he had[19] to þe inome."[20] 475
"De par Deus !"[21] quaþ þe King, "he is welcome,
Be he baroun, be he erl,
Be he burgeis,[22] be he cherl:
No man wil i forsake.
He þat winneȝ al sschal take." 480
Amorewe þe iustes was iset;
Þe King him purueid[23] wel þe bet,
And Degarré ne knew no man,
Ac al his trust is God vpon.
Erliche to churche þan wente he; 485
Þe masse he herde of þe Trinité.
To þe Fader he offreȝ hon[24] florine,
And to þe Sone anoþer al so fine,

---

[15] reflect. [16] hurt sorely. [17] lodging. [18] past. [19] would have; i.e., wishes to joust with you. [20] to "take a joust" is a common idiom for "joust." [21] by heaven. [22] townsman. [23] equipped. [24] one florin.

487. On this custom, see "Havelok" 1386.

And to þe Holi Gost þe þridde;
þe prest for him ful ȝerne gan bidde.   490
And þo þe seruise was idon,
To his in he wente wel son
And let him armi wel afin,[25]
In god armes to iusti in.
His gode stede he gan bistride;   495
His squier bar his sschaft biside;
In þe feld þe King he abide gan,
As he com ridend wiȝ mani a man,
Stoutliche out of þe cité toun,
Wiȝ mani a lord of gret renoun;   500
Ac al þat in þe felde beȝ
þat þe iustes iseȝ
Seide þat hi neuer ȝit iseȝe
So pert[26] a man wiȝ here egȝe
As was þis gentil Degarré,   505
Ac no man wiste whennes was he.
  Boþe þai gonne to iusti þan,
Ac Degarré can nowt þeron.
þe King haþ þe gretter schaft
And kan inowgh of þe craft.[27]   510
To breke his nekke he had iment:
In þe helm he set[28] his dent,
þat þe schaft al tosprong;[29]
Ac Degarré was so strong
þat in þe sadel stille he set,   515
And in þe stiropes held his fet;
For soþe i seie, wiȝoute lesing,
He ne couþe nammore[30] of iusting.
"Allas!" quaþ þe King, "allas!
Me ne fil neuere swich a cas,   520
þat man þat ich miȝte hitte
After mi strok miȝte sitte!"
He takeȝ a wel gretter tre[31]
And swor so he moste iþe,[32]

---

[25] presently.   [26] distinguished.   [27] art.   [28] aimed.   [29] splintered.   [30] no more.
[31] wood; i.e., shaft.   [32] prosper.

491. MS. *and to.*

"3if his nekke nel nowt atwo, 525
His rigg schal, ar ich hennes go!"
He rod eft wi3 gret raundoun[33]
And þought to beren him adoun,
And girt[34] Degarré anon
Ri3t a3ein þe brest-bon. 530
Þe schaft was stef and wonder god,
And Degarre stede astod,[35]
And al biforen he ros on hegh3,
And þo was he ifallen negh3;
But as God Almi3ti wold, 535
Þe schaft brak and mi3t nowt hold,
And Degarré his cours out ritte,
And was agramed[36] out of his witte.
"Allas!" quaþ he, "for vilaynie!
Þe King me haþ ismiten þrie, 540
And i ne touchede him nowt 3ete.
Nou i schal vise me bette!"[37]
He turned his stede wi3 herte grim,
And rod to þe King, and he to him,
And togider þai gert[38] ful ri3t, 545
And in þe scheldes here strokes pi3t[39]
Þat þe speres al toriue3[40]
And vp ri3t to here honde sliue3,[41]
Þat alle þe lordings þat þer ben
Þat þe iusting mi3te sen 550
Seiden hi ne se3e neuer wi3 eg3e
Man þat mighte so longe dregh3e,[42]
In wraþþe for noþing,[43]
Sitten a strok of here King;
"Ac he his doughti for þe nones, 555
A strong man of bodi and bones."

---

[33] force.   [34] thrust.   [35] reared.   [36] enraged.   [37] change my tactics.   [38] thrust.
[39] aimed.   [40] break.   [41] cleave; i.e., the shafts split along their whole length.
[42] continue.   [43] i.e., even in serious combat.

540. þrie is a mistake for twye.
542. Read me vise to improve the meter.
551. To improve the meter, read hi neuer se3e wi3 eg3e.

þe King wiȝ egre mod gan speke:
"Do bring me a schaft þat wil nowt breke,
And be mi trewþe, he sschal adoun,
þai he be strengere þan Sampson;   560
And þei he be þe bare qued,[44]
He sschal adoun, maugré his heued!"
He tok a schaft was gret and long,
þe schild[45] anoþer al so strong;
And to þe King wel euene he rit;[46]   565
þe King faileȝ, and he him smit;
His schaft was strong and god wiȝal,
And wel scharped þe coronal.[47]
He smot þe Kyng in þe lainer:[48]
He miȝt flit[49] noþer fer ne ner.   570
þe King was strong and harde sat;
þe stede ros vp biforn wiȝ þat,[50]
And Sire Degarre so þriste him þan
þat, maugré whoso grochche[1] bigan,
Out of þe sadel he him cast,   575
Tail ouer top, riȝt ate last.
þan was þer long houting[2] and cri;
þe King was sor asschamed forþi;
þe lordinges comen wiȝ miȝt and mein
And broughte þe King on horse aȝein,   580
An seide wiȝ o criing iwis,
"Child Degarré haþ wonne þe pris!"
þan was þe damaisele sori,
For hi wist wel forwhi:
þat hi scholde ispoused ben   585
To a kniȝt þat sche neuer had sen,
And lede here lif wiȝ swich a man
þat sche ne wot who him wan,[3]
No in what londe he was ibore;

---

[44] devil himself.   [45] child, knight.   [46] i.e., met him in mid-course.   [47] steel
head.   [48] thong by which shield was suspended from neck.   [49] betake himself.
[50] thereupon.   [1] grudge.   [2] hooting.   [3] begot.

561. *Qued*, evil one, is a common euphemism for the devil.   See note
to Layamon's "Brut" 27641.

Carful[4] was þe leuedi þerfore.   590
Þan seide þe King to Degarré,
"Min hende sone, com hider to me:
And þou were al so gentil a man
As þou semest wiȝ siȝt vpan,
And ase wel couþest wisdomes[5] do   595
As þou art staleworht man þe[r]to,
Me þouwte mi kingdoms wel biset:[6]
Ac be þou werse, be þou bet,
Couenaunt ich wille þe holde.
Lo, her biforn mi barons bolde,   600
Mi douwter i take þe bi þe hond,
And seise[7] þe her in al mi lond.
King þou schalt ben after me:
God graunte þe god man for to be!"
Þan was þe child glad and bliȝe,   605
And þonked þe Kyng mani a sithe.
Gret perueaunce[8] þan was þer iwrout:
To churche þai were togidere ibrout,
And spoused þat leuedi verraiment,
Vnder Holi Sacrement.   610
Lo, what chaunse and wonder strong[9]
Bitideȝ mani a man wiȝ wrong,
Þat comeȝ into an vncouþe þede[10]
And spouseȝ wif for ani mede[11]
And knowes noþing of hire kin,   615
Ne sche of his, neiþer more ne min,[12]
And beȝ iwedded togider to libbe
Par auentoure, and beȝ neghȝ sibbe!
So dede Sire Degarré þe bold,
Spoused þer is moder [hold],[13]   620
And þat hende leuedi also
Here owene sone was spoused to,
Þat sche vpon here bodi bar:
Lo, what auentoure fil hem þar!

---

[4] sorrowful.   [5] acts of wisdom.   [6] provided for.   [7] endow, seise.   [8] preparations.   [9] unpleasant misfortune.   [10] strange people.   [11] i.e., whatever the inducement.   [12] less.   [13] gracious.

599. MS. *covonaunt.*

But God, þat alle þingge mai stere,[14]   625
Wolde nowt þa[t] þai sinned ifere:
To chirche þai wente wiȝ barouns bolde;
A riche feste þai gonne to holde;
And wan was wel ipassed non
And þe dai was al idon,   630
To bedde þai sscholde wende, þat fre,
þe dammaisele, and Sire Degarré.
He stod stille and biþouwte him þan
Hou þe hermite, þe holi man,
Bad he scholde no womman take   635
For faired[15] ne for riches sake
But ȝhe miȝte þis gloues two
Liȝtliche on hire hondes do.
"Allas, allas!" þan saide he,
"What meschaunce is comen to me?   640
A, wai! witles wrechche ich am!
Iich hadde leuere þan þis kingdam
þat is iseised into min hond
þat ich ware faire out of þis lond!"
He wrang his hondes and was sori,   645
Ac no man wiste þerfore wi.[16]
   þe King parceyued and saide þo,
"Sire Degarré, wi farest þou so?
Is þer ani þing don ille,
Spoken or seid aȝen þi willc?"   650
"ȝa, sire," he saide, "bi Heuene-king!
"I chal neuer, for no spousing,
þerwhiles i liue, wiȝ wimman dele,
Widue ne wif ne dammeisele,
But ȝhe þis gloues mai take and fonde   655
And liȝtlich drawen vpon hire honde."
His ȝonge bride þat gan here,
And al for þout[17] chaunged hire chere,
And ate laste gan to turne here mod:
Here visage wex ase red ase blod: 660
ȝhe knew þo gloues þat were hire.

---

[14] guide.   [15] fairness.   [16] why.   [17] i.e., remembrance.

"Schewe hem hider, leue sire."
Sche tok þe gloues in þat stede
And liȝtliche on hire hondes dede,
And fil adoun wiȝ reuli[18] crie,   665
And seide, "God, mercy, mercie!
Þou art mi sone hast spoused me her,
And ich am, sone, þi moder der.
Ich hadde þe loren, ich haue þe founde;
Blessed be Ihesu Crist þat stounde!"   670
    Sire Degarre tok his moder þo
And helde here in his armes two,
Keste and clepte here mani a siþe;
Þat hit wa[s] sche, he was ful bliþe.
Þe Kyng gret wonder hadde   675
What þat noise þat þai made,
And meruaile of hire crying,
And seide, "Doughter, what is þis þing?"
"Fader," ȝhe seide, "þou schalt ihere:
Þou wenest þat ich a maiden were,   680
Ac certes, nay, sire, ich am non:
Twenti winter nou hit is gon
Þat mi maidenhed i les
In a fforest as i wes,
And þis is mi sone, God hit wot: 685
Bi þis gloues wel ich wot."
Ȝhe told him al þat soþe þer,
Hou þe child was geten and wher;
And when þat he was boren also,
To þe hermitage ȝhe sente him þo,   690
And seþthen herd of him noþing;
"But þanked be Ihesu, Heuene-king,
Iich haue ifounde him aliue!
Ich am his moder and ek his wiue."
    "Leue moder," seide Sire Degarré,   695
"Telle me þe sothe, par charité:

_____

[18] piteous.

676. _What_ for _why_.
683. This line and 684 are written as one in the MS.
689. MS. _And hou_.

Into what londe i mai terne
To seke mi fader, swithe and ȝerne?"
"Sone," ȝhe saide, "bi Heuene-kyng,
I can þe of him telle noþing   700
But þo þat[19] he fram me rauȝt,[20]
His owen swerd he me bitauȝt,
And bad ich scholde take hit þe forþan[21]
Ȝif þou liuedest and were a man."
Þe swerd sche fet forht anon riȝt,   705
And Degarré hit out pliȝt.[22]
Brod and long and heui hit wes:
In þat kyngdom no swich nes.
Þan seide Degarré forþan,
"Whoso hit auȝt,[23] he was a man!   710
Nou ich haue þat i[n] kepe,
Niȝt ne dai nel ich slepe
Til þat i mi fader see,
Ȝif god wile þat hit so be."
In þe cité he reste al niȝt.   715
Amorewe, whan hit was dai-lit,
He aros and herde his masse;
He diȝte him and forȝ gan passe.
Of al þat cité þan moste non
Neiþer wiȝ him riden ne gon   720
But his knaue, to take hede
To his armour and his stede.
Forȝ he rod in his wai
Mani a pas[24] and mani iurnai;
So longe he passede into west   725
Þat he com into þeld[25] fforest
Þer he was biȝeten som while.
Þerinne he rideȝ mani a mile;
Mani a dai he ride gan;
No quik best he fond of man,[26]   730
Ac mani wilde bestes he seghȝ,

---

[19] when. [20] went away. [21] straightway. [22] plucked.   [23] owned. [24] short distance. [25] the ancient. [26] i.e., no domestic beast.

708. MS. *hyngdom.*
719. See "Perceval" 1039.

And foules singen on heghȝ.
So longe hit drouwȝ[27] to þe niȝt,
Þe sonne was adoune riȝt.
Toward toun he wolde ride,   735
But he nist neuer bi wiche side.[28]
  Þenne he seȝ a water cler,
And amidde a riuer,
A fair castel of lim[29] and ston:
Oþer wonying was þer non.   740
To his knaue he seide, "Tide wat tide,[30]
O fote forþer nel i ride,
Ac here abide wille we,
And aske herberewe[31] par charité,
Ȝif ani quik man be here on liue."   745
To þe water þai come als swiþe;
Þe bregge[32] was adoune þo,
And þe gate open also,
And into þe castel he gan spede.
First he stabled vp his stede;   750
He taiede[33] vp his palefrai;
Inouȝ he fond of hote[34] and hai;
He bad his grom on heying
Kepen wel al here þing.
He passed vp into þe halle,   755
Biheld aboute, and gan to calle;
Ac neiþer on lond ne on heȝ[35]
No quik man he ne seȝ.
Amidde þe halle flore
A fir was bet, stark an store,[36]   760
"Par fai," he saide, "ich am al sure
He þat bette þat fure
Wil comen hom ȝit to-niȝt;

---

[27] persists.   [28] direction.   [29] mortar.   [30] betide what may betide!   [31] shelter.
[32] drawbridge.   [33] tied.   [34] oats.   [35] on the floor or above.   [36] kindled, strong and vigorous.

733. MS. *longe he.*
753. MS. *heþing.*
758. On the deserted castle, cf. "Perceval" 435; "Voyage of Mael Duin;" "Guingamor;" and see Loomis 90 ff.

Abiden ich wille a litel wiȝt."
He sat adoun vpon þe dais,   765
And warmed him wel eche wais,[37]
And he biheld and vndernam[38]
Hou in at þe dore cam
Four dammaiseles, gent and fre;
Ech was nakked[39] to þe kne.   770
Þe two bowen an arewen bere,
Þe oþer two icharged[40] were
Wiȝ venesoun, riche and god.
And Degarré vpstod
And gret hem wel fair apliȝt,[41]   775
Ac þai answerede no wiȝt,
But ȝede into chaumbre anon
And barred þe dore after son.
Sone þerafter wiȝ-alle
Þer com a dwerw[42] into þe halle.   780
Four fet of lengthe was in him;
His visage was stout and grim;
Boþe his berd and his fax[43]
Was crisp an ȝhalew as wax;
Grete sscholdres and quarré;[44]   785
Riȝt stoutliche loked he;
Mochele were hise fet and honde
Ase þe meste man of þe londe;
He was iclothed wel ariȝt,
His sschon icouped[45] as a kniȝt;   790

---

[37] every way. [38] perceived. [39] i.e., bare-legged. [40] laden. [41] indeed. [42] dwarf.
[43] hair. [44] square. [45] shoes slashed.

770. MS. *itakked.*
771. The messengers of fairies often bear some token to show their
office. In this land of women, the hunting must of course be done by
women.
776. The mortal is often kept waiting for the fairy, probably because
of some magical impediment to their meeting. Cf. "Partonope."
780. This description is closely paralleled in "Libeaus Desconus" 140 ff.
790. The upper part of the shoes was pierced in regular patterns so
that the bright color of the stocking would show through. See Kaluza's
"Libeaus" 143; Schleich's "Ywain" 260; and Skeat's "Piers Plowman"
C.xxi.12.

He hadde on a sorcot ouert,[46]
Iforred wiȝ blaundeuer apert.[47]
Sire Degarre him biheld and lowgȝ,
And gret him fair inowgȝ,
Ac he ne answerede neuere a word,   795
But sette trestles and laid þe bord,
And torches in þe halle he liȝte,
And redi to þe soper diȝte.
Þan þer com out of þe bour
A dammeisele of gret honour;   800
In þe lond non fairer nas;
In a diapre[48] cloþed ȝhe was.
Wiȝ hire come maidenes tene,
Some in scarlet, some in grene,
Gent of bodi, of semblaunt swete,   805
And Degarré hem gan grete;
Ac hi ne answerede no wiȝt,
But ȝede to þe soper anon riȝt.
"Certes," quaþ Sire Degarré,
"Ich haue hem gret, and hi nowt me;   810
But þai be domb, bi and bi
Þai schul speke first ar i."
Þe leuedi þat was of rode so briȝt,
Amidde ȝhe sat anon riȝt,
And on aiþer half[49] maidenes fiue.   815
Þe dwerw hem seruede al so bliue
Wiȝ riche metes and wel idiȝt;
Þe coppe he filleȝ wiȝ alle his miȝt.
Sire Degarre couþe of curteisie:
He set a chaier bifore þe leuedie,   820
And þerin himselue set,
And tok a knif and carf his met;
At þe soper litel at[50] he,
But biheld þe leuedi fre,
And seȝ ase feir a wimman   825
Als he heuere loked an,

---

[46] unfastened surcoat.   [47] nicely trimmed with white fur.   [48] cloth with woven figures.   [49] side.   [50] ate.

Þat al his herte and his þout
Hire to loue was ibrowt.
And þo þai hadde souped anowȝ,
Þe drew com, and þe cloþ he drouȝ;   830
Þe leuedis wessche euerichon
And ȝede to chaumbre quik anon.
Into þe chaumbre he com ful sone.
Þe leuedi on here bed set,
And a maide at here fet,   835
And harpede notes gode and fine;
Anoþer brouȝte spices and wine.
Vpon þe [bedde] he set adoun
To here of þe harpe soun.
For murthe of notes so sschille,[1]   840
He fel adoun on slepe stille;
So he slep al þat niȝt.
Þe leuedi wreiȝ[2] him warm apliȝt,[3]
And a pilewe vnder his heued dede,
And ȝede to bedde in þat stede.   845
    Amorewe whan hit was dai-liȝt,
Sche was vppe and redi diȝt.
Faire sche awaked him þo:
"Aris!" sche seide, "graiȝ þe, an go!"
And saide þus in here game: 850
"Þou art worþ to suffri[4] schame,
Þat al niȝt as a best[5] sleptest,
And non of mine maidenes ne keptest."[6]
"O gentil leuedi," seide Degarré,
"For Godes loue, forȝif hit me!   855
Certes þe murie harpe hit made:[7]
Elles misdo nowt [i] ne hade;
Ac tel me, leuedi so hende,

---

[1] pleasure at notes so agreeable.   [2] covered.   [3] indeed.   [4] suffer.   [5] beast.
[6] guarded.   [7] caused.

832. Probably some lines are missing after this.
841. The Celtic harpers counted lays of sleep among their most potent charms; in the older literature they can cause sleep almost at pleasure. Fairy harpers of course shared the power.
844. MS. *pilewer*.

Ar ich out of þi chaumber wende,
Who is louerd of þis lond?   860
And who þis castel haþ in hond?
Wether þou be widue or wif,
Or maiden ȝit of clene lif?
And whi her be so fele wimman
Allone, wiȝouten ani man?"   865
Þe dameisele sore siȝte,
And bigan to wepen anon riȝte.
"Sire, wel fain ich telle þe wolde,
Ȝif euere þe better be me sscholde.[8]
Mi fader was a riche baroun,   870
And hadde mani a tour and toun.
He ne hadde no child but me;
Ich was his air of þis cuntré.
In mené ich hadde mani a kniȝ[t]
And squiers þat were gode and liȝt,[9]   875
An staleworht men of mester,[10]
To serue in court fer and ner;
Ac þanne is þar here biside
A sterne kniȝt, iknawe ful wide.
Ich wene in Bretaine þer be non   880
So strong a man so he is on.[11]
He had iloue me ful ȝore;
Ac in herte neuere-more
Ne miȝte ich louie him aȝein;
But whenne he seghȝe þer was no gein,[12]   885
He was aboute wiȝ maistri[13]
For to rauisse[14] me awai;
Mine kniȝtes wolde defende me,
And ofte fowȝten hi an he;
Þe best he slowgh þe firste dai,   890

---

[8] if it will do me any good. [9] active. [10] skill. [11] one; cf. Int. VII.A.5. [12] i.e., it was to no purpose. [13] i.e., force. [14] ravish.

865. In numerous stories (e.g., "The Voyage of Bran") a country peopled only by women is under an enchantment which can be broken only by a hero whose father is unknown. The enchanter can overthrow every one else. Here the situation has been thoroughly rationalized, although some features of it puzzle the knight.

And seþen an oþe[r],[15] par ma fai,
And seþen þe þridde and þe ferþe,—
þe beste þat miȝte gon on erthe!
Mine squiers þat weren so stoute,
Bi foure, bi fiue, þai riden oute,   895
On hors armed wel anowȝ:
His houen[16] bodi he hem slough.
Mine men of mester he slough alle,
And oþer pages of mine halle.
þerfore ich am sore agast   900
Lest he wynne me ate last."
Wiȝ þis word sche fil to grounde,
And lai aswoue a wel gret stounde.
Hire maidenes to hire come
And in hire armes vp hire nome.   905
He beheld þe leuedi wiȝ gret pité.
"Loueli madame," quaþ he,
"On[17] of þine ich am here:
Ich wille þe help, be mi pouere."
"Ȝhe, sire," ȝhe saide, "þan al mi lond   910
Ich wil þe ȝiue into þin hond,
And at þi wille bodi mine,
Ȝif þou miȝt wreke me of hine."
þo was he glad al for to fiȝte,
And wel gladere þat he miȝte   915
Haue þe leuedi so briȝt
Ȝif he slough þat oþer kniȝt.
   And als þai stod and spak ifere,
A maiden cried, wiȝ reuful chere,
"Her comeȝ oure enemi, faste vs ate!   920
Drauwe þe bregge[18] and sschet þe ȝate,
Or he wil slen ous euerichone!"
Sire Degarré stirt vp anon
And at a window him seȝ,
Wel iarmed on hors hegh;   925
A fairer bodi þan he was on

---

[15] second. [16] own; i.e., his very self, with his own hand. [17] one. [18] bridge.

915. MS. A wel.

In armes ne segh he neuer non.
Sire Degarré armed him bliue
And on a stede gan out driue.
Wiჳ a spere gret of gayn,[19]   930
To þe kniჳt he rit aჳein.[20]
Þe kniჳte spere al tosprong,[21]
Ac Degarré was so strong
And so harde to him þrast,[22]
And þe kniჳt sat so fast,   935
Þat þe stede rigge tobrek
And fel to grounde, and he ek;
But anon stir[t][23] vp þe kniჳt
And drouჳ out his swerd briჳt.
"Aliჳt," he saide, "adoun anon;   940
To fiჳt þou sschalt afote gon.
For þou hast slawe mi stede,
Deჳ-dint[24] schal be þi mede;
Ac þine stede sle i nille,
Ac on fote fiჳte ich wille."   945
Þan on fote þai toke þe fiჳt,
And hewe togidere wiჳ brondes briჳt.
Þe kniჳt ჳaf Sire Degarré
Sterne strokes gret plenté,
And he him aჳen also,   950
Þat helm and scheld cleue[25] atwo.
Þe kniჳt was agreued sore
Þat his armour toburste þore:
A strok he ჳaf Sire Degarré,
Þat to grounde fallen is he;   955
But he stirt vp anon riჳt,
And swich a strok he ჳaf þe kniჳt
Vpon his heued so harde iset[26]
Þurh helm and heued and bacinet

---

[19] advantage, worth (at that moment).   [20] aჳein is redundant.   [21] broke in pieces.   [22] thrust.   [23] leaped.   [24] death-blow.   [25] parted in two.   [26] vigorously brought down.

935. MS. But þe. The breaking of the steed's back is common in French romance. Cf. "Chanson de Roland" 1205; also "Eger" 186.
959. MS. þat helm.

Þat ate brest stod[27] þe dent;   960
Ded he fil doun, verraiment.
Þe leuedi lai in o kernel,[28]
And biheld þe batail eueri del.
ȝhe ne was neuer er so bliþe:
Sche þankede God fele sithe.   965
Sire Degarre com into castel;
Aȝein him com þe dammaisel,
And þonked him swiþe of þat dede.
Into chaumber sche gan him lede,
And vnarmed him anon,   970
And set him hire bed vpon,
And saide, "Sire, par charité,
I þe prai dwel wiȝ me,
And al mi lond ich wil þe ȝiue,
And miselue, whil þat i liue."   975
"Grant merci, dame," saide Degarré,
"Of þe gode þou bedest me:
Wende ich wille into oþer londe,
More of hauentours for to fonde;
And be þis twelue moneþ be go,   980
Aȝein ich wil come þe to."
Þe leuedi made moche mourning
For þe kniȝtes departing,
And ȝaf him a stede, god and sur,
Gold and siluer an god armur,   985
And bitauȝt him Ihesu, Heuene-king,
And sore þei wepen at here parting.
   Forht wente Sire Degarré
Þurh mani a diuers cuntré;
Euer-mor he rod west.   990
So in a dale of o forest
He mette wiȝ a douȝti kniȝt
Vpon a stede, god and liȝt,[29]
In armes þat were riche and sur,
Wiȝ þe sscheld of asur[30]   995
And þre bor-heuedes þerin,

---

[27] i.e., stopped.   [28] battlement.   [29] active.   [30] azure.

Wel ipainted wiȝ gold fin.
Sire Degarré anon riȝt
Hendeliche grette þe kniȝt,
And saide, "Sire, God wiȝ þe be;"   1000
And þous aȝein answerede he:
"Velaun,[31] wat dost þou here,
In mi forest to chase mi dere?"
Degarre answerede wiȝ wordes meke:
"Sire, þine der nougt i ne seke: 1005
Iich am an aunterous kniȝt,
For to seche werre and fiȝt."
Þe kniȝt saide, wiȝouten fail,
"Ȝif þou comest to seke batail,
Here þou hast þi per ifounde: 1010
Arme þe swiþe in þis stounde!"
Sire Degarré and his squier
Armed him in riche atir,[32]
Wiȝ an helm riche for þe nones,
Was ful of precious stones   1015
Þat þe maide him ȝaf, saun fail,
For whom he did raþer[33] batail.
A sscheld he kest[34] aboute his swere
Þat was of armes[35] riche and dere,
Wiȝ þre maidenes heuedes of siluer briȝt,   1020
Wiȝ crounes of gold precious of siȝt.
A sschaft he tok þat was nowt smal,
Wiȝ a kene coronal.[36]
His squier tok anoþer spere;
Bi his louerd he gan hit bere.   1025
Lo, swich auentoure þer gan bitide—
Þe sone aȝein þe fader gan ride,
And noiþer ne knew oþer no wiȝt!
Nou biginneȝ þe firste fiȝt.
    Sire Degarre tok his cours þare;   1030
Aȝen his fader a sschaft he bare;

---

[31] villain.   [32] attire.   [33] earlier.   [34] slung.   [35] devices.   Cf. Int. III.D.   [36] steel
head.

1027. On the combat of father and son, cf. M. A. Potter's "Sohrab and
Rustum;" Bruce's note to "Mort Artu" 268; Loomis 77.

To bere him doun he hadde imint.
Riȝt in þe sscheld he set[37] his dint;
Þe sschaft brak to peces al,
And in þe sscheld lat þe coronal.　　　　1035
Anoþer cours þai gonne take;
Þe fader tok, for þe sones sake,
A sschaft þat was gret and long,
And he anoþer also strong.
Togider þai riden wiȝ gret raundoun,[38]　　　1040
And aiþer bar oþer adoun.
Wiȝ dintes þat þai smiten þere,
Here stede rigges toborsten were.
Afote þai gonne fiȝt ifere,
And laiden on wiȝ swerdes clere.　　　　1045
Þe fader amerueiled wes[39]
Whi his swerd was pointles,
And seide to his sone apliȝt,
"Herkne to me a litel wiȝt:
Wher were þou boren, in what lond?"　　　1050
"In Litel Bretaigne, ich vnderstond:
Kingges doughter sone, witouten les,
Ac i not wo mi fader wes."
"What is þi name?" þan saide he.
"Certes, men clepeȝ me Degarré."　　　　1055
"O Degarré, sone mine!
Certes ich am fader þine!
And bi þi swerd i knowe hit here:
Þe point is in min aumenere."[40]
He tok þe point and set þerto;　　　　1060
Degarré fel iswoue þo,
And his fader, sikerli,
Also he gan swony;
And whan he of swoue arisen were,
Þe sone cride[41] merci þere　　　　　1065
His owen fader of his misdede,

---

[37] aimed.　[38] force.　[39] was astonished.　[40] wallet.　[41] begged.

1063. MS. *swouþ*.
1064. MS. *whanne of*.

And he him to his castel gan lede,
And bad him dwelle wiȝ him ai.
"Certes, sire," he saide, "nai;
Ac ȝif hit ȝoure wille were,   1070
To mi moder we wende ifere;
For ȝhe is in gret mourning."
"Bleþelich," quaþ he, "bi Heuene-kyng."

Some leaves are torn out of the manuscript, and the conclusion is
lacking. From the prints of the later version, it is evident that the lost
part dealt with the usual matrimonial adjustments: Degaré rejoins the
lady of the castle; his parents are reunited.

SIR ORFEO

SIR ORFEO

The piece is in the southern dialect of about 1325. The text is numbered as in Zielke's critical edition, based on the Auchinleck Manuscript, with interesting interpolations from two later manuscripts; and with the kind permission of the Oxford Press, Sisam's readings of all manuscripts have been used.

The romance has been a favorite subject of study; the student is referred to Miss Hibbard's discussion, p. 195. Most of the standard histories of the literature of the period have something interesting to say about it. A very close parallel is in the tale of "Connla the Fair" (*Gaelic Journal* II. 307).

We redyn ofte and fynde ywryte,
As clerkes don us to wyte,
þe layes þat ben of harpyng
Ben yfounde[1] of frely þing.
Sum ben of wele and sum of wo,　　　　　　5
And sum of ioy and merþe also,
Sum of trechery and sum of gyle,
And sum of happes þat fallen by whyle,[2]
Sum of bourdys[3] and sum of rybaudry,[4]
And sum þer ben of þe feyré.[5]　　　　　　10
Off alle þing þat men may se,
Moost to lowe[6] forsoþe þey be.
In Brytayn[7] þis layes arne ywryte,
Furst yfounde and forþe ygete—
Of aventures þat fillen by dayes,[8]　　　　　15
Wherof Brytouns made her layes;
When þey myght owher[9] heryn

---

[1] composed.　[2] now and then.　[3] jests.　[4] ribaldry.　[5] faery.　[6] praise.　[7] Brittany.
[8] in bygone days.　[9] anywhere.

1–25 are lacking in the Auchinleck MS., and are supplied from the Harleian MS. 3810.

Of aventures þat þer weryn,
Þey toke her harpys wiþ game,[10]
Maden layes and ӡaf it name.　　　　　　20
Of aventures þat han befalle,
Y can sum telle, but nouӡt all.
Herken, lordyngys þat ben trewe,
And y wol ӡou telle of Sir Orphewe.
Orfeo was a king,　　　　　　25
In Inglond an heiӡe lording,
A stalworþ man and hardi bo,[11]
Large,[12] and curteys he was also.
His fader was comen of King Pluto
And his moder of King Iuno,　　　　　　30
Þat sum time were as godes yhold
For auentours þat þai dede and told.
Orpheo most of ony þing
Louede þe gle of harpyng;
Syker was euery gode harpoure　　　　　　35
Of hym to haue moche honoure.
Hymself loued for to harpe
And layde þeron his wittes scharpe;
He lernyd so, þer noþing[13] was
A better harper in no plas.　　　　　　40
[In] þe world was neuer man born
Þat euer Orpheo sat byforn,
And he myӡt of his harpyng here,
He schulde þinke þat he were
In one of þe ioys of paradys,　　　　　　45
Suche ioy and melody in his harpyng is.
Þis king soiournd in Traciens,
Þat was a cité of noble defens;[14]

---

[10] pleasure.　　[11] as well.　　[12] generous.　　[13] not at all.　　[14] power to resist.

30. MS. H. has *Yno*. "Doubtless the -*o* was evidence of masculinity to this scribe."—E. Rickert. The genealogy here given has no classical authority. 33–46 are lacking in the Auchinleck MS., and are supplied from Harleian MS. 3810.

47. Orpheus was son of a king of Thrace. For the confusion in the following lines, see *Speculum* II. 396, "Euhemerism."

48. The next two lines were omitted by Zielke, though they are in the

For Winchester was cleped þo
Traciens wiþouten no.
Þe King hadde a Quen of priis,
Þat was ycleped Dame Herodis, 50
Þe fairest leuedi for þe nones
Þat miȝt gon on bodi and bones,
Ful of love and godenisse,
Ac no man may telle hir fairnise.
Bifel so in þe comessing[15] of May, 55
When miri[16] and hot is þe day,
And oway beþ winterschours,
And euᵉri feld is ful of flours,
And blosme breme[17] on eueri bouȝ
Oueral wexeþ miri anouȝ, 60
Þis ich[18] Quen, Dame Heurodis,
Tok to maidens of priis
And went in an vndrentide[19]
To play bi an orchardside,
To se þe floures sprede and spring 65
And to here þe foules sing.
Þai sett hem doun al þre
Vnder a fair ympe-tre,[20]
And wel sone þis fair Quene
Fel on slepe opon þe grene. 70
Þe maidens durst hir nouȝt awake,
Bot lete hir ligge and rest take.
So sche slepe til afternone,
Þat vndertide was al ydone.
Ac as sone as sche gan awake, 75
Sche crid and loþli bere[21] gan make,
Sche froted[22] hir honden and hir fet,

---

[15] beginning. [16] merry. [17] fresh. [18] same. [19] morning time. [20] young tree.
[21] grievous cry. [22] rubbed; i.e., writhed.

MS. On Camelot as Winchester, see Bruce's note "Mort Artu" 15;
E. Brugger, "Beiträge zur Erklärung der Arthurischen Geographie"
(*Zeitschrift für Französischen Sprache und Literatur* 28.22). Malory says
(18.10) that Camelot was "that tyme called Wynchester;" see Mead's
note, p. 168.1.
68. Sleeping under a grafted tree put her in the power of the fairies.

And crached[23] hir visage; it bled wete.[24]
Hir riche robe hye al torett[25]
And was reuey[se]d[26] out of hir witt.   80
Þe tvo maidens hir biside
No durst wiþ hir no leng[27] abide,
Bot ourn to þe palays ful riȝt,
And told boþe squier and kniȝt
Þat her Quen awede[28] wold,   85
And bad hem go and hir at-hold.[29]
Kniȝtes vrn and leuedis also,
Damisels sexti and mo.
In þe orchard to þe Quen hye come
And her vp in her armes nome   90
And brouȝt hir to bed atte last
And held hir þere fine[30] fast.
Ac euer sche held in o cri[31]
And wold vp and owy.[32]
When Orfeo herd þat tiding,   95
Neuer him nas wers for no þing.[33]
He come wiþ kniȝtes tene
To chaumber riȝt bifor þe Quene
And biheld, and seyd wiþ grete pité:
"O lef liif, what is te[34]   100
Þat euer ȝete hast ben so stille,
And now gredest[35] wonder schille![36]
Þi bodi, þat was so white ycore,[37]
Wiþ þine nailes is al totore!
Alas, þi rode, þat was so red,   105
Is al wan as þou were ded!
And also þine fingers smale

---

[23] scratched.   [24] wet.   [25] tore.   [26] ravished.   [27] longer.   [28] go mad.   [29] seize.
[30] very.   [31] continued with her lament.   [32] away.   [33] i.e., he was never so unhappy.   [34] what is wrong with you.   [35] cry.   [36] wonderfully loud.   [37] of such
choice whiteness.

78. For this as a sign of distress, cf. "Seven Sages" 535.

79. Cf. "Mort Aymeri" 216: the queen *s'ascrie, Ront ses chevex, et sa robe descire*, as a sign of grief. Cf. also Geoffrey of Monmouth's "Vita Merlini" 360: [*Guendoloena*] *dolet, fletuque fluit, lamatque capillos, Et secat ungue genas.*

80. MS. *reueyd.*—Sisam's emendation.   •

Beþ al blodi and al pale!
Allas! þi louesum eyȝen to
Lokeþ so man doþ on his fo! 110
A dame, ich biseche, merci!
Lete ben al þis reweful[38] cri,
And tel me what þe is and hou,
And what þing may þe help now!"
Þo lay sche stille atte last 115
And gan to wepe swiþe fast
And seyd þus þe King to:
"Allas, mi lord, Sir Orfeo!
Seþþen we first togider were,
Ones wroþ neuer we nere; 120
Bot euer ich haue yloued þe
As mi liif, and so þou me.
Ac now we mot delen ato,[39]
Do þi best,[40] for y mot go!"
"Allas," quaþ he, "forlorn icham! 125
Whider wiltow go, and to wham?
Whider þou gost, ichil wiþ þe,
And whider y go, þou schalt wiþ me."
"Nay, nay, sir, þat nouȝt[41] nis,
Ichil þe telle al hou it is: 130
As ich lay þis vndertide
And slepe vnder our orchardside,
Þer come to me to fair kniȝtes
Wele yarmed al to riȝtes
And bad me comen an heiȝing[42] 135
And speke wiþ her lord þe King.
And ich answerd at wordes bold,
Y durst nouȝt no y nold.[43]
Þai priked oȝain, as[44] þai miȝt driue;
Þo com her King al so bliue 140
Wiþ an hundred kniȝtes and mo,

---

[38] piteous. [39] part. [40] i.e., act for yourself. [41] of no avail. [42] haste. [43] nor would I. [44] i.e., as fast as.

135. The mortal is usually summoned by a messenger into the presence of the fairy king or princess.

And damisels an hundred also,
Al on snowewhite stedes;
As white as milke were her wedes.
Y no seiȝe neuer ȝete bifore   145
So fair creatours ycore:[45]
Þe King hadde a croun on hed:
It nas of siluer no of gold red,
Ac it was of a precious ston:
As briȝt as þe sonne it schon.   150
And as son as he to me cam,
Wold ich, nold ich, he me nam
And made me wiþ him ride
Opon a palfray bi his side
And brouȝt me to his palays,   155
Wele atird in ich ways,[46]
And schewed me castels and tours,
Riuers, forestes, friþ[47] wiþ flours,
And his riche stedes ichon,
And seþþen me brouȝt oȝain hom   160
Into our owhen orchard
And said to me þus afterward:
'Loke, dame, to morwe þatow be
Riȝt here vnder þis ympe-tre,
And þan þou schalt wiþ ous go   165
And liue wiþ ous euer-mo.
And ȝif þou makest ous ylet,[48]
Whar þou be, þou worst yfet,
And totore þine limes al
Þat noþing help þe no schal;   170
And þei þou best so totorn,
Ȝete þou worst wiþ ous yborn.' "
When King Orfeo herd þis cas,
"O we," quaþ he, "allas, allas!
Leuer me were to lete mi liif   175
Þan þus to lese þe Quen mi wiif!"
He asked conseyl at ich man,
Ac no man him help no can.

---

[45] distinguished.   [46] ordered in every way.   [47] field.   [48] delay.

Amorwe þe vndertide is come,
And Orfeo haþ his armes ynome,   180
And wele ten hundred kniȝtes wiþ him,
Ich yarmed stout and grim;
And wiþ þe Quen wenten he
Riȝt vnto þat ympe-tre.
Þai made scheltrom[49] in ich a side   185
And sayd þai wold þere abide,
And dye þer euerichon,
Er þe Quen schuld fram hem gon.
Ac ȝete amiddes hem ful riȝt
Þe Quen was oway ytuiȝt,[50]   190
Wiþ fairi[6] forþ ynome,
Men wist neuer wher sche was bicome.
Þo was þer criing, wepe, and wo!
Þe King into his chaumber is go
And oft swoned opon þe ston[7]   195
And made swiche diol and swiche mon,[8]
Þat neiȝe his liif was yspent.
Þer was non amendement;[9]
He cleped togider his barouns,
Erls, lordes of renouns.   200
And when þai al ycomen were,
"Lordinges," he said, "bifor ȝou here
Ich ordainy[10] min heiȝe steward
To wite mi kingdom afterward;
In mi stede ben he schal,   205
To kepe mi londes oueral.
For now ichaue mi quen ylore,
Þe fairest leuedi þat euer was bore,
Neuer eft y nil no woman se:
Into wildernes ichil te[11]   210
And liue þer euer-more
Wiþ wilde bestes in holtes hore.
And when ȝe vnderstond[12] þat y be spent,
Make ȝou þan a parlement

---

[49] phalanx.   [50] snatched.   [6] magic.   [7] i.e., of the castle floor.   [8] such lament and such complaint.   [9] means of correction.   [10] appoint.   [11] hasten.   [12] i.e., believe me dead.

And chese ʒou a newe king.   215
Now doþ ʒour best[13] wiþ al mi þing!"
Þo was þer wepeing in þe halle
And grete cri among hem alle.
Vnneþe miʒt old or ʒong
For wepeing speke a word wiþ tong.   220
Þai kneled adoun al yfere
And praid him, ʒif his wille were,
Þat he no schuld nouʒt fram hem go.
"Do way,"[14] quaþ he, "it schal be so."
Al his kingdom he forsoke;   225
Bot a sclauin[15] on him he toke:
He no hadde kirtel[16] no hode,
Schert [ne] no noþer gode.
Bot his harp he tok algate
And dede him barfot[17] out atte ʒate: 230
No man most wiþ him go.
O way, what þer was wepe and wo,
When he þat hadde ben king wiþ croun
Went so pouerlich[18] out of toun!
Þurch wode and ouer heþ[19]   235
Into þe wildernes he geþ.
Noþing he fint þat him is ays,[20]
Bot euer he liueþ in gret malais.[21]
He þat hadde ywerd þe fowe and griis[22]
And on bed þe purper biis,[23]   240
Now on hard heþe he liþ,
Wiþ leues and gresse he him wriþ.[24]
He þat hadde had castels and tours,
Riuer, forest, friþ wiþ flours,
Now, þei it comenci to snewe[25] and frese,   245
Þis King mote make his bed in mese.[26]
He þat had yhad kniʒtes of priis
Bifor him kneland and leuedis,
Now seþ he noþing þat him likeþ,

---

[13] what seems best to you. [14] have done! [15] pilgrim's robe. [16] tunic. [17] barefoot. [18] poorly. [19] heath. [20] finds nothing that eases him. [21] distress. [22] worn
spotted fur and grey fur. [23] purple linen. [24] covers. [25] snow. [26] moss.

228. *ne* supplied from Ashmole MS.—Sisam.

Bot wilde wormes[27] bi him strikeþ.[28]   250
He þat had yhad plenté
Of mete and drink, of ich deynté,
Now may he al day digge and wrote,[30]
Er he finde his fille of rote.
In somer he liueþ bi wild frut   255
And berien bot gode lite;[31]
In winter may he noþing finde
Bot rote, grases, and þe rinde.[32]
Al his bodi was oway duine[33]
For missays, and al to-chine.[34]   260
Lord! who may telle þe sore
Þis King sufferd ten ȝere and more!
His here of his berd, blac and rowe,[35]
To his girdel-stede[36] was growe.
His harp, whereon was al his gle,   265
He hidde in an holwe tre;
And when þe weder was clere and briȝt,
He toke his harp to him wel riȝt
And harped at his owhen wille;
Into alle þe wode þe soun gan schille,[37]   270
Þat alle þe wilde bestes þat þer beþ,
For ioie abouten him þai teþ.[38]
And alle þe foules þat þer were
Come and sete on ich a brere,
To here his harping afine,[39]   275
So miche melody was þerin.
And when he his harping lete wold,
No best bi him abide nold.
He miȝt se him bisides[40]
Oft in hot vndertides,   280

---

[27] serpents.   [28] glide.   [30] grub in the soil.   [31] berries worth but little.   [32] bark.
[33] dwindled.   [34] discomfort, and all chapped.   [35] rough.   [36] waist.   [37] resound.
[38] hasten.   [39] at length.   [40] at hand, near.

280. The fairy hunt is fairly common in Celtic literature. Cf. the first
meeting in "Pwyll Prince of Dyved;" and the tradition in Gervase of
Tilbury's "Otia Imperialia" that both at high noon or at full moon King
Arthur and his retainers hunt with dogs, horns, and huntsmen. Cf. also
Hartland's "Science of Fairy Tales," Ch. IX.

þe King o fairy⁴¹ wiþ his rout
Com to hunt him al about
Wiþ dim⁴² cri, and bloweing,
And houndes also wiþ him berking.
Ac no best þai no nome,   285
No neuer he nist whider þai bicome.
And oþerwhile⁴³ he miȝt him se
As a gret ost bi him te,
Wele atourned⁴⁴ ten hundred kniȝtes,
Ich yarmed to his riȝtes,⁴⁵   290
Of cuntenaunce stout and fers,
Wiþ mani desplaid baners,
And ich his swerd ydrawe hold,
Ac neuer he nist whider þai wold.
And oþerwhile he seiȝe oþer þing: 295
Kniȝtes and leuedis com daunceing
In queynt atire, gisely,⁴⁶
Queynt pas⁴⁷ and softly;
Tabours and trunpes⁴⁸ ȝede hem bi
And al maner menstraci.⁴⁹   300
And on a day he seiȝe him biside
Sexti leuedis on hors ride,
Gentil and iolif as brid on ris,⁵⁰
Nouȝt o man amonges hem þer nis.
And ich a faucoun on hond bere   305
And riden on haukin¹ bi o riuere;
Of game þai founde wel gode haunt:²
Maulardes, hayroun, and cormeraunt.³
þe foules of þe water ariseþ,
þe faucouns hem wele deviseþ:⁴   310
Ich faucoun his pray slouȝ.

---

⁴¹ fairyland. ⁴² faint. ⁴³ then. ⁴⁴ attired. ⁴⁵ properly. ⁴⁶ skillfully. ⁴⁷ a strange step. ⁴⁸ trumpets. ⁴⁹ minstrelsy. ⁵⁰ gay as bird on a bough. ¹ a-hawking. ² resort. ³ mallards, heron, and cormorant. ⁴ dispose.

285. Fairies themselves could take the form of animals. See Wimberly, 57. But the ill-success of their hunting is not always insisted on.

287. On the fairy cavalcade, see Wimberly, 193; cf. "Echtra Cormaic i Tir Tairngiri" (*Ir. Texte* III.1.213); Hartland, Ch. V.

þat seiȝe Orfeo and louȝ.
"Parfay," quaþ he, "þer is fair game;
þider ichil, bi Godes name;
Ich was ywon[5] swiche werk to se."   315
He aros and þider gan te.[6]
To a leuedi he was ycome,
Biheld and haþ wele vndernome[7]
And seþ bi al þing þat it is
His owhen quen, Dam Heurodis.   320
Ȝern he biheld hir, and sche him eke,
Ac noiþer to oþer a word no speke.
For messais[8] þat sche on him seiȝe,
þat had ben so riche and so heiȝe,
þe teres fel out of her eiȝe.   325
þe oþer leuedis þis yseiȝe
And maked hir oway to ride;
Sche most wiþ him ho lenger abide.
"Allas," quaþ he, "now me is wo!
Whi nil deþ now me slo!   330
Allas wreche, þat y no miȝt
Dye now after þis siȝt!
Allas! to long last mi liif,
When y no dar nouȝt wiþ mi wiif,
No hye to me, o word speke.   335
Allas, whi nil min hert breke!
Parfay," quaþ he, "tide wat bitide,[9]
Whider-so þis leuedis ride,
þe selue way ichil streche:[10]
Of liif no deþ [y] me no reche!"   340
His sclauain[11] he dede on al so spac[12]
And henge his harp opon his bac
And had wel gode wil to gon—
He no spard[13] noiþer stub no ston.

---

[5] wont. [6] hasten. [7] perceived. [8] unhappiness. [9] befall what may. [10] proceed.
[11] robe. [12] quickly. [13] i.e., trod on many.

322. Speaking to fairies was supposed to be dangerous, unless one said the right thing.
331. MS. *wroche.*—Sisam.

In at a roche[14] þe leuedis rideþ,   345
And he after and nouȝt abideþ.
When he was in þe roche ygo,
Wele þre mile oþer mo,
He com into a fair cuntray,
As briȝt so sonne on somers day,   350
Smoþe and plain and al grene,
Hille no dale was þer non ysene.
Amidde þe lond a castel he siȝe,
Riche and real[15] and wonder heiȝe;
Al þe vtmast[16] wal   355
Was clere and schine as cristal.
An hundred tours þer were about
Degiselich and bataild stout;[17]
Þe butras[18] com out of þe diche,
Of rede gold yarched riche;   360
Þe vousour was anow[rn]ed[19] al
Of ich maner diuers animal.
Wiþin þer wer wide wones[20]
Al of precious stones.
Þe werst piler on to biholde   365
Was al of burnist gold.
Al þat lond was euer liȝt,
For when it schuld be þerk[21] and niȝt,
Þe riche stones liȝt gonne,
As briȝt as doþ at none þe sonne.   370
No man may telle no þenche in þouȝt
Þe riche werk þat þer was wrouȝt.
Bi al þing, him þink þat it is
Þe proude[22] court of paradis.
In þis castel þe leuedis aliȝt;   375
He wold in after, ȝif he miȝt.
Orfeo knokkeþ atte gate;
Þe porter was redi þerate

---

[14] cave.   [15] regal.   [16] outer.   [17] strangely and stoutly battlemented.   [18] buttress.
[19] the vaulting was ornamented.   [20] chambers.   [21] dark.   [22] splendid.

345. The entrance to the Celtic otherworld is often through a cave; cf. Chambers, Ch. VII.

And asked what he wold haue ydo:
"Parfay," quaþ he, "icham a minstrel, lo! 380
To solas þi lord wiþ mi gle,
ȝif his swete wille be."
Þe porter vndede þe ȝate anon
And lete him into þe castel gon.
Þan he gan bihold about al 385
And seiȝe liggeand wiþin þe wal
Of folk þat were þider ybrouȝt
And þouȝt[23] dede and nare nouȝt:
Sum stode wiþouten hade,[24]
And sum non armes nade, 390
And sum þurch þe bodi hadde wounde,
And sum lay wode, ybounde,
And sum armed on hors sete,
And sum astrangled as þai ete,
And sum were in water adreynt,[25] 395
And sum wiþ fire al forschreynt:[26]
Wiues þer lay on child-bedde,
Sum ded, and sum awedde;[27]
And wonder fele þer lay bisides,
Riȝt as þai slepe her vndertides; 400
Eche was þus in þis warld ynome,
Wiþ fairi[28] þider ycome.
Þer he seiȝe his owhen wiif,
Dame Heurodis, his luf luf,[29]
Slepe vnder an ympe-tre; 405
Bi her cloþes he knewe þat it was he.
And when he hadde bihold þis meruails alle,
He went into þe Kinges halle.
Þan seiȝe he þer a semly siȝt:
A tabernacle[30] blisseful and briȝt, 410
Þerin her maister King sete
And her Quen fair and swete.
Her crounes, her cloþes schine so briȝt,

---

[23] seemed.   [24] head.   [25] drowned.   [26] shrivelled.   [27] crazed.   [28] through enchantment.   [29] dear love.   [30] canopy.

386. MS. *seiȝe ful.*

þat vnneþe bihold he hem miȝt.

When he hadde biholden al þat þing, 415

He kneled adoun bifor þe King.

"O lord," he seyd, "ȝif it þi wille were,

Mi menstraci þou schust yhere."

Þe King answerd, "What man artow,

Þat art hider ycomen now? 420

Ich, no[31] non þat is wiþ me,

No sent neuer after þe.

Seþþen þat ich here regni gan,

Y no fond neuer so folehardi man,

Þat hider to ous durst wende, 425

Bot þat ichim wald ofsende."[32]

"Lord," quaþ he, "trowe ful wel,

Y nam bot a pouer menstrel,

And, sir, it is þe maner of ous

To seche mani a lordes hous; 430

Þei we nouȝt welcom no be,

Ȝete we mot proferi forþ our gle."

Bifor þe King he sat adoun

And tok his harp so miri of soun

And tempreþ[33] his harp, as he wele can, 435

And blisseful notes he þer gan,

Þat al þat in þe palays were

Com to him forto here,

And liggeþ adoun to his fete,

Hem þenkeþ his melody so swete. 440

Þe King herkneþ and sitt ful stille;

To here his gle he haþ gode wille:

Gode bourde[34] he hadde of his gle;

Þe riche Quen al so hadde he.

When he hadde stint[35] his harping, 445

Þan seyd to him þe King,

"Menstrel, me likeþ wele þi gle;

Now aske of me what[36] it be,

Largelich[37] ichil þe pay.

---

[31] neither I nor. [32] send for. [33] tunes. [34] enjoyment. [35] ceased. [36] whatever.

[37] generously.

Now speke, and tow miȝt asay."³⁸   450
"Sir," he seyd, "ich biseche þe
þatow woldest ȝiue me
þat ich leuedi, briȝt on ble,
þat slepeþ vnder þe ympe-tre."
"Nay" quaþ þe King, "þat nouȝt nere!³⁹   455
A sori couple of ȝou it were,
For þou art lene, rowe,⁴⁰ and blac,
And sche is louesum wiþouten lac.⁴¹
A loþlich þing it were forþi
To sen hir in þi compayni."   460
"O sir," he seyd, "gentil King,
ȝete were it a wele fouler þing
To here a lesing of þi mouþe;
So, sir, as ȝe seyd nouþe,⁴²
What i wold aski, haue y schold,   465
And nedes þou most þi word hold."
þe King seyd, "Seþþen it is so,
Take hir bi þe hond and go.
Of hir ichil þatow be bliþe."
He kneled adoun and þonked him swiþe;   470
His wiif he tok bi þe hond
And dede him swiþe out of þat lond,
And went him out of þat þede:⁴³
Riȝt as he come, þe way he ȝede.
So long he haþ þe way ynome,   475
To Winchester he is ycome,
þat was his owhen cité;
Ac no man knew þat it was he.
No forþer þan þe tounes ende
For knoweleche⁴⁴ he durst wende;   480
Bot wiþ a begger ybilt⁴⁵ ful narwe
þer he tok his herbarwe,⁴⁶

---

³⁸ if you can.   ³⁹ that would be unfitting.   ⁴⁰ rough.   ⁴¹ blemish.   ⁴² now.
⁴³ country.   ⁴⁴ recognition.   ⁴⁵ lodged.   ⁴⁶ lodging.

467. The scene may be rationalised, and the minstrel's words reduced from a threat to persuasion. Bards were once greatly feared, because their curses and lampoons were supposed to bring bad luck.

480. MS. *ne durst.*

To[47] him and to his owhen wiif,
As a minstrel of pouer liif,
And asked tidings of þat lond,   485
And who þe kingdom held in hond.
Þe pouer begger in his cote
Told him euerich a grot:[48]
Hou her Quen was stole owy,
Ten ȝer gon,[49] wiþ fairy,   490
And hou her King en exile ȝede,
Bot no man nist in wiche þede,[50]
And hou þe steward þe lond gan hold,
And oþer mani þinges him told.
Amorwe, oȝain none tide,   495
He maked his wiif þer abide;
Þe beggers cloþes he borwed[1] anon
And heng his harp his rigge opon,
And went him into þat cité,
Þat men miȝt him bihold and se: 500
Erls and barouns bold,
Buriays and leuedis him gun bihold.
"Lo," þai seyd, "swiche a man!
Hou long þe here hongeþ him opan!
Lo, hou his berd hongeþ to his kne!   505
He is yclongen[2] also a tre!"
And as he ȝede in þe strete,
Wiþ his steward he gan mete,
And loude he sett on him a crie:
"Sir steward," he seyd, "merci!   510
Icham an harpour of heþenisse;
Help me now in þis destresse!"
Þe steward seyd, "Hom wiþ me come:
Of þat ichaue, þou schalt haue some.
Euerich gode harpour is welcom me to   515
For mi lordes loue, Sir Orfeo."[3]
In þe castel þe steward sat atte mete,

---

[47] for.   [48] bit.   [49] ago.   [50] what country.   [1] borrowed.   [2] withered.   [3] i.e., love of my lord, Sir Orfeo.

513. MS. *Com wiþ.*—Schleich.

And mani lording was bi him sete.
Þer were trompour[s] and tabourers,
Harpours fele and crouders.[4]   520
Miche melody þai maked alle,
And Orfeo sat stille in þe halle
And herkneþ.   When þai ben al stille,
He toke his harp and tempred schille.[5]
Þe bli[sse]fulest notes he harped þere,   525
Þat euer ani man yherd wiþ ere;
Ich man liked wele his gle.
Þe steward biheld and gan yse
And knewe þe harp als bliue:
"Menstrel," he seyd, "so mot þou þriue,   530
Where hadestow þis harp and hou?
Y pray þat þou me telle now."
"Lord," quaþ he, "in vncouþe þede[6]
Þurch a wildernes as y ȝede,
Þer y founde in a dale   535
Wiþ lyouns a man totorn smale,
And wolues him froto[7] wiþ teþ so scharp
Bi him y fond þis ich harp;
Wele ten ȝere it is ygo."
"O," quaþ þe steward, "now me is wo!   540
Þat was mi lord, Sir Orfeo.
Allas wreche, what schal y do,
Þat haue swiche a lord ylore!
A way, þat ich was ybore!
Þat him was so hard grace yȝarked[8]   545
And so vile deþ ymarked!"
Adoun he fel aswon[9] to grounde;
His barouns him toke vp in þat stounde
And telleþ him hou it geþ:
It nis no bot of manes deþ!   550
King Orfeo knewe wele bi þan
His steward was a trewe man,

---

[4] fiddlers, players on crowd. [5] tuned musically. [6] strange lands. [7] ate. [8] prepared; that such misfortune was his lot and doomed to so vile a death. [9] swooning.

525. MS. *blifulest.*

And loued him as he auȝt to do,
And stont vp and seyt þus, "Lo,
Steward, herkne now þis þing:⁣   555
Ȝif ich were Orfeo þe King,
And hadde ysuffred ful ȝore
In wildernisse miche sore,
And hadde ywon mi quen owy
Out of þe lond of fairy,⁣   560
And hadde ybrouȝt þe leuedi hende
Riȝt here to þe tounes ende,
And wiþ a begger her in ynome,¹⁰
And were miself hider ycome
Pouerlich to þe, þus stille,⁣   565
For to asay þi gode wille;
And ich founde þe þus trewe,
þou no schust it neuer rewe:
Sikerlich for loue or ay¹¹
þou schust be king after mi day.⁣   570
And ȝif þou of mi deþ hadest ben bliþe,
þou schust haue voided¹² also swiþe."
þo al þo þat þerin sete
þat it was King Orfeo vnderȝete,¹³
And þe steward him wele knewe,⁣   575
Ouer and ouer þe bord he þrewe¹⁴
And fel adoun to his fet;
So dede euerich lord þat þer sete,
And al þai seyd at o criing:¹⁵
"Ȝe beþ our lord, sir, and our king!"⁣   580
Glad þai were of his liue.
To chaumber þai ladde him als biliue,¹⁶
And baþed him and schaued his berd
And tired him as a king apert.¹⁷
And seþþen wiþ gret processioun⁣   585
þai brouȝt þe Quen into þe toun,
Wiþ al maner menstraci.

---

¹⁰ took her lodgings. ¹¹ fear. ¹² left. ¹³ understood. ¹⁴ i.e., knocked the board
off its trestles in his haste. ¹⁵ shout. ¹⁶ very quickly. ¹⁷ distinguished.

576. A common sign of excitement. Cf. Child V.498.

Lord, þer was grete melody!
For ioie þai wepe wiþ her eiӡe,
Þat hem so sounde ycomen seiӡe.   590
Now King Orfeo newe coround[18] is
And his quen, Dame Heurodis,
And liued long afterward,
And seþþen was king þe steward.
Harpours in Bretaine after þan   595
Herd hou þis meruaile bigan,
And made herof a lay of gode likeing[19]
And nempned it after þe King.
Þat lay "Orfeo" is yhote;
Gode is þe lay, swete is þe note.   600
Þus com Sir Orfeo out of his care.
God graunt ous alle wele to fare!

---

[18] crowned.   [19] charm.

SIR LAUNFAL

SIR LAUNFAL

The poem is in the southern dialect of about 1350. The unique text of this version is in MS. Cotton Caligula AII. With the kind permission of the authorities of the British Museum Library, the text of this edition has been prepared from rotographs.

So much has been written on this charming work that the reader need only be referred to Wells's bibliography for full discussions. It is a fairly ornate and literary version of a story of which more primitive versions also survive. (See *Am. Journal of Phil.* 10. 1.) Probably it is not directly from Marie de France's lai. Parallels in Celtic literature are found in "The Debility of the Ultonian Warriors," Meyer and Nutt's text of "The Voyage of Bran" I. 2, and "The Destruction of Da Derga's Hostel" (*Rev. Celt.* 22.15). Other incidental parallels are mentioned in the notes.

The manuscript shows a curious mixture of dentals, especially of -d- and -þ-. (See E. Rickert's "Emaré" x.) Flourishes at the ends of words have been printed as -e, except when the last letters are -ll, -ʒth, and -gh, which invariably have a cross-stroke, and -ch, which is uncrossed only in l. 993. The flourish after -r has been expanded to -e only when it is elaborate.

For various references to the fairy world, see Miss Hibbard's chapter on "Partonope de Blois;" and on p. 197 she lists the most useful studies and general articles on the subject. Wimberly also has much information.

> Be douʒty Artours dawes
> Þat heldc Engelond yn good lawes,
> Þere fell a wondyre cas
> Of a ley þat was ysette,[1]
> Þat hyʒt Launual, and hatte ʒette;[2]
> Nów herkeneþ how hyt was:
>
> Douʒty Artoure som whyle
> Soiournede yn Kardeuyle,[3]

---

[1] composed. [2] is still so called. [3] Carlisle?

Heading. The title of the poem in the MS. is *Launfal Miles.*

Wythe ioye and greet solas;
And kny3tes þat were profitable[4]   10
With Artour of þe Rounde Table,
Neuere noon bettere þer nas:[5]

Sere Perseuall and Sere Gawayn,
Syr Gyheryes and Syr Agrafrayn[6]
And Launcelet du Lake;   15
Syr Kay and Syr Ewayn,
þat well couþe fy3te yn playn,
Bateles for to take;[7]

Kyng Banboo3t and Kyng Bos[8]—
Of ham þer was a greet los:[9]   20
Men sawe þo nowhere here make;[10]—
Syre Galafre and Syr Launfale,
Whereof a noble tale
Among vs schall awake.

With Artoure þer was a bachelere,   25
And hadde ybe well many a 3ere:
Launfal for soþ he hy3t;
He gaf gyftys largelyche[11]—
Golde and syluere and clodes ryche,
To squyer and to kny3t.   30

For hys largesse and hys bounté,
þe kynges stuward made was he
Ten yere, y you ply3t;
Of alle þe kny3tes of þe Table Rounde,
So large þer nas noone yfounde,   35
Be dayes ne be ny3t.

---

[4] serviceable. [5] i.e., he was surrounded with the best of his knights. [6] Agravayn. [7] assume. [8] Ban, King of Benwick in France; and Bors, his brother. [9] praise. [10] equals. [11] generously.

19. For conjectures on these names, cf. Loomis 146, 148.
22. Sir Galafre is not mentioned elsewhere in Arthurian romance. In French romance, several Saracens bear the name.
25. A bachelor was a young knight with too few followers or too little wealth to raise his own banner; he therefore followed the banner of another knight.

So hyt befyll yn þe tenþe ȝere,
Marlyn was Artours counsalere;
   He radde hym for to wende
To Kyng Ryon[12] of Irlond ryȝt,   40
And fette hym þer a lady bryȝt,
   Gwennere[13] hys douȝtyr hende.

So he dede, and hom her brouȝt;
But Syr Launfal lykede her noȝt,
   Ne oþer knyȝtes þat were hende;   45
For þe lady bar los of swych word[14]
Þat sche hadde lemannys vnþer here lord,[15]
   So fele þere nas noon ende.[16]

Þey were ywedded, as y you say,
Vpon a Wytsonday,   50
   Before princes of moch pryde;
No man ne may telle yn tale
What folk þer was at þat bredale,[17]
   Of countreys fere and wyde!

No noþer man was yn halle ysette   55
But he were prelat oþer baronette
   (In herte ys noȝt to hyde);
Yf þey satte noȝt alle ylyke,
Hare seruyse[18] was good and ryche,
   Certeyn yn ech a syde;[19]   60

And whan þe lordes hadde ete yn þe halle
And þe cloþes were drawen alle,
   As ye mowe her and lyþe,[20]
The botelers sentyn[21] wyn
To alle þe lordes þat were þeryn,   65
   With chere boþe glad and blyþe.

---

[12] Ryence. [13] Guinevere. [14] had the reputation. [15] i.e., courtiers. [16] so many that there was no end (of them). [17] bridal festivity. [18] attendance on them. [19] i.e., everywhere. [20] hear. [21] butlers served.

46. The unfavorable portrait of Guinevere is from a tradition or story form in which the fairy wife of a mortal is claimed by her former husband, an enchanter. Cf. Bruce I.203 ff.

56. A banneret was a knight who could bring followers into the field under his own banner.

Þe Quene yaf [g]yftes for þe nones,
Gold and seluere and precyous stonys,
 Here curtasye to kyþe;
Euerych knyȝt sche ȝaf broche oþer ryng,   70
But Syr Launfal sche yaf no þyng—
 Þat greuede hym many a syde.[22] ·

And whan þe bredale was at ende,
Launfal tok hys leue to wende
 At Artoure þe kyng,   75
And seyde a lettere was to hym come
Þat deþ hadde hys fadyr ynome:
 He most to hys beryynge.[23]

Þo seyde Kyng Artour, þat was hende,
"Launfal, yf þou wylt fro me wende,   80
 Tak with þe greet spendyng,[24]
And my sustere sones two:
Boþe þey schull with þe go,
 At hom þe for to bryng."

Launfal tok leue, withoute fable,[25]   85
With knyȝtes of þe Rounde Table,
 And wente forþ yn hys iourné
Tyl he com to Karlyoun,[26]
To þe Meyrys[27] hous of þe toune,
 Hys seruaunt þat hadde ybe.[28]   90

The Meyr stod, as ye may here,
And sawe hym come ryde vp anblere,[29]
 With two knyȝtes and oþer mayné;
Agayns hym he haþ wey ynome,
And seyde, "Syre, þou art wellcome;   95
 How faryþ oure Kyng, tel me."

Launfal answerede and seyde þan,
 "He faryþ as well as any man,

---

[22] time. [23] burying. [24] money for expenses. [25] deceit. [26] Caerleon-on-Usk.
[27] mayor's. [28] who had been Launfal's servant. [29] at an easy pace.

72. The scribe's spelling has been retained in *syde*, and in many similar
cases where the rhyme shows an incorrect form.

And elles greet ruþe hyt wore;
But, Syr Meyr, without lesyng, 100
I am þepartyþ[30] fram þe Kyng,
   And þat rewythe me sore;

Neþer þare[31] no man, beneþe ne aboue,
For þe Kyng Artours loue[32]
   Onowre[33] me neuer-more; 105
But, Syr Meyr, y pray þe, par amoure,
May y take with þe soioure?[34]
   Som tyme we knewe vs yore."[35]

Þe Meyr stod and beþoȝte hym þere
What myȝt be hys answere, 110
   And to hym þan gan he sayn:
"Syr, vii knyȝtes han here hare in ynom[e],[36]
And euer y wayte whan þey wyl come,
   Þat arn of Lytyll Bretayne."[37]

Launfal turnede hym self and lowȝ: 115
Þerof he hadde scorn inowȝ;
   And seyde to hys knyȝtes twcyno,
"Now may ye se, swych ys seruice
Vnþer a lord of lytyll pryse—
   How he may þerof be fayn!"[38] 120

Launfal awayward gan to ryde;
Þe Meyr bad he schuld abyde,
   And seyde yn þys manere:
"Syr, yn a chamber by my orchard syd[e],
Þer may ye dwelle, with ioye and pryde, 125
   ȝyf hyt your wyll were."

Launfal anoon ryȝtes,
He and hys two knytes,
   Soiournede þer yn fere.
So sauagelych hys good he besette[39] 130

---

[30] departed.   [31] need.   [32] i.e., to please Arthur.   [33] honor.   [34] lodging.   [35] i.e.,
we have long been acquainted.   [36] have taken their lodging here.   [37] Brittany.
[38] i.e., how a lord of little power cannot be happy at the lack of respect shown
him.   [39] such fierce inroads he made on his wealth.

130. MS. *sauragelych.*

þat he ward[40] yn greet dette
Ryȝt yn þe ferst yere.

So hyt befell at Pentecost,
Swych tyme as þe Holy Gost
   Among mankend[41] gan lyȝt,   135
þat Syr Huwe and Syr Ion
Tok here leue for to gon
   At Syr Launfal þe knyȝt;

þey seyd, "Sir, our robes beþ torent,
And your tresoure ys all yspent,   140
   And we goþ ewyll ydyȝt."[42]
þanne seyde Sir Launfal to þe knyȝtes fr[e],
Tellyd no man of my pouerté,
   Ffor þe loue of God Almyȝt."

þe knyȝtes answerede and seyde þo   145
þat þey nolde hym wreye neuir-mo,
   All þys world to wynne;
With þat word þey wente hym fro
To Glastyngbery, boþe two,
   þer Kyng Artoure was inne.   150

þe Kyng sawe þe knyȝtes hende,
And aȝens ham he gan wende,
   For þey were of hys kenne;
Noon oþer robes þey ne hadde
þan þey owt[42a] with ham ladde,   155
   And þo were totore and thynne.

þan seyde Quene Gwenore, þat was fel,[43]
"How faryþ þe prowde knyȝt Launfal?
   May he hys armes welde?"[44]
"Ȝe, madame," sayde þe knytes þan,   160

---

[40] came to be.   [41] mankind.   [42] poorly clothed.   [42a] i.e., away.   [43] malicious.
[44] can he (still) manage weapons?

140. MS. *tosoure.*
149. On the attachment of Arthur to Glastonbury, see E. K. Chambers, "Arthur of Britain" 112 ff.

"He faryþ as well as any man,
And ellys, God hyt schelde!"[45]

Moche worchyp and greet honour
To Gonnore þe Quene and Kyng Artoure
   Of Syr Launfal þey telde,[46]   165
And seyde, "He louede vs so
þat he wold vs euir-mo
   At wyll haue yhelde.[47]

But vpon a rayny day hyt befel
An-huntynge wente Syr Launfel,   170
   To chasy yn holtes hore;
In oure old robes we yede þat day,
And þus we beþ ywent[48] away,
   As[49] we before hym wore."

Glad was Artoure þe Kyng   175
þat Launfal was yn good lykyng;[50]
   þe Quene hyt rew well sore,
For sche wold, with all here myʒt,
þat he hadde be, boþe day and nyʒt,
   In paynys more and more.[1]   180

Vpon a day of þe Trinité,
A feste of greet solempnité
   In Carlyoun was holde;
Erles and barones of þat countré,
Ladyes and borieies[2] of þat cité,   185
   þyder come, boþe yongh and olde;

But Launfal, for hys pouerté,
Was not bede to þat scmblé:
   Lyte men of hym tolde.[3]
þe Meyr to þe feste was ofsent;[4]   190
þe Meyrys douʒter to Launfal went,
   And axede yf he wolde

---

[45] God forbid it should be otherwise. [46] spoke, said. [47] kept at his will; i.e., retained. [48] have gone; i.e., went. [49] (in such robes) as. [50] well suited. [1] in greater and greater pain. [2] burgesses. [3] men counted him as of little worth. [4] summoned.

In halle dyne with here þat day.
"Damesele," he sayde, "nay:
  To dyne haue i no herte;   195
Þre dayes þer ben agon,[5]
Mete ne drynke eet y noon,
  And all was fore pouert.[6]

To-day to cherche y wolde haue gon,
But me fawtede[7] hosyn and schon,   200
  Clenly brech[8] and scherte;
And fore defawte of clodynge,
Ne myȝte y yn with þe peple þrynge;[9]
  No wonþer douȝ me smerte![10]

But o þyng, damesele, y pray þe: 205
Sadel and brydel lene þou me
  A whyle for to ryde,
Þat y myȝte confortede be
By a launde[11] vnþer þys cyté,
  Al yn þys vndern[12]-tyde."   210

Launfal dyȝte hys courser
Withoute knaue oþer squyer;
  He rood with lytyll pryde;
Hys hors slod[13] and fel yn þe fen,[14]
Wherefore hym scornede many men   215
  Abowte hym fere and wyde.

Pouerly[15] þe knyȝt to hors gan sprynge;
For to dryue away lokynge,[16]
  He rood toward þe west.
Þe weþer was hot þe vndern-tyde;   220
He lyȝte adoun and gan abyde
  Vnder[17] a fayr forest;

---

[5] for the past three days. [6] poverty. [7] I lacked. [8] breeches. [9] press. [10] if
I feel the hurt. [11] on a heath. [12] morning. [13] slipped. [14] mud. [15] humbly.
[16] to avoid notice. [17] close by.

220. Mortals who slept under certain trees when the sun was hot
might fall into the power of the fairies. Cf. Child II.505, III.456; "Degaré" 70–2; and "Orfeo" 68 ff.

And for hete of þe wedere,
Hys mantell he felde[18] togydere,
   And sette hym doun to reste;   225
Þus sat þe kny3t yn symplyté,
In þe schadwe, vnþer a tre,
   Þer þat hym lykede best.

As he sat, yn sorow and sore,
He sawe come out of holtes hore   230
   Gentyll maydenes two;
Har kerteles were of Inde-sandel[19]
Ilased smalle, iolyf,[20] and well:
   Þer my3t noon gayere go.

Hare manteles were of grene felwet,[21]   235
Ybordured with gold, ry3t well ysette,
   Ipelured with grys and gro.[22]
Hare heddys were dy3t well withalle:
Euerych hadde oon a iolyf coronall[23]
   With syxty gemmys and mo.   240

Hare faces were whyt as snow on downe;
Har rode was red, here eyn were browne·
   I sawe neuir non swyche!
Þat oon barc of gold a basyn,
Þat oþer a towayle,[24] whyt and fyn,   245
   Of selk þat was good and ryche.

Hare kercheues were well schyre,[25]
Arayd with ryche golde wyre;[26]
   Launfal began to syche.[27]
Þey com to hym ouir þe heth:[28]   250
He was curteys, and a3ens hem geth,
   And greette hem myldelyche:

---

[18] folded.   [19] gowns were of rich silk from India.   [20] laced tight, attractively.
[21] velvet.   [22] trimmed with gray and gray-and-white squirrels' fur.   [23] diadem.
[24] towel.   [25] bright.   [26] ornamented with fine gold thread.   [27] sigh.   [28] heath.

244. The maidens are to offer these to the guests before the meal which
is about to take place (339).
250–1. MS. *hoth, goth.*

"Damesels," he seyde, "God yow se !"
"Syr kny3t," þey seyde, "well þe be !
Oure lady, Dame Tryamour,   255
Bad þou schuldest com speke with here,
3yf hyt were þy wylle, sere,
Withoute more soiour."²⁹

Launfal hem grauntede curteyslyche,
And wente with hem myldelyche;   260
þey wheryn³⁰ whyt as floure.
And when þey come in þe forest an hy3,
A pauyloun yteld³¹ he sy3,
With merthe and mochell honoure.

þe pauyloun was wrouth,³² fore soþe ywys,   265
All of werk of Sarsynys:
þe pomelles³³ of crystall;
Vpon þe toppe an ern³⁴ þer stod
Of bournede³⁵ golde, ryche and goode,
Iflorysched³⁶ with ryche amall;³⁷   270

Hys eyn were carbonkeles bry3t—
As þe mone þe[y] schon a-ny3t,
þat spreteþ³⁸ out ouyr all;
Alysaundre þe conqueroure
Ne Kyng Artoure yn hys most honour   275
Ne hadde noon scwych iuell !³⁹

He fond yn þe pauyloun
þe Kynges dou3ter of Olyroun,
Dame Tryamoure þat hy3te;

---

²⁹ delay. ³⁰ were. ³¹ pitched. ³² wrought. ³³ balls on the tops of poles. ³⁴ eagle.
³⁵ burnished. ³⁶ decorated. ³⁷ enamel. ³⁸ spreads. ³⁹ such jewel.

256. The coming of the hero is often expected by the fairy. Cf., e.g.,
"The Voyage of Maelduin" (Rev. Celt. 9.491).
265. The weaving and metal-work of the Saracens were admired
throughout Europe.
271. On carbuncles that shone at night, see "Havelok" 2145.

Here fadyr was kyng of fayrye 280
Of Occient, fere and nyȝe,
A man of mochell myȝte.

In þe pauyloun he fond a bed of prys
Iheled with purpur bys,[40]
þat semyle was of syȝte. 285
þerinne lay þat lady gent
þat aftere Sir Launfal hedde ysent,
þat lefsom lemede[41] bryȝt.

For hete her cloþes down sche dede
Almest to here gerdylstede;[42] 290
þan lay sche vncouert;
Sche was as whyt as lylye yn May
Or snow þat sneweþ yn wynterys day:
He seygh neuere non so pert.[43]

þe rede rose, whan sche ys newe, 295
Aȝens here rode nes nauȝt of hewe,[44]
I dar well say yn sert;[45]
Here here schon as gold wyre;
May no man rede[46] here atyre,
Ne nauȝt well þenke yn hert. 300

Sche seyde, "Launfal, my lemman swete,
Al my ioye for þe y lete,

---

[40] covered with purple linen. [41] lovely one shone. [42] waist. [43] attractive. [44] i.e.,
would seem of poor color. [45] surely. [46] read of.

278, 281. The two names may be substitutions: "Sir Landeval" has,
Amylione, That ys an ile of the fayré, In occian full faire to see. Possibly
Oléroun—an island off the west coast of France, famous for its maritime
code—was used for the less familiar Avalon (see *Am. Jour. of Philology*
10.13); and Occiant—a Saracen land mentioned in French poetry (cf.
"Chanson" 3246, 3474, 3517, etc.)—is for some reputed otherworld island
like the Orkneys. Cf. Loomis 214; *PMLA* 15.171.

302. This statement appears also in the "Lai of Graelent" (Barbazon
IV.57), from which Chester seems to have taken part of his material.

Swetyng[47] paramour:
Þer nys no man yn Cristenté
Þat y loue so moche as þe,   305
Kyng neyþer emperoure!"

Launfal beheld þat swete wyȝth—
All hys loue yn her was lyȝth—
And keste þat swete flour,
And sat adoun her bysyde,   310
And seyde, "Swetyng, what so betyde,
I am to þyn honoure."[48]

She seyde, "Sir Knyȝt, gentyl and hende,
I wot þy stat, ord and ende;[49]
Be nauȝt aschamed of[50] me.   315
Yf þou wylt truly to me take,
And alle wemen for me forsake,
Ryche i wyll make þe.

I wyll þe ȝeue an alner[1]
Imad of sylk and of gold cler,   320
With fayre ymages þre;
As oft þou puttest þe hond þerinne,
A mark of gold þou schalt wynne,
In wat place þat þou be."

Also sche seyde, "Syr Launfal,   325
I ȝeue þe Blaunchard, my stede lel,[2]
And Gyfre, my owen knaue;
And of my armes oo pensel,[3]
With þre ermyns ypeynted well,
Also þou schalt haue.   330

---

[47] beloved. [48] service. [49] state, first and last. [50] before. [1] purse. [2] loyal, true.
[3] a banner.

310. On the fairy's making the advances, see Bruce's "Mort Artu" 270;
Mead's "Malory," 297.
316. *To* is unnecessary to the construction in Modern English.
319. On the purse that is never empty, cf. Bela-Lazar, "Über das
Fortunatus-Märchen" (Leipzig, 1897) 34; *FF Communications* 74.224, 580.

In werre ne yn turnement,
Ne schall þe greue[4] no knyʒtes dent,
So well y schall þe saue."
Þan answerede þe gantyl[5] knyʒt,
And seyde, "Gramarcy, my swete wyʒt: 335
No bettere chepe[6] y haue."

Þe damesell gan here vp sette,
And bad here maydenes here fette
To hyr hondys watyr clere;
Hyt was ydo without lette.   340
Þe cloþ was spred, þe bord was sette,
Þey wente to hare sopere.

Mete and drynk þey hadde afyn,
Pyement, claré, and Reynysch[7] wyn,
And elles, greet wondyr hyt were.[8]   345
Whan þey had sowpeþ[9] and þe day was gon,
Þey wente to bedde, and þat anoon,
Launfal and sche yn fere.

For play lytyll þey sclepte[10] þat nyʒt,
Tyll on morn hyt was day lyʒt;   350
Sche badde hym aryse anoon.
Hy seyde to hym, "Syr gantyl Knyʒt,
And þou wylt speke with me any wyʒt,[11]
To a derne[12] stede þou gon:

Well priuyly i woll come to þe—   355
No man alyue ne schall me se—
As stylle as any ston."
Þo was Launfal glad and blyþe—
He cowde no man hys ioye kyþe[13]—
And keste here well good won.   360

---

[4] hurt.   [5] gentle.   [6] bargain.   [7] Rhenish.   [8] it would have been strange had
it been otherwise.   [9] supped.   [10] slept.   [11] amount; i.e., time.   [12] secluded.
[13] make known (because it was so great).

336. MS. *kepte.*

355. On the unwillingness of the fairy wife to appear to any mortal
but her husband, cf. *MPhil.* 12.622.   On her invisibility, cf. Cox, "Cinderella" 517; Wimberly 174.

"But of o þyng, Sir Kny3t, i warne þe:
þat þou make no bost[14] of me
   For no kennes mede;[15]
And yf þou doost, y warny þe before,
All my loue þou hast forlore!"   365
   And þus to hym sche seyde.

Launfal tok hys leue to wende;
Gyfre kedde þat he was hende,
   And brou3t Launfal hys stede.
Launfal lepte yn to þe arsoun[16]   370
And rood hom to Karlyoun
   In hys pouere wede.

þo was þe kny3t yn herte at wylle:[17]
In hys chaunber he hyld hym stylle
   All þat vndern-tyde.   375
þan come þer þorwgh þe cyté ten
Well yharneysyth[18] men,
   Vpon ten somers ryde,[19]

Some with syluer, some with golde;
All to Syr Launfal hyt scholde;[20]   380
   To presente hym wythe pryde
With ryche cloþes and armure bry3t,
þey axede aftyr Launfal, þe kny3t,
   Whare he gan abyde.

þe yong men wer clodeþ yn ynde;[21]   385
Gyfre he rood all behynde
   Vp[22] Blaunchard, whyt as flour.
þo seyde a boy þat yn þe market stod,
"How fere schall all þys good?[23]
   Tell vs, par amour."   390

---

[14] boast.   [15] i.e., on any consideration.   [16] saddle.   [17] pleased.   [18] armored.
[19] riding on ten pack-horses.   [20] sc. "go."   [21] Indian silk.   [22] upon.   [23] how far
(i.e., whither) shall this wealth (go)?

362. Fairy stories involving the union of a mortal and an immortal
commonly have some such prohibition. Cf. *MPhil.* 12.585; *HarvStN.*
viii (1903).

Þo seyde Gyfre, "Hyt ys ysent
To Syr Launfal yn present,
  Þat haþ leued yn greet doloure."
Þan seyde þe boy, "Nys he but a wrecche![24]
What þar[25] any man of hym recche?   395
  At þe Meyrys hous he takeþ soioure."

At þe Merys hous þey gon aly3te,
And presented þe noble Kny3te
  With swych good as hym was sent;
And whan þe Meyr sey3 þat rychesse[26]   400
And Syr Launfales noblenesse,[27]
  He held hymself foule yschent.

Þo seyde þe Meyr, "Syr, par charyté,
In halle to-day þat þou wylt ete with me;
  3esterday y hadde yment   405
At þe feste we wold han be yn same,
And yhadde solas and game,
  And erst þou were ywent."[28]

"Syr Meyr, God for3elde[29] þe:
Whyles y was yn my pouerté,   410
  Þou bede me neuer dyne;
Now y hauc more gold and fe
Þat myne frendes han sent me,
  Þan þou and alle dyne!"[30]

Þe Meyr for schame away 3ede;   415
Launfal yn purpure gan hym schrede,[31]
  Ipelured[32] with whyt ermyne.
All þat Launfal hadde borwyþ before,
Gyfre, be tayle and be score,[33]
  3ald[34] hyt well and fyne.   420

Launfal helde ryche festes,

---

[24] poor creature.   [25] why need.   [26] wealth.   [27] (new) state.   [28] first (i.e., before
I had opportunity) you were gone.   [29] reward.   [30] thine.   [31] array.
[32] trimmed.   [33] according to tally-stick and written account.   [34] repaid.

421. The minstrels admired liberal patrons; but Launfal's generosity is
exceptional even for a minstrel's hero.

Fyfty fedde pouere gestes,[35]
Þat yn myschef[36] were;
Fyfty bouȝte stronge stedes;
Fyfty yaf ryche wedes   425
    To knyȝtes and squyere;

Fyfty rewardede relygyons;[37]
Fyfty delyuerede pouere prysouns,[38]
    And made ham quyt and schere;[39]
Fyfty clodede gestours;[40]—   430
To many men he dede honours,
    In countreys fere and nere.

Alle þe lordes of Karlyoun
Lette crye[41] a turnement yn þe toun,
    For loue of Syr Launfel   435
And for Blaunchard hys good stede,
To wyte how hym wold spede,
    Þat was ymade so well.

And whan þe day was ycome
Þat þe iustes were yn ynome,[42]   440
    Þey ryde out also snell;
Trompours gon hare bemes[43] blowe,
Þe lordes ryden out arowe[44]
    Þat were yn þat castell;

There began þe turnement,   445
And ech knyȝt leyd on oþer good dent
    With mases[45] and with swerdes boþe.
Me myȝte yse some þerfore[46]
Stedes ywonne, and some ylore,
    And k[n]yȝtes wonþer wroȝth.   450

Sythe þe Rounde Table was,
    A bettere turnement þer nas,

---

[35] guests. [36] misfortune. [37] members of religious orders. [38] prisoners. [39] relieved
and clear (of debt). [40] minstrels. [41] proclaim. [42] on which the jousts were
held. [43] horns. [44] in order. [45] maces. [46] as a result.

422. The *fyfty* refers to the following nouns.
449. See "Havelok" 40 for note on the horse as a prize in combat.

I dare well say for soþe;
Many a lord of Karlyou[n]
þat day were ybore adoun,   455
Certayn, withouten oþe.[47]

Of Karlyoun þe ryche constable
Rod to Launfal, without fable:
He nolde no lengere abyde;
He smot to Launfal, and he to hym;   460
Well sterne strokes and well grym
þer were, yn eche a syde.

Launfal was of hym yware:[48]
Out of hys sadell he hym bare
To grounde þat ylke tyde;   465
And whan þe constable was bore adoun,
Gyfre lepte ynto þe arsoun,[49]
And awey he gan to ryde.

þe Erl of Chestere þerof segh;[50]
For wreþþe yn herte he was wod negh,   470
And rood to Syr Launfale,
And smot hym yn þe helm on hegh,
þat þe crest adoun flegh:
þus seyd þe Frenssche tale.

Launfal was mochel of myȝt: 475
Of hys stede he dede hym lyȝt
And bare hym doun yn þe dale.
þan come þer Syr Launfal abowte
Of Walssche knyȝtes a greet rowte,
þe numbre y not how fale.[1]   480

þan myȝte me se scheldes ryue,[2]
Speres tobreste and todryue,[3]
Behynde and ek before;[4]

---

[47] oath.   [48] aware; i.e., perceived him.   [49] saddle.   [50] saw.   [1] I know not how
many.   [2] broken.   [3] splintered and split.   [4] i.e., all about.

469. The Earl of Chester was long one of the most absolute and powerful lords in England, and hence is a stock character in romances.

474. The "French tale" was probably two tales. Cf. *PMLA* 15.121.

Þoruȝ Launfal and hys stedes dent,
Many a knyȝt, verement,   485
    To ground was ibore.

So þe prys of þat turnay
Was delyuered to Launfal þat day,
    Without oþ y swore.
Launfal rod to Karl[youn],   490
To þe Meyrys hous [of] þe toun,
    And many a lord hym before;

And þan þe noble knyȝt Launfal
Held a feste, ryche and ryall,
    Þat leste[5] fourtenyȝt;   495
Erles and barouns fale
Semely were sette yn sale,[6]
    And ryaly were adyȝt;

And euery day Dame Triamour,
Sche com to Syr Launfal boure,   500
    A-day[7] whan hyt was nyȝt;
Of all þat euer were þer þo,
Segh he[r] non but þey two,
    Gyfre and Launfal þe knyȝt.

A knyȝt þer was yn Lumbardye;   505
To Syr Launfal hadde he greet enuye:
    Syr Valentyne he hyȝte.
He herde speke of Syr Launfal,
How þat he couþ iusty[8] well,
    And was a man of mochel myȝte.   510

Syr Valentyne was wonþere strong;
Ffyftene feet he was longe:
    Hym þoȝte he brente bryȝte[9]

---

[5] lasted.   [6] hall.   [7] at an hour.   [8] joust.   [9] i.e., he was fired with a desire.

484. The strength of the horse and his willingness to charge an opponent were as important as the knight's own prowess.
505. Schofield thought this incident mere padding (*PMLA* 15.152).
509. MS. *þat þat.*—Kaluza.

But he myȝte with Launfal pleye
In þe feld, betwene ham tweye   515
   To iusty oþer to fyȝte.

Syr Valentyne sat yn hys halle;
Hys massengere he let ycalle,
   And seyde he moste wende
To Syr Launfal, þe noble knyȝt,   520
Þat was yholde so mychel of myȝt:
   To Bretayne he wolde hym sende;

"And sey hym, fore loue of hys lemman,
Yf sche be any gantyle woman,
   Courteys, fre, oþer hende,   525
Þat he come with me to iuste,
To kepe hys harneys[10] from þe ruste,
   And elles hys manhod schende."

Þe messengere ys forþ ywent;
To þo[11] hys lordys commaundcment,   530
   He hadde wynde at wylle.[12]
Whan he was ouer þe water ycome,
Þe way to Syr Launfal he haþ ynome,
   And grette hym with wordes stylle,

And seyd, "Syr, my lord, Syr Valentyne,   535
A noble werrour and queynte of gynne,[13]
   Haþ me sent þc tylle,
And praythe þe, for þy lemmanes sake,
Þou schuldest with hym iustes take."[14]
   Þo louȝ Launfal full stylle,   540

And seyde, as he was gentyl knyȝt,
Þylke day a fourtenyȝt
   He wold with hym play.
He yaf þe messengere, for þat tydyng,

---

[10] armor.   [11] do.   [12] favorable wind.   [13] cunning in his art.   [14] undertake, try.

528. The construction is elliptical: "that he come to joust . . . and [that if he does] otherwise, he will destroy his [reputation for] manliness."

A noble courser and a ryng,   545
And a robe of ray.[15]

Launfal tok leue at Triamoure,
Þat was þe bryȝt berde[16] yn boure,
And keste þat swete may;
Þanne seyde þat swete wyȝt,   550
"Dreed þe no þyng, syr gentyl Knyȝt:
Þou schalt hym sle þat day."

Launfal nolde noþyng with hym haue
But Blaunchard hys stede and Gyfre hys kna[ue],
Of all hys fayre mayné.   555
He schypede, and hadde wynd well good,
And wente ouer þe salte flod
Into Lumbardye.

Whan he was ouir þe watir ycome
Þer þe iustes schulde be nome[17]   560
In þe cyte of Atalye,
Syr Valentyn hadde a greet ost,[18]
And Syr Launfal abatede here bost[19]
Wythe lytyll companye.

And whan Syre Launfal was ydyȝt   565
Vpon Blaunchard, hys stede lyȝt,
With helm and spere and schelde,
All þat sawe hym yn armes bryȝt
Seyde þey sawe neuir swych a knyȝt,
Þat hym wythe eyen behelde.   570

Þo ryde togydere þes knyȝtes two,
Þat hare schaftes tobroste bo[20]
And toscyuerede[21] yn þe felde;
Anoþer cours togedere þey rod,

---

[15] striped cloth.   [16] woman.   [17] held.   [18] host.   [19] lessened their boasting.   [20] both
[21] splintered.

561. Atalye is a city described in "Otinel." It is built by the Saracens in Northern Italy. Charlemagne seizes it, and it becomes the capital of Otinel's domain.

Þat Syre Launfal helm of glod,[22]   575
  In tale as hyt ys telde.

Syr Valentyn logh and hadde good game:
Hadde Launfal neuer so moche schame
  Beforhond[23] yn no fyȝt!
Gyfre kedde he was good at nede,   580
And lepte vpon hys maystrys stede:
  No man ne segh with syȝt.

And er þan þay togedere mette,
Hys lordes helm he on sette,
  Fayre and well adyȝt.   585
Þo was Launfal glad and blyþe,
And donkede Gyfre many syde[24]
  For hys dede so mochel of myȝt.

Syr Valentyne smot Launfal soo
Þat hys scheld fel hym fro,   590
  Anoon ryȝt yn þat stounde;
And Gyfre þe scheld vp hente
And broȝte hyt hys lord to presente[25]
  Ere hyt cam þoune[26] to grounde.

Þo was Launfal glad and blyþe,   595
And rode ayen þe þrydde syde,[27]
  As a knyȝt of mochell mounde;[28]
Syr Valentyne he smot so þere
Þat hors and man boþe deed were,
  Gronyng with grysly wounde.   600

Alle þe lordes of Atalye
To Syr Launfal hadde greet envye
  Þat Valentyne was yslawe,
And swore þat he schold dye
Er he wente out of Lumbardye,   605
  And be hongede and todrawe.[29]

---

[22] fell off; i.e., was knocked off.   [23] before.   [24] thanked . . . time.   [25] to
present to his lord.   [26] down.   [27] time.   [28] power.   [29] torn apart.

582. Gyfre is a fairy, and hence invisible at will.

Syr Launfal brayde out hys fachon,[30]
And as lyȝt as dew[31] he leyde hem doune,
  In a lytyll drawe;[32]
And whan he hadde þe lordes sclayn,   610
He wente ayen yn to Bretayn,
  Withe solas and wyth plawe.[33]

Þe tydyng com to Artoure þe Kyng,
Anoon, without lesyng,
  Of Syr Launfales noblesse;   615
Anoon he let to hym sende
Þat Launfall schuld to hym wende
  At Seynt Ionnys Masse,

For Kyng Artoure wold a feste holde
Of erles and of barouns bolde,   620
  Of lordynges more and lesse.
Syr Launfal schud be stward of halle,
For to agye[34] hys gestes alle,
  For [he] cowþe of largesse.

Launfal toke leue at Triamoure   625
For to wende to Kyng Artoure,
  Hys feste for to agye;
Þer he fond merthe and moch honour,
Ladyes þat wer well bryȝt yn boure,
  Of knyȝtes greet companye.   630

Fourty dayes leste þe feste,
Ryche, ryall, and honeste:
  What help hyt for to lye?[35]
And at þe fourty dayes ende,
Þe lordes toke har leue to wende,   635
  Euerych yn hys partye;[36]

---

[30] sword.   [31] as lightly as (falls the) dew.   [32] space.   [33] merriment.   [34] manage.   [35] i.e., I do not exaggerate.   [36] direction.

616. MS. *Anoon a let.*
618. On June 21.

And aftyr mete Syr Gaweyn,
Syr Gyeryes and Agrafayn,
   And Syr Launfal also
Wente to daunce vpon þe grene,   640
Vnþer þe toure þer lay þe Quene,
   With syxty ladyes and mo.

To lede þe daunce Launfal was set:[37]
For hys largesse he was louede þe bet,
   Sertayn, of alle þo.   645
Þe Quene lay out and beheld hem alle;
"I se," sche seyde, "daunce large Launfalle:
   To hym þan wyll y go.

Of alle þe knyȝtes þat y se þere,
He ys þe fayreste bachelere: 650
   He ne hadde neuer no wyf.
Tyde[38] me good oþer ylle,
I wyll go and wyte hys wylle;
   Y loue hym as my lyf!"

Sche tok with here a companye,   655
Þe fayrest þat sch[e] myȝte aspye—
   Syxty ladyes and fyf—
And wente hem doun anoon ryȝtes,
Ham to pley[39] among þe knyȝtes
   Well stylle, withouten stryf.   660

Þe Quene yede to þe formeste[40] ende,
Betwene Launfal and Gauweyn þe hende;
   And after, here ladyes bryȝt,
To daunce þey wente alle yn same:
To se hem play, hyt was fayr game,   665
   A lady and a knyȝt.

Þey hadde menstrales of moch honours—
Fydelers, sytolyrs,[41] and trompours—
   And elles hyt were vnryȝt.

---

[37] appointed.   [38] betide.   [39] to disport themselves.   [40] top.   [41] players on the citole.

669. MS. *vnrryȝt.*

þere þey playde, for soþe to say,   670
After mete þe somerys day
All-what⁴² hyt was ney3 ny3t.

And whanne þe daunce began to slake,⁴³
Þe Quene gan Launfal to counsell take,
   And seyde yn þys mainere: 675
"Sertaynlyche, Syre Kny3t,
I haue þe louyd with all my my3t
   More þan þys seuen 3ere;

But-þat þou louye me,
Sertes y dye fore loue of þe,   680
   Launfal, my lemman dere!"
Þanne answerede þe gentyll Kny3t,
"I nell be traytoure, þay⁴⁴ ne ny3t,
   Be God, þat all may stere!"⁴⁵

Sche seyde, "Fy on þe, þou coward!   685
An-hongeþ⁴⁶ worþ þou hye and hard!
   Þat þou euir were ybore—
Þat þou lyuest, hyt ys pyté;
Þou louyst no woman, ne no woman þe;
   Þow were worþy forelore!"⁴⁷   690

Þe Kny3t was sore aschamed þo:
To speke ne my3te he forgo,⁴⁸
   And seyde þe Quene before,
"I haue loued a fayryr woman
Þan þou euir leydest þyn ey vpon,   695
   Þys seuen yere and more!

Hyre loþlokste⁴⁹ mayde, withoute wene,⁵⁰
My3te bet be a quene
   Þan þou, yn all þy lyue!"
Þerfore þe Quene was swyþe wro3t;   700
Sche takeþ hyre maydenes, and forþ hy go[þ]
   Into here tour also blyue;

---

⁴² until.   ⁴³ slacken.   ⁴⁴ day.   ⁴⁵ guide.   ⁴⁶ hanged.   ⁴⁷ would deservedly be destroyed (a euphemism for "killed").   ⁴⁸ refrain.   ⁴⁹ ugliest.   ⁵⁰ doubt.

And anon sche ley doun yn her bedde;
For wrethe, syk sche hyre bredde,[1]
   And swore, so moste[2] sche thryue,   705
Sche wold of Launfal be so awreke
Þat all þe lond schuld of hym speke
   Withinne þe dayes fyfe.

Kyng Artour com fro huntynge,
Blyþe and glad yn all þyng;   710
   To hys chambere þan wente he.
Anoon þe Quene on hym gan crye,
"But y be awreke, y schall dye!
   Myn herte wyll breke a-þre!"[3]

I spak to Launfal yn my game,   715
And he besofte[4] me of schame—
   My lemman fore to be!
And of a lemman hys yelp[5] he made,
Þat þe lodlokest mayde þat sche hadde
   Myȝt be a quene aboue me."   720

Kyng Artour was well wroþ,
And be God he swor hys oþ
   Þat Launfal schuld be sclawe.
He wente aftyr doȝty knyȝtes
To brynge Launfal anoon ryȝtes   725
   To be hongeþ and todrawe.

Þe knyȝtes softe[6] hym anoon,
But Launfal was to hys chaumber gon,
   To han hadde solas and plawe;
He softe hys leef, but sche was lore,
As sche hadde warnede hym before;   730
   Þo was Launfal vnfawe.[7]

---

[1] turned, made.   [2] as she might (i.e., hoped to).   [3] into three pieces.   [4] besought.
[5] boast.   [6] sought.   [7] unhappy.

721. MS. *worþ*.
724. Probably *wente* is an error for *sent*.

He lokede yn hys alnere,[8]
þat fond hym spendyng all plenere
   Whan þat he hadde nede;   735
And þer nas noon, for soþ to say;
And Gyfre was yryde away
   Vp Blaunchard, hys stede.

All þat he hadde before ywonne,
Hyt malt[9] as snow aȝens þe sunne,   740
   In romaunce as we rede;
Hys armur, þat was whyt as floure,
Hyt becom of blak coloure,
   And þus þan Launfal seyde:

"Alas!" he seyde, "my creature,[10]   745
How schall i from[11] þe endure,
   Swetyng Tryamoure?
All my ioye i have forelore,
And þe: þat me ys worst fore,[12]
   þou blyssfull berde[13] yn boure!"   750

He bet hys body and hys hedde ek,
And cursede þe mouþ þat he with spek,
   With care and greet doloure,
And for sorow yn þat stounde
Anoon he fell aswowe[14] to grounde;   755
   With þat come knyȝtes foure,

And bond hym, and ladde hym þo—
þo was þe Knyȝte yn doble wo!—
   Before Artoure þe Kyng.
þan seyde Kyng Artoure,   760
"Fyle ataynte traytoure,[15]
   Why madest þou swyche yelpyng?[16]

---

[8] purse. [9] melted. [10] dear one. [11] away from. [12] for that, I am the worst; i.e., that afflicts me most. [13] woman. [14] swooning. [15] vile outlawed traitor. [16] boast.

734. Lit., "that supplied him funds in plenty."
742. In Celtic literature, love-tokens change color when the love of either party is changed. See "King Horn" 564 (Hall's note).

Þat þy lemmannes lodlokest mayde
Was fayrer þan my wyf, þou seyde:
    Þat was a fowll lesynge!   765
And þou besoftest here before þan
Þat sche schold be þy lemman:
    Þat was mysprowd lykynge!"[17]

Þe Knyȝt answerede with egre mode,[18]
Before þe Kyng þer he stode,   770
    Þe[19] Quene on hym gan lye:
"Sethe þat y euere was yborn,
I besofte her here beforn
    Neuir of no folye!

But sche seyde y nas no man,   775
Ne þat me louede no woman,
    Ne no womannes companye;
And i answerede her, and sayde
Þat my lemmannes lodlekest mayde
    To be a quene was bettere wordye.   780

Certes, lordynges, hyt ys so;
I am aredy for to þo[20]
    All þat þe court wyll loke!"[21]
To say þe soþ, without les,
All togedere how hyt was,   785
    xii knyȝtis were dryue to boke;"

All þey seyde, ham betwene,
Þat knewe þe maners of þe Quene
    And þe queste toke,[23]
Þe Quene bar los of swych a word[24]   790
Þat sche louede lemmannes without her lord;
    Har neuir on hyt foresoke;[25]

---

[17] presumptuous desire.   [18] excitedly.   [19] (that) the.   [20] do.   [21] ordain.   [22] i.e.,
they were forced to consult books to say what was the law.   [23] (undertook
the) inquiry.   [24] such a reputation.   [25] never a one denied it of her.

777. The subject is shifted; sc. "nor did I enjoy."
791. Possibly *without* should be *under* (cf. 47).

Þerfor þey seyden alle
Hyt was long on²⁶ þe Quene, and not on Launfal;
    Þereof þey gonne hym skere;²⁷   795
And yf he myȝte hys lemman brynge,
Þat he made of swych ȝelpynge,²⁸
    Oþere þe maydenes were

Bryȝtere þan þe Quene of hewe,
Launfal schuld be holde trewe   800
    Of þat, yn all manere;
And yf he myȝte not brynge hys lef,
He schud be hongede as a þef:
    Þey seyden all yn fere.

All yn fere þey made proferynge²⁹   805
Þat Launfal schuld hys lemman brynge:
    Hys heed he gan to laye.³⁰
Þan seyde þe Quene, without lesynge,
"Ȝyf he bryngeþ a fayrere þynge,
    Put out my eeyn gray!"   810

Whan þat waiowr was take on honde,³¹
Launfal þerto two borwes³² fonde,
    Noble knyȝtes twayn:
Syre Perceuall and Syr Gawayn,
Þey were hys borwes, soþ to sayn,   815
    Tyll a certayn³³ day.

Þe certayn day, i ȝow plyȝt,
Was xii moneþ and fourtenyȝt,
    Þat he schuld hys lemman brynge.
Syr Launfal, þat noble knyȝt,   820
Greet sorow and care yn hym was lyȝt:
    Hys hondys he gan wrynge.

---

²⁶ to be imputed to; i.e., the fault of. ²⁷ acquit (i.e., of the first charge). ²⁸ boast.
²⁹proposal. ³⁰give as a pledge. ³¹wager was agreed upon. ³²sureties. ³³ established.

800. MS. *schild.*

812. On this procedure, see "Havelok" 2463. The accused found
hostages or sureties, who undertook to vouch both for his presence and
for the truth of his contention. If the latter were shown to be false, the
sureties were executed.

So greet sorowe hym was vpan,
Gladlyche hys lyf he wold forgon,
In care and in marnynge;[34] 825
Gladlyche he wold hys hed forego:
Euerych man þerfore was wo,
þat wyste of þat tydynde.

þe certayn day was nyȝyng:
Hys borowes hym broȝt befor þe Kyng; 830
þe Kyng recordede[35] þo,
And bad hym bryng hys lef yn syȝt;
Syr Launfal seyde þat he ne myȝt—
þerfore hym was well wo.

þe Kyng commaundede þe barouns alle 835
To yeue iugement on Launfal,
And dampny[36] hym to sclo.
þan sayde þe Erl of Cornewayle,
þat was with ham at þat counceyle,
"We wyllyd[37] naȝt do so. 840

Greet schame hyt wer vs allo vpon
For to dampny þat gantylman,
þat haþ be hende and fré:
þerfore, lordynges, doþ be my reed:
Oure Kyng we wyllyþ anoþer wey lede; 845
Out of lond Launfal schall fle."

And as þey stod þus spekynge,
þe barouns sawe come rydynge
Ten maydenes bryȝt of ble:
Ham þoȝte þey were so bryȝt and schene 850
þat þe lodlokest, without wene,[38]
Hare quene þan myȝte be.

---

[34] mourning. [35] recalled the case. [36] condemn. [37] will. [38] doubt.

824. MS. *wold a.*—Kaluza; though the manuscript *a* (= have) may be right.

847. A scene like the ensuing is in the "Tain Bo Cuailgne" (Miss Hull's selections, p. 120); three corps of soldiers come up, and the queen is asked whether each is Cormac's.

Þo seyde Gawayn, þat corteys knyȝt,
"Launfal, brodyr, drede þe no wyȝt:
  Here comeþ þy lemman hende." 855
Launfal answerede and seyde ywys,
"Non of ham my lemman nys,
  Gawayn, my lefly frende !"

To þat castell þey wente ryȝt;
At þe gate þey gonne alyȝt; 860
  Before Kyng Artoure gonne þey wende,
And bede hym make aredy[39] hastyly
A fayre chambere, for here lady,
  Þat was come of kynges kende.

"Ho ys your lady?" Artoure seyde; 865
"Ye schull ywyte," seyde þe mayde,
  "For sche comeþ ryde."
Þe Kyng commaundede, for here sake,
Þe fayryst chaunber for to take
  In hys palys þat tyde; 870

And anon to hys barouns he sente
For to yeue iugemente
  Vpon þat traytour, full of pryde.
Þe barouns answerede anoon ryȝt,
"Haue we seyn þe madenes bryȝt, 875
  Whe[40] schull not longe abyde."

A newe tale þey gonne þo,
Some of wele and some of wo,
  Har lord þe Kyng to queme;[41]
Some dampnede Launfal þere, 880
And some made hym quyt and skere:[42]
  Hare tales were well breme.[43]

---

[39] ready. [40] we. [41] please, placate. [42] represented him as free and blameless.
[43] fierce was their debate.

873. I.e., Launfal. Arthur does not connect the coming of the lady
with Launfal's predicament. The portraits of the king and queen are
unflattering. See *PMLA* 22.2.8; and E. F. Van Der Ven-Ten Bensel's
"Character of King Arthur in English Literature" (Amsterdam, 1925).
875. "When we have seen. . . ." They seek pretexts for delay.

Þo saw þey oþer ten maydenes bryȝt,
Fayryre þan þe oþer ten of syȝt,
   As þey gone hym deme;[44]   885
Þey ryd upon ioly moyles[45] of Spayne,
With sadell and brydell of Champayne;[46]
   Hare lorayns lyȝt gonne leme.[47]

Þey were yclodeþ yn samyt tyre,[48]
Ech man hadde greet desyre   890
   To se hare clodynge.
Þo seyde Gaweyn, þat curtayse knyȝt,
"Launfal, here comeþ þy swete wyȝt,
   Þat may þy bote brynge."

Launfal answerede with drery doȝt,[49]   895
And seyde, "Alas, y knowe hem noȝt,
   Ne non of all þe of sprynge!"[50]
Forþ þey wente to þat palys
And lyȝte at þe hye deys,
   Before Artoure þe Kynge,   900

And grette þe Kyng and Quene ek,
And oo mayde þys wordes spak
   To þe Kyng Artoure:
"Þyn halle agrayde, and hele[1] þe walles
With clodes and with ryche palles[2]   905
   Aȝens my lady Tryamoure."

Þe Kyng answerede bedene,
"Well come, ye maydenes schene,
   Be oure lord þe Sauyoure!"
He commaundede Launcelet du Lake to brynge
      hem yn fere   910
In þe chamber þere hare felawes were,
   With merthe and moche honoure.

---

[44] *hym* for *hem*; i.e., as they judged them to be.   [45] fine mules.   [46] leather from Champagne, in France.   [47] bridle-reins brightly glittered.   [48] silk attire. [49] thought.   [50] nor any one from whom they spring.   [1] prepare, and cover. [2] hangings.

889. *Samit* is usually a noun in Middle English.

Anoon þe Quene suppose[d] gyle:[3]
Þat Launfal schuld yn a whyle
　　Be ymade quyt and skere　　　　　　　915
Þoruȝ hys lemman, þat was commynge.
Anon sche seyde to Artoure þe Kyng,
　　"Syre, curtays yf [þou] were,

Or yf þou louedest þyn honoure,
I schuld be awreke of þat traytoure　　　920
　　Þat doþ me changy chere![4]
To Launfal þou schuldest not spare;
Þy barouns dryueþ þe to bysmare;[5]
　　He ys hem lef and dere!"

And as þe Quene spak to þe Kyng,　　　925
Þe barouns seyȝ come rydynge
　　A damesele alone,
Vpoon a whyt comely palfrey;
Þey saw neuere non so gay
　　Vpon þe grounde gone:　　　　　　　930

Gentyll, iolyf as bryd[6] on bowe,
In all manere fayre inowe
　　To wonye yn wordly wone.[7]
Þe lady was bryȝt as blosme on brere,[8]
With eyen gray, with louelych chere;　　935
　　Her leyre lyȝt schoone.

As rose on rys[9] here rode was red;
Þe here schon vpon here hed
　　As gold wyre þat schynyth bryȝt.
Sche hadde a crounne vpon here molde[10]　　940
Of ryche stones and of golde,
　　Þat lofsom lemede lyȝt.

Þe lady was clad yn purpere palle,[11]
With gentyll body and myddyll small,
　　Þat semely was of syȝt.　　　　　　　945

---

[3] suspected a trick.　[4] causes me to alter my countenance; i.e., makes me unhappy.　[5] contumely; i.e., mock you.　[6] bird.　[7] in worldly state.　[8] briar.　[9] bough.　[10] top of the head.　[11] rich cloth.

Her mantyll was furryþ with whyt ermyn,
Ireuersyd[12] iolyf and fyn;
   No rychere be ne myȝt.

Her sadell was semyly set:
Þe sambus[13] were grene feluet,   950
   Ipaynted with ymagerye;
Þe bordure was of belles
Of ryche gold, and noþyng elles,
   Þat any man myȝte aspye.

In þe arsouns, before and behynde,   955
Were twey stones of Ynde,
   Gay for þe maystrye;[14]
Þe paytrelle[15] of her palfraye
Was worþ an erldome stoute and gay,
   Þe best yn Lumbardye.   960

A gerfawcon[16] sche bar on here hond;
A softe pas[17] here palfray fond,
   Þat men here schuld beholde.
Þoruȝ Karlyon rood þat lady;
Twey whyte grehoundys ronne hyre by;   965
   Hare colers[18] were of golde.

And whan Launfal sawe þat lady,
To alle þe folk he gon crye an hy,
   Boþe to yonge and olde,
"Here," he seyde, "comyþ my lemman swete! 970
Sche myȝte me of my balys bete,
   Ȝef þat lady wolde."

Forþ sche wente ynto þe halle,
Þer was þe Quene and þe ladyes alle,
   And also Kyng Artoure;   975
Here maydenes come ayens here ryȝt,
To take here styrop whan sche lyȝt—
   Of þe lady Dame Tryamoure.

---

[12] trimmed.   [13] saddle-cloths.   [14] i.e., exceedingly gay.   [15] breast-trappings.
[16] hawk, gerfalcon. [17] at an easy pace. [18] collars.

963. MS. *shuld he beholde.*

Sche dede of here mantyll on þe flet,[19]
Þat men schuld here beholde þe bet,   980
Withoute a more soiour.[20]
Kyng Artoure gan here fayre grete,
And sche hym agayn, with wordes swete,
Þat were of greet valoure.[21]

Vp stod þe Quene and ladyes stoute,[22]   985
Her for to beholde all aboute,
How euene sche stod vpryʒt;[23]
Þan were þey with here also donne[24]
As ys þe mone ayen þe sonne,
A-day whan hyt ys lyʒt.   990

Þan seyde sche to Artour þe Kyng,
"Syr, hydyr i com for swych a þyng:
To skere[25] Launfal þe knyʒt:
Þat he neuer, yn no folye,
Besofte þe Quene of no drurye,[26]   995
By dayes ne be nyʒt.

Þerfor, Syr Kyng, good kepe þou myne:[27]
He bad naʒt here, but sche bad hym
Here lemman for to be;
And he answerede here, and seyde   1000
Þat hys lemmannes loþlokest mayde
Was fayryre þan was sche."

Kyng Artoure seyde, withouten oþe,
"Ech man may yse þat ys soþe,
Bryʒtere þat ye be."   1005
With þat, Dame Tryamour to þe Quene geþ,
And blew on here swych a breþ
Þat neuer eft myʒt sche se.

---

[19] floor. [20] delay. [21] good breeding. [22] stately. [23] i.e., how fine was her carriage. [24] dun, lusterless. [25] clear. [26] love-making. [27] take good heed.

999. MS. *lemmain.*
1008. For similar blindings, cf. the story of Mongan, in Nutt's "Voyage of Bran" I.78, 299; "Chevelere Assigne" 332; and Hartland's "Science of Fairy Tales," Ch. IV.

þe lady lep an hyre palfray
And bad hem alle haue good day: 1010
 Sche nolde no lengere abyde.
With þat com Gyfre, all so prest,
With Launfalys stede out of þe forest,
 And stod Launfal besyde.

þe knyȝt to horse began to sprynge, 1015
Anoon, without any lettynge,
 With hys lemman away to ryde;
þe lady tok here maydenys achon,[28]
And wente þe way þat sche hadde er gon,
 With solas and wyth pryde. 1020

þe lady rod dorþ[29] Cardeuyle,
Fere yn to a iolyf ile,
 Olyroun þat hyȝte;
Euery [y]ere, vpon a certayn day,
Me may here Launfales stede nay,[30] 1025
 And hym se with syȝt.

Hu þat wyll þer axsy iustus[31]
To kepe hys armes fro þe rustus,[32]
 In turnement oþer fyȝt,
Dare[33] he neuer forþer gon: 1030
þer he may fynde iustes anoon,
 With Syr Launfal þe knyȝt.

þus Launfal, withouten fable,[34]
þat noble knyȝt of þe Rounde Table,
 Was take yn to fayrye:[35] 1035
Seþþe saw hym yn þis lond no man,
Ne no more of hym telle y ne can,
 For soþe, withoute lye.

---

[28] each one. [29] through. [30] neigh. [31] demand combat. [32] rust. [33] need. [34] untruth. [35] faery.

1027. Launfal becomes a guardian of a fairy realm. Cf. A. C. L. Brown, *HarvStN*. VIII.46 ff., the ballad "Sir Cawline" (Child 61), "Fiachna's Sidh" (*Silva Gadelica* II.290).

Thomas Chestre made þys tale
Of þe noble knyȝt Syr Launfale,   1040
   Good of chyualrye;
Ihesus, þat ys Heuene-kyng,
Ȝeue vs alle Hys blessyng,
   And Hys Modyr Marye! AMEN.
                    EXPLICIT LAUNFAL.

1039. Thomas Chester's is one of the very few names of English adapters that has been preserved. Nothing further is known of him, however; that any of his other works have survived is disputed.

THE EARL OF TOULOUSE

THE EARL OF TOULOUSE

"The Earl of Toulouse" is in the dialect of the northeast midlands, and was written after 1350. Though sometimes grouped with the Breton lays, to which it professes to be related, it has little in common with them, and its true source is probably historical. The writer had a strong moral sense, and, to judge by his vocabulary, was probably a cleric.

The poem is as found in Cambridge University Library Manuscript FfII. 38. Through the kindness of the librarian and other authorities of the library, it has been possible to prepare this text from rotographs of the manuscript. Since Lüdtke's edition, which contains all the variant readings, is still useful, his line-numbering has been retained, although it involves the undesirable juggling in the passages 285–9 and 849–53.

For discussions and bibliographies, see Wells and Hibbard; an interesting discussion of the type is Greenlaw's, in *PMLA* 21.575.

The scribe often assimilated final *-n* to the next word: *no nodur* (none other), 459. Final *-ght* usually has a cross-stroke which has not been expanded. A flourish after *-d* or *-dd* is printed as *-e*. Other flourishes have been disregarded.

> Ihesu Cryste, yn Trynyté,
> Oonly God and persons thre,
>   Graunt vs wele to spede,
> And gyf vs grace so to do
> That we may come þy blys vnto,   5
>   On rode as thou can blede!
> Leue lordys, y schall you telle
> Of a tale, some tyme befelle
>   Farre yn vnkowthe lede:
> How a lady had grete myschefe,   10
> And how sche couyrd[1] of hur grefe;
>   Y pray yow take hede!

[1] recovered.

Heading. In the MS. is this title: *Here foloweth the Erle of Tolous.*

Some tyme þere was in Almayn[2]
An Emperrour of moche mayn;
  Syr Dyoclysyan he hyght;   15
He was a bolde man and a stowte;
All Crystendome of hym had dowte,
  So stronge he was in fyght;
He dysheryted[3] many a man,
And falsely ther londys wan,   20
  Wyth maystry[4] and wyth myght,
Tyll hyt befelle vpon a day,
A warre wakenyd,[5] as y yow say,
  Betwene hym and a knyght.

The Erle of Tollous, Syr Barnard,   25
The Emperrour wyth hym was harde,
  And gretly was hys foo.
He had rafte owt of hys honde
Thre c poundys worth be yere of londe:
  Therfore hys herte was woo.   30
He was an hardy man and a stronge,
And sawe þe Emperour dyd hym wronge,
  And other men also;[6]
He ordeyned[7] hym for batayle
Into the Emperours londe, saun ffayle;   35
  And þere he began to brenne and sloo.

Thys Emperour had a wyfe,
The fayrest oon that euyr bare lyfe,
  Saue Mary mekyll of myght,
And therto gode in all thynge,   40
Of almesdede[8] and gode berynge,
  Be day and eke be nyght;
Of hyr body sche was trewe
As euyr was lady that men knewe,

---

[2] Germany.   [3] deprived of inheritance.   [4] intrigue.   [5] arose.   [6] i.e., to other men.   [7] made ready.   [8] charitable works.

15. MS. *Dyaclysyon.*

And therto moost bryght.   45
To the Emperour sche can say:
"My dere lorde, y you pray,
    Delyuyr the Erle hys ryght."

"Dame," he seyde, "let that bee;
That day schalt thou neuyr see,   50
    Yf y may ryde on ryght,[9]
That he schall haue hys londe agayne;
Fyrste schall y breke hys brayne,
    Os y am trewe knyght!
He warryth faste in my londe;   55
I schall be redy at hys honde
    Wythyn thys xiiii nyght!"
He sente abowte euerywhare,
That all men schulde make þem yare
    Agayne the Erle to fyght.   60

He let crye in euery syde,
Thorow hys londe ferre and wyde,
    Bothe in felde and towne,
All that myght wepon bere,
Sworde, alablast,[10] schylde, or spere,   65
    They schoulde be redy bowne;
The Erle on hys syde also
Wyth xl thousand and moo
    Wyth spere and schylde browne.
A day of batayle there was sett;   70
In felde when they togedur mett,
    Was crakydde many a crowne.

The Emperour had bataylys[11] seuyn;
He spake to them wyth sterne steuyn
    And sayde, so mot he thryue,   75
"Be ye now redy for to fyght,
Go ye and bete them downe ryght
    And leueth non on lyue;

─────────────────
[9] properly.   [10] cross-bow.   [11] battalions.

69. The other MSS. have *swordys* for *schylde*.

Loke that none raunsonyd bee
Nothyr for golde ne for fee,   80
   But sle them wyth swerde and knyfe !''
For all hys boste he faylyd ʒyt;
The Erle manly[12] hym mett,
   Wyth strokys goode and ryfe.

They reryd[13] batayle on euery syde;   85
Bo[l]dely togedyr can they ryde,
   Wyth schylde and many a spere;
They leyde on faste as þey were wode,
Wyth swerdys and axes that were gode;
   Full hedeous hyt was to here.   90
There were schyldys and schaftys schakydde,[14]
Hedys thorogh helmys crakydde,
   And hawberkys all totore.[15]
The Erle hymselfe an axe drowe;
An c men that day he slowe,   95
   So wyght he was yn were !

Many a stede there stekyd[16] was;
Many a bolde baron in that place
   Lay burlande[17] yn hys own blode.
So moche blode there was spylte,   100
That the felde was ouyrhylte[18]
   Os hyt were a flode.
Many a wyfe may sytt and wepe,
That was wonte softe to slepe,
   And now can they no gode.[19]   105
Many a body and many a heuyd,
Many a doghty knyʒt þere was leuyd,[20]
   That was wylde and wode.

The Erle of Tollous wan þe felde;
The Emperour stode and behelde: 110
   Wele faste can he flee

---

[12] vigorously.   [13] joined.   [14] brandished.   [15] coats of mail torn in pieces.
[16] pierced.   [17] weltering.   [18] covered.   [19] i.e., are wretched.   [20] left lying.

79. MS. *raumsonyd.*

To a castell there besyde
(Fayne he was hys hedde to hyde),
   And wyth hym erlys thre;
No moo forsothe scapyd away,   115
But they were slayn and takyn þat day:
   Hyt myght non othyr bee.
The Erle tyll nyght folowed þe chace,
And syþen he þanked God of hys grace,
   That syttyth in Trynyté.   120

There were slayne in þat batayle
Syxty thousand, wythowte fayle,
   On the Emperours syde;
Ther was takyn thre c and fyfty
Of grete lordys, sekyrly,   125
   Wyth woundys grymly[21] wyde;
On the Erlys syde þer were slayne
But twenty, sothely to sayne,
   So boldely they can abyde![22]
Soche grace God hym sende   130
That false quarell comeþ to cuell ende
   For oght that may betyde.

Now the Emperour ys full woo:
He hath loste men and londe also;
   Sore then syghed hee;   135
He sware be Hym þat dyed on rode,
Mete nor drynke schulde do hym no gode,
   Or he vengedde bee.
The Emperes seyde, "Gode lorde,
Hyt ys better ye be acorde[23]   140
   Be oght that y can see;
Hyt ys grete parell, sothe to telle,
To be agayne þe ryght quarell;[24]
   Be God, thus thynketh me!"

   "Dame," seyde the Emperoure,   145

---

[21] terribly.   [22] face the foe.   [23] agreed.   [24] cause.

137. The vow is common among heroes of romance. Cf. "Havelok"
317. Lüdtke correctly omitted *no.*

"Y haue a grete dyshonoure;
Therfore myn herte ys woo;
My lordys be takyn, and some dede;
Therfore carefull ys my rede:
Sorowe nye wyll me sloo."   150
Then seyde Dame Beulybon:
"Syr, y rede, be Seynt John,
Of warre that ye hoo;[25]
Ye haue the wronge and he þe ryʒt,
And that ye may see in syʒt,   155
Be thys and othyr moo."[26]

The Emperour was euyll payde:
Hyt was sothe the lady sayde;
Therfore hym lykyd ylle.
He wente awey and syghed sore;   160
Oon worde spake he no more,[27]
But helde hym wonder stylle.
Leue we now þe Emperour in thoght:
Game ne gle lyked hym noght,
So gretly can he grylle![28]   165
And to the Erle turne we agayn,
That þanked God wyth all hys mayn,[29]
That grace had sende hym tylle.

The Erle Barnard of Tollous
Had fele men chyualrous   170
Takyn to hys preson;[30]
Moche gode[31] of them he hadde;
Y can not telle, so God me gladde,[32]
So grete was ther raunsome!
Among them [alle] had he oon,   175
Was grettest of þem everychon,
A lorde of many a towne,

---

[25] cease.   [26] i.e., by this (defeat) and more things beside.   [27] i.e., he said nothing.   [28] grieve.   [29] might.   [30] i.e., as captives.   [31] tribute.   [32] make to rejoice.

151. The name means "beautiful and good," and has been conjectured to be a translation of *dame belle et bonne* in a lost original.

174. The fortunes of medieval houses were sometimes founded on ransoms exacted after successful raids.

Syr Trylabas of Turky
(The Emperour hym louyd, sekurly),
 A man of grete renowne.   180

So hyt befelle vpon a day
The Erle and he went to play[33]
 Be a rever syde.
The Erle seyde to Trylabas,
"Telle me, syr, for Goddys grace,   185
 Of a thyng þat spryngyth wyde:[34]
That youre Emperour hath a wyfe,
The fayrest woman þat ys on lyfe,
 Of hewe and eke of hyde.[35]
Y swere by boke and by belle,   190
Yf sche be so feyre as men telle,
 Mekyll may be hys pryde."

Then sayde that lord anon ryght,
"Be the ordre y bere of knyght,
 The sothe y schall telle the: 195
To seeke the worlde more and lesse,[36]
Bothe Crystendome and hethynnesse,
 Ther ys none so bryght of blee.
Whyte as snowe ys hur coloure;
Hur rudde[37] ys radder þen þe rose-floure,   200
 Yn syght who may hur see;
All men þat evyr God wroght
Myght not thynke nor caste in þoȝt[38]
 A fayrer for to bee."

Then seyde the Erle, "Be Goddys grace,   205
Thys worde in mornyng me mas.[39]
 Thou seyest sche ys so bryght;
Thy raunsom here y the forgeue,[40]
My helpe, my loue, whyll y leue
 (Therto my trowthe y plyght),

---

[33] i.e., hawk.   [34] i.e., is widely known.   [35] of color and also of skin.   [36] though one should search everywhere in the world.   [37] complexion.   [38] imagine.   [39] makes me mourn.   [40] in both senses: remit, grant.

190. Cf. "Havelok" 186.

So that thou wylt brynge me
Yn safegarde[41] for to bee,
     Of hur to haue a syght,
An c pownde, wyth grete honoure,
To bye þe horses and ryche armoure,   215
     Os y am trewe knyght !"

Than answeryd Syr Trylabas,
"Yn that couenaunt in þys place
     My trowthe y plyght thee;
Y schall holde thy forward gode   220
To brynge the, wyth mylde mode,[42]
     In syght hur for to see;
And therto wyll y kepe counsayle
And neuyr more, wythowte fayle,
     Agayne yow to bee;   225
Y schall be trewe, be Goddys ore,
To lose myn own lyfe therfore;
     Hardely[43] tryste to mee !"

The Erle answeryd wyth wordys hende:
"Y tryste to the as to my frende,   230
     Wythowte any stryfe;
Anon that [we] were buskyd yare,
On owre iurney for to fare,
     For to see that wyfe;
Y swere be God and Seynt Andrewe,   235
Yf hyt be so y fynde the trewe,
     Ryches schall be to the ryfe."
They lettyd noþyr for wynde nor wedur,[44]
But forthe þey wente bothe togedur,
     Wythowte any stryfe.   240

These knyghtys neuyr stynte nor blanne,
Tyll to the cyté that þey wan,
     There the Emperes was ynne.
The Erle hymselfe for more drede

---

[41] safety.   [42] peaceably.   [43] firmly.   [44] storms.
232. *We* is inserted in a later hand.

Cladde hym in armytes wede,[45]   245
  Thogh he were of ryche kynne,
For he wolde not knowen bee.
He dwellyd there dayes three
  And rested hym in hys ynne.[46]
The knyght bethoght hym, on a day,   250
The gode Erle to betray;
  Falsely he can begynne.

Anone he wente in a rese[47]
To chaumbur to the Emperes,
  And sett hym on hys knee;   255
He seyde, "Be Hym that harowed helle,
He kepe yow fro all parelle,
  Yf that hys wylle bee!"
"Madam," he seyde, "be Ihesus,
Y haue the Erle of Tollous;   260
  Oure moost enemye ys hee."
"Yn what maner," the lady can say,
"Ys he comyn, y the pray?
  Anone telle thou me."

"Madam, y was in hys preson;   265
He hath forgeuyn me my raunsom,
  Be God full of myght—
And all ys for the loue of the!
The sothe ys, he longyth yow to see,
  Madam, onys in syght!   270
And c pownde y haue to mede,
And armour for a nobull stede;
  Forsothe y haue hym hyght
That he schall see yow at hys fylle,
Ryght at hys owne wylle;   275
  Therto my trowthe y plyght.

Lady, he ys to vs a foo;
Therfore y rede þat we hym sloo;
  He hath done vs grete grylle."[48]

---

[45] hermit's clothing.   [46] inn.   [47] haste.   [48] treated us severely.

272. Other MSS. *armour and a nobull sted.*

The lady seyde, "So mut y goo,   280
Thy soule ys loste yf thou do so;
  Thy trowthe þou schalt fulfylle.
Sythe he forgaf the thy raunsom
And lowsydd[49] the owt of preson,
  Do away thy wyckyd wylle!   285

To-morne when þey rynge þe masbelle,   289
Brynge hym into my chapelle,
  And þynke þou on no false sleythe;[50]
There schall he see me at hys wylle,
Thy couenaunt to fulfylle;
  Y rede the holde thy trowthe!
Certys, yf thou hym begyle,   295
Thy soule ys in grete paryle,
  Syn thou haste made hym othe;
Certys, hyt were a traytory,[1]
For to wayte[2] hym [wyth] velany;
  Me thynkyth hyt were rowthe!"   300

The knyght to the Erle wente;
Yn herte he helde hym foule schente
  For hys wyckyd thoght.
He seyde, "Syr, so mote y the,
To-morne þou schalt my lady see;   305
  Therfore, dysmay the noght:
When ye here the masbelle,
Y schall hur brynge to the chapelle;
  Thedur sche schall be broght.
Be the oryall[3] syde stonde þou stylle;   310
Then schalt þou see hur at þy wylle,
  That ys so worthyly wroght."

· The Erle sayde, "Y holde the trewe,
And that schall þe neuyr rewe,
  As farre forthe as y may:"[4]   315

---

[49] loosed.   [50] trick.   [1] treachery.   [2] lie in wait, ambush.   [3] a recess.   [4] as long as I may prevent it.

280. On the penalties for forswearing oneself, cf. "Havelok" 186.
291. Other MSS. *slouth.*

Yn hys herte he waxe gladde:
"Fylle⁵ the wyne," wyghtly he badde,
"Thys goyth to my pay!"⁶
There he restyd that nyght;
On the morne he can hym dyght   320
    Yn armytes⁷ array;
When they ronge to the masse,
To the chapell conne they passe,
    To see that lady gay.

They had stonden but a whyle,   325
The mowntaunse of halfe a myle,⁸
    Then came that lady free;
Two erlys hur ladde;
Wondur rychely sche was cladde,
    In golde and ryche perré.⁹   330
Whan the Erle sawe hur in syght,
Hym thoght sche was as bryght
    Os blossome on the tree;
Of all the syghtys that euer he sye,
Raysyd neuyr nonc hys hcrtc so hyc,   335
    Sche was so bryght of blee!

Sche stode stylle in that place
And schewed opynly hur face
    For loue of that knyght.
He behelde ynly¹⁰ hur face;   340
He sware there be Goddys grace,
    He sawe neuyr none so bryght.
Hur eyen were gray as any glas;
Mowthe and nose schapen was
    At all maner ryght;¹¹   345
Fro the forhedde to the too,
Bettur schapen myght non goo,
    Nor none semelyer yn syght.

---

⁵ pour.   ⁶ goes to my liking.   ⁷ hermit's.   ⁸ time required to ride half a mile.
⁹ jewels.   ¹⁰ closely.   ¹¹ rightly in every particular.

323. Probably the chapel was attached to the buildings of Diocletian's castle. The oriel seems to have opened off the vestibule. Cf. Int. III.A.1.
343. To-day this color of the eye is called blue.

Twyes sche turnyd hur abowte
Betwene the erlys þat were stowte,   350
   For the Erle schulde hur see.
When sche spake wyth mylde steuyn,
Sche semyd an aungell of heuyn,
   So feyre sche was of blee !
Hur syde longe, hur myddyll small;   355
Schouldurs, armes therwythall, [12]
   Fayrer myght non bee;
Hur hondys whyte as whallys bonne,
Wyth fyngurs longe and ryngys vpon;
   Hur nayles bryght of blee.   360

When he had beholden hur welle,
The lady wente to hur chapell,
   Masse for to here;
The Erle stode on þat odur syde;
Hys eyen fro hur myght he not hyde,   365
   So louely sche was of chere !
He seyde, "Lorde God, full of myght,
Leue [13] y were so worthy a knyght,
   That y myght be hur fere,
And that sche no husbonde hadde,   370
All the golde that euyr God made
   To me were not so dere !"

When the masse come to ende,
The lady, that was feyre and hende,
   To the chaumbur can sche fare;   375
The Erle syghed and was full woo
Owt of hys syght when sche schulde goo;
   Hys mornyng was the mare.
The Erle seyde, "So God me saue,
Of hur almes y wolde craue,   380
   Yf hur wylle ware; [14]

---

[12] as well.   [13] if only, granted.   [14] if she were willing.

380. MS. *he wolde.*—Lüdtke.

Myght y oght gete of that free,
Eche a day hur to see[15]
Hyt wolde couyr[16] me of my care."

The Erle knelyd down anon ryght   385
And askyd gode,[17] for God allmyght,
That dyed on the tree.
The Emperes callyd a knyght:
"xl floranse that ben bryght,
Anone brynge thou mee."   390
To that armyte sche hyt payde;
Of hur fyngyr a rynge she layde
Amonge that golde so free;
He thankyd hur ofte, as y yow say.
To the chaumbyr wente þat lady gay,   395
There hur was leueste to bee.

The Erle wente home to hys ynnys,[18]
And grete yoye he begynnys
When he founde the rynge;
Yn hys herte he waxe blythe   400
And hyt kyssyd fele sythe,
And seyde, "My dere derlynge,
On thy fyngyr thys was!
Wele ys me, y hauc thy grace
Of the to haue thys rynge!   405
Yf euyr y gete grace of þe Quene
That any loue betwene vs bene,
Thys may be oure tokenyng."

The Erle, also soone os hyt was day,
Toke hys leue and wente hys way   410
Home to hys cuntré;
Syr Trylabas he thanked faste:
"Of thys dede þou done me haste,
Well qwyt schall hyt bee."

[15] i.e., in which (symbol) to see her every day.   [16] restore.   [17] alms.   [18] lodgings.

382. MS. *y not.*—Lüdtke.
392. MS. *Of on.*
401. MS. *kyssyd hyt.*—Lüdtke.

They kyssyd togedur as gode frende;   415
Syr Trylabas home can wende,
   There euell mote he thee!
A traytory he thoght to doo
Yf he myght come thertoo;
   So schrewde[19] in herte was hee!   420

Anon he callyd two knyghtys,
Hardy men at all syghtys;[20]
   Bothe were of hys kynne.
"Syrs," he seyde, "wythowt fayle,
Yf ye wyl do be my counsayle,   425
   Grete worschyp schulde ye wynne;
Knowe ye the Erle of Tollous?
Moche harme he hath done vs;
   Hys boste y rede we blynne;
Yf ye wyll do aftur my redde,   430
Thys day he schall be dedde,
   So God saue me fro synne!"

That oon knyght Kaunters, þat odur Kaym;
Falser men myght no man rayme,[21]
   Certys, then were thoo;   435
Syr Trylabas was the thrydde;
Hyt was no mystur[22] þem to bydde
   Aftur the Erle to goo.
At a brygge they hym mett;
Wyth harde strokes they hym besett,   440
   As men that were hys foo;
The Erle was a man of mayn:
Faste he faght them agayne,
   And soone he slew two.

The thrydde fledde and blewe[23] owt faste;   445
The Erle ouyrtoke hym at þe laste:
   Hys hedd he clofe[24] in three.
The cuntrey gedyrd abowte hym faste,
And aftur hym ȝorne they chaste:
   An c there men myght see.   450

---

[19] mean.   [20] points of view.   [21] govern.   [22] need.   [23] panted.   [24] clove.

The Erle of them was agaste:
At the laste fro them he paste;
   Fayne he was to flee;
Fro them he wente into a waste;
To reste hym there he toke hys caste:[25]   455
   A wery man was hee.

All the nyght in that foreste
The gentyll Erle toke hys reste:
   He had no nodur woon.
When hyt dawed,[26] he rose vp soone   460
And thankyd God, that syttyþ in trone,
   That he had scapyd hys foon;
That day he trauaylyd many a myle,
And ofte he was in grete parylle,
   Be the way os he can gone,   465
Tyll he come to a fayre castell,
There hym was leuyst to dwelle,
   Was made of lyme and stone.

Of hys comyng hys men were gladde.
"Be ye mery, my men," he badde,   470
   "For nothyng ye spare;
The Emperour, wythowte lees,
Y trowe, wyll let vs be in pees
   And warre on vs no mare."
Thus dwellyd the Erle in þat place   475
Wyth game, myrthe, and grete solase,
   Ryght os hym leuyst ware.
Let we now the Erle ailoon,
And speke we of Dame Beulyboorr,
   How sche was caste in care.   480

The Emperoure louyd hys wyfe
Also so moche os hys own lyfe,
   And more, yf he myght;
He chose two knyghtys þat were hym dere,
Whedur that he were ferre or nere,   485
   To kepe hur day and nyght.

---

[25] tried his fortune.   [26] dawned.

That oon hys loue on hur caste:
So dud the todur at the laste;
  Sche was feyre and bryght!
Nothyr of othyr wyste ryght noght,[27]   490
So derne[28] loue on them wroght;
  To dethe they were nere dyght.

So hyt befelle vpon a day,
That oon can to þat othyr say,
  "Syr, also muste y thee,   495
Methynkyth þou fadyste all away,
Os man þat ys clongyn[29] in clay,
  So pale waxeth thy blee!"
Then seyde that oþer, "Y make avowe,
Ryght so, methynketh, fareste þou,   500
  Whysoeuyr hyt bee;
Telle me thy cawse, why hyt ys,
And y schall telle þe myn, ywys:
  My trouthe y plyght to thee."

"Y graunte," he seyde, "wythowt fayle,   505
But loke hyt be trewe counsayle!"
  Therto hys trowthe he plyght.
He seyde, "My lady the Emperes,
For loue of hur y am in grete dystresse;
  To dethe hyt wyll me dyght."   510
Then seyde that othyr, "Certenly,
Wythowte drede, so fare y
  For that lady bryght;
Syn owre loue ys on hur sett,
How myght owre bale beste be bett?   515
  Canste thou rede on ryght?"

Then seyde that oþyr, "Be Seynt Iohn,
Bettur counsayle can y noon,
  Methynkyth, then ys thys:

---

[27] neither knew of the other's love.   [28] secretly.   [29] shrivelled; i.e., one
dead.

487. On this episode, see *PMLA* 21.575 ff., where the type is discussed
at length.

Y rede that oon of vs twoo 520
Preuely to hyr goo
 And pray hur of hur blys;[30]
Y myselfe wyll go hyr tylle;
Yn case y may gete hur wylle,[31]
 Of myrthe schalt thou not mys; 525
Thou schalt take vs wyth the dede:
Leste thou vs wrye, sche wyll drede,
 And graunte the þy wylle, ywys."

Thus they were at oon assent;
Thys false thefe forthe wente 530
 To wytt the ladyes wylle.
Yn chaumbyr he founde hyr so free;
He sett hym downe on hys knee,
 Hys purpose to fulfylle.
Than spake that lady free, 535
"Syr, y see now well be the,
 Thou haste not all thy wylle;
On thy sekeness now y see;
Telle me now thy preuyté,
 Why thou mornyst so stylle." 540

"Lady," he seyde, "that durste y noght
For all the gode þat euyr was wroght,
 Be grete God invysybylle,
But on a booke yf ye wyll swere
That ye schull not me dyskere,[32] 545
 Then were hyt possybyll."
Then seyde þe lady, "How may þat bee?
That[33] thou darstc not tryste to mee,
 Hyt ys full orybylle.[34]
Here my trowthe to the y plyght: 550
Y schall heyle[35] the day and nyght,
 Also trewe as boke or belle."

---

[30] favor. [31] consent [32] disclose. [33] what. [34] horrible. [35] conceal.

523. MS. *telle.*

"Lady, in yow ys all my tryste;
Inwardely[36] y wolde ye wyste
   What payne y suffur you fore;   555
Y drowpe, y dare[37] nyght and day;
My wele, my wytt ys all away,
   But ye leue on my lore;
Y haue yow louyd many a day,
But to yow durste y neuyr say—   560
   My mornyng ys the more!
But ye do aftur my rede,
Certenly, y am but dede:
   Of my lyfe ys no store."[38]

Than answeryd þat louely lyfe: 565
"Syr, wele thou wottyst y am a wyfe:
   My lorde ys Emperoure;
He chase the for a trewe knyght,
To kepe me bothe day and nyght
   Vndur thy socowre;   570
To do that dede yf y assente,
Y were worthy to be brente
   And broght in grete doloure;
Thou art a traytour in thy sawe,
Worthy to be hanged and to-drawe   575
   Be Mary, that swete floure!"

"A, madam!" seyde the knyght,
"For the loue of God almyght,
   Hereon take no hede![39]
Yn me ye may full wele tryste[40] ay;   580
Y dud nothyng but yow to affray,[41]
   Also God me spede!
Thynke, madam, youre trowþe ys plyȝt
To holde counsayle bothe day and nyȝt
   Fully, wythowte drede;   585
Y aske mercy for Goddys ore!
Hereof yf y carpe more,
   Let drawe me wyth a stede!"

---

[36] earnestly.   [37] pine and lie motionless.   [38] quantity.   [39] i.e., overlook it.
[40] trust. [41] frighten.

The lady seyde, "Y the forgeue;
Also longe os y leue,   590
   Counsayle schall hyt bee;
Loke thou be a trewe man
In all thyng that thou can,
   To my lorde so free."
"ȝys, lady, ellys dyd y wronge,   595
For y haue seruyd hym longe,
   And wele he hath qwytt mee."
Hereof spake he no mare,
But to hys felowe can he fare,
   There euyll must they the!   600

Thus to hys felowe ys he gon,
And he hym frayned anon,
   "Syr, how haste thou spedde?"
"Ryght noght," seyde that othyr:
"Syth y was borne, lefe brothyr,   605
   Was y neuyr so adredde;
Certys, hyt ys a boteles bale
To hur to touche[42] soche a tale
   At borde or at bedde."
Then sayde þat odur, "Thy wytt ys thynne: 610
Y myselfe schall hur wynne:
   Y lay my hedde to wedde!"[43]

Thus hyt passyd ouyr, os y yow say,
Tyl aftur on the thrydde day
   Thys knyght hym bethoght: 615
"Certys, spede os y may,
My ladyes wylle, þat ys so gay,
   Hyt schall be thorowly soght."
When he sawe hur in beste mode,
Sore syghyng to hur he ȝode,   620
   Of lyfe os he ne roght.
"Lady," he seyde, "wythowte fayle,
But ye helpe me wyth yowre counsayle,
   Yn bale am y broght."

---

[42] mention.   [43] as a forfeit.

Sche answeryd full curtesly, 625
"My counsayle schall be redy.
Telle me how hyt ys;
When y wott worde and ende,
Yf my counsayle may hyt mende,
Hyt schall, so haue y blysse !" 630
"Lady," he seyde, "y vndurstonde[44]
Ye muste holde vp yowre honde
To holde counsayle, ywys."
"3ys," seyde the lady free,
"Thereto[45] my trouthe here to the, 635
And ellys y dudde amys."

"Madam," he seyde, "now y am in tryste;[46]
All my lyfe thogh ye wyste,
Ye wolde me not dyskeuere;[47]
For yow y am in so grete thoght, 640
Yn moche bale y am broght,
Wythowte othe[48] y swere;
And ye may full wele see,
How pale y am of blee:
Y dye nere for dere; 645
Dere lady, graunt me youre loue,
For þe loue of God, þat sytteþ aboue,
That stongen[49] was wyth a spere."

"Syr," sche seyde, "ys þat youre wylle?
Yf hyt were myne, þen dyd y ylle; 650
What woman holdyst thou me?
Yn thy kepeyng y haue ben:
What haste þou herde be me or sene
That touchyth to any velanye,
That thou in herte art so bolde 655
Os y were a hore or a scolde?
Nay, that schall neuyr bee !

---

[44] take it for granted. [45] sc. I give. [46] trust. [47] reveal. [48] i.e., on my word of honor. [49] pierced.

628. Possibly a blunder for the usual *orde and ende*.

Had y not hyght to holde counsayle,
Thou schouldest be honged, wythowt fayle,
   Vpon a galowe-tree."   660

The knyght was neuyr so sore aferde
Sythe he was borne into myddyllerde,[50]
   Certys, os he was thoo.
"Mercy," he seyde, "gode madam!
Wele y wott y am to blame;   665
   Therfore myn herte ys woo!
Lady, let me not be spylte;
Y aske mercy of my gylte!
   On lyue ye let me goo."
The lady seyde, "Y graunte wele;   670
Hyt schall be counseyle, euery dele,
   But do no more soo."

Now the knyght forthe yede
And seyde, "Felowe, y may not spede.
   What ys thy beste redde?   675
Yf sche telle my lorde of thys,
We be but dedde, so haue y blys:
   Wyth hym be we not fedde.[1]
Womans tonge ys euell to tryste;[2]
Certys, and my lorde hyt wyste,   680
   Etyn were all owre bredde.
Felow, so mote y ryde or goo,
Or sche wayte[3] vs wyth þat woo,
   Hurselfe schall be dedde!"

"How myght þat be?" þat othur sayde;   685
"Yn herte y wolde be wele payde,
   Myght we do that dede."
"Ʒys, syr," he seyde, "so haue y roo,[4]
Y schall brynge hur wele thertoo;
   Therof haue thou no drede.   690
Or hyt passe dayes three,
In mekyll sorowe schall sche bee:
   Thus y schall qwyte hur hur mede."

---

[50] the world.   [1] i.e., they will be outcasts.   [2] unsafe to trust in.   [3] inflict.   [4] peace.

Now are þey bothe at oon assente
In sorow to brynge þat lady gente: 695
   The deuell mote them spede!

Sone hyt drowe toward nyght;
To soper they can them dyght,
   The Emperes and they all;
The two knyghtys grete yapys⁵ made,   700
For to make the lady glade,
   That was bothe gentyll and small;
When the sopertyme was done,
To the chaumbyr they went soone,
   Knyghtys cladde in palle⁶   705
(They daunsed and revelyd, os þey noȝt dredde),
To brynge the lady to hur bedde:
   There foule muste them falle!

That oon thefe callyd a knyght
That was carver to þat lady bryght;   710
   An erleys sone was hee;
He was a feyre chylde and a bolde;
Twenty wyntur he was oolde:
   In londe was none so free.
"Syr, wylt thou do os we the say?   715
And we schall ordeygne vs a play,
   That my lady may see.
Thou schalt make hur to lagh soo,
Thogh sche were gretly thy foo,
   Thy frende schulde sche bee."   720

The chylde answeryd anon ryght:
"Be the ordur y bere of knyght,
   Therof wolde y be fayne,
And hyt wolde my lady plese,
Thogh hyt wolde me dysese,⁷   725
   To renne yn wynde and rayne."

---

⁵ jests.　⁶ fine cloth.　⁷ inconvenience.

710. The roast was set before the persons for whom it was intended,
but on the opposite side of the table; and the squires served the others.
Squires were often young noblemen.

"Syr, make the nakyd saue þy breke;[8]
And behynde the ȝondur curtayn þou crepe,
    And do os y schall sayne;
Then schalt þou see a yoly[9] play!"   730
"Y graunte," þys yonge knyȝt can say,
    "Be God and Seynte Iermayne."

Thys chylde thoght on no ylle:
Of he caste hys clothys stylle;
    And behynde þe curtayn he went.   735
They seyde to hym, "What so befalle,
Come not owt tyll we þe calle."
    And he seyde, "Syrs, y assente."
They reuelyd forthe a grete whyle;
No man wyste of ther gyle   740
    Saue they two, veramente.
They voyded[10] þe chaumber sone anon;
The chylde þey lafte syttyng alone,
    And that lady gente.

Thys lady lay in bedde on slepe;   745
Of treson toke sche no kepe,
    For þerof wyste sche noght.
Thys chylde had wonder euyr among
Why þese knyghtys were so longe:
    He was in many a thoght.   750
"Lorde, mercy! how may thys bee?
Y trowe þey haue forgeten me,
    That me hedur broght;
Yf y them calle, sche wyll be adredd,
My lady lyeth here in hur bedde,   755
    Be Hym þat all hath wroght!"

Thus he sate stylle as any stone:
He durste not store[11] nor make no mone
    To make the lady afryght.

---

[8] breeches.   [9] jolly.   [10] cleared.   [11] stir.

732. St. Germaine, bishop of Auxerre, led a British army against the Picts and Scots in 429 A.D. His name is preserved in several Welsh place-names.

755. I.e., my lady (who lies).

Thes false men (ay worthe þem woo!),   760
To ther chaumbur can they goo
   And armyd them full ryght;
Lordys owte of bedde can they calle
And badde arme þem, grete and smalle:
   "Anone that ye were dyght,   765
And helpe to take a false traytoure
That wyth my lady in hur bowre
   Hath playde hym all þys nyght."

Sone þey were armyd euerychone;
And wyth þese traytours can þey gone,   770
   The lordys that there wore.
To þe Emperes chaumber þey cam ryȝt
Wyth torchys and wyth swerdys bryght
   Brennyng them before.
Behynde the curtayne they wente;   775
The yonge knyght, verrament,
   Nakyd founde they thore.
That oon thefe wyth a swerde of were
Thorow þe body he can hym bere,
   That worde spake he no more.   780

The lady woke and was afryght,
Whan sche sawe the grete lyght
   Before hur beddys syde.
Sche seyde, "Benedycyté!¹²
Syrs, what men be yee?"   785
   And wonder lowde sche cryedd.
Hur enemyes mysansweryd¹³ þore
"We are here, thou false hore:
   Thy dedys we haue aspyedd!
Thou haste betrayed my lorde;   790
Thou schalt haue wonduryng¹⁴ in þys worde:
   Thy loos¹⁵ schall sprynge wyde!"

---

¹² bless us! ¹³ spoke abusively. ¹⁴ wandering. ¹⁵ fame.

761. MSS. *to hur*.
768. On the seneschal as accuser, cf. Miss Schlauch's "Constance" 95 ff.
770. MS. *traytour*.
773. The other MSS. have *swerdys* and *torchys* transposed.

The lady seyde, "Be Seynte Iohn,
Hore was y neuyr none,
    Nor neuyr thoght to bee."   795
"Thou lyest," þey seyde, "þy loue ys lorne"—
The corse þey leyde hur beforne—
    "Lo, here ys thy lemman free!
Thus we haue for þe hym hytt;
Þy horedam[16] schall be wele quytte: 800
    Fro vs schalt thou not flee!"
They bonde þe lady wondyr faste
And in a depe preson hur caste:
    Grete dele hyt was to see!

Leue we now thys lady in care,   805
And to hur lorde wyll we fare,
    That ferre was hur froo.
On a nyght, wythowt lette,
In hys slepe a sweuyn he mett,[17]
    The story telleth vs soo.   810
Hym þoght þer come ii wyldc berys[18]
And hys wyfe all toterys[19]
    And rofe[20] hur body in twoo;
Hymselfe was a wytty[21] man,
And be þat dreme he hopyd þan   815
    Hys lady was in woo.

3erly,[22] when þe day was clere,
He bad hys men all in fere
    To buske and make þem yare.
Somer horsys[23] he let go before   820
And charyettes stuffud wyth stoore[24]
    Wele xii myle and mare.
He hopud wele in hys herte
That hys wyfe was not in querte;[25]
    Hys herte therfore was in care;   825
He styntyd[26] not tyll he was dyght,

---

[16] prostitution.   [17] a dream he dreamed.   [18] bears.   [19] tore in pieces.   [20] rent.
[21] sensible.   [22] early.   [23] pack horses.   [24] chariots filled with supplies.   [25] safety.
[26] stopped.

Wyth erlys, barons, and many a knyght;
Homeward can they fare.

Nyght ne day neuyr they blanne,
Tyll to that cyté they came						830
	There the lady was ynne.
Wythowt þe cyté lordys þem kepyd;
For wo in herte many oon wepyd:
	There teerys myght þey not blynne.
They supposyd wele yf he hyt wyste				835
That hys wyfe had soche a bryste,[27]
	Hys yoye wolde be full thynne;
They ladden stedys to the stabyll,
And the lorde into the halle,
	To worschyp hym wyth wynne.					840

Anon to the chaumbur wendyþ he:
He longyd hys feyre lady to see,
	That was so swete a wyght.
He callyd them þat schoulde hur kepe:
"Where ys my wyfe? Ys sche on slepe?			845
	How fareth that byrde[28] bryght?"
The ii traytours answeryd anone,
"Yf ye wyste how sche had done,
	To dethe sche schulde be dyght."				849

"A, deuyll!"[29] he seyde, "how soo,				853
To dethe þat sche ys worthy to go?
	Telle me, in what manere."					855
"Syr," they seyd, "be Goddys ore,
The yonge knyght Syr Antore,
	That was hur keruere,
Be that lady he hath layne,
And þerfore we haue hym slayne;					860
	We founde them in fere;
Sche ys in preson, verrament;

---

[27] injury.		[28] lady.		[29] the devil!

856. MS. *he seyde.*

The lawe wyll þat sche be brente,
  Be God, that boght vs dere."

"Allas!" seyde the Emperoure,   865
"Hath sche done me thys dyshonoure?
  And y louyd hur so wele!
Y wende for all þys worldys gode
That sche wolde not haue turned hur mode:[30]
  My yoye begynnyth to kele."[31]   870
He hente a knyfe wyth all hys mayn;
Had not a knyȝt ben, he had hym slayn,
  And þat traytour haue broght owt of heele.[32]
For bale hys armes abrode he bredde[33]
And fell in swowne vpon hys bedde;   875
  There myght men see grete dele.

On the morne be oon assente,
On hur they sett a perlyament
  Be all the comyn[34] rede.
They myȝt not fynde in þer counsayle   880
Be no lawe, wythowt fayle,
  To saue hur fro the dede.
Then bespake an olde knyght,
"Y haue wondur, be Goddys myght,
  That Syr Antore thus was bestedde,[35]   885
In chaumbyr thogh he naked were;
They let hym gyf none answere,
  But slowe hym, be my hedde!

Ther was neuyr man, sekurly,
That be hur founde any velany,   890
  Saue they two, y dar wele say;
Be some hatered hyt may be;
Therfore doyth aftur me
  For my loue, y yow pray.

---

[30] been unfaithful. [31] cool. [32] corrupt: seems to mean, "had not a knight interfered, he would have slain his informant, and thus discomfited the traitor."
[33] threw up. [34] common. [35] set upon.

870. MS. *kelee*.
886. MS. *þey naked*.

No mo wyll preue[36] hyt but þey twoo;   895
Therfore we may not saue hur fro woo,
   For sothe, os y yow say,
In hyr quarell[37] but we myȝt fynde
A man þat were gode of kynde
   That durste fyght agayn þem tway."   900

All they assentyd to the sawe:
They thoght he spake reson and lawe.
   Then answeryd þe Kyng wyth crowne,
"Fayre falle the for thyn avyse."
He callyd knyghtys of nobyll pryce   905
   And badde them be redy bowne
For to crye thorow all þe londe,
Bothe be see and be sonde,
   Yf they fynde mowne[38]
A man þat ys so moche of myght,   910
That for þat lady dar take þe fyght,
   "He schall haue hys warison."[39]

Messangerys, y vndurstonde,
Cryed thorow all the londe
   In many a ryche cyté,   915
Yf any man durste proue hys myȝt
In trewe quarell for to fyght,
   Wele avaunsed schulde he bee.
The Erle of Tullous harde þys telle,
What anger[40] the lady befelle;   920
   Thereof he thoght grete pyté.
Yf he wyste that sche had ryght,
He wolde aventure hys lyfe to fyght
   For that lady free.

---

[36] testify.   [37] cause.   [38] could.   [39] reward.   [40] grief.

911. The champion must volunteer out of a conviction that the accusation is false; the accuser must meet him in the field. On the judicial duel, see George Neilson's "Trial by Combat" (London, 1890); notes to the "Chanson de Roland;" and Pollock and Maitland.

922. The champion of the right cause was sure of success and the champion of the wrong sure of failure; hence he is circumspect. Cf. the fate of the knight in "Amis and Amiloun."

For hur he morned nyȝt and day,   925
And to hymselfe can he say
   He wolde aventure hys lyfe:
"Yf y may wytt þat sche be trewe,
They þat haue hur accused schull rewe,
   But they stynte of ther stryfe."[41]   930
The Erle seyde, "Be Seynte Iohn,
Ynto Almayn wyll y goon,
   Where y haue fomen ryfe;
I prey to God full of myght
That y haue trewe quarell to fyȝt,   935
   Owt of wo to wynne þat wyfe."

He rode on huntyng on a day;
A marchand mett he be þe way,
   And asked hym of whens he was.
"Lorde," he seyde, "of Almayn."   940
Anon the Erle can hym frayne
   Of that ylke case:
"Whercforc ys yowre Emperes
Put in so grete dystresse?
   Telle me, for Goddys grace.   945
Ys sche gylté, so mote thou the?"
"Nay, be Hym þat dyed on tree,
   That schope man aftur hys face."[42]

Then seyde the Erle, wythowte lett,
"When ys the day sett   950
   Brente that sche schulde bee?"
The marchande seyde sekyrlyke,
"Euyn thys day thre wyke,[43]
   And therfore wo ys mee."
The Erle seyde, "Y schall the telle: 955
Gode horsys y haue to selle,
   And stedys two or thre:
Certys, myght y selle þem yare,

---

[41] cease their persecution. [42] created man in his likeness. [43] three weeks from to-day.

Thedur wyth the wolde y fare,
 That syght for to see."   960

The marchand seyd wordys hende:[44]
"Into the londe yf ye wyll wende,
 Hyt wolde be for yowre prowe,[45]
There may ye selle þem at your wylle."
Anon the Erle seyde hym tylle, 965
 "Syr, herkyn me nowe:
Thys yurney wylt þou wyth me dwelle
Twenty pownde y schall the telle
 To mede, y make avowe !"
The marchand grauntyd anon; 970
The Erle seyde, "Be Seynt Iohn,
 Thy wylle y alowe."[46]

The Erle tolde hym in þat tyde
Where he schulde hym abyde,
 And homeward wente hee. 975
He busked hym, þat no man wyste,
For mekyll on hym[47] was hys tryste.[48]
 He seyde, "Syr, go wyth mee !"
Wyth them they toke stedys seuyn—
Ther were no fayre vndyr heuyn 980
 That any man myght see.
Into Almayn þey can ryde:
As a coresur[49] of mekyll pryde
 He semyd for to bee.

The marchand was a trewe gyde;[50] 985
The Erle and he togedur can ryde,
 Tyll they came to that place.
A myle besyde[1] the castell
There the Emperoure can dwelle,
 A ryche abbey ther was; 990
Of the abbot leue they gatt
To soyorne and make þer horsys fatt;

---

[44] favorable. [45] advantage. [46] approve. [47] i.e., the merchant. [48] trust. [49] horse-dealer. [50] guide. [1] i.e., from.

That was a nobyll case!
The abbot was the ladyes eme;
For hur he was in grete wandreme,[2] 995
And moche mornyng he mase.

So hyt befelle vpon a day,
To churche the Erle toke þe way,
 A masse for to here.
He was a feyre man and an hye; 1000
When the abbot hym sye,
 He seyde, "Syr, come nere:
Syr, when the masse ys done,
Y pray yow, ete wyth me at noone,
 Yf yowre wylle were." 1005
The Erle grauntyd all wyth game;
Afore mete they wysche all same,
 And to mete they wente in fere.

Aftur mete, as y yow say,
Into an orchard þey toke þe way, 1010
 The abbot and the knyght.
The abbot seyde and syghed sare;
"Certys, syr, y leue in care
 For a lady bryght;
Sche ys accusyd—my herte ys woo!— 1015
Therfore sche schall to dethe goo,
 All agayne the ryght;
But sche haue helpe, verrament,
In fyre sche schall be brente
 Thys day seuenyght." 1020

The Erle seyde, "So haue y blysse,
Of hyr, meþynkyþ, grete rewþe hyt ys,
 Trewe yf that sche bee!"
The abbot seyde, "Be Seynte Poule,
For hur y dar ley[3] my soule 1025
 That neuyr gylté was sche;
Soche werkys neuyr sche wroght

---

[2] grief. [3] wager.

Neythyr in dede nor in thoght,
　　Saue a rynge so free
To þe Erle of Tullous sche gafe hyt wyth wynne, 1030
Yn ese of hym⁴ and for no synne:
　　In schryfte⁵ thus tolde sche me."

The Erle seyde, "Syth hyt ys soo,
Cryste wreke hur of hur woo,
　　That boght hur wyth Hys bloode!　　　　1035
Wolde ye sekyr⁶ me, wythowt fayle,
For to holde trewe counsayle,
　　Hyt myght be for yowre gode."
The abbot seyde be bokes fele
And be hys professyon, þat he wolde hele,⁷　　1040
　　And ellys he were wode.
"Y am he þat sche gaf the rynge
For to be oure tokenynge.
　　Now heyle hyt, for the rode!

Y am comyn, lefe syr,　　　　　　　　　　1045
To take the batayle for hyr,
　　There to stonde wyth ryght;
But fyrste myselfe y wole hur schryue,
And yf y fynde hur clene of lyue,
　　Then wyll my herte be lyght.　　　　　1050
Let dyght me in monkys wede
To þat place þat men schulde hyr lede,
　　To dethe to be dyght;
When y haue schreuyn hyr, wythowt fayle,
For hur y wyll take batayle,　　　　　　　1055
　　As y am trewe knyght!"

The abbot was neuyr so gladde;
Nere for yoye he waxe madde;
　　The Erle can he kysse;
They made meré and slewe care.⁸　　　　　1060
All that seuenyght he dwellyd þare
　　Yn myrthe wythowt mysse.⁹

---

⁴ for his comfort.　⁵ confession.　⁶ assure.　⁷ conceal.　⁸ i.e., had no sorrow.
⁹ interruption.

That day þat þe lady schulde be brent,
The Erle wyth the abbot wente
  In monkys wede, ywys;   1065
To the Emperour he knelyd blyue,
That he myght þat lady schryue:
  Anon resceyued he ys.

He examyned hur, wyttyrly,
As hyt seythe in the story;   1070
  Sche was wythowte gylte.
Sche seyde, "Be Hym þat dyed on tree,
Trespas was neuyr none in me
  Wherefore y schulde be spylte;
Saue oonys, wythowte lesynge,   1075
To the Erle of Tollous y gafe a rynge:
  Assoyle me[10] yf thou wylte;
But þus my destanye ys comyn to ende,
That in þys fyre y muste be brende;
  There Goddys wylle be fulfyllyt." 1080

The Erle assoyled hur wyth hys honde,
And syþen pertely[11] he can vp stonde
  And seyde, "Lordyngys, pese!
Ye that haue accused þys lady gente,
Ye be worthy to be brente."   1085
  That oon knyght made a rees:[12]
"Thou carle[13] monke, wyth all þy gynne,[14]
Thowe youre abbot be of hur kynne,
  Hur sorowe schalt thou not cees;
Ryght so thou woldyst sayne   1090
Thowe all youre couent[15] had be hyr layne;
  So are ye lythyr and lees!"[16]

The Erle answeryd, wyth wordys free,
"Syr, that oon y trowe thou bee
  Thys lady accused has.   1095
Thowe we be men of relygyon,

---

[10] absolve. [11] boldly. [12] rush, i.e., came forward. [13] i.e., rude. [14] trickery.
[15] monastery. [16] foul liars.

Thou schalt do vs but reson[17]
  For all the fare thou mas.
Y proue on hur þou sayst not ryght.
Lo, here my gloue wyth þe to fyght!   1100
  Y vndyrtake thys case;
Os false men y schall yow kenne;
Yn redde fyre for to brenne;
  Therto God gyf me grace!"

All þat stoden in that place   1105
Thankyd God of hys grace,
  Wythowte any fayle.
The two knyghtys were full wrothe:
He schulde be dedde, þey swere grete othe;
  But hyt myght not avayle.[18]   1110
The Erle wente there besyde
And armyd hym wyth mekyll pryde,
  Hys enemyes to assayle.
Manly[19] when they togedur mett,
They hewe thorow helme and basenet[20]   1115
  And martyrd[21] many a mayle.

They redyn togedur, wythowt lakk,[22]
That hys oon spere on hym brakk;
  That othyr faylyd thoo;
The Erle smote hym wyth hys spere;   1120
Thorow the body he can hym bere:
  To grounde can he goo.
That sawe that odyr, and faste can flee;
The Erle ouyrtoke hym vndur a tre
  And wroght hym mekyll woo;   1125
There þys traytour can hym ȝylde
Os recreaunt yn the fylde;[23]
  He myght not fle hym froo.

---

[17] i.e., you shall account to us. [18] i.e., their swearing was useless. [19] fiercely.
[20] steel cap. [21] ruined many a link of chain-mail. [22] fail. [23] i.e., yielded himself as fighting in a false cause.

1100. The glove thrown down was evidence of a public challenge; by picking it up, the opponent publicly accepted the challenge.

Before the Emperoure they wente
And there he made hym, verrament,   1130
  To telle for the noonys.
He seyde, "We thoght hur to spylle,
For sche wolde not do oure wylle,
  That worthy ys in wonnys."[24]
The Erle answeryd hym then,   1135
"Therfore, traytours, ye schall brenne
  Yn thys fyre, bothe at onys!"
The Erle anon them hente,
And in the fyre he þem brente,
  Flesche, felle,[25] and boonys.   1140

When þey were brent bothe twoo,
The Erle preuely can goo
  To that ryche abbaye.
Wyth yoye and processyon
They fett the lady into the towne,   1145
  Wyth myrthe, os y telle may.
The Emperoure was full gladde:
"Fette me the monke!" anon he badde,
  "Why wente he so awaye?
A byschoperyke y wyll hym geue,   1150
My helpe, my loue, whyll y leue,
  Be God that owyth[26] thys day!"

The abbot knelyd on hys knee
And seyde, "Lorde, gone ys hee
  To hys owne londe;   1155
He dwellyth wyth the pope of Rome;
He wyll be glad of hys come,[27]
  Y do yow to vndurstonde."
"Syr [abbot]," quod the Emperoure,
"To me hyt were a dyshonoure;   1160
  Soche wordes y rede thou wonde;[28]
Anone yn haste that y hym see,

---

[24] life, habits.   [25] skin.   [26] owns; i.e., guides events.   [27] arrival.   [28] cease from.

1138. MS. *anon hym.*

Or thou schalt neuyr haue gode of me,
And therto here myn honde !"[29]

"Lorde," he seyde, "sythe hyt ys soo   1165
Aftur hym þat y muste goo,
    Ye muste make me sewrté,[30]
Yn case he haue byn youre foo,
Ye schall not do hym no woo;
    And then, also mote y thee,   1170
Aftur hym y wyll wynde,
So that ye wyll be hys frende,
    Yf youre wylle bee."
"3ys," seyd the Emperoure full fayne,
"All my kynne þogh he had slayne,   1175
    He ys welcome to mee."

Then spake the abbot wordys free:
"Lorde, y tryste now on thee:
    Ye wyll do os ye sey;
Hyt ys Syr Barnard of Tollous,   1180
A nobyll knyght and a chyualrous,
    That hath done thys iurney."
"Now certys," seyde the Emperoure,
"To me hyt ys grete dyshonoure;[31]
    Anon, syr, y the pray   1185
Aftur hym þat thou wende:
We schall kysse and be gode frende,
    Be God, that owyth thys day !"

The abbot seyde, "Y assente."
Aftur the Erle anon he wente,   1190
    And seyde, "Syr, go wyth mee:
My lorde and ye, be Seynt Iohn,
Schull be made bothe at oon,
    Goode frendys for to bee."
Therof þe Erle was full fayne;   1195
The Emperoure came hym agayne
    And sayde, "My frende so free,

_____

[29] i.e., I swear it.   [30] assurance.   [31] (because an enemy saved the situation).

My wrath here y the forgeue,
My helpe, my loue, whyll y leue,
   Be Hym that dyed on tree!"   1200

Togedur louely can they kysse;
Therof all men had grete blysse:
   The romaunse tellyth soo.
He made hym steward of hys londe
And sesyd[32] agayne into hys honde   1205
   That he had rafte hym froo.
The Emperoure leuyd but yerys thre;
Be alexion[33] of the lordys free,
   The Erle toke they thoo.
They made hym ther Emperoure,   1210
For he was styffe yn stoure
   To fyght agayne hys foo.

He weddyd þat lady to hys wyfe;
Wyth yoye and myrthe þey ladde þer lyfe
   Twenty yere and three.   1215
Betwene þem had þey chyldyr xv,
Doghty knyghtys all bedene,
   And semely on to see.
Yn Rome thys geste cronyculyd ywys;
A lay of Bretayne callyd hyt ys,   1220
   And euyr more schall bee.
Ihesu Cryste to heuyn vs brynge,
There to haue owre wonnyng!
   Amen, amen, for charytee!

---

[32] gave over.   [33] choice.

1203. The "romaunse" has not survived.
1224. One MS. ends, *Amen q*[d] *Rate;* another, *Sic transit gloria mundi.*
The Cambridge MS. ends, *Here endyth the Erle of Tollous and begynneth
Syr Egyllamoure of Artas.*

EMARÉ

EMARÉ

"Emaré" is in the northeast midland dialect of the late fourteenth century. By permission of the authorities of the Department of Manuscripts of the British Museum, it has been edited from rotographs of the unique manuscript, Cotton Caligula A II (fifteenth century).

The story is a greatly rationalized version of a primitive form of the Constance-saga (cf. Chaucer's "Man of Law's Tale"). A good discussion of the type is to be found in Margaret Schlauch's "Chaucer's Constance and Accused Queens," and in *PMLA* 21.575.

Emendations not credited otherwise are Miss Rickert's (EETSES. xcix).

The following peculiarities are common in this manuscript: the interchange of *-th* or *-þ* with *-t* and *-d*(*swyde* for *swyþe*, 219; *whythe* for *white*, 66); the substitution of *-(g)ht* for *-th*, and of *-th* for *-ht* (*thawȝth* for *taught*, 58; *fryght* for *fryth*, 600); *þe* appears several times for *þey;* long *-a* is frequently retained where the midland ordinarily has long *-o* (*lawe: low*).

Stanza divisions are marked in the manuscript. Flourishes at the ends of words have been printed as *-e*. The cross-stroke always written through final *-ll* and *-ght* (except in ll. 817 and 937) has been disregarded.

Ihesu, þat ys kyng in trone,
As þou shoope boþe sonne and mone,
   And all shall dele and dyghte,
Now lene vs grace such dedus to done,
In þy blys þat we may wone;   5
   Men calle hyt heuen lyghte.
And þy modur Mary, Heuyn-qwene,·
Bere our arunde[1] so bytwene,
   That semely ys of syght,
To þy Sone þat ys so fre,   10

---

[1] message, prayer.

3. MS. *þat shalle.*—Holthausen emends.

In heuen wyth hym þat we may be,
That lord ys most of myght.

Menstrelles þat walken fer and wyde
Her and þer in euery a syde,
   In mony a dyuerse londe,
Sholde, at her bygynnyng,
Speke of þat ryghtwes Kyng
   That made bothe see and sonde.
Whoso wyll a stounde dwelle,
Of mykyll myrght y may ʒou telle,
   And mornyng þer amonge:[2]
Of a lady fayr and fre;
Her name was called Emaré,
   As i here synge in songe.

Her fadyr was an emperour
Of castell and of ryche towre;
   Syr Artyus was hys nome.
He hadde boþe hallys and bowrys,
Frythes[3] fayr, forestes wyth flowrys;
   So gret a lord was none.
Weddedde he had a lady
That was both fayr and semely,
   Whyte as whales bone.
Dame Erayne hette þat Emperes;
She was full of loue and goodnesse;
   So curtays lady was none.

Syr Artyus was þe best manne
In þe worlde þat lyuede þanne,
   Both hardy and þerto wyght;
He was curtays in all þyng
Bothe to olde and to ʒynge,
   And well kowth dele and dyght.
He hadde but on chyld in hys lyue
Begeten on hys weddedde wyfe;
   And þat was fayr and bryght.

15

20

25

30

35

40

45

---

[2] mingled with mourning.   [3] woodlands.

For soþe, as y may telle þe,
They called þat chyld Emaré,
   That semely was of syght.

When she was of·her modur born,
She was þe fayrest creature borne   50
   That yn þe lond was þoo.
The Emperes, þat fayr ladye,
Fro her lord gan she dye
   Or hyt[4] kowþe speke or goo.
The chyld, þat was fayr and gent,   55
To a lady was hyt sente
   That men kalled Abro.
She thawȝthe hyt curtesye and thewe,[5]
Golde and sylke for to sewe,
   Amonge maydenes moo.   60

Abro tawȝte þys mayden small
Nortur[6] þat men vsedene in sale,[7]
   Whyle she was in her bowre.
She was curtays in all thynge,
Bothe to olde and to ȝynge,   65
   And whythe as lylye-flowre.
Of her hondes she was slye;
All he[r] loued þat her sye,
   Wythe menske[8] and mychyl honour.
At þe maydene leue we,   70
And at þe lady fayr and fre,
   And speke we of þe Emperour.

The Emperour of gentyll blode
Was a curteys lorde and a gode,
   In all maner of thynge.   75
Aftur, when hys wyf was dede,
A[9] ledde hys lyf yn weddewede,[10]
   And myche loued playngc.

---

[4] i.e., the child. [5] behavior. [6] manners. [7] hall. [8] reverence. [9] he. [10] as a widower.

77. MS. *And;* cf. 989.

Sone aftur, yn a whyle,
The ryche Kynge of Cesyle[11]   80
To þe Emperour gane wende.
A ryche present wyth hym he browght,
A cloth þat was wordylye[12] wroght;
He wellcomed hym as þe hende.

Syr Tergaunte, þat nobyll knyȝte,   85
He presented þe Emperour ryght—
And sette hym on hys kne—
Wyth þat cloth rychyly dyght;
Full of stones þer hyt was pyght,[13]
As thykke as hyt myght be: 90
Off topaze and rubyes
And oþur stones of myche prys,
That semely wer to se;
Of crapowtes[14] and nakette,[15]
As thykke ar þey sette,   95
For sothe, as y say þe.

The cloth was dysplayed sone;
The Emperour lokede þervpone,
And myght hyt not se.
For glysteryng of þe ryche ston   100
Redy syghte had he none,
And sayde, "How may þys be?"
The Emperour sayde on hyghe,
"Sertes, þys ys a fayry,[16]
Or ellys a vanyté!"[17]   105
The Kyng of Cysyle answered þan,
"So ryche a iwelle[18] ys þer non
In all Crystyanté.

---

[11] Sicily. [12] worthily. [13] set. [14] toad-stones. [15] agates (?). [16] magic device.
[17] illusion. [18] jewel, treasure.

85. MS. knyȝte hyȝte (partially blotted).
94. Toad-stones were jewels found in toads' heads, or resembling toads;
cf. Century Dictionary, under "toadstone."
99. For clothes that give off light, cf. Wimberly 92.

The Amerayle dowȝter of heþennes
Made þys cloth, wythouten lees,   110
 And wrowȝte hyt all wyth pride;
And purtreyed hyt wyth gret honour,
Wyth ryche golde and asowr,[19]
 And stones on ylke a syde."
And, as þe story telles in honde,   115
The stones þat yn þys cloth stonde,
 Sowȝte þey wer full wyde.
Seuen wynter hyt was yn makynge,
Or hyt was browght to endynge;
 In herte ys not to hyde.   120

In þat on korner made was
Ydoyne and Amadas,
 Wyth loue þat was so trewe.
For þey loueden hem wyth honour,
Portrayed þey wer wyth trewe-loue-flour,[20]   125
 Of stones bryght of hewe;
Wyth carbunkull and safcrc,[21]
Kassydonys[22] and onyx so clere,
 Sette in golde newe;
Dcamondes and rubyes   130
And oþur stones of mychyll pryse
 And menstrellys wyth her gle[we].

In þat oþur corner was dyght
Trystram and Isowde so bryȝt,
 That semely wer to se;   135
And for þey loued hem ryght,
As full of stones ar þey dyght,
 As thykke as þey may be:
Of topase and of rubyes,
And oþur stones of myche pryse,   140
 That semely wer to se;
Wyth crapawtes and nakette,

---

[19] azure. [20] an herb whose leaves resemble a true-love knot. [21] sapphire.
[22] chalcedony.

Thykke of stones ar þey sette,
For sothe, as y say þe.

In þe thrydde korner, wyth gret honour,   145
Was Florys and Dam Blawncheflour,
As loue was hem betwene.
For þey loued wyth honour,
Purtrayed þey were wyth trewe-loue-flour,
Wyth stones bryght and shene: 150
Ther were kny3tus and senatowres,
Emerawdes of gret valowres,
To wyte wythouten wene;[23]
Deamoundes and koralle,
Perydotes[24] and crystall   155
And gode garnettes bytwene.

In the fowrthe korner was oon,
Of Babylone þe Sowdan sonne,
The Amerayles dow3tyr hym by.
For hys sake þe cloth was wrowght;   160
She loued hym in hert and thowght,
As testymoyeth[25] þys storye.
The fayr mayden here byforn
Was portrayed an vnykorn,
Wyth hys horn so hye;   165
Flowres and bryddes[26] on ylke a syde,
Wyth stones þat wer sowght wyde,
Stuffed wyth ymagerye.

When the cloth to ende was wrowght,
To þe Sowdan sone hyt was brow3t,   170
That semely was of sy3te.
"My fadyr was a nobyll man;

---

[23] doubt.   [24] chrysolite.   [25] testifies.   [26] birds.

152. MS. *vertues.* "(Depicted in) emeralds of great worth." Cf. 126.
168. Though here rationalized, the cloth is a love-charm—originally given to the fairy Emaré by supernatural well-wishers,—and explains the irresistible attraction of the emperor and, later, of the king of Galys. The unicorn is a symbol of virginity; ordinarily wild and fierce, it would lay its head in the lap of a maiden. Magic dresses occur in many variants of the Cinderella story. Cf. M. R. Cox's "Cinderella."

Of þe Sowdan he hyt wan
  Wyth maystrye and wyth myȝth.
For gret loue he ȝaf hyt me;   175
I brynge hyt þe in specyalté;[27]
  Thys cloth ys rychely dyght."
He ȝaf hyt þe Emperour;
He receyued hyt wyth gret honour,
  And þonkede hym fayr and ryȝt.   180

The Kyng of Cesyle dwelled þer
As long as hys wyll wer,
  Wyth þe Emperour for to play;
And when he wolde wende,
He toke hys leue at þe hende,   185
  And wente forth on hys way.
Now remeueth þys nobyll Kyng.
The Emperour aftur hys dowȝtur hadde longyng,
  To speke wyth þat may.
Messengeres forth he sent   190
Aftyr þe mayde fayr and gent,
  That was bryȝt as someres day.

Messengeres dyȝte hem in hye;
Wyth myche myrthe and melodye,
  Forth gon þey fare,   195
Both by stretes and hy stye,[28]
Aftur þat fayr lady,.
  Was godely vnþur gare.[29]
Her norysse,[30] þat hyȝte Abro,
Wyth her she goth forth also,   200
  And wer sette in a chare.[31]
To þe Emperour gan þé go;
He come aȝeyn hem a myle or two;
  A fayr metyng was there.

The mayden, whyte as lylye-flour,   205
Lyȝte aȝeyn her fadyr þe Emperour;
  Two knyȝtes gan her lede.

---

[27] as a token of regard.   [28] path.   [29] cloth.   [30] nurse.   [31] litter.

Her fadyr, þat was of gret renowne,
That of golde wered[32] þe crowne,
 Lyȝte of hys stede.   210
When þey wer bothe on her fete,
He klypped her and kyssed her swete,
 And bothe on fote þey ȝede.
They wer glad and made good chere;
To þe palys þey ȝede in fere,   215
 In romans as we rede.

Then þe lordes þat wer grete,
They wesh and seten don to mete,
 And folk hem serued swyde.
The mayden, þat was of sembelant swete,   220
Byfore her owene fadur sete,
 The fayrest wommon on lyfe,
That all hys hert and all hys þowȝth
Her to loue was ybrowght;
 He byhelde her ofte syþe.   225
So he was anamored hys þowȝtur tyll,[33]
Wyth her he þowȝth to worche hys wyll,
 And wedde her to hys wyfe.

And when þe metewhyle[34] was done,
Into hys chambur he wente sone,   230
 And called hys counseyle nere.
He bad þey shulde sone go and come
And gete leue of þe Pope of Rome
 To wedde þat mayden clere.
Messengeres forth þey wente—   235
They durste not breke hys commandement—
 And erles wyth hem yn fere.

---

[32] wore.   [33] enamored of.   [34] mealtime.

218. MS. *dou* or *don*, for *doun*.
224. MS. *yn browght*.
228. Usually procuring the fine garment is a task imposed on the inces-
tuous father.   Cf. M. R. Cox, "Cinderella," 189 ff. and Miss Schlauch's
'Constance."

They wente to þe courte of Rome,
And browȝte þe Popus bullus[35] sone,
   To wedde hys dowȝter dere.   240

Þen was þe Emperour gladde and blyþe,
And lette shape a robe swyþe
   Of þat cloth of golde;
And when hyt was don her vpon,
She semed non erþely wommon   245
   That marked[36] was of molde.
Then seyde þe Emperour so fre,
"Dowȝtyr, y woll wedde þe;
   Thow art so fresh to beholde."
Then sayde þat wordy[37] vnþur wede,   250
"Nay, syr, God of heuen hyt forbede
   Þat euer do so we shulde!

Ȝyf hyt so betydde þat ȝe me wedde
And we shulde play togedur in bedde,
   Bothe we were forlorne!   255
Þe worde shulde sprynge fer and wyde;
In all þe worlde on euery syde
   Þe worde shulde be borne.
Ȝe ben a lorde of gret pryce;
Lorde, lette neuur suche sorow aryce;   260
   Take God ȝou beforne![38]
That my fadur shulde wedde me,
God forbede þat i hyt so se,
   That wered þe crowne of þhorne!"[39]

The Emperour was ryght wrothe,   265
And swore many a gret othe
   That deed shulde she be.
He lette make a nobull boot
And dede her þeryn, God wote,

---

[35] pope's bulls.   [36] created.   [37] worthy lady.   [38] i.e., let God guide you.   [39] thorn.

245. A hint that Emaré is supernatural; cf. also 396, 443, 701.
268. Cf. "Man of Law's Tale" 439. On magic boats, cf. L. A. Paton's
"Fairy Mythology of Arthurian Romance" 16 n.1.

In þe robe of nobull ble.   270
She moste haue wyth her no spendyng,[40]
Noþur mete ne drynke,
But shate[41] her ynto þe se.
Now þe lady dwelled þore
Wythowte anker or ore,   275
And þat was gret pyté!

Ther come a wynd, y vnþurstonde,
And blewe þe boot fro þe londe;
Of her þey lost þe syght.
The Emperour hym beþowght   280
That he hadde all myswrowht,[42]
And was a sory knyʒte.
And as he stode yn studyynge,
He fell down in sowenynge;
To þe yrþe was he dyght.   285
Grete lordes stode þerby,
And toke vp þe Emperour hastyly,
And comforted hym fayr and ryght.

When he of sownyng kouered[43] was,
Sore he wepte and sayde, "Alas   290
For my dowhter dere!
Alas þat y was made man,
Wrecched kaytyf[44] þat i hyt am!"
The teres ronne by hys lere..
"I wrowght aʒeyn Goddes lay[45]   295
To her þat was so trewe of fay.
Alas, why ner she here!"[46]
The teres lasshed[47] out of hys yʒen;
The grete lordes þat hyt syʒen
Wepte and made yll chere.   300

---

[40] money.   [41] pushed.   [42] done amiss.   [43] recovered.   [44] villain.   [45] law.   [46] i.e., why is she not here?   [47] poured.

272. Ritson adds *givyng*.
287. MS. *toke vn*. Miss Rickert emends.

Ther was noþur olde ny ȝynge
That kowþe stynte[48] of wepynge
   For þat comely vnþur kelle.[49]
Into shypys faste gane þey þrynge[50]
For to seke þat mayden ȝynge,   305
   Þat was so fayr of flesh and fell.[1]
They her sowȝt ouurall yn þe see,
And myȝte not fynde þat lady fre;
   Aȝeyn þey come full snell.
At þe Emperour now leue we,   310
And of þe lady yn þe see
   I shall begynne to tell.

The lady fleted[2] forþ alone;
To God of heuen she made her mone,
   And to Hys Modyr also.   315
She was dryuen wyth wynde and rayn,
Wyth stronge stormes her agayn,
   Of þe watyr so blo.[3]
As y haue herd menstrelles syng yn sawe,[4]
Hows ny lond myȝth she non knowe;   320
   Aferd she was to go.
She was so dryuen fro wawe to wawe
She hyd her hede and lay full lawe;
   For watyr she was full woo.

Now þys lady dwelled þore   325
A good seuen-nyȝth and more,
   As hyt was Goddys wylle,
Wyth carefull herte and sykyng sore;
Such sorow was here ȝarked ȝore,[5]
   And euer lay she styll.   330
She was dryuen ynto a lond
Thorow þe grace of Goddes sond,
   That all þyng may fulfylle.
She was on þe see so harde bestadde,[6]

---

[48] cease. [49] netted cap.   [50] throng. [1] skin. [2] floated. [3] dark. [4] story. [5] long
ordained. [6] bestead.

For hungur and thurste almost madde; 335
Woo worth wederus yll![7]

She was dryuen into a lond
That hy3th Galys,[8] y vnþurstond,
That was a fayr countré.
þe Kyngus steward dwelled þer bysyde 340
In a kastell of mykyll pryde;
Syr Kadore hyght he.
Euery day wolde he go
And take wyth hym a sqwyer or two,
And play hym by þe see. 345
On a tyme he toke þe eyr[9]
Wyth two kny3tus gode and fayr;
The wedur was lythe of le.[10]

A boot he fond by þe brym,[11]
And a glysteryng þyng þeryn; 350
Therof þey hadde ferly.
They went forth on þe sond
To þe boot, y vnþurstond,
And fond þeryn þat lady.
She hadde so longe meteles be 355
That hym þowht gret dele to se;
She was yn poyn[t] to dye.[12]
They askede her what was her name;·
She chaunged hyt þer anone,
And sayde she hette Egaré. 360

Syr Kadore hadde gret pyté;
He toke vp þe lady of þe see,
And hom gan he[r] lede.
She hadde so longe meteles be,
She was wax lene as a tre, 365
That wordy vnþur wede.

---

[7] woe befall bad storms. [8] Galicia. [9] air. [10] peacefully calm. [11] shore. [12] about to die.

360. "Egaré" means "the outcast;" cf. Rickert xxix.

Into hys castell when she came,
Into a chawmbyr þey her namm,
   And fayr þey gan here fede
Wyth alle delycyus mete and drynke   370
That þey myȝth hem on þynke
   That was yn alle þat stede.

When þat lady fayr of face
Wyth mete and drynke keuered was,
   And had colour agayne,   375
She tawȝte hem to sewe and marke
All maner of sylkyn werke;
   Of her þey wer full fayne.
She was curteys yn all þyng,
Bothe to olde and to ȝynge,   380
   I say ȝow for certeyne.
She kowȝþe werke all maner þyng
That fell to emperour or to kyng,
   Erle, barowne, or swayne.

Syr Kadore lette make a feste   385
That was fayr and honeste,[13]
   Wyth hys lorde, þe Kynge.
Ther was myche menstralsé,
Trommpus, tabours, and sawtré,
   Bothe harpe and fydyllyng.   390
The lady þat was gentyll and small
In kurtull[14] alone serued yn hall,
   Byfore þat nobull Kyng.
Þe cloth vpone her shone so bryȝthe,
When she was þeryn ydyȝth,   395
   She semed non erdly þyng.

---

[13] honorable.   [14] servant's tunic.

377. MS. *sylky*, but a letter has been erased.   In the Irish "Tochmarc
Emere" ("Wooing of Emer"), the women at court learn needlework from
Emer; similarly in "The Destruction of Da Derga's Hostel" the heroine
is a good needlewoman.

The Kyng loked her vpone;
So fayr a lady he syȝ neuur none;
Hys herte she hadde yn wolde.[15]
He was so anamered of þat syȝth   400
Of þe mete non he myȝth,[16]
But faste gan her beholde.
She was so fayr and gent
The Kynges loue on her was lent,
In tale as hyt ys tolde.   405
And when þe metewhyle was done,
Into þe chambur he wente sone,
And called hys barouns bolde.

Fyrst he calle[d] Syr Kadore,
And oþur knyȝtes þat þer wore   410
Hastely come hym tyll.
Dukes and erles, wyse of lore,
Hastely come þe Kyng before,
And askede what was hys wyll.
Then spakke þe ryche yn ray;[17]   415
To Syr Kadore gan he say
Wordes fayr and stylle:
"Syr, whenns ys þat louely may
That yn þe halle serued þys day?
Tell me, ȝyf hyt be þy wyll."   420

Then sayde Syr Kadore, y vnþurstonde,
"Hyt ys an erles þowȝtur of ferre londe,
That semely ys to sene.
I sente aftur her, certeynlye,
To teche my chylderen curtesye,   425
In chambur wythe hem to bene.
She ys þe konnyngest wommon,
I trowe, þat be yn Crystendom,
Of werk þat y haue sene."

---

[15] power.   [16] i.e., could eat.   [17] striped cloth.

Then sayde þat ryche Raye,[18]   430
"I wyll haue þat fayr may,
And wedde her to my quene."

The nobull Kyng, verament,
Aftyr hys modyr he sent,
  To wyte what she wolde say.   435
They browȝt forthe hastely
That fayr mayde Egarye;
  She was bryȝth as someres day,
The clothe on her shon so bryght
Whenn she was þeryn dyght,   440
  And herself a gentell may;
The olde Qwene sayde anone,
"I sawe neuer wommon
  Haluendell so gay!"[19]

The olde Qwene spakke wordus vnhende,   445
And sayde, "Sone, þys ys a fende,
  In þys wordy wede!
As þou louest my blessynge,
Make þou neuur þys weddynge;
  Cryst hyt de forbede!"   450
Then spakke þe ryche Ray,
"Modyr, y wyll haue þys may;"
  And forth gan her lede.
The olde Qwene, for certayne,
Turnede wyth ire hom agayne,   455
  And wolde not be at þat dede.

The Kyng wedded þat lady bryght;
Grete puruyance[20] þer was dyȝth
  In þat semely sale.
Grete lordes wer serued aryght,   460

---

[18] king.   [19] *woman* half so gay, i.e., she is no mortal.   [20] provision.

430. The phrase is probably the same as *ryche yn ray* in 415; but as it
stands, it may be taken to mean "powerful king."
446. Cf. "Chevelere Assigne" 40 ff.

Duke, erle, baron, and kny3th,
Both of grete and smale.[21]
Myche folke forsoþe þer was,
And þerto an huge prese,
As hyt ys tolde in tale.   465
Ther was all maner þyng
That fell to a kyngus weddyng,
And mony a ryche menstrall.

When þe mangery[22] was done,
Grete lordes departed sone,   470
That semely were to se.
The Kynge belafte wyth þe Qwene;
Moch loue was hem betwene,
And also game and gle.
She was curteys and swete;   475
Such a lady herde y neuur of 3ete;
They loued both wyth herte fre.
The lady, þat was both meke and mylde,
Conceyued and wente wyth chylde,
As God wolde hyt sholde be.   480

The Kyng of France yn þat tyme
Was besette wyth many a Sarezyne,
And cumbered[23] all in tene;
And sente aftur þe Kyng of Galys
And oþur lordys of myche prys,   485
That semely were to sene.
The Kyng of Galys in þat tyde
Gedered men on euery syde,
In armour bryght and shene.
Then sayde þe Kyng to Syr Kadore   490
And oþur lordes þat ther wore,
"Take good hede to my qwene."

The Kyng of Fraunce spared none,
But sent for hem euerychone,

---

[21] i.e., with everything.   [22] feast.   [23] weighed down.

462. The more usual phrase would be "Both grete and smale;" i.e.,
everybody.

Both kyng, kny3th, and clerke.   495
The stward bylaft at home
To kepe þe Qwene whyte as fome;
    He com not at þat werke.[24]
She wente wyth chylde yn place[25]
As longe as Goddus wyll was,   500
    That semely vnþur serke;[26]
Thyll þer was of her body
A fayr chyld borne and a godelé;
    Hadde a dowbyll kyngus marke.[27]

They hyt crystened wyth grete honour,   505
And called hym Segramour;
    Frely was þat fode.[28]
Then þe steward, Syr Kadore,
A nobull lettur made he thore,
    And wrow3te hyt all wyth gode.   510
He wrow3te hyt yn hy3ynge
And sente hyt to hys lorde þe Kynge,
    That gentyll was of blode.
The messenger forth gan wende,
And wyth þe Kyngus modur gan lende,[29]   515
    And ynto þe castell he 3ode.

He was resseyued rychely,
And she hym askede hastyly
    How þe Qwene hadde spedde.
"Madame, þer ys of her yborne   520
A fayr man-chylde, y tell 3ou beforne,
    And she lyth in her bedde."
She 3af hym for þat tydynge
A robe and fowrty shylynge,
    And rychely hym cladde.   525
She made hym dronken of ale and wyne,

---

[24] i.e., he did not go to war. [25] i.e., there. [26] smock. [27] mark of royal birth.
[28] child. [29] tarry.

504. Cf. "Havelok" 604, 2139–47. Possibly this king-mark is double
because both father and mother are royal.

And when she sawe þat hyt was tyme,
Tho³⁰ chambur she wolde hym lede.

And when he was on slepe browȝt,
The Qwene, þat was of wykked þowȝt,   530
Tho chambur gan she wende:
Hys letter she toke hym fro;
In a fyre she brente hyt do;³¹
Of werkes she was vnhende!
Anoþur lettur she made wyth euyll,   535
And sayde þe Qwene had born a deuyll;
Durste no mon come her hende.³¹ᵃ
Thre heddes hadde he there,
A lyon, a dragon, and a beere—
A fowll, feltred³² fende.   540

On þe morn when hyt was day,
The messenger wente on hys way
Bothe by stye and strete,
In trwe story as y say,
Tyll he come þeras þe Kynge laye,   545
And speke wordus swete.
He toke þe Kyng þe lettur yn honde,
And he hyt redde, y vnþurstonde;
The teres downe gan he lete.
And as he stode yn redyng,   550
Downe he fell yn sowenyng;
For sorow hys herte gan blede.

Grete lordes þat stode hym by
Toke vp þe Kyng hastely;
In herte he was full woo.   555
Sore he grette and sayde, "Alas,
That y euur man born was!

---

³⁰ to. ³¹ then. ³¹ᵃ near. ³² with matted hair.

529. MS. *she.*

That hyt euur shullde be so !
Alas þat y was made a kynge,
And syghe[33] wedded þe fayrest þyng   560
    That on erþe myght go !
That euur Ihesu hymself wolde sende
Such a fowle loþly[34] fende
    To come bytwene vs[35] too !"

When he sawe hyt myȝt no bettur be,   565
Anoþur lettur þen made he,
    And seled hyt wyth hys sele.
He commanded yn all þynge
To kepe well þat lady ȝynge
    Tyll she hadde her hele;[36]   570
Bothe gode men and ylle
To serue her at here wylle,
    Bothe yn wo and wele.
He toke þys lettur of hys honde
And rode þorow þe same londe,   575
    By þe Kyngus modur castell.

And þen he dwelled þer all nyȝt;
He was resseyued and rychely dyȝt,
    And wyste of no tresou.
He made hym well at ese and fyne   580
Bothe of brede, ale, and wyne;
    And þat berafte hym hys reson.
When he was on slepe browȝt,
The false Qwene hys lettur sowȝt;
    Into þe fyre she kaste hyt downe.   585
Anoþur lettur she lette make:
That men sholde þe lady take
    And lede her out of towne,

And putte her ynto þe see,
    In þat robe of ryche ble,   590

33 afterwards. 34 detestable. 35 i.e., to be begotten by me. 36 health.

558. MS. *That hyt euur so shullde be.* Miss Rickert rearranges.

The lytyll chylde here wyth;
And lette here haue no spendyng
For no mete ny for drynke,
　　But lede here out of þat kyghe.[37]
"Vpone payne[38] of chylde and wyfe,   595
And also vpone ȝour owene lyfe,
　　Lette here haue no gryght !"[39]
The messenger knewe no gyle,
But rode hom mony a myle
　　By forest and by fryght.[40]   600

And when þe messengere come home,
The steward toke þe lettur sone
　　And bygan to rede.
Sore he syght and sayde, "Alas !
Sertes, þys ys a fowle case   605
　　And a defull[41] dede !"
And as he stode yn redyng,
He fell downe yn swonynge;
　　For sorow hys hert gan blede.
Ther was noþur olde ny ȝynge   610
That myȝte forbere of wepynge
　　For þat worþy vnþur wede.

The lady herde gret dele yn halle;
On þe steward gan she calle,
　　And sayde, "What may þys be?   615
Ȝyf any þyng be amys,
Tell me what þat hyt ys,
　　And lette not for me."
Then sayde þe steward, verament,
"Lo, her[42] a lettur my lord hath sente,   620
　　And þerfore woo ys me !"
She toke þe lettur and bygan to rede;

---

[37] land. [38] i.e., upon pain of losing. [39] security. [40] woods. [41] pitiful. [42] here.

593. Read: *For mete ny drynke ny oþer thyng?*
605. MS. *senrtes.*

Then fonde she wryten all þe dede,
How she moste ynto þe see.

"Be stylle, syr," sayde þe Qwene,   625
"Lette syche mornynge bene;
    For me haue þou no kare.
Loke þou be not shente,
But do my lordes commaundement;
    God forbede þou spare !   630
For he weddede so porely
On me, a sympull lady,
    He ys ashamed sore.
Grete well my lord fro me;
So gentyll of blode yn Cristyanté   635
    Gete he neuur more !"⁴³

Then was þer sorow and myche woo
When þe lady to shype shulde go;
    They wepte and wronge her hondus.
The lady, þat was meke and mylde,   640
In her arme she bar her chylde,
    And toke leue of þe londe.
When she wente ynto þe see
In þat robe of ryche ble,
    Men sowened on þe sonde.   645
Sore þey wepte and sayde, "Alas !
Certys, þys ys a wykked kase !
    Wo worth dedes wronge !"

The lady and þe lytyll chylde
Fleted⁴⁴ forth on þe watur wylde,   650
    Wyth full harde happes.
Her surkote,⁴⁵ þat was large and wyde,
Therwyth her vysage she gan hyde
    Wyth þe hynþur lappes;⁴⁶

She was aferde of þe see,   655
And layde her gruf[47] vponn a tre,
  The chylde to her pappes.
The wawes, þat were grete and strong,
On þe bote faste þey þonge,[48]
  Wyth mony vnsemely rappes.   660

And when þe chylde gan to wepe,
Wyth sory hert she songe hyt aslepe,
  And putte þe pappe yn hys mowth,
And sayde, "Myȝth y onus gete lond
Of þe watur þat ys so stronge,   665
  By northe or by sowthe,
Wele owth y to warye[49] þe see;
I haue myche shame yn the!"[50]
  And euur she lay and growht.[1]
Then she made her prayer   670
To Ihesu and Hys Modur dere,
  In all þat she kowþe.

Now þys lady dwelled thore
A full seuene-nyght and more,
  As hyt was Goddys wylle;   675
Wyth karefull herte and sykyng sore—
Such sorow was here ȝarked[2] ȝore—
  And she lay full stylle.
She was dryuen toward Rome,
Thorow þe grace of God yn trone,   680
  That all þyng may fulfylle.
On þe see she was so harde bestadde,
For hungur and thurste allmost madde;
  Wo worth chawnses ylle!

A marchaunte dw[el]led yn þat cyté,   685
A ryche mon of golde and fee;
  Iurdan was hys name.

---

[47] prone. [48] =*dong*, struck. [49] curse. [50] i.e., the sea. [1] lamented. [2] had long been preordained.

Euery day wolde he
Go to playe hym by þe see,
   The eyer for to tane.   690
He wente forth yn þat tyde,
Walkynge by þe see-syþe,[3]
   All hymselfe alone.
A bote he fonde by þe brymme,
And a fayr lady therynne,   695
   That was ryght wo-bygone.

The cloth on her shon so brythe
He was aferde of þat syght,
   For glysteryng of þat wede;
And yn hys herte he þowȝth ryght   700
That she was none erdyly wyght;
   He sawe neuur non such yn leede.
He sayde, "What hette ȝe, fayr ladye?"
"Lord," she sayde, "y hette Egarye,
   That lye her yn drede."   705
Vp he toke þat fayre ladye,
And þe ȝonge chylde her by,
   And hom he gan hem lede.

When he come to hys byggynge,[4]
He welcomed fayr þat lady ȝynge,   710
   That was fayr and bryght;
And badde hys wyf yn all þynge
Mete and drynke for to brynge
   To þe lady ryght.
"What þat she wyll craue   715
And here mowth wyll hyt haue,
   Loke hyt be redy dyght.
She hathe so longe meteles be
That me þynketh grette pyté;
   Conforte her ȝyf þou myght."   720

---

[3] seaside. [4] building, home.

688. MS. *eeuery*.
702. MS. *shuche*.

Now þe lady dwelles ther,
And alle mete[s] þat gode were
   She hedde at her wylle.
She was curteys yn all þyng,
Bothe to olde and to ӡynge;   725
   Her loued bothe gode and ylle.
The chylde bygan for to þryfe;
He wax þe fayrest chyld on lyfe,
   Whyte as flour on hylle;
And she sewed sylke-werk yn bour,   730
And tawӡte her sone nortowre;[5]
   But euyr she mornede stylle.

When þe chylde was seuen ӡer olde,
He was bothe wyse and bolde,
   And wele made of fleshe and bone;   735
He was worþy vnþur wede,
And ryght well kowþe prike a stede;
   So curtays a chylde was none.
All men louede Segramowre
Bothe yn halle and yn bowre,   740
   Wheresoeuur he gan gone.
Leue we at þe lady, clere of vyce,[6]
And speke of the Kyng of Galys,
   Fro þe sege when he come home.

Now þe sege broken ys;   745
The Kyng come home to Galys
   Wyth mykyll myrthe and pride.
Dukes and erles of ryche asyce,[7]
Barones and knyӡtes of mykyll pryse,
   Come rydynge be hys syde.   750
Syr Kodore, hys steward þanne,
Aӡeyn hym rode wyth mony a man,
   As faste as he myght ryde;

[5] manners. [6] beautiful of face. [7] great substance.

722. MS. *with alle.*   *Metes* is Gough's emendation.
730. MS. *shewed.*

He tolde þe Kyng aventowres
Of hys halles and hys bowres   755
   And of hys londys wyde.

The Kyng sayde, "By Goddys name,
Syr Kadore, þou art to blame
   For þy fyrst tellynge![8]
Thow sholdest fyrst haue tolde me   760
Of my lady Egaré
   I loue most of all þyng."
Then was þe stewardes herte wo,
And sayde, "Lorde, why sayst þou so?
   Art not þou a trewe kynge?   765
Lo, her, þe lettur ʒe sente me,
ʒowr owene self þe soþe may se;
   I haue don ʒour byddynge."

The Kyng toke þe lettur to rede,
And when he sawe þat ylke dede,   770
   He wax all pale and wanne.
Sore he grette and sayde, "Alas
That euur born y was,
   Or euur was made manne!
Syr Kadore, so mot y the,   775
Thys lettur come neuur fro me,
   I telle þe her anone!"
Bothe þey wepte and ʒaf hem ylle;
"Alas," he sayde, "saf[9] Goddys wylle!"
   And both þé sowened þen.   780

Grete lordes stode by,
And toke vp þe Kyng hastyly;
   Of hem was gret pyté;
And when þey both keuered[10] were,
The Kyng toke hym þe letter þer,   785
   Of þe heddys þre.[11]

---

[8] news. [9] without offense to, i.e., God's will be done. [10] recovered. [11] concerning the three heads.

"A, lord," he sayde, "be Goddus grace,
I sawe neuur þys lettur yn place![12]
Alas, how may þys be?"
Aftur þe messengere þer þey sente;   790
The Kyng askede what way he went.
"Lor[d], be ȝour modur fre."

"Alas!" þen sayde þe Kynge,
"Wheþur my modur were so vnhende
   To make þys treson?   795
By my krowne, she shall be brent,
Wythowten any oþur iugement;
   That thenketh me best reson!"
Grete lordes toke hem betwene
That þey wolde exyle þe Qwene   800
   And berefe here hyr renowne.
Thus þey exiled þe false Qwene
And byrafte here hyr lyfloþe[13] clene,
   Castell, towre, and towne.

When she was fled ouur þe see fome,   805
The nobull Kyng dwelled at home
   Wyth full heuy chere;
Wyth karefull hert and drury[14] mone,
Sykynges made he many on
   For Egarye þe clere;   810
And when he sawe chylderen play,
He wepte and sayde, "Wellawey
   For my sone so dere!"
Suche lyf he lyued mony a day
That no mon hym stynte[15] may   815
   Fully seuen yere,

Tyll a thowght yn hys herte come
How hys lady, whyte as fome,
   Was drowned for hys sake.
"Thorow þe grace of God yn trone,   820

---

[12] anywhere.   [13] revenue.   [14] dreary.   [15] stop.

I woll to þe Pope of Rome,
My penans for to take!"
He lette ordeyne shypus fele,
And fylled hem full of wordes wele,[16]
Hys men mery wyth to make.   825
Dolys[17] he lette dyȝth. and dele,
For to wynnen hym sowles hele;[18]
To þe shyp he toke þe gate.

Shypmen þat were so mykyll of price
Dyght here takull on ryche acyse,[19]   830
That was fayr and fre.
They drowȝ vp sayl and leyd out ore;
The wynde stode as here lust wore;[20]
The weþur was lyþe on le.
They sayled ouere þe salt fome,   835
Thorow þe grace of God in trone,
That most ys of powsté.[21]
To þat cyté when þé come,
At þe burgeys hous hys yn he nome[22]
Theras woned Emarye.   840

Emaré called he[r] sone
Hastely to here come,
Wythoute ony lettynge,
And sayde, "My dere sone so tre,
Do a lytull aftur me[23]   845
And þou sha[l]t haue my blessynge:
To-morowe þou shall serue yn halle,
In a kurtyll[24] of ryche palle,
Byfore þys nobull Kyng;
Loke, sone, so curtays þou be   850
That no mon fynde chalange[25] to þe.
In no manere þynge!

When þe Kyng ys serued of spycerye,[26]

---

[16] the world's wealth. [17] alms. [18] health, salvation. [19] manner. [20] i.e., as pleased them. [21] power. [22] took his lodging. [23] do as I bid you. [24] tunic, i.e., the magic cloth. [25] fault. [26] i.e., the dessert course; cf. Int. III.B.

Knele þou downe hastylye
    And take hys hond yn thyn;   855
And when þou hast so done,
Take þe kuppe of golde sone
    And serue hym of þe wyne;
And what þat he speketh to þe,
    Cum anone and tell me,   860
    On Goddus blessyng and myne!"
The chylde wente ynto þe hall
Among þe lordes, grete and small,
    That lufsumme were vnþur lyne.[27]

Then þe lordes þat were grete   865
Wyshe and wente to here mete;
    Men[s]trelles browȝt yn þe kowrs.
The chylde hem serued so curteysly,
All hym loued þat hym sy,
    And spake hym gret honowres.   870
Then sayde all þat loked hym vpone,
So curteys a chyld sawe þey neuur none,
    In halle ny yn bowres.
The Kynge sayde to hym yn game,
"Swete sone, what ys þy name?"   875
    "Lorde," he seyd, "y hyȝth Segramowres."

Then þat nobull Kyng
Toke vp a grete sykynge,
    For hys sone hyght so;
Certys, wythowten lesynge,   880
The teres out of hys yen gan wryng;
    In herte he was full woo.
Neuere-þe-lese, he lette be,
And loked on þe chylde so fre,
    And mykell he louede hym þoo.   885

---

[27] linen.

867. Minstrels often walked in before the course, playing. Cf.
Wright 152.
876. *He seyd* is superfluous.—Gough.

The Kyng sayde to þe burgeys anone,
"Swete syr, ys þys þy sone?"
The burgeys sayde, "3oo."

Then þe lordes þat were grete
Whesshen aӡeyn aftyr mete,   890
    And þen come spycerye.
The chyld, þat was of chere swete,
On hys kne downe he sete
    And serued hym curteyslye.
The Kynge called þe burgeys hym tyll   895
And sayde, "Syr, yf hyt be þy wyll,
    3yf me þys lytyll body!
I shall hym make lorde of town and towre,
Of hye halles and of bowre;
    I loue hym specyally."   900

When he had serued þe Kyng at wylle,
Fayr he wente hys modyr tyll
    And tellys her how hyt ys.
"Soone when he shall to chambur wende,
Take hys hond at þe grece²⁸ ende,   905
    For he ys þy fadur, ywysse;
And byd hym come speke wyth Emaré,
That changed here name to Egaré
    In the londe of Galys!"
The chylde wente aӡeyn to halle   910
Amonge þe grete lordes alle,
    And serued on ryche asyse.²⁹

When þey were well at ese afyne³⁰
Bothe of brede, ale, and wyne,
    They rose vp, more and myn.³¹   915
When þe Kyng shulde to chambur wende,
He toke hys hond at þe grece ende,
    And fayre he helpe hym yn;
And sayde, "Syr, yf ӡour wyll be,

---

²⁸ foot of the (dais) steps.   ²⁹ manner.   ³⁰ at last.   ³¹ less.

Take me ȝour honde and go wyth me;   920
For y am of ȝowr kynne.
Ȝe shull come speke wyth Emaré,
That chaunged here nome to Egaré,
That berys þe whyte chynne!"

The Kyng yn herte was full woo   925
When he herd mynge[32] þo
Of her þat was hys qwene,
And sayde, "Sone, why sayst þou so?
Where-to vmbraydest[33] þou me of my wo?
That may neuere bene!"   930
Neuurþeles wyth hym he wente;
Aȝeyn hem come þe lady gent,
In þe robe bryght and shene.
He toke here yn hys armes two;
For ioye þey sowened, both to,   935
Suche loue was hem bytwene.

A ioyfull metyng was þer þore
Of þat lady, goodly vnþur gore,[34]
Frely in armes to folde.
Lorde! gladde was Syr Kadore   940
And oþur lordes þat þere wore,
Semely to beholde,
Of þe lady þat was put yn þe see,
Thorow grace of God in Trinité,
Þat was keuered of cares colde.   945
Leue we at þe lady whyte as flour,
And speke we of here fadur þe Emperour,
That fyrste þys tale of y tolde.

The Emperour her fadyr þen
Was woxen an olde man,   950
And thowȝt on hys synne:

---

[32] recalled.   [33] upbraid.   [34] cloth.

943. MS. wat.
950. MS. wax.

Of hys þowȝtyr Emaré,
That was putte ynto þe see,
   That was so bryght of skynne.
He þowȝt that he wolde go   955
For hys penance to þe Pope þo,
   And heuen for to wynne.
Messengeres he sente forthe sone,
And þey come to þe kowrt of Rome
   To take her lordes inne.[35]   960

Emaré prayde her lord þe Kyng:
"Syr, abyde þat lordys komyng,
   That ys so fayr and fre.
And, swete syr, yn all þyng,
Aqweynte ȝou wyth þat lordyng;   965
   Hyt ys worshyp to þe."
The Kyng of Galys seyde þan,
"So grete a lord ys þer non
   In all Crystyanté."
"Now, swete syr, whateuur betyde,   970
Aȝayn þat grete lord ȝe ryde,
   And all þy knyȝtys wyth þe."

Emaré thawȝte her sone ȝynge.
Aȝeyn þe Emperour komynge
   How þat he sholde done: 975
"Swete sone, yn all þyng
Be redy wyth my lord þe Kyng,
   And be my swete sone!
When þe Emperour kysseth þy fadur so fre,
Loke ȝyf he wylle kysse the: 980
   Abowe[36] þe to hym sone,
And bydde hym come speke wyth Emaré,
That was putte ynto þe see;
   Hymself ȝaf þe dome."

Now kometh þe Emperour of pryse;   985
Aȝeyn hym rode þe Kyng of Galys
   Wyth full mykull pryde.

---

[35] i.e., to find a lodging for their lord. [36] bow to.

The chyld was worþy vnþur wede;
A[37] satte vpon a nobyll stede
   By hys fadyr syde;   990
And when he mette þe Emperour,
He valed hys hode[38] wyth gret honour,
   And kyssed hym yn þat tyde;
And oþur lordys of gret valowre,
They also kessed Segramowre;   995
   In herte ys not to hyde.

The Emperours hert anamered gretlye
Of þe chylde þat rode hym by
   Wyth so louely chere.
Segramowre, he s[t]ayde hys stede;   1000
Hys owene fadur toke good hede,
   And oþur lordys þat þer were.
The chylde spake to þe Emperour
And sayde, "Lord, for þyn honour,
   My worde þat þou wyll here: 1005
ȝe shull come speke wyth Emaré,
That changede her name to Egaré,
   That was þy þowȝþur dere."

The Emperour wax all pale,
And sayde, "Sone, why vmbraydest me of bale, 1010
   And þou may se no bote?"
"Syr, and ȝe wyll go wyth me,
I shall þe brynge wyth þat lady fre,
   þat ys louesom on to loke."
Neuur-þe-lesse, wyth hym he wente;   1015
Aȝeyn hym come þat lady gent,
   Walkynge on her fote.
And þe Emperour alyȝte þo
And toke her yn hys armes two,
   And clypte and kyssed her sote.[39]   1020

---

[37] he. [38] lowered his hood. [39] sweetly.

1000. Miss Rickert's emendation.

Ther was a ioyfull metynge
Of þe Emperour and of þe Kynge,
   And also of Emaré;
And so þere was of Syr [S]egramour,
That aftyr was emperour;   1025
   A full gode man was he.
A grette feste þer was holde
Of erles and barones bolde,
   As testymonyeth[40] þys story.
Thys ys on of Brytayne layes   1030
That was vsed by olde dayes;
   Men callys "Playn þe Garye."

Ihesus, þat settes yn þy trone,
So graunte vs wyth þe to wone
   In þy perpetuall glorye ! AMEN.   1035

EXPLICIT EMARÉ.

---

[40] witnesses.

1032. "Complaint of Egaré." Complaints are common in Celtic literature, and stories were often written around them to explain their existence and provide a setting.
1034. MS. *wene;* Miss Rickert emends.

ARTHURIAN PIECES

LAYAMON'S BRUT

Layamon, a priest of Arley Regis, on the Severn, composed the "Brut" at the close of the twelfth century. In recounting the legends of English history from the fall of Troy and the arrival in England of Brutus, Æneas' grandson, to the year 689, he told the story of Arthur for the first time in English. His chief source was Wace's "Brut," possibly in a lost version expanded from Breton tradition; he may also have drawn upon the "Historia Regum Britanniæ" and the "Vita Merlini" of Geoffrey of Monmouth. The theory that he collected and added to Wace Celtic legendary material has been largely abandoned.

The poem exists in two manuscripts in the British Museum; they have been edited by Sir Frederic Madden. The present text is from the older, C. (Cotton Caligula A IX.); words and lines in brackets have been supplied from O. (Cotton Otho C XIII.), wherever the sense demanded. Otherwise, lines missing from C. have been indicated with dots in order to conform to Madden's line-numbering. Through the kindness of the authorities of the British Museum, it has been possible to edit this text from photographs of the manuscript. Lines 27424 to 28650 are included in this selection.

Layamon's style is very like that of the Old English epic. It is somber, rugged, forceful. He likes parentheses, appositive or exclamatory (*Arður þat bihedde—þe king wes abolȝe—*); his word-order is loose (*him to cleopien*, call to him; *mid aðelen his folke*, with his noble folk). Like the author of "Beowulf," he frequently foreshadows (*þer weore monie uæie*, many were doomed).

It will be found useful to remember the following constructions: (1) An untranslatable reflexive often follows an intransitive verb; *hit* is sometimes used as the grammatical subject or object of a verb and is in apposition with the logical subject or object (cf. *he* in the vocabulary). (2) A complementary infinitive is frequent which must be translated as a participle (*come riden*, come riding; *funde liggen*, found lying).

Many inflexional endings besides those mentioned in the Introduction are retained, especially for adjectives and pronouns: in the singular, *-re*, gen. fem.; *-ne*, acc. masc.; *-(e)n*, dat. masc. and neut.;

459

in the plural, -re, gen. A superfluous -n is frequently added (nunna-tion), especially to verb forms. Old English grammatical gender is retained, although not with entire consistency.

Æ will usually be found under e (rarely a) in the vocabulary (næuere: neuer); eo under e; sc under sh. Nouns and verbs prefixed with a- or i- are listed under the second letter (iwillen under w). Since Layamon's dialect is southern, consonant u and v will frequently be found under f (uiht: fiht), and the vowel u under i (fur: fir).

Layamon's meter represents a breaking down of Old English alliter-ative verse, and a shift toward rhymed trimeter and tetrameter couplets. Hall recognizes two main types of line, with almost every conceivable variation and mixture. (See Hall's "Layamon" XV-XIX for a full discussion):

(1) The alliterative line, consisting of two half-lines, each con-taining two accented syllables, of which at least two alliterate—one in each half-line. The number of unaccented syllables varies. Some-times the half-lines are linked by alliteration only, sometimes by rhyme also.

He bigon to hewene   ·   hardliche swiðe   28030

(2) The rhymed line, which is roughly trimeter or tetrameter. These sometimes alliterate.

Twein kinges þere   ·   æuere weoren ifere   27434

Arður lette slæn an teld   ·   amidden ænne bradne ueld   27848

Accurate rhymes are not frequent in Layamon. Assonance suffices (eorles—beornes, 27868); he rhymes on weak beats (heolden—uallen, 27454); he is satisfied with the slightest similarity of sound (adradde—deðe, 27962).

The following words appear extensively in this selection alone, and should be learned at starting: forcuð(est), wicked(est); oht, brave; unimete, immeasurable; abolge, enraged; aneouste, quickly; liðen, go; mæi, kinsman; aðele, noble; ferde, army; beornes, men; halden, fall.

For material on the Arthurian legends, see Int. IV. C.

For material on the "Brut," see Madden; Joseph Hall's "Layamon's Brut" (selections), Oxford, 1924. See also the bibliography in Hall's "Selections from Early English," pp. 450-1.

The Emperor Lucius of Rome has claimed England as part of his feudal lands and has demanded homage and taxes from Arthur. Arthur rejects his demands and declares war. After several exploits, the two rulers meet in the final battle on the Continent, with which this selection opens.

Æfne þan worde[1] · þa sturede þa uerde;   27424
Bi þusend and bi þusende · heo þrunggen[2] to-somne;
Ælc king of his folke · ȝarkede ferde.[3]
Þa hit al was iset · and ferden isemed,[4]   27430
Þa weoren þar riht italde · fulle fiftene ferden.
Twein kinges þere · æuere weoren ifere,
Feouwer[5] eorles and a duc · dihten heom to-gadere,
And þe Kæisere him-seolf · mid ten þusend kempen.[6]
Þa gon þat folc sturien; · þa eo[r]ðen gon to dunien;[7]   27440
Bemen[8] þer bleowen, · bonneden ferden;[9]
Hornes þer aqueðen[10] · mid hæhȝere stefnen.[11]
Sixti þusende · bleowen to-somne;
Ma þer aqueðen · of Arðures iueren
Þene sixti þusende · segges[12] mid horne.   27450
Þa wolcne[13] gon to dunien; · þa eo[r]ðe gon to biuien.[14]
To-somne heo heolden · swulc heouene wolde uallen.
Ærst heo lette fleon to, · feondliche[15] swiðe,
Flan[16] al-swa þicke · swa þe snau[17] adun ualleð.
Stanes heo letten seoððen · sturnliche winden.[18]   27460
Seoððen speren chrakeden;[19] · sceldes brastleden;[20]
Helmes to-helden;[21] · heȝe men uellen;
Burnen to-breken; · blod ut ȝeoten;[22]
Ueldes falewe[23] wurðen; · feollen heore mærken.[24]
Wondrede ȝeond þat wald[25] · iwundede cnihtes ouer-al.   27470
Sixti hundred þar weoren · to-tredene mid horsen;
Beornes þer swelten;[26] · blodes at-urnen.[27]
Stræhten after stretes[28] · blodie stremes;
Balu wes on uolke; · þe burst[29] wes vnimete.
Swa al-swa suggeð writen · þæ witeȝen[30] idihten: 27480
Þat wes þat þridde mæste uiht · þe auere wes here idiht.
Þeo at þan laste · nuste nan kempe
Whæm he sculde slæn on, · and wham he sculde sparien;
For no icneou na man oðer þere · for vnimete blode.

---

[1] even with these words (a frequent formula). [2] thronged. [3] prepared his army.
[4] appointed. [5] four. [6] warriors. [7] the earth began to resound. [8] trumpets.
[9] armies made ready. [10] resounded. [11] sound, tone. [12] men. [13] heavens.
[14] tremble. [15] fearfully. [16] arrows. [17] snow. [18] fiercely fly. [19] cracked.
[20] clashed. [21] rolled away. [22] spouted. [23] discolored. [24] battle flags. [25] wood.
[26] died. [27] streams of blood ran away. [28] flowed through the paths. [29] uproar.
[30] wise men.

Þa hæf³¹ þat fiht of þan studen · þer heo ær fuhten, 27490
And bigunnen arumðe³² · ræsen³³ to-somne,
And neouwe ueht bi-gunnen, · narewe iþrungen.³⁴
Þer weoren Romleoden · reouliche iladde.³⁵
 Þa comen þer kinges þreo³⁶ · of hæðene londe.
Of Ethi[o]pe wes þe an; · þe oðer wes an Aufrican; 27500
Þe þridde wes of Libie, · of hæðene leode.
Heo comen to þere uerde · a þere æst ænde
And þene sceld-truma³⁷ breken. · Þe Bruttes³⁸ þer heolden,
And anan fælden · fiftene hundred
Baldere þeinen · of Arðures þeoden.³⁹ 27510
Þa wenden Bruttes · sone to þa rugges.⁴⁰
 Þa comen þer riden · tweien eorles kene,
Þat was Beduer and Kæi, · Arðures birle and his mæi.⁴¹
Heore Bruttes heo isehȝen · mid bronden to-hawen.⁴²
Þer iwurðen to-bursten⁴³ · eorles swiðe balden. 27520
Mid ten þusend cnihten · hælden to þan uihten,
Amidden þan þrunge · þer heo þihkest weoren,
And sloȝen Romleoden · reouliche swiðen,
And ȝeond þan uehte wenden · after heore iwillen.
Þa weoren heo to þriste,⁴⁴ · and to ufele heom biwusten.⁴⁵
 27530
Wala-wa! wala-wa! · þat heo neoren war þa,
Þat heo ne cuðen bi-witen heom⁴⁶ · wið heore wiðer-iwinnen;⁴⁷
For heo weoren to kene · and to ær-wene,⁴⁸
And to swiðe fuhten, · and to ueor wenden,
And spradden⁴⁹ to wide · ȝeond þat feht brade. 27540
 Þa com þe King of Mede · þe muchele and þe brade,
Heðene here-þring,⁵⁰ · þer he hærm wrohte.
He ladde to iueren · twenti þusend rideren;
He heold on his honde · ænne gare¹ swiðe stronge.
Þene gare he uorð strahte² · mið strongen his maine, 27550
And smat þene Eorl Beduer · forn a þan breoste,³

---

³¹ moved. ³² widely. ³³ rush. ³⁴ densely congested. ³⁵ inhabitants of Rome
were badly led. ³⁶ three. ³⁷ shield-troops. ³⁸ British. ³⁹ people. ⁴⁰ literally,
turned the backs to; i.e., retreated. ⁴¹ cup-bearer and his kinsman. ⁴² hewn to
pieces. ⁴³ enraged. ⁴⁴ bold. ⁴⁵ protected themselves too badly. ⁴⁶ guard
themselves. ⁴⁷ opponents. ⁴⁸ desperate. ⁴⁹ spread. ⁵⁰ army-chief. ¹ spear.
² thrust. ³ in front of his breast.

27544. MS. þrihng.

Þat þa burne to-barst sone, · biuoren and bihinde,
An opened wes his breoste; · þa blod com forð luke.[4]
Þer feol Beduer anan, · ded uppen uolden.[5]
Þer wes sarinesse, · sorreȝen[6] inoȝe.   27560
Þer Kai funde Beduer · ded liggen him þer,[7]
And Kai þat lich[8] wolde · leden mid him-seolue.
Mid twenti hundred cnihten · he hælde þer a-buten,
And feondliche feuhten · and falden Rom-leoden,
And of Medie þer sloȝen · moni hundred monnen.   27570
Þat ueht wes strong swiðe, · and heo·weoren þer to longe.

  Þa com þer liðen · a swiðe ladlic[9] King an
Mid sixti þusend monnen · sele[10] of his londen,
Setor þe kene, · þe com him from Libie.
Þer þe King stronge · wið Kæi him gon fehte   27580
And forwundede Kai swiðe · inne strongen þan fehte,
To þan bare deðe. · Reoulich wes þa dede.
His cnihtes þer rihte · hine ladden of þan uihte;
Mid muchelere strengðe · þurh þat feht stræhten.[11]
Wa wes Arðure Kinge · for þa tidinge.   27590
Þæt isch þc richc þcin— · Ridwaðelan wes ihaten,
Beduerres suster sune; · of heȝe Bruttes he wes icume—
Þat Boccus mid his spere stronge · Bedver hafde istunge.[12]
Wa wæs him on liue · þa·his æm wes an deðe,
For he of alle monnen · mæst hinc lufedc.   27600
He cleopede of his cunne · cnihtes swiðe gode,
And of þan alre leoteste · þe he on liue wuste
Fif hundred bi tale; · fusden[13] to-somne.
Riwaððlan þa sæide, · riche mon of Bruttene,[14]
"Cnihtes, ȝe beoð of mine cunne; · cumeð hidere to me, 27610
And wreke we Beduer, min æm, · þa bezst wes of ure cunne,
Þa Buccus hafd of-stungen[15] · mid his spere strongen.
Fuse we alle to-somne · and ure ifan feollen."

---

[4] lukewarm. [5] ground. [6] miseries. [7] lying dead there. [8] corpse. [9] loathsome.
[10] good. [11] penetrated. [12] struck. [13] advanced. [14] Britons. [15] pierced.

27559. MS. deð.
27572. Probably should read swiðe strong, for the rhyme.
27579. Him is untranslatable; cf. he in the vocabulary.
27581. MS. wid.

Æfne þan worde · forð he iwende,
And alle mid him anan · aðele his iueren, 27620
And Buccus þene King icneowen · þer he was i compen.[16]
Mid his spere and mid his scelde · monine king he acqu[a]lde.[17]
Riwæððlan braid ut his sweord sone, · and him to sweinde,[18]
And smat þane King a þene helm · þat he a twa to-ueol,[19]
And æc þere burne-hod[20] · þat hit at þe toðen at-stod;[21] 27630
And þe heðene King · hælde to grunde,
And his fule saule · sæh[22] in-to helle.
Riwæððlan þa seide— · ræh[23] he was on mode,—
"Boccus, nu þu hafst aboht; · Beduer þu sloȝe,
And þi saule scal to-ȝere[24] · beon þas Wurse iuere."[25] 27640
Æfne þan worde, · swulc hit þe wind weore,
He þraste[26] to þan fihte · swa þode[27] doð on felde
þenne he þat dust heȝe · aȝiueð[28] from þere eorðe.
Al-swa Riwaððlan · ræsde[29] to his feonden;
Al heo hit sloȝen · þat heo aneh comen 27650
þe while þe heo mihte walden · heoren kinewurðe[30] wepnen.
Neouren in al þan fihte · cnihtes nane betere
þe while þat heom ilaste · þat lif on heore breoste.
Boccus þene King heo of-sloȝen, · and a þusend of his cnihten.
þa wes Beduer awræken · wel mid þan bezsten. 27660
þer wes an oht eorl · aðeles cunnes,
Leir wes ihaten, · Lauerd of Buluine;
He isæh i þan fihte · enne ueond fusen
þat [wes] on admirail; · of Babiloine he wes ældere.[31]

---

[16] combat. [17] many a king he killed. [18] struck. [19] it fell in two. [20] corselet-hood. [21] it (the sword) stood still at the teeth. [22] sank. [23] furious. [24] now. [25] companion to the Worse; i.e., the devil. [26] pressed on. [27] whirlwind. [28] lifts. [29] rushed. [30] noble. [31] prince.

27625. O. reads *many cniht*.
27626. MS. *Riwædðlan*.
27630. Cf. Int. III.D.
27641. Euphemistic titles for the devil were common in the Middle Ages, for to speak his real name was to summon him. Cf. Edward Clodd's "Magic in Names" 97.
27650. *Hit* is untranslatable; cf. *he* in the vocabulary.
27664. Lear of Boulogne; not to be confused with King Lear, whose story is told in ll. 2902–3725.
27668. MS. *þat on.*—Madden. Babiloine was Cairo in Egypt.

Muchel uolc he aualde,[32] · uolde[33] to grunde, 27670
And þe Eorl þat bihædde;[34] · an heorte him wes unneðe.
He bræid an his breoste · ænne sceld bradne,
And he igrap an his hond · a sper þat wes swiðe strong,
And his hors muneʒeden[35] · mid alle his imaine,
And þene Admiral hitte · mid smærten[36] ane dunte 27680
Vnder þere breoste · þat þa burne gon to berste
Þat him þer bæfte[37] · þat sper þurh ræhte[38]
Fulle ane ueðme;[39] · þe ueond feol to grunde.
Þat isah sone · þeos Admirale sone—
Gecron is ihate,— · and his spere grap anan 27690
And smat Leir þene Eorl sære · a þa lift[40] side
Þurh-ut þa heorte; · þe Eorl adun halde.
    Walwain[41] þat bihedde[42] · þer he wes on uehte,
And he hine iwraðede · wunder ane swiðe.[43]
Þat isæh Howel, · hæh mon of Brutten, 27700
And he þider halde · mid fiftene hundred monnen;
Herde here-kempen[44] · mid Howele fusden,[45]
And Walwain heom uuenon,[46] · swiðe stið-imoded[47] mon.
He hefde to iferen · fif and twenti hundred
Baldere Brutten; · þa bigunnen heo to fehten. 27710
Þer weoren Rom-leoden · reouliche iledde.
Howel heom kepte; · Walwain heom imette.
Þer wes wunderlic grure:[48] · þa welcnen aqueðen;[49]
Þa eorðe gunnen to buuien;[50] · stanes þer bursten;
Urnen[1] stremes of blode · of ærmen[2] þan folke. 27720
Þat wel[3] wes unimete; · þa weoren Bruttes werie.
    Kinard, þe Eorle of Strugul, · bilefde þene King Howel
And inom mid him Labius, · Rimarc, and Boclouius.
Þis weoren þa keneste men · þat æi king ahte;
Þeos weoren on moncunne[4] · eorles main stronge.[5] 27730

<hr>

[32] felled. [33] dashed. [34] beheld. [35] spurred. [36] sharp. [37] behind. [38] reached.
[39] fathom. [40] left. [41] Gawain. [42] beheld. [43] wondrously much. [44] hardy warriors. [45] advanced. [46] towards. [47] proud spirited. [48] uproar. [49] heavens
resounded. [50] tremble. [1] ran. [2] wretched. [3] slaughter. [4] mankind. [5] very
strong.
27670. Perhaps should read *aqualde*, killed.
27700. Howel, or Hoel, Count of Flanders and Arthur's nephew.
27704. MS. *kenpen.*
27706. The meaning of *fusden* is carried over from 27705.

Heo nalden for heore mucle mode · fulien[6] Howele þan gode,
Ah bi heom seoluen heo slo3en · alle þe heo neh come.
Þat isæh a riche mon · of þan Rom-leoden,
Hu Kinard þe kene · heore uolc þer aqualde,[7]
And þe cniht gon him alihten · of leofuen his steden, 27740
And nom him on his honde · a spere imaked of stele,
And bi-walede[8] hine a blode, · and bihalues[9] him eode
Þat he com a þan ende · þer fæht Kinard þe stronge.
Kinardes burne he up ahof,[10] · and he þene Eorl þer of-sloh.
Þa 3eiden[11] lude · alle Rom-leode, 27750
And bu3en[12] to þan Brutten · and heore trume[13] breken
And feollen here-marken.[14] · Uolc adun helden;
Sceldes þer scenden;[15] · scalkes[16] þer feollen.
Þer ueollen to grunde · fiftene þusende
Baldere Brutten; · balu þer wes riue. 27760
Swa ilaste longe · þat uiht swiðe stronge.
    Walwain gon 3eonge · 3eond þat wæl muchele
And somnede[17] his cnihtes alle · þer he heom funde i fihte.
Aneouste þer com ride · Howel þe riche;
Heo somneden heore veire uolc anon, · and forð heo gunnen
    fusen 27770
And riden to Rom-leoden · mid ra3ere[18] wraððen,
And fastliche heom to bu3en · and breken þere Freinsce[19]
    trumen;
And Walwain forð rihte[20] · þer he ifunde
Luces þene Kaiser · leouien[21] under scelde;
And Walwain him to sweinde[22] · mid þe stelene[23] sweorde,
    27780
And þe Kaisere hine; · þat gome[24] wes swiðe sturne.[25]
Sceld a3ein scelden, · sciuren[26] þer wunden;
Sweord a3ein sweorde · sweinde wel ilome.[27]
Fur fleh of þe stelen; · þa ueond weoren abol3en.

---

[6] follow. [7] killed. [8] bathed. [9] aside. [10] lifted. [11] shouted. [12] turned.
[13] ranks. [14] battle-standards. [15] shivered. [16] warriors. [17] assembled. [18] great.
[19] French. [20] went. [21] to live; i.e., alive. [22] struck at. [23] steel. [24] man.
[25] merciless. [26] pieces. [27] often.

27770. MS. *beire.*—Madden.
27782. Understand "struck" from 27780.
27783. MS. *com wes swi.*—Madden.

Þer wes uiht swiðe strong; · stureden[28] al þa ferden. 27790
Þe Kaisere wende · Walwain to scende
Þat he mihte an uuere-daȝe[29] · ȝelpen[30] uor þere deden;
Ah Bruttes him þrungen to · þræfliche[31] swiðe,
And þa Romanisce men · arudden[32] heore Kæiseren,
And heo to-somne heolde · swulc heouene wolde ualle. 27800
Alle þene dai-liht · heo heolden seoððen þat fiht.
Ane lutle stunde · ær þe sunne eode to grunde,
Arður þa cleopede, · aðelest alre kinge:
"Nu we heom to alle,[33] · mine cnihtes ohte,
And Godd seolf us fulste[34] · ure feond to afallene." 27810
Æfne þan worden · þa bleou men þa bemen;[25]
Fiftene þusend anan · þraste[36] to blauwen
Hornes and bemen; · þa eorðe gon beouien[37]
For þan vnimcte blase,[38] · for þan mucle ibeote.[39]
Romleoden wenden · rug to þan feohten; 27820
Feollen here-marken;[40] · heȝe-men swulten.[41]
Fluȝen þa þe mihten; · þa ueie[42] þær feollen.
Muchel mon-slæht[43] wes þere; · [moche sorȝe, moche care.]
Ne mihte hit na man tellen · [ine boke ne in spelle]
Hu feole hundred monnen · to-heouwen[44] þer weoren 27830
I þan mucle þrunge,[45] · i þan mon-slæhte.
Wes þe Kaisere of-slæȝen · a seolcuðe wisen,[46]
Þat nuste hit nauer seoðen · na mon to sugen,
Of nauer nare cuððe,[47] · wha þene Kaisere qualde;[48]
Bute þa þet feht was al idon · and þat folc wes al iblissed,[49]
27840
Þa funde men þene Kaisere · of-stungen mid ane spere.
  Word com to Arðure, · þer he wes on telde,[50]
Þat þe Kaisere wes of-slaȝen · and idon of lif-dæȝen.

---

[28] moved quickly. [29] after-days. [30] boast. [31] boldly. [32] rescued. [33] now
at them, all of us! [34] aid. [35] trumpets. [36] pressed forward. [37] trembled.
[38] blast. [39] menace. [40] battle-standards. [41] perished. [42] fated. [43] slaughter of
men. [44] cut to pieces. [45] throng. [46] slain in strange manner. [47] never afterwards could any man of any race at all say. [48] killed. [49] stricken. [50] tent.

27808. Cf. Int. VII.A.3.
27827. O.: *moche . . . moche care;* Madden suggests *sorȝe.* Perhaps
the two lines are an addition by the later scribe for the sake of the
rhymes. Lines 27826, 27828 alliterate and make complete sense.
27838. MS. cuðde.

Arður lette slæn[1] an teld · a-midden ænne bradne ueld,
And þider iberen lette · Luces þene Kaisere, 27850
And lette hine bitillen · mid gold-faӡe pallen,[2]
And biwiten[3] hine þer lette · þreo daӡes fulle,
Þe while he wurchen lette · an werc swiðe riche,
Ane cheste longe; · and wreon[4] heo al mid golde,
And lette leggen þer-inne · Luces of Rome, 27860
Þat wes a swiðe duhti mon · þa while his daӡes ilasten.[5]
Þa ӡet dude Arður mære, · aðelest alre Brutte:
Arður asechen lette · alle þa riche
Kinges and eorles · and þa riccheste beornes
Þa i þan fehte weoren i-slaӡen · and idon of lif-dæӡen, 27870
He lette heom burien · mid baldere pruten;[6]
Buten þreo kinges he lette beren · to Luces þan Kaisere,
And lette makien beren[7] · riche and swiðe maren,[8]
And lette heom sone · senden to Rome,
And grette Rom-weren[9] alle · mid græten ane huxe,[10] 27880
And seide þat he heom sende · þat gauel[11] of his londe,
And efte wold heom alswa · senden heom gretinge ma
Ӡif heo ӡirnen wolden · of Arðures golden.[12]
"And þer-after wulle[13] sone · riden into Rome
And tellen heom tiðinge · of Brutlondes Kinge, 27890
And Rome-walles rihten,[14] · þe ӡare weoren to-fallen;
And swa ich wulle awelden · þe wode Rom-leoden."
Al þis ӡelp wes idel[15] ido, · for oðer-weis hit eode;
Al oðer hit itidde:[16] · þe leoden[17] he bilæfden
Al þurh Modred is mæin,[18] · for-cuðest alle monnen. 27900

---

[1] pitch. [2] cover with cloths decorated with gold. [3] be guarded. [4] covered.
[5] i.e., while he lived. [6] splendor. [7] bier. [8] beautiful. [9] Rome-dwellers. [10] a
great taunt. [11] tribute. [12] (some) of Arthur's gold. [13] will I. [14] repair. [15] in
vain. [16] happened. [17] i.e., the Roman people. [18] through Modred's power.

27857. MS. swid.
27874. MS. beren lette; O. lette bere.
27881. Boasting was the proper privilege of heroes, and sometimes a
sport. Cf. "The Pilgrimage of Charlemagne," in Miss Schlauch's "Medieval Narrative;" cf. also "The Avowing of Arthur."
27897. MS. eoðer.
27900. Madden reads: is mæi, his kinsman, a common phrase; but
"his" is also a common sign of the possessive; cf. 28048. MS. forcudest.

A þan muchele fihte, · Arður of his cnihtes losede
Fif and twenti þusend · a uolden to-havwen,[19]
Of Brutten swiðe balde · biræued at liue.
Kæi wes forwunded seore, · wunder ane swiðe.[20]
To Kinun he wes ilad, · and sone þer-after he wes ded. 27910
Bi-bured[21] he wes þere · bi-halue[22] þan castle
Imong heremiten,[23] · þat[24] wæs þe riche mon.
Kæi hehte þe Eorl; · Kinun, þe castel.
Arður ȝæf him þene tun, · and h[in]e þer-to tumde[25]
And sette þer þene nome · after him-seoluen; 27920
For Keies dæðe, · Kain[26] he hit hehte;
Nu and auere-mare · swa hit hehte þere.
Seoððen Beduer wes islæȝen · and idon of lif-dahȝen,
Arður hine beren lette · to Bæios[27] his castle;
And biburied he wes þere · inne þere burȝe. 27930
Wið-uten þan suð ȝæte · in eorðe me hine sette.
Howeldin iulut[28] wes · forð into Flandres,
And alle his bezste cnihtes · þer flutten uorð-rihtes
In-to þan eorldomen · þenne heo þer comen,
And alle þa dede · in corðc me heom leide. 27940
Inne Teruane[29] · heo liggeoð alle claue.
Leir þene Eorl me ladde · in-to Buluine,
And Arður þer-æfter seoððe · wunede in ane londe,
Inne Burguine,[30] · þer him bezst þuhte.
Þat lond he al biwuste[31] · and alle þe castles sette,[32] 27950
And seide þat he wolde · him-seolue þat lond holde;
    And seoððen he his beot[33] makede: · a sumere þat he wolde
Faren into Rome · and ahnien[34] al þa riche,

---

[19] cut to pieces on the ground. [20] wondrously much. [21] buried. [22] beside.
[23] hermits. [24] i.e., he who had been. [25] buried. [26] Caen. [27] Bayeux. [28] floated;
i.e., carried. [29] Therouanne, near Calais. [30] Burgundy. [31] ruled. [32] placed
guards in. [33] boast. [34] possess.

27903. MS. losesede.
27909. MS. a swiðe.
27922. Such etymologies, though popular in the Middle Ages, are
always to be mistrusted. Cf. Cormac's Glosses, and the frequent sus-
picious explanations of names in Celtic romances (Emaré, Degaré; on the
latter see Loomis 77). The real derivation of Caen is from Quentovicum.
MS. Keises.
27926. MS. Beðuer.
27957. MS. ahnienien.

And beon him-seolf kaisere · þe[35] Luces wuneden ære;
And monie of Rom-leoden · wolden þat hit swa eoden, 27960
For heo weoren adradde · to heore bare deðe,[36]
Þat monie þer awæi fluȝen · and heore castles bibuȝen,[37]
And monie sende sonde · to Arðure þan stronge,
And monie him speken wið, · and ȝirnden Arðures grið.
And summe heo wolde · aȝein Arðure halden 27970
And halden wið him Rome · and wer[i]en[38] þa leode,
And neoðeles heo auered[39] weoren · for heore uæie-siðen,[40]
Þat nusten heo under Criste · nenne ræd godne.
Þa wes hit itimed[41] þere · þat Merlin saide while,
Þat Rom-walles sculden · aȝein Arðure to-uallen. 27980
Þat was agan[42] þære · bi þan Kaisere,
Þa ueol þer inne fehte · mid fifti þusund monne;
Ruren[43] þer to grunde · riche Rom-leoden.
Þa Arður wende to soðe · to aȝen al Rome,
And wunede inne Burguine, · richest alre kinge. 27990
Þa com þer in are tiden · an oht mon riden,
And brohte tidinge · Arðure þan Kinge
From Moddrede, his suster sune. · Arðure he wes wilcume,
For he wende þat he brohte · boden[44] swiðe gode.
Arður lai alle longe niht · and spac wið þene ȝeonge cniht.
 28000
Swa nauer nulde he him sugge · soð hu hit ferde.[45]
Þa hit wes dæi a marȝen, · and duȝeðe[46] gon sturien,
Arður þa up aræs · and strehte[47] his ærmes.
He aras up and adun sat · swulc he weore swiðe seoc.[48]
Þa axede hine an uæir cniht, · "Lauerd, hu hauest þu iuaren
to-niht?" 28010
Arður þa andswarede— · a mode him wes uneðe:—
"To-niht a mine slepe, · þer ich læi on bure,
Me imætte a sweuen;[49] · þer-uore ich ful sa[ri] æm.

---

[35] where.   [36] to their very death.   [37] abandoned.   [38] defend.   [39] afraid.
[40] deaths.   [41] come to pass.   [42] begun.   [43] fell.   [44] tidings.   [45] i.e., the young
knight would not tell him the truth, how affairs stood.   [46] warriors.
[47] stretched.   [48] sick.   [49] dream.

27981. MS. *ardure*.
27989. MS. *aȝein*.—Madden.
28014. On prophetic dreams, cf. "Havelok" 1285.

Me imette þat mon me hof[50] · uppen are halle.
Þa halle ich gon bi-striden · swulc ich wolde riden. 28020
Alle þa lond þa ich ah, · alle ich þer ouer-sah,[1]
And Walwain sat biuoren me; · mi sweord he bar an honde.
Þa com Moddred faren þere · mid unimete uolke.
He bar an his honde · ane wiax[2] stronge;
He bigon to hewene · hardliche swiðe, 28030
And þa postes for-heou[3] alle · þa heolden up þa halle.
Þer ich iseh Wenheuer[4] eke, · wimmonnen leofuest me,
Al þere muche halle-rof · mid hire honden heo to-droh.[5]
Þa halle gon to hælden, · and ich hæld to grunden
Þat mi riht ærm to-brac. · Þa seide Modred, 'Haue þat !' 28040
Adun ueol þa halle, · and Walwain gon to ualle
And feol a þere eorðe; · his ærmes breken beine.[6]
And ich igrap mi sweord leofe · mid mire leoft[7] honde,
And smæt of Modred is hafd, · þat hit wond a þene ueld;
And þa Quene ich al to-snaðde[8] · mid deore mine sweorede,
28050
And seoððen ich heo adun sette · in ane swarte putte,[9]
And al mi uolc riche · sette to fleme,[10]
Þat nuste ich under Criste[11] · whar heo bicumen weoren;
Buten mi-seolf, ich gon atstonden[12] · uppen ane wolden,[13]
And ich þer wondrien[14] agon · wide ȝeond þan moren[15] 28060
Þer ich isah gripes[16] · and grisliche fuȝeles.
Þa com an guldene leo[17] · liðen ouer dune,
Deoren owiðc[18] honde · þa uro Drihton[19] makc[dc].
Þa leo me orn foren to[20] · and iueng me bi þan midle,
And forð hire gun ȝeongen · and to þere sæ wende; 28070
And ich isæh þæ vðen[21] · i þere sæ driuen,

---

[50] lifted. [1] looked over. [2] battle-axe. [3] cut to pieces. [4] Guinevere. [5] pulled
down. [6] both. [7] left. [8] cut in pieces. [9] black pit. [10] fled. [11] i.e., anywhere.
[12] take my stand. [13] wooded plain. [14] wander. [15] moorlands. [16] vultures.
[17] golden lioness. [18] most. [19] Lord. [20] up to me. [21] waves.

28045. MS. brekeen.
28048. Modred his; i.e., Modred's.
28052. MS. seoðen . . . adum.
28058. MS. gond.
28066. Layamon several times uses swiðe as an adj., meaning "most."
Cf. line 28613.

And þa leo i þan ulode[22] · iwende wið me-seolue.
Þa wit[23] i sæ comen, · þa vðen me hire binomen.[24]
Com þer an fisc[25] liðe · and fereden me to londe.
Þa wes ich al wet · and weri of sorȝen and seoc.[26]   28080
Þa gon ich iwakien; · swiðe ich gon to quakien.[27]
Þa gon ich to biuien[28] · swulc ich al for-burne,[29]
And swa ich habbe al niht · of mine sweuene swiðe iþoht;
For ich what to iwisse · agan is al mi blisse.
For a to mine liue, · sorȝen ich mot driȝe.[30]   28090
Wale, þat ich nabbe here · Wenhauer, mine Quene!"
    Þa andswarede þe cniht, · "Lauerd, þu hauest un-riht.[31]
Ne sculde me nauere sweuen · mid sorȝen arecchen.[32]
Þu ært þe riccheste mon · þa rixleoð[33] on londen
And þe alre wiseste · þe wuneð under weolcne.[34]   28100
Ȝif hit weore ilimpe[35]— · swa nulle hit ure Drihte[36]—
Þat Modred, þire suster sune, · hafde þine Quene inume
And al þi kineliche lond · isæt[37] an his aȝere hond
Þe þu him bitahtest · þa þu to Rome þohtest,[38]
And he hafde al þus ido · mid his swikedome,[39]   28110
Þa ȝet þu mihtest þe awreken · wurðliche[40] mid wepnen,
And æft þi lond halden · and walden þine leoden,
And þine feond fallen · þe þe ufel unnen,[41]
And slæn heom alle clane · þet þer no bilauen nane."
    Arður þa andswarede, · aðelest alre kinge,   28120
"Longe bið æuere;[42] · þat no wene ich nauere,
Þat æuere Moddred mi mæi · [þat man is me leouest]
Wolde me biswiken · for alle mine richen,
No Wenhauer mi Quene · wakien on þonke.[43]
Nulleð hit biginne · for nane weorld-monne."[44]   28130

---

[22] sea. [23] we two (the dual). [24] took me from her. [25] fish. [26] sick. [27] tremble.
[28] tremble. [29] were being burned up. [30] suffer. [31] you are wrong. [32] interpret sorrowfully. [33] reigns. [34] the heavens. [35] come to pass. [36] as our Lord forbid it should. [37] royal land seized. [38] thought (to go). [39] treachery.
[40] worthily. [41] who wished thee evil. [42] forever is a long time. [43] weaken in thought. [44] human being.

28074. MS. *þe leo*.—Madden.
28085. MS. *fur burne*. Hall emends to *for-burne*.
28087. MS. *sweueuene*.
28112. MS. *þe ȝet*.

Æfne þan worde forð-riht · þa andswarede þe cniht,
"Ich sugge þe soð, leofe King, · for ich æm þin vnderling.
Þus hafeð Modred idon: · þine Quene he hafeð ifon,
And þi wunliche⁴⁵ lond · isæt an his aȝere hond.
He is king, and heo is quene; · of þine kume⁴⁶ nis na wene.⁴⁷

28140
For no weneð heo nauere to soðe · þat þu cumen aȝain from
    Rome.
Ich æm þin aȝen mon · and iseh þisne swikedom,
And ich æm icumen to þe seoluen · soð þe to suggen.
Min hafued beo to wedde⁴⁸ · þat isæid ich þe habbe
Soð buten lese · of leofen þire quene   28150
And of Modrede, þire suster sune, · hu he hafueð Brutlond
    þe binume."⁴⁹
Þa sæt hit al stille · in Arðures halle;
Þa wes þer særinæsse · mid sele⁵⁰ þan Kinge;
Þa weoren Bruttisce men · swiðe vnbalde¹ uorþæn.
Þa umbe stunde · stefne þer sturede;²   28160
Wide me mihte iheren · Brutten iberen,³
And gunne to tellen · a feole cunne spellen,
Hu heo wolden for-deme⁴ · Modred and þa Quene
And al þat moncun⁵ for-don · þe mid Modred heolden.
    Arður þa cleopede, · hendest alre Brutte,   28170
"Sitteð adun stille, · cnihtes inne halle,
And ich eou telle wulle · spelles vncuðe.
Nu to-mærȝe þenne hit dæi bið, · and Drihten hine⁶ sende,
Forð ich wulle buȝe⁷ · in toward Bruttaine;
And Moddred ich wulle slean · and þa Quen for-berne, 28180
And alle ich wulle for-don · þa biluueden⁸ þen swikedom;
And her ich bileofuen wulle · me leofuest monne,
Howel, minne leofue mæi, · hexst of mine cunne;
And half mine uerde · ich bilæfuen a þissen ærde⁹
To halden al þis kine-lond¹⁰ · þa ich habbe a mire hond. 28190

---

⁴⁵ pleasant. ⁴⁶ coming. ⁴⁷ expectation. ⁴⁸ for a pledge. ⁴⁹ deprived of. ⁵⁰ good.
¹ dispirited. ² in a little while, voices arose. ³ clamor. ⁴ doom to death.
⁵ folk. ⁶ i.e., day. ⁷ turn, go. ⁸ delighted in. ⁹ country. ¹⁰ kingdom.

28140. MS. que.
28172. MS. sitted.
28180. MS. scaln.
28181. For the burning of unfaithful wives, cf. "Chevelere Assigne" 68.

And þenne þas þing beoð alle idone, · aȝan[11] ich wulle to
  Rome,
And mi wunliche lond bitæche · Walwaine, mine mæie,
And iuorþe mi beot[12] seoððe · bi mine bare[13] life;
Scullen alle mine feond · wæi-sið[14] makeȝe.''
  Þa stod him up Walwain, · þat wes Arðures mæi,   28200
And þas word saide— · þe Eorl wes abolȝe,—
''Ældrihten Godd, · domes waldend,
Al middel-ærdes mund![15] · whi is hit iwurðen
Þat mi broðer Modred · þis morð[16] hafueð itimbred?[17]
Ah to-dæi ich at-sake[18] hine here · biuoren þissere duȝeðe,[19]
                                                    28210
And ich hine for-demen wulle · mid Drihtenes wille.
Mi seolf ich wulle hine an-hon[20] · haxst alre warien;[21]
Þa Quene ich wulle mid Goddes laȝe[22] · al mid horsen to-
  draȝe,[23]
For ne beo ich nauere bliðe · þa wile ha beoð aliue
And þat ich habbe minne æm · awræke mid þan bezste.''   28220
Bruttes þa andswarede · mid baldere stefne,
''Al ure wepnen sunden ȝarewe; · nu to-marȝen we scullen
  uaren!''
  A-marȝen þat hit dæi wes · and Drihten hine senden,
Arður uorð him wende · mid aðelen his folke.
Half he hit bilæfde, · and half hit forð ladde.   28230
Forð he wende þurh þat lond · þat he com to Whit-sond.[24]
Scipen he hæfde sone, · monie and wel idone,
Ah feowertene-niht fulle · þere læi þa uerde
Þeos wederes abiden, · windes bi-delde.[25]
  Nu was sum[26] for-cuð kempe · in Arðures ferde;   28240
Anæn swa he demen iherde · of Modredes deðe,[27]

---

[11] go. [12] shall carry out my threat. [13] very; i.e., as surely as I live. [14] make their
death-journey. [15] almighty God, wielder of fate, guardian of the earth. [16] sin.
[17] wrought. [18] repudiate. [19] doughty (band). [20] hang. [21] villains. [22] according to God's law. [23] draw to pieces. [24] Wissant, near Calais (Emerson).
[25] awaiting a storm, deprived of winds. [26] a certain. [27] as soon as he heard
Modred's death determined upon.

28194. bitatæche.
28196. MS. seodðe.
28219. MS. a beoð.
28224. Such expressions of approval are common in French romances.
28228. MS. arðu.
28243. MS. ðeðe.

He nom his swein aneouste · and sende to þissen londe,
And sende word Wenhaueren · heou hit was iwurðen,
And hu Arður wes on uore[28] · mid muclere ferde,
And hu he wolde taken on[29] · and al hu he wolde don. 28250
Þa Quene com to Modred, · þat wæs hire leofuest monnen,
And talde him tidende · of Arðure þan Kinge,
Hu he wolde taken an, · and al hu he wolde don.
Modræd nom his sonde · and sende to Sexlond
After Childriche, · þe king wes swiðe riche, 28260
And bæd hine cume to Brutaine, · þer-of he bruke sculde.
Modræd bad Childriche, · þene stronge and þene riche,
Weide senden sonde · a feouwer half Sexlonde,[30]
And beoden[31] þa cnihtes alle · þat heo biзeten[32] mihte
Þat heo comen sone · to þissen kinedome, 28270
And he wolde Childriche · зeouen of his riche
Al biзeonde þere Humbre; · for he him scolde helpe
To fihten wið his æme, · Arðure þan Kinge.
Childrich beh[33] sone · in-to Brutlonde.
Þa Modred hafde his ferde · isomned[34] of monnen, 28280
Þa weoren þere italde · sixti þusende,
Here-kempen harde[35] · of heðene uolke,
Þa heo weoren icumen hidere · for Arðures hærme
Modred to helpen, · forcuðest monnen.
Þa þe uerde wes isome · of ælche mon-cunne,[36] 28290
Þa heo weoren þer on hepe[37] · an hunddred þusende,
Heðene and cristene, · mid Modrede Kinge.
   Arður lai at Whit-sond; · feouwertene-niht him þuhte to
      long,
And al Modred wuste · wat Arður þær wolde;
Ælche dai him comen sonde · from þas Kinges hirede.[38] 28300

---

[28] on the march.   [29] act.   [30] four corners of Saxony.   [31] summon.   [32] reach.
[33] went.   [34] assembled.   [35] powerful veterans.   [36] folk.   [37] in a company.   [38] retinue.

28253. MS. *monnes.*
28260. Childriche, a German emperor, invaded England as an ally of Uther's slayers. Arthur defeated him, but released him on the promise not to return to England.
28271. MS. *kinedone.*
28274. MS. *þerere.*
28277. MS. *arðuren kinge.*
28287. MS. *ardures.*

Þa ilomp[39] hit an one time · muchel rein[40] him gon rine,
And þæ wind him gon wende · and stod of þan æst ende,[41]
And Arður to scipe fusde[42] · mid alle his uerde
And hehte þat his scip-men · brohten hine to Romenel,[43]
Þer he þohte up wende · in-to þissen londe.   28310
Þæ he to þere hauene com, · Moddred him wes auornon.
Asc þe dæi gon lihte, · heo bigunnen to fihten.
Alle þene longe dæi · moni mon þer ded læi.
Summe hi fuhten a londe, · summe bi þan stronde;
Summe heo letten ut of scipen · scerpe garen scriþen.[44] 28320
Walwain bi-foren wende · and þene wæi rumde[45]
And sloh þere a-neuste · þeines elleouene.
He sloh Childriches sune, · þe was þer mid his fader icume.
To reste eode þa sunne; · wæ wes þa monnen!
Þer wes Walwain aslæзe · and idon of lif-daзe   28330
Þurh an eorl Sexisne— · særi wurðe his saule!
Þa wes Arður særi · and sorhful an heorte forþi,
And þas word bodede,[46] · ricchest alre Brutte:
"Nu ich ileosed[47] habbe · mine sweines leofe.
Ich wuste bi mine sweuene[48] · whæt sorзen me weoren
зeueðe.[49]   28340
I-slaзen is Augel þe King, · þe wes min aзen deorling,
And Walwaine [mi] suster sune. · Wa is me þat ich was mon
iboren!
Up nu of scipen biliue, · mine beornes ohte!"
Æfne þan worde · wenden to fihte
Sixti þusend anon · selere kempen[50]   28350
And breken Modredes trume,[1] · and wel neh him seolue wes
inome.
Modred bi-gon to fleon, · and his folc after teon.[2]
Fluзen ueondliche;[3] · feldes beoueden[4] eke;
зurren[5] þa stanes · mid þan blod-stremes.
Þer weore al þat fiht i-don · ah þat niht to raðe com.   28360

[39] happened. [40] rain. [41] from the east. [42] went. [43] Romney, in Kent (Em.).
[44] let sharp spears fly. [45] cleared. [46] spoke. [47] lost. [48] dream. [49] given.
[50] valiant warriors. [1] ranks. [2] hasten. [3] furiously. [4] trembled. [5] rumbled.

28309. MS. *romerel;* Emerson's emendation.

28342. Augusel, King of Albany (in Scotland), brother of Loth, who
married Arthur's sister Anna. MS. *Angel?*

ʒif þa niht neore,[6] · islaʒen hi weoren alle.
Þe niht heom to-delde[7] · ʒeond slades[8] and ʒeon[d] dunen,[9]
And Modred swa vorð com · þat he wes at Lundene.
Iherden þa burh-weren[10] · hu hit was al ifaren,
And warnden him inʒeong[11] · and alle his folke.   28370
Modred þeone wende · toward Winchastre,
And heo hine underuengen[12] · mid alle his monnen;
And Arður after wende · mid alle his mahte[13]
Þat he com to Winchestre · mid muchelere uerde
And þa burh al biræd,[14] · and Modred þer-inne abeod. 28380
Þa Modred isæh · ðat Arður him wes swa neh,
Ofte he hine biþohte · wæt he don mahte.
Þa a þere ilke niht, · he hehte his cnihtes alle
Mid alle heore iwepnen · ut of burhʒe wenden,
And sæide þat he weolde · mid fihte þer at-stonden.[15] 28390
He bi-hehte[16] þere burʒe-were · auer-mare freo laʒe[17]
Wið-þan þa heo him heolpen · at heʒere neoden.
Þa hit wes dæi-liht, · ʒaru þa wes heore fiht.
Arður þat bi-hedde[18]— · þe King wes abolʒe;—
He lette bemen[19] blawen · and beonnen[20] men to fihten; 28400
He hehte alle his þeines, · and aðele his cnihte[s]
Fon somed to fihten[21] · and his ueond auallen,
And þe burh alle for-don · and þat burh-folc ahon.
Heo to-gadere stopen[22] · and sturnliche fuhten.
Modred þa þohte · what he don mihte;   28410
And he dude þere, · alse he dude elles-whare,
Swikedom[23] mid þan mæste; · for auere he dude unwraste.[24]
He biswac his iueren · biuoren Winchestren,
And lette him to cleopien · his leofeste cnihtes anan
And his leoueste freond alle · of allen his folke,   28420
And bi-stal[25] from þan fihte— · þe feond hine aʒe !—

---

[6] if night had not come. [7] scattered. [8] valleys. [9] hills. [10] citizens. [11] denied entrance. [12] received. [13] force, army. [14] surrounded. [15] make a stand. [16] promised. [17] free law. [18] perceived. [19] trumpets. [20] prepared. [21] to fight the foes together. [22] advanced. [23] treachery. [24] wickedly. [25] stole away.

28383. MS. *hit wes*.
28393. A "free town" was one which had gained exemption from part or all of its feudal duties. Cf. H. W. C. Davis's "Medieval Europe," ch. IX.
28405. MS. *ueod*.

And þat folc gode lette · al þer for-wurðe.[26]
Fuhten alle dæi; · wenden þat heore lauerd þer læi
And weore heom aneouste[27] · at muchelere neode.
Þa heold he þene wai · þat touward Hamtone lai,   28430
And heolde touward hauene, · forcuðest hæleðe![28]
And nom alle þa scipen · þa þer oht weore
And þa steormen[29] alle · to þan scipen neodde,
And ferden into Cornwalen, · forcuðest kingen a þan daȝen.
And Arður Winchestre · þa burh bilai[30] wel faste   28440
And al þat moncun of-sloh. · Þer wes sorȝen inoh;
Þa ȝeonge and þa alde · alle he aqualde.[31]
Þa þat folc wes al ded, · þa burh al for-swelde,[32]
Þa lette he mid alle[33] · to-breken þa walles alle.
Þa wes hit itimed[34] þere · þat Merlin seide while: 28450
"Ærm[35] wurðest þu, Winchæstre! · Þæ eorðe þe scal for-
    swalȝe!"[36]
Swa Merlin sæide, · þe witeȝe wes mære.[37]
    Þa Quene læi inne Eouwerwic;[38] · næs heo næuere swa
    sarlic;
Þan wes Wenhauer þa Quene · særȝest wimmonne.
Heo iherde suggen · soððere worden   28460
Hu ofte Modred flah, · and hu Arður hine bibah.[39]
Wa wes hire þere while · þat heo wes on life.
Ut of Eouerwike · bi nihte heo iwende,
And touward Karliun[40] tuhte[41] · swa swiðe swa heo mahte.
. . . . 28470

Þider heo brohten bi nihte · of hire cnihten tweiȝe,
And me hire hafd bi-wefde[42] · mid ane hali rifte,[43]
And heo wes þer munechene · kare-fullest wife.[44]
Þa nusten men of þere Quene · war heo bicumen weore;
No feole ȝere seoððe, · nuste hit mon to soðe   28480
Whaðer heo weore on deðe . . . .

---

[26] perish.   [27] at hand.   [28] of men.   [29] pilots.   [30] besieged.   [31] killed.   [32] burned
down.   [33] wholly.   [34] come to pass.   [35] wretched.   [36] swallow.   [37] who was
a famous prophet.   [38] York.   [39] surrounded.   [40] Caerleon.   [41] drew.   [42] clothed.
[43] holy veil.   [44] most sorrowful woman among the nuns.

28430. Southampton, a chief seaport.
28456. MS. *que.*

Þa[45] heo here seolf weore · isunken in þe watere.
Modred wes i Cornwale · and somnede[46] cnihtes feole;
To Irlonde he sende · aneoste his sonde;
To Sex-londe he sende · aneouste his sonde; 28490
To Scotlonde he sende · aneouste his sonde.
He hehten heom to cume alle anan · þat wolde lond habben,
Oðer seoluer oðer gold, · oðer ahte[47] oðer lond.
On ælchere wisen · he warnede[48] hine seoluen
Swa deð ælc witer[49] mon · þa neode cumeð uuenan.[50] 28500
Arður þat iherde— · wraðest Kinge—
Þat Modred wæs i Cornwale · mid muchele monweorede,[1]
And þer wolde abiden · þat Arður come riden.
Arður sende sonde · ȝeond al his kine-londe,[2]
And to cumen alle hehte · þat quic wes on londe, 28510
Þa to uihte oht weoren · wepnen to beren.
. . . .
. . . .
And wha-swa hit for-sete[3] · þat þe King hete,
Þe King hine wolde a folden[4] · quic al for-bernen.[5] 28520
Hit læc[6] toward hirede[7] · folc vnimete,
Ridinde and ganninde · swa þe rein falleð adune.[8]
Arður for to Cornwale · mid unimete ferde;
Modred þat iherde · and him toȝeines heolde.
Mid vnimete folke; · þer weore monie uæie.[9] 28530
Uppen þere Cambre[10] · heo tuhten[11] to-gadere;
Þe stude hatte Camelford— · euer-mare ilast[12] þat ilke
    weorde!—

_____

[45] or. [46] assembled. [47] property. [48] guarded. [49] intelligent. [50] upon (him).
[1] army. [2] realm. [3] opposed. [4] ground. [5] burn to death. [6] rushed. [7] retinue.
[8] i.e., as thick as rain. [9] doomed. [10] the Camel, in North Cornwall. [11] drew.
[12] may endure.

28484. Might read "no more than if she were. . . ." Wace simply says
no one ever heard of her.
28497. MS. _oder . . . oder._
28518. MS. _wah swa._
28521. MS. _quid._
28525. MS. _rim falled._—Madden.
28527. MS. _unile._
28532. MS. _Tanbre_ for _Cambre._

And at Camelforde wes isomned · sixti þusend
And ma þusend þer-to; · Modred wes heore ælder.[13]
Þa þiderward gon ride · Arður þe riche   28540
Mid unimete folke, · uæie þah hit[14] weore.
Uppe þere Cambre · heo tuhte to-somne.[15]
Heuen here-marken;[16] · halden to-gadere;
Luken[17] sweord longe; · leiden[18] o þe helmen;
Fur ut sprengen.[19] · Speren brastlien;[20]   28550
Sceldes gonnen scanen;[21] · scaftes to-breken.
Þer faht al to-somne · folc vnimete;
Cambre wes on flode · mid vnimete blode.
Mon i þan fihte non þer ne mihte · ikenne nenne kempe,
No wha dude wurse no wha bet, · swa þat wiðe wes
    imenged;[22]   28560
For ælc sloh adun-riht, · weore he swein, weore he cniht.
Þer wes Modred of-slaʒe · and idon of lif-daʒe,
[And alle his cnihtes · islaʒe] in þan fihte.
Þer weoren of-slaʒe · alle þa snelle,
Arðures hered-men,[23] · heʒe [and lowe],   28570
And þa Bruttes alle · of Arðures borde,[24]
And alle his fosterlinges[25] · of feole kineriches,
And Arður forwunded · mid wal-spere[26] brade.
Fiftene he hafde · feondliche[27] wunden;
Mon mihte i þare lasten[28] · twa glouen iþraste.[29]   28580
Þa nas þer na mare · i þan fehte to laue,[30]
Of twa hundred þusend monnen · þa þer leien to-hauwen,[31]
Buten Arður þe King ane, · and of his cnihtes tweien.
    Arður wes for-wunded · wunder ane swiðe.[32]
Þer to him com a cnaue · þe wes of his cunne;   28590

---

[13] leader. [14] i.e., the folk. [15] assembled. [16] they raised the battle-standards.
[17] crossed. [18] hit. [19] caused to spring. [20] splintered. [21] break. [22] so confused was
that conflict. [23] warriors. [24] i.e., retinue. [25] princes being reared in his court.
[26] battle-spear. [27] horrible. [28] least (of the wounds). [29] thrust two gloves.
[30] remnant. [31] cut to pieces. [32] wondrously much.

28544, 28556. MS. *Tambre.*
28570. MS. *Ardures.*
28573. The chief obligation of a lord in times of peace was to feed his
retainers. The *borde* may be the Round Table, mentioned in Wace, but
first described at length by Layamon, l. 22737; cf. Hall.

He wes Cadores sune,   ·   þe Eorles of Cornwaile.
Constantin hehte þe cnaue;   ·   he wes þan Kinge deore.
Arður him lokede on,   ·   þer he lai on folden,
And þas word seide   ·   mid sorhfulle heorte:
"Constæntin, þu art wilcume;   ·   þu weore Cadores sone. 28600
Ich þe bitache here   ·   mine kineriche,
And wite mine Bruttes   ·   a to ende þines lifes,
And hald heom alle þa la3en³³   ·   þa habbeoð istonden a mine
da3en,
And alle þa la3en gode   ·   þa bi Vðeres da3en stode;
And ich wulle uaren to Aualun   ·   to uairest alre maidene, 28610
To Argante þere Quene,   ·   aluen swiðe sceone;³⁴
And heo scal mine wunden   ·   makien alle isunde;
Al hal me makien   ·   mid halewei3e drenchen.³⁵
And seoðe ich cumen wulle   ·   to mine kineriche
And wunien mid Brutten   ·   mid muchelere wunne."   28620
Æfne þan worden   ·   þer com of se wenden,
Þat wes an sceort bat³⁶ liðen,   ·   sceouen mid vðen,³⁷
And twa wimmen þer-innc   ·   wunderliche idihte;
And heo nomen Arður anan   ·   and aneouste hine uereden
And softe hine adun leiden   ·   and forð gunnen hi liðen. 28630
Þa wes hit iwurðen   ·   þat Merlin seide whilen:
Þat weore³⁸ unimete care   ·   of Arðures forð-fare.³⁹
   Bruttes ilcucð 3ete   ·   þat he beon on liue
And wunnien in Aualun   ·   mid fairest alre aluen,

---

³³ laws.   ³⁴ fairest of elves.   ³⁵ healing potions.   ³⁶ small boat.   ³⁷ tossing on the waves.   ³⁸ that there would be.   ³⁹ departure.

28592. Cador's relationship to Arthur is unknown, but Guinevere was reared in his court.
28593. MS. *Corwaile*.
28600. MS. *Costæntin*.
28605. MS. *to þines lifes*.
28610. Geoffrey omits mention of Avalon in the "Historia," but tells the story in his "Vita Merlini," where Argante is called Morgan. Morgan (in Malory, Morgan le Fay, Arthur's sister) lives there with her eight sisters.
28614. MS. *slal*.
28624. *Liðen* is a useless and untranslatable repetition of *wenden*.
28631. MS. *hine liðen*.
28637. MS. *bon on*.

And lokieð euere Bruttes ȝete · whan[40] Arður cumen liðe.

28640

Nis nauer þe mon iboren · of nauer nane burde icoren[41]
þe cunne of þan soðe · of Arðure sugen mare;
Bute while wes an witeȝe,[42] · Mærlin ihate.
He bodede[43] mid worde— · his quides[44] weoren soðe—
þat an Arður sculde ȝete · cum Anglen to fulste.[45]   28650

---

[40] look for (the time) when. [41] especially favored woman; i.e., there is no mortal man. [42] wiseman, prophet. [43] spoke. [44] sayings. [45] aid.

28649. MS. quiðes.

28650. Since Layamon says an Arthur, he may be inferring that the prophecy has been fulfilled in Arthur, Duke of Brittany (1187–1203), grandson of Henry II, who was so named in an effort to win the loyalty of the Welsh to the English crown. Moreover, Layamon here uses Anglen instead of his usual Bruttes.

YWAIN AND GAWAIN

YWAIN AND GAWAIN

The poem is in MS. Galba E IX, and has been prepared from rotographs, made with the permission and assistance of the Department of Manuscripts of the British Museum.

The studies of the story are so important in determining the relation of English and Celtic literature that the reader is referred directly to them. Especially interesting are A. C. L. Brown's essay (*Harvard Studies* viii) and R. S. Loomis's "Celtic Myth and Arthurian Romance," Bks. I and II. Bruce (I. 67 ff.) has bibliographies and summaries.

The dialect is northern of 1350 or after. Long -*a* is retained in many words in which it had already become -*o* in the midlands (*mane*, moan; *balde*, bold; *lath*, loath; etc.). Schleich's edition contains the whole poem.

HERE BEGYN[NETH] YWAINE AND GAWAIN

Almyghti God, [þat m]ade mankyn,
He schilde his [ser]vandes out of syn
And mayntene [þa]m with might and mayne,
Þat herkens [*Ywa*]*yne and Gawayne!*
Þai war knightes of þe Tabyl Rownde: 5
Þarfore listens a lytel stownde.
    Arthure, þe Kyng of Yngland,
Þat wan al Wales with his hand
And al Scotland, als sayes þe buke
(And mani mo, if men wil luke),[1]   10
Of al knightes he bare þe pryse:
In werld was none so war ne wise.
Trew he was in alkyn[2] thing,

---

[1] more (books), if one should investigate. [2] all sorts of.

9. The book is Chrétien de Troyes' "Yvain, ou Le Chevalier au Lion." The English poet condenses it, but follows it closely. In Schleich's edition, the corresponding line numbers in Chrétien are occasionally given.

Als it byfel to swilk a kyng.
He made a feste, þe soth to say,   15
Opon þe Witsononday,[3]
At Kerdyf, þat es in Wales;
And efter mete, þare in þe hales[4]
Ful grete and gay was þe assemblé
Of lordes and ladies of þat cuntré,   20
And als of knyghtes, war and wyse,
And damisels of mykel pryse.
Ilkane with oþer made grete gamin
And grete solace, als þai war samin;
Fast þai carped and curtaysly   25
Of dedes of armes and of veneri,[5]
And of gude knightes þat lyfed þen,
And how men might þam kyndeli ken[6]
By doghtines of þaire gude dede
On ilka syde, wharesum[7] þai ȝede;   30
For þai war stif in ilka stowre,
And þarfore gat þai grete honowre.
Þai tald of more trewth þam bitw[e]ne,
Þan now omang men here es sene;
For trowth and luf es al bylaft:[8]   35
Men uses now a noþer craft:
With worde men makes it trew and stabil,[9]
Bot in þaire faith es noght bot fabil;[10]
With þe mowth men makes it hale,[11]
Bot trew trowth es nane in þe tale.   40
Þarfore hereof now wil i blyn:
Of þe Kyng Arthure i wil bygin,
And of his curtayse cumpany.
Þare was þe flowre of cheuallry!
Swilk lose[12] þai wan with speres horde,[13]   45
Ouer al þe werld went þe worde.
   After mete went þe Ky[ng]

---

[3] Whitsunday. [4] halls. [5] hunting. [6] readily know. [7] wherever. [8] left behind.
[9] i.e., men seem by their words to be loyal and steadfast.   [10] falseness.
[11] sound; i.e., pretend frankness. [12] fame. [13] =ord, point.

17. Cardiff was a center for Celtic stories, and in them often serves as Arthur's capital.

Into chamber to s[le]peing,
And also went with him þe Quene.
Þat byheld[14] þai al bydene,   50
For þai saw þam neuer so
On high dayes to chamber go.
Bot sone, when þai war went to [slepe],
Knyghtes sat þe dor [to k]epe;
Sir Dedyne and Sir Segramore,   55
Sir Gawayn and Sir Kay sat þore,
And also sat þare Sir Ywaine,
And Colgreuance, of mekyl may[n.]
Þis knight þat hight Colgreuance
Tald his felows of a chance[15]   60
And of a stowre he had in bene;
And al his tale herd þe Quene:
Þe chamber-dore sho has vnshet,
And down omang þam scho hir set;
Sodainli sho sat down right,   65
Or ani of þam of hir had sight.
Bot Colgreuance rase vp in hy;
And þareof had Syr Kay enuy,
For he was of his tong a skalde,[16]
And for to boste was he ful balde.   70
"Ow, Colgreuance!" said Sir Kay,
"Ful light of lepes[17] has þou bene ay;
Þou wenes now þat þe sal tall
Forto be hendest of vs all;
And[18] þe Quene sal vnderstand,   75
Þat here es none so vnkunand.[19]

---

[14] noticed. [15] adventure. [16] scold; i.e., abusive. [17] ready to jump; i.e., ob-
sequious. [18] yet; the translator was puzzled by an ironical passage in Chrétien.
[19] boorish.

55. In Malory, these names and characters are Dodynas le Saveage
and Sagramore le Desyrus, who are struck down by Lancelot in a tournament (xviii. 11); Kay, Arthur's famous steward; Uwayne and Gawayn,
nephews of Arthur. Colgrevance, called by Chrétien Calogrenant, is an
unimportant figure in the prose romances, and has a principal rôle only
here. Loomis points out (*MLN* 43.215) that actually he is Kay under a
soubriquet (meaning The Grumbler) that Chrétien did not recognize.

72. The French says, *Molt vos voi or preu et saillant* (72).

Al if þou rase and we sat styll,
We ne dyd it for none yll
Ne for no manere of fayntise,[20]
Ne vs denyd noght forto rise,   80
Þat we ne had resen,[21] had we hyr sene."
"Sir Kay, i wote wele," sayd þe Quene,
"And it war gude þou left swilk sawes,
And noght despise so þi felawes."
"Madame," he said, "by Goddes dome,   85
We ne wist no thing of þi come;[22]
And if we did noght curtaysly,
Takes to no uelany,[23]
Bot pray ȝe now þis gentil man
To tel þe tale þat he bygan."   90
Colgreuance said to Sir Kay,
"Bi grete God, þat aw þis day,
Na mare manes me þi flyt[24]
Þan it war a flies byt.
Ful oft wele better men þan i   95
Has þou desspised desspytusely.[25]
It es ful semeli, als me think,
A brok[26] omang men forto stynk.
So it fars by þe, Syr Kay:
[Of we]ked wordes has þou bene ay;   100
And sen þi wordes er wikked and fell,
Þis time þarto na more i tell
Bot of the thing þat i bygan."
And sone Sir Kay him answerd þan,
And said ful tite vnto þe Quene,   105

---

[20] indifference.   [21] i.e., with the intention of not rising.   [22] coming.   [23] regard it as no discourtesy.   [24] attack.   [25] enviously.   [26] badger.

80. MS. *ne* for *vs;* probably a blunder for the French *Por ce que nos ne deignames.*
84. Shifts in tense and construction are common.
94. The MS. is damaged and almost illegible.
98. The badger was the symbol for what was malodorous and disgusting among beasts. The phrase means, A badger (Kay) must necessarily be offensive among men; so why be angry about it?
101–15. Beginnings of lines almost illegible.

"Madame, if ȝe had noght here bene,
We sold haue herd a selly[27] case;
Now let ȝe vs of oure solace:
Þarfore, madame, we wald ȝow pray,
Þat ȝe cumand him to say   110
And tel forth, als he had tyght."[28]
Þan answerd þat hende knight,
"Mi lady es so auysé,[29]
Þat scho wil noght cumand me
To tel þat towches me to ill:[30]   115
Scho es noght of so weked will."[31]
Sir Kai said þan ful smertli,
"Madame, al hale[32] þis cumpani
Praies ȝow hertly, now omell,[33]
Þat he his tale forth might tell.   120
If ȝe wil noght for oure praying,
For faith ȝe aw vnto þe Kyng
Cumandes him his tale to tell,
Þat we mai here how it byfell."
Þan said þe Quene, "Sir Colgreuance,   125
I prai þe, tak to no greuance
Þis kene karping of Syr Kay;
Of weked wordes has he bene ay,
So þat none may him chastise.
Þarfore i prai þe, on al wise,[34]   130
Þat þou let noght for his sawes,
At[35] tel to me and þi felawes
Al þi tale, how it bytid:
For my luf i þe pray and byd."
"Sertes, madame, þat es me lath;   135
Bot for i wil noght mak ȝow wrath,
Ȝowre cumandment i sal fulfill.
If ȝe wil listen me vntill,
With hertes and eres vnderstandes,
And i sal tel ȝow swilk tithandes,   140

---

[27] interesting. [28] intended. [29] discreet. [30] dishonors me. [31] mean spirit. [32] this
entire. [33] together. [34] by all means. [35] to.

135. *Me* is inserted over the line in another hand.

Þat ȝe herd neuer none slike
Reherced[36] in no kynges ryke.
Bot word fares als dose þe wind,
Bot if men it in hert bynd;
And wordes wo-so trewly tase,[37]   145
By þe eres into þe hert it gase;
And in þe hert þare es þe horde[38]
And knawing of ilk mans worde.
Herkens, hende, vnto my spell:
Trofels[39] sal i ȝow nane tell,   150
Ne lesinges, forto ger ȝow lagh;
Bot i sal say right als i sagh.
    Now als þis time sex ȝere[40]
I rade allane, als ȝe sal here,
Obout for to seke auenturs,   155
Wele armid in gude armurs.
In a frith i fand a strete,[41]
Ful thik and hard, i ȝow bihete,
With thornes, breres, and moni a quyn;[42]
Nerehand al day i rade þareyn,   160
And thurgh i past with mekyl payn.
Þan come i sone into a playn
Whare i gan se a bretise[43] brade,
And þederward ful fast i rade.
I saw þe walles and þe dyke,[44]   165
And hertly wele it gan me lyke;
And on þe drawbrig saw i stand
A knight with fawkon on his hand.
Þis ilk knight, þat be ȝe balde,[45]
Was lord and keper of þat halde.[46]   170
I hailsed[47] him kindly als i kowth;
He answerd me mildeli with mowth;
Mi sterap toke þat hende knight,
And kindly cumanded me to lyght.
His cumandment i did onane,   175

---

[36] repeated. [37] whoever takes words seriously. [38] hoard. [39] trifles. [40] six years ago. [41] wood I found a path. [42] whin, bramble. [43] wooden tower. [44] moat. [45] i.e., sure. [46] stronghold. [47] greeted.

And into hall sone war we tane.
He thanked God, þat gude man,
Seuyn sithes or euer he blan,
And þe way þat me þeder broght,
And als þe auenturs þat i soght.   180
Þus went we in—God do him mede![48]—
And in his hand he led my stede.
When we war in þat fayre palays
(It was ful worthly wroght always),
I saw no man of moder born.   185
Bot a burde[49] hang vs biforn,
Was nowther of yren ne of tre,
Ne i ne wist whareof it might be;
And by þat bord hang a mall.[50]
Þe knyght smate on þar with all   190
Thrise; and by þen might men se
Bifore him come a faire men3e,
Curtayse men in worde and dede.
To stabil sone þai led mi stede.
A damisel come vnto me,   195
Þe semeliest þat euer i se:
Lufsumer lifed neuer in land;
Hendly scho toke me by þe hand,
And sone þat gentyl creature
Al vnlaced myne armure.   200
Into a chamber sho me led,
And with a mantil scho me cled:
It was of purpure,[1] faire and fine,
And þe pane[2] of riche ermyne.
Al þe folk war went vs fra,   205
And þare was none þan bot we twa.
Scho serued me hendely te hend:[3]
Hir maners might no man amend;
Of tong sho was trew and renable,[4]
And of hir semblant soft and stabile.[5]   210
Ful fain i wald, if þat i might,

---

[48] God reward him! [49] board. [50] hammer. [1] purple cloth. [2] skirt. [3] to hand;
i.e., with ready courtesy. [4] fluent. [5] constant.

Haue woned with þat swete wight.
And when we sold go to sopere,
Þat lady with a lufsom chere
Led me down into þe hall. 215
Þare war we serued wele at all;[6]
It nedes noght to tel þe mese,[7]
For wonder wele war we at esse.[8]
Byfor me sat þe lady bright,
Curtaisly my mete to dyght; 220
Vs wanted nowþer baken[9] ne roste.
And efter soper, sayd myne oste
Þat he cowth noght tel þe day
Þat ani knight are with him lay,
Or þat ani auentures soght. 225
Þarfore he prayed me, if i moght,
On al wise, when i come ogayne,
Þat i sold cum to him sertayne.
I said, "Sir, gladly, yf i may."
It had bene shame haue said him nay. 230
Þat night had i ful gude rest
And mi stede esed of þe best.[10]
Alsone als it was dayes lyght,
Forth to fare sone was i dyght;
Mi leue of mine ost toke i þare 235
And went mi way withowten mare,
Auentures forto layt[11] in land.
A faire forest sone i fand.
Me thoght mi hap þare fel ful hard,[12]
For þare was mani a wilde lebard,[13] 240
Lions, beres, bath bul and bare,[14]
Þat rewfully gan rope and rare.[15]
Oway i drogh me, and with þat,
I saw sone whare a man sat
On a lawnd,[16] þe fowlest wight 245
Þat euer ʒit man saw in sy[ght];

---

[6] in all ways. [7] fare. [8] ease. [9] baked meats. [10] had the best of care. [11] seek.
[12] my luck here was bad. [13] leopard. [14] boar. [15] howl and roar. [16] heath.

244. On this figure, cf. Loomis 56; Dickman 174.

He was a lathly[17] creature,
For fowl he was out of mesure.
A wonder mace in hand he hade;
And sone mi way to him i made.   250
His heuyd, me thoght, was als gre[te]
Als of a rowncy or a nete:[18]
Vnto his belt hang his hare.
And efter þat byheld i mare:
To his forhede byheld i þan,   255
Was bradder þan twa large span;[19]
He had eres als ane olyfant[20]
And was wele more þan geant;
His face was ful brade and flat;
His nese was cutted als a cat;[21]   260
His browes war like litel buskes[22]
And his tethe like bare[23]-tuskes;
A ful grete bulge opon his bak;
Þare was noght made withowten lac;[24]
His chin was fast vntil his brest;   265
On his mace he gan him rest.
Also it was a wonder wede
Þat þe cherle yn ȝede;
Nowther of wol ne of line[25]
Was þe wede þat he went yn.   270
When he me sagh, he stode vp right;
I frayned him if he wolde fight,
For þarto was i in gude will;
Bot als a beste þan stode he still.
I hopid þat he no wittes kowth[26]   275
No reson forto speke with mowth.
To him i spak ful hardily
And said, "What ertow, belamy?"[27]
He said ogain, "I am a man."
I said, "Swilk saw i neuer nane."   280
"What ertow?" alsone said he.

---

[17] repulsive. [18] nag or ox. [19] two span, about nine inches. [20] elephant.
[21] slit like a cat's. [22] bushes. [23] boar-. [24] defect. [25] wool nor linen. [26] believed that he had not the sense. [27] good fellow.

I said, "Swilk als þou here may se."
I said, "What dose þou here allane?"
He said, "I kepe þir[28] bestes ilkane."
I said, "Þat es meruaile, think me;   285
For i herd neuer of man bot þe,
In wildernes ne in forestes,
Þat kepeing had of wilde bestes,
Bot þai war bunden fast in halde."[29]
'He sayd, "Of þire es none so balde,   290
Nowþer by day ne bi night,
Anes to pas out of mi sight."
I sayd, "How so? Tel me þi scill."[30]
"Parfay," he said, "gladly i will."
He said, "In al þis faire foreste,   295
Es þare none so wilde beste
Þat remu[31] dar, bot stil stand
When i am to him cumand.
And ay when þat i wil him fang
With mi fingers, þat er strang,   300
I ger him cri on swilk manere
Þat al þe bestes, when þai him here,
Obout me þan cum þai all,
And to mi fete fast þai fall
On þaire manere merci to cry.   305
Bot vnderstand now redyli,
Olyue es þare lifand no ma[32]
Bot i þat durst omang þam ga,
Þat he ne sold sone be al torent.
Bot þai er at my comandment: 310
To me þai cum when i þam call,
And i am maister of þam all."
Þan he asked onone right
What man i was. I said, a knyght
Þat soght auenturs in þat land,   315
"My body to asai and fande;[33]
And i þe pray, of þi kownsayle

---

[28] these. [29] confinement. [30] art, method. [31] stir. [32] more; i.e., other. [33] test and prove.

þou teche[34] me to sum meruayle."
He sayd, "I can no wonders tell;
Bot herebisyde es a well;   320
Wend þeder and do als i say:
þou passes noght al quite[35] oway.
Folow forth þis ilk strete,
And sone sum meruayles sal þou mete.
þe well es vnder þe fairest tre   325
þat euer was in þis cuntré;
By þat well hinges a bacyne[36]
þat es of gold gude and fyne,
With a cheyne, trewly to tell,
þat wil reche into þe well;   330
þare es a chapel nere þarby,
þat nobil es and ful lufely.
By þe well standes a stane;
Tak þe bacyn sone onane,
And cast on water with þi hand;   335
And sone þou sal se new tithand.
A storme sal rise, and a tempest,
Al obout, by est and west;
þou sal here mani thonor-blast
Al obout þe blawand fast;   340
And þare sal cum slik slete and rayne,
þat vnnese[37] sal þou stand ogayne;
Of lightnes sal þou se a lowe,[38]
Vnnethes þou sal þi seluen knowe;
And if þou pas withowten greuance,   345
þan has þou þe fairest chance
þat euer ȝit had any knyght
þat þeder come to kyth his myght."
    þan toke i leue and went my way,

---

[34] direct. [35] unscathed. [36] hangs a basin. [37] scarcely. [38] you shall see a flash of brightness.

344. Chrétien: *Se tu t'an puez departir* [come away]. The poet seems to have rendered "departir" by "distinguish," a sense it has in "Yvain" 2626. The sense of the passage in Chrétien is, "You will be fortunate to come thence unharmed." (Cf. next two lines in the English.)

And rade vnto þe midday. 350
By-þan i come whare i sold be,
I saw þe chapel and þe tre.
þare i fand þe fayrest thorne
þat euer groued sen God was born:[39]
So thik it was with leues grene, 355
Might no rayn cum þarbytwene,
And þat grenes[40] lastes ay,
For no winter dere yt may.
I fand þe bacyn, als he talde,
And þe wel with water kalde:
An amerawd[41] was þe stane— 360
Richer saw i neuer nane—
On fowre rubyes on heght standand;
þaire light lasted ouer[42] al þe land.
And when i saw þat semely syght, 365
It made me bath ioyful and lyght:
I toke þe bacyn sone onane
And helt[43] water opon þe stane.
þe weder wex þan wonder blak,
And þe thoner fast gan crak; 370
þare come slike stormes of hayl and rayn,
Vnnethes i might stand þareogayn;
þe store[44] windes blew ful lowd:
So kene come neuer are of clowd;
I was dreuyn[45] with snaw and slete: 375
Vnnethes i might stand on my fete;
In my face þe leuening smate,[46]
I wend haue brent, so was it hate.[47]
þat weder made me so will of rede[48]
I hopid sone to haue my dede; 380
And sertes, if it lang had last,
I hope i had neuer þeþin past.

---

[39] grew since Christ was born. [40] greenness. [41] emerald. [42] pervaded. [43] poured.
[44] fierce. [45] beaten. [46] lightning smote. [47] it was so hot that I expected
to burn. [48] storm made me bewildered.

353. MS. *tlorne*. The thorn was supposed to be a special favorite of
the fairies. See Wimberly for material.
360. On storm-producing springs, see Bruce II.77 for bibliography.

Bot thorgh His might þat tholed[49] wownd,
Þe storme sesed within a stownde;
Þan wex þe weder fayre ogayne,   385
And þareof was i wonder fayne,
For best comforth of al thing
Es solace efter myslikeing.[50]
Þan saw i sone a mery syght:
Of al þe fowles þat er in flyght   390
Lighted so thik opon þat tre
Þat bogh ne lefe none might i se;
So merily þan gon þai sing
Þat al þe wode bigan to ring;
Ful mery was þe melody   395
Of þaire sang and of þaire cry:
Þare herd neuer man none swilk,
Bot-if ani had herd þat ilk.
And when þat mery dyn was done,
A noþer noyse þan herd i sone,   400
Als it war of horsmen
Mo þan owþer nyen or ten.
    Sone þan saw i cum a knyght;
In riche armurs was he dight;
And sone when[1] i gan on him loke,   405
Mi shelde and spere to me i toke.
Þat knight to me hied ful fast,
And kene wordes out gan he cast:
He bad þat i sold tel him tite
Whi i did him swilk despite,[2]   410
With weders wakend him of rest,
And done him wrang in his forest;
"Þarfore," he said, "þou sal aby."
And with þat come he egerly,

---

[49] suffered.   [50] discomfort.   [1] as soon as.   [2] injury.

390. Probably a translation of the partitive in Chrétien's line, *branche ne fuelle Que tot ne fust covert d'oiseax.* The singing birds are regularly part of the scene. Cf. Bruce II.78.

412. In condensing a passage in Chrétien, the translator has shifted his tense as Chrétien did. Sc. "and that I had done."

And said, i had ogayn resowne   415
Done him grete destrucciowne,
And might it neuermore amend;
Þarfore he bad i sold me fend;[3]
And sone i smate him on þe shelde.
Mi schaft brac out in þe felde;   420
And þan he bare me sone bi strenkith
Out of my sadel my speres lenkith.[4]
I wate þat he was largely
By þe shuldres mare þan i;[5]
And bi þe ded þat i sal thole,[6]   425
Mi stede by his was bot a fole.[7]
For mate[8] i lay down on þe grownde,
So was i stonayd[9] in þat stownde.
A worde to me wald he noght say,
Bot toke my stede and went his way.   430
Ful sarily þan þare i sat;
For wa, i wist noght what was what.
With my stede he went in hy
Þe same way þat he come by;
And i durst folow him no ferr,   435
For dout me solde bite werr;[10]
And also ȝit, by Goddes dome,
I ne wist whare he bycome.
Þan i thoght how i had hight
Vnto myne ost, þe hende knyght,   440
And also til his lady bryght
To com ogayn, if þat i myght.
Mine armurs left i þare ilkane,
For els myght i noght haue gane.
Vnto myne in[11] i come by day;   445
Þe hende knight and þe fayre may,
Of my come war þai ful glade,
And nobil semblant[12] þai me made;

---

[3] defend. [4] i.e., backward a spear's length. [5] i.e., fully a head taller. [6] death I shall suffer; i.e., surely. [7] foal, colt. [8] weakness. [9] stunned. [10] for fear worse might befall me. [11] lodging. [12] appearance; i.e., preparations.

416. For a similar rebuke, cf. "Silva Gadelica" I.348; E. Clodd's "Tom Tit Tot" 20; the French "Chevalier au Cygne."

In al thinges þai haue þam born
Als þai did þe night biforn.   450
Sone þai wist whare i had bene,
And said þat þai had neuer sene
Knyght þat euer þeder come
Take þe way ogayn home.
On þis wise þat tyme i wroght: 455
I fand þe folies þat i soght."
　　"Now sekerly," said Sir Ywayne,
"Þou ert my cosyn iermayne;[13]
Trew luf suld be vs bytwene,
Als sold bytwyx breþer bene.   460
Þou ert a fole at[14] þou ne had are
Tald me of þis ferly fare;
For sertes i sold onone ryght
Haue venged þe of þat ilk knyght.
So sal i ȝit, if þat i may."   465
And þan als smertly sayd Syr Kay;
He karpet to þam wordes grete:
"It es scne, now es efter mete:
Mare boste es in a pot of wyne
Þan in a karcas of Saynt Martyne.   470
Arme þe smertly, Syr Ywayne,
And sone, þat þou war cumcn ogayne;
Luke þou fil wele þi panele,[15]
And in þi sadel set þe wele;
And when þou wendes, i þe pray,   475
Þi baner wele þat þou desplay;
And, rede i, or þou wende,
Þou tak þi leue at ilka frende:
And if it so bytide þis nyght
Þat þe in slepe dreche ani wight,[16]   480
Or any dremis mak þe rad,[17]

_____

[13] by blood.　[14] that.　[15] saddle-cloth (which was stuffed with soft material).
[16] any one troubles you.　[17] afraid.

470. Meaning a flitch of dried beef. St. Martin's Day, Nov. 11, was traditionally the time for drying meat for the winter.
472. Chrétien says merely, _Or tost_ [quickly], _por Deu, mes Sire Yvain!_

Turn ogayn and say i bad."[18]
þe Quene answerd with milde mode
And said, "Sir Kay, ertow wode?
What þe deuyl es þe withyn,   485
At[19] þi tong may neuer blyn
þi felows so fowly to shende?
Serte[s], Sir Kay, þou ert vnhende.
By Him þat for vs sufferd pine,
Syr, and þi tong war myne,   490
I sold bical[20] it tyte of treson;
And so might þou do, by gude reson:
þi tong dose þe grete dishonowre,
And þarefore es it þi traytowre."
And þan al sone Syr Ywayne   495
Ful hendly answerd ogayne
(Al if men sayd hym velany,
He karped ay ful curtaysly):
"Madame," he said vnto þe Quene,
"þare sold na stryf be vs bytwene: 500
Vnkowth men wele may he shende
þat to his felows es so vnhende.
And als, madame, men says sertayne
þat wo-so flites or turnes ogayne,[21]
He bygins al þe mellé,[22]   505
So wil i noght it far by me.[23]
Lates him say halely[24] his thoght:
His wordes greues me right noght."
    Als þai war in þis spekeing,
Out of þe chamber come þe Kyng;   510
þe barons þat war þare, sertayn,
Smertly rase þai him ogayne.
He bad þam sit down al bydene,
And down he set him by þe Quene.
þe Quene talde him fayre and wele,   515
Als sho kowth, euerilka dele
Ful apertly[25] al þe chance

---

[18] predicted it. [19] that. [20] accuse. [21] quarrels or turns about; i.e., shows resentment. [22] fight. [23] (that) it come about through me. [24] entirely. [25] openly.

Als it bifel Syr Colgreuance.
When sho had talde him how it ferd,
And þe King hyr tale had herd, 520
He sware by his owyn crowne
And his fader sowl, Vterpendragowne,²⁶
Þat he sold se þat ilk syght
By þat day þeþin a fowretenight,
On Saint Johns euyn, þe Baptist, 525
Þat best barn²⁷ was vnder Crist.
"Swith," he sayd, "wendes with me,
Who-so wil þat wonder se."
Þe Kynges word might noght be hid:
Ouer al þe cowrt sone was it kyd, 530
And þare was none so litel page
Þat he ne was fayn of þat vayage;
And knyghtes and swiers war ful fayne;
Mysliked none bot Syr Ywaine.
To himself he made grete mane, 535
For he wald haue went allane;
In hert he had grete myslykyng
For þe wending of þe Kyng,
Al for he hopid, withowten fayle,
Þat Sir Kay sold ask þe batayle 540
Or els Sir Gawayn, knyght vailant,
And owþer wald þe King grant:²⁸
Who-so it wald first craue
Of þam two, sone might it haue.
Þe Kynges wil wald he noght bide, 545
Worth of him what may bityde:²⁹
Bi him allane he thoght to wend
And tak þe grace þat God wald send.
He thoght to be wele on hys way
Or it war passed þe thryd day, 550

---

²⁶ the soul of his father, Uther Pendragon. ²⁷ man. ²⁸ to either would the king
have granted it. ²⁹ become of him what might.

523. MS. þar he.
525. June 23, Eve of Midsummer Day, was especially favorable for
the meeting of mortals and fairies.

And to asay[30] if he myght mete
With þat ilk narow strete,
With thornes and with breres set,
Þat mens way might lightli[31] let,
And also forto fynd þe halde[32]   555
Þat Sir Colgreuance of talde,
Þe knyght and þe mayden meke;
Þe forest fast þan wald he seke,
And als þe karl of Kaymes kyn,[33]
And þe wilde bestes with him—   560
Þe tre with briddes þareopon—
Þe chapel, þe bacyn, and þe stone.
His thoght wald he tel to no frende
Vntil he wyst how it wald ende.
    Þan went Ywaine to his yn;   565
His men he fand redy þareyn.
Vnto a swier gan he say,
"Go swith and sadel my palfray,
And so þou do my strang stede,
And tak with þe my best wede;   570
At ȝone ȝate i wil out ryde;
Withowten town i sal þe bide;
And hy þe smertly vnto me,
For i most make a iorné.
Ogain sal þou bring my palfra[y].   575
And forbede þe oght to say:
If þou wil any more me se,
Lat none wit of my preueté;
And if ani man þe oght frayn,
Luke now lely þat þou layn."[34]   580
"Sir," he said, "with ful gude will
Als ȝe byd, i sal fulfyll;
At ȝowre awyn wil may ȝe ride,
For me ȝe sal noght be ascryed."[35]

---

[30] try. [31] easily. [32] stronghold. [33] churl of Cain's kin. [34] dissemble loyally.
[35] discovered.

559. On Cain, see "Havelok" 2045.
575. MS. *brring*.

Forth þan went Sir Ywayne: 585
He thinkes, or he cum ogayne,
To wreke his kosyn at his myght.
Þe squier has his hernays[36] dyght;
He did right als his mayster red:
His stede, his armurs he him led. 590
When Ywayn was withowten town,
Of his palfray lighted he down
And dight him right wele in his wede,
And lepe vpon his gude stede.
Furth he rade onone right 595
Vntil it neghed nere þe nyght.
He passed many high mowntayne
In wildernes, and mony a playne,
Til he come to þat leþir sty[37]
Þat him byhoued pass by. 600
Þan was he seker for to se
Þe wel and þe fayre tre;
Þe castel saw he at þe last,
And þeder hyed he ful fast.
More curtaysi and more honowre 605
Fand he with þam in þat toure,
And mare conforth by mony falde,[38]
Þan Colgreuance had him of talde.
Þat night was he herberd[39] þare,
So wele was he neuer are. 610
At morn he went forth by þe strete,
And with þe cherel sone gan he mete
Þat sold tel to him þe way.
He sayned[40] him, þe soth to say,
Twenty sith, or euer he blan, 615
Swilk mcruayle had he of þat man;
For he had wonder þat nature
Myght mak so fowl a creature.
Þan to þe well he rade, gude pase,

---

[36] armor. [37] ugly path. [38] many times. [39] sheltered. [40] crossed.

603. MS. *chapel saw.*—Ritson.

And doun he lighted in þat place, 620
And sone þe bacyn has he tane
And kest water opon þe stane;
And sone þare wex, withowten fayle,
Wind and thonor, rayn and haile.
When it was sesed, þan saw he 625
Þe fowles light opon þe tre;
Þai sang ful fayre opon þat thorn,
Right als þai had done byforn;
And sone he saw cumand a knight,
Als fast so þe fowl in flyght, 630
With rude sembland and sterne chere;
And hastily he neghed nere.
To speke of lufe na time was þare,
For aiþer hated vþer ful sare;
Togeder smertly gan þai driue; 635
Þaire sheldes sone bigan to ryue;[41]
Þaire shaftes cheuerd to þaire hand,[42]
Bot þai war bath ful wele syttand.[43]
Out þai drogh þaire swerdes kene,
And delt strakes þam bytwene; 640
Al to peces þai hewed þaire sheldes:
Þe culpons flegh[44] out in þe feldes;
On helmes strake þay so with yre,
At ilka strake out brast þe fyre.
Aiþer of þam gude buffettes bede, 645
And nowþer wald styr of þe stede;
Ful kenely þai kyd þaire myght,
And feyned[45] þam noght for to fight;
[At] þaire hauberkes þat men myght ken.
Þe blode out of þaire bodyes ren; 650
Aiþer on oþer laid so fast,
Þe batayl might noght lang last.
Hauberkis er broken and helmes reuen,
Stif strakes war þare gyfen.

---

[41] break. [42] i.e., shivered along their whole length. [43] i.e., kept firmly in their seats. [44] bits flew. [45] i.e., did not merely pretend.

641. MS. *sleldes.*

Þai faght on hors stifly always; 655
Þe batel was wele more to prays.
Bot at þe last Syr Ywayne
On his felow kyd his mayne:
So egerly[46] he smate him þan,
He clefe[47] þe helme and þe hern-pan.[48] 660
  Þe knyght wist he was nere ded:
To fle þan was his best rede;
And fast he fled, with al hys mayne,
And fast folow[d] Syr Ywayne.
Bot he ne might him ouertake, 665
Þarfore grete murning gan he make;
He folowd him ful stowtlyk,
And wald haue tane him, ded or quik.
He folowd him to þe ceté:
Na man lyfand met he. 670
When þai come to þe kastel ȝate,
In he folowd faste þareate.
At aiþer entré was iwys
Straytly wroght a portculis,
Shod wele with yren and stele, 675
And also grunden[49] wonder wele;
Vnder þat þan was a swyke[50]
Þat made Syr Ywain to myslike:
His hors fote toched þareon,
Þan fel þe portculis onone, 680
Bytwyx him and his hinder-arsown;[1]
Thorgh sadel and stede it smate al down;
His spores of his heles it schare.[2]

---

[46] fiercely. [47] clove. [48] skull. [49] sharpened. [50] trap. [1] rear saddle-peak. [2] shore, cut.

656. Knights fought on foot only when one had been unhorsed; here, neither is unhorsed, and both combatants thus prove themselves masters of their art. This excites the poet's admiration.
670. Cf. other stories where the hero enters the castle of the fairies (e.g., "Eger," "Degaré"): the fairies remain invisible for a time. Chrétien may have added the city because the castles he knew had cities around them (cf. Brown's study, passim), but the deserted city became a fairly common part of the scene.

Þan had Ywaine murnyng mare;[3]
Bot so he wend haue passed quite,[4]　　685
Þan fel þe toþer bifore, als tyte.
A faire grace ȝit fel him swa,
Al if it smate his hors in twa
And his spors of aiþer hele,
Þat himself passed so wele!　　690
Bytwene þa ȝates now es he tane:
Þarfore he mase ful mykel mane;
And mikel murnyng gan he ma
For þe knyght was went him fra.
　　Als he was stoken in þat stall,[5]　　695
He herd byhind him in a wall
A dore opend, faire and wele,
And þareout come a damysel.
Efter hir þe dore sho stak;[6]
Ful hinde wordes to him sho spak.　　700
"Syr," sho said, "by Saint Myghell,
Here þou has a febil ostell:[7]
Þou mon be ded, es noght at laine,[8]
For my lord, þat þou has slayne.
Seker it es þat þou him slogh;　　705
My lady makes sorow ynogh,
And al his menȝe euerilkane.
Þare has þou famen many ane;
To be þi bane er þai ful balde.
Þou brekes noght out of þis halde;　　710
And for þai wate,[9] þai may noght fayl:
Þai wil þe sla in playn[10] batayl."
He sayd, "Þai ne sal, so God me rede,
For al þaire might, do me to dede,
Ne no handes opon me lay!"　　715
Sho said, "Na, sertes, if þat i may;[11]

---

[3] the greater grief.　[4] passed unhurt.　[5] caught in that enclosure.　[6] closed.
[7] poor lodging.　[8] it is not to be denied.　[9] are watching.　[10] open.　[11] sc.
'prevent it'.

686. MS. þat fel.—Schleich.
698. On the helpful damsel, cf. Griffith's "Sir Perceval" 100.
712. MS. þe wil.

Al if þou be here straytly stad,[12]
Me think þou ert noght ful adrad;
And sir," sho said, "on al wise,
I aw þe honore and seruyse. 720
I was in message at þe King
Bifore þis time, whils i was ȝing;
I was noght þan s[o] auesé[13]
Als a damysel aght to be.
Fro þe tyme þat i was lyght,[14] 725
In cowrt was none so hend knyght
Þat vnto me þan walde take hede,
Bot þou allane, God do þe mede!
Grete honore þou did to me,
And þat sal i now quite þe. 730
I wate, if þou be seldom sene,
Þou ert þe Kyng son Vriene,[15]
And þi name es Sir Ywayne.
Of me may þou be sertayne:
If þou wil my kownsail leue, 735
Þou sal find na man þe to greue.
I sal lene þe here mi ring;
Bot ȝelde it me at myne askyng:
When þou ert broght of al þi payn,
Ȝelde it þan to me ogayne. 740
Als þe bark hilles[16] þe tre,
Right so sal my ring do þe:
When þou in hand has þe stane,
Dere sal þai do þe nane;
For þe stane es of swilk myght, 745
Of þe sal men haue na syght."
Wit ȝe wele þat Sir Ywáyne
Of þir wordes was ful fayne.

---

[12] hard beset. [13] discreet. [14] alighted; i.e., arrived. [15] King Urien's son.
[16] hides.

731. In Chrétien, the couplet is: *Bien sai comant voz avez non* [name],
Et reconeu vos ai bien. Possibly the translator mistook *avez* for some
form like *savez*, and took the sense to be, "you are not known," and to
make the rhyme, gave as a paraphrase, "you are seldom seen."

In at þe dore sho him led,
And did him sit opon hir bed. 750
A quylt ful nobil lay þareon;
Richer saw he neuer none.
Sho said if he wald any thing,
He sold be serued at his liking.
He said þat ete wald he fayn; 755
Sho went and come ful sone ogain;
A capon rosted broght sho sone,
A clene klath and brede þarone,
And a pot with riche wine,
And a pece[17] to fil it yne; 760
He ete and drank with ful gude chere,
For þarof had he grete mystere.[18]
When he had eten and dronken wele,
Grete noyse he herd in þe kastele:
þai soght oueral him to haue slayn; 765
To venge þaire lorde war þai ful bayn,[19]
Or þat þe cors in erth was layd.
þe damysel sone to him sayd,
"Now seke þai þe fast for to sla;
Bot whosoeuer com or ga, 770
Be þou neuer þe more adred,
Ne styr þou noght out of þis stede;
In þis here[20] seke þai wyll,
Bot on þis bed luke þou be styll:
Of þam al mak þou na force.[21] 775
Bot when þat þai sal bere þe cors
Vnto þe kyrk for to bery,
þan sal þou here a sary cry,
So sal þai mak a doleful dyn.
þan wil þay seke þe eft herein; 780
Bot loke þou be of hert lyght,
For of þe sal þai haue no syght:
Here sal þou be, mawgré þaire berd;

---

[17] bowl. [18] need. [19] eager. [20] this (place) here. [21] pay no attention.

750. In women's apartments, the bed was usually the only piece of furniture on which one could sit. See note, "Havelok" 421; Wright 261.

And þarfore be þou noght aferd:
Þi famen sal be als þe blynd;   785
Both byfor þe and byhind,
On ilka side sal þou be soght.
Now most i ga; bot drede þe noght,
For i sal do þat þe es lefe,
If al it turn me to mischefe."   790
    When sho come vnto þe ȝate,
Ful many men fand sho þarate
Wele armed, and wald ful fayn
Haue taken and slane Sir Ywaine.
Half his stede þare fand þai,   795
Þat within þe ȝates lay;
Bot þe knight þare fand þai noght:
Þan was þare mekil sorow vnsoght.[22]
Dore ne window was þare nane
Whare he myght oway gane.   800
Þai said he sold þare be laft,
Or els he cowth of wechecraft,
Or he cowth of nygromancy,[23]
Or he had wenges for to fly.
    Hastily þan went þai all   805
And soght him in þe maydens hall,
In chambers high, es noght at[24] hide,
And in solers[25] on ilka side.
Sir Ywaine saw ful wele al þat,
And still opon þe bed he sat.   810
Þare was nane þat anes mynt[26]
Vnto þe bed at[27] smyte a dynt.
Al obout þai smate so fast
Þat mani of þaire wapins brast.
Mekyl sorow þai made ilkane   815
For þai ne myght wreke þaire lord[28] bane.
Þai went oway with dreri chere,
And sone þareefter come þe bere.

---

[22] i.e., vindictive rage.   [23] understood necromancy.   [24] to.   [25] upper rooms.
[26] thought.   [27] to.   [28] (genitive case).

788. MS. *neght.*

A lady folowd, white so mylk:
In al þat land was none swilk.   820
Sho wrang hir fingers—out brast þe blode;
For mekyl wa sho was nere wode.
Hir fayre hare scho al todrogh,[29]
And ful oft fel sho down in swogh;
Sho wepe with a ful dreri voice.   825
Þe hali water and þe croyce
Was born bifore þe procession;
Þare folowd mani a moder son;
Bifore þe cors rade a knyght
On his stede, þat was ful wight,   830
In his armurs wele arayd,
With spere and target gudely grayd.[30]
Þan Sir Ywayn herd þe cry
And þe dole of þat fayre lady;
For more sorow myght nane haue   835
Þan sho had when he went to graue.
Prestes and monkes on þaire wyse
Ful solempnly did þe seruyse.
    Als Lunet þare stode in þe thrang,
Vntil Sir Ywaine thoght hir lang.   840
Out of þe thrang þe wai sho tase;
Vnto Sir Ywaine fast sho gase.
Sho said, "Sir, how ertow stad?[31]
I hope ful wele þou has bene rad."[32]
"Sertes," he said, "þou sais wele þare!   845
So abayst[33] was i neuer are;"
He said, "Leman, i pray þe,
If it any wise may be,
Þat i might luke a litel throw[34]
Out at sum hole or sum window;   850
For wonder fayn," he sayd, "wald i
Haue a sight of þe lady."
Þe maiden þan ful sone vnshet[35]

---

[29] disheveled.   [30] shield well appointed; ie., suitable.   [31] placed; i.e., prospering.
[32] suppose you have been frightened.   [33] afraid.   [34] space, while.   [35] opened.

In a place a preué weket;[36]
Þare of þe lady he had a syght.   855
Lowd sho cried to God Almyght:
"Of his sins do hym pardowne!
For sertanly in no regyowne
Was neuer knight of his bewté,
Ne efter him sal neuer nane be;   860
In al þe werld, fro end to ende,
Es none so curtayse ne so hende.
God grant þe grace þou mai won
In heuyn, with His owyn Son!
For so large lifes none in lede,   865
Ne none so doghty of gude dede!"
When sho had þus made hir spell,[37]
In swowny[n]g ful oftsithes sho fell.
  Now lat we þe lady be,
And of Sir Ywaine speke we.   870
Luf, þat es so mekil of mayne,
Sare had wownded Sir Ywayne,
Þat whare-so he sal ride or ga,
His hert sho has, þat es his fa;
His hert he has set al bydene   875
Whare himself dar noght be sene.
Bot þus in langing bides he,
And hopes þat it sal better be.
Al þat war at þe enterement[38]
Toke þaire leue at þe lady gent,   880
And hame now er þai halely[39] gane,
And þe lady left allane,
Dweland with hir chamberere[40]
And oþer mo þat war hir dere.
Þan bigan hir noyes al new;   885
For sorow failed hir hide and hew.[41]
Vnto his sawl was sho ful hulde:[42]

---

[36] secret panel. [37] i.e., spoken. [38] burial. [39] entirely; i.e., all of them. [40] maid, confidante. [41] because of grief her color and skin grew pale. [42] faithful.

881. MS. *yane.*

Opon a sawter al of gulde[43]
To say þe salmes fast sho bigan,
And toke no tent[44] vnto no man.   890
Þan had Sir Ywain mekyl drede,
For he hoped noght to spede;
He said, "I am mekil to blame
Þat i luf þam þat wald me shame;
Bot ӡit i wite hir al with wogh,[45]   895
Sen þat i hir lord slogh.
I can noght se, by nakyn gyn,[46]
How þat i hir luf sold wyn.
Þat lady es ful gent and small,
Hir yghen clere als es cristall;   900
Sertes þare es no man oliue
Þat kowth hir bewtese[47] wele descriue."
Þus was Syr Ywayne sted[48] þat sesowne;
He wroght fu[l] mekyl ogayns resowne
To set his luf in swilk a stede   905
Whare þai hated him to þe dede.
He sayd he sold haue hir to wiue,
Or els he sold lose his lyue.
    Þus als he in stody[49] sat,
Þe mayden come to him with þat;   910
Sho sayd, "How hasto farn þis day,
Sen þat i went fro þe oway?"
Sone sho saw him pale and wan,
Sho wist wele what him ayled þan;
Sho said, "I wote þi hert es set;   915
And sertes i ne sal noght it let,
Bot i sal help þe fra presowne
And bring þe to þi warisowne."[50]
He said, "Sertes, damysele,
Out of þis place wil i noght stele;   920
Bot i wil wende by dayes lyght,
Þat men may of me haue sight
Opinly on ilka syde;

---

[43] book of psalms illuminated in gold.   [44] heed.   [45] blame her wrongly.   [46] any
sort of device.   [47] beauty.   [48] beset.   [49] perplexity.   [50] reward.

Worth of me what so bityde,
Manly[1] wil i heþin wende."   925
Þan answerd þe mayden hende,
"Sir, þow sal wend with honowre,
For þou sal haue ful gude socowre.
Bot, sir, þou sal be here sertayne
A while, vnto i cum ogayne."   930
  Sho [kend] al trewly his entent,
And þarfore es sho wightly went
Vnto þe lady, faire and bright.
For vnto hir right wele sho myght
Say what som hyr willes es,[2]   935
For sho was al hir maystres,[3]
Her keper and hir cownsaylere.
To hir sho said als ȝe sal here,
Bytwix þam twa in gude cownsayl.
"Madame," sho sayd, "i haue meruayl   940
Þat ȝe sorow þus euer onane.
For Goddes luf, lat be ȝowre mane:
Ȝe sold think, ouer alkyn[4] thyng,
Of þe Kinges Arthurgh cumyng.
Menes ȝow noght of þe message   945
Of þe Damysel Sauage,
Þat in hir lettre to ȝow send?
Allas, who sal ȝow now defend,
Ȝowre land, and al þat es þareyn,
Sen ȝe wil neuer of wepeing blyn?   950
A, madame, takes tent[5] to me:
Ȝe ne haue na knyght in þis cuntré
Þat durst right now his body bede
For to do a doghty dede,
Ne for to bide þe mekil boste[6]   955
Of King Arthurgh and of his oste;
And if he find none hym ogayn,

---

[1] courageously.   [2] part of her wishes.   [3] confidante.   [4] every other.   [5] heed.
[6] stand firm in the face of the menace.

946. Mentioned aimlessly by Chrétien.   Malory gives the name as a
soubriquet of Lynette.

ʒowre landes er lorn, þis es sertayn."
Þe lady vnderstode ful wele
How sho hyr cownsaild ilka dele;　　960
Sho bad hyr go hir way smertly,
And þat sho war na more hardy
Swilk wordes to hyr at speke;
For wa hir hert wold al to-breke.
Sho bad, "Go wightly heþin oway."　　965
Þan þe maiden þus gan say,
"Madame, it es oft wemens will
Þam for to blame þat sais þam scill."[7]
Sho went oway als sho noght roght;
And þan þe lady hyr bythoght　　970
Þat þe maiden said no wrang,
And so sho sat in stody lang.
　In stody þus allane sho sat;
Þe mayden come ogayn with þat.
"Madame," sho said, "ʒe er a barn![8]　　975
Þus may ʒe sone ʒowre self forfarn;"
Sho sayd, "Chastise þi hert, madame;
To swilk a lady it es grete shame
Þus to wepe and make slike cry.
Think opon þi grete gentri;　　980
Trowes þou þe flowre of cheualry
Sold al with þi lord dy,
And with him be put in molde?[9]
God forbede þat it so solde!
Als gude als he and better bene."　　985
"Þou lyes," sho sayd, "by Heuyn-quene!
Lat se, if þou me tel kan,
Whare es any so doghty man
Als he was þat wedded me."
"ʒis, and ʒe kun me na mawgré,[10]　　990
And þat ʒe mak me sekernes[11]
Þat ʒe sal luf me neuer þe les."

---

[7] wisdom.　[8] child.　[9] earth.　[10] bear me no ill will.　[11] assurance.

987. MS. *þoue*.

Sho said, "Þou may be ful sertayn
Þat for na thing þat þou mai sayn
Wil i me wreth on nane manere." 995
"Madame," sho said, "þan sal ȝe here.
I sal ȝow tel a preueté,
And na ma sal it wit bo[t] we.
Yf twa knyghtes be in þe felde
On twa stedes, with spere and shelde. 1000
And þe tane¹² þe toþer may sla,
Wheþer es þe better of þa?"
Sho said, "He þat has þe bataile."¹³
"Ȝa," said þe mayden, "sawnfayle,
Þe knyght þat lifes es mare of maine 1005
Þan ȝowre lord þat was slayne.
Ȝowre lord fled out of þe place,
And þe toþer gan hym chace
Heder into his awyn halde:¹⁴
Þare¹⁵ may ȝe wit he was ful balde." 1010
Þe lady said, "Þis es grete scorne
Þat þou neuyns¹⁶ him me biforne!
Þou sais nowþer soth ne right;
Swith out of myne eghen syght!"
Þe mayden said, "So mot i the, 1015
Þus ne hight ȝe noght me,
Þat ȝe sold so me myssay."¹⁷
With þat sho turned hir oway,
And hastily sho went ogayn
Vnto þe chameber to Sir Ywayne. 1020
Þe lady thoght þan al þe nyght
How þat sho had na knyght,
For to seke¹⁸ hir land thorghout,
To kepe Arthurgh and hys rowt;
Þan bigan hir for to shame, 1025
And hirself fast forto blame;
Vnto hirself fast gan sho flyte,¹⁹
And said, "With wrang now i hir wite:²⁰

---

¹² one. ¹³ i.e., victory. ¹⁴ castle. ¹⁵ thereby. ¹⁶ name. ¹⁷ abuse. ¹⁸ i e., even should she seek. ¹⁹ contend. ²⁰ blame.

Now hopes sho i wil neuer-mare
Luf hir als i haue done are.   1030
I wil hir luf with main and mode!
For þat sho said was for my gode."
    On þe morn þe mayden rase,
And vnto chamber sone sho gase.
Þare sho fyndes þe faire lady,   1035
Hingand[21] hir heuyd ful drerily,
In þe place whare sho hir left;
And ilka dele sho talde hir eft
Als sho had said to hir bifore.
Þan said þe lady, "Me rewes sore   1040
Þat i missayd þe ʒisterday:
I wil amend, if þat i may.
Of þat knyght now wald i here—
What he war, and wheþen he were.
I wate þat i haue sayd omys: 1045
Now wil i do als þou me wys.
Tel me baldely, or þou blin,
If he be cumen of gentil kyn."
"Madame," sho said, "i dar warand[22]
A genteler lord es none lifand;   1050
Þe hendest man ʒe sal him fynde
Þat euer come of Adams kynde."
"How hat he? Sai me for sertayne."
"Madame," sho said, "Sir Ywayne;
So gentil knight haue ʒe noght sene: 1055
He es þe Kin[g]s son Vryene."
Sho held hir paid of þat tiþ[y]ng,
For þat his fader was a kyng;
"Do me haue him here in my sight
Bitwene þis and þe thrid night;   1060
And are, if þat it are myght be:
Me langes sare him for to se.—
Bring him, if þou mai, þis night!"
"Madame," sho sayd, "þat i ne might,
For his wonyng es heþin oway   1065

---

[21] hanging.   [22] warrant.

More þan þe iorné of a day.
Bot i haue a wele rinand page
Wil stirt þider right in a stage,[23]
And bring him by to-morn at nyght."
Þe lady saide, "Loke yf he myght   1070
To-morn by euyn be here ogayn."
Sho said, "Madame, with al his mayn."
"Bid him hy on alkyn wyse;
He sal be quit wele his seruyse:
Avancement sal be hys bone   1075
If he wil do þis erand sone."
"Madame," sho said, "i dar ӡow hight
To haue him here or þe thrid nyght.
Towhils,[24] efter ӡowre kownsayl send,
And ask þam wha sal ӡow defend—   1080
Ӡowre well,[25] ӡowre land, kastel and towre—
Ogayns þe nobil King Arthure;
For þare es nane of þam ilkane,
Þat dar þe batel vndertane.
Þan sal ӡe say, 'Nedes bus[26] me take   1085
A lorde, to do þat ӡe forsake.'[27]
Nedes bus ӡow haue sum nobil knyght
Þat wil and may defend ӡowre right;
And sais also, to suffer ded,[28]
Ӡe wil noght do out of þaire rede.   1090
Of þat worde sal þai be blyth,
And thank ӡow ful many siþe."
Þe lady said, "By God of myght,
I sal areson[29] þam þis night.
Me think þou dwelles ful lang here: 1095
Send forth swith þi messangere!"
    Þan was þe lady blith and glad:
Sho did al als hir mayden bad.
Efter hir cownsail sho sent onane,
And bad þai sold cum sone ilkane.   1100
Þe maiden redies hyr ful rath;

---

[23] space of time; i.e., quickly.   [24] meanwhile.   [25] spring.   [26] it behooves.
[27] avoid.   [28] even at the cost of death.   [29] summon to council.

Biliue sho gert Syr Ywaine bath,
And cled him seþin in gude scarlet,
Forord[30] wele, and with gold fret;[31]
A girdel ful riche for þe nanes,   1105
Of perry[32] and of preciows stanes.
Sho talde him al how he sold do
When þat he come þe lady to.
And þus, when he was al redy,
Sho went and talde to hyr lady   1110
Þat cumen was hir messagere.
Sho said smertly, "Do lat me here:
Cumes he sone, als haue þou wyn?"[33]
"Medame," sho said, "i sal noght blin
Or þat he be byfor ȝow here."   1115
Þan said þe lady, with light chere,
"Go bring him heder preuely,
Þat none wit bot þou and i."
Þan þe maiden went ogayn
Hastily to Sir Ywayn;   1120
"Sir," sho sayd, "als haue i wyn,
My lady wate þou ert hereyn.
To cum bifore hir luke þou be balde,
And tak gode tent[34] what i haue talde."
    By þe hand sho toke þe knyght   1125
And led him vnto chamber, right
Byfor hir lady (es noght at layne);[35]
And of þat come[36] was sho ful fayne.
Bot ȝit Sir Ywayne had grete drede
When he vnto chamber ȝede.   1130
Þe chamber flore and als þe bed
With klothes of gold was al ouerspred.
Hir thoght he was withowten lac,[37]
Bot no word to him sho spak;
And he, for dred oway he drogh!   1135
Þan þe mayden stode and logh;
Sho sayd, "Mawgre[38] haue þat knyght

---

[30] furred. [31] adorned. [32] jewels. [33] may have joy; i.e., on your honor. [34] heed.
[35] to hide (a tag). [36] coming. [37] defect. [38] ill luck.

Þat haues of swilk a lady syght,
And can noght shew to hir his nede.
Cum furth, sir; þe thar[39] noght drede   1140
Þat mi lady wil þe smyte:
Sho loues þe wele, withouten lite.[40]
Pray to hir of hir mercy,
And for þi sake right so sal i,
Þat sho forgif þe in þis stede   1145
Of Salados þe Rouse ded,
Þat was hir lord, þat þou has slayne."
On knese him set þan Syr Ywaine:
"Madame, i ȝelde me ȝow vntill,
Euer to be at ȝowre wyll;   1150
Yf þat i might, i ne wald noght fle."
Sho said, "Nay, whi sold so be?
To ded yf i gert do þe now,
To me it war ful litel prow.[41]
Bot for i find þe so bowsum,[42]   1155
Þat þou wald þus to me cum,
And for þou dose þe in my grace,
I forgif þe þi trispase.
Syt down," sho said, "and lat me here
Why þou ert þus debonere."[43]   1160
"Madame," he said, "anis[44] with a luke
Al my hert with þe þou toke;
Sen i first of þe had syght,
Haue i þe lufed with al my might.
To mo þan þe, mi lady hende,   1165
Sal neuer more my luf wende;
For þi luf euer i am redy
Lely[45] forto lif or dy."
Sho said, "Dar þou wele vndertake
In my land pese for to make   1170
And for to maintene al mi rightes
Ogayns King Arthure and his knyghtes?"
He said, "Þat dar i vndertane

---

[39] need.   [40] defect, fail.   [41] profit.   [42] obedient.   [43] meek.   [44] i.e., completely.
[45] loyally.

Oganyes ilka lyfand man."
Swilk kownsail byfore had sho tane;   1175
Sho said, "Sir, þan er we at ane."⁴⁶
    Hir barons hir ful rathly red
To tak a lord hir for to wed.
Þan hastily sho went to hall.
Þare abade hir barons all   1180
For to hald þaire parlement
And mari hir by þaire asent.
Sho sayd, "Sirs, with an acorde,
Sen me bus nedely haue a lord
My landes for to lede and ȝeme,   1185
Sais me sone howe ȝe wil deme."
"Madame," þai said, "how so ȝe will,
Al we sal assent þartyll."
Þan þe lady went ogayne
Vnto chameber to Sir Ywaine.   1190
"Sir," sho said, "so God me saue,
Oþer lorde wil i nane haue;
If i þe left, i did noght right,
A king son and a noble knyght."
Now has þe maiden done hir thoght—   1195
Sir Ywayne out of anger broght.
Þe lady led him vnto hall;
Ogains him rase þe barons all,
And al þai said, ful sekerly,
"Þis knight sal wed þe lady."   1200
And ilkane said, þamself bitwene,
So faire a man had þai noght sene:
"For his bewté in hal and bowre,
Him semes to be an emparowre.
We wald þat þai war trowth-plight⁴⁷   1205
And weded sone þis ilk nyght."
Þe lady set hir on þe dese
And cumand al to hald þaire pese,
And bad hir steward sumwhat say

⁴⁶ agreed.   ⁴⁷ betrothed.
1175–6. Possibly these lines should be transposed.

Or men went fra cowrt oway.   1210
Þe steward said, "Sirs, vnderstandes
Were es waxen in þir⁴⁸ landes:
Þe King Arthure es redy dight
To be here byn⁴⁹ þis fowretenyght;
He and his menȝe ha thoght   1215
To win þis land, if þai moght;
Þai wate ful wele þat he es ded
Þat was lord here in þis stede.
None es so wight wapins to welde
Ne þat so boldly mai vs belde;⁵⁰   1220
And wemen may maintene no stowre:
Þai most nedes haue a gouernowre.
Þarfor mi lady most nede
Be weded hastily for drede;
And to na lord wil sho tak tent   1225
Bot if it be by ȝowre assent."
Þan þe lordes al on raw¹
Held þam wele payd of þis saw;
Al assented hyr vntill
To tak a lord at hyr owyn wyll.   1230
Þan said þe lady onone right,
"How hald ȝe ȝow paid of þis knight?
He profers hym on al wyse
To myne honore and my seruyse;
And sertes, sirs, þe soth to say,   1235
I saw him neuer or þis day;
Bot talde vnto me has it bene
He es þe Kyng son Vriene;
He es cumen of hegh parage²
And wonder doghty of vasselage,³   1240
War and wise and ful curtayse.
He ȝernes me to wife alwayse,
And nereþelese, i wate he might
Haue wele better; and so war right."
With a voice halely⁴ þai sayd,   1245
"Madame, ful wele we hald vs payd.

---

⁴⁸ these.   ⁴⁹ within.   ⁵⁰ hearten.   ¹ row.   ² lineage.   ³ valor.   ⁴ unanimously.

Bot hastes fast, al þat ȝe may,
Þat ȝe war wedded þis ilk day;"
And grete prayer gan þai make
On al wise þat sho suld hym take.   1250
Sone vnto þe kirk þai went,
And war wedded in þaire present;[5]
Þare wedded Ywaine in pleuyne[6]
Þe riche Lady Alundyne,
Þe Dukes doghter of Landuit;   1255
Els had hyr lande bene destruyt.
Þus þai made þe maryage
Omang al þe riche barnage;
Þai made ful mekyl mirth þat day,
Ful grete festes on gude aray.   1260
Grete mirthes made þai in þat stede,
And al forgetyn es now þe ded
Of him þat was þaire lord fre;
Þai say þat þis[7] es worth swilk thre,
And þat þai lufed him mekil more   1265
Þan him þat lord was þare byfore.
   Þe bridal sat, for soth to tell,
Til Kyng Arthure come to þe well,
With al his knyghtes euerilkane;
Byhind leued þare noght ane.   1270
Þan sayd Sir Kay, "Now whare es he,
Þat made slike bost here for to be
For to venge his cosyn germayne?
I wist his wordes war al in vayne;
He made grete boste bifor þe Quene,   1275
And here now dar he noght be sene!
His prowd wordes er now al purst,[8]
For in fayth ful ill he durst
Anes luke opon þat knyght
Þat he made bost with to fyght."   1280
Þan sayd Gawayn hastily,

---

[5] presence.   [6] pledge.   [7] i.e., the new lord is worth three of the old.   [8] withdrawn.

"Syr, for Goddes luf, mercy!⁹
For i dar hete þe for sertayne
Þat we sal here of Sir Ywayne
Þis ilk day, þat be þou balde,¹⁰   1285
Bot he be ded or done in halde;¹¹
And neuer in no cumpany
Herd i him speke þe velany."
Þan sayd Sir Kay, "Lo, at þi will
Fra þis time forth i sal be still."   1290
    Þe King kest water on þe stane;
Þe storme rase ful sone onane,
With wikked weders kene and calde,
Als it was byforehand talde.
Þe King and his men ilkane   1295
Wend þarwith to haue bene slane,
So blew it store,¹² with slete and rayn!
And hastily þan Syr Ywayne
Dight him graythly¹³ in his gere,
With nobil shelde and strong spere.   1300
When he was dight in seker¹⁴ wede,
Þan he vmstrade¹⁵ a nobil stede:
Him thoght þat he was als lyght
Als a fowl es to þe flyght.
Vnto þe well fast wendes he,   1305
And sone, when þai myght him se,
Syr Kay—for he wald noght fayle—
Smertly askes þe batayl;
And alsone þan said þe Kyng,
"Sir Kay, i grante þe þine askyng."   1310
    Þan Sir Ywayn neghed þam nere,
Þaire cowntenance to se and here;
Sir Kay þan on his stede gan spring.
"Bere þe wele now," sayd þe Kyng.
Ful glad and blith was Syr Ywayne   1315
When Sir Kay come him ogayn;

⁹ your pardon. ¹⁰ i.e., can safely say. ¹¹ confinement. ¹² hard. ¹³ suitably.
¹⁴ sure, durable. ¹⁵ mounted.

Bot Kay wist noght wha it was;
He findes his fere now, or he pas![16]
Syr Ywaine thinkes now to be wroken
On þe grete wordes þat Kay has spoken.　　1320
Þai rade togeder with speres kene:
Þare was no reuerence[17] þam bitwene.
Sir Ywayn gan Sir Kay bere
Out of his sadel lenkith of his spere;
His helm vnto þe erth smate:　　1325
A fote depe þarein yt bate.[18]
He wald do him na more despite,[19]
Bot down he lighted als tyte;
Syr Kay stede he toke in hy,
And presand þe King ful curtaysly.　　1330
Wonder glad þan war þai all
Þat Kay so fowl a shame gan fall,
And ilkone sayd til oþer þen,
"Þis es he þat scornes al men;"
Of his wa war þai wele paid.　　1335
Syr Ywain þan to þe Kyng said,
"Sir Kyng, i gif to þe þis stede,
For he may help þe in þi nede;
And to me war it grete trispas
For to withhald þat ʒowres was."　　1340
"What man ertow?" quod þe Kyng;
"Of þe haue i na knawyng
Bot-if þou vnarmed were,
Or els þi name þat i might here."
"Lord," he sayd, "i am Ywayne."　　1345
Þan was þe King ferly fayne;
A sari man þan was Sir Kay,
Þat said þat he was stollen oway!
Al descumfite he lay on grownde;
To him þat was a sary stownde.　　1350
Þe King and his men war ful glad

---

[16] match before he goes.　[17] forbearance.　[18] cut.　[19] humiliation.

1317. The Welsh version explains that Ywain wore the slain knight's armor.

Þat þai so Syr Ywayne had,
And ful glad was Sir Gawayne
Of þe welefare of Sir Ywayne,
For nane was to him half so dere   1355
Of al þat in þe court were.
Þe King Sir Ywayn sone bisoght
To tel him al how he had wroght;
And sone Sir Ywaine gan him tell
Of al his fare, how it byfell: 1360
With þe knight how þat he sped,
And how he had þe lady wed,
And how þe mayden hym helped wele;
Þus tald he to him ilka dele.
    "Sir Kyng," he sayd, "i ȝow byseke,   1365
And al ȝowre menȝe, milde and meke,
Þat ȝe wald grante to me þat grace
At wend with me to my purchace,²⁰
And se my kastel and my towre.
Þan myght ȝe do me grete honowre."   1370
Þe Kyng granted him ful right
To dwel with him a fowretenyght;
Sir Ywayne thanked him oft sith;²¹
Þe knyghtes war al glad and blyth
With Sir Ywaine for to wend.   1375
And sone a squier has he send:
Vnto þe kastel þe way he nome,
And warned þe lady of þaire come,
And þat his lord come with þe Kyng;
And when þe lady herd þis thing,   1380
It es no lifand man with mowth
Þat half hir cumforth²² tel kowth.
    Hastily þat lady hende
Cumand al hir men to wende
And dight þam in þaire best aray,   1385
To kepe²³ þe King þat ilk day.
Þai keped him in riche wede,
Rydeand on many a nobil stede;

²⁰ possession, property.   ²¹ many a time.   ²² pleasure.   ²³ receive.

þai hailsed him ful curtaysly,
And also al his cumpany; 1390
þai said he was worthy to dowt²⁴
þat so fele folk led obowt.
þare was grete ioy, i ȝow bihete,
With clothes spred in ilka strete,
And damysels danceand ful wele 1395
With trompes, pipes, and with fristele.²⁵
þe castel and þe ceté rang
With mynstralsi and nobil sang.
þai ordand þam, ilkane in fere,
To kepe þe King on faire manere. 1400
þe lady went withowten towne,
And with hir many bald barowne,
Cled in purpure and ermyne,
With girdels al of gold ful fyne.
þe lady made ful meri chere: 1405
Sho was al dight with drewries²⁶ dere;
Abowt hir was ful mekyl thrang;
þe puple cried and sayd omang,
"Welkum ertou, Kyng Arthoure!
Of al þis werld þou beres þe flowre, 1410
Lord Kyng of all kynges;
And blissed be he þat þe brynges."
When þe lady þe Kyng saw,
Vnto him fast gan sho draw
To hald his sterap whils he lyght. 1415
Bot sone when he of hir had syght,
With mekyl myrth þai samen met.
With hende wordes sho him gret,
"A thowsand sithes welkum," sho says,
"And so es Sir Gawayne þe curtayse." 1420
þe King said, "Lady, white so flowre,
God gif þe ioy and mekil honowre,
For þou ert fayre with body gent."
With þat he hir in armes hent,
And ful faire he gan hir falde:²⁷ 1425

²⁴ should be feared. ²⁵ flute. ²⁶ love-tokens. ²⁷ embrace.

þare was many to bihalde.
It es no man with tong may tell
þe mirth þat was þam omell.[28]
Of maidens was þare so gude wane
þat ilka knight myght tak ane.   1430
Ful mekil ioy Syr Ywayn made
þat he þe King til his hows hade;
þe lady omang þam al samen
Made ful mekyl ioy and gamen.
In þe kastel þus þai dwell;   1435
Ful mekyl myrth wase þam omell.
þe King was þare with his knyghtes
Aght dayes and aght nyghtes,
And Ywayn þam ful mery made
With alkyn gamyn, þam for to glade.   1440
He prayed þe Kyng to thank þe may
þat hym had helpid in his iornay;
And ilk day had þai solace sere[29]
Of huntyng and als of reuere;[30]
For þare was a ful fayre cuntré,   1445
With wodes and parkes grete plenté,
And castels wroght with lyme and stane,
þat Ywayne with his wife had tane.

---

[28] together.   [29] various entertainment.   [30] river; i.e., hawking.

The rest of the poem is a tangle of adventures in which Ywain is aided by a friendly lion.

Middle English
Metrical Romances

Middle English Metrical Romances

edited by

Walter Hoyt French

and

Charles Brockway Hale

TWO VOLUMES BOUND AS ONE

VOLUME II

NEW YORK / RUSSELL & RUSSELL

FIRST PUBLISHED IN 1930
REISSUED, 1964, BY RUSSELL & RUSSELL
A DIVISION OF ATHENEUM PUBLISHERS, INC.
BY ARRANGEMENT WITH WALTER H. FRENCH
L. C. CATALOG CARD NO: 64-18606
PRINTED IN THE UNITED STATES OF AMERICA

SIR PERCEVAL OF GALLES

SIR PERCEVAL OF GALLES

Few pieces have occasioned so much discussion as this, because it has been taken into consideration by every student of the Grail-legend. But if the author knew the courtly poems on that legend, he broke away from them, and emphasized the spectacular and picturesque elements in his material. He also preserved some primitive features not found in the courtly pieces. Since he only half understood his original material, references to other versions have been given in the hope of making some of the lines clear.

The poem is in the northern dialect of the second half of the fourteenth century. The expression is frequently stumbling and awkward and the grammatical constructions loose. The second parts of compound expressions show frequent ellipsis, especially the omission of relatives. The genitive is often without -s. The scribe often writes s- for sh- (sall, shall); aa- for a- or -o; adds inorganic -e; and uses a superfluous initial h- (habyde).

The text follows Sir Frederick Madden's transcript (now in the Harvard University Library) of the Thornton Manuscript, with corrections from Halliwell's edition.

HERE BYGYNNES THE ROMANCE OFF
SIR PERCYUELL OF GALES

Lef, lythes[1] to me,
Two wordes or thre,
Off one þat was faire and fre
 And fell in his fighte.
His righte name was Percyuell,   5
He was ffosterde in the felle,[2]

---

[1] friends, listen. [2] wilds.

1. On the stanza, see E. Rickert's "Emaré" xviii; cf. also "The Avowing of Arthur."

He dranke water of þe welle:[3]
And ȝitt was he wyghte.
His ffadir was a noble man;
Fro þe tyme þat he began,[4]   10
Miche wirchippe he wan
    When he was made knyghte;
In Kyng Arthures haulle
Beste byluffede[5] of alle:
Percyuell þay gan hym calle,   15
    Whoso redis ryghte.

Who þat righte can rede,
He was doughty of dede,
A styffe body on a stede
    Wapynes to welde;   20
Þarefore Kyng Arthoure
Dide hym mekill honoure:
He gaffe hym his syster Acheflour,
    To haue and to holde
Fro thethyn till his lyues ende,   25
With brode londes to spende;[6]
For he þe knyght wele kende,
    He bytaughte hir to welde;
With grete gyftes to fulfill,
He gaffe his sister hym till—   30
To þe knyght, at þer bothers will,[7]
    With robes in folde.[8]

He gaffe hym robes in folde,
Brode londes in wolde,[9]

_____

[3] spring. [4] i.e., began to engage in warfare. [5] beloved. [6] enjoy the revenue of.
[7] with the consent of both of them. [8] in plenty; cf. Sd. 2070. [9] in his possession.

7. In the primitive versions of the story, Perceval's mother seems to
have been a water-fairy; thus their life beside a spring is insisted on in
this version, from which the fairies have almost disappeared. See A. C. L.
Brown's articles in *Modern Philology* xvi ff., "The Grail and the English
Sir Percival" (hereafter referred to as Brown).
    23. Usually Blanchefleur. Bruce (I.310) thought the form in the text
a corruption; viz., [Bl]a[n]chefleur.

Mony mobles vntolde,[10]   35
    His syster to take.
To þe kirke þe knyghte ȝode
For to wedde þat frely fode,[11]
For þe gyftes þat ware gude
    And for hir ownn sake.   40
Sythen, withowtten any bade,[12]
A grete brydale[13] þay made,
For hir sake þat hym hade
    Chosen to hir make;[14]
And after, withowtten any lett,   45
A grete iustyng þer was sett;
Off all þe kempes[15] þat he mett
    Wolde he none forsake.[16]

Wolde he none forsake,
The Rede Knyghte ne þe Blake,   50
Ne none þat wolde to hym take[17]
    With schafte ne with schelde;
He dose als a noble knyghte,
Wele haldes þat he highte;
Faste preues he his myghtc: 55
    Deres hym none clde.
Sexty schaftes, i say,
Sir Percyuell brake þat ilke day,
And euer þat riche lady lay
    One walle and byhelde.   60
Þofe þe Rede Knyghte hade sworne,[18]
Oute of his sadill is he borne
And almoste his lyfe forlorne,
    And lygges in the felde.

---

[10] countless furnishings.   [11] lovely maid.   [12] delay (a tag common in this poem).
[13] wedding festival.   [14] mate.   [15] warriors.   [16] refuse battle.   [17] come.   [18] i.e.,
sworn the contrary.

46. On the custom of holding tournaments at the wedding of a lord or
the birth of an heir, see W. C. Meller, "The Knight's Life in the Days of
Chivalry," 134.

50. A Red Knight and a Black Knight are two of the villains of the
piece; but possibly this line means merely "knights of all sorts."

There he lygges in the felde— 65
Many men one hym byhelde—
Thurgh his armour and his schelde
    Stoneyde[19] þat tyde.
Þat arghede[20] all þat þer ware,
Bothe þe lesse and þe mare, 70
Þat noble Percyuell so wele dare
    Syche dynttys habyde.
Was þer nowthir more ne lasse
Off all þose þat þer was
Þat durste mete hym one þe grasse, 75
    Agaynes hym to ryde.
Þay gaffe Sir Percyuell þe gree:
Beste worthy was he;
And hamewardeʒ þan rode he,
    And blythe was his bryde. 80

And þofe þe bryde blythe be
Þat Percyuell hase wone þe gree,
ʒete þe Rede Knyghte, es he
    Hurte of his honde;
And þerfore gyffes he a gyfte[21] 85
Þat if he euer couere[22] myghte
Owthir by day or by nyghte,
    In felde for to stonde,
Þat he scholde qwyte hym þat dynt
Þat he of his handes hynte; 90
Sall neuer þis trauell be tynt,[23]
    Ne tolde in þe londe
Þat Percyuell in the felde
Schulde hym schende þus vndire schelde,

---

[19] stunned.   [20] made fearful.   [21] assurance.   [22] recover.   [23] labor be lost; i.e., his effort be in vain.

74. *Was* and *þat* agree with the singular subject of the main clause, not with their real antecedent *þose*.
78. Holthausen emended to *was þat fre.* The text lacks a stressed syllable.
83. MS. *kynghte.*

Bot he scholde agayne it ȝelde,   95
If þat he were leueande.

Now þan are þay leueande bathe;
Was noȝte þe Rede Knyghte so rathe
For to wayte hym with skathe[24]
    Er þer þe harmes felle;[25]   100
Ne befelle þer no stryffe
Till Percyuell had in his lyffe
A son by his ȝonge wyffe,
    Aftir hym to duelle.
When þe child was borne,   105
He made calle it one þe morne
Als his ffadir highte byforne—
    Ȝonge Percyuell.
The knyghte was fayne, a feste made
For a knaue[26]-childe þat he hade;   110
And sythen, withowtten any bade,
    Offe justyngeȝ þay telle.[27]

Now of justyngeȝ þay tell:
Þay sayne þat Sir Percyuell,
Þat he will in þe felde duelle,[28]   115
    Als he hase are done.
A grete justynge was þer sett
Of all þe kempes[29] þat þer mett,
For he wolde his son were gette
    In þe same wonne.[30]   120
Þeroff þe Rede Knyghte was blythe,

---

[24] bring violence upon him. [25] before dissension occurred. [26] male. [27] announce. [28] i.e., await all comers. [29] warriors, champions. [30] brought into the same habit; i.e., would grow up enjoying combat.

95. MS. *it scholde agayne be ȝolden.* Holthausen's emendation.
100. *þer*, abbreviated in the MS., may be a mistake for *þat*.
106. The baptising and christening of infants was never long delayed; the child was thus enabled at once to enjoy the benefits of the sacrament, which purged it of original sin. Cf. Gautier, Ch. V. He was also protected against being carried off by monsters or demons or fairies. Cf. Hartland's "Science of Fairy Tales," Ch. V.

When he herde of þat justynge kythe,[31]
And graythed hym armour ful swythe,
And rode thedir riȝte sone.
Agayne Percyuell he rade,   125
With schafte and with schelde brade,[32]
To holde his heste[33] þat he made,
Of maistres to mone.[34]

Now of maistres to mone,
Percyuell hase wele done,   130
For þe loue of his ȝonge sone,
One þe firste day.
Ere þe Rede Knyghte was bownn,
Percyuell hase borne downn
Knyght, duke, erle, and baroun,   135
And vencusede the play.[35]
Right als he hade done þis honour,
So come þe Rede Knyghte to þe stowre;
Bot "Wo worthe wykkyde armour!"
Percyuell may say;   140
For þer was Sir Percyuell slayne,
And þe Rede Knyghte fayne
(In herte is noȝte for to layne),
When he went on his way.

When he went on his way,   145
Durste þer no man to hym say,[36]
Nowþer in erneste ne in play,
To byd hym habyde;
For he had slayne riȝte þare
The beste body at[37] þare ware: 150
Sir Percyuell, with woundeȝ sare,

---

[31] lit., when he heard (it) made known concerning the jousting.   [32] broad.
[33] promise.   [34] call to mind injuries; i.e., his past disgrace.   [35] vanquished in
the sport.   [36] speak.   [37] person that.

139. "A curse on faulty armor!" The references to untrustworthy arms
are numerous. When a sword proved trustworthy, the knight often gave
it a name, and prized it greatly, for his very life might depend on its
durability. Cf. Meller, *op. cit.*, 73 ff.

And stonayed þat tyde.
And þan þay couthe no better rede
Bot put hym in a preuee stede,
Als þat men dose with þe dede— 155
In erthe for to hyde.
Scho þat was his lady
Mighte be full sary,
Þat lorne hade siche a body:
Hir aylede no pryde. 160

And now is Percyuell þe wighte
Slayne in batelle and in fyghte,
And þe lady hase gyffen a gyfte,[38]
Holde if scho may,
Þat scho schall neuer mare wone 165
In stede, with hir ʒonge sone,
Þer dedeʒ of armeʒ schall be done,
By nyghte ne be daye;
Bot in þe wodde schall he be:
Sall he no thyng see 170
Bot þe leues of the tree
And þe greues graye;[39]
Schall he nowþer take tent[40]
To justeʒ ne to tournament,
Bot in þe wilde wodde went,[41] 175
With besteʒ to playe.

With wilde besteʒ for to playe,
Scho tuke hir leue and went hir waye,
Bothe at baron and at raye,[42]
And went to þe wodde. 180
Byhynde scho leued boure and haulle;
A mayden scho tuke hir withalle,
Þat scho myʒte appon calle
When þat hir nede stode.

_____

[38] assurance.   [39] grey groves.   [40] i.e., know.   [41] go about.   [42] king.

160. Holthausen suggested [v]aylede, availed; as an idiom, it is much more common than aylede.

Oþer gude3 wolde scho nonne nayte,[43]   185
Bot with hir tuke a tryppe of gayte,[44]
With mylke of þam for to bayte[45]
     To hir lyues fode.[46]
Off all hir lordes faire gere,
Wolde scho no3te with hir bere   190
Bot a lyttill Scottes spere,
     Agayne hir son 3ode.[47]

And when hir 3ong son 3ode,
Scho bade hym walke in þe wodde,
Tuke hym þe Scottes spere gude,   195
     And gaffe hym in hande.
"Swete modir," sayde he,
"What manere of thyng may þis bee
Þat 3e nowe hafe taken mee?
     What calle 3ee this wande?"[48]   200
Than byspakke the lady:
"Son," scho sayde, "sekerly,
It is a dart doghty;
     In þe wodde i it fande."
The childe es payed, of his parte,   205
His modir hase gyffen hym þat darte;
Þerwith made he many marte[49]
     In that wodde-lande.

Thus he welke in þe lande,
With hys darte in his hande;   210
     Vnder þe wilde wodde-wande[50]

---

[43] use, have.   [44] flock of goats.   [45] feed.   [46] as sustenance for their lives.   [47] in anticipation of (the time when) her son should walk.   [48] staff.   [49] slaughtered animal.   [50] branches.

191. The weapon is obviously a dart, which might be cast at a mark or animal, but was unsuitable for tilting or thrusting. For much material on this and other details of the plot, see R. H. Griffith's "Sir Perceval of Galles" (University of Chicago thesis); he points out (22) that the weapon is elsewhere described as short (478), and suggests that the word in the text is a corruption of this. The word also bears a resemblance to *schot*, cast. Evidently it is a talismanic spear, which alone can accomplish the death of the Red Knight.

He wexe and wele thrafe.[1]
He wolde schote[2] with his spere
Bestes and oþer gere,
As many als he myghte bere;   215
   He was a gude knaue!
Smalle birdes wolde he slo,
Hertys, hyndeȝ also;
Broghte his moder of thoo:
   Thurte hir none craue.[3]   220
So wele he lernede hym to schote,
Þer was no beste þat welke one fote
To fle fro hym was it no bote,
   When þat he wolde hym haue—

Euen when he wolde hym haue.   225
Thus he wexe and wele thraue,
And was reghte a gude knaue
   Within a fewe ȝere.
Fyftene wynter and mare
He duellede in those holtes hare;   230
Nowþer nurture ne lare[4]
   Scho wolde hym none lere.
Till it byfelle, on a day,
Þe lady till hir son gun say,
"Swete childe, i rede þou praye   235
   To Goddeȝ Sone dere,
Þat he wolde helpe the—
Lorde, for his poustee[5]—
A gude man for to bee,
   And longe to duelle here."   240

"Swete moder," sayde he,
"Whatkyns[6] a godd may þat be
Þat ȝe nowe bydd mee
   Þat i schall to pray?"
Then byspakke þe lady euen:[7]   245
   "It es þe grete Godd of heuen:

---

[1] throve. [2] strike by casting. [3] she had not to beg for any. [4] manners nor learning. [5] power. [6] what manner of. [7] straightway.

This worlde made he within seuen,
Appon þe sexte day."
"By grete Godd," sayde he þan,
"And i may mete with þat man,   250
With alle þe crafte þat i kan,
Reghte so schall i pray !"
There he leuede in a tayte[8]
Bothe his modir and his gayte,[9]
The grete Godd for to layte,[10]   255
Fynde hym when he may.

And as he welke in holtes hare,
He sawe a gate, as it ware;[11]
With thre knyghtis mett he þare
Off Arthurs in.[12]   260
One was Ewayne fytz Asoure,
Anoþer was Gawayne with honour,
And Kay, þe bolde baratour,[13]
And all were of his kyn.
In riche robes þay ryde;   265
The childe hadd no thyng þat tyde
Þat he my3te in his bones hyde,[14]
Bot a gaytes skynn.
He was burely[15] of body, and þerto ri3t brade;
One ayther halfe[16] a skynn he hade;   270
The hode[17] was of þe same made,
Juste to þe chynn.

His hode was juste to his chyn,
Þe flesche halfe[18] tourned within.

---

[8] left with joy, eagerness. [9] goats. [10] seek. [11] it befell that he saw a path.
[12] household. [13] bully. [14] in which to hide his bones. [15] powerful. [16] i.e., back
and front. [17] hood. [18] skin side.

247. Seems corrupt. It may have read, *This worlde made in dayes seuen.*
260. MS. *Arthrus.*
264. In this poem, in which the relationships are considerably confused
(cf. Loomis, Ch. 27), the mothers of Perceval and Gawain are sisters of
Arthur; hence the knights are cousins. Ywain was cousin to Gawain,
but not to Perceval; Kay was Arthur's foster brother. But these relationships were altered by medieval writers, and in Malory are not as
stated here.

The childes witt was full thyn   275
When he scholde say oughte.
þay were clothede all in grene;
Siche hade he neuer sene:
Wele he wened þat thay had bene
    þe Godd þat he soghte.   280
He said, "Wilke of ȝow alle three
May þe grete Godd bee
þat my moder tolde mee,
    þat all þis werlde wroghte?"
Bot þan ansuerde Sir Gawayne   285
Faire and curtaisely agayne,
"Son, so Criste mote me sayne,[19]
    For swilke are we noghte."

Than saide þe fole one þe filde,[20]
Was comen oute of þe woddeȝ wilde,   290
To Gawayne þat was meke and mylde
    And softe of ansuare,
"I sall sla ȝow all three
Bot ȝe smertly now telle mee
Whatkyns thyngeȝ þat ȝe bee,   295
    Sen ȝe no goddes are."
Then ansuerde Sir Kay,
"Who solde we than say
þat hade[21] slayne vs to-day
    In this holtis hare?"   300
At Kayes wordes wexe he tene:
Bot a grete bukke had bene—

---

[19] bless.   [20] fool in the field.   [21] would have.

289. In Middle English, "fool" was not so strong a word as to-day; probably the most satisfactory translation is "fellow."

302. MS. *Bot he a. Bukke* may mean "body," "bulk," and *he* = Gawain; it may mean "stag." Stags appear in legends in various capacities: (1) As messengers to bring a mortal to a fairy; they are usually killed as the meeting occurs (see *Am. Jour. Phil.* 37.399). (2) Because they are under an enchantment that they are seeking to dissolve (see *Folklore* 17.435.n.6). In the French lai of "Tyolet," which closely resembles the first part of "Sir Perceval," a stag leads the boy to a river, and is disenchanted when his pursuer kills a roebuck that comes between them. (3) As trophies proving that the hero had arrived at manhood. (Cf. Griffith 33, *PMLA* 32.598.) The second of these possibilities seems to fit best here.

Ne hadd he stonde þam bytwene,—
He hade hym slayne þare.

Bot þan said Gawayn to Kay,   305
"Thi prowde wordes pares²² ay;
I scholde wyn þis childe with play,²³
And þou wolde holde the still.
Swete son," þan said he,
"We are knyghtis all thre;   310
With Kyng Arthoure duelle wee,
þat houyn es on hyll."²⁴
Then said Percyuell þe lyghte,
In gayte-skynnes þat was dyghte,
"Will Kyng Arthoure make me knyghte,   315
And i come hym till?"
þan saide Sir Gawayne riȝte þare,
"I kane gyffe þe nane ansuare;
Bot to þe Kynge i rede þou ffare,
To wete his awenn will!"   320

To wete þan þe Kynges will
þare þay houen ȝitt still;
The childe hase taken hym till²⁵
For to wende hame.
And als he welke in þe wodde,   325
He sawe a full faire stode²⁶
Offe coltes and of meres²⁷ gude,
Bot neuer one was tame;
And sone saide he, "Bi Seyne John,
Swilke thyngeȝ as are ȝone   330
Rade þe knyghtes apone;
Knewe i thaire name,
Als euer mote i thryffe or thee,
The moste of ȝone²⁸ þat i see
Smertly schall bere mee   335
Till i come to my dame."

---

²² do harm.   ²³ i.e., by gentle means.   ²⁴ who has remained on the hill; i.e., in the open country.   ²⁵ set about.   ²⁶ stud.   ²⁷ mares.   ²⁸ largest of (those) yonder.

312. The commoner form is *houande*.

He saide, "When i come to my dame,
And i fynde hir at hame,
Scho will telle [me] þe name
    Off this ilke thynge."   340
The moste mere he þare see
Smertly ouerrynnes[29] he,
And saide, "Þou sall bere me
    To-morne to þe Kynge."
Kepes[30] he no sadill-gere,   345
Bot stert vp on the mere:
Hamewarde scho gun hym bere,
    Withowtten faylynge.
The lady was neuer more sore bygone:[31]
Scho wiste neuer whare to wonne,[32]   350
When scho wiste hir ȝonge sonne
    Horse hame brynge.

Scho saw hym horse hame brynge;
Scho wiste wele, by þat thynge,
Þat þe kynde wolde oute sprynge   355
    For thynge þat be moughte.[33]
Þan als sone saide þe lady,
"Þat euer solde i sorowe dry[34]
For loue of þi body,
    Þat i hafe dere boghte!   360
Dere son," saide scho hym to,
"Þou wirkeste th[is]elfe mekill vnroo;[35]
What will þou with þis mere do,
    That þou hase hame broghte?"
Bot the boye was neuer so blythe   365
Als when he herde þe name kythe
Of þe stode-mere stythe:[36]
    Of na thyng þan he roghte.

Now he calles hir a mere,
Als his moder dide ere;   370

---

[29] runs down.   [30] pays attention to.   [31] overwhelmed.   [32] dwell; i.e., knew not what to do.   [33] despite anything.   [34] suffer.   [35] unrest.   [36] hardy.

339. *Me* supplied by C.

He wened all oþer horseȝ were
And hade bene callede soo.
"Moder, at ȝonder hill hafe i bene,
Þare hafe i thre knyghtes sene,
And i hafe spoken with þam, i wene,   375
Wordes in throo;[37]
I haue highte þam all thre
Before þaire Kyng for to be:
Siche on[38] schall he make me
As is one of tho !"   380
He sware by grete Goddeȝ myȝte,
"I schall holde þat i hafe highte;
Bot-if þe Kyng make me knyghte,
To-morne i sall hym sloo !"

Bot than byspakke þe lady,   385
Þat for hir son was sary—
Hir thoghte wele þat scho myȝt dy—
And knelyde one hir knee:
"Sone, þou has takyn thi rede,
To do thiselfe to þe dede !   390
In euerilke a strange stede,
Doo als i bydde the:
To-morne es forthirmaste[39] ȝole-day,
And þou says þou will away
To make the knyghte, if þou may,   395
Als þou tolde mee.
Lyttill þou can of nurtoure:
Luke þou be of mesure[40]
Bothe in haulle and in boure,
And fonde to be fre."[41]   400

Than saide þe lady so brighte,
"There þou meteste with a knyghte,

---

[37] anger.   [38] such a one.   [39] first.   [40] moderate in conduct.   [41] try to be well-mannered.

393. Probably Christmas Day itself, although sometimes the Yule season began at the winter solstice.   It lasted about twelve days.
397. MS. *nuttoure.*

Do thi hode off, i highte,
  And haylse[42] hym in hy."
"Swete moder," sayd he then,   405
"I saw neuer ȝit no men;
If i solde a knyghte ken,
  Telles me wharby."
Scho schewede hym þe menevaire[43]—
Scho had robes in payre;[44]—   410
"Sone, þer þou sees this fare[45]
  In thaire hodes lye."
"Bi grete God," sayd he,
Where þat i a knyghte see,
Moder, as ȝe bidd me,   415
  Righte so schall i."

All þat nyȝte till it was day,
The childe by þe modir lay,
Till on þe morne he wolde away,
  For thyng[46] þat myȝte betyde.   420
Brydill hase he righte nane;
Seese he no better wane,[47]
Bot a wythe[48] hase he tane,
  And keuylles[49] his stede.
His moder gaffe hym a ryng,   425
And bad he solde agayne it bryng:
"Sonne, þis sall be oure takynnyng,[50]
  For here i sall þe byde."
He tase þe rynge and þe spere,
Stirttes vp appon þe mere: 430
Fro þe moder þat hym bere,
  Forthe gan he ryde.

---

[42] greet. [43] cloth or fur worn under helmet. [44] sets. [45] thing. [46] despite anything.
[47] means. [48] withy, willow-shoot. [49] bridles, puts a bit on. [50] sign of recognition.

406. In the early versions of the story, Perceval's fairy-mother probably
lived in a land of women, to which men did not have access. French
poets generally rationalized this detail, because it was so contrary to the
social conditions with which they were familiar; but a trace of it is preserved in this line, which contradicts l. 310, etc. See "Degaré" 865.

410. This contradicts 185 ff.; but the expression seems cognate with
in folde (32).

432. In the MS. the division of a fitte is marked here.

One his way as he gan ryde,
He fande an haulle þer besyde;
He saide, "For oghte þat may betyde,   435
    Thedir in will i."
He went in withowtten lett;
He fande a brade borde sett,
A bryghte fire, wele bett,[1]
    Brynnande þerby.   440
A mawnger[2] þer he fande,
Corne þerin lyggande;
Þerto his mere he bande
    With the withy.
He saide, "My modir bad me   445
Þat i solde of mesure bee;
Halfe þat i here see
    Styll sall it ly."

The corne he pertis[3] in two,
Gaffe his mere þe tone of þoo,   450
And to þe borde gan he goo,
    Certayne that tyde.
He fande a lofe of brede fyne
And a pychere with wyne,
A mese[4] of the kechyne,   455
    A knyfe þer besyde.
The mete þer þat he fande,
He dalte it euen with his hande,
Lefte þe halfe lyggande
    A felawe[5] to byde.   460
Þe toþer halfe ete he;
How myȝte he more of mesure be?

---

[1] kindled.   [2] manger.   [3] divides.   [4] dinner.   [5] i.e., some one else.

433. Griffith (29 and 108) gives a detailed analysis of this episode, which is here so compressed as to be almost unintelligible. Cf. Brown 125, also; he conjectures that in the original form of the story the mother advises Perceval to exchange rings with a damsel, because the mother, a fairy, knows that she can so direct him that he will secure a ring making him invulnerable.

456. A knife was the only utensil given a banqueter.

Faste he fonded to be free,
þofe he were of no pryde.[6]

þofe he were of no pryde,   465
Forthir more gan he glyde
Till a chambir þer besyde,
    Moo sellys[7] to see.
Riche clothes fande he sprede,
A lady slepande on a bedde;   470
He said, "Forsothe, a tokyn to wedde[8]
    Sall þou lefe with mee."
þer he kyste þat swete thynge;
Of hir fynger he tuke a rynge;
His awenn modir takynnynge[9]   475
    He lefte with þat fre.
He went forthe to his mere,
Tuke with hym his schorte spere,
Lepe on lofte, as he was ere;
    His way rydes he.   480

Now on his way rydes he,
Moo selles to see;
A knyghte wolde he nedis bee,
    Withowtten any bade.
He come þer þe Kyng was,   485
Seruede of þe firste mese:[10]
To hym was þe maste has[11]
    þat þe childe hade;
And þare made he no lett
At ȝate, dore, ne wykett,   490
Bot in graythely[12] he gett—
    Syche maistres he made.[13]
At his firste in-comynge,
His mere, withowtten faylynge,

---

[6] tried to be mannerly, though not out of pride.   [7] wonders.   [8] as a pledge.
[9] mother's token.   [10] course.   [11] greatest purpose; i.e., fixed intention.
[12] readily.   [13] violence he did.

490. For the wicket, cf. Int. III.A.1.
493. Riding a steed into the hall is a common incident in romance.
Cf. Child's notes, II.510; III.508.

Kyste þe forheuede of þe Kynge—   495
So nerehande he rade!

The Kyng had ferly þaa,
And vp his hande gan he taa
And putt it forthir hym fraa,
   The mouthe of the mere.   500
He saide, "Faire childe and free,
Stonde still besyde mee,
And tell me wythen[14] þat þou bee,
   And what þou will here."
Than saide þe fole of þe filde,   505
"I ame myn awnn modirs childe,
Comen fro þe woddeȝ wylde
   Till Arthure the dere.[15]
ȝisterday saw i knyghtis three:
Siche on sall þou make mee   510
On þis mere byfor the,
   Thi mete or þou schere!"[16]

Bot þan spak Sir Gawayne,
Was þe Kynges trenchepayne,
Said, "Forsothe, is noȝte to layne,   515
   I am one of thaa.
Childe, hafe þou my blyssyng
For þi feres folowynge![17]
Here hase þou fonden þe Kynge
   Þat kan þe knyghte maa."   520
Than sayde Percyuell þe free,
"And this Arthure þe Kyng bee,
Luke he a knyghte make mee:
   I rede[18] at it be swaa!"
Þofe he vnborely[19] were dyghte,   525
He sware by mekill Goddes myȝte:
"Bot if þe Kyng make me knyghte,
   I sall hym here slaa!"

---

[14] whence.   [15] great.   [16] cut.   [17] following thy fellows.   [18] i.e., demand.   [19] meanly.

514. Cutter of trenchers. (See Int. III.B.) This was as much an art and duty for the accomplished gentleman as carving.

All þat þer weren, olde and ȝynge,
Hadden ferly[20] of þe Kyng,   530
Þat he wolde suffre siche a thyng
    Of þat foull wyghte
On horse houande[21] hym by.
The Kyng byholdeȝ hym on hy;
Than wexe he sone sory   535
    When he sawe þat syghte.
The teres oute of his eghne glade:
Neuer one anoþer habade.[22]
"Allas," he sayde, "þat i was made,
    Be day or by nyghte,   540
One lyue i scholde after hym[23] bee
Þat me thynke lyke the:
Þou arte so semely to see,
    And þou were wele dighte !"

He saide, "And þou were wele dighte,   545
Þou were lyke to a knyghte
Þat i louede with all my myghte
    Whills he was one lyue.
So wele wroghte he my will
In all manere of skill,   550
I gaffe my syster hym till,
    For to be his wyfe.
He es moste in my mane;[24]
Fiftene ȝere es it gane,
Sen a theffe hade hym slane   555
    Abowte a littill stryffe ![25]
Sythen hafe i euer bene his fo,
For to wayte[26] hym with wo;
Bot i myȝte hym neuer slo,
    His craftes are so ryfe."   560

He sayse, "His craftes are so ryfe,
Þer is no man apon lyfe,
With swerde, spere, ne with knyfe
    May stroye[27] hym allan,

---

[20] wonder. [21] staying. [22] one did not wait for another. [23] that I should survive him
(Perceval's father). [24] remembrance. [25] disagreement. [26] afflict. [27] destroy.

Bot if it were Sir Percyuell son,   565
Whoso wiste where he ware done![28]
The bokes says þat he mon
    Venge his fader bane."
The childe thoghte he longe bade
Þat he ne ware a knyghte made,   570
For he wiste neuer þat he hade
    A ffader to be slayne;
The lesse was his menynge.[29]
He saide sone to þe Kynge,
"Sir, late be thi iangleynge![30]   575
    Of this kepe i nane."[31]

He sais, "I kepe not to stande
With thi iangleyn[ge]s to[32] lange;
Make me knyghte with thi hande,
    If it sall be done!"   580
Than þe Kyng hym hendly highte
Þat he schold dub hym to knyghte,
With-thi-þat[33] he wolde doun lighte
    And ete with hym at none.
The Kyng biholdeȝ þe vesage free,   585
And euer more trowed hee
Þat þe childe scholde bee
    Sir Percyuell son:
It ran in the Kynges mode,
His syster Acheflour þe gude—   590
How scho went into þe wodde
    With hym for to wonn.

The childe hadde wonnede in þe wodde:
He knewe noþer euyll ne gude;
The Kynge hymselfe vnderstode   595
    He was a wilde man.

---

[28] put; i.e., is. [29] grief, moaning. [30] rambling talk. [31] to this pay I no heed.
[32] too. [33] provided.

567. Possibly a relic of an older version in which the son is fated to slay the father's enemy. Cf. Brown, and cf. also the prophetic passages in "King Horn" and "Havelok."
578. MS. *iangleyns*.

So faire he spakke hym withall,
'He lyghtes doun in he haulle,
Bonde his mere amonge þam alle,
And to þe borde wann.   600
Bot are he myghte bygynn
To þe mete for to wynn,
So commes þe Rede Knyghte in
Emangeȝ[34] þam righte þan,
Prekande one a rede stede;   605
Blode-rede was his wede.
He made þam gammen full gnede,[35]
With crafteȝ[36] þat he can.

With his craftes gan he calle,
And callede þam recrayhandes[37] all,   610
Kynge, knyghtes within walle,
At þe bordes þer þay bade.
Full felly þe coupe[38] he fett,
Bifore þe Kynge þat was sett;
Þer was no man þat durste hym lett,   615
Þofe þat he were ffadde.[39]
The couppe was filled full of wyne;
He dranke of þat þat was þerinn.
All of rede golde fyne
Was þe couppe made.   620
He tuke it vp in his hande,
Þe coupe that he there fande,
And lefte þam all sittande,
And fro þam he rade.

---

[34] amongst. [35] sorry sport. [36] arts, spells. [37] traitors, cowards. [38] fiercely the cup. [39] bold.

605. The Red Knight seems to be an enchanter. His red armor, etc., are common marks of the supernatural being. Every one is put under a spell that prevents his resisting the knight. Cf. *Rev. Celt.* 22.36.

611. MS. *in with.*

613. Brown and Loomis think the cup very important, in spite of its suppression here. It is some sort of talisman, without which Arthur's realm cannot prosper.

Now fro þam he rade, 625
Als he says þat þis made:[40]
The sorowe þat þe Kynge hade
  Mighte no tonge tell.
"A! dere God," said þe Kyng þan,
"Þat all this wyde werlde wan, 630
Whethir i sall euer hafe þat man
  May make ȝone fende duelle?
Fyve ȝeres hase he þus gane,
And my coupes fro me tane,
And my gude knyghte slayne, 635
  Men calde Sir Percyuell;
Sythen taken hase he three,
And ay awaye will he bee,
Or i may harnayse[41] me
  In felde hym to felle." 640

"Petir!"[42] quod Percyuell þe ȝynge,
"Hym þan wil [i] down dynge
And þe coupe agayne brynge,
  And þou will make me knyghte."
"Als i am trewe kyng," said he, 645
"A knyghte sall i make the,
Forthi þou will brynge mee
  The coupe of golde bryghte."
Vp ryses Sir Arthoure,
Went to a chamboure 650
To feche doun armoure,
  Þe childe in to dyghte;
Bot are it was doun caste,[43]

---

[40] i.e., the poet's original. [41] arm. [42] by St. Peter! [43] i.e., taken from the hooks.

633. Campion emended to *fyftene*. The other versions do not help in establishing the right reading; but it seems that the knight takes a cup every fifth year (637); and the poet may have confused this with the fifteen-year period elapsing after the death of Perceval's father. Cf. Griffith 49.n.1.

653. The construction *are . . . ere*, the second correlative being redundant, is fairly common.

Ere was Percyuell paste,
And on his⁴⁴ way folowed faste   655
Þat he solde with fyghte.

Wi[t]h his foo for to fighte,
None oþergates⁴⁵ was he dighte,
Bot in thre gayt-skynnes righte,
    A fole als he ware.   660

He cryed, "How,⁴⁶ man on thi mere!
Bryng agayne þe Kynges gere,
Or with my dart i sall þe fere⁴⁷
    And make þe vnfere!"⁴⁸
And after þe Rede Knyghte he rade,   665
Baldely, withowtten bade:
Sayd, "A knyght i sall be made
    For som of thi gere."
He sware by mekill Godde₃ payne,
"Bot if þou brynge þe coupe agayne,   670
With my dart þou sall be slayne
    And slongen of thi mere."
The knyghte byhaldes hym in throo,⁴⁹
Calde hym fole þat was hys foo,
For he named hym soo—   675
    Þe stede þat hym bere.

And for to see hym with syghte,
He putt his vmbrere¹ on highte,
To byhalde how he was dyghte
    Þat so till hym spake;   680
He sayde, "Come i to the, appert² fole,
I sall caste þe in þe pole,
For all þe heghe days of ₃ole,
    Als ane olde sakke."

---

⁴⁴ i.e., the Red Knight's.   ⁴⁵ otherwise.   ⁴⁶ stop.   ⁴⁷ terrify.   ⁴⁸ infirm.   ⁴⁹ anger.
¹ visor.   ² impudent.

682. Apparently a common way of disposing of dead wretches was to throw them into marshes and pools; cf. "Havelok" 2110.

683. The Yule-season lasted about twelve days, and during this period all fighting was forbidden. See Brand, on Yule.

Than sayd Percyuell þe free, 685
"Be i fole, or whatte i bee,
Now sone of þat sall wee see
Whose browes schall blakke."³
Of schottyng was þe child slee:⁴
At þe knyghte lete he flee, 690
Smote hym in at þe eghe
And oute at þe nakke.

For þe dynt þat he tuke,
Oute of sadill he schoke,⁵
Whoso þe sothe will luke,⁶ 695
And þer was he slayne.
He falles down one þe hill;
His stede rynnes whare he will.
Þan saide Percyuell hym till,
"Þou art a lethir swayne."⁷ 700
Then saide þe childe in þat tyde,
"And þou woldeste me here byde,
After þi mere scholde i ryde
And brynge hir agayne:
Þen myȝte we bothe with myȝte 705
Menskfully⁸ togedir fyghte,
Ayther of vs, as he were a knyghte,
Till tyme þe tone ware slayne."

Now es þe Rede Knyghte slayne,
Lefte dede in the playne; 710
The childe gon his mere mayne⁹
After þe stede.
Þe stede was swifter þan þe mere,
For he hade no thynge to bere
Bot his sadill and his gere, 715
Fro hym þofe he ȝede.
The mere was bagged with fole;¹⁰
And hirselfe a grete bole;¹¹

---

³ grow pale. ⁴ the boy was skillful at casting at a mark. ⁵ tumbled. ⁶ examine; i.e., in truth. ⁷ evil knave. ⁸ honorably; i.e., as befits us. ⁹ ride. ¹⁰ heavy with foal. ¹¹ i.e., swelled.

716. I.e., "Though he was being pursued;" but possibly þofe = þaa.

For to rynne scho myȝte not thole,[12]
Ne folowe hym no spede.   720
The childe saw þat it was soo,
And till his fete he gan hym too;
The gates þat he scholde goo
Made he full gnede.[13]

The gates made he full gnede   725
In þe waye þer he ȝede;
With strenght tuke he þe stede
And broghte to þe knyghte.
"Me thynke," he sayde, "þou arte fele[14]
Þat þou ne will away stele;   730
Now i houppe þat þou will dele
Strokes appon hyghte.[15]
I hafe broghte to the thi mere
And mekill of thyn oþer gere;
Lepe on hir, as þou was ere,   735
And þou will more fighte !"
The knyghte lay still in þe stede:
What sulde he say, when he was dede?
The childe couthe no better rede,
Bot down gun he lyghte.   740

Now es Percyuoll lyghte
To vnspoyle[16] þe Rede Knyghte,
Bot he ne couthe neuer fynd righte
The lacynge of his wede;
He was armede so wele   745
In gude iryn and in stele,
He couthe not gett of[17] a dele,
For nonkyns nede.

_____
[12] bear.   [13] stingy; i.e., took no extra steps, ran straight.   [14] trusty.   [15] i.e.,
from on horseback.   [16] despoil.   [17] off.

720. too, for taa; take, get.
738. Cf. "Ogier de Danemarche" 8474.   The dead men on the walls are
addressed by Charlemagne: Cil sont tot qoi qe nus n'a mot soné: Com
parlera qi ne puet ne ne set?

He sayd, "My moder bad me,
When my dart solde broken be,   750
Owte of þe iren bren þe tree:[18]
   Now es me fyre gnede."[19]
Now he getis hym flynt,
His fyre-iren[20] he hent,
And þen, withowtten any stynt,   755
   He kyndilt a glede.[21]

Now he kyndils a glede:
Amonge þe buskes[22] he ȝede
And gedirs, full gude spede,
   Wodde, a fyre to make.   760
A grete fyre made he þan,
The Rede Knyghte in to bren,
For he ne couthe nott ken
   His gere off to take.
Be þan was Sir Gawayne dyght,   765
Folowede after þe fyghte
Betwene hym and þe Rede Knyghte,
   For þe childes sake.
He fande þe Rede Knyght lyggand,
Slayne of Percyuell hande,   770
Besyde a fyre brynnande
   Off byrke and of akke.[23]

Þer brent of birke and of ake
Gret brandes and blake.[24]
"What wylt þou with this fyre make?"   775
   Sayd Gawayne hym till.
"Petir!" quod Percyuell then,
"And i myghte hym þus ken,[25]
Out of his iren i wòlde hym bren
   Righte here on this hill."   780
Bot þen sayd Sir Gawayne,
"The Rede Knyghte for þou has slayne,
I sall vnarme hym agayne,
   And þou will holde þe still."

---

[18] burn the wood out of the iron (head). [19] lacking. [20] steel, to strike on flint.
[21] fire of coals. [22] bushes. [23] birch and oak. [24] charred. [25] i.e., get to see.

Þan Sir Gawayn doun lyghte,   785
Vnlacede þe Rede Knyghte;
The childe in his armour dight
    At his awnn will.

When he was dighte in his atire,
He tase þe knyghte bi þe swire,[26]   790
Keste hym reghte in the fyre,
    Þe brandes to balde.[27]
Bot þen said Percyuell on bost,
"Ly still þerin now and roste!
I kepe nothynge of þi coste,[28]   795
    Ne noghte of thi spalde!"[29]
The knyghte lygges þer on brede;[30]
The childe es dighte in his wede,
And lepe vp apon his stede,
    Als hymselfe wolde.   800
He luked doun to his fete,
Saw his gere faire and mete:
"For a knyghte i may be lete[31]
    And myghte be calde."

Then sayd Sir Gawayn hym till,   805
"Goo we faste fro this hill!
Þou hase done what þou will;
    It neghes nere nyghte."
"What! trowes þou," quod Percyuell þe ȝynge,
"Þat i will agayn brynge   810
Vntill Arthoure þe Kynge
    Þe golde þat es bryghte?
Nay, so mote i thryfe or thee,
I am als grete a lorde als he;
To-day ne schall he make me   815
    None oþer gates[32] knyghte.
Take þe coupe in thy hande
And mak þiselfe þe presande,[33]

---

[26] neck. [27] embolden; i.e., replenish. [28] care nothing for your (evil) ways.
[29] shoulder; i.e., strength of arm. [30] sprawling. [31] may pass. [32] in any other
wise. [33] presentation.

For i will forthire into þe lande,
Are i doun lyghte." 820

Nowþer wolde he doun lyghte,
Ne he wolde wende with þe knyght,
Bot rydes forthe all þe nyghte:
So prowde was he than.
Till on þe morne at forthe dayes,[34] 825
He mett a wyche, as men says;
His horse and his harnays
Couthe scho wele ken.
Scho wende þat it hade bene
Þe Rede Knyghte þat scho hade sene, 830
Was wonnt in þose armes to bene,
To gerre þe stede rynne.
In haste scho come hym agayne,
Sayde, "It is not to layne,
Men tolde me þat þou was slayne 835
With Arthours men.

Ther come one of my men:
Till ʒonder hill he gan me kenne,[35]
There þou sees þe fyre brene,
And sayde þat þou was thare." 840
Euer satt Percyuell stone-still,
And spakke no thynge hir till
Till scho hade sayde all hir will,
And spakke lesse ne mare.[36]
"At ʒondere hill hafe i bene: 845
Nothynge hafe i there sene
Bot gayte-skynnes, i wene—
Siche ill-farande fare.[37]
Mi sone, and þou ware thare slayne
And thyn armes of drawen, 850

---

[34] late in the morning. [35] show. [36] i.e., neither less nor more. [37] poor stuff.

826. On the witch, see Griffith, Ch. III. By healing him after a disastrous encounter, she prevents the enchanter's enemies from vanquishing him.

I couthe hele the agayne
Als wele als þou was are."

Than wist Percyuell by thatt,
It seruede hym of somwhatt,[38]
The wylde[39] fyre þat he gatt 855
When þe knyghte was slayne;
And righte so wolde he, thare
Þat þe olde wiche ware.
Oppon his spere he hir bare
To þe fyre agayne; 860
In ill wrethe[40] and in grete,
He keste þe wiche in þe hete;
He sayde, "Ly still and swete[41]
Bi þi son, þat lyther[42] swayne !"
Thus he leues thaym twoo, 865
And on his gates gan he goo:
Siche dedis to do moo
Was þe childe fayne.

Als he come by a wodd-syde,
He sawe ten men ryde; 870
He said, "For oughte þat may betyde,
To þam will i me."[43]
When þose ten saw hym bare,
Þay wende þe Rede Knyghte it ware,
Þat wolde þam all forfare, 875
And faste gan þay flee;
For he was sogates[44] cledde,
Alle belyffe fro hym þay fledde;
And euer þe faster þat þay spedde,
The swiftlyere sewed[45] hee, 880
Till he was warre of a knyghte,
And of þe menevaire[46] he had syght;
He put vp his vmbrere[47] on hight,
And said, "Sir, God luke[48] thee !"

---

[38] was of some use. [39] fierce, great. [40] raging anger. [41] sweat. [42] evil.
[43] will I [hie] me. [44] in such wise. [45] followed. [46] helm-lining. [47] visor.
[48] may God be propitious.

The childe sayde, "God luke þe!" 885
The knyght said, "Now wele þe be!
A, lorde Godd, now wele es mee
    þat euer was i made!"
For by þe vesage hym thoghte
The Rede Knyȝte was it noȝte, 890
þat hade them all bysoughte;[49]
    And baldely he bade.[50]
It semede wele bi þe syghte
þat he had slayne þe Rede Knyȝt:
In his armes was he dighte, 895
    And on his stede rade.
"Son," sayde þe knyghte tho,
And thankede þe childe full thro,[1]
"þou hase slayne þe moste foo
    þat euer ȝitt i hade." 900

Then sayde Percyuell þe free,
"Wherefore fledde ȝee
Lange are, when ȝe sawe mee
    Come rydande ȝow by?"
Bot þan spake þe olde knyghte, 905
þat was paste out of myghte
With any man for to fyghte:
    He ansuerde in hy;
He sayde, "Theis children nyne,
All are þay sonnes myne. 910
For ferde or[2] i solde þam tyne,[3]
    þerfore fledd i.
We wende wele þat it had bene
þe Rede Knyȝte þat we hade sene;
He walde hafe slayne vs bydene, 915
    Withowtten mercy.

Withowtten any mercy
He wolde hafe slayne vs in hy;

---

[49] searched for. [50] stopped, waited. [1] effusively. [2] fear that. [3] lose.

To my sonnes he hade envy
  Moste of any men.   920
Fiftene ȝeres es it gane
Syn he my brodire hade slane;
Now hadde þe þeefe vndirtane
  To sla vs all then:
He was ferd lesse[4] my sonnes sold hym slo   925
When þay ware eldare and moo,[5]
And þat þay solde take hym for þaire foo
  Where þay myȝte hym ken;
Hade i bene in the stede
þer he was done to þe dede,   930
I solde neuer hafe etyn brede
  Are i hade sene hym bren."

"Petir!" quod Percyuell, "he es brende:
I haffe spedde better þan i wend
Euer at þe laste ende."   935
  The blythere wexe þe knyghte;
By his haulle þaire gates felle,[6]
And ȝerne he prayed Percyuell
þat he solde þer with hym duelle
  And be þer all þat nyghte.   940
Full wele he couthe a geste calle;[7]
He broghte þe childe into þe haulle;
So faire he spake hym withalle
  That he es doun lyghte;
His stede es in stable sett   945
And hymselfe to þe haulle fett,
And þan, withowtten any lett,
  To þe mette þay þam dighte.

Mete and drynke was þer dighte,
And men to serue þam full ryghte;   950
þe childe þat come with þe knyghte,
  Enoghe þer he fande.

---

[4] afraid lest. [5] i.e., larger. [6] way lay. [7] invite a guest.

920. In other versions and similar stories, the sons are under an enchantment which dooms them to fight every day against the enchanter.

At þe mete as þay beste satte,[8]
Come þe portere fro þe ȝate,
Saide a man was þeratte　　　　　955
　　Of þe Maydenlande;
Saide, "Sir, he prayes the
Off mete and drynke, for charyté;
For a messagere es he
　　And may nott lange stande."　　　　960
The knyght badde late hym inn,
"For," he sayde, "it es no synn,
The man þat may þe mete wynn[9]
　　To gyffe þe trauellande."

Now þe trauellande man　　　　　965
The portere lete in þan;
He haylsede[10] þe knyghte as he can,
　　Als he satt on dese.
The knyghte askede hym þare
Whase man þat he ware,　　　　　970
And how ferre þat he walde so fare,
　　Withowtten any lese.[11]
He saide, "I come fro þe Lady Lufamour,
Þat sendes me to Kyng Arthoure,
And prayes hym, for his honoure,　　975
　　Hir sorowes for to sesse.[12]
Vp resyn es a sowdane:
Alle hir landes hase he tane;
So byseges he that woman
　　That scho may hafe no pese."　　980

He sayse þat scho may haue no pese,
The lady, for hir fayrenes,
And for hir mekill reches.
　　"He wirkes hir full woo;

---

[8] when the feast was at its height.　[9] i.e., for one who has food.　[10] greeted.
[11] lie.　[12] put an end to.

956. Cf. note to 406.　On fairy countries inhabited only by women,
see Brown's "Iwain" 30 ff.

He dose hir sorow all hir sythe,[13]   985
And all he slaes doun rythe;[14]
He wolde haue hir to wyfe,
    And scho will noȝte soo.
Now hase þat ilke sowdane
Hir fadir and hir eme[15] slane,   990
And hir brethir[16] ilkane,
    And is hir moste foo.
So nere he hase hir now soughte[17]
þat till a castelle es scho broghte,
And fro þe walles will he noghte,   995
    Ere þat he may hir too.[18]

The sowdane sayse he will hir ta;
The lady will hirselfe sla
Are he, þat es hir maste fa,
    Solde wedde hir to wyfe.   1000
Now es þe sowdan so wyghte,
Alle he slaes doun ryghte:
þer may no man with hym fyghte,
    Bot he were kempe ryfe."[19]
þan sayde Percyuell, "I þe praye,   1005
þat þou wolde teche me þe waye
Thedir, als þe gates laye,[20]
    Withowtten any stryfe;
Mighte i mete with þat sowdan
þat so dose to þat woman,   1010
Alsone he solde be slane,
    And i myȝte hafe þe lyfe !"[21]

The messangere prayed hym mare[22]
þat he wolde duell still þare:
"For i will to þe Kynge fare,   1015
    Myne erandeȝ for to say."
"For þen mekill sorowe me betyde,
And i lenger here habyde,

---

[13] time; i.e., days. [14] straight. [15] uncle. [16] (plural). [17] closely has he pursued her. [18] take. [19] renowned warrior. [20] the roads lie. [21] if I may live (to do it). [22] rather.

Bot ryghte now will i ryde,
Als so faste als i may."   1020
[T]he knyghte herde hym say so;
3erne he prayes hym to too
His nyne sonnes, with hym to goo;
He nykkes²³ hym with nay.
Bot so faire spekes he   1025
þat he takes of þam three,
In his felawchipe to be—
The blythere were þay.

þay ware blythe of þer bade,²⁴
Busked þam and forthe rade;   1030
Mekill myrthes þay made:
Bot lyttill it amende.²⁵
He was paste bot a while—
The montenance of a myle²⁶—
He was bythoghte of a gyle²⁷   1035
Wele werse þan þay wende.
þofe þay ware of þaire fare fayne,
Forthwarde²⁸ was þaire cheftayne;
Euer he sende one agayne
At ilke a myle ende,   1040
Vntill þay ware alle gane;
þan he rydes hym allane
Als he ware sprongen of a stane,
þare na man hym kende,

For he walde none sold hym ken.   1045
Forthe ryde3 he then,

---

²³ refuses.   ²⁴ these tidings.   ²⁵ did good.   ²⁶ space of a mile.   ²⁷ trick.
²⁸ ahead.

1029. þer for þir, these.
1039. Probably this was done so that the hero could encounter the enemy unaided—the only terms on which success was possible. Cf. Maelduin's troubles in numbering his crew, and the breaking of the charm by foster brothers who insist on accompanying him (*Rev. Celt.* 9.447, 10.50). The precise number is not always known, and the hero must discover it by chance.
1043. Cf. note on "King Horn" 1025.

Amange3 vncouthe men
   His maystres[29] to make.
Now hase Percyuell in throo[30]
Spoken with his emes twoo,   1050
Bot neuer one of thoo
   Took his knawlage.[31]
Now in his way es he sett
Þat may hym lede, withowtten lett,
Þare he and þe sowdan sall mete,   1055
   His browes to blake.[32]
Late we Percyuell þe 3ynge
Fare in Goddes blyssynge,
And vntill Arthoure þe Kynge
   Will we agayne take.   1060

The gates agayne we will tane;
The Kyng to care-bedd es gane;
For mournynge es his maste mane:[33]
   He syghes full sore.
His wo es wansome[34] to wreke,   1065
His hert es bownn for to breke,
For he wend neuer to speke
   With Percyuell no more.
Als he was layde for to ly,[35]
Come þe messangere on hy   1070
With lettres fro þe lady,
   And schewes þam righte þare.
Afote my3te þe Kyng no3t stande,
Bot rede þam þare lyggande,
And sayde, "Of thyne erande   1075
   Thou hase thyn answare."

---

[29] deeds of valor.   [30] haste, a short time.   [31] recognised him.   [32] make pale.
[33] his greatest lament is mourning (for one dead).   [34] wretched; i.e., so great
as to be hard to avenge.   [35] was put to bed preparatory to lying ill.

1050. Cf. 23, 922.
1062. The king's illness may be an enchantment. (Cf. Brown 127;
"The Debility of the Ultonian Warriors"; *Romania* 40.628.)   The phrase
occurs in the ballad "Sir Cawline."

He sayde, "Þou wote thyne ansuare:
The mane þat es seke and sare,
He may full ill ferre fare
  In felde for to fyghte."   1080
The messangere made his mone:
Saide, "Wo worthe wikkede wone![36]
Why ne hade i tournede and gone
  Agayne with the knyghte?"
"What knyghte es þat," said þe Kyng,   1085
"Þat þou mase of thy menynge?
In my londe wot i no lordyng
  Es worthy to be a knyghte."
The messangere ansuerd agayne,
"Wete ȝe, his name es for to layne,   1090
Þe whethir[37] i wolde hafe weten fayne
  What þe childe highte.

Thus mekill gatt i of þat knyght:
His dame[38] sonne, he said, he hight.
One what maner þat he was dight   1095
  Now i sall ȝow telle:
He was wighte and worthly,[39]
His body bolde and borely,[40]
His armour bryghte and blody—
  Hade bene late in batell;   1100
Blode-rede was his stede,
His akton[41] and his oþer wede;
His cote of þe same hede[42]
  Þat till a knyghte felle."
Than comanded þe Kyng   1105
Horse and armes for to brynge:
"If i kan trow thi talkynge,
  That ilke was Percyuell."

---

[36] woe befall unwise conduct.   [37] although.   [38] mother's.   [39] fine.   [40] goodly.
[41] jacket.   [42] quality.

1105. The mere mention of Perceval seems enough to dissolve the enchantment.   On the incident, cf. Griffith 82; Wimberly 345.   On the magic of names, see bibliography and E. Clodd's *Tom Tit Tot* 169.

For þe luffe of Percyuell,
To horse and armes þay felle;   1110
Þay wolde no lengare þer duelle:
    To fare ware þay fayne.
Faste forthe gan þay fare;
Þay were aferde full sare,
Ere þay come whare he ware,   1115
    Þe childe wolde be slayne.
The Kyng tase with hym knyghtis thre:
The ferthe wolde hymselfe be;
Now so faste rydes hee,
    May folowe hym no swayne.   1120
The Kyng es now in his waye;
Lete hym come when he maye!
And i will forthir in my playe[43]
    To Percyuell agayne.

Go we to Percyuell agayne!   1125
The childe paste oute on þe playne,
Ouer more[44] and mountayne,
    To þe Maydenlande;
Till agayne þe euen-tyde,
Bolde bodys[45] sawe he byde,   1130
Pauelouns[46] mekill and vnryde[47]
    Aboute a cyte stonde.
On huntyng was þe sowdane;
He lefte men many ane:
Twenty score þat wele kan,   1135
    Be þe ȝates ȝemande—
Ell[even] score one the nyghte,
And ten one þe daye-lighte,
Wele armyde at alle righte,[48]
    With wapyns in hande.   1140

---

[43] performance, narration.   [44] moor.   [45] fellows.   [46] tents, temporary shelters.
[47] ugly.   [48] particulars.

1127. The fairy world always has barriers.   Cf. the dangerous pass in
"Iwain;" the ford in "Eger;" the island in "Launfal;" the cave in "Orfeo."

With þaire wapyns in þaire hande,
There will þay fight þer þay stande,
Sittande and lyggande,
    Elleuen score of men.
In he rydes one a rase,⁴⁹   1145
Or þat he wiste where he was,
Into þe thikkeste of þe prese
    Amanges þam thanne.
And vp stirt one þat was bolde,
Bygane his brydill to holde,   1150
And askede whedire⁵⁰ þat he wolde
    Make his horse to rynne.
He said, "I ame hedir come
For to see a sowdane;
In faythe, righte sone he sall be slane,   1155
    And i myghte hym ken.

If i hym oghte ken may,
To-morne, when it es lighte daye,
Then sall we togedir playe
    With wapyns vnryde."   1160
They herde þat he had vndirtane
For to sle þaire sowdane;
Thay felle aboute hym, euerilkane,
    To make þat bolde¹ habyde.
The childe sawe þat he was fade,²   1165
Þe body þat his bridill hade:
Euen ouer hym he rade,
    In gate þere bisyde.
He stayred³ about hym with his spere;
Many thurgh gane he bere:⁴   1170
Þer was none þat myȝt hym dere,
    Perceuell, þat tyde.

Tide in townne who will telle,⁵
Folkes vndir his fete felle;

---

⁴⁹ rush.   ⁵⁰ whither.   ¹ brave (knight).   ² determined.   ³ thrust.   ⁴ strike.
⁵ whoever would tell in town (i.e., anywhere) the course of events (would say), etc.

The bolde body Perceuelle,   1175
 He sped, þam to spill.
Hym thoghte no spede at his spere:
Many thurgh gane he bere,
Fonde folke in the here,[6]
 Feghtyng to fill.[7]   1180
Fro that it was mydnyghte
Till it was euen[8] at daye-lighte,
Were þay neuer so wilde ne wighte,
 He wroghte at his will.
Thus he dalt with his brande,[9]   1185
There was none þat myght hym stande
Halfe a dynt of his hande
 Þat he stroke till.[10]

Now he strykes for þe nonys,
Made þe Sarazenes hede-bones   1190
Hoppe als dose hayle-stones
 Abowtte one þe gres;[11]
Thus he dalt þam on rawe[12]
Till þe daye gun dawe:[13]
He layd þaire lyues full law,   1195
 Als many als there was.
When he hade slayne so many men,
IIe was so wery by thon,
I tell ȝow for certen,
 He roghte wele þe lesse   1200
Awþer of lyfe or of dede,
To medis þat he were[14] in a stede
Þar he myghte riste hym in thede[15]
 A stownde in sekirnes.[16]

Now fonde he no sekirnes,   1205
Bot vnder þe walle þer he was,
A faire place he hym chese,
 And down there he lighte.

---

[6] foolish folk of the enemy.   [7] to (his own) fill.   [8] just.   [9] dealt (blows) with his sword.   [10] upon.   [11] grass.   [12] in turn.   [13] dawn.   [14] if only he could be in the midst of.   [15] people; i.e., there.   [16] security.

He laide hym doun in þat tyde;
His stede stode hym besyde: 1210
The fole was fayne for to byde—
  Was wery for þe fyght.
Till one þe morne þat it was day,
The wayte[17] appon þe walle lay:
He sawe an vggly play[18]   1215
  In þe place dighte;
3itt was þer more ferly:[19]
Ther was no qwyk man left þerby;
Thay called vp þe lady
  For to see þat sighte.   1220

Now commes þe lady to þat sight,
The Lady Lufamour, þe bright;
Scho clambe vp to þe walle on hight
  Full faste scho behelde;
Hedes and helmys þer was   1225
(I tell 3ow withowtten lese),
Many layde one þe gresse,
  And many brode schelde.
Grete ferly thaym thoghte
Who þat wondir[20] had wroghte,   1230
That had þam to dede broghte,
  That folke in the felde,
And wold come none innermare[21]
For to kythe what he ware,
And[22] wist þe lady was þare,   1235
  Thaire warysoune[23] to 3elde.

Scho wold þaire warysone 3elde:
Full faste forthe þay bihelde
If þay myghte fynde in þe felde

---

[17] sentinel, watcher.   [18] performance; i.e., sight.   [19] marvel.   [20] destruction.
[21] no further within (the castle).   [22] even though he.   [23] reward.

1224. Holthausen's emendation for MS. *to beholde.*
1228. MS. *schelde brode.*

Who hade done þat dede.   1240
Þay luked vndir þair hande,[24]
Sawe a mekill horse stande,
A blody knyghte liggande
    By a rede stede.
Then said þe lady so brighte,   1245
"Ʒondir ligges a knyghte
Þat hase bene in þe fighte,
    If i kane righte rede;
Owthir es ʒone man slane,
Or he slepis hym allane,   1250
Or he in batelle es tane,
    For blody are his wede."

Scho says, "Blody are his wede,
And so es his riche stede;
Siche a knyght in this thede   1255
    Saw i neuer nane.
What-so he es, and he maye ryse,
He es large there he lyse,
And wele made in alle wyse,
    Ther als man sall be tane."[25]   1260
Scho calde appon hir chaymbirlayne,
Was called hende Hatlayne—
The curtasye of Wawayne
    He weldis in wane;[26]—
Scho badd hym, "Wende and see   1265
Ʒif ʒon man on lyfe be.
Bid hym com and speke with me,
    And pray hym als þou kane."

Now to pray hym als he kane,
Vndir þe wallis he wane;   1270
Warly[27] wakend he þat mane:
    Þe horse stode still.

---

[24] i.e., just below.   [25] in which a man is judged.   [26] manners.   [27] cautiously.

1262. *Hatlayne* possibly from *chatelain*, the governor or chief-of-staff in a castle.—Holthausen.

Als it was tolde vnto me,
He knelid down on his kne;
Hendely hailsed[28] he þat fre,   1275
   And sone said hym till,
"My lady, lele[29] Lufamour,
Habyddis the in hir chambour,
Prayes the, for thyn honour,
   To come, ʒif ʒe will."   1280
So kyndly takes he þat kyth[30]
Þat vp he rose and went hym wyth,
The man þat was of myche pyth,[31]
   Hir prayer to fulfill.

Now hir prayer to fulfill,   1285
He folowed þe gentilmans will,
And so he went hir vntill,
   Forthe to that lady.
Full blythe was þat birde[32] brighte
When scho sawe hym with syghte,   1290
For scho trowed þat he was wighte,
   And askede[33] hym in hy:
At þat fre gan scho frayne,
Þoghe he were lefe for to layne,[34]
If he wiste who had þam slayne—   1295
   Þase folkes of envy.
He sayd, "I soghte none of tho;
I come the sowdane to slo,
And þay ne wolde noghte late me go;
   Þaire lyfes there refte i."   1300

He sayd, "Belyfe þay solde aby."
And Lufamour, þat lele lady,
Wist ful wele therby
   The childe was full wighte.
The birde was blythe of þat bade[35]   1305
Þat scho siche an helpe hade:

---

[28] greeted.   [29] worthy.   [30] announcement.   [31] force.   [32] lady.   [33] questioned.
[34] desirous of dissembling.   [35] tidings.

Agayne þe sowdane was fade[36]
    With alle for to fighte.
Faste þe lady hym byhelde:
Scho thoght hym worthi to welde,[37]   1310
And he myghte wyn hir in felde,
    With maystry and myghte.
His stede þay in stabill set
And hymselfe to haulle was fet,
And than, withowtten any let,   1315
    To dyne gun thay dighte.

The childe was sett on þe dese,
And serued with reches[38]
(I tell ȝow withowtten lese)
    Þat gaynely was get[39]—   1320
In a chayere of golde
Bifore þe fayrest, to byholde
The myldeste mayden one molde,[40]
    At mete als scho satt.
Scho made hym semblande so gude,[41]   1325
Als þay felle to þaire fude—
The mayden mengede[42] his mode
    With myrthes at þe mete,—
Þat for hir sake righte tha
Sone he gane vndirta   1330
The sory sowdane to sla,
    Withowtten any lett.

He sayd, withowtten any lett,
"When þe sowdane and i bene mett,
A sadde[43] stroke i sall one hym sett,   1335
    His pride for to spyll."
Then said þe lady so free,
"Who þat may his bon[44] be
Sall hafe þis kyngdome and me,
    To welde at his will."   1340

---

[36] determined. [37] govern. [38] dainties. [39] were properly served. [40] earth. [41] looked on him so pleasantly. [42] mingled; i.e., entertained. [43] severe, hard. [44] bane, death.

He ne hade dyned bot smalle[45]
When worde come into þe haulle
Þat many men with alle
    Were hernyste[46] one the hill;
For tene[47] þaire felawes were slayne,   1345
The cité hafe þay nere tane;
The men þat were within þe wane[48]
    The comon-belle gun knylle.[49]

Now knyllyn þay þe comon-belle.
Worde come to Perceuell,   1350
And he wold there no lengere duelle,
    Bot lepe fro the dese—
Siche wilde gerys hade he mo;[50]—
Sayd, "Kynsmen, now i go.
For alle ȝone sall i slo   1355
    Longe are i sese!"
Scho kiste hym withowtten lett;
The helme on his hede scho sett;
To þe stabill full sone he gett,
    There his stede was.   1360
There were none with hym to fare;
For no man þen wolde he spare![1]—
Rydis furthe, withowtten mare,
    Till he come to þe prese.

When he come to þe prese,   1365
He rydes in one a rese;[2]
The folkes, þat byfore hym was,
    Thaire strenght[3] hade þay tone;
To kepe hym þan were þay ware;
Þaire dynttis deris hym no mare   1370
Þen whoso hade strekyn sare
    One a harde stone.
Were þay wighte, were þay woke,[4]
    Alle þat he till stroke,

---

[45] eaten but a little. [46] armed. [47] anger that. [48] stronghold. [49] did toll the alarm-bell. [50] i.e., of such impulsive ways had he very many. [1] forbear, stop. [2] rush. [3] full force. [4] weak.

He made þaire bodies to roke:[5]   1375
Was þer no better wone.[6]
I wote, he sped hym so sone
Þat day, by heghe none
With all þat folke hade he done:
One life lefte noghte one.   1380

When he had slayne all tho,
He loked forthir hym fro,
If he myghte fynde any mo
With hym for to fyghte;
And als þat hardy bihelde,   1385
He sese, ferre in the felde,
Fowre knyghtis vndir schelde
Come rydand full righte.
One was Kyng Arthour,
Anothir Ewayne, the floure,   1390
The thirde Wawayne with honoure,
And Kay, þe kene knyghte.
Perceuell saide, withowtten mare,
"To ȝondir foure will i fare;
And if the sowdane be thare,   1395
I sall holde þat i highte."

Now to holde þat he hase highte,
Agaynes thaym he rydis righte,
And ay lay the lady brighte
One þe walle, and byhelde   1400
How many men þat he had slane,
And sythen gane his stede mayne[7]
Foure kempys[8] agayne,
Forthir in the felde.

---

[5] fall back.   [6] manner; i.e., fate.   [7] ride.   [8] warriors.

1380. MS. lefe.
1387. I.e., in armor.   A knight frequently removed his armor when riding on a peaceful mission.
1390. For Ewayne fitz-Asoure, as in 261?   The sequence of rhymes is much the same.

Then was the lady full wo 1405
When scho sawe hym go
Agaynes foure knyghtys tho,
    With schafte and with schelde.
They were so mekyl and vnryde[9]
Þat wele wende scho þat tyde 1410
With bale þay solde gare hym byde
    Þat was hir beste belde.[10]

Þofe he were beste of hir belde,
As þat lady byhelde,
He rydes forthe in þe felde, 1415
    Euen[11] þam agayne.
Then sayd Arthoure þe Kyng,
"I se a bolde knyghte owt spryng;
For to seke feghtyng,
    Forthe will he frayne. 1420
If he fare forthe to fighte
And we foure kempys agayne one knyght,
Littill menske[12] wold to vs lighte
    If he were sone slayne."
They fore forthward right faste, 1425
And sone keuells[13] did þay caste,
And euyr fell it to frayste[14]
    Vntill Sir Wawayne.

When it felle to Sir Wawayne
To ryde Perceuell agayne, 1430
Of þat fare was he fayne,
    And fro þam he rade.
Euer þe nerre hym he drewe,
Wele þe better he hym knewe,
Horse and hernays of hewe, 1435
    Þat þe childe hade.
"A, dere God!" said Wawayne þe fre,
"How-gates[15] may this be?
If i sle hym, or he me,

---

[9] huge. [10] reliance. [11] straight. [12] honor. [13] lots. [14] try. [15] by what chance.

þat neuer ȝit was fade,   1440
And we are sister sones two,
And aythir of vs othir slo,
He þat lifes will be full wo
     þat euer was he made."

Now no maistrys[16] he made,   1445
Sir Wawayne, there als he rade,
Bot houyde[17] styll and habade,
     His concell to ta.
"Ane vnwyse man," he sayd, "am i,
þat puttis myselfe to siche a foly;   1450
Es þere no man so hardy
     þat ne anothir es alswa.[18]
þogfe Perceuell hase slayne þe Rede Knyght,
Ȝitt may anoþer be als wyghte,
And in þat gere be dyghte,   1455
     And taken alle hym fra.
If i suffire[19] my sister sone,
And anothir in his gere be done,[20]
And gete þe maystry me appon,
     þat wolde do me wa;   1460

It wolde wirke me full wa!
So mote i one erthe ga,
It ne sall noghte betyde me swa,
     If i may righte rede!
A schafte sall i one hym sett,   1465
And i sall fonde firste to hitt;
þen sall i ken be my witt
     Who weldys þat wede."
No more carpys he þat tyde,
Bot son togedyr gon þay ryde—   1470
Men þat bolde were to byde,[21]

---

[16] warlike manœuvers. [17] remained. [18] i.e., that another may not be his
match. [19] i.e., deal gently with. [20] arrayed. [21] were courageous in waiting (for
an enemy).

1440. In all four instances in the poem, *fade* seems to mean "eager for
trouble."

And styff appon stede;
Þaire horse were stallworthe and strange,[22]
Þair scheldis were vnfailande;
Þaire speris brake to þaire hande,[23]   1475
Als þam byhoued nede.[24]

Now es broken þat are were hale,[25]
And þan bygane Perceuale
For to tell one a tale
    Þat one his tonge laye.   1480
He sayde, "Wyde-whare[26] hafe i gane;
Siche anothir sowdane
In faythe sawe i neuer nane,
    By nyghte ne by daye.
I hafe slayne, and i þe ken,   1485
Twenty score of thi men;
And of alle þat i slewe then,
    Me thoghte it bot a playe
Agayne[27] þat dynt þat i hafe tane;
For siche one aughte i neuer nane   1490
Bot i qwyte two for ane,
    Forsothe, and i maye."

Then spake Sir Wawayne—
Certanely, is noghte to layne,
Of þat fare was he fayne,   1495
    in felde there thay fighte:
By the wordis so wylde
At the fole one the felde,
He wiste wele it was þe childe,
    Perceuell þe wighte—   1500
He sayse, "I ame no sowdane,
Bot i am þat ilke man
Þat thi body bygan

---

[22] strong. [23] along their whole length. [24] they needs must. [25] whole. [26] far and wide. [27] in comparison with.

1476. If both knights sat firm, and their shields held, the spears must be the parts to break.

In armours to dighte.
I giffe the prise to thi pyth;[28]   1505
Vnkyndely[29] talked thou me with:
My name es Wawayne in kythe,[30]
 Whoso redys righte."

He sayes, "Who þat will rede the aryghte,
My name es Wawayne þe knyghte."   1510
And þan þay sessen of þaire fighte,
 Als gude frendes scholde.
He sayse, "Thynkes þou noghte[31] when
þat þou woldes þe knyghte brene,
For þou ne couthe noghte ken   1515
 To spoyle[32] hym alle colde?"
Bot þen was Perceuell þe free
Als blythe als he myghte be,
For þen wiste he wele þat it was he,
 By takens[33] þat he tolde.   1520
He dide þen als he gane hym lere:
Putt vp hys vmbrere;[34]
And kyste togedir with gud chere
 Þose beryns[35] so bolde.

Now kissede the beryns so bolde—   1525
Sythen, talkede what þay wolde
Be then come Arthour þe bolde,
 Þat there was knyghte and kyng—
Als his cosyns hadd done,
Thankede God also sone.   1530
Off mekill myrthis þay mone[36]
 At þaire metyng.
Sythen, withowtten any bade,
To þe castelle þay rade
With þe childe þat thay hade,   1535
 Perceuell þe ȝynge.
The portere was redy þare,

[28] acknowledge your spirit.   [29] rudely.   [30] among my people.   [31] do you not recall.   [32] plunder.   [33] tokens.   [34] visor.   [35] warriors.   [36] recall.

Lete þe knyghtis in fare;
A blythere lady þan . . .

. . . .   1540

"Mi grete socour at[37] þou here sende,
Off my castell me to diffende,
Agayne þe sowdane to wende,
    Þat es my moste foo."
Theire stedis þay sett in þe stalle;   1545
Þe Kyng wendis to haulle;
His knyghtis ʒode hym with alle,
    Als kynde was to go.[38]
Þaire metis was redy,
And þerto went þay in hy,   1550
The Kyng and þe lady,
    And knyghtis also.

Wele welcomed scho þe geste
With riche metis of þe beste,
Drynkes of þe derreste,   1555
    Dightede bydene.
Þay ete and dranke what þay wolde,
Sythen talked and tolde
Off othir estres[39] full olde,
    Þe Kyng and þe Qwene.   1560
At þe firste bygynnyng,
Scho frayned Arthour þe Kyng
Of childe Perceuell þe ʒyng,
    What life he had in bene.
Grete wondir had Lufamour   1565
He was so styffe in stour
And couthe so littill of nurtour
    Als scho had there sene.

Scho had sene with þe childe

---

[37] that.   [38] as was their habit.   [39] stories.

1539. The missing words are torn out of the MS. The scribe omitted a few lines telling of the lady's welcome to Arthur.

No thyng bot werkes wylde;[40] 1570
Thoghte grete ferly on filde
Of þat foly fare.[41]
Þen said Arthour þe Kyng
Of bold Perceuell techyng,[42]
Fro þe firste bygynnyng 1575
[Ti]ll þat he come thar:
[How] his ffadir was slayne,
[And his modi]r to þe wode gane
[For to be t]here hir allane
[In þe holtis har]e, 1580
Fully feftene ȝere
To play hym with þe wilde dere:
Littill wonder it were
Wilde if he ware!

When he had tolde this tale 1585
To þat semely in sale,[43]
He hade wordis at wale[44]
To þam ilkane.
The[n] said Perceuell þe wighte,
"ȝif i be noghte ȝitt knyghte, 1590
Þou sall halde þat þou highte,
For to make me ane."
Than saide þe Kyng full sone,
"Ther sall oþer dedis be done,
And þou sall wynn thi schone[45] 1595
Appon þe sowdane."
Þen said Perccuell þe fre,
"Als sone als i þe sowdane see,
Righte so sall it sone be,
Als i hafe vndirtane." 1600

He says, "Als i hafe vndirtane

---

[40] acts of violence. [41] unusual conduct. [42] training. [43] hall. [44] choice. [45] i.e., spurred knight's-shoes.

1576 ff. The words in brackets were supplied by Halliwell and Holthausen; the corner of the leaf is missing.

For to sla þe sowdane,
So sall i wirke als i kanne,
    Þat dede to bygynn."
Þat day was þer no more dede   1605
With those worthily in wede,
Bot buskede þam and to bedde ȝede,
    The more and the mynn;[46]
Till one þe morne erely
Comes þe sowdane with a cry,[47]   1610
Fonde all his folkes hym by
    Putt vnto pyn.[48]
Sone asked he wha
Þat so durste his men sla
And wete hym one lyfe gaa,   1615
    The maystry to wynn.

Now to wynn þe maystry,
To þe castell gan he cry,
If any were so hardy,
    The maistry to wynn,   1620
A man for ane;[49]
Þoghe he hadd all his folke slane,
"Here sall he fynde Golrotherame
    To mete hym full ryghte,
Appon siche a couenande   1625
Þat ȝe hefe[50] vp ȝour hande:
Who þat may þe better stande
    And more es of myghte
To bryng þat oþer to þe dede,
Browke wele þe londe on brede,[1]   1630
And hir þat is so faire and rede—
    Lufamour þe brighte."

---

[46] less.   [47] noise.   [48] pain; i.e., dead.   [49] man for man.   [50] raise.   [1] throughout.

1606. *Worthily* is an adjective.
1615. I.e., knew the sultan to be alive, and hence sure to resent it.
Saracens are always boastful in the romances.
1620. Probably the right reading is: *With hym for to fyghte*.

Then þe Kyng Arthour
And þe Lady Lufamour
And all þat were in þe towre   1635
   Graunted þerwith.
Thay called Perceuell þe wight;
Þe Kyng doubbed hym to knyghte.
Þofe he couthe littill insighte,[2]
   The childe was of pith.[3]   1640
He bad he solde be to prayse,[4]
Þerto hende and curtayse;
Sir Perceuell the Galayse
   Þay called hym in kythe.
Kyng Arthour in Maydenlande   1645
Dubbid hym knyghte with his hande,
Bad hym, þer he his fo fande,
   To gyff hym no grythe.

Grith takes he nane:
He rydes agayne þe sowdane   1650
Þat highte Gollerotherame,
   Þat felle was in fighte.
In þe felde so brade,
No more carpynge þay made,
Bot sone togedir þay rade,   1655
   Theire schaftes to righte.[5]
Gollerotheram, þofe he wolde wede,[6]
Perceuell bere hym fro his stede
Two londis one brede,
   With maystry and myghte.   1660
At þe erthe þe sowdane lay;
His stede gun rynn away;

---

[2] formal learning. [3] spirited. [4] i.e., act worthily. [5] well aimed. [6] rage.

1659. The distance traversed by the unfortunate Sultan is uncertain. A land was the part of a field between dead furrows, and was apparently a stable unit of measure. Heroes in romance often cause the weapons of opponents and even the opponents themselves to fly long distances. Cf. "Bevis" A. 1906, where a shield flies three acres. More conservative poets are content with a spear's length.

Þan said Perceuell one play,
"Þou haste þat i the highte."

He sayd, "I highte the a dynt,   1665
And now, me thynke, þou hase it hynt.
And i may, als i hafe mynt,
    Þou schalt it neuer mende."
Appon þe sowdan he duelled[7]
To þe grownde þer he was felled,   1670
And to þe erthe he hym helde
    With his speres ende.
Fayne wolde he hafe hym slayne,
This vncely[8] sowdane,
Bot gate couthe he get nane,   1675
    So ill was he kende.
Þan thynkes þe childe
Of olde werkes full wylde:
"Hade i a fire now in this filde,
    Righte here he solde be brende."   1680

He said, "Righte here i solde þe brene,
And þou ne solde neuer more then
Fighte for no wymman,
    So i solde the fere !"[9]
Þen said Wawayne þe knyghte,   1685
"Þou myghte, and þou knewe righte,
And þou woldes of þi stede lighte,
    Wynn hym one were."
The childe was of gamen gnede;[10]
Now he thynkes one thede,[11]   1690
"Lorde ! whethir this be a stede
    I wende had bene a mere?"
In stede righte there he in stode,
He ne wiste noþer of euyll ne gude,[12]
Bot then chaunged his mode   1695
    And slaked[13] his spere.

---

[7] blocked, pressed. [8] luckless. [9] terrify. [10] chary of banter. [11] land; i.e., there.
[12] sc. "manners." [13] released.

When his spere was vp tane,
The[n] gan this Gollerothiram,
This ilke vncely sowdane,
    One his fete to gete.   1700
Than his swerde drawes he,
Strykes at Perceuell the fre;
The childe hadd no powsté[14]
    His laykes[15] to lett.
The stede was his awnn will:[16]   1705
Saw þe swerde come hym[17] till,
Leppe vp ouer an hill,
    Fyve stryde mett.[18]
Als he sprent forby,[19]
The sowdan keste vp a cry;   1710
The childe wann owt of study[20]
    þat he was inn sett.

Now ther he was in sett,
Owt of study he gett,
And lightis downn, withowtten lett,   1715
    Agaynes hym to goo.
He says, "Now hase þou taughte me
How þat i sall wirke with the."
Than his swerde drawes he
    And strake to hym thro [21]   1720
He hitt hym euen one þe nekk-bane,
Thurgh ventale and pesane;[22]
The hede of the sowdane
    He strykes the body fra.
þen full wightly he ȝode   1725
To his stede, þere he stode;
The milde mayden in mode,
    Mirthe may scho ma!

Many mirthes then he made;
In to þe castell he rade,   1730

---

[14] ability. [15] sword play. [16] i.e., own master. [17] Perceval. [18] and measured
five strides. [19] raced past. [20] preoccupation. [21] fiercely. [22] visor and neck
armor.

And boldly he there habade
With þat mayden brighte.
Fayne were þay ilkane
Þat he had slane þe sowdane
And wele wonn þat wymman,   1735
With maystry and myghte.
Þay said Perceuell þe ȝyng
Was beste worthy to be kyng,
For wele withowtten lesyng
He helde þat he highte.   1740
Ther was no more for to say,
Bot sythen, appon þat oþer day,
He weddys Lufamour þe may,
This Perceuell þe wighte.

Now hase Perceuell þe wight   1745
Wedded Lufamour þe bright,
And is a kyng full righte
Of alle þat lande brade.
Than Kyng Arthour in hy
Wolde no lengare ther ly: 1750
Toke lefe at the lady:
Fro þam þan he rade:
Left Perceuell the ȝyng
Off all þat lande to be kyng,
For he had [wedded] with a ryng   1755
Þe mayden þat it hade.
Sythen, appon þe toþer day,
The Kyng went on his way,
The certane sothe, als i say,
Withowtten any bade.   1760

Now þan ȝong Perceuell habade
In those borowes so brade
For hir sake, þat he hade
Wedd with a ryng.
Wele weldede he þat lande,   1765
Alle bowes to his honde;

Þe folke, þat he byfore fonde,[23]
  Knewe hym for kyng.
Thus he wonnes in þat wone[24]
Till that the twelmonthe was gone,   1770
With Lufamour his lemman:
  He thoghte on no thyng,
Nor on his moder þat was,
How scho leuyde with þe gres,[25]
With more drynke and lesse,   1775
  In welles, þere þay spryng;

Drynkes of welles, þer þay spryng,
And gresse etys, withowt lesyng!
Scho liffede with none othir thyng
  In þe holtes hare;   1780
Till it byfelle appon a day,
Als he in his bedd lay,
Till hymselfe gun he say,
  Syghande full sare,
"The laste ȝole-day þat was,   1785
Wilde wayes i chese:
My modir all manles[26]
  Leued i thare."
Þan righte sone saide he,
"Blytho ȝall i neuor bo   1790
Or i may my modir see,
  And wete how scho fare."

Now to wete how scho fare,
The knyght busked hym ȝare;
He wolde no lengare duelle thare   1795
  For noghte þat myghte bee.
Vp he rose in þat haulle,

---

[23] came.   [24] place.   [25] grass.   [26] i.e., unprotected.

1770. A year is a conventional period for a mortal to remain in fairy-land without recalling his old life. On the subject, see Hartland's "Science of Fairy Tales," Ch. 7.

1775. MS. *with moste.*—Holthausen.

Tuke his lefe at þam alle,
Bot[h] at grete and at smalle;
   Fro thaym wendis he.   1800
Faire scho prayed hym euen than,
Lufamour, his lemman,
Till þe heghe dayes of ȝole were gane,
   With hir for to bee;
Bot it serued hir of no thyng:[27]   1805
A preste he made forthe bryng,
Hym a messe for to syng,
   And aftir rode he.

Now fro þam gun he ryde;
Þer wiste no man þat tyde   1810
Whedirwarde he wolde ryde,
   His sorowes to amende.
Forthe he rydes allone;
Fro þam he wolde euerichone:
Mighte no man with hym gone,   1815
   Ne whedir he wolde lende.[28]
Bot forthe thus rydes he ay,
Þe certen sothe als i ȝow say,
Till he come at a way
   By a wode-ende.   1820
Then herde he faste hym by
Als it were a woman cry:
Scho prayed to mylde Mary
   Som socoure hir to sende.

Scho sende hir socour full gude,   1825
Mary, þat es mylde of mode:
As he come thurgh the wode,
   A ferly he fande.
A birde,[29] brighteste of ble,
Stode faste bonden till a tre   1830

---

[27] i.e., did her no good.   [28] arrive.   [29] lady.

1812, 1816. Holthausen transposed these lines; but they may be left as in the MS. if the second is an ellipsis for "nor (know) whither," etc.

(I say it ӡow certanly),
    Bothe fote and hande.
Sone askede he who,
When he sawe hir tho,
Þat had serued hir so,   1835
    Þat lady in lande.
Scho said, "Sir, þe Blake Knyghte
Solde be my lorde with righte;
He hase me thusgates[30] dighte
    Here for to stande."   1840

Scho says, "Here mon i stande
For a faute[31] þat he fande,
Þat sall i warande,
    Is my moste mone.
Now to the i sall say: 1845
Appon my bedd i lay
Appon þe laste ӡole-day—
    Twelue monethes es gone.
Were he knyghte, were he kyng,
He come one his play[y]nge: 1850
With me he chauugede[32] a ryng,
    The richeste of one.[33]
The body myght i noghte see
Þat made þat chauugyng with me,
Bot what þat euer he be,   1855
    The better hase he tone!"

Scho says, "Þe better hase he tane;
Siche a vertue es in þe stane,
In alle this werlde wote i nane
    Siche stone in a rynge;   1860
A man þat had it in were[34]
One his body for to bere,
There scholde no dyntys hym dere,

---

[30] in this wise. [31] fault. [32] exchanged. [33] i.e., finest of all. [34] war.

1863. On protective stones, cf. Dickman 181; Joan Evans, "Magical Jewels of the Middle Ages," 111 ff.

Ne to þe dethe brynge."
And then wiste Sir Perceuale   1865
Full wele by the ladys tale
þat he had broghte hir in bale
Thurgh his chaungyng.
Than also sone sayd he
To that lady so fre,   1870
"I sall the louse[35] fro þe tre,
Als i am trewe kyng."

He was bothe kyng and knyght:
Wele he helde þat he highte;
He loused the lady so brighte,   1875
Stod bown to the tre.
Down satt the lady,
And ȝong Perceuall hir by;
Forwaked[36] was he wery:
Rist hym wolde he.   1880
He wende wele for to ryst,
Bot it wolde nothyng laste:
Als he lay althir best,[37]
His hede one hir kne,
Scho putt on Perceuell wighte,   1885
Bad hym fle with all his myghte,
"For ȝonder comes þe Blake Knyghte;
Dede mon ȝe be !"

Scho sayd, "Dede mon ȝe be,
I say ȝow, sir, certanly: 1890
ȝonder out comes he
þat will vs bothe sle!"
The knyghte gan hir answere,
"Tolde ȝe me noghte lang ere

---

[35] let loose.   [36] exhausted from being awake.   [37] i.e., most comfortably.

1864. MS. *ne the to.*
1873. This is a preliminary to the enchanter's entrance. Cf. Wimberly 348.
1885. Possibly the right reading is *pull on,* pushed away.

Ther solde no dynttis me dere,   1895
  Ne wirke me no woo?"
The helme on his hede he sett;
Bot or he myght to his stede get,
The Blak Knyght with hym mett,
  His maistrys to mo.   1900
He sayd, "How! hase þou here
Fonden now thi play-fere?[38]
ȝe schall haby it full dere
  Er þat i hethen go !"

He said, "Or i hethyn go,   1905
I sall sle ȝow, bothe two,
And all siche othir mo,
  Þaire waryson[39] to ȝelde."
Than sayd Perceuell þe fre,
"Now sone þan sall we see   1910
Who þat es worthy to bee
  Slaync in the felde."
No more speke þay þat tyde,
Bot sone togedir gan þay ryde,
Als men þat wolde were habyde,[40]   1915
  With schaftc and with schelde.
Than Sir Perceuell þe wight
Bare down þe Blake Knyght;
Þan was þe lady so bright
  His best socour in telde:[41]   1920

Scho was þe beste of his belde:[42]
Bot scho had there bene his schelde,
He had bene slayne in þe felde,
  Right certeyne in hy.
Euer als[43] Perceuell the kene   1925

---

[38] paramour.   [39] reward.   [40] i.e., readily engage in war.   [41] tent.   [42] reliance.
[43] just as.

1900. *Mo* is a copyist's substitution; he probably confused the *ma* (make) of the original with *ma* (more), and put in the midland form.

1920. Probably the line should end *in belde*, in relief, defense. The expression in the text is a tag of little meaning.

Sold þe knyghtis bane hafe bene,
Ay went þe lady bytwene
    And cryed, "Mercy!"
Than þe lady he forbere,[44]
And made þe Blak Knyghte to swere   1930
Of alle euylls þat þere were,
    Forgiffe the lady;
And Perceuell made þe same othe
Þat he come neuer vndir clothe
To do þat lady no lothe[45]   1935
    Þat pendid[46] to velany.

"I did hir neuer no velany;
Bot slepande i saw hir ly:
    Þan kist i þat lady—
I will it neuer layne;—   1940
I tok a ryng þat i fande;
I left hir, i vndirstande[47]
    (Þat sall i wele warande),
    Anothir ther-agayne."[48]
Þofe it were for none oþer thyng,   1945
He swere by Ihesu, Heuen-kyng,
To wete withowtten lesyng,
    And here to be slayne;
"And all redy is the ryng;
And þou will myn agayne bryng,   1950
Here will i make þe chaungyng,
    And of myn awnn be fayne."

He saise, "Of myn i will be fayne."
Þe Blak Knyghte ansuers agayne:
Sayd, "For sothe, it is noghte to layne,   1955
    Thou come ouer-late.
Als sone als i þe ryng fande,
I toke it sone off hir hande;

---

[44] spared.   [45] injury.   [46] pertained.   [47] believe.   [48] i.e., as a substitute.

1948. I.e., called on heaven to slay him if he spoke falsely. On swearing by one's life, see "Havelok" 186.

To the lorde of this lande
   I bare it one a gate.[49]   1960
Þat gate with grefe hafe i gone:
I bare it to a gude mone,[50]
The stalwortheste geant of one[1]
   Þat any man wate.
Es it nowþer knyghte ne kyng   1965
Þat dorste aske hym þat ryng,
Þat he ne wolde hym down dyng[2]
   With harmes full hate."[3]

Be þay hate, be þay colde,
Than said Perceuell þe bolde—   1970
For þe tale þat he tolde
   He wex all tene—
He said, "Heghe on galous mote he hyng
Þat to þe here giffes any ryng,
Bot þou myn agayne brynge,   1975
   Thou haste awaye geuen!
And ʒif it may no noþer be,
Righte sone þan tell þou me
The sothe: whilke þat es he
   Thou knawes, þat es so kene?   1980
Ther es no more for to say,
Bot late me wynn it ʒif i may,
For þou hase giffen thi part of bothe away,
   Þof thay had better bene."[4]

He says, "Þofe þyn had better bene."   1985
The knyghte ansuerde in tene,
"Þou sall wele wete, withowtten wene,[5]
   Wiche[6] þat es he!
If þou dare do als þou says,
Sir Perceuell de Galays,   1990
   In ʒone heghe palays,

---

[49] i.e., straight. [50] man. [1] all. [2] strike. [3] i.e., fearful injuries. [4] had been even more valuable. [5] doubt. [6] which.

1976. *Geuen* is for the northern form *gein, gen.*

Therin solde he be—
The riche ryng with þat grym![7]
The stane es bright and nothyng dym;
For sothe, þer sall þou fynd hym: 1995
  I toke it fro me;[8]
Owthir within or withowt,
Or one his play þer abowte,
Of the he giffes littill dowte,[9]
  And that sall thou see."   2000

He says, "That sall þou see,
  I say the full sekirly."
And than forthe rydis he
  Wondirly swythe.
The geant stode in his holde,[10]   2005
That had those londis in wolde:[11]
Saw Perceuell, þat was bolde,
  One his lande dryfe;
He calde one his portere:
"How-gate[12] may this fare?   2010
I se a bolde man ʒare
  On my lande ryfe.[13]
Go reche me my playlome,[14]
And i sall go to hym sone;
Hym were better hafe bene at Rome,   2015
  So euer mote i thryfe!"

Whethir he thryfe or he the,
Ane iryn clobe takes he;
Agayne Perceuell the fre
  He went than full right.   2020
The clobe wheyhed[15] reghte wele
Þat a freke[16] myght it fele:
The hede was of harde stele,

---

[7] fearful (creature).   [8] gave it away.   [9] has little fear.   [10] castle.   [11] power.
[12] by what means.   [13] arrive, come.   [14] fighting-implement, weapon.   [15] weighed.
[16] man, knight.

2018. Cf. "Degaré" 385.

Twelue stone weghte.
Þer was iryn in the wande,[17]   2025
Ten stone of the lande,[18]
And one was byhynde his hande,[19]
For holdyng was dight.
Þer was thre and twenty in hale;[20]
Full euyll myght any men smale,   2030
Þat men telles nowe in tale,
With siche a lome[21] fighte.

Now are þay bothe bown,
Mett one a more[22] brown,
A mile withowt any town,   2035
Boldly with schelde.
Þan saide þe geant so wight,
Als sone als he sawe þe knyght,
"Mahown, loued be thi myght!"
And Perceuell byhelde.   2040
"Art thou hym, that," saide he than,
"That slew Gollerothirame?
I had no brothir bot hym ane,
When he was of elde."[23]
Than said Perceuell the fre,   2045
"Thurgh grace of God so sall i the,
And siche geantes as ʒe
Sle thaym in the felde!"

Siche metyng was seldom sene;
The dales dynned thaym bytwene[24]   2050
For dynttis þat þay gaffe bydene

---

[17] shaft. [18] i.e., by English standards. [19] i.e., the handle is bound in iron weighing one stone. [20] all. [21] implement. [22] moor. [23] full-grown (a tag). [24] the walls of the valleys reëchoed.

2024. A stone was about 14 lb., but varied because of lack of standards.

2031. Writers often represented the men of former times as of unusual stature and strength. Even this poet admits that his own heroes belong to a past age. Ossian, returning from the otherworld, finds the men of the day small and puny, and remarks that they are no such fellows as composed the Fenian band.

2042. On the name, cf. *MPhil.*, 18.220.

When þay so mett.
The gyant with his clobe-lome²⁵
Wolde hafe strekyn²⁶ Perceuell sone,
Bot he þervnder wightely²⁷ come,   2055
A stroke hym to sett.
The geant missede of his dynt;
The clobe was harde as þe flynt:
Or he myght his staffe stynt²⁸
    Or his strengh lett,   2060
The clobe in þe erthe stode:²⁹
To þe midschafte it wode.³⁰
The[n] Perceuell the gode,
    Hys swerde owt he get.

By then hys swerde owt he get,   2065
Strykes þe geant withowtten lett,
Merkes euen³¹ to his nekk,
    Reght euen þer he stode;
His honde he strykes hym fro,
His lefte fote also;   2070
With siche dyntis as tho
    Nerre³² hym he ȝode.
Þen sayd Perceuell, "I vndirstande³³
Þou myghte with a lesse wande³⁴
Hafe weledid better thi hande   2075
    And hafe done the some gode;
Now bese it neuer for ane³⁵
The clobe of þe erthe tane;
I tell þi gatis alle gane,³⁶
    Bi the gude rode !"   2080

He says, "By þe gud rode,
As euyll als þou euer ȝode,³⁷

---

²⁵ lit., club-weapon.   ²⁶ struck.   ²⁷ actively.   ²⁸ withhold.   ²⁹ pierced and remained fixed.   ³⁰ i.e., went half its length.   ³¹ thrusts straight.   ³² nearer.
³³ believe, ween.   ³⁴ smaller shaft.   ³⁵ will never by one (man).   ³⁶ count your
roads all traveled; i.e., your career ended.   ³⁷ However awkwardly you walk
hereafter; i.e., since you are badly crippled.

2064. MS. *He swerde.*

Of þi fote þou getis no gode;
  Bot lepe[38] if þou may !''
The geant gan þe clobe lefe,   2085
And to Perceuell a dynt he ȝefe
In þe nekk with his nefe:[39]
  Sone neghede[40] þay.
At þat dynt was he tene:
He strikes off þe hande als clene   2090
Als þer hadde neuer none bene:
  Þat oþer was awaye.
Sythen his hede gan he off hafe;[41]
He was ane vnhende[42] knaue
A geantberde so to schafe,   2095
  For sothe, als i say !

Now for sothe, als i say,
He lete hym ly there he lay,
And rydis forthe one his way
  To þe heghe holde.[43]   2100
The portare saw his lorde slayne;
Þe kayes[44] durste he noght layne:
He come Perceuell agayne;
  Þe ȝatis he hym ȝolde.
At þe firste bygynnyng,   2105
He askede þe portere of the ryng—
If he wiste of it any thyng;
  And he hym than tolde:
He taughte[45] hym sone to þe kiste[46]
Þer he alle þe golde wiste,[47]   2110
Bade hym take what hym liste
  Of that he hafe wolde.

Perceuell sayde, hafe it he wolde,
And schott owtt all þe golde

---

[38] hop. [39] fist. [40] closed. [41] take. [42] rude. [43] high castle (cf. 1991). [44] keys.
[45] showed. [46] chest. [47] knew (to be).

2092. MS. *alwaye.*—Campion.
2095. Cf. the alliterative "Morte Arthure" 2095; "Ywain" 2400.

Righte there appon þe faire molde;[48]   2115
The ryng owte glade.[49]
The portare stode besyde,
Sawe þe ryng owt glyde,
Sayde ofte, "Wo worthe þe tyde
   þat euer was it made!"   2120
Perceuell answerde in hy,
And asked wherefore and why
He banned it so brothely,[50]
   Bot-if he cause hade.
Then alsone said he,   2125
And sware by his lewté:[1]
"The cause sall i tell the,
   Withowten any bade."

He says, withowtten any bade,
"The knyghte þat it here hade,   2130
þeroff a presande he made,
   And hedir he it broghte.
Mi mayster tuke it in his hande,
Ressayued faire þat presande:
He was chefe lorde of þis lande,   2135
   Als man þat mekill moghte.[2]
þat tyme was here fast by
Wonna[n]de a lady,
And hir wele and lely[3]
   He luffede, als me thoghte.   2140
So it byfelle appon a day,
Now þe sothe als i sall say,
Mi lorde went hym to play,
   And the lady bysoghte.[4]

Now þe lady byseches he   2145
þat scho wolde his leman be;
Fast he frayned þat free,

---

[48] ground, turf.   [49] flew.   [50] cursed it so violently.   [1] fealty.   [2] had great power.
[3] truly.   [4] importuned.

2138. Campion's emendation.

For any kyns aughte.[5]
At þe firste bygynnyng,
He wolde hafe gyffen hir þe ryng;   2150
And when scho sawe þe tokynyng,
    Then was scho vn-saughte.[6]
Scho gret and cried in hir mone;
Sayd, 'Thefe, hase þou my sone slone
And the ryng fro hym tone,   2155
    þat i hym bitaughte?'
Hir clothes ther scho rafe[7] hir fro,
And to þe wodd gan scho go;
Thus es þe lady so wo,
    And this is the draghte.[8]   2160

For siche draghtis als this,
Now es þe lady wode, iwys,
And wilde in þe wodde scho es,
    Ay sythen þat ilke tyde.
Fayne wolde i take þat free,   2165
Bot alsone als scho sees me,
Faste awaye dose scho flee:
    Will scho noghte abyde."
Then sayde Sir Perceuell,
"I will assaye full snelle   2170
To make þat lady to duelle;
    Bot i will noghte ryde:
One my fete will i ga,
þat faire lady to ta.
Me aughte to bryng hir of wa: 2175
    I laye in hir syde."[9]

Ile sayse, "I laye in hir syde;
I sall neuer one horse ryde
Till i hafe sene hir in tyde,[10]

---

[5] i.e., wealth being no object; on any terms. [6] distressed. [7] tore. [8] course (of fate), bad luck. [9] i.e., she was my mother. [10] time; at once.

2162. On the mother's madness, see Loomis, Ch. 27.
2175. On the impersonal construction, cf. Int. VII.A.1.

Spede if i may;   2180
Ne none armoure þat may be
Sall come appone me
Till i my modir may see,
    Be nyghte or by day.
Bot reghte in þe same wode   2185
Þat i firste fro hir 3ode,
That sall be in my mode
    Aftir myn oþer play;[11]
Ne i ne sall neuer mare
Come owt of 3one holtis hare   2190
Till i wete how scho fare,
    For sothe, als i saye."

Now for sothe, als i say,
With þat he helde one his way,
And one þe morne, when it was day,   2195
    Forthe gonn he fare.
His armour he leued þerin,
Toke one hym a gayt-skynne,
And to þe wodde gan he wyn,
    Among þe holtis hare.   2200
A seuenyght long hase he soghte;
His modir ne fyndis he noghte;
Of mete ne drynke he ne roghte,
    So full he was of care.
Till þe nynte day, byfell[12]   2205
Þat he come to a welle
Þer he was wonte for to duelle
    And drynk take hym thare.

When he had dronken þat tyde,
Forthirmare[13] gan he glyde;   2210
Than was he warre, hym besyde,
    Of þe lady so fre;
Bot when scho sawe hym thare,
Scho bygan for to dare,[14]

---

[11] deeds; i.e., despite anything.   [12] it chanced.   [13] farther.   [14] hide.

And sone gaffe hym answare,   2215
þat brighte was of ble.
Scho bigan to call and cry:
Sayd, "Siche a sone hade i!"
His hert lightened in hy,
    Blythe for to bee.   2220
Be þat he come hir nere
þat scho myght hym here,
He said, "My modir full dere,
    Wele byde &yogh;e me !"

Be that, so nere getis he   2225
þat scho myghte nangatis[15] fle;
I say &yogh;ow full certeynly,
    Hir byhoued þer to byde.
Scho stertis appon hym in tene;
Wete &yogh;e wele, withowtten wene,   2230
Had hir myghte so mekill bene,[16]
    Scho had hym slayne þat tyde !
Bot his myghte was þe mare,
And vp he toke his modir thare;
One his bake he hir bare: 2235
    Pure[17] was his pryde.
To þe castell, withowtten mare,
þe righte way gon he fare;
The portare was redy &yogh;are,
    And lete hym in glyde.   2240

In with his modir he glade,
Als he sayse þat it made;
With siche clothes als þay hade,
    þay happed[18] hir forthy.
þe geant had a drynk wroghte;   2245
þe portere sone it forthe broghte—
For no man was his thoghte
    Bot for that lady.

_____
[15] in no wise. [16] strength been great enough. [17] poor, little. [18] clad.

2242. ' As he says who composed the tale."

þay wolde not lett long thon,
Bot lauede[19] in hir with a spone;   2250
Þen scho one slepe fell also sone,
    Reght certeyne in hy.
Thus the lady there lyes
Thre nyghttis and thre dayes,
And þe portere alwayes   2255
    Lay wakande hir by.

Thus þe portare woke [hir by]—
Ther whills[20] hir luffed se[kerly],—
Till at þe laste the lady
    Wakede, als i wene.   2260
Þen scho was in hir awenn [state][21]
And als wele in hir gate[22]
Als scho hadde nowthir arely ne late
    Neuer þerowte bene.
Thay sett þam down one þaire kne,   2265
Thanked Godde, alle three,
That he wolde so appon þam see[23]
    As it was there sene.
Sythen aftir gan þay ta[24]
A riche bathe for to ma,   2270
And made þe lady in to ga,
    In graye and in grene.

Than Sir Perceuell in hy
Toke his modir hym by,
I say ȝow than certenly,   2275
    And home went hee.

---

[19] poured, dosed. [20] all the while (he). [21] right mind. [22] way; i.e., sane. [23] look graciously. [24] set about.

2257. A corner of the page is missing. Halliwell's conjectures.
2261. Campion's conjecture.
2270. On medieval notions of the properties of colors, cf. W. G. Black, "Folk Medicine," Ch. 7. Cf. also "Eger and Grime." Green was especially effective in soothing and restoring. Grey is the traditional color of wild vegetation; cf. *holtes hore.*
2275. MS. *centenly.*

Grete lordes and the Qwene
Welcomed hym al bydene;
When þay hym one lyfe sene,
    Þan blythe myghte þay bee.   2280
Sythen he went into þe Holy Londe,
Wanne many cités full stronge,
And there was he slayne, i vndirstonde;
    Thusgatis endis hee.
Now Ihesu Criste, heuens Kyng,   2285
Als he es lorde of all thyng,
Grante vs all His blyssyng!
    Amen, for charyté!

QUOD ROBERT THORNTON. EXPLICIT SIR PERCEUELL DE
GALES. HERE ENDYS ÞE ROMANCE OF SIR PERCEVELL OF
GALES, COSYN TO KYNG ARTHOURE.

2279. *Sene* is preterite plural, *saw.*

THE AVOWING OF ARTHUR

THE AVOWING OF KING ARTHUR, SIR GAWAIN, SIR KAY, AND BALDWIN OF BRITAIN

This romance is in the dialect of the northwest midlands of before 1400. The manuscript is in the possession of Colonel R. Ireland Blackburne; through his kindness and that of the late H. B. Melville, it has been possible to prepare the text from photographs. Robson's edition for the Camden Society, however, is very exact; for convenience, his numbering of the stanzas has been retained. Final -*ll* is expanded to -*lle* only when the cross-stroke is very plain. Final -*h* is crossed except in lines 51 and 474, but since the stroke evidently has little significance (in lines 237, 510, 1036, and others, it is followed by an -*e*), it has usually been ignored. Flourishes after -*n* and other letters have been disregarded.

The story is a skillful compilation: it introduces popular heroes, and blends several familiar anecdotes and traditional practical jokes in a narrative that is by turns swaggering, heroic, comic, and extremely cynical. In all these particulars, it is like the Latin prose tale "Arthur and Gorlagon" (*Harv. St. N.* viii), and may very well have been adapted from a Welsh original. The sources and discussions of the different incidents are indicated in the notes to the text.

On the verse, see *Rom. Rev.* 7.243.

The poem shows several dialectal peculiarities: the omission of relatives, the assimilation of -*n* by pronouns (*thi none*, thine own), plurals in -*us*, preterites in -*ut*, an extra -*u* after -*w* (*doun; Rown Tabull*), singular forms where plurals seem called for, and the spelling *qu-* for *wh-* or *w-*. For a careful discussion of the dialect, see *Review of English Studies* 3.54, 186, and especially 328.

I

He þat made vs on þe mulde[1]
And fare fourmet þe folde[2]
Atte his will as he wold,
The see and the sande,

---

[1] earth. [2] formed the dry land.

Giffe hom ioy þat wille here   5
Of duȝti men and of dere,
Of haldurs³ þat before vs were,
   þat lifd in this londe!
One was Arther the Kinge,
Withowtun any letting;   10
With him was mony lordinge
   Hardi of honde;
Wice and war ofte þay were,
Bold vndur banere,
And wiȝte weppuns wold were,⁴   15
   And stifly wold stond.

II

þis is no fantum ne no fabulle:
Ȝe wote wele of þe Rowun Tabull,
Of prest men and priueabulle,⁵
   Was holdun in prise: 20
Cheuetan⁶ of chiualry,
Kyndenesse of curtesy,⁷
Hunting full warly,⁸
   As wayt⁹ men and wise.
To þe forest þa[y] fare   25
To hunte atte buk and atte bare,¹⁰
To þe herte¹¹ and to þe hare,
   þat bredus in þe rise.¹²
þe King atte Carlele he lay;
þe hunter cummys on a day: 30
Sayd, "Sir, þer walkes in my way
   A well grim gryse.¹³

III

He is a balefulle bare;
Seche on segh i neuyr are;

---

³ elders. ⁴ bear. ⁵ meritorious. ⁶ chief lord. ⁷ i.e., (chief of) courteous kindness. ⁸ alertly. ⁹ brave. ¹⁰ boar. ¹¹ hart. ¹² thickets. ¹³ horror.

29. In northern poems, Carlisle was confused with Caerleon, and became one of Arthur's principal seats.

30. Attached to each court was a professional huntsman, who attended
to the mechanical details of the chase.

He hase wroȝte me myculle care,   35
    And hurte of my howundes:
Slayn hom downe slely[14]
    With feȝting full furcely;
Wasse þer none so hardi
    Durste bide in his bandus.[15]   40
On him spild i my spere
    And mycull of my nothir gere;
þer mone no dintus him dere,
    Ne wurche him no wowundes.
He is masly[16] made,   45
    All of fellus[17] þat he bade;
þer is no bulle so brade
    That in frith[18] foundes.

IV

He is heȝer þenne a horse,
    That vncumly corse;[19]   50
In fayth him faylis no force
    Quen þat he shalle feȝte!
And þerto blake as a bere,
    Feye folk will he fere:[20]
þer may no dyntus him dere,   55
    Ne him to dethe diȝte.
Quen he quettus[21] his tusshes,
    Thenne he betus on þe busshes:
All[22] he rinnes and he russhes,
    þat þe rote is vnryȝte.[23]   60
He hase a laythelych luffe:[24]
    Quen he castus vppe his stuffe,[25]

---

[14] craftily.   [15] stay in his neighborhood.   [16] massively.   [17] hide.   [18] field.
[19] bulk.   [20] cowardly folk will he frighten.   [21] whets.   [22] so.   [23] torn up.   [24] i.e.,
a violent rage.   [25] dust cloud.

46. *Bade* for *hade?* But then the tense is wrong.

55. Destructive boars are found in many Celtic pieces, but were not
peculiar to them (cf. "Auberi"). Cf. "Kilhwch and Olwen," "Gawain and
the Green Knight" 1440, "Guy of Warwick" 6417, and "Sir Eglamoure."
Wordsworth is said to have written Cunningham a letter including a
rhyme that "Arthur's boar" was loose and was ravaging the land. (*Rom.
Rev.* 3.192.)

Quo durst abide him a buffe,[26]
Iwisse he were wiȝte."

V

He sais, "In Ingulwode is hee."   65
Þe toþer[27] biddus, "Lette him bee;
We schall þat satnace[28] see,
   Giffe þat he be þare."
Þe King callut on knyȝtis thre:
Himseluun wold þe fuyrthe be;   70
He sayd, "Þere schalle no mo mené
   Wynde to þe bore."
Bothe Kay and Sir Gauan
And Bowdewynne of Bretan,
Þe hunter and þe howundus-squayn[29]   75
   Hase ȝarket[30] hom ȝare.
Þe Kinge hase armut him in hie,
And þo thre buirnes[31] hym bie;
Now ar þay fawre alle redie,
   And furthe conne þay fare.   80

VI

Vnto þe forest þay weynde
Þat[32] was hardy and heynde;
Þe huntur atte þe northe ende
   His bugulle con he blaw,
Vncoupult kenettis[33] as he couthe;   85
Witturly þay soȝte þe southe—
Raches[34] with opon mouthe,
   Rennyng on a raw,[35]
Funde fute[36] of þe bore,
   Faste folutte to him thore.   90

---

[26] blow.   [27] i.e., the king.   [28] fiend.   [29] master of hounds.   [30] made ready.
[31] men.   [32] those men who.   [33] loosed the small dogs.   [34] dogs.   [35] row; i.e.,
pack.   [36] scent.

65. Inglewood is a forest in Cumberland, south of Carlisle.

74. Baldwin appears as a knight in Malory, the Morte Arthur poems,
and here. As a bishop, he appears in several Gawain poems and the
Mabinogion. He seems to have been a Celtic hero. Cf. Loomis 172.

83. I.e., as they entered the forest; they were going south.

Quen þat he herd, he hade care;
　To þe denne conne he draw:
He sloȝe hom downe slely
With feȝting full fuyrsly;
But witte ȝe sirs, witturly,   95
　He stode butte litull awe.[37]

VII

Þay held him fast in his hold;[38]
He brittunt bercelettus[39] bold,
Bothe þe ȝunge and þe old,
　And rafte hom þe rest.[40]   100
Þe raches comun rennyng him by,
And bayes[41] him full boldely,
Butte þer was non so hardy
　Durste on þe fynde fast.[42]
Þenne þe huntur sayd, "Lo, him þare!   105
ȝaw þar such[43] him no mare;
Now may ȝe sone to him fare;
　Lette see quo dose beste!
ȝaw þar such him neuyr more:
I sette my hed opon a store[44]   110
Butte-giffe he slaey ȝo alle fawre,
　Þat griselich geste!"[45]

VIII

Þenne þe hunter turnes home agayn;
Þe King callut on Sir Gauan,
On Bawdewin of Bretan,   115
　And on kene Kay.
He sayd, "Sirs, in ȝour cumpany,
Myne avow make i,
Were he neuyr so hardy,
　ȝone satenas to say;[46]   120

---

[37] had little fear.　[38] den.　[39] cut hounds to pieces.　[40] took away their comfort.
[41] bring him to bay.　[42] seize the fiend.　[43] need seek.　[44] as I value my head.
[45] fearful stranger.　[46] attempt, attack.

100. MS. *raste*.
110. MS. *Butte sette*, anticipating the next line.
111. "Slay" has been altered to "flay" in the MS.

To brittun[47] him and downe bringe
Withoute any helpinge,
And i may haue my leuynge[48]
Hentill to morne atte day!
And now, sir, i cummaunde ʒo   125
To do as i haue done nowe:
Ichone make ʒour avowe."
Gladdely grawuntutte þay.

IX

Þen vnsquarut Gauan
And sayd godely agayn,   130
"I avowe to[49] Tarne Wathelan
To wake hit[50] all nyʒte."
"And i avow," sayd Kaye,
"To ride[1] þis forest or daye,
Quo so wernes[2] me þe waye,   135
Hym to dethe diʒte."
Quod Baudewyn, "To stynte[3] owre strife,
I avow bi my life
Neuyr to be ielus of my wife,
Ne of no birde[4] bryʒte;   140
Nere werne[5] no mon my mete
Quen i gode may gete;
Ne drede my dethe for no threte,
Nauthir of king ner knyʒte."

X

Butte now þay haue þayre vowes made,   145
Þay buskute hom and furth rade

---

[47] cut to pieces. [48] if I live. [49] at. [50] keep watch. [1] i.e., patrol. [2] contests.
[3] make an end of. [4] woman. [5] refuse.

127. On the practice of vowing, cf. Koschwitz's later editions of "Karls des Grossen Reise nach Jerusalem," Introduction; *STS* 17, xxxv; and 21, Preface; cf. "Bricriu's Feast," and "The Tournament of Tottenham." It was usually a sort of literary exercise; but here the vows are actually carried out. Cf. *ESt*. 36.337; also *MPhil*. 25.349.

131. The Tarn Wadling was a small lake about ten miles southeast of Carlisle. Arthur's knights often found adventures on its shores. It was drained long ago.

To hold þat þay heȝte hade,
  Ichone sere[6] way.
The King turnus to þe bare;
Gauan, with[oute] any more,   150
  To þe tarne[7] con he fore,
    To wake hit to day.
Þenne Kay, as i conne roune,[8]
He rode þe forest vppe and downe.
Boudewynne turnes to toune   155
  Quer þat his gate lay,
And sethun to bed bownus he;
Butte carpe we now of þer[9] othir thre,
How þay preuyd hor wedde-fee,[10]
    Þe sothe for to say.   160

XI

Furst, to carpe of oure Kinge,
Hit is a kyndelich thinge—
  Atte his begynnyng,
    Howe he dedde his dede.
Till his houndus con he hold;[11]   165
The bore, with his brode schilde,[12]
  Folut hom fast in þe filde
    And spillutte on hom gode spede.[13]
Þen þe Kinge con crye,
And carputte of venerie;[14]   170
  To make his howundus hardi,
    Houut[15] on a stede.
Als sone as he come þare,
Aȝaynus him rebowndet[16] þe bare:
  He se neuyr no syȝte are   175
    So sore gerutte him to drede.

----

[6] separate.   [7] lake.   [8] tell (a tag).   [9] these.   [10] justified their wager.   [11] look at.
[12] hide at the shoulder.   [13] worked havoc rapidly.   [14] cried out hunting terms.
[15] rode up.   [16] rebounded, dashed.

156. MS. *Sum þat.*
160. MS. *þo sothe.*
165. The rhyme-word should probably be *hilde.*   Cf. 330.
171. Some of the right words to use to dogs are given in Lord Berners'
"Boke of St. Albans," under the hunting of the hare; all are French.

XII

He hade drede and doute
Of him þat was sturun[17] and stowte;
He began to romy and rowte,[18]
   And gapes and gones.[19]   180
Men myȝte noȝte his cowch kenne
For howundes and for slayn men
Þat he hade draun to his denne
   And brittunt all to bonus.[20]
Þenne his tusshes con he quette,[21]   185
Opon þe Kinge for to sette;
He liftis vppe, withoutun lette,
   Stokkes[22] and stonis.
With wrathe he begynnus to wrote:[23]
He ruskes[24] vppe mony a rote   190
With tusshes of iii fote,
   So grisly he gronus.[25]

XIII

Þenne þe Kinge spanus[26] his spere,
Opon þat bore for to bere;
Þer may no dyntus him dere,   195
   So seker was his schilde.[27]
Þe grete schafte þat was longe,
All to spildurs[28] hit spronge;
Þe gode stede þat was stronge
   Was fallun in þe filde.   200
As þe bore had mente,
He gaue þe King such a dinte,
Or he myȝte his bridull hente,
   Þat he myȝte euyr hit fele.
His stede was stonet[29] starke ded: 205
He sturd neuyr owte of þat sted.

---

[17] fierce, stern.   [18] roar and rumble.   [19] yawns; i.e., comes on with open mouth. [20] stripped to the bones.   [21] whet.   [22] tree trunks.   [23] root (with his tusks). [24] tears.   [25] rages.   [26] seizes.   [27] tough his hide.   [28] splinters.   [29] struck, stunned.

181. I.e., his lair was concealed by the bones, etc.
193. MS. *span os*.
204. To restore rhyme, read, *That euyr he hit felde*.

To Ihesu a bone he bede,
Fro wothes hym weylde.[30]

XIV

Þenne þe King in his sadul sete
And wiȝtely wan on his fete;   210
He prays to Sayn Margarete
    Fro wathes him ware:[31]
Did as a duȝty knyȝte:
Brayd oute a brand bryȝte
And heue[32] his schild opon hiȝte,   215
    For spild was his spere.
Sethun he buskette him ȝare,
Squithe, withoutun any mare,
Aȝaynus þe fynde for to fare
    That hedoes was of hiere.[33]   220
So þay cowunturt[34] in þe fild,
For all þe weppuns þat he myȝte weld,
Þe bore brittunt his schild
    On brest he conne bere.

XV

Þere downe knelus he   225
And prayus till Him þat was so fre,
"Send me þe victoré!
    Þis satanas[35] me sekes."
All wroth wex þat sqwyne,
Blu and brayd vppe his bryne;[36]   230
As kylne[37] oþer kechine,
    Þus rudely he rekes.[38]
Þe Kynge myȝte him noȝte see,
Butte lenyt[39] him doune bi a tree,

---

[30] perils him to protect. [31] guard. [32] raised. [33] whose hair was hideous. [34] encountered. [35] devil. [36] snorted and raised his brows (rolled his eyes). [37] maltfurnace. [38] vilely he smells. [39] bent.

209. I.e., recovered his balance.

211. St. Margaret is probably the Scotch saint of that name (d. 1093).

224. The relative which should introduce this line is omitted; the construction is common in northern poems.

232. In "The Master of Game" (W. A. and F. Baillie-Grohman), the strong odor of the boar is especially mentioned.

So nyȝe discumford[40] was hee   235
  For smelle oþer smekis.[41]
And as he neghet bi a noke,[42]
þe King sturenly him stroke,
That both his brees con blake;[43]
  His maistry he mekes.[44]   240

XVI

Thus his maistry mekes he
With dyntus þat werun duȝté;
Were he neuyr so hardé,
  þus bidus þat brothe.[45]
þe Kinge, with a nobull brande,   245
He mette þe bore comande:
On his squrd till his hande
  He rennes full rathe.
He bare him inne atte þe throte;
He hade no myrth of þat mote:[46]   250
He began to dotur and dote[47]
  Os he hade keghet scathe.[48]
With sit siles[49] he adowne.
To brittun him þe King was bowne,
And sundurt in þat sesun   255
  His brode schildus bothe.

XVII

þe King couthe of venery,[50]
Colurt[1] him full kyndely:
þe hed of þat hardy
  He sette on a stake.   260
Sethun brittuns he þe best
As venesun in forest;

---

[40] discomfited.   [41] odors.   [42] drew near an oak.   [43] brows grew pale; i.e., he was stunned.   [44] gets the upper hand.   [45] pauses that fierce (creature).   [46] joy of that encounter.   [47] stagger and reel.   [48] received injury.   [49] pain sinks.   [50] hunting.   [1] cut out the neck.

256. The "schilds" were the shoulder quarters. The boar was to be cut up into thirty-two pieces ("Book of St. Albans"): *The fyrst of theym is the hede, whatteuer befall; An oþer is the coler, and so ye schall hitt call; The sheldys on the sholderis, thereof shall ii be.*

Bothe þe ȝonge and lees[2]
He hongus on a noke.[3]
Þere downe knelys hee   265
Þat loues Hur þat is free:
Says, "Þis socur þou hase send me
For þi Sune sake !"
If[4] he were in a dale depe,
He hade no knyȝte him to kepe: 270
For-werré[5] slidus he on slepe:
No lengur myȝte he wake.

XVIII

The King hase fillut his avowe;[6]
Of Kay carpe we nowe;
How þat he come for his prowe[7]   275
Ȝe schall here more.
Als he rode in þe nyȝte,
In þe forest he mette a knyȝte,
Ledand a brede[8] bryȝte;
Ho[9] wepputte wundur sore.   280
Ho sayd, "Sayn Maré myȝte me spede
And saue me my madunhede,[10]
And giffe þe knyȝte for his dede
Bothe soru and care !"

XIX

Þus ho talkes him tille,   285
Quille[11] ho hade sayd alle hur wille;
And Kay held him full stille,
And in þe holte houes.[12]
He prekut oute prestely[13]
And aure-hiet[14] him radly,   290

---

[2] strips and slices. [3] oak. [4] though. [5] overweary. [6] made good his boast.
[7] came to seek his advantage. [8] maiden. [9] she. [10] maidenhood. [11] until. [12] remains. [13] dashed out speedily. [14] overtook.

263. Ȝonge for þonge, strip; cf. Layamon 14227.
274. This episode is familiar. See "Ywain and Gawain" for bibliography.
275. MS. fro his.
280. MS. he.

And on þe kny3te conne cry,
  And pertely him repreues,
  And sayd, "Recraiand[15] kny3te,
  Here i profur þe to fi3te
Be chesun[16] of þat biurde bri3te!   295
  I bede þe my glouus."
Þe toþer vnsquarut him with skille
  And sayd, "I am redy atte þi wille
  Þat forward to fulfille
    In alle þat me behouus."   300

XX

"Now quethun art þou?" quod Kay,
  "Or quethur[17] is þou on way?
  Þi ri3te name þou me say!
    Quere wan þou þat wi3te?"
Þe toþur vnsquarut him agayn,   305
  "Mi ri3te name is no3te to layn:
Sir Menealfe of þe Mountayn
  My gode fadur hi3te;
And this lady sum[18] i þe telle:
  I fochet[19] hur atte Ledelle,   310
  Þer hur frindus con he felle
    As foes in a fi3te.
So i talket hom tille
  Þat muche blode conne i spille,
  And all a3aynus þayre awne wille   315
    Þere wan i this wi3te."

XXI

Quod Kay, "Þe batell i take
  Be chesun[20] of þe birdus sake,

---

[15] treacherous. [16] cause. [17] whither. [18] something. [19] got. [20] cause.

296. On the glove as a challenge, see Hall's note to "King Horn" 793.
300. MS. þe me.
307. If this is the same character as the Meleagant of Chrétien's
"Charette," his father's name was Baudemagus. The poet seems confused. See Loomis 211 ff.
311. He may possibly refer to the father; but more probably this is a
relapse into indirect discourse. MS. hur selle is expuncted, and he felle
written over the line.

And i schalle wurch þe wrake,"[21]
And sqwithely con squere.[22]   320
Þenne þay rode togedur ryȝte
As frekes[23] redy to fiȝte
Be chesun of þat birde bryȝte,
    Gay in hor gere.
Menealfe was þe more myȝty: 325
He stroke Kay stifly,
Witte ȝe sirs, witturly,
    With a scharpe spere;
All to-schildurt[24] his schilde,
And aure his sadull gerut him to held,[25]   330
And felle him flatte in þe filde,
    And toke him vppeon werre.[26]

XXII

Þus hase he wonnen Kay on werre,
And all to-spild[27] is his spere;
And mekill of [his] othir gere   335
    Is holden to þe pees.[28]
Þenne vnsquarut Kay aȝayn
And sayd, "Sir, atte Tarne Wathelan
Bidus me Sir Gauan,
    Is derwurthe[29] on dese;   340
Wold ȝe thethur be bowne[30]
Or ȝe turnut to þe towne,
He wold pay my rawunsone
    Withowtyn delees."
He sayd, "Sir Kay, þi lyfe i þe heȝte   345
For a cowrce[31] of þat knyȝte !"
Ȝette Menealfe, or þe mydnyȝte,
    Him ruet all his rees.[32]

---

[21] mischief. [22] swore it. [23] men. [24] shattered. [25] sink. [26] i.e., won him as a captive. [27] broken. [28] forfeited when he desired a truce. [29] prized; i.e., an intimate of nobles. [30] betake yourself. [31] encounter. [32] regretted his haste.

344. The form *delees*, delays, is not found in the N.E.D., but the rhymes with *pees* (>*pais*) and *dese* (>*dais*) indicate that this is the sense (>*delai*).

XXIII

þus þay turnut to þe torne[33]
With þe thriuand thorne;[34]   350
Kay callut on Gauan ʒorne:
    Asshes[35] quo is there.
He sayd, "I, Kay, þat þou knawes,
þat owte of tyme bostus and blawus;[36]
Butte þou me lese with þi lawes,   355
    I lif neuyr more;
For as i rode in þe nyʒte,
In þe forest i mette a knyʒte
Ledand a birde bryʒte;
    Ho wepput wundur sore.   360
þere togedur faʒte we
Be chesun[37] of þat lady free;
On werre þus hase he wonun me,
    Gif þat me lothe ware.

XXIV

þis knyʒte þat is of renowun   365
Hase takyn me to presowun,[38]
And þou mun pay my rawunsun,
    Gawan, with þi leue."
þen vnsquarutte Gauan
And sayd godely agayn,   370
"I wille, wundur fayne:
    Quatt schall i geue?"
"Quen þou art armut in þi gere,
Take þi schild and þi spere
And ride to him a course on werre;[39]   375
    Hit schall þe noʒte greue."
Gauan asshes, "Is hit soe?"
To toþer knyʒt grauntus, "ʒoe;"
He sayd, "þen togedur schull we goe
    Howsumeuyr hit cheuis!"[40]   380

---

[33] lake. [34] thriving thorn-tree. [35] (Gawain) asks. [36] brag and boast unseasonably. [37] cause. [38] as prisoner. [39] tilting-bout. [40] befalls.

350. Not previously mentioned; but apparently a trysting place.

354. Usually the idiom is "blows boasts."

355. The phrase seems to mean, "unless you release me by acting as surety."

XXV

And these kny3tus kithun hor crafte,
And aythir gripus a schafte
Was als rude as a rafte;[41]
　So runnun þay togedur.
So somun[42] conne þa[y] hie　　　　　　385
þat nauthir scaput forbye;[43]
Gif Menealfe was þe more my3tie,
　3ette dyntus gerut him to dedur:[44]
He stroke him sadde[45] and sore.
Squithe squonut he thore;　　　　　　390
þe blonke[46] him aboute bore,
　Wiste he neuyr quedur.[47]
Quod Kay, "þou hase þat þou hase so3te!
Mi raunnsum is all redy bo3te;
Gif þou were ded, i ne ro3te;　　　　　　395
　Forþi come i hedur."

XXVI

þus Kay scornus þe kny3te,
And Gauan rydus to him ry3te;
In his sadul sette him on hi3te,
　Speke[48] gif he may.　　　　　　400
Of his helme con he draw,
Lete þe wynde on him blaw;
He speke with a vois law,
　"Delyueryt hase þou Kay:
With þi laa hase made him leyce;[49]　　　　405
Butte him is lothe to be in pece,
And þou was aye curtase
　And prins of ich play.[50]
Wold þou here a stowunde bide,
A noþer course wold i ride;　　　　　　410

---

[41] rough as a beam (hewn by hand).　[42] close.　[43] i.e., slipped past.　[44] tremble.
[45] severely.　[46] horse.　[47] whither.　[48] let him speak.　[49] by accepting the contest, you have freed him.　[50] contest.

381. MS. *kithiun*.

þis þat houes[1] by my side,
In wedde[2] i wold hur lay."

XXVII

Thenne vnsquarut Gauan,
Sayd godely agayn,
"I am wundur fayn   415
For hur for to fiȝte."
These knyȝtus kithun þay[re] gere
And aythir gripus a spere;
Runnun togedure on werre
Os[3] hardy and wiȝte.   420
So somen þer þay ȝode
þat Gauan bare him from his stede,
þat both his brees[4] con blede
On growunde qwen he liȝte.
Thenne Kay con on him calle   425
And sayd, "Sir, þou hade a falle
And þi wench lost withalle,
Mi trauthe i þe pliȝte!"

XXVIII

Quod Kay, "þi leue hase þou loste
For all þi brag or þi boste;   430
If þou haue oȝte on hur coste,[5]
I telle hit for tente."[6]
Thenne speke Gauan to Kay,
"A mons happe is notte ay;[7]
Is none so sekur of asay[8]   435
Butte he may harmes hente."
Gauan rydus to him ryȝte
And toke vppe þe toþer knyȝte
þat was dilfully dyȝte[9]
And stonet in þat stynte;[10]   440
Kay wurdus tenut[11] him mare
þenne all þe hapnes[12] þat he hente þare;

---

[1] this (maiden) who rides. [2] as a prize. [3] like. [4] brows. [5] spent. [6] I count it lost. [7] (good) fortune does not last. [8] surely proved (by test). [9] in evil plight. [10] check; i.e., collision, onset. [11] Kay's words angered. [12] misfortune.

421. MS. *somen þat.*

He sayd, "And we allone ware,
    þis stryf schuld i stynte."[13]

XXIX

"ȝe, hardely,"[14] quod Kay,   445
"Butte þou hast lost þi fayre may
And þi liffe, i dare lay."[15]
    þus talkes he him tille.
And Gauan sayd, "God forbede,
For he is duȝti in dede;"   450
Prayes þe knyȝte gud spede[16]
    To take hit to none ille
If Kay speke wurdes kene.
"Take þou þis damesell schene;
Lede hur to Gaynour þe Quene,   455
    þis forward to fulfille;
And say þat Gawan, hur knyȝte,
Sende hur þis byurde briȝte;
And rawunsun þe[17] anon riȝte
    Atte hur awne wille."   460

XXX

þerto grawuntus þe knyȝte
And truly his trauthe pliȝte,
Inne saue-ward[18] þat byurde bryȝte
    To Carlele to bringe.
And as þay houet[19] and abode,   465
He squere on þe squrd brode.
Be he his othe hade made,
    þenne waknut þe King.
þenne þe day beganne to daw;[20]
þe Kinge his bugull con blaw;   470

---

[13] put a stop to this abuse. [14] surely. [15] wager. [16] i.e., earnestly. [17] i.e.,
obtain your own ransom. [18] safe keeping. [19] waited. [20] dawn.

455. Gawain was the queen's special attendant. In another poem in
this manuscript, "The Awntyrs of Arthur," he is her escort when she is
admonished by the spirit of her mother.

466. The sword was sworn upon because it was iron, which was a magic
substance; because it might be the abode of a spirit; or because of its
slight resemblance to a cross. See Wimberly 92.

His kny3tus couth hitte welle knaw
His was a sekur thinge.[21]
Sethun þay busket hom 3are,
Sqwith withowtun any mare,
To wete þe Kingus wele-fare,   475
Withowtun letting.   PRIMUS PASSUS.

XXXI

To þe forest þay take þe way;
Bothe Gawan and Kay,
Menealfe, and þe fare may
Comun to þe Kinge.   480
Þe bore brittunt[22] þay fande,
Was colurt[23] of the Kingus hande;
If he wore lord of þat londe,[24]
He hade no horsing.
Downe þay take þat birde bry3te,   485
Sette hur one behinde þe kny3te;
Hur horse for þe King was dy3te,
Withoutun letting;
Gaue Kay þe venesun to lede,
And hiet hamward gode spede;   490
Bothe þe birde and þe brede[25]
To Carlele þay bringe.

XXXII

Now as þay rode atte þe way,
Þe Kynge himseluun con say
Bothe to Gauan and to Kay,   495
"Quere wan 3e þis wi3te?"
Þenne Kay to þe King spake;
He sayd, "Sir, in þe forest as i con wake[26]
Atte þe anturus hoke,[27]
Þer mette me this kny3te;   500

---

[21] i.e., he had accomplished his aim. [22] butchered. [23] cut in sections. [24] i.e.,
but king though he was, etc. [25] cuts of meat. [26] watch. [27] adventurous oak.

481–2. In the MS., -a and -u are much alike. Though here the reading
is clearly *funde . . . hunde*, the rhyme shows that the vowels have been
confused, possibly in copying from a similar MS.

Þer togedur faȝte we
Be chesun of this lady fre;
On werre hase he þus wonnen me,
   With mayn and wyth myȝte;
And Gawan hase my rawunsun made   505
For a course þat he rode
And felle him in þe fild brode;
   He wanne þis buirde bryȝte.

XXXIII

He toke him þere to presunnere;"
Þen loghe þat damesell dere   510
And louet[28] with a mylde chere
   God and Sir Gawan.
Þenne sayd þe King, opon hiȝte,
All sqwithe to þe knyȝte,
"Quat is þi rawunsun, opon ryȝte?[29]   515
   Þe soth þou me sayn."
Þe tothir vnsquarut him with skille,
"I conne notte say þe þertille:
Hit is atte þe Quene wille;
   Qwi schuld i layne?   520
Bothe my dethe and my lyfe
Is inne þe wille of þi wife,
Quethur ho wulle stynte me of my strifc[30]
   Or putte me to payne."

XXXIV

"Grete God," quod þe King,   525
"Gif Gawan gode endinge,
For he is sekur[31] in alle kynne thinge
   To cowuntur with a knyȝte!
Of all playus he beris þe prise,[32]
Loos of þer ladise;[33]   530

---

[28] praised.   [29] truly.   [30] relieve me of my trouble (release me).   [31] to be depended upon.   [32] contests he carries off the honors.   [33] praise of ladies.

530. In constructions felt to be genitive or dative, the poet often uses þer for the more usual þe (cf. Norse þeirra).

Menealfe, and þou be wise,
　Hold þat þou beheʒte,
And i schall helpe þat i maye,"
The King himseluun con saye.
To Carlele þay take þe waye,　　　　　535
　And inne þe courte is liʒte.[34]
He toke þis damesell gente;
Before þe Quene is he wente,
And sayd, "Medame, i am hedur sente
　Fro Gawan, ʒour knyʒte."　　　　　540

XXXV

He sayd, "Medame, Gawan, ʒour knyʒte,
On werre hase wonun me to-nyʒte,
Be chesun of this birde briʒte;
　Mi pride conne he spille,
And gerut me squere squyftely　　　　545
To bringe the this lady
And my nowne body,
　To do hit in þi wille.
And i haue done as he me bade."
Now quod þe Quene, "And i am glad;　　550
Sethun þou art in my wille stade,[35]
　To spare or to spille,
I giffe þe to my lord þe Kinge,—
For he hase mestur[36] of such a thinge:
Of knyʒtus in a cowunturinge[37]—　　　555
　þis forward to fullfille."

XXXVI

Now þe Quene sayd, "God almyʒte
Saue me Gawan, my knyʒte,
That þus for wemen con fiʒte;
　Fro wothus him were !"[38]　　　　560
Gawan sayd, "Medame, as God me spede,
He is duʒti of dede,

---

[34] have alighted.　[35] put.　[36] need.　[37] battle.　[38] perils him shield.

A blithe burne[38a] on a stede,
  And grayth[39] in his gere."
Þenne þay fochet[40] furth a boke,   565
All þayre laes[41] for to loke;
Þe Kinge sone his[42] othe toke
  And squithely gerut him squere;
And sekirly, withouten fabull,
Þus dwellus he atte þe Rowun Tabull,   570
As prest knyȝte and priueabull,[43]
  With schild and with spere.

XXXVII

Nowe gode frindus are þay;
Þen carpus Sir Kay:
To þe King con he say: 575
  "Sire, a mervaell[44] thinke me
Of Bowdewyns avouyng,
Ȝustur-euyn in þe eunyng,
Withowtun any lettyng,
  Wele more thenne we thre."   580
Quod þe King, "Sothe to sayn,
I kepe no lengur for to layn:
I wold wete wundur fayn
  How best myȝte be."
Quod Kay, "And ȝe wold gif me leue,   585
And sithun take hit o no greue,[45]
Now schuld i propurly preue,
  As euyr myȝte i thee !"

XXXVIII

"Ȝisse," quod þe King, "on þat comande,[46]
Þat o payn on life and on londe   590

[38a] man.   [39] ready, fitly arrayed.   [40] brought.   [41] laws.   [42] Menealfe's.   [43] deserving.   [44] marvel.   [45] as no injury.   [46] these terms.

567. MS. *þo kinge.*
590. More usual is "on pain of life and of land," i.e., on pain of losing them.

Þat ȝe do him no wrunge,
  Butte saue wele my knyȝte.
As men monly[47] him mete,
And sithun forsette him þe strete:[48]
ȝe fynde him noȝte on his fete![49]   595
  Bewarre, for he is wyȝte.
For he is horsutte full wele
And clene clad in stele;
Is none of ȝo but þat he mun fele[50]
  Þat he may on lyȝte.   600
ȝe wynnun him noȝte owte of his way,"
Þe King himseluun con say;
"Him is lefe, i dar lay,
  To hald þat he heȝte."

XXXIX

Þenne sex ar atte on assente,[1]   605
Hase armut hom and furthe wente,
Brayd owte aure a bente,[2]
  Bawdewyn to mete,
With scharpe weppun and schene,
Gay gowuns of grene   610
To hold þayre armur clene,
  And were hitte[3] fro þe wete.
Thre was sette on ich side
To werne[4] him þe wayus wide:
Quere þe knyȝte schuld furth ride,   615
  For-sette[5] hym þe strete.
Wyth copus[6] couert þay hom thenne,
Ryȝte as þay hade bene vncowthe men,
For þat þay wold noȝte be kennet
  Euyn downe to þayre fete.   620

---

[47] manfully. [48] refuse him the road. [49] i.e., he will be mounted and ready to
fight. [50] feel; i.e., be injured. [1] agreed. [2] over a field. [3] protect it. [4] contest.
[5] blocked. [6] capes.

591. To restore the rhyme, read *schonde*.
612. Chaucer's Knight also wore a cloth over his armor to preserve its
luster (Pro. 75).

XL

Now as þay houut and þay hyild,[7]
þay se a schene vndur schild
Come prekand fast aure þe filde
    On a fayre stede;
Wele armut, and dyȝte   625
As freke[8] redy to fyȝte,
Toward Carlele ryȝte
    He hies gode spede.
He see þer sixe in his way;
þenne to þaymseluun con þay say,   630
"Now he is ferd, i dar lay[9]
    And of his lyfe dredus."
þen Kay crius opon heȝte,
All squyth to þe knyȝte,
"Othir flee or fiȝte: 635
    þe tone behouus þe nede !"[10]

XLI

þenne þay kest þayre copus hom fro;
Sir Bawdewyn se þat hit wasse so,
And sayd, "And ȝe were als mony mo,
    Ȝe gerutte me notte to flee.   640
I hauue my ways for to weynde
For to speke with a frynde;
As ȝe ar herdmen hinde,[11]
    Ȝe marre[12] notte me !"
þenne þe sex sembult[13] hom in fere   645
And squere by Him þat boȝte vs dere,
"þou passus neuyr away here
    Butte gif þou dede be !"
"Ȝisse, hardely,"[14] quod Kay,
"He may take anothir way—   650

---

[7] waited and went about. [8] man. [9] afraid, I dare wager. [10] the one (or the other) is incumbent on you. [11] gentle retainers. [12] hinder (subjunctive). [13] gathered. [14] surely.

622. MS. *þay so.* The form here given is the usual spelling in the poem.
632. Probably for *adrede.*
650. The point of view is hastily shifted; Kay addresses first the company, then Baldwin.

And þer schall no mon do nere say[15]
þat schall greue þe !"

XLII

'Gode þe forȝilde,"[16] quod þe knyȝte,
"For i am in my wais riȝte;
ȝistur euyn i þe King hiȝte   655
To cumme to my mete.
I warne ȝo, frekes, be ȝe bold,[17]
My ryȝte ways wille i holde !"
A spere in fewtre he foldes,[18]
A gode and a grete.   660
Kay stode nexte him in his way:
He iopput[19] him aure on his play;
þat heuy horse on him lay;
He squonet in þat strete.
He rode to þere othir fyue: 665
þayre schene schildus con he riue,[20]
And faure felle[21] he belyue,
In hie in þat hete.[22]

XLIII

Hardely, withouten delay,
þe sex[23] to hom hase takyn vppe Kay;   670
And thenne Sir Baw[d]ewin con say,
"Will ȝe any more?"
þe toþer vnsquarutte him þertille,
Sayd, "þou may weynd quere þou wille,
For þou hase done vs noȝte butte skille,[24]   675
Gif we be wowundut sore."

---

[15] do or say (anything).   [16] reward; an exclamation of impatience.   [17] you may
be confident (that).   [18] places in rest.   [19] dashed down, pushed over.   [20] split.
[21] four did he fell.   [22] rage.   [23] sixth.   [24] right.

664. MS. *þat squete*. The initial combinations look much alike in the
MS. But *squate* (cf. "Ipomadon" 4352) means "heavy tumble."

665. At several points in the manuscript, words have been scrawled on
the margin. On fol. 48, at the bottom, are two lines: *Per me Rychardum
Lathum; Thomas Yrlond*. After each, in another hand, has been added:
scripsit hoc.

He brayd aure to þe Kinge,
Withowtun any letting;
He asshed if he hade herd any tithing
    In þayre holtus hore.   680
Þe kny3te stedit[25] and stode;
Sayd, "Sir, as i come thro 3ondur wode,
I herd ne se[26] butte gode
    Quere i schuld furthe fare."

XLIV

Thanne was þe Kinge ameruaylet þare   685
That he wold telle him no more.
Als squithur[27] þay ar 3are,
    To masse ar thay wente.
By þe masse wasse done,
Kay come home sone,   690
Told þe King before none,
    "We ar all schente
Of Sir Baudewyn, 3our kny3te:
He is nobull in þe fi3te,
Bold, hardy, and wi3te   695
    To bide on a bente.[28]
Fle wille he neuyr more:
Him is much leuyr dee þore.
I may banne[29] hur þat him bore,
    Suche harmes haue i hente!"   700

XLV

Noue þe King sayd, "Fle he ne can,
Ne werne his mete to no man;
Gife any buirne[30] schuld him ban,
    A mcruail hit ware."
Þenne þe King cald his mynstrelle   705
And told him holly[31] his wille:
Bede him layne atte hit were[32] stille:
    Þat he schuld furth fare

---

[25] pondered. [26] neither heard nor saw. [27] soon as. [28] field. [29] curse. [30] man.
[31] entirely. [32] so that it should be.

To Baudewins of Bretan:
"I cummawunde þe, or þou cum agayne,   710
Faurty days, o payne,[33]
  Loke þat þou duelle þere,
  And wete me preuely to say
If any mon go meteles[34] away;
  For þi wareson for ay,   715
  Do þou me neuyrmore."[35]

XLVI

Þen þe mynstrell weyndus on his way
Als fast as he may;
  Be none of þe thryd day,
  He funde þaym atte þe mete,   720
Þe lady and hur mené
And gestus grete plenté;
  Butte porter none funde he
  To werne[36] him þe ȝate,
Butte rayket[37] in to þe halle   725
Emunge þe grete and þe smalle,
And loket aboute him aure-alle:
  He herd of no threte,[38]
  Butte riall[39] seruys and fyne:
In bollus birlutte[40] þay þe wyne,   730
And cocus[41] in þe kechine
  Squytheli con squete.[42]

XLVII

Þen þe ladi conne he loute,[43]
And þe buirdes all aboute;
  Both withinne and withoute,   735
  No faute he þer fonde.
Knyȝte, squyer, ȝoman, ne knaue,
Hom lacket noȝte þat þay schuld haue;
Þay nedut notte aftur hit to craue:
  Hit come to hor honde.   740

---

[33] on penalty. [34] unfed. [35] on your eternal welfare, do no more (than this).
[36] deny. [37] made his way. [38] threat, constraint. [39] splendid. [40] passed.
[41] cooks. [42] sweat, toil. [43] bow.

Þenne he wente to þe dece,
Before þe pruddust[44] in prece;
Þat lady was curtase,
　　And bede him stille stonde.
He sayd he was knoun and couthe,   745
And was comun fro bi southe,[45]
And ho had myrth of his mouthe
　　To here his tithand.

XLVIII

A sennyჳte[46] duellut he þare;
Þer was no spense for to spare:[47]   750
Burdes[48] þay were neuyr bare,
　　Butte euyr couurt clene;
Bothe knyჳte and squiere,
Mynstrelle and messyngere,
Pilgreme and palmere   755
　　Was welcum, i wene.
Þer was plenty of fode:
Pore men hade þayre gode,[49]
Mete and drinke or þay ჳode,
　　To wete wythoutyn wene.   760
Þe lord lenge[50] wold noჳte,
Butte come home qwen him gode thoჳte,
And both he hase with him broჳte
　　The Kinge and þe Quene.   A FITTE.

XLIX

Now þer come fro þe kechine   765
Riall seruice and fine;
Ther was no wonting[1] of wine
　　To lasse ne to mare.
Þay hade atte þayre sopere
Riche metes and dere;   770
Þe King, with a blythe chere,
　　Bade hom sle care.[2]

---

[44] proudest.　[45] the south.　[46] week.　[47] spending spared.　[48] tables.　[49] i.e., their needs were filled.　[50] Baldwin tarry (in Arthur's court).　[1] lack.　[2] kill care, be merry.

Þan sayd þe Kinge opon hiȝte,
All sqwithe to þe knyȝte,
"Such a seruice on a nyȝte   775
    Se i neuyr are."
Þenne Bawdewyn smylit and on him logh;
Sayd, "Sir, God hase a gud pluȝe;
He may send vs all enughe:
    Qwy schuld we spare?"   780

L

"Now i cummawunde þe," quod þe King,
"To-morne in þe mornyng
Þat þou weynde on huntyng,
    To wynne vs þe dere.
Fare furthe to þe fenne;[3]   785
Take with þe howundus and men,
For þou conne hom best kenne:
    Þou knoes best here.
For all day to-morne will i bide,
And no forthir will i ride,   790
Butte with þe lades of pride
    To make me gud chere."
To bed bownut[4] þay þat nyȝte,
And atte þe morun, atte days liȝte,
Þay blew hornys opon hiȝte   795
    And ferd furthe in fere.

LI

Þenne þe Kynge cald his huntere,
And sayd, "Felaw, come here!"
Þe toþer, with a blithe chere,
    Knelet on his kne: 800
Dowun to þe Kinge con he lowte.[5]
"I commawunde þe to be all nyȝte oute;

---

[3] swamp. [4] went. [5] bow.

778. "God has a good plough," i.e., he has the means of sending us
enough food.

Bawdewyn, þat is sturun and stowte,
   With þe schall he be.
Erly in þe dawyng[6]   805
Loke þat ȝe come fro huntyng;
If ȝe no venesun bring,
   Full litille reche me."
Þe toþer vnsquarut him þertille,
Sayd, "Sir, þat[7] is atte ȝour aune wille,   810
Þat hald i resun and skille,
   As euyr myȝte i the."

LII

And atte euyn þe King con him dyȝte,
And callut to him a knyȝte,
And to þe chambur full riȝte   815
   He hiees gode waye,[8]
Qwere þe lady of þe howse
And maydyns ful beuteowse,
Were curtase and curiowse,[9]
   Forsothe in bed lay.   820
The Kyng bede, "Vndo;"
Þe lady asshes, "Querto?"[10]
He sayd, "I am comun here, loe,[11]
   In derne[12] for to play."
Ho sayd, "Haue ȝe notte ȝour aune quene here,   825
And i my lord to my fere?
To-nyȝte more neȝe ȝe me nere,[13]
   In fayth, gif i may !"[14]

LIII

"Vndo þe dore," quod þe Kinge,
"For bi Him þat made all thinge,   830

---

[6] dawning.   [7] whatever.   [8] directly.   [9] attentive.   [10] why.   [11] lo!   [12] secret.
[13] nearer shall you not be to me.   [14] i.e., if I have my way.

813. On this incident, see *PMLA* 21.575, where its relationship to "The Earl of Toulouse" is discussed.
821. MS. *Vnto.*
825. As in other passages, *Ho sayd* is hypermetrical.

þou schall haue no harmynge
Butte in þi none[15] wille."
Vppe rose a damesell squete,
In þe Kinge þat[16] ho lete;
He sette him downe on hur beddus fete,   835
And talkes so hur tille:
Sayd, "Medame, my kny3te
Mun lye with þe all ny3te
Til to-morne atte days li3te;
Take hit on non ille;[17]   840
For als euyr my3te i the,
þou schall harmeles[18] be:
We do hit for a wedde-fee,[19]
The stryue for to stylle."[20]

LIV

Thenne þe Kyng sayd to his kny3te,   845
"Sone þat þou were vndy3te,[21]
And in 3ondur bedde ry3te!
Hie þe gud spede."
þe kny3te did as he him bade,
And qwenne ho se him vnclad,   850
þen þe lady wex drede,
Worlyke in wede.[22]
He sayd, "Lye downe preuely hur by,
Butte neghe no3te þou þat lady;
For and þou do, þou schall dey   855
For þi derfe[23] dede;
Ne no3te so hardy þou stur,[24]
Ne onus turne þe to hur."
þe toþer sayd, "Nay, sur."
For him hade he drede.   860

LV

Thenne þe Kyng asshet a chekkere,[25]
And cald a damesel dere;

---

[15] thine own.   [16] that she should.   [17] i.e., do not be vexed.   [18] unharmed.
[19] wager.   [20] to settle a dispute.   [21] undressed.   [22] prudent one.   [23] presumptuous.   [24] be not so bold as to move.   [25] asked for chess board.

851. Read *adrade*, fearful.

Downe þay sette hom in fere
    Opon þe bed-syde.
Torches was þer mony liȝte,   865
And laumpus brennyng full bryȝte;
Butte notte so hardy was þat knyȝte
    His hede onus to hide.
Butte fro þay began to play
Quyle[26] on þe morun þat hit was day,   870
Euyr he lokette as he lay,
    Baudewynne to byde.
And erly in þe dawyng
Come þay home from huntyng,
And hertis[27] conne þay home bring,   875
    And x buckes of pride.

LVI

Þay toke þis venesun fyne
And hade hit to kechine;
Þe Kinge sende aftur Bawdewine,
    And bede him cum see.   880
To þe chaumbur he takes þe way;
He fyndus þe King atte his play;
A knyȝte in his bedde lay
    With his lady.
Þenne sayd þe King opon hiȝte,   885
"To-nyȝte myssutte[28] i my knyȝte,
And hithir folut i him ryȝte;
    Here funden is hee;
And here i held hom bothe stille
For to do hom in þi wille;[29]   890
And gif þou take hit now till ille,
    No selcouthe thinge[30] me !"

LVII

Þen þe King asshed, "Art þou wroth?"
"Nay, sir," he sayd, "withouten othe,

---

[26] till.   [27] harts.   [28] missed.   [29] put at your disposal.   [30] no marvel seems it to me.

876. The x is a doubtful reading.
879. MS. *sonde.* *O-* and *e-* are much alike in the MS.

Ne wille þe lady no lothe;[31]   895
I telle ʒo as quy:
For hitte was atte hur awen wille;
Els thur[s]t[32] no mon comun hur tille;
And gif i take hitte þenne to ille,
    Muche maugreue[33] haue y.   900
For mony wyntur togedur we haue bene,
And ʒette ho dyd me neuyr no tene,
And ich syn schall be sene
    And sette full sorely."[34]
Þe King sayd, "And i hade þoʒte[35]   905
Quy þat þou wrathis þe noʒte
And fyndus him in bed broʒte
    By þi laydy?"

LVIII

Quod Bawdewyn, "And ʒe will sitte,
I schall do ʒo wele to witte."   910
"ʒisse!" quod þe King, "I þe hete,
    And þou will noʒte layne."
"Hit befelle in ʒour fadur tyme,
Þat was þe Kyng of Costantyne,
Puruayed a grete oste[36] and a fyne   915
    And wente into Spayne.
We werrut on a sawdan
And all his londus we wan,
And himseluun, or we blan;   920
    Þen were we full fayn.
I wos so lufd with þe King,
He gafe me to my leding[37]

---

[31] wish her harm. [32] durst. [33] trouble. [34] if each sin is to be given attention and sternly judged(?). [35] i.e., I marvelled. [36] gathered a large host. [37] under my leadership.

914. In the prose "Merlin," Constant is Uther's father. In Layamon's "Brut," a Constantine, son of Cador, is Arthur's successor. The reference here may be due to a confusion with one of these. Two of Arthur's predecessors were said by Geoffrey of Monmouth to have become emperors of Rome.

Lordus atte my bidding,
Was buxum and bayne.[38]

LIX

He gafe me a castell to gete,[39]   925
With all þe lordschippus[40] grete;
I hade men atte my mete,
    Fyue hundryth and mo,
And no wemen butte thre,
Þat owre seruandis schild be.   930
One was bryȝtur of ble
    Þen þer othir toe.
Toe were atte one assente:[41]
Þe thrid felow haue þay hente;
Vnto a well ar þay wente,   935
    And says hur allso:
"Sithin all þe loce in þe lise,[42]
Þou schall tyne þine aprise;"[43]
And wurchun as þe vnwise,
    And tite conne hur sloe.   940

LX

And for þo workes were we wo,
Gart threte þo othir for to slo.[44]
Þenne says þe tone of þo,
    "Lette vs haue oure life,
And we schall atte ȝour bidding be   945
As mycull as we all thre;
Is none of ȝaw in preueté
    Schall haue wontyng of wyfe."

---

[38] obedient and ready.   [39] guard.   [40] i.e., supervision of the vassals.   [41] agreed.
[42] praise resides in thee.   [43] fail in thy undertaking.   [44] caused the others to be
threatened with death.

929. This strange story has two analogues: see A. de Montaiglon and
G. Reynaud, "Recueil Général . . . des Fabliaux" I. xxvi; and Johannes
de Garlandia, "Poetria" (a Latin tragedy). Cf. *MLN.* 8.251. For similar
cynicism about women, cf. "Salomon and Marcolf," and "Kittredge Anniversary Volume" 209.

Þay held vs wele þat þay heȝte,
And diȝte⁴⁵ vs on þe day-liȝte,   950
And þayre body vche nyȝte,
   Withoutun any stryue.
Þe tone was more louely,
Þat þe toþer hade enuy;
Hur throte in sundur preuely,   955
   Ho cutte hitte with a knyfe.

LXI

Muche besenes⁴⁶ hade we
How þat best myȝte be;⁴⁷
Þay asshed cowuncell atte me
   To do hur to dede.   960
And i vnsquarut and sayd, "Nay!
Loke furst qwatt hur seluun will say,
Queþer ho may serue vs all to pay;
   Þat is a bettur rede."
Þer ho hette vs in þat halle   965
To do all þat a woman schild falle,⁴⁸
Wele for to serue vs alle
   Þat stode in þat stede.
Ho held vs wele þat ho heȝte,
And diȝte vs on þe day-liȝte,   970
And hur body iche nyȝte
   Intill oure bed beed.⁴⁹

LXII

And bi this tale i vndurstode,
Wemen þat is of mylde mode
And syne giffes hom⁵⁰ to gode,   975
   Mecull may ho mende;¹
And þo þat giffus hom to þe ille,
And sithin þayre folis² will fullfill,

---

⁴⁵ waited on us. ⁴⁶ perplexity. ⁴⁷ what was best to do. ⁴⁸ work befitting a woman. ⁴⁹ offered. ⁵⁰ devote themselves. ¹ greatly improve (herself).
² foolish.

965. MS. þer.
974. For *evyll mode?* As in other passages the numbers are confused.

I telle ʒo wele, be propur skille,[3]
   No luffe will inne hom lenge.[4]   980
With gode wille grathely hom gete,
Meke and mylde atte hor mete;
[And] thryuandly, withoutun threte,
   Ioy atte iche ende.
Forthi ieluis[5] schall i neuer be   985
For no siʒte þat i see,
Ne no buirdes briʒte of ble;
   Ich ertheli thinke[6] hase ende."

LXIII

þe King sayd, "þou says wele.
Sir," he sayd, "as haue i sele,[7]   990
I will þou wote hit iche dele;
   þerfore come y.
þi lady gret me to squere squyftelé,
Or i myʒte gete entré,
þat ho schuld harmeles[8] be,   995
   And all hire cumpany.
þen gerut i my knyʒte
To go in bed with þe buirde bryʒte,
On þe far[9] syde of þe liʒte,
   And lay hur dowun by.   1000
I sette me doune hom besyde,
Here þe for to abide;
He neʒhit neuyr no naked syde
   Of þi lady.

LXIV

Forthi, of ielusnes, be þou bold,[10]   1005
Thine avow may þou hold;

---

[3] true reasoning.   [4] dwell.   [5] jealous.   [6] thing.   [7] happiness.   [8] unharmed.
[9] right.   [10] concerning jealousy you may be assured.

981 ff. I.e., select those of good disposition, who are good natured at
the table; and spiritedly, without threatening, be happy at whatever befalls.
   984. MS. *And ioy.*
   999. Probably a lamp or candle was set in a stick attached to the bed;
but the meaning is not clear.

Butte of þo othir thingus þat þou me told
I wold wete more:
Quy þou dredus notte þi dede[11]
No non þat bitus on þi brede? 1010
As [eu]yr brok i my hede,
　þi ȝatis are euyr ȝare !"[12]
Quod Bawdewyn, "I schall ȝo telle:
Atte þe same castell
Quere þis antur befelle, 1015
　Besegitte we ware.
On a day we vsshet[13] oute
And toke presonerus stoute;
þe tone of owre feloys[14] hade doute,
　And durst notte furthe fare. 1020

LXV

þe caytef crope into a tunne[15]
þat was sette þerowte[16] in þe sunne;
And þere come fliand a gunne,[17]
　And lemet as þe leuyn;[18]
Lyȝte opon hitte,[19] atte þe last, 1025
þat was fastnut so fast;
All in sundur hit brast,
　In six or in seuyn.
And there hit sluȝe him als
(And his hert was so fals !); 1030
Sone þe hed fro þe hals,[20]
　Hit lyputt full euyn.[21]
And we come fro þe feȝting
Sowunde,[22] withoutun hurting,
And þen we louyd[23] þe King 1035
　þat heghhest was in heuyn.

LXVI

þen owre feloys con say,
"Schall no mon dee or his day,

---

[11] death.　[12] i.e., open.　[13] issued.　[14] fellows.　[15] barrel.　[16] outside.　[17] projectile.
[18] gleamed like the lightning.　[19] alighted on the cask.　[20] neck.　[21] i.e., was
entirely severed.　[22] sound.　[23] praised.
　1019. MS. foloys.

Butte he cast himselfe away
Throȝhe wontyng of witte." 1040
And þere myne avow made i—
So dyd all þat cumpany—
For dede neuyr to be drery;[24]
Welcum is hit:
Hit is a kyndely thing." 1045
"Þou says soth," quod þe King,
"Butte of þi thryd avowyng
Telle me quych is hit:
Quy þi mete þou will notte warne[25]
To no leuand barne?" 1050
"Ther is no man þat may hit tharne;[26]
Lord, ȝe schall wele wete.

LXVII

For þe sege aboute vs lay stille;
We hade notte all atte oure wille
Mete and drinke vs to fille: 1055
Vs wontutte þe fode.
So come in a messyngere,
Bade, "Ȝild vppe all þat is here!"—
And speke with a sturun schere[27]
I nyll, by þe rode!— 1060
I gerutte him bide to none,
Callud þe stuard sone,
Told him all as he schuld done,
As counsell is gud;[28]
Gerutte trumpe[29] on the wall, 1065
And couerd burdes[30] in þe hall;
And i myself cmunge hom all
As a king stode.

---

[24] unhappy. [25] refuse. [26] lack. [27] =chere; i.e., I will never speak harshly. [28] as is a good plan. [29] blow trumpets. [30] set tables.

1053. For parallels, etc., to this story, see *Revue Hispanique* 12.281, especially 296 ff.; and I. P. McKeehan's "St. Edmund of East Anglia" (*Colorado Studies* 15.55 ff.).

LXVIII

I gerut hom wasshe, to mete wente;
Aftur þe stuard þen i sente;   1070
I bede þat he schuld take entente[31]
    That all schuld well fare:
Bede bringe bred plenté,
And wine in bollus of tre,[32]
Þat no wontyng schuld be   1075
    To lasse ne to mare.
We hade no mete butte for on day;
Hit come in a nobull aray.
Þe messungere lokit ay
    And se hom sle care.[33]   1080
He toke his leue atte me;
We gerutte him drinke atte þe ȝate,
And gafe him giftus grete,
    And furthe con he fare.

LXIX

But quen þe messyngere was gone,   1085
Þese officers ichone
To me made þay grete mone,
    And drerely con say;
Sayd, "In this howse is no bred,
No quyte wine nere[34] red;   1090
Ȝo behoues ȝild vppe þis stid
    And for oure lyuys pray."
Ȝette God helpus ay his man!
Þe messyngere come agayn þan
Withoute to þe cheuytan,[35]   1095
    And sone conne he say:
"Þoȝhe ȝe sege þis seuyn ȝere,
Castelle gete ȝe none here,
For þay make als mury chere
    Als hit were ȝole-day!"   1100

---

[31] attend to it. [32] wooden bowls. [33] saw them make merry. [34] nor. [35] chief.

1081. To restore the rhyme, read *me atte.*

1082. The stirrup-cup and the reward were attentions that only people well supplied with food and money could afford.

1090. MS. *nyf red.*

LXX

Þen þe messyngere con say,
"I rede 3o, hie 3o heþinn away,
For in 3our oste is no play,
  Butte hongur and thurst."
Þenne þe King con his kny3tis calle;   1105
Sethinn to cowunsell wente þay alle;
"Sythinn no bettur may befalle,
  This hald i þe best."
Euyn atte þe mydny3te,
Hor lordis sembelet to a sy3te,[36]   1110
Þat were hardy and wi3te:
  Þay remuyt of hor rest.[37]
Mete laynes mony lakke,
And þere mete hor sege brake,
And gerut hom to giffe vs þe bake:[38]   1115
  To preke þay were full preste.

LXXI

And þen we lokit were þay lay
And see oure enmeys away;
And þen oure felawis con say,
  þe lasse and þe maro,   1120
"He þat gode may gete,
And wernys men of his mete,
Gud Gode þat is grete
  Gif him sory care!
For the mete of þe messyngere,   1125
Hit mendutte[39] alle oure chere."
Þen sayd þe King, þat þay my3te here,
  And sqwythely con squere,
"In the conne we fynde no fabull;[40]
Þine avowes arne profetabull;"   1130
And þus recordus[41] þe Rownde Tabulle,
  þe lasse and þe more.

---

[36] in plain view (a tag).   [37] left their sleep.   [38] turn their backs on us.
[39] mended.   [40] weakness.   [41] publicly agree.

LXXII

Thenne þe Kinge and his knyȝtis alle,
þay madun myrthe in þat halle,
And þen þe lady conne þay calle,   1135
    The fayrist to fold;[42]
Sayd Bawdewyn, "And þou be wise,
Take þou þis lady of price,
For muche loue in hur lyce;[43]
    To þine hert hold.   1140
Ho is a buirde full bryȝte,
And þerto semely to þy siȝte,
And þou hase holdinn all þat þou hiȝte,
    As a kniȝte schulde!"
Now Ihesu Lord, Heuyn-kynge,   1145
He graunt vs all his blessynge,
And gife vs alle gode endinge,
    That made vs on þe mulde.[44]   AMEN.

---

[42] to embrace. [43] lies. [44] earth.

1137. *Bawdewyn* is a dative.
1140. The -*d* of *hold* is expuncted.
1148. Ending a poem with the same line with which it begins is a Celtic device (*Rom. Rev.* 7.243).

COMPOSITES

IPOMADON

This piece is probably more like the erroneous conception of romance generally current than any other in Middle English. The youthful knight falls in love with a princess of a neighboring kingdom without having seen her; spends years in her service without revealing his high rank; wins a tournament of which she is the prize, though he remains in disguise by changing his armor each day; proves himself in many adventures in far lands; and at last appears, still disguised, to champion the lady against an undesired suitor. The complications are numerous; the situations, even those without magic, are wildly improbable; and the pace of the story is deliberate, in spite of the great plenty of incidents.

The English poem is a translation, slightly altered, of the French of Hue de Rotelande, an Englishman (fl. 1190). He made free with the best effects in other romances, but combined them with great literary skill. References to the French are to the edition of Koelbing and Koschwitz.

The dialect is north midland, of the middle of the fourteenth century. The word *fere*, which occurs frequently, is a translation of the French, meaning "proud one" (cf. mod. Fr. *fière*). The scribe often wrote *-ey* where the midland spelling was *-e* (*deyre*, harm). A plural subject sometimes has a singular verb (cf. 390). Final *-ll*, which has a cross-stroke except in a few lines (353, 389, 430, 1137, 1189, 3043, 3138, and 3179), is printed as *-ll*. Final crossed *-h*, which rarely has the stroke, is printed *-he*. The flourish after final *-f* has been printed as *-fe*. Other flourishes (after final *-d*, *-m*, *-n*, and *-g*) have been disregarded.

Through the kindness of the Rev. C. T. E. Phillips and the other authorities of Chetham's Library, it has been possible to prepare the text from rotographs. The numbering is as in Koelbing's edition, which also contains many emendations adopted here; only the less obvious ones are credited to him. Those marked H. are Holthausen's; those marked Z., Zupitza's.

Ipomadon at the Court

After a long journey, the youth and his tutor, Tholomew, arrive at the lady's court. She has been holding a parliament, to reconcile two knights who have quarreled.

That day the fere hade made hem frende,
And broughte that grette debate[1] to ende:
    So ys she ware and wyce!
Ladyes, witte that she wille not
Abowtte hur suffyr no debatte,   350
    So grette goodenes in her lyethe.
Her meyny lovyd her euerilke one.
Into the hall comys Ipomadon,
    Amonge thes lordys of price;
An ewen[2] pase forthe he paste,   355
Nother to softe[3] ne to ffaste,
    But at his owne devyce.[4]

Lordys, laydys in the hall
Lokis on hym, men and all,
    And grette mervaylle they þought: 360
He was large of lyme and lythe,[5]
And made so wonder [fayre] therwythe;
    Of ffetter faylyd hym not.[6]
A llyttell wax he rede, for shame;
Full welle that coloure hym became;   365
    Before that high he sowghtte.[7]
His dobelett was of red welvet,
Off bryght golde botuns ibete,[8]
    That worthely was wrovghte.

---

[1] war, contention. [2] even, easy. [3] slow. [4] inclination. [5] limb and joint (a tag).
[6] he lacked nothing in his features; i.e., had good features. [7] went before that high (princess). [8] covered over with bright gold buttons.

349. Koelbing proposed, *Ladyes wote that she wille nat Abowtte*, etc. Koeppel suggested, *That she wille not (ladyes wate!)*, etc. MS. *Ladyes wille that she not wote*. The poem has several admonitions to proud ladies.
351. To help the meter, read *soche* for *so grette*.
362. MS. *then wythe*.

His mantell was of skarlett[9] fyne,   370
Furryd with good armyne:
   Ther myght no better been:
The bordoure all of red sendell;[10]
That araye became hym wele,
   To wete withouten wene.[11]   375
A noble countenavnce he hade:
A blyther and a better made,
   Before they had not sayne,
Also bryght his coloure shone.
All hym lovyd that lokyd hym one,   380
   Bothe lord and lady shene.

And longe he beheldis the fere,
But nothynge chaunges her chere
   For carpynge[12] of the crowde:
[Her] hertte is sett so mekyll of wyte,   385
With love it is not sammyd yte,[13]
   Thowȝe she be shene in schcrovde;[14]
But aftur sore it bande the fre[15]—
And so i wold that all ye shuld be,
   That is of love so prowde!—   390
The chyld before her knclys than,
And to the lady he began
   To tell his tale on lowde.

He sayd, "Dereworthy[16] damysell,
Grette God kepe the in hele,[17]   395
   And all thy ffayre menye:
Vnder heyvyn is holdyn none
So worthy a lady as thow arte on,
   Ne of so grette beweté.
Ofte sythes this haue i harde saye: 400
A noble[r] courte then thyne allwaye
   There may non holdyn bee.

---

[9] scarlet cloth. [10] silk. [11] doubt. [12] i.e., praise. [13] her heart is so devoted to reasoning that it has not yet joined with love. [14] clothing (a tag). [15] fettered that noble (one). [16] precious; i.e., splendid. [17] health.

376. MS. *countenavaunce.*
398. For the construction, see Int. VII. 5.

The to serve haue i thowghte;
Thereffore haue i hedyr sought,
 Oute of ffarre contraye.   405

What-as[18] thou wilte put me tow
That longis a gentyll man to doo,
 Gladlye do wille i;
Thereffore i praye the me tell
Whedur thow [wilte] i with the dwell,   410
 Or wynde thedyr i come ffroo;
On asay[19] now shall i see
Yff it be as men say of the
 In countreys many and fell."
The lady satt and hym behylde,   415
And lykyd full wele the tale he tolde,
 When she hym hard[20] say soo,

That he wold hur servand be.
She behylde his grette bewté,
 And in her hertt she thought   420
That he myghte with grette honoure
Haue seruyd kynge or emperoure,
 He was so worthy wroughte.
A thynge in her hert gan ryse,
That she shuld lyke wele hes seruyce: 425
 Forgoo hym wold she note.
She answeryd hym full curtesly,
"Thou arte welcome, Belamye;[21]
 I thanke hym that the browghte.

Syn thou to seruys will be sett,   430
What ys thy name, þou stravnge valete?[22]

---

[18] whatever.   [19] by proof.   [20] heard.   [21] good friend.   [22] attendant.

408, 410. Koelbing's emendations. MS. *do i wille.* Koelbing emended
414 to *and mo* for the rhyme. Since the poet does not elsewhere use
alternate rhyme in the short lines, and since other rhymes are considerably
altered by the scribe, an emendation is necessary.
419. MS. *behyldys.*
430 ff. Willert suggested omitting 432, and deleting *name* in 433.
431. The Oxford Dictionary has no example of "valet" in this sense

Anon that thou tell mee."
"I was callyd at home by the same name,
And borne i was in ferre contré;
　Forther watte ye not for me,　　　　　435
Wheddyr ye blysse[23] or blame!"
The lady att his wordys lough:
She sayd sone, "This holde i good inowe:
　It is a noble name!
And thou artte welcome, securly."　　　440
His mayster sayd, that stode hym by,
　"Gravnte mercy,[24] madame."

The lady callyd hur botelere:
"This cupe of gold þou shalte take here,
　And gyffe hit to younde man;　　　　445
To buttrey dore lede hym with the,
Therwith of wyne to serue me:
　We shall se yf he can."
The butteler hym the cuppe betoke,
And he was fayne, and not foresoke;[25]　　450
　To the chylde sayd he thanne,
"It ys my ladyes byddynge
That off wyne thou shall here bring."
　In covrte thus he began.

Rightte in his mantell, as he stode,　　455
With the botteler forthe he youde;
　The cupe on hande he bare.
All that lovyd þat chyld beforne
For that dede lovghe hym to skorne,
　Bothe the lesse and the more:　　　　460

─────────
[23] approve.　[24] thanks.　[25] did not refuse.

for the Middle English period. In the French, the hero describes himself
to the lady: *Dame, un estrange valet sui* (463).

433. I.e., at home his name was Belamye. Cf. "Perceval," "Libeaus
Desconus."

438. As often in this MS., *She sayd* is inserted, to the detriment of
the meter.

453. MS. *That thou off wyne shall serue here.*

Yffe that he shuld serue one,
It were semande,[26] they sayd ylkone,
  Away his mantell were;
But littill knewe þey his entente:
To the buttery-dore he went,   465
  And offe he caste hit yare.

To the boteler than went hee:
"Syr, this mantell gyffe i the,
  As i haue happe or sele;[27]
And thow wilte take þis sympull gyfte,   470
It shall be mendyd, be my thryfte,
  With efte so good a wille."[28]
The butteler thankyd hym curtesly,
And sayd, "Gentyll syr, gramercy
  Off this ffrenshipe ifelle.[29]   475
In awght þat i can do or saye,
Be grette God, that oweth this day,
  It shall be quytte full wele.

For this vii yere, be my thryfte,
Was not gevyne me suche a gyfte!"   480
  The mantyll he toke hym tille.
All they that thowght skorne before
Thought themselfe folys therefore:
  They satt and held them stille,
And sayden it was a gentill dede;   485
There may no man, so God vs spede,
  Otherwyse say be skylle![30]
All they spake in prevyté,
"A hundyrd men a man may se,
  Yet wott not one his wille."   490

---

[26] fitting.   [27] fortune.   [28] it shall be pieced out (as I hope for good fortune!) with just as much good will.   [29] act of friendship performed.   [30] intelligently.

463. When serving, the squire wore his tunic, but no mantle. Cf. the cuts in Wright. Only the marshal wore a mantle.
476. MS. *An in.*—H.
482. MS. *all them.*
489. MS. *men may a man se.*—H.

Ipomadon's Soliloquy

The hero's accomplishments make him a favorite; but his preference of hunting to more manly sports excites surprise. The princess finally reproves him, saying that no knight is worthy of a lady's love until he has proved his valor. Not knowing that she returns his love, he goes home in despair. The following soliloquy is typical of the method of the piece. Much of it is a debate between the knight's reason and his heart.

When the chyld his leve had tane,
To his in[ne] he is ganne   1050
    With sorowys and sykynge sare.
He saw right nought þat was hym leffe:
All thynge he þought dyd hym greffe
    In ye,[31] bothe lesse and more.
His maystur Thelamewe he prayed   1055
That his bedde were redy arayde:
    "Therein i wold i were !"
Off all the nyght he slepyd noþinge,
But lay with many a sore sykynge,
    And mornyethe aye more and more.   1060

"Alas, foule, what alysse[32] the
Soo farre oute of thy owne contré
    Heddur for to come?
Thou dyd as many haue done ayre:[33]
Come to seke sorye care—   1065
    And therof hathe þou sum !
Thou myghttis no man but þiselffe blame:
Thyne owne wille made þe come fro hame;
    Thereffore no man wille the moone.
As euer haue i happe or selle,   1070
That ma[r]kis[34] þat lady, eueri deyle;
    Yet love makis me so dome ![35]

---

[31] eye. [32] ails. [33] before. [34] notices. [35] dumb.

1069. Read *none* for *no man.*—H.; so also in 1067.
1070 ff. MS. *or skylle; þan lady; so deme. Selle* is Kaluza's proposal; *dome* is Koelbing's.

Be God of heyvyn, now i wott well
That she percevys hit, euery dealee,
   How i with love was tane.   1075
And thoo she gaffe me þat vpbrayde,[36]
Hit was for gode þat she me sayde,
   Thowȝe i toke hit with none.[37]
Therefore spake she all þat þing,
To make me leve my long lokynge,   1080
   That i caste hur vppon!

Thereatt i wotte welle she gave tene
Yet be hur owne cosyn, as i wene;
   She blamyd me forthye!
And sayd it was a skorne, perdé,   1085
That anny suche brothels[38] as we
   Anny ladyes love shuld trye,
That nought þinkyth for to thryve,
Nor neuer gyffys[39] in oure lyve
   To no chevalrye;   1090
But ther was anoþur þinge:
On me she cast an longe lokynge:
   I toke good hede therebye.

A, dere God! what myghte þat meane?
I shall tell the all bedene: 1095
   Younde lady is so whyce,[40]
In fayth, she holdythe me but a foole,
That shuld me melle of lovys scole[41]
   That neuer wanne losse[42] ne price;

---

[36] rebuke.   [37] i.e., badly.   [38] knaves.   [39] devote ourselves.   [40] wise.   [41] busy me in the school of love.   [42] praise.

1076. MS. *gyffe me with vpbrayde.*

1080. Ipomadon had looked very intently at the lady, who perceived the state of his heart. She thereupon rebuked his friend Jason for an imaginary offense of the sort; but all knew that it was intended for Ipomadon.

1083. The meter may be improved by deleting *yet* or *owne.*

1087. Read *A ladyes?*—H. MS. *shuld they.* The French (1150) supports the emendation in the text.

1095. MS. *the tell.*—H.

Now sertys, þat trowe i well, forthy: 1100
She lokyd and spake so angurlye,
   And callyd vs euer full nyce.[43]
Of helle yt is the hottis[t] payne
To love and be not lovyd agayne!
   Thereon no wysdome lyethe.   1105

Now, hertte, i praye the, lett hur be!
Nay, þat maye i not, pardé,
   Yf thow wylte i were[44] slayne!
Yes! Nay, in faythe, i;
For thou, hertte, artte sett[45] so sodenly   1110
   Thou wilte not turne agayne.
Why? I watte neuer whereffore;
But dede i had leuer i wore
   Than longe to dryȝe[46] this payne!
Dyd neuer love man so deyre;   1115
Had she perte, yet rovghte i neyre;[47]
   In faythe then were i ffayne.

We, leef,[48] what dyd thou in this londe?—
I came to seke, and i hur favnde
   That aye wille do me deyre.—   1120
He fallythe that puttis hymselfe so farre,
That all his lyffe lon[g]ythe to warre.
   Thus darre i savely[49] swerê.
Yet is ther non that wotte that,
Ne whens he come, ne what he hatte,   1125
   So prevely i am here. . . .
Shalte thou tell them? Sertis, naye!
   And gette the schyld and spere,

---

[43] foolish.   [44] even though you would have me.   [45] fixed.   [46] suffer.   [47] if she shared it, I should never regret it.   [48] alas, my good friend!   [49] safely.

1110. Omit *hertte?*—H.
1114. MS. *dryve.*—Z.
1121. The couplet is not in the French, but seems to mean, "He falls who is so distant from other resources that his life (and reputation) depend entirely on ability in war."
1127. The sense of the missing line is, "I shall disclose who I am and whence I come!" (Cf. French 1184.) He at once gives up this course of action, and resolves on proving himself.

And wen the price; and þen may þou
Acordynge be to her avowe,   1130
   For thou have gotten losse![50]
Yet in her cowrte there ys none
That so mekyll of bowrdyng[1] can,
   Ne of all gamus that goothe,
Bothe[2] with schyld and schafte to ryde;   1135
But so that love[3] ys all thy pryde,
   Thereffore all men be thy foos.
In erthe ys none so worthy a knyght
But yf his dede be shewyde in syght,
   Men will no good sopose.   1140

And vnder pryde so arte thow hyde[4]
That for a cowarde art thou kyde
   Bothe with lesse and more;
And yf thou now thyselfe shuld rose,[5]
Men wold say, "All this he dos   1145
   His spendyng[6] for to spare;
Of suche dedis have we not sene
As awauntis hym of bedene;
   Hym semes of bownté[7] bare!"
Therefore thy way i rede the gange;   1150
In faythe, and thou dwell here lange,
   It moo the sorow full sore.

Foole, wille thou lyghttly goo
Fro thy love and lovys the soo?[8]—
   Be God, i may not byde!—   1155

---

[50] honor. [1] entertaining. [2] as well as. [3] i.e., being distinguished in love.
[4] hidden. [5] vaunt. [6] i.e., to avoid the actual practice. [7] i.e., he gives no
evidence of wealth of deeds. [8] i.e., and are so in love.

1130. She had vowed that she would have only the best knight in the
world.

1131. MS. *gotton.*

1139. From the French, it is clear that the passage means, ". . . that
if he brags about his deeds, men will think ill of him." The French further says that prowess must be established in other ways than by talk.

1147. MS. *not sere.*

May thou goo?—Sertis naye.—
Yes, in faythe, i hoope i maye,
  Suche harmys in hertte i take!
To-morowe thou goos, yf þou haue quarte;[9]
Yea, and thou hauc anny hertte,   1160
  Thou turnys[10] not that tyde;
Here has thou take thy leve for aye
That nedys behovys the love allway,
  Where thou shalte goo or ryede.

And here shall thou wynne noþinge   1165
But many a skorne of old and younge.—
  Lo, here[11] this foole forthi![12]
Whoso maye be nere hys love,
Sumtyme love it comys above,[13]
  Be they neuer so slyc;   1170
And fere therefro yf he be browghte,
Then shall no man witte his thought
  But his hertte and hee.
On thynge ys, yf he takc kcpe:[14]
Sore is he bett that darre not wepe,   1175
  Be God and be my lewté.[15]

He hathe no myghle þat mornyngc gos,
Ne no ese that sorowe hathe,
  This darre i trewly tclle."
Thus lythe he wrynggyng[16] tow and fro   1180
With many a sory syghyng so,
  And mewsus ay in mell;[17]
A while to go he ys in wille,
Anoþur stovnde to hold hym stille
  With þat gay damysell.   1185

---

[9] health; i.e., if you can.   [10] turn back.   [11] listen to.   [12] i.e., on the subject.
[13] wins.   [14] one thing is true, if one notices it.   [15] faith.   [16] writhing.   [17] in the
midst (of the sighs) he muses.

1167. MS. *for the.*

1174. The French says, "There is another point;" the next line states
it: *mal est batu qe plurer n'ose*—sore is his punishment who dare not
weep, i.e., cannot relieve his sorrow by weeping. The hero must keep
up appearances if he stays in Calabria; in distant countries he may appear
melancholy without exciting attention.

To hymselfe he told þis tale:
"Might i byde, i were all hale—
Be God, i may nought dwell!

For love my herte hathe bovnde so faste
That euermore love will with me last,   1190
To tyme that i shall dye.
It ys full swete to enter in sele,[18]
But ay more and more it bryngys above[19]
To sorowe, and that i se.
Whoso euer ys takyne þerwith   1195
Or wytheinne hem he lyghte,
Full sore schall bovnden be.
Wyth a sorovfull hertte i mon wende,
And sche in quarte[20] mon leve behynde,
And haue no maynde[21] on me!"   1200

The Tournament

To the lady's dismay, Ipomadon leaves her court and returns to his
father. He is knighted, and soon acquires a great reputation for valor.
Meanwhile the lady's vassals insist that she marry some warrior who
will defend her kingdom and keep the lords from quarreling. She is
reluctant because of her love for Ipomadon; but after much debate,
agrees to make herself the prize of a three-day tournament. The hero
appears incognito in the retinue of the Queen of Sicily, whose special
attendant he has become; and again he feigns indifference to deeds of
arms and the impending contest.

Leve we now this folke there,
And offe the knyght speke we more
That dwellys with the Quene.
To serue hur welle he dyd his tente;[22]
No semblaunte made he to turnament;   2995
Thereat was ladyes tene.

---

[18] happiness.   [19] leads on.   [20] untouched,   heart-whole.   [21] interest.   [22] gave
his attention.

1196. *Lyghte* for *lyethe.*
2993. The queen is the Queen of Sicily.
2996. MS. *there as.*

The maydans hym to skorne lou3ghe:
Thereoffe had þey ioye inowghe,
  For he the sothe had sene.
The Quene to hur mete he fett,   3000
And seruyd hyr when she was sett
  Right worthely, i wene.

And sythen vp agayne her ledde,
And kyssyd that lady before her bedde;
  To speke he gan hym spede: 3005
"Madame, lett them turnay to-morn:
I will hunte with hounde and horne,
  And bryng vs home a brayd.[24]
I hold it bettur amonge þe akys[25]
Then in turnament to take strokys;   3010
  I kepe[26] no blod to blede !"
The maydons hym to skorne loughe,
And seyd, "Loo, madam, your drew[27]
  Spekys offe doughtty dedis !"

The Quene cursyd his desteny,[28]   3015
Withoute prowes þat he shuld be,
  That was so fayre offe face;
But sothe ys sayd in olde sawe:
Whedur þat eucr love will drawe,
  Lake no lettyng mase.[29]   3020
She louyd hym well for his service,
But oþur damysels of pryse
  Grette skorne at hym have.

---

[24] roast.   [25] oaks.   [26] intend.   [27] lover.   [28] evil lot.   [29] whoever is in the toils of
love, faults are no drawback (to him).

2999. The French (3495) has: *li vilains dist veir* (speak the truth).   The
English translator seems to have perceived this, and then to have confused *veir* with *veoir* (see).   The line is therefore unintelligible.

3003. MS. *agayne vp.*—H.

3004. In accepting the post of special attendant to the Queen, he had
stipulated that he be allowed to kiss her each night, and that he be known
as the "dru la reine" (queen's lover).   These conditions were deliberately
strange because he wishes a reputation for eccentricity.

3006. MS. *thy turnay.*

3020. MS. *Lake ne.*

To there skorne toke he no hede,
But toke his leve and forth he yede;   3025
   To the porter he goose.

He gafe the porter a grette gold rynge,
And he sayd, "Sir, i love huntyng
   At rayne-dere and at roos.[30]
And as well wott thow as i,   3030
He that ys not there erlye,
   His best tyde mvst he lose.
Therefore of o thyng i þe praye:
Lett me forthe before the daye."
   "In faythe, sir, i sopposse   3035
Whyles this offyce shall be myn,
Entré and issue shall be thyne,
   For ffrenshipe or for foos!"

Ipomadon to bede goos,
And in the mornyng erly he roosse,   3040
   Or day began to sprynge.
He gerte aray his whyȝte stede,
And all his armore that hym nede,
   Belyve he lett vp brynge.
Soune was covpled all his houndis;   3045
With lowde blowyng forthe he wendis,
   That wakyd ladys yonge.
They sayd, "Lo, madame, your drewe
With horne and hounde se ye may now:
   He hyes to turnayeng!"   3050

The Quene þerto wold take no kepe,[31]
But laye in bedde purposyd to slepe,
   And sore forthought[32] þat tyde

---

[30] roes. [31] pay no attention. [32] regretted.

3042. MS. gette.
3046. To restore the rhyme, K. suggested foundis, goes.

That he ne was man of prowes;
Whedur³³ she loved hym neuerthelesse: 3055
   In hertt she it hyde.
In the thykest place of all þat woode,
A ermytage he wyst þer stode,
   And thedur gan he ryde.
There he gret araye hym tyte,   3060
His stede and hym all in white:
   He wold no lengur byde.

"Mayster," quod Ipomadon,
"To-day on huntynge mvste ye goone:
   For Goddis love, i you praye,   3065
Yffe God will send you any dere,
Agayne the nyght abyde me here:
   I shall come while i maye."
Fro then vnto the iustyng plase
A full depe dale [betwene] ther was,   3070
   In a deerne³⁴ waye.
Couyrd-heddyd³⁵ myght men ryde:
No man myght se hym on no syde
   Yf it were lyghte of day.

His mayster dyd his comaundement;   3075
Ipomadon his waye is went
   Thorow the thike woode.
No man take with hym he lyst
But a chyld þat he on tryste,³⁶
   Whiche was bothe fayre and goode: 3080
Of his lond a barons sone,
That wele hym serue con,
   And ofte in stedde hym stoode.³⁷

---

³³ yet therefore. ³⁴ hidden. ³⁵ i.e., concealed. ³⁶ trusted. ³⁷ aided him.

3063. The master is the faithful Tholomew. During the day he kills three harts, and thus Ipomadon is able to keep up the fiction of having spent the time in the forest.
3070. *Betwene.*—H. MS. *dede dale.* In the French, it is a *fosse.*

The semely chylde Egyon
Was cosyn[38] to Ipomadon,　　　　　　　　3085
Right nere sib of his blode.

In the mornynge erly,
He passyd thorow the derne sty
Be þat the day gan dawe.[39]
He hovis[40] before that fayre castell;　　　3090
The wynd wavyd his whyght pensell,[41]
And waytis[42] began to blowe;
And ouer the walle þey behylde,
And sawe hym hove in the feld,
As whyȝte as any snowe.　　　　　　　3095
He[43] cryed, "Wake, lady bryghte!
For sothe younder hovis a knyghte,
The feyrest that euer i sawe.

His stede and he is all in whyȝte;
That syght to se is grette delyȝte,　　　　3100
Fro bale as i be broughte!"
The lady weyndis to a wyndowe,
And saw hym hove, as white as snowe;
In grette care is she broughte.
Sone she wyst at that day　　　　　　　3105
On whome she shuld her love laye,
For in hur h[e]rtte she thought
She wold not the valet chaunge
For emperoure nor for kyng stronge,
Gette hym and she movghte.　　　　　　3110

She beholdys the knyght in whyte,
But what he was, she wot but lite:
The more care had the maye.

---

[38] relative.　[39] dawn.　[40] rides.　[41] pennon.　[42] sentinel-minstrels.　[43] i.e., a sentinel.

3098. MS. *i the.*
3109. Koeppel proposed *valet straunge,* and *kyng chaunge,* to make a good rhyme. The former is a common epithet for Ipomadon.

The sonne was vpon lofte be thanne;
All the feld was full of men,   3115
  There armys to assaye.[43]
The Kynge of Spayne, Sir Ottynore,
Sawe the white knyght hove thore
  In armys good and gaye;
To all his folke he sayde syne,[44]   3120
"The fyrste iuste to-day is myne,
  And i hold comnaunte aye!"[45]

With hym was Sir Amfyon;
The Kyng comaundyd hys men ilkone
  Stille they shuld abyde.   3125
He sayd, "Younder is for the fers love
A kyng in white, wele dothe hove;[46]
  And to hym will i ryde!"
A grette spere in honde he nome;
Ipomadon was ware he come   3130
  And blemesshyd on anoþur syde.[47]
Ayther on other brake þer speris:
Ipomadon behynde hym beyris[48]
  Twenty foote þat tyde!

The Kyng laye waltrand[49] in his wede;   3135
Egyon of his hors toke hede,
  And lyghttly lepte þerone.
For all the strengh þat he weldyþe,
The riche Kyng of Spayne hym eldyþe[50]
  To Ipomadon.   3140
Ioyfull was þat lady clere:
How she ordayned[1] now shall ye here:
  Hyr owne cosyne Iosane,

---

[43] try. [44] straightway. [45] keep my agreement. [46] who rides well. [47] crossed the field. [48] strikes him over the back of his steed. [49] writhing. [50] yields. [1] commanded.

3122. In the French (3623): *Kar jo lai assez cuveitee* (craved).
3127. For *kyng* read *knyght*.—K.

That he shuld serue² þerfore [of] speyres,
To what man that best hym beyres   3145
To the iii dayes were goone.

And þerfore trewly she hym highte
The thryd day he shuld be knyghte,
His good dedys to alowee.³
A spere to Ipomadon he bare;   3150
As he hadde neuer sene hym ayre,
He sayd, "Sir, what artt thou?"
"I am the laydis cosyn, sir,
That thus is ordayned here be hur,
Trewly for to trowe,   3155
That i shall serue here of speris
Two⁴ what man that hym best beris;
And sertis, that i hold you.

For the man that was of grettis[t] boste
And hym that my lady hatyd moste   3160
In ffeld here haue ye felde;"
For wele he wyst it was reson.⁵
But he knewe not Ipomadon,
Togeddur that they had dwellyd;
Togedyr, but it was long beffore.   3165
Ipomadon likyd the more
The tale that he hym tolde,
And he sayd, "Sir, so God me spede,
My presonere to thy lady lede;
I wold þat she hym hylde.⁶   3170

Thou shalt haue to þi lady gent
His hors, and saye þat i hit sent—
The Kyng to hur presone."

---

² furnish. ³ reward. ⁴ to. ⁵ the truth. ⁶ held.

3145. MS. *And what.* ˙The French has *celui ke.*
3152. MS. *And sayd.* Koelbing emends.
3156. The *of* is a result of a literal translation of the French *de lances servir* (3691).
3158. MS. *sertus.*

Syr Attynore than sorow hade,
But vp he wanne, as he hym bade,   3175
　And rydythe forthe with Iasone.
Whan he came to þat lady bry3te,
"Madame," he sayd, "younde white kny3te
　That berythe all oþer downe,
The Kyng offe Spayne takyn hath he,   3180
And he send hym for to bee
　Att your byddyng bowne."

Whereffore was þat lady fayne;
But eft she sayd to Imayne,
　"For ought þat i can see,   3185
Alas! this is a grett myscheffe!
For welle i wott þat my leeffe
　Ys not in this contré.
Certenly he had byn here,
Iosane hym knewe, þat was his fere;   3190
　Now wotte i well, perdé,
That othere [failis] hym manhode
Or he is dede, so God me spede;
　Thereffore full woo is me.

Younde knyght to myne avowe will corde;   3195
And yffe i take hym to my lorde,
　I losse my love, alas!". . .

Ipomadon continues successful, changing the color of his arms each
day, and thus avoiding recognition. Though judged the victor, he does
not reveal himself, and seeks many more adventures before claiming his
reward.

3176. To improve the meter, omit *forthe.*—H.
3184. Imayne is the proud lady's confidante.
3185. MS. *gan see.*
3192. Koelbing's emendation; the rhyme-word is *manhede.*
3195. To avoid hasty marriage proposed by her barons, she had told
her lords that she had vowed to marry only the best knight in the world.
The White Knight fulfills the condition.

EGER AND GRIME

EGER AND GRIME

This poem appears in two versions, one in The Percy Folio Manuscript, c. 1650, and the other in a chapbook printed in Aberdeen in 1711.[1] Of these, the latter is longer by about 1,400 lines, but seems to be a corrupt and expanded version of the source of the former.[2] The present text is from the Percy Folio Manuscript. Through the kindness of the authorities of the British Museum it has been possible to print this text from rotographs of the original.

The earliest mention of the poem is in 1497, when two fiddlers sang it to James IV of Scotland. Its original dialect was northern of the middle or early fifteenth century, but the forms have been greatly altered. It was probably written in and about Linlithgowshire on the Firth of Forth.

The story is of mixed Celtic and Teutonic origins, the latter element being slight and apparently ancient. In Teutonic legend, Grime seems to have been a giant-god who threw up immense dykes; as many as fifteen are ascribed to him in Great Britain. He may possibly be the same person as the Grim in "Havelok," who, according to Skeat's introduction, is said to have thrown down churches. Possibly Eger is the Ægir of Teutonic mythology, god of angry seas, with whose name the fishermen of England were familiar even in Carlyle's time.[3] A Grime's Dyke—an old Roman wall—stretches across the northern part of Linlithgow; the adjacent Firth knew Ægir's wrath sufficiently well. The Teutonic part of the story is thus possibly related to an ancient nature-myth.

With this Teutonic plot has been combined a Celtic account of the Otherworld, similar in many details to the story of Ywain. Gray-steel's country has the usual perilous entrance—a ford defended against invasion—, is located on an island, and is inhabited entirely by women. Gray-steel is the defender of a "perilous princess," and Grime is led to his land by a guide, here rationalized into a squire.

For much useful material on this romance, see the manuscript

---

[1] Edited by Laing, who also had an earlier version printed in 1687 and lacking the name of the printer or place. [2] For the opposite opinion see *ESt.* 19.4ff. [3] See "Heroes and Hero Worship," *Hero as Divinity.*

thesis of Elizabeth Willson (1914) in the University of Chicago Library, Hibbard, and Loomis, many of whose remarks on the Ywain story apply to this. Uncredited emendations are mostly those of Furnivall and Hales.

Off frequently appears for *of;* here it is printed *of.*

It ffell sometimes in the land of Beame
There dwelled a lord within that realme;
The greatest he was of renowne
Eccept the King that ware the crowne.
Thé[4] called him to name Erle Bragas;   5
He marryed a ladye was fayre of face.
They had noe child but a daughter younge;
In the world was none soe fayre thing.
They called that ladye Winglayne.
Husband wold she neuer haue none,   10
Neither for gold nor yett for good
Nor for noe highnese of his blood,
Without he would with swords dent
Win euery battell where he went.
Soe there were many in that realme rich,   15
But they cold find but few such;
For the Erle rydeth with such a route
Of lords and knights hardye and stout.
There was in that same time
A curteous knight called Sir Grime,   20
And of Garwicke lord was hee;
He was a wise man and a wittye.
Soe there was in that same place
A young knight men called Egace,

[4] *the* for *they; they* for *the,* frequent in the P. F. MS.

1. The land of Beame is a conventional land of romance, now unidentifiable. It has been supposed to be Bohemia. Malory says (XX 18) that Benwyck is Bourges in France; and that *somme men calle it Bayen and somme men colle it Beaume, where the wine of Beaume is.*

9. MS. *winglanye.*

15–6. Laing: *Als there was men in that kinrick Many one, but very few sik* [as she demanded].

21. Garwicke is said by Sir Walter Scott to be Carrick.

24. This form, evidently French, appears only here.

But his name was Sir Eger;   25
For he was but a poore bachlour;[5]
For his elder brother was liuande
And gouerned all his fathers land.
Egar was large of blood and bone,
But broad lands had hee none;   30
But euermore he wan the honour
Through worshipp of his bright armour;
And for loue that he was soe well taught,
Euer he iusted and hee fought.
And because he was soe well proued,   35
The Erles daughter shee him loued.
They ladye granted her good will;
Her father sented[6] there soone till.
He was glad that shee wold,
That shee wold in hart fold[7]   40
For to take vntill her fere
A barun or else a bacheleere.
These knights, Sir Egar and Sir Grime.
They were fellowes good and fine.
They were nothing sib of blood,   45
But they were sworne bretheren good.
They keeped a chamber together att home;
Better loue loved there never none.
Vpon a time Egar he wold forth fare
To win him worshippe as he did ere,   50
Wherby that he might praysed bee
Aboue all knights of high degree.
Soe hee came home vpon a night,
Sore wounded, and ill was he dight:
His kniffe was forth; his sheath was gone;   55

---

[5] young knight, candidate for knighthood.   [6] assented.   [7] determine.

26. Laing: *And he.* The Percy scribe has probably copied the *for* of l. 27.

39–40. Corrupt. MS. illegible. Laing: *Her friends were fain that she would Once in her heart it for to hold, That she would have to her a pier.*

42. MS. *baru.*

55–6. Laing: *His knife was tint, his sheath was tane, His scabert by his thigh was gane.*

His scaberd by his thigh was done;
A truncheon[8] of a speare hee bore,
And other weapons he bare noe more.
On his bedside he sett him downe;
He siked sore, and fell in swoone.   60
Sir Grime of Garwicke shortlye rose
And ran to Sir Egar and said, "Alas,
For thee, Egar, my hart is woe
That euer I were soe farr thee froe!
For when wee parted att yonder yate,   65
Thou was a mightye man and milde of state;
And well thou seemed, soe God me speede,
To proue thy manhood on a steede.
And now thou art both pale and greene,[9]
And in strong battell thou hast beene.   70
Thou hast beene in strong battell;
It was neuer litle that made thee fayle."
"Now as it hath behappned mee,
God let it neuer behappen thee
Nor noe other curteous knight   75
That euer goeth to the feild to fight
For to win worshipp as I haue done!
I haue bought it deare and lost it soone!
For other lords haue biddn att home
And saued their bodyes forth of shame   80
And kepeed their manhood faire and cleane
Will brook my loue before mine eyen.
And I am hurt and wounded sore,
And manhood is lost for euermore."
Then said Grime to Sir Egar,   85
"Ye greeue you more then meete were;
For that man was neuer soe well cladd,
Nor yett soe doughtye in armes dread,
But in battell place he may be distayned.[10]

---

[8] shaft of a spear.   [9] sickly.   [10] dishonored.

79. Read: "other lords who. . . ."   The relative is often omitted.
82. MS. *well broked;* Laing, *will brook.*

Why shold his manhood be reproued,   90
Or his ladye or his loue repine?"
Then said Egar, "Lett be, Sir Grime!
For fairer armour then I had
Was neuer Cristian knight in cladd.
I had a body that seemed well to doe   95
And weapons that well longed therto;
Well I trusted my noble steed,
Soe that I did my good rich weed;
And well I trusted my noble brand.
The best of all I trusted my hart and my hand.   100
I heard tell of a venterous knight
That kept a fforbidden countrye bath day and night
And a fresh iland by the sea,
Where castles were with towers hye.
Ouer the riuer were ryding frythes 2,[11]   105
And soone I chose to the one of tho.
In short while had I rydden
In that land that was fforbidden,
But I heard mouing in the greete[12]
As itt had beene of a steeds feete.   110
My horsse gladedd with that cheere,
Cast vp his head, and was a-steere.
He crope[13] together as he wold haue runen;
I hearkned when more din had comen.
I looked on the way nye before   115
And see a knight come on a sowre.[14]
Red was his sheild, red was his speare,
And all of fresh gold shone his geere;

---

[11] fords to be crossed on horseback. [12] gravel. [13] crept, gathered himself. [14] sorrel.

100. Lines 100 and 102 are hypermetrical. In 100 the first three syllables are probably light, and in 102 the first four. Such lines are common in the P. F. MS.

103. *Iland* illegible in MS. Percy reads *strand*.

113. MS. *groped.*

And by the death that I must thole,[15]
My steed seemed to his but a fole.[16]   120
His speare that was both great and long,
Faire on his brest he cold itt honge;
And I mine in my rest[17] can folde;
I gaue my horsse what head he wold.
Our steeds brought vs together soone.   125
Alas! that meeting I may mone!
For through coate-armour and acton,[18]
Through brest-plate and habergion,[19]
Through all my armour lesse and more,
Cleane through the body he me bore;   130
And I still in my sadle sate;
My good spere on his brest I brake.
The 2[d] time he came againe,
He fayled of me, and my steede he has slaine.
Then I gott vpp deliuerlye,[20]   135
Not halfe soe soone as need had I;
I thought to haue wrocken my steeds bane,
But that great outrage myself hath tane.
I drew a sword of mettle bright,
And egerlye I sought vnto that knight.   140
I stroke at him with all my maine;
I failed of him, and his steed has slaine.
When hee see that itt was soe,
To counter on ffoote he was full throe.[21]

---

[15] suffer. [16] foal. [17] = arest, socket for a spear. [18] stuffed jacket under the coat
of mail. [19] coat of mail. [20] quickly. [21] bold.

119. Cf. "Ywain and Gawain," 425–6: *And, bi the ded that i sal
thole, Mi stede by his was but a fole.* Laing lacks these lines. A supernatu-
rally large horse belongs to the fairy huntsman in "Geraint, Son of Er-
bin" in the "Mabinogion"; also in the "Voyage of Mael Duin," *Rev. Celt.*
9.467, and Tale 155 of the "Gesta Romanorum."

122–3. Eger has to rest the butt of his spear in the leather socket at
his side. His opponent can stand the encounter with his spear braced
against his breast.—Rickert.

127. MS. *ffro.*

137–8. Laing: *For to revenge my steeds bane, The great defoul myself
hath tane.*

142. *Has,* northern form of the first person singular.

Hee drew a sword, a worthy weapon; 145
The first dint that on me did happen,
'Throug[h] all my armour, lesse and more,
7 inches into the sholder he me shore.[22]
And I hitt him with whole pith[23]
Aboue the girdle, that he groned with, 150
And with that stroke I cold him lett
Whiles another shortlye on him I sett;
And well I wott I had him gotten,[24]
But with that stroke my sword was broken.
Then I drew a kniffe—I had noe other,— 155
The wh[ich] I had of my owne borne brother,
And he another out of sheath hath tane;
And neerehand together are we gone.
First he wounded me in the face;
My eyen were safe; that was my grace. 160
Then I hitt him vpon the head,
That in his helme my blade I leade.[25]
God lett neuer knight soe woe begon[26]
As I was when all my false weapons were gone!
Yett with the haft that was left in my hand, 165
Fast vpon his face I dange,[27]
That the blood sprang out from vnder the steele.
He lost some teeth; that wott I weele.
My habergion that was of Millaine fine
First my fathers and then was mine, 170
And itt had beene in many a thrust,
And neuer a maile[28] of itt wold burst.
My acton was of Paris worke
Saued me noe more than did my sarke,[29]
For his sword was of noble steele; 175
He strake hard—and it lasted[30] weele—
Through all my armour more and lesse,
And neuer ceaced but in the fleshe.

---

[22] cut. [23] strength. [24] killed, conquered. [25] left. [26] be so downcast. [27] struck.
[28] ring. [29] shirt. [30] penetrated.
162. Original rhymes were probably *heued—leued*.
163. Cf. *sore bygone*, "Perceval" 349.
169. The famous Milanese steel was a precious possession and heirloom.

Then, fore-foughten,[31] I waxed wearye,
For blood as drye as any tree.   180
I fought soe long, I ffell in swoone,
Till betweene his hands I fell downe.
When I came to myself, my steed was away;
I looked on the land where he lay.
My steed lay slaine a litle me froe,   185
And his backe striken in tow.
Then I was ware of a runing strand,[32]
And thither I crope on foot and hand,
And from my eyen I washt the blood.
All was away shold have done me good.   190
Then I looked on my right hand;
My litle fingar was lackand.
Then I went further on the greene,
Where more strong battells hadden beene.
A slaine knight and spoyled[33] lay;   195
His litle fingar was away,
And by that knight I might well see
That one man had delt both with him and me.
Then of a sadled horsse I gatt a sight,
And by him lay a slaine knight;   200
His steede was both good and fine,
But not halfe soe good as mine.
All that day did I ryde
Till itt was in the euen-tide.
The moone shone fayre; the starres cast light;   205
Then of a castle I gott a sight,
Of a castle and of a towne,
And by an arbour side I light downe;
And there I saw fast me by
The fairest bower that euer saw I.   210
A litle while I tarryed there,

---

[31] tired with fighting.   [32] stream.   [33] plundered.
179. MS. *sore foughten.*
196. The cutting off of a finger may have been done to ensure recognition. The victor wants to be able to recognize the vanquished. Cf. Campbell, "Popular Tales," 1.31, 2.451; "Book of Taliesin" ("Mabinogion"); McInnes and Nutt, "Folk and Hero Tales," 303.

And a lady came forth of a fresh arbor.
Shee came forth of that garden greene,
And in that bower faine wold haue beene.
Shee was cladd in scarlett redd,   215
And all of fresh gold shone her heade;
Her rud was red as rose in raine;
A fairer creature was neuer seene.
Methought her coming did me good,
And straight vpon my feete I stoode.   220
"Good Sir," quoth shee, "what causes you here to lenge?
For ye had me[s]tter of great easmend,[34]
And heere beside is a castle wight,
And there be leeches of great sleight,[35]
Cuning men with for to deale,   225
And wonderous good happ haue for to heale;
And there is the gentlest lady att will
That euer man came in misery till.
Therfore I councell you thither to wend,
For ycc had neede of great easmend."   230
"Lady," said Egar, "as itt behappened mee,[36]
I irke to come in any companye.
I beseeche you, lady faire and sweete,
Helpe that I were sounded[37] with one sleepe
And some casment for me and my hackney."   235
"Sir," sayd shee, "I will doe the best I may.
Sir, sith I am first that with you mett,
I wold your neede were the better bett."[38]
Then a faire maid, shee tooke my steede,

---

[34] you have need of relief.   [35] skill.   [36] because of what happened.   [37] made
sound.   [38] remedied.

222. MS. meetter.
224. But no physician later appears, and it was usual in the romances
for wounded knights to be treated by ladies.
227. This is the lady Loosepaine. The account is confused, so that it
is not clear when Eger leaves his guide, one of Loosepaine's attendants,
and meets the lady herself.
231. Logically the line should read, *said I*. The meter shows the
expression has been added, as it frequently is in this version.

And into a stable shee did him leade;   240
And into a chamber both faire and light,
I was led betweene 2 ladyes bright.
All my bloodye armour of me was done;
The lady searched my wounds full soone.
Shee gaue me drinke for to restore,   245
For neerehand was I bled before;
There was neuer alle nor wine
Came to mee in soe good a time.
A siluer bason she cammanded soone,
And warme water therin to be done.   250
The ladye louesome vnde[r] line,[39]
With her white hands shee did wash mine;
And when shee saw my right hand bare,
Alas! my shame is much the more.
The gloue was whole, the hand was nomen;   255
Therby shee might well see I was ouercomen.
And shee perceiued that I thought shame;
Therfore shee would not aske me my name,
Nor att that word[40] shee sayd noe more,
But all good easments I had there.   260
Then till a bed I was brought;
I sleeped neuer halfe soe soft.
The ladye fayre of hew and hyde,
Shee sate downe by the bedside;
Shee laid a souter[41] vpon her knee;   265
Theron shee plaid full louesomlye.
And yett for all her sweet playinge,
Oftimes shee had full still mourninge;
And her 2 maydens sweetlye sange,
And oft thé weeped, and their hands wrange.   270
But I heard neuer soe sweet playinge,
And euer amongst, soe sore siking.

---

[39] linen.   [40] on that subject.   [41] psaltery.

240. It was courtesy for a lady to disarm a tired knight and attend his wounds, but unusual for her to stable his horse. An instance does occur in the "Mabinogion" in a tale of Ywaine, "The Lady of the Fountain."
255. Laing: *My gloue was hail, my finger was tint.*

In the night shee came to me oft,
And asked me whether I wold ought,
But alwayes I said her nay   275
Till it drew neerr to the breake of day.
Then all my bloodye tents[42] out shee drew;
Againe shee tented my wounds anew.
Wott yee well itt was noe threede,[43]
The tents that into my wounds yeede.   280
They were neither of lake nor line,[44]
But they were silke both good and fine.
Twise the tenting of my wounds
Cost that ladye 20 pounds,
Without spices and salues that did me ease   285
And drinkes that did my body well please.
And then shee gaue me drinke in a horne;
Neuer since the time that I was borne
Such a draught I neuer gatt;
With her hand shee held me after thatt.   290
The drinke shee gaue mee was grasse greene;
Soone in my wounds itt was seene;
The blood was away, the drinke was there,
And all was soft[45] that erst was sore.
And methought I was able to run and stand,   295
And to haue taken a new battell in hand.
The birds sange in the greene arbor;
I gate on foote and was on steere.[46]
The layde came to me where I lay;
These were the words shee to me did say: 300
"I rede you tarry a day or towe

---

[42] dressings of the wounds.   [43] thread, cheap cloth.   [44] both words mean linen;
lake was the finer.   [45] soothed.   [46] astir.

286–92. According to a common medieval belief, only if the medicine
appears in the wounds will the patient live.   Green was the favorite color
for potions and salves.   One of the best known of the latter was composed
chiefly of verdigris.   *Take pimpernole also called self-heal and stampe hit
and temper hit with water and gif hym to drinke, and ʒif hit go out at ye
wonde, he schal live.*   Cf. "Sir Ferumbras" 510; "Merveilles de Rigomer"
16,954, for similar use of ointment.

Till you be in better plight to goe."
But I longed soe sore to be at home
That I wold needlye[47] take leaue to gone.
Shee gaue me 2 shirts of Raines[48] in fere,   305
Put them next my body; I haue them here.
And my owne shee did abone,[49]
And my bloudye armour on me hath done
Saue my heauy habergion; shee was afrayd
Lest they wold haue mad my wounds to bleede.   310
That ladye with her milke-white hand
To the arson[50] of my saddell shee it bound
With 2 bottels of rich wine,
And therof haue I liued euer sinne.
I sayd, "A! deare, good madam, how may this be?   315
The coningest leeche in this land be yee;
For all my wounds lesse or more,
Of them I feele noe kind of sore,
As I had neuer beene wounded with sword nor speare,
Nor neuer weapon had done mee deere."   320
"Wold God," said shee, "that itt were soe!
But I know well for a day or 2
Froe that loue make you once agast,[1]
Your oyntments may noe longer last.
Sith you will not abyde with mee,   325
Lett your ladye in your countrye
Doe to your wounds as I wold haue done;
Then they will soft and heale full soone."
One thing did my hart great greeffe;
I had nothing that ladye to giue,   330
But my golden beades[2] forth I drew
That were of fine gold fresh and new.
Shee wold not receiue them at my hand,
But on her bedside I lett them liggand.
I tooke leaue of that ladye bright,   335

---

[47] earnestly. [48] of Rennes, Brittany. [49] put above. [50] saddle-bow. [1] when
your love stirs you again. [2] rosary, prayer-beads.

305. Cf. "Squire" 842.
312. MS. *rason*.

And homewards rid both day and night.
I fared full well all that while
Till I came home within 2 mile;
Then all my wounds wrought[3] att once
As kniues had been beaten thorrow my bones.   340
Out of my sadle I fell that fraye;[4]
When I came to myselfe, my steed was away.
Thus haue I beene in this ffarr countrye;
Such a venterous knight mett with mee.
Men called him Sir Gray-steele;   345
I assayd[5] him, and he ffended weele."

2D PARTE

Then spake Grime to Sir Egar
With soft words and faire,
"That man was neuer soe wise nor worthye,
Nor yet soe cuning proued in clergye,[6]   350
Nor soe doughtye of hart nor hand,
Nor yett so bigg in stowre to stand,
But in such companye he may put in[7]
But he is as like to loose as win.
And euer I bade you to keepe you weele   355
Out of the companye of Sir Gray-steele,
For he is called by command[8]
The best knight in any land.
Sith the matter is chanced soe,
Wee will take the choice of wayes 2.   360
From your loue and laydye lained this shal bee;
Shee shall know nothing of our priuitye."
But litle wist Egar nor Sir Grime
Where the lady was that same time;
For the lady that Egars loue was,   365

---

[3] worked, acted . . . as if.   [4] at that seizure.   [5] tested.   [6] learning.   [7] enter.
[8] covenant, general agreement.

354. The scribe may have copied the *but* from line 353. Perhaps read:
that he. . . .
357. Laing: *For he is called uncannand.* Cf. *N.E.D.*, *covenant*.
360. MS. *wayes of choice 2.*

Her chamber was within a litle space;
Of Sir Egar shee soe sore thought
That shee lay wakened, and sleeped nought.
A scarlett mantle hath shee tane;
To Grimes chamber is shee gone.   370
Shee heard them att a priuie dain;[9]
Shee stayd without and came not in.
When shee heard that Egars bodye was in distresse,
She loued his body mickle the worse.
Words this lady wold not say,   375
But turned her backe and went awaye;
Yett soe priuilye shee is not gone,
But Grime perceived that there was one.
An vnfolded[10] window opend hee
And saw the way-gate[11] of that ladye.   380
"What is that," said Egar, "maketh that dain?"
Grime sayd, "My spanyell hound wold come in."
To his fellow Sir Egar he said noe more,
But he repented that she came there.
Gryme hath gotten that same night   385
Leeches that beene of great sleight,[12]
Coning men with for to deale
That had good happ wounds to heale;
Yett long ere day word is gone
That Egar the knight is comen home,   390
And hath moe wounds with sword and kniffe
Then had euer man that bare liffe.
17 wounds hee hath tane;
7 beene thorrow his body ran.
The leeches cold doe him noe remede,   395
But all said Egar wold be dead.
In the morning the Erle and the Countesse,
To Grymes chamber can thé passe.

_____

[9] din, dispute; cf. 381.   [10] unfastened.   [11] departure.   [12] skill.

371. Laing: _She heard him with a privy din._ MS. one stroke of _u_ in
priuie is lacking.
379. Windows generally opened with a lateral swing and were held in
place by a pin.

The Erle said, "How doth Sir Egar the knight?"
Then answered Grime both wise and wight,   400
"He doth, my lord, as you may see."
"Alas!" said the Erle, "how may this bee?"
Grime answered him hastilye,
"My lord, I shall tell you gentleye:
An vncoth land he happened in,   405
Where townes were both few and thinn.
Giffe he rode neuer soe fast,
7 dayes the wildernesse did last.
He heard tell of a venterous knight
That kept a forbbidden countrye day and night,   410
And a mile by the salt sea,
Castles fayre, and towers hye;
On the other side a fayre strand,
A faire fforrest on the other hand.
On the one side run a fresh riuere;   415
There might noe man nighe him nere.[13]
For he that ouer that riuer shold ryde
Strange aventures shold abyde;
Hee shold either fight or flee,
Or a weed[14] in that land leaue shold hee.   420
The wedd[15] that he shold leaue in this land
Shold be the litle ffingar of his right hand;
And or he knew himselfe to slowe,[16]
His litle fingar he wold not forgoe.
Boldlye Egar gaue him battell tho;   425
His helme and his hawberckes he tooke him fro.
Soe did he his sword and his spere
And much more of his golden gayre;
And homewards as he rode apace

---

[13] approach closely.   [14] forfeit.   [15] forfeit.   [16] about to be slain.

405. MS., &, for *an*, as commonly.
406. MS. *where both few.*
410. Gray-steel's land is separated from Earl Bragas's by a river over which are two fords.   Before crossing the ford, one can see the ocean shore, fair castles, high towers, seven towns, and an island.   Cf. 102–5, 933 ff., Laing 122–8 and 1447.
423. *He* refers to Eger; above (417–22) it is general.

Thorrow the wylde forrest and the wyldenesse,   430
He thought to haue scaped withouten lett.
Then 15 theeves with Egar mett;
They thought Egar for to haue him sloe,
His gold and his good to haue tooke him froe.
Thrise through them with a spere he ran;   435
7 he slew, and the master man.[17]
Yett had hee scaped[18] for all that dread,
They shott att him, and slew his steed.
Hee found a steed when they were gone,
Wheron Sir Egar is come home;   440
For if Sir Egar dye this day,
Farwell flower of knighthoode for euer and aye."
Then the Erle proferred 40^{li}[19] in land
For a leeche that wold take Egar in hand.
9 dayes were comen and gone   445
Or any leeche wold Egar vndertane.
It was 9 dayes and some deale more
Or his ladye wold come there;
And att the coming of that fayre ladye,
Her words they were both strange and drye.[20]   450
Shee saies, "How doth that wounded knight?"
Then answered Gryme both wise and wight,
"He doth, madam, as yee may see."
"In faith," said the lady, "that's litle pittye.
He might full well haue bidden att home;   455
Worshipp in that land gatt he none.
He gaue a ffingar to lett him gange;
The next time he will offer vp the whole hand."
Gryme was euer wont to gange
In councell with the ladye to stand,   460
And euer told Egar a fayre tale
Till the knight Sir Egar was whole;
For and her want[21] and will had beene to him lenging,[22]
It wold have letted him of his mending.
Soe long the leeches delt with Sir Egar   465

---

[17] chief robber. [18] would have escaped . . . (but) they shot . . . [19] pounds. [20] caustic, unsympathetic. [21] for if her desire. [22] delayed, denied.

Till he might stoutlye goe and stirr;
Till itt once beffell vppon a day
Gryme thought the ladye to assaye
Whether shee loued Sir Egar his brother
As well as euer shee did before.   470
Grime said, "Madame, by Godds might,
Egar will take a new battell with yonder knight.
He is to sore wounded yett for to gone;
Itt were worshipp to cause him to abyde at home,
For he will doe more for you then mee."   475
Then answered that fayre lady,
"All that while that Egar was the knight
That wan the degree in euery fight,
For his sake verelye
Manye a better I haue put by;   480
Therfor I will not bidd him ryde,
[Nor att] home I will not bid him abyde,
Nor of his marriage I haue nothing adoe;[23]
I wott not, Gryme, what thou saist therto."
Gryme turned his backe of the ladye faire,   485
And went againe to his brother Sir Egar,
Sett him downe on his bed side,
And talked these words in that tyde:
"Egar," he said, "thou and I are brethren sworne;
I loued neuer better brother borne.   490
Betwixt vs tow let vs make some cast,[24]
And find to make our foemen fast;
For of our enemies wee stand in dread,
And wee lye sleeping in our bedd."
Egar said, "What mistrust haue yee with mee?[25]   495
For this 7 months if I here bee,
Shall neuer man take my matter in hand

---

[23] regret, perturbation.   [24] devise some plan.   [25] doubt . . . of me.

477. MS. *while Egar y^t was.*
478. Cf. "Sir Triamore," P. F. MS., II, p. 103, l. 674, and note.
492. MS. *formen.* Perhaps the line should read: *And fand to make our foemen gast.*
497. *M* of *matter* illegible; Laing: *Shall no man take that deed on hand.*

Till I bee able to auenge myselfe in land."
A kinder knight then Gryme was one
Was neuer bredd of blood nor bone.   500
"Methinke you be displeased with mee,
And that is not your part for to bee;
For sith the last time that ye came home,
I haue knowen priuie messengers come and gone
Betwixt your ladye and Erle Olyes,   505
A noble knight that doughtye is,
Of better blood borne then euer were wee,
And halfe more liuings[26] then such other 3."
Then Egar vp his armes sprang,[27]
And ffast together his hands dange   510
With still mourning and siking sore.
Saith, "Alas! my loue and my ladye fayre,
What haue I done to make you rothe[28]
That[28a] was euer leeue, and now soe lothe?"
Gryme had of him great pittye.   515
"Brother," he said, "be councelled by mee.
If you will doe after my counsaile,
Peraduenture it will greatly prevaile.
Another thing; my liffe I dare lay
That yee shall wed that ladye within this monthes day."[29] 520
"How now?" quoth Egar; "how may that bee?"
"Peace!" said Gryme, "and I shall tell thee.
I haue a brother that men call Palyas,
A noble squier and worthye is.
He is wel beloued within this court   525
Of all the lords round about.
Wee will him call to our councell;
Peraduentur he will vs prevayle,[29a]
And I myselfe will make me sicke at home
Till a certen space be comen and gone,   530
And that such a disease hath taken mee
That I may noe man heare nor noe man see.
Palyas my brother shall keepe you att home,

---

[26] landed estates, sources of income. [27] threw up. [28] angry. [28a] you who. [29] a month from this day. [29a] transitive: be of use to.

And I myselfe will to that battell gone;
And I shall feitch[30] Gray-steeles right hand,   535
Or I shall leaue another fingar in that land."

3D PARTE

They called Pallyas to their councell,
And he assented soone withouten fayle;
For he loued Sir Egar both euen and morne
As well as he did Gryme his brother borne.   540
"And iff you will to this battell goe,
Yee had neede of good councell betwene vs 2.
Gryme, if thou wilt fight with Sir Gray-steele,
Thou had neede of weapons that stand wold weele;
For weapons may be both fresh and new,   545
Fikle, false, and full vntrue.
When a weapon faileth when a man hath need,
All the worse then may hee speede;
And all I say by Sir Egar,
Where was a better knight knowen any where?   550
When his weapon faild him att most need,
All the worse then did he speede."
Palyas said, "There was sometime in this countrye,
Egar, your vnckle, Sir Egramie;
And when that Egramye was liuand,   555
He had the guiding of a noble brand.
The name of itt was called Erkyin;
Well were that man had it in keeping.[31]
First when that sword was rought,
To King Ffundus it was brought   560

---

[30] fetch.   [31] well were it for that man who . . .

553. MS. *somtimes.*
557. Good swords were named and handed down from generation to generation. It was not unusual to ascribe a sword to foreign or supernatural workmanship; cf. "Beowulf" 1557 ff. Erkyin appears here only; otherwise called Egeking, king of swords. Not named in Laing.
560. Fundus is not found in Langlois's index, but Forre (the name in Laing) is the name of several Saracens in the chansons de geste.

Full far beyond the Greekes sea
For a iewell of high degree.
When the King departed this world hence,
He left it with the younge prince;[32]
And some sayd that Egramye   565
Shold loue that ladye in priuitye;
He desired the sword in borrowing.
The King deceased at that time;
And when that Egrame was liuande,
He had the guiding of that noble brand.   570
That man was neuer of a woman borne
Durst abyde the winde his face beforne.[33]
The ladyes dwelling is heere nye;
She saith there is noe man that sword shall see
Till her owne sonne be att age and land,[34]   575
And able to welde his fathers brande."
Grime sayd, "I will goe thither to-morrow at day
To borrow that sword if that I may."
On the morrow when the sun shone bright,
To Egrames ladie went Grime the knight;   580
Kindley he halcht[35] that ladye faire.
She saith, "How doth my cozin, Sir Egar?"
"Hee will forth, maddam, with all his might
To take a new battell on yonder knight.
He prayeth you to lend him his vnckeles brand,   585
And there he hath sent you the deeds of his land,
And all mine I will leaue with you in pawne
That your sword shall safelye come againe."
Soe he desired that sword soe bright
That shee was loth to withsay[36] that knight;   590
Then shee feitched him forth that noble brand,
And receiued the deeds of both their lands.

---

[32] princess.   [33] endure the wind of the sword on his face.   [34] of age and in possession of his land.   [35] greeted.   [36] deny.

564. Prince frequently feminine throughout the Middle English period.
Laing: *Then he betauht it to the queen.*

574. Possibly the weapon is left by a fairy for his son; cf. "Degaré."
If so, the situation is rationalized.

She said, "There was noe fault with Egeking
But for want of grace and gouerninge;
For want of grace and good gouerninge   595
May loose a kingdome and a king;
For there is neither lim nor lith[37]
That Egeking my sword meeteth with,
But gladlye it will through itt gone,
That biting sword, vnto the bone.   600
But I wold not for both your lands
That Egeking came in a cowards hands."
And yett was faine Sir Gryme the knight;
To Egar he went againe that night.
Pallyas, he said,[38] "I read you be councelled by mee,   605
And take some gifts to that faire ladye,
To that ladye faire and bright
That lodged Sir Egar soe well the first night."
"The best tokens," said Sir Egar,
"Beene her sarkes of Raines;[39] I haue them here."   610
He tooke broches and beads in that stondc
And other iewells worth 40[li]
To reward that fayre ladye
And thanke her of her curtesie.
"Wherby," sayd Gryme, "shall I her know   615
Amongst other ladyes that stands on a row?"
"I shall tell you tokens," sayd Sir Egar,
"Wherby you may know that ladye faire.
Shee hath on her nose, betweene he[r] eyen,
Like to the mountenance[40] of a pin;   620
And that is red, and the other is white.
There is noe other ladye her like;
For shee is the gentlest of hart and will
That euer man came vntill."

---

[37] limb, i.e., arm nor leg. [38] i.e., Pallyas said. [39] shirts from Rennes. [40] amount.

597. MS. *lin nor light.* Laing: *Whether that were shank or arm.*
613. MS. *and to.*
619–21. Cf. Laing, 947–51: *Betwixt her een and eke her neise There is the greatness of a peise A spot of red, the lave is white.* This is a "love-spot"; cf. Hibbard, 316.

Early on the other day 625
Theese 2 knights did them array;
Into a window Sir Egar yeede
Bookes of romans for to reede
That all the court might him heare.
The knight was armed and on steere;[41] 630
He came downe into the hall
And tooke his leaue both of great and small.
The Erle tooke Egars hand in his fist;
The Countesse comlye[42] cold him kisse.
His oune lady stood there by; 635
Shee wold bere the knight noe companye.
He sayd, "Ffarwell, my lady faire."
Shee sayd, "God keepe you better then he did ere!"
And all that euer stoode her by
Did marueill her answer was soe dry.[43] 640
He went to the chamber, or he wold blin;
Sir Gryme came forth as he went in,
Stepped into the stirropp that stiffe were in warr,
And Palyas his brother wrought[44] him a spere.
Then wold he noe longer abyde, 645
But towards Gray-steele can he ryde;
To the walls went Winglaine, that lady faire,
For to see the waygate of her loue Sir Egar.
And Gryme the spurres spared not; soe weele
To the steeds sides he let them feele,[45] 650
His horsse bouted[46] forth with noble cheere;
He spowted[47] forward as he had beene a deere
Till he was passed out of her sight.
To Grymes chamber went that ladye bright;
Yett long time or shee came there, 655
Palyas had warned Sir Egar,
Drawen double curtaines in that place
That noe man of Sir Egar noe knowledg hath.

---

[41] astir.   [42] courteously.   [43] caustic.   [44] reached.   [45] be felt.   [46] bolted.
[47] bounded.

650. Laing: *But his steeds sides he made them feel.*
657. The canopy and curtains of his bed.

Palyas was full of curtesie,
And sett a chaire for that faire ladye. 660
Shee said, "At the walls, Palyas, I haue beene there
To see the ryding forth of Sir Egar;
He rydeth feircely out of the towne
As he were a wild lyon.
Alas! hee may make great boast and shoure[48] 665
When there is noe man him before,
But when there is man to man and steed to steede,
To proue his manhood then were it neede!"
Oftentimes Egar both cruell and keene
For her in strong battells oft hath beene, 670
And oftentimes had put himselfe in warr;
And lay and heard her lowte[49] him like a knaue.
He wist not how he might him wrecke,
But cast vp his armes, and thought to speake;
And Palyas was perceiued[50] of that, 675
And by the sholders he him gatt.
He held him downe both sad and sore
That he lay still and sturrd noe more.
Palyas was full of curtesie,
And thus answered that faire ladye: 680
He said, "Maddame, by Gods might,
Egar is knowne for the noblest knight
That euer was borne in the land of Beame,
And most worshipp hath woon to that relme.
That was well proued in heathenesse 685
When the King of Beame did thither passe;
Soe did the lords of this countrye
And alsoe your father, that Erle soe free.
There came a sowdan to a hill
That many Christen men had done ill; 690
The name of him was Gornordine,
That many a Christen man had put to pine;
And he becalled[1] any Cristen knight
Or any 5 that with him wold fight.
500 knights were there that day, 695

---

[48] clamor. [49] abuse. [50] aware. [1] challenged.

And all to that battell they saydden nay.
Egar thought on you att home
And stale to that battell all alone;
They fought together, as I heard tell,
On a mountaine top till Gornordine fell.   700
60 hethen were in a busment[2] neere,
And all brake out vpon Sir Egar;
Or any reskew came to him then,
He had kild Gornordine and other ten.
Then was he rescewed by a noble knight   705
That euer was proued both hardye and wight;
The name of him was Kay of Kaynes;[3]
A northeren knight I trow he is.
There were but Egar and other ten,
And thé killed 60 or more of the heathen men;   710
Thus they reschewd the noble Egar
And brought him to the host, as you shall hear.
The King of Beame in that stage
Offered Sir Egar his daughter in marryage;
Yet that gentle knight wold not doe soe;   715
He loued you best [that] now be his foe.
You be his foe; he knowes that nowe
When he standeth in dread, I know."
The lady was soe wroth with Palyas
Shee tooke her leaue and forth shee goth.   720
Now lett vs leaue chyding att home
And speake of Sir Gryme that is to the battell gone.

4D PARTE

All the wildernesse that there bee,
Grime rode it in dayes 3.
He mett a squier by the way;   725
With fayre words Grime can to him say:

---

2 ambush.   3 Caen(?).

707. On the attachment of Kay to Caen, see the selections from the
"Brut."

"Sir," he said, "who is lord of this countrye?"
The squier answered him gentlye,
"It is a lord most worthyest in waine;[4]
Erle Gares is his name."   730
Grime sayd, "How highteth that lords heyre?"
He sayd, "He hath none but a daughter fayre."
Gryme saith, "Who hath that ladye wedd?"
The knight sayd, "Shee neuer came in mans bedd;
But Sir Attelston, a hardye knight,   735
Marryed that lady fayre and bright;
For he gaue battell, that wott I weele,
Vpon a day to Sir Gray-steele.
A harder battell then there was done tho
Was neuer betwixt knights 2;   740
But Gray-steele killed Sir Attelstone,
A bolder knight was neuer none.
Erle Gares sonne and his heyre—
In all the world was none more goodlyere—
He was soe sorry Attelstone was dead   745
He thought to quitt Gray-steele his meede.
Boldlye he gaue him battell vpon a day;
Therfor many a man sayd wellaway,
And there thé both ended att this bane[5]
As many another knight hath done;   750
Ffor I haue wist that tyrant with his hands 2
Kill a 100 knights and some deale moe;
Shamfulye hath driuen them to dead
Withouten succour or any remed."
For all the words he spake in that time,   755
Nothing it feared[6] the knight, Sir Grime.
Gryme sayd, "How ffarr haue wee[7] to that citye
Wheras that ladyes dwelling doth bee?"
The knight said, "But miles 2;

---

[4] customs, character. [5] at (the hands of) this murderer. [6] frightened. [7] have
we (to go).

734. Obviously the line should read: *"The squire sayd. . . ."*
758. MS. *deth.*
759. Again *knight* should be *squier.* Cf. Laing 1167–9.

The one of them I will with you goe."   760
They talked together gentlye
Till he had brought Grime to that citye;
Att a burgesse house his ine⁸ he hath tane·
To seeke the ladye Sir Grime is gone.
Then he went into a garden greene   765
Where he saw many ladyes sheene;
Amongst them all he knew her there
By the tokens of Sir Eger.
Egar was hurt vnder the eare;
An oyntment Gryme had drawen there.⁹   770
He held the gloue still on his hand
Where Egers fingare was lackand;
And when that knight came her nye,
He kneeled downe vpon his knee
And thanked her with humble cheere—   775
"Sith the last time, madam, that I was heere."
"Sir," said shee, "excused you must hold mee,
Thus avised¹⁰ I did you neuer see."
Then hee gaue her the shirts of Raines in that stond
And other iewells worth 40li,   780
And thus rewarded that fayre ladye
And thanked her of her curtesie.
"Now sir," sayd shee, "soe haue I blisse,
How fareth the knight that sent me this?"
"I doe, madam, as yee see now;   785
Therof I thanke great God and you."
"Why, sir," said shee, "but is it yee
That in such great perill here did bee?
I am glad to see you so sound in sight."
Hastilye shee rose and kist that knight.   790
Gryme looke vpon that ladye faire:
"Soe faire a creature saw I neuer ere."
For shee was cladd in scarlett redd,
And all of fresh gold shone her head;

---

⁸ lodging.   ⁹ applied (under his own ear as a disguise).   ¹⁰ in this guise.

772. MS. *fingars.*
791. MS. *ladyes.*

Her rud was red as rose in raine;   795
A fairer creature was neuer seene.
As many men in a matter full nice[11]—
But all men in louing shall neuer be wise—,
His mind on her was soe sett
That all other matters he forgett;   800
And as thé stood thus talkeand,
Shee stale the gloue besids his hand.
When shee saw his right hand bare,
Softlye shee said to him there:
"Sir," said shee, "it was noe marueill though you hidd your
      hand,   805
For such leeches in this land are none!
There is noe leeche in all this land
Can sett a fingar to a hand
To be as well and as faire
As neuer weapon had done it dere;   810
But game and bourd let goe together;[12]
Scorning I can well conssider.
It was neuer that knights commandement
Noe scorne hither to mee to send;
If thou be comen to scorne mee,   815
Ffull soone I can scorne thee."
Before, shee was mild of state;
Now is shee high[13] and full of hate;
And of all the iewells that he hath brought,
Shee curset[14] them to the ground, and wold them naught.   820
Grime was neuer soe sore in all his day;
He wist neuer a word what he shold say,
And as shee was to the chamber passand,
Grime tooke that ladye by the hand.
Saith, "I beseech you, lady free,   825
A word or 2 to hearken mee,
And, soe helpe me God and Holy Dame,
I shall tell you how all this matter was done:

[11] particular.   [12] make an end of sport and jest.   [13] proud.   [14] cast(?).

800. An illegible word inserted above line before *forgett*. Furnivall
printed *quite*.

The knight that was heere, he was my brother,
And hee thought me more abler then any other   830
For to take that matter in hand.
He loueth a ladye within his land;
If not in euery fight he win the gree,
Of his loue forsaken must he bee."
Shee sayd, "Yee seeme a gentle knight   835
That answereth a ladye with soe much right."
The iewells the mayden hath vpp tane,
And shee and the knight to chamber are gone.
Shee sent vnto that burgesse place
A mayden that was faire of face;   840
What cost soeuer his steed did take,
Twice double shee wold it make.
A rich supper there was dight
And shortlye sett before that knight;
Meate nor drinke none wold hee,   845
He was soe enamored of that fayre ladye.
He longed sore to [bee] a-bedd,
And to a chamber shee him led,
And all his armour of was done,
And in his bed he was layd soone.   850
The ladye louesome of hew and hyde[15]
Sett her downe by his bedside;
Shée layd a sowter vpon her knee,
And theron shee playd full louesomlye;
And her 2 mayds full sweetlye sang,   855
And euer they wept, and range their hands.
Then spake Gryme to that ladye fayre:
"Of one thing, madam, I haue great marueile,
For I heard neuer soe sweet playinge
And ofetimes soe sore weepinge."   860
Shee commanded her sowter to be taken her froe,
And sore shee wrange her hands 2.

---

[15] skin.

841. "The cost of stabling his steed she offered to pay four times over."
MS. *cast.*
848–63. Largely a repetition of 339 ff.

"Sir," shee sayd, "I must neuer be weele
Till I be auenged on Sir Gray-steele;
For he slew my brother, my fathers heyre,   865
And alsoe my owne lord both fresh and fayre;
For Sir Attelstone shold me haue wedd,
But I came neuer in his bedd.
He gaue a battell, that wott I weele,
Vpon a day to Sir Gray-steele;   870
A harder battell then was done thoe
Was neuer betweene knights 2.
Gray-steele killed Attelstone;
Therfor many a knight made great moane.
Then my brother that was my fathers heyre—   875
In all the world was none more goodlyer—
He was soe sorry for my husband indeed
He thought to haue quitt Gray-steele his meede.
Boldlye he gaue him battell vpon a day;
Therfore many a man sayd wellaway,   880
And there they both ended all that bone
As many another knight hath done.
For I haue wist that tyrant with his hands 2
To haue killed a 100 knights and moe,
And shamefully driuen them to dead   885
Withouten succour or any remed;
And if thou be comen to fight with that knight,
Iesu defend thee in thy right!
There is noe woman aliue that knoweth so weele
As I doe of the condic[i]ouns[16] of Sir Gray-steele; 890
For euerye houre from midnight till noone
Eche hower he increaseth the strenght of a man,
And euery houer from noone till midnight

---

[16] characteristics.

881. *Bone* for *bane;* cf. 749.   878–86 are a repetition of 746–54.
884. MS. *haue a killed a.*
886. MS. *remedeye.*
891–4. Sir Gray-steel here represents the Celtic sun-hero, whose strength grew and diminished each day with the sun.   Cf. Miss J. L. Weston's "Gawaine."

Euery hower he bateth[17] the strenght of a knight.
Looke thou make thy first counter[18] like a knight,   895
And enter into his armour bright;
Looke boldlye vpon him thou breake thy spere
As a manfull knight in warr;
Then light downe rudlye[19] for thy best boote;
The tyrant is better on horsbacke then on foote.   900
Presse stiflye vpon him in that stoure
As a knight will thinke on his paramoure;
But I will not bid you thinke on me,
But thinke on your ladye whersoeuer shee bee.
And let not that tyrant, if that he wold,   905
Lett you of that couenant that ladye to holde."
Then shee tooke leaue of that gentle knight;
To her chamber shee is gone with her maidens bright.
Sir Gryme longed sore for the day;
The ostler[20] soone can him arraye.   910
He armed the knight and brought him his steede,
And he gaue him red gold for his meede.
A rich breakfast there was dight,
And shortlye sett before that knight;
But meate nor drinke none wold hee   915
But a cuppe of wine and soppes 3.[21]
He tooke leaue of that ladye cleare
And rydeth towards the fresh riuer.

5D PARTE

Early in that May morning
Merrely when the burds can sing,   920
The throstlecocke, the nightingale,
The laueracke,[22] and the wild woodhall,[23]
The rookes risen in euery riuer,
The birds made a blissfull bere.[24]
It was a heauenly melodye   925

---

[17] grows weaker by. [18] attack. [19] quickly. [20] groom of the chamber. [21] bread dipped in wine. [22] lark. [23] witwall. [24] noise.
  919–30. A conventional medieval May morning.
  925. MS. *molodye.*

For a knight that did a louer bee
On the one side to heare the small birds singing,
On the other side the flowers springing.
Then drew forth of the dales the dun deere;
The sun it shone both fresh and cleere;   930
Phebus gott vp with his golden beames,
Ouer all the land soe light it gleames.
Hee looked vpon the other side,
See parkes and palaces of mickle pryde,
With 7 townes by the salt sea   935
With castles fayre and towers hyee.
Ouer the riuer were ryding places 2,
And soone Grime chose to the one of tho;
And then he wold noe longer abyde,
But into Gray-steeles land can he ryde.   940
And yett was feared Sir Gryme the knight
Lest he wold haue tarryed him[25] till night;
But, God wott, he had noe cause to doe soe,
For Gray-steele had euer waches[26] 2.
They went and told their master anon right: 945
"Into your land is comen a knight,
And 3st he hath rydden about the [plaine],
And now is he bowne to turne home againe."
"Nay," sayd Gray-steele, "by St. Iohn!
This one yeere he shall not goe home,   950
But he shall either fight or flee,
Or a wed in this land leaue shall hee."
They brought him red sheeld and red spere,
And all of fresh gold shone his geere;
His brest plate was purpelye pight;[27]   955
His helmett itt shone with gold soe bright,
Was sett with gold and precious stone;

---

[25] waited (reflexive). [26] watchmen. [27] decorated with purple.

926. *For* is abbreviated in the MS.

942. If Gray-steel waited until night, Grime would not have the honor
of fighting him at his strongest.

947. Last word illegible.

955. Read: *purpel ypight?*

957–8 are reversed in the MS.

His shankes full seemlye shone;
His armes with plate and splents[28] dight
Were sett with gold and siluer bright,   960
With his sheelde on his brest him beforne.
Theron was a dragon and a vnicorne;
On the other side a beare and a wyld bore,
In the middest a ramping lyon[29] that wold byte sore.
About his necke, withouten fayle,   965
A gorgett[30] rought with rich mayle,[31]
With his helme sett on his head soe hye;
A mase[32] of gold, full royallye
On the top stoode a carbunckle[33] bright;
It shone as moone doth in the night.   970
His sadle with selcamoure[34] was sett,
With barrs of gold richlye frett;[35]
His petrill[36] was of silke of Inde;
His steed was of a furley[37] kinde
With raines of silke raught to his hand,   975
With bells of gold theratt ringand.
He stepped into his stirropp well armed in war;
A knight kneeled and raught him a spere;
And then wold he noe longer abyde,
But straight to Sir Grime cold he ryde.   980
When Grime was ware of Gray-steele,
Through comfort his hart came to him weele.
He sayd, "Thou wounded my brother Sir Egar;
That deed, traytor, thou shalt buy full sore."
Gray-steele answered neuer a word,   985
But came on Sir Grime as he was woode.
They smoten their steeds with spurres bright
And ran together with all their might,
But Gray-steele came on Sir Grime
Like a lyon in his woodest time;   990
Soe did Grime vpon Sir Gray-steele,

---

[28] splints, overlapping plates for a joint in the armor. [29] lion rampant. [30] armor to protect the neck. [31] chain-mail. [32] mace, war-club. [33] ruby, or any red stone. [34] rich silk. [35] decorated. [36] breast plate. [37] wonderful.

969–70. On shining gems, cf. "Havelok" 2145.

And attilde[38] him a dint that bote[39] full weele.
Thorrow all his armour lesse and more,
Cleane thorrow the body he him bore,
That all his girthers[40] burst in sunder;   995
The knight and salle[41] and all came vnder.
Through the strenght of Gryime and his steede,
He smote downe Gray-steele, and ouer him yeede;
And well perceiued Gray-steele then
That he was macht with a noble man.   1000
Then young Grime start out of stray,[42]
And from his stirropps he light that day.
He thought on that ladye yore,
How shee had taught him to doe before;
He shooke out his sword Egeking;   1005
The other mett him manffully without leasing.
Grime sought[43] him on one side
And raught him with a wound full wyde;
A 100^d mailes[44] he shore assunder
And all the stuffe that was therevnder.   1010
Throughout all his armour bright,
5 inch into the sholder, the sword light,[45]
But Gray-steele neuer with noe man mett
That 2 such dints did on him sett.
Then thought Gray-steele, that warryour wight,   1015
To quitt Sir Grime that noble knight;
He hytt him on the helme on hye
That the fire as flynt out can flye.
Or euer he cold handle Egeking againe,
3 doughtye dints he sett on him certaine   1020
That almost Sir Gryme was slaine;
The least of them might haue beene a mans bane.
Thus these noble burnes[46] in battele
Hacked and hewed with swords of mettle;

---

[38] aimed at him. [39] cut. [40] girths. [41] saddle. [42] astray; jumped clear of his stirrups. Cf. *N.E.D.*, *stray*, sb. II. [43] attacked. [44] links of chain-mail. [45] cut, hit (alighted). [46] men.

1003. In the scribe's source, *yore* may have been *þore*. Rhyme frequently indicates this form. Or the *y* may have been carried over from *ladye; ladye ore*, the favors of the lady.

Through rich mail and myny plee,[47]   1025
The red blood blemished both their blee.
Sir Grime was learned in his childhood
Full noblye to handle a sworde;
With an arkward[48] stroke ffull slee
He hitt Sir Gray-steele on the knee;   1030
If he were neuer soe wight of hand,
On the one foote he might but stand.
"Thou wounded my brother, Sir Egar;
That deed thou shalt abuy full sore."
Then answered Gray-steele, that warryour wight: 1035
"Wherfore vpbraydest thou me with that knight?"
"For he neuer went by watter nor lande,
But he was as good as he, both of hart and hand;
And hee had beene weaponed as well as I,
He had beene worth both thee and mee."   1040
He hitt Sir Gryme on the cainell bone;[49]
A quarter of his sheeled away is gone.
The other he claue in tow
That it ffell into the feyld soe far him froe.
His noble sword, Egeking,   1045
Went from him, without leasing,
But Grime was wight vpon the land;
He followed fast after and gatt his brand.
But-on Gray-steele had had his other foote
To haue holpen him in neede and boote,   1050
I cold not thinke how Gryme the knight
Shold haue comen againe to that lady bright.
When he had gotten againe Egeking,
Fell were the dints he sett on him;
With an arkeward stroke full sore,   1055
Through liuer and longs Gray-steele he bore.

---

[47] many folds (of armor).   [48] backward.   [49] neck-bone.

1025. MS. *many and myny plee.*
1033. MS. *brorther.*
1037-8. No one ever went by water or land (i.e., existed), but Eger
was as good as he.
1042. MS. *his gone.*

Gray-steele went walling⁵⁰ woode
When his sydes fomed of his harts blood;
Then perceiued the knight Sir Grime
That Gray-steele was in poynt of time.¹   1060
Grime sayd, "Yeeld thee, Sir Gray-steele,
For thou can neuer doe soe weele."
The other said, "Thou mayst lightlye lye;
That man shall I neuer see,
That man was neuer of woman borne   1065
Shall make me yeelde, one man to one."
He was soe angry att Grimes word
That both his hands he sett on his sword;
And with all his strenght that was in him leade,²
He sett itt on Sir Grimes heade   1070
That such a stroke he neuer gate
Nor noe knight that was his mate.
He thought his head roue³ assunder;
His necke cracked that was vnder;
His eares brushed⁴ out of blood;   1075
The knight stackered with that stroke, and stoode.
For and he had once fallen to the ground,
The lady had neuer seene him sound.
Thus they fought together fell and sore
The space of a mile and somthing more;   1080
Gray-steele bled withouten fayle;
His visage waxed wan and pale.
Grime att his gorgett he gate a gripe,
And fast he followed in after itt,
And backward to the ground he him bare;   1085
He let him neuer recouer more;
His brest-plate from him he cast,
And thrise to the hart he him thrust.
Thus vngracious deeds without mending
Can neuer scape without an ill endinge.   1090

---

⁵⁰ boiling.   ¹ at the point of death.   ² for *leafde;* left.   ³ rived.   ⁴ burst.

1060. Possibly read: *in poynt to tyne.*
1077. MS. *for and he and had.*
1082. MS. *pan and wale.*

All this I say by Sir Gray-steele,
For fortune had led him long and weele.
I haue wist that knight with his hands tow
Slay a 100 knights and moe,
Shamefullye driuen them to dead 1095
Without succour or any remed;
And he lyeth slaine with[5] a poore knight
That for his sworne brother came to fight.
Then Gryme looked by him soone;
They steeds were fighting, as they had done. 1100
In sonder he parted the steeds 2;
To Gray-steeles sadle can he goe;
He right[6] the girthes and sadled the steed,
And againe to the dead body he yeede
And pulled forth his noble brand 1105
And smote of Sir Gray-steeles hande.
"My brother left a fingar in this land with thee;
Therfore thy whole hand shall he see."
Hee looked vp to the castle of stone
And see ladyes manye a one 1110
Wringing,[7] and wayling, and riuing there heare;
Striking, and crying with voices full cleere:
"Wight men, they wold not blin
Horsse and harnesse for to win."
It was euer Sir Gray-steeles desiring 1115
That for his death shold be made noe chalishing.[8]
Grime leapt on Sir Gray-steeles steed;
His owne by the bridle he cold him leade,
And he rode towards the fresh riuer.
There was noe man durst nye him nere; 1120
Yett it was an howre within the night

---

[5] by. [6] righted. [7] wringing their hands. [8] mourning(?).

1100. For fighting horses, cf. "Chevelere Assigne" 321; also "Fled Bricrend" (Bricriu's Feast) *Irish Texts Society* 2.89.
1113. The women praise Gray-steel's bravery while mourning him: "Brave men never cease fighting."
1114. *For* is abbreviated in the MS.
1116. Only known occurrence of the word; Laing has *challenging*, i.e., attempted revenge.

Before he came againe to that ladye bright.
He rode strayght to the burgesse dore;
The ostler mett him on the flore.
"O master," he sayd, "now is come that knight 1125
That went hence when the day was light;
He hath brought with him Sir Gray-steeles steede
And much more of his golden weede;
He hath brought with him his chaine of gold—
His sadle harnes is fayre to behold— 1130
With other more⁹ of his golden geere;
In all this land is none such to were."
Then to the dore fast cold they hye
Bold men and yeamanrye;
The burgesse asked the knight 1135
Whether he wold lodg with him all night.
Grime sayd, "To lye in a strange land,
And here is a strong castle att hand,
Methinke itt were a great follye;
I wott not who is my freind or my enemye." 1140
Hee tooke the hand and the gloue of gold soe gay;
To the ladyes chamber he tooke the way
Att supper where shee was sett,
But neuer a morsell might shee eate.
"A!" shee sayd, "now I thinke on that knight 1145
That went from me when the day was light!
Yesternight to the chamber I him ledd;
This night Gray-steele hath made his bed!
Alas! he is foule lost on him;
That is much pittye for all his kine! 1150
For he is large of blood and bone,
And goodlye nurture lacketh he none;
Woe is me for his loue in his countrye!
Shee may thinke longe or she him see,
And he is fayre in armes to fold; 1155

⁹ more things besides.
1123. Cf. 763.
1130. MS. *behorld.*
1153–4. These lines follow 1156 in the MS.
1155. MS. *his fayre;* cf. 1227.

He is worth to her his waight in gold."
With that shee thought on her Lord Attelstone
That they water out of her eyen ran.
With that Grime knocked att the chamber dore,
And a maiden stoode ther on the flore.   1160
"O madam!" shee said, "now is come that knight
That went hence when the day was light."
And hastilye from the bord she rise
And kissed him 20 sithe.
"How haue you farren on your iourney?"   1165
"Full well, my loue," Sir Grime did say;
"For I haue taken such a surtye[10] on yonder knight
That pore men in his country may haue right;
Merchants may both buy and sell
Within the lands where they doe dwell."   1170
He gaue her the hand and the gloue gay
And sayd, "Lay vp this till itt be day."
Shee tooke the gloue att him,
But shee wist not that they hand was in;
And as they stoode still on the ground,   1175
The hand fell out ther in that stond.
And when shee looked on that hand
That had slaine her brother and her husband,
Noe marueill though her hart did grisse;[11]
The red blood in her face did rise.   1180
It was red rowed[12] for to see,
With fingars more then other three;
On euerye fingar a gay gold ring,
A precious stone or a goodly thing;
And yet shee hath it vp tane   1185
And put into the gloue againe,
And vnto a coffer did shee goe
And vnlocked lockes one or 2.
A rich supper there was dight
And sett before that worthye knight,   1190

---

[10] surety, pledge. [11] tremble (with horror). [12] colored.

1179. *Grisse* has been altered to *griffe*.
1182. Cuchulainn's hands had seven fingers.

But meate nor drinke he might none;
He was soe furbrished,[13] body and bone,
He longed sore to be a-bedd;
And to a chamber shee him ledd,
And all his armour of was done,   1195
And the lady searched his wounds soone.
The ladye was neuer soe sounde
When shee saw hee had no death wound,
For euer thought that fayre ladye
His wedded wife that shee shold bee;   1200
And when shee had this done,
To her owne chamber shee went soone.
She tooke out the hand and the gloue of gold;
To her fathers hall shee sayd shee wold
Att supper when he was sett,   1205
And many lords, withouten lett.
And when shee came into the hall,
Finely shee halched[14] on them all:
"I can tell you tydings, father, will like you well;
Slaine is your enemye Sir Gray-steelee."   1210
Then they laughed all ffull hastilye;
Said, "Maddam, it seemeth to be a lye.
That man was neuer borne of a woman
Cold neuer kill Gray-steele, one man to one."
She cast out[15] the hand and the gloue of gold;   1215
All had marueill did it behold,
For it was red rowed for to see
With fingars more then other 3;
And on euerye fingar a fine gold ring,
A precious stone or a goodlye thing.   1220
The Erle sayd, "Daughter, wher dwelleth that knight?"
Then answered that ladye both faire and bright
And sayth, "Father, his name I cannott myn,[16]
But he was borne in the land of Beame.
He is large of blood and bone,   1225

---

[13] severely bruised, broken. [14] greeted. [15] threw in their midst. [16] tell.

1197. MS. *ladyes . . . soe soe sounde.*
1222. MS. omits *and.*

And goodlye nurture lacketh none.
He is faire in armes to fold;
He is worth his waight in gold;
But he rydeth in the morning when it is day."
"That I sett Gods forbott,"[17] the Erle can say;   1230
"For I wold [not] for a 1000[li]
Of florences red and rounde
Vnrewarded of me that he shold goe
That soe manfully hath uenged mee on my foe."
Earlye on the other day   1235
Sir Gryme radylye can him array;
And as hee was his leaue takeand,
The Erle came att his hand.
And when the Erle came him nye,
Sir Gryme sett him on his knee   1240
And thanked him with humble cheerre
For the great refreshing he had there.
The Erle tooke Gryme by the hand
And said, "Gentle knight, doe thou vpp stand;
And as thou art a warriour wight,   1245
Tarry with me this day and this night."
"My lord," hee said, "I am at your will,
All your commandement to fulfill."
Then a squier tooke the steeds tow,
And to a stable then can he goe.   1250
The Erle tooke Gryme by the hand;
To the pallace thé yode leadand.[18]
A rich dinner ther men might see;
Of meate and drinke was great plentye—
The certaine sooth if I shold say   1255
He was meate-fellow[19] for the ladye gay.
And when the dinner was all done,
The Erle tooke Grime into a chamber soone
And spurred[20] him gentlye,
"Sir, beene you marryed in your countrye?"   1260

---

[17] prohibition.   [18] went hand in hand.   [19] dinner companion.   [20] asked.

1255–7. It is not unlikely that a pun is intended on *meat* (dinner companion) and *meet* (proper fellow). Cf. 1375–6.

Grime answered him hastilye,
"I had neuer wiffe nor yett ladye.
I tell you truly, by Saint Iohn;
I had neuer wiffe nor yett lemman."
The Erle sayd, "I am glad indeed,   1265
For all the better here may you speede;
For I haue a daughter that is my heyre
Of all my lands, that is soe faire;
And if thou wilt wed that ladye free,
With all my hart I will giue her thee."   1270
Great thankes Gryme to him can make;
Saith, "I loue her to well to forsake."
And afore the Erle and bishopps 3,
Gryime handfasted[21] that faire ladye.
The day of marryage itt was sett,   1275
That Gryme shold come againe without let.
The Erle feitched him in that stonde
2 robes was worth 400^{li};
They were all beaten gold begon.[22]
He gaue Egar the better when he came home.   1280
He tooke leaue of the Erle and the ladye,
And rydes home into his countrye.

6D Parte

He came to a forrest a priuye way,
And leaueth his steed and his palfray;
And when he had soe doone,   1285
He went to his chamber right soone,
And priuylye knocked on the dore;
Palyas his brother stood on the flore.
Palyas was neuer more glad and blyth
When he see his brother come home aliue.   1290
"How fareth Sir Egar?" Sir Grime can say.
"The better that you haue sped on your iourney."
"Rise, Sir Egar, and arme thee weele
Both in iron and in steele,

---

[21] betrothed.   [22] adorned, trimmed.

And goe into yonder forreste free, 1295
And Pallyas my brother shall goe with thee;
And there thou shalt find Sir Gray-steeles steed
And much more of his golden weede.
There thou shalt find his chaine of gold,
His sadle harnesse full fayre to behold 1300
With other more of his golden geere;
In all this land is none such to weare.
To-morrow when the sunn shineth bright,
Looke thou gett into thy ladyes sight,
And looke thou as strange to her bee 1305
As shee in times past hath beene to thee;
For and thou doe not as shee hath done before,
Thou shalst loose my loue for euermore."
Then forth went Egar and Pallyas
Where the steeds and steuen²³ was. 1310
A scarlett mantle Grime hath tane;
To the Erles chamber hee is gone
With still mourning and sighing sore,
"Alas! slaine is my brother, Sir Egar!
For 7 dayes are comen and gone 1315
Sith he promised me to bee att home;
He rode forth wounded verry sore;
Alas! my sorrow is much the more.
The great pride of thy daughter free
Made him in this great perill to bee. 1320
Alas that euer shee was borne!
The best knight that euer was in this world is forlorne!"
Gryme vpon his way can goe;
The Erle and the Countesse were full woe.
Then they bowned them both more and lesse 1325
To the parish church to hear a masse.
When the masse was all done,
To the pallace thé went full soone.
One looked betwene him and the sunn;

---

²³ stuff, goods.

1312. MS. *his gone.*
1319. MS. *thy.*

Sais, "Methinkes I see tow armed knights come." 1330
Another sayd, "Nay indeed,
It is an armed knight ryding, and leads a steede."
And when they knight came them neere,
All wist it was Sir Egar;
But Gryme was the first man 1335
That euer welcomed Sir Egar home.
The Erle tooke Egars hand in his;
The Countesse cold him comlye kisse.
His owne lady Winglaine wold haue done soe;
He turned his backe and rode her froe, 1340
And said, "Parting is a priuye payne,
But old freinds cannott be called againe.
For the great kindnesse I haue found att thee,
Fforgotten shalt thou neuer bee."
He turned his steede in that tyde 1345
And said to Garnwicke he wold ryde.
The lady sooned when he did goe;
The Erle and the Countesse were full woe.
The Erle profered Gryme 40^{li} of land
Of florences that were fayre and round 1350
For to gett the good will of Egar his daughter to;
I hope[24] that was ethe to doe.
Grime went forth on his way
And faire words to Egar can he say.
"Brother," he said, "for charitye, 1355
Abyde and speake a word with mee."
Egar sayd, "Here I am att your will;
Whatere you command, Ile fulfill."
A squier tooke his steeds tow,
And to a stable can he goe. 1360
Gryme tooke Egar by the hand;
To their owne chamber they went leadand,
And all his armour off hath done
And laid it downe where he put it on.
Gryme feitched forth tow robes in that stond; 1365

---

[24] expect.

1354. MS. now illegible after *faire*.

The worse was worth 400^{li};
Thé were all of beaten gold begon.
He put the better Egar on;
Then was Egar the seemlyest man
That was in all christendoume.   1370
Gryme tooke him by the hand;
To the palace thé yode leadand.
A rich dinner there men might see;
Meate and drinke there was plentye—
Certaine sooth if I shold say   1375
He was meate fellow with the ladye gay.
And when the dinner was all done,
Grime tooke the Erle to councell soone:
"As my lord Egar is the knight
That winneth the worshipp in euery fight,   1380
And if hee shall haue your daughter free,
Att your owne will I haue gotten him to bee.
I read anon that it were done."
The Erle and the Countesse accorded soone;
The Erle sent forth his messenger   1385
To great lords both far and neere
That they shold come by the 15 day
To the marryage of his daughter gay.
And there Sir Egar, that noble knight,
Married Winglayne, that ladye bright.   1390
The feast it lasted fortye dayes,
With lords and ladyes in royall arrayes;
And att the 40 dayes end
Euery man to his owne home wend,
Eche man home into his countrye.   1395
Soe did Egar, Grime, and Pallyas, all 3;
They neuer stinted[25] nor blan
To Earle Gares land till thé came.
The Erle wist [t]hé wold be there;
He mett them with a royal fere,   1400
With a 100 knights in royall array

[25] stopped.

1372. MS. *yod*, followed by an erasure.

Mett Egar and Grime in the way
With much myrth of minstrelsye,
And welcomed them into that countrye;
And there Sir Gryme, that noble knight,   1405
Marryed Loosepine, that ladye bright.
Why was shee called Loospaine?
A better leeche was none certaine.
A royall wedding was made there,
As good as was the other before;   1410
And when 5 dayes done did bee,
Egar desired all the Erles meanye
To ryde with him into Gray-steeles land
To resigne all into his brothers hand.
They chose Pallyas to be their captain wight;   1415
The Erle dubd him and made a knight,
And by councell of lords with him did bee,
Hee gaue him a 100^{li} of fee.
Then wold they noe longer abyde,
But into Gray-steeles land can they ryde;   1420
They brake his parkes and killed his deere,
Rasen[26] his hauens and shipps soe cleere;
They tooken townes and castles of stone.
Gray-steele had neuer a child but one
That was a daughter fayre and free;   1425
Vntill that castle shee did flee.
Egar tooke that lady, as I vnderstand,
And brought her into Earle Gares land.
When that ladye the Earle did see,
Shee kneeled downe vpon her knee   1430
And said, "If my father were a tyrant and your enemye,
Neuer take my land froe me."
The Erle sayd, "For thy curtesye,
All the better the matter may bee.
For to weld thy land and thee,   1435

---

[26] razed.
1411. MS. *did hee.*
1435. According to feudal law, an overlord might compel the heiress
of his vassal's land to marry whom he pleased as a protection to his
interests.

Choose thee any knight that thou here see."
Amongst all that there was
Shee chose vnto Pallyas.
Glad and blythe was baron and knight;
Soe were Egar and Gryme that were soe wight; 1440
And there Sir Pallyas, that noble knight,
Marryed Emyas that was soe bright.
A royall wedding was made thore,
As good as was the other before.
I neuer wist man that proued[27] soe weele 1445
As did Sir Grine vpon Sir Gray-steele;
For he gate to his brother Sir Egar
An erles land and a ladye faire;
He gate himselfe and erles lande,
The fairest lady that was liuande; 1450
He gate his brother Pallyas
A barrons daughter and a barronage.
Winglaine bare to Sir Egar
15 children that were fayre;
10 of them were sonnes wight 1455
And 5 daughters fayre in sight.
And Loosepine bare to Sir Grime
10 children in short time;
7 of them sonnes was,
And 3 were daughters faire of face. 1460
Emyeas bare to Sir Pallyas
3 children in short spacee;
2 of them sonnes were;
The 3 was a daughter faire and cleere.
After, shee was marryed to a knight 1465
That proued both hardye and wight.
There was noe man in noe countrye
That durst displease those brethren 3;
For 2 of them were erles free;
The 3ᵈ was a barron in his countrye. 1470

[27] came out well with.

1436. MS. *hee see.*
1465. "Afterwards she, the daughter, was married. . . ."

And thus they liued and made endinge:
To the blisse of heauen their soules bringe!
I pray Iesus that wee soe may;
Bring vs the blisse that lasteth aye.

FFINS.

1471. MS. *an end.*

THE SQUIRE OF LOW DEGREE

THE SQUIRE OF LOW DEGREE

"The Squire of Low Degree" exists complete only in Copland's print of the middle of the sixteenth century. Several leaves of Wynkyn de Worde's edition also exist, and a corrupt version called "The Squier" in the Percy Folio Manuscript. Dialect and date of composition are doubtful, but are probably midland of the late fifteenth century. Through the kindness of the authorities of the British Museum, it has been possible to prepare this text from rotographs of the original.

The poem was carefully edited by W. E. Mead (Ginn and Company, 1904); and the publishers have kindly allowed the use of several of his notes. Emendations not otherwise credited are his.

No source of the story is known. It is probable that the poet assembled such well-known medieval motives and devices as pleased him. Notable among them are the love of persons of unequal rank, the probation of seven years, the wickedness of the steward, and the long descriptive lists. A more unusual motive, the preservation of the body, has a parallel in Keats's "Isabella," derived from Boccaccio's "Decameron" iv. 5.

The, which is sometimes abbreviated in Copland, is always spelled out in this text.

It was a squyer of lowe degre
That loued the Kings doughter of Hungré.
The squir was curteous and hend,
Ech man him loued and was his frend;
He serued the Kyng, her father dere,   5
Fully the tyme of seuen yere;
For he was marshall of his hall,
And set the lords both great and smal.
An hardy man he was, and wight,
Both in batayle and in fyght;   10
But euer he was styll[1] mornyng,

---

[1] secretly.

7–8. The marshal, master of ceremonies, must arrange the king's guests in order of their rank. Cf. "Babees' Book."

721

And no man wyste for what thyng;
And all was for that lady,
The Kynges doughter of Hungry.
There wyste no wyghte in Christenté   15
Howe well he loued that lady fre;
He loued her more then seuen yere,
Yet was he of her loue neuer the nere.
He was not ryche of golde and fe;
A gentyll man forsoth was he.   20
To no man durst he make his mone,
But syghed sore hymselfe alone.
    And euermore, whan he was wo,
Into his chambre would he goo;
And through the chambre he toke the waye,   25
Into the gardyn, that was full gaye;
And in the garden, as i wene,
Was an arber fayre and grene,
And in the arber was a tre,
A fayrer in the world might none be;   30
The tre it was of cypresse,
The fyrst tre that Iesu chose;
The sother-wood[2] and sykamoure,
The reed rose and the lyly-floure,
The boxe, the beche, and the larel-tre,   35
The date, also the damyse,[3]
The fylbyrdes hangyng to the ground,
The fygge-tre, and the maple round,
And other trees there was mané one,
The pyany, the popler, and the plane,   40
With brode braunches all aboute,
Within the arbar and eke withoute;
On euery braunche sate byrdes thre,

---

[2] wormwood.   [3] damson-plum.

15. C. *chrinstente.*
32. Possibly Christ was supposed to have selected the cypress first before cedar and pine as the materials for the cross. Cf. Mead's long note, pp. 50–7.
33. C. *lykamoure.*

Syngynge with great melody,
The lauorocke[4] and the nightyngale,   45
The ruddocke,[5] the woodwale,[6]
The pee[7] and the popiniaye,
The thrustele saynge both nyght and daye,
The marlyn,[8] and the wrenne also,
The swalowe whippynge to and fro,   50
The iaye iangled[9] them amonge,
The larke began that mery songe,
The sparowe spredde her on her spraye,
The mauys[10] songe with notes full gaye,
The nuthake[11] with her notes newe,   55
The sterlynge set her notes full trewe,
The goldefynche made full mery chere,
Whan she was bente vpon a brere,
And many other foules mo,
The osyll,[12] and the thrusshe also;   60
And they sange wyth notes clere,
In confortynge that squyere.
    And euermore, whan he was wo,
Into that arber wolde he go,
And vnder a bente[13] he layde hym lowe,   65
Ryght euen vnder her chambre wyndowe;
And lened hys backe to a thorne,
And sayd, "Alas, that i was borne!
That i were ryche of golde and fe,
That i myght wedde that lady fre!   70
Of golde good, or some treasure,
That i myght wedde that lady floure!
Or elles come of so gentyll kynne,
The ladyes loue that i myght wynne.
Wolde God that i were a kynges sonne,   75
That ladyes loue that i myght wonne![14]
Or els so bolde in eche fyght,

---

[4] lark. [5] robin. [6] woodpecker. [7] magpie. [8] merlin-hawk. [9] chattered. [10] mavis, song-thrush. [11] nuthatch. [12] blackbird. [13] grassy slope. [14] win.

69. C. *goldy.*

As was Syr Lybius that gentell knyght,
Or els so bolde in chyualry
As Syr Gawayne, or Syr Guy;   80
Or els so doughty of my hande
As was the gyaunte Syr Colbrande.
And [it] were put in ieope[r]de[14]
What man shoulde wynne that lady fre,
Than should no man haue her but i,   85
The Kinges doughter of Hungry."
But euer he sayde, "Wayle a waye!
For pouerte passeth[15] all my paye!"
And as he made thys rufull chere,
He sowned downe in that arbere.   90
    That lady herde his mournyng all,
Ryght vnder the chambre wall;
In her oryall[16] there she was
Closed well with royall glas;
Fulfylled[17] it was with ymagery   95
Euery wyndowe by and by;
On eche syde had there a gynne,[18]
Sperde[19] with many a dyuers pynne.
Anone that lady, fayre and fre,
Undyd a pynne of yueré,   100
And wyd the windowes she open set.
The sunne shone in at her closet;[20]
In that arber fayre and gaye
She sawe where that squyre lay.
The lady sayd to hym anone,   105
"Syr, why makest thou that mone?
And whi thou mournest night and day?

---

[14] jeopardy, to trial. [15] disappears my joy. [16] oriel window opening from a recess in the chamber. [17] covered. [18] device (for keeping the windows closed). [19] fastened. [20] chamber.

78. Lybeaus Desconus, Gawain's son, is the hero of a popular romance mentioned in Chaucer's "Sir Thopas."

82. Colbrand is a giant and Guy the hero in the romance "Guy of Warwick."

83. Ritson supplies *it*.

86. C. *goughter*.

Now tell me, squyre, i thee pray;
And as i am a true lady,
Thy counsayl shall i neuer dyscry;   110
And yf it be no reprefe to thee,
Thy bote of bale yet shall i be."
And often was he in wele and wo,
But neuer so well as he was tho.

    The squyer set hym on hys kne   115
And sayde, "Lady, it is for thee:
I haue thee loued this seuen yere,
And bought thy loue, lady, full dere.
Ye are so ryche in youre aray
That one word to you i dare not say,   120
And come ye be of so hye kynne,
No worde of loue durst i begynne.
My wyll to you yf i had sayde,
And ye therwith not well apayde,[21]
Ye might haue bewraied me to the Kinge,   125
And brought me sone to my endynge.
Therfore, my lady fayre and fre,
I durst not shewe my harte to thee;
But i am here at your wyll,
Whether ye wyll me saue or spyll;   130
For all the care i haue in be,
A worde of you might comfort me;
And yf ye wyll not do so,
Out of this land i must nedes go;
I wyll forsake both lande and lede,   135
And become an hermyte in vncouth stede;
In many a lande to begge my bread,

---

[21] pleased.

124. C. þan ye.

137 ff. The squire threatens to become a pilgrim, not a hermit. Pilgrims went to all spots where the Lord or His mother were thought to have revealed themselves (138). The staff (139) was obligatory if he went on foot; he went barefoot (144) to obtain more merit in heaven; he was sustained (137) by various charitable organizations, and had no business or trade to maintain him. He wore a distinctive habit of rough grey wool (140). Cf. Mead's note.

To seke where Christ was quicke and dead;
A staffe i wyll make me of my spere,
Lynen cloth i shall none were;   140
Euer in trauayle i shall wende,
Tyll i come to the worldes ende;
And, lady, but thou be my bote,
There shall no sho come on my fote;
Therfore, lady, i the praye,   145
For Hym that dyed on Good Frydaye,
Let me not in daunger²² dwell,
For His loue that harowed hell."
Than sayd that lady milde of mode,
Ryght in her closet there she stode,   150
"By Hym that dyed on a tre,
Thou shalt neuer be deceyued for me;
Though i for thee should be slayne,
Squyer, i shall the loue agayne.
Go forth, and serue my father the Kynge,   155
And let be all thy styll mournynge;
Let no man wete that ye were here,
Thus all alone in my arbere;
If euer ye wyll come to your wyll,²³
Here and se, and holde you styll.   160
Beware of the stewarde, i you praye:
He wyll deceyue you and he maye;
For if he wote of your woyng,
He wyl bewraye you vnto the Kynge;
Anone for me ye shall be take   165
And put in pryson for my sake;
Than must ye nedes abyde the lawe,
Perauenture both hanged and drawe.
That syght on you i would not se
For all the golde in Christenté.   170
For and ye my loue should wynne,

---

²² uncertainty. ²³ wish to achieve your desire.

140. I. e., such fine cloth as linen.
150. C. closed.
158. C. arbery.

With chyualry ye must begynne,
And other dedes of armes to done,
Through whiche ye may wynne your shone;[24]
And ryde through many a peryllous place   175
As a venterous man, to seke your grace,
Ouer hylles and dales and hye mountaines,
In wethers wete, both hayle and raynes,
And yf ye may no harbroughe[25] se,
Than must ye lodge vnder a tre,   180
Among the beastes wyld and tame,
And euer you wyll gette your name;
And in your armure must ye lye,
Eeuery nyght than by and by,[26]
And your meny euerychone,   185
Till seuen yere be comen and gonc;
And passe by many a peryllous see,
Squyer, for the loue of me,
Where any war begynneth to wake,
And many a batayll vndcrtake,   190
Throughout the land of Lumbardy,
In euery cytie by and by.
And be auised,[27] when thou shalt fight,
Loke that ye stand aye in the right;
And yf ye wyll, take good hede,   195
Yet all the better shall ye spede;
And whan the warre is brought to ende,
To the Rodes then must ye wende;
And, syr, i holde you not to prayes
But ye there fyght thre Good Frydayes;   200

---

[24] shoes, i.e., win your spurs.   [25] shelter.   [26] one after the other.   [27] cautious.

183. It was usual not to disarm when in hostile territory.
198. Rhodes was the stronghold of the Hospitallers, one of whose duties it was to shelter a pilgrim on his way to Palestine.
200. According to the "Truce of God" (partially adopted in Europe in the eleventh century; confirmed by the Lateran Council in the twelfth), it was an offence against Holy Church to fight on Friday, Saturday, and Sunday of each week, and during Lent, Advent, and certain other major festivals. But it might be considered commendable to fight heathen on Good Friday as symbolical revenge for Christ's death.

And if ye passe the batayles thre,
Than are ye worthy a knyght to be,
And to bere armes than are ye able,
Of gold and goules[28] sete with sable;[29]
Then shall ye were a shelde of blewe,   205
In token ye shall be trewe,
With vines of golde set all aboute,
Within your shelde and eke without,
Fulfylled with ymagery,
And poudred with true loues by and by.   210
In the myddes of your sheld ther shal be set
A ladyes head, with many a frete;[30]
Aboue the head wrytten shall be
A reason[31] for the loue of me:
Both O and R shall be therin: 215
With A and M it shall begynne.
The baudryke[32] that shall hange therby
Shall be of white, sykerly;
A crosse of reed therin shall be,
In token of the Trynyté.   220
Your basenette[33] shall be burnysshed bryght,
Your ventall[34] shal be well dyght;
With starres of golde it shall be set
And couered with good veluet.
A coronall[35] clene coruen[36] newe,   225
And oy[s]tryche fethers of dyuers hewe.
Your plates[37] vnto you[r] body shal be enbraste,[38]
Sall syt full semely in your waste.
Your cote-armoure[39] of golde full fyne,
And poudred well with good armyne.   230
Thus in your warres shall you ryde,
With syxe good yemen by your syde,

---

[28] gules, heraldic term for red.   [29] heraldic term for black.   [30] ornament.
[31] motto.   [32] belt.   [33] light steel headpiece.   [34] visor.   [35] circlet on helmet.
[36] carved.   [37] back and front of armor.   [38] fastened securely.   [39] tabard, coat worn over armor.

207. C. *yet.* Mead alters.
210. "Covered with true-love knots, one after the other." Cf. "Emaré."

And whan your warres are brought to ende,
More ferther behoueth to you to wende,
And ouer many perellous streme,   235
Or ye come to Ierusalem,
Through feytes[40] and feldes and forestes thicke,
To seke where Christe were dead and quycke.
There must you drawe your swerde of were;[41]
To the sepulchre ye must it bere,   240
And laye it on the stone,
Amonge the lordes euerychone;
And offre there florences fyue,
Whyles that ye are man on lyue;
And offre there florences thre,   245
In tokenyng of the Trynyté;
And whan that ye, syr, thus haue done,
Than are ye worthy to were your shone;
Than may ye say, syr, by good ryght,
That you ar proued a venturous knyght.   250
I shall you geue to your rydinge
A thousande pounde to your spendinge;
I shall you geue hors and armure,
A thousande pounde of my treasure,
Where-through that ye may honoure wynn   255
And be the greatest of your kynne.
I pray to God and Our Lady,
Sende you the whele of vyctory,
That my father so fayne may be,
That he wyll wede me vnto thee,   260
And make the king of this countré,
To haue and holde in honesté,
Wyth welth and wynne to were the crowne,
And to be lorde of toure and towne,

---

[40] fights (for *frithes*, fields?).   [41] war.

235. Thus his pilgrimage is from Hungary, through Lombardy (northern Italy) and Rhodes, to the Holy Land.
245. On this practice, cf. "Havelok" 1386.
258. A confusion of the usual medieval metaphor, "the Wheel of Fortune," i.e., unstable luck.   Cf. Mead's note.

That we might our dayes endure 265
In parfyte loue that is so pure.
And if we may not so come to,[42]
Other wyse then must we do;
And therfore, squyer, wende thy way,
And hye the fast on thy iournay, 270
And take thy leue of Kinge and Quene,
And so to all the courte bydene.
Ye shall not want at your goyng
Golde nor syluer nor other thyng.
This seuen yere i shall you abyde, 275
Betyde of you what so betyde;
Tyll seuen yere be comen and gone
I shall be mayde all alone."
The squyer kneled on his kne,
And thanked that lady fayre and fre; 280
And thryes he kyssed that lady tho,
And toke his leue, and forth he gan go.
The Kinges steward stode full nye
In a chambre fast them bye,
And hearde theyr wordes wonder wele, 285
And all the woyng euery dele.
He made a vowe to Heauen-kynge
For to bewraye that swete thynge,
And that squyer taken shoulde be
And hanged hye on a tre; 290
And that false stewarde full of yre,
Them to betraye was his desyre.
He bethought hym nedely,[43]
Euery daye by and by,
How he myght venged be 295
On that lady fayre and fre,
For he her loued pryuely,
And therfore dyd her great enuye.

---

[42] achieve our purpose. [43] zealously.

271. C. *quenen*.
283. The steward in romances was usually a villain.

Alas! it tourned to wrother heyle[44]
That euer he wyste of theyr counsayle.   300
  But leue we of the stewarde here,
And speke we more of that squyer,
Howe he to his chambre went
Whan he past from that lady gente.
There he araied him in scarlet reed   305
And set his chaplet vpon his head,
A belte about his sydes two,
With brode barres to and fro;
A horne about his necke he caste,
And forth he went at the last   310
To do hys office in the hall
Among the lordes both great and small.
He toke a white yeard[45] in his hande;
Before the Kynge than gane he stande,
And sone he sat hym on his knee   315
And serued the Kynge ryght royally
With deynty meates that were dere,
With partryche, pecoke, and plouere,
With byrdes in bread ybake,
The tele, the ducke, and the drake,   320
The cocke, the curlewe, and the crane,
With fesauntes fayre—theyr were no wane,[46]—
Both storkes and snytes[47] ther were also,
And venyson freshe of bucke and do,
And other deyntes many one,   325
For to set afore the Kynge anone.
And when the squyer had done so,
He serued the hall to and fro.
Eche man hym loued in honesté,

---

[44] misfortune.   [45] staff of office (as marshal).   [46] lack.   [47] snipes.

299. C. *wroth her heyle.* Mead's emendation.
316. C. *kyuge.*
318. The Middle Ages inherited from Rome the practice of cooking in their feathers the swan and the peacock, not very palatable birds, as a display of wealth. Cf. Wright on feasts, especially on cooking birds in their plumage, Ch. XVI.
328. C. *they.*

Hye and lowe in theyr degre;   330
So dyd the Kyng full sodenly,
And he wyst not wherfore nor why.
The Kynge behelde the squyer wele
And all his rayment euery dele;
He thought he was the semylyest man   335
That euer in the worlde he sawe or than.
Thus sate the Kyng and eate ryght nought,
But on his squyer was all his thought.
  Anone the stewarde toke good hede,
And to the Kyng full soone he yede,   340
And soone he tolde vnto the Kynge
All theyr wordes and theyr woynge;
And how she hyght hym lande and fe,
Golde and syluer great plentye,
And how he should his leue take   345
And become a knight for her sake:
"And thus they talked bothe in fere,
And i drewe me nere and nere.
Had i not come in, verayly,
The squyer had layne her by;   350
But whan he was ware of me,
Full fast away can he fle.
That is sothe: here my hand
To fight with him while i may stand."
  The Kyng sayd to the steward tho,   355
"I may not beleue it should be so;
Hath he be so bonayre[48] and benyngne,
And serued me syth he was younge,
And redy with me in euery nede,
Bothe true of word and eke of dede,   360
I may not beleue, be nyght nor daye,
My doughter dere he wyll betraye,
Nor to come her chambre nye,

---

[48] courteous, debonair.

353. C., *here my;* W., *here is.*
358. C., *I was.*

That fode[49] to longe[50] with no foly;
Though she would to hym consente,   365
That louely lady fayre and gente,
I truste hym so well, withouten drede,
That he would neuer do that dede
But yf he myght that lady wynne
In wedlocke to welde, withouten synne;   370
And yf she assent him tyll,
The squyer is worthy to haue none yll;
For i haue sene that many a page
Haue become men by mariage;
Than it is semely that squyer   375
To haue my doughter by this manere,
And eche man in his degre
Become a lorde of ryaltye,
By fortune and by other grace,
By herytage and by purchace:[13]   380
Therfore, stewarde, beware hereby;
Defame hym not for no enuy:[14]
It were great reuth he should be spylte,
Or put to death withouten gylte
(And more ruthe of[15] my doughter dere,   385
For[16] chaungyng of that ladyes chere.
I woulde not for my crowne so newe
That lady chaunge hyde or hewe);
Or for to put thyselfe in drede,
But thou myght take hym with the dede.   390
For yf it may be founde in thee
That thou them fame[17] for enmyté,
Thou shalt be taken as a felon
And put full depe in my pryson,

---

[49] child. [50] desire. [13] the acquiring of property in any way other than by inheritance. [14] malice (as usual in Middle English). [15] in the case of. [16] on account of. [17] defame.

364. Perhaps *longe* should be read *fonge*, seize.
375. C. *that the;* Mead emends.
389. *Or for to put* is in parallel structure with ll. 383–4. "It would be a pity to put yourself in jeopardy."
392. C. *enuyte.* Mead emends.

And fetered fast vnto a stone　　　　　395
Tyl xii yere were come and gone,
And drawen wyth hors throughe the cyté,
And soone hanged vpon a tre.
And thou may not thyselfe excuse:
This dede thou shalt no wise refuse;[18]　　　400
And therfore, steward, take good hed
How thou wilt answere to this ded."
The stewarde answered with great enuy,
"That i haue sayd, that i wyll stand therby;
To suffre death and endlesse wo,　　　　405
Syr Kynge, i wyl neuer go therfro;
For yf that ye wyll graunt me here
Strength of men and great power,
I shall hym take this same nyght
In the chambre with your doughter bright;　410
For i shall neuer be gladde of chere
Tyll i be venged of that squyer."
　　Than sayd the Kynge full curteysly
Unto the stewarde, that stode hym by,
"Thou shalte haue strength ynough with the,　415
Men of armes xxx and thre,
To watche that lady muche of pryce,
And her to kepe fro her enemyes.
For there is no knyght in Chrystenté
That wolde betray that lady fre,　　　　420
But he should dye vnder his shelde,
And i myght se hym in the feldde;
And therfore, stewarde, i the pray,
Take hede what i shall to the say;
And if the squiere come to-night　　　　425
For to speke with that lady bryght,
Let hym say whatsoeuer he wyll,
And here and se and holde you styll;
And herken well what he wyll say

---

[18] escape responsibility for this deed.

398. C. *vopn.*
425. C. *come not;* Mead emends.

Or thou with him make any fray;   430
So he come not her chambre win,[19]
No bate[20] on hym loke thou begyn;
Though that he kysse that lady fre
And take his leaue ryght curteysly,
Let hym go, both hole and sounde,   435
Without wemme[21] or any wounde;
But-yf he wyl her chamber breke,
No worde to hym that thou do speke.
But yf he come with company
For to betraye that fayre lady,   440
Loke he be taken soone anone,
And all his meyné euerychone,
And brought with strength to my pr̃yson
As traytour, thefe, and false felon;
And yf he make any defence,   445
Loke that he neuer go thence,
But loke thou hew hym also small
As flesshe whan it to the potte shall.
And yf he yelde hym to thee,
Brynge him bothe saufe and sounde to me: 450
I shall borowe,[22] for seuen yere
He shall not wedde my doughter dere.
And therfore, stewarde, i thee praye
Thou watche that lady nyght and daye."
The stewarde sayde the Kyng vntyll,   455
"All your byddyng i shall fulfyll."
    The stewarde toke his leaue to go.
The squyer came fro chambre tho:
Downe he went into the hall.
The officers sone can he call,   460
Both vssher,[23] panter,[24] and butler,
And other that in office were;

---

[19] within (a contraction).   [20] strife.   [21] injury.   [22] guarantee.   [23] keeper of the door.   [24] keeper of the pantry.

430. C. *made*.
431. For *bin?*   There is a dot over the *w* of *win* in C.
452. C. *uot*.
456. C. *bydgdyng*.

There he them warned sone anone
To take vp the bordes euerychone.
Than they dyd his commaundement,   465
And sythe vnto the Kyng he went;
Full lowe he set hym on his kne,
And voyded his borde[25] full gentely;
And whan the squyre had done so,
Anone he sayde the Kynge vnto,   470
"As ye are lorde of chyualry,
Geue me leue to passe the sea,
To proue my strenthe with my ryght hande
On Godes enemyes in vncouth land,
And to be knowe in chyualry,   475
In Gascoyne, Spayne, and Lumbardy,
In eche batayle for to fyght,
To be proued a venterous knyght."
The Kyng sayd to the squyer tho,
"Thou shalt haue good leue to go;   480
I shall the gyue both golde and fe
And strength of men to wende with thee;
If thou be true in worde and dede,
I shall thee helpe in all thy nede."
The squyer thanked the Kyng anone   485
And toke his leue and forth can gone,
With ioye and blysse and muche pryde,
Wyth all his meyny by his syde.
He had not ryden but a whyle,
Not the mountenaunce[26] of a myle,   490
Or he was ware of a vyllage.
Anone he sayde vnto a page,
"Our souper soone loke it be dyght:
Here wyll we lodge all to-nyght."

---

[25] removed the king's table.   [26] amount.

464. Cf. Int. III. B.

480. The vassal was looked upon with suspicion if he left the domain of his lord for long; the supposition was that he would attach himself to someone else. Hence the requirement that he be granted formal leave of absence; otherwise he might be treated as an enemy. Cf. Fundenburg 96.

They toke theyr ynnes in good intente,[27]   495
And to theyr supper soone they wente.
Whan he was set and serued at meate,
Than he sayd he had forgete
To take leue of that lady fre,
The Kynges doughter of Hungré.   500
  Anone the squyer made him yare,
And by hymselfe forth can he fare;
Without strength of his meyné,
Vnto the castell than went he.
Whan he came to the posterne[28] gate,   505
Anone he entred in thereat,
And his drawen swerd in his hande.
There was no more with him wolde stande:
But it stode with hym full harde,
As ye shall here nowe of the stewarde.   510
He wende in the worlde none had bene
That had knowen of his pryuité;
Alas! it was not as he wende,
For all his counsayle the stewarde [kende].
He had bewrayed him to the Kyng   515
Of all his loue and his woyng;
And yet he layc hcr chambrc by,
Armed with a great company,
And beset it one eche syde,
For treason walketh wonder wyde.   520
The squyer thought on no mystruste;[29]
He wende no man in the worlde had wyste;
But yf he had knowen, ne by Saynt Iohn,
He had not come theder by his owne![30]
Or yf that lady had knowen his wyll,   525
That he should haue come her chamber tyll,
She would haue taken hym golde and fe,
Strength of men and royalté.

---

[27] took shelter with good will. [28] rear. [29] suspicion. [30] alone.

501. C. *ayre.*
511. M. emended to *be.*
514. Ritson supplies *kende.*

But there ne wyst no man nor grome
Where that squyer was become,   530
But[31] forth he went hymselfe alone,
Amonge his seruauntes euerychone.
Whan that he came her chambre to,
Anone he sayde, "Your dore vndo!
Undo," he sayde, "nowe, fayre lady!   535
I am beset with many a spy.
Lady as whyte as whales bone,
There are thyrty agaynst me one.
Undo thy dore, my worthy wyfe!
I am besette with many a knyfe.   540
Undo your dore, my lady swete!
I am beset with enemyes great;
And, lady, but ye wyll aryse,
I shall be dead with myne enemyes.
Vndo thy dore, my frely[32] floure!   545
For ye are myne, and i am your."
    That lady with those wordes awoke;
A mantell of golde to her she toke;
She sayde, "Go away, thou wicked wyght:
Thou shalt not come here this nyght,   550
For i wyll not my dore vndo
For no man that cometh therto.
There is but one in Christenté
That euer made that forwarde with me;
There is but one that euer bare lyfe,   555
That euer i hight to be his wyfe;
He shall me wedde, by Mary bryght,
Whan he is proued a venterous knyght,
For we haue loued this seuen yere:
There was neuer loue to me so dere.   560
There lyeth on[33] me both kyng and knyght,
Duke, erles, of muche might.
Wende forth, squyer, on your waye,
For here ye gette none other praye;[34]
For i ne wote what ye should be,   565

---

[31] except that.   [32] lovely.   [33] importune, woo.   [34] prey, booty.

That thus besecheth loue of me."
"I am your owne squyr," he sayde,
"For me, lady, be not dysmayde.
Come i am full pryuely
To take my leaue of you, lady." 570
"Welcome," she sayd, "my loue so dere,
Myne owne dere heart and my squyer;
I shall you geue kysses thre,
A thousand pounde vnto your fe,
And kepe i shall my maydenhede ryght 575
Tyll ye be proued a venturous[35] knyght.
For yf ye should me wede anone,
My father wolde make slee you soone.
I am the Kynges doughter of Hungré,
And ye alone that haue loued me, 580
And though you loue me neuer so sore,
For me ye shall neuer be lore.
Go forth, and aske me at my kynne,
And loke what graunt[36] you may wynne;
Yf that ye gette graunt in faye, 585
Myselfe therto shall not say nay;
And yf ye may not do so,
Otherwyse ye shall come to.[37]
Ye are bothe hardy, stronge, and wight;
Go forth and be a venterous knight. 590
I pray to God and our Lady
To send you the whele of victory,
That my father so leue ye be,
That [he] wyll profer me to thee.
I wote well it is lyghtly sayd, 595
'Go forth, and be nothyng afrayde.'
A man of worshyp may not do so:

---

[35] bold, tried. [36] concession, favor. [37] gain your will.

571–636. Kittredge regards these lines as an interpolation because there "is no proper place for love talk or any kind of conversation after l. 570. The Lady at that point learns that it is *her* Squire and that he is in horrible danger." Cf. Mead lxxxiii.
593. C. *he be.*

He must haue what neds him vnto;
He must haue gold, he must haue fe,
Strength of men and royalté.   600
Golde and syluer spare ye nought
Tyll to manhode ye be brought;
To what batayll soeuer ye go,
Ye shall haue an hundreth pounde or two;
And yet to me, syr, ye may saye   605
That i woulde fayne haue you awaye,
That profered you golde and fe
Out of myne eye syght for to be.
Neuerthelesse it is not so:
It is for the worshyp of vs two.   610
Though you be come of symple[38] kynne,
Thus my loue, syr, may ye wynne:
Yf ye haue grace of victory,
As euer had Syr Lybyus or Syr Guy,
Whan the dwarfe and mayde Ely   615
Came to Arthoure, kyng so fre.
As a kyng of great renowne
That wan the lady of Synadowne,
Lybius was graunted the batayle tho;
Therfore the dwarfe was full wo,   620
And sayd, 'Arthur, thou arte to blame.
To bydde this chylde go sucke his dame
Better hym semeth, so mote i thryue,
Than for to do these batayles fyue
At the chapell of Salebraunce!'   625
These wordes began great distaunce;[39]

---

[38] humble. [39] dissensions.

614–32. The references are to the romance "Libeaus Desconus." Libeaus, always victorious (614), is selected by Arthur to accompany a maid Elene and a dwarf to free the lady of Sinadoune; they mock him (620); but when after five preliminary encounters (624), he overcomes the knight of Salebraunce (625), they confess their error (628). *Syr Guy* is Guy of Warwick.

617. Mead suggests that *kyng* should be *knyght*. Very possibly ll. 617–8. should follow l. 614.

The[y] sawe they had the victory;
They kneled downe and cryed mercy;
And afterward, syr, verament,
They called hym knyght absolent:[40]   630
Emperours, dukes, knyghtes, and quene,
At his commaundement for to bene.
Suche fortune with grace now to you fall,
To wynne the worthyest within the wall,
And thynke on your loue alone,   635
And for to loue that ye chaunge none."
    Ryght as they talked thus in fere,
Theyr enemyes approched nere and nere,
Foure and thyrty armed bryght
The steward had arayed hym to fyght.   640
The steward was ordeyned to spy
And for to take them vtterly.
He wende to death he should haue gone;
He felled seuen men agaynst hym one;
Whan he had them to grounde brought,   645
The stewarde at hym full sadly[41] fought.
So harde they smote together tho,
The stewardes throte he cut in two,
And sone he fell downe to the grounde
As a traitour vntrewe, with many a wound.   650
The squyer sone in armes they hente,
And of they dyd his good garmente,
And on the stewarde they it dyd,
And sone his body therin th[e]y hydde,
And with their swordes his face they share,[42]   655
That she should not knowe what he ware;
They cast hym at her chambre dore,
The stewarde that was styffe[43] and store.[44]
Whan they had made that great affraye,
Full pryuely they stale awaye;   660
In arme the[y] take that squyer tho

---

[40] finished, perfect (only occurrence; cf. *N.E.D.*).   [41] determinedly.   [42] cut.
[43] strong.   [44] sturdy.

627. C. *wictory*.

And to the Kynges chambre can they go,
Without wemme[45] or any wounde,
Before the Kynge bothe hole and sounde.
As soone as the Kynge him spyed with eye,   665
He sayd, "Welcome, sonne, sykerly!
Thou hast cast[46] thee my sonne to be;
This seuen yere i shall let thee."
  Leue we here of this squyer wight,
And speake we of that lady bryght,   670
How she rose, that lady dere,
To take her leue of that squyer.
Also naked as she was borne,
She stod her chambre dore beforne.
"Alas," she sayd, "and weale away!   675
For all to long nowe haue i lay;"
She sayd, "Alas, and all for wo!
Withouten men why came ye so?
Yf that ye wolde haue come to me,
Other werninges there might haue be.   680
Now all to dere my loue is bought,
But it shall neuer be lost for nought;"
And in her armes she toke hym there,
Into the chamber she dyd hym bere;
His bowels soone she dyd out drawe,   685
And buryed them in Goddes lawe.[47]
She sered[48] that body with specery,
Wyth wyrgin[49] waxe and commendry;[50]
And closed hym in a maser[1] tre,
And set on hym lockes thre.   690
She put him in a marble stone
With quaynt gynnes many one,
And set hym at hir beddes head;
And euery day she kyst that dead.
Soone at morne, whan she vprose,   695
Unto that dead body she gose;

---

[45] bruise. [46] decided, planned. [47] according to religious practice. [48] covered.
[49] pure. [50] dry cummin (?), an aromatic plant; cf. Mead. [1] maple.

690. C. *lackes.*

Therfore² wold she knele downe on her kne
And make her prayer to the Trynité,
And kysse that body twyse or thryse,
And fall in a swowne or she myght ryse.   700
Whan she had so done,
To chyrche than wolde she gone;
Than would she here masses fyue,
And offre to them whyle she myght lyue:
"There shall none knowe but Heuen-kynge   705
For whome that i make myne offrynge."
  The Kyng her father anone he sayde:
"My doughter, wy are you dysmayde,
So feare³ a lady as ye are one,
And so semely of fleshe and bone?   710
Ye were whyte as whales bone;
Nowe are ye pale as any stone.
Your ruddy⁴ read as any chery,
With browes bent⁵ and eyes full mery;
Ye were wont to harpe and syng,   715
And be the meriest in chambre comyng;
Ye ware both golde and good veluet,
Clothe of damaske with saphyres set;
Ye ware the pery⁶ on your head,
With stones full oryent,⁷ whyte and read;   720
Ye ware coronalles of golde,
With diamoundes set many a foulde;⁸
And nowe ye were clothes of blacke;
Tell me, doughter, for whose sake?
If he be so poore of fame   725
That ye may not be wedded for shame,
Brynge him to me anone ryght:
I shall hym make squyer and knight;
And yf he be so great a lorde
That your loue may not accorde,   730
Let me, doughter, that lordynge se;
He shall have golde ynoughe with thee."
  "Gramercy, father, so mote i thryue,

---

² on account of it. ³ fair. ⁴ complexion. ⁵ arched. ⁶ jewels. ⁷ shining. ⁸ row.

For i mourne for no man alyue.
Ther is no man, by Heuen-kyng,   735
That shal knowe more of my mournynge."
  Her father knewe it euery deale,
But he kept it in counsele:
"To-morowe ye shall on hunting fare,
And ryde, my doughter, in a chare;[9]   740
It shal be couered with veluet reede,
And clothes of fyne golde al about your hed,
With dam[a]ske white and asure-blewe,
Wel dyapred[10] with lyllyes newe;
Your pomelles[11] shal be ended with gold,   745
Your chaynes enameled many a folde;
Your mantel of ryche degre,
Purpyl palle[12] and armyne fre;
Jennettes[13] of Spayne, that ben so wyght,
Trapped[14] to the ground with veluet bright; 750
Ye shall haue harpe, sautry, and songe,
And other myrthes you amonge;
Ye shall haue rumney and malmesyne,
Both ypocrasse and vernage wyne,
Mountrose and wyne of Greke,   755
Both algrade and respice eke,
Antioche and bastarde,
Pyment also and garnarde;
Wyne of Greke and muscadell,
Both claré, pyment, and rochell.   760
The reed your stomake to defye,[15]

---

[9] litter.   [10] embroidered with a pattern, especially a diamond-shaped one.
[11] ornamental knobs on the litter.   [12] fine cloth.   [13] small horses (considered
suitable for a lady).   [14] caparisoned.   [15] make active in digestion.

753–62. All the names of kinds of wine. Rumney was a white Spanish
wine; Malmsey, a sweet wine; ypocrasse (Hippocrates), a spiced cordial;
vernage, an Italian white wine; mountrose appears only here; algrade, a
Cretan wine; raspis, "deepe redde enclining to black;" bastarde, a sweet
Spanish wine; pyment, wine with honey; garnarde, wine of Granada (or
possibly, pomegranates); muscadel, a rich sweet wine; claré, wine mixed
with honey and spices; rochelle, wine from La Rochelle; osey, Alsatian wine.
    754. C. ypocraffe.

And pottes of osey set you by.
You shall haue venison ybake,
The best wylde foule that may be take.
A lese[16] of grehound with you to streke[17]   765
And hert and hynde and other lyke.
Ye shal be set at such a tryst[18]
That herte and hynde shall come to your fyst,
Your dysease[19] to dryue you fro,
To here the bugles there yblow   770
With theyr bugles in that place,
And seuenscore raches[21] at his rechase;[22]
Homward thus shall ye ryde,
On haukyng by the ryuers syde,
With goshauke and with gentyll fawcon,   775
With egle-horne and merlyon.[23]
Whan you come home, your men amonge,
Ye shall haue reuell, daunces, and songe;
Lytle chyldren, great and smale,
Shall syng as doth the nyghtyngale.   780
Than shall ye go to your euensong,
With tenours and trebles among;
Threscore of copes,[24] of damaske bryght,
Full of perles th[e]y shal be pyght;[25]
Your aulter clothes[26] of taffata,   785
And your sicles[27] all of taffetra.
Your sensours[28] shal be of golde,
Endent[29] with asure many a folde.
Your quere nor organ songe shall wante
With countre-note[30] and dyscant,[31]   790
The other halfe on orgayns playeng,

---

[16] a leash. [17] move quickly. [18] a station past which game was driven. [19] discomfort; i.e., unhappiness. [21] dogs hunting by scent. [22] recall. [23] kinds of hawks. [24] vestments (of her choir and priests). [25] decorated. [26] altar-cloths. [27] women's tunics. [28] censers. [29] ornamented. [30] counterpoint. [31] descant.

765. C. *hrehound.*
768. Possibly read *lyst*, pleasure.
771. In 770 *bugles* means "horns;" here, "beagles."
786. Evidently a scribe's mistaken recopying of the preceding line; *taffetra* unknown; possibly read *camaca* as in 835.

With yonge chyldren full fayre syngyng.
Than shall ye go to your suppere,
And sytte in tentes in grene arbere,
With clothes of Aras[32] pyght to the grounde,   795
With saphyres set and dyamonde.
A cloth of golde abought your heade,
With popiniayes pyght, with pery read,
And offycers all at your wyll:
All maner delightes to bryng you tyll.   800
The nightingale sitting on a thorne
Shall synge you notes both euen and morne.
An hundreth knightes truly tolde
Shall play with bowles in alayes colde,
Your disease to driue awaie: 805
To se the fisshes in poles[33] plaie;
And then walke in arbere vp and downe,
To se the floures of great renowne:
To a draw-brydge than shall ye,
The one halfe of stone, the other of tre;   810
A barge shall mete you full ryght
With xxiiii ores full bryght,
With trompettes and with claryowne,
The fresshe water to rowe vp and downe.
Than shall ye go to the salte fome,   815
Your maner[34] to se, or ye come home,
With lxxx shyppes of large towre,
With dromedaryes[35] of great honour,
And carackes[36] with sayles two,
The sweftest that on water may goo,   820
With galyes good vpon the hauen,
With lxxx ores at the fore stauen.[37]
Your maryners shall synge arowe[38]
'Hey, how, and rumbylawe.'[39]

---

[32] Arras, i.e., tapestry.   [33] pools.   [34] manor.   [35] large ships.   [36] galleons.   [37] stem.
[38] in a row.   [39] "a very favorite burden to an ancient sea-song."—M.

804. "Bowling in alleys cooled."   They were covered grass alleys.
817. Small castellated towers were sometimes built on battleships; cf. Mead's note.

Than shall ye, doughter, aske the wyne,   825
With spices that be good and fyne,
Gentyll pottes with genger grene,
With dates and deynties you betwene,
Forty torches, brenynge bryght,
At your brydges to brynge you lyght.   830
Into your chambre they shall you brynge,
With muche myrthe and more lykyng.
Your costerdes[40] couered with whyte and blewe,
And dyapred[41] with lyles newe.
Your curtaines of camaca[42] all in folde,   835
Your felyoles[43] all of golde.
Your tester-pery[44] at your heed,
Curtaines with popiniayes white and reed.
Your hyllynges[45] with furres of armyne,
Powdred with golde of hew full fyne.   840
Your blankettes shall be of fustyane,[46]
Your shetes shall be of clothe of Rayne.[47]
Your head-shete[48] shall be of pery pyght,
With dyamondes set and rubyes bryght.
Whan you are layde in bedde so softe,   845
A cage of golde shall hange alofte,
With longe peper[49] fayre burnning,
And cloues that be swete smellyng,
Frankensence and olibanum,[50]
That whan ye slepe the taste may come.   850
And yf ye no rest may take,
All night minstrelles for you shall wake."
"Gramercy, father, so mote i the,
For all these thinges lyketh not me."
Vnto her chambre she is gone,   855
And fell in sownyng sone anone
With much sorow and sighing sore;

---

[40] hangings for a bed. [41] adorned. [42] a rich silk cloth. [43] posts of bed. [44] jeweled
canopy over bed. [45] coverings. [46] cloth of linen and cotton. [47] Rennes. [48] sheet
covering the pillow. [49] pepper used as incense. [50] aromatic gum for incense.

835. C. *curtianes.*
837. C. *fester;* Mead emends.

Yet seuen yeare she kept hym thore.
But leue we of that lady here,
And speake we more of that squyer,   860
That in pryson so was take
For the Kinges doughters sake.
The Kyng hymselfe, vpon a daye,
Full pryuely he toke the waye;
Vnto the pryson sone he came;   865
The squyer sone out he name,
And anone he made hym swere
His counsayl he should neuer discure.[1]
The squyer there helde vp his hande
His byddyng neuer he should withstande: 870
The Kyng him graunted ther to go
Upon his iorney to and fro,
And brefely to passe the sea,
That no man weste but he and he;
And whan he had his iurnay done,   875
That he wolde come full soone;
"And in my chambre for to be,
The whyles[2] that i do ordayne for thee;
Than shalt thou wedde my doughter dere
And haue my landes, both farre and nere."   880
The squyer was full mery tho,
And thanked the Kynge, and forth gan go.
The Kyng hym gaue both lande and fe.
Anone the squyer passed the se.
In Tuskayne and in Lumbardy,   885
There he dyd great chyualry.
In Portyngale nor yet in Spayne
There myght no man stan[d] hym agayne;
And where that euer that knyght gan fare,
The worshyp with hym away he bare.   890
And thus he trauayled seuen yere
In many a land, both farre and nere;

---

[1] disclose. [2] times.

869. I. e., "swore that he should never . . ."

Tyll on a day he thought hym tho
Unto the Sepulture for to go;
And there he made his offerynge soone,   895
Right as the Kinges doughter bad him don.
Than he thought hym on a day
That the Kynge to hym dyd saye.
He toke his leue in Lumbardy,
And home he came to Hungry.   900
Unto the Kynge soone he rade,
As he before his couenaunce³ made,
And to the Kyng he tolde full soone
Of batayles bolde that he had done,
And so he did the chyualry   905
That he had sene in Lumbardy.
To the Kynge it was good tydande;
Anone he toke him by the hande,
And he made him full royall chere,
And sayd, "Welcome, my sonne so dere!   910
Let none wete of my meyné
That out of prison thou shuldest be,
But in my chamber holde the styll,
And i shall wete my doughters wyll."
   The Kynge wente forth hymselfe alone   915
For to here his doughters mone,
Right vnder the chambre window,
There he might her counseyle knowe.
Had she wyst, that lady fre,
That her father there had be,   920
He shulde not, withouten fayle,
Haue knowen so muche of her counsayle;
Nor nothing she knew that he was there.
   Whan she began to carke and care,⁴
Unto that body she sayd tho,   925
"Alas that we should parte in two!"
Twyse or thryse she kyssed that body,

---

³ covenant. ⁴ worry and lament.

894. Christ's tomb at Jerusalem.
923. For *nor* read *but?*

And fell in sownynge by and by.
"Alas!" than sayd that lady dere,
"I haue the kept this seuen yere; 930
And now ye be in powder small,
I may no lenger holde you with all.
My loue, to the earth i shall the brynge,
And preestes for you to reade and synge.
Yf any man aske me what i haue here, 935
I wyll say it is my treasure.
Yf any man aske why i do so,
'For no theues shall come therto':
And, squyer, for the loue of the,
Fy on this worldes vanyté! 940
Farewell golde, pure and fyne;
Farewell veluet and satyne;
Farewell castelles and maners also;
Farewell huntynge and hawkynge to;
Farewell reuell, myrthe, and play; 945
Farewell pleasure and garmentes gay;
Farewell perle and precyous stone;
Farewell my iuielles euerychone;
Farewell mantell and scarlet reed;
Farewell crowne vnto my heed; 950
Farewell hawkes and farewell hounde;
Farewell markes and many a pounde;
Farewell huntynge at the hare;
Farewell harte and hynde for euermare.
Nowe wyll i take the mantell and the rynge 955
And become an ancresse[5] in my lyuynge:
And yet i am a mayden for thee,
And for all the men in Chrystenté.
To Chryst i shall my prayers make,
Squyer, onely for thy sake; 960
And i shall neuer no masse heare
But ye shall haue parte in feare:[6]

---

[5] anchoress, nun.   [6] together; i.e., you shall share the mass.

955. When a nun finished her probation, she was formally married to
the church with bridal costume and ring.

And euery daye whyles i lyue,
Ye shall haue your masses fyue,
And i shall offre pence thre,   965
In tokenynge of the Trynyté."
And whan this lady had this sayde,
In sownyng she fel at a brayde.[7]
  The whyle she made this great mornynge,
Vnder the wall stode har[8] father the Kynge.   970
"Doughter," he sayde, "you must not do so,
For all those vowes thou must forgo."
"Alas, father, and wele awaye!
Nowe haue ye harde what i dyde saye."
"Doughter, let be all thy mournynge: 975
Thou shalt be wedede to a kynge."
"Iwys, father, that shall not be
For all the golde in Christenté;
Nor all the golde that euer God made
May not my harte glade."   980
"My doughter," he sayde, "dere derlynge,
I knowe the cause of your mourny[n]g:
Ye wene this body your loue should be.
It is not so, so mote i the!
It was my stewarde, Syr Maradosc,   985
That ye so longe haue kept in close."[9]
"Alas! father, why dyd ye so?"
"For he wrought you all thys wo.
He made reuelation vnto me
That he knewe all your pryuyté,   990
And howe the squyer, on a day,
Unto your chambre toke the way,
And ther he should haue lyen you bi,
Had he not come with company;
And howe ye hyght hym golde and fe,   995
Strengthe of men and royalté;
And than he watched your chambre bryght,

---

[7] suddenly.   [8] her.   [9] confinement.

982. C. *mournyg.*
992. C. *her chambre;* Mead emends.

With men of armes hardy and wyght,
For to take that squyer,
That ye haue loued this seuen yere;   1000
But as the stewarde strong and stout
Beseged your chambre rounde about,
To you your loue came full ryght,[10]
All alone about mydnight.
And whan he came your dore vnto,   1005
Anone 'Lady,' he sayde, 'vndo,'
And soone ye bade hym wende awaye,
For there he gate none other praye:
And as ye talked thus in fere,
Your enemyes drewe them nere and nere;   1010
They smote to him full soone anone.
There were thyrty agaynst hym one:
But with a bastarde large and longe
The squyer presed into the thronge;
And so he bare hym in that stounde,   1015
His enemyes gaue hym many a wounde.
With egre mode and herte full throwe,[11]
The stewardes throte he cut in two;
And than his meyné all in that place
With their swordes they hurte his face,   1020
And than they toke him euerichone
And layd him on a marble stone
Before your dore, that ye myght se,
Ryght as your loue that he had be.
And sone the squier there they hent,   1025
And they dyd of his good garment,
And did it on the stewarde there,
That ye wist not what he were.

---

[10] directly.   [11] bold.

1006. C. *and lady;* cf. 534.
1008. Cf. 564.
1009. C. *he talked thys.*   Mead emends.
1013. M. suggests *baslarde*, dagger, since *bastard* usually means a cannon
and appears with sword only as a modifying adjective, "large."
1015. C. *bate.*

Thus ye haue kept your enemy here
Pallyng[12] more than seuen yere;   1030
And as[13] the squyer there was take
And done in pryson for your sake.
And therfore let be your mourning;
Ye shal be wedded to a kyng,
Or els vnto an emperoure,   1035
With golde and syluer and great treasure."
"Do awaye,[14] father, that may not be,
For all the golde in Chrystenté.
Alas! father," anone she sayde,
"Why hath this traytour me betraid?   1040
Alas!" she sayd, "i haue great wrong
That i haue kept him here so long.
Alas! father, why dyd ye so?
Ye might haue warned me of my fo;
And ye had tolde me who it had be,   1045
My loue had neuer be dead for me."
Anone she tourned her fro the Kyng,
And downe she fell in dead sownyng.
    The Kyng anone gan go,
And hente her in his armes two.   1050
"Lady," he sayd, "be of good chere:
Your loue lyueth and is here;
And he hath bene in Lombardy,
And done he hath great chyualry,
And come agayne he is to me;   1055
In lyfe and health ye shall him se.
He shall you wede, my doughter bryght:
I haue hym made squier and knyght;
He shal be a lorde of great renowne,
And after me to were the crowne."   1060
"Father," she sayd, "if it so be,
Let me soone that squyer se."

---

[12] fading, decaying.   [13] so.   [14] cease.

1057. On the succession of a foreigner to the throne by marrying the
princess, cf. Frazer ii.280.
1061. C. *it be so;* Mead alters.

The squyer forth than dyd he brynge,
Full fayre on lyue an[d] in lykynge.
As sone as she saw him with her eye,   1065
She fell in sownyng by and by.
The squyer her hente in armes two,
And kyssed her an hundreth tymes and mo.
There was myrth and melody
With harpe, getron,[15] and sautry,   1070
With rote,[16] ribible,[17] and clokarde,[18]
With pypes, organs, and bumbarde,[19]
Wyth other mynstrelles them amonge,
With sytolphe and with sautry songe,[20]
With fydle, recorde, and dowcemere,[21]   1075
With trompette and with claryon clere,
With dulcet pipes of many cordes;[22]
In chambre reuelyng all the lordes
Unto morne, that it was daye.
    The Kyng to his doughter began to saye,   1080
"Haue here thy loue and thy lyking,
To lyue and ende in Gods blessinge;
And he that wyll departe[23] you two,
God geue him sorow and wo!
A trewe[r] louer than ye are one   1085
Was neuer [yet of] fleshe ne bone;
And but he be as true to thee,
God let him neuer thryue ne thee."
The Kyng in herte he was full blithe;
He kissed his doughter many a sithe,   1090
With melody and muche chere;
Anone he called his messengere,
And commaunded him soone to go
Through his cities to and fro
For to warne his cheualry   1095
That they should come to Hungry,
That worthy wedding for to se,

---

[15] gittern, sort of guitar.   [16] zither, played guitar-fashion.   [17] lute with two strings.   [18] bells.   [19] bassoon.   [20] song accompanied by citoles and psalteries.   [21] flageolet and dulcimer.   [22] harmonies.   [23] separate.

1085. C. *that ye.*
1086. Additions by Kittredge.

And come vnto that mangeré.[24]
That messenger full sone he wente
And did the Kinges commaundemente.   1100
Anone he commaunded bothe olde and yonge
For to be at that weddyng,
Both dukes and erles of muche myght,
And ladyes that were fayre and bryght.
As soone as euer they herde the crye,[25]   1105
The lordes were full soone redy;
With myrth and game and muche playe
They wedded them on a solempne daye.
A royall feest there was holde,
With dukes and erles and barons bolde,   1110
And knyghtes and squyers of that countré,
And sith with all the comunalté.[26]
And certaynly, as the story sayes,
The reuell lasted forty dayes;
Tyll on a day the Kyng himselfe   1115
To hym he toke his lordes twelfe,
And so he dyd the squyer
That wedded his doughter dere;
And euen in the myddes of the hall,
He made him kyng among them al;   1120
And all the lordes euerychone,
They made him homage sone anon;
And sithen they reuelled all that day
And toke theyr leue and went theyr way,
Eche lorde vnto his owne countré,   1125
Where that hym [semed] best to be.
That yong man and the Quene his wyfe,
With ioy and blysse they led theyr lyfe;
For also farre as i haue gone,
Suche two louers sawe i none:
Therfore blessed may theyr soules be,   1130
Amen, Amen, for charyté!

FINIS. THUS ENDETH UNDO YOUR DOORE, OTHERWISE
CALLED THE SQUYER OF LOWE DEGRE.

IMPRENTED AT LONDON, BY ME WYLLYAM COPLAND.

---

[24] feast. [25] announcement. [26] common folk.

THE MATTER OF THE ORIENT

THE SEVEN SAGES OF ROME

The "Seven Sages of Rome" is the chief Middle English representative among romances of the "framework" story adopted by medieval Europe from the Orient. In such stories—the "Thousand and One Nights," the "Decameron," the "Canterbury Tales," the "Confessio Amantis"—many unrelated tales are linked together through being told by one or more characters of a tenuous main plot. For a full discussion of the legend of the Seven Sages, cf. Campbell's edition, Wells, and Hibbard.

The selections include part of the prologue; two tales of the Sages— the second, "Canis," and the twelfth, "Vidua," with its prologue— and part of the epilogue. For a discussion and bibliography of "Canis," see G. L. Kittredge, *HarvStN.* 8.222, and Campbell lxxviii; of "Vidua," Campbell ci. Ginn and Company have kindly permitted the use of some of Campbell's notes.

After each tale is a "process" carrying on the main plot, then a prologue to the next tale.

The selections in this book are from MS. Cotton Galba E IX (early fifteenth century), edited from rotographs by the kind permission of the authorities of the Department of Manuscripts of the British Museum. Final *-ll* is always crossed.

The story deals with a familiar theme in Oriental literature—the unscrupulousness of women.. The Emperor Diocletian, before he marries a second time, places his only son under the tuition of seven philosophers, who instruct him strenuously for seven years. The selections begin with the end of the sixth year.

Þe sext ȝere, his maisters thoght	215
For to asay him, yf þai moght;	
Þai puruaid[1] þam leues sextene,	
Þat war of iubarb[2] gude and grene.	
Þe child lay in a bed o-loft,	
Made ful esely and soft;	220
Vnder ilka corner of þe bed,	

---

[1] procured. [2] house-leek.

Foure leues þe maysters spred,
Ilkane on oþer, als þam thoght;
Bot þe maisters werk ne wist he noght.
Þe childe went to his bed þat night,   225
And sone him thoght it raised on hight.
Þarfore þat night he sleped noght,
Bot euer in his hert he thoght
Þat þe firmament was satteld³ doun
Wele lawer þan it was won,   230
Or els þe erth was raised bidene
Þe thiknes of foure leues grene.
Þus lay he thinkand al þat night,
And sone, when it was dayes light,
He redied him and went to hall.   235
Þarin he fand his maisters all;
He hailsed⁴ þam, and hendly stode
Al bareheuid, withouten hode.⁵
    Þe childe luked obout him fast;
And hastily his maisters ast⁶   240
What thing he persaiued in þat place.
"Parfay," he said, "a ferly case,
For owþer am i mad or drunken,
Or els þe heuen es sumdel sonken,
Or els raised es þis grounde   245
Þe thiknes of foure leues rounde;
Þis night so mekill higher i lay
More þan it was ȝisterday."
Þe maisters þan wele vnderstode
Þe childes wit was wonder gode.   250
Or þe seuin ȝere war gane,
He past his maisters euerilkane.
    Togeder had þai grete solace,
Bot sone þan fel a ferly case.
Of þe riche Emperoure of Rome   255
I sal ȝow tel, if i haue tome;⁷
Þarfore þe childe now lat we be,
And of his fader speke wil we.

---

³ settled.   ⁴ saluted.   ⁵ bareheaded, without hood.   ⁶ asked.   ⁷ leisure.

His knightes com to him on a day,
And þir[8] wordes gan þai say: 260
"Sir, ȝe lif an anly[9] life;
We wald ȝow rede to wed a wife,
To haue solace bitwix ȝow twa,
And fandes[10] to get childer ma,
For ȝe haue werldes welth, gude wane,   265
To mak þam riche men ilkane."
  Hereof þe Emperowre was payd,
And sone asented als þai said.
Þai puruaid him an emperise,
A gentil lady of mekil prise,   270
Ful lufsom and of high lenage.[11]
Þe Emperoure asked þe mariage;
Þe barnage al þarto asent
Þat he sold wed þat ladi gent.
Þan war þai wed by comun dome;[12]   275
Þat was þe custum þan in Rome.
Þai made grete mirth and mangcry,[13]
And samin lufed þai ful trewly.
Þare was grete welth at þaire wedyng,
Als scmly was to swilk a thing.   280
  Sone efter þat fel ferly case;
I sal ȝow tel how þat it wase;
For nathing mai ay vnkid[14] be
Bot anely Goddes awin preueté.
Opon a day a seriant nyce[15]   285
Tald vnto þe Emperice
Of þe Emperoure son ful euyn,[16]
And how he wond with maisters seuyn,
And how he sal be emperowre
Efter his fader of þat honowre,   290
And how hir barnes sal be bastardes,

---

[8] these. [9] solitary. [10] attempt. [11] lineage. [12] general consent. [13] feasting.
[14] hidden. [15] foolish servant. [16] entirely; i.e., everything.

283. MS. *vnhid; vnkid* suggested by W. H. Browne; cf. Campbell 154.

291. "According to the canonists, bigamy consisted in marrying two virgins successively, one after the death of the other; or in once marrying a widow." *Amer. and Eng. Encyc. of Law,* 2.192, note 1.

And how he sal haue al þe wardes,[17]
And how he sal haue in his hand
Al þe lordship of þat land.
    When þe Emperice herd of þis childe,   295
Hir thoght þat sho was euil bigild,
And in hir hert sho thoght ful sone,
With wichecraft sold he be vndone.
Sho puruaid hir a counsailoure,
A wiche[18] þat cowth hir wele socoure.   300
Þai made couenant bitwen þam twa
Þe Emperours son for to sla.
Þai ordand[19] þus bi þaire asent
A maner of experiment:
Þat if þe childe spak les or mare[20]   305
Fra he into court entred ware
To seuyn daies war went fully,
At þe first word sold he dy;
And if he seuyn daies hald him still,
Efter may he speke at will.   310
Þus was þaire purpose and þaire thoght:
Þe childe sone to dede haue broght;
Bot mani wald greue oþer sare[21]
And to þamself turnes al þe care;
On þe same wise fel it here;   315
Herkins now on what manere.
    Þe Emp[er]oure and his faire wife,
Þat he lufed euer als his life,
On a day þai played þam samen;
And als þai war best in þaire gamen,   320
"Sir," sho said, "bi Heuin-king,
I luf ȝow ouer al oþer thing,
And ȝe luf me noght so trewly;
I sal ȝow say encheson[22] why.
Vntil þis court when þat i come,   325
Ȝe made me Emperice of Rome,

---

[17] guardianships. [18] witch. [19] ordained. [20] i.e., at all. [21] many intend to grieve
other people sorely. [22] reason.

323. MS. lul.

To be with ʒow at bed and borde,
And wit ʒowre cownsail ilka worde.
Bot a thing haue ʒe hid fra me
Þat i haue moste desire to se.   330
    ʒe haue a son þat es ʒow dere,
With seuyn maisters for to lere;
He es þi son, sir, and þine ayre,
And als i here say, whise[23] and fayre.
I wald se him bifor me stand,   335
Þat es so wise and so cunand;[24]
I luf him wele, for he wil thriue;
Al samyn i wald we led oure liue;
For sertes, sir, sen he es þine,
Me think also he sold be myne;   340
For sertes, sir, it mai fal swa
Þat neuer gettes þou childer ma.
If þou wil euer haue ioy of me,
Þi faire son þou lat me se!"
Son answerd þe Emperoure,   345
And said, "Dame, by Saint[25] Sauiore,
Þou sal him se, yf þat i may,
Tomorn by vnderon[26] of þe day."
    Sho answerd þan with semblant blith,
"Gramercy, syr, a hundereth sith;   350
I sal him honore at my myght,
Als i am halden wele by right."[27]
    Þe Emperoure cald currurs[28] twa
And bad þam swith þat þai sold ga
His erand to þe Seuyn Sages,   355
And to þam tald he his message[s]:
"ʒe sal þam prai, on al manere,
Send hame my son, þat es me dere;
For i wil wit tomorn by prime
How þat he has set[29] his tyme;   360
Miself sal bath se and here
What he has lered þis seuyn ʒere."

---

[23] wise. [24] knowing, learned. [25] blessed. [26] 9 A.M. [27] according to my power
as I am rightly bound to do. [28] couriers. [29] employed.

Þe messagers er wightly went
To do þaire lordes cumandment.
Vnto þe place smertly þai come   365
Whare þai wond, withouten Rome.
Into þe hal þai went ful euyn,[30]
And þare þai fand þe Maisters Seuyn
Faire desputand in Latyne
With þe ȝung childe, Florentine.   370
Þe messagers on knese þam set,
And þe maysters faire þai gret;
Þe child also þai gret ful faire,
Als prince of Rome and kindest[31] ayre.
Þai said, "Þe Emperoure of Rome   375
Cumand vs heder to come;
He biddes ȝe sal send hame his son,
And hastily þat it be done,
Þat he cum in his awin presens;
And for ȝowre trauail and ȝowre spens[32]   380
He wil ȝow quite on al manere,
And mak aseth[33] for þis seuyn ȝere."
Þe messagers war welkum þare
With þa maisters, les and mare:
Vnto þe sopere war þai sett,   385
And riche fode bifor þam fett;
Ful wele at ese þare war þai made,
With al gamyns þat men might glade.
Þare þai soiornd al þat night;
Þe mone and sternes bath shined bright.   390
Forth þan went þe maisters all,
And þe childe with þam gan þai call
Preuely to a gardine;
And þare þai teched Florentine
How þat he sold do and say,   395
His lord þe Emperowre to pay.

---

[30] straightway.   [31] most natural, probable.   [32] expense.   [33] recompense.

394. MS. *Floreentine*.

And in þat time þai toke entent[34]
And loked vp to þe fyrmament;
Þai saw þe constellaciowne;
Þareof a wise man was Catoun;   400
He luked þe sternes[35] and þe mone,
And what he saw he said ful sone:
   "Felous, ʒe sal vnderstand
Slike ferlies neuer bifore i fand;
Þe Emperoure has til vs sent   405
To bring him hame his son so gent;
And if we bring him to his lord,
I se þare sal be sone discord;
For if he speke with man or wyfe,
At þe first word he loses his life;   410
And if him swilk vnhap[36] bifall,
Þe Emperoure wil ger sla vs all.
And þat it sal þusgat be done
May ʒe se in sternes and mone."
Þan þai biheld þe sternes ilkane,   415
And al acorded þai vntil ane:[37]
Þat al was soth þat Caton talde.
And Florentine þan gan byhalde
Vnto þe sternes and to þe mone,
And what he saw he said ful sone: 420
He said, "Sirs, se ʒe noght þis tide
A litel stern þe mone bisyde?
Can ʒe me tel, þis pray i ʒow,
What ʒone stern bitakins now?"
Þan sayd þe maisters, mare and myn,[38]   425
"Tel vs what þou sese þareyn."
   "Sirs," he said, "i sal ʒow tell
What þe mone and þe sternes menes omel.[39]

---

[34] heed.   [35] stars.   [36] misfortune.   [37] unanimously.   [38] less.   [39] together.

398. For a discussion of astrology in the Middle Ages, see *YaleSt.* 60.103.

399. A "constellation" is a particular astrological position or arrangement of the stars.

þe mone sais i sal dy with wreke[40]
At þe first word þat i speke;   430
þe litel stern þan tels me till
If i mai seuyn dayes hald me still
And answer vnto þam nathing,
þan sal i lif in gude liking,
And i sal be of grete renowne,   435
And saue ჳow fra destrucciowne."
þe maisters vnderstode ful wele
þat he said soth ilka dele.
    þan spak Maister Bausillas,
And said, "þis es a ferly case.   440
I rede we tak oure kounsail sone
On what maner es best to done."
þe childe [said], "Sirs, saun fayle,
I sal tel ჳow my counsayle.
Seuen daies sal i hald me still   445
And speke na word, gude ne ill;
And sen ჳe er Seuyn Maysters wise,
In al þe werld maste of prise,
By ჳowre wit me think ჳe may
Ilka man saue me a day,   450
And warand[41] me with ჳowre wisdom
Bifor mi fader, Emperoure of Rome;
And seþin i sal speke for vs all,
And ger oure famen al doun fall;
þan sal we wele venged be   455
Of þam þat ordans[42] þus for me."
    þan spak Maister Bausillas,
And said, "Son, by Saint Nicholas,
A dai for þe i sal be bowne."
"And i anoþer," said Maister Caton;   460
And al halely to him þai hight
For to saue him at þaire might
Fra alkin shame and velany;
And he said, "Maisters, gramercy;

---

[40] violence.   [41] guard.   [42] plot.

443. Campbell adds *said*.

ᛁ mun suffer ful grete turmentes 465
Bot-if ȝe haue gude argumentes."
After þir wordes rase þai all
And went ogayn into þe hall.
It was wele passed of þe night;[43]
Vnto bed al went þai right. 470
Þe childes thoght was euer in one:[44]
How þat him was best to done,
And how he sold be war and wise,
And answer noght þe Emperice;
For wele he wist and vnderstode 475
Þat scho wald him litel gude.
    When day was cumen and nyght gane,
Þe maisters rase ful sone ilkane;
Þai cled þe childe in riche wede
And horsed him on a gude stede, 480
And forth þai went fra þat gardyne,
Þat was kald Boys[45] Saynt Martine.
Þai broght þe childe furth in his way,
And at þaire parting gan þai pray
Þat he sold speke wordes nane 485
Til seuyn dayes war cummen and gane:
"Þan sal þou pas fro al þi payne."
When þis was said, þai turned ogayn;
Þe messagers and þe childe hende,
Toward þe court gan þai wende. 490
    When þe Emperiȝ herd tiþand
Þat þe childe was nere cumand,
A desterer[46] sone gert sho dyght,
And keped him with many a knyght.
He louted[47] hir and þam ilkane, 495
Bot wordes wald he speke right nane.
In court þai come within a while;
Þe Emperice thoght euer on gile;[48]
Sho toke þe child, þat was so hende,
And vnto chamber gan þai wende, 500

---

[43] i.e., the night was far gone. [44] on one matter. [45] wood. [46] war horse.
[47] bowed to. [48] trickery.

And doun sho set him on hir bed,
And Florentine was ful adred.
Sho said, "Þou ert of mekil prise,
Hende and curtays, war and wise;'
And sen þi fader has wedded me, 505
Gude reson es þat i luf þe;
And so i do, þe soth to say,
And þarfore, par amore⁴⁹ i þe pray
Þat þou me kys and luf me;
And, sir, þi soiet⁵⁰ sal i be: 510
Vnto þe, sir, so God me rede,
Haue i keped my maydenhed."¹
 Sho toke þe childe obout þe hals,²
Bot al þat fageing³ was ful fals.
Þe childe made ay ful heuy chere, 515
And wald noght speke on no manere;
He turned oway with al his might;
And als-sone þan þe lady bryght
Saw sho might noght turn his mode,
And for wa sho was nere wode. 520
"Sir," sho said, "what ayles þe?
Whi wiltou noght speke with me?
And al þi wil, syr, wil i do."
He answerd nothing hir vnto.
 Sho saw þir gaudes⁴ might noght gain; 525
Þarfore sho toke anoþer trayn:⁵
Sho lete⁶ als sho war wode for wrath,
And sone sho rafe⁷ euerilka klath,
And als þe forors⁸ of ermyne,
And couercheues⁹ of silk gude and fyne. 530
Hir smok¹⁰ also sone rafe sho it,
Als sho wer wode out of hir wit.
Hir faire hare sho al to-drogh;¹¹
And sari noys sho made inogh.
Sho al to-raced¹² hir vesage, 535

---

⁴⁹ in the name of love. ⁵⁰ subject. ¹ maidenhood. ² neck. ³ feigning. ⁴ tricks.
⁵ stratagem. ⁶ behaved. ⁷ tore each garment. ⁸ furs. ⁹ kerchiefs. ¹⁰ under-
garment. ¹¹ disheveled. ¹² scratched severely.

525. End of line illegible in MS.

And cried "Harrow!"[13] in grete rage.
Þe Emperoure was in þe hall,
Carpand with his knightes all;
And when þai herd slike nois and cri,
Fast to chamber gan þai hy.   540
Þai fand þe Emperice al to-rent;[14]
Hir hare, hir face was fouly shent.
Þe Emperoure was ful euil payd,
And vnto hir ful sone he said,
"Tel me wha did þis dishonowre,   545
And sertes it sal be boght ful soure!"
"Þis deuil," sho said, "þat here standes
Has me shent þus with his handes;
Had ȝe noght titter[15] cumen me till,
With me he had done al his will!   550
Þus he haues me al to-rent,
Mi body for he wolde haue shent.
He was neuer cumen, sir, of þi blode;
Ger bind him fast, for he es wode!
He es a deuil, withowten drede!   555
Þarfore, to preson gers him lede;
I tine[16] mi wit—þat wele wit ȝe!—
And i lenger opon hym se."
Þan hastily þe Emperowre
Cald vnto his turmentoure,[17]   560
And bad þe traitur sold als-sone
Be nakend[18] and in preson done,
And beten als with skowrges sare
For his misdedis and his lare;[19]
"And ger him speke if þat þou may;   565
Here says he nowþer 'ȝa' ne 'nay.'
Bot-if he speke, by God in heuyn,
I sal ger sla his Maisters Seuyn!"
Alsone þan þe turmentoure
Led þe childe fra þe Emperowre   570
Hastily þe preson vntill;
Þat lyked many a man ful ill;

---

[13] help.   [14] torn to pieces.   [15] very quickly.   [16] lose.   [17] torturer, executioner.
[18] stripped naked.   [19] evil thoughts.

þe knyghtes asked whi it was;
þe turmentoure tald þam þe case:
þai bad þe child sold haue na skath,[20]   575
Bot plenté of mete and drink bath.
þe turmentoure said, "Lattes me allane;
Mete ne drink sal him want nane."
þan þe knightes of grete valure
Went tite vnto þe Emperowre;   580
þai blamed him for þat owtrage,
Withowten cownsail of his barnage;
þai praied him to ses[21] of his sorow
And gif þe childe respite til þe morow,
And þan ger sla him, or els bren,   585
By kownsail of his wisest men.
þat dai þe Emperoure spared his son
And bad no harm þai sold him done,
Bot gif him mete and drink at will,
And hald him so in presown still.   590
Ful wrath he was, þe soth to say;
Bot þus his son was saued þat day.

That evening the Empress tells the Emperor that his son will supplant him, and relates a story to prove her assertion. He arises next morning determined to kill his son, but is dissuaded by the first Sage, who tells the following story.

Þe Secund Tale, of Maister Bausillas.

He said, "Sir, in þis same ceté,   775
On a day of þe Trinité,[22]
Was ordand to be a bowrdice[23]
Of nobil knightes of mekil prise:
In a medow þai made þaire play.
And þus bifel on þat same day,   780
þe knight þat i of tel þis stownde
Had at hame a faire grehownde.
Biside þe medow was his manere,
Al vmclosed[24] with a reuere;

---

[20] harm.   [21] cease.   [22] Trinity Sunday, which follows Pentecost.   [23] festival.
[24] surrounded.

Of ald werk was ilka wall,   785
Ful of creuices and holes ouer-all.
Þe knight had wed a faire lady;
A faire childe sho haued him by.
Þare war thre norices[25] it to ȝeme;
An gaf at sowke,[26] als it wald seme;   790
Þe toþer wasshes it and bathes,
Makes þe bed, and dons þe clathes;
Þe thrid wasshes þe shetes oft
And rokkes it on slepe soft.
    Þis grehund þat i are of talde   795
Was wonder wight and þarto balde,
And þarto was he so wele taght,
Þe knight wald gif him for none aght.[27]
Þe knight was armed in nobil wede,
And sone lepe vp on his stede,   800
With sheld on sholder and shaft in hand,
To iust with knightes of þe land.
Sone he come into þe feld:
Þe lady lay euer and byhelde,
Vp in þe kastell on a vice,[28]   805
Whare sho might se þe faire bourdice.
Þe norices said þat þai wald ga
For to se þe gamyn alswa,
And al þai went out of þo hull
And set þe credil[29] vnder a wall;   810
Þe childe þarein slepand it lay.
Al thre þai went to se þe play,
At a preué place bisyde;
And in þat time þus gan bitide:
A nedder was norist[30] in þe wall,   815
And herd þe noys of riding all;
He loked out to se þat wonder
And saw þe childe stand him vnder.
Vnto þe erth he went onane;
Þe childe he hopid to haue slane.   820

---

[25] nurses. [26] one suckled (the child). [27] possession; i.e., would not give him away for anything. [28] winding stairway. [29] cradle. [30] adder was nourished.

809. *iii* is written above *þai* in the MS.

Þe grehund wanders þareobout
And sese how þe nedder crepis out;
And sone þan gan he him asail,
And toke him ful tite bi þe tayl;
And sone þe nedder bate[31] him sare, 825
Þat he durst hald him na mare.
Out of his mowth when he was gane,
Vnto þe credel he crepis onane;
He fanded fast þe childe to styng;
Þe grehund ogayn to him gan flyng; 830
And sone he hentes [him] by þe bak,
And al obout his eres gan shak.
Bitwix þe nedder and þe grehownd,
Þe credil welterd[32] on þe grownd
Vp-so-down,[33] with þaire fyghting, 835
So þat þe childe lay grouelyng.
Þe foure stulpes[34] held vp þe childe,
Þat he was nowþer hurt ne filde.[35]
Þe nedder bate þe grehund sare
Bath bak and side and eueraywhare. 840
Þe grehund bledes, þe nedder alswa;
Grete batail was bitwix þam twa.
At þe last þe grehund þe neder slogh,
And al to peces he hym drogh.
 By þai had done, withouten dout, 845
Al was blody þam obout.
When þe bourdice was broght til ende,
Þe knightes wald no lenger lende,[36]
Bot ilka man his hernayse[37] hent,
And hastily hame er þai went. 850
Þe norices went to hall in hy,
And ful sone þai war sary;
Þe credel with þe childe þai fand:
Turned on þe stulpes þai saw it stand.

---

[31] bit. [32] overturned. [33] upside down. [34] posts (on top the cradle). [35] dirtied.
[36] remain. [37] armor.

830. Campbell supplies *him.*
840. MS. *buth* (?).

Þai wend þe childe ware ded for ay;   855
Þarfore þai luked noght how it lay;
Al obout þare saw þai blode;
Þai had slike wa þai wex nere wode;
Grete sorow had þai in þaire hert.
Þe grehund cried, so euyl him smert;   860
Þai wend he had bene wode and wilde,
And in his wodnes slane þe childe.
Þe lady oft in swown gan fall
Euin[38] omang þam in þe hall.
"Allas," sho said, "þat i was born!   865
Es my faire childe no[w] f[ra] me lorn?"
Þe knight hame come in þat tyde,
And his men on ilka side;
He sese þam wepe and sorow make,
Ilkane for þe childes sake;   870
Þe knight þam asked w[hat] þam was;[39]
And son þai tald him al þe cas.
    Þe lady said, "Sir, þi grehunde
Has etin oure childe on þis grownde.
Bot-if þou reue him sone his life,   875
Miself i sal sla with my knyfe."
Þe knight went withowten let;
His fayre grehund sone him met;
He ran obout both here and þare,
And berked fast, so felde[40] he sare.   880
Of rinyng might he haue no rest:
Þe nedder had venum on him kest.
He fawned[41] his lord fast with his tail;
And þe knyght—for he wald noght fayl—
With his swerd on þe rig he hittes,   885
And sone in sonder he him slittes.[42]
    Þe grehund es ded in þat place;
Þe knight vnto þe credil gase;

---

[38] right.   [39] what was the matter with them.   [40] felt, i.e., out of sympathy.
[41] fawned upon.   [42] cuts.

866. Letters in brackets inserted above line.
883. Cf. "Piers Plowman," B.xv.295, *fauhnede wiþ þe tailes.*

Ay lay þe childe fast slepeand,
And þe wemen sare wepeand.   890
Þe knyght findes þe nedder ded,
In peces casten in þat stede;
Þe credil was blody and þe grund,
Of þe nedder and þe grehund.
Þe credel es turned, þe child es quik;   895
Þareof haue þai grete ferlik.
He sese þe hund þe nedder slogh;
Þan þe knight had sorow inogh;
Ful grete greuance to him bigan:
He said, "Sorow cum to þat man,   900
And sertanly right so it sale,
Þat euer trowes any womans tale!
Allas," he said, "for so did i!"
Þarwith he murned and made grete cri;
He kald his menȝe, les and mare,   905
And shewed þam his sorow sare:
How his childe was hale and sownde,
And slane was his gude grehound
For his prowes and his gude dede,
And also for his wiues rede.   910
    "A!" he said, "sen i þe slogh,
I miself sal by þe wogh;[43]
I sal ken oþer knightes, sanȝ fail,
To trow noght in þaire wife counsail."
He set him down þare in þat thraw,[44]   915
And gert a grome[45] his gere of draw;
Al his gay gere he gaf him fra,[46]
And al barfote forth gan he ga,
Withowten leue of wife or childe.
He went into þe woddes wilde,   920
And to þe forest fra al men,
Þat nane sold of his sorow ken:
Þare tholed[47] he mani a sari stownde
For sorow of his gude grehownde.

---

[43] atone for the evil deed.   [44] (space of) time.   [45] groom, servant.   [46] i.e., gave away.   [47] suffered.

And for þe kounsail of his wife   925
In sorow þus he led his life!
　So mai þou haue, Sir Emperoure,
Sorow and shame and dishonoure,
To sla þi son ogains þe right,
Als þe grehund was with þe knyght;   930
For he was fel and ouer hastif,
And wroght´by kounsayl of his whif."
　þe Emperoure: "By Ihesu fre,
So sal noght bifal to me!
And, maister, i hete þe hardily,   935
þis day sal noght my son dy."
"Sir," said Maister Bausillas,
"Trowes my kownsail in þis cas;
For al þis werld wil þe despise,
To trow þi whif and leue þe wise."[48]   940
þe Emperowre said, "þat ware reson;
I sal noght by hir kownsayl done."
þe childe ogayn to preson es sent;
þe court departes, þe maister es went.

But that evening the Empress tells another tale, and the Emperor changes his mind again until he sees one of the Sages in the morning. So it goes for seven days. The following tale is told by one of the Sages on the sixth day.

HERE BIGINS þE XII PROLOUG.

　Sone at morn, bifor þe sun,
þe Emperoure rase, als he was won.
He come omang his knyghtes all,   2785
And gert his turmentowre furth call.
He bad his son þat he sold bring,
And on þe galows high him hyng.
For mani knightes and burias come
For to here þe childes dome.   2790

---

[48] forsake the wise.

941. MS. *roson.*
2789. *For* a mistake for *and?*

Þe Emperoure wald haue no rede,
Bot said algates[49] he sold be ded;
And right so cumes into þe hall
Þe sest[50] maister omang þam all.
He said, "Sir Emperoure, lord of prise,   2795
In þi werkes þou ert noght wise;
Ilk man has mater[1] þe to blame;
Þarof þe burd think mekil shame.[2]
Sen þat þou wil trow na whise rede,
Bot wrang[3] wil ger þi son be ded,   2800
Þat ilk chance bifal to þe
Als fel a knyght of þis cuntré,
Þat hurt his whife finger with a knif,
And for þat sorow lost hys life."
Þe Emperoure said, "On al manere,   2805
Maister, þat tale most i here."
He said, "Sir, grant þi son respite,
And i sal tel it þe ful tite."
Þe Emperoure said blethly he sale;
And þan þe mayster tald his tale.   2810

Þe XII Tale Sayd Maister Iesse.

Þe maister said, "Bi God of might,
In þis cuntré woŋd a knight
Þat wedded had a ful faire whif,
And lufed hir more þan his life,
And sho lufed him wele, als him thoght,   2815
For efter his wil ai sho wroght.
So on a day, bifore his whife,
To þe knight was gifen a fetyce[4] knife;
And als þai plaied with þe knif bare,
A litel in hir fynger he share;[5]   2820
And when he saw þe blude rede,
For sorow he said he sold be ded;
And so he was, sone on þe morow.
Þan þe whife made mekyl sorow:
Sho wrang hir hend and made il chere.   2825

---

[49] in any case.   [50] sixth.   [1] cause.   [2] thereof you should be ashamed.   [3] wrongfully.   [4] well-fashioned.   [5] cut.

Þe cors was sone broght on a bere,
With torches and series[6] faire brinand,
And prestes and freres fast singand.
For him þai delt seluer and golde,
And sone he was broght vnder molde.[7]   2830
    When þe knight þus grauen[8] was,
Þe lady cried and sayd "Allas!"
And hardily sho said na man
Sold mak hir fra þat graue to gane,
Bot on þat graue ai wald sho ly,   2835
And for hir lordes luf wald sho dy.
Al hir frendes gederd þare
For to cumforth hir of care.
"Dame," þai said, "par charité,
Of þiself þou haue peté.   2840
Þou ert faire of hide and hew;
Þou may haue knightes nobil inowe;
And sen þou ert both ȝong and fayre,
Þou mai haue childer to be þine aire.
It es na bote to mak murning;   2845
Al sal we dy, bath ald and ȝing."
Þe lady said oft siþes, "Allas!
Out of þis place sal i neuer pas,
Til i be ded with him alswa!"
Þan hir frendes was ful wa: 2850
    Na man might, for na preching,
Þe lady fra þe graue bring;
And euil þam thoght þare to dwell.
Þarfore þai did als i sal tell:
Þai made a loge[9] þe graue biside,   2855
Fra rain and hayl hir for to hide.
Þai couerd it ouer ilka dele,
And made a fire þarin ful wele;
Mete and drink þai broght plenté,
And bad þe lady blith sold be.   2860
Bot ett ne drink wald sho nothing.

---

[6] candles.   [7] ground.   [8] buried.   [9] lodge.

Euer sho cried, and made murning.
Hir frendes went oway ilkane,
And þus þe lady leued allane.
    Þat ilk day war outlaws thre   2865
Dampned[10] and hanged on galow-tre,
And knightes war þai euerilkane;
Ful many had þai robbed and slane;
Þarfore war þai hastily hent
And hanged so, by right iugement.   2870
Anoþer knyght of þat cuntré
Fel for to kepe þa theues thre
On þe galows al þat nyght,
Als it was resown and right.
For, sirs, ȝe sal wele vnderstand   2875
He gaf na ferm[11] els for his land
Bot for to kepe þe galows a-night,
When þare hang gentel men or knight;
And if ani þan war oway,
His landes sold he lose for ay.   2880
    Þe knight him cled in nobil wede,
And set him on a stalworth stede,
And went to kepe þe knightes thre
Þat hanged on þe galow-tre.
Þe frost fresed fast þarout;   2885
Þe knight rides euer obout
Biside þe galows, vp and down,
So was he dredand of tresown.
So grete cald[12] come him vnto
Þat he ne wist what he might do.   2890
Toward þe toun luked þe knyght;
He saw a fire brin faire and bright
In þe kirk-ȝerd of þe town,
And þeder fast he made hym boun.

---

[10] condemned. [11] rental. [12] cold.

2862. MS. *sho shied;* Campbell emends.
2867. Knights and barons often turned bandits; cf. Jusserand 150 ff.
2876. This was his feudal duty; cf. Int. III.E.

Vnto þe loge he come onane;   2895
Þe lady þare he fyndes allane.
To cal and speke wald he noght spare.
Þe lady sais sone, "Wha es þare?"
"I am a knyght þat wald me warm
And wend my way withowten harm."   2900
Þe lady said, "By Him me boght,
Herin, sir, ne cumes þou noght!"
"Lat me cum in, dame, i þe pray."
Þe lady said ful sadly,[13] "Nay."
"A, dame," he said, "me es ful kalde;   2905
A litel while wharm me i walde."
"Sir," sho said, "bi Him me boght,
In þis close[14] ne cumes þou noght!"
"A, dame," he said, "par charyté,
Þare sal na man wit bot we."   2910
Þe knyght spak so with þe lady
Þat in he come, and sat hir by,
And warmed him wele at his will.
Þe lady gret and gaf hir ill.[15]
Þan said þe knight to hir in hy,   2915
"Dame, whi ertou so sary,
And whi ertou þus here allane,
And so with murni[n]g makes þi mane?
Tel me, gude dame, i þe pray,
And i sal help þe if i may."   2920
Sho said, "Sir, i am wil of rede,[16]
For my lord es fra me dede,
And right here es he laid in graue;
Swilk a lord mun i neuer haue.
He lufed me euer ful stedfastly;   2925
Þarfore here wil i lif and dy."
Þe knyght said, "Dame, þou ert a fole
Þat þou makes so mekyl dole!
What helpes it so to sorow þe
For thing þat may noght mended be?   2930

13 firmly.   14 enclosure, shelter.   15 lamented.   16 at a loss for advice.

2929. MS. go.

Þiseluen mai þou so forfare,
And him ogayn gettes þou na mare.
I rede þou morn na mare þarfore;
Þou may haue ane worth twenti score.[17]
Þarfore, dame, do efter me,   2935
And lat now al þi murning be:
I rede þou luf som oþer knyght,
Þat may þe cumforth day and night."
"Nay," sho said, "sir, by Saint Iohn,
Swilk a lord get i neuer none   2940
Þat so mekil wil mensk[18] me
Ne suffer my will als did he;
For to seke fra hethin till Ynde,
Swilk a lord sold i neuer finde."
When þe knight had warmed him a while,   2945
He dred þat men sold do him gile
To stele som of þe hanged men
And ger him lose his landes þen.
He toke his leue of þe lady
And went to his hors hastily.   2950
Vnto þe galows rides he,
And sone he myssed ane of þe thre.
Þan was þe knyght ful sary man:
He hopid to tyne[19] his landes ilkane;
He thoght wemen kowth gif gud rede   2955
Vnto men þat had grete nede;
He was noght fer fro þe lady:
Ogayn he rides ful hastily.
He cald als he bifore had done,
And in þan was he laten sone.   2960
He said he had more sorow þan sho,
And assed[20] wat was best to do;
Al þe soth he gan hir say,
How his o knight was stollen oway.
Þan spak þe lady to þe knight: 2965
"Say me þe soth, sir, if þou myght,
If þou has any whif at hame?"

---

[17] i.e., worth twenty score like him. [18] honor. [19] lose. [20] asked.

"Nay," he said, "by swete Saint Iame,
Whif no leman had i neuer."
"Sir," sho said, "so es me leuyr;[2] 2970
Ful wele sal þou helped be
If þat þou wil wed me."
"ȝis, dame," he said, "by swete Ihesus !"
When þai had made þaire cownand[22] þus,
"Sir, tak we vp þis cors," sho sayd,— 2975
"Þis ilk day here was he layd—
And hang him vp for him þat failes."
Þe knight was paid of þir counsailes:
Out of þe graue þai toke þe cors;
Þe knight him led opon his hors. 2980
Þan said þe knyght to hir in hy,
"Dame, þou most hang him sertanli,
For if þat i hanged a knight,
Mine honore war lorn by þat vnright."[23]
Þe lady said, "So haue i sele,[24] 2985
I sal hang hym wonder wele."
Sho did þe rape obout his hals[25]—
In hir faith sho was ful fals!—
Sho drogh him vp and fest him fast.
"Lo," sho said, "now sal þis last." 2990
"Dame," said þe knight, "habide a stound:
He þat here hanged had a wounde
In þe forheuyd,[26] wele to knaw;[27]
Swilkane on þis byhoues vs shew,
Or els tomorn, in lytel while, 2995
Wil be percayued al oure gile."
"Sir," sho said, "draw owt þi swerde;
To smite him thar þe noght be lered.[28]
Smite my lord wharesom þe list;
Þan sal noght þi man be mist." 3000

[21] i.e., I am the better pleased. [22] covenant, agreement. [23] misdeed. [24] happiness. [25] rope about his neck. [26] forehead. [27] i.e., in truth. [28] you need not be taught how.

2978. *þir*, these; cf. "The Avowing of Arthur" 530.
2983. He is bound by his oath of knighthood not to injure except in fair combat.

"Nay, dame," he said, "for al þis rike,
A ded knyght wald i noght strike."
Sho said, "Tak me þi swerd þe fra,
And i sal merk him or we ga."
He tald hir whare þat sho sold smyte,   3005
And on þe heuyd sho hit him tite.
   Þan þe knyght wele vnderstode
Þat sho was cumen of vnkind blode.
"Dame," he said, "by heuen-rike,
ȝit es noght þis þat oþer lyke;   3010
His forteth[29] war al smeten out."
"Sir," sho said, "þarof no dowt;
Smites out his teth; biliue lat se!"
"Nay, dame," he said, "so mot i the
I wil do him no velany;   3015
He was a knyght, and so am i."
   Þan þe whif sone toke a stane
And smate his fortheth out ilkane
When sho had on þis wise done,
Sho said vnto þe knight ful sone,   3020
"Sir, now sal þou wed me."
"Nay, dame," he sayd, "so mot i the,
Are wald i swere to wed na wife
Or i with þe sold lede my lyfe,
For þou wald hang me with a cord   3025
Right als þou has done þi lord;
Swilk sorow has þou shewed me now
Þat i sal neuer no wemen trow."
   Þan said þe maister to þe Emperowre,
"I pray Ihesu, our Sauiowre,   3030
Þat to þe fal slike velany
Als did þis knyght of his lady,
If þou for kownsail of þi whife
Reues þi faire son his life.
Spare him, sir, vntil tomorow;   3035
Vnto hir sal fal al þe sorow;
For, sertes, sir, þi son sall speke;

---

[29] front teeth.

By righ[t]wis[30] dome þan þou him wreke."
Þe Emperoure said, "So mot i gang,
And i mai wit wha haues þe wrang,   3040
And wha þe right, sir, þan sal i
Deme þam bath ful rightwisly."
Þan þe mayster went hys way;
Þus was þe clerk saued þat day.

After the seventh day, the child tells the final tale of a king's son who,
from overhearing the conversation of some ravens, prophesies he will be
served by his father. The king casts him into the sea; but he survives
to fulfill the prophecy.

Þus þis tale was broght til ende,
And Florentine, with wordes hende   4240
And with reuerence and grete honowre,
Sayd to his fader, þe Emperowre,
"Fader, on þis wise wald ȝe
Ogayns þe right haue gert sla me,
And fully haue ȝe bene my fa.   4245
Dere fader, why do ȝe swa?
I trispast[31] na mare þan did he,
Þe childe þat was kast in þe se;
And if i myght come to honowre
For to be king or emperowre,   4250
Wene ȝe þat i wald greue ȝow?
Nay, sir, þat sal ȝe neuer trow.
Drawen and brend are wald i be
Or i wald greue my fader fre!
And, fader, ȝowre wife, weterly,   4255
Wald haue gert me lig hir by;
Bot i had leuer haue died als-sone
Þan þat dede to ȝow haue done."
When þe Emperoure herd how he sayd,
Of þat poynt he was noght payd,   4260
And sone he sent efter his whife,
Þat him had made so mekil strife.

---

[30] righteous.   [31] offended.

"Dame," he sayd, "es þis soth thing?"
"ʒa, syr," sho sayd, "by Heuyn-kyng;
He says al soth in þis sesowne,³²   4265
And i sal say by what resowne,
For he sold do na harm þe till;
And also for þis sertayn skyll:³³
Þat mi sons sold be na bastardes,
Bot haue þi landes and be grete lardes.   4270
    And, sir, i dred me ʒit alswa
Þat he sold haue þe empire þe fra,
Hereefter when þou cums on elde
And may noght wele þiseluen welde;
Þarfore i wald haue had him dede,   4275
Þat my barnes might be in þi stede.
And on þis wise, sir, haue i soght
To ger hym vnto ded be broght."
    "A, dame!" said þe Emperowre,
"Þou haues bene a fals gilowre,³⁴   4280
And with þi treson done me tene;
Þat sal now on þiself be sene;
For þi gaudes and þi gilry³⁵
I gif þis dome: þat þou sal dy.
Sakles³⁶ þou wald my son haue slayne: 4285
Þiself sal haue þe same payne;
Þi witchecraft and þi sorceri
Sal þou now ful dere aby.
Þou grantes þiself here al þe gilt;
Þarfore es reson þou be spilt.   4290
If þou lifed lenger, it war wath,³⁷
For ful sone wald þou shend vs bath;
And sen þou grantes þi werkes wrang,
It nedes no quest on þe to gang.³⁸
Þou ert worthy þe ded to take,   4295
By rightwis dome, for my son sake."
    Þe Emperoure gert bifor hym call
His knightes and hys menʒe all,

---

³² at this time.   ³³ reason.   ³⁴ deceiver.   ³⁵ tricks and deceptions.   ³⁶ guiltless.
³⁷ harm.   ³⁸ no jury need examine you.
4294. Cf. "Gamelyn" 840.

And sayd, "Sirs, smertly for my sake,
A grete fire þat ȝe ger make,   4300
Hastily at þe towns end;
For þaryn sal þis whif be brend,
With mekyl dole, þis day or none,[39]
For þe tresown þat sho has done;
And loke ȝe spare hyr neuer a dele,   4305
For sho has serued[40] it ful wele."
Þe barons war al of ane asent
Þat sho sold haue þat same iugement,
And al þe knyghtes fast gan cri,
"Do to ded þat fals lady,   4310
Þat with hir wichecraft and hir rede
Wald haue gert þe childe be ded!"
    Sone þai made, onane right,
A faire fire, brinand ful bright.
Þan þai tok þat faire lady;   4315
Yt helpid hyr noght to ask mercy:
Þai band hir fast, bath fote and hand,
Þat sho myght nowþer rise ne stand.
Hir fete þai fest vnto hir swyre,
And lete hir flye in myddes þe fire.   4320
Þus was þe ladies ending-day,
And þus was sho quit hir iornay.[41]
Þe childe lifed with grete honowre,
And efter his fader was emperoure,
And led his life with werkes wise,   4325
And ended seþn in Goddes seruyse.
Þusgate endes al þis thing;
Ihesu grante vs his blyssyng!
                                    AMEN.

---

[39] before noon.   [40] deserved.   [41] repaid her for pains.

KING ALEXANDER

KING ALEXANDER

In the Middle Ages, the history of Alexander the Great suffered the same fate as the Troy-legend: it was known only through a late Latin romance, considerably expanded by French writers of the twelfth century. (See Wells, and M. Schlauch's "Medieval Narrative" 281; the different rescensions are discussed by G. L. Hamilton in *Speculum* 2.113.) The source of the English poem is Thomas of Kent's "Roman de Toute Chevalerie," which has not yet been printed entire. A few passages, including an index to the divisions, are in Meyer's selections. Those quoted here are from a rotograph of the Durham Cathedral MS. (Library of Congress, Modern Language Association Deposit No. 59).

The text is from Hale MS. 150, and is prepared from a rotograph, made with the kind permission of the Librarian and Library Committee of Lincoln's Inn Library. The right numbering of the lines in the two extracts is 3835–4261 and 5418–5467; but here Weber's numbering has been followed, both as likely to be serviceable and because a forthcoming edition of the poem will follow the same practice.

The dialect is southern, of the early fourteenth century. The language shows two common southern peculiarities: -e- is often broken into -eo- (*beo*, *þreo*); and -u- often is written where the midland form had -i- (*hulle*, hill; *fuf*, five). The sense often suffers from the writer's attempt to compress the French original and preserve its idiom, and hence several passages are obscure. In the manuscript, final -*ll* always has a cross-stroke; final -*g* and -*k* always, and final -*r* sometimes, are followed by a flourish.

There is only a mild undercurrent of history in the story. Alexander invades the east and encounters King Darius on the banks of the Tigris, where a bloody battle takes place. The following incident illustrates the generosity and magnanimity for which Alexander's name was a byword in the Middle Ages.

Darie fauȝte wel douȝtyliche
And dude swiþe muche wo;
To on side he drough him to;
He blew his horn, saun doute;[1]   3860
His folk come swiþe aboute,
And he heom saide wiþ voys clere,
"Y bidde, freondes, ȝe me here!
Alisaundre is ycome in þis lond
Wiþ stronge knyȝtis and myȝty of hond;   3865
Ȝef he passeþ[2] wiþ honour,
Oure is þe deshonour!
Y am of Perce deschargid,[3]
Of Mede and of Assyre aquyted;[4]
Ac ȝef þer is among vs   3870
Ony knyȝt so vertuous[5]
Þat Alisaundre myȝte slen,
We scholde parten ows bytweon
Alle my londis, euen atwo,[6]
And ȝet he schal haue þerto   3875
Cristaline, my douȝter flour,[7]
And þoruȝ and þoruȝ[8] al my tresour.
Now let seo ȝef ony is so hardy
Þat durste hit him afyȝe!"[9]
Þey þouȝten þoruȝ,[10] noþeles,   3880
Ȝef he myȝte come on cas[11]

---

[1] indeed.   [2] goes through.   [3] deprived of Persia.   [4] relieved of Media and Assyria.
[5] valorous.   [6] right in two.   [7] white.   [8] i. e., quite.   [9] trust himself at it.   [10] unanimously.   [11] be in a situation.

3857. In the margin is a gloss: *Quomodo Darius viviter pugnauit cum Alex.* The last word has a flourish. The passage is a translation of sections LXV ff. in the French.

3859. The second *to* for *tho?*

3860. Weber's numbering contains some errors, and this number is assigned by him to the line beginning *And dude.* He corrects the numbering later. Except for minor differences such as this, his numbering is followed.

3866. The French has *ist*, comes away, for *passeth.*

3876. The French has, *ma fille au gent corps.*

Wher he myȝte yseo him abaye,[12]
Oþir bygile oþir bytreye.
Lord Crist, þat þis world eyȝte,[13]
Is lyf[14] to duyk and to knyȝte: 3885
Þer nys non so slow[15] wiþinne,
And he wiste to haue muche wynne,[16]
Þat he no wolde for gret tresour
Don himseolf in antoure![17]
Among þo of Perce was a knyȝt,   3890
Hardy and stalworþe, queynte and lyȝt;[18]
A knyȝt of Grece sone he slowe,
And his armure of he drowe,
And quyk armed him þerynne,
And þouȝte Alisaundre wynne.   3895
Alisaundre of him nouȝt ȝaf,[19]
Ac Perciens tofore him he drof:
Somme he kyt[20] of þe arme
And somme þe hed, and dude heom harm.
He bad his folk fyȝte harde   3900
Wiþ spere, mace, and sweord,
And he wolde, after fyȝt,
Rome londis to heom dyȝt.[21]
Þis forsaide knyȝt rod him by
As he weore his amy;[22]   3905
Whan he Alisaunder besy[23] seoþ,
To him anon he geþ;
He tok a launce, so y fynde,
And rod Alisaundre byhynde;
He smot him harde on þe hawberk.[24]   3910
Hit was mad of strong werk;
Þe Kyng was sumdel agast;
He huld faste: þeo spere tobarst:

---

[12] brought to bay. [13] owns. [14] gracious. [15] sluggish. [16] profit. [17] risk himself. [18] clever and spirited. [19] paid no heed. [20] cut. [21] make over. [22] comrade. [23] busy. [24] coat of mail.

3882. MS. *akaye*. The construction is loose: they preferred seeing him at bay, or beguiled, etc. (to engaging him openly). It is an addition by the English poet.

He sat faste, and lokid aȝeyn,
And saw on armed so hit weore his men.[25]   3915
"Fy!" he saide, "apon þe, lechour![26]
þow schalt dye as a traytour!"
"Certis," quod þe aliene knyȝt,
"Y am no traytour, ac an aliene knyȝt;
Y dude a gyn,[27] þe to slene;   3920
And ded þow hadest for soþe ybeon;
At auenture for þe fyȝt,[28]
Þis victorie is þe ydyȝt.
Of Perce y am, feor by west;[29]
Þis hardinesse y dude for a byheste[30]   3925
Þat Darie byheyȝte, to whom þat myȝte,
Þe to slene in þis fyȝte:
He scholde haue half his kynriche,
And his douȝter, sikirliche.
Þis was, Kyng, al my chesoun;[31]   3930
No myȝt þou fynde here no treson
Ac þat y me putte in dedly cas
For to haue þat faire byheste!"
Þe Kyng by chyn him schoke,
And his seriauns he him toke   3935
And bad him loke[32] in prisoun:
He nolde him sle bote by resoun.[33]
He was don in god warde,[34]
And bounde faste in bondis harde.
Þe Kyng brouȝte forþ Bulsifall,[35]   3940
And metiþ of Perce an admyrall;
He smot him þoruȝ body and scheld,
And cast him ded in to þe felde.

---

[25] one armed as were his men.   [26] wretch.   [27] performed a trick.   [28] by the chances of war.   [29] to the west.   [30] bold act I did because of a promise.   [31] reason.   [32] lock.   [33] according to law.   [34] safe-keeping.   [35] Bucephalus.

3922. MS. *Ac.*
3924. The French says, *Ainz sui nee de Perse, al chef vers orient* (at the end of the orient).
3934. I.e., handled him roughly. The Fr. has only *Alixandre prist le Persanz.*
3943. þe not clearly written; may be þeo.

Þer myȝte men in heorte reowe[36]
How noble knyȝtis ouerþreowe;[37]   3945
Hors totraden þeo boukes[38]
Of noble barouns and dukis.
Þicke weore þe stretis[39] of knyȝtis yslawe,
And medewe and feld, hyȝ and lowe.
Non no myȝte heom bytweone   3950
Wite who scholde maister beon;
In boþe halue,[40] wiþ sweord and spere
Was ydo gret lore:[41]
Mony faire knyȝt þat day was schent,
Hors totorn, hauberke torent;   3955
Mony fair eyȝe wiþ deþ yblent,[42]
And mony a soule to helle went.
Þeo day failiþ, þeo nyȝt is come;
Wery buþ þe gentil gome.[43]
In boþe halue, mony gent   3960
Wenten hom to heore tent
And tokyn reste til amorwe,
Makyng ful gret sorwe
For heore lordis and for heore kyn
Þat laien yslayn in þe fen.[44]   3965
Alisaundre arisen is,
And sittiþ on his hyȝ deys:
His duykes and his barouns, saun doute,
Stondiþ and sittiþ him aboute.
He hette brynge forþ þat felawe   3970
Þat him wolde haue yslawe;
He is forþ brouȝt, and þe Kyng
Ȝeueþ him acoysyng:[45]
"Þow," he saide, "traytour,
Ȝursturday þow come in aunture,   3975
Yarmed so on of myne;[46]
Me byhynde at my chyne[47]
Smotest me wiþ þy spere;
No hadde myn hawberk beo þe strengore,

---

[36] regret.   [37] fell.   [38] bodies.   [39] roads.   [40] sides.   [41] caused great loss.   [42] blinded.
[43] fine warriors.   [44] mud.   [45] accusation.   [46] armed like one of my men.
[47] back.

Þou hadest me vyly[48] yslawe. 3980
Þou schalt beo honged and todrawe,
And beo tobrent al to nouʒt,
For þou soche traytory wrouʒtest."
"Sire," quoþ þeo Perciens knyʒt,
"ʒef ʒe doþ me lawe and ryʒt, 3985
No worþ y todrawe no anhonge,
For hit weore[49] al wiþ wronge.
Darie byhette to eche of his
To make pere to him, ywis,
Who þat myʒte þe wynne, 3990
Oþir by gile oþir by gynne.
Darie was my ryʒte lord:
Y fonded to do his word—
His fɔ to quelle in eche manere;[50]
And of treson me wol y skere;[1] 3995
ʒef ony wol oþer preoue,
Aʒeyns him, lo, here my gloue!"
Antiochus saide, "Þow no myʒt þe skere!
Þow hast denied[2] þyself here
Þo þow for mede or byhotyng 4000
Stal[3] byhynde on oure Kyng,
Him to slen so þeofliche![3a]
Founde[4] þow schalt beon openliche:
Þow schalt sterue[5] on soche deþ hard!
Þis dom y ʒeue to þe-ward!"[6] 4005
Tholomeus þeo marchal vpstod,
Wyʒt in bataile and in counsail god,
And saide, "Þe Kyng may do his wille,
Saue þat Percien knyʒt or spille;
Ac he no haþ no ryʒt cheson,[7] 4010

---

[48] basely. [49] would be. [50] kill in any wise. [1] clear, acquit. [2] i.e., contradicted
(by stealing). [3] stole. [3a] like a thief. [4] confounded. [5] die. [6] upon thee.
[7] cause.

3989. MS. þere.
3997. On the glove as a challenge, cf. Hall's note on "Horn" 793;
"Avowing" 296; "Earl of Toulouse" 1100.
4003. In the French, Antiochus accepts the challenge; this line is his
defiance.

For he no dude no treson.
His dede nas bote honest,[8]
For he dude his lordes hest:[9]
Euery man to sle his fo,
Diuers gyn[10] he schal do.   4015
For his lord, nymeþ god cure,[11]
He dude his lif in aunture;
He nas nouȝt sworn to my lord,
Bote wiþ spere and wiþ sweord
Lefliche[12] is euery fo   4020
How he may oþir slo.
Ȝe mowe wel him do brenne and honge,
Ac y sigge hit where wiþ wrong!"
Vp stode Sire Mark of Rome
And entermetyd[13] of þis dome: 4025
"Certes," he saide, "he dude wowȝ
Þat he a knyȝt of Grece slowȝ
And dispoyled him of his armes
By treson, to oure harmes,
And ioyned him vs among   4030
So on of al þis was wrong,[14]
And so stal on oure Kyng,
Him to brynge to eyndyng!
Y iugge he schal anhonged beo!
Barouns of court, what sey ȝe?"   4035
Eueriche saide, "He schal beo slawe,
Forbrent,[15] hongid, and todrawe!"
Non no spak him on word fore[16]
Bote þat he scholde beo lore.
Þo Alisaunder say þis,   4040
Heriþ what he saide, ywis

---

[8] honorable. [9] command. [10] sleight. [11] note carefully. [12] every fighter may practice any sleight to slay another. [13] interposed. [14] so this (act) was wholly wrong. [15] burned up. [16] one word in his favor.

4020. *Lefliche* for *lefful?* The French has, *Car de son enemy deust prendre vengeison En tot manere sanz fere traison.*
4031. The French has, *M'est auis de donc en fist tres malement* (I think that in it all he did very evilly).

(Hit is ywrite, euery þyng
Himseolf schewiþ in castyng;[17]
So hit is of lewed[18] and clerk:
Hit schewiþ in his werk):　　　　　　　4045
He saw þat no knyȝt hende
Nul more þat knyȝt schende,
And saide, "Knyȝt, he weore wod
Þat wolde do þe ouȝt bote god;
Treson þou no dudest, no feyntise,[19]　　4050
Ac hardy dede, in queyntise.[20]
For þat dede, by myn hod,[21]
Ne schaltow haue bote god!"
Richeliche he deþ him schrede[22]
In spon-neowe[23] knytis wede,　　　　4055
And sette him on an hyȝ corsour,[24]
And ȝaf him muche of his tresour,
And lette him to Darie wende hom;
No ȝaf he him non oþir dom.[25]
　　Mury[26] hit is in þe dawenyng[27]　　4060
Whan þe foules bygynneþ to syng,
And iolyf[28] heorte bygynneþ to spryng;
In muche loue is gret mornyng;
To sone hit þenkiþ þeo slowe gadelyng;[29]
In muche nede is gret þankyng.　　　　4065

. . . .

　　Erly þe Kyng ariseþ, and makiþ bost,
And hoteþ quyk arme al his host;

[17] under trial.　[18] ignorant.　[19] nor cowardice.　[20] ingeniously.　[21] order (rank as king).　[22] clothe.　[23] newly spun.　[24] charger.　[25] sentence.　[26] merry.　[27] dawn.　[28] joyous.　[29] sluggish knave.

4042. MS. *ywrite in*. Most of the passage is not in the French.

4047. *Shend* is a translation of the French *defent*, defend. Although the Oxford Dictionary gives no example of its use in this sense before 1530, this is evidently an early occurrence of it.

4060. The different sections of the poem are not indicated in the MS. by capitals, but each has a little preface constructed like this one: an observation on the season, then some disconnected reflections or proverbs.

4068. Before this line, Weber has two others not in this manuscript. The numbering is made to conform to his, though the lines are omitted. The phrase *makith bost* probably means that he announces his intention of doing something surprising.

þey beon alle armed quykliche, 4070
And alle him sywiþ,[30] sikirliche,
Ouer a water, into a forest,
And alle doþ heore lordes hest:
Bowes of diuers treoes þey kyttiþ[31]
And to heore hors tayl kneottiþ.[32] 4075
To Darie-ward[33] alle þey fariþ;
Þeo bowes þeo dust areriþ;[34]
Of drawyng of bowes and stikke,
Þeo eyr bycam þo trouble[35] and þikke,
Þat to Daries ost[36] hit ferde 4080
So on heom com þe myddelerd.[37]
Anon þey tolden hit Darie,
And bad him he scholde warye,[38]
"For Alisaundre comeþ wiþ his pray:[39]
His folk srediþ al þe contray." 4085
Darie hyȝt al his men
Remuwe his tentis of þe fen[40]
And setten his bysyde Estrage,
A cold water and a sauage;
A castel he hadde in þat ryue:[41] 4090
Nas non strenger in al his lyue.
Anon was alle Darios ost
Ylogged by Estrages acost,[42]
Þere þey wolde fonde aspye
Al Alisaundres folye. 4095
Alisaunder þis tellen herd;
Wiþ his ost he after ferd,
And þere he loggiþ anon
Þer Darie hadde beon erst apon.[43]
Now is ywrye[44] al þe contray 4100
Bytweone heom as feole myle way.[45]
Ofte þer was bytweone heom rydyng,[46]
And mony a wyȝt batailyng.

---

[30] follow. [31] cut. [32] tie. [33] toward Darius. [34] the boughs raise the dust.
[35] murky. [36] host. [37] as if the earth were descending on them. [38] beware.
[39] company. [40] remove his tents from the flats. [41] river. [42] shore. [43] i.e.,
had camped. [44] hidden, covered. [45] for many a mile. [46] i.e., scouting, etc.

Þeo whiles[47] [of] Alisaunder þe Kyng
Listeniþ now a woundur þyng: 4105
In a more-tyde[48] hit was;
Þeo dropes hongyn on þe gras;
Þeo maydenes lokyn in þe glas,
For to tyffen[49] heore fas.
Kyng Alisaundre is out yride,   4110
And þreo noble kny3tis him myde,
Pryueliche, in a gret myst;
His grete ost hit no wist.
He doþ þeo þreo, wiþoute reuþe,[50]
Ply3te to him heore treowþe,   4115
"Þat 3e ne schal me bywry3en[1]
Of þat y wol to 3ow sayn."
Þey doþ al his wille,
And he heom gan telle
He wolde wende swiþe snel   4120
To Darye þe feolle,
To seo þe contynaunce[2]
Of Daries court, saun demorrance.[3]
No kny3t no rod wiþoute stede,
No wiþouten yren wede;   4125
To þe water þey come ry3t:
Of his stede þe Kyng aly3t,
And of dude al his armure,
And dude on a robe of peolour![4]
Apon a palfray he leope,[5]   4130
And saide, "Kny3tis, nymeþ kepe[6]
To Bulsifall, my destrere,[7]
And abideþ me ry3t here:
Y wol come whan y may."
Quyk he doþ him in his way.   4135
Þeo þreo kny3tis of whom y saide,
Þat on het Amas of Cartage,
Þat oþir hette Philotas,

---

[47] meanwhile. [48] morning. [49] adorn. [50] i.e., severely. [1] betray. [2] appearance.
[3] delay. [4] fur. [5] leapt. [6] take care. [7] charger.

4104. *Of* supplied by Weber from other MSS.

And þe þridde Perditas:
Þer nere better kny3tis þreo 4140
In al þe Kyngis maigné;
Þis þreo Alisaundre abyde,
Wel yarmed, by þe water syde.
Now sit Darye on an hulle,[8]
Folk of his ost to telle; 4145
Alisaunder to him comeþ and nou3t stet,[9]
And saide, "Kyng Alisaunder þe Gret,
He is ycome to þe parlement
For to 3ulde þe þy rent.[10]
Tweyes he haþ þe ouercome, 4150
Þy wif and þy children ynome:
Feole þow hast yslawe of his.
He sent þe sigge[11] þus ywis:
'Hit schal beo ful deore abou3t,
Þeo tole[12] þat was in Grece ysou3t! 4155
Greyþeþ armes and 3arkiþ[13] scheldis:
He 3ow abideþ in þe felde!' "
Darie was ful sore anoyed
Of þat Alisaunder haþ to him saide,
And saide, "Of tale beo [þou] smart![14] 4160
Alisaundre þyseolf þow hit art!"
Alisaundre saide, "Hit is nou3t so:
He is whitter, wiþowte no,[15]
And his lokkes buþ nou3t so crolle;[16]
Ac he is waxe more to þe fulle.[17] 4165
Ac y am hoten Antygon,
Þat mony a message haue ydon."
Darie saide, "Messanger, aly3t,
And go we eten anon ry3t,
And after mete þow schalt beore 4170

---

[8] hill. [9] did not hasten. [10] tribute. [11] he sends to say to thee. [12] tribute.
[13] make ready. [14] your speech is impudent. [15] fairer, unquestionably. [16] curly.
[17] attained a better growth.

4160. MS. *table*. Possibly for *fable*, lie? The other MSS. read *tale*.
The French has, *Et ly dit, D'un rien* (thing) *me sui aperceuz: Vous estes
Alixandre: as dis la y entenduz* (by your words it is known).

To þy lord aȝeyn onswere."
. . . .
Alisaundre, wiþoute fable,
He set at his owne table.   4175
þey weore serued wiþ gret plenté:
Wiþ fresch and salt and alle deynté,
And dronke wyn and eke pyment,[18]
Whyt and red, al to talent.[19]
þere was coppes riche ywrouȝt;   4180
Alisaunder him byþouȝt
How he myȝte do sum þyng
Of to speke wiþoute eyndyng.
þer of a coppe to him he dronk;
He hit afongiþ wiþ muche þonk.   4185
He dronk of þat wyn rede;
þe coppe he putte vndur his grede.[20]
þeo coppe was of red gold;
A botileir hit haþ al byholde,
And tolde Darie al þe soþe,   4190
And he bycom ryȝt wroþe,
And saide, "Haþ he do me þat schond?[21]
Men schal speke of Grece-londe
Of þe vengaunce þat he schal þole,[22]
Haue he my coppe ystole!"   4195
þeo botiler takiþ vp his grede
And fynt þeo coppe of gold rede.
Darie to Alisaunder gan to sigge,
"Ey, felaw! theof! þow schalt abygge!
Y set þe at table myn   4200
For reuerence of lord þyn:
My coppe þow hast ystole,
And vndur þy barm hole![23]

---

[18] spiced wine.   [19] desire.   [20] bosom; i.e., under his robe.   [21] injury.   [22] suffer.
[23] concealed in thy bosom.

4171. After this line, Weber inserted two more, so that the numbering
is disturbed.

4185. "He accepts it gratefully."   Darius drinks to Alexander from a
cup, then hands it to him to complete the ceremony; Alexander takes it
and drinks to Darius.

þow art ynome hond-habbyng;[24]
þow schalt honge wiþ þe wynd!"   4205
Quoþ Alisaundre, þe Kyng so heynde,
"Of þefþe[25] y wol me defende
Aȝeyn knyȝt, swayn, and baroun,
þat y no am no laroun:[26]
Y come to ȝow on message,   4210
And wende ȝe hadde soche an vsage
So haueþ my lord in court his—
For þy richesse and for þy pris,
þat þow hast oþer tofore;[27]
Ac þat honour þou hast lore,   4215
For ȝef kyng sente, or kayser,
To my lord a messanger,
And he beo worþy, saun fable,
He schal sitte at his table,
And whan my lord him drynkiþ to,   4220
þe coppe he schal to wille[28] vp do;
Y wende ȝe hadde also here
Of oure court þe manere!
Y am repentand, seþ ȝe no doþ:[29]
For harme no dude y hit, forsoþ."   4225
Darie, þauȝ he weore agramed,[30]
Of his[31] onswar he was aschamed;
Stille sate ȝonge and olde,
And heo gonne him byholde.
A knyȝt þer was þat hyȝte Pertage: 4230
Alisaundre he kneow in þe vysage:
. . . .
He saw Alisaundre vnder his hod.
Wel Alisaunder hit vndurstod: 4235

---

[24] i.e., red-handed.   [25] theft.   [26] thief.   [27] which you have in excess of other rulers.   [28] at his pleasure.   [29] sorry, since you do not do so.   [30] angered.   [31] Alexander's.

4218. The MS. has, *And ha* (flourish) *worþy*. Weber's emendation.
4230. MS. *Percage?* The French has, *Qui fu tenu per sage* (who was thought a wise man). The English translator takes this as a proper name.
4232. Weber here inserted two lines from the Auchinleck MS.

Hit ran in Alisaundres corage
Þat qued of him reumed³² Per[t]age,
And þat he of him to Darie spak.
Ouer þeo table he leop arape;³³
Quyk in his way he him dyȝt,³⁴   4240
Darie after wiþ al his myȝt.
A sweord Alisaunder hadde, certes,
Þat was to him faste ygurd;³⁵
Out he brayd hit in hond;
Non nolde in his way stonde.   4245
He mette a knyȝt wiþ a spere,
So God wolde, on a iustere;³⁶
He smot him swyftly in þe swyre,
Þat he laide his hed to hyre;³⁷
He schof him quycly adoun   4250
And leop himseolf in þe arsoun;³⁸
He smot þe stede, and he forþ glyt;³⁹
Alisaunder quyk away ryt:⁴⁰
Þat day no schole þey him take!
Darie gynneþ after schake:⁴¹   4255
Prynce and duyk, knyȝt and swayn
Dasscheþ after wiþ gret mayn.
Euerichon þey doþ for nouȝt:
Alisaunder haþ þeo water cauȝt.⁴²
Hit was brod, and eke Estrage   4260
Deope stremes and sauage:
He smot þe hors and in he leop.
Hit was swiþe brod and deop:
Hors and Kyng, wiþ alle hater,⁴³
Was auntred vndur þe water.   4265
Alisaunder tofore⁴⁴ no seoþ:
He was sore adred of deþ.
Noþeles his hors was god,

---

³² whispered evil of him. ³³ in haste. ³⁴ i.e., started away. · ³⁵ girded.
³⁶ charger. ³⁷ left his head as a forfeit. ³⁸ saddle. ³⁹ rushed. ⁴⁰ =rideth.
⁴¹ dash. ⁴² attained. ⁴³ trappings. ⁴⁴ ahead.

4260. This seems to mean, "and likewise was Estrage a deep stream,"
etc. The French has, *Venuz est a l' Estrage, dont le ewe* (water) *fu bruant*
(roaring).

And keouerid[45] vp abowe þe flod,
And swam to þat oþir syde, 4270
Þere his kny3tis him dude abyde.
Þay halp him vp, and his stede,
And anon chaungeþ his wede.
3ette he hadde þe coppe in hond
Þat he on Daries table fond; 4275
To his ost he fariþ, god schour,[46]
And tolde heom his auenture.
Þeo 3onge þerof hadden game:
Þeo olde wyse nome hit agrame,[47]
And saiden wel, þat cas 4280
Of gret folye don hit was.

When Alexander passes through her territory, Candace, a queen, falls
in love with him, though she has never seen him. She sends him this
letter:

"To Alisaundre þe Emperour, ·
Of alle kayseris pris kyng and flour: 6685
Þe Quene Candace, wiþ alle honour,
Sendiþ þe gretyng par amour.
O, Alisaundre, dure[48] sire,
Ouer alle men y þe desyre!
Tak me tofore alle to þy qwene! 6690
Riche schal þy mede beone:
Y wol charge,[49] saun faile,
Wiþ besauns[50] a þousand camailes;
Y wol 3eue þe 3ymmes and by3es[1]
Ten þousand caries;[2] 6695
Y wol cha[r]gen al þe bestis
Wiþ pellis and siglatouns[3] honeste;
Y wol þe 3eue gentil men—

---

[45] recovered, got. [46] at a good speed. [47] were angered. [48] dear. [49] load.
[50] gold coins. [1] gems and rings. [2] pack-horses. [3] fur garments and genuine
satins.

6684. This episode is adapted from § CCV of the French.
6695. The French has *somer*, pack-horses, for *caries*.

Ten þousand wyȝte Ethiopen,
ȝonge knyȝtis, flumbardynges,[4]   6700
Wyȝte in euery batalynges,
And an C þousand noble knyȝtis
To þy seruyse, gode and wyȝte;
And of gold a coroune bryȝt,
Ful of preciouse stones ypyȝt:[5]   6705
Gold no seoluer, so y sigge,
No myȝte þe stones to worþ bugge.[6]
ȝet þou schalt haue six hundred rinoceros,
And V C olifauns and VII C pardos,[7]
And two hundred vnycornes,   6710
And fuf M boles wiþ on hornes,[8]
And four hundred lyouns whyte,
And a þousand þat wel can byte
Olifans, and in playn,
Stronge houndis of Albayne,   6715
And fyf hundred ceptres[9] of gold,
And my lond to þy wold,[10]
And an C þousand gentil sqwyers
Þat konne þe serue in eche mesters,[11]
And þrytty þousand maidenes bryȝt,   6720
For to serue þyne knyȝtis—
Alle eorlis, duykes, and barouns,
Ful of cortely wones![12]

---

[4] fiery warriors.   [5] adorned.   [6] buy at their true worth.   [7] panthers.   [8] with one horn.   [9] scepters.   [10] power.   [11] art.   [12] ways.

6699. The French has *blauns Ethiopiens.*

6700. The French has, "beardless youths."

6709. The French also has *pardos;* the usual English form is *pardes.*

6711. The French has, *Mil blanc tors que ont les corns lusanz.* The last word may have puzzled the English translator, so that he took it to be some form of the word *sanz,* without.

6713. This line is misplaced by the English translator; it belongs after 6715, as the French shows.

6714. Other MSS. read *and lyouns in playn,* following the French.

6719. Plurals should not be taken too seriously in the work of this scribe.

6723. MS. *cortesy?* This may be an error for the familiar phrase *corteys wones.*

O, Alisaundre, riche Kyng,
Beo my lord and my derlyng!   6725
Y wol þe serue to hond and fot,
By nyȝt and day, ȝef y mot."
Of þis lettres was muche pris[13]
Wiþ Alisaundre and alle his;
Þe messangers aȝeyn heom dyȝtis,   6730
And ȝaf heom riche ȝeftis,
And wiþ wordes bonere[14]
Heom answeriþ swiþe faire.
Þer was ycome wiþ þe messangers
A queynte[15] mon, a metal ȝeoter,[16]   6735
Þat couþe caste in alle þyng.[17]
He avysed[18] þan þe Kyng,
And þo he com hom, sykirliche,
He caste a forme þe Kyng yliche:
In face, in eyȝnen, in nose, in mouþ,   6740
In leynthe,[19] in membres, þat is selcouþ;[20]
Þe Qwene sette him in hire boure,
And kepiþ hit in gret honour.

---

[13] was highly regarded. [14] courteous. [15] skillful. [16] caster. [17] i.e., any sort
of thing. [18] looked closely at. [19] length. [20] marvelous.

THE DESTRUCTION OF TROY

THE DESTRUCTION OF TROY

This piece, the full title of which is "The Gest Historiale of the Destruction of Troy," is in a manuscript in the Hunterian Museum at Glasgow. Mr. W. R. Cunningham, Librarian of Glasgow University, and Keeper of the Hunterian Books and Manuscripts, has very kindly compared the proof of the text with the manuscript.

The Troy-legend was known to the Middle Ages, not through the work of Homer, but through Latin versions of the Christian era. (For a brief account, see C. H. A. Wager's "Seege of Troy," Introduction.) These were distinguished by sympathy for the cause of the Trojans, from whom many western races thought themselves descended; and this preference is apparent in every medieval version. Achilles is reduced from a hero to a cowardly murderer; Helen's conduct is made the occasion for a disapproving sermon; the gods are carefully suppressed; war is conducted in terms of medieval chivalry, with castles, cavalry, captives, cross-bows, mining, etc.

The immediate source, which the Middle English poem follows closely, is the "Historia Destructionis Troiæ" of Guido della Colonne. The dialect is northern of before 1400. Few pieces in Middle English can approach the poem in sustained excellence; there is scarcely a dull passage in its 14,000 lines. The three selections below show the peculiar merits and point of view of the piece.

On the verse, see Introduction VI.B.2.

The vocabulary contains several words common in alliterative poetry and rare elsewhere. The most useful of these are the following: *wegh, shalk, lede, buern, gome*—man; *wees*—men; *bent*—field; *stithe, dern*—fierce; *euyn*—right, quite; *gird*—strike, rush; *braid*—rushed; *hor*—their; and *greme*—rage. The participles often end in *-it*.

Prologue

Maistur in Magesté, Maker of alle,
Endles and on,[1] euer to last !

---

[1] one.

1. The prologue is a paraphrase of Guido's own.

809

Now, God, of þi grace graunt me þi helpe,
And wysshe me with wyt þis werke for to end
Off aunters ben[2] olde, of aunsetris nobill   5
And slydyn vppon shlepe by slomeryng of age;[3]
Of stithe men in stoure, strongest in armes,
And wisest in wer to wale[4] in hor tyme,
þat ben drepit[5] with deth and þere day paste,
And most out of mynd for þere mecull age.   10
Sothe stories ben stoken vp and straught[6] out of mynd
And swolowet into swym[7] by swiftenes of yeres
For new, þat ben now, next at our hond,
Breuyt[8] into bokes for boldyng of hertes,—
On lusti to loke, with lightnes of wille,[9]   15
Cheuyt[10] throughe chaunce and chaungyng of[11] peopull;
Sum tru for to traist, triet[12] in þe end,
Sum feynit o fere,[13] and ay false vnder.
Yche wegh as he will warys[14] his tyme
And has lykyng to lerne þat hym list after;   20
But olde stories of stithe þat astate helde[15]
May be solas to sum þat it segh neuer:[16]
Be writyng of wees þat wist it in dede—
With sight for to serche of hom þat suet after[17]—
To ken all the crafte how þe case felle,   25
By lokyng of letturs þat lefte were of olde.
    Now of Troy for to telle is myn entent euyn:[18]
Of the stoure and þe stryff when it distroyet was;
þof fele yeres bene faren syn þe fight endid
And it meuyt[19] out of mynd, myn[20] hit i thinke   30

---

[2] events that are.   [3] lapsed into sleep in the slumbering (oblivion) of age.
[4] choose, who could be chosen.   [5] struck down.   [6] locked away and gone out.
[7] swallowed up in confusion.   [8] written.   [9] i.e., agreeable as light reading.
[10] gained, come by.   [11] exchanging among.   [12] trust, tried.   [13] altogether fictitious.   [14] spends.   [15] fierce (men) who were prominent.   [16] i.e., do not know the
story.   [17] followed; i.e., to read the work of their successors.   [18] plain.   [19] moved,
removed.   [20] to recall.

5. Historians thought the English descendants of the Trojans.

13. This prologue is like that of the "Cursor Mundi" in its recognition
of the power and attractiveness of the new fiction and its distrust of the
influence of that fiction.

23. Dares and Dictys professed to have been eye-witnesses of the
struggle.

Alss wise men haue writen the wordes before—
Left it in Latyn for lernyng of vs.
But sum poyetis full prist[21] þat put hom þerto
With fablis and falshed fayned þere speche,
And made more of þat mater þan hom maister[22] were; 35
Sum lokyt ouer-little, and lympit[23] of the sothe.
Amonges þat menye, to myn hym be nome,
Homer was holden haithill[24] of dedis
Qwiles his dayes enduret, derrist of other,[25]
þat with the Grekys was gret and of Grice comyn. 40
He feynet myche fals was neuer before wroght,
And turnet[26] þe truth, trust ye non other.[27]
Of his trifuls[28] to telle i haue no tome[29] nowe,
Ne of his feynit fare þat he fore with:
How goddes foght in the filde, folke as þai were, 45
And other errours vnable,[30] þat after were knowen,
That poyetis of prise have preuyt vntrew—
Ouyd, and othir þat onest were ay—
Virgill þe virtuus, verrit for nobill—:
Thes dampnet his dedys, and for dull[31] holdyn. 50
But þe truth for to tell, and þe text euyn,
Of þat fight, how it felle in a few yeres,
þat was clanly compilet with a clerk wise—
On[32] Gydo, a gome þat graidly[33] hade soght
And wist all þe werkes by weghes[34] he hade, 55
That bothe were in batell while the batell last,
And euþer sawte and assembly[35] see with þere een.
Thai wrote all þe werkes wroght at þat tyme,

---

[21] i.e., officious. [22] i.e., authority. [23] i.e., were inattentive, and failed.
[24] worthy. [25] finest of all. [26] distorted. [27] i. e., else. [28] inaccuracies. [29] leisure. [30] unfortunate. [31] condemned his deeds and thought them unfortunate. [32] one. [33] thoroughly. [34] i.e., authorities. [35] every assault and meeting.

44. "The fictitious material with which he dealt;" medieval poets were willing to concede that the gods of Greece had existed, but thought they were merely men and women elevated by poets and priests to the dignity of gods after their deaths. Cf. article on Euhemerism, *Speculum* II.396.

49. Maybe *verrit* for *verdit*, attested; but the Oxford Dictionary gives no example of the verb so early.

In letturs of þere langage, as þai lerned hade:
Dares and Dytes were duly þere namys.   60
Dites full dere was dew[36] to the Grekys—
A lede of þat lond, and loged[37] hom with;
The tothyr was a tulke[38] out of Troy selfe—
Dares, þat duly the dedys behelde.
Aither breuyt[39] in a boke, on þere best wise,   65
That sithen at a sité somyn were founden—
After at Atthenes, as aunter befell;—
The whiche bokes barely,[40] bothe as þai were,
A Romayn ouerraght,[41] and right[42] hom hymseluyn,
That Cornelius was cald to his kynde name.   70
He translated it into Latyn, for likyng to here;
But he shope it so short þat no shalke might
Haue knowlage by course[43] how þe case felle;
For he brought it so breff, and so bare leuyt,[44]
þat no lede might have likyng to loke þerappon,   75
Till þis Gydo it gate, as hym grace felle,
And declaret it more clere, and on clene wise.
In this shall faithfully be founden, to the fer ende,
All þe dedes bydene, as þai done were:
How þe groundes[45] first grew and þe grete hate;   80
Bothe of torfer[46] and tene þat hom tide aftur.
And here fynde shall ye faire of þe felle peopull:
What kynges þere come of costes[47] aboute;
Of dukes full doughty and of derffe[47a] crlcs
That assemblid to þe citie þat sawte to defend;[48]   85
Of þe Grekys þat were gedret, how gret was þe nowmber—
How mony knightes þere come, and kynges enarmed;[49]
And what dukes thedur droghe for dedis of were;
What shippes þere were shene and shalkes within,
Bothe of barges and buernes[50] þat broght were fro Grese;   90

---

[36] belonged.   [37] lodged, stayed.   [38] warrior.   [39] wrote.   [40] entirely.   [41] recovered.
[42] corrected.   [43] duly.   [44] left it so bare.   [45] causes.   [46] injury.   [47] regions.
[47a] fierce.   [48] repulse.   [49] under arms.   [50] warriors.

59. The book of Dictys was said to have been written in Phoenician
characters; but it survives only in a Latin abridgment of the fourth century A.D. Dares' book is also preserved only in a Latin summary, declared to be by Cornelius Nepos, but actually by a later writer.

And all the batels on bent, þe buernes betwene—
What duke þat was dede throughe dyntes of hond;
Who falin was in ffylde, and how it fore after;
Bothe of truse and of trayne[1] þe truthe shall þou here,   95
And all the ferlies þat fell, vnto the ferre ende.[2]
Fro this prologe i passe, and part me þerwith:
Frayne will i fer, and fraist[3] of þere werkes:
Meue[4] to my mater, and make here an ende.

Explicit Prologus

The Taking of Tenedos

The island of Tenedos was one of the outposts of Troy, and was taken by the Greeks before they attacked the city.

Þai past fro þat port with pillage þai hade
And turnyt vnto Tenydon, taryt no lengur.   4700
Þere arof[5] all the rowte with þere ranke[6] shippes;
Cast ancres with cables þat kene were of byt;[7]
Lete sailes doune slide; slippit into botis;
Festnet with fuerse[8] ropis the flete in þe hauyn,
And buskit vnto banke, the boldist ay first.   4705
At this Tenydoun truly was a tried[9] castell,
Wele wroght for the werre, with walles full stronge,
Evyn[10] fild full of folke, fuerse men and noble,
And riches full rife; rank[11] men within;
Wele viteld,[12] iwisse, for winturs ynoghe.   4710
Hit was sothely but sex myle fro the cité euyn,
As i told haue tomly[13] in a tale here before.
The folke in þat fuerse hold[14] were ferde of hom selfe;[15]
Arait hom full radly, right to the werre;

---

[1] truce and treachery.   [2] to the very last.   [3] make trial.   [4] proceed.   [5] arrived.
[6] proud.   [7] holding power, grip.   [8] strong.   [9] strong.   [10] quite.   [11] powerful.
[12] provisioned.   [13] at length.   [14] castle.   [15] feared for their lives.

4699. For information about the tactics, cf. Charles Oman, "A History of the Art of War in the Middle Ages," especially VI.vii.3.

4704. The ships were tied together, instead of being separately berthed, for security against storms and attacks.

In defense[16] of hor fos, þat on flete[17] lay,   4715
Wenton out wightly wale[18] men of armys,
And bateld hom on the banke, as hom best thught.
When the Grekes were gethurt and to ground comen,
Mony fightyng folke in a fuerse nowmbur,
The pepull with hor power put[19] hom agayne,   4720
And foght with hom felly, þof þai few were.
Bold was þat biker[20] opon bothe haluys:[21]
Mony deid bydene of the derfe[22] Grekes,
And Troiens with tene tynt[23] of hor pepull,
But not so fele at þe first as of the ferre side.[24]   4725
The Grekes full greatly greuyt þerat,
Oppresset hom with payne and preset þere faster,
Fought full felly, and fele were þere slayne.
Of the Troiens þat tyme tynt were þe mo;
The fresshe[25] was so felle of the furse Grekes,   4730
And the nowmber so noyous[26] þat neghed in hast,
That the Frigies[27] floghen, and the fild leuyt:
Turnyt vnto Troy, and the toune entrid.
And þo at fore[28] not to flight ne of forse[29] were,
The Grekes gird[30] hom to gro[u]nd with hor grym swerdes,   4735
And brittenit[31] on the bent þat abide wold;
Comyn to the castell, vnclosit[32] it aboute,
Foghten with the folke þat defens made;
Shottyn[33] vp sharply at the shene wallis
With glayues and gonnes;[34] girdyn doun toures;   4740
Dryuen vp dartes, gyffen depe woundes.
With alblasters also, amyt[35] full streght,
Whappet in wharels, whellit[36] of the pepull;
With speris full dispitiously spurnit[37] at the yates;
Dongen on dernly,[38] with mony dede-hurttes   4745
In diffens[39] of þe folke þat affroi[40] made.

---

[16] to repel.   [17] afloat.   [18] picked.   [19] with all their might thrust them back.
[20] struggle.   [21] sides.   [22] fierce.   [23] lost.   [24] i.e., their opponents.   [25] ferocity.
[26] grievous.   [27] Phrygians, Trojans.   [28] those who took.   [29] strong.   [30] struck.
[31] butchered.   [32] encircled.   [33] cast.   [34] spears and missiles.   [35] cross-bows
aimed.   [36] shot in bolts, killed.   [37] violently beat.   [38] struck angrily.   [39] attacking.   [40] resistance.

4728. MS. *were þere þai slayne.*
4740. MS. *gomes.*

But the wallis thé were, for all the wo yet,[41]
And fele of hor fos fellyn without.
Þen gone furthe the Grekes, graithet engynes,
Batold[42] hom all abrode vmbe[43] the bare walles,   4750
Layn ladders alenght,[44] and oloft wonnen.
At yche cornell[45] of þe castell was crusshyng of weppon;
Fell was the feght þo fuerse men amonge:
Mony Greke in þere gremþ gird[46] on the hed,
Till þai lept of the ladder, light in the dyke,   4755
The brayne out-brast, and the brethe leuyt;
And mony dongen[47] to dethe with dynttes of hond.
The Troiens full tit were terghit[48] for fight:
Wondit and weré, þat þai were noght;[49]
And the Grekes in so grete nowmber gedrit hom till,   4760
Wonyn on the wallis wightly with ladders,
At wyndous on yche wiss[50] a wondurfull nombur.
The grete toures þai toke, tiruyt[1] the pepull:
Was no lede opon lyfe þat alofte stode.
Thé chefe[2] into chambers and oþer chere[3] hallis,   4765
And yche freke þat þai found, felly þai slogh,
Old men and other, with ournyng[4] to dethe,
Tyll no lede of þat lynage[5] vpon lyfe was.
All the caves[6] in the castell clenly þai sought,
Robbit the riches and the rife goodes,   4770
Prayet and piket þat[7] proffet was in,
And wonnyn[8] it wightly þe wallis withoute,
Till all was bare as a bast, to þe bigge woghes![9]
Mynours than mightely the moldes[10] did serche;

---

[41] protect, despite all their misfortune. [42] drew up. [43] about. [44] end to end. [45] battlement. [46] fury (were) struck. [47] beaten. [48] exhausted. [49] so that they had no strength. [50] staircase. [1] threw over. [2] make their way. [3] fine. [4] running down (like beasts of the chase). [5] race. [6] vaults. [7] plundered and looted whatever. [8] took. [9] wand, to the strong walls. [10] earthworks.

4755. Castles were usually set on mounds, formed by heaping up earth; the resulting excavation around the mound was called the ditch, or moat, and was a part of the defenses.

4766. The Greeks are always represented as butchers by Guido. They succeed only because of overwhelming numbers (cf. 4758), not superior valor.

Ouertyrnet the toures and the tor[11] walles;   4775
All dusshet[12] into the diche, doll to beholde;
Betyn doun the buyldynges and brent[13] into erthe
Tyll the place was playne[14] and out of plite broght[15]
And hegh Tenydon with tourys tyrnyt all vnder.
When þai hade wasted the won and wonen the gre,   4780
All the tresour thay toke and turnyt to ship.
This fight is the first, and firre vs behouus.[16]

The Death of Hector

Though his wife has dreamed that he will die and his father has therefore kept him from the battle, Hector cannot restrain himself when one
of his brothers is killed by the Greeks.

Ector, wode of his wit for woo of his brother,
Haspit[17] on his helme and his horse toke,
Went out wightly, vnwetyng[18] his fader.
Two dukes full derne he to dethe broght,   8595
And manly with mayn mellit[19] with other;
Kyld[20] downe knightes, karve hom in sondur.
Mony wondet the weghe and to woo caste,[21]
Britnet hom on bent, and on bake[22] put.
The Grekes for his greffe girdyn[23] hym fro: 8600
Thay knew hym full kyndly be caupe[24] of his sword.
Then the Troiens full tyte to the towne floghen,
Issuet out egurly Ector to helpe,
Gird evyn to the Grekes, and hor ground toke;[25]
Foghten full felly, and hor fos harmyt.   8605
Polidamas the pert[26] was presset so fast
Þat he was wonen in wer, and away led.
Than Ector in yre egerly faght,
And the Grekes in his grem gird[27] he to dethe—

---

[11] strong.   [12] dashed.   [13] burnt to the ground.   [14] levelled.   [15] i.e., rendered
harmless.   [16] it behooves us to proceed further.   [17] fastened.   [18] without the
knowledge of.   [19] and manfully with might contended.   [20] struck.   [21] made sorrowful.   [22] i.e., overthrew.   [23] because of the harm he did, fled.   [24] blow.
[25] took up a position.   [26] brave.   [27] rage struck.

4775. Undermining walls was the easiest way of destroying them. The
miners removed the earth at key-points, and the walls fell of themselves.
8606. Polydamas was the son of the Trojan prince Antenor.

Two hundreth in hast, þat the hend led[28]— 8610
And deliuert the lede with his lyfe hole!
This a grete[29] of the Grekes graidly[30] beheld,
Had meruell full mekyll, macchet hym to Ector:
Liochydes the large, so þe lord hight;
He wend the prinse in the prese haue put out of lyue. 8615
Ector wrathit hym with,[31] and the wegh hit
þat he deghit of the dynt er he doun fell.
Achilles this chaunse choisly[32] beheld,
þat so mony of þaire men were marrid by hym;[33]
He hopit but if happely þat hardy were slayne, 8620
þat neuer Greke shuld haue grace the ground for to wyn,
Ne neuer Troye for to take, terme of hor lyue.[34]
He bethoght hym full thicke,[35] in his thro[36] hert,
And all soteltie soght, serchit his wit
On all wise in this world þat werke for to end, 8625
And the prinse with his power put vnto dethe.
As he stode þus in stid, starit hym vpon,
Policenes—a pert duke þat in prese rode,
þat was chere[37] to Achilles, cherisit with loue,
And thidur soght for his sake his sistur to haue; 8630
A mon he was of More Ynde, mighty of godes,—
þere hit auntrid full euyn þat Ector hym met,
And the lede with a launse out of lyue broght.
Achilles the chaunse cheuit[38] for to se,
Vne[39] wode of his wit, walt[40] into angur: 8635
The dethe of þat duke he dight hym to veng.
To Ector full egurly he etlit[41] anon;
Ector keppit[42] the kyng er he caupe[43] might,

---

[28] who led Polydamas (as captive). [29] great (hero). [30] completely; i.e., saw it all. [31] raged against him. [32] especially. [33] Hector. [34] during their lives. [35] hard. [36] fierce. [37] dear. [38] managed; happened. [39] even, quite. [40] burst. [41] rushed. [42] struck. [43] give a blow.

8610. For such feats in battle see "Havelok" 1919.

8628. The sentence is never completed; the following four lines are in apposition with *hym* (8632).

8631. Greater India was the eastern part, around the Bay of Bengal; Lesser India was along the western coast.

8638-9. Most of the principal warriors are described as kings by Guido, and hence have some right to the title; but the poet also calls them princes, dukes, lords, barons, or men, if these words suit the alliteration.

Drof at hym with a dart, and þe duke hit.
Hit was keruond[44] and kene, and the kyng hurt,   8640
And woundit hym wickedly thurght the waist euyn,
Þat he sesit of his sute;[45] soght he no ferre!

The Dethe of Ector, By Achilles Traturly Slayn

Achilles for the chop cherit[46] hym not litle:
Braid out of batell, bound vp his wounde,
Stoppet the stremys stithly[47] agayne,   8645
Lep vp full lyuely, launchit on swithe,
To þat entent truly, as the trety[48] sais,
To deire Ector with dethe or degh þere hymseluyn.
As Ector faght in the fild fell[49] of þe Grekes,
He caupit[50] with a kyng, caght hym anon,   8650
Puld[1] hym as a prisoner of prise for to wyn
With strenght thurgh the stoure, as the story tellus.
His sheld on his shulders shot[2] was behynd
And his brest left bare: so the buerne rode
To weld hym more winly[3] þat worthy to lede.   8655
Achilles grippit a gret speire with a grym wille;
Vnpersayuit of the prince, prikit hym to;
Woundit hym wickedly as he away loked,
Thurgh the body with the bit of the bright end,[4]
That he gird to þe ground and the gost yald.   8660
This Sedymon segh, þat soght out of Troy;
Evyn wode for þat worthy was of lyue done,
He cheuet[5] to Achilles with a chop felle,
Þat he braid to þe bent with a brem[6] wound,
And for ded of þat dynt the duke þere hym leuit.   8665

---

[44] penetrating. [45] ceased in his pursuit. [46] blow altered his course. [47] strongly.
[48] book, history. [49] encountered . . . many. [50] engaged. [1] drew, led away.
[2] slung. [3] manage more readily. [4] cutting edge of the bright point. [5] reached.
[6] terrible.

8643. Heading—The text is full of such headings, which also appeared
in the Latin MSS. (See George Neilson's "Huchowne of the Awle Riale"
25 and *Speculum* II.114.n.9.)

8651. Prisoners were desired because large ransoms could be exacted
for their return.

The Myrmaidons,[7] his men, þaire maistur can take,
Bere hym on his brade sheld to his big tent,
There left hym as lyueles, laid hym besyde;[8]
But yet deghit not the duke, þof hym dere tholet.[9]
Then the Troiens with tene turnyt them backe,   8670
Soghten to þe citie with sorow in hert,
Entrid al samyn, angardly[10] fast,
And the body of the bold prinse broghtyn hom with.

---

[7] Myrmidons.   [8] to one side.   [9] suffered great injury.   [10] very.

8673. The scene in which Priam begs his son's body of Achilles is not in Guido's version.

MISCELLANEOUS

FLORIS AND BLANCHEFLOUR

The romance has the two peculiarities of having been current in English at an early date (c. 1250) and of dealing well with sentiment, a merit not common in early romances. On the history of the legend, see Hibbard 184 ff. For a complete introduction, see A. B. Taylor's edition (Oxford, 1927).

The text given here is that of the Trentham Manuscript (now Egerton 2862), which is reproduced from rotographs taken and used with the kind permission of the officials of the Department of Manuscripts of the British Museum. Though not the earliest or best text, this is nearly complete, and is hence most suitable for literary study.

The dialect is that of the east midlands; but late and northern forms have been freely substituted. The scribe seems not to have been familiar with the use of final -e in the earlier dialects, and ends many words with a flourish that might be expanded into -e; but in transcribing, this has usually been disregarded after final -n or -m, and expanded after -d. In other occurrences, it has been invariably disregarded.

The numbering is as in McKnight's edition for the Early English Text Society, and the work of Hausknecht and Taylor has also been consulted; but only the more ingenious emendations and conjectures have been carefully credited. References to the French are to Du Meril's edition, usually to his first text.

The beginning of the story is lost in all the English manuscripts; from the French, it may be summarized as follows: A Christian woman of high rank, taken by a heathen king during a raid, bears a daughter at the same time that the queen, her mistress, gives birth to a son. In honor of the feast of Pasque-florie (Palm Sunday), they are named Florie and Blanceflor. They are brought up together, the Christian mother being nurse to both.

Heading. The MS. has *Fflorence and Blanchefloure.*

Ne thurst[1] men neuer in londe
After feirer children fonde.
Þe Cristen woman fedde hem þoo;
Ful wel she louyd hem boþ twoo.
So longe she fedde hem in feere   5
þat þey were of elde of seuen ȝere.
Þe Kyng behelde his sone dere,
And seyde to him on this manere:
Þat harme it were muche more
But his son were sette to lore   10
On þe book letters to know,
As men don, both hye and lowe.
"Feire sone," she seide, "þou shalt lerne;
Lo, þat þou do ful ȝerne!"
Florys answerd with wepyng,   15
As he stood byfore þe Kyng;
Al wepyng seide he,
"Ne schal not Blancheflour lerne with me?
Ne can y noȝt to scole goon
Without Blaunchefloure," he seide þan,   20
"Ne can y in no scole syng ne rede
Without Blauncheflour," he seide.
Þe King seide to his soon,
"She shal lerne, for þy loue."
To scole þey were put;   25
Boþ þey were good of wytte.
Wonder it was of hur lore,
And of her loue wel þe more.[2]
Þe children louyd togeder soo
Þey myȝt neuer parte a twoo.   30
When þey had v ȝere to scoole goon,
So wel þey had lerned þoo,
Inowȝ þey couþ of Latyne,
And wel wryte on parchemyne.[3]
Þe Kyng vnderstod þe grete amoure[4]   35
Bytwene his son and Blanchefloure,

---

[1] need.   [2] i.e., the greater wonder.   [3] parchment.   [4] love.

3. In the French, the Christian mother acts as nurse for both children.

And þouȝt when þey were of age
Þat her loue wolde noȝt swage,[5]
Nor he myȝt noȝt her loue withdrawe
When Florys shuld wyfe[6] after þe lawe.   40
Þe King to þe Queene seide þoo
And tolde hur of his woo—
Of his þouȝt and of his care
How it wolde of Floreys fare.
"Dame," he seide, "y tel þe my reed: 45
I wyl þat Blaunchefloure be do to deed.
When þat maide is yslawe
And brouȝt of her lyf-dawe,[7]
As sone as Florys may it vnderȝete,[8]
Rathe he wylle hur forȝete.   50
Þan may he wyfe after reed."[9]
Þe Queene answerde þen and seid,
And þouȝt with hur reed
Saue þe mayde fro þe deed.
"Sir," she seide, "we auȝt to fonde   55
Þat Florens lyf with menske[10] in londe,
And þat he lese not his honour
For þe mayden Blauncheflour.
Who so myȝt [reue] þat mayde clene,
Þat she were brouȝt to deþ bydene,   60
Hit were muche more honour
Þan slee þat mayde Blancheflour."
Vnneþes þe King g[ra]unt þat it be soo:
"Dame, rede vs what is to doo."
"Sir, we shul oure soon Florys   65
Sende into þe londe of Mountargis;
Blythe wyl my suster be,
Þat is lady of þat contree;
And when she woot for whoom
Þat we haue sent him vs froom,   70
She wyl doo al hur myȝt,

---

[5] abate. [6] marry. [7] days of life, life. [8] realize. [9] i.e., advisedly. [10] honor.

59. Hausknecht's emendation: in l. 289, *reve* is used to translate *tolir*, which also occurs here in the corresponding French passage.

Boþ by day and by nyʒt,
To make hur loue so vndoo
As it had neuer ben soo.
And, sir," she seide, "y rede eke   75
Þat þe maydens moder make hur seeke.[11]
Þat may be þat other resoun
For þat ylke encheson,[12]
Þat she may not fro hur moder goo."
Now ben þese children swyþ woo,   80
Now þey may not goo in fere;
Drewryer[13] þinges neuer noon were.
Florys wept byfore þe Kyng
And seide, "Sir, without lesyng,
For my harme out ʒe me sende,   85
Now she ne myʒt with me wende;
Now we ne mot togeder goo,
Al my wele is turned to woo!"
Þe King seide to his soon aplyʒt,[14]
"Sone, withynne þis fourtenyʒt,   90
Be her moder quykke or deede,
Sekerly," he him seide,
"Þat mayde shal com þe too."
"ʒe, sir," he seid, "y pray ʒow it be soo.
ʒif þat ʒe me hur sende,   95
I rekke neuer wheder y wende."
Þat þe child graunted, þe Kyng was fayn,
And him betauʒt his chamburlayn.
With muche honoure þey þeder coom,
As fel to[15] a ryche kynges soon.   100
Wel feire him receyuyd þe Duke Orgas,
Þat king of þat castel was,
And his aunt wiþ muche honour;
But euer he þouʒt on Blanchefloure.
Glad and blythe þey ben him withe;   105
But for no ioy þat he seith
Ne myʒt him glade game ne gle,
For he myʒt not his lyf[16] see.

---

[11] feign sickness.   [12] cause.   [13] sadder.   [14] straightway.   [15] befitted.   [16] dear one.

His aunt set him to lore
Þere as other children wore, 110
Boþ maydons and grom;
To lerne mony þeder coom.
Inowȝ he sykes, but noȝt he lernes;
For Blauncheflour euer he mornes.
Yf eny man to him speke, 115
Loue is on his hert steke.[17]
Loue is at his hert roote,
Þat no þing is so soote:[18]
Galyngale[19] ne lycorys
Is not so soote as hur loue is, 120
Ne no thing ne non other.[20]
So much he þenkeþ on Blancheflour,
Of oo day him þynkeþ þre,
For he ne may his loue see;
Þus he abydeth with muche woo, 125
Tyl þe fourtenyȝt were goo.
When he saw she was nouȝt ycoome,
So muche sorow he haþ noome
Þat he loueth mete ne drynke,
Ne may noon in his body synke.[21] 130
Þe chamberleyn sent þe King to wete[22]
His sones state, al ywrete.
Þe King ful sone þe waxe to-brake
For to wete what it spake;
He begynneth to chaunge his moode, 135
And wel sone he vnderstode,
And with wreth he cleped þe Queene,
And tolde hur alle his teene,
And with wraþ spake and sayde,
"Let do bryng forþ þat mayde! 140
Fro þe body þe hcued shal goo."
Þenne was þe Quene ful woo;
Þan spake þe Quene, þat good lady,

---

[17] fastened. [18] sweet. [19] a spice. [20] no other person. [21] consume. [22] advise of.

111. "Grom" is the masculine equivalent of "maiden"; i.e., an unmarried youth.

"For Goddes love, sir, mercy!
At þe next hauen þat here is,   145
Þer ben chapmen[23] ryche, ywys,
Marchaundes of Babyloyn ful ryche,
Þat wol hur bye blethelyche.
Than may ȝe for þat louely foode[24]
Haue muche catell[25] and goode;   150
And soo she may fro vs be brouȝt
Soo þat we slee hur nouȝt."
Vnneþes[26] þe King grauntet þis,
But forsoth, so it is.
Þe King let sende after þe burgeise,   155
Þat was hende and curtayse,
And welle selle and bygge couth,
And moony langages had in his mouth.
Wel sone þat mayde was him betauȝt,
An to þe hauen was she brouȝt;   160
Ther haue þey for þat maide ȝolde[27]
xx mark of reed golde,
And a coupe good and ryche;
In al þe world was non it lyche.
Þer was neuer noon so wel graue;[28]   165
He þat it made was no knaue.
Þer was purtrayd on, y weene,
How Paryse ledde awey þe Queene;
And on þe couercle[29] aboue
Purtrayde was þer bother[30] love;   170
And in þe pomel[31] þeron
Stood a charbuncle stoon:
In þe worlde was not so depe soler[32]
Þat it nolde lyȝt þe botelere
To fylle boþ ale and wyne;   175
Of syluer and golde boþ good and fyne.
Enneas þe King, þat nobel man,

---

[23] merchants.   [24] maid.   [25] chattels.   [26] not readily.   [27] given.   [28] engraved, decorated.   [29] lid.   [30] of them both.   [31] knob on the lid.   [32] cellar.

147. Babyloyn is Old Cairo in Egypt.—Taylor.
170. MS. *þer both her.*
176. A condensation of several lines of description in the French.

At Troye in batayle he it wan,
And brouȝt it into Lumbardy,
And gaf it his lemman, his amy.   180
Þe coupe was stoole fro King Cesar;
A þeef out of his tresour-hous it bar;
And sethe þat ilke same þeef
For Blaunchefloure he it ȝeef;
For he wyst to wynne suche þree,[33]   185
Myȝt he hur bryng to his contree.
Now þese marchaundes saylen ouer þe see
With þis mayde, to her contree.
So longe þey han vndernome[34]
Þat to Babyloyn þey ben coom.   190
To þe Amyral of Babyloyne
Þey solde þat mayde swythe soone;
Rath and soone þey were at oon:
Þe Amyral hur bouȝt anoon,
And gafe for hur, as she stood vpryȝt,   195
Seuyn sythes of golde her wyȝt,[35]
For he þouȝt without weene
Þat faire mayde haue to Queene;
Among his maydons in his bour
He hur dide, with muche honour.   200
Now þese merchaundes þat may belete,[36]
And ben glad of hur byȝete.[37]
    Now let we of Blancheflour be,
And speke of Florys in his contree.
Now is þe bu[r]gays to þe King coom   205
With þe golde and his garyson,[38]
And haþ take þe King to wolde[38a]
Þe seluer and þe coupe of golde.
They lete make in a chirche
A swithe feire graue wyrche,[39]   210
And lete ley þervppon

---

[33] three as good.   [34] persisted.   [35] weight.   [36] abandoned the maid.   [37] their
profit from her.   [38] payment.   [38a] in keeping.   [39] made a fine tomb.

180. *Amy*, beloved. She was Lavinia, daughter of Latinus.—Taylor.
210. MS. *as swithe*.

A new feire peynted ston,
With letters al aboute wryte
With ful muche worshippe.
Whoso couth þe letters rede,   215
Þus þey spoken and þus þey seide:
"Here lyth swete Blaunchefloure,
Þat Florys louyd par amoure."
Now Florys haþ vndernome,[40]
And to his ffader he is coome: 220
In his ffader halle he is lyʒt.
His ffader him grette anoon ryʒt,
And his moder, þe Queene also,
But vnneþes myʒt he þat doo[41]
Þat he ne asked where his lemman bee;   225
Nonskyns[42] answere chargeþ[43] hee.
So longe he is forth noome,[44]
In to chamber he is coome.
Þe maydenys moder he asked ryʒt,
"Where is Blauncheflour, my swete wyʒt?"   230
"Sir," she seide, "forsothe ywys,
I ne woot where she is."
She beþouʒt hur on þat lesyng
Þat was ordeyned byfoore þe King.
"Þou gabbest[45] me," he seyde þoo;   235
"Þy gabbyng doþ me muche woo!
Tel me where my leman be!"
Al wepyng seide þenne shee,
"Sir," shee seide, "deede." "Deed!" seide he.
"Sir," sche seide, "for sothe, ʒee."   240
"Allas, when died þat swete wyʒt?"
"Sir, withynne þis ffourtenyʒt
Þe erth was leide hur aboute,

---

[40] journeyed.   [41] scarcely might he perform that act without, etc.   [42] no sort of answer.   [43] awaits.   [44] made his way.   [45] mock.

226. *Chargeþ* is a result of confusion for the French: *Il* (his parents) *se tardent de respons rendre.* The Cotton MS. has *targeþ*, and the rest of the context is more like the French. The idiom "charge to answer," demand an answer, may have been intended.

243. The rhyme requires *hur above*.

And deed she was for thy loue."
Flores, þat was so feire and gent, 245
Sownyd þere, verament.
Þe Cristen woman began to crye
To Ihesu Crist and Seynt Marye.
Þe King and þe Queene herde þat crye;
Into þe chamber þey ronne on hye, 250
And þe Queene seʒe her byforne[46]
On sowne þe childe þat she had borne.
Þe Kinges hert was al in care,
Þat sawe his son for loue so fare.
When he awooke and speke moʒt, 255
Sore he wept and sore he syʒt,
And seide to his moder ywys,
"Lede me þere þat mayde is."
Þeder þey him brouʒt on hyʒe;
For care and sorow he wolde dyʒe. 260
As sone as he to þe graue com,
Sone þere behelde he þen
And þe letters began to rede,
Þat þus spake and þus seide:
"Here lyth swete Blauncheflour, 265
Þat Florys louyd par amoure."
Þre sithes Florys sownydde nouth,[47]
Ne speke he myʒt not with mouth.
As sone as he awoke and speke myʒt,
Sore he wept and sore he syʒt. 270
"Blauncheflour!" he seide, "Blauncheflour!
So swete a þing was neuer in boure!
Of Blauncheflour is þat y meene,[48]
For she was com of good kyn.
Lytel and muche loueden þe 275
For þy goodnesse and þy beauté.
Ʒif deþ were dalt aryʒt,
We shuld be deed boþ on oo nyʒt.
On oo day born we were;

---

[46] saw that before her her own child was swooning, etc. [47] now. [48] bemoan.

251. MS. *Queene herde her.* *Herde* is carelessly repeated from l. 249.

We shul be ded boþ in feere.   280
Deeþ," he seide, "ful of enuye
And of alle trechorye,
Refte þou hast me my lemman;
For soth," he seide, "þou art to blame.
She wolde haue leuyd, and þou noldest,   285
And fayne wolde y dye, and[49] þou woldest.
After deeþ clepe no more y nylle,
But slee my selfe now y wille."
His knyfe he braide[50] out of his sheth;
Himself he wolde haue doo to deth   290
And to hert he had it smeten,
Ne had his moder it vnderȝeten;
Þen þe Queene fel him vppon,
And þe knyfe fro him noom:
She reft him of his lytel knyf,   295
And sauyd þere þe childes lyf.
Forþ þe Queene ranne, al wepyng,
Tyl she come to þe Kyng.
Þan seide þe good lady,
"For Goddes loue, sir, mercy!   300
Of xii children haue we noon
On lyue now but þis oon;
And better it were she were his make[1]
Þan he were deed for hur sake."
"Dame, þou seist soþ," seide he;   305
"Sen it may noon other be,
Leuer me were she were his wyf
Þan y lost my sonnes lyf."
Of þis word þe Quene was fayne,
And to her soon she ran agayne.   310
"Floryes, soon, glad make the:
Þy lef þou schalt on lyue see.
Florys, son, þrouȝ engynne[2]
Of þy ffaders reed and myne,
Þis graue let we make,   315
Leue sone, for þy sake.

---

[49] if.   [50] plucked.   [1] mate.   [2] device.

ȝif þou þat maide forgete woldest,
After oure reed wyf þou sholdest."
Now euery worde she haþ him tolde
How þat þey þat mayden solde. 320
"Is þis soth, my moder dere?"
"For soth," she seide, "she is not here."
Þe rowȝ³ stoon adoun þey leyde
And sawe þat [þere] was not þe mayde.
"Now, moder, y þink þat y leue may. 325
Ne shal y rest nyȝt ne day—
Nyȝt ne day ne no stounde—
Tyl y haue my lemmon founde.
Hur to seken y woll wende,
Þauȝ it were to þe worldes ende!" 330
To þe King he goþ to take his leue,
And his ffader bade him byleue.⁴
"Sir, y wyl let for no wynne;⁵
Me to bydden it it were grete synne."
Þan seid þe King, "Seth it is soo, 335
Seþ þou wylt noon other doo,
Al þat þe nedeþ we shul þe fynde.
Ihesu þe of care vnbynde!"
"Leue ffader," he seide, "y telle þe
Al þat þou shalt fynde me: 340
Þou mast me fynde, at my deuyse,⁶
Seuen horses al of prys;
And twoo ycharged⁷ vppon þe molde⁸
Boþ with seluer and wyþ golde;
And twoo ycharged with moonay 345
For to spenden by þe way;
And þree with clothes ryche,
Þe best of al þe kyngryche;⁹
Seuen horses and seuyn men,
And þre knaues without hem;¹⁰ 350
And þyne owne chamburlayne,
Þat is a wel nobel swayne:¹¹

³ rough.   ⁴ remain.   ⁵ pleasure.   ⁶ disposal.   ⁷ loaded.   ⁸ ground (a tag).
⁹ realm.   ¹⁰ in addition.   ¹¹ fellow.

He can vs both wyssh[12] and reede,
As marchaundes we shull vs lede."
His ffader was an hynde king;   355
Þe coupe of golde he dide him bryng,
Þat ilke selfe coupe of golde
Þat was Blauncheflour for ȝolde.[13]
"Haue þis, soon," seide þe King,
"Herewith þou may þat swete þing   360
Wynne, so may betyde[14]—
Blauncheflour with þe white syde,
Blauncheflour, þat faire may."
Þe King let sadel a palfray,
Þe oone half[15] so white so mylke,   365
And þat other reed so sylke.
I ne can telle nouȝt
How rychely þat sadel was wrouȝt.
Þe arson[16] was of golde fyn;
Stones of vertu[17] stode þeryne,   370
Bygon aboute wit orfreys.[18]
Þe Queene was kynde and curtays:
Cast hur toward þe Kyng,
And of hur fynger she brayde a ryng:
"Haue now þis ylke ryng: 375
While is it þyne, douȝt no þyng
Of fire brennyng ne water in þe see;
Ne yren ne steele shal dere thee."
He took his leue for to goo;
Þer was ful muche woo;   380
Þey made him noon other chere
Þan her soon were leide in bere.[19]
Furþ he went with al his mayne;[20]
With him went þe chamberlayne.
So haue þey her hauyn nome   385
Þat þey ben to þe hauyn come
Þere Blaunchefloure was al nyȝt.

---

[12] guide.   [13] given in payment for.   [14] as may befall.   [15] side.   [16] saddle-peak.
[17] worth.   [18] fringed with gold fringe.   [19] bier.   [20] might.

385. Probably *hauyn* is an error for *wey*.

Wel rychely þey ben dyʒt;
Þe lord of þe ynne was welle hende;
Þe childe he sette next þe ende 390
In al þe feirest seete.
Alle þey dronken and al þey ʒete:²¹
Ete ne drynke myʒt he nouʒt;
On Blaunchefloure was al his þouʒt.
Þe lady of þat vnderʒat²² 395
Þat þe childe mornyng sat,
And seide to her lord with styl dreme,²³
"Sir, nym now goode ʒeme²⁴
How þe childe mournyng syttes:
Mete and drynke he forʒetes; 400
Lytel he eteþ, and lasse he drynkeþ;
He is no marchaund, as me þynkeþ."
To Flores þen seide she,
"Al ful of mournyng y the see.
Þer sate þer þis sender day²⁵ 405
Blauncheflour, þat swete may.
Heder was þat mayde brouʒt
With marchaundes þat hur had bouʒt;
Heder þey brouʒt þat mayde swete;
Þey wold haue solde hur for byʒete;²⁶ 410
To Babyloyn þey wylle hur bryng,
Boþ of semblant and of mornyng."
When Florys herd speke of his lemman,
Was he neuer so glad a man,
And in his hert bygan to lyʒt;²⁷ 415
Þe coupe he let fulle anoon ryʒt:
"Dame," he seide, "þe fessel²⁸ is þyne,
Boþ þe coupe and þe wyne—
Þe wyne and þe gold eke,

---

²¹ ate.   ²² perceived.   ²³ quiet voice.   ²⁴ heed.   ²⁵ recently.   ²⁶ profit.   ²⁷ grow
lighter.   ²⁸ vessel.

390. This table was not on a dais, but a single long one, the carver
sitting at one end, and the seat of honor being at his right.
402. MS. *He is a.* The reading is from the Cambridge MS.
405. For *þis ender*, a recent.
412. For this line the Cambridge MS. has, *þou art hire ilich of alle þinge.*

For þou of my leman speke. 420
On hur y þouȝt; for hur y syȝt;
I ne wyst where i hur fynde myȝt.
Wynde ne weder shal me assoyne²⁹
Þat y ne shal seche hur in Babyloyne."
Now Florys resteþ him al a nyȝt. 425
At morn, when it was day lyȝt,
He dide him into þe wylde floode.
Wynde and weder with him stoode;
Sone so Florys com to londe,
Þere he þanked Goddes sonde³⁰ 430
To þe londe þer his lyf ynne is:
Him þouȝt he was in paradyse.
Sone to Florys tydyng men tolde
Þat þe Amyral wold ffest holde;
His erls, barons, comyn sholde, 435
And al þat wolde of him lond holde,
For to herkyn his hest,
And for to honoure his ffeest.
Glad was Florys of þat tydyng.
He hoped to com to þat gestnyng,³¹ 440
Ȝif he myȝt in þat halle
His lemman see among hem alle.
    Now to þat citee Florys is come;
Feire he hath his ynne ynoome
At a palaise; was non it lyche; 445
Þe lord of þat ynne was fulle ryche;
He hadde ben ferre and wyde.
Þe childe he set next his syde
In al þe feirest seete.
Alle þey dronken and ete, 450
Al þat þerynne were:
Al þey made good chere;
Þey ete and dronke echoon with other;
But Florys þouȝt al another:
Ete ne drynke he myȝt noȝt; 455
On Blauncheflour was al his þouȝt.

---

²⁹ provide excuse.   ³⁰ sending (him).   ³¹ entertainment.

Þan spake þe burgays,
Þat was hende and curtays:
"Ow,[32] child, me þynkeþ welle
Þat muche þou þynkest on my catelle."　　　460
"Nay, sir, on catel þenke y nouȝt"
(On Blauncheflour was al his þouȝt),
"But y þynke on al wyse
For to fynde my marchaundise;
And ȝit it is þe most woo,　　　465
When y it fynd, y shal it forgoo."
Þan spak þe lord of þat ynne,
"Þis sender day, þer sate hereyn
Þat faire maide Blauncheflour,
Boþ in halle and in boure.　　　470
Euer she made mornyng chere,
And bement[33] Florys, her lyf fere;
Ioye ne blis made she noon,
But for Florys she made her moon."
Florys toke a coupe of syluer clere,　　　475
A mantyl of scarlet with menyuere:[34]
"Haue þis, sir, to þyn honour:
Þou may þonke it Blauncheflour.
He myȝt make myn hert glade
Þat couþ me tel wheder she is ladde."　　　480
"Child, to Babyloyn she is brouȝt;
Þe Amyral hur haþ bouȝt:
He gafe for hur, as she stood vpryȝt,
Seuen sithes of gold hur wyȝt;
For he þenkeþ, without weene,　　　485
Þat feire may haue to Queene.
Among his maydons in his toure
He hur dide, with muche honoure."
Now Flores resteþ him þere al nyȝt,
Tyl on þe morow þe day was lyȝt;　　　490

---

[32] oh.　[33] bemoaned.　[34] fur.

461. Such riddling replies were common in romances. Cf. "Horn,"
"Havelok," "Beryn."
477. MS. *Houe.*

He roos on þe morownyng.
He gaf his ost an hundryd shelyng,
To his ost and to his ostesse,
And toke his leue, and feire dide kysse;
And ȝerne his ost he besouȝt,   495
Þat he him help, ȝif he myȝt ouȝt[35]—
Ȝif he myȝt, with any gynne,[36]
Þat feire may to him wynne.
"Childe," he seide, "to a brygge[37] þou shalt com;
The senpere fynde at hoom: 500
He woneth at þe brygges ende;
Curtays man he is, and hende;
We arn bretheren, and trouthes plyȝt:
He can þe wyssh[38] and rede aryȝt.
Þou shalt bere him a rynge   505
Fro myself, to tokenynge,
Þat he help þe in boure and halle
As it were my self befalle."
Florys takeþ þe rynge and nemeþ leue,
For longe wolde he nouȝt beleue.[39]   510
By þat it was vndern hyȝe,
Þe brygge com he swyth nye.
Þe senperes name was Darys:
Florys gret him wel feire, ywys,
And he him þe rynge arauȝt,[40]   515
And ful feire it him betauȝt.
Þrowȝ þe token of þat ilk ryng
Florys had ful faire gestnyng[41]
Off ffyssh and flessh and tender breede,
Of wyn, both white and reede: 520
And euer Florys sate ful colde,
And Dares bygan þe childe behȯlde:
"Leue child, what may þis be,
Þus þouȝtful, as y the see?

---

[35] could in any way. [36] trick. [37] bridge. [38] direct. [39] tarry. [40] handed over.
[41] entertainment.

500. *Senpere* translates *pontonnier* and *portier* in the French. But other English translations show that their French source had *burgeis;* and this may account for the peculiar *senpere*, man of good rank.

Art þou nou3t al in feere,[42]   525
Þat þou makist þus sory chere,
Or þou lykkest no3t þis yn?"
Þan Floreys answerd him:
"3is, sir, by Goddes ore,
So good ne had y mony day 3ore;   530
God let me abyde þat daye
Þat y þe quyte wel may!
But y þenke on al wyse
Most vppon my marchaundyse;
And 3it it is most woo,   535
When y hit ffynde, y shal it forgoo."
"Childe, woldest þou telle me þy gryf,[43]
To hele[44] þe, me were ful lyf."
Euery word he haþ him tolde—
How þe mayde was fro him solde,   540
And how he was of Spayn a kynges son,
For grete loue þeder ycome
To fonde, with quayntyse and with gyn,[45]
Blauncheflour for to wynne.
"Now," seith Dares, "þou art a ffolt"[46]—   545
And ffor a ffoole þe childe he halt—;
"Now y woot how it gooth:
Þou desirest þyn own deeth.
Þe Amyral haþ to his iustinges[47]
Oþer[48] half hundred of ryche kinges;   550
And þe alder-rychest king
Durst not begynne suche a þing.
3if Amyral my3t it vnderstonde,
He shulde be drawe in his owne londe.
About Babyloyn, y wene,   555
Six longe myle and tene;
At euery myle is a walle þerate,

<hr>

[42] well. [43] grief. [44] heal. [45] slyness and trickery. [46] dunce. [47] tournaments.
[48] half a hundred other.

543. MS. *quanytyse.*

555. The scribe has condensed without noting that this is a description
of the city: "it is six and ten long miles around the city."

557. The Cambridge MS. has, *Abute þe walle þer buþ ate Seue siþe
tuenti 3ates.* The passage is different in the French.

Seuen sithes twenty ȝate;[49]
And xx toures þer ben ynne,
Þat euery day chepyng[50] is ynne;   560
Euery day and nyȝt þrouȝout þe ȝere
Þe chepyng is ylyche plenere;[1]
And þauȝ al þe men þat ben bore
Had on hur lyf swore
To wynne þat maide feire and free,   565
Al shul þey die, so moot y the.
In þat bour, in mydward ryȝt,
Stondeþ a toure, y the plyȝt:[2]
An hundryd fathum it is hye;
Whosoo beholdeþ hit, fer or nere,   570
An hundred fathum it is yfere;
It is made without pere,[3]
Of lyme and of marbul stone;
In al þis world is suche noone.
Now is þe morter made so wele,   575
Ne may it breke iren ne steele.
Þe pomel[4] þat aboue is leide,
It is made with muche pride,
Þat man ne þar[4a] in þe tour berne
Nouther torche ne lanterne,   580
Suche a pomel was þer bygone:[5]
Hit shyned anyȝt so doþ þe soone.
Now arn in þat ilke toure
Twoo and fourty nobell boure;
Wel were þat ilke man   585
Þat myȝt woon in þat oon!
Ne durst him neuer more, ywys,
Couete after more blysse.
Naw arn þer seriauntes in þat stage[6]
Þat seruen þe maydons of hyȝe parage:[7]   590

---

[49] gates. [50] trading. [1] in full progress. [2] assure. [3] equal. [4] ornamental globe on top. [4a] need. [5] set. [6] set of apartments. [7] lineage.

561. MS. þrouȝtout.
570. The rhyme requires nye for nere.
580. MS. torthee.

But no serieaunt may serue þerynne
þat bereþ in his breche þat gynne[8]
To serue hem day and ny3t,
But he be as a capoun[9] dy3t.
At þe 3ate is a 3atewarde;   595
He is not a cowarde:
He is wonder proude withalle;
Euery day he goþ in ryche palle.[10]
And þe Amyral haþ a wonder woon,
þat he þat is com of Cristendom,   600
Euery 3ere to haue a new wyf;
þen he louiþ his Queene as his lyf.
Then shul men bryng doun of þe toure
Al þe maidens of grete honoure,
And bryng hem into an orcharde,   605
þe feirest of al mydlerde:[11]
þeryn is mony fowles song;
Mcn my3t leue þeryn ful long.
About þe orchard is a walle;
þe fowlest stone is cristall;   610
And a well spryngcþ þerynne
þat is made with muche gynne:
þe wel is of muche prys:
þe stremcs com froo Paradyse;
þe grauel of þe ground is precious stoones,   615
And al of vertu[12] for þe noones.
Now is þe well of muche au3t:[13]
3if a woman com þat is forlau3t
And she be doo to þe streeme
For to wesshe her honndes clene,   620
þe water wylle 3elle as it were woode
And bycome red as bloode.
On what maide þe water fareþ soo,

---

[8] i.e., has manhood.   [9] eunuch.   [10] rich cloth.   [11] the earth.   [12] peculiar power.
[13] power.

600. Apparently interpolated without meaning. It is not in the French
or the other MSS.

618. *Forlau3t* seems to be a bad form, made on the analogy of *au3t* (in
other MSS. *eye,* fear), from *forleie,* unchaste.

Sone she shal to deþ be doo;
Þoo þat ben maidens clene, 625
Þey may wessh þeryn, y wene;
Þe water woll stonde feire and clere;
To hem makeþ it no daungere.[14]
At þe walles hed stondeþ a tree—
Þe feirest þat on erthe may be; 630
It is cleped þe Tree of Loue;
Floures and blossomes spryngen aboue.
Þen þey þat maydons clene bene,
Þei shul be brouȝt vnder þe trene,
And which so falleþ þe floure[15] 635
Shal be queene with muche honour.
Ȝif any mayden þer is
Þat þe Amyral telleþ of more pris,
Þe flour shal be to her sent
Þrouȝ art of enchauntement. 640
Þe Amyral cheseþ hem by þe flour,
And euer he herkeneþ after Blaunchefloure."
Thre sithes Flores sownyd anoon
Riȝt byfore hem euerychoon.
When he awoke and speke myȝt, 645
Sore he wept and sore he syȝt,
And seide, "Dares, y worth now deede,
But þat y hope of þe som reede."
"Leue soon, wyl ȝe see
Þat þy trust is muche on me. 650
Þen is þe best reed þat y can—
Other reed ne can y noon—
Wende to-morn to þe toure
As þou were a good gynoure;[16]
Take on þy honde squyer and scantlon[17] 655
As þou were a freemason.

---

[14] resistance. [15] the one upon whom, etc. [16] craftsman. [17] square and measure (mason's tools).

642. The French says, *Blanceflor dist qu'adont prendra* (1837). The English means, "He listens eagerly for the announcement that it will be Blancheflour."

649. "Dear son, well you see that," etc.; but *ȝe* should be *i*.

Behold þe tour vp and doun;
Þe porter is cruel and ffeloun;
Wel sone he wyl com to the
And aske what maner man þou be,   660
And bere[18] on þe ffelonye,
And sey þou art com to be a spye.
And þow shalt answere swetlyche,
And sey to him myldelyche;
Sey þou art a gynoure   665
To beholde þat feire toure,
For to loke and for to fonde
To make suche another in þy londe.
Wel sone he wyl com þe nere
And wyl byd þe pley at þe chekere.[19]   670
When þou art at cheker brou3t,
Without seluer [be] þou nou3t;
Þou shalt haue redy with the
xx marke beside þy knee.
3if þou wynne ou3t of his,   675
Þow tel þerof lytel prys;
And yf he wynne ou3t of þyn,
Loke þow leue it with hym.
So þou shalt, al with gynne,[20]
Þe porters loue forsoth wynne,   680
Þat he þe help on þis day:
But he þe helpe, no man may.
Wel 3erne he wyl þe bydde and pray
Com anoþer day to playe;
Þou shalt seye þou wylt soo;   685
Þou shalt take with þe suche twoo.
Þe þrydde day, take an hundred pound
And þy coupe hool and sound;
3eue him markes and poundes of þy male;[21]
Of þy tresoure tel þou no tale.[22]   690
Wel 3erne he wyl þe bydde and pray
To lay[23] þy coupe, and to play;

---

[18] impute.   [19] chess.   [20] a trick.   [21] wallet.   [22] keep no account.   [23] wager.

686. I.e., "twice as much money."

þou shalt answere alþerfirst,[24]
Lenger to play þe ne lyst.
Ful muche he wylle for þe coupe bede,   695
ʒif he myʒt þe better spede;[25]
þou shalt it blethly ʒeue him,
ʒif[26] it be of gold fyne;
And he wol ful muche loue þe,
And to þe bowe also, pardé,   700
þat he wyl falle to þy foote
And becom þyn, ʒif he moote;
And homage þou shalt fonge,
And þe trouþ[27] of his honde."
As he seide, he dide ywys;   705
And as he ordeyned, so it is:
þe porter ys Florys man bycom
For his gold and his warysone.[28]
Florys seide, "Now art þou my moon,[29]
Al my trust is þe vppon;   710
Now my consel y wyl þe shewe;
Rede me ryʒt, ʒif þou be trew."
Now euery word he haþ him tolde—
How þe mayde was fro him solde,
And how he was of Spayn a kynges soon,   715
For grete loue þeder ycoom
To fonden, with some gynne,
þat feire mayde for to wynne.
þe porter þat herde, and sore syʒt,
And seide, "Y am betrayde aryʒt;   720
þrouʒ þy catel y am dismayde;
þerfore y am wel euyl apayde.[30]
Now y woot how it gooþ;
For þe shal y suffer deth!
I shal þe faile neuermoo,   725
þe while y may ryde and goo;

---

[24] at the very first.   [25] i.e., in the hope of succeeding better.   [26] though.
[27] pledge of faith.   [28] reward.   [29] companion, fellow.   [30] little pleased.

711. MS. *new.*
714. MS. *sholde.*

Þy fforwardes shal y holde alle,
Whatsoeuer may befalle.
Wynde now hoom to þyn ynne,
While y beþenke me of sum gynne;   730
Bytwene þis and þe þrydde day,
Fonde[31] y shal what y do may.''
Flores spake and wept among,[32]
And þou3t þe terme al to long.
Þe porter þou3t þe best reed,   735
And let geder floures in a meede;
He wist it was þe maydons wylle.
To lepes[33] he lete of floures fylle:
Þat was þe best reed, as him þou3t þoo,
Floures in þat oon lep to doo.   740
Twoo maydens þe lepe bore;
So heuy charged[34] neuer þey wore,
And bade God 3eue hem euyl fyne[35]—
To[36] mony floures he dide þerynne!
To Blaunchefloures chamber þey shulde tee;[37]   745
Þey 3ede to anoþer, and let þat be;
Þey shuld haue gon to Blauncheflour,
And 3ede to swete Clarys boure,
And cursed him[38] so fele brou3t to honde;
Þey 3ede hoom, and lete hem stonde.   750
Clarys to þe lepe com wolde,
Þe flores to hondel and to beholde;
Florys wende it hadde be his swete wy3t;
Of þe lepe he stert vpry3t,
And þe mayde, al for drede,   755
Bygan to shrelle and to grede.[39]
When he saw3 it was not shee,
Into þe lepe a3en stert he,
And held him betrayde clene;
Of his lyf tolde[40] he not a beene.   760
Þer com maydons, and to Clarys lepe
By ten, by twelf, on an heepe,[41]

[31] try.   [32] as well.   [33] baskets.   [34] loaded.   [35] an evil end.   [36] too.   [37] hasten.
[38] him who.   [39] shriek and cry.   [40] thought worth.   [41] group, body.

And þey asked what hur were,[42]
And why she made suche a bere.[43]
Clarys byþou3t hur anoon ry3t   765
Þat hit was Blauncheflour þe white,
And gaue þe maydons answere anoon,
Þat to her chamber were goon,
Þat to þe lepe com she wolde,
Þe fflowres to hondel and to beholde;   770
"And or y it e[ue]re wyst,
A botterfleye [cam] ageynst my brest!
I was so soore adrad þan
Þat y loude crye can."
Þe maydons þerof hadden glee,   775
And turned hem and lete hur be.
As sone as þe maydons were gone,
To Blauncheflour she 3ede anoon,
And seide boldly to Blauncheflour,
"Felow, come and see a feire fflour!   780
Suche a flour þe shal wel lyke,
Haue þou it sene a lyte."
"Awey, Clarys!" quod Blauncheflour;
"To scorne me, it is none honoure.[44]
I here, Clarys, without gabbe,[45]   785
Þat þe Amyral wyl me to wyf habbe;
But þat day shal neuer be
Þat he shal euer haue me—
Þat y shal be of loue so vntrewe,
Ne chaunge my loue for no newe;   790
For no loue, ne for noon aye,[46]
Forsake Florys in his contraye.
Now[47] y shal swete Florys mysse,

---

[42] what was wrong with her.   [43] outcry.   [44] to mock me is a small distinction.   [45] mockery.   [46] fear.   [47] i.e., since.

765–6. A careless translation of the French: *Cele se fu rasseuree, Et de Blanceflor porpensee; Ce fu ses amis, bien le sot.* . . . *Blauncheflour* is a genitive; but the reading proposed by Taylor, *Blauncheflour swete wi3t,* is better than the text.

772. MS. *An otter fley3.* The reading is conjectured from the other MSS., which do not rhyme on the same words found here.

Ne shal noon other of me haue blysse."
Clarys stood and beheld þat rewth 795
And þe trewnesse of hur trewth,[48]
And seide, "Lady Blaunchefloure,
Goo we see þat ilke floure."
To þe lepe þey went both;
Ioyful man was Florys þoo, 800
For he had herde al þis.
Of þat lepe he stert ywys;
Wel sone Blaunchefloure chaunged hewe;
Ayther of hem other knewe:
Withoute speche togeder þey lepe, 805
And klippt[49] and kyst wonder swete.
Clarys beheld al this,
Her countenaunce and her blysse,
And seide þen to Blaunchefloure,
"Felow, knowist þou auʒt þis flour? 810
She shul konne ful muche of art
Þat þou woldest þerof geue part."[50]
Now Blaunchefloure and Florys,
Boþ þese swete þinges ywys,
Cryen her mercy, al wepyng, 815
Þat she ne wrey hem to þe King.
"Ne douʒt no more of me in alle
Þan it were myself byfalle:
Wete ʒe wel weturly,
Heele[51] y wyl ʒoure drury."[21] 820
To a bedde þey ben brouʒt
Þat is of palle and of sylke wrouʒt,
And þere þey sette hem doun
And drowʒ hemself al aroom:[22]
Þer was no man þat myʒt radde[23] 825
Þe ioye þat þey twoo madde.
Florys þen to speke bygan,
And seide, "Lord, þat madest man,

---

[48] trustworthiness of her pledged word.   [49] embraced.   [50] i.e., only a most artful woman could induce you to share him.   [51] conceal.   [21] love.   [22] aside.   [23] express.

799. MS. *loþe*. The rhyme-word should be *bo*.

I it þonke Goddes Sone
Þat al my care i haue ouercome;   830
Now my leue i haue yfounde,
Of al my care y am vnbounde."
Clarys hem seruyd al at wylle,
Boþ dernlyche²⁴ and stylle.

Clarys with þe white syde   835
Rose vp on morne tyde,
And cleped after Blaunchefloure
To wende with her in to þe toure.
She²⁵ seide, "Y am commaunde;"²⁶
But her answere was slepaunde.²⁷   840
Þe Amyral had suche a woone
Þat euery day shulde com
Twoo maydons of hur bour
Vp to him in to þe toure
With water and clooth and basyn   845
For to wesshe his hondes ynne:
Þat day þey seruyd him feire;
Anoþer day com another peire;
But most were wonyd²⁸ into þe toure
Clarys and Blaunchefloure.   850
Clarys come þenne aloon:
Þe Amyral asked anoon,
"Where is Blauncheflour so free?
Why comeþ she not heder with þe?"
"Sir," she seide anoon ryȝt,   855
"She haþ wakyd²⁹ al þis nyȝt,
And ycryde and yloke³⁰
And yredde on hur booke,
And ybede to God her orysone³¹
Þat He geue þe his benysone,   860
And þat He holde long þy lyf;
And now þe mayde slepeþ swyth;
She slepeþ so fast, þat mayde swete,

---

²⁴ secretly. ²⁵ Blancheflour. ²⁶ coming. ²⁷ given sleepily. ²⁸ used (to go).
²⁹ been awake. ³⁰ gazed (in meditation). ³¹ offered her prayer.

838. MS. *with him.*

þat she may not com ȝete."
"Certes," seide þe Kyng, 865
"Now is she a swete þing:
Wel auȝt me ȝerne³² her to wyf
þat so preyeth for my lyf."
Anoþer day Clarys erly aryst,
þat Blauncheflour well wyst, 870
And seide, "Y com anoone,"
When Clarys her clepe bygan,
And fel in a slepe newe;
Sone after it made hem to rewe!
Clarys to þe pyler cam; 875
A basyn of gold in hond she nam,
And cleped after Blaunchefloure
To wende with hur into þe toure.
þe Amyral asked after Blauncheflour,
"What! is she not com ȝet? 880
Now she me douteþ al t[o lyte."]
Forþ he cleped his chamburlayne
And bade him wende with his mayne
"To wete why she wyl not com
As she was wonyd to doon." 885
þe chamburlayn is forth noom;
In to chamber he is coom,
And stondeþ byfore hur hedde,
And fyndeþ þere, nebbe to nebbe,³³
Nebbe to nebbe, and mouþ to mouþ. 890
To þe Amyral it was sone couþ;
Vp in to þe toure he steyȝ³⁴
And told his lord al þat he seyȝ.
þe Amyral lete him his swerd bryng,
For wete³⁵ he wolde of þat tydyng. 895
He went to hem þere þey lay:
Ȝit was she aslepe þere ay.³⁶

---

³² desire. ³³ face. ³⁴ ascended. ³⁵ learn the truth. ³⁶ ever, still.

875. In a passage preserved in the French and other MSS., it is explained that the water supply of the castle is circulated through a pipe of brass, here called a pillar.

The Amyral lete þe clothes doun cast
A lytel bynethe hur brest,
And sone he knew anoon   900
þat oon was woman, and þat oþer groom.
He quaked for tene þere he stood;
Hem to sloon was in his moode;
ȝit he þouȝt, or he hem quelde,
What þey were, þey shuld him telle,   905
And seth he wyl with dome hem done.[37]
þe children wakyd swyth soone,
And saw þe swerde ouer hem drawe;
þey ben adrad and in awȝe.
þan seide Florys to Blauncheflour,   910
"Of oure lyf is no socour."
But þey cryde him mercy swyth,
For to length[38] her lyue.
Vp he bade hem sytte booth,
And do on boþ her cloþ;   915
Seþ he dide hem bynde fast
And in prison lete hem be cast.
Now haþ he after his barons sent,
To wreke him after iugement.[39]
Now han þe barons vndernome,[40]   920
And to þe Amyral þey ben coom.
He stood vp among hem al
With semblaunt wroþ withalle,
And seide, "Lordynges with much honour,
ȝe herde speke of Blauncheflour: 925
þat y bouȝt hur dere aplyȝt[41]
For seuen sithes of golde hur wyȝt;[42]
For y wende, without wene,
þat feire mayde to haue had to quene.
Among my maydons in my toure   930
I hur dide, with muche honoure;

---

[37] bring judgment on them.   [38] prolong.   [39] avenge him according to law.
[40] set out.   [41] indeed.   [42] weight.

904. The rhyme shows that the right form is the present: *quelle*, kill.
917. On the judicial procedure, cf. notes to the trial in "Havelok."

Byfore her bedde my self y coom;
I fonde þeryn a naked man.
Þan were þey to me so looþ,
I þouȝt to haue sleyn hem booþ,   935
I was so wroþ and so woode;
Ȝit y withdrowȝ myn hoot bloode[43]
Tyl y haue sende after ȝow, by assent,
To wreke me with iugement.
Now ȝit ȝe woot how it is goone;   940
Wreke me soon of my foon."
Þan spake a kyng of þat londe,
"We haue herd al þis shame and shonde;[44]
But or we hem to deth deme,
Lat vs hem see, ȝif it þe queeme,[45]   945
What þey wolde speke or sygge,[46]
Ȝif þey wyl auȝt ageyn vs legge:[47]
Hit were nouȝt ryȝt iugement
Without answere make acoupement.[48]
Til þis is herde of more and lasse,   950
What myster is to bere wytnesse?"[49]
After þe children haue þey sent—
To brenne hem was his entent—;
Two serieauntes hem gan bryng
Toward hur [deþ] al wepyng.   955
Drery booþ þese children goo;
Ayther bemeneþ[50] oþeris woo.
Þan seide Florys to Blauncheflour,
"Of oure lyf is no socour:
Yf kinde of man it þole myȝt,[1]   960
Twyes y shuld dye with ryȝt,
Oones for myself, anoþer for the,
For þy deeþ þou hast for me."
Blauncheflour seyde þoo,
"Þe gylt is myn of oure woo."   965

---

[43] withheld my rage. [44] injury. [45] please. [46] say. [47] set forth against our decree. [48] accusation. [49] what is the use of passing judgment? [50] laments. [1] if man's nature were such as to endure it.

955. *Deþ* supplied from other MSS.

Florys drou3 forþ þat ryng
Þat his moder him gaff at her partyng:
"Haue þis ryng, lemman myn;
Þou shalt not dye while it is þyn."
Blaunchefloure seide þoo, 97ᴜ
"So ne shal it neuer goo²
Þat þis ryng shal help me,
And þe deed on þe see."
Florys þat ryng hur rau3t,
And she it him agayn betau3t: 975
Nouther ne wyl other deed seene;
Þey let it falle hem bytwene.
A king com after; a ryng he fonde,
And brou3t it forth in his honde.
Þus þe children wepyng com 980
To þe fire and hur doom;
Byfore þe folk þey were brou3t.
Drery was her bothes³ þou3t;
Þere was noon so stern man
Þat þe children loked oon, 985
Þat þey ne wolde, al wel fawe,⁴
Her iugement haue withdrawe,
And with grete catel hem bygge,
3if þey durst speke or sygge;
For Flores was so feire a 3onglyng,⁵ 990
And Blaunchefloure so swete a þing,
Þer wyst no man whor⁶ hem were woo
For no semblaunt þat þey made þoo.
Þe Admyral was so woode,
Ne my3t he nou3t kele⁷ his hoot bloode. 995
He bade þe children fast be bound
And in to þe fire slong.⁸
Þat ilke king þat þe ryng fonde,

---

² be done, come to pass. ³ of both of them. ⁴ gladly. ⁵ youth. ⁶ whether.
⁷ cool. ⁸ cast.

973. The construction is confused: "The ring shall not help me (if) I
am to see you dead."
992. Another MS. says that they in their sorrow seemed more fair than
others who were glad.

To Amyral he spake and rounde,[9]
And wolde hem saue to þe lyf, 1000
And told how for þe ryng þey gon stryf.
Þe Amyral lete hem ageyn clepe,[10]
For he wolde here hem speke,
And asked Florys what he heete,
And he tolde him ful skeete:[11] 1005
"Sir," he seide, "yf it were þy wylle,
Þou ne getest not þat maide to spylle;[12]
But, goòd sir, quel[13] þou me,
And late þat maide on lyue be."
Blauncheflour seide byne,[14] 1010
"Þe gylt of oure dedes is myn."
Þe Admyral seide þoo,
"Iwys, ȝe shul dye boo !"[15]
His swerd he breide[16] out of his sheeth,
Þe children to haue don to deeth. 1015
Blaunchefloure put forþ hur swire,[17]
And Florys dide her agayn to tyre,[18]
And seide, "I am man; i shal byfore:
With wrong hast þou þy lyf loore !"
Florys forth his swere putte, 1020
And Blauncheflour agayn him tytte.[19]
Þe king seide, "Drery mot ȝe be,[20]
Þis rouþ by þis children to see !"
Þe king þat þe ryng hadde,
For routh of hem sone he radde,[21] 1025
And at þe Amyral wyl he spede[22]
Þe children fro þe deþ to lede.
"Sir," he seide, "it is lytel prys
Þese children for to slee, ywys;
And it is wel more worship 1030

---

[9] whispered. [10] be called back. [11] quickly. [12] kill. [13] kill. [14] within, i.e., interjected. [15] both. [16] plucked. [17] neck. [18] draw. [19] drew back. [20] i.e., bad luck to you. [21] spoke. [22] succeeded.

1007. Other MSS. have, *þu nauȝtest*, you should not.
1020. MS. *swerd*.
1022. MS. *dredry*.
1027. *Amyral* is a genitive.

Florys counsel þat ȝe weete:
Who him tauȝt þat ilke gynne,
Þy toure for to com ynne,
And who him brouȝt þare,
And other,[23] þat ȝe may be ware."   1035
Þan seide þe Amyral, "As God me saue,
Florys shal his lyf haue
Ȝif he me telle who him tauȝt þerto.". . .
. . . . Of Florys, "Þat shal y neuer doo."
Now þey bydden al ywys   1040
Þat þe Admyral graunted þis,
To forȝeue þat trespas
Ȝif Florys told how it was.
Now euery word he haþ him tolde:
How þat maide was for him solde,   1045
And how he was of Spayn a kynges sone,
For grete loue þeder ycom
For to fonde, with sum gynne,
Þat feire maide for to wynne,
And how þe porter was his man bycom   1050
For his gold and for his warysoun,[24]
And how he was in þe fflorys borne;
Alle þe lordinges lowȝ þerforne.
Now þe Admyral—wol him tyde![25]—
Florys setteþ next his syde,   1055
And efte he made him stonde vpryȝt
And dubbed him þere knyȝt,
And bade he shulde with him be
Þe furthermast[26] of his meyné.
Florys falleþ doun to his feet   1060
And prayeþ geue[27] him his sweet.
Þe Amyral gaf him his lemman:
Al þat þere were þankyd him þanne.
To a chirche he let hem bryng,
And dede let wed hem with a ryng.   1065

---

[23] more things too. [24] reward. [25] good luck to him! [26] foremost. [27] that he give.

1039. This is all that is left of a speech in which Floris refuses to betray his accomplices unless they are pardoned.

Boþ þese twoo swete þinges, ywys,
Fel his feet for to kysse;
And þrouȝ consel of Blauncheflour,
Clarys was fet doun of þe toure,
And Amyral wedded hur to queene.   1070
Þere was fest swythe breeme;[28]
I can not telle al þe sonde,[29]
But rycher fest was neuer in londe.
Was it nouȝt longe after þan
Þat to Florys tydyng cam   1075
Þat þe King his ffader was deed.
Þe baronage gaf him reed
Þat he shuld wende hoom
And fonge his feire kyngdoom.
At þe Amyral þey toke leue,   1080
And he byddeþ þem byleue.[30]
Hom he went with royal array,
And was crownyd within a short day.

---

[28] fine.   [29] dishes, viands.   [30] remain.

1083. The end of the story is not found in the MS.; but in another version are found the usual benediction of the hearers and the assurance that the couple lived happily.

CHEVELERE ASSIGNE

CHEVELERE ASSIGNE

The romance is in the east midland dialect (with some northern forms) of the late fourteenth century. With the consent of the Department of Manuscripts of the British Museum, it has been edited from rotographs of the unique manuscript, Cotton Caligula A II.

The story is apparently a condensation of about the first 1100 lines of the French "Chevalier au Cygne," a 6000-line composite of the late twelfth century. A long English prose version was printed by Copland and again by Wynkyn de Worde.

This romance is related to the cycle of Godfrey of Bouillon, famous crusader and one of the Nine Worthies, who was reputed to have descended from a swan—a legend which attached itself to some noble English families also. The changing of a human being into a swan is a well-known theme in folklore; its origin may be traced to totemism (cf. Lang, "Myth, Ritual, and Religion," 1.168; also E. S. Hartland, "The Science of Fairy Tales," last chapters).

The manuscript is peculiar in its interchange of -th and -d (*swyde* for *swythe*, 158; *bygyleth* for *bygyled*, 78) so that many preterites and past participles resemble the present tense. These forms have been retained. Because of doubt of the scribe's intentions, final -*m* and -*n* with a flourish and final crossed -*ll* and -*th* have not been doubled or expanded to -*lle*, etc.

Gibbs's edition (*EETS.*) is referred to in the notes as G.

All-weldynge[1] God · whenne it is His wylle,
Wele He wereth[2] His werke · with His owne honde;
For ofte harmes were hente · þat helpe we ne myȝte,
Nere þe hyȝnes[3] of Hym · þat lengeth in heuene.
For this i saye by a lorde · was lente[4] in an yle   5
That was kalled Lyor— · a londe by hymselfe.
The Kynge hette Oryens · as þe book telleth,

[1] omnipotent.   [2] protects.   [3] were it not for the supremacy.   [4] dwelt.

6. A corruption of the Lillefort of the French poem, where it is no island. Possibly the scribe took it to be some form of *l'île forte*. Cf. Krüger, *Arch.* 77.169.

859

And his Qwene, Bewtrys[5] · þat bryȝt was and shene.
His moder hyȝte Matabryne · þat made moche sorwe,
For she sette her affye[6] · in Sathanas of helle.   10
This was chefe of þe kynde · of Cheualere Assygne;[7]
And whenne þey sholde into a place— · it seyth full wele
      where,—
Sythen aftur his lykynge · dwellede he þere
With his owne Qwene · þat he loue myȝte;
But all in langour he laye · for lofe of here one   15
That he hadde no chylde · to cheuenne[8] his londis,
But to be lordeles of his[9] · whenne he þe lyf lafte;
And þat honged in[10] his herte · i heete þe for sothe.
   As þey wente vpon a walle · pleynge hem one,
Bothe þe Kynge and þe Qwene · hemselfen togedere,   20
The Kynge loked adowne · and byhelde vnder
And seyȝ a pore womman · at þe ȝate sytte
With two chylderen her byfore · were borne at a byrthe;
And he turned hym þenne · and teres lette he falle.
Sythen sykede he on hyȝe · and to þe Qwene sayde,   25
"Se ȝe þe ȝonder pore womman · how þat she is pyned
With twynlenges[11] two · and þat dare i my hedde wedde."[12]
   The Qwene nykked hym with nay[13] · and seyde, "It is
      not to leue:
Oon manne for oon chylde · and two wymmen for tweyne,
Or ellis hit were vnsemelye þynge · as me wolde þenke,   30
But eche chylde hadde a fader · how manye so þer were."
   The Kynge rebukede here · for her worþes ryȝte þere,
And whenne it drowȝ towarde þe nyȝte · þey wenten to bedde;
He gette on here þat same nyȝte · resonabullye manye.
The Kynge was witty[14] · whenne he wysste her with chylde,35
And þankede lowely our Lorde · of his loue and his sonde;
But whenne it drowȝe to þe tyme · she shulde be delyuered,

---

[5] Beatrice.   [6] trust.   [7] Knight of the Swan.   [8] possess.   [9] without a lord of
his blood.   [10] weighed on.   [11] twins.   [12] wager.   [13] contradicted.   [14] overjoyed.

17. Violation of parallel structure is common in the romances.
28–31. I.e., the same man did not father both children. Twins were
considered infallible sign of adultery; cf. Westermarck, "Origin and De-
velopment of Moral Ideas," I. 408.

Ther moste no womman come her nere · but she þat was
   cursed,
His moder Matabryne · þat cawsed moche sorowe;
For she thow3te to do[15] þat byrthe · to a fowle ende. 40
   Whenne God wolde þey were borne · þenne brow3te she
   to honde
Sex semelye sonnes · and a dow3ter, þe seueneth,
All safe and all sounde · and a seluer cheyne[16]
Eche on of hem hadde abowte · his swete swyre;
And she lefte[17] hem out · and leyde hem in a cowche. 45
And þenne she[18] sente aftur a man · þat Markus was called
That hadde serued herseluen · skylfully longe;
He was trewe of his feyth · and loth for to tryfull.
She knewe hym for swych · and triste[19] hym þe better,
And seyde, "þou moste kepe counsell · and helpe what þou
   may. 50
The fyrste grymme watur · þat þou to comeste,
Looke þou caste hem þerin · and lete hem forth slyppe;
Sythen seche to þe courte · as þou now3te hadde sene,
And þou shalt lyke full wele · yf þou may lyfe aftur."
Whenne he herde þat tale · hym rewede þe tyme, 55
But he durste not werne[20] · what þe Qwene wolde.
The Kynge lay in langour · sum gladdenou to here,
But þe fyrste tale þat he herde · were tydynges febull.[21]
   Whenne his moder Matabryne · brow3te hym tydynge,
At a chamber dore · as she forth sow3te, 60
Seuenne whelpes she sawe · sowkynge þe damme;
And she kaw3te out a knyfe · and kylled þe bycche.

---

[15] bring. [16] silver chain. [17] lifted. [18] i.e., Matabryne. [19] trusted. [20] refuse.
[21] unpleasant.

40. In the French version, the king ravishes his bride from the other-world, a fact which explains Matabryne's hostility. Cf. "Emaré."

42. A similar story is told about Irmentrude, Countess of Altorfe, ancestress of the Guelphs (whelps), who bore twelve sons at a birth after having accused the mother of triplets of adultery. Cf. Gibbs xi. For a full discussion and parallels of this incident, see M. Schlauch, "Chaucer's Constance and Accused Queens," 21.

52. MS. hym forth.

57. In the French story, the children are born during the king's absence.

She caste her þenne in a pytte · and taketh þe welpes
And sythen come byfore þe Kynge · and vpon hy3e she seyde,
"Sone, paye þe with þy Qwene · and se of her berthe !"²² 65
Thenne syketh þe Kynge · and gynnyth to morne,
And wente wele it were sothe · all þat she seyde.
Thenne she seyde, "Lette brenne her anone · for þat is the
beste."
"Dame, she is my wedded wyfe · full trewe as i wene
As i haue holde her er þis · our Lorde so me helpe !" 70
"A, kowarde of kynde," quod she · "and combred²³ wrecche,
Wolt þou werne wrake²⁴ · to hem þat hit deserueth?"
"Dame, þanne take here þyselfe · and sette her wher þe
lyketh,
So þat i se hit no3te · what may i seye elles?"
   Thenne she wente her forth · þat God shall confounde, 75
To þat febull,²⁵ þer she laye · and felly she bygynneth,
And seyde, "Aryse, wrecched Qwene · and reste þe her no
lengur;
Thow hast bygyleth²⁶ my sone · it shall þe werke sorowe.
Bothe howndes and men · haue hadde þe a wylle;²⁷
Thow shalt to prisoun fyrste · and be brente aftur." 80
Thenne shrykede þe 3onge Qwene · and vpon hy3 cryeth.
"A, lady," she seyde · "where ar my lefe chylderen?"
Whenne she myssede hem þer · grete mone she made.
   By þat come tytlye · tyrauntes²⁸ tweyne,
And by þe byddynge of Matabryne · anon þey her hente, 85
And in a dymme prysoun · þey slongen here deepe
And leyde a lokke on þe dore · and leuen here þere.
Mete þey caste here adowne · and more God sendeth.
And þus þe lady lyuede þere · elleuen 3ere,
And mony a fayre orysoun · vnto þe Fader made 90

---

²² see what she has borne. ²³ troubled. ²⁴ deny punishment. ²⁵ wretched
woman. ²⁶ beguiled. ²⁷ at their pleasure. ²⁸ evildoers.

65. For information and parallels to the old queen's accusation against
the young, cf. M. R. Cox's "Cinderella" 199, 486.

68. "Burning for adultery is common in the romances, but appears to
have no basis in medieval custom," Child 2.113. Cf. J. D. Bruce, "Mort
Artu," 282; W. Foerster, "Ywain," 3rd. ed., ix; Pio Rajna, "Le Fonti dell'
Orlando Furioso," 2nd ed., 154. Cf. also "Layamon" 28,181; "Emaré" 533.

That saued Susanne fro sorowefull domus · [her] to saue als.
Now leue we þis lady in langour and pyne
And turne aȝeyne to our tale · towarde þese chylderen
And to þe man Markus · þat murther hem sholde,
How he wente þorow a foreste · fowre longe myle   95
Thyll he come to a water · þer he hem shulde in drowne,
And þer he keste vp þe cloth · to knowe hem bettur;
And þey ley and lowȝe on hym · louelye all at ones.
"He þat lendeth wit," quod he · "leyne[29] me wyth sorowe
If i drowne ȝou to-day · thowgh my deth be nyȝe."   100
Thenne he leyde hem adowne · lappedde in þe mantell,
And lappede hem and hylyde[30] hem · and hadde moche rewthe
That swyche a barmeteme[31] as þat · shulde so betyde.
Thenne he taketh hem to Cryste · and aȝeyne turneth,
But sone þe mantell was vndo · with mengynge[32] of her
legges.   105
They cryedde vpon hyȝe · with a dolefull steuenne;
They chyuered[33] for colde · as cheuerynge chyldrenn.
They ȝoskened[34] and cryde out · and þat a man herde;
An holy hermyte was by · and towarde hem cometh.
Whenne he come byfore hem · on knees þenne he fell, 110
And cryede ofte vpon Cryste · for somme sokour hym to
sende
If any lyfe were hem lente[35] · in þis worlde lengur.
Thenne an hynde kome fro þe woode · rennynge full swyfte
And fell before hem adownne · þey drowȝe to þe pappes.[36]
The heremyte prowde[37] was þerof · and putte hem to
sowke;[38]   115
Sethen taketh he hem vp · and þe hynde foloweth,
And she kepte hem þere · whyll our Lorde wolde.
Thus he noryscheth hem vp   and Criste hem helpe sendeth.
Of sadde[39] leues of þe wode · wrowȝte he hem wedes.
Malkedras þe fostere[40]— · þe fende mote hym haue !— 120

---

[29] reward. [30] concealed. [31] progeny. [32] entangling. [33] shivered. [34] sobbed.
[35] remained in them. [36] teats. [37] gratified. [38] suck. [39] fallen. [40] forester.

91. The apocryphal story of the saving of Susannah from the false charges of the elders was popular in the Middle Ages. G. supplies her.
99. MS. lendeth w^t the usual contraction for with.

That cursedde man for his feyth[41] · he come þer þey weren,
And was ware in his syȝte— · syker[42] of þe chyldren.
He turnede aȝeyn to þe courte · and tolde of þe chaunce,
And menede byfore Matabryne · how many þer were.
"And more merueyle þenne þat · dame, a seluere cheyne 125
Eche on of hem hath · abowte here swyre."
She seyde, "Holde þy wordes in chaste[43] · þat none skape
     ferther;
I wyll soone aske hym · þat hath me betrayed."
     Thenne she sente aftur Markus · þat murther hem sholde,
And askede hym in good feyth[44] · what fell of þe chyldren. 130
Whenne she hym asked hadde · he seyde, "Here þe sothe:[45]
Dame, on a ryueres banke · lapped in my mantell
I lafte hem lyynge there · leue þou for sothe.
I myȝte not drowne hem for dole · do what þe lykes!"
Thenne she made here all preste · and out bothe hys yen.135
Moche mone was therfore · but no man wyte moste.
     "Wende þou aȝeyne, Malkedras · and gete me þe cheynes,
And with þe dynte of þy swerde · do hem to deth;
And i shall do þe swych a turne— · and þou þe tyte hyȝe—
That þe shall lyke ryȝte wele · þe terme[46] of þy lyue." 140
     Thenne þe hatefull thefe · hyed hym full faste;
The cursede man in his feyth · come þer þey were.
By þenne was þe hermyte go into þe wode · and on of þe
     children,
For to seke mete · for þe other sex
Whyles þe cursed man · asseylde þe other.   145
And he out with his swerde · and smote of þe cheynes;
They stoden all stylle · for stere[47] þey ne durste.
And whenne þe cheynes fell hem fro · þey flowenn vp swannes
To þe ryuere bysyde · with a rewfull steuenne;

---

[41] i.e., accursed because of his allegiance (to a wicked woman). [42] sure. [43] box,
i.e., be secret. [44] i.e., to tell in good faith. [45] here is the truth; cf. "Alex." 3997.
[46] for the length of. [47] stir.

127. Hypermetrical *she seyde*, added by a copyist; fairly common in
later romances. Cf. "Eger and Grime."
135. MS. has *putt* in different ink, but much the same hand, and a
caret between *and* and *out*. Verbs of motion are frequently omitted.
Cf. 146. Cf. also Int. VII.A.3.

And he taketh vp þe cheynes · and to þe cowrte turneth, 150
And come byfore þe Qwene · and here hem bytaketh;
Thenne she toke hem in honde · and heelde ham full stylle.
She sente aftur a goldesmyȝte[48] · to forge here a cowpe,[49]
And whenne þe man was comen · þenne was þe Qwene blythe.
She badde þe wessell were made · vpon all wyse,[50] 155
And delyuered hym his weyȝtes[1] · and he from cowrte wendes.
 The goldesmyȝth gooth and beetheth[2] hym a fyre · and
  breketh a cheyne,
And it wexeth in hys honde · and multyplyeth swyde.
He toke þat oþur fyue · and fro þe fyer hem leyde
And made hollye þe cuppe · of haluendell þe sixte; 160
And whenne it drowȝe to þe nyȝte · he wendeth to bedde,
And thus he seyth to his wyfe · in sawe[3] as i telle:
"The olde Qwene at þe courte · hath me bytaken
Six cheynes in honde · and wolde haue a cowpe,
And i breke me a cheyne · and halfe leyde in þe fyer, 165
And it wexedde in my hande · and wellede[4] so faste
That i toke þe oþur fyve · and fro þe fyer caste,
And haue made hollye þe cuppe · of haluendele þe sixte."
"I rede þe," quod his wyfe · "to holden hem stylle.
Hit is þorowe þe werke of God · or þey be wronge wonnen; 170
For whenne here mesure is made · what may she aske more?"
And he dedde as she badde · and buskede hym at morwe.
He come byfore þe Qwene · and bytaketh here þe cowpe,
And she toke it in honde · and kepte hit full clene.
"Nowe lefte ther ony ouur vnwerketh[5] · by þe better
  trowthe?"[6] 175
And he recheth her forth · haluenndele a cheyne,
And she rawȝte hit hym aȝeyne · and seyde she ne rowȝte,
But delyuered hym his seruyse[7] · and he out of cowrte
 wendes.

---

[48] goldsmith. [49] cup. [50] at all hazards. [1] amount of gold. [2] mended. [3] speech.
[4] boiled up. [5] unused. [6] to the best of your belief. [7] pay.

155 and 156 are reversed in the MS. The first four words in 157 probably should be replaced with *He*. The word "mended," rather than "kindled," is generally used of fires, since fires were kept banked because of the difficulty of lighting them.

"The curteynesse of Criste," quod she · "be with þese oþur
cheynes.
They be delyuered out of þis worlde · were þe moder eke! 180
Thenne hadde i þis londe · hollye to myne wyll;
Now all wyles[8] shall fayle · but i here deth werke."
    At morn she come byfore þe Kynge · and byganne full
keene,
"Moche of þis worlde, sonne, · wondreth on þe allone,
That thy Qwene is vnbrente · so meruelows longe 185
That hath serued[9] þe deth · if þou here dome wyste.[10]
Lette sommene þy folke · vpon eche a syde,
That þey bene at þy syȝte · þe xi day assygned."
And he here graunted þat · with a grymme herte,
And she wendeth here adown · and lette hem anone warne.
                                                        190
    The nyȝte byfore þe day · þat þe lady shulde brenne,
An angell come to þe hermyte · and askede if he slepte.
The angell seyde, "Criste sendeth þe worde · of þese six
chyldren,
And for þe sauynge of hem · þanke[11] þou haste serueth.
They were þe Kynges Oriens · —wytte þou forsothe— 195
By his wyfe Betryce · she bere hem at ones
For a worde on þe wall · þat she wronge seyde,
And ȝonder in þe ryuer · swymmen þey swannes.
Sythen Malkedras þe forsworn þefe · byrafte hem her cheynes,
And Criste hath formeth þis chylde · to fyȝte for his moder."
                                                        200
"Oo lyuynge God þat dwellest in heuene," · quod þe her-
myte þanne,
"How sholde he serue for suche a þynge · þat neuer none
syȝe?"
"Go brynge hym to his fader courte · and loke þat he be
cristened—
And kalle hym Enyas to name · for awȝte þat may befalle—
Ryȝte by þe mydday · to redresse his moder; 205

___

[8] tricks. [9] deserved. [10] i.e., knew what her doom should be. [11] thanks.

179. The line seems to mean: "Now heaven's blessing go with these
other chains"; i.e., "good riddance to."

For Goddes wyll moste be fulfylde · and þou most forth
    wende."
The heremyte wakynge lay · and thow3te on his wordes.
Soone whenne þe day come · to þe chylde he seyde,
"Criste hath formeth þe, sone, · to fy3te for þy moder."
He asskede hymm þanne · what was a moder.   210
"A womman þat bare þe to man · sonne, and of here re-
    redde."[12]
"3e, kanste þou, fader, enforme me · how þat i shall fy3te?"
"Vpon a hors," seyde þe heremyte · "as i haue herde seye."
"What beste is þat," quod þe chylde · "lyonys wylde?
Or elles wode · or watur?"[13] quod þe chylde þanne.   215
"I sey3e neuur none," quod þe hermyte · "but by þe mater[14]
    of bokes.
They seyn he hath a feyre hedde · and fowre lymes hye,
And also he is a frely beeste · forthy he man serueth."
"Go we forth, fader," quod þe childe · "vpon Goddes
    halfe."[15]
Thé grypte eyþur a staffe in here honde · and on here wey
    straw3te.[16]   220
Whenne þe heremyte hym lafte · an angell hym suwethe,[17]
Euur to rede þe chylde · vpon his ry3te sholder.
    Thenne he seeth in a felde · folke gaderynge faste,
And a hy3 fyre was þer bette · þat þe Qwene sholde in brenne,
And noyse was in þe cyté · felly lowde,   225
With trumpes and tabers · whenne þey here vp token,
The olde Qwene at here bakke · betynge full faste.
The Kynge come rydynge afore · a forlonge and more.
The chylde stryketh[18] hym to · and toke hym by þe brydell.
"What man arte þou," quod þe chylde · "and who is þat þe
    sveth?"[19]   230
"I am þe Kynge of þis londe · and Oryens am kalled,
And þe 3ondur is my Qwene— · Betryce she hette—

---

[12] i.e., nourished, fed thee.   [13] i.e., wood-beast or water-beast—G.   [14] con-
tents.   [15] behalf, i.e., in God's name.   [16] set forth.   [17] follows.   [18] ran.   [19] follows.

210 ff. Cf. "Perceval."

In þe ȝondere balowe-fyre[20] · is buskedde[21] to brenne.
She was sklawnndered[22] on hyȝe · þat she hadde taken howndes,
And ȝyf she hadde so done · here harm were not to charge."[23]

235

"Thenne were þou noȝt ryȝ[t]lye sworne,"[24] quod þe chylde ·
"vpon ryȝte iuge,
Whenne þou tokest þe þy crowne— · kynge whenne þou made were—
To done aftur Matabryne · for þenne þou shalt mysfare;
For she is fowle, fell, and fals · and so she shall be fownden,
And bylefte with þe fend · at here laste ende."   240
That styked styffe in here brestes[25] · þat wolde þe Qwene brenne.
"I am but lytull and ȝonge," quod þe chylde · "leeue þou forsothe,
Not but[26] twelfe ȝere olde · euenn at þis tyme;
And i woll putte my body · to better and to worse
To fyȝte for þe Qwene · with whome þat wronge seyth."[27] 245
Thenne graunted þe Kynge · and ioye he bygynneth,
If any helpe were þerinne · þat here clensen myȝte.
By þat come þe olde Qwene · and badde hym com þenne:
"To speke with suche on as he · þou mayste ryȝth loth thenke."
"A, dame!" quod þe Kynge · "thowȝte ȝe none synne? 250
Thow haste forsettc[28] þe ȝonge Qwene · þou knoweste well þe sothe.
This chylde þat i here speke with · seyth þat he woll preue
That þou nother þy sawes · certeyne be neyther."[29]
And þenne she lepte to hym · and kawȝte hym by þe lokke[30]
That þer leued in here honde · heres an hondredde.   255

---

[20] blazing fire. [21] prepared. [22] accused. [23] of no importance. [24] badly advised; see note. [25] this remark stuck in the breasts of those who. [26] only. [27] against whoever makes the accusation. [28] opposed. [29] thou nor thy sayings, neither is trustworthy. [30] hair.

233. The scribe has confused the bale-fire (blazing, outdoor fire) of his original with the adjective *balwe*, deadly. Cf. 344.

236. The second half is a mistranslation of the French: *Nas pas a droit iugé comme roy loyaument.*

"A, by lyuynge God," quod þe childe · "þat bydeste in heuene!

Thy hedde shall lye on þy lappe · for þy false turnes.[31]

I aske a felawe anone · a fresh knyȝte aftur,[32]

For to fyȝte with me · to dryue owte þe ryȝte."[33]

"A, boy," quod she, "wylt þou so? · þou shalt sone mys-
karye; 260

I wyll gete me a man · þat shall þe sone marre."

She turneth her þenne to Malkedras · and byddyth hym take armes,

And badde hyme bathe his spere · in þe boyes herte;

And he of suche one · gret skorne he þowȝte.

An holy abbot was þer by · and he hym þeder boweth[34] 265

For to cristen þe chylde · frely and feyre.

The abbot maketh hym a fonte · and was his godfader;

The Erle of Aunnthepas · he was another;

The Countes of Salamere · was his godmoder.

They kallede hym Enyas to name · as þe book telleth. 270

Mony was þe ryche ȝyfte · þat þey ȝafe hym aftur.

Alle þe bellys of þe close[35] · rongen at ones

Withoute ony mannes helpe · whyle þe fyȝte lasted;

Wherefore þe[y] wyste well · þat Criste was plesed with here dede.

Whenne he was cristened · frely and feyre, 275

Aftur þe Kynge dubbede hym knyȝte · as his kynde wolde.[36]

Thenne prestly he prayeth þe Kynge · þat he hym lene wolde

An hors with his harnes · and blethelye he hym graunteth.

Thenne was Feraunce fette forth · þe Kynges price stede,

And out of an hyȝe towre · armour þey halenne,[37] 280

And a whyte shelde with a crosse · vpon þe posse honged,

And hit was wryten þer vpon · þat to Enyas hit sholde;[38]

And whenne he was armed · to all his ryȝtes,

Thenne prayde he þe Kynge · þat he hym lene wolde

Oon of his beste menne · þat he moste truste 285

---

[31] tricks. [32] (I ask) for a strong knight. [33] bring out the truth by fighting. [34] goes. [35] abbey grounds. [36] i.e., as befitted his condition. [37] bring. [38] i.e., should belong.

281. As Gibbs noted, *posse* is probably an error for *poste.*

To speke with hym but · a speche-whyle.[39]
A kny3te kaw3te hym by þe hande · and ladde hym of þe
    rowte.
  "What beeste is þis," quod þe childe · "þat i shall on
    houe?"[40]
"Hit is called an hors," quod þe kny3te · "a good and an
    abull."
"Why eteth he yren;" quod þe chylde · "wyll he ete no3th
    elles?   290
And what is þat on his bakke · of byrthe or on bounden?"[41]
"Nay, þat in his mowth · men kallen a brydell,
And that a sadell on his bakke · þat þou shalt in sytte."
"And what heuy kyrtell[42] is þis · with holes so thykke;
And þis holowe on my hede · i may no3t here?"   295
"An helme men kallen þat on · and an hawberke[43] þat other."
"But what broode on[44] is þis on my breste? · Hit bereth
    adown my nekke."
"A bry3te shelde and a sheene · to shylde þe fro strokes."
"And what longe on is þis · that i shall vp lyfte?"
"Take þat launce vp in þyn honde · and loke þou hym hytte,
                                          300
And whenne þat shafte is schyuered · take scharpelye[45]
    another."
"3e, what yf grace be · we to grownde wenden?"
"Aryse vp ly3tly on þe fete · and reste þe no lengur,
And þenne plukke out þy swerde · and pele[46] on hym faste,
Allwey eggelynges[47] down · on all þat þou fyndes.   305
His ryche helm nor his swerde · rekke þou of neyþur;
Lete þe sharpe of þy swerde · schreden[48] hym small."
"But woll not he smyte a3eyne · whenne he feleth smerte?"[49]
"3ys—i knowe hym full wele— · both kenely and faste.
Euur folowe[50] þou on þe flesh · tyll þou haste hym falleth, 310
And sythen smyte of his heede · i kan sey þe no furre."

---

[39] time for conversation. [40] remain. [41] i.e., is it natural or bound on. [42] shirt.
[43] body-armor. Cf. Int. III.D. [44] i.e., thing. [45] quickly. [46] strike. [47] edge-
wise. [48] shred. [49] the sting. [50] keep on striking.

295. Originally *holowe on on;* one *on* assimilated by the other.—G.

"Now þou haste tawȝte me," quod þe childe · "God i þe
beteche;
For now i kan of þe crafte · more þenne i kowthe."
Thenne þey maden raunges[1] · and ronnen togedere
That þe speres in here hondes · shyuereden to peces, 315
And for rennenge aȝeyn · men rawȝten hem other
Of balowe[2] tymbere and bygge · þat wolde not breste;
And eyther of hem · so smer[t]lye smote other
That all fleye in þe felde · þat on hem was fastened,
And eyther of hem topseyle[3] · tumbledde to þe erthe. 320
Thenne here horses ronnen forth · aftur þe raunges,
Euur Feraunnce byforne · and þat other aftur.
Feraunnce launces[4] vp his fete · and lasscheth out his yen.
The fyrste happe other hele[5] was þat · þat þe chylde hadde
Whenne þat þe blonk[6] þat hym bare · blente[7] hadde his
fere. 325
Thenne thei styrte vp on hy · with staloworth shankes,
Pulledde out her swerdes · and smoten togedur.
"Kepe þy swerde fro my croyse" · quod Cheuelyre Assygne.
"I charge[8] not þy croyse," quod Malkedras · "þe valwe of
a cherye;[9]
For i shall choppe it full small · ere þenne þis werke ende."
330
An edder[10] spronge out of his shelde · and in his body
spynneth;[11]
A fyre fruscheth[12] out of his croys · and [f]rapte[13] out his yen.
Thenne he stryketh a stroke— · Cheualere Assygne—
Euenn his sholder in twoo · and down into þe herte,

---

[1] marked off a tilting course. [2] deadly. [3] upside down. [4] kicks. [5] advantage. [6] horse. [7] blinded. [8] value. [9] amount of a cherry. [10] adder. [11] hurls
itself. [12] rushes. [13] struck.

316. MS. *rennenne*.
323. For fighting horses, cf. "Eger and Grime" 1100.
325. MS. *þe chylde þat.* Obviously wrong; G. suggests *blonk*.
328. MS. *cheuelrye*.
329. MS. *charde*.
332. Cf. *A fire þan fro þe crosse gane frusche*, "Sege of Melayne" 469.
Here the fire burns the eyes of a Saracen who has attempted to destroy
the cross.
334. Understand *stryketh* from 333.

And he boweth hym down · and ȝeldeth vp þe lyfe. 335
"I shall þe ȝelde," quód þe chylde · "ryȝte as þe knyȝte me
 tawȝte."
He trusseth his harneys[14] fro þe nekke · and þe hede wynneth;
Sythen he toke hit by the lokkes · and in þe helm leyde.
Thoo thanked he our Lorde lowely · þat lente hym þat grace.
 Thenne sawe þe Qwene Matabryne · her man so mur-
 dered, 340
Turned her brydell · and towarde þe towne rydeth;
The chylde foloweth here aftur · fersly[15] and faste.
Sythen browȝte here aȝeyne · wo for to drye,[16]
And brente here in þe balowe-fyer[17] · all to browne askes.[18]
The ȝonge Qwene at þe fyre · by þat was vnbounnden. 345
The childe kome byfore þe Kynge · and on hyȝe he seyde,
And tolde hym how he was his sone · "and oþur sex childeren
By þe Qwene Betryce · she bare hem at ones
For a worde on þe walle · þat she wronge seyde,
And ȝonder in a ryuere · swymmen þey swannes 350
Sythen þe forsworne thefe Malkadras · byrafte hem her
 cheynes."
"By God," quod þe goldsmythe · "i knowe þat ryȝth wele.
Fyve cheynes i haue · and þey ben fysh-hole."[19]
 Nowe with þe goldsmyȝth · gon all þese knyȝtes;
Toke þey þe cheynes · and to þe watur turnen 355
And shoken vp[20] þe cheynes · þer sterten vp þe swannes;
Eche on chese to his[21] · and turnen to her kynde,
But on was alwaye a swanne · for losse of his cheyne.
Hit was doole for to se · þe sorowe þat he made:
He bote[22] hymself with his byll · þat all his breste bledde, 360
And all his feyre federes · fomede vpon blode
And all formerknes[23] þe watur · þer þe swanne swymmeth.
There was ryche ne pore · þat myȝte for rewthe

---

[14] plucks the armor. [15] fiercely. [16] suffer. [17] blazing fire. [18] ashes. [19] as sound
as a fish. [20] rattled. [21] chose his own. [22] bit. [23] darkens.

358. In the French poem, also, the sixth son remains a swan, who
guides his brother, the Chevelere, on many adventures; but in the English
prose story, Queen Beatrice, following the guidance of a dream, restores
him to his true form by having a mass said over him and over the two
cups which were made from his chain.

Lengere loke on hym · but to þe courte wenden.
Thenne þey formed a fonte · and cristene þe children, 365
And callen Vryens þat on, · and Oryens another,
Assakarye þe thrydde · and Gadyfere þe fowrthe;
The fyfte hette Rose · for she was a mayden.
The sixte was fulwedde[24] · —Cheuelere Assygne—
And þus þe botenynge of God · browȝte hem to honde.[25] 370

EXPLICIT.

---

[24] had been baptized. [25] the succour of God saved them.

369. *Cheuelere Assygne* must be in apposition with *sixte*, since he was christened Enyas.

SIR CLEGES

SIR CLEGES

"Sir Cleges" is in the north midland dialect of the late fourteenth, or possibly very early fifteenth, century. The poem exists in two manuscripts of the fifteenth century: (1) the Edinburgh manuscript, 19.1.11* in the National Library of Scotland (formerly the Advocates' Library), from rotographs of which this text is printed with the kind permission and assistance of the authorities of the Library; (2) the Oxford manuscript, Ashmole 61. The two versions can be compared in Treichel's edition, *ESt.* 22.345.

Both of the main incidents, the miraculous fruit and the choosing of blows as a reward, were very popular in the Middle Ages (for variants and parallels, cf. G. H. McKnight's edition of the Oxford manuscript in his "Middle English Humorous Tales in Verse," lxi ff.); but the actual source of the romance is unknown. It is both a fabliau—a comic tale—and an exemplum—a moral tale to be used in sermons. In its present form it is clearly also a Christmas tale which minstrels told "to encourage liberality at Yule-tide feasts" (McKnight lxiii).

The following spellings peculiar to this manuscript should be noted: *nere* for *nor*, *ar* for *or*, *will* for *well*, and the intrusion of an inorganic -ʒ (*prowʒd*, proud, 448).

Plurals of nouns are abbreviated in the manuscript in the usual fashion; they have been expanded as -*is*, which seems to be the scribe's favorite form. The scribe is prodigal with *ff*-. At the beginning of lines, this has been printed *F-;* elsewhere, *ff*-. The following final letters are always crossed or flourished in the manuscript, but have not been expanded: -*ll*, -*ch*, -*m*, (except in *hym*, 123), -*n* (except in *in*, where it is never flourished). Final -*ng* and -*t*, which are nearly always crossed or flourished, have not been expanded; nor has -*d*, which is flourished in about half its occurrences. Final flourished -*r* has been expanded to -*re*.

* Formerly Jac.V.6.21; the editors are grateful to Mr. H. W. Meikle of the National Library of Scotland for this correction.

Will ye lystyn, and ye schyll here
Of eldyrs that before vs were,
    Bothe hardy and wyʒt,

In the tyme of kynge Vtere,
That was ffadyr of kynge A[r]thyr,   5
   A semely man in siȝt.
He hade a knyȝt, þat hight Sir Cleges;
A dowtyar was non of dedis
   Of the Rovnd Tabull right.
He was a man of hight¹ stature   10
And therto full fayre of ffeture,
   And also of gret myȝt.

A corteysear knyȝt than he was on
In all the lond was there non;
   He was so ientyll and fre.   15
To men þat traveld in londe of ware²
And wern fallyn in pouerté bare,
   He yaue both gold and ffee.
The pore pepull he wold releve,
And no man wold he greve;   20
   Meke of maners was hee.
His mete was ffre to euery man
That wold com and vesite hym than;
   He was full of plenté.

The knyȝt hade a ientyll wyffe;   25
There miȝt non better bere life,
   And mery sche was on siȝte.
Dame Clarys hight þat ffayre lady;
Sche was full good, sekyrly,
   And gladsum both day and nyȝte.   30
Almus³ gret sche wold geve,
The pore pepull to releue;
   Sche cherisschid many a wiȝt.
For them hade no man dere,
Rech ar pore wethyr they were;   35
   They ded euer ryght.

---

¹ tall.   ² suffered in a war-swept country.   ³ alms.

21. MS. *manres.*

Euery yer Sir Cleges wold
At Cristemas a gret ffest hold
   In worschepe of þat daye,
As ryall in all thynge   40
As he hade ben a kynge,
   Forsoth, as i you saye.
Rech and pore in þe cuntré abouȝt
Schuld be there, wythoutton douȝtt;
   There wold no man say nay.   45
Mynsstrellis wold not be behynde,
For there they myȝt most myrthis fynd;
   There wold they be aye.

Mynsstrellys, whan þe ffest was don,
Wythoutton yeftis schuld not gon,   50
   And þat bothe rech and good:
Hors, robis, and rech ryngis,
Gold, siluer, and othyr thyngis,
   To mend wyth her modde.[4]
Ten yere sech ffest he helde   55
In the worschepe of Mari myld
   And for Hym þat dyed on the rode.
Be that, his good began to slake[5]
For the gret ffestis that he dede make,
   The knyȝt ientyll of blode.   60

To hold the feste he wold not lett;
His maners he ded to wede sett;[6]
   He thowȝt hem out to quyȝtt.
Thus he ffestyd many a yere
Many a knyȝt and squire   65
   In the name of God all-myȝt.
So at the last, the soth to say,
All his good was spent awaye;
   Than hade he but lyȝt.
Thowe his good were ner[h]and leste,   70

---

[4] to cheer their spirits with.   [5] decrease.   [6] he put up his estates as security.

Yet he thow3t to make a feste;
In God he hopyd ryght.

This rialté[7] he made than aye,
Tyll his maneris wern all awaye;
Hym was lefte but on,   75
And þat was of so lytyll a value
That he and his wyffe trewe
Mi3t not leve thereon.
His men that wern mekyll of pride
Gan slake[8] awaye on euery syde;   80
With hym there wold dwell non
But he and his childyrn too;
Than was his hart in mech woo,
And he made mech mone.

And yt befell on Crestemas evyn,   85
The kny3t bethow3t hym full evyn;[9]
He dwellyd be Kardyfe syde.[10]
Whan yt drowe toward the novn,
Sir Cleges fell in svounnyng sone,
Whan he thow3t on þat tyde   90
And on his myrthys þat he schuld hold
And howe he hade his maners sold
And his renttis wyde.[11]
Mech sorowe made he there;
He wrong his handis and wepyd sore,   95
And ffellyd was his pride.

And as he walkyd vpp and dovn
Sore sy3thyng, he hard a sovne
Of dyvers mynstrelsé:
Of trompus, pypus, and claraneris,[12]   100

---

[7] magnificence.   [8] disappear.   [9] pondered deeply.   [10] near Cardiff.   [11] large income.   [12] trumpeters.

82. O. *Bot hys wife and.* . . .
86. MS. *kynge.*
99. MS. *mynstrelses;* Treichel emends.
100. Most of these instruments are illustrated in Wright.

Of harpis, luttis, and getarnys,
   A sitole and sawtré,[13]
Many carellys[14] and gret davnsyng;
On euery syde he harde syngyng,
   In euery place, trewly.   105
He wrong his hondis and wepyd sore;
Mech mone made he there,
   Syghynge petusly.

"Lord Ihesu," he seyd, "Hevyn-kynge,
Of now₃t Thou madyst all thynge;   110
   I thanke The of Thy sond.
The myrth that i was wonte to make!
At thys tyme for Thy sake,
   I fede both fre and bond.
All that euer cam in Thy name   115
Wantyd neythyr wyld nere tame[15]
   That was in my lond;
Of rech metis and drynkkys good
That my₃t be gott, be the rode,
   For coste i wold not lend."[16]   120

As he stod in mornyng soo,
His good wyffe cam hym vnto,
   And in hyr armys hym hent.
Sche kyssyd hym wyth glad chere;
"My lord," sche seyd, "my trewe fere,   125
   I hard what ye ment.
Ye se will, yt helpyth now₃t
To make sorowe in youre thow₃t;
   Therefore i pray you stynte.[17]
Let youre sorowe awaye gon,   130

---

[13] lutes and gitterns, a citole and psaltery.   [14] carols.   [15] lacked neither game nor domestic animal.   [16] hesitate.   [17] cease.

102. MS. *sotile;* O. *sytall.*
103. Carols were dances accompanied by singing; cf. the famous example in "Handlyng Synne" 8987 ff.
128. MS. *your hart;* O. *thou₃ht.*

And thanke God of hys lone[18]
Of all þat He hath sent.

For Crystis sake, i pray you blyne[19]
Of all the sorowe þat ye ben in,
　In onor of thys daye.　　　　　　　　　　　　135
Nowe euery man schuld be glade;
Therefore i pray you be not sade;
　Thynke what i you saye.
Go we to oure mete swyth
And let vs make vs glade and blyth,　　　　　140
　As wele as we may.
I hold yt for the best, trewly;
For youre mete is all redy,
　I hope, to youre paye."

"I asent," seyd he tho,　　　　　　　　　　145
And in with hyr he gan goo,
　And sumwatt[20] mendyd hys chere.
But neuerþeles hys hart was sore,
And sche hym comforttyd more and more,
　Hys sorewe away to stere.[21]　　　　　　150
So he began to waxe blyth
And whypyd[22] away hys teris swyth,
　That ran dovn be his lyre.
Than they wasschyd and went to mete
Wyth sech vitell[23] as they myзt gett　　　　155
　And made mery in fere.

Whan they hade ete, the soth to saye,
Wyth myrth they droffe þe day away,
　As will as they myзt.
Wyth her chyldyrn play they ded　　　　　160
And after soper went to bede,
　Whan yt was tyme[24] of nyзt.
And on the morowe they went to chirch,

---

[18] gift.　[19] stop.　[20] somewhat.　[21] guide.　[22] wiped.　[23] food.　[24] i.e., the proper time.

Godis service for to werch,
　　As yt was reson and ryȝt.　　　　　　165
[Up þei ros and went þeþer,
They and þer chylder togeþer,
　　When þei were redy dyȝht.]

Sir Cleges knelyd on his kne;
To Ihesu Crist prayed he　　　　　　170
　　Becavse of his wiffe:
"Gracius Lord," he seyd thoo,
"My wyffe and my chyldyrn too,
　　Kepe hem out of stryffe !"
The lady prayed for hym ayen　　　　175
That God schuld kepe hym fro peyne
　　In euerlastyng lyf.
Whan service was don, hom they went,
And thanked God with god entent,
　　And put away penci[ffe].[25]　　　　180

Whan he to hys place cam,
His care was will abatyd than;
　　Thereof he gan stynt.
He made his wife afore hym goo
And his chyldyrn both to;　　　　　185
　　Hymselfe alone went
Into a gardeyne there besyde,
And knelyd dovn in þat tyde
　　And prayed God veramend,
And thanked God wyth all hys hartt　　190
Of his dysese and hys povertt,[26]
　　That to hym was sent.

As he knelyd on hys knee
Vnderneth a chery-tre,
　　Makyng hys preyere,　　　　　195
He rawȝt a bowe ouer hys hede

---

[25] pensiveness, melancholy.　[26] poverty.

166. The three lines in brackets are supplied from O.

And rosse vpe in that stede;
  No lenger knelyd he there.
Whan þe bowe was in hys hand,
Grene leves thereon he fonde,   200
  And rovnd beryse in fere.
He seyd, "Dere God in Trenyté,
What manere of beryse may þis be,
  That grovyn[27] þis tyme of yere?

Abowȝt þis tyme i sey neuer ere,   205
That any tre schuld frewȝt[28] bere,
  As for[29] as i haue sowȝt."
He thowȝt to taste yf he cowþe;
And on he put in his mowth,
  And spare wold he nat.   210
After a chery þe reles[30] was,
The best þat euer he ete in place,
  Syn he was man wrowȝt.
A lytyll bowe he gan of-slyve,[31]
And thowȝt to schewe yt to his wife,   215
  And in he yt browȝt.

"Loo! dame, here ys newelté;[32]
In oure gardeyne of a chery-tre
  I fond yt, sekerly.
I am aferd yt ys tokynnyng   220
Of more harme that ys comynge;
  For soth, thus thynkkyth me."
[His wyfe seyd, "It is tokenyng
Off mour godness þat is comyng;
  We schall haue mour plenté.]   225
But wethyr wee haue les or more,
Allwaye thanke we God therefore;
  Yt ys best, trewly."

---

[27] grow.   [28] fruit.   [29] far.   [30] taste.   [31] cut off.   [32] novelty.

208. MS. *caste;* O. *tayst.*
222. The lines in brackets are supplied from O.
226. MS. *more or les;* Tr. alters.

Than seyd the lady with good chere,
"Latt vs fyll a panyer[33]   230
    Of þis þat God hath sent.
To-morovn, whan þe day doþe spryng,
Ye schill to Cardyffe to þe kynge
    And yeve hym to present;
And sech a yefte ye may haue there   235
That þe better wee may fare all þis yere,
    I tell you, werament."
Sir Cleges gravntyd sone thereto:
"To-morovn to Cardiffe will i goo,
    After youre entent."   240

On the morovn, whan yt was lyȝt,
The lady hade a panere dyght;
    Hyr eldest son callyd sche:
"Take vpp thys panyere goodly
And bere yt forth esyly   245
    Wyth thy fadyr fre !"
Than Sir Cleges a staffe toke;
He hade non hors—so seyth þe boke—
    To rydc on hys iorny,
Neythyr stede nerc palfray,   250
But a staffe was hys hakenay,[34]
    As a man in pouerté.

Sir Cleges and his son gcnt
The right waye to Cardiffe went
    Vppon Cristemas daye.   255
To the castell he cam full right,
As they were to mete dyȝt,
    Anon, the soth to saye.
In Sir Cleges thowȝt to goo,
But in pore clothyng was he tho   260
    And in sympull araye.

---

[33] basket. [34] horse.

248. The source is unknown; for analogues, see McKnight.
258. O. *at none.*

The portere seyd full hastyly,
"Thou chorle, withdrawe þe smertly,
  I rede the, without delaye;

Ellys, be God and Seint Mari,   265
I schall breke thyne hede on high;
  Go stond in beggeris rowȝt.[35]
Yf þou com more inward,
It schall þe rewe afterward,
  So i schall þe clowȝt."[36]   270
"Good sir," seyd Sir Cleges tho,
"I pray you, lat me in goo
  Nowe, without dowȝt.
The kynge i haue a present browȝtt
From Hym þat made all thynge of nowȝt;   275
  Behold all abowȝt!"

The porter to the panere went,
And the led[37] vppe he hentt;
  The cheryse he gan behold.
Will he wyst, for his comyng   280
Wyth þat present to þe kyng,
  Gret yeftis haue he schuld.
"Be Hym," he seyd, "that me bowȝt,
Into thys place comste þou nott,
  As i am man of mold,[38]   285
The thyrde part but þou graunte me
Of þat the kyng will yeve þe,
  Wethyr yt be syluer or gold."

Sir Cleges seyd, "I asent."
He yaue hym leve, and in he went,   290
  Wythout more lettyng.
In he went a gret pace;
The vsschere at the hall-dore was

---

[35] crowd.   [36] beat.   [37] lid.   [38] earth; i.e., mortal man.

266. MS. *higȝt;* Tr. emends.
267. Cf. Int. III.A.2 and "Horn" 1080.

Wyth a staffe stondynge,
In poynte[39] Cleges for to smyȝt: 295
"Goo bake, þou chorle," he seyd, "full tyȝt,
  Without teryyng!
I schall þe bette euery leth,[40]
Hede and body, wythout greth,
  Yf þou make more pressynge."[41]   300

"Good sir," seyd Sir Cleges than,
"For Hys loue þat made man,
  Sese[42] youre angrye mode!
I haue herr a present browȝt
From Hym þat made all thynge of nowȝt,   305
  And dyed on the rode.
Thys nyȝt in my gardeyne yt grewe;
Behold wethyr it be false or trewe;
  They be fayre and good."
The vsschere lyfte vp þe lede smartly   310
And sawc the cheryse verily;
  He marveld in his mode.

The vsschere seyd, "Be Mari swet,
Chorle, þou comste not in yctt,
  I tell þe sekyrly,   315
But þou me graunte, without lesyng,
The thyrd part of þi wynnyng,
  Wan þou comste ayen to me."
Sir Cleges sey non othyr von;[43]
Thereto he grauntyd sone anon;   320
  It woll non othyr be.
Than Sir Cleges with hevi chere

---

[39] ready. [40] limb. [41] importunity. [42] cease. [43] supposition; i.e., no alternative.

295. Ushers were attendants at the doors who kept the rabble from annoying guests at a feast; cf. Wright, Ch. V.
296. MS. transfers *full tyȝt* to the beginning of l. 297.
306. MS. *on rode tre;* Tr. emends.
315-6. These lines are written as one in the MS.; also 333-4.

Toke hys son and hys panere;
Into the hall went he.

The styward walkyd there withall 325
Amonge the lordis in þe hall,
  That wern rech on wede.
To Sir Cleges he went boldly
And seyd, "Ho made the soo hardi
  To com into thys stede? 330
Chorle," he seyd, "þou art to bold!
Wythdrawe the with thy clothys old
  Smartly, i the rede!"
"I haue," he seyd, "a present browȝt
From oure Lord, that vs dere bowȝt 335
  And on the rode gan blede."

The panyere he toke the styward sone,
And he pullyd out the pyne[44] [anon],
  As smertly as he myȝt.
The styward seyd, "Be Mari dere, 340
Thys sawe i neuer thys tyme of yere,
  Syn i was man wrowȝt.
Thou schalt com no nere the kynge,
But yf thowe graunt me myn askyng,
  Be Hym þat me bowȝt: 345
The thyrd partt of the kyngis yefte,
That will i haue, be my threfte,[45]
  Ar forthere gost þou nott!"

Sir Cleges bethowȝt hym than,
"My part ys lest bethwyxt þes men, 350
  And i schall haue no thynge.
For my labor schall i nott get,
But yt be a melys mete."[46]
  Thus he thouȝt syynge.

---

[44] pin, fastener. [45] thrift. [46] a meal's food.

338. Tr. supplies *anon* from O.

He[47] seyd, "Harlot, hast þou noo tonge?   355
Speke to me and terye nat longe
  And graunte me myn askynge,
Ar wyth a staffe i schall þe wake,
That thy rebys schall all toquake,[48]
  And put þe out hedlynge."[49]   360

Sir Cleges sey non othyr bote,
But his askyng graunte he most,
  And seyd with syynge sore,
"Whatsoeuer the kyng reward,
Ye schyll haue the thyrd part,   365
  Be yt lesse ar more."
[When Sir Cleges had seyd þat word,
The stewerd and he wer acorde
  And seyd to hym no more.]
Vpe to the desse Sir Cleges went   370
Full soborly and with good entent,
  Knelynge the kynge beforn.

Sir Cleges oncowyrd[50] the panyere
And schewed the kynge the cheryse clere,
  On the grovnd knelynge.   375
He seyd, "Ihesu, oure savyore,
Sent the thys frewȝt with honore
  On thys erth growynge."
The kynge sye thes cheryse newe;
He seyd, "I thanke Cryst Ihesu;   380
  Thys ys a fayre neweynge."[1]
He commaunndyd Sir Cleges to mete,
And aftyrward he thowȝt with hym to speke,
  Wythout any faylynge.

The kynge thereof made a present   385
And sent yt to a lady gent
  Was born in Cornewayle.

---

[47] i.e., the steward.   [48] that your ribs shall be shattered.   [49] headlong.   [50] uncovered. [1] novelty.

362. *Most* for *mote*.

Sche was a lady bryght and schene
And also ryght will besene,[2]
   Wythout any fayle.   390
The cheryse were servyd thorowe þe hall;
Than seyd þe kynge, þat lord ryall:
   "Be mery, be my cunnsell!
And he þat browȝt me þis present,
Full will i schall hym content;   395
   Yt schall hym will avayle."

Whan all men were mery and glade,
Anon the kynge a squire bade,
   "Brynge nowe me beforn
The pore man þat the cheryse browȝt!"   400
He cam anon and teryde natt,
   Wythout any skorn.
Whan he cam before the kynge,
On knese he fell knelynge,
   The lordis all beforn.   405
To the kyng he spake full styll;
"Lord," he seyd, "watte ys your will?
   I am youre man fre-born."

"I thanke the hartyly," seyd þe kynge,
"Of thy yeft and presentynge,   410
   That þou haste nowe idoo.
Thowe haste onowryd[3] all my fest,
Old and yonge, most and lest,
   And worschepyd me also.
Wattsooeuer þou wolt haue,   415
I will the graunnte, so God me saue,
   That thyne hart standyth to.[4]
[Wheþer it be lond our lede
Or oþer gode, so God me spede,
   How-þat-euer it go."]   420

---

[2] circumspect.   [3] honored.   [4] desires.

388. O. says that afterwards this lady was his queen, a reminiscence of
the story of Uther and Ygerne.

He seyd, "Gramarcy, lech[5] kynge !
Thys ys to me a comfortynge,
   I tell you sekyrly.
For to haue lond or lede
Or othyr reches, so God me spede,   425
   Yt ys to mech for me.
But seth i schall chese myselfe,
I pray you graunt me strokys xii
   To dele were lykyth me;
Wyth my staffe to pay hem all   430
To myn aduerseryse in þe hall,
   For Send[6] Charyté."

Than aunsswerd Hewtar[7] þe kynge,
"I repent my grauntynge
   That i to þe made.   435
God!" he seyd, "so mott i thee,
Thowe haddyst be better[8] haue gold or fee;
   More nede thereto þou hade."
Sir Cleges seyd with awaunt,[9]
"Lord, yt ys youre owyn graunte;   440
   Therefore i am full gladc."
The kynge was sory therefore,
But neuer the lesse he grauntyd hym there;
   Therefore he was full sadc.

Sir Cleges went into þe hall   445
Amonge þe gret lordis all,
   Without any more.
He sowȝt after the prowȝd styward,
For to yeve hym hys reward,
   Becavse he grevyd hym sore.   450
He yaffe the styward sech a stroke,
That he fell dovn as a bloke[10]
   Before all þat therein were,

---

[5] liege.   [6] saint.   [7] Uther.   [8] it would be better for you to.   [9] boast; i.e., boldly.
[10] block.

434. MS. *grauntetynge.*
436. MS. *Good.*
437. Written as two lines in the MS.

And after he yafe hym othyr thre;
He seyd, "Sire, for thy corteci,   455
    Smyȝte me no more!"

Out of the hall Sir Cleges went;
Moo to paye was hys entent,
    Wythout any lett.
He went to þe vsschere in a breyde:[11]   460
"Haue here sum strokys!" he seyde,
    Whan he wyth hym mete,
So þat after and many a daye
He wold warn[12] no man þe waye,
    So grymly he hym grett.   465
Sir Cleges seyd, "Be my threft,
Thowe haste the thyrd part of my yefte,
    As i the behight."

Than he went to the portere,
And iiii strokys he yaue hym there;   470
    His part hade he tho,
So þat after and many a daye
He wold warn no man þe waye,
    Neythyr to ryde nere goo.
The fyrste stroke he leyde hym on,   475
He brake in to hys schuldyr bon
    And his on arme thereto.
Sir Cleges seyd, "Be my threfte,
Thowe haste the thyrd parte of my yefte;
    The comnaunnte[13] we made soo."   480

The kynge was sett in hys parlore[14]
Wyth myrth, solas, and onor;
    Sir Cleges thedyr went.
An harpor sange a gest[15] be mowth
Of a knyȝt there be sowth,   485

---

[11] rush. [12] deny. [13] agreement. [14] small, private audience-room. [15] tale.

455. MS. *sore;* O. *sir.*
471. MS. *there;* O. *tho.*

Hymselffe, werament.
Than seyd the kynge to þe harpor,
"Were ys kny3t Cleges, tell me here;
    For þou hast wyde iwent.
Tell me trewth, yf þou can: 490
Knowyste þou of þat man?"
    The harpor seyd, "Yee, iwysse:

Sum tyme forsoth i hym knewe;
He was a kny3t of youris full trewe
    And comly of gesture.   495
We mynstrellys mysse hym sekyrly,
Seth he went out of cunntré;
    He was fayre of stature."
The kynge sayd, "Be myn hede,
I trowe þat Sir Cleges be dede,   500
    That i lovyd paramore.[16]
Wold God he were alyfe;
I hade hym levere than othyr v,
    For he was stronge in stowre."

Sir Cleges knelyd before þe kynge;   505
For he grauntyd hym hys askynge,
    He thanked hym cortesly.
Specyally the kynge hym prayed,
To tell hym whye tho strokis he payed
    To hys men thre.   510
He seyd þat he my3t nat com inward,
"Tyll euerych i graunttyd þe thyrd·partt
    Of þat ye wold yeve me.
With þat i schuld haue now3t myselfe;
Werefore i yaue hem strokis xii;   515
    Me thowt yt best, trewly."

The lordes lowe, both old a[nd] yenge,
And all that wern with þe kynge,

<hr>

[16] fervently.

488. MS. *herere.*

They made solas inowe.
The kynge lowe, so he my3t nott [sitte];　　　　520
He seyd, "Thys ys a noble wy3t,[17]
　　To God i make a wove."[18]
He sent after his styward:
"Hast þou," he seyd, "thy reward?
　Be Cryst, he ys to lowe."[19]　　　　525
The styward seyd with lokes grym,
["I thynke neuer to haue ado[20] with hym;]
　The dewle hym born on a lowe !"[21]

The kynge seyd to hym than,
"What ys thy name? tell me, good man,　　　　530
　Nowe anon rygh[t] !"
"I hig3t Sir Cleges, soo haue i blysse;
My ryght name yt ys iwysse;
　I was 3oure owyn kny3t."
"Art thou Sir Cleges, þat servyd me,　　　　535
That was soo ientyll and soo fre
　And so stronge in fyght?"
"Ye, sir lord," he seyd, "so mott i thee;
Tyll God in hevyn hade vesyte[22] me,
　Thus pouerte haue me dy3t."[23]　　　　540

The kynge yaue hym anon ry3t
All þat longed to a kny3t,
　To rech[24] hys body wyth;
The castell of Cardyffe he yaue hym thoo
[With all þe pourtenans[25] þerto,　　　　545
　To hold with pes and grythe.
Than he made hym hys stuerd
Of all hys londys afterwerd,
　Off water, lond, and frythe.[26]

---

[17] wit, jest.　[18] vow.　[19] be praised.　[20] to do.　[21] may the devil burn him in a fire.　[22] blessed.　[23] afflicted.　[24] enrich.　[25] appurtenances.　[26] woods.

520. O. *sytte;* Tr. supplies.

A cowpe[27] of gold he gafe hym blythe, 550
To bere to Dam Clarys, hys wyfe,
Tokenyng of ioy and myrthe.]

The last page of the Edinburgh manuscript is lacking. The Oxford manuscript has two more stanzas. The king makes Sir Cleges' son a squire. They return to Dame Clarice and live long and happy lives thereafter.

---

[27] cup.

THE TALE OF BERYN

THE TALE OF BERYN

This piece is one of the spurious Canterbury Tales in the Duke of Northumberland's manuscript (after 1400), where it is assigned to the Merchant on the return journey. The text is that of the edition of Furnivall and Stone for the Early English Text Society (*Extra Series* 105), with normalized capitals and punctuation and restoration of many readings of the manuscript. A flourish at the end of a word has been transcribed as *-e*. Most of the purely metrical emendations of previous editors have been removed.

The meter is that of "Gamelyn": a doggerel line tending to seven stresses and an iambic cadence.

The poem is very like a French romance, "L'Histoire du Chevalier Berinus," known in a manuscript of the fifteenth century and in a print of the sixteenth. This, in turn, has several oriental analogues, and, despite the Roman names and setting, the source of the tale is certainly oriental. Discussions of the story are in the edition mentioned above, and in "The Book of Sindibad," E. Comparetti (*Folk Lore Society* 1882), and by W. A. Clouston (privately printed, Glasgow, 1884), who lists eight oriental versions and one Spanish. Like most oriental pieces, this has been unduly neglected.

The scribe's most troublesome mannerism is omission of relatives (2924, etc.).

The extract is the trial scene, the first of its kind in the English romances. Beryn's father, Faunus, turns against him because of his profligacy and the enmity of a stepmother. As a parting gift, Beryn receives five merchant ships and their cargoes. After a storm, the fleet lands at Falsetown, where the inhabitants make a business of swindling strangers. In their courts, no matter how preposterous the testimony, no rebuttal or negative evidence is permitted; and they abet each other in swearing to falsehoods. They find Beryn easy prey: as the loser in a game of chess, he must drink all the salt water in the sea or give up his ships; a merchant, Hanybald, offers to exchange for the cargo five shiploads of such goods as Beryn shall find in his house, but removes all the goods before Beryn can seize them; a blind man accuses him of having stolen his eyes; a woman of the town asks damages because he has deserted her; and another knave, Macaigne, sells Beryn a knife, and then accuses him

of having murdered Macaigne's father with it. Beryn is indicted
on each count, and is in sore straits when Geffrey, a Roman exile
a hundred years old, so abused by the Falsetowners that he must
masquerade as a crippled beggar, offers his services. Beryn accepts,
and the accusers, fearful that he will put to sea before the trial,
appear before his ships to summon him.

When Beryn hem aspied: "Now, Geffrey, in thy honde　2910
Stont lyff and goodis; doth with vs what the list;
For all our hope is on the—comfort, help, and trist;[1]
For we must bide aventur such as God woll shape,
For nowe i am in certen we mow no wise scape."[2]
"Have no dout," quod Geffrey, "beth mery; let me aloon:　2915
Getith a peir sisours,[3] sherith my berd anoon;
And aftirward lete top[4] my hede, hastlych and blyve."
Som went to with sesours, som with a knyfe;
So what for sorowe and hast, and for lewd tole,[5]
There was no man alyve bet like to[6] a fole　　2920
Then Geffrey was. By þat tyme þey had al ido,
Hanybald clepid out Beryn, to motehall[7] for to go,
And stood oppon the brigg, with an huge route.[8]
Geffrey was the first to Hanybald gan to loute,[9]
And lokid out a-fore-shipp. "God bles ȝew, sir!" quod he.　2925
"Where art þow now, Beryn? com nere! behold and se!
Here is an huge pepill irayd and idight;[10]
All these been my children, þat been in armys bryȝte.
Ȝistirday i gate[11] hem: [is it] nat mervaill
That þey been hidir icom, to be of oure counsaill,　　2930
And to stond by vs, and help vs in oure ple.
A, myne owne childryn, blessid mut ye be!"
Quod Geffrey, with an hiȝe voise, and had a nyce[12] visage,
And gan to daunce for ioy, in the fore-stage.[13]
Hanybald lokid on Geffrey as he were amasid,[14]　　2935
And beheld his contenaunce, and howe he was irasid;[15]

---

[1] trust.　[2] escape.　[3] scissors.　[4] cut hair off the top.　[5] unsuitable instruments.
[6] more like.　[7] assembly-hall, court.　[8] throng.　[9] bow.　[10] crowd dressed up and
ready.　[11] begot.　[12] silly.　[13] forecastle.　[14] dazed.　[15] shaved.

2917. This is done to show that he is a professional jester. Cf. "Robert
of Sicily" 170 ff.
2927. MS. *in dight.*

But evir-more he þouȝt þat he was a fole,
Naturell of kynde, and had noon othir tool,[16]
As semed by his wordis and his visage both;
And þouȝt it had been foly to wex with hym wroth,   2940
And gan to bord[17] ageyn, and axid hym in game,
"Sith þow art oure ffadir, who is then oure dame?
And howe and in what plase were wee begete?"
"ȝistirday," quod Geffrey, "pleying in the strete
Att a gentill game þat clepid is the quek:[18]   2945
A longe peny-halter was cast about my nekk,
And iknet[19] fast with a ryding-knot,[20]
And cast ovir a perche and hale[d][21] along my throte."
"Was þat a game," quod Hanybald, "for to hang þyselve?"
"So þey seyd about me, a Ml[22] ech by hymselff."   2950
"How scapiddist þow," quod Hanybald, "þat þow were nat
     dede?"
"Thereto can i answere, without eny rede:
I bare thre dise[23] in myne owne purs—
For i go nevir without, fare i bettir or wors;
I kist[24] hem forth al thre, and too fil amys-ase,[25]   2955
But here now what fill aftir—riȝt a mervelouse case!—
There cam a mows lepe forth, and ete þe þird boon,[26]
That puffid out hire skyn, as grete as she myȝt goon;
And in this manere wise, of þe mouse and me
All yee be icom, my childien fulre and fre.   2960
And ȝit, or it be eve, fall wol such a chaunce,
To stond in my power ȝew alle to avaunce;
For and wee plede wele to-day, we shull be riche inowȝe."
Hanybald of his wordis hertlich louȝe,

---

[16] silly by nature and without other device (intent). [17] jest. [18] checkers. [19] tied.
[20] slip-knot. [21] projection, and drawn. [22] thousand. [23] dice. [24] cast. [25] double-
aces (the lowest possible throw). [26] bone, die.

2945. Geffrey's answers are deliberately silly; the force of this one is,
"We were playing a harmless game: they were about to hang me." *Quek*
means checkers, and is also used in the morality play "Mankind" (801)
to imitate the sound of a man strangling.
2956. MS. *mervolouse*.
2962. The infinitive stands for a complement of *such*, this fortune:
namely, to advance you, etc.

And so did al þat herd hym, as þey myʒte wele,   2965
And had grete ioy with hym for to telle,
For þey knewe hym noon othir but a fole of kynde;
And al was his discrecioune; and þat previd þe ende.[27]
    Thus whils Geffrey iapid[28], to make hire hertis liʒte,
Beryn and his company were rayid and idiʒte,   2970
And londit hem in botis, ferefull howe to spede;
For all hir þouʒtis in balance stode betwene hope and drede.
But ʒit they did hir peyn[29] to make liʒtsom chere,
As Geffrey hem had enfourmed, of port[30] and al manere
Of hire governaunce,[31] al the longe day,   2975
Tyll hir plee were endit. So went they forth hire wey,
To the court with Hanybald. Then Beryn gan to sey,
"What nedith this, Sir Hanybald, to make such aray,
Sith wee been pese-marchantis, and vse no spoliacioune?"[32]
"For soth, sire," quod Hanybald, "to me was made relacioune
Yee were in poynt to void;[33] and yef ye had do so,   2981
Yee had lost yeur lyvis, without wordis mo."
Beryn held hym still; Geffrey spak anoon;
"No les wed þen lyvis![34] whi so, good Sir Iohne?
That were somwhat to much, as it semeith me!   2985
But ye be ovir-wise þat dwell in this ceté:
For[35] yee have begonne a thing makith ʒewe riʒte bold;
And ʒit, or it be eve, as folis shul ye be hold.
And eke yee devyne;[36] for in shipmannys crafft,
Wotith litill what longith to afore-þe-shipp and bafft;[37]   2990
And namelich[38] in the dawnyng, when shipmen first arise."
"My good ffrend," quod Hanybald, in a scornyng wise,
"Ye must onys enfourme me, þurh yeur discrecioune;
But first ye must answer to a questioune:

---

[27] it was all ingenuity on his part, and the outcome proved it. [28] jested. [29] i.e., did their best. [30] demeanor. [31] conduct. [32] practice no robbery. [33] leave. [34] forfeit not only bail, but life too. [35] that. [36] make guesses. [37] the front and stern of a vessel. [38] especially.

2984. "Sir John" is a jesting name for a priest. It was first a name very commonly assumed by members of the priesthood; then it became a soubriquet for "priest;" and at length it was often used disparagingly. See Skeat's Chaucer, "Pro." 1172.

2990. MS. *and wotith.*

Why make men cros-saill in myddis of þe mast?"   2995
[Gef.] "For to talowe þe shipp, and fech[e] more last."[39]
[Han.] "Why goon the ȝemen[40] to bote, ankirs to hale?"[41]
[Gef.] "For to make hem redy to walk to þe ale."
[Han.] "Why hale they vp stonys by the crane-lyne?"
[Gef.] "To make the tempest sese, and the sonne shyne."   3000
[Han.] "Why close they the port with the see-bord?"[42]
[Gef.] "For the mastir shuld awake atte first word."[43]
[Han.] "Thow art a redy reve,"[44] quod Hanybald, "in fay."
[Gef.] "Yee sir trewly, for sothe is þat yee sey."
Geffrey evir clappid[45] as doith a watir myll,   3005
And made Hanybald to lauȝe al his hert fell.[46]
"Beryn," quod this Geffrey, "retourn thy men ageyne;
What shull they do with the[m] at court? No men on hem
     pleyne.[47]
Plede thy case thyselve, riȝt as þow hast iwrouȝt;
To bide with the shippis my purpos is and þouȝt."   3010
"Nay, for soth," quod Hanybald, "þow shalt abyde on lond;
Wee have no folis but the," and toke hym by þe hond,
"For thow art wise in lawe to plede al the case."
"That can i bettir," quod Geffrey, "þen eny man in this plase!
What seyst þow therto, Beryn? shall i tell thy tale?"   3015
Hanybald likid his wordis welc, and forward gan hym hale.[48]
Beryn made hym angry,[49] and siȝhid wondir sore,
For Geffrey hym had enfourmyd of euery poynt tofore,
How he hym shuld govern all the longe day.
     Geffrey chas[t]id[50] hym ageyne: "Sey me ȝe or nay!   3020
Maystowe nat ihere speke som maner word?"
"Leve thy blab, lewd[1] fole! me likith nat thy bord![2]

---

[39] grease the bottom and give more displacement.   [40] sailors.   [41] haul up.   [42] a plank to cover the ports.   [43] i.e., quickly.   [44] overseer.   [45] rattled on.   [46] heart's fill.   [47] accuse them.   [48] draw.   [49] feigned grief.   [50] rebuked.   [1] ignorant, stupid.   [2] humor.

2995 ff. The cross-sail is the square sail used in going rapidly before the wind. The anchors were dropped at some distance from the ship, often in shallow water; and hence at least one had to be dislodged and recovered from a small boat. The stones are being put in for ballast, Beryn's cargo having been removed by Hanybald's men.
3008. MS. *man.*

I have anothir þouȝt," quod Beryn, "whereof þowe carist lite."[3]
"Clepeist þow me a fole," quod Geffrey; "al þat i may þe wite?[4]
But first, when wee out of Rome saillid both in fere,   3025
Tho i was thy felawe and thy partynere;
For tho the marchandise was more þen halff myne;
And sith þat þowe com hidir, þowe takeist al for thyne.
But ȝit or it be eve, i woll make oon behest:[5]
But þowe have my help, thy part shal be lest."   3030
"Thyn help!" quod Beryn; "lewde fole, þow art more þen
    masid![6]
Dres the to þe shippis ward,[7] with thy crowne irasid,
For i myȝt nevir spare the bet! trus, and be agoo!"[8]
"I wol go with the," quod Geffrey, "where þow wolt or no,
And lern to plede lawe, to wyn both house and londe."   3035
"So þow shalt," quod Hanybald, and led hym by the honde,
And leyd his hond oppon his nek; but, and he had iknowe
Whom he had led, in sikirnes he had wel levir in snowe
Have walkid xl myle, and rathir then faill more;[9]
For he wisshid that Geffrey had ibe vnbore   3040
Ful offt-tyme in that day, or the ple were do;[10]
And so did al þat wrouȝt Beryn shame and woo.
    Now yee þat list abide and here of sotilté[11]
Mow knowe how þat Beryn sped in his ple,
And in what aray to the court he went;   3045
And howe Hanybald led Geffrey, disware[12] of his entent.
But ȝit he axid of Geffrey, "What is þy name, i prey?"
"Gylhochet," quod Geffrey, "men clepid me ȝistirday."
"And where weer þow ibore?" "I note, i make avowe,"
Seyd Geffrey to this Hanybald; "i axe þat of ȝewe;   3050
For i can tell no more, but here i stond nowe."
Hanybald of his wordis hertlich lowȝe,
And held hym for a passing[13] fole to serve eny lord.
Thus þey romyd ianglyng[14] into þe court ward;

---

[3] i.e., his impending trial.   [4] though I may protect you.   [5] vow.   [6] befuddled.
[7] hasten to the ship.   [8] get out and begone!   [9] and (walked) many more (even)
more readily.   [10] suit was completed.   [11] trickery.   [12] unaware.   [13] excellent.
[14] bandying words.

But or they com ther, the Steward was iset, 3055
And the grettest of þe towne, a company imet
And gon to stryve fast who shuld have þe good
That com was with Beryn ovir þe salt flood.
Som seyd oon, and som seyde anothire;
Som wold have the shippis, þe parell, and þe rothir;[15] 3060
Som his eyen, som his lyff wold have, and no les;
Or els he shuld for hem fyne,[16] or he did pas.
And in the mene-whils[17] they were in this afray,
Beryn and these Romeyns were com, in good aray
As myȝt be made of woll and of coloure greynyd;[18] 3065
They toke a syde-bench þat for hem was ordeyned.
   When all was husst[19] and still, Beryn rose anoon
And stode in the myddis of þe hal, tofore hem everychone,
And seyd, "Sir Steward, in me shall be no let:
I am icom to answere as my day is set. 3070
Do me ryȝte and reson: i axe ȝewe no more."
"So shall [i]," quod the Steward, "for þerto i am swore."
   "He shall have ryȝt," quod Geffrey, "where þow wolt or no.
For, and þow mys onys thy iugement on do,[20]
I woll to þe Emperour of Rome, my cosyne; 3075
For of o cup he and i ful offt have dronk þe wyne,
And ȝit wee shull hereaftir, as offt as wee mete,
For he is long[21] the gladdere when i send hym to grete "
Thus Geffrey stode oppon a fourme,[22] for he wold be sey
Above all the othir the shuldris and the cry,[23] 3080
And starid al aboute, with his lewd[24] berd,
And was ihold a verry[25] fole of ech man [þat] hym herd.
   The Steward and þe officers and þe burgeyssis alle

---

[15] tackle and rudder.   [16] pay ransom.   [17] while.   [18] wool and fast-dyed colors.
[19] hushed.   [20] impose your judgment wrongly.   [21] by far.   [22] bench.   [23] above
the shoulders and tumult of all the others.   [24] absurd.   [25] true.

3055. Evander the Steward is in league with the accusers, and has
already given decisions against Beryn.
3056. The right reading probably is *town in company imet*. The loose
syntax of the next clause is of no importance.—F.
3083. The various accusations and the solutions are all in the French
original; but the English story is more ingenious in not disposing of each
accusation as it is made, but waiting until the charges are complete.

Lauȝhid at hym hertlich; the crioure gan to calle
The burgeys þat had pleyd with Beryn atte ches;   3085
And he aros quiklich, and gan hym for to dres²⁶
Afore the Steward atte barr, as þe maner is.
He gan to tell his tale with grete redynes;
"Here me, Sir Steward! þis day is me set,
To have ryght and reson—i ax ȝewe no bet,—   3090
Of Beryn, þat here stondith, þat with me ȝistirday
Made a certen covenaunt, and atte ches we did pley:
That whoso were imatid²⁷ of vs both too
Shuld do the todirs byddyng; and yf he wold nat so,
He must drynke al the watir þat salt were in the se;   3095
Thus i to hym surid,²⁸ and he also to me."
To preve my tale trewe, i am nat al aloon."
Vp rose x burgeysis quyklich anoon,
And affermyd evir[y] word of his tale soth;
And made hem al redy for to do²⁹ hire othe.   3100
    Evandir the Steward, "Beryn, now," quod he,
"Thow must answere nede; it wol noon othir be;
Take thy counsell to the: spede on! have i doon."
Beryn held hym still: Geffrey spak anoon:
    "Now be my trowith," quod Geffrey, "i mervell much of
        ȝewe   3105
To bid vs go to counsell, and knowith³⁰ me wise inowȝ,
And evir ful avisid, in twynkelyng of an eye,
To make a short answere, but yf my mowith be dry.
Shuld wee go to counsell for o word or tweyne?
Be my trowtith we nyl! let se mo that pleyne!³¹   3110
And but he be ianswerd, and þat riȝt anoon,
I ȝeve ȝewe leve to rise and walk out, everychoon,
And aspy redely yf ye fynd me there.
In the meen-whils, i wol abide here.
Nay, i telle trewly, i am wiser þen yee ween;   3115

---

²⁶ go. ²⁷ mated, beaten. ²⁸ assured. ²⁹ take. ³⁰ knowing me to be. ³¹ i.e.,
produce other complainants.

3103. Line 3102 is repeated after this.
3113. I.e., if the plaintiffs are not answered, it will be because Geffrey
is out of the courtroom.

For þere nys noon of ʒewe woot redely what i meen."
Every man gan lawʒe al his hert fill
Of Geffrey and his wordis; but Beryn held hym still,
And was cleen astonyd,—but ʒit, nere-þe-lattir,[32]
He held it nat al foly þat Geffrey did clatir,[33]   3120
But wisely hym governyd, as Geffrey hym tauʒte,
For parcell of his wisdom tofore he had smaught.[34]
"Sire Steward," quod Beryn, "i vndirstond wele
The tale of þis burgeyse; now let anothir tel,
That i may take counsell, and answer al att onys."   3125
"I graunt," quod the Steward, "thyn axing, for þe nonys,
Sith þow wolt be rewlid by þy folis rede;
For he is ryʒte[35] a wise man to help the in thy nede !"
     Vp arose the accusours, queyntlich[36] anoon;
Hanybald was the first of hem evirichone,   3130
And gan to tell his tale with a proud chere:
"ʒistirday, soverens, when i was here,
Beryn and thes burgeyse gon to plede[37] fast
For pleying atte ches; so ferforth,[38] atte last,
Thurh vertu of myne office, þat i had in charge   3135
Beryns fyve shippis, for[39] to go at large,
And to be in answere here þis same day.
So, walkyng to the strond ward, wee bargeynyd by the wey
That i shuld have the marchaundise þat Beryn with hym brouʒte
(Wherof i am sesid,[40] as ful sold and bouʒte),   3140
In covenaunt that i shuld his shippis fill ageyne
Of my marchaundise, such as he tofore had seyne
In myne owne plase, howsis to or thre,
Ful of marchandise as they myʒt be.
And i am evir redy: when-so-evir he woll,   3145
Let hym go or sende, and charge[41] his shippis full
Of such marchandise as he fyndith there:
For in such wordis wee accordit[42] were."
     Vp rose x burgeysis—not tho þat rose tofore,
But oþir,—and made hem redy to have swore   3150

---

[32] nevertheless. [33] babble. [34] for he had tasted a bit of his wisdom before.
[35] indeed. [36] with alacrity. [37] have a dispute over. [38] to such an extent. [39] i.e.,
so as to permit him. [40] in possession. [41] load. [42] agreed.

That every word of Hanybald, from þe begynnyng to þe ende,
Was soth and eke trewe; and with all hir mende[43]
Ful prest they were to preve; and seyd þey were present
Atte covenaunte makeing, by God omnipotent.
    "It shall nede," quod Geffrey, "whils þat i here stonde;   3155
For i woll preve it myself with my riȝt honde.
For i have been in foure batellis heretofore,
And this shall be the ffifft; and therfor i am swore;
Beholdith and seith !" and turnyd hym aboute.
The Steward and þe burgeyse gamyd[44] al aboute;   3160
The Romens held hem still, and lawuȝid but a lite.
    With that cam the blynd man, his tale to endite,[45]
That God hym graunte wynnyng riȝte as he hath aservid.[46]
Beryn and his company stood al astryvid
Betwene hope and drede, riȝte in hiȝe distres;   3165
For of wele or of woo þey had no sikirnes.[47]
"Beryn," quod this blynd, "þouȝe i may nat se,
Stond nere ȝit the barr: my comyng is for the:
That wrongfullich þowe witholdist my both to eyen,[48]
The wich i toke the for a tyme, and quyklich to me hyen,   3170
And take hem me ageyn, as our covenant was.
Beryn, i take no reward[49] of othir mennys case,
But oonlich of myne owne, that stont me most an hond.[50]
Nowe blessid be God in heven, þat brouȝt þe to this lond !
For sith our laste parting, many bittir teris   3175
Have i lete for thy love, þat som tyme partineris[1]
Of wynnyng and of lesing[2] were, ȝeris fele;
And evir i fond the trewe, til at the last þow didist stele
Awey with my too eyen that i toke to the

---

[43] memory. [44] jested. [45] say over. [46] deserved. [47] certainty. [48] both my two
eyes. [49] regard. [50] is especially pressing to me. [1] partners. [2] losing.

3158. I.e., he jestingly proposes a tríal by combat, and offers himself
as experienced in such affairs.
3164. The rhyme-word is probably *asterued*, in bad condition, nearly
dead.
3170. The construction is: "Which I gave you (so that you might)
come soon to me and give them back, as we agreed."
3176. Though the syntax is involved, the meaning is clear. The antecedent of *þat* is *our*.

To se the tregitour[i]s pley,[3] and hir sotilté, 3180
As ʒistirday here in this same plase
Tofore ʒewe, Sir Steward, rehersid as it was.
Ful trewe is that byword,[4] 'a man to seruesabill
Ledith offt Beyard from his owne stabill.'
Beryn, by the i meen, þouʒe þowe make it straunge;[5] 3185
For þow knowist trewly þat i made no chaunge[6]
Of my good eyen for thyne, þat badder[7] were."
Therewith stood vp burgeys four, witnes to bere.

Beryn held hym still, and Geffrey spak anoon:
"Nowe of þy lewde[8] compleynt and thy masid moon,[9] 3190
By my trowith," quod Geffrey, "i have grete mervaill.
For þouʒe þow haddist eyen-sight, [y]it shuld it litil availl:
Thow shuldist nevir fare þe bet, but þe wors, in fay;
For al thing may be stil nowe for the[10] in house and way;
And yf thow haddist þyn eyen, þowe woldist no counsell hele.[11]
I knowe wele by thy fisnamy,[12] thy kynd were to stele; 3196
And eke it is thy profite and thyne ese also
To be blynd as þowe art; for nowe, whereso þow go,
Thow hast thy lyvlode,[13] whils þow art alyve;
And yf þowe myʒtist see, þow shuldist nevir thryve." 3200
Al the house þurhout, save Beryn and his feris,
Lawʒid of[14] Geffrey, þat watir on hire leris
Ran downe from hir eyen, for his masid[15] wit.

With that cam þe vomman—hir tunge was nat sclytt[16]—
With xv burgeysis and vommen also fele[17] 3205
Hir querell[18] for to preve, and Beryn to apele,[19]
With a feire knave-child iloke[20] within hir armys;
And gan to tell hir tale of wrongis and of armys,[21]

---

[3] jugglers' performance. [4] proverb. [5] of you I complain though you feign lack of acquaintance. [6] exchange. [7] worse. [8] stupid. [9] muddled lament. [10] for all that you can do. [11] hide; i.e., use discretion. [12] face. [13] sustenance. [14] at. [15] perverse. [16] slit; i.e., she was not dumb. [17] as many. [18] complaint. [19] accuse. [20] clasped. [21] injuries.

3183. Bayard was a common name for a horse; and since horses were valuable property, "Bayard" was often used as a symbol of treasure or wealth. The proverb means that a man too kind to others will assist them to take his own best treasure.

3200. I.e., he would be hanged for stealing.

And eke of vnkyndnes, vntrowith,[22] and falshede
That Beryn had iwrouȝt to hire, þat queyntlich[23] from hire ȝede
Anoon oppon hire wedding, when he his will had doon,　　3211
And brouȝt hir with child, and lete her sit aloon
Without help and comfort from þat day; "and noweȝ
He proferid me nat to kis onys with his mowith,
As ȝistirday, Sir Steward, afore ȝewe eche word　　3215
Was rehersid here; my pleynt is of record,
And this day is me set for to have reson:[24]
Let hym make amendis, or els tell encheson[25]
Why hym ouȝt nat fynd[26] me, as man ouȝt his wyffe."
These fifftene burgeysis, quyklich also blyve,　　3220
And as fele vymmen as stode by hire there,
Seyd that they were present when they weddit were,
And that every word þat þe vomman seyde
Was trewe, and eke Beryn had hire so betrayd.
　　"Benedicite!" quod Geffrey, "Beryn, hast þowe a wyff?　　3225
Now have God my trowith, the dayis of my lyff
I shall trust the þe las! Þow toldist me nat tofore
As wele of thy wedding and of thy sone ibore.
Go to, and kis hem both, thy wyff and eke thyn heire!
Be þow nat ashamyd, for þey both be feyr!　　3230
This wedding was riȝt pryvy, but i shal make it couthe:
Behold, thy sone, it semeth, crope[27] out of þy mowith,
And eke of thy condicioune both sofft and some.
Now am i glad þyne heir shall with vs to Rome;
And i shall tech hym as i can whils þat he is ȝong,　　3235
Every day by the strete to gadir houndis doung,[28]
Tyll it be abill of prentyse to crafft of tan[e]ry,[29]
And aftir i shall teche hym for to cache a fly,
And to mend mytens[30] when they been to-tore,
And aftir to cloute shoon,[31] when he is elder more:　　3240

---

[22] untruth.　[23] craftily.　[24] reckoning.　[25] cause.　[26] provide for.　[27] crept; i.e., the resemblance is strong.　[28] dung.　[29] till the child is able to be apprenticed to the business of tanning.　[30] mittens.　[31] patch shoes.

3223. MS. *vommen*.
3233. The more usual spelling is *saught and some* (accordant and fitting).
3237. *Taury*, as printed by Urry, means whitening leather. Either reading makes nonsense.

ʒit, for his parentyne, to pipe as doith a mowse,
I woll hym tech, and for to pike a snayll out of his house,
And to berk as doith an hound, and sey 'Baw bawe!'
And turne round aboute, as a cat doith with a strawe;
And to blete as doith a shepe, and ney as doith an hors,   3245
And to lowe as doith a cowe; and as myne owne corps[32].
I woll cherissh hym every day, for his modirs sake;"
And gan to stapp[33] nere, the child to have itake,
As semyd by his contenaunce, alþouʒe he þouʒt nat so.

Butte modir was evir ware, and blenchid[34] to and fro,   3250
And leyd hire hond betwene, and lokid somwhat wroth;
And Geffrey in pure wrath beshrewid[35] hem al bothe;
"For by my trowith," quod Geffrey, "wel masid is thy pan![36]
For i woll teche thy sone the craftis þat i can,
That he in tyme to com myʒt wyn his lyvlood.   3255
To wex therfor angry, þow art verry wood!
Of husbond, wyff, and sone, by the Trynyté,
I note wich is the wisest of hem al[le] thre!"
"No, sothly," quod the Steward, "it liith al in þy noll,[37]
Both wit and wisdome, and previth by þy poll."[38]   3260
For al be that Geffrey wordit[39] sotilly,
The Steward and þe burgeysis held it for foly,
Al that evir he seyd, and toke it for good game,
And had ful litill knowlech he was Geffrey þe lame

Beryn and his company stode still as stone,   3265
Betwene hope and drede, disware[40] how it shuld goon;
Saff Beryn trist in party[41] þat Geffrey wold hym help;
But ʒit into þat houre he had no cause to ʒelpe,[42]
Wherfor þey made much sorow, þat dole was, and peté.
Geffrey herd hym siʒe sore; "What devill is[43] ʒewe?" quod he;
"What nede ʒew be sory, whils i stonde here?   3271

---

[32] body.   [33] step.   [34] twisted.   [35] cursed, abused.   [36] head.   [37] pate.   [38] (shaven)
crown.   [39] spoke.   [40] uncertain.   [41] except that Beryn trusted in part.   [42] boast.
[43] is (wrong with).

3241. The only examples of *parentyne* in the *Oxford Dictionary* are from
this poem, where it is glossed "parentage." It seems rather to mean
"training."
3249. MS. *nat nat.*
3264. Geffrey was well known to them; they had robbed him of all
'.is money, and he had pretended to be a cripple so as to escape death.

Have i nat enfourmyd ȝewe how and in what manere
That i ȝew wold help, and bryng hem in the snare?
Yf yee coude plede as wele as i, ful litill wold yee care.
Pluke[44] vp thy hert!" quod Geffrey; "Beryn, i speke to the!"
"Leve þy blab leude!"[45] quod Beryn to hym a-ye,   3276
"It doith nothing availl þat[46] sorowe com on thy hede!
It is nat worth a fly, al þat þowe hast seyde!
Have wee nat els nowe for to thynk oppon,
Saff here to iangill?"[47] Machyn rose anoon,   3280
And went to the barr, and gan to tell his tale:
He was as fals as Iudas, þat set Criste at sale.

   "Sir Steward," quod this Machyn, "and þe burgeysis all,
Knowith wele howe Melan, with purpill and with pall,[48]
And othir marchandise, seven ȝere ago   3285
Went toward Rome; and howe þat i also
Have enquerid sith, as reson woll, and kynde,
Syth he was my ffadir, to knowe of his ende.
For ȝit sith his departyng, til it was ȝistirday,
Met i nevir creature þat me coude wissh[49] or say   3290
Reedynes[50] of my ffadir, dede othir alyve.
But blessid be God in heven, in this thevis sclyve,[1]
The knyff i gaff my ffadir was ȝistirday ifound.
Sith i hym apele,[2] let hym be fast ibound.
The knyff i knowe wel inowe; also þe man stont here   3295
And dwellith in this towne, and is a cotelere,[3]
That made þe same knyff with his too hondis,
That wele i woot þere is noon like, to sech al Cristen londis;
For iii preciouse stonys been within the hafft[4]
Perfitlych icouchid, and sotillich by crafft[5]   3300
Endendit[6] in the hafft, and þat riȝt coriously:[7]

---

[44] pluck.   [45] ignorant babble.   [46] i.e., to prevent.   [47] except here to have words.
[48] rich cloth.   [49] inform.   [50] sure knowledge.   [1] sleeve.   [2] accuse.   [3] cutler.
[4] handle.   [5] set and expertly by skill.   [6] fixed.   [7] with careful art.

3283. A close parallel to this incident is in the Irish "Echtra Cormaic i Tir Tairngiri," which otherwise is little like the "Tale of Beryn."

3292. The sleeve was a convenient place for carrying small articles. Cf. the proverb, "The friar preached against stealing when he had a pudding up his sleeve."

A saphir and a salidone and a rich ruby."
The cotelere cam lepeing forth with a bold chere,
And seyd to the Steward, "Þat Machyn told now here,
Every word is trew: so beth the stonys sett; 3305
I made þe knyff myselff—who myȝt know it bet?—
And toke the knyff to Machyn, and he me payd wele:
So is this felon gilty; there is no more to tell."
Vp arose burgeysis, by to, by iii, by iiii,
And seyd þey were present, þe same tyme and houre, 3310
When Machone wept sore, and brouȝt his ffadirs gownd,[8]
And gaff hym þe same knyff oppon the see stronde.
 "Bethe there eny mo pleyntis of record?"
Quod Geffrey to the Steward. And he ageynward:
"How semeth the, Gylhoget? beth þere nat inowȝe? 3315
Make thyne answere, Beryn, case[9] þat þow mowe;
For oon or othir þow must sey, alþouȝe it nat availl;
And but þowe lese or þowe go, me þinkith grete mervaill."
 Beryn goith to counsell, and his company;
And Geffrey bode behynde, to here more, and se, 3320
And to shewe the burgeyse somwhat of his hert,
And seyd, "But i make the pleyntyfs for to smert,
And al þat hem meyntenyth, for auȝt þat is iseyd,
I woll graunte ȝewe to kut þe eris fro my hede.
My mastir is at counsell, but counsell hath he noon; 3325
For but i hym help, he is cleen vndoon.
But i woll help hym al þat i can, and meynten hym also
By my power and connyng; so i am bound thereto.
For i durst wage batell[10] with ȝewe, þouȝe yee be stronge,
That my mastir is in the trowith, and yee be in the wrong: 3330
For and wee have lawe,[11] i ne hold ȝew but distroyed
In yeur owne falshede, so be ye now aspied;[12]
Wherfor, ȝit or eve i shall abate yeur pride,
That som of ȝew shall be riȝt feyne to sclynk[13] awey and hyde."

---

[8] gown. [9] if. [10] agree to a judicial duel. [11] i.e., right judgment. [12] found out. [13] slink.

3302. A celidony was red or black, and was thought to come from the stomach of a swallow. Cf. "Anglo-Norman Lapidaries," P. Studer and J. Evans.

The burgeysis gon to lawȝe, and scornyd hym thereto.   3335
"Gylochet," quod Evander, "and þow cowdist so
Bryng it þus about, it were a redy way."[14]
"He is a good fool," quod Hanybald, "in fay,
To put hymselff aloon in strengith, and eke in witt,
Ageyns al the burgeysis þat on þis bench sit."   3340
   "What clatir is this," quod Machyn, "al day with a fole?
Tyme is nowe to worch with som othir tole.
For i am certeyn of hir answere þat they wolle faill;
And lyf for lyf of my ffadir,[15] what may þat availl?
Wherfor beth avisid, for i am in no doute,   3345
The goodis been sufficient to part al aboute;
So may euery party-pleyntyff have his part."
"That is reson," quod the blynd; "a trew man þow art;
And eke it were vntrowith, and eke grete syn,
But ech of vs þat pleynyth myȝt somwhat wyn."   3350
   Hanybald bote[16] his lyppis, and herd hem both wele:
"Towching the marchandise, o tale i shall ȝew tell,
And eke make avowe, and hold my behest:[17]
That of the marchandise yeur part shall be lest;
For i have made a bargeyn þat may nat be vndo;   3355
I woll hold his covenaunt, and he shall myne also."
   Vp roos quyklich the burgeyse Syrophanes:
"Hanybald," quod he, "the lawe goith by no lanys,[18]
But hold forth the streyt wey, even as doith a lyne;
For ȝistirday when Beryn with me did dyne,   3360
I was the first persone þat put hym in arest;
And for he wold go large, þow haddist in charge and hest[19]
To sese both shipp and goodis, til i were answerid;
Then must i first be servid: þis knowith al men ilerid."
   The vomman stode besidis, and cried wondir fast: 3365
"Ful soth is þat byword,[20] 'to pot who comyth last,
He worst is servid;' and so it farith by me:
Ȝit nethirles, Sir Steward, i trust to yeur leuté,[21]
That knowith best my cause and my trew entent;
I ax ȝewe no more but riȝtfull iugement.   3370

---

[14] easy way (out of trouble).   [15] i.e., if Beryn is killed in reprisal.   [16] bit.
[17] promise.   [18] by-paths.   [19] command.   [20] proverb.   [21] uprightness.
   3358. L. 3352 is repeated here in the MS.

Let me have part with othir, sith he my husbond is:
Good sirs, beth avisid: i axe ȝew nat amys."
  Thus they gon to stryve, and were of hiȝe[22] mode
For to depart[23] among hem othir mennys good,
Where they tofore had nevir properté,   3375
Ne nevir shuld þereaftir, by doom of equyté,
But they had othir cause þen þey had tho.
  Beryn wȧs at counsell; his hert was ful woo,
And his meyny sory, distrakt, and al amayide;[24]
For tho they levid noon othir but[25] Geffrey had hem trayde: 3380
Because he was so long, they coude no maner rede;
But everich by hymselff wisshid he had be dede:
"O myȝtfull God!" þey seyd, "i trow, tofore this day
Was nevir gretter tresoun, fere, ne affray[26]
Iwrouȝt onto mankynde, þen now is to vs here;   3385
And namelich[27] by this Geffrey, with his sotil chere!
So feithfulle he made it[28] he wold vs help echone;
And nowe we be imyryd,[29] he letith vs sit aloon!"
"Of Geffrey," quod Beryn, "be as it be may:
Wee mut answere nede;[30] ther is noon oþir way;   3390
And therfor let me know yeur wit and yeur counsaille."
They wept and wrong hire hondis, and gan to waille
The tyme þat they were bore; and shortly, of þe lyve
The[y] wisshid þat þey were. With þat cam Geffrey blyve,
Passing hem towardis, and began to smyle.   3395
Beryn axid Geffrey wher he had be al the while;
"Have mercy oppon vs, and help vs as þowe hiȝte!"
"I woll help ȝew riȝt wele, þurh grace of Goddis myȝte;
And i can tell ȝew tyding of hir governaunce:
They stond in altircacioune and stryff in poynt to praunce[31] 3400
To depart[32] yeure goodis, and levith verryly
That it were impossibill ȝewe to remedy.
But hire hiȝe pryde and hir presumpcioune
Shal be, ȝit or eve, hir confusioune,
And to make amendis, ech man for his pleynt.   3405
Let se therfor yeur good avise, howe þey myȝt be ateynt."[33]

[22] angry. [23] divide. [24] dismayed. [25] nothing else except that. [26] fear or
fright. [27] especially. [28] professed. [29] stuck in the mire. [30] must needs answer.
[31] on the verge of swaggering away. [32] share. [33] convicted.

The Romeyns stode still, as who had shore hire hed.[34]
"In feith," quod Beryn, "wee con no maner rede;
But in God and 3ewe we submit vs all,
Body, lyffe, and goodis, to stond or to fall;   3410
And nevir for to travers[35] o word þat þow seyst:
Help vs, good Geffrey, as wele as þow maist!"
"Depardeux,"[36] quod Geffrey, "and i wol do me peyn
To help 3ewe, as my connyng wol strech and ateyne."

The Romeyns went to barr, and Geffrey al tofore,   3415
With a nyce contenaunce, barefote, and totore,
Pleyng with a 3erd[37] he bare in his honde,
And was evir wistlyng[38] att euery pase comyng.

The Steward and the burgeysis had game inow3e
Of Geffreyis nyce comyng, and hertlich low3e,   3420
And eche man seyd, "Gylhochet, com nere:
Thowe art ry3t welcom, for þowe makist vs chere."
"The same welcom," quod Geffrey, "þat yee wol vs,
Fall oppon yeur hedis, i prey to God, and wers!"
They held hym for a verry fole, but he held hem wel more:[39] 3425
And so he made hem in breff tyme, alþou3 þey wer nat shore.

"Styntith[40] nowe," quod Geffrey, "and let make pese!
Of myrthis and of iapis[41] tyme is now to cese,
And speke of othir mater þat wee have to doon,
For and wee hewe amys eny maner spone,[42]   3430
We knowe wele in certeyn what pardon wee shull have.
The more is our nede vs to defend and save.
My mastir hath bee at counsell, and ful avisid is
That i shall have the wordis,—speke i wele or mys.[43]
Wherfor, Sir Steward and yee burgeysis all,   3435
Sittith vpry3t and wriith nat,[44] for auntris þat may fall.
For and yee deme vntrewly or do vs eny wrong,
Wee shull be refourmyd,[45] be ye nevir so strong,

---

[34] cut their heads off. [35] oppose. [36] by heaven. [37] stick. [38] whistling. [39] greater
(fools). [40] stop. [41] jesting. [42] chip; i.e., make any sort of mistake. [43] badly.
[44] conceal nothing. [45] redressed.

3407. See the note to line 3779.
3425. MS. *hym wel.* I.e., he held them greater fools than himself, and
made them appear so, although their heads were not shorn like his own.
3438. MS. *Yee shull.*

Of euery poynt and iniury, and þat in grete hast,
For he is nat vnknowe to vs þat may ȝewe chast.[46]   3440
Hold forthe the riȝt wey, and by no side-lanys!
    And as towching the first pleyntyfe Syrophanes,
That pleyde with my mastir ȝistirday atte ches
And made a certen covenaunte, who þat had þe wers
In the last game (alþouȝe i were nat there)   3445
Shuld do the todirs bidding, whatsoevir it were,
Or drynk al the watir þat salt were in the see;
Thus, i trowe, Sir Steward, ye woll record þe ple:
And yf i have imyssid[47] in lettir or in word
The lawe, wol i be rewlid aftir yeure record;[48]   3450
For we be ful avisid in this wise to answere."
    Evander þe Steward and al men þat were there
Had mervill much of Geffrey, þat spak so redely,
Whose wordis ther[to]for semyd al foly,
And were astonyed cleen, and gan for to drede;   3455
And euery man til othir lenyd with his hede,
And seyd, "He reportid the tale riȝt formally;[49]
He was no fool in certen, but wise, ware, and scly:[50]
For he hath but iiapid[1] vs, and scornyd heretofore,
And wee have hold hym a fole; but wee be wel more!"[2]   3460 .
Thus they stodied[3] on Geffrey, and lauȝid þo riȝt nauȝt.
    When Geffrey had aspied they were in such þouȝt,
And hir hertis trobelid, pensyff, and anoyed,
Hym list to dryv in bet þe nayll, til they were fully cloyid.[4]
"Soveren sirs," he seyd, "sith þat it so is   3465
That in reportyng of our ple yee fynd nothing amys—
As previth wele yeur scilence,—eke yee withseyith[5] not
O word of our tale, but [fynde it] clene without spot;[6]
Then to our answere i prey ȝewe take hede,
For wee wol sey al the trowith, riȝt as it is indede.   3470
For this is soth and certeyne: it may nat be withseyd:
That Beryn, þat here stondith, was þus ovirpleid[7]

---

[46] chastise. [47] misstated. [48] corrected by your remembrance. [49] in good form.
[50] cunning. [1] made fun of. [2] i.e., greater fools. [3] pondered. [4] sharply pricked.
[5] deny. [6] defect. [7] outdone.

3440. A reference to the wise Isope, the ruler of the country.
3468. Words supplied by Furnivall.

In the last game, when wagir was opon;
But þat was his sufferaunce,[8] as ye shul here anoon.
For in al this ceté ther nys no maner man   3475
Can pley bettir atte ches þen my mastir can;
Ne bet þen i, þouȝe i it sey, can nat half so much.
N[ow]e how he lost it be his will, the cause i wol teehe:
For ye wend, and ween, þat ye had hym engyned;[9]
But yee shul fele in every veyn þat ye be vndirmyned   3480
And ibrouȝt at ground, and eke ovirmusid.[10]
   And aȝenst the first[11] þat Beryn is acusid,
Hereith nowe entyntyflich:[12] when wee were on the see,
Such a tempest on vs fill þat noon myȝt othir se,
Of þundir, wynd, and liȝtenyng, and stormys ther among; 3485
xv dayis duryng[13] the tempest was so strong,
That ech man til othir began hym for to shryve,
And made hire avowis, yf þey myȝte have þe lyve,
Som to sech the Sepulkir, and som to oþir plase,
To sech holy seyntis, for help and for grace;   3490
Som to fast and do penaunce, and som do almys-dede;
Tyl atte last, as God wold, a voise to vs seyde,
In our most turment, and desperate of mynde,
That yf we wold be savid, my mastir must hym bynde
Be feith and eke by vowe, when he cam to londe,   3495
To drynke al the salt watir within the se-stronde,
Without drynkyng any sope[14] of þe fressh watir,
And tauȝt hym al the sotilté: how and in what manere
That he shuld wirch by engyne[15] and by a sotill charme
To drynk al the salt watir, and have hymselff no harme: 3500
But stop the ffressh ryvers by euery cost side,
That they entir nat in the se þurh þe world wyde!

---

[8] condescension. [9] tricked. [10] bewildered. [11] with regard to the first (charge).
[12] attentively. [13] lasting; i.e., continuously. [14] bit. [15] trickery.

3477. [Nor can anyone play] better than I, though I say it, [who]
know, etc.
3489. MS. *se the the.* Vipan's emendation. The Holy Sepulcher at
Jerusalem was the most famous of medieval shrines, and pilgrimages to
it were thought especially meritorious; but many had to be content with
visits to the less distant shrines of the saints (3490).
3493. The usual word is *desperaunce,* despair.

The voyse we herd, but nauȝt wee sawe, so were our wittis
    ravid:[16]
For this was [the] end fynally,[17] yf we lust be savid.
Wherfor my mastir Beryn, when he cam to this port,   3505
To his avowe and promys he made his first resort,[18]
Ere that he wold bergeyne[19] any marchandise.
And riȝt so doith these[20] marchandis in the same wise,
That maken hir avowis in saving of hire lyvis:
They completyn hire pilgremagis or þey se hir wyvis.   3510
So mowe ye vndirstond þat my mastir Beryn
Of fre will was imatid, as he þat was a pilgrym,
And myȝt nat perfourme by many-þowsand part[21]
His avowe and his hest, without riȝt sotil art,
Without help and strengith of many mennys myȝte.   3515
Sir Steward and Sir Burgeyse, yf we shul have riȝte,
Sirophanes must do [the] cost and aventur[22]
To stopp al the ffressh ryvers into þe see þat entir.
For Beryn is redy in al thing hym to quyte;
Ho-so be in defaute must pay for the wite.[23]   3520
Sith yee been wise all, what nede is much clatir?[24]
There was no covenaunte hem betwen to drynk fressh water."
    When Sirophanes had iherd al Geffreyis tale,
He stode al abasshid, with coloure wan and pale,
And lokid oppon the Steward with a rewful chere   3525
And on othir frendshipp and neyȝbours he had there,
And preyd hem of counsell, the answere to reply.
    "These Romeyns," quod the Steward, "been wondir scly,[25]
And eke riȝt ynmagytyff, and of sotill art,
That i am in grete dowte howe yee shull depart   3530
Without harm in oon side.[26] Our lawis, wel þowe wost,
Is to pay damagis and eke also the cost
Of euery party-plentyff þat fallith in his pleynt.

---

[16] taken away. [17] i.e., final terms. [18] i.e., gave his first attention. [19] barter.
[20] i.e., all. [21] by the many-thousandth part. [22] must pay for the expense and
the risk. [23] whosoever is in arrears must pay for his offense. [24] rambling
talk. [25] clever. [26] i.e., in either event.

3520. MS. *So ho.*
3529. *Ynmagytyff* is not in the *Oxford Dictionary*, but is intended for
imaginatif, inventive.

Let hym go quyte, i counsell, yf it may so be queynt."[27]
"I merveill," quod Syrophanes, "of hir sotilté;   3535
But sith þat it so stondith and may noon othir be,
I do woll be[28] counsell;" and grauntid Beryn quyte.
But Geffrey þou3t anothir, and without respite,
"Sirs," he seyd, "wee wetith wele þat yee wol do vs ri3te,
And so ye must nedis, and so yee have vs hi3te;   3540
And therfor, Sir Steward, ye occupy [y]our plase;
And yee knowe wele what law woll in this case.
My mastir is redy to perfourme his avowe."
"Geffrey," quod the Steward, "i can nat wete howe
To stop all the ffressh watir were possibilité."   3545
"3is, in soth," quod Geffrey, "who had of gold plenté
As man coude wissh, and it my3t wel be do.
But þat is nat our defaute he hath no tresour to.[29]
Let hym go to[30] in hast, or fynd vs suerté
To make amendis to Beryne for his iniquité,   3550
Wrong, and harm, and trespas, and vndewe wexacioune,
Loss of sale of marchandise, disese and tribulacioune,
That wee have sustenyd þurh his iniquité.
What vaylith it to tary[31] vs? for þou3 [ye] sotil bee,
Wee shull have reson, where yee woll or no.   3555
So wol wee þat ye knowe what þat wee wol do:
In certen, ful avisid to Isope for to pase,
And declare euery poynt, þe more and eke the lase,
That of yeur opyn errours hath pleyn[32] correccioune;
And ageyns his iugement is noon proteccioune!   3560
He is yeur lord riall, and soveren iugg and lele;[33]
That, and ye wrie in eny poynt,[34] to hym liith oure apele."
 So when the Steward had iherd, and þe burgeysis all,
Howe Geffrey had isteryd, þat went so ny3e the gall,[35]

---

[27] settled. [28] will act according to. [29] for the purpose. [30] set about his task.
[31] hinder. [32] full. [33] judge and worthy. [34] go amiss in any particular.
[35] managed, who came so near to the sore spot.

 3547. The syntax is poor, but the sense apparent. Render *who* (3546) as "[grant that] some one."
 3552. MS. *lost*.
 3554. MS. *þou3 sotil pry*. The emendation is on analogy with 3592.—Vipan.
 3562. MS. *ye work*. Cf. 3436.

What for shame and drede of more harme and repreff,[36]   3565
They made Syrophanes, weer hym looth or leffe,
To take Beryn gage,[37] and plegg fynd also,
To byde þe ward[38] and iugement of þat he had mysdo.
    "Nowe ferthermore," quod Geffrey, "sith þat it so is
That of the first pleyntyff wee have sikirnes,   3570
Nowe to the marchant wee must nedis answere,
That bargayned[39] with Beryn al þat his shippis bere,
In covenaunte þat he shuld his shippis fill ageyne
Of othir marchandise, þat he tofore had seyne
In Hanybaldis plase, howsis too or thre,   3575
Ful of marchandise as they my3t be.
Let vs pas thidir, yf eny thing be there
At our lust and likeing, as they accordit were."[40]
"I graunt wele," quod Hanybald; "þow axist but ri3te."
Vp arose these burgeysis,—"þowe axist but ri3te:"—   3580
The Steward and his comperis[41] entrid first þe house,
And sawe nothing within, strawe ne leffe ne mowse,
Save tymbir and þe tyle-stonys and þe wallis white.
"I trowe," quod the Steward, "the wynnyng woll be but lite
That Beryn wol nowe gete in Hanybaldis pleynte;   3585
For i can se noon othir but they wol be atteynt."[42]
And clepid hem in echone, and went out hymselve.
As soon as they were entrid, they sawe no maner selve[43]
For soris of hir hert; but as tofore is seyd,
The house was cleen iswept. þen Geffrey feir þey preyde   3590
To help [hem] yf he coude.   "Let me aloon!" quod he,
"3it shull they have the wors, as sotill as þey bee."
    Evander the Steward in the mene while
Spak to the burgeyse, and began to smyle:
"Thou3e Syrophanes by ihold these Romeyns for to curs,   3595

---

[36] shame.   [37] pledge.   [38] award.   [39] exchanged.   [40] i.e., under the terms of the
agreement.   [41] fellows.   [42] convicted; i.e., refused a decree.   [43] salve.

3567. "To give Beryn a pledge," usually a glove.   This served as a
public acknowledgment of the debt.
3580. Recopied from the preceding line.
3595. The reading is bad, the usual expression being *be biholden*, be
constrained.

ȝit i trow þat Hanybald woll put hym to þe wers;
For i am suyr and certeyn, within they shul nat fynde."
  "What sey yee be my pleynt, sirs?" quod the blynde,
"For i make avowe i wol nevir cese
Tyl Sirophanes have of Beryn a pleyn[44] relese,   3600
And to make hym quyte of his submyssioune;[45]
Els woll i have no peté of his contricioune,
But folow hym also fersly as i can or may,
Tyl i have his eyen, both to, away."
  "Now in feith," quod Machyn, "and i wol have his lyffe! 3605
For þouȝe he scape ȝewe all, with me wol he nat stryffe,
But be riȝt feyn in hert al his good forsake[46]
For to scape with his lyff, and to me it take."
  Beryn and his feleshipp were within the house,
And speken of hir answere, and made but litill rouse;   3610
But evir preyd Geffrey to help yf he coude ouȝt.[47]
  "I woll nat faill," quod Geffrey, and was tofore beþouȝt[48]
Of too botirfliis, as white as eny snowe:
He lete hem flee within the house, þat aftir on the wowe[49]
They clevid[50] wondir fast, as hire kynde woll,   3615
Aftir they had flowe, to rest anothir quile.
  When Geffrey sawe the botirfliis cleving on þe wall,
The Steward and þe burgeys in he gan call:
"Lo, sirs," he seyde, "whosoevir repent,[1]
Wee have chose marchandise most to oure talent,[2]   3620
That wee fynd herein. Behold, Sir Hanyball,
The ȝondir bottirflyis, þat clevith on þe wall:
Of such yee must fille oure shippis al fyve.
Pluk vp thy hert, Beryn, for þow must nedis thryve!
For when wee out of Rome, in marchantfare went,   3625
To purchase buttirflyes was our most entent.[3]
ȝit woll i tell the cause especial and why:

---

[44] complete. [45] i.e., relieved of his obligation. [46] relinquish. [47] i.e., any means.
[48] had before thought (to bring). [49] wall. [50] clung. [1] regret it. [2] liking.
[3] principal purpose.

3597. *Nat find* is used absolutely for "not find anything."
3610. The *Oxford Dictionary* lists *rouse* as an isolated occurrence. The
senses under *roose*, boast, flatter, are satisfactory in this poem.
3616. MS. *anothir pull.*

There is a leche in Room þat hath imade a cry[4]
To make an oyntement to cure al tho been blynde
And all maner infirmytees þat growith in man-kynde.　　3630
The day is short, the work is long: Sir Hanyball, ye mut hy !"
　　When Hanybald herd this tale, he seyd pryuely
In counsell to the Steward, "In soth i have þe wors:
For i am sikir by þis pleynt þat i shal litil purs."[5]
"So me semeth," quod the Steward, "for in þe world rounde 3635
So many botirflyis wold nat be founde,
I trowe, o shipp to charge.[6]　Wherfor me þinkith best,
Lete hym have his good ageyn, and be in pese and rest.
And ȝit is an auntir and[7] þowe scape so,
Thy covenaunt to relese without more ado."　　　　　3640
　　The burgeysis everichon þat were of þat ceté
Were anoyid sore when they herd of þis plee.
Geffrey with his wisdom held hem hard and streyte,[8]
That they were accombrit[9] in hire owne disceyte.
　　When Hanybald with his ffrendis had spoke of þis matere, 3645
They drowe hem toward Beryn, and seid in þis manere:
"Oonly for botirflyes ye com fro yeur contrey;
And wee ȝewe tell in sikirnes, and opon oure fey,
That so many botirflyes wee shul nevir gete:
Wherfor we be avisid othirwise to trete:[10]　　　　　3650
That Hanybald shall relese his covenaunt þat is makid,
And delyvir the good ageyn þat from ȝewe was ransakid,[11]
And wexe[12] ȝewe no more, but let ȝew go in pese."
"Nay, for soth," quod Geffrey, "vs nedith no relese !
Yee shull hold oure covenaunt, and wee shul yeurs also, 3655
For wee shull have reson, where ye wol or no.
Whils Isope is alyve, i am nothing aferd;
For i can wipe al this ple cleen from yeur berd

---

[4] publicly announced his intention.　[5] be in pocket.　[6] load.　[7] mere chance
that.　[8] tight.　[9] overwhelmed.　[10] we should be wise to make another agreement.　[11] taken as loot.　[12] vex.

3658. The expression apparently means, "I can take the case out of
your hands (and before Isope)." Cf. the proverbial phrases "wipe some
one's nose" (take by fraud) and "shave some one's beard" (defraud, do
out of); the line in the text may be a mixture of the two.

And ye blench[13] onys out of the hy-wey."
Thé proferid hym plegg and gage,[14] without more deley.   3660
   "Now ferthirmore," quod Geffrey, "vs ouȝt to procede,
For to the blynd mannys poynt we must answere nede:
That for to tel trowith, he lyvith al to long;
For his owne fawte and his owne wrong
On Beryn he hath surmysid,[15] as previth by his ple;   3665
And þat yee shulle opynlich knowe wele and se.
For as i vndirstod hym, he seyd þat fele ȝeris,
Beryn, þat here stondith, and he were pertyneris
Of wynnyng and of lesyng, as men it vse and doith;
And that þey chaungit eyen; and ȝit þis is sothe.   3670
But the cause of chaunging ȝit is to ȝewe onknow;[16]
Wherfor i wol declare it, both to hiȝe and lowe.
In that same tyme þat þis burgeys blynde
And my mastir Beryn, as fast as feith myȝt bynde,
Were marchaundis in comyn[16a] of al þat þey myȝt wyn,   3675
Saff[17] of lyffe and lyme and of dedely synne,
There fill in tho marchis[18] of al thing such a derth
That ioy, comfort, and solas, and al maner myrth
Was exilid cleen, saff oonly molestacioune,
That abood contenuell, and also dispiracioune.   3680
So when þat the pepill were in most myscheff,
God þat is above, þat al thing doith releve,
Sent hem such plenté of mony, fruyte, and corne,
Wich turned al to ioy hire mournyng al toforne.
Then gaff they hem to myrth, revel, pley, and song;   3685
And þankid God above, evir-more among,[19]
Of hire relevacioune[20] from woo into gladnes:
For aftir soure when swete is com, it is a plesant mes.[21]
So in the meen-while[22] of this prosperité,
There cam such a pleyer into þe same contré,   3690
That nevir theretofore was seyn such anothir;

---

[13] flinch, shy.   [14] surety and bond.   [15] blamed.   [16] unknown.   [16a] common.
[17] except.   [18] that region.   [19] continually.   [20] relief.   [21] course (at dinner).
[22] midst.

3661. On the impersonal verb, cf. Int. VII.A.1.
3676. I.e., neither shared the other's bodily organs or worst sins; an
important point in the case.

That wele was the creature þat born was of his modir
That myȝt se the mirthis²³ of this iogeloure;
For of the world wyde tho dayis he bare þe floure.²⁴
For there nas man ne vomman in þat regioune   3695
That set of hymselff the store of a boton²⁵
Yf he had nat sey his myrthis and his game.
  So oppon a tyme, this pleyer did proclame
That alle maner of pepill [þat] his pleyis wold se
Shuld com oppon a certen day to þe grete ceté.   3700
Then among othir, my mastir here, Beryn,
And this same blynd, þat pledith now with hym,
Made a certen covenaunt þat þey wold see
The mervellis of this pleyer and his sotilté.
So what for hete of somyr, age and febilnes,   3705
And eke also þe long way, this blynde for werynes
Fil flat adowne to the erth: o foot ne myȝt he go;
Wherfor my mastir Beryn in hert was ful woo,
And seyd, 'My ffrend, how nowe? mowe ye no ferþer pas?'
'No,' he seyd, 'by Hym þat first madc mas!²⁶   3710
And ȝit i had levir, as God my soule save,
Se these wondir pleyis þen al the good i have!'
'I can nat els,' quod Beryn, 'but yf it may nat be
But þat yee and i mut retourn aȝe,
Afftir yee be refresshid of yeur werynes;   3715
For to leve ȝewe in this plyte, it were no gentilnes.'
  Then seyd this blynd, 'I am avisid bet:
Beryn, yce shull wend thidir without eny let,
And have myne eyen with ȝewe, þat they þe pley mowe se,
And i woll have yeurs tyll ye com aȝe.'   3720
Thus was hir covenaunt made, as i to ȝewe report,
For ese²⁷ of this blynd, and most for his comfort.
But wotith wele the hole science of al surgery
Was vnyd,²⁸ or the chaunge was made of both [hir] eye,
With many sotill enchauntours, and eke nygramancers,²⁹ 3725
That sent were for the nonys, mastris and scoleris;

²³ entertainment. ²⁴ bore the flower, was preëminent. ²⁵ worth of a button.
²⁶ the service of the mass. ²⁷ relief from trouble. ²⁸ united. ²⁹ magicians.

3713. Probably *but* is superfluous and anticipates the construction in
the next line.

So when al was complete, my mastir went his way
With this mannys eyen, and sawe al the pley,
And hastly retourned into that plase aye,
And fond this blynd seching, on hondis and on kne   3730
Grasping al aboute to fynd þat he had lore—
Beryn his both eyen,[30] þat he had tofore!
But as sone as Beryn had pleyne knowleche
That his eyen were ilost, vnneth he myȝt areche[31]
O word, for pure anguyssh þat he toke sodenly,   3735
And from þat day till nowȝe ne myȝt he nevir spy
This man in no plase there lawe was imevid;[32]
But nowe in his presence the soth is ful iprevid,
That he shall make amendis or he hen[ny]s pas,
Riȝte as the lawe wol deme, ethir more or les.   3740
For my mastris eyen were bettir and more clere
Then these þat he hath nowe, to se both fer and nere;
So wold he have his owne, þat propir[33] were of kynde;
For he is evir redy to take to the blynde
The eyen þat he had of hym, as covenaunt was,   3745
So he woll do the same. Nowe, soverens, in this cas
Ye mut take hede for to deme riȝte;
For it were no reson my mastir shuld lese his siȝte
For his trew hert and his gentilnes."
    "Beryn," quod the blynd tho, "i woll the relese   3750
My quarell,[34] and my cause, and fal[35] fro my pleynt."
    "Thow mut nede," quod Geffrey, "for þow art atteynt![36]
So mut þow profir gage, and borowis[37] fynd also,
For to make amendis, as othir have ido.
Sire Steward, do vs lawe,[38] sith wee desire but riȝte!   3755
As wee been pese-marchandis, vs longith nat to fiȝte,
But pleyn vs to the lawe, yf so wee be agrevid."
    Anoon oppon that Geffrey þese wordis had imevid,[39]
The blynd man fond borowis for al his maletalent,[40]
And were ientrid[41] in the court to byde þe iugement;   3760
For þouȝe þat he blynd were, ȝit had he good plenté,
And more wold have wonne, þurh his iniquité.

---

[30] Beryn's two eyes.   [31] command.   [32] pleaded.   [33] suitable.   [34] complaint.
[35] withdraw.   [36] convicted.   [37] sureties.   [38] give us justice.   [39] spoken as a plea.
[40] malevolence.   [41] (they) were entered (on the records).

"Nowe herith, sirs," quod Geffrey, "th[r]e pleyntyfs been
    assurid:
And as anenst þe ferth this vomman hath arerid,[42]
That pleynyth here on Beryn, and seyith she is his wyff,   3765
And þat she hath many a day led a peynous[43] lyff,
And much sorowe endurid, his child to sustene;
And al is soth and trewe. Nowe riȝtfullich to deme,
Whethir of hem both shal othir obey,
And folow wil[44] and lustis, Sir Steward, ye mut sey."   3770
   And þerewith Geffrey lokid asyde on this vomman,
Howe she chaungit colours, pale, and eke wan:
"Al for nouȝt," quod Geffrey, "for yee mut with vs go,
And endur with yeur husbond both wele and woo;"
And wold have take hir by þe hond; but she awey did breyde,
And with a grete sighing, þese wordis she seyd: 3776
That ageyns Beryn she wold plede no more:
But gagid with too borowis,[45] as othir had do tofore.
   The Steward sat as still as who had shore his hede,
And specially the pleyntifs were in much drede: 3780
Geffrey set his wordis in such manere wise
That wele they wist þe[y] myȝt nat scape in no wise
Without los of goodis, for damage and for cost,
For such were hir lawis where pleyntis were ilost.
   Geffrey had ful perseyte of hire encombirment;[46]   3785
And eke he was in certen þat the iugement
Shuld pas[47] with his mastir; wherfor he anoon,
"Soveren sirs," he seyd, "ȝit must wee ferþer goon,
And answere to this Machyn, þat seith þe knyff is his
That found was on Beryn: thereof he seith nat amys.   3790
And for more pryve[48] he seith in this manere:

---

[42] as for the fourth (suit that) this woman has brought. [43] troubled. [44] i.e.,
which shall follow the other's will. [45] gave bail through two suretics. [46] per-
ception of their embarrassment. [47] be given in favor of. [48] proof.

3763. Vipan's emendation.
3771. MS. *aseyd*. "Geffrey noticed, with a sidelong glance. . . ."
3779. See *Oxford Dictionary, shave*, v., 5.c. A jocular way of saying,
"as if some one had cut off his head." After splitting an opponent's skull,
Ipomadon says (8087): *A monke ye may be when ye will, For ye be shavynne
wile þertill, And right wele be ye crownde . . . For ye be shavyne rounde.*
3791. MS. *pryvy*.

That here stondith present the same cotelere
That þe knyffe made, and þe precious stonys thre
Within the hafft been couchid, þat in Cristyanité,
Thouʒe men wold of purpose make serch and siche,[49]   3795
Men shuld nat fynd in al thing a knyff þat were it lich:
And more opyn pryue[50] þan mannys owne knowlech,
Men of lawe ne clerkis con nat tell ne teche.
Now sith wee be in this manere thus ferforth[1] ago,
Then were spedful[2] for to knowe howe Beryn cam first t[h]o   3800
To have possessioune of the knyff þat Machyn seith is his:
To ʒewe vnknowe, i shall enfourme þe trowith as it is.
    Nowe vii yeer be passid, oppon a Tuysday
In the Passion-Woke,[3] when men leven pley
And vse more devosioune, fastyng, and preyere   3805
Then in othir tyme or seson of þe ʒeer,
This Beryns ffadir erlich wold arise,
And barefote go to chirch, to [don] Goddis service,
And lay hymselff aloon, from his owne wyff,
In reverence of þe tyme and mending of his lyff.   3810
So on the same Tuysday þat i tofore nempt,[4]
This Beryn rose and rayd hym, and to þe chirch went,
And mervelid in his hert his ffadir was nat there,
And homward went ageyn, with drede and eke fere.
Into his ffadirs chambir sodenlich he rakid,[5]   3815
And fond hym ligg, stan-dede,[6] oppon the strawe al nakid,
And the clothis halyd[7] from the bed away.
'Out, alas!' quod Beryn, 'that evir i sawe this day!'
The meyné herd the noyse, how Beryn cried 'Allas!'
And cam into the chambir, al þat therin was.   3820
But the dole and the sorowe and anguyssh þat was there,
It vaylith nat at this tyme to declare it here;
But Beryne had most of all, have ye no doute.
And anoon they serchid the body al aboute,
And fond this same knyff, þe poynt riʒt at his hert   3825

---

[49] seek.   [50] proof.   [1] far.   [2] profitable.   [3] Holy Week.   [4] named, mentioned.
[5] rushed.   [6] stone-dead.   [7] dragged.

3797. MS. þat mannys.
3803. MS. vii yeer and passid.

Of Beryns ffadir, whose teris gan outstert
When he drow3 out the knyff of his ffadirs wound:
Then stan-dede[8] i sawe hym fal doun to þe ground,
In si3te of the most part þat beth with hym nowe here."
(And they affermyd it for sothe, as Geffrey did hem lere:) 3830
"And 3it had i nevir suspecioun, from þat day til noweth,[9]
Who did þat cursid dede, till Machyn with his mowith
Afore 3ewe hath knowlechid þat the knyff is his:
So mut he nedis answere for his deth, iwis."
    When Machyn had iherd al Geffreyis tale, 3835
He rose of bench sodynly, with coloure wan and pale,
And seyd onto Beryn, "Sir, ageyn the
I wolle plete no more; for it were gret peté
To combir 3ewe with accions,[10] þat beth of nobill kynde."
"Graunte mercy, sir!" quod Geffrey, "but 3it yee shulle fynde
Borowis, or yee pas, amendis for to make 3841
For our vndewe vexacioune, and gage also vs take
In signe of submissioun for yeur iniury,
As lawe woll and resone; for wee woll vttirly[11]
Procede, tyll wee have iugement finall. 3845
And therfor, Sir Steward, what þat evir fall,
Delay vs no lenger, but gyve us iugement!
For tristith ye noon othir but we be fullich bent[12]
To Isope for to wend, and in his hi3e presence
Reherce all oure plees, and have his sentence;[13] 3850
Then shul yee make[14] ffynys, and hi3lich be agrevid."
    And as sone as the Steward herd these wordis mevid,[15]
"Reson, ry3te, and lawe," seyd the Steward tho,
"Yee mut nedis have, where i woll or no.
And to preve my full will, or wee ferþer goon," 3855
Quiklich he comaundit, and sparid nevir oon,
xxiiii burgeysis in lawe best ilerid,
Rehersyng hem the plees, and how Geffrey answerid;
And on lyffe and lym and forfetur of good,
And as they wold nat lese the ball within hire hood,[16] 3860
To drawe apart togidir, and by hire al assent,
Spare no man on lyve, to gyve trewe iugement.

---

[8] i.e., fainting. [9] now. [10] load you with lawsuits, who are. [11] to the end.
[12] determined. [13] opinion. [14] pay. [15] uttered. [16] i.e., their heads.

And when these xxiiii burgeysis had iherd
The charge of the Steward, riȝt sore þey were aferd
To lese hire owne lyvis, but they demyd trowith;   3865
And eke of hire neyȝbours þey had grete rowith,
For they perseyvid clerelich, in þe plee þurhoute,
Hire ffrendis had þe wors side; þerof þey had no doute:
"And yff wee deme trewly, þey wol be sore anoyid;
Ȝit it is bettir then wee be shamyd and distroyed."   3870
And anoon þey were accordit, and seyd with[17] Beryn,
And demed euery pleyntyff to make a grete fyne
With Beryn, and hym submyt hoolich[18] to his grace
Body, good, and catell, for wrong and hire trespase,
So forforth, till atte last it was so boute[19] ibore   3875
That Beryn had the dobill good[20] þat he had tofore,
And with ioy and myrth, with al his company,
He drouȝe hym to his shippis ward,[21] with song and melody.
    The Steward and þe burgeyse from þe court bent[22]
Into hir owne placis; and evir as they went,   3880
They talkid of þe Romeyns, howe sotil thé were
To aray hym like a fole þat for hem shuld answere.
"What vaylith it," quod Hanybald, "to angir or to curs?
And ȝit i am in certen i shall fare the wers
All the dayis of my lyff for þis dayis pleding.   3885
And so shall al the remnaunt, and hir hondis wryng,
Both Serophanus, and þe blynde, þe vomman, and Machayne,
And be bet avisid er they efftsonys pleyne;
And all othir personys within this ceté,
Mell[23] the les with Romeyns, whils þey here be.   3890
For such anothir fole was nevir ȝit iborne,
For he did nauȝt ellis but evir with vs scorne,
Tyl he had vs cauȝt, even by the shyn,[24]
With his sotill wittis, in our owne gren."[25]

The great Isope is so well pleased with Beryn's success in outwittng
the Falsetowners that he induces him to live with him and marry his
daughter. "May we all find as good a friend in need!"

---

[17] judged in favor of. [18] entirely. [19] to such an extent . . . that it was brought
about. [20] twice the goods. [21] toward his ships. [22] went. [23] meddle. [24] shin,
leg. [25] snare.

3868. *þerof* is repeated in the MS.

3894. At the end of the tale is this note: *Nomen autoris presentis
cronica Rome, Et translatoris filius ecclesie Thome* (i.e., Canterbury).

ROBERT OF SICILY

ROBERT OF SICILY

Strictly speaking, this is a pious legend, told to edify rather than to amuse. It is included in a vólume of romances as an example of a literature that borders on fiction and often uses its methods, but differs from it in being supposedly founded on fact. Its style is simple, severe, and reverent.

The writer's original is unknown, although many analogues have been discovered. For these, see Hibbard 58, and Wells 162. The poem was composed before 1370, probably in the south midlands. The scribe frequently writes *ou* for *you*, and uses *-u-* for *-i-* (*gult*, *guilt*).

Through the kindness of the authorities of the Bodleian Library, it has been possible to prepare the text from a rotograph of the Vernon Manuscript, MS. English Poetry A.1, fol. 300 ff. The divisions in the poem are as marked in the manuscript.

> Princes proude þat beþ in pres,[1]
> I wol ou telle þing not lees.[2]
> In Cisyle was a noble kyng,
> Fair and strong and sumdel ȝyng;
> He hedde a broþer in grete Roome,　　　5
> Pope of al Cristendome;
> Anoþer he hedde in Alemayne,[3]
> An emperour, þat Saraȝins wrouȝte payne.
> Þe kyng was hote Kyng Robert;
> Neuer mon ne wuste him fert.[4]　　　10
> He was kyng of gret honour,
> For þat he was conquerour;
> In al þe world nas his peer,
> Kyng ne prince, fer ne neer;
> And for he was of chiualrie flour,　　　15

---

[1] who are proud amid the throng.　[2] false.　[3] Germany.　[4] afraid.

Heading. The MS. has, *Her is of Kyng Robert of Cicyle, Hou pride dude him begyle.*

His broþer was mad emperour;
His oþer broþer, Godes vikere,[5]
Pope of Rome, as i seide ere.
Þe pope was hote Pope Vrban:
He was good to God and man.   20
Þe emperour was hote Valemounde;
A strengur weorreour nas non founde
After his broþer of Cisyle,
Of whom þat i schal telle a while.

    Þe Kyng þhouȝte he hedde no peer   25
In al þe world, fer no neer,
And in his þouȝt he hedde pryde,
For he was nounpeer[6] in vch a syde.

    At midsomer, a[7] Seynt Iones Niht,[3]
Þe Kyng to churche com ful riht   30
For to heeren his euensong.
Hym þouhte he dwelled þer ful long:
He þouhte more in worldes honour
Þen in Crist, vr saueour.
In *Magnificat* he herde a vers;   35
He made a clerk hit him rehers
In langage of his owne tonge;
In Latyn he nuste what heo songe.
Þe vers was þis, i telle þe:
"Deposuit potentes de sede,   40
Et exaltauit humiles."
Þis was þe vers, wiþouten les.

    Þe clerk seide anon riht,
"Sire, such is Godes miht
Þat he may make heyȝe lowe   45
And lowe heiȝe, in luytel þrowe;[9]
God may do, wiþoute lyȝe,
His wil, in twynklyng of an eiȝe."

---

[5] vicar. [6] umpire, judge in disputes; hence a person of importance. [7] on.
[8] June 24, St. John's Night. [9] space.

35. The Magnificat (Luke 1:46) was a psalm sung by the Virgin Mary.
It is used in the vesper service.

41. "He hath put down the mighty from their seats, and exalted them
of low degree" (52). MS. *exultauit*.

þe Kyng seide, wiþ herte vnstable,[10]
"Al ȝor song is fals and fable;[11] 50
What mon haþ such pouwer
Me to bringe lowe in daunger?[12]
I am flour of chiualrye;
Myn enemys i may distruye;[13]
No mon lyueþ in no londe 55
þat me may wiþstonde;
þen is þis a song of nouht!"
þis errour he hedde in þouȝt,
And in his þouht a sleep him tok
In his pulput,[14] as seiþ þe bok. 60
　Whon þat euensong was al don,
A kyng ilyk[15] him out gan gon,
And alle men wiþ hym gan wende;
Kyng Robert lafte out of mynde.[16]
　þe newe kyng was, as i ou telle, 65
Godes angel, his pruide to felle.
　þe angel in halle ioye made,
And alle men of hym weore glade.
þe Kyng wakede þat lay in churche:
His men he þouhte wo to worche 70
For he was laft þer alon
And derk niht him fel vppon.
He gan crie after his men:
þer nas non þat spak aȝen;
But þe sexteyn, atten eende,[17] 75
Of þe churche to him gan wende,
And seide, "What dost þou nouþe[18] her,
þou false þef, þou losenger?[19]
þou art her wiþ ffelenye,
Holy churche to robbye!"[20] 80
　He seide, "Foule gadelyng,[21]
I am no þef; i am a kyng!

---

[10] inconstant.　[11] a lie.　[12] power.　[13] destroy.　[14] royal pew.　[15] like.　[16] was quite forgotten.　[17] at last.　[18] now.　[19] lying knave.　[20] rob.　[21] rascal.

60. The book is unknown.

Opene þe churche-dore anon,
Þat i mowe to my paleis gon!"
  Þe sexteyn þouhte anon wiþ-þan[22]   85
Þat he was sum wood man,
And wolde þe chirche dilyueret were
Of hym, for he hedde fere,
And openede þe chirche-dore in haste.
Þe Kyng bygon to renne out faste,   90
As a mon þat was wood.
At his paleys ȝate he stood,
And heet þe porter gadelyng,
And bad hym come in hiȝing,[23]
Anon þe ȝates vp to do.   95
Þe porter seide, "Ho clepeþ so?"
He onswerde anon þo,
"Þou schalt witen ar i go:
Þi kyng i am: þou schalt knowe!
In prison þou schalt ligge lowe,   100
And ben anhonged and todrawe
As a traytur bi þe lawe.
Þou schalt wel witen i am kyng!
Open þe ȝates, gadelyng!"
  Þe porter seide, "So mot i þe,   105
Þe Kyng is mid his meyné!
Wel i wot, wiþoute doute,
Þe Kyng nis not now wiþoute."
Þe porter com into halle,
Bifore þe newe kyng aknes[24] gan falle,   110
And seide, "Þer is atte ȝate
A nyce fool[25] icome late;[26]
He seiþ he is lord and kyng,
And clept me foule gadelyng.
Lord, what wol ȝe þat i do: 115
Leten him in, or leten him go?"
  Þe angel seide in haste,
"Do him come in swiþe faste,
For my fol i wole him make

---

[22] thereupon.   [23] haste.   [24] on his knees.   [25] silly fool.   [26] just now.

Forte[27] he þe nome of kyng forsake." 120
 Þe porter com to þe ʒate,
And him he called, in to late.[28]
He smot þe porter whon he com in
Þat blod barst out of mouþ and chyn.
Þe porter ʒeld him his trauayle:[29] 125
Him smot aʒeyn, wiþouten fayle,
Þat neose and mouþ barst a-blood;
Þenne he semed almost wod.
 Þe porter and his men in haste
Kyng Robert in a podel[30] caste; 130
Vnsemely heo maden his bodi þan,
Þat he nas lyk non oþer man,
And brouht him bifore þe newe kyng
And seide, "Lord, þis gadelyng
Me haþ smyte withoute decert:[31] 135
He seiþ he is vr kyng apert.[32]
Þis harlot[33] ouʒte, for his sawe,[34]
Ben ihonged and todrawe,
For he seiþ non oþer word
Bote þat he is boþe kyng and lord." 140
 Þe angel seide to Kyng Robert,
"Þou art a fol, þat art not ffert
Mi men to don such vilenye;
Þi gult þou most nede abuye.
What art þou?" seide þe angel. 145
Qwath Robert, "Þou schalt wite wel
Þat i am kyng, and kyng wol be!
Wiþ wronge þou hast my dignité.[35]
Þe Pope of Roome is my broþer,
And þe Emperour myn oþer: 150
Heo wol me wreke, for soþ to telle;
I wot heo nulle not longe dwelle!"
 "Þow art my fol," seide þe angel;
"Þou schal be schoren,[36] euerichdel,
Lych a fool, a fool to be. 155

[27] until. [28] let. [29] repaid him for his pains. [30] puddle. [31] deserving. [32] openly. [33] vagabond. [34] speech, assertion. [35] dignity; i.e., usurp my state. [36] shaved.

Wher is now þi dignité?
Þi counseyler schal ben an ape,
And o cloþing ou worþ ischape:[37]
I schal him cloþen as þi broþer
Of o cloþing: hit is non oþer.[38]   160
He schal beo þin owne feere:
Sum wit of him þou miht lere!
Houndes, how so hit falle,
Schulen eten wiþ þe in halle;
Þou schalt eten on þe ground;   165
Þin assayour[39] schal ben an hound,
To assaye þi mete bifore þe.
Wher is now þi dignité?"
He heet a barbur him bifore,
Þat as a fool he schulde be schore   170
Al around, lich a frere,
An honde-brede[40] boue eiþer ere,
And on his croune make a crois.
He gan crie and make nois:
He swor þei schulde alle abuye,   175
Þat him dude such vileynye;
And euere he seide he was lord,
And vche mon scorned him for þat word,
And vche mon seide he was wod;
Þat proued wel he couþe no good,[41]   180
For he wende in none wyse
Þat God Almihti couþe deuyse
Him to bringe to lower stat;[42]—
Wiþ o drauht he was chekmat![43]
Wiþ houndes eueri niht he lay,   185
And ofte he criȝede weylaway
Þat he euere was ibore,
For he was a mon forlore.
Þer nas in court grom ne page

---

[37] the same sort of clothes shall be made for both of you. [38] it shall not be otherwise. [39] taster (to provide against poison or bad cooking). [40] hand-breadth. [41] had no wisdom. [42] state. [43] move he was checkmated.

166. An assayer was also one who placed the food before the diner. Probably both functions are included in the term here.

þat of þe Kyng ne made rage,[44]   190
For no mon ne mihte him knowe:
He was defygured[45] in a þrowe.
So lowe er þat was neuer kyng;
Allas, her was a deolful[46] þing,
þat him scholde for his pryde   195
Such hap among his men betyde!
Hunger and þurste he hedde grete,
For he ne moste no mete ete
But houndes eeten of his disch,
Wheþer hit weore fflesch or ffisch.   200
He was to deþe neiȝ ibrouht
For hunger, ar he miht eten ouht
Wiþ houndes þat beþ in halle;
How miȝt him hardore bifalle?
And whon hit nolde non oþur be,[47]   205
He eet wiþ houndes gret plenté.
    þe angel was kyng, him þhouȝte long;[48]
In his tyme was neuer wrong,
Tricherie, ne falshede, ne no gyle
Idon in þe lond of Cisyle.   210
Alle goode þer was gret plenté:
Among men loue and charité;
In his tyme was neuer strif
Bitwene mon and his wyf;
Vche mon louede wel oþer: 215
Beter loue nas neuere of broþer.
þenne was þat a ioyful þing
In londe to haue such a kyng;
Kyng he was þreo ȝeer and more.—
Robert ȝeode as mon forlore.   220
    Seþþe hit fel vppon a day
A luytel bifore þe moneþ of May,
Sire Valemound, þe Emperour,
Sende lettres of gret honour

---

[44] sport. [45] altered in appearance. [46] sorry. [47] would not be otherwise. [48] it seemed long to him; cf. 407. He wishes to return to heaven.

195. MS. *þat he.*

To his broþer, of Cisyle Kyng, 225
And bad him come withouten lettyng,
Þat heo mihten beo boþe isome
Wiþ heore broþer, Pope of Rome.
Hym þhouȝte long heo weore atwinne;[49]
He bad him lette for no wynne,[50] 230
Þat he neore of good aray[1]
In Roome an Holy þoresday.[2]
   Þe angel welcomede þe messagers
And ȝaf hem cloþes riche of pers,[3]
Furred al wiþ ermyne; 235
In Cristendom is non so fyne;
And al was chouched mid perré.[4]
Better was non in Cristianté.
Such cloþ, and hit weore to dihte,
Al Cristendom hit make ne mihte. 240
Of þat wondrede al þat lond,
Hou þat cloþ was wrouȝt wiþ hond;
Wher such cloþ was to selle,
Ne ho hit maade, couþe no mon telle.
   Þe messagers wenten with þe Kyng 245
To grete Rome, wiþoute lettyng.
Þe ffool Robert also went,
Cloþed in lodly garnement,[5]
Wiþ ffoxes tayles mony aboute:
Men miht him knowen in þe route! 250
   Þe angel was cloþed al in whit;
Nas neuer seyȝe such samyt;[6]
And al was chouched[7] myd perles riche:
Neuer mon seiȝ none hem liche.
Al was whit, atyr and steede; 255
Þe steede was feir þer he ȝede;

---

[49] apart. [50] gain; i.e., consideration. [1] clothing; ie., festival attire. [2] Ascension Day, ten days before Whitsunday. It usually comes in May (cf. 222). [3] sky-blue material. [4] set with jewels. [5] hideous clothing. [6] rich silk. [7] adorned.

255. MS. *Al whit atyr was.* Horstmann's emendation.
256. Another MS. has *place* for *steede.*

So feir a steede as he on rod
Nas neuer mon þat euer bistrod.
  Þe angel com to Roome sone,
Real, as fel a kyng to done;[8]   260
So real kyng com neuere in Rome;
Alle men wondrede wheþen he come.
His men weore realliche[9] diht:
Heore richesse con seye no wiht.
Of cloþus, gurdeles, and oþer þing,   265
Eueriche sqyȝer þhouȝte a kyng,
And alle ride of riche aray
Bote Kyng Robert, as i ow say:
Alle men on him gon pyke,[10]
For he rod al oþer vnlyke: 270
An ape rod of his cloþing,[11]
In tokne þat he was vnderlyng.
Þe Pope and þe Emperour also
And oþer lordes mony mo
Welcomede þe angel as for kyng,   275
And made ioye of his comyng.
Þeose þreo breþeren made cumfort;[12]
Þe angel was broþer mad bi sort;[13]
Wel was þe Pope and Emperour
Þat hedden a broþur of such honour!   280
  Forþ con sturte Kyng Robert
As ffol and mon þat nas not fert,
And criȝede wiþ ful egre speche
To his breþeren to don him wreche
Of him þat haþ with queynte gyle[14]   285
His coroune and lond of Cisyle.
Þe Pope ne þe Emperour nouþer
Þe ffol ne kneuȝ not for heor broþer.
Þo was he more fol iholde,
More þen er a þousend folde,   290
To cleyme such a breþerhede:

___

[8] royally as befitted a king. [9] royally. [10] peer. [11] i.e., clad as he was. [12] merriment. [13] destiny. [14] through a clever trick.

281. MS. *com.*

Hit was holde a foles dede.
Kyng Robert bigon to maken care,[15]
Muche more þen he dude are,
Whon his breþeren nolde him knowe;　　　　295
"Allas," quaþ he, "nou am i lowe!"
For he hopede, bi eny þing,[16]
His breþeren wolde ha mad him kyng;
And whon his hope was al ago,
He seide allas and weilawo!　　　　300
He seide allas þat he was bore,[17]
For he was a mon forlore:
He seide allas þat he was mad,
For of his lyf he was al sad.[18]
Allas! allas! was al his song:　　　　305
His heer he tar,[19] his hondes wrong,
And euere he seide, "Allas, allas!"—
And þenne he þouȝte on his trespas:
He þouȝte on Nabugodonosore,[20]
A noble kyng was him bifore:　　　　310
In al þe world nas his peer,
Forte acounte,[21] fer ne neer.
Wiþ him was Sire Olyferne,[22]
Prince of knihtes stout and steorne.
Olyferne swor euermor　　　　315
By God Nabugodonosor,
And seide þer nas no God in londe
But Nabugodonosor, ich vnderstonde;
þerfore Nabugodonosor was glad
þat he þe name of God had,　　　　320
And louede Olofern þe more;
And seþþe hit greued hem boþe sore.
Olofern dyȝede in dolour:
He was slaye in hard schour.[23]
Nabugodonosor lyuede in desert;　　　　325
Dorst he nouȝwher ben apert;[24]

---

[15] be sorrowful.　[16] in any event.　[17] born.　[18] weary.　[19] tore.　[20] Nebuchadnezzar.　[21] according to record.　[22] Holofernes.　[23] pain.　[24] openly.

315. See the Book of Judith, vi.

Fyftene ʒer he liuede þare,
With rootes, gras, and euel fare,
And al of mos[25] his cloþing was;
"Al com þat bi Godes gras: 330
He criʒede merci with delful chere:
God him restored as he was ere!
Nou am i in such caas,
And wel worse þen he was.
Whon God ʒaf me such honour   335
þat i was clepet conquerour,
In eueri lond of Cristendome
Of me men speke wel ilome,[26]
And seiden nouʒwher was my peer
In al þe world, fer ne neer.   340
For þat name i hedde pride:
And angels þat gonne from ioye glyde,[27]
And in twynklyng of an eiʒe
God binom[28] heore maystrie,
So haþ he myn, for my gult;   345
Now am i wel lowe ipult,[29]
And þat is riht þat i so be!
Lord, on þi fool þow haue pité!
I hedde an errour in myn herte,
And þat errour doþ me smerte;   350
Lord, i leeued not on þe.
On þi fol þou haue pité!
Holy Writ i hedde in dispyt;
For þat[30] is reued my delyt—
For þat is riht a fool i be!   355
Lord, on þi fool þou haue pité!
Lord, i am þi creature;
þis wo is riht þat i dure,[31]
And wel more, ʒif hit may be.[32]

---

[25] moss.   [26] often.   [27] i.e., angels who fell from heaven.   [28] took away.
[29] brought down.   [30] therefore.   [31] endure.   [32] i.e., greater suffering would be justified, if it were possible.

343. The construction is faulty, the sense clear. Nuck read *As in.*
354. In all MSS. the lines begin as here or with *Therefore;* the second *For þat* is hence correct.

Lord, on þi fool þou haue pité!   360
Lord, i haue igult[33] þe sore!
Merci, Lord: i nul no more;
Euere þi fol, Lord, wol i be.
Lord, on þi fol [þou] haue pité!
"Blisful Marie, to þe i crie,   365
As þou art ful of cortesye;
Preye þi Sone, þat dyed for me;
On me, his fol, þow haue pité.
Blisful Marie, ful of graas,
To þe i knowe[34] my trespas;   370
Prey þi Sone, for loue of þe,
On me, his fool, he haue pité!"
He seide no more, "Allas, allas!"
But þonked Crist of his gras,
And þus he gon himself stille,[35]   375
And þonked Crist mid good wille.
Þen Pope, Emperour, and Kyng
Fyue wikes[36] made heore dwellyng.
Whon fyue wykes weore agon,
To heore owne lond heo wolden anon,   380
Boþe Emperour and þe Kyng;
Þer was a feir departyng.[37]
  Þe angel com to Cisyle,
He and his men in a while.[38]
Whon he com into halle,   385
Þe fool anon he bad forþ calle;
He seide, "Fool, art þow kyng?"
"Nay, sire," quaþ he, "wiþoute lesyng."
"What artou?" seide þe angel.
"Sire, a fol; þat wot i wel,   390
And more þen fol, ʒif hit may be;
Kep[39] i non oþer dignité."
Þe angel into chaumbre went,
And after þe fol anon he sent;
He bad his men out of chaumbre gon: 395
Þer lafte no mo but he alon

[33] sinned against. [34] acknowledge. [35] calm. [36] weeks. [37] leave-taking. [38] after a time. [39] assume.

And þe fol þat stod him bi.
To him he seide, "Þou hast merci:
Þenk, þou weore lowe ipult,[40]
And al was for þin owne gult.   400
A fool þou weore to Heuene-kyng;
Þerfore þou art an vnderlyng.
God haþ forʒiuen þi mysdede;
Euere herafter þou him drede!
I am an angel of renoun,   405
Isent to kepe þi regioun;
More ioye me schal falle
In heuene, among my feren alle,
In an houre of a day,
Þen in eorþe, i þe say,   410
In an hundred þousend ʒeer,
Þeiʒ al þe world fer and neer,
Weore myn at my lykyng!
I am an angel, þou art kyng."
He went in twynklyng of an eʒe;   415
No more of him þer nas seʒe.
    Kyng Robert com into halle;
His men he bad anon forþ calle.
And alle weore at his wille
As to heore lord, as hit was skille.[41]   420
He louede God and holi churche,
And euere he þouhte wel to worche.
He regned after two ʒer and more,
And louede God and his lore.
Þe angel ʒaf him in warnyng   425
Of þe tyme of his diʒing.
Whon tyme com to dyʒe son,
He let write hit riht anon—
Hou God myd his muchel miht
Made him lowe, as hit was riht.   430
Þis storie he sende eueridel
To his breþeren vnder his seel;[42]
And þe tyme whon he schulde dye

---

[40] brought down, thrust.   [41] i.e., as if he had been their (true) lord, as was right.
[42] seal.

Þat tyme he diȝede as he gon seye.
Al þis is writen, withouten lyȝe,   435
At Roome, to ben in memorie
At Seint Petres Chirche, i knowe;
And þus is Godes miht isowe,[43]
Þat heiȝe beoþ lowe, þeiȝ hit be ille,[44]
And lowe heiȝe, at Godes wille.   440
Crist, þat for vs gon dye,
In his kynereche let vs ben heiȝe,
Euermore to ben aboue,
Þer is ioye, cumfort, and loue.   AMEN.

---

[43] disseminated.   [44] though they dislike it.

435. The "Gesta Romanorum," which has a story like this, was long thought to have been compiled from Roman records. Probably this allusion is to the "Gesta," although it is not the immediate source. Cf. Miss Rickert's "Emaré" xviii, n.2.
    439. MS. ben.

KING EDWARD AND THE SHEPHERD

KING EDWARD AND THE SHEPHERD

The poem is in the Cambridge University Library Manuscript Ff V 48 (fifteenth century), fols. 40b to 56b. Through the kindness of the authorities of the library, it has been possible to prepare the text from photographs of the manuscript, and to correct the numbering of the folios. In transcribing, *Ff* is printed *F* at the beginning of lines; *S* in the long form has been expanded at the ends of words to *-is* or *-ys;* the abbreviation for *-er, -ar,* and *-ur* has been expanded according to the customary spelling in the manuscript.

The poem has been printed only once before—by C. H. Hartshorne, in "Ancient Metrical Tales" (1829). It has never been carefully studied. For various information, other versions, and analogues, see Child V.67 ff; *FF Communications* No. 42.5, 17; Wells under "Rauf Coilȝear"; W. A. Clouston's "Group of Eastern Romances and Stories" 425, etc.; J. Bolte and G. Polivka, "Anmerkungen zu den Kinder- und Hausmärchen der Brüder Grimm" (1913) 15.18, III. 214–233. ⟨G. Liebau's "König Edward III in Lichte Europäischer Poesie" has summaries and material. The closest parallel is "The King and the Hermit" (W. C. Hazlitt's "Remains of the Early Popular Poetry of England" I.11). Cf. especially the details in 253 ff., 421 ff., and 436 ff.

Whatever the origin of the story, it found great favor in England, being told of four kings: Henry II (by Giraldus Cambrensis), Edward II, Edward III, and Edward IV. Analogous stories are attached to Henry IV and John.

Probably it was composed at about the end of the fourteenth century. The words in the vocabulary are suitable to that time; it occurs in a manuscript of antiquarian pieces; and its style is that of ordinary romance. The chronology is sufficiently inexact to prove that it was written long after the events it relates; but it must have been written for an audience that knew something of the life of Edward III, and could appreciate the humor of passages such as 43 ff. and 98 ff. From references to the Black Prince (928, 972) and Warenne, the very date of the fictitious adventure can be set as not long after 1340. Thomas Hoccleve knew a tradition that Ed-

949

ward III liked to go about in disguise ("Regement of Princes" 2556; cf. also Child V. 71. n.2); hence the tradition must have been persistent.

The dialect is northern, though it has been altered by the copyist (cf. rhymes such as *ʒong—knoyng, countenence—Fraunce*). Probably it was written down from recitation, because mistakes like those in ll. 340 and 350 seem to be a result of imperfect memory rather than of careless copying. Flourishes at the ends of words have been printed as -*e*, with the following exceptions: final -*ll*, which is crossed everywhere but in ll. 110 and 446, is not expanded; final -*ch* has a cross-stroke everywhere except in ll. 783, 862, and 916, and is not expanded; final -*g* sometimes has a tag, which has been disregarded.

The truth of the social conditions reflected in the poem is attested in many documents. Complaints about the prevalence of marauding bands and the corruptness of officials are often addressed to Parliament; the constant poaching is evident from the many statutes directed against it; outlaws were numerous in the forest. Cf. in this volume "Gamelyn" and "Havelok"; Furnivall's note on the bondman in "John de Reeve," Percy Folio Manuscript II.xxxiii; R. D. French's "Chaucer Handbook" 14, 30; W. H. Clawson's "Geste of Robin Hood" 102 ff.; and Jusserand. For facts about the forest laws, mostly of an earlier time, see Pollock and Maitland; *Publications of the Selden Society*, xiii, "Select Pleas of the Forest," especially the introduction; and John Manwood's "Treatise of the Forest Laws," especially the article on hunting.

> God, þat sittis in Trinité,
> Gyffe thaym grace wel to the
>   That listyns me a whyle!
> Alle þat louys of melody,
> Off heuon blisse God graunte þaim party:[1]   5
>   Theyre soules shelde fro peryle.
> At festis and at mangery,[2]
> To tell of kyngys, þat is worthy—
>   Talis þat byn not vyle.
> And ʒe wil listyn how hit ferd   10
> Betwene Kyng Edward and a scheperd,
>   Ʒe shalle lawghe of gyle.[3]

[1] share. [2] banquets. [3] deceit (practised by Edward).

Oure Kyng went hym in a tyde
To pley hym be a ryver side[4]
 In a mornyng of May;   15
Kny3t ne squyer wold he non
But hym self and a grome,[5]
 To wende on þat iorney.
With a scheperde con he mete,
And gret hym with wordis swete,   20
 Without any delay.
þe scheperde louyd his hatte so well,
He did hit of neuer a dele,
 But seid, "Sir, gud-day."

The Kyng to þe herde[6] seid þan,   25
"Off whens art þou, gode man,
 Also mot i the?"
"In Wynsaure was i borne;
Hit is a myle but here beforne;[7]
 þe towne þen maist þou see.   30
I am so pylled[8] with þe Kyng
þat i most fle fro my wonyng,
 And therfore woo is me.
I hade catell; now haue i non;
Thay take my bestis and don þaim slone,   35
 And payen but a stik of tre."

---

[4] i.e., hawking. [5] groom. [6] shepherd. [7] only a mile ahead. [8] robbed by.

16. Versions in which the king is unaccompanied are few. Usually a bishop or knight is with him.

22. This episode is also peculiar to this one version.

35. Cf. the letter written to Edward III about 1333: "The harbingers of your court and various grooms and servants take many goods by violence from their owners: bread, beer, eggs, poultry, beans, peas, oats, etc., for which scarcely any payment is made," D. A. Hughes, "Illustrations of Chaucer's England" 173. See also Simon Islip's "Speculum Regis Edwardi III" (ed. J. Moisant, 1891), a long complaint.

36. Wooden tally-sticks were exchanged between buyer and seller as memoranda of indebtedness in credit transactions. These could be mislaid or altered by the buyer; the practice caused much trouble. Cf. *Archæologia* 74.289.

The Kyng seid, "Hit is gret synne
Þat þei of sich werkis wil not blynne,
    And Edward wot hit noȝt;
But come to-morne when it is day: 40
Þou shal be seruyd of⁹ þi pay;
    Therof haue þou no thoȝt.
For in your towne borne i was;
I haue dwellid in diuerse place
    Sithe i thens was broght;   45
In þe courte i haue sich a frende:
Þe treserer, or þen i wende,
    For þi luffe shalle be soght."

Þis gret lord þe herd con frayne,
"What wil men of your Kyng seyne?   50
    Wel litull gode, i trowe!"
The herd onsweryd hym riȝt noȝt,
But on his schepe was all his thoȝt,
    And seid agayn, "Char, how!"¹⁰
Þen loogh oure Kyng and smyled stille:¹¹   55
"Þou onsweris me not at my will;
    I wolde þai were on a lowe!¹²
I aske þe tythyngys of oure Kyng,
Off his men and his wyrkyng;
    For sum¹³ i haue sorow.   60

I am a marchant and ride aboute,
And fele sithis i am in doute¹⁴
    For myn owne ware.
I tell it þe in priueté,
Þe Kyngys men oon¹⁵ to me   65
    A M pounde and mare.
Owe he ouȝt mycull¹⁶ in þis cuntré?

---

⁹ presented with.   ¹⁰ stop, ho! A common cry of shepherds to their flocks.
¹¹ i.e., to himself.   ¹² in the mire.   ¹³ i.e., some of his deeds.   ¹⁴ fear.   ¹⁵ owe.
¹⁶ any great sum.

43. Edward III was born at Windsor November 13, 1312.
57. Possibly a proverbial trope; cf. "Leave a scold in a ley and let
the devil get her out."

What siluer shall he pay the,
  For Goddis haly are?
Sith þou art neghtbur myne,   70
I wil my nedis do and thyne;
  Tharof haue þou no care."

"Sir," he seid, "be Seynt Edmonde,
Me is owand iiii pounde
  And odde[17] twa schillyng.   75
A stikke i haue to my witnesse—
Off hasill[18] i mene þat hit is;—
  I ne haue no noþer thyng.
And gif þou do as þou has me hote,
Then shall i gif þe a cote,[19]   80
  Withowt any lesyng;
Seuen schelyng to-morne at day
When i am siruyd of my pay."
  "Graunte,"[20] seid oure Kyng.

"Tel me, sir, what is þi name,   85
Þat i for þe haue no blame,
  And wher þi wonnyng is."
"Sir," he seid, "as mot i the,
Adam þe scheperde men callen me,
  For certan sotho iwynno."   90
Þe scheperde seid, "Whos son art þou of oure towne?
Hat not þi fadur Hochon,
  Also haue þou blisse?"
"No, for God," seid oure Kyng,
"I wene þou knowist me nothyng;   95
  Þou redis alle amysse."[21]

"My fadur was a Walsshe knyȝt;

---

[17] in addition. [18] hazel. [19] coat. [20] agreed. [21] guess all wrong.

73. Cf. preface to "Athelston."
91. The first three words are probably an insertion.
92. *Hochon* was a common name in the North; it is a form of *Hugh.*
97. Edward II was born at Carnarvon, Wales, and was said by tradition to have been presented to the Welsh as their king.

Dame Isabell my modur hyȝt,
For sothe as i tell the.
In þe castell was hir dwellyng, 100
Thorow commaundment of þe Kyng;
Whene[22] she þar shuld be;
Now wayte[23] þou wher þat i was borne.
The toþer Edward here beforne,
Full well he louyd me, 105
Sertanly withowte lye.
Sum tyme i live be marchandye,
And passe well ofte þe see.

I haue a son is with þe Whene;
She louys hym well, as i wene; 110
That dar i sauely say.
And he pray hir of a bone,
ȝif þat hit be for to done,[24]
She will not onys say nay;
And in þe courte i haue sich a frende, 115
I shal be seruyd or i wende,
Withowt any delay.
To-morne at vndern[25] speke with me:
þou shal be seruyd of þi moné[26]
Er þan hye mydday." 120

"Sir, for Seynt Thomas of Ynde,
In what place shall i þe fynde,
And what shalle i þe calle?"
"My name," he seid, "is Ioly Robyn;
Ilke man knowes hit well and fyne, 125
Bothe in bowrs and halle.
Pray þe porter, as he is fre,
þat he let þe speke with me,
Soo faire hym mot befalle.[27]

---

[22] queen.   [23] know.   [24] i.e., if it be possible.   [25] morning.   [26] money.   [27] as
he may prosper (with your blessing).

98. Isabella of France was the Queen of Edward II.

109. Edward III's queen was Philippa of Hainault.

121. The apostle Thomas was traditionally the founder of Christianity
in India.

For fer owtward[28] shall i not be;   130
Sumquer[29] i trow þou shall me see,
  Within þe castell wall.

For þou and oþer þat lene your thyng,[30]
Wel ofte sithes ye banne[31] þe Kyng,
  And ȝe are not to blame;   135
Hit er oþer[32] þat do þat dede;
Þei were worthy, so God me spede,
  Therfor to haue gret shame.
And if i wist whilke þei were,
Hit shulde come þe Kyng to ere,[33]   140
  Be God and be Seynt Iame.
Þen durst i swere þei shold abye
Þat dose oure Kyng þat vilanye,
  For he berys all þe fame."[34]

The herd onswerd to þe Kyng,   145
"Sir, be Seynt Iame, of þis tithyng
  Þou seist þerof right well:
Þei do but gode, þe Kyngus men;[35]
Þei ar worse þen sich ten,
  Þat bene with hym no dell.   150
Þei goo aboute be viii or nyne
And done þe husbondys mycull pyne,[36]
  Þat carfull is theire mele.[37]
Thai take geese, capons, and henne,
And alle þat euer þei may with renne,   155
  And reves vs oure catell.

---

[28] distant.   [29] somewhere.   [30] lend your property.   [31] curse.   [32] other persons;
stewards, etc.   [33] to the king's ear.   [34] infamy.   [35] the king's men do only good.
[36] do farmers much mischief.   [37] full of sadness is their speech.

141. The shrine of St. James at Compostella in Galicia, Northern
Spain, was an object of pilgrimage and very famous.

148. Statute of the twenty-fifth year of Edward III: "No forester nor
keeper of forest or chase, nor none other minister shall make or gather
sustenance, nor any other gathering of victuals nor other things by color
of his office . . . but what is due of ancient right." Possibly this explains
his popularity and that of his retainers among the people of Windsor
Forest, though the statute was not often enforced.

Sum of þeim was bonde sore,
And afturwarde hanget þerfore,
  For sothe, as i yow say.
ȝet ar þer of þeim nyne moo,   160
For at my hows þei were also
  Certis ȝisturday.
þei toke my hennes and my geese
And my schepe with all þe fleese,
  And ladde þem forthe away.   165
Be my doȝtur þei lay alnyȝt;
To come agayne þei haue me hyȝt;
  Off helpe i wolde yow pray.

With me þei lefte alle þeire thyng,
þat i am sicur of þeire comyng,   170
  And þat me rewes soore.
I haue fayre chamburs thre,
But non of þeim may be with me
  While þat þei be þore.
Into my carthaws[38] þei me dryfe;   175
Out at þe dur þei put my wyfe,
  For[39] she is olde gray hore.
Had i helpe of sum lordyng,
I shulde make with þeim recknyng;
  þei shulde do so no more.   180

For oþer iii felowes and i,
We durst wel take party[40]
  These nyne for to mete.
I haue slyngus[41] smert and gode
To mete with þeim ȝif þei were wode,   185

---

[38] cart-house.   [39] on the ground that.   [40] take a side in a combat.   [41] slings.

157. Cf. "Havelok" 2440 ff.

160. No matter how severe the punishment of outlaws, their ranks were constantly recruited, partly from rogues, partly from men outlawed for trivial offenses, and partly from small landowners and nobles who improved their income by robbing travelers. See Pollock and Maitland I.476.

168. MS. *i y wolde.*

178. MS. *lordyngys.*

And reve hem her lyves swete.
þe best archer of ilkon,[42]
I durst mete hym with a stone,
And gif hym leve to schete.[43]
þer is no bow þat shall laste   190
To draw[44] to my slynges caste,
Nought be fele fete.

þer is non archer in þis lande,
And i haue my slyng in hande;
For i dar lay with hym ale[45]   195
þat whoso sonyst hittys a bauke,
For to haue þe toþer haut
To what thyng he will hale;[46]
þat whoso furst smytys a thyng
Off[47] his bow or my slyng—   200
Vndirstande my tale—,
Be þe deth þat i shall dye,
þerto my hed þen dar i ley,
Now sone in þis swale."[48]

With talis he made þe Kyng to dwell,   205
With mony moo þen i can tell,
Till hit was halfe gan prime.
His hatte was bonde vndir his chyn;
He did hit nothyng of[49] to hym:
He thoȝt hit was no tyme.[50]   210
"Robyn," he seid, "i pray the,
Hit is þi will, come hom with me,

---

[42] of them all.   [43] shoot.   [44] fly as far as.   [45] wager him a drink.   [46] drink.
[47] this depends on *whoso*.   [48] shade.   [49] did not remove it.   [50] i.e., there was no occasion.

192. MS. *feel.*

196. Corrupt.   The rhyme-words may have been *benke . . . shenke.*
An archery bank was a butt, a pyramidal mound of earth on which a
paper bull's-eye was fixed; and shots which hit the mound and missed
the bull's-eye counted as misses.   The general sense may have been,
"I propose as terms that whoever first hits the bank (misses) is to order
poured out for the other whatever he will drink."

199. Present tense for future: "shall strike."   The sense is "I am
ready to bet my head as to who will first hit a mark."

A morsell for to dyne."
The Kyng list of his bourdis lere;[1]
"Gladly," he seid, "my lefe fere,   215
I wil be on of thyne."[2]

As þei hamward can gon,
Þe Kyng saw conyngys[3] mony on;
Þerat he can smyle.
"Adam," he seid, "take vp a ston   220
And put hit in þi slyng anon;
Abyde we here a while.
Gret bourde it wold be
Off þeim to slee twoo or thre,
I swere þe be Seynt Gyle."[4]   225
"Do way!"[5] quod Adam, "let be þat!
Be God, i wolde not for my hat
Be takyn with sich a gyle.[6]

Hit is alle þe Kyngus waren;[7]
Ther is nouþer kny3t ne sqwayne   230
Þat dar do sich a dede,
Any conyng here to sla
And with þe trespas awey to ga,
But his sidis shulde blede.
The warner[8] is hardy and fell;   235
Sirtanly, as i þe tell,
He will take no mede.
Whoso dose here sich maistrye,[9]
Be þou wel sicur he shall abye
And vnto prison lede.   240
Þer is no wilde foule þat will flyne
But i am sicur hym to hittyne;

---

[1] wished to hear his jokes.   [2] one of your company.   [3] rabbits.   [4] Saint Giles.
[5] stop.   [6] trick.   [7] warren.   [8] keeper of the warren.   [9] evil deed.

229. Forest game was under the king's protection. Poaching was punishable by imprisonment, and poachers were often roughly handled. Illegally killing a rabbit remained a serious offense until late in the nineteenth century.
242. Cf. note 425.

Sich mete i dar þe hote.
ȝif hit be so my slyng will last,
ȝif i fayle of hym a caste,   245
    Brok[10] þan welle my cote.
When we come and sittes in same,
I shalle tech þe a gamme;
    I can hit wel be rote.
Þen shal þou se my slyng-slaght,[11]   250
And of þe best take vs a draght,
    And drynk well right be note."[12]

The scheperde hows ful mery stode
Vndir[13] a forest fayre and gode,
    Of hert and hynde gret mynde.[14]   255
Þe Kyng seid, "Be God Almyght,
In thy hert þou may be liȝt
    Hamward when þou shall wende;
I the swere, be Goddis grace,
And i had here sich a place,   260
    I shulde haue of þat kynde;[15]
Ouþer on euen or on morneng,
Sum of þeim shuld come to ryng,[16]
    Þerwith to make me a frende."[17]

Þe herd bade, "Let soch wordis be!   265
Sum man myȝt here the;
    Þe were bettir be still.
Wode has erys, fylde has siȝt;
Were þe forster here now right,
    Thy wordis shuld like þe ille.   270
He has with hym ȝong men thre;
Þei be archers of þis contré,
    Þe Kyng to serue at wille,[18]
To kepe þe dere boþe day and nyȝt,
And for þeire luf a loge[19] is diȝt   275
    Full hye vpon an hill.

---

[10] i.e., take my coat. [11] game taken by my sling. [12] i.e., with a song to guide us. [13] close beside. [14] numbers. [15] sort (venison). [16] to hand. [17] i.e., with gifts. [18] at his pleasure. [19] lodge.

I wolde haue here no standyng,
But ride now forthe in my blessy[ng],
   And make vs wel at ese.
I am glad þou come with me;   280
Goo sit now wher þi willes be,
   Right at þine owne ese;
Þoughe sumdel of my gode be lorne,
I shall haue more; and God beforne,[20]
   He may hit wel increse;   285
And i shall tech þe play—
When tyme comys, þou shalt asay—
   Whilke play be not lese."[21]

A fayre cloth on þe borde he leyd;
Into þe boure he made abrayde,[22]   290
   Gode mete for to fette.
Brede of whete bultid[23] smalle,
ii peny ale he brouȝt with all:
   Therof wolde he not lett;
A ffesaunde[24] brid and þerwith a crane—   295
Oþer fowles were þer gode ane[25]—
   Before þe Kyng he sette.
"Adam," quod þe Kyng, "blessed þou be:
Here is better þen þou heȝtist me,
   To-day when þat we mette."   300

"Sir," he seid, "do now gladly;
Ȝet haue i mete þat were worthy
   A gret lord for to fech."
He broȝt a heron with a poplere,[26]
Curlews, boturs,[27] boþe in fere,   305
   Þe maudlart[28] and hur mech;[29]
And a wylde swan was bake.
"Sich fowle con my slyng take;
Þeroff am i no wrech;[30]
   I bade felowes to my dynere;   310
And sithen þei wil not cum here,

---

[20] with God's guidance. [21] in vain. [22] incursion. [23] sifted. [24] pheasant. [25] number. [26] spoonbill. [27] bitterns. [28] mallard. [29] mate. [30] niggard.

A devoll haue who þat rech!

3if þou wilt ete, þou shall non waue;[31]
But gif þou will any drynk haue,
    þou most con thy play;   315
When þou seest þe cuppe anon,
But þou sei 'passilodion,'
    þou drynkis not þis day.
Sely Adam shall sitt þe hende,[32]
And onswere with 'berafrynde,'   320
    Leue vpon my ley."[33]
Þe Kyng seid þat he wold lere:
"Me þink it bourde for to here:
    Teche me, i þe pray."

"Passilodyon, þat is þis: 325
Whoso drynkys furst, iwys,
    Wesseyle þe mare dele![34]
Berafrynde also, i wene,
Hit is to make þe cup clene,
    And fylle hit ofte full wele.   330
Thus shal þe game go aboute,
And who so falys of þis route,[35]
    I swere be Seynt Mighell,
Get hym drynk wher he will,
He getys non here—þis is my skill[36]—   335
    Noȝt to a noþer sele."[37]

Þe Kyng seid, "Let se þat drynke;
I shall say riȝt þat i thynke:
    Me thirstis swythe sore."
The scheperde bade þe cup fill;   340
Þe Kyng to drynk hade gode will,
    With passilodion more. . . .

---

[31] hesitate.   [32] worthy Adam shall sit near thee.   [33] statement.   [34] the more health to him!   [35] rote, formula.   [36] opinion.   [37] another occasion.

313. *Non* for *not?*

317. *Passilodion* and *berafrynde* are nonsense-words. On the custom, see Brand, under "Pledging."

340. The scribe has inadvertently omitted most of this stanza, and has replaced part of it with ll. 350-5, below.

"I can riȝt wel my lore."
"Berafrynde," iseid Adam,
"Iwysse þou art a wytty man;   345
    þou shalt wel drynk þerfore."

Thus þei sate withoute strife,
Þe Kyng with Adam and his wyfe,
    And made hym mery and glad.
The scheperde bade þe cuppe fill;   350
The Kyng to drynke hade gode will;
    His wife did as he bade.
When þe cuppe was come anon,
Þe Kyng seid "passylodion,"
    When he þe cuppe hade.   355
Hit was a game of gret solas;
Hit comford[38] all þat euer þer was;
    Therof þai were noght sade.

Þe scheperde ete till þat he swatte,[39]
And þan nou erst he drew[40] his hatt   360
    Into þe benke-ende.[41]
And when he feld[42] þe drynk was gode,
He wynkid and strokyd[43] vp his hode,
    And seid, "Berafrynde."
He was qwyte as any swan;   365
He was a wel begeten man,
    And comyn of holy kynde.[44]
He wold not ete his cromys drye:
He louyd nothyng but it were trie,[45]
    Neþer fer ne hende.[46]   370

Þen seid þe Kyng in his reson,[47]
"Whoso were in a gode town,
    þis wold ha costed dere,

---

[38] comforted.   [39] sweat.   [40] removed.   [41] end of the bench.   [42] felt.   [43] pushed.
[44] worthy parents.   [45] choice.   [46] near.   [47] speech.

348. In some versions the wife is an important character; in others she
is entirely omitted.
365. A white skin was a mark of gentility.

In þis maner to be fed
With alkyn dentethe wel bested,[48]   375
  As we haue had now here.
I shalle þe whyte,[49] be hode myne.
Now hade i leuer a conyne[50]
  Diȝt in my manere;
But-ȝif hit were of buk or doo,   380
Þer is no mete i louyd soo,
  And i come[1] þer hit were."

Þe scheperde seid, "So mot þou the,
  Can þou heyle[2] a priueté?
And þou shalt se gode game."   385
"Ȝe!" seid þe Kyng, "be my levté,[3]
And ellis haue i mycul maùgré[4]
  Ȝif hit be for my frame.[5]
What man þat wrye[6] a gode frende,
Þouȝ he were riȝt sibbe of my kynde,[7]   390
  He were worthy gret shame."
Þen seid Adam, "Þou seis sothe;
Ȝet i haue a morsel for þi tothe,
  And ellis i were to blame."

He went and fett conyngys thre,   395
Alle baken well in a pasty,[8]
  With wel gode spicerye,[9]
And oþer baken mete alsoo,
Boþe of hert[10] and of roo;
  Þe venyson was full trye.[11]   400
"Sir," he seid, "asay of this:
Þei were ȝisterday qwyk, iwysse,
  Certan, withouten lye;
Hider þei come be mone-liȝt.
Eete þerof well apliȝt,[12]   405
  And schewe no curtasye."

---

[48] dainties well set out.   [49] requite.   [50] rabbit.   [1] if I should come.   [2] conceal.
[3] honor.   [4] mischance.   [5] profit.   [6] betrays.   [7] blood-relative.   [8] pie.   [9] spices.
[10] hart.   [11] choice.   [12] straightway.

379. MS. *maners.*

To þe scheperd seid þe Kyng,
"Þe forsters[13] luf þis ouer al thyng;
   Þou art alle þaire felawe:
To þaire profett þou con foulis slyng,[14]   410
And þei will venyson to þe bryng:
   Þerof stande þei non awe.[15]
Were þou as perfete in a bowe,[16]
Þou shulde haue moo dere, i trowe,
   Sothe to say in sawe.[17]   415
Ȝet i rede þat þou fande[18]
Þan any forster in þis land
   An arow for to drawe."

Þen seid þe scheperde, "Noþing soo:
I con a game worthe þei twoo[19]   420
   To wynne me a brede:[20]
Þer is no hert ne bucke so wode
Þat i ne get without blode,
   And i of hym haue nede.
I haue a slyng for þe nones   425
Þat is made for gret stonys;
   Therwith i con me fede.
What dere i take vnder þe side,[21]
Be þou siker he shall abide
   Til i hym home will lede.   430

Conyngus with my noþer slyng
I con slee and hame bryng,
   Sumtyme twoo or thre;
I ete þaim not my self alon:
I send presandes[22] mony on,   435
   And fryndes make i me,

---

[13] wardens. [14] kill with a sling. [15] they are not afraid. [16] with a bow. [17] as one remarks (a tag). [18] are readier. [19] two of that. [20] roast. [21] i.e., hit in the ribs. [22] presents.

421. MS. *bridde*, which fits neither the rhyme nor the sense.
425. Strutt (II.ii) devotes part of a chapter to the Saxon practice of hunting with a sling. Slings might be of two kinds: leather thongs, which were whirled about before the missile was released; and sticks over the ends of which stones could be flipped.

Til gentilmen and ȝemanry;
Thei haue þaim all þat ar worthy,—
　Those þat ar priué.
Whatso þai haue, it may be myne,　　　　　　　　　　440
Corne and brede, ale and wyne,
　And alle þat may like me.

Do now gladly, Ioly Robyne:
Ȝet shall þou drynk a drauȝt fyne
　Off gode drynk, as i wene;　　　　　　　　　　　　445
Off Lanycoll þou shall proue:[23]
Þat is a cuppe to my behoue;[24]
　Off maser[25] it is ful clene.
Hit holdis a gode thryden dele[26]
Ful of wyne euery mele;　　　　　　　　　　　　　450
　Before me it is sene.
Fil þe cuppe," he seid anon,
"And play we passilodion,
　Sith no moo þat we bene."[27]

When þe drynk was filled,　　　　　　　　　　　　455
Þe wife askid, "Who shuld begynne,
　Þe godeman, sir, or ȝe?"
"Take my gcyst,"[28] seid Adam þan,
"Sithe he his gamme con;
　I wil þat it so be."　　　　　　　　　　　　　　460
Þe Kyng toke þe cuppe anon
And seid, "Passilodion!"
　Hym thoȝt it was gode gle.
Þe sheperde seid certanly,
"Berafrynd shal be redy,　　　　　　　　　　　　465
　Also mot i the."

He drank and made þe cuppe ful clene,
And sithe he spake wordis kene,

---

[23] taste, try.　[24] profit.　[25] maple-wood.　[26] i.e., enough for three.　[27] i.e., since there are but two of us.　[28] give to my guest.

438. MS. þei ar.
448. Glass vessels were uncommon at the tables of peasants.

Þat gamme was to here:
"This cuppe hit hat Lonycoll;   470
I luf it wel, for it is holl;²⁹
    It is me lefe and dere;
Fil it efte to Ioly Robyn;
Iwisse, he drank no better wyne
    Off alle þis seuen ʒere!   475
To alle þat wil my gamme play,
Fill it be þe ee,³⁰ i þe pray,
    My bourdis þat wil lere."

Then dranke oure Kyng and toke his leue;
Þe sheperd seid, "Sir, not þe greue,   480
    And it þi wille be:
I shalle þe schew, Ioly Robyn,
A litull chaumber þat is myne,
    Þat was made for me."
Þe Kyng þerof was ful glad,   485
And did as þe scheperde bad:
    Moo bourdis wold he se.
He lad hym into a priué place
Ther venyson plenté in was,
    And þe wyne so claré.³¹   490

Vnder þe erth it was diʒt;
Feire it was, and clene of syʒt,
    And clergially³² was hit wroʒt.
The Kyng seid, "Here is feyre ese:
A man myʒt be here wel at ese,   495
    With gamme ʒif he were sauʒt."³³
The Kyng seid, "Gramercy, and haue goday!"³⁴
Þe scheperde onswerid and said, "Nay,
    ʒet ne gose þou noughte;
Þou shalle preue³⁵ furst of a costrell tre³⁶   500
    Þat gode frendis send to me,

---

²⁹ hollow, capacious. ³⁰ eye; i.e., full. ³¹ like claré. Probably *so* is a scribal error. ³² learnedly; i.e, cleverly. ³³ contented. ³⁴ farewell. ³⁵ taste. ³⁶ wooden bottle.

470. Probably the words are addressed to his wife. Cf. 348.

þe best þat myght be bouȝt.

Telle me now, whilke is þe best wyne
Off Lonycoll, cuppe myne,
   Als þou art gode and hynde?   505
Play onys passilodion,
And i shall onswer sone anon,
   Certes, 'berafrynde.'
This chamber hat Hakderne, my page;
He kepis my thyng and takis no wage,   510
   In worde[37] wher þat i wende.
þer is no man þis place con wrye
But thiself, ȝif þou will sey,[38]
   And þan art þou vnkynde.[39]

Ther is no man of þis contré   515
So mycull knowes of my priueté
   Als þou dose, Ioly Robyn;
Whil þat i liff, welcum to me;
Wyne and ale i dar hete þe,
   And gode flesshe for to dyne."   520
þe Kyng his stede he can stride,
And toke his leue for to ride;
   Hym þoȝt it was hye tyme.
þe schepcrde seid, "I will with þe goo:
I dar þe hete a foule or twoo,   525
   Paraunter with a conyne."

þe Kyng rode softely on his way;
Adam folowyd, and wayted his pray;
   Conyngus saw he thre.
"Ioly Robyn, chese þou which þou wylt;[40]   530
Hym þat rennys er hym þat sitt,
   And i shall gif hym the."
"He þat sittis and wil not lepe:
Hit is þe best of alle þe hepe,
   For soth so thynkithe me."   535
þe scheperde hit hym with a stone

---

[37] world; i.e., wherever I go (a tag).   [38] if you should tattle.   [39] disloyal.   [40] want.

And breke in two his brest-bon;
Thus sone ded was he.

þe Kyng seid, "þou art to alow:[41]
Take hym als þat rennyth now,   540
And þan con þou thy crafte."[42]
"Be God," quod Adam, "here is a ston
þat shalle be his bane anon;"
Thus sone his life was rafte.
What fowle þat sittis or flye,   545
Wheþer it were ferre or nye,
Sone with hym it lafte.
"Sir," he seid, "for sothe i trowe
This is bettur þen any bowe,
For alle þe fedurt schafte.[43]   550

Ioly Robyn, brok wel my pray
þat i haue wone here to day:
I vouchesafe wele more:
I pray þe telle it to no man
In what maner þat i hit wan: 555
I myȝt haue blame therfore;
And gif þou do my errand of riȝt,[44]
þou shalle haue þat i þe hyȝt,
I swere be Goddis ore."
þe Kyng seid, "Take me thy tayle;[45]   560
For my hors, i wolde not þe fayle,
A peny þat þou lore."

The Kyng to court went anon,
And Adam to his schepe con gon;
His dogge lay ther fulle stille.   565
Home er nyȝt come he noȝt;
New mete with hym he broȝt:
For defaute wolde he not spill.[46]
"Wife," he seid, "be not sory:
I wil to courte certanly;   570

---

[41] be praised.   [42] (then I shall admit) you know your art.   [43] feathered
arrow.   [44] rightly.   [45] tally-stick.   [46] he would never die of want.

I shalle haue alle my will.
Ioly Robyn, þat dynet with me,
Hase behette me my moné,
As he can lawe and skill.[47]

He is a marchande of gret powere: 575
Many man is his treserere;
Men awe hym mony a pounde.
The best frend he had sith he was borne
Was þe toþer Edwart here beforne,
Whil he was holl and sounde.   580
He hase a son is with þe Qwene;
He may do more þen oþer fyftene,[48]
He swerys be Seynt Edmonde.
Thouȝ he shuld gif of his càtell,
I shalle haue myne, euery dell,   585
Off penys holl and rownde."

On morow when he shuld to court go,
In russet clothyng he tyret[49] hym þo,
In kyrtil[50] and in curtebye,[1]
And a blak furred hode   590
Þat wel fast to his cheke stode,
Þe typet[2] myght not wrye.[3]
Þe mytans clutt[4] forgate he noȝt;
Þe slyng cumys not out of his thoȝt,
Wherwith he wrouȝt maystrie.   595
Toward þe court he can goo;
His doȝter lemman met he thoo,
And alle his cumpanye.

---

[47] means.   [48] than any other fifteen men.   [49] attired.   [50] tunic.   [1] short cloak
of coarse material.   [2] fur muffler.   [3] conceal.   [4] cloth mittens.

586. Coins were frequently clipped, so that whole and round pennies
were hard to obtain.
588. From the Rolls of Parliament for 1363: "Cowherds, shepherds
. . . and all manner of men engaged in husbandry, and other people who
have not goods and chattels worth forty shillings, shall wear no cloth save
blanket and russet [coarse brown material], twelve pence the yard,"
Hughes 165. The statute proved unenforceable, and was soon withdrawn.
589. MS. surstbye.

He tho3t more þen he seyde;
Towarde þe court he gaf a brayde,[5]   600
   And 3ede a well gode pas,
And when he to þe 3atis come,
He askid þe porter and his man
   Wher Ioly Robyn was.
He was warned what he shuld sayn;   605
Off his comyng he was fayne,
   I swere be Goddis grace.
"Sir, i shall tel þe wher he is;"
And þan be[gan] þaire gammen, iwis,
   When he come forthe in place.   610

The Kyng seid to erles tweyne,
"3e shall haue gode bourd,[6] in certayne,
   3if þat 3e will be stille,
Off[7] a scheperde þat i see
Þat is hider come to me   615
   For to speke his wille.
I pray yow alle, and warne betyme,[8]
Þat 3e me calle Ioly Robyne,
   And 3e shalle law3 your fille.
He wenys a marchand þat i be;   620
Men owe hym siluer here for fe:[9]
   I shalle hym helpe þertille.

But a wager i dar lay,
And 3e will as i yow say,
   A tune[10] of wyne, iwysse: 625
Þer is no lorde þat is so gode,
Þou3 he avayle[11] to hym his hode,
   Þat he wil do of his.
Sir Raufe of Stafforde, i pray the,
Goo wete what his wil! be,   630

---

[5] proceeded rapidly. [6] fun. [7] at the expense of. [8] betimes. [9] in payment.
[10] large measure. [11] lower, remove.

629. Ralph de Stafford (d. 1372) was a well-known courtier, who distinguished himself in war and was made earl in 1351. This gives an early limit for the composition of the piece. (Cf. 644.)

And telle me how hit is."
"Gladly, lord, so mot i the,
Sich bourdis i wolde ful fayne se,
    Off thyngus þat fallis amysse."

And whan he to þe herde came,   635
He seid, "Al hayle, godeman:
    Whider wiltow goo?"
He onsweryd as he thouȝt gode,
But he did not of his hode
    To hym neuer þe moo: 640
"Ioly Robyn, þat i yonder see,
Bid hym speke a worde with me,
    For he is not my foo."
þen onswerid þat Erle balde,
"Take þe porter þi staffe to halde,   645
    And þi mytens also."

"Nay, felow," he seid, "so mot i the,
My staffe ne shal not goo fro me:
    I wil hit kepe in my hande;
Ne my mytans getis no man   650
Whil þat i þaim kepe can,
    Be Goddis Sone alweldand;[12]
Ioly Robyn, þat i yonder see,
Goo bidde hym speke a worde with me,
    I pray the, for Goddis sande: 655
I wolde wete how hit is:
I am aferd my schepe go mysse[13]
    On oþer mennys lande."

And when he to þe Kyng came,
þen seid þe Kyng, "Welcum, Adam,   660

---

[12] almighty.   [13] astray.

631. In the MS. line 633 follows here. But probably the whole passage
is corrupt, and ll. 657-8 are echoed.
    633. MS. *whilke bourdis*.
    645. It was customary for guests to surrender all their weapons to the
attendants. The shepherd's failure to do so is a sign of his unfamiliarity
with court etiquette.

As to my powere !"[14]
"Ioly Robyn," he seid, "wel mot þou be !
Be God, so shuld þou to me
   On oþer stede þan here.[15]
I am commyn, þou wat wherfore;   665
Þi trauayle shal not be forlore:
   Þou knowis wel my manere."
"For God," seid þe Kyng þo,
"Þou shal be seruyd er þou goo;
   Forthy make glad chere."[16]   670

"Ioly Robyn," he seid, "i pray the
Speke with me a worde in priueté."
   "For God," quod þe Kyng, "gladly !"
He freyned þe Kyng in his ere
What lordis þat þei were   675
   "Þat stondis here þe bye?"
"The Erle of Lancaster is þe ton,
And þe Erle of Waryn, Sir Iohn,
   Bolde and as hardy;
Þei mow do mycull with þe Kyng: 680
I haue tolde hem of þi thyng."
   Þen seid he, "Gremercy !"

Þe scheperde seid, "Sir[s], God blesse ȝew !
I know yow not, be swete Ihesu !"
   And swere a wel gret oth.   685
"Felaw," they seid, "i leve þe well:
Þou haȿe sene Robyn or þis sell;[17]
   Ȝe ne ar nothyng wrothe."[18]
"No, sirs," he seid, "so mot i the,
We ar neghtburs, i and he;   690
   We were neuer lothe."
As gret lordis as þei ware,

---

[14] as far as is in my power.   [15] i.e., anywhere.   [16] i.e., look happy.   [17] time, moment.   [18] i.e., are friendly.

677. See introduction to this poem. All the persons named were important noblemen. Lancaster (d. 1361) was the king's chief adviser. Warenne was the earl of Surrey. Since he died in 1347, the poet is in error in representing Ralph de Stafford as an earl at this time (cf. l. 629).

He toke of his hode neuer þe mare,
  But seid, "God saue yow bothe."

þe lordis seid to hym anon,   695
"Ioly Robyn, let hym noȝt gon
  Till þat he haue etyn.
Hym semys a felow[19] for to be;
Moo bourdis ȝet mow we se
  Er his errand be gettyn."   700
þe Kyng to þis scheperde con say,
"Fro me ne gost þou not away
  Tille we togeder haue spokyn;
An errande i hyȝt þe for to done;
I wolde þat þou were seruyd sone,   705
  þat hit be not forgetyn.

Goo we togeder to þe marshalle,
And i myself shall tel þe tale—
  The better may þou spede."
"Robyn," he seid, "þou art trwe;   710
Iwis, it shalle þe neuer rew:
  þou shalt haue thy mede."
To þe hall he went, a ful gode pase,
To seke wher þe stuarde was;
  þe scheperde with hym ȝede.   715
Long hym thouȝt, til mydday
þat he ne were seruyd of his pay;
  He wolde haue done his dede.[20]

When he into þe hall came,
þer fande he no maner of man;   720
  þe Kyng hym bade abyde:
"I wil go aboute þi nede,
For to loke gif i may spede,
  For þing þat may betide."[21]
"Robyn, dwel not long fro me: 725
I know no man here but the;

---

[19] eccentric, "character." [20] finished the business. Cf. 657. [21] happen what may.

This court is noȝt but pride;[22]
I ne can of no sich fare:
These hye halles, þei ar so bare!
Why ar þei made so wyde?"   730

Then lowȝ þe Kyng, and began to go,
And with his marsshale met he tho;
He commaundit hym aȝeyne;
"Felaw," he seid, "herkyn a liȝt,
And on myne errand go þou tyte,   735
Also mot þou thynne:
A scheperde abides me in hall:
Off hym shall we laȝ alle,
At þe meyte when þat we bene.
He is cum to aske iiii pounde;   740
Goo and fech it in a stounde,
Þe sothe þat i may sene.

Twey schelyng þer is more:[23]
Forgete hem not, be Goddis ore,
Þat he ne haue alle his pay.   745
I wolde not for my best stede
But he were seruyd er he ȝede,
Er þen hye mydday.
He wenys a marchande þat i be;
Ioly Robyn he callis me,   750
For sertan soþe to say.
Now sone to mete when i shall goo,
Loke he be noȝt fer me fro."
"Lorde," he seid þen, "nay."

Forþe þe marshale can gon,   755
And brouȝt þe stuard sone anon,
And did adowne his hode.
"Herstow, felow, hast þou do

---

[22] ostentation.   [23] in addition.

742. The king means to see that the steward withholds none of the money; cf. "Sir Cleges."
758. These lines are spoken by the king.

þe thyng þat i seid þe to,
  For þe gode rode?" 760
"Sir," he seid, "it is redy;
I know hym not, be oure Lady,
  Before me þoȝ he stode."
"Goo, take ȝond man and pay betyme,[24]
And bidde hym thonke Ioly Robyne; 765
  We shall sone haue gamme gode."

Forþe þei went all thre,
To pay þe scheperde his moné
  þer he stode in þe halle.
þe stiward at hym frayned tho, 770
"What askis þou, felaw, er þou goo?
  Telle me, among vs alle."
"Sir," he seid, "so mot i the,
Foure pounde ȝe owe to me,
  So fayre mot me befalle![25] 775
Twey schillyngis is þer odde:
I haue wytnesse þerof, be God,
  With in þis castell wall.

Hit is skorid here on a tayle;[26]
Haue; brok[27] hit wel withowt fayle: 780
  I haue kepte hit lang enoȝ!"
þe stiwarde: "þerof i ne rech:
Iwisse, i haue þerto no mech!"[28]
  At hym ful fast þei looȝ;
"Ne were[29] Ioly Robyn, þat i here se, 785
To-day [ȝe] gate no moné of me,
  Made þou it neuer so towȝ;[30]
But for his luf, go tel[31] it here."
þen made þe scheperde right glad chere,
  When he þe siluer drowȝ.[32] 790

---

[24] at once. [25] as I hope for good luck. [26] tally-stick. [27] here: enjoy. [28] mate.
[29] were it not for. [30] tough; i.e., no matter how much you complained. [31] count
it out. [32] reckoned.

785. Said by the steward. Destroying the mate to a tally-stick was an
easy way of evading payment.
786. MS. illegible.

He did it vp, þe sothe to say,
But sum þerof he toke away
   In his hand ful rathe.
"Ioly Robyn," he seid, "herkyn to me:
A worde or tweyne in preueté   795
   Togedir betwene vs bathe:
I hiȝt þe ȝistirday seuen shyllyng;
Haue: brok it wel to þi clothyng:
   Hit wil do þe no skathe.
And for þou hast holpyn me now,   800
Euermore felowes i and thow,
   And mycull þanke, sir, now haue ȝe."

"Graunt mercy, sir," seid þan he,
"But siluer shalt þou non gif me,
   I swere be Seynt Martyne!"   805
"Be God," seid þe scheperde, "ȝys!"
"Nay," seid oure Kyng, "iwys,
   Noȝt for a tune[33] of wyne;
For þi luf, i wolde do more
Then speke a worde or ii þe fore;[34]   810
   Þou may preue sum tyme.[35]
Ȝif þou be fastyng, cum with me
And take a morsell in preueté;
   Togedir þen shalle we dyne."

"Nay, sir," he seid, "so God me spede!   815
To þe Kyngis meyte haue i no nede:
   I wil þerof no dele.
Þer is non of his proud meny
Þat hase alway so gode plenté
   [As] i haue euery sele."[36]   820
Þe Kyng bare wittnesse, and seid, "Ȝa!
But þou myȝt onys, er þou ga,
   Etyn with me a mele!
Þe grettist lordis of þis lande

---

[33] cask. [34] for you. [35] test my friendship some time. [36] at every season.

802. This line begins a page, and seems to be a copyist's error.
820. MS. (apparently) ha ne.

Haue bidde þe tary, i vndirstonde,   825
And þerfore bere þe well."

"For þi luff, Robyn, i wil gladly;
Today þen mett i myne enmye,
    For sothe as i the tell—
He þat be my doȝtir lay;   830
I tolde þe of hym ȝistirday—
    I wolde he were in hell!
At my howse is alle þe rowte;
They wil do harme whil i am owte;
    Full yuel þen dar i dwell.   835
Wold þou speke for me to þe Kyng,
He wolde avow[37] me my slyngyng;
    Thaire pride þen shulde i fell!"

Kyng Edwart onswerid agayne,
"I wil go to these erles twane   840
    þat stode lang ore be me;
þai ar aperte,[38] of my knowyng;
þei shall speke for þe to þe Kyng,
    þat wrokyn shal þou be.
In þis courte þai ar twenty   845
At my biddyng to bidde redy[39]
    To do a gode iornay;
When þou comys home, make no bost:
þei shal be takyn er þou it wost,
    þouȝ þai were sech thre."[40]   850

Thus þe Kyng held hym with tale,
þat alle þat euer was in þe sale[41]
    Off hym hade gret ferly.
Togedir þei ȝede vp and downe
As men þat seid þaire orison,   855
    But no man wist why.
þe scheperde keppid his staf ful warme,
And happid[42] it euer vndir his harme[43]

---

[37] sanction.   [38] bold.   [39] ready to be commanded at my order.   [40] i.e., three times as many.   [41] hall.   [42] wrapped.   [43] arm.

As he romyd hym by;
He wold no man toke it hym fro   860
Til þat he shulde to meyte goo;
    Sich was his curtasy!

The Kyng commaundit al his[44]
þat no man speke to hym amysse,
    As þei wolde be his frynde.   865
When tablys were layd and cloþes sprad,
þe scheperde into þe hall was lad
    To begynne a bordis ende.[45]
His mytans hang be his spayre,[46]
And alway hodit[47] like a frere,   870
    To meyte when he shulde wende;
And when þe waytis blew lowde hym be,
þe scheperde þo3t, "What may þis be?"
    He wende he hade herd a fende.[48]

And alle þat hym aboute stode   875
Wende þat man hade bene wode,
    And low3 hym to hethyng[49]
For he so nycely[50] 3ede in halle,
And bare a staffe among þaim alle,
    And wolde take[1] it nothyng.   880
þe stwarde seid to Ioly Robyn,
"Goo wesshe, sir, for it is tyme,
    At þe furst begynyng;
And for þat odir Edwart loue,
þou shalt sitte here aboue,   885
    Instidde alle of þe Kyng."

When he had wasshen and fayre isett,
þe Qwene anon to hym was fett,
    For sche was best worthy.
At euery ende of the deyse   890

---

[44] his company.   [45] sit at the head of a table.   [46] slit in clothing near the waist.   [47] hooded.   [48] devil. Devils made hideous sounds.   [49] scorn.   [50] foolishly.   [1] yield.

872. Waits were minstrels who blew trumpets or pipes at stated hours. Their signal here is for the bringing on of the first course.

Sate an erle, withowt lese,
   And a fayre lady.
Þe Kyng commandet þe stuard þo
To þe scheperde for to goo
   And pray hym specially   895
A tabul dormant[2] þat he begynne;
"Þen shal we lawȝ, þat be hereine,
   Off his rybaudy."[3]

"Adam," he seid, "sit here downe,
For Ioly Robyn of þis towne,   900
   He gifis þe gode worde.[4]
And for þou art of his knoyng,[5]
We vouchsafe, olde and ȝong,
   Þat þou begynne þe borde."
"Perdy," seid þe scheperde "nowe![6]   905
What shal be þouȝt, if þat i mow,
   Hit is wel kept in horde![7]
But-if i do Robyn a gode iorné,
Ellis mot i hangyt be
   With a hempyn corde!"   910

And when þe hall was rayed out,[8]
Þe scheperde lokid al aboute,
   How þat hit myȝt bene.
Surketis[9] oueral he con holde;[10]
Off knyȝtis and of persons bolde,   915
   Sich hade he non sene.
Þe Prince was feched to þe borde
To speke with þe Kyng a worde,
   And also with þe Qwene.
Then he frayned hym in his ere   920
If he wolde 'passilodion' lere,

---

[2] table fixed to the floor. [3] uncouth blunders. [4] speaks well of you. [5] acquaintance. [6] no. [7] secret; i.e., better left unsaid. [8] decked out. [9] outer coats. [10] behold.

896. The *Oxford Dictionary* cites Chaucer's use of *tabul dormant* in 1386 as the earliest.
906. MS. *Hit shal.*
911. MS. *rayed oȝt.*

And 'berafrende' bedene.

"Lorde," he seid, "what may þat be?
I know it not, be Goddis tre!
　It is a new language."　　　　　　　　　925
"I leue þe well," seid þe Kyng,
"Þou may not know al thyng:
　Þou þerto ne has non age.
Þer is a mon in þis towne
Þat will it preue gode reson[11]　　　　　930
　To kyng, squyer, and page;
And gif þou wille gif any mede,
I shal do þe to hym lede,
　Vnto his scole a stage.[12]

Hit is a scheperde þat i of mene;　　　　935
At his howse þen haue i bene
　Within þis seuen-ny3t;
A dosan[13] kny3tis, and þai had cum with me,
Þei shulde haue had mete plenté
　Off þat i fonde redy dy3t."　　　　　940
Then he tolde hym alle þe case,
Off 'passilodion,' what it was,
　And 'berafrynde' ipli3t.[14]
"He sittis yonde, in a furred hode;
Goo, bere hym here a golde ryng gode,　945
　And þat anon right,

And þank hym mycul for Ioly Robyn:
He wenys þat it be name myne,
　For soth as i þe say.
He wot i haue a son here,　　　　　　950
Þat is þe Quene lefe and dere:
　I tolde hym so 3isterday.
As ofte as þou wilt to hym gan,
Name 'passilodian,'

---

[11] sense.　[12] (to pùrsue) a study in his school.　[13] dozen.　[14] as well.

934. *Stage* in this sense is given in the *Oxford Dictionary* as first occurring in "The Pearl."

And wete what he will say."   955
"Lorde," he said, "i wil gladly:
I can hit wel and parfitely;[15]
Now haue i lornyd a play."[16]

When he to þe scheperde came,
He seid, "Do[17] gladly, gode Adam,   960
And mycull gode hit þe doo!
Micul þanke for Ioly Robyn,
Þat þou did[18] my lorde to dyne;
And oþer[19] þer is also:
Whi playes þou not 'passilodion,'   965
As þou did ʒisterday at home?
I wil onswer þerto:
I know þi gamme to þe ende,
For to say 'berafrynde,'
As haue i rest and roo."[20]   970

Þen looʒ þe herd, and liked ille,
And seid, "Lefe childe, be stille,
For Goddis swete tre!
Go sei þi fadir he is to blame
Þat he for[21] gode dose me schame!   975
Why has he wryed me?
Haue i maugré[22] for my god dede,
Shall i neuer more marchand fede,
Ne telle my pryueté!"
He stroked vp his hud for tene,   980
And toke a cuppe and mad it clene;
A gret drauʒt þen drank he.

Þe Prynce seid, "Þat was wel done:
Hit shal be filled aʒeyne ful sone,
Alle of the best wyne.   985
Play 'passilodion,' and ha no drede,
And haue a gold ryng to þi mede,

---

[15] perfectly. [16] diversion. [17] eat. [18] caused, invited. [19] another matter. [20] peace.
[21] in return for. [22] bad treatment.

972. The Black Prince was born in 1330.
986. MS. *drade*.

And were²³ it for luf myne."
"I wil it not, for sothe to sey:
Hit shulde not laste me halfe a day,   990
Be Goddis swete pyne!²⁴
When it were brokyne, farewell he!²⁵
An hatte were bettir þen sech thre
For reyne and sonneschyne."

When þe Prince hade hym beholde,   995
He ȝede and sate hym where he wolde,
As skille and reson is;
And alle þe lordyngis in þe halle
On þe herd þei lowgen alle
When any cuppe ȝede amys.   1000
When þei hade etyne and cloþis draw,
And wasshen, as hit is landis lawe,
Certan sothe iwysse,
Þan dranke þai aftir sone anon,
And played passilodion   1005
Tille ilke man hade his.

Þe lordis anon to chawmber went;
Þe Kyng after þe scheperde sent;
He was broȝt forth full sone.
He clawed his hed, his hare he rent,   1010
He wende wel to haue be schent:
He ne wyst what was to done.
When he French and Latyn herde,
He hade mervell how it ferde,²⁶
And drow hym euer alone.   1015
"Ihesu," he seid, "for þi gret grace,
Bryng me fayre out of þis place!
Lady, now here my bone!

---

²³ wear.   ²⁴ suffering (on the cross).   ²⁵ farewell to it!   ²⁶ what was happening.

990. Possibly a reference to the robbers.
1007. The chamber was a room adjoining the banquet-hall where the men gathered. The women went to their apartments, usually on another floor.
1015. MS. *alove.*

"What eyled²⁷ me? Why was i wode,
þat i cowth so litell gode   1020
    Myseluen for to wrye?
A, Lord God! þat i was vnslye!²⁸
Alasse, þat euer he come so nye,
    þe sothe þat i shulde seye!
Wolde God, for His Modirs luf,   1025
Bryng me onys at myne abofe²⁹—
    I were out of þeire eye,—
Shuld i neuer, for no faire spech,
Marchande of my cowncell teche,
    Soo aferde i am to dye!"   1030

The Kyng saw he was sory;
He had þer of gret myrth forþi,
    And seid, "Come nere, Adam;
Take þe spices and drynk þe wyne
As homely³⁰ as i did of thyne,   1035
    So God þe gif þe dame!"³¹
Fulle carfully in he ȝede;
"Haue i þis for my gode dede?
    Me rewes þat i here came!"
He toke þe wyne and laft þe spice;   1040
Then wist þei wel þat he was nyce;
    Wel carfull was þat man.

He ete þe spyce, the wyne he drank;
Oure Kyng on þe scheperde wanke³²
    Priuely with his eye.   1045
"Ioly Robyn," he þoȝt, "wo þou³³ be
þat tyme þat i euer met with þe,
    Er euer þat i þe seye!
Be God," he þouȝt, "had i þe nowe
þer were ȝisturday i and þow,   1050
    Paynes þen shulde þou drye!³⁴
I shulde chastis þe so with my slyng,

---

²⁷ ailed. ²⁸ guileless. ²⁹ into a better state. ³⁰ familiarly. ³¹ judgment. ³² winked.
³³ i.e., may the time be evil to you. ³⁴ suffer.

1026. On *abofe*, see Koelbing's note, "Ipomadon" 5.

þou shulde no moo tythyngis bryng,
    On horse þouȝ þou were hye !"

The Kyng commaundit a squyer tere,[35]   1055
"Goo telle þe scheperde in his ere
    þat i am þe Kyng,
And þou shall se sich cowntenence
þat hym had leuer be in Fraunce,
    When [he] heris of þat tythyng !   1060
He has me schewid his priueté:
He wil wene ded to be,
    And make þerfore mornyng.
Hit shalle hym mene al to gode:
I wolde not ellis, be þe rode,   1065
    Nouȝt for my best gold ryng !"

The squyer pryuely toke his leue
And plucked þe scheperde be þe sleue
    For to speke hym with:
"Man," he said, "þou art wode !   1070
Why dose þou not down þi hode?
þou art all out of kithe ![36]
Hit is þe Kyng þat spekis to þe,
May do þe what his willis be,
    Berefe þe lym and lithe;[37]   1075
And gif þou haue do any trespas,
Fall on knees and aske grace,
    And he will gif þe grithe."

þen was þat herd a carful man,
And neuer so sory as he was þan,   1080
    When he herd þat sawe;
He wist not what hym was gode,
But þen he putte doune his hode;
    On knees he fel downe lawe.
"Lorde," he seid, "i crye þe mercy !   1085

---

[35] fine.   [36] company; i.e., your conduct is inappropriate.   [37] a tag, both words meaning limb.

1060. MS. not clear.

I knew þe not, be oure Lady,
   When i come into þis sale,[38]
For had i wist of þis sorowe
When þat we met ȝister-morowe,
   I had not bene in þis bale."   1090
         NON FINIS SED PUNCTUS.

In other versions of the story, the king makes his host a knight and rewards him well.

---

[38] hall.

1086. MS. *know.*

THE TOURNAMENT OF TOTTENHAM

THE TOURNAMENT OF TOTTENHAM

This burlesque, in the dialect of the north of about 1400–1440, is less famous than Chaucer's "Sir Thopas," but shows the same familiarity with the machinery of chivalry and the same unwillingness to take it seriously. It survives in two MSS., Harleian 5306 (H.), dated 1456, and Cambridge University Library MS. Ff. II 38 (C.), after 1431. C. was first printed in 1631 by William Bedwell, rector of Tottenham, who published a text with modernized spellings. Several antiquaries reprinted this version, evidently subscribing to Bedwell's opinion that it had historical value. Percy printed it in the first and second editions of his "Reliques of Ancient English Poetry" (1765, 1767); but was then informed by Tyrwhitt of the existence of H.; and, perceiving its superiority to Bedwell's text, he used it in subsequent editions, with a few of Bedwell's readings where H. was obscure. In "Ancient Songs and Ballads" (1790), Joseph Ritson attacked Percy venomously for tampering with the texts in the "Reliques," and, as a part of the rebuke, edited this poem from H.; but his work contains several inaccuracies and unwarrantable emendations. In 1836, Thomas Wright edited the text from C.; this was reprinted by Hazlitt in "Remains of the Early Popular Poetry of England," vol. iii, with readings from H. and Bedwell's edition. No critical text has been attempted.

The stanza is a variation of a type common in the north; but, because of the state in which this poem has survived, it is nearly impossible to tell whether the normal line was iambic or doggerel. In either event, variations are numerous.

Through the kindness of the authorities of the Department of Manuscripts of the British Museum and of the Library of Cambridge University, it has been possible to prepare the text from rotographs of both manuscripts. Since H., which has the better version, is wretchedly copied and in many places almost illegible, the readings of C. furnish many valuable clues.

The incidents in the piece are very like those in other pieces involving boasts. Especially close is the parallel with "The Avowis of Alexander" (*STS*. 21): they boast in the presence of a lady; they threaten to capture each other's horses and swords (5440); two of them dispute as to their prowess; the prize is a peacock (not a hen);

and one boast is generally granted to be better than all the rest.
Some of the words in the Scotch poem also occur in this.

Why a poem written in the northern dialect should deal so familiarly with the topography of the district about London that
Tottenham antiquaries have included it in their histories of the
parish is something of a puzzle. Long -a is frequently retained where
the midland form had -o (ga, go); the plurals of verbs and nouns are
often in -ys, and so are the third singulars of many verbs (stonys,
getis). For a discussion of the language, see PMLA. 43. 124.

Of all þes kene conquerours to carpe it were kynde:
Of fele feꝫtyng-folk ferly we fynde;
The Turnament of Totenham haue we in mynde:
It were harme¹ sych hardynes were holden byhynde,²
    In story as we rede—   5
Of Hawkyn, of Herry,
Of Tomkyn, of Terry,
Of þem þat were dughty
And stalworth in dede.

It befel in Totenham, on a dere³ day,   10
Þer was mad a schurtyng⁴ be þe hyway.
Þeder com al þe men of þe contray—
Of Hyssyltoun, of Hygate, and of Hakenay,⁵
    And all þe swete swynke[rs].⁶
Þer hopped Hawkyn,   15
Þer davnsed Dawkyn,
Þer trumped Tomkyn;
    And all were trewe drynkers,

Tyl þe day was gon, and euyn-song past,
Þat þay schuld rekyn þer scot and þer contes cast;⁷   20
Perkyn þe potter in to þe press past,
And sayd, "Rondol þe refe,⁸ a doꝫter þou hast,

---

¹ would be evil. ² concealed. ³ i.e., memorable. ⁴ festival. ⁵ Islington, High-
gate, Hackney. ⁶ blessed workmen. ⁷ reckon their bill and cast up their
accounts. ⁸ reeve, bailiff.

Title. Tottenham and the other towns mentioned were at this time
separate parishes just north of London.
    8. MS. dughyt.
    21. MS. prest, probably a miscopying of long double -s.

Tyb, þe dere:
Þer-for wyt wold i
Whych of all þys bachelery[9]   25
Were best worthy
To wed hur to hys fere."

Vp styrt þes gadelyngys[10] with þer long staues,
And sayd, "Randal þe refe, lo! þis lad raues!
Baldely amang us þy duȝter he craues,   30
And we er rycher men þe[n] he, and more god haues,
  Of catell and corn."
Þen sayd Perkyn, "To Tybbe i haue hyȝt
Þat i schal be alway redy in my ryȝt,[11]
If þat it schuld be þys day seuenyȝt,[12]   35
Or ell[is] ȝet to-morn."

Þen sayd Randolfe þe refe, "Euer be he waryed[13]
Þat about þys carpyng lenger wold be taryed!
I wold not þat my doȝter þat scho were myscaryed,[14]
But at hur most worschyp[15] i wold scho were maryed.   40
  Þer-for a turnament schal begin
Þys day seuenyȝt,
With a flayl for to fyȝt,
And [he] þat ys of most myght
  Schall brouke hur with wynne.   45

"Whoso berys hym best in þe turnament,
Hym schall be granted þe gre, be þe comon assent,
For to wynne my doȝter with dughty[nes] of dent,
And Coppeld, my brode[16]-henne, was broȝt out of Kent,
  And my donnyd[17] kowe.   50

---

[9] company of young men. [10] rogues. [11] to defend my rights. [12] week. [13] cursed.
[14] should do badly. [15] to her greatest honor. [16] brood. [17] brown.

23. In the MS., *dere* has been altered in other ink to *devoll*.
38. MS. *atryed*.
39. *þat* is carelessly doubled.
47. MS *camon*.
49. Copple, meaning "crested," seems to have been a common name
for a hen. Cf. "Townley Mysteries" p. 99. A bird is often the prize
of such a contest.

F[or] no spens[18] wyl i spare,
For no catell wyl i care:
He schal haue my gray mare,
    And my spottyd sowe !"

Þer was many bold lad þer bodyes to bede;[19]   55
Þan þay toke þayr leue, and homward þay ȝede,
And all þe woke[20] afterward þay grayþed þer wede,
Tyll it come to þe day þat þay suld do þer dede.
    Þay armed ham in mattis:[21]
    Þay set on þer nollys,[22]   60
    For to kepe þer pollys,[23]
    Gode blake bollys,
        For[24] batryng of battis.

Þay sowed þam in schepe-skynnes, for[25] þay suld not brest;
Ilkon toke a blak hat insted of a crest,   65
A harow brod as a fanne[26] aboune on þer brest,
And a flayle in þer hande, for to fyght prest.
    Furth gon þay fare !
    Þer was kyd mekyl fors[27]
    Who schuld best fend his cors;[28]   70
    He þat had no gode hors,
        He gat hym a mare.

Sych anoþer gadryng haue i not sene oft !
When all þe gret cumpany com rydand to þe croft,[29]
Tyb on a gray mare was set upon loft,   75
On a sek ful of sedys, for scho schuld syt soft,
    And led hur to þe gap.[30]

---

[18] expenditure. [19] i.e., undertake it. [20] week. [21] mattings. [22] heads. [23] crowns.
[24] to prevent. [25] so that. [26] an arrow broad as a fan. [27] much might shown.
[28] defend his body. [29] field. [30] opening in the hedge.

62. MS. *bellys*.
64. I.e., sewed themselves in securely.
67. MS. *syght*.
72. By preference, knights used chargers. Cf. Perceval's early adventures.
76. C. has *senvye*, mustard seed.
77. MS. *cap*.

For cryeng of al þe men,
Forþer wold not Tyb þen
Tyl sche had hur gode brode-hen   80
    Set in hur lap.

A gay gyrdyl Tyb had on, borwed for þe nonys,
And a garland on hur hed, ful of rounde bonys,
And a broche on hur brest, ful of safer[31] stonys—
With þe holy rode tokenyng was wrethyn[32] for þe nonys: 85
    No catel was þer spared!
When ioly Gyb saw hure þare,
He gyrd[33] so hys gray mere
þat sche lete a faucon-fare[34]
    At þe rereward.   90

"I wow to God," quod Herry, "i schal not lefe behende!
May i mete with Bernard, on Bayard þe blynde,
Ich man kepe hym out of my wynde;[35]
For whatsoeuer þat he be befor[36] me i fynde,
    I wot i schal hym greue!"   95
"Wele sayd!" quod Hawkyn;
"And i avow," quod Dawkyn,
"May i mete with Tomkyn,
    His flayl hym refe."

"I vow to God," quod Hud, "Tyb, sone schal þou se   100
Whych of all þis bachelery grant is þe gre!
I schal scomfet[37] þaym all, for þe loue of þi;
In what place so i come, þay schal haue dout of me,
    Myn armes ar so clere:[38]

---

[31] sapphire. [32] it was worked with the sign of the cross. [33] struck. [34] broke wind. [35] course. [36] be (whom) before, etc. [37] discomfit. [38] shining (!).

85. MS. wrotyn. The inscription gave the jewel its power.
89. MS. þe sche.
92. Bayard was a common name for a horse; the original Bayard was the marvelous steed of the four sons of Aymon, and was popularly reputed to have been blind.
104. Possibly a reference to the light-giving power of the arms of heroes. See Wimberly 92.

I bere a reddyl[39] and a rake,   105
Poudred with a brenand drake,[40]
And iii cantell[41] of a cake
   In ycha cornare."

"I vow to God," quod Hawkyn, "yf i haue þe gowt,[42]
Al þat i fynde in þe felde presand[43] here aboute,   110
Haue i twyes or thryes redyn þurgh þe route,[44]
In ycha stede þer þay me se, of me þay schal haue doute
   When i begyn to play.
I make a vow þat i ne schall,
But-yf Tybbe wyl me call,   115
Or i be thryes doun fall,
   Ryȝt onys com away."

þen sayd Terry, and swore be hys crede,
"Saw þou neuer ȝong boy forþi hys body bede,
For when þay fyȝt fastest, and most ar in drede,   120
I schal take Tyb by þe hand and hur away lede.
   I am armed at þe full:
In myn armys[45] i bere wele
A doȝ trogh and a pele,[46]
A sadyll withouten a panell,[47]   125
   With a fles of woll."

"I vow to God," quod Dudman, "and swor be þe stra,[48]
Whyls me ys left my mere, þou getis hur not swa;
For scho ys wele schapen, and lyȝt as þe ro:[49]
þer ys no capul[50] in þys myle befor hur schal ga;   130
   Sche wil me noȝt begyle.

---

[39] gardener's hedging-stick.   [40] with figures of a fiery dragon sprinkled over it.
[41] sections.   [42] although I have the gout.   [43] rushing.   [44] throng.   [45] coat of arms.
[46] dough-trough and baker's-shovel.   [47] saddle-cloth.   [48] straw.   [49] roe.   [50] horse.

105 ff. The items enumerated are all painted on his coat of arms; they
are not weapons.
   109. MS. *yf he.*
   110. MS. *felte.*
   119. *For þi* may be a mistake for *forþer,* i.e., more recklessly.
   128. MS. *sws; has* is written over *ys.*
   131. Nearly illegible. *Wil ne?*

She wyl me bere, i dar wele say,
On a lang somerys day,
Fro Hyssyltoun to Hakenay,
   No3t oþer half myle!"[1]   135

"I vow to God," quod Perkyn, "þou spekis of cold rost![2]
I schal wyrch wyselyer, withouten any bost:
V of þe best capullys[3] þat ar in þys ost,[4]
I wot i schal þaym wynne, and bryng þaym to my cost;[5]
   And here i graunt þam Tybbe.   140
Wele, boyes, here ys he
þat wyl fy3t and not fle,
For i am in my iolyté,[6]
   With io forth, Gybbe!"[7]

When þay had þer vowes [made], furth [g]an þey hye,   145
With flayles and hornes and trumpes mad of tre.
þer were all þe bachelerys of þat contré:
þay were dy3t i[n] aray as þamselfe wold be.
   þayr baners were ful bry3t,
   Of an old roten fell;[8]   150
þe cheuerone, of a plow-mell[9]
And þe schadow[10] of a bell,
   Poudred with mone-ly3t.[11]

I wot it ys no chylder-game whan þay togedyr met!

---

[1] i.e., no more and no less. [2] roast; i.e., your news is late. [3] horses. [4] host.
[5] side. [6] in good spirits. [7] keep on, Gilbert! i.e., let's be doing something.
[8] rotten hide. [9] the chevron (pointed ornament) is in the likeness of a mallet carried by plowmen for breaking clods. [10] silhouette. [11] moons being sprinkled over the field.

133. MS. *sonerys*.
134. The distance is some three miles.
137. MS. *swyselyer*.
138. MS. *of þo*.
146. Wooden horns and trumpets were common in the Middle Ages, and were still sometimes used in England as late as the eighteenth century. Though their tone was satisfactory, they were discarded because of their clumsiness.
150 ff. The heraldic terms were confusing both to this scribe and to the scribe of MS. C. Hence the exact meaning of some of the phrases is conjectural. MS. *raton*.

When icha freke in þa feld on hys felay be[t],   155
And layd o[n] styfly; for noþyng wold þay let!
And faght ferly fast, tyll þer horses swet,
 And fewe wordys spoken.
þer were flayles al to-slatred,[12]
þer were scheldys al to-clatred,[13]   160
Bollys and dysches al to-schatred,
 And many hedys brokyn.

þer was clynkyng of cart-sadellys and clattiryng of cannes;[14]
Of fele frekis in þe feld, brokyn were þer fannes;[15]
Of sum were þe hedys brokyn, of sum þe brayn-panes;[16]   165
And yll ware i[t] be sum or þay went þens,
 With swyppyng of swepyllys.[17]
þe boyes were so wery for-fught[18]
þat þay myʒt not fyʒt mare oloft,[19]
But creped þen about in þe [c]roft   170
 As þey were croked crepyls.[20]

Perkyn was so wery þat he began to loute;[21]
"Help, Hud! i am ded in þys ylk rowte![22]
A hors for xl pens, a gode and a stoute,
þat i may lyʒtly come of my noye out![23]   175
 For no cost wyl i spare."
He styrt up as a snayle
And hent a capul be þe tayle,
And raʒt[24] Dawkyn hys flayle,
 And wan þer a mare.   180

Perkyn wan v and Hud wan twa;
Glad and blyþe þay ware þat þay had don sa:

---

[12] split. [13] smashed. [14] metal pots. [15] winnowing shovels. [16] skulls. [17] blows
from the leather of flails. [18] fought out. [19] i.e., on horseback. [20] broken cripples.
[21] sink. [22] throng. [23] easily come out of my vexation. [24] seized from.

159 ff. MS. *flatred . . . flatred.* The emendation is suggested by the
readings of C.
 163. MS. *chaltitryng.*
 166. MS. illegible in part.
 172. MS. *louter.*
 173. MS. *rowet.*
 178. MS. *be þo.*

Þay wold haue²⁵ þam to Tyb and present hur with þa.
Þe capull were so wery þat þay my3t not ga,
    But styl gon þay stand.   185
"Allas !" quod Hudde, "my ioye i lese !
Me had leuer þen a ston²⁶ of chese
Þat dere Tyb had al þese,
    And wyst it were my sand."²⁷

Perkyn turnyd hym about in þat ych thrange;   190
Among þes wery boyes he wrest and he wrang:²⁸
He threw þam doun to þe erth, and þrast þaim amang,²⁹
When he saw Tyrry away with Tyb fang,³⁰
    And after hym ran.
Of hys hors he hym drogh,   195
And gaf hym of hys flayl inogh.
"We, te-he !" quod Tyb, and lugh,³¹
    "3e er a dughty man."

Þus þay tugged and rugged³² tyl yt was nere ny3t.
All þe wyues of Totenham come to se þat sy3t,   200
With wyspes and kexis and ryschys³³ þer ly3t,
To fech hom þer husbandes, þat were þam trouth-ply3t;
    And sum bro3t gret harwes,³⁴
Þer husbandes hom for to fech;
Sum on dores and sum on hech,³⁵   205
Sum on hyrdyllys and sum on crech,³⁶
    And sum on welebaraws.

Þay gaderyd Perkyn about, euerych syde,
And graunt hym þer [þe gre]; þe more was hys p[r]ide.
Tyb and he, with gret merthe homward con þay ryde,   210
And were al ny3t togedyr, tyl þe morn-tyde;
    And þay in fere assent:³⁷
So wele hys nedys he has sped³⁸

---

²⁵ bring. ²⁶ stone, fourteen pounds. ²⁷ sent by me. ²⁸ twisted and jerked. ²⁹ i.e., jabbed with his flail. ³⁰ start. ³¹ laughed. ³² scuffled. ³³ twists of straw and flax and rushes. ³⁴ sledges, hurdles. ³⁵ gratings. ³⁶ lattices. ³⁷ agree with one another. ³⁸ brought to a successful issue.

210. MS. *mothe.*

þat dere Tyb he has wed;
þe pryse folk þat hur led 215
Were of þe turnament.

To þat ylk fest com many, for þe nones:
Some come hyp-halt,[39] and sum tryppand[40] on þe stonys;
Sum a staf in hys hand, and sum two at onys:[41]
Of sum were þe hedys to-broken, and sum þe schulder-bonys: 220
With sorow com þay þedyr!
Wo was Hawkyn, wo was Herry;
Wo was Tomkyn, wo was Terry;
And so was al þe bachelary,
When þay met togedyr. 225

At þat fest þay were seruyd with a ryche aray:
Euery v and v had a cokenay;[42]
And so þay sat in iolyté al þe lang day,
And at þe last þay went to bed, with ful gret deray.[43]
Mekyl myrth was þem amang: 230
In euery corner of þe hous
Was melody delycyous,
For to here precyus,
Of vi menys sang.[44]

EXPLICIT.

---

[39] limping. [40] stumbling. [41] i.e., staves in both hands. [42] cf. note. [43] unsteadiness. [44] contrapuntal song for six voices.

214. MS. *had.*
215. MS. *prayse.*
219. MS. *þys þay.*
227. The *Oxford Dictionary* cites this passage as an illustration of the word *cockney* in the sense of "small egg"; but that sense is obviously unsatisfactory. The word seems to mean "cook." See "King Lear" II. iv. 120.

VOCABULARY

INTRODUCTION

Only common words are included, and only a few references for each. Words neither glossed nor included here have the sense of their phonetic equivalents in Modern English. Compounds (e.g., *aslaghe, dore-barr*) are hastily dealt with; for spellings and derivations, see the root-form of the words (*slaghe, dore,* etc.).

The following conventions in spelling have been observed:

When *y-* is equivalent to *i-*, the word is listed under *i*, regardless which letter is used (*ynne* under *in*). But participles in *i-* are listed under the letter immediately following the *i-*.

Æ is listed as if it were *a*, not *æ*.

The character *þ* is not used, and is replaced with *th*.

C and *k*, which were used interchangeably in Middle English for the hard sound of *c*, are listed according to the modern spellings of the words, so far as possible (*karpe* under *c*). For *cw-, kw-,* see *qu-*.

For Old English and Old French *-u-*, see *-ou-*. Scribes used *u* and *v* interchangeably; here all are listed under *u*, except a few initial *v's*. They also did not discriminate between *ȝ* and *z*; and their practice has been followed here.

F, which between vowels was often voiced, has been replaced with *u*.

Forms of a word that differ only by the addition of final *e* have usually not been distinguished, except when the *-e* is a case ending.

For *ȝ*, see *y-* or *g-*.

Cases and modes are not always noted unless their forms have peculiarities. Verbs are in the indicative mode unless otherwise noted. The persons of pronouns and verbs are indicated by the figures, 1, 2, 3, etc.

The following abbreviations for grammatical terms are used:

a., accusative
adj., adjective
adv., adverb
comp., compound
conj., conjunction
cp., comparative
d., dative
f., feminine gender
g., genitive
imp., imperative
inf., infinitive
int., interrogative
interj., interjection
m., masculine and neuter genders
n., { noun
     { nominative case
OE, Old English

OF, Old French
ON, Old Norse
plu., plural
pp., past participle
pr., present tense
prep., preposition
pro., pronoun
prp., present participle
pt., preterite
rel., relative
sb., adjective as noun
sg., singular
sj., subjunctive
sup., superlative
vbl., verbal
vs., strong verb
vw., weak verb

1001

In the vocabulary, entries are followed by a reference to poem and line. Titles of poems are abbreviated as follows:

Al, "Alexander"
At, "Athelston"
Av, "The Avowing of Arthur"
B, "The Tale of Beryn"
CA, "Chevelere Assigne"
Cl, "Sir Cleges"
D, "Sir Degaré"
EG, "Eger and Grime"
Em, "Emaré"
ET, "The Earl of Toulouse"
FB, "Floris and Blancheflour"
G, "Gamelyn"
Hr, "King Horn"
Hv, "Havelok the Dane"
Ip, "Ipomadon"

K, "King Edward and the Shepherd"
Lv, "Sir Launfal"
Ly, Laymon's "Brut"
O, "Sir Orfeo"
P, "Sir Perceval of Galles"
R, "Robert of Sicily"
Sd, "The Sultan of Babylon"
Sq, "The Squire of Low Degree"
SS, "The Seven Sages of Rome"
Tr, "The Destruction of Troy"
TT, "The Tournament of Tottenham"
Yw, "Ywain and Gawain"

VOCABULARY

A

a, *cf.* **an, on, ai, at.**

abide, *vs.*, (OE abīdan), (1) dwell, remain. *inf.*, **abyde,** G 742, D 479; *pt.˙sg.*, **abood,** B 3680; **abeod,** Ly 28381; **habade,** P 1731; *pp.*, **abide,** G 337. (2) await. *inf.*, G 24; *pr.*, **habyddis,** P 1278; *pt.*, **abood,** At 753. (3) wait, delay, stop. *pt.*, **abod,** D 48; *imp. sg.*, **habide,** SS 2991. (4) endure. *inf.*, EG 418; **abide,** Hr 1048; **habyde,** P 72.

abie, abegge, *vs.*, (OE abycgan), pay for, atone for. G 816; **aby,** SS 4288; **haby,** P 1903; **abugge,** Hr 75; **abeie,** Hr 110; **abygge,** Al 4199; *pt. sg.*, **abought,** G 76; **aboht,** Ly 27638. *Used absolutely,* Yw 413, Sd 1793.

aboute, *prep. and adv.*, (OE onbutan), about, around, near. **aboute,** Tr 83; **abute,** Hr 1081; **abuten,** Ly 27567; **abouȝt,** Cl 43.

ac, *conj.*, (OE ac, ah), but. Hr 523; D 29; Ly 27734.

adight, *cf.* **dight.**

admiral, *n.*, (OF amiral), Saracen viceroy or officer. Ly 27680; **admirail,** Ly 27668; **admirad,** Hr 89; *g. sg.*, **admirale,** Ly 27689; **amerayle,** Em 109.

adoun, *adv.*, (OE of dūne), down. Hr 428; **adun,** Ly 27459; Hr 1488.

adred, *adj.*, (OE ofdrædd), afraid, terrified. SS 502; Hr 291; **adrad,** G 562; **adradde,** Ly 27962.

afered, *adj.*, (OE afæran), frightened. ET 661; D 101.

afore, aforn, *prep. and adv.*, before. G 656, 806; **auorne,** Ly 28313.

after, (OE æfter), (1) *prep.*, next in order. Hv 171. (2) (sent) for. G 17; **aftur,** CA 129. (3) (name) for. Ly 27921. (4) in accordance with, according to. Ly 27529; EG 517; **efter,** SS 2816.

(5) in pursuit of. Hr 880.

(6) *adv.*, afterwards. Tr 81; Sd 1877; SS 310; aftir, P 1808.

(7) *conj.*, according as. Hv 2810.

again, (OE ongēn, ongegn), (1) *adv.*, back, in return. ET 52; aȝen, D 267; ayein, D 931; agen, Hr 582, aye, B 3276.

(2) once more. ogayn, SS 468; aȝeyn, CA 316; aȝe, B 3720.

(3) *prep.*, against. aȝaynns, Av 219; aȝaynus, Av 315.

(4) toward, nearing (*of place and time*). aȝeyn, Em 203; P 1129; D 967.

(5) until. Ip 3067.

(6) in anticipation of. Ip 3217; Hv 1106.

(7) before, in the face of. Em 206; aȝein, Ly 27980; ayen, Lv 989.

(8) *conj.*, in preparation for the time when. P 198.

comp. as *adv.*, ageynward, in return. B 3314.

agast, *adj.*, (OE agæstan), afraid, in awe of. D 900; G 7; ET 451.

aȝe, back; *cf.* again.

ah, *cf.* ac, but; awe, owe, own.

ahon, *v.*, hang. Ly 28407.

ai, ay, (OE ā, ō), (1) *adv.*, always, ever. SS 2816; Tr 18; æi, Ly 27729; a, Ly 28090.

(2) *adj.*, eternal. Av 434.

comp., for ay, forever, SS 855; Ip 1162.

air, *cf.* heir.

aither, *cf.* either.

al, alle, (OE eall, all), (1) *adj. and adj.-pro.*, all. Hr 756; Hv 35. *old g.*, aller, of us all, G 321; our alther, of us all, G 256; alther best, best of all, Hv 182; althir best, P 1883; alther leste, least of all, Hv 1978; alre, of all. Ly 27807; alder, FB 551.

(2) *adv.*, wholly, entirely. Ly 27840.

comp., alkyn, all sorts of, Yw 1073; algate, any way, G 115; always, yet, O 229 .

ælc, *cf.* ilk.

alighte, alighted; *cf.* light.

als, also, *cf.* as.

alsone, *adv.*, (OE al swa sōna), (1) straightway. P 1011; alssone, SS 518.

(2) as soon (as). Yw 233.

amis, *adv. and adj.*, wrong, wrongly. D 60.

amorwe, a-marȝen, to-morrow; *cf.* morne.

an, *adj.*, (OE ān), one. Hv 114; a, Cl 521; on, Sd 1582; *d.f.*, are, Ly 27992; *d.m.*, ane, Ly 27947; *a.m.*, enne, Ly 27667; ænne, Ly 27549.

an, *cf.* on, one, and.

and, an, *conj.*, (OE ond), (1) and. Hr 699; Hv 4; an, Ly 27556; D 153.

(2) if. At 403; Av 443.

ani, *adj. and pro.*, (OE ænig), any. Hv 10; anny, Ip 1086; eni, G 260.

anon, *adv.*, (OE on ān), at once, quickly. D 79; anone, ET 253; anan, Ly 27508; onane, SS 819.

comp., anon right, straightway, G 734; anæn swa, as soon as, Ly 28242.

another, (OE ān oðer), (1) *adj. and pro.*, another. Hr 578.

(2) *adv.*, otherwise. B 3538.

anowȝ, enough; *cf.* inogh.

answer, *vw.*, (OE ondswerian), answer. *pt.*, answarede, Hr 42; andswarede, Ly 28094; vnsquarut, Av 129; *pt. pl.*, ansuereden, Hv 176.

aplight, *adv.*, (OE on pliht), (1) at once. D 1048.

(2) indeed. D 775.

are, (OE ǣr), (1) *conj.*, before. G 605; or, Ip 3041; are, P 653; er, G 568; ar, Hr 546.

(2) *adv.*, earlier, formerly. Lv

1019; ær, Ly 27491; ære, Ly
27959; ayre, Ip 1064; *sup.*, arst,
first, formerly, G 538; ærst, Ly
27456.
(3) sooner, rather, SS 3023, 4253.
(4) *prep.*, before, earlier than.
SS 4303.
comp., er thane, before the time
when. Hr 1435.
aright, *adv.*, (OE on riht), (1)
rightly. G 29.
(2) straightway (*often used merely
to intensify*). Hr 457.
arise, *vs.*, (OE arīsan), arise, get up.
pt., aros, Hr 1313; aræs, Ly
28006; *imp. plu.*, ariseth, G 643.
armed, *pp.*, *adj.*, armed. iarmed,
Hr 803; armut, Av 77; yarmed,
O 134.
as, als, also, (OE alswa), (1) *conj.*
as, as if. P 2263; ase, D 272; os,
ET 613.
(2) as (*correlative*). D 1039; ET
409; alswa (. . swa), Ly 27458.
(3) when. Hv 2120.
(4) in such manner. Hr 538; Ly
27648; alse, Ly 28413.
(5) as surely as (*followed by subj.*).
Hr 775.
(6) however, in whatever manner.
Hr 543.
(7) *adv.*, thus, so, likewise. Yw
839.
(8) also. CA 91; Ly 27884.
(9) very (*in phrases, such as:* also
swithe, *etc.*). D 746; Hr 471.
(10) *prep.*, like. Hv 319.
(11) *expletive, untranslatable.* Av
896; Tr 8668.
aslaghe, slain. asla3en Hr 897,
1491.
astonied, stunned. Sd 2057.
aswoue, aswowe, swooning. D 903;
Lv 755.
at, *prep.*, (OE æt), (1) in (a place).
Hr 253; a, Ly 27505.

(2) with. O 138; Hr 1033.
(3) of, from. P 179; Em 185;
atte, Av 1081.
(4) according to (*in the phrase:*
at will). Av 3.
(5) to. B 3481.
comp., atte, at the. B 3002; ate,
D 576.
aueden, had; *cf.* haue.
auenture, aunter, (OF aventure),
(1) *n.*, adventure. G 777; antur,
Av 1015.
(2) fate, chance, luck. auentoure,
D 624; Tr 67.
(3) occurrence, happening. auntris, B 3436; aventowres, Em 754.
(4) *vv.*, take a risk. auntre, G
217; aventure, ET 927.
(5) happen. *pt.*, auntrid, Tr
8632.
aught, (OE āwiht, āuht, āht), (1)
pro., anything. awght, Ip 476;
aw3te, CA 204; oght, Sd 2713;
o3te, Av 431; ou3t, B 3611.
(2) *adv.*, at all. Hr 976; P 1157.
auter, awter, altar.
awe, owen, *vs.*, (OE āgan), (1) own,
have. Hv 1292; a3en, Ly 27989;
1 sg. pr., ah, Ly 28022; *3 sg. pr.*,
oweth, Ip 477; *pr. sj.*, a3e, Ly
28423; *pt.*, aute, Hv 743; awcte,
Hv 207; ahte, Ly 27729; au3t,
D 710 *pr. sj.*, hawe, Hv 1188.
(2) ought, should. *pt. as pr.*,
aughte, P 2175; aucte, Hv 2787;
auhte, Hv 2800; *pr.*, owth, Em
667.
(3) owe. K 577; *pr. sg.*, aw, Yw
92; *pr. plu.*, owe, K 621; *pt.*,
aughte, P 1490.
awe, *n.*, fear. aw3e, FB 909.
awen, awin, a3en, *cf.* own.
awreke, avenge; *cf.* wreke.
axe, axid, ask, asked. B 2941,
3372.
ayen, aye, a3e, *cf.* again.

B

bac, back, *n.*, (OE bæc), back. Hv 47; bake, P 2235; Tr 8599; bakke, CA 291.

bald, bold, *adj.*, (OE beald, bald), (1) bold. Hr 90; *g. plu.*, baldere, Ly 27510.
(2) fine, spirited. D 394; *d.f.sg.*, baldere, Ly 27873.
comp., baldelike, boldly. Hv 53; boldelych, G 717.

bale, *n.*, (OE bealu), (1) sorrow, evil, trouble. P 1411; Ip 3101; *pl.*, balys, Lv 971; *often in the following phrases:* bale bett, repair an injury, rescue from trouble, ET 515; balys bete, Lv 971; boteles bale, irreparable injury, ET 607.
(2) destruction. balu, Ly 27478.

band, bond, *pt. of* bind. Ip 388; G 818.

bane, *n.*, (OE bana), (1) ruin, death. Yw 709; EG 137; P 568.
(2) murderer, slayer. P 1926.

barnage, group of barons. SS 273; barronage, the lands of a baron, EG 1452.

bath, see both.

be-. *For all forms with the prefix* be-, *cf.* bi-.

be, ben, *vs.*, (OE bēon, wesan), *inf.*, EG 545; Hr 8; bee, Av 66; beo, Hr 1285; bene, Em 626; beon, Ly 27641. *pr. 1 sg.*, am, D 98; ame, P 1501; *2 sg.*, art, B 2926; ert, SS 503; ært, Ly 28098; *(with enclitic pronoun)* ertou, SS 2916. *3 sg.*, is, D 78; his, Hv 279; es, P 205, SS 245; beth, B 3315. *As future*, bese, P 2077; beth, Hv 1261; bi3, D 127. *1 plu.*, aren, Hv 619; ben, G 162; be3, D 104. *2 plu.*, ar, Av 643; beoth, Ly 27610. *3 plu.*, arne, Av 1130;

be, D 980; beth, O 57; ben, Hv 2599; sunden, Ly 28224; er, SS 363; bethe, B 3313; byn, K 9; buth, Al 3959. *subj. 1 sg. pr.*, be, Ip 3101. *3 sg.*, beo, Ly 28148; *(with nunnation)* beon, Ly 28637; be, D 811. *pt. 1 sg.*, was, D 873; wos, Av 921. *2 sg.*, were, Av 846; P 544; wore, Hv 684. *3 sg.*, wasse, Av 638; was, D 302. wes, Ly 27478. *plu.*, war, SS 218; wore, Em 410; ware, Av 400; was, Av 865; weoren, Ly 27432; werun, Av 242; wern, Cl 17; weryn, O 18; wheryn, Lv 261. *sj. sg.*, were, CA 180; ware, P 150; weer, B 3566; weore, Ly 27643; wore, Hv 1938. *imp. sg.*, beo, Hr 541; be, Hv 683. *plu.*, bes, Hv 2246. *pp.*, be, Sd 2440; bene, P 2231; ybeon, Al 3921; byn, Ip 3189; iben, D 232; ibe, B 3040. *Used for auxiliary of intransitive v. in pt.*, is wente, Av 538; er went, SS 363.
Negative forms, nas (ne was), G 29, D 11; nam (ne am), O 428; nis (ne is), O 129; nes, (ne wes), D 708; neoren, neoruen (ne weoren), Ly 27533, 27654.

bede, *vs.*, (OE bēodan), (1) offer, present *(sometimes of blows)*. TT 119; *pr. 1 sg.*, bede, Av 296; *(with enclitic pronoun)* biddi, Hv 484.
(2) command, summon, invite. *pr. 2 sg.*, bedes, Hv 2392; *pt.*, bede, Av 744; bed, Hr 504; *pp.* ybede, FB 859.
The forms were gradually superseded by forms of bidde *(q.v.)*, pray, beg. *They were often confused in M.E. times.*

beie, bye, *vs.*, (OE bycgan), (1) buy, redeem. Hv 53. *pt. 3 sg.*, bo3te, Av 646; bow3t, Cl 335.
(2) pay for, atone for, suffer for. bo3te, Hr 1388; bouthe, Hv

875. *pp.*, **boght,** SS 546; **bouth,** Hv 883.

bere, *vs.*, (OE **beran**), (1) carry, bear. D 771; **beor,** Al 4170; **iberen,** Ly 27850. *pt. 3 sg.*, **bar,** D 247. *pp.*, **borne,** Em 258; **yboren,** Hv 2557. (2) comport oneself. *pr. 3 sg.*, **berys,** TT 46. (3) ride down, strike down. *pr. 3 sg.*, **berythe,** Ip 3179; *pt. 3 sg.*, **bare,** Av 422; **bore,** EG 130. (4) give birth to. *pt. 1 sg.*, **bere,** CA 196; **bare,** CA 211; *pp.*, **bore,** Sd 2195; **ibore,** D 181, Hr 138; *pt. sj.*, **bere,** Hv 974. (5) *in idiomatic senses:* wear, Hr 1286; have, Em 924; weigh down, CA 297.

berst, brest, *vs.*, (OE **berstan**), burst, break. *inf.*, CA 317; Ly 27683. *sj. 2 sg. pr.*, **berste,** Hr 1192. *pt.*, **brast,** Yw 814; Av 1027.

beste, beeste, *n.*, (OE **beste**), beast. Hv 279; CA 214, 218; *plu.*, **besteȝ,** P 176.

bet, bette, better; *cf.* **gode.**

bete, *vs.*, (OE **bēatan**), beat, strike. D 348; *pr. 3 sg.*, **betus,** Av 58; *pt. 3 sg.*, **bet,** TT 155; *plu.*, **beten,** Hv 1876; *imp. plu.*, **beteth,** G 111; *pp.*, **beten,** G 115.

bethe, *cf.* **both.**

beȝst, best; *cf.* **gode.**

bi, by, be, (OE **be, bi**), (1) *prep.*, beside. Hr 35; D 1025. (2) by means of. Tr 23; Hr 436. (3) in the name of. B 3105; Ip 471. (4) to the extent of. D 909. (5) concerning. B 3598; CA 5. (6) during. G 65. (7) about (*of time*). Hr 1431. (8) in groups of. D 895. (9) *adv.*, near. CA 109.

(10) *conj.*, by the time that. Av 689; SS 845. *comp.*, **be that,** then, when. Cl 58; D 273; **by that,** CA 248, At 496.

bicome, *vs.*, (OE **bicuman**), (1) become, happen. *pt. plu.*, **bicomen,** Hv 2257. *imp. plu.*, **bicomes,** Hv 2303. (2) betake oneself, go. *pr. 3 sg.*, **bicomeȝ,** D 178; *pt. 3 sg.*, **bycome,** Yw 438; *pp.*, **bicumen,** Ly 28057; **bicome,** O 192.

bidde, *vs.*, (OE **biddan**), (1) ask, beg, pray, invite. Hr 457; D 490. *pr. 1 sg.*, **bidde,** G 744; **biddus,** Av 66; *pt. 3 sg.*, **bade,** Av 549; **bad,** G 238, Hr 1069. (2) command. *pr. 3 sg.*, **byddyth,** CA 262. *pt. sg.*, **bad,** Hr 273; Cl 398; **badde,** CA 155; *imp. plu.*, **biddeȝ,** D 212.

bide, *vs.*, (OE **bīdan**), (1) remain, delay. Av 409; *pt.*, **bod,** At 405; **bade,** P 569; *pp.*, **biddn,** EG 79. (2) await. *pr. 3 sg.*, **bidus,** Av 244.

bidene, bedene, *adv.*, (OE ?), (*usually following* **al**), at once, at the same time, together. Lv 907; Yw 50; SS 231.

bifore, biforn, (OE **biforan**), (1) *prep.*, in the presence of. **biuore,** Hr 233; **biuoren,** Ly 28417. (2) in front of. Cl 399; Ly 28024. (3) earlier than. Hv 246. (4) *adv.*, earlier, in front of, *etc.* P 107; **beforne,** Ip 458; Ly 27555.

biginne, *vs.*, (OE **biginnan**), begin, do. *inf.*, Hr 1277. *pt. plu.*, **bigunnen,** Ly 28315, Hr 1433; *sg.*, **byganne,** CA 183. *The preterit is frequently equivalent to the past tense of the following verb:* **bigan,** to flow, flowed, Hr 117.

bihald, biheld, *vs.*, (OE **bihaldan, bihealdan**), look at, look about.

Hr 1147. *pr. sg.*, behylde, Ip 419; byholdeʒ, P 534; byhaldes, P 673; *pt. sg.*, biheld, D 756, FB 262; *plu.*, byhelde, P 66.

bihate, bihete, *vs.*, (OE behātan), promise. *pr. 1 sg.*, bihete, Yw 158; *pt.*, bihet, Hr 470; behight, Cl 468; byheyʒte, Al 3926; beheʒte, Av 532; byheet, G 418; byhette, Al 3988; *pp.*, bihoten, Hv 564; behette, K 573; *vb.n.*, byhotyng, Al 4000.

bihoue, *vw.*, (OE bihōfian), behoove (*always impersonal*), befit. *pr.*, bihoueth, Hr 178; behovys, Ip 1163; behouus, Av 300; *pt.*, byhoued, P 2228.

bileue, *vw.*, (OE belǣfan), (1) remain, survive. Hr 363; *pr. 3 plu.*, bilauen, Ly 28119; *pt. 3 sg.*, belaftc, Em 472; bilefte, Hv 2963. (2) leave, relinquish. bileofuen, Ly 28184; bilæfuen, Ly 28189. *pt. sg.*, bilæfden (*with nunnation*), Ly 27899; *pp.*, bylcfte, CA 240; bileued, G 98.

bileue, *vw.*, (OE gelyfan), believe. Hr 1321; *etc.*

bilinnc, *vs.*, hcsitate. G 552.

biliue, quickly; *cf.* bliue.

bireue, *vs. and w.*, (OE bereafian), deprive of, take away. *pt.*, byrafte, CA 199; *pp.*, byreeued, G 85; byreued, G 97; biræued, Ly 27907.

biswike, *vs.*, (OE biswīcan), beguile, cheat, betray. *inf.*, Hr 290; biswiken, Ly 28126; *pt. sg.*, biswac, Ly 28416; *pp.*, biswike, Hv 1249.

biteche, bitake, *vs.*, (OE betǣcan), commit, entrust, give. *pr. 1 sg.*, beteche, CA 312; bitache, Ly 28602; *3 sg.*, bytaketh, CA 151; *pt. 2 sg.*, bitahtest, Ly 28108; *3 sg.*, bitaughte, P 2156; betoke, Ip 449; bitaucte, Hv 206; bitawt,

D 331. *pp.*, bytaken, CA 163. *Very common in the phrase:* to Gode bitechen, farewell; CA 312, G 338.

biwreie, *vw.*, (OE -wregan), reveal, betray. Sd 1580; *pr. sj.*, Hr 362.

ble, blee, *n.*, (OE blēo), complexion, hue. Lv 849; ET 198; Em 270.

blethelye, *cf.* blithe.

blinne, *vs.*, (OE blinnan), stop, cease, put an end to. Sd 2442; bylynne, G 557; blin, EG 641; *pt.*, blan, Av 919; blanne, ET 241; blunne, Hv 2670.

blithe, *adj. and adv.*, (OE blīðe), happy, happily. Hr 274; blethelye, CA 278; bliʒe, D 171; blethelyche, FB 148.

bliue, *adj. and adv.*, (OE bi līfe), quick, quickly. ET 1066; belyffe, P 878; biliue, SS 3013; Ly 28346.

blow, *vs.*, (OE blāwan), blow. Hv 587; blauwen, Ly 27815; *pt. plu.*, bleou, Ly 27813; bleowen, Ly 27442; *imp. sg.*, blou, Hv 585; *prp.*, blawand, Yw 340.

bonc, *n.*, (OE bān), bone. D 16; bonus, Av 184.

bone, *n.*, (ON bōn), request, a request granted, reward. At 731; G 153; Yw 1075.

bord, *n.*, (OE bord), (1) board. Hv 2106; burde, Yw 186. (2) table. P 438; ET 609; *d. sg.*, borde, Ly 28573; burdes, Av 751.

boru, borow, *n.*, (OE burh, burg), city, town. burh, Ly 28380; burhʒc, Ly 28389; borw, Hv 847; borowes, P 1762; burwes, Hv 55.

bote, *n.*, (OE bōt), remedy, help, welfare. P 223; boote, EG 1050, 899; Lv 894.

bote, *n.*, (OE bāt), boat. Hr 202; boot, Em 268; botis, B 2971.

both, (ON bāðir), (1) *adj. and pro.*, both. Hr 1523; bothen, G 625; bethe, Hv 1680. *In the phrase:*

both two, both of them, Em 935, Cl 185.

(2) *adv.*, as well. G 843.

(3) *correlative*, bath, SS 361; Tr 56.

bouhte, bouthe, bought, *cf.* **beie.**

boun, bowne, *adj.*, (ON **būinn**), ready, prepared. ET 66; Av 254; **bownn,** P 1066. *In the phrase:* made him boun, he went, SS 2894.

braid, breid, *vs.*, (OE **bregdan**), (1) draw (a sword). *pt. sg.*, **braid,** Ly 27626; Av 214; *plu.*, Sd 1795.

(2) start, jump, rush. **braid,** Tr 8644; Av 607; **bræid,** Ly 27674; **breyde,** B 3775.

brand, brond, *n.*, (OE **brand, brond**), sword. P 1185; D 947; Av 214; *d. plu.*, **bronden,** Ly 27519.

breke, *vs.*, (OE **brecan**), break. *pt. sg.*, **brake,** Ip 3132; **breke,** CA 165; **brakk,** ET 1118; **brak,** Hr 681; *plu.*, **breken,** Ly 27506.

brenne, berne, *vw.*, (ON **brenna**), burn. CA 68; ET 36; **bren,** SS 585; *pt. 3 sg.*, **brent,** P 773; **brente,** CA 344; *plu.*, **brenden,** Hv 594; *pp.*, **brent,** Tr 4777; ET 572; **brend,** SS 4253; *prp.*, **brynnande,** P 440; SS 2827; **brennyng,** Av 866.

bri3t, bright, *adj. and adv.*, (OE **bryht**), bright, shining (*often of beauty*). B 2928; CA 8; **brythe,** Em 697.

bringe, *vs.*, (OE **bringan**), bring. Hr 338; **brenge,** D 43; *pt. 3 sg.*, **browght,** Em 82; **bro3te,** Hr 466; **brow3te,** CA 59; **brouth,** Hv 336; (*by nunnation*) **brohten,** Ly 28472; *plu.*, **brohten,** Ly 28309; **brouthen,** Hv 2791; *pp.*, **brow3tt,** Cl 274; **ibrout,** D 102; **ybrowght,** Em 224.

brinie, corslet; *cf.* **brunie.**

brode, *adj.*, (OE **brād**), broad. **broode,** CA 297; **brade,** P 126; *a.m.*, **bradne,** Ly 27675.

brouht, brouth, brouct, *cf.* **bringe.**

brouke, *vs.*, (OE **brūcan**), enjoy, use (*word used mostly in emphatic sentences, in subjunctive*). TT 45; **brook,** EG 82; **bruke,** Ly 28263; *sj.*, **brouk,** G 273; **brok,** Av 1011; **browke,** P 1630; *imp.*, **brok,** K 551.

brunie, burnie, *n.*, (OE **byrne**), corslet. Hr 841; **brinie,** Hv 1775; **burne,** Ly 27748; *plu.*, **burnen,** Ly 27466.

brygge, bridge. ET 439.

bure, bur, apartment, room. Hr 269.

burgeis, *n.*, (OF **burgeis**), burgess, townsman. Sd 1748; *plu.*, **burgeys,** B 3188; **burgeysis,** B 3149; **burias,** SS 2789; **buriays,** O 502.

burh, bur3e, town; *cf.* **boru.**

burn, *cf.* **brenne.**

buske, *vw.*, (ON **būask**), (1) adorn, prepare, get ready. ET 819; *pt.*, **busked,** P 1030; **buskyd,** ET 232; **buskute,** Av 146.

(2) hasten, go. *pt.*, **buskit,** Tr 4705.

bute, (OE **būtan**), (1) *conj.*, but, yet. Hr 193; Ly 27840; **buten,** Ly 27874; **bot,** P 2213.

(2) unless. D 214; **butte,** Av 1039.

(3) *prep.*, except. **bote,** D 74; **butte,** Av 1077.

(4) without. **buten,** Ly 28150.

(5) *adv.*, only. Hr 198; ne but, B 3331.

comp., **butte,** but the. B 3250; **bot-if,** unless, P 383; **butte-giffe,** Av 111; **but-3if,** D 31; **but-on,** except that, provided that, if, Hv 505; EG 1049; Hv 962; **but-that,** unless, Lv 679.

C

can, *vs.*, (OE cunnan, conne), (1) know, know how, be able. *pr. 1 sg.*, kane, P 318; kan, CA 313; *2 sg.*, kane, P 1268; (*with enclitic pronoun*) canstu, Hr 1206; *3 sg.*, can, ET 252; cunne, Ly 28644; *plu.*, kan, P 1135; conne, G 63; con, B 3408; kunne, Hv 435; *pt. sg.*, kan, D 510; can, D 508; cowthe, Cl 208; coude, B 3611, G 4; cowdist, B 3336; couthe, Av 257; *plu.*, couthen, D 58; couth, Av 471; *pr. sj. sg.*, cone, Hv 622; cunne, Hv 568; *pt.*, couthest, D 595.
(2) did (*used with infinitive to make the equivalent of a preterit, a result of confusion with gan, q.v.*), EG 123; con, Av 84; conne, Av 92; cold, EG 122, 634; con, D 45.
In the phrases: als he can, as best he can, in his best manner, P 967; that wele kan, who know their business, P 1135.
carbuncle, *cf.* Hv 2145.
care, *n.*, (OE cearu), grief, sorrow, distress. Hr 1244; Ly 28634; kare, Em 627. carefull, wretched, Em 328.
carpe, *vw.*, (ON karpa), speak, say. TT 1; ET 587; *pr. 3 sg.*, carpys, P 1469; carpus, Av 574; *sj. plu.*, carpe, Av 158; *pt.*, carputte, Av 170; karped, Yw 498; *prp.*, carpand, Sd 538.
cas, case, *n.*, (OF cas). *Used loosely for any* matter, chance, case, *or* condition of affairs. O 173; B 2956; Tr 25.
caste, *vs.*, (ON kasta), cast, throw. *pt. sg.*, caste, G 237; kist, B 2955; keste, P 1710; *plu.*, kest, Av 637; *pp.*, kest, SS 882; casten, SS 892.

catel, (OF catel, chatel), (1) goods, property. TT 32; Hv 225.
(2) cattle, beasts. K 156.
certes, surely; *cf.* sertes.
charbocle, *cf.* Hv 2145.
chaunce, *n.*, (OF cheance), circumstance, fortune (good or bad). CA 123; Em 684.
chere, (OF chere), (1) *n.*, countenance. B 3525; Av 658.
(2) expression of face. cheere, G 319; *in the phrases:* make heavy chere and make ill chere, lament. SS 515; Em 300.
(3) mood, state of mind. Sd 2032.
(4) kind act, friendliness. Sd 2023; EG 111; Sd 2781.
(5) *adj.*, Sd 3030.
cherl, *n.*, (OE ceorl), churl, rustic (*a term of reproach*), bumpkin. D 478; chorle, Cl 296; cherel, Yw 612; carl, Hv 1789.
chese, *vs.*, (OE cēosan), choose. Cl 427; *pr.*, Sd 2934; cheose, Hr. 664; *pl.*, chese, P 1207; chase, ET 568; ches, At 110; chose, EG 938; *pp.*, icoren, Ly 28643; *as adj.*, chosen, choice; ycore, O 103.
child, *n.*, (OE cild), (1) child, youth. Ip 3079; *plu.*, chyldyrn, Cl 160; *g. plu.*, children, Hv 499.
(2) aspirant to knighthood. Hr 25; Ip 391.
claré, wine mixed with honey and spices, and then strained clear (*not* claret). Lv 344.
clene, clane, *adj. and adv.*, (OE clǣne). (1) clean. Av 611.
(2) correct, true. Tr 53, 57.
(3) thoroughly, entirely. Av 598; Ly 27943; cleane, EG 130; cleen, B 3326.
clepe, *vw.*, (OE cleopian, clypian), cry, call, summon. cleopien, Ly 28418; *pr. 2 sg.*, clepeist, B 3024; *3 sg.*, clepeth, G 106; *pt. sg.*,

clepede, D 49; clupede, Hr 225; clepid, B 2922; cleopede, Ly 27602; *pp.*, clepid, B 2945; ycleped, O 50; clepet, R 336.

clere, *adj.*, (OF cler), of attractive appearance, shining.   Cl 374; cleare, EG 917.

clerk, scholar, student.   D 285; Tr 53.

clippe, *vw.*, (OE clyppan), embrace. *pt.*, clipped, Sd 1935; Em 212; clepte, D 673; klippt, FB 806.

cniht, knight. Ly 28563.

come, *vs.*, (OE cuman), (1) come. At 305; cume, Ly 28262; cumme, Av 656; *pr. 2 sg.*, comste, Cl 284; *3 sg.*, cummys, Av 30, Ip 353; comth, G 602; *pt. sg.*, come, CA 110, 113; com, Hr 1365; kam, Hv 766; *plu.*, comen, G 23; comyn, Tr 4737; icom, Hr 1318; comun, Av 480; keme, Hv 1208; *pr. sj. 1 sg.*, come, P 681; *2 sg.*, (*by nunnation*) cumen, Ly 28143; *3 sg.*, come, Ly 28507; *imp. plu.*, cumeth, Ly 27611; comes, Hv 1798; *pp.*, comen, D 207; comyn, ET 263; icome, D 63, Hr 176; icomen, Hr 202; icume, Ly 27595; *prp.*, comande, Av 246; cumand, SS 592.

conne, *cf.* can.

corune, crowne, *n.*, (OF corône, ON krūna), (1) king's crown. corune, Hv 1319; crune, Hr 475; corowne, At 270.
(2) top of the head. crowne, ET 72; Hr 1487.

counsail, *n.*, (OF cunseil), (1) advice. SS 582; counseil, Sd 1772.
(2) secret, secrets. ET 1037; SS 328.

couthe, knew; *cf.* can.

couthe, known, Av 745; *cp.* uncouthe.

crepe, *vs. and w.*, (OE crēopan), creep. Hv 68; *pr. 3 sg.*, crepis,

SS 822; *pt. sg.*, crope, EG 188; Av 1021; crepe'd, TT 170.

croise, *n.*, cross. Hv 1263; CA 328; Hr 1309; croyce, Yw 826.

cume, *cf.* come.

cunne, cunde, *cf.* kin, kind.

curteis, *adj.*, (OF courtois), well-mannered, courteous.   D 92; curtays, Em 64; curtase, Av 743; *cp.*, corteysear, Cl 13.

curteisye, courtesy. Hv 194; corteci, Cl 455.

D

dai, *n.*, (OE dæg), day, lifetime. G 12; dawes, Lv 1; daȝes, Ly 27863; *d. pl.*, daȝen, Ly 28439.

dais, *n.*, (OF deis), a raised platform at the end of a hall. D 765; dese, Yw 1207; P 968; dece, Av 741; deys, Lv 899; deyse, K 890.

dalt, dealt; *cf.* dele.

dece, *cf.* dais.

ded, *adj. and sb.*, (OE dēad), dead, the dead. P 155; deed, Em 267.

dede, *n.*, (OE dǽd), deed. Em 456; Ly 27585; *plu.*, dedes, Hr 537; dede, Ip 1139; dedus, Em 4; dedys, Tr 50; deden, Ly 27795.

dede, *cf.* dethe, ded, do.

defaut, defawte, lack. Lv 202.

degre, prize; *cf.* gre.

deie, *vw.*, (ON deyja), die. Hr 109; dey, Av 855; dye, Ip 1191; dyȝe, R 427; dee, Av 698; degh, Tr 8648; *pt. sg.*, deyde, G 68; dyȝede, R 323; deghit, Tr 8617; *plu.*, deid, Tr 4723; *pp.*, dyyd, At 32; *vb.n.*, diȝing, R 426.

dele, *n.*, (OE dæl), part, share, bit. ET 671; Sd 2024; deel, G 635; deyle, Ip 1071; deale, EG 447; *in the phrases:* ilka del, Sd 2016; some deale, somewhat, EG 447; neuer a dele, no dell, not at all, K 150.

dele, *vw.*, (OE **dælan**), share, associate with, divide, give (*of blows*). D 653; G 18; *pt. sg.*, **delt**, SS 2829; **dalte**, P 458; *plu.*, **dalten**, G 45; *imp. plu.*, **deleth**, G 37; *pp.*, **deled**, G 49.

dele, sorrow; *cf.* dole.

deme, *vw.*, (OE **dēman**), judge, pass sentence on, adjudge. Yw 1186; *pr. plu.*, **deme**, B 3437.

dent, blow; *cf.* dint.

dere, *n.*, (OE **dēor**), beast, animal. *plu.*, **dere**, Ip 3066; *g. plu.*, **deoren**, Ly 28066.

dere, *adj.*, *sb.*, *and adv.*, (OE **dēore**), (1) beloved, dear. Av 6; **deore**, Ly 28051; *sup.*, **derrist**, Tr 39. (2) expensive, precious. Sd 1902; *sup.*, **derreste**, P 1555.

dere, *n.*, (OE **daru**), injury, harm, grief. Yw 744; EG 810; **deere**, EG 320; **deyre**, Ip 1120; **der**, D 1005.

dere, *vw.*, (OE **derian**), injure, afflict, harm. P 1171; **derie**, Hr 786; **deyre**, Ip 1115; **deire**, Tr 8648; *pr. plu.*, **deris**, P 1370.

dethe, *n.*, (OE **dēað**, O Frisian dād) death. Tr 4757; **dæthe**, Ly 27922; **dede**, P 390; Yw 906; At 180; **dead**, EG 753; **deȝ**, D 463.

dighte, *vs. and w.*, (OE **dihtan**), (1) arrange, prepare, ordain, get ready, put (*a word of vague meaning, roughly equivalent to the various senses of "set"*). Sd 2763; *pt. sg.*, **diȝte**, D 718; *plu.*, **dyȝte**, Em 193; **dihten**, Ly 27437; **idihten**, Ly 27481; *pp.*, **dyght**, Em 133; **dightede**, P 1556; **adight**, G 731. (2) dress, accouter. **diȝte**, Av 813; *pt. sg.*, **dight**, P 787; *pp.*, **idiȝte**, B 2970; **idihte**, Ly 28627; **ydyȝth**, Em 395. *In the following special phrases and compounds:* to dethe dyght, kill. ET 492; yuel

dight, badly treated, G 87; to yrthe dyght, fall, Em 285.

dint, *n.*, (OE **dynt**), blow, stroke. CA 138; D 338; **dent**, TT 48; **dunte**, Hr 609, Ly 27681; *plu.*, **dynttys**, P 72; **dintus**, Av 43.

disese, *n.*, (OF **desaise**), discomfort, annoyance. Sd 2318; B 3552.

do, don, *vs.*, (OE **dōn**), (1) cause to happen (*followed by an active infinitive in the passive sense*). D 558; *pt.*, **dede**, G 866; *plu.*, **dyd**, Ip 1053; **deden**, Hv 242; *imp. plu.*, **doth**, Hv 2037; *pp.*, **do**, G 144. (2) act, perform, do. **doon**, G 207; **done**, D 244; *pr. 2 sg.*, **doost**, Lv 364; *pr. 3 sg.*, **dose**, D 53; **dos**, Hv 2390; *pt. 3 sg.*, **dude**, Hr 1247, Ly 27864; **dedde**, CA 172; *imp.*, **do**, CA 138; **doyth**, ET 893; *pp.*, **ido**, Ly 28110; *pt. sj.*, **dudde**, ET 636; **doon**, G 211. (3) put, place, put on, take off. *pt. 3 sg.*, **dede**, D 664; *imp. sg.*, **do**, G 269; *pp.*, EG 849. (4) complete, finish. *pp.*, **idoon**, G 270. (5) *in emphatic conjugations, used for other verbs:* *pr. 3 sg.*, **deth**, Ly 28500; **doith**, B 3005. (6) *in the following special phrases:* don of liue, kill, Hr 180; idon of lif-dæȝen, killed, Ly 27847; do to ded, kill, SS 4310.

dole, *n.*, (OF **doel**), (1) sorrow, sorrowful sight. B 3269; **diol**, O 196; **deole**, Hr 1050; **dool**, At 367; **dele**, ET 876; **doll**, Tr 4776; *comp.*, **delful**, pitiful, R 331. (2) compassion, pity. CA 134; Em 356. (3) lamenting. SS 2928; Em 613.

dome, *n.*, (OE **dōm**), judgment, doom, verdict. At 562; SS 2790; **dom**, Hv 2473; *plu.*, **domus**, CA 91.

doughter, *n.*, (OE dohtor), daughter. D 47; dow3ter, Em 109; doghter, Hr 994; dowter, D 440; douwter, D 601; thow3tur, Em 226.

doughti, dughti, *adj.*, (OE dyhtig), powerful, brave. D 364; TT 8; doghty, P 203; do3ty, Lv 724; du3ti, Av 6; duhti, Ly 27862; *cp.*, dowtyar, Cl 8.

doun, *adv.*, (OE a dūne), down. Hv 901; dowun, Av 801.

dout, *n.*, (OF doute), (1) doubt. douthe, Hv 1331; dou3tt, Cl 44. (2) fear. Av 1019; SS 3012; TT 103.

doute, *vw.*, (OF douter), doubt, fear. *pr. 1 sg.*, dute, Hr 344; *pt. sg.*, doutede, Hv 708; *plu.*, doutiden, G 78; *imp. sg.*, dowt, G 517.

drawe, *vs.*, (OE dragan), (1) draw, drag, pull. *pt. 3 sg.*, drogh, SS 844; TT 195; drou3, D 830; drowe, ET 94; *pp.*, drawe, ET 575; drawen, P 850.
(2) withdraw, go, come. Av 92; dra3e, Hr 1289; *pt.*, dro3e, Hr 1006; droghe, Tr 88; *pt. sg.*, drow3, CA 33.
(3) disembowel (*usually in connection with hanging*).
(4) remove (*of a table-cloth*). *pt.*, drou3, D 830; *pp.*, draw, K 1001.
(5) portray. *pp.*, ydrawe, Hr 1303.

drede, *n.*, (OE ondrǣdan, *vb.*), fear, dread. Av 860; ET 233; dread, EG 718; *especially in the phrase:* wythoute drede, beyond doubt. ET 512.

drede, *vw.*, (OE ondrǣdan), dread, fear. Av 143; *pr. 3 sg.*, dredus, Av 632; *pt.*, dred, SS 2946; dradde, Hr 120; dredden, Hv 2289; *prp.*, dredand, SS 2888.

driue, *vs.*, (OE drīfan), (1) push along, drive, force. *pt. sg.*, drof, Tr 8639; G 124; *plu.*, droffe, Cl 158; *pr. sj.*, driue, Hr 1333.
(2) rush, ride. D 929; dryfe, P 2008; driuen, Ly 28073; *prp.*, driuende, Hv 2702.

dubbe, *vw.*, (OE dubbian), dub, confer knighthood (*a ceremony which could be performed by a knight or head of a monastery*). Hr 458; *pt.*, doubbede, P 1638; dubd, EG 1416. *In the phrase:* dub to knight, D 414; *vb.n.*, dubbyng, At 233.

dune, doune, meadow, down. Ly 28065.

dwelle, *vw.*, (OE dwellan), (1) live in a place. *pr. 3 sg.*, dwelles, Em 721.
(2) tarry, linger, remain for a short time. Hr 374; *pt. 3 sg.*, duellut, Av 749.

E

eche, *adj. and pro.*, (OE ǣlc, ylc), (1) every, each. Hr 1087; D 403; ich, TT 93; vche, Av 951. *comp.* echone, each one, B 3387; ychon, Sd 2778; icha, TT 155. (2) same, very; ich, O 538.

een, eghne, *cf.* eie.

eft, *adv.*, (OE eft, æft), afterwards, again. D 527; æft, Ly 28114. *comp.*, efftsonys, soon again, B 3888.

efter, *cf.* after.

eie, *n.*, (OE ēage), eye. *sg.*, Hv 2545; i3e, Hr 755; *plu.*, eyen, Lv 570; yen, CA 135; een, Tr 57; eghne, P 537; y3en, Em 298; eg3e, D 504; ey3en, O 109; eeyn, Lv 810; ey3nen, Al 6740.

eir, *cf.* heir.

either, other, (OE ǣgðer), (1) *adj. pro.*, either, each. aither, Tr 65;

Ip 3132; euther, Tr 57; aythur, CA 220; eythir, Av 382.

(2) *conj.*, or. owther, SS 243; outher, K 262; other, CA 324; *correlative*, other . . . other, Ly 28496.

eke, ok, *adv.*, (OE ēac; ON auk), also. D 26; eeke, G 480; hec, Hv 2348; æc, Ly 27630.

elde, *n.*, (OE eldo), age. SS 4273; G 649.

elles, *adv.*, (OE elles), else, otherwise. Hr 246; D 253; CA 215; ellis, TT 36.

eme, *n.*, (OE ēam), uncle. ET 994; eemes, At 29; æm, Ly 27599.

eni, any. Hr 316, G 318.

enoghe, *cf.* **inoghe.**

enuye, *n.*, *commonly* hatred, wrath; *rarely* envy.

eode, went; *cf.* **yede.**

eow, you; *cf.* **thou.**

er, ere, before; *cf.* **are.**

erst, first; *cf.* **are.**

ethe, *adj. and adv.*, (OE ēaðe), easy, easily. Hr 835.

euer, *adv.*, (OE ǣfre), ever. Hr 79; aure, Av 662; auere, Ly 27483; *in the phrase:* euyr among, continually, ET 748.

eueri, *adj. and pro.*, (OE ǣfre ǣlc), every. Em 14; eurech, Hr 216; euerilk, Hv 2258; euereche, Hr 934; *comp.*, euerichon, every one, B 3068; D 138; euerilkane, SS 252; P 1163.

F

fai, faith, *n.*, (OF fei, feid), faith, word. Em 296. *Usually in the phrases:* par fay, SS 242; in faye, Sd 1970.

faile, *vw.*, (OF faillir), **(1)** fail (in an undertaking). *pt. 3 sg.*, faylyd, ET 1119.

(2) be lacking, disappoint (*usu-*

ally impersonal). Hr 638; *pr. 3 sg.*, faylis, Av 51; SS 2977.

fain, *adj. and adv.*, (OE fægn), glad, gladly. ET 723; Yw 1346; feyn, B 3334.

fair, *adj.*, *sb.*, *and adv.*, (OE fæger), **(1)** comely. CA 217; veire, Ly 27770; uæir, Ly 28010; *cp.*, fairer, Hr 10; fayre, ET 980; *sup.*, fayrist, Av 1136; færȝest, Ly 28459.

(2) justly, well. Tr 82; CA 266.

(3) readily. D 144.

falle, *vs.*, (OE feallan). (*The forms are often substituted, through confusion, for those of* felle, knock down.) **(1)** fall. uallen, Ly 27455; *pt. sg.*, fell, Em 551; fil, D 375; feol, Hr 428; ffil, B 3707; *plu.*, fillen, D 73; fellyn, Tr 4748; feollen, Ly 27469; uellen, Ly 27465; *pp.*, fallun, Av 200; falin, Tr 94; ifallen, D 534.

(2) occur, befall, happen. fal, SS 341; *pt. sg.*, fil, D 624, B 2956.

(3) befit, appertain to (*usually impersonal*). falle, Av 966; *pt. sg.*, fell, Em 383; SS 2872; *pt. plu.*, fillen, O 15. *In the phrase:* felle to, P 1104.

fare, *n.*, (OE faru), **(1)** behavior. G 199.

(2) journey. Hv 1337; uore, Ly 28248.

(3) encounter, adventure. P 1431, Yw 462.

fare, *vw. and s.*, (OE faran; *by confusion*, fēran), **(1)** go, march. At 330; fore, Av 151; *pr. 2 sg.*, farst, Hr 793; *pt. sg.*, ferde, Hr 649; *plu.*, ferd, Av 796; fore, P 1425; *pp.*, faren, Tr 29.

(2) prosper, get on, behave. D 648; *pp.*, ifare, Hr 468; fare, Hr 1355; farren, EG 1165; farn, Yw 911; iuaren, Ly 28011.

(3) happen, befall. *pt. 3 sg.*, Tr 94; *pp.*, ifaren, Ly 28369.

fast, *adj. and adv.*, (OE fæste), (1) rapid, rapidly. Em 659. (2) firmly, fixedly, attentively. feste, Av 1026; SS 2989; Hv 2148.

faute, fault, lack, Av 736, B 3664.

fe, *n.*, (OE feoh), property, wealth, fief. Sd 1749; fee, Cl 437.

fecche, *vw.*, (OE feccan), fetch, bring. TT 204, Hr 351; *pt. sg.*, feched, K 917; *pt. plu.*, fett, ET 1145; fochet, Av 565; *pp.*, fette, CA 274; fet, Sd 3188; yfet, O 168; *imp. plu.*, fetteth, G 643.

fei, feith, *cf.* fai.

feire, *cf.*, fair.

fel, *adj. and adv.*, (OE fel), fierce, cruel, savage. G 151; SS 931; fele, TT 2; felle, Tr 8663; feolle, Al 4121.

felawe, *n.*, (ON fēlagi), (1) companion, comrade. fellow, Av 934; fela3e, Hr 996; felay, TT 155; *plu.*, felawis, Av 1119. (2) servant (*often a term of reproach*). G 227, Av 798.

feld, *n.*, (OE feald, feld), field (*often battlefield*). D 10; fild, Av 507; ffylde, Tr 94; *plu.*, ueldes, Ly 27468.

fele, *adj. and adv.*, (OE fela, feolu, etc.) many, frequent. Em 823; Hr 1329; ET 170; feole, Ly 27830; fale, Lv 496; fell, Ip 414.

felede, followed; *cf.* folwe.

felle, *vw.*, (OE fellan), knock down, cause to fall. *pr. 3 sg.*, feollen, Ly 27617; *pt. sg.*, felde, Ip 3161; fulde, Hr 1488; G 593; *plu.*, fælden, Ly 27508; *pp.*, fellyd, Cl 96; *by confusion with* falle: *inf.*, auallen, Ly 28405; afallene, Ly 27811; *pt.*, felle, Av 331, 667; feollen, Ly 27754; *pp.*, falleth, CA 310; fall, TT 116.

fend, *n.*, (OE fēond), (1) enemy. feond, Ly 28116; ueond, Ly 27667; *plu.*, feonden, Ly 27649. (2) devil, fiend, the Devil. fende, Em 540; *in the phrase:* the fende mote hym haue, CA 120; fynde, Av 104.

fer, *adj. and adv.*, (OE feorr), far, distant. D 77; ffarre, Ip 405; fere, Ip 1171; ferre, ET 485; feor, Hr 769; ueor, Ly 27539; *cp.*, fer, Tr 78; ferre, Tr 96; furre, CA 311; (*by confusion with* forth) forthir, Av 790; ferther, CA 127.

fere, *n.*, (OE gefēra), fellow, comrade, wife. TT 27; feere, R 161; *plu.*, feris, B 3201; feiren, Hr 237; ferin, Hr 1242; ifere, Hr 102; iueren, Ly 27449. *In the phrase:* in fere, together, TT 212; ifere, D 67; in feere, G 667.

fere, go, fare; *cf.* fare.

fereden, uereden, carried, conveyed. Ly 28079, 28629.

ferli, ferlik, *adj., sb., and adv.*, (OE fǣrlīc), marvel, marvelous, marvelously; amazement. SS 896; TT 2; Em 351; *plu.*, ferlies, Tr 96; SS 404.

ferthe, fourth. B 3764, Hv 1810.

fest, *cf.* fast.

feste, *n. and v.*, (OF feste), feast. Hr 477, Cl 61.

ff-. For words beginning with ff, see f.

fighte, *vs.*, (OE feohtan), fight. Hr 514; fehten, Ly 27711; fe3te, Av 52; fy3te, CA 200; *pt. sg.*, faght, Tr 8608; faugt, D 122; faht, Ly 28554; *plu.*, foghten, Tr 4738; faght, Yw 655; fuhten, Ly 27491; fa3te, Av 361; *prp. sb.*, fe3ting, Av 38.

fiht, uiht, *n.* fight; *d.s.*, feohten, Ly 27821.

finde, *vs.*, (OE findan), find. O 257;

fynd, Yw 1051; *pr. 3 sg.*, fint, O 237; *pt.*, fond, O 424; ifunde, Ly 27777; fande, K 720; favnd, Ip 1119; fonde, P 1611; *pp.*, yfounde, Lv 35; fonden, P 519; ifunde, Hr 955; fownden, CA 239.

fir, fur, fyer, fire. CA 159; Ly 27788; ffeer, At 631.

fle, *vs.*, (OE flēon), flee (*forms confused with* fleie). fleon, Ly 28354; *pt. 3 sg.*, fley, G 127; flah, Ly 28462; *plu.*, floghen, Tr 4732; fluȝen, Ly 27824; *pp.*, flowe, G 133.

fleie, *vs.*, (OE flēogan), fly. fleon, Ly 27456; flyne, K 241; *pt. sg.*, fleye, CA 319; flegh, Lv 473; fleh, Ly 27788; *plu.*, flowenn, CA 148; *pp.*, flowe, B 3616; *prp.*, fliand, Av 1023.

florine, *n.*, (OF florin), florin (*a coin containing 55 grains of gold, issued at Florence and much used in trade. In 1343, an English coin of the same name, worth six shillings, was struck.*) D 295; floranse, ET 389, floiences, EG 1232.

fo, *n.*, (OE fāh), foe, enemy. Fa, SS 4245; *plu.*, fos, Tr 4715; foon, ET 462, G 541; ifan, Ly 27617. *comp.*, foomen, G 682; famen, SS 454.

fole, *n.*, (OF fol), fool, eccentric. B 2937; SS 2927; foule, Ip 1061; *plu.*, folis, B 2988.

folwe, *vw.*, (OE folgian), follow, pursue. fulien, Ly 27733; *pt. sg.*, felede, Hv 67; folut, Av 167; *plu.*, folutte, Av 90.

fonde, *vw.*, (OE fundian), seek, search, try, go. D 2; funde, Hr 133; founde, At 702; *pt.*, fond, Lv 962; fonded, Al 3993.

fonge, *vs.*, (OE fōn, ON fangen), seize, receive, catch. Hr 327; fang, Yw 299; *pt. sg.*, iueng,

Ly 28069; *pp.*, ifon, Ly 28137.

for, *prep. and conj.*, (OE for), *Only the unusual senses are here given:* (1) *prep.*, by reason of. Hr 1104; Tr 13.
(2) by the agency of. Ip 435.
(3) on account of. Em 618; Hr 69.
(4) *as sign of infinitive.* Hr 280; Hv 38.
(5) in spite of. Sd 1686; P 356.
(6) *conj.* because, for. Cl 489; Sd 2008.
(7) in order that, lest (*with negatives*). SS 4267; B 3002.
(8) on condition that. Ly 28275.

for-, *prefix*, (OE for-). *Indicates a destructive sense or the intensifying of a bad sense in the verb which follows it:* forwunded, Ly 27908; forwurthe, perish, Ly 28425; forloren, D 84; forsworn, CA 199; fordon, kill, Ly 28168; forfare, perish, G 74; destroy, SS 2931; forfarn, Yw 976.

forȝ, forht, forth. D 56; D 227.

forthan, uorthæn, because of this, for this reason, Ly 28159.

forthi, *adv. and conj.*, (OE for þī, because, therefore, provided that. P 647; Av 985; CA 218; Hv 2043.

forward, *n.*, (OE foreweard), agreement. ET 220; forthward, G 747; foreward, Hr 452.

fot, *n.*, (OE fōt), foot. Hr 758; fout, Hr 134; *plu.*, fete, Av 595; fote, Av 191; Ip 3134.

foule, foȝel, *n.*, (OE fugel), bird. D 732; Hr 1398; *plu.*, fuȝeles, Ly 28063; foȝeles, Hr 129.

foule, *adj. and adv.*, (OE fūl), foul, vicious, ugly. CA 239; G 485; fule, Ly 27634.

fraine, *vw.*, (OE fregnan), ask, inquire, question. ET 941; Yw 579; Tr 98; *pt.*, 94. *Often used with the prepositions to and at.*

fre, *adj. and sb.*, (OE frēo), (1) free.
Hv 262; freo, Ly 28393.
(2) generous, noble (*a term of
general commendation*). ET 382;
Sd 1615; fri, Hv 1072.
freli, *adv. and adj.*, (OE frēolīc),
goodly, worthy, worthily (*sometimes used in the sense of* freely).
CA 218; Em 507; P 38.
frend, *n.*, (OE frēond), friend.
frynde, Av 642; *plu.*, frindus,
Av 211; freond, Ly 28420; frende,
Ip 346.
fro, from, *prep. and conj.*, (OE
fra, fram). (1) *prep.*, from. CA
159; Hr 72.
(2) *conj.*, from the time when.
SS 306; Av 869.
ful, *adj. and adv.*, (OE full), quite,
very, very greatly. (*Often used
as a metrical filler, not to be taken
seriously in translation.*) Hr 429;
D 372.
fur, fire; *cf.* fir.

G

galow-tre, gallows. SS 2866.
game, *n.*, (OE gamen), sport, enjoyment, playfulness, content-
ment, jest. ET 164; B 3263;
Hr 198; gamyn, SS 808; *plu.*,
gamus, Ip 1134; gamyns, SS 388;
gammen, K 609.
gange, *vs.*, (OE gangan), go, walk.
Ip 1150; EG 457; ʒeongen, Ly
28070; *prp.*, gangande, Hv 2283.
(*The preterit is usually supplied
from* yede, *q.v.*)
gate, *n.*, (OE geat, ON gatt), (1)
road, path. P 258; Em 828.
(2) gate, wicket. ʒate, CA 22;
ʒæte, Ly 27932; yate, EG 65.
(3) means. P 1675. *Especially
in the phrases:* so-gates, thusgates, in this wise, P 877; 1839.
gent, *adj.*, (OF gent), of good an-

cestry, well bred. ET 695; Ip
3171.
gere, gare, *vw.*, (OE gearwian),
prepare, cause. At 477; SS 412;
gerre, P 832; yaren, Hv 1350;
pt., gerutte, Av 176; gerut, Av
330; gert, Yw 1102; garte, At
251; (*with metathesis*) gret, Ip
3060; *imp. sg.*, gers, SS 556.
gere, *n.*, (OE gearwe), equipment
of any sort, things, clothes, armor. P 189; Av 324; gayre, EG
428.
gete, *vs.*, (OE -gietan), (1) get, obtain. *pt. sg.*, gate, Tr 76; gatt,
EG 456; *pp.*, gotten, Ip 1131;
ygete, O 14.
(2) beget. *pr.for fut. sg. 2*, gettes,
SS 342; *pt.*, gette, CA 34; *pp.*,
geten, D 688.
gethurt, gedrit, gadred, gathered.
gif, *cf.* if *and* give.
ginne, *vs.*, (OE ginnan), (1) begin,
start. Hr 546; *pr. 3 sg.*, gynnyth,
CA 66; *pt. sg.*, agon, Ly 28060;
gun, Ly 28070; *plu.*, gonnen, Ly
28552.
(2) *in preterit, frequently means*
"did." gan, Hr 1047; goon, G
236; gun, P 740; *plu.*, gon, G
236; gonne, D 628.
giue, ʒiue, *vs.*, (OE giefan), give.
giffe, Av 283; Ip 445; gif, K 932;
pr. 1 sg., gyff, Ip 468; *3 sg.*, ʒiffes,
P 85; *plu.*, gyffen, Tr 4741;
giffus, Av 977; gifis, K 901; *pt.
sg.*, ʒaf, D 326; ʒæf, Ly 27918;
ʒefe, P 2086; ʒeef, FB 184; yaf,
Hv 1635; *plu.*, gafe, Av 1083;
imp. sg., yif, Hv 674; giffe, Av
5; *pp.*, gifen, SS 2818; yʒeue, G
870; gevyne, Ip 480; yoven, Hv
1643; *in the phrase:* ʒaf him ylle,
lamented. Em 778.
gle, glewe, *n.*, (OE glēow), mirth,
amusement, singing. O 381; Em
132; gleu, Hv 2333.

go, *vs.*, (OE gān), go, walk. D 720;
goo, ET 280; gon, D 80; gone,
Em 741; ga, SS 354; *pr. 3 sg.*,
gooth, CA 157; gos, Ip 1177;
goose, Ip 3026; gase, SS 888;
goht, D 77; goʒ, D 82; geth, O
236; *imp.*, gowe, G 661; *plu.*,
goth, G 36; *pp.*, agoo, B 3033;
agan, Ly 28089; igoon, G 347;
go, Sd 2760; gane, SS 251; ago,
R 299; gon, D 682; *prp.*, ganninde, Ly 28524. (*The preterit
is supplied from* yede, *q.v.*)
gode, *adj. and adv.*, (OE gōd), (1)
good. gude, Yw 83; *a. m.*, godne, Hr 720; *cp.*, bet, betere, Lv
698; Hr 567; bctte, Sd 1716; *sup.*,
beste, Hr 174; Av 958; beʒst, Ly
27613.
(2) *sb.*, property, goods; profit,
advantage. Hr 770; gudeʒ,
P 185; best warriors, *d. plu.*,
beʒsten, Ly 27661.
grace, *n.*, (OF grace), grace, heav-
enly favor; *hence* chance, fortune,
luck, destiny. Tr 76; Em 944;
Yw 548; graas, R 369; gras, R
374.
graithe, *vw.*, (ON greiða), prepare,
make ready. graiʒ, D 849;
pt., graythed, TT 57; graithet,
Tr 4749; *imp.*, graiʒ, D 849;
greytheth, Al 4156.
gramarcy, great thanks! Cl 421;
gramercy, Ip 474; grant merci,
D 976.
graunte, *vw.*, (OF granter), (1) agree,
accede, admit. *pr. 2 sg.*, grantes,
SS 4293; *3 sg.*, grawuntus, Av
461; *pt.*, grauntede, Lv 259; Av
128.
(2) grant, give. *pr 3 sg.*, graunteth, CA 278; *pr. sj. 2 sg.*, graunte,
Cl 286; *pp.*, grant, TT 101.
gre, degre, *n.*, (OF gre), (1) victor's title, prize. TT 47; EG
478; Tr 4780.

(2) excellence, rank. EG 562;
Sq 1.
gret, *cf.* gere, prepare.
grete, *vs.*, (OE grǣtan), weep, wail.
pt. sg., gret, SS 2914; grette,
Em 556.
grette, greeted. D 468; G 668;
gret, D 810.
greue, *vs.*, (OF grever), grieve, injure. TT 95; *pt.*, greuyt, Tr
4726.
gripe, *vw. and vs.*, (OE grīpan),
grasp, seize. *pr. 3 sg.*, gripus,
Av 382; *pt. 3 sg.*, grippit, Tr
8656; igrap, Ly 27676.
grisli, grisliche, *adv. and adj.*, (OE
grislic), fearful, horrible. Lv
600; Ly 28063; Av 192.
grith, *n.*, (OE gri ð), peace, security.
Sd 2850, P 1648; greth, Cl 299.

H

H-. *For the following words spelled
with* h- *in the text, cf. the second
letter:* hec, heke, *also;* heie, *eye;*
helde, heldest, *old;* his, is; hun-
till, hentill, to, until; habydes,
awaits; her, *before;* herl, *earl;*
hete, *eat;* heuere, *ever;* hi, hic,
I; hold, *old;* hure, *our;* hore,
grace; haby, atone for; hoc, *also;*
hawe, awe.
ha, han, *cf.* haue. ha, *cf.* he.
halp, helped. G 60.
haluendel, half. G 272.
hap, *n.*, (ON happ), chance, fate,
luck. Yw 229; happe, Av 434;
Em 651.
harrow Helle, to despoil Hell.
(*According to the late Gospel of
Nicodemus, Christ, between his
crucifixion and resurrection, descended into Hell and liberated
the souls of patriarchs, prophets,
and saints.*) At 422; Sq 148.
haue, *vw.*, (OE habban), have, own.

hauen, D 27; ha, K 373; han, Lv
406; *pr. 1 sg.*, habbe, Ly 28086;
hafe, P 1961; has, EG 142; *2
sg.*, hase, Av 267; hathe, Ip 1066;
hafst, Ly 27638; haste, P 1664;
3 sg., hafeth, Ly 28136; haues,
SS 551; *plu.*, habbeӡ, D 64;
haues, TT 31; habbeoth, Ly
28607; *pt. sg.*, hauede, Hr 48;
hafde, Ly 27597; hefde, Ly
27708; hade, Tr 54; *plu.*, hadden,
EG 194; *pt. sj.*, hadde, CA 181;
pp., hadde, Hr 9; ihad, G 357;
negative forms, nabbe, Ly 28092;
nade, O 390; nadde, Hr 863.
With enclitic pro., hadestow, hadst
thou, O 531; hasto, hast thou,
Yw 911; *negative with enclitic
pro.*, nastu, Hr 1193.

he, heo, hem, hit, *pro.*, (OE he,
etc.), (1) he, he. *n.*, Hr 127; *g.*,
his, Sq 4; is, Ly 27900; hes, Ip
425; *d. and a.*, him, D 170; hine,
D 913, Hr 1028; *reflexive*, him;
often used after intransitive verb:
Ly 27563.
(2) heo, she. *n.*, Hr 69; he, Hr
71; hye, O 79; ha, Ly 28219; ho,
Av 281; hi, D 80; *g.*, Sq 585;
here, Em 830; hyr, Em 803; hire,
D 49; hure, Hr 1121; *d. and a.*,
here, Em 164; hure, Hr 1103;
hyr, Cl 146.
(3) hit, it, there. *n. and a.*, Hr 6;
hitte, Av 471; *g. and d. as masculine*, him, Hr 570. *Used to postpone the true subject*, Em 716;
*also superfluously in apposition
with the object*, Ly 27650.
(4) they. *n.*, Hv 54; hi, Hr 22;
hye, O 89; hii, D 48; heo, Ly
27454; *g.*, her, Em 211; hir, B
3343; hare, Lv 59; hore, Hr 854;
hor, Tr 4715; hur, FB 564;
heore, Ly 27518; *d. and a.*, hem,
CA 52; hom, Tr 24; heom, Ly
27885; ham, Lv 20; hym, B 3425.

hed, heued, *n.*, (OE hēafod), head.
Av 110; ET 113; hafd, Ly 28048;
hafued, Ly 28148; hedde, CA
27; heed, G 430.

heie, heghe, *adj.*, *adv.*, *and sb.*,
(OE hēah), high, noble, tall,
great. D 925; P 683; hiӡe, B
3165; heiӡe, O 203; hye, CA 217;
cp., hæhӡer, Ly 27445; heӡer,
Av 49; *sup.*, hexte, Hv 1080;
heghhest, Av 1036. *Especially
in the phrases:* on hyӡe, aloud,
CA 25, 64; on heghӡ, on high, up,
D 533; *cf. also* hight *and* hie.

heir, *n.*, (OF heir), heir. G 365;
air, D 873; SS 333; *plu.*, aire,
SS 2844; heyre, EG 731.

hem, them; *cf.* he.

hende, *adj.*, *sb.*, *and adv.*, (OE
gehende), (1) lovely, gracious.
At 224; hinde, Yw 700; heende,
G 663.
(2) well trained, proficient. Tr
8610; heynde, Av 82.
adv., *also* hendeliche, hendly, D
999, SS 237.

hende, hands.

henne, *adv.*, (OE heonan), hence.
D 130; Hr 46; hennys, Sd 1922.

hente, *vw.*, (OE -hentan), seize,
grasp, receive. Av 203; *pr. sg.*,
hint, P 754; *pt.*, hent, SS 849;
hente, CA 85; *pp.*, hynt, P 1666;
hente, CA 3.

heo, she; *cf.* he.

herte, *n.*, (OE heorte), heart. D
543; hartt, Cl 190; heort, Ly
27673; heorte, Hr 263.

hest, *n.*, command. Al 4073.

hethen, *adv.*, (ON heðan), hence.
P 1905; hethinn, Av 1102.

hethennes, heathendom. Em 109;
hethenisse, O 511.

hexte, tallest; *cf.* heie.

hider, *adv.*, (OE hider), hither. D
470; hedur, Av 396.

hie, *vw.*, (OE higean), hasten, hie. Av 1102; hiȝe, Hr 880; hy, Yw 1073; *pr. 3 sg.*, hiees, Av 816; *pt.*, hiet, Av 490; *sj. pr.*, hyȝe, CA 139; *vbl.n.*, hyȝynge, Em 511; *esp. in the phrase:* on heying, in haste, D 753.

hie, *n.* (*from the verb*), haste. P 1550; hyȝ, At 716. *Especially in the phrases:* on *or* in hie, in haste; on hy, CA 326, P 534; on high, Cl 266. *Cf. also* hight *and* heie.

hie, she, they; *cf.* he.

hight, *n.*, (OE hēahȱo), height. *Especially in the phrase:* on hight, *meaning:* (1) on high, up. SS 226; opon hiȝte, Av 215.
(2) aloud; opon hiȝte, Av 513; opon heȝte, Av 633.
(3) in haste (*by confusion with* hie, *q.v.*); in hiȝte, D 136.

highte, *vs. and w.*, (OE hātan), (1) command, issue commands. *pr. 1 sg.*, P 403; *3 sg.*, hoteth, Al 4069; *pt. sg.*, hehte, Ly 28308; hete, Ly 28519.
(2) promise. *pr. 1 sg.*, heȝte, Av 350; hete, SS 935; heete, CA 18; *pt. 2 sg.*, heȝtist, K 299; *3 sg.*, heȝte, Av 604; highte, Ip 3147; hette, Av 965; *plu.*, heȝte, Av 147.
(3) call, be called, named (*originally from a different stem, but confused with this verb*). *pr. 1 sg.*, hote, Hr 767; *3 sg.*, hehte, Ly 27916; hat, Yw 1053; *pt.*, hatte, Ly 28534; heet, R 93; hyȝte, CA 9; het, Hr 25; *pp.*, ihaten, Ly 27593; ihote, Hr 201; hoten, Al 4166.

hinge, hang. SS 2788.

ho, *cf.* he *and* who.

holde, *vs.*, (OE healdan), (1) keep in one's possession. D 390; *by assimilation,* halt, FB 546;

helde, Hr 902; halden, D 30; *pt. 3 sg.*, heeld, CA 152; hylde, Ip 3170.
(2) repute, account, consider. *pr. 1 sg.*, hold, Ip 3158; *pt. plu.*, heelden, G 553; *pp.*, holde, CA 70; holdyn, Ip 402; yholde, Lv 521.
(3) keep to (a road, course of conduct, etc.) *pt. sg.*, heold, Ly 28430; *plu.*, held, Av 949; halden, Ly 28547; *pr. sj.*, holde, Hr 452; *pp.*, holdunn, Av 1143.
(4) go, advance. *pt. sg.*, halde, Ly 27702; *plu.*, hælden, Ly 27523.

holpen, helped, EG 1050; holpyn, K 800.

holt, *n.*, (OE holt), wood, forest. Av 288. *Especially in the phrase:* holtis hore, grey woods. O 212; Lv 171.

honde, hand, hands. Ly 28037.

honge, hang. EG 122.

hope, *vw.*, (OE hopian), believe, expect, fear. houppe, P 731; *pl.*, hopid, SS 820.

hors, horse. *plu.*, hors, At 628; horsen, Ly 27473.

hu, how. Hr 468; heou, Ly 28247.

hw-. *See* wh-.

hwat, *cf.* quath *and* what.

hwor, *cf.* whether.

I

I, ich, *pro.*, (OE ic), I. *n.*, y, Hr 344; ich, D 6; ihc, Hr 149; iich, D 98. *g.*, min, Hr 1281; my, CA 27. *d. and a.*, me, SS 343; *frequently attached to a verb:* ichave, I have; ichil, I will; icham, I am; ichim, I plus him, O 426. *In older pieces, the genitive* min *is inflected like an adjective.* mire, *d.f.*, Ly 28047; minne, *a.m.*, Ly 28186 *plu. n.*, we. wee, CA 302. *g.*

owre, Av 1037; ure, Hr 132;
vre, Hr 516. *d. and a.*, us. Hr
682; ous, D 922.
ientyll, gentle.
if, *conj.*, (OE gif), if, whether, although. CA 192; yff, Ip 413;
giffe, Av 68; ȝif, D 203; yef, B
2981; ȝhif, D 312.
ifan, foes; *cf.* fo.
ifere, *adj.*, together; *sb.*, comrade;
cf. fere.
ilke, *adj. and pro.*, (OE ylca, ǽlc),
each, same. P 340; ilka, SS 450;
vlke, Hr 1199; ælchere, *d.f.*, Ly
28498. *In the phrases:* ilkone,
each one, Ip 3124; thilke, *for
that* ilke, Lv 542.
in, *prep. and adv.*, (OE innan), in,
within, into, on, among, *etc.* Em
257; Hr 17; i, Ly 27623; ynne,
ET 243.
inogh, inowe, *adj. and adv.*, (OE
genōh), enough. TT 196; Ip
438; inowȝe, B 2963; inowgh,
Ip 2998; inoh, Ly 28443; inoȝe,
Hr 1228; anouȝ, O 60; enoȝ,
K 781.
intil, *prep.*, to, into.
ioie, *n.*, (OF joie), joy. Ip 2998;
ioy, B 2966; yoye, ET 1144.
iorné, iurnai, *n.*, (OF jornée), (1)
trip. D 425, 724; yurney, ET
967.
(2) day's work. iornay, SS 4322.
is, *cf.* be, he.
isome, isame, together; *cf.* samen.
isunde, *cf.* sound.
iswoue, iswoȝe, swoon; *cf.* sowne, *n.*
iwis, *adv.*, (OE gewis), certainly.
ET 1065; D 77; iwisse, Av 64.
iȝe, eye; *cf.* eie.

K

kene, *adj.*, *sb.*, *and adv.*, (OE cēne),
(1) spirited, brave, fierce. TT
1; P 1980.

(2) sharp (*of a weapon*). Tr
8640.
kenne, *vw.*, (OE cennan), recognize, discern, know, make known,
instruct. D 129; ken, SS 913;
ikenne, Ly 28559; *pt.*, kend, Yw
931; *pp.*, kende, P 1676; kennet,
Av 619.
kepe, *vw.*, (OE cēpan), (1) guard,
restrain, watch, care for. Yw
1024; *pt.* kepte, Hv 879; keped,
SS 494.
(2) pay attention to. P 576;
sg., keptest, D 853.
(3) intend. *pr. sg.*, kepe, Ip
3011; Av 582.
kin, *n.*, (OE cynn), (1) kindred.
Hv 393; kunne, Hr 865; kynne,
ET 246; kenne, Lv 153; ken, D
319.
(2) kind, sort. cunne, Ly 28165.
In the phrase: none kines, Hv
861, 2691.
kinde, *n.*, (OE cynd), (1) nature,
disposition. B 3196; Sd 2228.
(2) family, race, rank. cunde,
Hr 421.
(3) sort, variety. B 3615.
kinde, *adj. and adv.*, (OE cynde),
(1) natural, real. Tr 70; kinde-
liche, Av 162; *adv.*, kyndely, Av
258.
(2) proper, fitting. TT 1; Tr 70.
(3) kind.
kineriche, kingeriche, kinerike, *n.*,
kingdom.
kithe, *vw.*, (OE cȳðan), show, make
known, display. P 366; *imp.
plu.*, kithe, Sd 1947; *pt.*, kedde,
Lv 368; kyd, Yw 647; *pp.*, kid,
Hv 1060; kyde, Ip 1142.
knaue, *n.*, (OE cnapa), servant,
boy, fellow. B 3207; Av 737;
cnaue, Ly 28590.
knowe, *vs.*, (OE gecnāwan), (1)
know. knawe, Hv 2785; *pr. 2
sg.*, knoes, Av 788; *pt.*, icneou,

icneouwen, Ly 27488; kneuʒ, R 288; kneow, Al 4231.
(2) acknowledge. R 295.

L

laie, to lay; *cf.* lege.

laine, *vw.*, (OE lēgnian), conceal. P 143; Av 306; *pr. 3 sg.*, laynes, Av 1113; *pp.*, lained, EG 361.

large, *adj.*, (OF large), (1) liberal, generous. Hv 97.
(2) at liberty. B 3136; 3362.
(3) of great size. las, lasse, less. Av 768.

lauʒh, lagh, *vs. and vw.*, (OE hlehhan), smile, laugh. B 3006; ET 718; laʒ, K 738; *pt.*, loughe, Sd 2602; louʒgh, Ip 2997; loghe, Av 510; lawʒe, B 3335; lowe, Cl 517; lugh, TT 197; lowgʒ, D 793; lawuʒid, B 3161; louʒ, O 312; loogh, K 55.

leche, *n.*, (OE lǽce), physician. G 614; *plu.*, leeches, EG 224.

lede, *vw.*, (OE lǽdan), (1) lead, govern. Hr 908; *pt.*, ladde, CA; *prp.*, ledande, Av 279; *pp.*, iledde, Ly 27713.
(2) carry, take. Hr 1393; *pp.*, ilad, G 528.

lede, *n.*, (OE leod), people, subjects. Yw 865; leede, Em 702; G 61; leode, Ly 27503.

lefe, *adj., adv., and sb.*, (OE lēof), (1) beloved, dear. Av 603; leue, D 695; lef, P 1; lyfe, ET 565; leof, Hr 708; leef, Ip 1118; liif, O 404.
(2) willing, willingly. leeue, EG 514; Hv 261.
(3) pleasing. leffe, Ip 1052; leofen, *d.s.*, Ly 28151.
(4) *cp.*, rather. leuer, SS 4257; levir, B 3038. *sup.*, leueste, ET 396; leofeste, Ly 27604.

lege, *vw.*, (OE lecgan). (*Forms confused with those of* lie.)

(1) to lay, put. legge, Hr 1057; *pt. plu.*, layn, Tr 4751; leien, D 71; laid, D 185.
(2) strike (with a sword, *etc.*) *pt.*, leid, D 357; *plu.*, leiden, Ly 28549.

leie, to lay; *cf.* lege.

lemman, *n.*, (OE lēofman), lover (of either sex). Hr 433; ET 798.

lene, *vw.*, (OE lǽnan), (1) lend. At 4; CA 277; *pt.*, lente, CA 239.
(2) give, bestow. *pp.*, lent, Em 404.

lengore, *cp. adv.*, longer. D 226; leng, longer, O 82.

lep, leaped. D 421; leop, Al 4239.

lere, *n.*, (OE hlēor), face, countenance. Sd 2289; leyre, Lv 936; lyre, Cl 153; *plu.*, leris, B 3202.

lere, *vw.*, (OE lǽran), teach, instruct; learn. SS 332; At 707; *pp.*, lered, SS 362; ilerid, B 3857.

lese, lesing, *adj. and sb.*, (OE lēas, lēasung), false, falsehood. lees, ET 472; lesynges, G 385; At 83; leasing, EG 1006. *Especially in the phrase:* withoute lese, *or* lesing, truly, D 517.

lese, *vs.*, (OE lēosan), lose. Sd 1683; leose, Hr 663; *pr. 1 sg.*, lese, TT 186; losse (*as future*), Ip 3197; *pt.*, les, D 23; *pp.*, lore, G 202; ilore, G 301; lorn, Yw 958; loren, D 669; lest, Cl 70; ylore, O 543.

lete, *vs.*, (OE lǽtan), (1) allow, permit, let fall. Av 402; late, G 722; *pt.*, Hr 1222; *imp.*, lates, Yw 507; *in imperative and hortatory phrases:* lat we be, SS 257; *with inf.*, bewiten hine lette, let him be guarded, Ly 27854.
(2) leave, relinquish, lose. Sd 1510; *pt.*, lett, EG 334; *imp. plu.*, lattes, SS 577; *pp.*, laten, Hv 240.

(3) remain. *pt.*, **lat**, D 1035.
(4) cause, put. *pt.*, **let**, Hr 1381;
G 311.
lete, *vw.*, (OE **lettan**), (1) delay,
hinder. **lette**, Sd 2610; **leten**,
Hr 929; EG 151; *pp.*, **letted**,
EG 464; *vbl. n.*, **letting**, Av 10;
Cl 291.
(2) deprive. Sd 1510.
(3) cease. TT 156; **lett**, Cl 61.
(4) forbear. *pr. sj.*, **let**, Yw 131.
lete, *n.* (*from the verb*), hindrance,
delay. *Usually in the phrase:*
withouten lette, P 45; Av 187.
leue, *vw.*, (OE **lǣfan**), (1) stay
behind, remain. *pt.*, **leued**, Yw
1270; **lefte**, Hr 647; **lefde**, Hr
1378; Sd 2734; **lafte**, K 547.
(2) forsake, give up. **lefe**, Sd
1896; *pr. plu.*, **leuen**, CA 87;
pt., **leuyt**, Tr 4732; *pp.*, **leued**,
Hv 225.
leue, *cf.* **lefe**, dear.
leue, *vw.*, (OE **lēfan**), believe, trust.
CA 28; *pr. plu.*, **ileueth**, Ly
28636; *pt.*, **levid**, B 3380; *imp.*,
leeve, Sd 2636; CA 242.
leuedi, lefdi, lady. D 229, Hr 335.
lewed, *adj.*, (OE **lǣwede**), un-
learned, unlettered, common. G
505.
libbe, *cf.* **liue**.
lich, like, similar. B 3796. *Also
used as a suffix, meaning* "in
like manner, like."
lie, *n.*, falsehood. **ly3e**, R 47.
lie, *vs.*, (OE **licgan**). (*Forms confused with those of* **lege**.) (1)
recline. **lien**, G 598; **ligge**, Hr
1275; At 527; **li3e**, Hr 1158;
lig, SS 4256; *pr. 3 sg.*, **lise**, Av
937; **lyce**, Av 1139; **lis**, D 209;
liggeth, Hv 330; **lyethe**, Ip 351;
lygges, P 64; **lith**, O 241. *plu.*,
liggeoth, Ly 27943; *pt.*, **lay**, Hr
1303; **lӕi**, Ly 28015; **ley**, CA 98;
leyen, Hv 475; **laien**, Al 3965;

prp., **liggande**, EG 334; **liggeand**,
O 386.
(2) dwell, remain. *pt.*, **lay**, SS
804; **lӕi**, Ly 28427.
lie, *vw.*, (OE **lēogan**), tell a falsehood. *pr. 2 sg.*, **lixte**, G 297;
pr. sj., **leye**, Hv 2010.
life, *in the idioms:* **on liue**, alive,
P 541; **of the lyve**, dead, B 3393;
have the lyve, live, B 3488.
lighte, *vw.*, (OE **līhtan**), alight, get
down. **alihten**, Ly 27740; *pr.*,
lyghte, Ip 1196; **li3te**, Hr 519;
pp., **ly3th**, Lv 308.
liking, *n.*, (OE **līcung**), pleasure,
comfort, ease. Tr 71, CA 13.
liste, *vs.*, (OE **lystan**), (1) wish,
desire. *pt.*, **lust**, B 3504; **lyst**,
Ip 3078.
(2) please (*usually impersonal*).
pt., **liste**, P 2111; **luste**, Hr 406;
pr. sj., **leste**, Hr 862.
lite, little. Hv 276; **ly3t**, Cl 69.
liue, *vw.*, (OE **libban**, **lifian**), live.
Sd 3031; **libbe**, Hr 63; **lyfe**, CA
54; *pr. as f.*, **lif**, Av 356; *pt.*,
leuyd, P 1774; **leuede**, P 253;
liffede, P 1779; *prp.*, **leuand**,
Av 1050; **lyfand**, Yw 670; **leueande**, P 46.
longe, *vw.*, (OE **langian**), befit, appertain to (*usually impersonal*).
pr., **longith**, B 2990; **longis**, Ip
407.
lore, *n.*, (OE **lār**), counsel, wisdom,
training. P 231; Em 412.
lore, loren, *cf.* **lese**, lose.
loth, *adj.*, (OE **lāð**), (1) reluctant,
unwilling. CA 48; *often in the
tag:* **looth and leffe**, unwilling
and willing; *i.e.*, every one, B 3566.
(2) hateful, hated, displeasing,
hostile. **lath**, Yw 135; **loth**, CA
249.
loue, *vw.*, love, praise. Ip 458.
louerd, *n.*, (OE **hlāford**), lord,
feudal superior. D 470; **lauerd**,

Ly 27665; lardes, SS 4270; lordys, Ip 354; lordyng, gentleman, Em 965.

lufsome, *adj. and sb.*, lovely; lofsom, Lv 942.

M

ma, *cf.* make, more.

Mahoun, *lit.*, Mahomet, *but supposed to be a Saracen god and idol.*

mai, *vs.*, (OE magan), may, can. *pr. 1 sg.*, Hr 562; *2 sg.*, mayt, Hv 845; *(with enclitic pro.)* maistow, Sd 1826, B 3021; mowe, B 3316; *3 sg.*, mowe, IIv 175; *plu.*, mowe, G 675; mowne, ET 909; mone, Av 43; *(confused in form with* mun, *q.v.*); *pt.*, miȝte, D 521; movghte, Ip 3110; mahte, Ly 28385; maght, Hv 1348; moucthe, Hv 376; *plu.*, micten, Hv 516; mouthen, Hv 1183; *(with enclitic pro.)* miȝtou, D 319.

maic, maiden. Ip 3113.

main, *n.*, (OE mægen), strength, power, might. EG 141; imaine, Ly 27679; mein, D 579.

make, *vw.*, (OE macian), make, force, display. Hr 358; ma, P 1728; maa, P 520; *pr. 2 sg.* *(with enclitic pro.)*, makestow, G 199; *3 sg.*, mekes, Av 241; mase, ET 996; *pt. sg.*, maked, D 384; *plu.*, makede, Hr 1234; madun, Av 1134; *pp.*, mad, TT 11; maad, At 778; *pr. sj.*, moo, Ip 1152.

manere, *in the phrases:* some maner thing, some sort of thing; all maner thyng, every sort of thing, B 3021, Em 466; on al manere, by all means; in this maner wise, thus, SS 2805; B 2959.

maugré, *prep.*, (OF maugré), de-

spite *(usually in phrases of anger or contempt).* Yw 783; D 562.

me, men *(often used impersonally).* Hr 366; Ly 27933.

mede, *n.*, (OE mēd), (1) reward, deserts. Hr 470; EG 746; *in the phrase:* God do thee mede, God reward you, Yw 728. (2) bribe, gratuity. Hv 1635.

meiné, *n.*, (OF maisonnée), household, troop, retinue, company. Sd 1981; mayne, Sd 2022; menye, Tr 37; menȝe, SS 905; mene, Av 71; meny, K 818; meyny, Ip 352; maigne, Al 4141.

mekill, *cf.* muchel, much.

mene, mone, *vw.*, (OE mænan), (1) signify, intend. *pr sg.*, manes, Yw 93; menes, Hv 597; *plu.*, menes, SS 428; *pp.*, mynt, P 1667; iment, D 511; mente, Av 201; imint, D 1032. (2) speak, tell. K 935; *pt.*, menede, CA 124; ment, Cl 126. (3) moan, complain, lament. *(Same stem as preceding in OE, though senses have always been different.)* mone, EG 126; moone, Ip 1069.

mete, *n.*, (OE mete), food, meal. Av 720; CA 88; meyte, K 739; met, D 822.

mete, *vw.*, (OE mætan), dream. Hr 1408; imætte, Ly 28016.

mete, *vw.*, (OE mētan), meet, encounter. *pr.*, mette, Hr 1027; imette, Ly 27715.

miche, mech, much.

mid, *prep.*, (OE mid), with. Hr 220; Ly 27661; mide, D 217; myde, Al 4111.

misfare, *vw.*, do amiss, go astray. CA 238.

moche, much.

mochel, much; *cf.* muchel.

mode, *n.*, (OE mōd), mind, state of mind, pride, courage. ET

619; Ip 1031; **moode**, Sd 2077.
mone, *n.* (*from the vb.*), moan,
lament. Av 1087; **mane**, P
1063; **moon**, B 3190.
mone, moon. Em 2.
monnen, men. Ly 27830.
moo, *cf.* more, make.
more, *cp. adj., adv., and sb.*, (OE
māra, mā), more, greater. Hr
554; **mo**, Hr 808; **moo**, ET 156;
mære, Ly 27864; **ma**, SS 264.
morne, morwen, *n.*, (OE **morgen**),
morrow. **morun**, Av 794; *often
in the following phrases, meaning
"to-morrow"*: **amorewe**, D 481;
to-morn, Ip 3006; **a marʒen**, Ly
28004; **a moreʒe**, Hr 645.
moste, *sup. adj., sb., and adv.*, (OE
mǣst, mest), most, greatest.
P 899; **mest**, Hr 250; **maste**, SS
448; **mæste**, Ly 27482.
mote, moste, *vs.*, (OE *pr.*, **mōte**,
pt., **mōste**) may, shall, must.
pr. and pt., G 233; **mut**, B 2932;
moot, G 577; **moste**, CA 50;
plu., **mot**, G 131; **moten**, Hv 18.
muchel, *adj., sb., and adv.*, (OE
mycel), much, great. Hr 83;
mochel, D 10; **mycull**, Av 35;
mucle, Ly 27732; **mekill**, Av 335.
cp., **more**, *q.v.*; *sup.*, **moste**.
mun, mon, *vs.*, (OE **mon**; ON
mun), must, shall (*forms confused with* **mai**, *q.v.*) Av 367,
SS 465; **mon**, Ip 1198, P 567.

N

N-. *For the following negative
compounds, see the word indicated:* **nas, nis, nes, nam, neoren,
næs**, *cf.* be; **not, note, niste**, *cf.*
wite; **nabben, nastu, nafte, nade,
nauede**, *cf.* haue; **nalde, nulde,
nolde, nil, null, nel**, *cf.* wille.
nauthir, neither.
ne, *adv. and conj.*, (OE **ne**), (1) not,

nor (*correlative*, **ne . . . ne**). Hr
46; D 253; **ny**, Em 320.
(2) only (*correlative*, **ne . . . but**).
Hr 198.
nede, *n.*, (OE **nēad**), need, necessity. Hr 48; **neoden**, *d.s.*,
Ly 28395; **neodde**, Ly 28437;
d. as adv., **nede**, necessarily, B
3102; *g. as adv.*, **nedys**, Ip 1163.
negh, *adj., adv., and prep.*, (OE
nēah), nigh, near, almost. **negʒ**,
D 255; **neghʒ**, D 534; **ny**, ET
150; **neʒ**, Hr 252; **nyʒe**, B 3564;
neh, Ly 28353; **neyh**, G 626;
aneh, Ly 27651; **neiʒ**, R 201.
neghe, *vw.*, (OE **nēhwan**), approach,
draw near. **nyʒhe**, Sd 2100;
newhen, Hv 1866; *pr.*, **neghes**,
P 808; **neh**, Ly 27735; **neʒe**, Av
827; *pt.*, **neʒhit**, Av 1003;
neghed, Tr 4731; *imp.*, **neghe**,
Av 854; *prp.*, **nyʒyng**, Lv 829.
nemnede, named. D 252; **nempned**,
O 598.
nere, *adj., adv., and prep.*, (OE
nēah), near. SS 520; **neerr**, EG
276. *cp.*, **nerre**, P 2072; **ner**,
G 109; **neer**, G 138. *comp.*,
nerhand, nearly, Cl 70, At 327;
nerehonde, Sd 2998; **neerehand**,
EG 158.
netheles, *adv.*, nevertheless. Hv
1658; **neotheles**, Ly 27974; **nethirles**, B 3368.
nice, *adj.*, foolish. B 3416.
nime, *vs.*, (OE **niman**), (1) take,
seize. *pt.*, **nam**, Hr 585; **nome**,
Hr 1173; **inom**, Ly 27726; **neme**,
Hr 60; *pp.*, **inome**, G 119;
nomen, EG 255.
(2) go, take the road. *pr. sj.*,
nimen, Hv 1336; *pt.*, **nom**, D
368; **ynome**, Lv 94.
nith, nicth, niht, night. Hv 575.
no, *adv., adj., and conj.*, (OE **nā, nō**),
(1) no (*opposite of* "yes"). (2)
not any, not. Hr 11; **na**, Hr 1193.

(3) nor. SS 2969, Av 1010.
In the phrase: withouten no;
beyond denial, O 48. *comp.*, nouȝwher, nowhere. R 326.
none, *pro. and adj.*, (OE nān),
none, no one, not any. non,
Hr 8; CA 250; nane, SS 485;
a.m., nenne, Ly 27977; *d.f.*,
nare, Ly 27838.
none, nones, *n.*, (OE nōn), nones
(*originally the sixth* canonical
hour, *coming about three p.m.
But, when the Church required
fasting until* nones *on fast-days,
which were increasingly numerous
in the later Middle Ages, the time
drifted toward midday. In the
romances, the time can be determined only from the context, if at
all.*) SS 4303; novn, Cl 88.
nonis, *in the phrase:* for the nonis,
a tag of slight meaning; lit., for
that occasion, just then; *often
best translated* "indeed." TT 82;
nones, D 1014.
nought, *pro., adj., and adv.*, (OE
nāwiht, naht), (1) naught, nothing. Ip 1052; nowȝt, Cl 110;
nott, Cl 352; nowt, D 253; noȝt,
Hr 937; noȝth, CA 290.
(2) not, not at all. nat, G 158;
note, Ip 426; noȝt, CA 236;
nougt, D 1005.
nowther, nother, noither, nouther,
neither.
nowȝe, noweȝ, now. B 3213, 3736.

O

O, written for a, on, one, or, of.
of, off, *prep.*, (OE of). *Only the
more unfamiliar senses are noted:*
(1) by (*agency*). Av 693.
(2) from, out of. CA 287.
(3) from, at the hands of. Hr
365.
of, *a common spelling for* off. Tr
4755.

olde, *adj. and sb.*, (OE eald), old.
K 177; G 79; eld, D 210; alde,
Ly 28444; *sup.*, heldeste, Hv
1396.
on, an, one.
on, *prep. and adv.*, (OE on), on (*in
most of the senses of Modern
English*). one, P 60; o, Hv 1251;
an, D 411; a, Ly 27744.
one, *pro., adj., and adv.*, (OE ān),
(1) one. oon, ET 778; o, B 3076;
on, CA 143; tone (*by assimilation
from* that one), P 708; ton, K 677.
(2) *Used to complete a comparison:*
A kinder knight then Grime was
one (*i.e.*, than G. was), EG 499.
(3) alone. CA 15; ane, P 2043.
ones, *adv.*, (OE ānes), once. onys,
B 2993; onus, Av 868; anes, Yw
292; ones, CA 196.
or, *conj.* (*contraction of* other; *cf.*
either), or. CA 30; ꜵr, Cl 35;
our, Cl 418; er, Sd 2732.
or, before; *cf.* are.
ore, *n.*, (OE ār), mercy, favor,
grace. ET 226; are, K 69.
orn, ourn, ran; *cf.* runne.
os, *cf.* as.
other, *pro., adj., and adv.*, (OE
ōðer), (1) other, the other. Hr
238; vther, Yw 634; odur, ET
610; odir, K 884.
(2) next, second. D 228; EG
625; Hr 187.
(3) otherwise. othyr, ET 117;
Ly 27898.
Assimilations: no nodur, no other,
ET 459; my nothir, mine other,
Av 42; tother, the other, Av 297;
todirs, other's, B 3094.
other, or; *cf.* either.
ouer, *prep. and adv.*, (OE ofer),
over. Hv 293; ouur, CA 175;
aure, Av 623.
comp., oueral, everywhere, Ly
27471, O 206.
our, *cf.* I *and* or.

owe, ought, *cf.* awe.

own, *pro. and adj.*, (OE āgen), own. awin, SS 284; awne, Av 315; oȝene, Hr 249; *d.f.*, aȝere, Ly 28107; owyn, Cl 534; owhen, O 161; oȝe, Hr 984.

P

paie, *n.*, pleasure. Cl 144.

paie, *vw.*, (OF paier), (1) pay. K 36. (2) please. pay, SS 396; *pp.*, payde, ET 157; paid, Yw 1057.

palefrai, *n.*, (OF palefrei), saddle-horse (*as distinguished from steed, or war-horse*). Cl 250; Hv 2060.

par (*in oaths*), in the name of, by. par charité, in the name of charity; pardy, perdé, by God, Ip 1085; parauenture, by chance, D 127; par fai, by my faith, D 761; par ma foy, by my faith, G 367.

paramour, *n.*, (OF par amour), lover. Lv 303; *as adv.*, fervently. Lv 106.

pas, *n.*, pace; *especially in the phrase:* ful gode pase, rapidly. K 713; gude pase, Yw 619.

passe, *vw.*, (OF passer), (1) pass, go. pas, SS 2848. (2) escape, go away. B 3062; SS 487.

pere, *n.*, (OF per), (1) peer, noble. Hv 989. (2) an equal. At 33; per, D 1010.

piment, spiced wine. Sq 758; pyement, Lv 344.

pine, *n.*, (OE pīn), pain, suffering. CA 92; EG 692; Sd 2030.

pine, *vw.*, (OE pīnian), torment, cause pain. Hr 635; *pp.*, pyned, CA 26.

plight, *vw.*, (OE plihtan), pledge, assure. pliȝte, Hr 305; *pr.*, Av 428; plyght, ET 210.

pouer, poor, power; pouerlich, poorly.

prese, *n.*, (*fr.* OF presser), throng, tumult. Em 464; press, TT 21; prece, Av 742.

prest, priest.

prest, *adj. and adv.*, (OF prest), ready, quick. At 745; TT 67; Av 19.

preue, *cf.* proue.

price, prise, *n.*, (OF pris), (1) worth, esteem, excellence. Em 92; Av 20; priis, O 49. (2) judgment of superiority, prize. D 582; Av 529; Ip 1099. (3) *as adj.*, worthy, noble. TT 215, CA 279.

prike, *vw.*, (OE prician), spur, ride rapidly. Em 737; preke, Av 1116; *pt.*, prikit, Tr 8657; prekut, Av 289; *prp.*, prekand, Av 623.

prime, *n.*, beginning of the day (*strictly, the canonical hour after sunrise; extended to cover the period between six and nine a.m.*) SS 359.

priué, *adj.*, (OF privé), secret. prevée, P 154; priuyé, EG 1341.

priueli, *adv.*, secretly. B 3632; preuely, Av 853; Ip 1126.

priueté, *n.*, (OF priveté), secret counsels, secrecy. preueté, SS 284; Av 947; Ip 488.

proue, *vw.*, (OF prover), (1) prove. preue, CA 252; *pr.*, preues, P 55; *pp.*, preuyt, Tr 47. (2) make trial of. proue, Hr 545.

Q

Qu-, Qw-. *For northern words beginning with this combination, see* Wh-.

quath, quod, *vs.*, (OE cweðan). *Only in preterit:* said, quoth. Hr 127; quod, CA 99; quad, D 175; hwat, Hv 1650; quoth, Al 3984.

quik, *adj., sb., and adv.*, (OE cwic),

(1) alive, living. D 164; SS 895; quic, Hr 86; qwyk, K 402.
(2) quick. D 832.

quite, *vw.*, (OF quiter), (1) repay, requite. B 3519; *pt.*, qwyte, P 1491; *pp.*, quytte, Ip 478; *in the phrase:* quite him his mede, give him his deserts, ET 693; Sd 1921.
(2) acquit, redeem, clear. quyȝtt, Cl 63; *pp.*, quyte, B 3534.

R

rape, *adj. and adv.*, quick. G 101.

ras, rase, roos, rose.

rathe, *adj. and adv.*, (OE hræð, hrædlīce), quick, impatient. P 98; Av 248; radlye, EG 1236; radly, Tr 4714.

rawghte, *cf.* recchen, reach.

reche, rekke, *vs.*, (OE rēcan), care, take heed. *pr. 1 sg.*, recche, Hr 366; *2 sg.*, rekke, CA 306; *3 sg.*, reche, Av 808; *pt.*, rowȝte, CA 177; roght, Sd 1878; *pt. sj.*, roght, Yw 969.

recche, *vw.*, (OE rǣccan), (1) reach, grasp. *pt.*, rawȝt, Cl 196.
(2) hand over, deal (a blow). *pr. sg.*, recheth, CA 176; rawȝte, CA 177; raught, EG 978; *plu.*, rawȝten, CA 316.

rede, *n.*, (OE rǣd), advice, counsel, plan. SS 910; Av 964; G 432; ræd, Ly 27977; redd, ET 430; *in the phrase:* couthe no rede, was uncertain what to do, P 153.

rede, *vs. and w.*, (OE rǣdan), read. *pt.*, radde, D 243.

rede, *vs.*, (OE rǣdan), advise, counsel, direct. *pr. 1 sg.*, CA 169; Ip 1150; read, EG 605; *pt.*, radde, Lv 39; rathe, Hv 1335.

reson, *n.*, (OF raison), good sense, due cause, justice. ET 902.

reue, *vw.*, (OE rēafian), take away, deprive of. SS 875; refe, TT 99; *pt.*, rafte, Av 100; *pp.*, rafte, ET 1206; reued, G 704.

rewe, *vs. and w.*, (OE hrēowan), (1) regret (*often impersonal*). Hr 378; Cl 269; *pt.*, rewed, CA 55; rew, Lv 177.
(2) pity. rewythe, Lv 102; *pt.* (*with prep.*), rued on, Sd 1561.

rewthe, *n.*, (OE hrēowð), pity, sorrow. O 112; ruthe, Hr 673; routhe, G 677.

riall, *adj.*, splendid, royal.

riche, *adj. and sb.*, (OF riche), wealthy, powerful, well born; sumptuous, expensive. Em 416; Hr 314; B 2963.

riche, rike, *n.*, (OE rīce), kingdom, realm. SS 3001; Yw 142; Ly 28273.

ride, *vs.*, (OE rīdan), ride. Hr 34; rith, Hv 2690; *pt.*, rade, Av 146; rid, EG 336; rood, G 190; rod, Hr 32; ritte, D 537; *pp.*, redyn, TT 111; ride, G 191; iriden, D 56; *prp.*, rydand, TT 74; ridinde, Ly 28524.

rife, *adj.*, (OE rīf), thick, numerous, crowded, frequent. P 560; Tr 4770; ryue, G 783.

rigge, *n.*, (OE hrycg), back. Hr 1058; rig, SS 885; rug, Ly 27821; rigg, D 526.

right, *n.*, (OE riht), that which is fitting, proper, or just. Cl 36; riȝte, D 52; *g. as adv.*, rightis, Sd 2278; *in the phrase:* on ryght, aright, ET 516.

right, *adj. and adv.*, (1) right, proper, just, immediate, direct. Cl 254; rith, Hv 2235; *adv.*, *often a mere filler, meaning* "indeed": right, Cl 9; ryȝth, CA 352; reght, P 227.
(2) right (*as opposed to left*). rith, Hv 604.

rode, *n.*, (OE rōd), the cross of Christ. Hr 328; roode, G 639; rod, ET 1044.

rode, *n.*, (OE rudu), complexion. D 813; rud, EG 217; ruddy, Sq 713.

rowte, *n.*, (OF route), throng, crowd, turmoil. G 285; Tr 4701; rowt, Yw 1024; row3t, Cl 267; rout, O 281.

runne, *vs.*, (OE irnan), run. rynn, P 1662; vrn, Hr 878; *pr. sg.*, rinnes, Av 59; *pt. sg.*, orn, Ly 28068; ourn, O 83; *pt. plu.*, runnun, Av 384; vrn, O 87; ronnen, CA 314; *pp.*, iorne, Hr 1146; *prp.*, rinyng, SS 881; rennynge, CA 113; rinand, Yw 1067.

S

sagh, saw; *cf.* se.

sai, say, *cf.* seie.

samen, *adj. and adv.*, (ON saman), together, in company. samyn, SS 338; samin, Yw 24; somyn, Tr 66; somun, Av 385; in same, At 754; Sd 1938; isome, R 227.

sand, sond, *n.*, (OE sand), shore, strand (*especially in the phrase:* see and sonde, sea and land). Em 18, Hv 708.

Saresyns, *n.*, Saracens, Turks. Sd 3103; Sarazins, Hr 1319; Sarezyne, Em 482; Sarsynys, Lv 266.

saunfail, without fail. Yw 1004; D 1016; san3 fail, SS 913.

sawe, *n.*, (OE sagu), (1) speech, talk, remark, proverb. ET 574; Ip 3018.

(2) story, tale. Em 319; CA 162.

sayne, seen, say; *cf.* se *and* seie.

sc-, sch-, *cf.* sh-.

scl-, *cf.* sl-.

scape, *vw.*, (OF escaper), escape.

skape, G 576; *pt.*, scapyd, ET 115.

sceldes, shields. Ly 27463; scelden, Ly 27784.

scipen, ships, Ly 28234; *g. plu.*, scipen, Ly 28437.

se, *vs.*, (OE sēon), see, look upon. seen, Sd 1588; seon, Hr 1345; yseo, Al 3882; ise, Ly 28470; yse, O 528; *pr. 1 sg.*, see, ET 538; *2 sg.*, sese, SS 426; sest, Hv 534; *3 sg.*, sese, SS 822; seese, P 422; seth, O 249. *plu.*, sen, Hv 168; sayne, P 114; *pt. sg.*, sa3, Hr 777; sagh, Yw 152; segh, D 87; sye, ET 1001; se3, D 335; saugh, Sd 2985; isi3e, Hr 1157; seigh, G 120; segh3, D 731; si3e, O 353; saye, Sd 1998; sey, G 330; se, Av 776; sey3, CA 22; sei3e, O 295; isæh, Ly 28382; *plu.*, seghen, D 139; ysei3e, O 326; see, Tr 57; sy3en, Em 299; sy, Em 869; ise3e, D 503; sowen, Hv 1055; iseh3en, Ly 27518; *pt. sj.*, isi3e, Hr 976; *imp. plu.*, seith, B 3159; *pp.*, seyn, B 3574; sen, D 586; sey, B 3697; sene, CA 53; sayne, Ip 378; se3e, R 416. *In the phrase:* God you see, God be gracious to you, Sd 2707; Lv 253.

seche, seken, *vw.*, (OE sēcan), (1) seek, look for. sech, B 3298; seke, Ip 1065; siche, B 3795; *pr. with enclitic pro.*, sechestu, Hr 942; *pt.*, sow3t, Em 307; soght, Tr 8624.

(2) come, go. *pt.*, sowghtte, Ip 366; sow3te, CA 60; soghten, Tr 8671; *imp.*, seche, CA 53; *pp.*, sought, Ip 404; sow3t, Cl 207.

(3) attempt. *pp.*, soght, ET 618.

segh, saw; *cf.* se.

seie, *vw.*, (OE secgan), say, speak, tell (*often used absolutely*). CA 311; sigge, Al 4198; sayne, Sd

1736; sugen, Ly 27837; sai, D 166; *pr. 1 sg.*, sigge, Al 4023; *pr. 2 sg.*, seyst, Hv 2008; *3 sg.*, saise, P 1953; seyt, O 554; *plu.*, seyn, CA 217; suggeth, Ly 27480; says, Av 936; *pt.*, seide, D 431; Hr 271; sede, Hr 531; iseid, K 344; *pp.*, seyd, Hv 1281.

self, selue, *pro. and adj.*, (OE self), self, same. seluun, Av 70; seoluen, Ly 28146. *Often used without preceding personal pronoun.*

semblaunt, *n.*, (OF semblant), (1) expression of countenance. Yw 631; sembelant, Em 220; sembland, Yw 631. (2) show, display. Ip 2995.

semeli, *adj. and adv.*, (ON sœmiligr), (1) handsome, pleasant, attractive. CA 12; P 543; semyle, Lv 285. (2) fitting, proper. *cp.*, semelyer, ET 348.

sen, since, see; *cf.* sithen, se.

sertes, *adv.*, (OF certes), surely. SS 339; sertis, Ip 1127; certys, Em 647.

shaft, *n.*, (OE sceaft), shaft, (*by metonymy*) spear, arrow. SS 801; schafte, P 52; scaftes, Ly 28553.

shal, *vs.*, (OE sceal), shall, will, be expected to, be supposed to. *pr. 1 sg.*, schal, Hr 544; sal, Yw 465; chal, D 652; *2 sg.*, shalst, EG 1308; *3 sg.*, sall, P 91; sale, SS 901; sschal, D 30; *plu.*, shole, Hv 562; schuln, G 842; schulle, Hr 847; schul, G 587; scullen, Ly 28198; *pt. sg.*, sholde, CA 94; sold, SS 274; schust, O 418; sulde, P 738; schud, Lv 803; *plu.*, schuld, Av 780; sholden, Hv 1020; sculden, Ly 27980; schild, Av 930; *pr. sj.*, sschulle, D 86; *with enclitic pro.*, shaltow,

schaltu, D 318.

shape, *vs. and w.*, (OE scieppan), form, create, give shape to. Em 242; *pt.*, shope, Tr 72; ET 948; shoope, Em 2; shaped, Hv 424.

she, *pro.* (*origin uncertain*), she. *For oblique cases, see* he. ssche, D 54; ʒhe, D 23; ʒe, D 78; sho, SS 519.

shende, *vw.*, (OE scendan), (1) injure, disgrace. Sd 1682; scende, Ly 27793; *pp.*, schente, Av 692; ishente, Sd 2286. (2) abuse, reprove. *pp.*, schente, ET 302; G 704.

shene, *adj.*, (OE scēne), shining, lovely, beautiful. Em 150; schene, Av 454; schine, O 356; sheene, CA 298; *in the phrase:* schene vndur schild (*tag for a warrior*), Av 622.

shewe, *vw.*, (OE scēawian), (1) show, reveal. shauwe, Hv 2206; Hr 1311; *pr. sg.*, schewes, P 1072; *pp.*, shewed, Hv 2056; schewid, K 1060. (2) declare. sheue, Hv 1401. (3) look at, gaze upon. shewe, Hv 2136.

shir, bright, shining. Hv 1253.

shitte, *cf.* shut.

shole, should; *cf.* shal.

shon, shoon, *plu. of* sho, shoe. G 212.

showe, *cf.* shewe.

shul, *cf.* shal.

shut, *vw.*, (OE scyttan), shut. schitte, G 286; *pt.*, shet, Sd 2960; *pp.*, ischet, G 292; shit, Sd 2963.

sibbe, *n. and adj.*, (OE sibb), kin, blood-relation. D 618; sib, Ip 3086; EG 45.

sike, *vw.*, (OE sīcan), sigh, lament. Hv 291; siʒe, B 3270; syche, Lv 249; *pt.*, siʒte, D 866; siʒhid, B 3017; sykede, CA 25; *prp.*, sikend, D 133; syʒthyng, Cl 98;

syghynge, Cl 108; *vbl. n.*, sykynge,
Ip 1051; Em 328.
siker, *adj. and adv.*, (OE siker),
sure. D 115; B 3634; seker,
Yw 601; sicur, K 170; *adv.*,
securly, P 202; Ip 440; Cl 219;
sekerlike, ET 952.
sin, since; *cf.* sithen.
sithe, *n.*, (OE sīð), time, occasion.
Hr 356; P 985; *plu.*, sithe, EG
1164; At 585; sythis, At 783.
sithen, *adv., conj., and prep.*, (OE
seoððan,ᶜsiððan), (1) since, after
(*of time*), afterwards. CA 25;
sethin, SS 453; sethun, Av 157;
sythinn, Av 1107; sith, B 3175;
sen, P 296; seoththen, Ly 27803;
syn, Cl 213; sethn, SS 4326;
suththe, Hr 1078.
(2) because, since (*of cause*).
sithin, Av 937; sith, B 3288; sen,
SS 339.
sitte, *vs.*, (OE sittan), sit. *pr. sg.*,
sitte, G 749; *pt. sg.*, seet, G 790;
set, D 157; *plu.*, seten, Em 218;
sete, G 681; *pp.*, sette, G 805;
iset, B 3055.
sle, slo, sla, *vs.*, (OE slēan), (1)
slay, kill. slee, G 822; sla, P
293; sloo, ET 150; sclo, Lv 837;
sloe, Av 940; slean, Ly 28180;
slone, K 35; slen, D 922; *pr. sg.*,
slos, Hv 2706; *pt. sg.*, sluȝe, Av
1029; slogh, SS 843; slouȝ, O 312;
slowgh, D 890; *plu.*, slogh, Tr
4766; *pr. sj.*, slaey, Av 111; slos,
Hv 2596; *pp.*, slane, P 1774;
sloe, EG 433; slawe, At 705;
islæȝen, Ly 27926; aslæȝe, 28330;
sclayn, Lv 610; sclawe, Lv 723;
slone, P 2154; slawene, Sd 2802.
(2) strike, beat on. slæn, Ly
27486; *pt. plu.*, slowe, Sd 2565.
slike, such; *cf.* swilk.
slo, slay, strike; *cf.* sle.
slogh, slew, struck; *cf.* sle.
snell, *adj., sb., and adv.*, (OE snell),

quick, active. Em 309; Lv 441.
so, *cf.* swa.
soghte, sowȝte, sought; *cf.* seche.
solas, *n.*, (OF solaz), enjoyment,
comfort. Lv 407, G 328; solace,
SS 253.
sonde, *n.*, (OE sond), (1) message.
Hr 271.
(2) providence, mercy. CA 36,
Em 332; sande, K 655.
(3) messenger. Hr 933; *plu.*,
sonde, Ly 27966.
sone, *adv.*, (OE sona), at once,
straightway, speedily. Hr 42;
Em 230; soune, Ip 3045.
sone, sune, *n.*, (OE sunu), son. Ip
3081, D 592; *g. sg.*, sune, Av 268;
son, SS 4296; *plu.*, sonnes, CA
42.
sonne, sunne, sone, sun.
sore, (OE sār, sāre), (1) *n.*, sorrow,
pain. Hv 152, EG 318.
(2) *adj. and adv.*, sad, wretched,
painful. EG 847; sare, SS 563,
ET 1012; sor, D 578; soure, SS
546; *cp.*, sorrere, At 565; sarlic,
Ly 28457.
sori, *adj. and adv.*, (OE sārig), (1)
sad, wretched. Hv 151; særi,
Ly 28333; sorye, Ip 1065; særȝest, Ly 28459.
(2) regretful. sary, SS 852.
sorwe, sorghe, *n.*, (OE sorg), sorrow. Hv 57; sorow, SS 3027;
plu., soreȝe, Hr 261; sorȝen, Ly
28443; sorhful, sorrowful, Ly
28335.
soth, *adj. and sb.*, true, the truth.
SS 4263, ET 158; south, Sd 1689;
cp., soththere, Ly 28461. *In the
phrases:* forsothe, to sothe, be
sothe, in truth, CA 18, Ly
28142, Cl 485.
soun, *n.*, sound, noise.
sound, *adj.*, (OE gesund), sound,
unhurt, in good health. EG 789;
sund, Hr 1341; sowunde, Av

1034; isunde, Ly 28615.

sowdan, sultan. P 977; sawdan, Av 917; sowdon, Sd 2095.

sowne, swoone, n. (from the verb), swoon, daze. EG 60; swown, SS 863; swoue, D 1064; iswoue, D 1061; swogh, Yw 824.

sowne, swone, vw., swoon, be dazed. inf., swony, D 1063; pt., sooned, EG 1347; sowened, Em 780; squonut, Av 390; swoned, O 195; swownyd, At 604; pp., iswoʒe, Hr 428; prp. as noun, sowenynge, Em 284; svounnyng, Cl 89; swownyng, Yw 868.

spede, vw., (OE spēdan), (1) hasten, speed. D 749, Ip 3005; pr. plu., spede, Sd 2842.

(2) prosper, progress, succeed. Sd 2433; pr. sg., spette, G 806; pt., spedde, P 934. Especially in the phrase: God us spede, God give us success, Ip 486.

spede, n, (OE spēd), (1) speed, P 759; d. as adv., gode spede, fast, Av 628.

(2) success, Sd 1737.

spell, n., (OE spell), (1) tale, news. Yw 149, Hr 1030; pl., spelles, Ly 28175.

(2) language. pl., spellen, Ly 28165.

spille, vw., (OE spillan), (1) destroy, kill, spill blood. Av 314, ET 1132; pp., spild, Av 216; spilt, SS 4290.

(2) perish. Hr 194, Hv 2422.

squ-, sqw-, cf. sw-.

squete, sweet; Av 833.

stande, vs., (OE standan), (1) stand, stand up, stand still. stonde, Hr 399; pr. sg., stant, G 814; stont, B 3173; pt., stod Hr 529.

(2) stop, delay. stande, P 960.

(3) in various idiomatic senses: issue out (of light). pt, stod,

Hv 591; blow (of wind); pt., stod, Ly 28305, Em 833.

staleworth, adj. (origin uncertain), stalwart, valiant, strong. D 288; stalworthi, Hv 24; staloworth, CA 326.

stede, n., (OE stēda), horse, steed (generally used of a war-horse). D 408; d. sg., (by nunnation) steden, Ly 27741.

stede, n., (OE stede, styde), place, location. P 154; stid, Av 1091, Tr 8627; stude, Ly 28534; in the phrase: stand in stedde, be an aid to, Ip 3083.

sterte, vs., (ON sterta), jump, rush. sturte, R 281; pr. sg., stertis, P 2229; stirttes, P 430; pt., sterte, G 219, Sd 1606; styrte, CA 326; stirt, D 923.

sterue, vs., (OE steorfan), die, perish. pr., sterue, Hr 910; pp., isterue, Hr 1167.

steuen, n., (OE stefn), voice. Sd 2258; steuyn, ET 74; steuenne, CA 106.

sti, n., (OE stīg), path. Ip 3088, Hv 2618.

stiffe, adj. and adv., (OE stif), valiant, stubborn, strong. P 1472, EG 643; stif, D 9; stef, D 531; stifly, Av 326, TT 156.

stiward, n., (OE stigweard), steward. (This official was seldom popular with minstrels, as he discouraged prodigality toward wayfarers.) Hr 227; stuard, Av 1070; stward, Em 496.

stounde, n., (OE stund), time, period of time, occasion. SS 2991; stonde, EG 611; stunde, Hr 739; stowunde, Av 409; d. as adv., this stownde, on this occasion, now, SS 781.

stowre, n., (OF estour), tumult, uproar, combat. Yw 1221, P 138; stoure, Tr 8652. Especially *in the phrase:* **stiffe in stowre,** valiant in battle.

sturien, stir. Ly 27440; *pt.,* **sturede,** Ly 27424.

sugge, say; *cf.* seie.

sumdel, *adj. and adv.,* somewhat. K 283.

sunden, be; *cf.* be.

suthe, very; *cf.* swithe.

suththe, afterwards; *cf.* sithen.

swa, so, *adv., and conj.,* (OE swa). *The senses are as in Modern English except:* (1) since, because, as. Ip 1136; Hr 590. (2) as if, provided that. B 3746; Hr 718.

swein, swain, *n.,* (ON sveinn), (1) peasant, servant *(often an epithet).* P 700, G 527, Em 384; sqwayne, K 230. (2) retainer, soldier. Ly 28339.

swerd, *n.,* (OE sweord), sword. sweord, Ly 27626; **squrd,** Av 247.

swere, *vs.,* (OE swerian), swear, take oath. squere, Av 320; *pr.,* **suereth,** Hv 647; *pt.,* swor, Hv 398; **squere,** Av 466; **sworen,** Hr 1249; *pp.,* swore, G 302.

swilk, swich, slike, (OE swylc, ON slīkr), (1) *pro., adj., and sb.,* such. CA 49; SS 404; Yw 820; **seche,** Av 34; **swihc,** Hr 166; **sich,** P 159; *comp.,* swilkane, SS 2994. (2) *conj. and prep.,* as if, like. Hv 2123; **swulc,** Ly 27455.

swire, swere, *n.,* (OE swīra), neck. CA 44, D 1018; **sweere,** G 273.

swithe, *adv.,* (OE swið, swȳð), (1) quickly. Hr 273; **swyde,** CA 158, Em 219; *(by nunnation)* swithen, Ly 27527; **squith,** Av 218; **sqwithely,** Av 320; **swiʒe,** D 305. (2) very, very much. Hr 174; **suthe,** Hr 178; **squytheli,** Av 732.

swone, swoone, swoue, swoon; *cf.* sowne.

T

taa, tan, *cf.* take.

take, *vs.,* (ON taka), (1) take, seize, receive, lift. Hv 409; too, P 1022; tan, At 495; taa, P 498; *pr. sg.,* tase, P 790; *pt. sg.,* tok, D 1036; tuke, P 186; *pt. plu.,* token, CA 226; *pp.,* itake, G 350; token, Hv 1194; tone, P 2155; take, Ip 1162; tane, Ip 1049; *prp.,* takeand, EG 1237. (2) entrust, give. B 3608; *pr., 1 sg.,* take, G 747; *3 sg.,* taketh, CA 104; *pt.,* tok, D 295; toke, Em 547; tuke, P 195; *imp. sg.,* tak, SS 3003. (3) *in various idiomatic senses:* take no keep, have no regard for, ET 746; toke hem bitwene, decided between them, Em 799, Hv 1833; take, tane, take oneself, go, P 1060; the ded to take, receive the death-penalty, SS 4295.

tale, *n.,* (OE tæl), (1) speech, tale, story. Hv 3, Hr 311. (2) number, count. Hv 2026, Ly 27606.

teche, *vs.,* (OE tǣcan, tæcean), teach. *pt.,* tauʒt, D 285; taʒte, Hr 244; tauhte, Hv 2214; thawʒth, Em 58; thawʒte, Em 973; *pp.,* tawʒte, CA 312; taght, SS 797.

telle, *vs.,* (OE tellan), (1) talk, tell, relate. B 2966; *pt.,* tolde, Hr 467; talde, Ly 28254. (2) enumerate, count. Hr 617; *pp.,* italde, Ly 27432. (3) count out (money), pay. ET 968.

tene, *n.,* (OE tēona), (1) injury, sorrow. Sd 2896, Ip 1082, Av 902.

(2) wrath, anger. P 1986, Tr 4724; *as adj.*, angry, P 301, 1972, Ip 2996.

tha, those, then, when; *cf.* **tho.**

thanne, thenne, *adv. and conj.*, (OE *þanne*), (1) then. Ip 451, Hr 439; **than**, Tr 8608; **thon**, P 2249. (2) than, than if. Hv 944; **thane**, Hr 13; **thene**, Ly 27450; **then**, B 3027. (3) when, the time when. CA 330, Sd 2527. (4) *correlative.* **thanne** . . . **thanne**, then . . . when, Hv 1203.

that, (OE *þæt*). *Only uses fairly uncommon in Modern English are given:* (1) *rel. adj.*, that which, who, whoever, what. Sd 2489; D 244; that of which, B 3482. (2) *conj.*, that, so that, in order that. ET 780; **thet**, Ly 28119. (3) *conj.*, until, when. Av 870, Ly 27746. (4) because. Hv 161. (5) *used with other conjunctives; not to be translated:* **whenne that**, when; **yif that**, if; **what that**, what, *etc.* Em 617; (*with enclitic pro.*) **thatow**, that thou, O 452.

thaw3th, thaw3te, taught; *cf.* **teche.**

the, *adj.*, (OE *þe*), (1) the (*definite article*). Hr 27; **theo**, Al 3946; *n.f.*, **tha**, Ly 28068; *d.f.*, **there**, Ly 27931; *d.m.*, **than**, Ly 27932; *a.f.*, **tha**, Ly 28022; *a.m.*, **thane**, Ly 27628; **thene**, Ly 27506; **then**, Ly 28183; *plu.*, *n. and a.*, **thæ**, Ly 28072; **tha**, Ly 27806; *d.*, **than**, Ly 27490. (2) *relative pro.* (*indeclinable*), who, which. **the**, Ly 28169; **tha**, Ly 27613; **thæ**, Ly 27481.

thee, *vs.*, (OE *þēon*), prosper, thrive. ET 417; **the**, K 2;

then, Sd 1593; **thynne**, K 736; *especially in the oath:* so mote i thee, as I hope to prosper, Av 812, Cl 538.

thei, thai, *pro.*, (ON *þeir*), they. D 65, Hv 414; **the**, Em 202, EG 270; *g.*, **there**, Hv 1350; **thayre**, Av 145; *d. and a.*, **tham**, SS 230; **theim**, K 160; **thaym**, Av 630; *cf.* **he.**

thei, although; *cf.* **thouh.**

thein, thain, *n.*, (OE *þegn*), thane (*a land-holding freeman, not noble*). Hv 1327; *plu.*, **theines**, Ly 28325; **theinen**, Ly 27510.

thenche, thenke, thinke, *vs.*, (OE *þencan, þyncan, which became confused in Middle English*), (1) think, be mindful of, believe, intend. D 455; *pr. 2 sg.*, (*with enclitic pro.*) **thenkestu**, Hv 578; *pt.*, **thow3te**, CA 250; **tho3te**, Hr 1274; **thoucte**, Hv 691; **thhou3te**, R 25; **thow3th**, Em 227; *pp.*, **thouth**, Hv 312; **ithoht**, Ly 28087; *prp.*, **thinkand**, SS 233. (2) *seem* (*impersonal*). Hr 1151; **thenke**, CA 30; *pr.*, think, SS 449; *pt.*, **thu3te**, Hr 278; **thouthe**, Hv 1286; **thught**, Tr 4717; **thuhte**, Ly 28297; *pt. sj.*, **thouwte**, D 597.

thenne, *cf.* **thanne**, then, when; *and* **thethin**, thence.

theo, *cf.* **the** *and* **tho.**

there, thore, *adv. and conj.*, (OE *þær, þār*), (1) there, in that place. Hr 298; **thore**, Av 90; **thar**, Hr 505; **thare**, Av 749; **thær**, Ly 27825. (2) where, wherever. Hv 142; to the place where, **ther**, Ly 27777; Hr 936. (3) *comp.*, **ther-at**, thereat, Ip 2996; **ther-as**, where, Em 545; **ther-uore**, for which, Ly 28017;

there-on, in this, Ip 1105; ther-
tille, concerning that, Av 518;
there-to, in addition, D 596, SS
796, Sd 2193; to or concerning
this, B 2952, 3328; therwhile,
while, D 156; ther-whiles, while,
D 653.

thethen, *adv.*, (OE þeþan, þanan),
thence. Hv 2498; thethin, Yw
382; thenne, CA 248; thennes,
G 545.

thider, *adv. and conj.*, (OE þider),
(1) thither. Hr 699; theder,
CA 265; thedur, Ip 3058; thether,
Cl 166; thuder, Hr 1424.
(2) to the place from which.
thedyr, Ip 411.

thilke, this same, that same; *cf.*
ilk.

thinge, *plu.*, things, creatures. Av
830, Em 333.

this, *pro. and adj.*, (OE þys, þes),
this. thes, Hr 804; *g.m.sg.*,
theos, Ly 27689; *g. and d.f.sg.*,
thissere, Ly 28211; *d.m.sg.*, this-
sen, Ly 28189; *a.m.sg.*, thisne,
Ly 28145; *plu.*, this, D 655;
thes, Tr 50; theos, Ly 27730;
theis, P 909; *g.*, theos, Ly 27689;
a., thas, Ly 28202.

tho, tha, *pro.*, (OE þā), those.
tho, Av 977; tha, TT 183; thoo,
P 219; thaa, P 516.

tho, *adv. and conj.*, (OE þā), (1)
then, when. Cl 145; thoo, Em
51; thaa, P 497; tha, Ly 28446;
theo, Ly 27489.
(2) although. thoo, Ip 1076;
cf. thouh.

thonked, ʒonked, *pt.*, thanked,
D 246, 384.

thore, *cf.* there.

thou, *pro.*, (OE þu, ge, ēow), thou,
you. *n. sg.*, thou, G 145; thu,
Hr 91; tu, Hv 2903; tow, O 450;
thw, Hv 1316; *g.*, thy, G 142;
thine, G 241; thi, Av 268; *g.*

and *d.f.*, thire, Ly 28104; *a.*,
the, G 140; te, O 100; de, Em
450; *pl.* (*used also as polite form
of the singular*), *n. and a.*, ye,
Sd 2478; ʒe, G 170; ʒo, Av 111;
ʒaw, Av 106; ʒew, B 2962; eou,
Ly 28174; *g.*, yeur, B 2982;
ʒowre, SS 449; ʒoure, Hr 814;
ʒor, R 50; ou, R 65.

thouh, thei, *adv. and conj.*, (OE
þēah, þēh, ON þō), although,
though. thouʒe, B 3167; thowʒe,
Ip 1078; thoghe, P 1622; thofe, P
616; thowe, Cl 70; thah, Ly
28543; thei, D 461; thai, D 560;
thou, Hv 124; theʒ, Hr 317;
douʒ, Lv 204; thauʒ, Al 4226;
theiʒ, R 412; thogfe, P 1453.

thowʒtur, daughter; *cf.* doughter.

thridde, *adj. and pro.*, (OE þridda),
third. D 489, ET 614; thrid,
SS 793, Av 1047.

thurgh, thorow, *prep. and adv.*,
(OE þurh), through (*with senses
as in Modern English*). Em
332, Tr 8652; thorrowe, EG 340;
thurh, B 3502; throʒhe, Av 1040;
thureʒ, Hr 875; thorw, Hv 264;
thuruth, Hv 52; thoruth, Hv
1065; thoruʒ, Lv 484; thourgh,
D 334; thurght, Tr 8641; thurch,
O 534; *comp.*, thorwʒout, At 611;
thurhout, B 3201.

tide, *n.*, time, hour. Hr 849, Cl
188; *d. as adverb*, that tyde, then,
Ip 1161; this tyde, now, SS 421.
Especially in the phrase: in are
tiden, once on a time, Ly 27992.

tide, *v.*, betide. *pt.*, tide, Tr 81.

til, *prep. and conj.*, (ON til), (1)
to, towards. Hr 938; tille, Sd
1640; tylle, ET 523.
(2) for. til, Hv 761.
(3) until. Hr 124; thyll, Em 502.

tite, *adv.*, (ON tīðr), speedily. Yw
409, Ip 3060; tit, Tr 4758; tytlye,
CA 84.

tithande, tidinge, *n.*, (ON tīðindi), news, tidings. Av 748; tithandes, Yw 140; tydynge, CA 59; tithing, Av 679.

to, (OE tō), (1) *adv.*, too. G 398. (2) *adv.*, to, towards. Ly 27456; tow, Ip 406. (3) *prep.*, to. *Examples of senses unusual in Modern English:* te, to, Yw 207; to, during, Ly 28090; to, until, Av 1061; to name, by name, CA 204; to, as, Ly 27546, Hv 575; to, according to, Ly 28437; to, in consideration of, Hv 486. (4) *conj.*, until. Ip 3146, SS 307.

to, two; *cf.* tweie.

to-. *A prefix, with the force of* "violently" *or* "apart": tobarst, burst to pieces, G 537; tobreste, Lv 482; toborsten, D 1043; tofallen, fallen to ruins, Ly 27893; torent, torn to pieces, D 353; togrinde, grind to pieces, D 85; todrawe, torn apart, Lv 606; tobreke, broke in two, D 986; tobrent, burned up, Al 3982.

tofore, toforn, *adj.*, *adv.*, *and prep.*, former, formerly, before. B 3018, 3684.

toȝeines, towards. Ly 28529.

tone, *cf.* one, take.

tosomne, together. Ly 27424.

tothir, todir, *cf.* other.

toune, *n.*, (OE tūn), town. Hv 2911; tun, Ly 27918; tune, Hr 153.

tour, *n.*, (OF tour), tower. D 871; tur, Hr 1453.

toward, *commonly separated in Middle English:* to himward, toward him.

tre, *n.*, (OE trēo), (1) wood. Yw 187, Av 1074. (2) beam, plank. Em 656. (3) tree. D 72; *plu.*, treoes, Al 4074; trene, FB 634.

(4) the Cross. ET 387.

treuthe, trowthe, *n.*, (OE trēowð), truth, troth, pledged word. Hr 672, At 155; trowith, B 3105; trauthe, Av 428; trowthe, ET 276; truthe, Hr 674.

trone, throne. Em 1.

trowe, *vw.*, (OE trēowian), believe, trust. P 1107; tro, Hv 2862; trowes, Yw 981; *pt.*, trowed, P 586; *imp. sg.*, trowes, SS 938; *especially in the phrase:* for to trowe, surely, Ip 3155.

tryste, trust, reliance. ET 553.

tuke, *cf.* take.

tweie, twa, *adj. and pro.*, (OE twā, twegen), two. G 202; twa, SS 263; tweiȝe, Ly 28473; tway, ET 900; too, B 3179; to, B 3169; tow, EG 491; toe, Av 932; tvo, O 81.

U

uncouthe, *adj.*, (OE uncūð), strange, unfamiliar, unknown. P 1047; vncowthe, Av 618; vncuthe, Hr 729; vncoth, EG 405.

underȝete, *vs.*, understand, perceive. D 165.

unethe, *adj. and adv.*, (OE unēaðe), (1) *adj. as sb.*, discomfort. Ly 27673. (2) *adv.*, scarcely, with difficulty. onnethe, Sd 3000; vnnethes, Yw 372.

unkinde, *adj. and adv.*, (OE uncynde), unnatural. SS 3008; unkindelike, Hv 1250.

until, *prep.*, *adv.*, *and conj.*, (OE un + till), to, unto, until. Hv 2913; hentill, Av 124.

unto, to, unto, until. Yw 930.

upon, (OE up on), upon. *Only senses unusual in Modern English are:* (1) *prep.*, in the course of, during. Hr 1097, Hv 468;

against, Hv 2689; **uppen**, above, Ly 28019.
(2) *adv.*, above, from above. Hr 11.
ure, vre, our; *cf.* **I.**
urn, vrn, ran; *cf.* **runne.**

V

venesun, *n.*, (OF **veneisun**), meat of any game-animal. Av 262; **venesoun**, D 773; **ueneysun**, Hv 1726.
verrament, *adv.*, (OF **veraiment**), truly. ET 862; **varraiment**, D 11; **veramend**, Cl 189; **werament**, Cl 237; **verement**, Lv 485.
vnsquarut, answered; *cf.* **answer.**
vomen, *cf.* **wimman.**

W

w-. *The following words are spelled in* **w-** *for* **wh-**: **wo**, who; **wich**, which; **were**, where; **wan**, when; **wat**, what; **wether**, whether; **wilke, whilk**, which.
wa, wai, walawa, *cf.* **wo.**
wan, *cf.* **when** *and* **winne.**
ware, *adj.*, (OE **wær**), **(1)** aware, conscious. CA 122, Ip 3130; **warre**, P 881.
(2) wary, resourceful. **war**, Av 13, Yw 1241.
wasche, *vs. and vw.*, (OE **wascan, wescan**), wash. **washen**, Hv 1233; *pt. plu.*, **wasschyd**, Cl 154; **wessh**, Sd 1871; **wyshe**, Em 866; **wesh**, Em 218; **wessche**, D 831; **wisschen**, G 542; **whesshen**, Em 890; *pp.*, **waisschen**, G 439; **wasshen**, K 887.
wat, *cf.* **what** *and* **wite.**
waxe, wexe, *vs.*, (OE **weaxan**), grow, become. Cl 151; **wex**, B 2940; *pr.*, **wexeth**, CA 158; *pt.*, **wax**, Ip 364; **wexe**, P 212; **waxe**,

ET 400; *pp.*, **woxe**, G 232; **woxen**, Em 950; **wax**, Em 365; **waxen**, Yw 1212.
we, *cf.* **I** *and* **wo.**
wede, *n.*, (OE **wæde**), garment, clothing, armor. ET 245, SS 799; **weed**, EG 98; *especially in the complimentary rhyme-tag:* **wordy vnthur wede**, worthy under weeds, Em 250.
wei, weilawei, *cf.* **wo.**
wel, welle, *adv.*, (OE **wel**), **(1)** well, excellently. Hr 484, CA 352.
(2) quite, fully; very, very much (*often used as a metrical filler*). Hr 808; **wele**, SS 230; **will**, Cl 127; **vel**, Hr 445.
welde, *vw.*, (OE **geweldan**), wield, manage, have power over, govern, protect. SS 4274; **walden**, Ly 27652; **awelden**, Ly 27894; *pr. sg.*, **weldythe**, Ip 3138.
wele, wealth, prosperity. *Especially in the phrase:* **yn wo and wele**, in ill and good, Em 573.
wende, *vw.*, (OE **wendan**), go, turn. Ip 1198; **weynde**, Av 641; *pr. sg.*, **weyndes**, Ip 3102; *pt. sg.*, **wente**, ET 1190; **wende**, Sd 2958; **iwende**, Ly 27619; *pt. plu.*, **wenten**, G 609; **wenden**, Ly 27512; **wenton**, Tr 4716; **wenden**, CA 364; **weynde**, Av 81; *pp.*, **went,** Ip 3076; **iwent**, Hr 440; **wente**, Av 538; *vb.n.*, **wending**, Yw 538; *imp.*, **went**, Hr 325.
wene, *vw.*, (OE **wēnan**), think, expect, believe. *pr.*, **wene**, Av 756; **ween**, B 3479; (*with enclitic pro.*) **wenestu**, Hv 1787; *pr. as future*, **wene**, Ly 28123; *pt.*, **wende**, D 81; **wente**, CA 67; **wend**, B 3479.
wepe, *vw. and vs.*, (OE **wēpan**), weep. *pr.*, (*with enclitic pro.*) **wepestu**, Hr 656; *pt. sg.*, **wep**, D

108; **weop**, Hr 69; **wepputte**, Av 280; *plu.*, **wepen**, D 987; *prp.*, **wepeand**, SS 890; **wepende**, D 132.

wepen, wepne, *n.*, (OE **wæpen**), weapon. Hv 89; *plu.*, **weppun**, Av 609; **weppon**, Tr 4752; **wapynes**, P 20; **iwepnen**, Ly 28388.

wer, were, werre, war, combat. Av 332, Tr 88.

werche, *cf.* **wirche**.

werd, world; *cf.* **werld**.

werk, *n.*, (OE **weorc**), (1) deed, work. Tr 8625, Av 941. (2) construction, fortification. Hr 1432; **werc**, Ly 27857.

werld, world, *n.*, (OE **weorold**, *etc.*), world. **weorld**, Ly 28131; **werd**, Hv 1290; **worl**, At 136; *g.*, **wordes**, Em 824.

what, (OE **hwæt**), (1) *adj. and pro.;* what, which. **wat**, D 6, Hr 942. (2) *relative and interrogative pro.;* what, whatever. Hr 765; **wat**, SS 2962; **wæt**, Ly 28385; **hwat**, Hv 590; **qwatt**, Av 962. why, what, D 676, B 2978. (3) *interjection*, what! lo! **hwat**, Hv 2547. *comp.*, **what-so**, whatsoever, P 1257.

what, *cf.* **wite**.

whennes, *adv. and conj.*, (OE **hwanan**), whence. **whenns**, Em 418; **whannes**, Hr 161.

when, whan, *adv. and conj.*, (OE **hwanne**), when. **whan**, Cl 49; **whanne**, Hr 915; **quen**, Av 52; **qwen**, Av 424; **hwan**, Hv 408; **wan**, D 629; **wanne**, Hr 913.

where, *adv. and conj.*, (OE **hwǣr**, **hwār**), where. **whar**, Ly 28057; **quere**, Av 304; **were**, Av 1117; **hwere**, Hv 1083; **hware**, Hv 1881; **war**, Ly 28479; **wer**, D 462. *comp.*, **whereto**, why, Em 929;

wharesom, wheresoever, SS 2999; **hworeso**, Hv 1349.

where, *cf.* **whether** *and* **be**.

whesshen, washed; *cf.* **wasche**.

whethen, *adv. and conj.*, (ON **hvaðan**), whence. Yw 1044; **quethun**, Av 301.

whether, (OE **hwæðer**), (1) *conj.*, whether, whether or not. **whedur**, Ip 410; **quether**, Av 963; **wher**, B 3034; **hwere**, Hv 549; **wether**, D 862. (2) *adj. and pro.*, which, whichever. **whether**, G 249; Yw 1002. (3) *untranslatable expletive, sign of a question*. **whethir**, P 1691; **wher**, G 430; **whethur**, Em 794; **hwor**, Hv 1119; **wether**, Hv 292.

whether, wheder, whither, FB 96.

whi, qui, qwi, hwi, why.

while, (OE **hwīl**), (1) *n.*, space of time. Hr 1317; **hwile**, Hv 722; **quile**, B 3616. (2) *d. as adv.*, formerly. **whilen**, Ly 28633; **while**, Ly 27979. (3) *oblique cases as conj.*, while, during the time that. **the while** **the**, Ly 27652; **tha wile**, Ly 28219; **hwile**, Hv 301; **whils**, B 2969; **whyles**, CA 145; **quille**, Av 286; **qwiles**, Tr 39.

whilk, which, who, P 1979; **wilke**, P 281.

white, *adj.*, (OE **hwīt**), white. **why3te**, Ip 3095; **whyght**, Ip 3091; **qwyte**, K 365; **quyte**, Av 1090; **whythe**, Em 66; **hwit**, Hv 1729; **with**, Hv 48.

who, *rel. and int. pro.*, (OE **hwa**), who, whoever. D 311; **hwo**, Hv 296; **wo**, D 1053; *d. and a.*, **wham**, Hr 352; **whæm**, Ly 27486; **quo**, Av 108; **ho**, Cl 329. *comp.*, **wha-swa**, whosoever, Ly 28518; **quo-so**, Av 135.

wife, *n.*, (OE **wīf**), (1) woman.

SS 409.

(2) wife. **wif,** Hr 553; **whif,** SS
932; *g.sg.,* **whife,** SS 2803; **wiif,**
O 496.

wight, *adj. and adv.,* (ON vīgt),
valiant, powerful, active, quick.
Sd 2077, ET 96; **wicth,** Hv 344;
with, Hv 1008; **wiȝte,** Av 15;
wightly, Sd 2682, Tr 4716.

wight, *n.,* (OE **wiht**), (1) whit,
particle, bit. **wicth,** Hv 97;
with, Hv 1763, **wiȝt,** Hr 503, D
776.

(2) person, creature. **wiȝte,** Hr
671, Av 304; **wihȝte,** D 97; **wyȝth,**
Lv 307.

wille, *n.,* (OE **willa**), pleasure, wish,
will. Hr 288; **will,** P 843; **iwulle,**
Av 315; *plu.,* **iwillen,** Ly 27529;
in wille, desirous, Ip 1183.

wille, *vs.,* (OE **willan**), will, wish,
desire, be willing. *pr. 1 sg.,*
wille, D 6; **wole,** Sd 1910; **wulle,**
Ly 27888; **woll,** Em 248; *2,* **wolt,**
G 182; *(with enclitic pro.)* **wiltu,**
Hv 681; **wilte,** Hv 528; *3,* **wile,**
Hr 811; **wulle,** Av 523; **wol,** B
2961; **wole,** Sd 1906; *pr. plu.,*
wille, D 742; **wulleȝ,** Hr 603;
wol, B 3423; **wele,** Sd 2633; *pt.,*
wolde, Hv 367; **wald,** SS 262;
weolde, Ly 28390; **wolden,** D 57;
pr. sj., **wile,** D 714. *Negative
forms compounded with* **ne:** *pr.,*
nel, D 525; **nulleth,** Ly 28130;
nyl, B 3110; **null,** Hr 1144; **nyll,**
Av 1060; *pt.,* **nolde,** D 194;
nold, O 138; **nulde,** Ly 28002;
nalden, Ly 27732.

wimman, woman, *n.,* (OE **wīfman**),
woman. **wimman,** Hv 1720;
vomman, B 3204; **wommon,** Em
245; *plu.,* **wymmanne,** Hr 67;
wemen, Av 559; **vommen,** B 3205;
g. plu., **wimmonne,** Ly 28459;
wimmonnen, Ly 28035.

winde, *vs.,* (OE **windan**), go, turn,
roll. Ip 411, Av 72; *pt. sg.,* **wond,**
Ly 28049; *plu.,* **wunden,** Ly
27785.

winne, *n.,* (OE **wynn**), joy. TT
45, ET 840; **wunne,** Ly 28621.

winne, *vs.,* (OE **winnan**), (1) attain,
win, conquer. Hr 1357; **wen,**
Ip 1129; **wyn,** B 3255; *pt. sg.,*
wan, TT 181; **wonn,** P 1735;
wann, Ip 1099; *pt. plu.,* **wonen,**
Tr 4780; *pp.,* **wonnen,** CA 170;
wonen, Tr 8607; **wonun,** Av 542;
woon, EG 684; **ywon,** O 559.

(2) make one's way, go, get up.
Sd 2969; **wyn,** P 2199; *pt. sg.,*
wan, Av 210; **wane,** P 1270;
wann, Ip 3175; *pt. plu.,* **wan,**
ET 242; **wonnen,** Tr 4751;
wonyn, Tr 4761.

wirche, *vw.,* (OE **wyrcan**), (1) do,
work, perform. **werch,** Cl 164;
wirke, P 1718; **worch,** B 3342;
worche, G 500; *pr. plu.,* **wurchun,**
Av 939; *pp.,* **iwrouȝt,** B 3009;
wrouth, Hv 1352.

(2) cause, make, build, create.
wurchen, Ly 27856; **werke,** CA
78; **wirchen,** Hv 510; *pt.,* **wrowȝte,**
CA 119; **wroghte,** P 284; *pp.,*
wroght, ET 312; **rought,** EG 559;
iwrout, D 607; **wrouth,** Lv 265.
In the phrase: **syn he was man
wrowȝt,** since he was born, Cl
213.

wise, *adj. and adv.,* (OE **wīs**), wise,
sage. Hr 989; **wyce,** Ip 348;
whise, SS 2799; *sup.,* **wiseste;**
cp. adv., **wyselyer,** more wisely,
TT 137.

wise, *n.,* (OE **wīse**), manner, means,
way. Yw 1073, Hr 360; *d. sg.,*
wisen, Ly 27835.

wisse, *vw.,* (OE **wissian**), direct,
guide, advise. Hv 104, At 661;
wise, D 267; *pr. sg.,* **wys,** Yw
1046; *imp.,* **wysshe,** Tr 4.

wite, *vs.,* (OE **witan** *and* **wītan**; *the*

forms become confused in Middle English), (1) know, learn. Lv 653; **wit,** SS 3040; **iwite,** D 201; **witte,** Ip 1172; **wete,** B 3544; **witen,** Hr 288; *pr. plu.*, **wetith,** B 3539; **wite,** Hv 2808; **witen,** Hv 2208; *pt. with the force of pr.*, **wott,** Ip 1073; **wate,** At 108; **woot,** B 3116; **wost,** Hv 527; **wot,** D 84; **watte,** Ip 1112; *as future,* **watte,** Ip 435; *pt.*, **wot,** D 78; **what,** Ly 28088; **wiste,** Tr 23; **wisste,** CA 35; **wuste,** Ly 28298; *pp.*, **wist,** EG 751; *imp. sg. and plu.*, **witte,** Av 327; CA 195; *pt. sj.*, **wyst,** TT 189. *Negative forms compounded with* **ne;** *pr.*, **note,** B 3049; **not,** D 254; *pt.*, **nist,** D 69; **nuste,** Ly 27604.
(2) guard, guard against, decree. **wite,** CA 136; *imp.*, **wite,** Hv 1316, Ly 28604.

with, *prep.*, (OE wiδ), with. **wiȝ,** D 44. *Senses unusual in Modern English are:* (1) against. Ly 27581, Hr 830.
(2) by. P 836, Tr 53.
(3) *in the phrase:* with **wronge,** unjustly. Hr 905.
(4) *comp.*, **with-thi,** if, on condition, P 584; **with-than,** provided that, Hv 532.

with, *cf.* **wight,** courageous; white; and **wight,** person, particle.

withoute, *prep. and adv.*, (OE wiδūtan), (1) without, lacking. **withute,** Hr 188; **withouten,** Ip 375; **withowtun,** Av 10; **wiȝouten,** D 320.
(2) except. **withuten,** Hv 425.
(3) outside, outside of. **withoute,** Av 1095; **withouten,** SS 366.
(4) *in the following rhyme-tags meaning* "surely": **withouten les,** without lies; **withouten wene,** beyond doubt; **withouten faile,**

without fail; **withouten let(ting),** without hindrance; **withouten drede,** beyond doubt; **withouten othe,** beyond the necessity of taking oath.

witterly, *adv.*, (ON vitrliga), surely. At 80; **witturly,** Av 86; **weterly,** SS 4255; **wyttyrly,** ET 1069.

wo, wa, wei, *adj., n., and interj.*, (OE wā, wēa; ON vei), (1) alas, woe, sorrow. **wa,** Yw 432; **way,** O 232; **wo,** Hr 115; **woo,** Tr 8592; **we,** Ip 1118; **wæ,** Ly 28329; **wowȝ,** Al 4026.
(2) sad, sorrowful, wretched. **wa,** SS 2850; **woo,** Em 324; At 81.
(3) *comp.*, **walawai,** alas! woe is me! Hr 956; **walawa,** Ly 27532; **wale,** Ly 28092; **wellaway,** EG 748; **weilawei,** Hv 462.

wod, *adj.*, (OE wōd), (1) mad, insane. Lv 470; **wood,** At 250; **woode,** EG 986.
(2) fierce, raging. **wode,** Ly 27895, ET 108.

wode, *n.*, (OE wudu), (1) wood, fuel. Hv 940.
(2) a wood, woods. **wude,** Hr 361; **wode,** D 59.

wolde, *cf.* **wille.**

won, *n. and adj.*, (OE ȝewuna), (1) accustomed. SS 230; **wone,** Hv 2151.
(2) dwelling, place. **woon,** ET 459; **wone,** At 238; **won,** Tr 4780; **wane,** P 1347.

won, *n.*, (OE wēn, ON vān), plenty, quantity. Sd 2093; **woon,** Sd 2478; **wane,** SS 265. *Especially in the phrases:* **ful god wone,** plenty, plentiful, plentifully, G 125; Hv 1024; **well good won,** repeatedly, Lv 360.

wonder, wunder, *n.*, (OE wundor), (1) marvel, wonderful or terrible occurrence. Hr 1247.

(2) as *adj.*, strange, wonderful. Yw 267; **wondir**, Sd 1697.

(3) as *adv.*, very, wonderfully. ET 162; **wondir**, B 3017; **won-there**, Lv 511.

wone, *vw.*, (OW **wunian**), (1) dwell, inhabit. P 165; **wune**, Hr 731; **wunien**, Ly 28620; *pr.*, **wonnes**, P 1769; **wuneth**, Ly 28101; *pt. sg.*, **wond**, SS 288; **wonede**, Hr 917; **wunede**, Ly 27947; (*by nunnation*) **wuneden**, Ly 27959; *prp.*, **wonnande**, P 2138; *prp. as noun.*, **wonnyng**, dwelling, ET 1223; **woniyng**, D 223. (2) be accustomed. *pp.*, **woned**, Hr 34; **wonte**, Cl 112. (3) delay, remain. At 716; *pp.*, **woned**, Yw 212.

worche, wurche, wro3te, *cf.* **wirche**.

word, *n.*, (OE **word**), word, fame, report. **weorde**, Ly 28535; *plu.*, **word**, Ly 28202; **worden**, Ly 28461; **wurdus**, Av 441; **worthes**, CA 32.

word, world; *cf.* **werld**.

worschip, *vw. and n.*, honor, praise. ET 840, EG 456.

worthe, *vs.*, (OE **weorðan, wyrðan**), be, become (*often as auxiliary for passive*). G 491; *pr. as future*, **worst**, O 168; **wurth**, Hr 684; **wurthest**, Ly 28452; (*with enclitic pro.*) **wurstu**, Hr 324; **worht**, D 115; *pt.*, **wurthen**, Ly 27468; **iwurthen**, Ly 27520; *pp.*, **iwurthen**, Ly 28207; *sj.*, *especially in the exclamations and oaths:* **worthe them woo!** woe be to them, ET 760; **særi wurthe his saule!** wretched be his soul, Ly 28333; **wo worth dedes wronge!** woe come to wrong deeds, Em 648.

wrathe, *vw.*, (OE **gewrāðian**), grow angry, make angry, vex. **wrath-the**, G 80; **wreth**, Yw 995; *pr.*, **wrathis**, Av 906; *pt.*, **wraththed**,

G 91; **iwrathede**, Ly 27698; *pp. as adj.*, **wro3t**, Lv 700.

wrathe, wrath; *d. sg.*, (*by nunnation*) **wraththen**, Ly 27773; **wreth-the**, Lv 470.

wreie, *vw.*, (OE **wrēgan**), betray. *pr.*, **wrye**, K 389; *pt.*, **wryed**, K 976; *pr. sj.*, **wrye**, ET 527.

wreke, *vs.*, (OE **wrecan**), avenge. D 913, Yw 587; **wreche**, Hr 1284; **awreken**, Ly 28112; **wrecke**, EG 673; *pr.*, **wreke**, Ly 27612; *pt.*, **wrak**, G 303; *pp.*, **wreke**, G 346; **iwroken**, G 541; **awræken**, Ly 28221; **wrocken**, EG 137; **awreke**, Lv 706; **wrokyn**, K 844.

writ, *n.*, (OE **writ**), writing, letter. Hr 930; *plu.*, **writes**, Hv 2275; **writen**, Ly 27480.

write, *vs.*, write. *pp.*, **wryte**, FB 213; **ywrete**, FB 132.

wrong. *Especially in the phrase:* **with wronge**, unjustly, wrongfully.

wroth, *adj. and adv.*, (OE **wrāð**), angry. B 2940; **wro3th**, Lv 450; **wro3t**, Lv 700; **wrothe**, Hr 348; **wroth**, EG 719; *sup.*, **wrathest**, Ly 28503.

wunde, *n.*, (OE **wund**), wound. Hr 640; **wonde**, SS 2992; *plu.*, **wowundes**, Av 44; **wounde3**, P 151; *g.*, **wunden**, Ly 28579.

wunien, wunede, dwell, dwelt; *cf.* **wone**.

Y

yare, *adj. and adv.*, (OE **gearu, geare, gearwe**), ready, fast, quick. Sd 1720; **3are**, P 1537; **3aru**, Ly 28397; **3arewe**, Ly 28224.

ye, ya, *adv.*, (OE **gēa**, ON **jā**), yes (*usually confirmatory; cf.* **yis**). Hr 100; **3e**, CA 302; **ya**, Hv 2607; **3oe**, Av 378; **3a**, SS 566; **3oo**, Em 888.

yede, yode, *v. defective*, (OE ēode), went (*in preterit only; cf.* go). *sg.*, ʒeode, Hr 381; yede, Ip 3025; ʒode, ET 620; youde, Ip 456; eode, Ly 27805; (*by nunnation*) eoden, Ly 27961; *plu.*, ʒeeden, G 510; ʒode, Av 421; yeede, EG 280; ʒede, TT 56.

yeftes, yiftes, gifts. Cl 50.

yelde, *vs.*, (OE geldan), (1) yield, give up. Hv 2712; ʒild, Av 1058; ʒulde, Al 4149; ʒylde, ET 1126; *pr. sg.*, ʒeldeth, CA 335; eldythe, Ip 3137; *pt.*, yald, Tr 8660; ʒolde, P 2104. (2) repay, requite. ʒelde, CA 336; *pt.*, ʒald, Lv 420; *pp.*, iʒolde, Hr 460.

yeme, *vw.*, (OE gēman), govern, guard, protect. SS 789; *pr.*, ʒemeʒ, D 151; *pt.*, yemede, G 267; *pp.*, yemed, Hv 305; *prp.*, ʒemande, P 1136.

yen, eyes; *cf.* eie.

yere, *n.*, (OE gēar), year. ʒer, D 103; *plu.*, ʒer, Em 733; ʒere, P 228; ʒeris, B 3177.

yerne, yorne, *adv.*, (OE georne), (1) eagerly, earnestly, violently. ʒerne, Hr 1085; ʒorne, ET 449. (2) speedily. ʒerne, D 82.

yerne, *vw.*, (OE gyrnan), yearn for, desire. ʒerne, Hr 915; ʒirnen, Ly 27886; *pr.*, ʒernes, Yw 1242; *pt.*, ʒirnden, Ly 27969.

yet, *adv.*, (OE giet, gyt, *etc.*), yet, nevertheless. ʒete, D 541; ʒet, G 272; ʒit, B 2961; ʒute, Hr 70; ʒette, Av 347; ʒyt, ET 81; ʒhit, D 187.

yeue, yaf, *cf.* giue.

yghen, yʒen, eyes; *cf.* eie.

yif, *cf.* if and giue.

yis, *adv.*, (OE gise), yes (*usually contradictory; cf.* ye). ʒis, SS 2973; ʒys, CA 309; ʒisse, Av 589.

yon, yond, *adj., adv., and prep.*, (OE geon, geond), (1) yonder. ʒone, P 330, Av 120; ʒound, Ip 445; younde, Ip 3178. (2) through, throughout. ʒeond, Ly 27470.

yong, ying, *adj. and sb.*, (OE geong, iung), young. ʒong, B 3235; ʒing, SS 2846; yenge, Cl 517; ʒeonge, Ly 28001; yongh, Lv 186.

yore, yare, *adv.*, (OE gēara), (1) long ago. ʒore, D 882; ʒare, Hr 1356. (2) for a long time. ʒore, O 557.

you, ʒowre, ye, *cf.* thou.